WILLS, TRUSTS, AND ESTATES

Fourth Edition

WILLS, TRUSTS, AND ESTATES

Jesse Dukeminier
Richard C. Maxwell Professor of Law
University of California, Los Angeles

Stanley M. Johanson
Fannie Coplin Regents Professor of Law
University of Texas

Little, Brown and Company
Boston   Toronto   London

Library of Congress Catalog Card No. 89-63644
ISBN No. 0-316-19519-7

Fourth Edition

Second Printing

MV NY

Published simultaneously in Canada
by Little, Brown & Company (Canada) Limited

Printed in the United States of America

To
J.J.D., L.W.D.
and G.J.

SUMMARY OF CONTENTS

CONTENTS

Chapter 2. Intestacy: An Estate Plan by Operation of Law   75

Chapter 4. Will Substitutes: Avoidance of Probate

271

Chapter 5. Wills: Construction Problems   **319**

PREFACE

This book is designed for use in a course in decedents' estates and trusts and as an introduction to estate planning. Our basic aim in this fourth edition remains as before: to produce not merely competent practitioners in the estates and trusts field, but lawyers who think critically and comparatively about problems and probe alternative solutions.

We start with inheritance and its limitations, then move to wills and will substitutes. Since the 1960s, the law of wills has been undergoing major renovation. Initially, change was brought on by a swelling public demand for cheaper and simpler ways of transferring property at death. Then imaginative scholars began to ventilate this ancient law of the dead hand, challenging assumptions and suggesting judicial and legislative innovation. Finally, during the Reagan presidency, Congress decided that it was going to tax away about half the wealth of millionaires transferred from one generation to the next. The ensuing changes in both law and practice have been many, and they are far from over.

After dealing with the law of wills, we turn to trusts. During the last quarter century lawyers have come to regard the trust as the best solution to all sorts of client problems. As a result, trusts have proliferated — large trusts, small trusts, even trusts of one dollar or less. The fiduciary obligation has come to be the most useful and important principle in our society for managing and allocating resources of all types, public as well as private. In this expansion, the law of private trusts has annexed the law of future interests and powers of appointment, reducing these two subjects largely to problems in drafting and construing trust instruments and to the Rule against Perpetuities — a rule that curbs overlong trusts.

Our final chapter on taxation of donative transfers is designed to give the student basic knowledge about estate, gift, and generation-skipping taxes, so that the student as lawyer can (1) handle the usual situations and know when further expert advice is called for or (2) build upon this foundation to become a tax planner. The chapter also serves a unifying function of bringing back together the various kinds of donative transfers analyzed separately in earlier chapters of the book and exploring their different tax costs.

Throughout the book we emphasize the basic theoretical structure and the general philosophy and purposes that unify the field of donative transfers. To this end we have pruned away mechanical matters (such as a step-by-step discussion of how to probate a will and settle an estate, which is essentially local law, easily learned from a local practice book). So too we have omitted old technical learning and disappearing distinctions of little contemporary importance. At the same time we have sought historical roots of modern law. Understanding how the law became the way it is illuminates both the continuing growth of the law and the sometimes exasperating peculiarities of thought inherited from the past.

While we organize the book around theory, we have set our mind to undermine it with details. We believe interesting students in family wealth transfers requires cultivation of curiosity and compassion; details are the stuff of a humanistic perspective. They hook your interest in a way ideas never can. So we have included details about cases and relevant persons, where we have been able to dig them up. Not only do details give students insights into the incertitude of theory; they make it easier to identify with — and thus better understand — all these people quarreling about money.

We said in the first edition of this book, in 1972,

> In this book we deal with people, the quick as well as the dead. There is nothing like the death of a moneyed member of the family to show persons as they really are, virtuous or conniving, generous or grasping. Many a family has been torn apart by a botched-up will. Each case is a drama in human relationships — and the lawyer, as counselor, draftsman, or advocate, is an important figure in the dramatis personae. This is one reason the estates practitioner enjoys his work, and why we enjoy ours.

This observation remains true for students preparing themselves to counsel clients in the twenty-first century. Some things in this fascinating, evolving field never change.

Many persons have sent us valuable suggestions for improving the book. We particularly want to thank Joel S. Lee, John and Mary Ann Tally, Mark Reutlinger, and Valerie Vollmar. We are indebted to Linda Maisner and Fred Smith of the UCLA Law Library for helping to run down some of our cast of characters, and to our editor, Alistair Nevius of Little, Brown and Company, for his careful and intelligent editing. Finally, and most of all, we thank Dorothe Brehove of the UCLA Law School for her superlative work in typing and assembling the manuscript of this book.

Jesse Dukeminier
Stanley M. Johanson

March 1, 1990

Editor's Note: Throughout the book, footnotes to the text and to opinions and other quoted materials are numbered consecutively from the begining of each chapter. Some footnotes in opinions and secondary authorities are omitted. Editors' footnotes added to quoted materials are indicated by the abbreviation: — Eds.

ACKNOWLEDGMENTS

Anthropophagy: Swift Reprisal, 279 New Eng. J. Med. 890 (1968). Copyright © 1968 by The New England Journal of Medicine. Reprinted by permission.

Blum, Walter & Harry Kalven, The Uneasy Case for Progressive Taxation, 19 U. Chi. L. Rev. 417 (1952). Copyright © 1952 by The University of Chicago. Reprinted by permission of Professor Blum and The University of Chicago Law Review.

Buck, Beryl H. Photograph. Reproduced by permission of Marin Community Foundation.

Buck, Estate of. California Superior Court Opinion, 21 U.S.F.L. Rev. 691 (1987). Reprinted by permission of the University of San Francisco Law Review.

Casner, Andrew James, Estate Planning, vol. 5 (5th ed. 1983). Copyright © 1983 by A. James Casner. Reprinted by permission of the author and Little, Brown & Co.

Dukeminier, Jesse, A Modern Guide to Perpetuities, 74 Calif. L. Rev. 1867 (1986). Copyright © 1986 by Jesse Dukeminier. Reprinted by permission of the author.

——, & James E. Krier, Property (2d ed. 1988). Copyright © 1988 by Jesse Dukeminier and James E. Krier. Reprinted by permission of Professor Dukeminier and Little, Brown & Co.

Eliot, Thomas Stearns, Burnt Norton, *in* Four Quartets (1943). Copyright © 1943 by T.S. Eliot. Reprinted by permission of Harcourt Brace Jovanovich Inc. and Faber and Faber Ltd.

Evicted Couple Leave Pictures of Son Who Threw Them Out. Los Angeles Times, Dec. 10, 1977, pt.1, p.24. Copyright © 1977 by United Press International. Reprinted by permission of United Press International.

Rev. 521 (1982). Copyright © 1982 by The University of Pennsylvania Law Review. Reprinted by permission of Professor Langbein and The University of Pennsylvania Law Review.

Langdell Lyrics, compiled by W. Barton Leach and privately published by The Foundation Press, Inc., in 1938. Reprinted by permission of Professor Leach.

Leach, W. Barton & James K. Logan, Future Interests and Estate Planning (1961). Copyright © 1961 by W. Barton Leach & James K. Logan. Reprinted by permission of Judge Logan.

Legal Challenges to AIDS Patients' Wills Seen on Rise. L.A. Daily Journal, Aug. 16, 1988, p.1. Copyright © 1988 by the Daily Journal Corporation. Reprinted by permission of the Los Angeles Daily Journal.

Megarry, Robert E. & Henry W.R. Wade, The Law of Real Property (5th ed. 1984). Copyright © 1984 by R.E. Megarry & H.W.R. Wade. Reprinted by permission of the authors.

New Yorker, The. The New Yorker Magazine, Inc. holds copyrights for the following: drawing by Peter Arno, copyright © 1940, 1968; drawing by Peter Arno, copyright © 1942, 1970; drawing by Wm. Hamilton, copyright © 1977; drawing by Handelsman, copyright © 1981; drawing by Saul Steinberg, copyright © 1970; drawing by Weber, copyright © 1988. Reprinted by permission of The New Yorker Magazine, Inc.

Norfolk, Duke of. Painting by Gerald Soest, 1677. Reproduced by permission of The Tate Gallery, London.

Note, The Regulation of Risky Investments, 83 Harv. L. Rev. 603 (1970). Copyright © 1970 by The Harvard Law Review Association. Reprinted by permission of The Harvard Law Review.

Nottingham, Lord Chancellor. Painting after Godfrey Kneller, 1680. Reproduced by permission of The National Portrait Gallery, London.

O'Connor, Sandra Day. Photograph. Reproduced by permission of Justice O'Connor.

Playboy, Cartoon by M. Tannenberg. Copyright © 1966 by Playboy. Reproduced by special permission of PLAYBOY Magazine.

Posner, Richard, Economic Analysis of Law (3d ed. 1986). Copyright © 1986 by Richard A. Posner. Reprinted by permission of the author and Little, Brown & Co.

Rothko, Mark. Number 22. Oil on Canvas, 9'9"(h) × 8'11⅛"(w). 1949. Collection, The Museum of Modern Art, New York. Gift of the artist. Photograph by Jeffrey Clements Photography. Reproduced by permission of The Museum of Modern Art.

Scott, Austin W., The Law of Trusts, vol. 4 (W. Fratcher 4th ed. 1989). Copyright © 1989 by Estate of Austin Wakeman Scott. Reprinted by permission of Little, Brown & Co.

Scott, Austin W. Photograph. Reproduced by permission of the Harvard Law School Art Collection.

Sharp, Susie. Photograph. Reproduced by permission of the Greensboro (N.C.) News and Record. Photograph by Burnie Batchelor Studio.

Simes, Lewis, Public Policy and the Dead Hand (1955). Copyright © 1955 by The University of Michigan. Reprinted by permission of the author and The University of Michigan Law School.

Simon, John, American Philanthropy and the Buck Trust, 21 U.S.F.L. Rev. 641 (1987). Reprinted by permission of the author and The University of San Francisco Law Review.

Table of Consanguinity, *in* California Decedent Estate Administration, vol. 1, at 805 (1971). Copyright © 1971, 1990 by the Regents of the University of California. Reproduced with permission from the California Continuing Education of the Bar practice book California Decedent Estate Administration.

Wellman, Richard, Punitive Surcharges Against Disloyal Fiduciaries — Is *Rothko* Right?, 77 Mich. L. Rev. 95 (1978). Copyright © 1978 by The Michigan Law Review. Reprinted by permission of the author and The Michigan Law Review.

Wells, Eleazer M.P. Photograph. Reproduced from The Church Militant, April 1944, at 4, with the permission of The Episcopal Diocese of Massachusetts.

Young, Raymond & John Lombard, Fiduciary Responsibility in Investments, 124 Tr. & Est., June 1985, at 14. Reprinted from Trusts and Estates. Copyright © 1985 by Communication Channels, Inc., Atlanta, Ga. U.S.A. Reprinted by permission.

WILLS, TRUSTS, AND ESTATES

1

A FOUNDATION FOR ESTATE PLANNING: SOCIETY'S CONTROL OF INHERITANCE

SECTION A. PROLOGUE

These materials on wills, trusts, and estates are intended to provide a basic course in estate planning and estate and trust administration. The materials bring together problems that traditionally have been discussed under separate titles and often in separate law school courses. The subject matter deals principally with what is conventionally known as the law of wills, gifts, future interests, trusts, estate administration, and estate and gift taxation. Practically all the legal doctrines and practices that are found under these rubrics are functionally related to the disposition of private wealth in two ways. First, the social process with which we are concerned is the allocation and transmission of wealth under conditions where the claimants have not given consideration that can be valued in money or money's worth. In most, but not all, cases these conditions arise where the claimants are members of the prior owner's family or where there is a donative transfer. The doctrines relating to wealth transmission can be broken down, for convenient handling, into the law of wills, the law of trusts, the law of future interests, and so forth. But from a functional viewpoint all this law interrelates as part of one wealth transmission process. The social values sought in this process give rise to community policies. The same community policies run (or ought to run) through all this law.

The second way in which this law is functionally interrelated can easily be seen if we shift our perspective to that of the estate planner. A competent attorney must understand how this law functions as part of the social process; to give sound advice the attorney must have insight into which doctrines are dying, which are growing, and which, from a policy perspective, are functional equivalents. But the role of a competent estate planner requires much more than this. The estate planner must examine alternative methods for disposing of property to carry out the client's objectives. The planner must consider the advantages and disadvantages of various kinds of inter vivos dispositions and of various kinds of testamentary dispositions and must assess the tax implications of the alternatives. These problems cannot be compartmentalized as problems solely involving wills or gifts or trusts. Proper estate planning requires moving in and out of, and comparing, all these areas of the law.

The materials in this book place special emphasis on two ways of thinking that correspond with the ways in which this law is functionally interrelated. The first is *policy thinking;* the second is *alternative thinking.* Policy thinking requires the clarification of community values; the examination of how or whether these values are served by specific practices, doctrines, and other conditions; the projection of future developments and trends; and the invention and evaluation of alternative policies. Alternative thinking requires the careful analysis of different methods of accomplishing one given objective. You should be concerned both with the ends and means of the social process as well as with the ends and means of clients.

Although we have generally arranged the material so that it can be dealt with from a planner's perspective, the lawyer's contact with this area of the law is, of course, not restricted to the planner's role alone. The lawyer may represent an interested party seeking a favorable interpretation of obscure language in a poorly drafted will or a fiduciary who needs guidance because the will or trust makes no provision for a contingency that has occurred. The lawyer may represent a disappointed relative who seeks to set the transfer aside, a creditor who wishes to reach estate assets or property settled in a trust, or a fiduciary charged with the duty of administering the trust or estate. In order to provide a comprehensive understanding of the wealth transmission process, the materials include a large number of cases, text notes, and problems not directly related to an estate planning perspective.

SECTION B.   INHERITANCE AND ITS LIMITATIONS

T. JEFFERSON, 7 JEFFERSON'S WORKS 454 (Monticello ed. 1904):   "The earth belongs in usufruct to the living; the dead have neither powers nor rights over it. The portion occupied by any individual

ceases to be his when he himself ceases to be, and reverts to society."
(Letter to James Madison dated Sept. 6, 1789.)

2 W. Blackstone, Commentaries
*10-13

The right of inheritance, or descent to the children and relations of the deceased, seems to have been allowed much earlier than the right of devising by testament. We are apt to conceive, at first view, that it has nature on its side; yet we often mistake for nature what we find established by long and inveterate custom. It is certainly a wise and effectual, but clearly a political, establishment; since the permanent right of property, vested in the ancestor himself, was no *natural,* but merely a *civil* right. . . . It is probable that [the right of inheritance arose] . . . from a plainer and more simple principle. A man's children or nearest relations are usually about him on his death-bed, and are the earliest witnesses of his decease. They become, therefore, generally the next immediate occupants, till at length, in process of time, this frequent usage ripened into general law. And therefore, also, in the earliest ages, on failure of children, a man's servants, born under his roof, were allowed to be his heirs; being immediately on the spot when he died. For we find the old patriarch Abraham expressly declaring that "since God had given him no seed, his steward Eliezer, one born in his house, was his heir."[1]

While property continued only for life, testaments were useless and unknown: and, when it became inheritable, the inheritance was long indefeasible, and the children or heirs at law were incapable of exclusion by will; till at length it was found, that so strict a rule of inheritance made heirs disobedient and headstrong, defrauded creditors of their just debts, and prevented many provident fathers from dividing or charging their estates as the exigencies of their families required. This introduced pretty generally the right of disposing of one's property, or a part of it, by *testament;* that is, by written or oral instructions properly *witnessed* and authenticated, according to the *pleasure* of the deceased, which we, therefore, emphatically style his *will.* This was established in some countries much later than in others. With us in England, till

---

1. Genesis 15:3. [The words put in quotation marks are Blackstone's paraphrase of two verses of the Bible, which no one has yet translated from the original Hebrew to everyone's satisfaction. Blackstone's statement that servants took as heirs in the absence of children has been disputed by many scholars. "Israel does not know a general rule like this for regulating the inheritance." G. Von Rad, Genesis 178 (J. Marks trans. 1961). Cf. E. Neufeld, Ancient Hebrew Marriage Laws 262 (1944). Abraham's declaration was never put to the test for thereafter, when Abraham was 100 years old and his wife Sarah was 90, Sarah gave birth to a son, Isaac. Genesis 17:15. — Eds.]

modern times, a man could only dispose of one-third of his movables from his wife and children; and in general, no will was permitted of lands till the reign of Henry VIII; and then only of a certain portion: for it was not till after the Restoration that the power of devising real property became so universal as at present.

Wills, therefore, and testaments, rights of inheritance and successions, are all of them creatures of the civil or municipal laws, and accordingly are in all respects regulated by them; every distinct country having different ceremonies and requisites to make a testament completely valid; neither does anything vary more than the right of inheritance under different national establishments.

IRVING TRUST CO. v. DAY, 314 U.S. 556, 562 (1942): "Rights of succession to the property of a deceased, whether by will or by intestacy, are of statutory creation, and the dead hand rules succession only by sufferance. Nothing in the Federal Constitution forbids the legislature of a state to limit, condition, or even abolish the power of testamentary disposition over property within its jurisdiction."

Hodel v. Irving

Supreme Court of the United States, 1987
481 U.S. 704

O'CONNOR, J.   The question presented is whether the original version of the "escheat" provision of the Indian Land Consolidation Act of 1983, Pub. L. 97-459, Tit. II, 96 Stat. 2519, effected a "taking" of appellees' decedents' property without just compensation.

I

Towards the end of the 19th century, Congress enacted a series of land Acts which divided the communal reservations of Indian tribes into individual allotments for Indians and unallotted lands for non-Indian settlement. This legislation seems to have been in part animated by a desire to force Indians to abandon their nomadic ways in order to "speed the Indians' assimilation into American society," Solem v. Bartlett, 465 U.S. 463, 466 (1984), and in part a result of pressure to free new lands for further white settlement. Ibid. Two years after the enactment of the General Allotment Act of 1887, ch. 119, 24 Stat. 388, Congress adopted a specific statute authorizing the division of the Great Reservation of the Sioux Nation into separate reservations and the allotment of specific tracts of reservation land to individual Indians, conditioned on the consent of three-fourths of the adult male Sioux. Act of Mar. 2, 1889, ch. 405, 25 Stat. 888. Under the Act, each male

Justice Sandra Day O'Connor

Sioux head of household took 320 acres of land and most other individuals 160 acres. 25 Stat. 890. In order to protect the allottees from the improvident disposition of their lands to white settlers, the Sioux allotment statute provided that the allotted lands were to be held in trust by the United States. Id., at 891. Until 1910 the lands of deceased allottees passed to their heirs "according to the laws of the State or Territory" where the land was located, ibid., and after 1910, allottees were permitted to dispose of their interests by will in accordance with regulations promulgated by the Secretary of the Interior. 36 Stat. 856, 25 U.S.C. §373. Those regulations generally served to protect Indian ownership of the allotted lands.

The policy of allotment of Indian lands quickly proved disastrous for the Indians. Cash generated by land sales to whites was quickly dissipated and the Indians, rather than farm the land themselves, evolved into petty landlords, leasing their allotted lands to white ranchers and farmers and living off the meager rentals. Lawson, Heirship: The Indian Amoeba, reprinted in Hearing on S. 2480 and S. 2663 before the Senate Select Committee on Indian Affairs, 98th Cong., 2d Sess., 82-83 (1984). The failure of the allotment program became even clearer as successive generations came to hold the allotted lands. Thus 40-, 80-, and 160-acre parcels became splintered into multiple undivided interests in land, with some parcels having hundreds and many parcels having dozens of owners. Because the land was held in trust and often could not be alienated or partitioned the fractionation problem grew and grew over time.

A 1928 report commissioned by the Congress found the situation administratively unworkable and economically wasteful. L. Meriam, Institute for Government Research, The Problem of Indian Administration 40-41. Good, potentially productive, land was allowed to lie fallow, amidst great poverty, because of the difficulties of managing property held in this manner. Hearings on H.R. 11113 before the Subcommittee on Indian Affairs of the House Committee on Interior and Insular Affairs, 89th Cong., 2d Sess., 10 (1966) (remarks of Rep. Aspinall). In discussing the Indian Reorganization Act of 1934, Representative Howard said:

> It is in the case of the inherited allotments, however, that the administrative costs become incredible. . . . On allotted reservations, numerous cases exist where the shares of each individual heir from lease money may be 1 cent a month. Or one heir may own minute fractional shares in 30 or 40 different allotments. The cost of leasing, bookkeeping, and distributing the proceeds in many cases far exceeds the total income. The Indians and the Indian Service personnel are thus trapped in a meaningless system of minute partition in which all thought of the possible use of land to satisfy human needs is lost in a mathematical haze of bookkeeping. 78 Cong. Rec. 11728 (1934) (remarks of Rep. Howard).

In 1934, in response to arguments such as these, the Congress acknowledged the failure of its policy and ended further allotment of Indian lands. Indian Reorganization Act of 1934, ch. 576, 48 Stat. 984, 25 U.S.C. §461 et seq.

But the end of future allotment by itself could not prevent the further compounding of the existing problem caused by the passage of time. Ownership continued to fragment as succeeding generations came to hold the property, since, in the order of things, each property owner was apt to have more than one heir. In 1960, both the House and the Senate undertook comprehensive studies of the problem. See House Committee on Interior and Insular Affairs, Indian Heirship Land Study, 86th Cong., 2d Sess. (Comm. Print 1961); Senate Committee on Interior and Insular Affairs, Indian Heirship Land Survey, 86th Cong., 2d Sess. (Comm. Print 1960–1961). These studies indicated that one-half of the approximately 12 million acres of allotted trust lands were held in fractionated ownership, with over 3 million acres held by more than six heirs to a parcel. Id., at pt.2, p. x. Further hearings were held in 1966, Hearings on H.R. 11113, supra, but not until the Indian land Consolidation Act of 1983 did the Congress take action to ameliorate the problem of fractionated ownership of Indian lands.

Section 207 of the Indian Land Consolidation Act — the escheat provision at issue in this case — provided:

> No undivided fractional interest in any tract of trust or restricted land within a tribe's reservation or otherwise subjected to a tribe's jurisdiction shall descendent [sic] by intestacy or devise but shall escheat to that tribe if such interest represents 2 per centum or less of the total acreage in such tract and has earned to its owner less than $100 in the preceding year before it is due to escheat. 96 Stat. 2519.

Congress made no provision for the payment of compensation to the owners of the interests covered by §207. The statute was signed into law on January 12, 1983, and became effective immediately.

The three appellees — Mary Irving, Patrick Pumpkin Seed, and Eileen Bissonette — are enrolled members of the Oglala Sioux Tribe. They are, or represent, heirs or devisees of members of the Tribe who died in March, April, and June 1983. Eileen Bissonette's decedent, Mary Poor Bear-Little Hoop Cross, purported to will all her property, including property subject to §207, to her five minor children in whose name Bissonette claims the property. Chester Irving, Charles Leroy Pumpkin Seed, and Edgar Pumpkin Seed all died intestate. At the time of their deaths, the four decedents owned 41 fractional interests subject to the provisions of §207. The Irving estate lost two interests whose value together was approximately $100; the Bureau of Indian Affairs placed total values of approximately $2,700 on the 26 escheatable interests in the Cross estate and $1,816 on the 13 escheatable interests in the Pumpkin Seed estates. But for §207, this property would have passed, in the ordinary course, to appellees or those they represent.

Appellees filed suit in the United States District Court for the District of South Dakota, claiming that §207 resulted in a taking of property without just compensation in violation of the Fifth Amendment. The District Court concluded that the statute was constitutional. It held that appellees had no vested interest in the property of the decedents prior to their deaths and that Congress had plenary authority to abolish the power of testamentary disposition of Indian property and to alter the rules of intestate succession.

The Court of Appeals for the Eighth Circuit reversed. Irving v. Clark, 758 F.2d 1260 (1985). Although it agreed that appellees had no vested rights in the decedents' property, it concluded that their decedents had a right, derived from the original Sioux allotment statute, to control disposition of their property at death. The Court of Appeals held that appellees had standing to invoke that right and that the taking of that right without compensation to decedents' estates violated the Fifth Amendment. . . .

II

The Court of Appeals concluded that appellees have standing to challenge §207. 758 F.2d, at 1267-1268. The Government does not contest this ruling. As the Court of Appeals recognized, however, the existence of a case or controversy is a jurisdictional prerequisite to a federal court's deliberations. Id., at 1267, n.12. We are satisfied that the necessary case or controversy exists in this case. Section 207 has deprived appellees of the fractional interests they otherwise would have inherited. This is sufficient injury-in-fact to satisfy Article III of the Constitution. See Singleton v. Wulff, 428 U.S. 106, 112 (1976).

III

The Congress, acting pursuant to its broad authority to regulate the descent and devise of Indian trust lands, Jefferson v. Fink, 247 U.S. 288, 294 (1918), enacted §207 as a means of ameliorating, over time, the problem of extreme fractionation of certain Indian lands. By forbidding the passing on at death of small, undivided interests in Indian lands, Congress hoped that future generations of Indians would be able to make more productive use of the Indians' ancestral lands. We agree with the Government that encouraging the consolidation of Indian lands is a public purpose of high order. The fractionation problem on Indian reservations is extraordinary and may call for dramatic action to encourage consolidation. The Sisseton-Wahpeton

Sioux Tribe, appearing as amicus curiae in support of the Secretary of the Interior is a quintessential victim of fractionation. Forty-acre tracts on the Sisseton-Wahpeton Lake Traverse Reservation, leasing for about $1,000 annually, are commonly subdivided into hundreds of undivided interests, many of which generate only pennies a year in rent. The average tract has 196 owners and the average owner undivided interests in 14 tracts. The administrative headache this represents can be fathomed by examining Tract 1305, dubbed "one of the most fractionated parcels of land in the world." Lawson, Heirship: The Indian Amoeba, reprinted in Hearing on S. 2480 and S. 2663 before the Senate Select Committee on Indian Affairs, 98th Cong., 2d Sess., 85 (1984). Tract 1305 is 40 acres and produces $1,080 in income annually. It is valued at $8,000. It has 439 owners, one-third of whom receive less than $.05 in annual rent and two-thirds of whom receive less than $1. The largest interest holder receives $82.85 annually. The common denominator used to compute fractional interests in the property is 3,394,923,840,000. The smallest heir receives $.01 every 177 years. If the tract were sold (assuming the 439 owners could agree) for its estimated $8,000 value, he would be entitled to $.000418. The administrative costs of handling this tract are estimated by the Bureau of Indian Affairs at $17,560 annually. Id., at 86, 87. See also Comment, Too Little Land, Too Many Heirs — The Indian Heirship Land Problem, 46 Wash. L. Rev. 709, 711-713 (1971).

This Court has held that the Government has considerable latitude in regulating property rights in ways that may adversely affect the owners. See Keystone Bituminous Coal Assn. v. DeBenedictis, 480 U.S. 470, 491-492 (1987); Penn Central Transportation Co. v. New York City, 438 U.S. 104, 125-127 (1978); Goldblatt v. Hempstead, 369 U.S. 590, 592-593 (1962). The framework for examining the question of whether a regulation of property amounts to a taking requiring just compensation is firmly established and has been regularly and recently reaffirmed. See, e.g., Keystone Bituminous Coal Assn. v. DeBenedictis, supra, at 485; Ruckelshaus v. Monsanto Co., 467 U.S. 986, 1004-1005 (1984); Hodel v. Virginia Surface Mining and Reclamation Assn., Inc., 452 U.S. 264, 295 (1981); Agins v. Tiburon, 447 U.S. 255, 260-261 (1980); Kaiser Aetna v. United States, 444 U.S. 164, 174-175 (1979); Penn Central Transportation Co. v. New York City, supra, at 124. As The Chief Justice has written:

> [T]his Court has generally "been unable to develop any 'set formula' for determining when 'justice and fairness' require that economic injuries caused by public action be compensated by the government, rather than remain disproportionately concentrated on a few persons." [Penn Central Transportation Co. v. New York City, 438 U.S.], at 124. Rather, it has examined the "taking" question by engaging in essentially ad hoc, factual

inquiries that have identified several factors — such as the economic impact of the regulation, its interference with reasonable investment backed expectations, and the character of the governmental action — that have particular significance. Ibid. Kaiser Aetna v. United States, supra, at 175.

There is no question that the relative economic impact of §207 upon the owners of these property rights can be substantial. Section 207 provides for the escheat of small undivided property interests that are unproductive during the year preceding the owner's death. Even if we accept the Government's assertion that the income generated by such parcels may be properly thought of as de minimis, their value may not be. While the Irving estate lost two interests whose value together was only approximately $100, the Bureau of Indian Affairs placed total values of approximately $2,700 and $1,816 on the escheatable interests in the Cross and Pumpkin Seed estates. These are not trivial sums. There are suggestions in the legislative history regarding the 1984 amendments to §207 that the failure to "look back" more than one year at the income generated by the property had caused the escheat of potentially valuable timber and mineral interests. S. Rep. No. 98-632, p.12 (1984); Hearing on H.J. Res. 158 before the Senate Select Committee on Indian Affairs, 98th Cong., 2d Sess., 20, 26, 32, 75 (1984); Amendments to the Indian Land Consolidation Act: Hearing on H.J. Res. 158 before the Senate Select Committee on Indian Affairs, 98th Cong., 1st Sess., 8, 29 (1983). Of course, the whole of appellees' decedents' property interests were not taken by §207. Appellees' decedents retained full beneficial use of the property during their lifetimes as well as the right to convey it inter vivos. There is no question, however, that the right to pass on valuable property to one's heirs is itself a valuable right. Depending on the age of the owner, much or most of the value of the parcel may inhere in this "remainder" interest. See 26 CFR §20.2031-7(f) (Table A) (1986) (value of remainder interest when life tenant is age 65 is approximately 32% of the whole).

The extent to which any of appellees' decedents had "investment-backed expectations" in passing on the property is dubious. Though it is conceivable that some of these interests were purchased with the expectation that the owners might pass on the remainder to their heirs at death, the property has been held in trust for the Indians for 100 years and is overwhelmingly acquired by gift, descent, or devise. Because of the highly fractionated ownership, the property is generally held for lease rather than improved and used by the owners. None of the appellees here can point to any specific investment-backed expectations beyond the fact that their ancestors agreed to accept allotment only after ceding to the United States large parts of the original Great Sioux Reservation.

Also weighing weakly in favor of the statute is the fact that there is something of an "average reciprocity of advantage," Pennsylvania Coal Co. v. Mahon, 260 U.S. 393, 415 (1922), to the extent that owners of escheatable interests maintain a nexus to the Tribe. Consolidation of Indian lands in the Tribe benefits the members of the Tribe. All members do not own escheatable interests, nor do all owners belong to the Tribe. Nevertheless, there is substantial overlap between the two groups. The owners of escheatable interests often benefit from the escheat of others' fractional interests. Moreover, the whole benefit gained is greater than the sum of the burdens imposed since consolidated lands are more productive than fractionated lands.

If we were to stop our analysis at this point, we might well find §207 constitutional. But the character of the Government regulation here is extraordinary. In Kaiser Aetna v. United States, supra, at 176, we emphasized that the regulation destroyed "one of the most essential sticks in the bundle of rights that are commonly characterized as property — the right to exclude others." Similarly, the regulation here amounts to virtually the abrogation of the right to pass on a certain type of property — the small undivided interest — to one's heirs. In one form or another, the right to pass on property — to one's family in particular — has been part of the Anglo-American legal system since feudal times. See United States v. Perkins, 163 U.S. 625, 627-628 (1896). The fact that it may be possible for the owners of these interests to effectively control disposition upon death through complex inter vivos transactions such as revocable trusts, is simply not an adequate substitute for the rights taken, given the nature of the property. Even the United States concedes that total abrogation of the right to pass property is unprecedented and likely unconstitutional. Moreover, this statute effectively abolishes both descent and devise of these property interests even when the passing of the property to the heir might result in consolidation of property — as for instance when the heir already owns another undivided interest in the property. Cf. 25 U.S.C. §2206(b) (1982 ed., Supp. III). Since the escheatable interests are not, as the United States argues, necessarily de minimis, nor, as it also argues, does the availability of inter vivos transfer obviate the need for descent and devise, a *total* abrogation of these rights cannot be upheld. But cf. Andrus v. Allard, 444 U.S. 51 (1979) (upholding abrogation of the right to sell endangered eagles' parts as necessary to environmental protection regulatory scheme).

In holding that complete abolition of both the descent and devise of a particular class of property may be a taking, we reaffirm the continuing vitality of the long line of cases recognizing the States', and where appropriate, the United States', broad authority to adjust the rules governing the descent and devise of property without implicating the guarantees of the Just Compensation Clause. See, e.g., Irving Trust

Co. v. Day, 314 U.S. 556, 562 (1942); Jefferson v. Fink, 247 U.S., at 294. The difference in this case is the fact that both descent and devise are completely abolished; indeed they are abolished even in circumstances when the governmental purpose sought to be advanced, consolidation of ownership of Indian lands, does not conflict with the further descent of the property.

There is little doubt that the extreme fractionation of Indian lands is a serious public problem. It may well be appropriate for the United States to ameliorate fractionation by means of regulating the descent and devise of Indian lands. Surely it is permissible for the United States to prevent the owners of such interests from further subdividing them among future heirs on pain of escheat. See Texaco, Inc. v. Short, 454 U.S. 516, 542 (1982) (Brennan, J., dissenting). It may be appropriate to minimize further compounding of the problem by abolishing the descent of such interests by rules of intestacy, thereby forcing the owners to formally designate an heir to prevent escheat to the Tribe. What is certainly not appropriate is to take the extraordinary step of abolishing both descent and devise of these property interests even when the passing of the property to the heir might result in consolidation of property. Accordingly, we find that this regulation, in the words of Justice Holmes, "goes too far." Pennsylvania Coal Co. v. Mahon, 260 U.S., at 415. The judgment of the Court of Appeals is Affirmed.[2]

NOTES AND QUESTIONS

1. Observe that almost all the controlling cases cited by Justice O'Connor involve governmental regulation of land use. Does abolishing descent or devise of fractional interests effect either physical invasion of private property (as in *Kaiser Aetna*) or interference with the possession or use of property (as in *Keystone, Penn Central,* and *Pennsylvania Coal*)? Why should tests that were designed to determine when compensation should be given for land use regulation be used when inheritance is regulated? A fundamental issue in the former area is whether the government is "forcing some people alone to bear public burdens which, in all fairness and justice, should be borne by the public as a whole." Armstrong v. United States, 364 U.S. 40, 49 (1960). Is this relevant to regulation of inheritance? See Michelman, Takings, 1987, 88 Colum. L. Rev. 1600, 1621-1625 (1988); Kmiec, The Original Understanding of the Taking Clause Is Neither Weak nor Obtuse, id. at 1630, 1662-1665.

2. Noted in 26 Am. Bus. L.J. 729; 88 Colum. L. Rev. 1581; 18 Envtl. L. 597.

In land use regulation cases the government's regulation devalues the property in the owner's hands. Does the prohibition against descent and devise in *Irving* devalue the property while in the owner's hands? How much? The court says, at page 10, "There is no question, however, that the right to pass on valuable property to one's heirs is itself a valuable right." But all the court cites as evidence of value is the value of a remainder interest, which is the value of the *right to receive*, not the value of the *right to transmit*.

With Hodel v. Irving, compare Andrus v. Allard, 444 U.S. 51 (1979), where the Court upheld, against a taking claim, the prohibition of the right to *sell or trade* artifacts made from eagle feathers and parts under the Bald Eagle Protection Act. The plaintiff Allard, an Indian, had legally killed the birds before the act took effect. The Court (per Brennan, J.) held that "where an owner possesses a full 'bundle' of property rights, the destruction of one 'strand' of the bundle is not a taking, because the aggregate must be viewed in its entirety." Since the right to donate or devise the artifacts remains, "the simple prohibition of the sale of lawfully acquired property . . . does not effect a taking in violation of the Fifth Amendment." Id. at 65-68.

In an omitted brief concurring opinion in Hodel v. Irving, Justice Scalia declared that *Allard* must be limited to its facts because the statutes in the two cases were in principle indistinguishable. A significant "strand" of property — conceptually severed — was rendered valueless in both cases. The Chief Justice and Justice Powell joined Justice Scalia's concurrence. Justice Brennan replied to Scalia in a brief concurrence. Brennan stated that *Irving* did not limit *Allard* to its facts. In *Irving,* he thought, "the unique negotiations giving rise to the property rights and expectations at issue here make this case the unusual one." Justices Marshall and Blackmun joined Brennan's concurrence.

2. If devise and descent of property generally were abolished, but inter vivos transfers permitted (as under the statute struck down in *Irving*), would the value of property decline? Or would people shift their property into other forms: transfer a remainder away, reserving a life estate and general power of appointment; transfer into a joint tenancy; establish a revocable trust; put a payable-on-death beneficiary on a deed or contract? (These other forms of ownership, which avoid probate, will be dealt with in later chapters in this book.) And would they consume more, rather than save, and spend more on the education of their children, thus creating human capital in the next generation? For a stimulating discussion, see S. Munzer, A Theory of Property 380-418 (1990).

3. In many societies wills are not permitted. With respect to Indian tribal lands, for example, wills were unknown until Congress forced individual allotments on the Indians. Even then, before 1910, Indian allottees were not permitted to devise their lands. Under Moslem law,

Moslems generally may not make wills disinheriting their children. They may only give directions relating to administration of the estate or management of property inherited by their children. 2 Manual of German Law 109 (B. Cohn ed. 1971).

In Anglo-American history, the right to devise property has always been in uneasy tension with forced succession. As Friedman, The Law of the Living, The Law of the Dead: Property, Succession, and Society, 1966 Wis. L. Rev. 1, 14 (1966), observes, "Practically speaking, forced succession means succession within the family — to the wife, children and other dependents. Forced succession . . . converts private property at death to family property." In early feudal times forced succession had the upper hand. Prior to 1540, when the Statute of Wills was enacted, a will of land was not permitted at law in England (though by the time of Henry VIII, chancery had developed a way to bypass forced primogeniture, infra page 436). Land owned at death passed to the eldest son, subject to the surviving spouse's dower or curtesy. In the United States, married women could not devise land without the consent of their husbands until the enactment of Married Women's Property Acts in the late nineteenth century. By the twentieth century, forced succession reappeared when statutes were enacted giving the surviving spouse a forced share of one-third or one-half of the decedent's estate, which the surviving spouse may not be deprived of by the decedent spouse's will. In Louisiana, where the civil law of France was introduced, minor or handicapped children may not be disinherited. (On protection of spouse and children, see Chapter 6, infra.)

Under Uniform Probate Code §2-402, the surviving spouse or children of the decedent are entitled to $3,500 worth of household goods and personal effects, or to these chattels and the difference in cash if the value of these chattels is less then $3,500. The decedent cannot destroy this right by bequeathing the chattels to another. In any state enacting this Uniform Probate Code provision, is this provision an unconstitutional taking of a right to devise chattels? How does it differ from what Congress did in Hodel v. Irving? Is forced succession by a tribe constitutionally permissible? See, generally, Kornstein, Inheritance: A Constitutional Right?, 36 Rutgers L. Rev. 741 (1984).

4. Suppose that Congress, recognizing that allotment of Indian lands to individual Indians has been a failure, decides to reestablish tribal ownership. To this end, it enacts a statute prohibiting inter vivos transfer of allotments and providing for escheat to the tribe of each allotment upon the death of the present tribal owner. Would this be a taking? See Choate v. Trapp, 224 U.S. 665, 674 (1912). Is there any way to change back to tribal ownership without paying individuals for their allotted lands? Is there any way to get the genie back in the bottle?

> They asked us to divide the land,
>   to divide our mother
> upon whose bosom we had been born,
> upon whose lap we had been reared.

Nez Perce chief, explaining why his tribe warred with the white man, as related by Senator Teller in 1881. H.R. Rep. No. 1576, 46th Cong., 2d Sess., 11 Cong. Rec. 781-782 (1881).

> As long as Indians live in villages they will retain many of their old and injurious habits. Frequent feasts, community in food, heathen ceremonies, and dances, constant visiting — these will continue as long as the people live together in close neighborhoods and villages.

Agent for the Yankton Sioux, writing in 1877, Reports of the Commissioner of Indian Affairs 75, 76 (1877), reprinted in F. Cohen, Handbook of Federal Indian Law 208 (1986 reprint).

Both quotations above were found in Note, Hodel v. Irving, 18 Envtl. L. 597, 598, 607 n.48 (1988).

5. *Inheritance in the Soviet Union.* In 1918 the Soviet Bolsheviks, carrying out the teaching of Marx and Engels, abolished inheritance. The 1918 law, translated into English, read: "Inheritance, testate and intestate, is abolished. Upon the death of the owner his property (movable and immovable) becomes the property of the R.S.F.S.R." [1918] 1 Sob. Uzak., RSFSR, No. 34, item 456, Apr. 26, 1918. Within four years, however, inheritance was reestablished. The abolition of inheritance proved unpopular, and the Soviet rulers, on second thought, decided it was an institution encouraging savings and an incentive to work. Inheritance was also viewed as a method of providing for dependents of the deceased, relieving the state of this burden, and of furthering family unity and stability. Today the Soviet law of inheritance does not substantially differ from the civil law of inheritance found in western Europe. Similarly, the Chinese inheritance system differs little from those in effect in civil law countries. See Foster-Simons, The Development of Inheritance Law in the Soviet Union and the People's Republic of China, 32 Am. J. Comp. Law 33 (1985); Comment, Soviet Inheritance Law: Ideological Consistency or a Retreat to the West?, 23 Gonz. L. Rev. 593 (1988).

6. For further reading on the changing institution of inheritance in this country, from its earliest days to the present, see C. Shammas, M. Salmon & M. Dahlin, Inheritance in America from Colonial Times to the Present (1987); T. Shaffer, Death, Property and Lawyers (1970); M. Sussman, J. Cates & D. Smith, The Family and Inheritance (1970); Langbein, The Twentieth-Century Revolution in Family Wealth Transmission, 86 Mich. L. Rev. 722 (1988).

J. BENTHAM, THE THEORY OF LEGISLATION 184 (C. Ogden ed. 1950): "[W]hen we recollect the infirmities of old age, we must be satisfied that it is necessary not to deprive it of this counterpoise of factitious attractions [prospects of inheritance]. In the rapid descent of life, every support on which man can lean should be left untouched, and it is well that interest serve as monitor to duty."

Halbach, An Introduction to Death, Taxes and Family Property
Death, Taxes and Family Property 3, 5-7 (E. Halbach ed. 1977)*

Many arguments are offered in support of the institution of inheritance. One is simply that, in a society based on private property, it may be the least objectionable arrangement for dealing with property on the owner's death.

Another is that inheritance is natural and proper as both an expression and a reinforcement of family ties, which in turn are important to a healthy society and a good life. After all, a society should be concerned with the total amount of happiness it can offer, and to many of its members it is a great comfort and satisfaction to know during life that, even after death, those whom one cares about can be provided for and may be able to enjoy better lives because of the inheritance that can be left to them. Furthermore, it is argued, giving and bequeathing not only express but beget affection, or at least responsibility. Thus, society is seen as offering a better and happier life by responding to the understandable desire of an individual to provide for his or her family after death.

Just as individuals may be rewarded through this desire, it can also be used by society, via inheritance rights, to serve as an incentive to bring forth creativity, hard work, initiative and ultimately productivity that benefits others, as well as encouraging individual responsibility — encouraging those who can to make provision that society would otherwise have to make for those who are or may be dependents. Of course, some doubt the need for such incentives, at least beyond modest levels of achievement and wealth accumulation, relying on the quest for power (or for recognition) and other motivations — not to mention habit. Long after these forces have taken over to stimulate the industry of such individuals, however, society may continue to find it important to offer property inducements to the irrepressibly productive to save rather than to consume, and to go on saving long after their own lifelong future needs are provided for. And what harm is there if

---

individuals, through socially approved channels, pursue immortality and psychological satisfactions? The direct and indirect (e.g., through life insurance and through corporate accumulations) savings of individuals are vital to the economy's capital base and thus to its level of employment and to the productivity of other individuals.

Consequently, it is concluded, inheritance may grant wealth to *donees* without regard to their competence and performance, but the economic reasons for allowing inheritance are viewed in terms of proper rewards and socially valuable incentives to the *donor*. In fact, some philosophers would insist, these rewards are required by ideals of social justice as the fruits of one's labors.

Still another argument is made to justify inheritance, at least inheritance by immediate family members, and even to justify (at the risk of a two-edged sword) a certain amount of freedom of testation. This is the idea that other individuals will normally have contributed to the wealth accumulated and held by the property owner or owners within the family unit. Support at home and help on the job, reinforced by a happy life in union with an understanding and loving family (and maybe other relatives and even friends), are the essence of this argument. In combination with other rationales for inheritance and testation, this argument is not seriously undermined by the difficulty — and, in fact, the undesirability (at least for others than a spouse) — of attempting to sort out the contributions and thus alleged entitlements of various individuals.

Ultimately, it is not at all easy to weigh against these and other claimed justifications the charges of unjustified inequalities of means and power, and of associated societal divisiveness and conflict. The charges extend to include economic inefficiencies that may result from allowing wealth to be allocated by the chance and caprice of inheritance, especially where testamentary freedom permits broad, long-term and potentially intrusive use of trusts.

The most powerful argument against permitting transmission of wealth is that the transfer of great fortunes perpetuates wide disparities in the distribution of wealth, rigid class distinctions, and the concentration of economic power in the hands of a few. It also tends not to reward merit and productivity of the recipients but the chance of fortunate birth. See J. Brittain, Inheritance and the Inequality of Material Wealth (1978); R. Chester, Inheritance, Wealth and Society (1982); L. Thurow, Generating Inequality: Mechanisms of Distribution in the U.S. Economy (1975). In the United States this argument has found a receptive ear in Congress, which, for over half a century, has imposed estate and gift taxes on the rich. Under current law, these taxes are imposed on individuals transferring property worth $600,000 or more, with rates varying from 37 percent to 55 percent. Federal estate, gift, and generation-skipping taxes are dealt with in Chapter 13 of this book.

Even though inequality may result from inherited wealth, inequality may also result from the creation of human capital in children. The following excerpt makes this point brilliantly and raises the following question: If economic inheritance were abolished, would it be even more difficult to break up an upper class?

Blum & Kalven, The Uneasy Case for Progressive Taxation
19 U. Chi. L. Rev. 417, 501-504 (1952)

There is still another road leading to the problem of equality. Almost everybody professes to be in favor of one kind of equality — equality of opportunity. What remains to be investigated is the relationship between this kind of equality and economic equality. . . . In terms of the justice of rewards, the point is that no race can be fair unless the contestants start from the same mark. . . .

It might simplify matters somewhat to go directly to the heart of the problem — the children. . . . The important inequalities of opportunity are inequalities of environment, in its broadest sense, for the children. It is the inequalities in the worlds which the children inherit which count, and this inheritance is both economic and cultural.

. . . The critical economic inheritance consists of the day to day expenditures on the children; it is these expenditures which add up to money investments in the children's health, education and welfare which in the aggregate are, at least in our society, gravely disparate. No progressive inheritance tax, or combination of gift and inheritance taxes, can touch this source of economic inequalities among children. On the other hand a progressive income tax can, as one of its effects, help to minimize this form of unequal inheritance. It is income, not wealth, which is the important operative factor here, and by bringing incomes closer together the tax tends to bring money investments in children closer together.

But the gravest source of inequality of opportunity in our society is not economic but rather what is called cultural inheritance for lack of a better term. Under modern conditions the opportunities for formal education, healthful diet and medical attention to some extent can be equalized by economic means without too greatly disrupting the family. However, it still remains true that even today much of the transmission of culture, in the narrow sense, occurs through the family, and no system of public education and training can completely neutralize this form of inheritance. Here it is the economic investment in the parents

"Having a fine old name really has been enough for me."

and the grandparents, irrevocably in the past, which produces differential opportunities for the children. Nor is this the end of the matter. It has long been recognized that the parents make the children in their own image, and modern psychology has served to underscore how early this process begins to operate and how decisive it may be. The more subtle and profound influences upon the child resulting from love, integrity and family morale form a kind of inheritance which cannot, at least for those above the minimum subsistence level, be significantly affected by economic measures, or possibly by any others. If these influences on the members of the next generation are to be equalized, nothing short of major changes in the institution of the family can possibly suffice. At a minimum such changes would include socializing decisions not only about how children are to be raised but who is to raise them. And this in turn would call into question the very having of children.

———

During life, a person can use his wealth to influence the conduct of another person. To what extent should a person be able to use wealth to influence behavior after death? Hobhouse wrote over 100 years ago, in condemning the "cold and numbing influence of the Dead Hand,"

A clear, obvious, natural line is drawn for us between those persons and events which the Settlor knows and sees, and those which he cannot know and see. Within the former province we may push his natural affections and his capacity of judgment to make better dispositions than any external Law is likely to make for him. Within the latter, natural affection does not extend, and the wisest judgment is constantly baffled by the course of events. . . . What I consider to be not conjectural, but proved by experience in all human affairs, is, that people are the best judges of their own concerns; or if they are not, that it is better for them, on moral grounds, that they should manage their own concerns for themselves, and that it cannot be wrong continually to claim this liberty for every Generation of mortal men. [A. Hobhouse, The Dead Hand 188, 183-185 (1880).]

The following case introduces you to the power of the dead hand and its limitations. The limitations society places — or ought to place — on the dead hand will be a recurring theme in this book.

Shapira v. Union National Bank

Ohio Court of Common Pleas, Mahoning County, 1974
39 Ohio Misc. 28, 315 N.E.2d 825

HENDERSON, J.   This is an action for a declaratory judgment and the construction of the will of David Shapira, M.D., who died April 13, 1973, a resident of this county. By agreement of the parties, the case has been submitted upon the pleadings and the exhibit.

The portions of the will in controversy are as follows:

Item VIII.   All the rest, residue and remainder of my estate, real and personal, of every kind and description and wheresoever situated, which I may own or have the right to dispose of at the time of my decease, I give, devise and bequeath to my three (3) beloved children, to wit: Ruth Shapira Aharoni, of Tel Aviv, Israel, or wherever she may reside at the time of my death; to my son Daniel Jacob Shapira, and to my son Mark Benjamin Simon Shapira in equal shares, with the following qualifications: . . .

(b)   My son Daniel Jacob Shapira should receive his share of the bequest only, if he is married at the time of my death to a Jewish girl whose both parents were Jewish. In the event that at the time of my death he is not married to a Jewish girl whose both parents were Jewish, then his share of this bequest should be kept by my executor for a period of not longer than seven (7) years and if my said son Daniel Jacob gets married within the seven year period to a Jewish girl whose both parents were Jewish, my executor is hereby instructed to turn over his share of my bequest to him. In the event, however, that my said son Daniel Jacob is unmarried within the seven (7) years after my death to a Jewish girl whose both parents were Jewish, or if he is married to a non Jewish girl, then his share of my estate, as provided in item 8 above should go to The State of Israel, absolutely.

The provision for the testator's other son Mark, is conditioned substantially similarly. Daniel Jacob Shapira, the plaintiff, alleges that the condition upon his inheritance is unconstitutional, contrary to public policy and unenforceable because of its unreasonableness, and that he should be given his bequest free of the restriction. Daniel is 21 years of age, unmarried and a student at Youngstown State University.

CONSTITUTIONALITY

Plaintiff's argument that the condition in question violates constitutional safeguards is based upon the premise that the right to marry is protected by the Fourteenth Amendment to the Constitution of the United States. Meyer v. Nebraska (1923), 262 U.S. 390; Skinner v. Oklahoma (1942), 316 U.S. 535; Loving v. Virginia (1967), 388 U.S. 1. In Meyer v. Nebraska, holding unconstitutional a state statute prohibiting the teaching of languages other than English, the court stated that the Fourteenth Amendment denotes the right to marry among other basic rights. In Skinner v. Oklahoma, holding unconstitutional a state statute providing for the sterilization of certain habitual criminals, the court stated that marriage and procreation are fundamental to the very existence and survival of the race. In Loving v. Virginia, the court held unconstitutional as violative of the Equal Protection and Due Process Clauses of the Fourteenth Amendment an antimiscegenation statute under which a black person and a white person were convicted for marrying. In its opinion the United States Supreme Court made the following statements, 388 U.S. at page 12.

"There can be no doubt that restricting the freedom to marry solely because of racial classifications violates the central meaning of the Equal Protection Clause.

". . . The freedom to marry has long been recognized as one of the vital personal rights essential to the orderly pursuit of happiness by free men.

"Marriage is one of the 'basic civil rights of man,' fundamental to our very existence and survival. . . . The Fourteenth Amendment requires that the freedom of choice to marry not be restricted by invidious racial discriminations. Under our Constitution, the freedom to marry, or not marry, a person of another race resides with the individual and cannot be infringed by the State."

From the foregoing, it appears clear, as plaintiff contends, that the right to marry is constitutionally protected from restrictive state legislative action. Plaintiff submits, then, that under the doctrine of Shelley

v. Kraemer (1948), 334 U.S. 1, the constitutional protection of the
Fourteenth Amendment is extended from direct state legislative action
to the enforcement by state judicial proceedings of private provisions
restricting the right to marry. Plaintiff contends that a judgment of this
court upholding the condition restricting marriage would, under Shelley
v. Kraemer, constitute state action prohibited by the Fourteenth Amendment as much as a state statute.

In Shelley v. Kraemer the United States Supreme Court held that
the action of the states to which the Fourteenth Amendment has
reference includes action of state courts and state judicial officials. Prior
to this decision the court had invalidated city ordinances which denied
blacks the right to live in white neighborhoods. In Shelley v. Kraemer
owners of neighboring properties sought to enjoin blacks from occupying properties which they had bought, but which were subjected to
privately executed restrictions against use or occupation by any persons
except those of the Caucasian race. Chief Justice Vinson noted, in the
course of his opinion at page 13: "These are cases in which the purposes
of the agreements were secured only by judicial enforcement by state
courts of the restrictive terms of the agreements."

In the case at bar, this court is not being asked to enforce any
restriction upon Daniel Jacob Shapira's constitutional right to marry.
Rather, this court is being asked to enforce the testator's restriction
upon his son's inheritance. If the facts and circumstances of this case
were such that the aid of this court were sought to enjoin Daniel's
marrying a non-Jewish girl, then the doctine of Shelley v. Kraemer
would be applicable, but not, it is believed, upon the facts as they are.

Counsel for plaintiff asserts, however, that his position with respect
to the applicability of Shelley v. Kraemer to this case is fortified by two
later decisions of the United States Supreme Court: Evans v. Newton
(1966), 382 U.S. 296, and Pennsylvania v. Board of Directors of City
Trusts of the City of Philadelphia (1957), 353 U.S. 230.

Evans v. Newton involved land willed in trust to the mayor and city
council of Macon, Georgia, as a park for white people only, and to be
controlled by a white board of managers. To avoid the city's having to
enforce racial segregation in the park, the city officials resigned as
trustees and private individuals were installed. The court held that such
successor trustees, even though private individuals, became agencies or
instrumentalities of the state and subject to the Fourteenth Amendment
by reason of their exercising powers or carrying on functions governmental in nature. The following comment of Justice Douglas seems
revealing: "If a testator wanted to leave a school or center for the use
of one race only and in no way implicated the State in the supervision,
control, or management of that facility, we assume arguendo that no
constitutional difficulty would be encountered." 382 U.S. 300.

The case of Pennsylvania v. Board, as the full title, above, suggests, is a case in which money was left by will to the city of Philadelphia in trust for a college to admit poor white male orphans. The court held that the board which operated the college was an agency of the state of Pennsylvania, and that, therefore, its refusal to admit the plaintiffs because they were negroes was discrimination by the state forbidden by the Fourteenth Amendment.

So, in neither Evans v. Newton nor Pennsylvania v. Board was the doctrine of the earlier Shelley v. Kraemer applied or extended. Both of them involved restrictive actions by state governing agencies, in one case with respect to a park, in the other case with respect to a college. Although both the park and the college were founded upon testamentary gifts, the state action struck down by the court was not the judicial completion of the gifts, but rather the subsequent enforcement of the racial restrictions by the public management.

Basically, the right to receive property by will is a creature of the law, and is not a natural right or one guaranteed or protected by either the Ohio or the United States constitution. . . . It is a fundamental rule of law in Ohio that a testator may legally entirely disinherit his children. . . . This would seem to demonstrate that, from a constitutional standpoint, a testator may restrict a child's inheritance. The court concludes, therefore, that the upholding and enforcement of the provisions of Dr. Shapira's will conditioning the bequests to his sons upon their marrying Jewish girls does not offend the Constitution of Ohio or of the United States. United States National Bank of Portland v. Snodgrass (1954), 202 Or. 530, 275 P.2d 860, 50 A.L.R.2d 725; Gordon v. Gordon (1955), 332 Mass. 197, 124 N.E.2d 228; 54 Mich. L. Rev. 297 (1955); cf. 39 Minn. L. Rev. 809 (1955).

PUBLIC POLICY

The condition that Daniel's share should be "turned over to him if he should marry a Jewish girl whose both parents were Jewish" constitutes a partial restraint upon marriage. If the condition were that the beneficiary not marry anyone, the restraint would be general or total, and, at least in the case of a first marriage, would be held to be contrary to public policy and void. A partial restraint of marriage which imposes only reasonable restrictions is valid, and not contrary to public policy: . . . The great weight of authority in the United States is that gifts conditioned upon the beneficiary's marrying within a particular religious class or faith are reasonable. . . .

Plaintiff contends, however, that in Ohio a condition such as the one in this case is void as against the public policy of this state. . . . Plaintiff's position that the free choice of religious practice cannot be circumscribed or controlled by contract is substantiated by Hackett v. Hackett (C.A. Lucas 1958), 78 Ohio Law Abs. 485, 150 N.E.2d 431. This case held that a covenant in a separation agreement, incorporated in a divorce decree, that the mother would rear a daughter in the Roman Catholic faith was unenforceable. However, the controversial condition in the case at bar is a partial restraint upon marriage and not a covenant to restrain the freedom of religious practice; and, of course, this court is not being asked to hold the plaintiff in contempt for failing to marry a Jewish girl of Jewish parentage. . . .

It is noted, furthermore, in this connection, that the courts of Pennsylvania distinguish between testamentary gifts conditioned upon the religious faith of the beneficiary and those conditioned upon marriage to persons of a particular religious faith. In In re Clayton's Estate (1930), 13 Pa. D. & C. 413, the court upheld a gift of a life estate conditioned upon the beneficiary's not marrying a woman of the Catholic faith. In its opinion the court distinguishes the earlier case of Drace v. Klinedinst (1922), 275 Pa. 266, 118 A. 907, in which a life estate willed to grandchildren, provided they remained faithful to a particular religion, was held to violate the public policy of Pennsylvania.[3] In *Clayton's Estate,* the court said that the condition concerning marriage did not affect the faith of the beneficiary, and that the condition, operating only on the choice of a wife, was <u>too remote to be regarded as coercive of religious faith</u>. . . .

The only cases cited by plaintiff's counsel in accord with [plaintiff's contention] are some English cases and one American decision. In England the courts have held that partial restrictions upon marriage to persons not of the Jewish faith, or of Jewish parentage, were not contrary to public policy or invalid. Hodgson v. Halford (1879 Eng.) L.R. 11 Ch. Div. 959, 50 A.L.R.2d 742. Other cases in England, however, have invalidated forfeitures of similarly conditioned provisions for children upon the basis of uncertainty or indefiniteness. . . . Since the foregoing decisions, a later English case has upheld a condition precedent that a granddaughter-beneficiary marry a person of Jewish faith and the child of Jewish parents. The court distinguished the cases cited above as not applicable to a condition precedent under which the legatee must qualify for the gift by marrying as specified, and there were found

---

3. In In re Estate of Laning, 462 Pa. 157, 339 A.2d 520 (1975), the court stated that the *Drace* case was correctly decided on the ground that the testator sought to require his grandchildren to "remain true" to the Catholic religion, and that the enforcement of a condition that they remain faithful Catholics would require the court to determine the doctrines of the Catholic church. "Such questions are clearly improper for a civil court to determine." The court went on to uphold a provision in Laning's will that the gift be distributed to certain relatives who held "membership in good standing" in the Presbyterian church; the court construed the provision to mean only a formal affiliation with the specified church, thus avoiding improper inquiry into church doctrine.

Restatement (Second) of Property, Donative Transfers §8.1 (1983), says that a provision calling for forfeiture of property if the transferee fails to adhere to certain religious beliefs is valid. — Eds.

to be no difficulty with indefiniteness where the legatee married unquestionably outside the Jewish faith. Re Wolffe, [1953] 1 Week. L.R. 1211, [1953] 2 All Eng. 697, 50 A.L.R.2d 747.[4]

The American case cited by plaintiff is that of Maddox v. Maddox (1854), 52 Va. (11 Grattan's) 804. The testator in this case willed a remainder to his niece if she remain a member of the Society of Friends. When the niece arrived at a marriageable age there were but five or six unmarried men of the society in the neighborhood in which she lived. She married a non-member and thus lost her own membership. The court held the condition to be an unreasonable restraint upon marriage and void, and that there being no gift over upon breach of the condition, the condition was in terrorem, and did not avoid the bequest. It can be seen that while the court considered the testamentary condition to be a restraint upon marriage, it was primarily one in restraint of religious faith. The court said that with the small number of eligible bachelors in the area the condition would have operated as a virtual prohibition of the niece's marrying, and that she could not be expected to "go abroad" in search of a helpmate or to be subjected to the chance of being sought after by a stranger. . . . The other ground upon which the Virginia court rested its decision, that the condition was in terrorem because of the absence of a gift over, is clearly not applicable to the case at bar, even if it were in accord with Ohio law, because of the gift over to the State of Israel contained in the Shapira will.

In arguing for the applicability of the Maddox v. Maddox test of reasonableness to the case at bar, counsel for the plaintiff asserts that the number of eligible Jewish females in this county would be an extremely small minority of the total population especially as compared with the comparatively much greater number in New York, whence have come many of the cases comprising the weight of authority upholding the validity of such clauses. There are no census figures in

4. The most recent English case is In re Tuck's Settlement Trusts, [1977] 2 W.L.R. 411. In this case a trust was set up by the first Baron Tuck, a Jew, for the benefit of his successors in the baronetcy. Anxious to ensure that his successors be Jewish, he provided for payment of income to the baronet for the time being if and when and as long as he should be of the Jewish faith and married to a wife of Jewish blood and of the Jewish faith. The trust also provided that in case of any dispute the decision of the Chief Rabbi of London would be conclusive. The court held that the conditions were not void for uncertainty. Lord Denning was of the view that if there was any uncertainty, it was cured by the Chief Rabbi clause. The other two judges declined to reach that issue. Determining who is Jewish has provoked continuing controversy in Israel. See Note, Who Is a Jew? A Determination of Ethnic Status for Purposes of the Israeli Population Registry Act, 10 Colum. J. Transnatl. L. 133 (1971).

See generally Butt, Testamentary Conditions in Restraint of Religion, 8 Sydney L. Rev. 400 (1977); Nevins, Testamentary Conditions: The Principle of Uncertainty and Religion, 18 St. Louis U.L.J. 563 (1974). — Eds.

evidence. While this court could probably take judicial notice of the fact that the Jewish community is a minor, though important segment of our total local population, nevertheless the court is by no means justified in judicial knowledge that there is an insufficient number of eligible young ladies of Jewish parentage in this area from which Daniel would have a reasonable latitude of choice. And of course, Daniel is not at all confined in his choice to residents of this county, which is a very different circumstance in this day of travel by plane and freeway and communication by telephone, from the horse and buggy days of the 1854 Maddox v. Maddox decision. Consequently, the decision does not appear to be an appropriate yardstick of reasonableness under modern living conditions.

Plaintiff's counsel contends that the Shapira will falls within the principle of Fineman v. Central National Bank (1961), 87 Ohio Law Abs. 236, 175 N.E.2d 837, 18 O.O.2d 33, holding that the public policy of Ohio does not countenance a bequest or device conditioned on the beneficiary's obtaining a separation or divorce from his wife. Counsel argues that the Shapira condition would encourage the beneficiary to marry a qualified girl just to receive the bequest, and then to divorce her afterward. This possibility seems too remote to be a pertinent application of the policy against bequests conditioned upon divorce. . . . Indeed, in measuring the reasonableness of the condition in question, both the father and the court should be able to assume that the son's motive would be proper. And surely the son should not gain the advantage of the avoidance of the condition by the possibility of his own impropriety.

Finally, counsel urges that the Shapira condition <u>tends to pressure</u> <u>Daniel, by the reward of money</u>, to marry within seven years without opportunity for mature reflection, and jeopardizes his college education. It seems to the court, on the contrary, that the seven year time limit would be a most reasonable grace period, and one which would give the son ample opportunity for exhaustive reflection and fulfillment of the condition without constraint or oppression. Daniel is no more being "blackmailed into a marriage by immediate financial gain," as suggested by counsel, than would be the beneficiary of a living gift or conveyance upon consideration of a future marriage — an arrangement which has long been sanctioned by the courts of this state. Thompson v. Thompson (1867), 17 Ohio St. 649.

In the opinion of this court, the provision made by the testator for the benefit of the State of Israel upon breach or failure of the condition is most significant for two reasons. First, it distinguishes this case from the bare forfeitures in . . . Maddox v. Maddox (including the technical in terrorem objection), and, in a way, from the vagueness and indefiniteness doctrine of some of the English cases. Second, and of greater importance, it demonstrates the depth of the testator's conviction. His purpose was not merely a negative one designed to punish his son for not carrying out his wishes. His unmistakable testamentary plan was that his possessions be used to encourage the preservation of the Jewish faith and blood, hopefully through his sons, but, if not, then through the State of Israel. Whether this judgment was wise is not for this court to determine. But it is the duty of this court to honor the testator's intention within the limitations of law and of public policy. The prerogative granted to a testator by the laws of this state to dispose of his estate according to his conscience is entitled to as much judicial protection and enforcement as the prerogative of a beneficiary to receive an inheritance.

It is the conclusion of this court that public policy should not, and does not preclude the fulfillment of Dr. Shapira's purpose, and that in accordance with the weight of authority in this country, the conditions contained in his will are reasonable restrictions upon marriage, and valid.

NOTES AND QUESTIONS

1. What social objectives are accomplished by honoring control of a beneficiary's behavior by the dead hand, a hand that does not have a live mind controlling it and making a continuously informed, intelligent judgment as circumstances change, that can no longer be affected by the opinions of mankind, and that does not suffer the consequences? See R. Posner, Economic Analysis of Law §18.5 (3d ed. 1986); Browder, Conditions and Limitations in Restraint of Marriage, 39 Mich. L. Rev. 1288 (1941).

2. Restatement (Second) of Property, Donative Transfers §6.2 (1983), provides that a restraint to induce the transferee to marry within a designated religious faith, or to refrain from marrying a person of such faith, is valid "if, and only if, under the circumstances, the restraint does not unreasonably limit the transferee's opportunity to marry. If the restriction is invalid, the donative transfer takes effect as though the restriction had not been imposed." Comment a provides that, "The restraint unreasonably limits the transferee's opportunity to marry if a marriage permitted by the restraint is not likely to occur. The likelihood of marriage is a factual question, to be answered from the circumstances of the particular case." Comment c goes on to say that whether or not the transferee is unreasonably limited "frequently depends upon the type and strength of the religious beliefs of the transferee. If marriage within the permitted sphere would be so contrary to those beliefs that it is unlikely that such marriage will ever occur, the restraint is . . . invalid." The Restatement gives an illustration:

    3. *O*, by an otherwise effective will, bequeaths $100,000 to *T* in trust to pay the income thereof "to my son *S* for life, provided that, if he ever marries a person not of the Catholic faith at the time of the marriage, then said income is to be paid to my daughter *D* for her life." *S* is a Protestant and his strong religious beliefs would most likely prevent him from marrying a person who did not share such beliefs. This fact makes it highly unlikely that he would marry any person of the Catholic faith. The restraint is invalid, and *S*'s income interest under the trust will not end if he marries a person who is not of the Catholic faith.

Under the Restatement (Second) of Property, motive or purpose apparently is irrelevant where the testator is forbidding a particular marriage; the factual likelihood of the permitted marriage is controlling.[5] Should motive be relevant?

    3.   Provisions encouraging separation or divorce have usually been held invalid, unless the dominant motive of the testator is to provide support in the event of separation or divorce. See Restatement (Second) of Property, supra note 2, §7.1.

Conditions not directly related to divorce have sometimes been held invalid as tending to disrupt the family unit. In Holmes v. Connecticut Trust & Safe Deposit Co., 92 Conn. 507, 103 A. 640 (1918), the testator devised property in trust for his two granddaughters, provided that the granddaughters and their husbands abstain from the use of tobacco and intoxicating beverages. The court held that, as applied to the husbands, the condition was invalid on the grounds that the beneficiaries would be penalized by conduct out of their control and that the husbands, by threatening to smoke or take a drink of liquor, could so intimidate their wives as to cause marital discord and, possibly, divorce. The court saw no reason to invalidate the condition as it applied to the granddaughters' conduct. Hence, the granddaughters could not smoke or drink (and keep their trust income) but their husbands could!

In Girard Trust Co. v. Schmitz, 129 N.J. Eq. 444, 20 A.2d 21 (1941), the court held invalid a condition that the testator's brothers and sisters must not communicate, either orally or in writing, with a brother and sister disliked by the testator. The court said it would not "lend its hand to help the testator use the power of his wealth to disrupt this family. . . . [S]ociety condemns all acts, be they contractual or testamentary, which tend to disturb the peace and harmony of families and to make inharmonious that which the state is interested in creating and preserving. 'As are families, so is society,'" Id. at 471, 20 A.2d at 37.

---

5. Comment b to Restatement §6.2 provides that a restraint excluding a particular named person as the spouse of the transferee ("to *A*, but if *A* marries *B*, to *C*") is subject to the same probability test. If *A* was engaged to marry *B* at the time the restraint was imposed, the restraint is invalid since a marriage permitted by the restraint is not likely to occur.

Provisions requiring a beneficiary to change his name have usually been upheld, unless the dominant purpose is to separate the beneficiary from his family. Thus a provision that a beneficiary change his name from his adoptive father to that of his natural father would probably be held void. See Restatement (Second) of Property, supra note 2, §7.2, Reporter's Notes 5 & 6.

4. Compare restraints relating to marriage and disruption of the family with restraints relating to personal habits or requiring the transferee to pursue a particular education. With practically no hesitation or fretting over public policy, courts have upheld the latter. However, cases involving restraints of these types often have at issue the question of whether the beneficiary has satisfied the condition. In Keating v. Keating, 182 Iowa 1056, 165 N.W. 74 (1917), for example, the testator left a farm to his eldest child, a lawyer, in trust for the testator's youngest child Charles, to be turned over to Charles should "he prove to be a careful and prudent man." Twenty years after the testator's death, Charles, over 40 years old, married, and practicing osteopathy, sued for the farm, alleging he was a careful and prudent person. The trustee defended that Charles was "not mentally right" because of his practice of masturbation "that had commenced when he was about 10 years of age, and also through the past years." Agreeing that masturbation was a "vicious and degrading habit," the court nonetheless generously held that "self-abuse" alone would afford no justification for refusing to convey the trust property to Charles.

SECTION C.   THE PROBATE PROCESS

1. Introduction and Terminology

Though the general pattern of administering decedents' estates is quite similar in all jurisdictions, there are widespread variations in the procedural details. In each state the procedure is governed by a collection of statutes and court rules giving meticulous instructions for each step in the process. Happily, this precludes our being concerned about specific rules and procedures and enables us to advise you that you can safely postpone any concern about the mechanics of probating a will and administering an estate until you can "learn by doing" when that first estate file comes across your desk. When that day comes you will find that there are available in most jurisdictions excellent probate practice books, which will be of assistance. The purpose of this section is to provide background information necessary for estate planning.

When a person dies, and probate is necessary, the first step is the appointment of a personal representative to oversee the winding up of the decedent's affairs. The principal duties of the personal representative are (1) to inventory and collect the assets of the decedent, (2) to manage the assets during administration, (3) to receive and pay the claims of creditors and tax collectors, and (4) to distribute the remaining assets to those entitled.

If the decedent dies testate and in the will names the person who is to execute (i.e., carry out the terms of) the will and administer the estate, such person is called an *executor*. When the person in charge of administering the estate is not named in the will, the person is called an *administrator*. These persons are appointed by, under the control of, and accountable to a court, generally referred to as a probate court.

One of the advantages of writing a will is that the testator can designate who is to administer the estate.[6] If a person dies intestate or leaves a will that fails to name an executor who qualifies, the administrator is selected from a statutory list of persons who are to be given preference, typically in the following order: surviving spouse, children, parents, siblings, creditors.

The person appointed as administrator must give bond. In most states, if the will names an individual rather than a corporate fiduciary as executor, the executor also must give bond unless the will waives the bond requirement. Thus another reason for writing a will is that the requirement and expense of a fiduciary bond can be eliminated if that appears desirable.

Historically, in England, three courts had jurisdiction over probate. The king's common law courts controlled succession to land, which was the base of power in the feudal system. The ecclesiastical courts controlled succession to personal property, which, before the time of the Tudors and the rise of England as a trading power, was of little value (cows, sheep, utensils, personal ornaments, and such made up the personal property of medieval life). During the course of the sixteenth century, under Tudor rule, the ecclesiastical courts declined drastically in power. When Parliament attempted to strengthen the ecclesiastical courts a hundred years later by enacting the Statute of Distributions (1670), it was too late. A basic shift in the public's attitude toward the proper role of the church in secular affairs had already occurred, and the common law courts and chancery continued to

6. In a number of states nonresident corporate fiduciaries cannot be appointed as executor, and in a few states this prohibition extends to nonresident individuals. These restrictions have been held constitutional. In re Estate of Greenberg, 390 So. 2d 40 (Fla. 1980), appeal dismissed for want of substantial federal question, 450 U.S. 961 (1981).

A court may refuse to appoint as executor the person named in the will if the person has an interest adverse to the will or the estate. See Annot., 11 A.L.R.4th 638 (1982).

impede the clergy's control of administration of personal property. With its flexible procedure and its power to enforce personal duties, chancery gradually took over the administration of personal property. Ecclesiastical jurisdication over decedents' estates was finally abolished in 1857, when a court of probate was established in chancery. However, the common law courts' jurisdiction over the succession to land continued. Not until 1925, with the Administration of Estates Act, was one English court given sole jurisdiction over succession to real and personal property.

Today, in this country, one court in each county has jurisdiction over administration of decedents' estates. The name of the court varies from state to state. It may be called the surrogate's court, the orphan's court, the probate division of the district court or chancery court, or something else. But all of these differently named courts are referred to collectively as probate courts. And "to go through probate" means to have an estate administered by one of these courts.

One needlessly complicating factor in this field is that we have two legal vocabularies — one applicable to real property, the other to personal property. It is often suggested that these parallel vocabularies are traceable to the historic fact that the English common law courts had jurisdiction over succession to real property whereas ecclesiastical courts controlled succession to personal property in England until the nineteenth century. But in most instances this is not provable. Take *last will and testament*. A common belief is that this phrase arose because a *will* disposed of real property and a *testament* disposed of personal property; therefore one instrument disposing of both was a will and testament. The belief that *testament* referred to personal property is based on its Latin origin (testamentum). It is assumed that the Latin-trained ecclesiastical courts introduced *testament* into the language to refer to an instrument disposing of property over which they had jurisdiction. It is then assumed that *will*, an old English word, was used by the common law courts and by a process of association came to relate to the type of property over which these courts had jurisdiction. The evidence does not support these assumptions. As far back as the records go, the words have been used interchangeably. To speak of a testament disposing of land, or of a will disposing of a cow, would not have sounded strange to the medieval ear. Professor Mellinkoff believes the phrase last will and testament is traceable to the law's habit of doubling Old English words with synonyms of Old French or Latin origin (e.g., had and received, mind and memory, free and clear), "helped along by a distinctive rhythm." D. Mellinkoff, The Language of the Law 331 (1963). In any case, the myth that a will disposes of land and a testament disposes of chattels dies terribly, terribly slowly. Today it is perfectly proper to use the single word will to refer to an instrument disposing of both real and personal property.

A person dying testate *devises* real property to *devisees* and *bequeaths* personal property to *legatees*. Using devise to refer to land and bequest to refer to personalty became a lawyerly custom little more than a hundred years ago,[7] although the distinction, like that between will and testament, is sometimes erroneously thought to have had more ancient roots in the different courts handling the decedent's property. Although these linguistic distinctions still have currency, there are signs that synonymous usage is returning in respectable circles. The Restatement of Property applies devise to both realty and personalty. In drafting wills, "I give" is an excellent substitute for "I devise," "I bequeath," and "I give, devise, and bequeath." "I give" will effectively transfer any kind of property, and no fly-specking lawyer can ever fault you for using the wrong verb.

When intestacy occurs we use different words to describe what happens to the intestate's real property and what happens to his personal property. We say real property *descends to heirs;* personal property is *distributed to next-of-kin*. At common law, heirs and next-of-kin were not necessarily the same. For example, when primogeniture, which applied only to land, was in effect, real property descended to the eldest son, but personal property was distributed equally among all the children. Today in almost all states a single *statute of descent and distribution* governs intestacy. The same persons are named as intestate successors to both real and personal property. Thus today the word heirs usually means those persons designated by the applicable statute to take a decedent's intestate property real and personal. Next-of-kin usually means exactly the same thing.

At common law a spouse was not an heir; he or she had only curtesy or dower rights. Today in all states the statutes of descent and distribution name the spouse as a possible intestate successor, depending upon who else survives, and a spouse thus may be an heir.

In this book we do not use the Latin suffix indicating feminine gender for women playing important roles in our cast: Testator, executor, and administrator. Although testatrix, executrix, and administratrix are still in current fashion, other *-trix* forms either have disappeared from use (e.g., donatrix, creditrix, creatrix[8]) or would sound odd to the contemporary ear (e.g., public administratrix). And of course it does not matter whether the person in the given role is a man or a woman.[9] We have tried to avoid words that assign a role to one sex, but we dare not hope that we have succeeded in a field so

---

7. Cf. W. Shakespeare, King John, act I, scene 1, line 109: "Upon his death-bed he by will bequeath'd/His lands to me. . . ."

8. See *-trix* in Oxford English Dictionary (1989).

9. The Supreme Court has held unconstitutional a statute giving preference to a male to serve as executor or administrator. Reed v. Reed, 404 U.S. 71 (1971).

long dominated by assumptions of male superiority in property management. We believe it was Bentham who observed, "Error is never so difficult to be destroyed as when it has its root in language."

2. Is Probate Necessary?

Much is heard nowadays about the excessive cost of probate — or, as some have put it, the high cost of dying. The administrative costs of probate are mainly probate court fees, the commission of the personal representative, the attorney's fee, and sometimes appraiser's and guardian ad litem's fees.[10] In most states the personal representative's commission is set by statute at a fixed percentage of the probate estate. The fee of the attorney for the personal representative is sometimes set by statute, but more often it is determined by the court by reference to a number of factors (including customary charges for probate work, complexity of the estate, and time and labor required).

In an article by Earl Gottschalk in the Wall Street Journal, Revocable Living Trusts Become Popular Option in Estate Planning, Wall St. J., Feb. 4, 1987, §2, at 27, col. 4, the author gives the following figures for probate costs in California, which he says are about average among the states:

Assets	Minimum Fees
$ 200,000	$ 10,300
300,000	14,300
400,000	18,300
500,000	22,300
750,000	32,300
1,000,000	42,300
2,000,000	62,300
3,000,000	82,300
5,000,000	122,300

10. In many jurisdictions it is necessary to appoint a guardian ad litem if a minor or incompetent person is beneficially interested in the estate. Critics in New York have long contended that the surrogate's courts' power to appoint guardians has been abused. Mayor Fiorello H. LaGuardia called the surrogate's court "the most expensive undertaking establishment in the world" when, during his anti-Tammany administration, he found himself unable to cut off that source of patronage to Tammany lawyers. "What most disturbs critics is that political figures seem to enjoy a preferred position. Often, the patronage can be blatant. In one extreme case 11 years ago, Joseph A. Cox, who was retiring as Surrogate, said he had named as special guardian to a large estate the son of his fellow Manhattan Surrogate, S. Samuel DiFalco. The assignment was a 'wedding present' for the younger DiFalco, Mr. Cox said."

"More recently, in last year's Brooklyn race for surrogate, Bernard M. Bloom pledged he would give court assignments to 'all my friends who are qualified and competent.' Mr. Bloom, who won, asked of an opponent who had been critical: 'Who is he going to appoint — his enemies?'" Goldstein, Once More, Surrogate Talk, N.Y. Times, Sept. 4, 1977, §E, at 5, col. 2.

The fee figures include both the lawyer's fee and the executor's commission. If a member of the family serves as executor and waives the commission, the fees can be cut in half. These fees to settle an estate in court do not include additional lawyer's fees (called "extraordinary fees") charged for selling real property, preparing tax returns, operating a business, and litigation. Bear in mind that these fees are deductible for federal estate tax or income tax purposes. Federal estate taxes begin on estates of $600,000 at a rate of 37 percent and go up to 55 percent. Hence the net cost of probate fees in large estates may be substantially less than appears. See also Stein & Fierstein, The Role of the Attorney in Estate Administration, 68 Minn. L. Rev. 1107 (1984).

In most jurisdictions a lawyer who serves as executor is entitled to fees for serving in both offices. See Estate of Hackett, 51 Ill. App. 3d 474, 366 N.E.2d 1103 (1977); cf. Estate of Thron, 139 Misc. 2d 1045, 530 N.Y.S.2d 951 (Sur. Ct. 1988) (fees to each of two law partners named coexecutors plus fee for legal services not allowed on ground law firm failed to fully disclose to testator financial impact of double commissions). In a minority of jurisdictions the lawyer who receives an executor's commission is not entitled to an attorney's fee as well. This is viewed as prohibited self-dealing by a fiduciary. See Estate of Downing, 134 Cal. App. 3d 256, 184 Cal. Rptr. 511 (1982). See W. McGovern, S. Kurtz & J. Rein, Wills, Trusts and Estates §14.5 at 631 (1988).

In view of the costs of probate and the attendant delays, the question is often asked: Can probate be avoided? One of the primary functions of the probate process is to provide evidence of *transfer of title* to the decedent's heirs or devisees. Suppose that *O*, owner of Blackacre, dies leaving *H* as her heir. *H* can take possession of Blackacre, but unless there is administration of *O*'s estate, *H* may have difficulty in selling Blackacre. The record owner is *O*, and *H* has no documentary evidence that *H* is the new owner. *H* cannot convey marketable title without such evidence. If *O*'s estate is administered, the decree of distribution will show (either by itself describing the tract or by referring to the inventory, which includes a legal description) that *O* owned the tract, that *H* is *O*'s heir, and that title is now vested in *H*. Similarly, if *O* had devised Blackacre to *A*, *A* would not have a clear record title unless the will were probated. Hence the probate records become a link in the chain of title, evidence that *O*'s title has passed to another.

From this explanation, it should be easy to see that the key to avoiding probate is to transfer title to property during life. Three common ways of avoiding probate are taking title in joint tenancy, creating a trust during life, and putting a payable-on-death beneficiary designation on a life insurance contract or other contract. The title passes to the beneficiaries under these inter vivos instruments and not under the decedent's will. These and other will substitutes are treated in Chapters 4 and 7 of this book.

Even with respect to property owned at death, however, probate is not always necessary. As a practical matter, establishment of the transferee's title is not necessary for many items of personal property, such as furniture or personal effects. A purchaser will assume that the possessor has title. But for items of personal property for which ownership is evidenced by a document, such as an automobile certificate of title or a stock certificate, the transferee needs some official recognition of his rights thereto in order to transfer those rights.

Statutes in all states permit heirs to avoid probate where the amount of property involved is small, but the states differ as to what kind of, and how much, property can be transferred without a formal administration. Among statutes commonly found are statutes permitting collection of small bank accounts or wage claims, or transfer of an automobile certificate of title to the decedent's heirs, upon affidavit by the heirs. By filling out the appropriate forms and presenting them to the bank, the employer, or the department of motor vehicles, the heir is able to collect the decedent's property or acquire a new certificate of title.

In addition, many states permit close relatives of the decedent to collect the decedent's personal property by presenting an affidavit to the holder of the property if the estate does not exceed a certain figure. The figure defining a *small estate,* which can be collected upon affidavit, ranges from $5,000 to $100,000. The affidavit procedure authorized by these *collection statutes* does *not* give title to the recipient of the property. It merely permits those presumptively entitled to the decedent's property to collect it expeditiously and without a cumbersome estate proceeding.

Finally, statutes in some states permit filing a will for probate solely as a title document, with no formal administration to follow. And in some states title insurance companies will insure real property sold by heirs if a certificate of death and affidavit of heirship is filed; probate proceedings are not required.

When the heirs or devisees pay the debts of the decedent and any real property is held in joint tenancy, there may be no need for probate of the estate. Indeed, a recent study of five states found that the percentage of decedents' estates that underwent estate administration ranged from 20 percent in California to 34 percent in Massachusetts. Stein & Fierstein, The Demography of Probate Administration, 15 U. Balt. L. Rev. 54 (1985). Thus, by one way or another, the large majority of decedents manage to avoid probate.

PROBLEMS

1.   Aaron Green died three weeks ago. His wife has come to your law firm with Green's will in hand: The will devises Green's entire

estate "to my wife, Martha, if she survives me; otherwise to my children in equal shares." The will names Martha Green as executor. An interview with Mrs. Green reveals that the Green family consists of two adult sons and several grandchildren and that Green owned the following property:

Furniture, furnishings, other items of tangible personal property (estimated value)	$10,000
Savings account in name of Aaron Green	5,000
Joint checking account on which Aaron and Martha Green were both authorized to write checks	1,500
Employer's pension plan, naming Martha Green for survivor's benefits	Life Annuity
Checking account on which Mr. and Mrs. Green were both authorized to write checks	1,500
Government bonds, payable to "Aaron or Martha Green"	5,000
Ordinary life insurance policy naming Martha Green as primary beneficiary	25,000
Oldsmobile car	7,500

not prob.

Green owned no real property; he and his wife lived in a rented apartment. Green's debts consisted of last month's utility bills ($40) plus the usual consumer charge accounts: Sears Roebuck ($300 balance), the local department store ($125), Shell Oil ($35). There is also a funeral bill ($825) and the cost of a cemetery lot ($300). Mrs. Green wants your advice: What should she do with the will? Must it be offered for probate? Must there be an administration of her husband's estate?

2. Same facts as in Problem 1 except that Green died intestate, and the state's statute of descent and distribution provides that where a decedent is survived by a spouse and children, one-half of his real and personal property shall descend to the spouse, and the remaining one-half shall descend to the children.

3. Same facts as in problem 1 except that Green also owned a house and lot worth $85,000 and another lot worth $8,000. The deeds to both tracts name Aaron Green as grantee. The residential property is subject to a mortgage with a current balance of $42,000; title to the other lot is free of encumbrances. Must (should?) Green's will be probated and his estate formally administered? See Tex. Prob. Code Ann. §§49, 89 (1980).

4. Let us look at Aaron Green's problem from another perspective. Suppose Green comes to you during his lifetime. He tells you that he does not have a will. He describes his family situation and the assets owned by him: the assets listed in Problem 1 but not the real estate

described in Problem 3. His question: In view of his family situation and his modest estate, does he really need a will?

3.   A Summary of Probate Procedure

a.   Opening Probate

The will should first be probated, or letters of administration should first be sought, in the jurisdiction where the decedent was domiciled at the time of death. This is known as the *primary* or *domiciliary* jurisdiction. If real property is located in another jurisdiction, *ancillary administration* in the jurisdiction is required. The purpose of requiring ancillary administration is to prove title to real property in the situs state's recording system and to subject those assets to probate for the protection of local creditors. Ancillary administration may be costly because the state may require that a resident be appointed personal representative, with a local attorney. Executor's commissions and attorney's fees will be paid to them on the value of the ancillary assets; the domiciliary representative and attorney also are entitled to fees based on the ancillary assets.

Each state has a detailed statutory procedure for issuance of *letters testamentary* to an executor or *letters of administration* to an administrator authorizing the person to act on behalf of the estate. Several states, mainly east of the Mississippi, follow the procedure formerly used by the English ecclesiastical courts in distinguishing between contentious and noncontentious probate proceedings. Under the English system, the executor had a choice of probating a will *in common form* or *in solemn form*. Common form probate was an ex parte proceeding in which no notice or process was issued to any person. Due execution of the will was proved by the oath of the executor or such other witnesses as might be required. The will was admitted to probate at once, letters testamentary were granted, and the executor began administration of the estate. If no one raised any questions or objections, this procedure sufficed. However, within a period of years thereafter an interested party could file a caveat, compelling probate of the will in solemn form. Under probate in solemn form, notice to interested parties was given by citation, due execution of the will was proved by the testimony of the attesting witnesses, and administration of the estate involved greater court participation. Ex parte or common form procedure is recognized in many states, sometimes preserving the common form/solemn form terminology, but more often not.

The majority of states do not permit ex parte proceedings but require prior notice to interested parties before the appointment of a personal representative or probate of a will. In these states the petition for letters must be accompanied by an affidavit stating that the statutory notice requirements have been met (personal service, mailing, or publishing). At the hearing, if a will is to be probated, it must be proved by the testimony or affidavits of the witnesses. The hearing may be before the probate judge or a clerk.

The Uniform Probate Code provides for both ex parte probate and notice probate. The former is called *informal probate,* the latter *formal probate.* The person asking for letters can choose informal or formal probate; the theory is that one may be more useful in a particular estate than another and a choice should be available. Uniform Probate Code §3-301 sets forth the requirements for informal probate. Without giving notice to anyone, the representative petitions for appointment; the petition contains pertinent information about the decedent and the names and addresses of the spouse, the children or other heirs, and, if a will is involved, the devisees. If the petition is for probate of a will, the original will must accompany the petition; the executor swears that, to the best of his knowledge, the will was validly executed; proof by the witnesses is not required. A will that appears to have the required signatures and that contains an attestation clause showing that requirements of execution have been met is probated by the registrar without further proof. UPC §3-303. Within 30 days *after the letters are issued,* the personal representative has the duty of mailing notice to every interested person, including heirs apparently disinherited by a will. UPC §3-306. The representative also has a duty to publish a newspaper notice for creditors once each week for three weeks. UPC §3-801. It has been argued that the no-prior-notice provisions of informal probate under the code are unconstitutional, and because of this changes in the notice provisions for informal probate have been made by several states adopting the code. See Note, The Constitutionality of the No-Notice Provisions of the Uniform Probate Code, 60 Minn. L. Rev. 317 (1976).

Formal probate under the Uniform Probate code is a judicial determination *after notice* to interested parties. Any interested party can demand formal probate. A formal proceeding may be used to probate a will, to block an informal proceeding, or to secure a declaratory judgment of intestacy. Formal proceedings become final judgments if not appealed.

No proceeding, formal or informal, may be initiated less than five days or more than three years from the date of death. UPC §3-108. If no will is probated within three years after death, the presumption of intestacy is conclusive. The three-year statute of limitations of the Uniform Probate Code changes the common law, which permits a will to be probated at any time, perhaps many years after the testator's death. See Annot., 2 A.L.R.4th 1315 (1980).

For a description of estate administration under the Uniform Probate

Code, see P. Haskell, Preface to Wills, Trusts and Administration 162-206 (1987).

Tulsa Professional Collection Services, Inc. v. Pope
Supreme Court of the United States, 1988
485 U.S. 478

O'CONNOR, J.   This case involves a provision of Oklahoma's probate laws requiring claims "arising upon a contract" generally to be presented to the executor or executrix of the estate within 2 months of the publication of a notice advising creditors of the commencement of probate proceedings. Okla. Stat., Tit. 58, §333 (1981). The question presented is whether this provision of notice solely by publication satisfies the Due Process Clause.

I

Oklahoma's probate code requires creditors to file claims against an estate within a specified time period, and generally bars untimely claims. Ibid. Such "nonclaim statutes" are almost universally included in state probate codes. See Uniform Probate Code §3-801, 8 U.L.A. 351 (1983); Falender, Notice to Creditors in Estate Proceedings: What Process is Due?, 63 N.C.L. Rev. 659, 667-668 (1985). Giving creditors a limited time in which to file claims against the estate serves the State's interest in facilitating the administration and expeditious closing of estates. See, e.g., State ex rel. Central State Griffin Memorial Hospital v. Reed, 493 P.2d 815, 818 (Okla. 1972). Nonclaim statutes come in two basic forms. Some provide a relatively short time period, generally 2 to 6 months, that begins to run after the commencement of probate proceedings. Others call for a longer period, generally 1 to 5 years, that runs from the decedent's death. See Falender, supra, at 664-672. Most States include both types of nonclaim statutes in their probate codes, typically providing that if probate proceedings are not commenced and the shorter period therefore never is triggered, then claims nonetheless may be barred by the longer period. See, e.g., Ark. Code Ann. §28-50-101(a), (d) (1987) (3 months if probate proceedings commenced; 5 years if not); Idaho Code §15-3-803(a)(1), (2) (1979) (4 months; 3 years); Mo. Rev. Stat. §473.360(1), (3) (1986) (6 months; 3 years). Most States also provide that creditors are to be notified of the requirement to file claims imposed by the nonclaim statutes solely by publication. See Uniform Probate Code §3-801, 8 U.L.A. 351 (1983); Falender, supra, at 660, n.7 (collecting statutes). Indeed, in most jurisdictions it is the publication of notice that triggers the nonclaim statute. The Uniform Probate Code, for example, provides that creditors have 4 months from publication in which to file claims. Uniform Probate Code §3-801, 8 U.L.A. 351 (1983). See also, e.g., Ariz. Rev. Stat. Ann. §14-3801 (1975); Fla. Stat. §733.701 (1987); Utah Code Ann. §75-3-801 (1978).

The specific nonclaim statute at issue in this case, Okla. Stat., Tit. 58, §333 (1981), provides for only a short time period and is best considered in the context of Oklahoma probate proceedings as a whole. Under Oklahoma's probate code, any party interested in the estate may initiate probate proceedings by petitioning the court to have the will proved. §22. The court is then required to set a hearing date on the petition, §25, and to mail notice of the hearing "to all heirs, legatees and devisees, at their places of residence," §§25, 26. If no person appears at the hearing to contest the will, the court may admit the will to probate on the testimony of one of the subscribing witnesses to the will. §30. After the will is admitted to probate, the court must order appointment of an executor or executrix, issuing letters testamentary to the named executor or executrix if that person appears, is competent and qualified, and no objections are made. §101.

Immediately after appointment, the executor or executrix is required to "give notice to the creditors of the deceased." §331. Proof of compliance with·this requirement must be filed with the court. §332. This notice is to advise creditors that they must present their claims to the executor or executrix within 2 months of the date of the first publicaton. As for the method of notice, the statute requires only publication: "[S]uch notice must be published in some newspaper in [the] county once each week for two (2) consecutive weeks." §331. A creditor's failure to file a claim within the 2-month period generally bars it forever. §333. The nonclaim statute does provide certain exceptions, however. If the creditor is out of State, then a claim "may be presented at any time before a decree of distribution is entered." §333. Mortgages and debts not yet due are also excepted from the 2-month time limit.

This shorter type of nonclaim statute is the only one included in Oklahoma's probate code. Delays in commencement of probate proceedings are dealt with not through some independent, longer period running from the decedent's death, see, e.g., Ark. Code Ann. §28-50-101(d) (1987), but by shortening the notice period once proceedings have started. Section 331 provides that if the decedent has been dead for more than 5 years, then creditors have only 1 month after notice is published in which to file their claims. A similar 1-month period applies if the decedent was intestate. §331.

II

H. Everett Pope, Jr. was admitted to St. John Medical Center, a hospital in Tulsa, Oklahoma, in November 1978. On April 2, 1979, while still at the hospital, he died testate. His wife, appellee JoAnne Pope, initiated probate proceedings in the District Court of Tulsa County in accordance with the statutory scheme outlined above. The court entered an order setting a hearing. After the hearing the court entered an order admitting the will to probate and, following the designation in the will, named appellee as the executrix of the estate. Letters testamentary were issued, and the court ordered appellee to fulfill her statutory obligation by directing that she "immediately give notice to creditors." Appellee published notice in the Tulsa Daily Legal News for 2 consecutive weeks beginning July 17, 1979. The notice advised creditors that they must file any claim they had against the estate within 2 months of the first publication of the notice.

Appellant Tulsa Professional Collection Services, Inc., is a subsidiary of St. John Medical Center and the assignee of a claim for expenses connected with the decedent's long stay at that hospital. Neither appellant, nor its parent company, filed a claim with appellee within the 2-month time period following publication of notice. In October 1983, however, appellant filed an Application for Order Compelling Payment of Expenses of Last Illness. In making this application, appellant relied on Okla. Stat., Tit. 58, §594 (1981), which indicates that an executrix "must pay . . . the expenses of the last sickness." Appellant argued that this specific statutory command made compliance with the 2-month deadline for filing claims unnecessary. The District Court of Tulsa County rejected this contention, ruling that even claims pursuant to §594 fell within the general requirements of the nonclaim statute. Accordingly, the court denied appellant's application.

The District Court's reading of §594's relationship to the nonclaim statute was affirmed by the Oklahoma Court of Appeals. Appellant then sought rehearing, arguing for the first time that the nonclaim statute's notice provisions violated due process. In a supplemental opinion on rehearing the Court of Appeals rejected the due process claim on the merits.

Appellant next sought review in the Supreme Court of Oklahoma. That court granted certiorari and, after review of both the §594 and due process issues, affirmed the Court of Appeals' judgment. With respect to the federal issue, the court relied on Estate of Busch v. Ferrell-Duncan Clinic, Inc., 700 S.W.2d 86, 88-89 (Mo. 1985), to reject appellant's contention that our decisions in Mullane v. Central Hanover Bank & Trust Co., 339 U.S. 306 (1950), and Mennonite Board of Missions v. Adams, 462 U.S. 791 (1983), required more than publication notice. 733 P.2d 396 (1987). The Supreme Court reasoned that the function of notice in probate proceedings was not to "'make a creditor a party to the proceeding'" but merely to "'notif[y] him that he may become one if he wishes.'" Id., at 400 (quoting *Estate of Busch,* 700 S.W.2d, at 88). In addition, the court distinguished probate proceedings because they do not directly adjudicate the creditor's claims. 733 P.2d, at 400-401. Finally, the court agreed with *Estate of Busch* that nonclaim statutes were self-executing statutes of limitations, because they "ac[t] to cut off potential claims against the decedent's estate by the passage of time," and accordingly do not require actual notice. 733 P.2d, at 401. See also Gibbs v. Estate of Dolan, 146 Ill. App. 3d 203, 100 Ill. Dec. 61, 496 N.E.2d 1126 (1986) (rejecting due process challenge to nonclaim statute); Gano Farms, Inc. v. Estate of Kleweno, 2 Kan. App. 2d 506, 582 P.2d 742 (1978) (same); Chalaby v. Driskell, 237 Or. 245, 390 P.2d 632 (1964) (same); William B. Tanner Co. v. Estate of Fessler, 100 Wis. 2d 437, 302 N.W.2d 414 (1981) (same); New York Merchandise Co. v. Stout, 43 Wash. 2d 825, 264 P.2d 863 (1953) (same). This conclusion conflicted with that reached by the Nevada Supreme Court in Continental Insurance Co. v. Moseley, 100 Nev. 337, 683 P.2d 20 (1984), after our decision remanding the case for reconsideration in light of *Mennonite,* supra. 463 U.S. 1202 (1983). In *Moseley,* the Nevada Supreme Court held that in this context due process required "more than service by publication." Id., at 338, 683 P.2d, at 21. We noted probable jurisdiction, 484 U.S. 813 (1987), and now reverse and remand.

III

Mullane v. Central Hanover Bank & Trust Co., supra, 339 U.S., at 314, established that state action affecting property must generally be accompanied by notification of that action: "An elementary and fundamental requirement of due process in any proceeding which is to be accorded finality is notice reasonably calculated, under all the circumstances, to apprise interested parties of the pendency of the action and afford them an opportunity to present their objections." In the years since *Mullane* the Court has adhered to these principles, balancing the "interest of the State" and "the individual interest sought to be protected by the Fourteenth Amendment." Ibid. The focus is on the reasonableness of the balance, and, as *Mullane* itself made clear, whether a

particular method of notice is reasonable depends on the particular circumstances.

The Court's most recent decision in this area is *Mennonite,* supra, which involved the sale of real property for delinquent taxes. State law provided for tax sales in certain circumstances and for a 2-year period following any such sale during which the owner or any lienholder could redeem the property. After expiration of the redemption period, the tax sale purchaser could apply for a deed. The property owner received actual notice of the tax sale and the redemption period. All other interested parties were given notice by publication. 462 U.S., at 792-794. In *Mennonite,* a mortgagee of property that had been sold and on which the redemption period had run complained that the State's failure to provide it with actual notice of these proceedings violated due process. The Court agreed, holding that "actual notice is a minimum constitutional precondition to a proceeding which will adversely affect the liberty or property interests of *any* party, whether unlettered or well versed in commercial practice, if its name and address are reasonably ascertainable." Id., at 800 (emphasis in original). Because the tax sale had "immediately and drastically diminishe[d] the value of [the mortgagee's] interest," id., at 798, and because the mortgagee could have been identified through "reasonably diligent efforts," id., at 798, n.4, the Court concluded that due process required that the mortgagee be given actual notice.

Applying these principles to the case at hand leads to a similar result. Appellant's interest is an unsecured claim, a cause of action against the estate for an unpaid bill. Little doubt remains that such an intangible interest is property protected by the Fourteenth Amendment. As we wrote in Logan v. Zimmerman Brush Co., 455 U.S. 422, 428 (1982), this question "was affirmatively settled by the *Mullane* case itself, where the Court held that a cause of action is a species of property protected by the Fourteenth Amendment's Due Process Clause." In *Logan,* the Court held that a cause of action under Illinois' Fair Employment Practices Act was a protected property interest, and referred to the numerous other types of claims that the Court had previously recognized as deserving due process protections. See id., at 429-431, and nn.4-5. Appellant's claim, therefore, is properly considered a protected property interest.

The Fourteenth Amendment protects this interest, however, only from a deprivation by state action. Private use of state sanctioned private remedies or procedures does not rise to the level of state action. See, e.g., Flagg Bros., Inc. v. Brooks, 436 U.S. 149 (1978). Nor is the State's involvement in the mere running of a general statute of limitation generally sufficient to implicate due process. See Texaco, Inc. v. Short, 454 U.S. 516 (1982). But when private parties make use of state procedures with the overt, significant assistance of state officials, state action may be found. See, e.g., Lugar v. Edmondson Oil Co, 457 U.S. 922 (1982); Sniadach v. Family Finance Corp., 395 U.S. 337 (1969). The question here is whether the State's involvement with the nonclaim statute is substantial enough to implicate the Due Process Clause.

Appellee argues that it is not, contending that Oklahoma's nonclaim statute is a self-executing statute of limitations. Relying on this characterization, appellee then points to *Short, supra.* Appellee's reading of *Short* is correct — due process does not require that potential plaintiffs be given notice of the impending expiration of a period of limitations — but in our view, appellee's premise is not. Oklahoma's nonclaim statute is not a self-executing statute of limitations.

It is true that nonclaim statutes generally possess some attributes of statutes of limitations. They provide a specific time period within which particular types of claims must be filed and they bar claims presented after expiration of that deadline. Many of the state court decisions upholding nonclaim statutes against due process challenges have relied upon these features and concluded that they are properly viewed as statutes of limitations. See, e.g., Estate of Busch v. Ferrell-Duncan Clinic, Inc., 700 S.W.2d, at 89; William B. Tanner Co. v. Estate of Fessler, 100 Wis. 2d 437, 302 N.W.2d 414 (1981).

As we noted in *Short,* however, it is the "self-executing feature" of a statute of limitations that makes *Mullane* and *Mennonite* inapposite. See 454 U.S., at 533, 536. The State's interest in a self-executing statute of limitations is in providing repose for potential defendants and in avoiding stale claims. The State has no role to play beyond enactment of the limitations period. While this enactment obviously is state action, the State's limited involvement in the running of the time period generally falls short of constituting the type of state action required to implicate the protections of the Due Process Clause.

Here, in contrast, there is significant state action. The probate court is intimately involved throughout, and without that involvement the time bar is never activated. The nonclaim statute becomes operative only after probate proceedings have been commenced in state court. The court must appoint the executor or executrix before notice, which triggers the time bar, can be given. Only after this court appointment is made does the statute provide for any notice; §331 directs the executor or executrix to publish notice "immediately" after appointment. Indeed, in this case, the District Court reinforced the statutory command with an order expressly requiring appellee to "immediately give notice to creditors." The form of the order indicates that such orders are routine. Finally, copies of the notice and an affidavit of publication must be filed with the court. §332. It is only after all of these actions take place that the time period begins to run, and in every one of these actions, the court is intimately involved. This involvement is so pervasive and substantial that it must be considered state action subject to the restrictions of the Fourteenth Amendment.

Where the legal proceedings themselves trigger the time bar, even if those proceedings do not necessarily resolve the claim on its merits, the time bar lacks the self-executing feature that *Short* indicated was necessary to remove any due process problem. Rather, in such circumstances, due process is directly implicated and actual notice generally is required. Cf. *Mennonite,* 462 U.S., at 793-794 (tax sale proceedings trigger 2-year redemption period); Logan v. Zimmerman Brush Co., supra, 455 U.S., at 433, 437 (claim barred if no hearing held 120 days after action commenced); City of New York v. New York, N.H. & H.R. Co., 344 U.S. 293, 294 (1953) (bankruptcy proceedings trigger specific time period in which creditors' claims must be filed). Our conclusion

that the Oklahoma nonclaim statute is not a self-executing statute of
limitations makes it unnecessary to consider appellant's argument that
a 2-month period is somehow unconstitutionally short. See Tr. of Oral
Arg. 22 (advocating constitutional requirement that the States provide
at least 1 year). We also have no occasion to consider the proper
characterization of nonclaim statutes that run from the date of death,
and which generally provide for longer time periods, ranging from 1
to 5 years. See Falender, 63 N.C.L. Rev., at 667-669. In sum, the
substantial involvement of the probate court throughout the process
leaves little doubt that the running of Oklahoma's nonclaim statute is
accompanied by sufficient government action to implicate the Due
Process Clause.

Nor can there be any doubt that the nonclaim statute may "adversely
affect" a protected property interest. In appellant's case, such an adverse
affect is all too clear. The entire purpose and effect of the nonclaim
statute is to regulate the timeliness of such claims and to forever bar
untimely claims, and by virtue of the statute, the probate proceedings
themselves have completely extinguished appellant's claim. Thus, it is
irrelevant that the notice seeks only to advise creditors that they may
become parties rather than that they are parties, for if they do not
participate in the probate proceedings, the nonclaim statute terminates
their property interests. It is not necessary for a proceeding to directly
adjudicate the merits of a claim in order to "adversely affect" that
interest. . . .

In assessing the propriety of actual notice in this context consideration
should be given to the practicalities of the situation and the effect that
requiring actual notice may have on important state interests. As the
Court noted in *Mullane*, "[c]hance alone brings to the attention of even
a local resident an advertisement in small type inserted in the back
pages of a newspaper." Id., at 315. Creditors, who have a strong interest
in maintaining the integrity of their relationship with their debtors, are
particularly unlikely to benefit from publication notice. As a class,
creditors may not be aware of a debtor's death or of the institution of
probate proceedings. Moreover, the executor or executrix will often
be, as is the case here, a party with a beneficial interest in the estate.
This could diminish an executor's or executrix's inclination to call
attention to the potential expiration of a creditor's claim. There is thus
a substantial practical need for actual notice in this setting.

At the same time, the State undeniably has a legitimate interest in
the expeditious resolution of probate proceedings. Death transforms
the decedent's legal relationships and a State could reasonably conclude
that swift settlement of estates is so important that it calls for very short
time deadlines for filing claims. As noted, the almost uniform practice
is to establish such short deadlines, and to provide only publication
notice. See, e.g., Ariz. Rev. Stat. Ann. §14-3801 (1975); Ark. Code Ann.

§28-50-101(a) (1987); Fla. Stat. §733.701 (1987); Idaho Code §15-3-803(a) (1979); Mo. Stat. §473.360(1) (1986); Utah Code Ann. §75-3-801 (1978). See also Uniform Probate Code §3-801, 8 U.L.A. 351 (1983); Falender, supra, at 660, n.7 (collecting statutes). Providing actual notice to known or reasonably ascertainable creditors, however, is not inconsistent with the goals reflected in nonclaim statutes. Actual notice need not be inefficient or burdensome. We have repeatedly recognized that mail service is an inexpensive and efficient mechanism that is reasonably calculated to provide actual notice. See, e.g., *Mennonite*, supra, 462 U.S., at 799, 800; *Mullane*, supra, 339 U.S., at 319. In addition, *Mullane* disavowed any intent to require "impracticable and extended searches . . . in the name of due process." 339 U.S., at 317-318. As the Court indicated in *Mennonite*, all that the executor or executrix need do is make "reasonably diligent efforts," 462 U.S., at 798, n.4, to uncover the identities of creditors. For creditors who are not "reasonably ascertainable," publication notice can suffice. Nor is everyone who may conceivably have a claim properly considered a creditor entitled to actual notice. Here, as in *Mullane*, it is reasonable to dispense with actual notice to those with mere "conjectural" claims. 339 U.S., at 317.

On balance then, a requirement of actual notice to known or reasonably ascertainable creditors is not so cumbersome as to unduly hinder the dispatch with which probate proceedings are conducted. Notice by mail is already routinely provided at several points in the probate process. In Oklahoma, for example, §26 requires that "heirs, legatees, and devisees" be mailed notice of the initial hearing on the will. Accord Uniform Probate Code §3-403, 8 U.L.A. 274 (1983). Indeed, a few States already provide for actual notice in connection with short nonclaim statutes. See, e.g., Calif. Prob. Code Ann. §§9050, 9100 (Supp. 1988); Nev. Rev. Stat. §§147.010, 155.010, 155.020 (1987); W. Va. Code §§44-2-2, 44-2-4 (1982). We do not believe that requiring adherence to such a standard will be so burdensome or impracticable as to warrant reliance on publication notice alone. . . .

Whether appellant's identity as a creditor was known or reasonably ascertainable by appellee cannot be answered on this record. Neither the Oklahoma Supreme Court nor the Court of Appeals nor the District Court considered the question. Appellee of course was aware that her husband endured a long stay at St. John Medical Center, but it is not clear that this awareness translates into a knowledge of appellant's claim. We therefore must remand the case for further proceedings to determine whether "reasonably diligent efforts," *Mennonite*, supra, 462 U.S., at 798, n.4, would have identified appellant and uncovered its claim. If appellant's identity was known or "reasonably ascertainable," then termination of appellant's claim without actual notice violated due process.

IV

We hold that Oklahoma's nonclaim statute is not a self-executing statute of limitations. Rather, the statute operates in connection with Oklahoma's probate proceedings to "adversely affect" appellant's property interest. Thus, if appellant's identity as a creditor was known or "reasonably ascertainable," then the Due Process Clause requires that appellant be given "[n]otice by mail or other means as certain to ensure actual notice." *Mennonite,* supra, at 800. Accordingly, the judgment of the Oklahoma Supreme Court is reversed and the case is remanded for further proceedings not inconsistent with this opinion.

It is so ordered.[11]

QUESTION

Would it be better to extend the rights of unnotified creditors to permit them to file a claim within a year or to require the personal representative to make a reasonable search and give notice? Would a one-year statute of limitations for unnotified creditors be constitutional? See Falender, Notice to Creditors in Estate Proceedings: What Process Is Due?, 63 N.C.L. Rev. 659, 673-677 (1985); Waterbury, Notice to Decedents' Creditors, 73 Minn. L. Rev. 763 (1989).

b.   Supervising the Representative's Actions

In many states the actions of the personal representative in administering the estate are supervised by the court. This supervision can be time-consuming and costly. The court must approve the inventory and appraisal, payment of debts, family allowance, granting options on real estate, sale of real estate, borrowing of funds and mortgaging of property, leasing of property, proration of federal estate tax, personal representative's commissions, attorney's fees, preliminary and final distributions, and discharge of the personal representative. The sale of real estate may require several trips to the courthouse to get an order to sell, to file notice of all offers received, to give notice that a previous low bidder has overbid the previous high bid, and, finally, to get approval of the terms of the sale to the highest bidder.

In some states the practice is for the personal representative to handle all these matters informally without court order, provided the interested parties are adults and will approve the fiduciary's account and release

---

11. Noted in 58 Miss. L.J. 193; 54 Mo. L. Rev. 189; 18 Stetson L. Rev. 471.

the fiduciary from liability. If minors are involved, judicial supervision is necessary.

The Uniform Probate Code authorizes unsupervised administration as well as supervised administration. If any interested party demands supervised administration, the probate court supervises the personal representative. But if no party demands it, administration is independent of the court. Under independent administration, after appointment, the personal representative administers the estate without going back into court. The representative has the broad powers of a trustee in dealing with the estate property, and may collect assets, sell property, invest in other assets, pay creditors, continue any business of the decedent, and distribute the estate — all without court approval. UPC §3-715. The estate may be closed by the personal representative filing a sworn statement that he has published notice to creditors, administered the estate, paid all claims, and sent a statement and accounting to all known distributees. UPC §3-1003. If at any time during independent administration an interested party is dissatisfied with the personal representative's actions, he may compel the representative to obtain court supervision. UPC §3-501.

Although unsupervised administration may be a useful reform, something more radical may be desirable. This is *universal succession,* a concept of the civil law invented by the Romans and followed on the continent of Europe. Under universal succession *there is no personal representative;* the heirs or the residuary devisees succeed to the title of the decedent. The heirs or the residuary devisees step into the shoes of the decedent at the decedent's death, taking the decedent's title and assuming all the decedent's liabilities and the obligation of paying legacies according to the decedent's will. If, for example, *O* dies intestate, leaving *H* as *O*'s heir, *H* succeeds to ownership of *O*'s property and must pay all of *O*'s creditors and any taxes resulting from *O*'s death. If *O* has three heirs, they hold as tenants in common at *O*'s death, with the ordinary rights of tenants in common. The payment of a commission to a fiduciary is not necessary, and a lawyer need not be employed unless the heirs decide they need legal advice. A system of universal succession can have enormous advantages where the heirs or the residuary devisees are all adults.

In 1982 the National Conference of Commissioners on Uniform State Laws approved amendments to the Uniform Probate Code authorizing universal succession. Under these new sections (UPC §§3-312 to 3-322) the heirs or the residuary devisees may petition the court for universal succession. If the court ascertains that the necessary parties are included and that the estate is not subject to any current contest or difficulty, it issues a written statement of universal succession. The universal successors then have full power of ownership to deal with the assets of the estate. They assume the liabilities of the decedent to creditors, including tax liability. The successors are personally liable to other heirs omitted from the petition or, in the case of residuary devisees, to other devisees for the amount of property due them. See Scoles, Succession Without Administration: Past and Future, 48 Mo. L. Rev. 371 (1983).

Universal succession is already available to a limited extent in the United States. Under California law, property that passes to the surviving spouse is not subject to administration unless the surviving spouse elects to have it administered. If the surviving spouse chooses not to have the property administered, the surviving spouse takes title to the property and assumes personal liability for the decedent's debts chargeable against the property. Cal. Prob. Code §§13500-13650 (1989). This exemption from probate raises an interesting question: If probate is not necessary for property passing to a surviving spouse, why is it necessary for property passing to children?

In Georgia something like universal succession is recognized by a procedure that permits the heirs of a decedent to petition for an order stating that no administration is necessary because the estate owes no debts and the heirs amicably agree upon a division of the estate among themselves. Ga. Code Ann. §113-1232 (Supp. 1988).

PROBLEMS

1. The testator's will directs his executor to tear down the testator's house, as he does not want anyone else to live in it. If probate is unsupervised, can the executor tear down the house? If probate is supervised, should a court order the house destroyed? See Brown v. Burdett, 21 Ch. D. 667 (1882); Eyerman v. Mercantile Trust Co., 524 S.W.2d 210 (Mo. App. 1975), noted in 41 Mo. L. Rev. 309 (1976).

2. Justice Hugo L. Black of the United States Supreme Court was of the view that private notes of the justices relating to Court conferences should not be published posthumously. Justice Black feared publication might inhibit free and vigorous discussion among the justices. Black was struck ill, destroyed his conference notes, resigned from the Court, and died a few weeks later. Suppose that Justice Black had died suddenly while on the bench and that his will had directed his executor to destroy his conference notes. Could the executor do this without a court order? Should a court order destruction of the notes, which might have enormous value to a Court historian? Who would have standing to object?

Franz Kafka bequeathed his diaries, manuscripts, and letters to his friend Max Brod, directing him to burn everything. Brod declined to do so on the ground that Kafka's unpublished work was of great literary value. Should Brod have ordered a bonfire? See M. Brod, Postscript, *in* F. Kafka, The Trial 326 (1925, Mod. Lib. ed. 1956), discussed in W. Bishin & C. Stone, Law, Language, and Ethics 1-9 (1972). Suppose that Franz Schubert and Giacomo Puccini had ordered their unfinished works destroyed at death, thus depriving the world of Schubert's unfinished Symphony in B Minor and Puccini's unfinished opera Turandot. Should a court order destruction?

c. Closing the Estate

The personal representative of an estate is expected to complete the administration and distribute the assets as promptly as possible. Even if all the beneficiaries are amicable, several things that must be done may prolong administration. Creditors must be paid. Taxes must be paid and tax returns audited and accepted by the appropriate tax authorities. Real estate or a sole proprietorship may have to be sold.

Judicial approval of the personal representative's action is required to relieve the representative from liability, unless some statute of limitations runs upon a cause of action against the representative. The representative is not discharged from fiduciary duties until the court grants discharge.

The high cost and delays of probate have come in for considerable criticism in the last 20 years. The Uniform Probate Code, first promulgated in 1969, has attempted to meet some of these criticisms. It has been adopted in many jurisdictions and has been a catalyst for reform in others. But the probate process remains expensive and the urge to bypass it remains strong. See Langbein, The Nonprobate Revolution and the Future of the Law of Succession, 97 Harv. L. Rev. 1108 (1984); Pennell, Introduction: Whither Estate Planning, 24 Idaho L. Rev. 339 (1988).

4. Contest of Wills

The right to contest a will is largely dependent upon statutes in the particular jurisdiction. Statutes usually control the procedure for contest, the period in which contest is allowed, the grounds for contest, and the parties who have standing to contest. Although some states permit contest before probate, the usual procedure is for a will to be admitted to probate upon proof of its due execution. This raises a presumption of validity. Then, within the period allowed by statute, complainants may petition to revoke probate upon grounds of mental incapacity, undue influence, fraud, or duress.

The period of limitations for filing a will contest is ordinarily jurisdictional and is not tolled by any fact not provided by statute. After the period passes, the probate court no longer has jurisdiction to entertain an action to revoke probate. Probate of the will thereby becomes final. See Larkin v. Ruffin, 398 So. 2d 676 (Ala. 1981) (holding order admitting will to probate cannot be set aside three and one-half years later when evidence is discovered showing will had been revoked). If the constitutional and statutory requirements for notice are complied with, generally no one can contest the will after probate becomes final.

PROBLEM

Testator died survived by his son Ervin and four brothers and sisters. His will bequeathed $1 to Ervin and the balance of the estate to 32 other beneficiaries. Ervin was in Leavenworth Penitentiary in Kansas. The application for letters testamentary named Ervin as a beneficiary and stated: "Address unknown. Last known confined to Federal Prison." Notice of letters testamentary was published in a local newspaper. No other effort was made to give Ervin any notice of the probate proceeding. Eighteen months later, Ervin filed a contest of the will. Mo. Rev. Stat. §473.083 (1969) provides that a will contest must be filed within six months of publication of notice of letters testamentary; otherwise the will is binding. Should Ervin be permitted to contest the will under the principle of Mullane v. Central Hanover Bank & Trust Co., 339 U.S. 306 (1949), reaffirmed in Tulsa Professional Services, Inc. v. Pope, 485 U.S. 478 (1988), supra page 39? See Haas v. Haas, 504 S.W.2d 44 (Mo. 1973), noted in 40 Mo. L. Rev. 552 (1975).

In re Estate of Getty

California Court of Appeal, Second District, 1978
85 Cal. App. 3d 755, 149 Cal. Rptr. 656

FLEMING, J. Petition by Anne Catherine Getty to contest the 21st codicil to the September 1958 will of her grandfather, Jean Paul Getty.[12]

---

12. Jean Paul Getty, one of the world's richest men, died June 6, 1976, aged 83, at Sutton Place, his 72-room country home in Surrey, England. Reared in California, and a graduate of Oxford with a degree in politics and economics, Getty started in the oil business in Oklahoma in 1914, made his first million within two years, and went on to become a billionaire after hitting enormous quantities of oil in Saudi Arabia in 1953.

In Sutton Place Getty installed a pay telephone booth so that his guests, as he explained, would not need to feel they were imposing on their host. At luncheon or dinner with friends, waiters automatically handed him the bill. "It's not the money I object to, it's the principle of the thing that bothers me — to say nothing of the monotony of it." He received 3,000 letters a month from strangers, all seeking money. But he gave no money to individuals, because, he said, accepting handouts was corrupting.

Getty was linked romantically with a succession of women. He had five marriages and an equal number of divorces, but most of his former wives had a good word to say for him and he for them. In his will he left substantial bequests to 12 women with whom he had had romances during his life. N.Y. Times June 6, 1976, at 1, col. 6; id., June 15, 1976, at 9, col. 1. — Eds.

J. Paul Getty

Reproduced by permission of the J. Paul Getty Museum.

Petitioner does not contest the will and its first 20 codicils, but asserts that decedent lacked testamentary capacity when he executed the 21st codicil on 11 March 1976, or in the alternative that he executed the codicil under the undue influence of his close advisers. The trial court *proc.* ruled petitioner was not an interested person within the meaning of Probate Code Sections 370 and 380 and sustained respondents' general demurrer without leave to amend. Petitioner appeals the judgment of dismissal.

The 1958 Getty will set forth a general plan of distribution which gave real property in Pacific Palisades and Getty's art collection to the trustees of the J. Paul Getty Museum (museum). After individual bequests, the will left the residue of the estate directly to the museum trustees to become part of the museum's endowment fund. If for any reason the bequest were invalidated, the residue of the estate would go to a trust created under the will, with income payable to specified universities. The will named decedent's four sons, George F. Getty II, Jean Ronald Getty, Eugene Paul Getty, and Gordon Peter Getty, as trustees of all trusts created under the will.

In November 1967 decedent executed a 9th codicil to the 1958 will. This codicil left the residue of his estate in trust to trustees under the will, with all income payable to the museum. It eliminated Gordon Peter Getty as a trustee and named decedent's other three sons — George F. Getty II, Jean Ronald Getty, and Eugene Paul Getty — as trustees, with the added provision that when the last of them ceased to act as trustee, whether from death or otherwise, the three oldest (over 21) lineal descendants of the testator would succeed and serve as co-trustees. Petitioner Anne, the daugher of George F. Getty II, is the eldest of decedent's grandchildren. The 14th codicil executed in July 1971 eliminated Eugene Paul Getty as a trustee of trusts under the will. The 16th codicil executed in June 1973 eliminated George F. Getty II, by then deceased, as a trustee of trusts under the will, and named Jean Ronald Getty and a bank as trustees of trusts under the will. In the 19th codicil executed in January 1975 Gordon Peter Getty was reinstated as a trustee of trusts under the will, joining Jean Ronald Getty and Title Insurance and Trust Company as trustees; and the number of contingent successor trustees was reduced to the testator's two oldest lineal descendants (with specified exceptions).

On 11 March 1976 decedent executed the 21st (and last) codicil, which eliminated the trust under the will as recipient of the residue of his estate and reinstated the museum trustees as residuary legatees of the estate for the benefit of the museum's endowment fund. Decedent died 6 June 1976, approximately three months after executing the 21st codicil. Both Jean Ronald Getty and Gordon Peter Getty, the named individual trustees and executors under the 21st codicil, survived decedent, and in conjunction with Title Insurance and Trust Company they serve as executors and trustees of trusts under the will.

The residue of the estate, approximately twenty percent of all outstanding shares of Getty Oil Company, has an estimated value in excess of $700,000,000.

The sole issue on appeal is whether petitioner, a contingent trustee for all trusts created under the will, is an "interested person" within the meaning of Probate Code sections 370 and 380, and thus authorized by statute to contest the validity of the 21st codicil. We hold she is not and affirm the trial court's ruling.

Probate Code sections 370 and 380 allow an "interested person" to contest the validity of a will. In the absence of a legislative definition, the courts have construed the term to mean that a person is "interested" within the meaning of these sections when the person's interest in the estate would be "'. . . impaired or defeated by the probate of the will, or benefited by setting it aside.'" (Estate of Plaut (1945) 27 Cal. 2d 424, 425-26, 164 P.2d 765, 766.) The right of a person to contest a will is based upon the loss of property or property rights that would result from recognition of an invalid instrument which deprives the person of those rights. Illustrative of interested persons are: decedent's heirs, who take by intestate succession if a will is invalid (Estate of Robinson (1963) 211 Cal. App. 2d 556, 27 Cal. Rptr. 441; Estate of Emery (1960) 199 Cal. App. 2d 22, 18 Cal. Rptr. 86); contingent remaindermen under a testamentary trust (Estate of Plaut, supra); judgment lien creditors of a disinherited heir (Estate of Harootenian (1951) 38 Cal. 2d 242, 238 P.2d 992); beneficiaries of a decedent's tax-liened life insurance policy (Estate of Kovacs (1964) 227 Cal. App. 2d 308, 38 Cal. Rptr. 612).

The crux of the dispute here centers on the general conception that a person must have a *pecuniary* interest in an estate to contest a will. Respondents claim that the necessity for a pecuniary interest absolutely precludes a trustee, in this case a contingent trustee, of a superseded testamentary instrument from attacking the validity of the document presented for probate. Petitioner, citing cases from other jurisdictions, asserts that a contingent trustee is necessarily an interested person with standing to contest a subsequent codicil which eliminates a trust. We think both sides overstate.

Initially, we note petitioner does not contest the validity of the 1958 will and its first 20 codicils, but takes issue solely with the validity of the 21st codicil. Petitioner asserts no basis for an "interest" predicated on possible intestate succession since: (a) she does not assert a lack of testamentary capacity prior to the 21st codicil, and (b) the prior, presumably valid will and codicils provide a complete scheme of charitable bequests — contingent upon the failure or invalidity of the initial museum bequest — which renders any reversionary interest in the intestate heirs so remote as to preclude standing to contest on that basis. We also note that, according to the briefs, petitioner is the recipient of a princely income from her grandmother's trust, the Sarah C. Getty Trust of 1934, and enjoys an expectancy of a royal fortune in principal on the termination of that trust.

Petitioner, therefore, must claim an interest in the estate solely by virtue of her asserted position under the 19th and 20th codicils as a contingent trustee of a trust created under the will to hold the residue of the estate.[13]

A testamentary trustee takes legal title to the trust corpus, with equitable title and the right to enforce performance of the trust vested in the beneficiary. Clearly, a trustee's naked legal title to the trust corpus is not a pecuniary interest, since he takes title solely for the benefit of the named beneficiaries. However, lack of direct pecuniary interest does not absolutely foreclose an omitted trustee's right to contest a will. In appropriate circumstances an executor omitted from a later will has a right to contest the subsequent will to insure that the testator's intent, as expressed in bequests to the beneficiaries under the will, is not impaired or thwarted by probate of a testamentary document which is not genuine or which is the end-product of undue influence or mental disability. (Estate of Costa (1961) 191 Cal. App. 2d 515, 518, 12 Cal. Rptr. 920; Jay v. Superior Court (1970) 10 Cal. App. 3d 754, 758, 89 Cal. Rptr. 466.) By direct analogy a testamentary trustee is the representative of his beneficiaries and the guardian of their interests, and, where appropriate, he may contest a subsequent testamentary document which impairs the pecuniary interests of the beneficiaries in the estate property. Therefore, a trustee's standing to contest a will does not depend strictly on a personal pecuniary interest in the bequeathed corpus under the prior instrument, but may be made determinate by impairment of the pecuniary rights of the beneficiaries by the probate of the subsequent testamentary document.

Thus, in the abstract, petitioner is correct in asserting that a testamentary trustee, in this case a contingent trustee, may contest a subsequent will. However, analysis of the ultimate effect of the contested change on the beneficiary here — the museum — does not disclose any impairment of its interest as a result of the subsequent codicil. Quite the contrary. Under both the 20th and 21st codicils the museum is entitled to receive all income from the residue of the estate. The sole difference under the 21st codicil is that control of the assets, primarily stock, is shifted from a trust under the will to the museum trustees and

---

13. Under the rationale of Estate of Plaut the contingent nature of petitioner's asserted interest does not in itself preclude standing for a will contest. (Estate of Plaut (1945) 27 Cal. 2d 424, 428-40,164 P.2d 765.)

the income now goes directly to museum purposes. The subsequent change has the effect of enhancing the museum's income by eliminating the sizeable trustee fees of the intermediate trust under the will, which, under earlier codicils, would become payable to the testamentary trustees.[14] Hence the museum will profit financially by elimination of the intermediate trust. The right to control the trust res and receive statutory fees for administration of the trust, though admittedly legal interests which stem from management of the corpus, are not rights to the estate res that constitute sufficient pecuniary interest to give standing to the omitted trustees to contest the codicil without reference to the effect of the subsequent codicil on the beneficiary. (Cf. Jay v. Superior Court, supra, 10 Cal. App. 3d 759, 89 Cal. Rptr. 466.) Since the pecuniary interest of the beneficiary of the residue of decedent's estate is not impaired but is enhanced by the 21st codicil's elimination of the intermediate trust, petitioner does not qualify as an interested person within the meaning of Probate Code sections 370 and 380.

The right to contest a will is purely statutory. (Jay v. Superior Court, supra, 10 Cal. App. 3d 758, 89 Cal. Rptr. 466, summarizing cases.) Petitioner's additional contentions about the testator's intent to retain family control over the Getty Oil Company stock that constituted the bulk of decedent's estate, and about his desire to have his lineal descendants act as financial watchdogs for the museum, are irrelevant and do not provide a substitute for petitioner's lack of pecuniary interest

14. The 19th codicil, like earlier codicils, directed that executors and trustees "shall serve for the statutory commissions provided by the applicable laws of the State of California." With respect to the compensation of trustees, California law provides only that trustees shall be entitled to reasonable compensation fixed by the court (Prob. Code, §1122), but in a trust with a corpus of $700,000,000 even amounts of "reasonable compensation" are bound to be staggering.

In January 1977, seven months after Getty's death $3,000,000 was paid to the executors of the Getty estate as partial allowance on statutory commissions of over $7,000,000, and $2,000,000 was paid to the attorneys for the executors as partial allowance on statutory fees of over $7,000,000. (Prob. Code, §§901, 910). The statute specifies amounts of commissions and fees in regressive percentages for estates up to $500,000, and then states a rate of 1 percent "for all above $500,000." Query: did the legislative scheme ever contemplate or visualize an estate of this size, and, if it did not, is there a gap in statutory rates which the court should fill by fixing reasonable compensation? (Church of the Holy Trinity v. United States (1892) 143 U.S. 457, 36 L. Ed. 226.) Ordinarily, the museum trustees would be the ones to take action on behalf of the charitable beneficiary to challenge this monumental windfall of commissions and fees to executors and their attorneys for administering what is essentially a liquid, one-asset estate. However, the composition of the museum's board of trustees makes it doubtful that the board could impartially consider this question, let alone take vigorous action, by reason of the conflicts of interest present between the trustees' duties as guardians of a charitable trust and their personal welfare as executors of the estate, affiliates of attorneys for the estate, and officers and employees of Getty Oil Company. When charitable trustees are unable to act to protect the interests of their beneficiary, the duty to act devolves upon the Attorney General of California. (Gov. Code, §§12511, 12591.) We invite the Attorney General to consider, negotiate, and take appropriate action.

or for the beneficial representation that would entitle her to contest the will.

Our decision on petitioner's lack of standing to contest renders moot respondents' contentions of untimely filing of the petition and improper joinder of parties.

The judgment is affirmed.

NOTES AND PROBLEMS

1. Prior to the execution of the twenty-first codicil, Getty's will and codicils devised his residuary estate to three trustees to pay the income to the Getty Museum. Those three trustees were Jean Ronald Getty, Gordon Peter Getty, and Title Insurance and Trust Company. The will and codicils also provided that the testator's two oldest lineal descendants (except Eugene Paul Getty and J. Paul Getty III) should succeed Jean Ronald Getty and Gordon Peter Getty as trustees. As the oldest grandchild, Anne stood next in line to act as trustee of the testamentary trust. By the twenty-first codicil Getty eliminated the testamentary trust and provided that his residuary estate be paid directly to the museum. Thus the fight in the *Getty* case was whether $700 million would be managed by the two oldest descendants of Getty (plus the corporate trustee), giving them — as owners of 20 percent of the stock — substantial say in the running of the Getty Oil Company and a good bit of deferential treatment by the richest art museum in the world, or by the museum itself. Anne Getty wanted to set aside the twenty-first codicil because of the alleged mental incapacity of Getty and the alleged undue influence by the museum director and one of Getty's lawyers, who was named to become a successor trustee of the Sarah C. Getty Trust upon Getty's death. The Sarah C. Getty Trust held 42 percent of the stock of the Getty Oil Company and hence held assets worth more than double Getty's probate estate. Anne Getty's theory was that Getty's lawyer wanted to take effective control of the Getty Oil Company from the Getty family and put it in his own hands at Getty's death. See N.Y. Times, Nov. 7, 1976, at 26, col. 6.

In the third from last paragraph of the opinion the court characterized as "irrelevant" Anne Getty's argument about Getty's intent to retain family control of the Getty Oil Company. Is it? Suppose that *T* executes a will naming *A* as trustee for the benefit of Podunk University. Subsequently, through the exercise of undue influence, *B* persuades *T* to execute a codicil naming *B* as trustee for the benefit of Podunk. Does *A* have standing to contest? Suppose that instead of *B* exercising undue influence, the president of Podunk exercises undue influence (by promising an honorary degree, among other things) and persuades

T to eliminate *A* as trustee and give the bequest directly to Podunk. Does *A* have standing to contest? Cf. Succession of Kilpatrick, 356 So. 2d 1083 (La. App. 1978); Reed v. Home National Bank, 297 Mass. 222, 8 N.E.2d 601, 112 A.L.R. 657 (1937).

If Anne Getty does not have standing, who may contest the twenty-first codicil? The two eldest lineal descendants eligible to serve as family trustees (Jean Ronald Getty and Gordon Peter Getty) and Title Insurance and Trust Company are named executors; their duty is to defend the will and all its codicils. By choosing to serve as executors, and collect millions in commissions, they put themselves in a position where they cannot contest the will.

In March 1982 the executors of the Getty estate distributed $1.2 billion to the trustees of the Getty Museum in Los Angeles, making it the richest art museum in the world. By 1989 the Getty trust fortune had swollen to $3 billion. To maintain its charitable status under federal tax laws, the Getty trust is required to spend annually a sum equal to 5 percent of its capital, or about $150 million a year.

In footnote 14 in In re Estate of Getty, the court invited the attorney general, as supervisor of charities, to take appropriate action to try to reduce the executors' commissions and attorneys' fees from the amounts specified in the state statutory fee schedules. In the proceeding to close the estate, the executors and attorneys were unwilling to agree to take less than they were entitled to by statute, and the attorney general objected to their accounts. The court held that the attorney general did not have the power to depart from the statutory fee schedules and had no authority to impose a standard of reasonableness in such a matter, and the court approved statutory executors' commissions in the amount of $13,589,923 and statutory attorneys' fees in an equal amount, for a total of $27,179,846. Estate of Getty, 143 Cal. App. 3d 455, 191 Cal. Rptr. 897 (1983).

2. If all the devisees oppose probate of a will, does the executor have standing to proceed to probate the will? See Uniform Probate Code §3-720, Comment. But cf. In re Estate of Harper, 202 Kan. 150, 446 P.2d 738 (1968).

3. Perry Pearson is senile and only occasionally knows relatives and old friends who come to visit him. Perry's will, executed while in sound mind, devises his property to his son, Dean. After Dean and his wife have marital difficulties, Dean — forseeing divorce ahead — persuades his father to execute a new will that leaves his property to a bank as trustee to pay the income to Dean for life, with remainder over to Dean's children. The trust has a spendthrift clause, which prevents creditors, including divorced spouses, from reaching Dean's life estate to satisfy claims. Perry dies. Dean's wife sues for divorce and petitions to set aside the will on the grounds of mental incapacity and undue influence. (If the will is set aside, Dean will take all his father's property

under the prior will, which then will be divided between Dean and his wife upon divorce.) Does Dean's wife have standing to contest? See In re Estate of Pearson, 319 N.W.2d 248 (Iowa 1982).

SECTION D.   AN ESTATE PLANNING PROBLEM

1.   *The Client's Letter and Its Enclosures*

September 15, 19—

Dear_____:

For some time now, Wendy and I have been considering the rewriting of our wills since we now have very simple wills giving all our property to each other in case of death and then to our three children when the survivor of us dies. However, in this day of air crashes where Wendy and I might die simultaneously, the problems of settling our estate might be complicated.

These, in general, are the assets with which we are concerned:

Residence	$160,000	($30,000 mtge.)
Lot, cabin, Lake Murray	75,000	
Chevrolet station wagon	5,000	
Toyota	3,000	
Household furniture, etc.	???	
Checking account	2,000 to 4,000	
Savings account	7,000	
Certificate of deposit	20,000	
Stocks	170,000	
Mutual funds	70,000	
Life insurance	175,000	
Group life insurance	125,000	

Wendy and I think our main objectives should be to avoid probate and to eliminate as many inheritance taxes as possible. I am enclosing copies of our present wills. These are some of the questions we would like your help on:

1.   It may be that we do not need wills at all. Can we let our property pass by inheritance or by joint and survivor arrangements? Our bank accounts and some of our stocks are set up to pass by a joint and survivor arrangement.

2.   As a sort of corollary to that first question, we have read in various places that it would be a good idea to set up a trust to pass our house, cars, etc. With the use of a trust plus the joint and survivor arrangements, could we avoid the need for wills and probate entirely?

3.   If you think we should have wills, are our present ones all right? If not, how should they be changed?

4. In case of simultaneous death most of our estate would go to our three young children. Should we name a trustee as well as a guardian? What is the difference between the two?

Any advice you have for us will be appreciated. I will be expecting to hear from you in the near future.

Sincerely yours,

/s/ Howard

Howard Brown

Last Will and Testament of Howard Brown

I, Howard Brown, of the city of Arlington, County of _____, and State of _____, do hereby make, publish, and declare this to be my Last Will and Testament, hereby revoking any and all other wills and codicils thereto, which I have heretofore made.

FIRST: I hereby direct that all of my just debts, funeral expenses, and expenses of administration of my estate be paid out of my estate as soon as may be practicable after my death.

SECOND: I name and appoint my beloved wife, Wendy Brown, to be the executor of this my Last Will and Testament, and I direct that she not be required to give bond or other security.

THIRD: I give, devise, and bequeath all of my property, both real and personal, of whatever kind and nature and description, and wherever located, including household furniture and equipment, and personal effects of which I now have or may die seised and possessed of or be entitled to, to my beloved wife, the aforesaid Wendy Brown, should she survive me. Should she not survive me, I then give, devise, and bequeath all of my property, as aforesaid, to my children.

FOURTH: I authorize and empower my said Executor, or anyone appointed to administer this my Last Will and Testament, to sell and convert into cash any and all of my personal property without a court order and to convey any such real estate by deed without the necessity of a court order authorizing such conveyance or approving such deed.

FIFTH: In the event that my beloved wife, the aforesaid Wendy Brown, predeceases me, I name and appoint my beloved wife's sister, Lucy Preston Lipman, of San Francisco, California, as legal guardian of my children during their respective minorities.

IN TESTIMONY WHEREOF I have hereunto set my hand and seal this 27th day of November, 19____.

_____
/s/ Howard Brown

Howard Brown

The above instrument, consisting of two typewritten pages, of which this is the second, with paragraphs FIRST through FIFTH, inclusive, was on the 27th day of November, 19____, signed by Howard Brown, in our presence, and he did then declare this to be his Last Will and Testament, and we at his request and in his presence and in the presence of each other, did sign this instrument as witnesses thereunto and as witnesses to his signature thereto.

WITNESSES: _____/s/ Michael Wong_____

                                     _____/s/ Patricia Muñoz Garcia_____

[Wendy Brown's will contains reciprocal provisions. Wendy leaves everything to Howard if he survives and if he does not survive her to her children.]

2.   Some Preliminary Questions Raised by Brown's Letter

From time to time we shall refer back to the Brown estate planning situation in the context of the substantive areas being considered. But before we embark on our studies, it may be profitable to reflect on some of the questions raised in, and by, Brown's letter.

PROBLEMS

1. Examine Howard Brown's present will in the context of the asset and family situation described in his letter. Can you detect any problems that may be raised, or any contingencies that are not provided for, by the will provisions? Here are a few:

Article FIRST: Does the "just debts" clause authorize the executor to pay debts barred by the statute of limitations?

Does the clause require the executor to pay off the mortgage on the Brown's home? Would this be desirable? See In re Estate of Miller, 127 F. Supp. 23 (D.D.C. 1955); In re Estate of Keil, 51 Del. 351, 145 A.2d 563 (1958). See also discussion of exoneration of liens, infra page 364.

Would death taxes incurred at Brown's death be "just debts," making this a tax apportionment clause requiring payment of all taxes out of Brown's residuary estate? See Thompson v. Thompson, 230 S.W.2d

376, 380 (Tex. Civ. App. 1950); Estate of Kyreazis, 701 P.2d 1022 (N.M. App. 1985); Internal Revenue Code of 1986, §§2206, 2207.

Suppose that Howard and Wendy Brown had signed an antenuptial agreement providing that in exchange for Wendy's giving up her job and working within the home, Howard promised to devise to Wendy one-half of his net estate. Suppose further that Howard's will contained a "just debts" clause and devised to Wendy $20,000, less than one-half of his net estate. Is Wendy entitled to both one-half of the estate under the contract and the $20,000 legacy? See Hammer v. Atchison, 536 P.2d 151 (Wyo. 1975).

Articles SECOND and FOURTH: Has suitable provision been made for appointment of an executor in case Wendy Brown dies before Howard? Does the executor have sufficiently broad powers to enable her to administer the estate effectively?

Article THIRD: Is the dispositive plan provided by Brown's will a sound one? Should he make an outright distribution of his entire estate to Mrs. Brown, or should he consider making some other distribution?

Which of the assets listed in Brown's letter will be governed by his will and which will pass as "nonprobate assets" unaffected by the will?

Article FIFTH: If Mr. and Mrs. Brown both die before their children attain majority, a guardianship administration will be required. Is this desirable? See infra page 103.

2.   What do you think of Brown's stated planning objectives? Why should he want to "avoid probate"? Should this be one of "our main objectives" in formulating an estate plan for the Browns? What functions does probate serve, and if probate is "avoided" how are these functions satisfied? See Martin, The Draftsman Views Wills for a Young Family, 54 N.C.L. Rev. 277 (1976).

3.   In view of the Browns' fairly straightforward asset and family situation, do they need wills at all? Will the intestacy laws of their home state provide a satisfactory distributive scheme for their assets at death? If so, doesn't this dispense with the need for a will? Can a will serve any function other than designating the takers of one's property at death?

4.   Should the Browns consider alternatives to a will or intestacy, such as joint and survivor arrangements and inter vivos trusts, as a means of transferring their property at death?

5.   One can readily understand the Browns' desire to eliminate as many inheritance taxes as possible. But in view of the size of the Browns' estate, will tax considerations be a factor in preparing their wills? In general, when should tax savings be one of the main objectives in estate planning?

6.   Perhaps it has occurred to you by now that we don't really know very much about the Brown family or the assets they own. What further

information should we obtain from the clients before we can proceed further?

3. Additional Data on the Browns' Family and Assets

Following receipt of the letter from Howard Brown asking for a review of the present wills of Mr. and Mrs. Brown, a conference was held with the clients, and the following additional information was obtained.

a. Family Data

Members of immediate family		Age	Birth date	Health	Insurable?
Husband	Howard Brown	43	7/12/—	good	yes
Wife	Wendy Brown	41	6/1/—	"	yes
Child	David Adam	16	9/25/—	"	
Child	Susan Jane	14	11/19/—	"	
Child	Barbara Carolyn	11	8/22/—	"	

None of the children has any special health or physical problem. Mrs. Brown stated that she and her husband do not intend to have any more children.

Residence

Home address: 2220 Casino Lane, Arlington.   477-5882
Period of residence in this state: all of life since college.
Note: No problems regarding domicile. Also, note that none of present assets acquired while residing in another state. Does not own property located in any other state.

Parents; collateral relatives

Mr. Brown's father, Burton, died of heart attack at age 60. Mother, Mrs. Alice Brown, is 63 years old, is in good health, and lives in Arlington. Brown stated that his mother has a modest but comfortable income from property left by her husband and from social security. When I asked whether he would inherit property from his mother at her death, he indicated that any such inheritance would be modest in amount. His father's will left all property to mother outright; Brown has no interest under the will.

Brown estimated that his mother owns property worth about $140,000, of which $75,000 is represented by a residence, which is owned outright. Brown is familiar with the terms of his mother's will; it provides for an equal distribution between himself and his brother and sister. Brown is named as executor under the will.

Mr. Brown is the oldest member of his family. A brother, Bruce M. Brown, lives in Salem. He is married to Ava Brown, has two children, and is a cashier at the Salem First National Bank. A sister, Carol Gould, a biochemist, is married to Douglas Gould. She has one child.

Wendy Brown's parents (Robert Preston, age 65, and Rachel Preston, age 62) are both living. Mrs. Brown stated that her father is a well-known doctor in Boston and is quite well off. When asked how well off, Mrs. Brown said he is probably "worth" around $500,000 (probably a conservative estimate). Mrs. Brown has a brother and two sisters, all younger than she is. From this it would appear that Mrs. Brown may acquire a substantial inheritance upon the death of her parents.

Mrs. Brown's collateral relatives: Sister, Lucy Preston Lipman, a writer, lives in San Francisco with her husband, Jonathan Lipman. They have two children. Brother, John Preston, is married to Stacy Preston, has no children, and is a certified public accountant. Sister, Ruth Preston, unmarried, is a professor of history at Boston University.

Mrs. Brown also has two maternal aunts, Fanny d'Alessandro and Polly O'Reilly. They both live in Somerville, New Jersey. Aunt Fanny is a rich widow without children and has a large house full of antiques, paintings, silver — things she and her husband collected during their marriage. Aunt Polly is also a widow without children, who lives comfortably but modestly about a mile from Aunt Fanny. Wendy Brown will likely inherit some of Aunt Fanny's things and possibly a substantial sum of money.

Special family problems

None.

b. Assets

The Browns have lived in Arlington since they were married 18 years ago. Since neither brought into the marriage any property of substantial value, there appears to be no problem in establishing their marital rights in the property they now own. All life insurance policies were taken out after the Browns married.

Tangible personal property

Tangible personalty consists of the usual furnishings in a family residence, two automobiles, outboard motor boat, personal effects such as clothing and jewelry, and other miscellaneous items. No items of unusual value. Estimated value: $20,000

Real estate

(1) Family residence: The Browns purchased their home at 2220 Casino Lane, Arlington, eleven years ago. Although the purchase price for the property was $55,000, Brown believes that it is now worth around $160,000. Present balance on mortgage loan (note held by Arlington Federal Savings & Loan Assn.) is $30,000. The deed shows that title to the property was taken by "Howard Brown and Wendy Brown, as joint tenants with right of survivorship and not as tenants in common."   160,000

(2) Lot and cabin, Lake Murray. Twelve years ago the Browns purchased a lot and cabin on Lake Murray for $20,000. Title to the land was taken in Howard Brown's name alone. Based on current values, the Browns believe they could sell the property for at least $75,000. No mortgage indebtedness.   75,000

Bank accounts

(1) Checking account, Arlington National Bank. The account balance fluctuates from around $1,000 to $4,000 each month. Mr. and Mrs. Brown are both authorized to draw checks on the account; the balance is payable to the survivor.   3,000

(2) Savings account, Arlington Federal Savings & Loan Assn. The account is in the name of "Howard Brown and Wendy Brown, payable on death to the survivor."   7,000

(3) Certificate of deposit, Arlington Federal Savings & Loan Assn, at $9\frac{1}{2}$ percent for four years. CD was issued in the name of "Howard Brown and Wendy Brown, as joint tenants with right of survivorship."   20,000

Securities

(1)   1600 shares, General Corporation common stock. Given to Mr. Brown under his aunt's will six years ago. Current value: $50 per share. Registered in the name of Howard Brown as owner.   80,000

(2)   1000 shares, Varoom Mutual Fund. When Mr. Brown's father died five years ago, his mother gave each of her children $7,500. Brown used all of this money to purchase 400 shares of the Varoom Fund, which has appreciated in value since his purchase. Brown has reinvested the ordinary income and capital gains dividends paid by the fund and now owns an additional 600 shares. Present value is $30 per share. Registered in the name of Howard Brown as owner.   30,000

(3)   1000 shares, American Growth Mutual Fund. Over the years the Browns have invested in the American Growth Fund under some form of monthly investment plan. Their objective was to establish an educational fund for their children. The purchase price has fluctuated over the years from $28 to $42 a share. Present price is $40 a share. Brown says that he has kept records on the price of the shares as purchased. Registered in the name of "Howard Brown and Wendy Brown, as joint tenants with right of survivorship and not as tenants in common."   40,000

(4)   1200 shares, Union National Bank common stock. Was given to Mrs. Brown by her parents. Registered in the name of Wendy Brown as owner.   90,000

Life insurance

(1)   Mutual of New York policy #624-05-91, ordinary life, participating, acquired 14 years ago. Annual premium $2050. Cash surrender value this year $20,500; CSV is increasing at about $1600/year.   100,000

(2)   Metropolitan Life policy #2,313,506T, five-year-renewable term, participating, guaranteed convertible, acquired 10 years ago. Premium this year and the next four years is $400/year.   50,000

(3)   Aetna Life Group policy, group term. Premiums are paid by Howard Brown's employer.   25,000

(4)   Prudential Life policy, group term. Premiums are paid by Wendy Brown's employers.   100,000

Note: Policy (2) (Metropolitan Life) contains double and triple indemnity provisions: double indemnity in case of accidental death, and triple indemnity in case of accidental death while riding on public conveyance.

Policies (1), (2), and (3) name Howard Brown as "insured" and "owner." The policies name Wendy Brown as primary beneficiary and "the insured's children, in equal shares" as contingent beneficiaries. Policy (4) names Wendy Brown as "insured" and "owner." The policy names Howard Brown as beneficiary. It names the estate of Wendy Brown as secondary beneficiary.

Employee benefits of Howard Brown

Mr. Brown is an industrial design engineer and manager of a department at Tresco Machine Tool Company in Arlington. He has been with this firm for the past eight years and feels that he has a secure and responsible position with the firm. His annual salary is $75,000.

In addition to the group insurance mentioned above, Brown's employer provides Blue Cross/Blue Shield coverage, disability insurance, and a qualified pension plan. The plan is "contributory": Brown contributes 4 percent of his annual salary (up to a maximum salary level of $35,000) to the plan and his employer contributes 8 percent. The plan will provide substantial retirement benefits to Brown, under a formula based on his years of service and his average annual salary (to the $35,000 maximum salary level). The present projection is that Brown would be able to retire at age 65 with an annuity of about $20,000.

The pension plan is primarily designed to give retirement benefits; it does not have substantial death benefits. Upon Brown's death before retirement, his wife would receive a lump-sum payment representing Brown's contributions to the plan. At the present time, the portion of the fund represented by Brown's contributions is about $10,000.

Mrs. Brown would have an option of (1) receiving the fund in a lump-sum payment or (2) settling it under an annuity. Because of the small size of the fund and Mrs. Brown's long life expectancy if Brown were to die in the next few years, it would probably be advisable for Mrs. Brown to select the lump-sum payment.

Employee benefits of Wendy Brown

Wendy Brown has a degree in Modern Languages and during the early years of their marriage taught German and French at a secondary school in Arlington. She then worked for several years only in the home. Four years ago Wendy Brown decided to go to law school. Last year she finished law school and received a J.D. degree. (She did *not* take a course in wills and trusts.) Wendy Brown has just accepted a position as an associate of Hanlon and Putz, a medium-size law firm. Her annual salary is $45,000.

In addition to the group insurance mentioned above, Hanlon and Putz provides group medical coverage. There are no pension benefits for associates, only for partners. Wendy Brown has been in practice for only a month. It is likely that her income will exceed Mr. Brown's in a few years.

c. Liabilities

Real estate mortgages: $30,000 mortgage loan, Arlington Federal Savings & Loan Assn.
Other notes to banks, etc.:   None.
Loans on insurance policies: None.
Accounts to others: "Usual" store, etc. accounts.
Other: None.

d. Assets and Liabilities: Summary

(1) Estate of Howard and Wendy Brown[15]

Tangible personalty	$ 20,000
Reality:	
Residence (joint tenancy)	160,000
Lake Murray property (in Howard Brown's name)	75,000
Bank accounts:	
Checking (joint and survivor)	3,000
Savings (joint and survivor)	7,000
Certificate of deposit (joint tenancy)	20,000
Securities:	
Varoom Mutual Fund (in Howard Brown's name)	30,000*

15. Items marked by asterisk were acquired by gift from Howard's and Wendy's respective relatives. All other assets are attributable to Howard Brown's earnings during their marriage. In a common law property state, the source of contributions may be relevant in determining inheritance taxes or the spouse's right to dissent from the will. See, e.g., N.C. Gen. Stat. §30-1(b) (1976). In a community property state, property acquired with a spouse's earnings is community property unless the spouses have changed it into another form of ownership.

General Corp. common (in Howard Brown's name)	80,000*
American Growth Mutual Fund	40,000
Union Natl. Bank common (in Wendy Brown's name)	90,000*
Life insurance on Howard Brown	175,000
Life insurance on Wendy Brown	100,000
Tresco pension plan (Howard Brown's contributions)	10,000
	$810,000

(2) Liabilities

Mortgage loan, Arlington Federal Savings & Loan Assn. $ 30,000

(3) Other factors:

Probable inheritance by Mr. Brown of about $50,000 from his mother. Probability of substantial inheritance by Mrs. Brown from her parents and her Aunt Fanny — but no knowledge of whether this would be outright or in some form of trust arrangement.

e. Planning Objectives

Copies of the Browns' wills are in the file. Mr. Brown's will leaves all property outright to his wife if she survives; otherwise to the children. Her will contains reciprocal provisions. Although there are defects in the dispositive and administrative provisions of the wills, they are not critically deficient; hence no need to draft interim wills.

The Browns stated that the dispositive provisions in their present wills accurately reflect their desires as to how they would like their property to pass at death. At the conference there was no opportunity to discuss this subject further, nor was there any discussion with the Browns about any alternative plans that they might consider. These topics will be discussed at the next conference.

4. Professional Responsibility

MILLER, FUNCTIONS AND ETHICAL PROBLEMS OF THE LAWYER IN DRAFTING A WILL, 1950 U. Ill. L.F. 415, 423: "Indeed, it would be no exaggeration to say that of all the moral obligations of the lawyer who undertakes to prepare a will the obligation of competence is paramount. . . . No lawyer should prepare a will unless he considers himself competent to do so. He should approach this question with a realization that to the client the will is probably the most important document of his life. . . . The property may be the result of a lifetime of effort. Its disposition will have lasting and significant effect both upon those included as beneficiaries and upon those excluded who might naturally expect or hope to be included. . . . If the lawyer doubts his ability to produce the best possible will for the client, he should decline to prepare one."

Ogle v. Fuiten

Supreme Court of Illinois, 1984
102 Ill. 2d 356, 466 N.E.2d 224

GOLDENHERSH, J.   Plaintiffs, James Elvin Ogle and Leland W. Ogle, initiated this action in the circuit court of Sangamon County against defendants, Lorraine Fuiten, as executrix of the estate of William F. Fuiten, and Robert G. Heckenkamp, who, under the name of Heckenkamp and Fuiten, had been associated with William F. Fuiten in the practice of law. In a two-count complaint plaintiffs alleged that William F. Fuiten had negligently drafted wills for Oscar H. Smith and Alma I. Smith, respectively an uncle and aunt of plaintiffs, and alternatively, that Fuiten failed to properly perform his contract with the Smiths to fulfill their testamentary intentions, and in so doing, failed to benefit the plaintiffs. Defendants moved to dismiss for failure to state a cause of action. The circuit court allowed the motion, and plaintiffs appealed. The appellate court reversed and remanded (112 Ill. App. 3d 1048, 68 Ill. Dec. 491, 445 N.E.2d 1344), and we allowed defendants' petition for leave to appeal (87 Ill. 2d R. 315).

The appellate court summarized the allegations contained in the complaint as follows:

> Count I essentially alleges: (1) Testators employed defendant Fuiten and the law firm of Heckenkamp and Fuiten to prepare wills in accordance with the testators' intentions; (2) the wills were prepared; (3) neither testator intended their property to devolve by the law of intestate succession; (4) it was their intention that their property be left to plaintiffs if neither testator survived the other by 30 days; (5) this contingency occurred; (6) Fuiten owed plaintiffs the duty of ascertaining the testators' intentions in all foreseeable events and to draft wills which would effectuate these intentions; (7) Fuiten breached this duty and negligently drafted the subject wills; and (8) plaintiffs suffered damage as a direct result of this breach.
>
> Count II essentially alleges the first five allegations noted above and

additionally alleges: (6) the purpose of the employment of Fuiten and the firm was to draft wills not only for the benefit of testators, but for the benefit of these plaintiffs; (7) Fuiten and the firm were paid the agreed consideration under the employment agreement; (8) Fuiten and the firm knew plaintiffs were intended beneficiaries of the wills and the employment agreement; (9) Fuiten and the firm had agreed to draft wills leaving the property to plaintiffs in the event neither testator survived the other by 30 days; (10) Fuiten breached this agreement in that the wills failed to fulfill the testators' intentions; and (11) plaintiffs suffered foreseeable, direct damage as a consequence of this breach. 112 Ill. App. 3d 1048, 1053, 68 Ill. Dec. 491, 445 N.E.2d 1344.

The wills of Oscar H. Smith and Alma I. Smith contained the following provisions:

> SECOND: I give, devise and bequeath all of my estate, real, personal and mixed wheresoever situated to my wife, ALMA I. SMITH, if she [my husband, OSCAR H. SMITH, if he] shall survive me within thirty (30) days from the date of my death.
>
> THIRD: I direct that if my wife, ALMA I. SMITH, [my husband, OSCAR H. SMITH] and I die in or from a common disaster that my estate be equally divided between my nephews, JAMES ELVIN OGLE, and LELAND OGLE, share and share alike. (In re Estate of Smith (1979), 68 Ill. App. 3d 30, 31, 24 Ill. Dec. 451, 385 N.E.2d 363.)

These wills were construed in In re Estate of Smith (1979), 68 Ill. App. 3d 30, 24 Ill. Dec. 451, 385 N.E.2d 363, and it was held that because Oscar Smith died suddenly of a stroke on April 10, 1977, and his wife, Alma, died 15 days later from a lingering cancer illness, and neither will contained any other dispositive provisions, their estates passed by intestacy to persons other than plaintiffs.

Because the judgment appealed from was entered upon allowance of defendants' motion to dismiss, all facts properly pleaded in the complaint must be taken as true. [A cause of action should not be dismissed on the pleadings unless it clearly appears that no set of facts can be proved which will entitle plaintiffs to recover.]

Conceding that under Pelham v. Griesheimer (1982), 92 Ill. 2d 13, 64 Ill. Dec. 544, 440 N.E.2d 96, privity is not a prerequisite to an action by a nonclient against an attorney, defendants argue that the complaint fails to allege a duty owed plaintiffs. They argue that the only duty owed by defendants was to provide each testator "with a valid testamentary instrument that disposes of the testators' property at his death in the manner expressly stated in his will." They argue that to permit persons unnamed in the will, or persons named with a precondition which fails to occur, to bring an action against the attorney "creates an unlimited and unknown class of potential plaintiffs." They contend, too, that in order to recover from an attorney, a nonclient must allege and prove "that the primary purpose and intent of the attorney-client relationship itself was to benefit or influence the third party." (92 Ill. 2d 13, 21, 64 Ill. Dec. 544, 440 N.E.2d 96.) Defendants argue that under this "intent to directly benefit" test, plaintiffs' cause fails because the testators' intent, as defined in the will-construction action, shows that plaintiffs were to benefit only under certain circumstances which did not occur. Thus, defendants contend, the intent of the testators to benefit plaintiffs is not, as required by *Pelham,* "clearly evident."

Also citing *Pelham,* plaintiffs contend that they have alleged facts which show that the testators, in obtaining the services of the defendants in the preparations of the wills, intended to "directly benefit" plaintiffs and that, as held by the appellate court, they have stated a cause of action in both counts of the complaint.

In support of their argument that the complaint states a cause of action, plaintiffs cite a number of cases from other jurisdictions. In Heyer v. Flaig (1969), 70 Cal. 2d 223, 449 P.2d 161, 74 Cal. Rptr. 225, an attorney was employed to draft a will, passing the client's entire estate to her daughters, but negligently failed to include a provision in the will specifically excluding the client's fiance. The client then married and thereafter died without changing her will. As a post-testamentary spouse, her husband claimed a portion of the estate. The California Supreme Court held the attorney liable to the daughters for failing to include in the will a provision excluding the prospective husband from any share in the estate, or to advise his client of the consequences of failing to so provide.

In Lucas v. Hamm (1961), 56 Cal. 2d 583, 364, P.2d 685, 15 Cal. Rptr. 821, the California Supreme Court indicated that an attorney might be held liable to the intended beneficiaries who had been damaged by the attorney's negligence, for the consequences of his negligent drafting of his client's will. The court, however, did not permit recovery because it determined that the attorney, in including in the will a provision which violated the rule against perpetuities, was not negligent.

Plaintiffs also cite to other jurisdictions which have permitted intended beneficiaries to recover from an attorney for his negligence in preparing a will or advising the testator. See Licata v. Spector (C.P. 1966), 26 Conn. Sup. 378, 225 A.2d 28 (will held invalid because of lack of statutory requisites as to attesting witnesses); McAbee v. Edwards (Fla. App. 1976), 340 So. 2d 1167 (erroneously advising testator that no change in her will necessary because of her marriage); Succession of Killingsworth (La. App. 1972), 270 So. 2d 196 (attorney's failure to comply with statute); Auric v. Continental Casualty Co. (1983), 111 Wis. 2d 507, 331 N.W.2d 325 (negligent failure to properly supervise execution and attestation of will).

Defendants attempt to distinguish these cases, contending that in each instance, unlike the situation here, the intent of the testator was expressly shown by the will. Defendants argue that to state a cause of action plaintiffs should be required to show, from the express terms of the will, that the plaintiff was an intended beneficiary of the relationship between the defendant attorney and the testator. They argue that this would protect against a flood of litigation. Defendants have cited no authority which has applied the rule which they espouse, and we found no basis in the cases which we have examined for imposing such a requirement.

We agree with the appellate court that "the allegations of count I sufficiently state the traditional elements of negligence in tort and count II sufficiently states the traditional elements of a third-party beneficiary/ breach of contract theory." (112 Ill. App. 3d 1048, 1053, 68 Ill. Dec. 491, 445 N.E.2d 1344.) We note parenthetically that, unlike *Pelham,* the defendants' representation of the testators here was of a nonadversarial nature and consisted only of the drafting of the wills which plaintiffs alleged were for their benefit as intended beneficiaries. See Pelham v. Griesheimer (1982), 92 Ill. 2d 13, 22, 64 Ill. Dec. 544, 440 N.E.2d 96. . . .

We note further that if plaintiffs here are successful in their action, the orderly disposition of the testator's property is not disrupted, and the provisions of the wills, and the probate administration, remain unaffected. On these facts, the present action is not a collateral attack on the wills. . . .

For the foregoing reasons, the judgment of the appellate court is affirmed.

Judgment affirmed.

NOTES AND QUESTIONS

1. Ogle v. Fuiten is representative of the modern trend to hold an attorney liable for negligence to intended will beneficiaries even though there is no privity of contract between them. In a few jurisdictions the privity barrier still exists, but most of the recent cases have swept it aside. In England will beneficiaries can sue the drafting attorney for negligence. See Bauman, Damages for Legal Malpractice: An Appraisal of the Crumbling Dike and the Threatening Flood, 61 Temp. L.Q. 1127 (1988); Adams & Abendroth, Malpractice Climate Heats Up for Estate Planners, 126 Tr. & Est., April 1987, at 41; Johnston, Legal Malpractice in Estate Planning — Perilous Times Ahead for the Practitioner, 67 Iowa L. Rev. 629 (1982); Comment, General Practitioners Beware: The Duty to Refer an Estate Planning Client to a Specialist, 14 Cum. L. Rev. 103 (1984).

2. Can the defendant lawyers in *Ogle* get reimbursement from the intestate successors? A trustee who delivers property to the wrong person can claim reimbursement from the payee. See Langbein & Waggoner, Reformation of Wills on the Ground of Mistake, 130 U. Pa. L. Rev. 521, 589 (1982).

3. When a lawyer learns of new information — either changes in the client's family or changes in the tax laws — that suggests revision of the will is desirable, does the lawyer have the duty to advise the client? A.B.A. Committee on Professional Ethics, Formal Opinion 210 (1941): "It is our opinion that where the lawyer has no reason to believe that he has been supplanted by another lawyer, it is not only his right, but it might even be his duty to advise his client of any change of fact or law which might defeat the client's testamentary purpose as expressed in the will."

4. In a comprehensive article covering many of the estate planning problems in this course, Professor Roger Andersen argues that lawyers have a duty to allow clients to make informed decisions on the large majority of issues. Andersen, Informed Decisionmaking in an Office Practice, 28 B.C.L. Rev. 225 (1987). Too often in estate planning the lawyer thinks he or she knows what is best for the client and the beneficiaries. And too often the lawyer uses standard forms without presenting the client with enough information for the client to determine whether those forms carry out the client's wishes. As you go through the cases in this book, appraise the work of the lawyer in disclosing choices to the client.

2

INTESTACY: AN ESTATE PLAN BY OPERATION OF LAW

SECTION A. INTESTATE SUCCESSORS: SPOUSE AND DESCENDANTS

1. *Introduction*

Studies indicate that the large majority of people dies intestate, forsaking wills and legal advice. The richer and older a person is, the more likely he or she has a will. Why do people of moderate wealth not seek legal advice and make wills? One reason of course is that most people cannot accept and plan for the fact of their own death; insurance salesmen are careful to omit the word "death" from their discussions with clients ("If anything should happen to you. . . ." *If*, indeed!). As Freud wrote, "Our own death is indeed unimaginable, and whenever we make the attempt to imagine it we can perceive that we really survive as spectators. Hence . . . at bottom no one believes in his own death, or to put the same thing in another way, in the unconscious every one of us is convinced of his own immortality." S. Freud, Our Attitude Towards Death, *in* 4 Collected Papers 304 (1925).

Another reason why people do not make wills is the cost involved. It seems like a "big deal" to go to a lawyer. Whatever the reason, a person who dies intestate necessarily accepts the intestacy laws as his estate plan, even though this might not be as satisfactory as an individually designed will could be.

Distribution of the property of a person who dies without a will, or whose will does not make a complete disposition of the estate, is governed by the statute of descent and distribution of the pertinent state. Generally speaking, the law of the state where the decedent was domiciled at death governs the disposition of personal property, and the law of the state where the decedent's real property is located governs the disposition of such real property.

Since it is a safe bet that the law of intestacy is not exactly the same in all details in any two states, it is essential that you become familiar with the intestacy statutes of the state in which you intend to practice. It is quite impossible to answer any specific question as to who succeeds to property without looking at the statutes of a particular state. We reproduce here the intestacy provisions of the Uniform Probate Code. The UPC, promulgated in 1969, has been adopted in about one-third of the states, and it has served as a catalyst for probate reform in many others. See Andersen, The Influence of the Uniform Probate Code in Nonadopting States, 8 U. Puget Sound L. Rev. 599 (1985). It should be profitable for you to compare the code provisions with those of your own state, which probably differ in several details.

Uniform Probate Code (1983)

§2-101   [INTESTATE ESTATE]

Any part of the estate of a decedent not effectively disposed of by his will passes to his heirs as prescribed in the following sections of this Code.

§2-102   [SHARE OF THE SPOUSE][1]

The intestate share of the surviving spouse is:

(1) if there is no surviving issue or parent of the decedent, the entire intestate estate;

(2) if there is no surviving issue but the decedent is survived by a parent or parents, the first [$50,000], plus one-half of the balance of the intestate estate;

(3) if there are surviving issue all of whom are issue of the surviving spouse also, the first [$50,000], plus one-half of the balance of the intestate estate;

(4) if there are surviving issue one or more of whom are not issue of the surviving spouse, one-half of the intestate estate.

---

1. The Uniform Probate Code's alternate section for community property states (§2-102A) provides for the same distribution of separate property as is provided in §2-102, and further provides that all community property passes to the surviving spouse whether or not the decedent is survived by issue or parents. — Eds.

§2-103   [SHARE OF HEIRS OTHER THAN SURVIVING SPOUSE]

The part of the intestate estate not passing to the surviving spouse under Section 2-102, or the entire intestate estate if there is no surviving spouse, passes as follows:

(1)   to the issue of the decedent; if they are all of the same degree of kinship to the decedent they take equally, but if of unequal degree, then those of more remote degree take by representation;

(2)   if there is no surviving issue, to his parent or parents equally;

(3)   if there is no surviving issue or parent, to the issue of the parents or either of them by representation;

(4)   if there is no surviving issue, parent or issue of a parent, but the decedent is survived by one or more grandparents or issue of grandparents, half of the estate passes to the paternal grandparents if both survive, or to the surviving paternal grandparent, or to the issue of the paternal grandparents if both are deceased, the issue taking equally if they are all of the same degree of kinship to the decedent, but if of unequal degree those of more remote degree take by representation; and the other half passes to the maternal relatives in the same manner; but if there be no surviving grandparent or issue of grandparent on either the paternal or the maternal side, the entire estate passes to the relatives on the other side in the same manner as the half.

§2-105   [NO TAKER]

If there is no taker under the provisions of this Article, the intestate estate passes to the [state].

§2-106   [REPRESENTATION]

If representation is called for by this Code, the estate is divided into as many shares as there are surviving heirs in the nearest degree of kinship and deceased persons in the same degree who left issue who survive the decedent, each surviving heir in the nearest degree receiving one share and the share of each deceased person in the same degree being divided among his issue in the same manner.

2.   *Spouse*

What policies are involved in framing an intestacy statute? Does the statute carry out the expectations of the *average decedent* and of the recipients? How does one determine who is the average decedent?[2]

---

2.   For an exploration of the thesis that intestate succession laws should reflect a person's (subconscious genetic) desire to pass his property to genetically close relatives (the *selfish gene* theory), see Beckstrom, Sociobiology and Intestate Wealth Transfers, 76 Nw. U.L. Rev. 216 (1981).

As the above questions indicate, framing an intestacy statute to give effect to the probable intent of the decedent requires that we decide what persons who do not have wills would most likely want. In the last 20 years a number of empirical studies have been made of popular preferences as to intestate succession. Although these studies do not always agree, they unanimously support the conclusion that the spouse's share is too small. They show that most persons want the entire estate to go to the surviving spouse when there are no children from a prior marriage, thus excluding parents and brothers and sisters. This preference is particularly strong among persons with moderate estates, who believe the surviving spouse will need the entire estate for support. The richer the person, the greater the desire that children or collaterals share with the spouse in the estate. See Fellows, Simon & Rau, Public Attitudes About Property Distribution at Death and Intestate Succession Laws in the United States, 1978 A.B.F. Res. J. 319, 348-364; Fellows, Simon, Snapp & Snapp, An Empirical Study of the Illinois Statutory Estate Plan, 1976 U. Ill. L.F. 717, 725-736; Comment, A Comparison of Iowans' Dispositive Preferences with Selected Provisions of the Iowa and Uniform Probate Codes, 63 Iowa L. Rev. 1041, 1078-1100 (1978). Earlier studies are cited in these publications. An empirical study by Price, The Transmission of Wealth at Death in a Community Property Jurisdiction, 50 Wash. L. Rev. 277 (1975), supports giving the spouse all of the decedent's interest in community property.

The Uniform Probate Code provision for the surviving spouse (§2-102), which is supported by the empirical studies, is more generous than that presently provided in the intestacy laws of most states.[3] The single most common statutory provision is to give the surviving spouse a one-half share if only one child or the issue of one child survives, and a one-third share if more than one child or one child and the issue of a deceased child survive. But there are variations, such as giving the surviving spouse one-half or one-third regardless of the number of children or issue (as the UPC provides) or giving the surviving spouse a child's share.

If there is no issue, most states provide, as does the Uniform Probate Code, that the spouse shares with the decedent's parents, if any. If no parent survives, the spouse usually takes all to the exclusion of collateral

---

3. A 1988 draft of a revised UPC §2-102, not yet approved by the National Conference of Commissioners on Uniform State Laws, provides even more generously for the surviving spouse. It gives the surviving spouse the entire intestate estate if the decedent leaves no issue or if all the decedent's issue are issue of the spouse and the spouse has no other issue. (The rationale of the latter provision is that the decedent's issue are likely to be the exclusive beneficiaries of the spouse's estate, and the decedent's property will be passed on to them when the spouse dies.) It further provides that in all other cases, the surviving spouse takes the first $150,000, plus one-half of any balance of the intestate estate.

kin, but in a number of states the spouse shares with brothers and sisters and their issue.

PROBLEM

Henry dies intestate. Anne, with whom he has been living, claims a spouse's share. Is Anne entitled to such if she married Henry, but the marriage is bigamous? If she did not marry Henry, but common law marriage is recognized? See W. McGovern, S. Kurtz & J. Rein, Wills, Trusts and Estates §2.3 (1988). If Anne and Henry did not marry because they perceived, as did the Princess of Cleves long ago, that there's nothing like marriage to spoil a perfect love, but Henry promised to take care of Anne? See infra page 271, dealing with contracts to make wills. Suppose that Henry and Anne had married, but Henry had moved out and filed for divorce. What result?

Simultaneous death.   A person succeeds to the property of an intestate or testate decedent only if the person survives the decedent for an instant of time. With the development of the automobile and the airplane came an increase of deaths of closely related persons in common disasters. Thus the question arose: When a person dies simultaneously with his heir or devisee, does the heir or devisee succeed to the person's property? The Uniform Simultaneous Death Act, drafted to deal with this problem, provides that where "*there is no sufficient evidence*" of the order of deaths, the beneficiary is deemed to have predeceased the benefactor. The act further provides that if two joint tenants, *A* and *B*, die simultaneously, one-half of the property is distributed as if *A* survived and one-half is distributed as if *B* survived. The same rule is applied to property held in tenancy by the entirety or community property. With respect to life insurance, when the insured and the beneficiary die simultaneously the proceeds are distributed as if the insured survived the beneficiary. The decedent may, of course, provide for a different distribution in a will or insurance contract.

Janus v. Tarasewicz
Illinois Appellate Court, 1985
135 Ill. App. 3d 936, 482 N.E.2d 418

O'CONNOR, J. This non-jury declaratory judgment action arose out of the death of a husband and wife, Stanley and Theresa Janus, who died after ingesting Tylenol capsules which had been laced with cyanide by an unknown perpetrator prior to its sale in stores. Stanley Janus was pronounced dead shortly after he was admitted to the hospital. However, Theresa Janus was placed on life support systems for almost two days before being pronounced dead. Claiming that there was no sufficient evidence that Theresa Janus survived her husband, plaintiff Alojza Janus, Stanley's mother, brought this action for the proceeds of Stanley's $100,000 life insurance policy which named Theresa as the primary beneficiary and plaintiff as the contingent beneficiary. Defendant Metropolitan Life Insurance Company paid the proceeds to defendant Jan Tarasewicz, Theresa's father and the administrator of her estate. The trial court found sufficient evidence that Theresa survived Stanley Janus. We affirm.

The facts of this case are particularly poignant and complex. Stanley and Theresa Janus had recently returned from their honeymoon when, on the evening of September 29, 1982, they gathered with other family members to mourn the death of Stanley's brother, Adam Janus, who had died earlier that day from what was later determined to be cyanide-laced Tylenol capsules. While the family was at Adam's home, Stanley and Theresa Janus unknowingly took some of the contaminated Tylenol. Soon afterwards, Stanley collapsed on the kitchen floor.

Theresa was still standing when Diane O'Sullivan, a registered nurse and a neighbor of Adam Janus, was called to the scene. Stanley's pulse was weak so she began cardiopulmonary resuscitation (CPR) on him. Within minutes, Theresa Janus began having seizures. After paramedic teams began arriving, Ms. O'Sullivan went into the living room to assist with Theresa. While she was working on Theresa, Ms. O'Sullivan could hear Stanley's "heavy and labored breathing." She believed that both Stanley and Theresa died before they were taken to the ambulance, but she could not tell who died first.

Ronald Mahon, a paramedic for the Arlington Heights Fire Department, arrived at approximately 5:45 P.M. He saw Theresa faint and go into a seizure. Her pupils did not respond to light but she was breathing on her own during the time that he worked on her. Mahon also assisted with Stanley, giving him drugs to stimulate heart contractions. Mahon later prepared the paramedic's report on Stanley. One entry in the report shows that at 18:00 hours Stanley had "zero blood pressure, zero pulse, and zero respiration." However, Mahon stated that the times in the report were merely approximations. He was able to say that Stanley was in the ambulance en route to the hospital when his vital signs disappeared.

When paramedic Robert Lockhart arrived at 5:55 P.M., both victims were unconscious with non-reactive pupils. Theresa's seizures had ceased but she was in a decerebrate posture in which her arms and legs were rigidly extended and her arms were rotated inward toward her body, thus, indicating severe neurological dysfunction. At that time, she was breathing only four or five times a minute and, shortly thereafter, she stopped breathing on her own altogether. Lockhart intubated them both by placing tubes down their tracheae to keep their air passages open. Prior to being taken to the ambulance, they were put on "ambu-bags" which is a form of artificial respiration whereby the paramedic respirates the patient by squeezing a bag. Neither Stanley nor Theresa showed any signs of being able to breathe on their own while they were being transported to Northwest Community Hospital in Arlington Heights, Illinois. However, Lockhart stated that when Theresa was turned over to the hospital personnel, she had a palpable pulse and blood pressure.

The medical director of the intensive care unit at the hospital, Dr. Thomas Kim, examined them when they arrived in the emergency room at approximately 6:30 P.M. Stanley had no blood pressure or pulse. An electrocardiogram detected electrical activity in Stanley Janus' heart but there was no synchronization between his heart's electrical activity and its pumping activity. A temporary pacemaker was inserted in an unsuccessful attempt to resuscitate him. Because he never developed spontaneous blood pressure, pulse or signs of respiration, Stanley Janus was pronounced dead at 8:15 P.M. on September 29, 1982.

Like Stanley, Theresa Janus showed no visible vital signs when she was admitted to the emergency room. However, hospital personnel were able to get her heart beating on its own again, so they did not insert a pacemaker. They were also able to establish a measurable, though unsatisfactory, blood pressure. Theresa was taken off the "ambu-bag" and put on a mechanical respirator. In Dr. Kim's opinion, Theresa was in a deep coma with "very unstable vital signs" when she was moved to the intensive care unit at 9:30 P.M. on September 29, 1982.

While Theresa was in the intensive care unit, numerous entries in her hospital records indicated that she had fixed and dilated pupils. However, one entry made at 2:32 A.M. on September 30, 1982, indicated that a nurse apparently detected a minimal reaction to light in Theresa's right pupil but not in her left pupil.

On September 30, 1982, various tests were performed in order to assess Theresa's brain function. These tests included an electroencephalogram (EEG) to measure electrical activity in her brain and a cerebral blood flow test to determine whether there was any blood circulating in her brain. In addition, Theresa exhibited no gag or cord reflexes, no response to pain or other external stimuli. As a result of these tests, Theresa Janus was diagnosed as having sustained total brain death, her life support systems then were terminated, and she was pronounced dead at 1:15 P.M. on October 1, 1982.

Death certificates were issued for Stanley and Theresa Janus more than three weeks later by a medical examiner's physician who never examined them. The certificates listed Stanley Janus' date of death as September 29, 1982, and Theresa Janus' date of death as October 1, 1982. Concluding that Theresa survived Stanley, the Metropolitan Life Insurance Company paid the proceeds of Stanley's life insurance policy to the administrator of Theresa's estate.

On January 6, 1983, plaintiff brought the instant declaratory judgment action against the insurance company and the administrators of Stanley and Theresa's estates, claiming the proceeds of the insurance policy as the contingent beneficiary of the policy. Also, the administrator of Stanley's estate filed a counterclaim against Theresa's estate seeking a declaration as to the disposition of the assets of Stanley's estate.

During the trial, the court heard the testimony of Ms. O'Sullivan, the paramedics, and Dr. Kim. There was also testimony that, while Theresa was in the intensive care unit, members of Theresa's family requested that termination of her life support system be delayed until the arrival of her brother who was serving in the military. However, Theresa's family denied making such a request.

In addition, Dr. Kenneth Vatz, a neurologist on the hospital staff, was called as an expert witness by plaintiff. Although he never actually examined Theresa, he had originally read her EEG as part of hospital routine. Without having seen her other hospital records, his initial evaluation of her EEG was that it showed some minimal electrical activity of living brain cells in the frontal portion of Theresa's brain. After reading her records and reviewing the EEG, however, he stated that the electrical activity measured by the EEG was "very likely" the result of interference from surrounding equipment in the intensive care unit. He concluded that Theresa was brain dead at the time of her admission to the hospital but he could not give an opinion as to who died first.

The trial court also heard an evidence deposition of Dr. Joseph George Hanley, a neurosurgeon who testified as an expert witness on behalf of the defendants. Based on his examination of their records, Dr. Hanley concluded that Stanley Janus died on September 29, 1982. He further concluded that Theresa Janus did not die until her vital signs disappeared on October 1, 1982. His conclusion that she did not die prior to that time was based on: (1) the observations by hospital personnel that Theresa Janus had spontaneous pulse and blood pressure which did not have to be artificially maintained; (2) the instance when Theresa Janus' right pupil allegedly reacted to light; and (3) Theresa's EEG which showed some brain function and which, in his opinion, could not have resulted from outside interference.

At the conclusion of the trial, the court held that the evidence was sufficient to show that Theresa survived Stanley, but the court was not prepared to say by how long she survived him. Plaintiff and the administrator of Stanley's estate appeal. In essence, their main contention is that there is not sufficient evidence to prove that both victims did not suffer brain death prior to their arrival at the hospital on September 29, 1982.

Dual standards for determining when legal death occurs in Illinois were set forth in the case of In Re Haymer (1983), 115 Ill. App. 3d 349, 71 Ill. Dec. 252, 450 N.E.2d 940. There, the court determined that a comatose child attached to a mechanical life support system was legally dead on the date he was medically determined to have sustained total brain death, rather than on the date that his heart stopped functioning. The court stated that in most instances death could be determined in accordance with the common law standard which is based upon the irreversible cessation of circulatory and respiratory functions. . . . If these functions are artificially maintained, a brain death standard of death could be used if a person has sustained irreversible cessation of total brain function. . . . In a footnote, the court stated that widely accepted characteristics of brain death include: (1) unreceptivity and unresponsivity to intensely painful stimuli; (2) no spontaneous movement or breathing for at least one hour; (3) no blinking, no swallowing, and fixed and dilated pupils; (4) flat EEGs taken twice with at least a 24-hour intervening period; and (5) absence of drug intoxication or hyperthermia. . . . See Report of the Ad Hoc Committee of the Harvard Medical School to Examine the Definition of Brain Death: A Definition of Irreversible Coma, 205 J.A.M.A. 337 (1968); . . . see also Report of the Medical Consultants on the Diagnosis of Death to the President's Commission for the Study of Ethical Problems in Medicine and Biomedical and Behavioral Research, 246 J.A.M.A. 2184 (proposing other criteria). However, the court refused to establish criteria for determining brain death because it noted that the advent of new research and technologies would continue to change the tests used for determining cessation of brain function. . . . Instead, the court merely required that the diagnosis of death under either standard must be made in accordance with "the usual and customary standards of medical practice." 115 Ill. App. 3d 349, 355, 71 Ill. Dec. 252, 450 N.E.2d 940.

Even though *Haymer* was decided after the deaths of Stanley and Theresa, we find that the trial court properly applied the *Haymer* standards under the general rule that a civil case is governed by the law as it exists when judgment is rendered, not when the facts underlying the case occur. . . . The application of *Haymer* is not unfair since the treating physicians made brain death diagnoses at the time of the deaths, and the parties presented evidence at trial regarding brain death.

Regardless of which standard of death is applied, survivorship is a fact which must be proven by a preponderance of the evidence by the party whose claim depends on survivorship. (In Re Estate of Moran

(1979), 77 Ill. 2d 147, 150, 32 Ill. Dec. 349, 395 N.E.2d 579.) The operative provisions of the Illinois version of the Uniform Simultaneous Death Act provides in pertinent part:

> If the title to property or its devolution depends upon the priority of death and there is no sufficient evidence that the persons have died otherwise than simultaneously and there is no other provision in the will, trust agreement, deed, contract of insurance or other governing instrument for distribution of the property different from the provisions of this Section:
>
> (a) The property of each person shall be disposed of as if he had survived. . . .
>
> (d) If the insured and the beneficiary of a policy of life or accident insurance have so died, the proceeds of the policy shall be distributed as if the insured had survived the beneficiary.

Ill. Rev. Stat. 1981, ch. 110½, par. 3-1.

In cases where the question of survivorship is determined by the testimony of lay witnesses, the burden of sufficient evidence may be met by evidence of a positive sign of life in one body and the absence of any such sign in the other. (In Re Estate of Lowrance (1978), 66 Ill. App. 3d 159, 162, 22 Ill. Dec. 895, 383 N.E.2d 703; Prudential Insurance Co. v. Spain (1950), 339 Ill. App. 476, 90 N.E.2d 256.) In cases such as the instant case where the death process is monitored by medical professionals, their testimony as to "the usual and customary standards of medical practice" will be highly relevant when considering what constitutes a positive sign of life and what constitutes a criteria for determining death. (See In Re Haymer (1983), 115 Ill. App. 3d 349, 71 Ill. Dec. 252, 450 N.E.2d 940.) Although the use of sophisticated medical technology can also make it difficult to determine when death occurs, the context of this case does not require a determination as to the exact moment at which the decedents died. Rather, the trial court's task was to determine whether or not there was sufficient evidence that Theresa Janus survived her husband. Our task on review of this factually disputed case is to determine whether the trial court's finding was against the manifest weight of the evidence. . . . We hold that it was not.

In the case at bar, both victims arrived at the hospital with artificial respirators and no obvious vital signs. There is no dispute among the treating physicians and expert witnesses that Stanley Janus died in both a cardiopulmonary sense and a brain death sense when his vital signs disappeared en route to the hospital and were never reestablished. He was pronounced dead at 8:15 P.M. on September 29, 1982, only after intensive procedures such as electro-shock, medication, and the insertion of a pacemaker failed to resuscitate him.

In contrast, these intensive procedures were not necessary with

Theresa Janus because hospital personnel were able to reestablish a spontaneous blood pressure and pulse which did not have to be artificially maintained by a pacemaker or medication. Once spontaneous circulation was restored in the emergency room, Theresa was put on a mechanical respirator and transferred to the intensive care unit. Clearly, efforts to preserve Theresa Janus' life continued after more intensive efforts on Stanley's behalf had failed.

It is argued that the significance of Theresa Janus' cardiopulmonary functions, as a sign of life, was rendered ambiguous by the use of artificial respiration. In particular, reliance is placed upon expert testimony that a person can be brain dead and still have a spontaneous pulse and blood pressure which is indirectly maintained by artificial respiration. The fact remains, however, that Dr. Kim, an intensive care specialist who treated Theresa, testified that her condition in the emergency room did not warrant a diagnosis of brain death. In his opinion, Theresa Janus did not suffer irreversible brain death until much later, when extensive treatment failed to preserve her brain function and vital signs. This diagnosis was confirmed by a consulting neurologist after a battery of tests were performed to assess her brain function. Dr. Kim denied that these examinations were made merely to see if brain death had already occurred. At trial, only Dr. Vatz disagreed with their finding, but even he admitted that the diagnosis and tests performed on Theresa Janus were in keeping with the usual and customary standards of medical practice.

There was also other evidence presented at trial which indicated that Theresa Janus was not brain dead on September 29, 1982. Theresa's EEG, taken on September 30, 1982, was not flat but rather it showed some delta waves of extremely low amplitude. Dr. Hanley concluded that Theresa's EEG taken on September 30 exhibited brain activity. Dr. Vatz disagreed. Since the trier of fact determines the credibility of expert witnesses and the weight to be given to their testimony . . . , the trial court in this case could have reasonably given greater weight to Dr. Hanley's opinion than to Dr. Vatz'. In addition, there is evidence that Theresa's pupil reacted to light on one occasion. It is argued that this evidence merely represents the subjective impression of a hospital staff member which is not corroborated by any other instance where Theresa's pupils reacted to light. However, this argument goes to the weight of this evidence and not to its admissibility. While these additional pieces of neurological data were by no means conclusive, they were competent evidence which tended to support the trial court's finding, and which also tended to disprove the contention that these tests merely verified that brain death had already taken place.

In support of the contention that Theresa Janus did not survive Stanley Janus, evidence was presented which showed that only Theresa Janus suffered seizures and exhibited a decerebrate posture shortly after ingesting the poisoned Tylenol. However, evidence that persons with these symptoms tend to die very quickly does not prove that Theresa Janus did not in fact survive Stanley Janus. Moreover, the evidence introduced is similar in nature to medical presumptions of survivorship based on decedents' health or physical condition which are considered too speculative to prove or disprove survivorship. (See In Re Estate of Moran (1979), 77 Ill. 2d 147, 153, 32 Ill. Dec. 349, 395 N.E.2d 579.) Similarly, we find no support for the allegation that the hospital kept Theresa Janus on a mechanical respirator because her family requested that termination of her life support systems be delayed until the arrival of her brother, particularly since members of Theresa's family denied making such a request.

In conclusion, we believe that the record clearly established that the treating physicians' diagnoses of death with respect to Stanley and Theresa Janus were made in accordance with "the usual and customary standards of medical practice." Stanley Janus was diagnosed as having sustained irreversible cessation of circulatory and respiratory functions on September 29, 1982. These same physicians concluded that Theresa Janus' condition on that date did not warrant a diagnosis of death and, therefore, they continued their efforts to preserve her life. Their conclusion that Theresa Janus did not die until October 1, 1982, was based on various factors including the restoration of certain of her vital signs as well as other neurological evidence. The trial court found that these facts and circumstances constituted sufficient evidence that Theresa Janus survived her husband. It was not necessary to determine the exact moment at which Theresa died or by how long she survived him, and the trial court properly declined to do so. Viewing the record in its entirety, we cannot say that the trial court's finding of sufficient evidence of Theresa's survivorship was against the manifest weight of the evidence.

Because of our disposition of this case, we need not and do not consider whether the date of death listed on the victims' death certificates should be considered "facts" which constitute prima facie evidence of the date of their deaths. See Ill. Rev. Stat. 1981, ch. 111½, par. 73-25; People v. Fiddler (1970), 45 Ill. 2d 181, 184-86, 258 N.E.2d 359.

Accordingly, there being sufficient evidence that Theresa Janus survived Stanley Janus, the judgment of the circuit court of Cook County is affirmed.

Affirmed.

PROBLEMS

1. Suppose that *H* and *W* both drown in a boating accident. The evidence shows that *W* was a better swimmer and in better health than

H. In addition, the autopsy shows W drowned after a violent death struggle while H passively submitted to death. Is there sufficient evidence of survival? See In re Estate of Campbell, 56 Or. App. 222, 641 P.2d 610 (1982).

2. To remedy the "no sufficient evidence" problem, Uniform Probate Code §§2-104 and 2-601 provide that an heir or devisee who fails to survive by 120 hours (5 days) is deemed to have predeceased the decedent. Suppose that in Janus v. Tarasewicz, Theresa Janus's family had required that she remain on a mechanical respirator until her brother arrived from the military and that he arrived on October 5th, after which the doctors turned off the respirator. What result?

3. Is it a good idea to avoid the "no sufficient evidence" problem by providing in a will that "If any person dies with me in a common disaster, any property given to such person by this will shall pass as if such person predeceased me"? See Silver v. Schroeder, 474 So. 2d 857 (Fla. App. 1985).

3. Descendants

a. Taking by Representation: Per Stirpes Distribution

In all jurisdictions in this country, after the spouse's share is set aside, children and issue of deceased children take the remainder of the property to the exclusion of everyone else. When one of several children has died before the decedent, leaving issue, all states provide that the issue shall *represent* the child and divide the child's share among themselves.

The following diagram involves this situation. Assume that the intestate decedent, A, a widow, has three children. One of her three children, C, dies before A, survived by a husband and two children. The decedent is survived by two children, B and D, and by five grandchildren, E, F, G, H, and I. Thus:

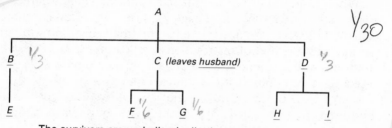

The survivors are underlined: all others are dead

C's children take *C*'s share by *representation* of their dead parent. Therefore *A*'s heirs are *B* (⅓), *D* (⅓), *F* (⅙) and *G* (⅙). Observe that *E*, *H*, and *I* take nothing because their parents are living. Observe also that *C*'s spouse takes nothing.

In other, more complicated contexts there are some disputes about what taking by representation means (or ought to mean). The fundamental question in these disputes is whether the division into shares should begin at the generational level immediately below the decedent *or* at the closest generational level where issue of the decedent is alive. To see this, take this case: *A* has two children, *B* and *C*. *B* predeceases *A*, leaving a child *D*. *C* predeceases *A*, leaving two children, *E* and *F*. *A* dies intestate leaving no surviving spouse, and survived by *D*, *E*, and *F*. Thus:

The survivors are underlined; all others are dead.

How is *A*'s estate distributed?

Uniform Probate Code §2-103(1), supra page 77, provides that if the issue of decedent "are all of the same degree of kinship to the decedent they take equally, but if of unequal degree, then those of more remote degree take by representation." Since *D*, *E*, and *F* are all grandchildren, of equal degree of kinship to *A*, each takes a one-third share of *A*'s estate. This is a *per capita* ("by the head") method of distribution. Under a *per stirpes* ("by the stocks") distribution followed in some states, *A*'s property is divided into two shares at the level of *A*'s children, and *D* takes *B*'s one-half by representation and *E* and *F* split *C*'s one-half by representation. (Observe that if *B* had survived *A*, the estate would have been split into two shares under both systems; *C*'s share would be divided between *C*'s two children.)

When all the issue of decedent are not of equal degree, Uniform Probate Code §2-106, supra page 77, provides for taking by representation. The stocks are determined at the first generation with any takers living. This method of distribution is called *per capita with representation* to distinguish it from a straight per stirpes distribution where the stocks are always determined at the children's level.

CAVEAT: In many jurisdictions what we call "per capita with representation" is called "per stirpes." The courts have merely defined the term per stirpes to mean that the stocks are divided at the generational level with any takers alive. Thus, one way to view this matter is to say there is a minority definition of per stirpes (meaning division of stocks at the children's level) and a majority definition (meaning division at the level where the closest descendant is alive). To avoid confusion, many commentators now speak of "per stirpes" and "per capita with representation." When a will devises property "to the issue of A per stirpes," the will may or may not be interpreted to call for the same representational system provided by the intestacy laws. The states differ on this. See infra pages 678-681.

PROBLEM

A has two children, B and C. B predeceases A, leaving a child D. C predeceases A, leaving two children, E and F. E predeceases A, leaving two children, G and H, who survive A. Thus:

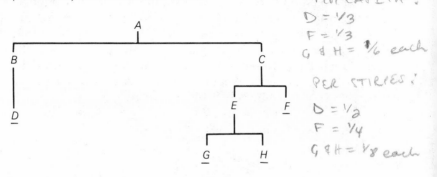

PER CAPITA:
D = 1/3
F = 1/3
G & H = 1/6 each

PER STIRPES:
D = 1/2
F = 1/4
G & H = 1/8 each

A dies intestate leaving no surviving spouse. How is A's estate distributed under the Uniform Probate Code? Under the intestacy statute of your state?

Two studies have indicated that an overwhelming majority of people prefers the per capita with representation system, dividing the stocks at the level where someone is alive. See Fellows, Simon, Snapp & Snapp, an Empirical Study of the Illinois Statutory Estate Plan, 1976 U. Ill. L.F. 717, 741 (95 percent of the persons interviewed); Comment, A Comparison of Iowans' Dispositive Preferences with Selected Provisions of the Iowa and Uniform Probate Codes, 63 Iowa L. Rev. 1041, 1111 (1978) (87 percent).

In a few states, a variation on the per capita with representation method of distribution exists. It is known as *per capita at each generation.* Under this method, the initial division of shares is made at the highest level of issue alive (as under UPC §2-106), but the shares of deceased persons on that level are treated as one pot and are dropped down and divided equally among the representatives on the next generational level. Thus in the situation pictured below, *D* takes a one-third share; the two-thirds that would have passed to *B* and *C* had they been living is divided equally among all the children of *B* and *C*. *E*, *F*, and *G* each take a two-ninth's share.

This method of distribution is recommended in Waggoner, A Proposed Alternative to the Uniform Probate Code's System for Intestate Distribution Among Descendants, 66 Nw. U.L. Rev. 626 (1971). Professor Waggoner believes that rejection of the per stirpes method of distribution logically requires that persons of the same degree of kinship take equally, even though the takers are in two generations. A 1988 revised draft of UPC §2-106, which may be adopted by The National Conference of Commissioners on Uniform State Laws, provides for per capita distribution at each generation.

NOTE: POSTHUMOUS CHILDREN

Where, for purposes of inheritance or of determining property rights, it is to a child's advantage to be treated as in being from the time of conception rather than from the time of birth, the child will be so treated if born alive. See Comment, When Is Child En Ventre Sa Mere Regarded as in Being, 33 Mich. L. Rev. 414 (1935). The principle is an ancient one. See 1 W. Blackstone, Commentaries *130.

If, at common law, a man died without children and his widow claimed to be pregnant, the person who would be the heir if there were no child could obtain a writ de ventre inspiciendo for a jury to determine if the widow was in fact pregnant. "The writ directs that, in the presence of knights and women, the female tractari per uberem et ventrem, — the presumed necessity of the case dispensing at once with common decency and with respectful deference to sex." 1 W. Blackstone, Commentaries *456 n.19. Courts have established a rebuttable presumption that the normal period of gestation is 280 days (ten lunar months). If the child claims that conception dated more than 280 days before birth, the burden of proof is usually upon the child.[4]

b.   Adopted Children

Hall v. Vallandingham
Maryland Court of Special Appeals, 1988
75 Md. App. 187, 540 A.2d 1162

GILBERT, C.J.   Adoption did not exist under the common law of England,[5] although it was in use "[a]mong the ancient peoples of Greece, Rome, Egypt and Babylonia." M. Leary and R. Weinberg, Law of Adoption (4th Ed. 1979) 1; Lord Mackenzie, Studies in Roman Law, 130-34 (3rd ed. 1870); American and English Encyclopaedia of Law (1887) 204, n.9. The primary purpose for adoption was, and still is, inheritance rights, particularly in "France, Greece, Spain and most of Latin America." Leary and Weinberg, Law of Adoption, 1. Since adoption was not a part of the common law, it owes its existence in this State, and indeed in this nation, to statutory enactments.

The first two general adoption statutes were passed in Texas and Vermont in 1850. Leary and Weinberg, Law of Adoption, 1. Maryland first enacted an Adoption Statute in Laws 1892, Ch. 244, and that law has continued in existence, in various forms, until the present time. The current statute, Maryland Code, Family Law Article Ann. §5-308 provides, in pertinent part:

> (b) [A]fter a decree of adoption is entered:
>   (1) the individual adopted:
>   (i) is the child of the petitioner for all intents and purposes;[6] and

---

4. On supposed periods of gestation beyond 280 days, the modern record for a protracted pregnancy apparently belongs to a woman from North Carolina. In Byerly v. Tolbert, 250 N.C. 27, 108 S.E.2d 29 (1959), a child was born to the decedent's widow 322 days after his death. The child (through a guardian ad litem, of course) claimed an intestate share. The trial court held as a matter of law that the infant was not the decedent's child. On appeal, the case was reversed. Although there is a presumption that a child born more than 280 days after death is not the decedent's child, the presumption is not irrebuttable, and the child was entitled to have the issue submitted to a jury. For older cases see Annot., 7 A.L.R. 329 (1920).

Uniform Parentage Act §4 presumes that a child born to a woman within 300 (rather than 280) days after the death of her husband is a child of that husband.

5. According to J.W. Madden, Handbook of the Law of Persons and Domestic Relations (Wash. 1931) §106, adoption in the sense of the term as used in this country was not a part of the English law until 1926.

6. Notwithstanding Maryland law, a child who is eligible for social security survivor's benefits through a deceased natural parent under Federal law does not lose eligibility for the continuation of those benefits because of a subsequent adoption. 42 U.S.C., §402(d).

(ii) is entitled to all the rights and privileges of and is subject to all the obligations of a child born to the petitioner in wedlock;

(2) each living natural parent of the individual adopted is:

(i) relieved of all parental duties and obligations to the individual adopted; and

(ii) divested of all parental rights as to the individual adopted; and

(3) *all rights of inheritance between the individual adopted and the natural relations shall be governed by the Estates and Trusts Article."* (Emphasis supplied.)

The applicable section of the Md. Estates and Trusts Code Ann., §1-207(a), provides:

An adopted child shall be treated as a natural child of his adopted parent or parents. On adoption, a child no longer shall be considered a child of either natural parent, except that upon adoption by the spouse of a natural parent, the child shall be considered the child of that natural parent.[7]

With that "thumbnail" history of adoption and the current statutes firmly in mind, we turn our attention to the matter sub judice.

Earl J. Vallandingham died in 1956, survived by his widow, Elizabeth, and their four children. Two years later, Elizabeth married Jim Walter Killgore, who adopted the children.

In 1983, twenty-five years after the adoption of Earl's children by Killgore, Earl's brother, William Jr., died childless, unmarried, and intestate. His sole heirs were his surviving brothers and sisters and the children of brothers and sisters who predeceased him.

Joseph W. Vallandingham, the decedent's twin brother, was appointed Personal Representative of the estate. After the Inventory and First Accounting were filed, the four natural children of Earl J. Vallandingham noted exceptions, alleging that they were entitled to the distributive share of their natural uncle's estate that their natural father would have received had he survived William. Est. & Trusts Art. §3-104(b).

The Orphan's Court transmitted the issue to the Circuit Court for St. Mary's County. That tribunal determined that the four natural children of Earl, because of their adoption by their adoptive father, Jim Walter Killgore, were not entitled to inherit from William M. Vallandingham Jr.

Patently unwilling to accept that judgment which effectively disinherited them, the children have journeyed here where they posit to us:

7. Although the statute speaks in terms of the "adopted child," the person who is adopted need not be a minor child. *See* Family Law Art. §5-307(a).

Did the trial court err in construing Maryland's current law regarding natural inheritance by adopted persons so as to deny the Appellants the right to inherit through their natural paternal uncle, when said Appellants were adopted as minors by their stepfather after the death of their natural father and the remarriage of their natural mother?

When the four natural children of Earl J. Vallandingham were adopted in 1958 by Jim Killgore, then Md. Ann. Code art. 16, §78(b) clearly provided that adopted children retained the right to inherit from their natural parents and relatives.[8] That right of inheritance was removed by the Legislature in 1963 when it declared: "Upon entry of a decree of adoption, the adopted child shall lose all rights of inheritance from its parents and from their natural collateral or lineal relatives." Laws 1963, Ch. 174. Subsequently, the Legislature in 1969 enacted what is the current, above-quoted language of Est. & Trusts Art. §1-207(a). Laws 1969, Ch. 3, §4(c).

The appellants contend that since the explicit language of the 1963 Act proscribing dual inheritance by adoptees was not retained in the present law, Est. & Trusts Art. §1-207(a) implicitly permits adoptees to inherit from natural relatives, as well as the adoptive parents.

The right to receive property by devise or descent is not a natural right but a privilege granted by the State. . . . Every State possesses the power to regulate the manner or term by which property within its dominion may be transmitted by will or inheritance and to prescribe who shall or shall not be capable of receiving that property. A State may deny the privilege altogether or may impose whatever restrictions or conditions upon the grant it deems appropriate. Mager v. Grima, 49 U.S. 490, 8 How. 490, 12 L. Ed. 1168 (1850).[9]

Family Law Art. §5-308(b)(1)(ii) entitles an adopted person to all the rights and privileges of a natural child insofar as the adoptive parents are concerned, but adoption does not confer upon the adopted child *more* rights and privileges than those possessed by a natural child. To construe Est. & Trusts Art. §1-207(a) so as to allow dual inheritance would bestow upon an adopted child a superior status. That status was removed in Laws 1963, Ch. 174 which, as we have said, expressly disallowed the dual inheritance capability of adopted children by providing that "the adopted child shall lose all rights of inheritance from its parents and from their natural collateral or lineal relatives." We think that the current statute, Est. & Trusts Art. §1-207(a), did not alter the substance of the 1963 act which eliminated dual inheritance.

8. "[N]othing in this subtitle shall be construed to prevent the person adopted from inheriting from his natural parents and relatives. . . ."

9. Since the Legislature is elected by the people, it is answerable to the people, and that is the best safeguard against unreasonable laws concerning inheritance.

Rather, §1-207(a) merely "streamlined" the wording while retaining the meaning.

Family Law Art. §5-308 plainly mandates that adoption be considered a "rebirth" into a completely different relationship. Once a child is adopted, the rights of both the natural parents and relatives are terminated. L.F.M. v. Department of Social Services, 67 Md. App. 379, 507 A.2d 1151 (1986). Est. & Trusts Art. §1-207(a) and Family Law Art. §5-308 emphasize the clean-cut severance from the natural blood-line. Because an adopted child has no right to inherit *from* the estate of a natural parent who dies intestate, it follows that the same child may not inherit *through* the natural parent by way of representation. What may not be done directly most assuredly may not be done indirectly. The elimination of dual inheritance in 1963 clearly established that policy, and the current language of §1-207(a) simply reflects the continuation of that policy.

We hold that because §1-207(a) eliminates the adopted child's right to inherit from the natural parent it concomitantly abrogated the right to inherit through the natural parent by way of representation.

"The Legislature giveth, and the Legislature taketh away."

Judgment affirmed.

Uniform Probate Code (1983)

§2-109 [MEANING OF CHILD AND RELATED TERMS]

If, for purposes of intestate succession, a relationship of parent and child must be established to determine succession by, through, or from a person,

(1) an adopted person is the child of an adopting parent and not of the natural parents except that adoption of a child by the spouse of a natural parent has no effect on the relationship between the child and either natural parent. . . .

§2-114 [PERSONS RELATED TO DECEDENT THROUGH TWO LINES]

A person who is related to the decedent through 2 lines of relationship is entitled to only a single share based on the relationship which would entitle him to the larger share.

NOTES AND PROBLEMS

1. Whether a child should continue to have inheritance rights from both natural parents (and their relatives) when the child is adopted by

a stepparent is a matter of some disagreement among the states. Would you have the same or different results in these two cases? (1) *H* and *W*, parents of *A*, divorce. *W* remarries. *H* consents to the adoption of *A*, a minor, by *W*'s new husband. (2) *H* and *W* are parents of *A*. *H* dies. *W* remarries. *W*'s new husband adopts *A*, a minor. Should *A* be able to inherit from *H*'s relatives or, in the first case, from *H*? Should *H* or *H*'s relatives be able to inherit from *A*? See Jones, Stepparent Adoption and Inheritance: A Suggested Revision of the Uniform Probate Code Section 2-109, 8 W. New Eng. L. Rev. 53 (1986); Note, Intestate Succession and Stepparent Adoptions, 1988 Wis. L. Rev. 321. See generally, W. McGovern, S. Kurtz & J. Rein, Wills, Trusts and Estates §2.2 (1988); Rein, Relatives by Blood, Adoption, and Association: Who Should Get What and Why, 37 Vand. L. Rev. 711 (1984).

2.   *H* and *W* have a child *A*, a minor. *H* and *W* are killed in a plane crash. *A* is adopted by *W*'s sister, a single woman. Does *A* inherit from *H*'s relatives? See Estate of Mills, 374 N.W.2d 675 (Iowa 1985).

3.   *Adult adoption.*   Only a few adoption or inheritance statutes draw any distinction between adoption of a minor and adoption of an adult. Occasionally, the adoption of an adult may be useful in preventing a will contest. The only persons who have standing to challenge the validity of a will are those persons who would take if the will were denied probate. If the testator adopts a child, testator's collateral relatives may not be able to contest the will since ordinarily they now can inherit nothing by intestacy. Hence, if a person wishes to leave property to a friend, under some circumstances it might be wise to adopt the friend as a child. In Greene v. Fitzpatrick, 220 Ky. 590, 295 S.W. 896 (1927), a wealthy bachelor adopted a married woman who had been his secretary for many years and with whom, it was alleged, the bachelor had a sexual relationship. In Collamore v. Learned, 171 Mass. 99, 50 N.E. 518 (1898), a 70-year-old man adopted three persons of ages 43, 39, and 25 respectively. In both cases it was held that the adoptions could not be set aside by the persons who would have been the heirs but for the adoptions. In the second case, Holmes, J., remarked that adoption for the purpose of preventing a will contest was "perfectly proper."

On the other hand, in at least one jurisdiction adoption of an adult lover is not possible. In In re Robert Paul P., 63 N.Y.2d 233, 471 N.E.2d 424, 481 N.Y.S.2d 652, 42 A.L.R.4th 765 (1984), the court held that a homosexual male, age 57, could not legally adopt his lover, age 50, although New York statutes permit the adoption of adults. The court thought it was "absurd" and a "cynical distortion of the function of adoption" to permit one lover, homosexual or heterosexual, to "enjoy the sanction of the law on their feigned union as parent and child." (But cf. Braschi v. Stahl Associates Co., 74 N.Y.2d 201, 543 N.E.2d 49, 544 N.Y.S.2d 784 (1989), holding that the surviving man of a 10-year homosexual domestic partnership was a "family member" and entitled to continue living in a rent-controlled apartment.) See also W. Mc-Govern, S. Kurtz & J. Rein, supra, §2.2 at 53 for other restrictions on adult adoptions in a few states.

Should a person adopted as an adult be able to inherit *through* the adoptive parent from the adoptive parent's collateral relatives?

4. *Stepchildren.* In a few states stepchildren inherit if an intestate has no close blood relatives. California permits a stepchild to take a child's share if (1) the relationship of parent and child "began during the person's minority and continued throughout the parties' joint lifetimes and (2) it is established by clear and convincing evidence that the foster parent or stepparent would have adopted the person but for a legal barrier." Cal. Prob. Code §6408(b) (1989). Suppose that *H* and *W* have a child *A*. They divorce; *H* assumes custody of *A* and remarries. *H*'s second wife wants to adopt *A*, but *W* refuses to allow it. Several years after *A* reaches majority, *H*'s second wife dies. Inasmuch as the legal barrier (*W*'s objection) ceases to exist when *A* reaches majority, and *H*'s second wife did not thereafter adopt *A*, does *A* inherit from *H*'s second wife? See generally Mahoney, Stepfamilies in the Law of Intestate Succession and Wills, 22 U.C. Davis L. Rev. 917 (1989).

Estate of Riggs

New York Surrogate's Court, New York County, 1981
109 Misc. 2d 644, 440 N.Y.S.2d 450

MIDONICK, S. In this accounting proceeding a hearing was held before a Law Assistant-Referee. Objectants claim to be nieces and nephews of Leon Corey Riggs, a stepfather of decedent who allegedly adopted her. Previously, one objectant had sought an advance payment of a distributive share and had submitted evidence to establish an adoption, but no adoption record was presented. This court found that the petitioner therein had not sustained his burden of proof (Matter of Riggs, 68 Misc. 2d 760, 763, 328 N.Y.S.2d 138). No adoption record has been found since then but now objectants claim that there was an equitable adoption under the laws of New Jersey which allow objectants to inherit from decedent.

The first issue to be resolved is whether the relatives of an alleged adoptive father can inherit from the adoptee. Clearly, if the adoption takes place pursuant to the statute, the adoptee is considered the same as a natural child and his or her distributees are determined from those related in the adoptive family. (EPTL 4-1.1, subd. [f]; Domestic Relations Law, §117). New Jersey similarly so provides (NJSA 9:3-30 [B]).

Objectants' position is that an equitable adoption creates the same rights for inheritance purposes as if adopted statutorily. For the purposes of the discussion hereinafter, the court accepts the allegations of objectants to be true that Leon Corey Riggs, who died in 1920, equitably adopted in New Jersey the decedent, who was his stepdaughter.

What is an equitable adoption? The courts in New Jersey do not specifically use that term, although others, who have interpreted the laws of New Jersey have described the applicable doctrine as an "equitable adoption." (In re Jarboe's Estate, 235 F. Supp. 505, 507). Using the language of a leading case in New Jersey, the rule applied is best stated as follows:

> . . . [A]n oral agreement to adopt, where there has been a full and faithful performance on the part of the adoptive child, but which was never consummated by formal adoption proceedings during the life of the adoptive parent, will, upon the death of the latter, and when equity and justice so requires, be enforced to the extent of decreeing that such child occupies in equity the status of an adopted child, entitled to the same right of inheritance from so much of his foster parent's estate that remains undisposed of by will or otherwise, as he would have been had he been a natural born child. [Burdick v. Grimshaw, 113 N.J. Eq. 591, 595, 168 A. 186, 188].

Therefore, the doctrine to be applied is an oral, written or implied contract right which is enforced in equity (id.; Ashman v. Madigan, 40 N.J. Super. 147, 122 A.2d 382; Hendershot v. Hendershot, 135 N.J. Eq. 232, 37 A.2d 770). By granting specific performance the court of equity is "considering as done that which ought to be done. . . ." (Burdick v. Grimshaw, supra). As a result the term equitable adoption is a shorthand way of describing an equitable result. However, each of these cases involved a claim by or on behalf of the alleged adopted child against the alleged adoptive parent's estate. No case from the courts of the State of New Jersey has been cited, found by this court or referred to by objectants' expert witness, who is a former Judge in New Jersey and leading authority in this area of the law, which decides the issue of whether the contract can be enforced by others, so as to permit the relatives of the alleged adoptive parent to inherit from the alleged adoptee. The testimony of this expert witness, referring to the above cases as well as others in the New Jersey courts, was that a court in New Jersey would permit the relatives of the adoptive parent to inherit. However, that issue was never decided therein and there are no dicta which so indicate.

This equitable principle which is sought to be enforced is or has been applied or acknowledged in numerous other states, including New York (e.g., Middleworth v. Ordway, 191 N.Y. 404, 84 N.E. 291; Robinson v. Robinson, 283 Ala. 257, 215 So. 2d 585; Matter of Lamfrom, 90 Ariz. 363, 368 P.2d 318; Chavez v. Shea, 185 Colo. 400, 525 P.2d 1148; Sheffield v. Barry, 153 Fla. 144, 14 So. 2d 417; Baker v. Henderson,

208 Ga. 698, 69 S.E.2d 278; Monahan v. Monahan, 14 Ill. 2d 449, 153
N.E.2d 1; Matter of Van Cleave, 610 S.W.2d 620 [Mo.]; Heien v.
Crabtree, 369 S.W.2d 28 [Tex.]; Whitchurch v. Perry, 408 A.2d 627
[Vt.]; Wheeling Dollar Savings & Trust Co. v. Singer, 250 S.E.2d 369
[W.V. App.]). Even the federal courts have acknowledged the enforcement of contracts for adoption under the state laws which are applicable. . . . However, no jurisdiction has permitted the adoptive parent
or the heirs of the adoptive parent to claim the estate of the alleged
adoptee, such a request having been denied each time (In re Estate of
Jarboe, supra; Baker v. Henderson, supra; Heien v. Crabtree, supra;
Adler v. Moran, 549 S.W.2d 760 [Tex. Civ. App.], revd. on other
grounds 570 S.W.2d 883 [Tex.]; Moorman v. Hunnicutt, 325 S.W.2d
941 [Tex. Civ. App.]; Rumans v. Lighthizer, 363 Mo. 125, 249 S.W.2d
397). Some courts have stated as dicta that the adoptive parent or his
heirs cannot make a claim . . . and others have denied an alleged
adoptive parent the right to bring a wrongful death cause of action
(Whitchurch v. Perry, supra), the right of the alleged adoptive parent
to workmen's compensation benefits (Servantez v. Aguirre, 456 S.W.2d
467 [Tex. Civ. App.]) or the right of the alleged adoptive parent to aid
for dependent children (Chavez v. Shea, supra; Tellis v. Saucier, 133
Ga. App. 779, 213 S.E.2d 39).

The rationale of each of the courts in denying relief, other than in
favor of the alleged adoptee against the alleged adoptive parent or the
estate, was that the enforcement of a contract right by specific performance, in equity, does not alter the status of the child and does not
create a parent-child relationship with all of its legal consequences.
Clearly, the alleged adoptee cannot compel an adoption (Matter of
Bamber, 147 Misc. 712, 265 N.Y.S. 798) and a legal adoption is not
created by the enforcement of a contract right, although the alleged
adoptee has an interest in the intestate share of the property of the
alleged adoptive parent. The purpose of the equitable principle is to
estop the relatives from denying an adoption by the adoptive parent.
Courts will enforce that which the adoptive parent should have done
but failed to do. On the other hand, the parent who breached the
agreement, by not adopting formally, cannot claim to be entitled to
equity and his or her relatives have no greater rights (Heien v. Crabtree,
supra p.30; In re Jarboe's Estate, supra, pp. 508-509). Such parent
cannot claim that the adoptee is estopped from denying the adoption
by the adoptee's acts, promises or conduct (id.). It seems plain that a
petition for adoption by a proposed adoptee does not lie.

All of the above cases as well as others indicate that the right to
enforce the equitable adoption rule is limited to the alleged adoptee
and is only as against the property of the alleged adoptive parent. The
cases in New Jersey are no different from these cases. To say that a
court in New Jersey would permit heirs of the alleged adoptive parent

to claim the property of the alleged adoptee is not a correct analysis of the case law. New Jersey courts would look to the decisions in sister states for support as the New Jersey Supreme Court did in the case of Burdick v. Grimshaw (supra). As evidenced by the decisions in other states and in the federal courts, collaterals of the alleged adoptive parent would not have any rights to the adoptee's property.

Consequently, this court finds that objectants have no rights to the decedent's property on the theory of being related because of an equitable adoption or any equivalent principle or rule. The only way in which they can demonstrate their status is to submit a copy of the order of adoption Leon Corey Riggs purportedly obtained. Absent proof of adoption they are mere strangers to this estate.

Accordingly, the objections by alleged distributees are not sustained and are dismissed without prejudice to their right to prove a valid adoption and to establish their relationship to Leon Corey Riggs. The objections of the guardian ad litem to the account shall proceed to settlement.

NOTE AND PROBLEM

1. In First National Bank in Fairmont v. Phillips, 344 S.E.2d 201 (W. Va. 1985), the court held that an equitably adopted child could inherit from another child of the adoptive parent. The court said it left "to another day the more troublesome question of whether the equitably adopted child would inherit from collateral kindred of the adoptive parent(s)."

2. Who would inherit in the following case? *H* and *W* do not formally adopt *A*, three months old, but they take *A* into their home and represent to the public that *A* is their son. At age 40, *A* dies intestate, unmarried, and very rich from some lucky real estate investments. *H* and *W* survive *A*. Who takes *A*'s property? Will it be easy to find out who are *A*'s natural relatives? See generally Note, Equitable Adoption: They Took Him Into Their Home and Called Him Fred, 53 Va. L. Rev. 727 (1972).

c. Illegitimate Children

Although innocent of any sin or crime, children of unmarried parents were given harsh, pitiless treatment by the common law.[10] A child born

---

10. For a description of the legal position of the illegitimate child at common law, see 1 W. Blackstone, Commentaries *454 ff.; 2 id. *247 ff. In the first book of Blackstone (1 id. *457) you may find out, if you care to, how a child could be "more than ordinarily legitimate."

out of wedlock was *filius nullius*, the child of no one, and could inherit from neither father nor mother. Only the child's spouse and issue could inherit from the child. If the child died intestate and left neither spouse nor issue, the child's property escheated to the king or other overlord. Even though the father married the mother after the child's birth, he or she remained the child of no one, without blood relations (except issue). Such was the law of England until the Legitimacy Act of 1926. Only recently did the English abolish the Civil Service office devoted to "The Escheated Estates of Intestate Bastards."[11]

All of our states have alleviated this unsympathetic treatment of children born out of wedlock. All jurisdictions permit inheritance from the mother, but the rules respecting inheritance from the father vary. In Trimble v. Gordon, 430 U.S. 762 (1977), the Supreme Court held unconstitutional, as a denial of equal protection, an Illinois statute denying an illegitimate child inheritance rights from the father. The Court held that state discrimination against illegitimate children, although they are not a suspect classification subject to the strict scrutiny test, must have a substantial justification as serving an important state interest. The state interest recognized by the Court is the desirability of establishing accurate and efficient methods for the orderly disposition of property at death — in this context, reliable proof of paternity. The Court found that total statutory disinheritance was not rationally related to this objective. A year later, in Lalli v. Lalli, 439 U.S. 259 (1978), the Court upheld a New York Statute permitting inheritance from the father only if the father had married the mother or had been formally adjudicated the father by a court during the father's lifetime. "Fraudulent assertions of paternity will be much less likely to succeed, or even to arise, where the proof is put before a court of law at a time when the putative father is available to respond, rather than first brought to light when the distribution of the assets of an estate is in the offing." Id. at 271-272.

In the wake of these two cases, most states have amended their intestacy statutes to liberalize inheritance by illegitimates from fathers. (The New York statutes were considerably broadened after the *Lalli* case. See N.Y. Est., Powers & Trusts Law §4-1.2 (Supp. 1989).) Most states have adopted the provisions in Uniform Probate Code §2-109, set out below. These permit paternity to be established by evidence of

---

11. In 1969, English law was changed to provide that an illegitimate child, and issue of such child, shall be entitled to the same interest in the child's father's and mother's estates as if the child were legitimate. Family Law Reform Act, 1969, §14(2). Where there is reference in a will to a "child" or to "children" of a person, illegitimates are presumed to be included, but not where the reference is to the "heirs" of a person. Id. §15. The Family Law Reform Act of 1987 goes further and seeks to give an illegitimate child exactly the same rights as one born to married parents.

the subsequent marriage of the parents, by an adjudication during the life of the father, or by clear and convincing proof after his death. Other states permit paternity to be established after death only by an acknowledgment of paternity by the father while alive; still others permit paternity to be established after the father's death by either an acknowledgment of paternity or clear and convincing evidence. See Comment, Inheritance Rights of Illegitimate Children in Kentucky: A Need for Reform, 71 Ky. L.J. 665, 676-677 (1982).

The Uniform Parentage Act, adopted in a few states, does not distinguish between "legitimate" and "illegitimate" children but enacts the concept of a "parent and child relationship," on which the law confers rights and obligations. The parent and child relationship extends to every child and parent, regardless of the marital status of the parents. When the father and mother do not marry or attempt to marry, a parent-child relationship is presumed to exist between a father and a child if (1) while the child is a minor, the father receives the child into his home and openly holds out the child as his natural child or (2) the father acknowledges his paternity in a writing filed with an appropriate court or administrative agency. Uniform Parentage Act §4 (1977). If a father and child relationship is presumed to exist, an action to determine its existence may be brought at any time; if a child has no presumed father, an action to establish a parent and child relationship must be brought before the estate has been closed in order to inherit. Id. §§6, 7.

Uniform Probate Code (1983)

§2-109   [MEANING OF CHILD AND RELATED TERMS]

If, for purposes of intestate succession, a relationship of parent and child must be established to determine succession by, through, or from a person, . . .

(2) In cases not covered by Paragraph (1) [dealing with adopted children], a person born out of wedlock is a child of the mother. That person is also a child of the father, if:

(i) the natural parents participated in a marriage ceremony before or after the birth of the child, even though the attempted marriage is void; or

(ii) the paternity is established by an adjudication before the death of the father or is established thereafter by clear and convincing proof, but the paternity established under this subparagraph is ineffective to qualify the father or his kindred to inherit from or though the child unless the father has openly treated the child as his, and has not refused to support the child.

QUESTIONS AND NOTE

1. Is the provision in the Uniform Probate Code depriving the father of the right to inherit from his illegitimate child if he refuses to support the child constitutional? The mother is not barred from inheriting from a child she has neglected. Does this distinction have a rational basis?

2. Should state courts develop an equitable legitimation doctrine (similar to equitable adoption) so that where a formal adjudication of paternity is required by statute for inheritance, an illegitimate child can inherit from the father if there is clear and convincing evidence of paternity and of the father's intent that the child be treated as an heir? See Prince v. Black, 256 Ga. 79, 344 S.E.2d 411 (1986) (announcing equitable legitimation doctrine); Note, Davis v. Jones: A Case for Equitable Legitimation, 23 S. Tex. L.J. 250 (1982).

3. In Alexander v. Alexander, 42 Ohio Misc. 2d 30, 537 N.E.2d 1310 (1988), the plaintiff alleged he was the illegitimate son and sole heir of David Summers, who had been buried. He petitioned the court for an order to disinter Summers so that paternity might be proven by a genetic (DNA) test performed on the remains of Summers. The court granted the petition over the objection of Summers's other relatives.

d. Transfers to Minors

Transfers to minors at death raise special problems. Minors do not have the legal capacity to manage property. It is now time to speak of guardians and of the property management alternatives available to parents of minors.

A *guardian of the person* has responsibility for the child's custody and care. As long as one parent of the child is living and competent, that parent is the natural guardian of the child's person. If both parents die while a child is a minor, and their wills do not designate a guardian, a court will appoint a guardian from among the nearest relatives. This person may not be the person the parents would want to have custody of the child. For a parent with a minor child, one of the principal reasons for having a will is to designate a guardian of the person in case both parents die during the child's minority.

The second principal reason a parent with a minor child needs a will relates to management of the child's property. If the child is to inherit property, the issue of management should be dealt with. A guardian of the person has no authority to deal with the child's property.

There are three alternatives for property management: guardianship, custodianship, and trusteeship. The latter two are available only to persons who die testate, creating these arrangements by will. If a parent dies intestate, leaving property to a minor child, a guardian of the property must be appointed by a court.

A *guardian of the property* is charged with possession and management of the child's property. The guardian of the property may be the same individual as is guardian of the person, or the guardians may be different individuals. A guardian of property, appointed by a court, is subject to supervision by that court, which traditionally has been strict in holding the guardian to straitjacketing rules. First, the guardian cannot change investments without a court order. The guardian has the duty of preserving the specific property and delivering it to the ward upon majority, unless the court approves a sale, lease, or mortgage. Second, the guardian ordinarily can use only the income from the property to support the ward; the guardian has no authority to go into principal to support the ward, unless the court approves. Strict court supervision over many of the guardian's acts is burdensome and time-consuming, and the resulting court costs and attorney's fees may constitute a substantial expense — leaving the ward with less property at the end of a guardianship than at the beginning.

intestate

Article V of the Uniform Probate Code adopts simplified procedures for managing a ward's property. Restricting the term guardian to guardian of the person, the code renames the guardian of a ward's property *conservator of a protected person*. A conservator is given powers and duties comparable to those of a trustee. Appointment and supervision by a court is still required, but the conservator has far more flexible powers than a guardian and only one trip to the courthouse annually for an accounting may be necessary.

In states without modern guardianship or conservatorship laws such as the UPC provides, the only effective way to handle guardianship administrations is to avoid them. And, indeed, we conclude that even in states with modern guardianship laws, the alternative arrangements of custodianship or trusteeship for a minor are preferable.

A *custodian* is a person who is given property to hold for the benefit of a minor under the state Uniform Transfers to Minors Act. A custodian is given statutory powers similar to those of a trustee. The custodian can spend income or principal for the support of the child. The custodian is not under the supervision of a court — as is a guardian or conservator — and no accounting to the court annually or at the end of the custodianship is necessary. The custodian can account directly to the ward when the ward attains majority. For discussion of the Uniform Transfers to Minors Act, see infra page 454.

will

The third alternative for property management on behalf of a minor is to establish a *trust* for a child. A trust is the most flexible of all property arrangements, and a good part of this book will later be devoted to it. The testator can tailor the trust specifically to the family

will

circumstances and the testator's particular desires. And it may be possible to account to the beneficiaries, and not to a court, at the termination of the trust.

If the testator wants to make a cash bequest to a beneficiary who is now a minor, the will might include a clause providing that any cash bequest to a minor beneficiary can be distributed to the beneficiary's parents. A bequest to a minor can be paid to the minor's parents if the will so authorizes. States often have laws permitting the personal representative to pay small sums from the decedent's estate without requiring the appointment of a guardian or conservator. See Uniform Probate Code §5-101 (sums not exceeding $5,000 per year).

PROBLEMS

1. Assume that Howard Brown dies intestate (see supra pages 59-69). After payment of debts, taxes, and expenses of administration, the assets of his estate include:

	Property acquired from H's earnings during marriage[12]	*H's property acquired by gift*[12]
Tangible personalty:	$ 20,000	
Real estate:		
Residence (title is in "Howard Brown and Wendy Brown, as joint tenants with right of survivorship and not as tenants in common"); subject to mortgage of $30,000	160,000	
Lot and cabin, Lake Murray (title is in Howard Brown alone)	75,000	
Bank accounts:		
Checking (joint and survivor account with wife)	3,000	
Savings ("Howard Brown and Wendy Brown, payable on death to the survivor")	7,000	

---

12. The source of the property is irrelevant for intestate distribution in common law property states; how title is held at death is controlling. In community property states, property acquired from a spouse's earnings during marriage is community property and at the spouse's death passes under a different intestate scheme than separate property.

Certificate of deposit ("Howard Brown and Wendy Brown, as joint tenants with right of survivorship")	20,000	
Securities:		
General Corp. stock (registered in Howard Brown's name alone)		$ 80,000
Varoom Mutual Fund (registered in Howard Brown's name alone)		30,000
American Growth Mutual Fund ("Howard Brown and Wendy Brown, as joint tenants with right of survivorship and not as tenants in common")	40,000	
Life insurance:		
(Wendy Brown is named primary beneficiary; "the insured's children in equal shares" are named contingent beneficiaries)	175,000	
	$500,000	$110,000

Brown is survived by his wife and their three minor children. How is Brown's estate distributed under the Uniform Probate Code? Under the intestacy statute of your state?

2. Based on the distribution that would result if Howard Brown were to die intestate (Problem 1 above), and in view of Brown's planning objectives, would you recommend that he should have a will?

3. If Howard Brown were to die intestate, who would take care of his children and manage their property?

Howard Brown wishes to leave everything to his wife, but his will should provide what happens to his property if his wife predeceases him. We recommend that his will contain a provision for a trust to be created for the benefit of his children if his wife predeceases him (see infra page 490). Brown should also make sure that his nonprobate assets (especially his life insurance proceeds) are made payable to the trustee of this trust if Wendy predeceases him. Under this arrangement, all his property will be administered by a trustee for the benefit of his children.

e. Advancements

If any child wishes to share in the intestate distribution of a deceased parent's estate, the child must permit the administrator to include in the determination of the distributive shares the value of any property that the decedent, while living, gave the child by way of an *advancement*. At common law, any lifetime gift to a child was presumed to be an advancement — in effect, a prepayment — of the child's intestate share. To avoid application of the doctrine, the child had the burden of establishing that the lifetime transfer was intended as an absolute gift that was not to be counted against the child's share of the estate. The doctrine is based on the assumption that the parent would want an equal distribution of assets among the children and that true equality can be reached only if lifetime gifts are taken into account in determining the amount of the equal shares. When a parent makes an advancement to the child and the child predeceases the parent, the amount of the advancement is deducted from the shares of such child's issue if other children of the parent survive.

If a gift is treated as an advancement, the donee must allow its value to be brought into *hotchpot* if the donee wants to share in the decedent's estate. Here is how hotchpot works: Assume decedent leaves no spouse, three children, and an estate worth $50,000. One daughter, A, received an advancement of $10,000. To calculate the shares in the estate, the $10,000 gift is added to the $50,000, and the total of $60,000 is divided by three. A has already received $10,000 of her share; thus she receives only $10,000 from the estate. Her siblings each take a $20,000 share.

PROBLEMS

1. Suppose, in the example immediately above, A had been given property worth $34,000 as an advancement. How should the $50,000 estate be distributed? Would A have to give back a portion of her $34,000?

2. Oliver, an elderly widower, has six children. Oliver's unmarried daughter Anna lives with Oliver and takes care of him. Oliver gives Anna a house worth $40,000; at Oliver's death the house is worth $60,000. Is this an advancement? If so, in what amount?

Oliver gives a farm to his married daughter Betty. Betty has ten children and a husband unable to work. Is this an advancement?

Oliver gives another farm to his married son Carl who has nine children. Oliver tells the son that his large brood would be better off living on a farm than in the city. Is this an advancement? See Miller v. Richardson, 85 S.W.2d 41 (Mo. 1935), which involved three gifts similar to these hypotheticals.

———

Largely because of problems of proof engendered by the advancements doctrine (What do you do with large birthday or Christmas presents or graduate school tuition fees expended on behalf of one child and not the other?), many states have reversed the common law presumption of advancement. In these states a lifetime gift is presumed *not* to be an advancement unless it is shown to have been intended as such. In other states, statutes declare that a gift is not an advancement unless it is declared as such in a writing signed by the grantor or grantee. If the decedent leaves a will, the doctrine does not come into play even though there is a partial intestacy. (Why should this be so?) See Bratt, Kentucky's Doctrine of Advancements: A Time for Reform, 75 Ky. L.J. 341 (1987).

Uniform Probate Code (1983)

§2-110 [ADVANCEMENTS]

If a person dies intestate as to all his estate, property which he gave in his lifetime to an heir[13] is treated as an advancement against the latter's share of the estate only if declared in a contemporaneous writing by the decedent or acknowledged in writing by the heir to be an advancement. For this purpose the property advanced is valued as of the time the heir came into possession or enjoyment of the property or as of the time of death of the decedent, whichever first occurs. If the recipient of the property fails to survive the decedent, the property is not taken into account in computing the intestate share to be received by the recipient's issue, unless the declaration or acknowledgement provides otherwise.

For criticism of the Uniform Probate Code, see Fellows, Concealing Legislative Reform in the Common-Law Tradition: The Advancements Doctrine and the Uniform Probate Code, 37 Vand. L. Rev. 671 (1984).

SECTION B.   INTESTATE SUCCESSORS: ANCESTORS AND COLLATERALS

When the intestate is survived by descendants, parents and collaterals do not take in any jurisdiction. When there are no descendants, after

---

13. UPC §2-110 applies to advancements made to collaterals (such as nephews and nieces) as well as to lineal descendants. In most states, gifts to collateral relations are not considered advancements. T. Atkinson, Wills 722 (2d ed. 1953). — Eds.

deducting the spouse's share (which may be all the property but is more commonly one-half), the intestate's property is usually distributed to parents.

If there are no parents, we must turn to more remote ancestors and collateral kindred to find the statutory heirs. All persons who are related by blood to the decedent but who are not descendants or ancestors are called collateral kindred. Descendants of the decedent's parents, other than the decedent and the decedent's issue, are called first-line collaterals. Descendants of the decedent's grandparents, other than decedent's parents and their issue, are called second-line collaterals. The reason for this terminology can be seen by a glance at the Table of Consanguinity on the facing page.

If the decedent is not survived by a spouse, descendants, or parents, intestate property passes to brothers, sisters, their descendants, or other collateral relatives. When property passes to collateral relatives, the property passes to issue of the decedent's parents, if any, excluding all other collaterals. The issue take *by representation*, that is, the issue of deceased brothers and sisters (nephews and nieces) represent their deceased parents and take their parent's share if other brothers or sisters survive. See, e.g., Uniform Probate Code §2-103(3), supra page 77. On how representation works, see supra pages 87-90.

If there are no first line collaterals, the states differ as to who is next in the line of succession. Two basic schemes are used: the *parentelic* system and the *degree-of-relationship* system. Under the parentelic system, the intestate estate passes to grandparents and their issue, and if none to great-grandparents and their issue, and if none to great-great-grandparents and their issue, and so on down each line (*parentela*) descended from an ancestor until an heir is found. Under the degree-of-relationship system, the intestate estate passes to the closest of kin, counting degrees of kinship. To ascertain the degree of relationship of the decedent to the claimant you count the steps (counting one for each generation) up from the decedent to the nearest common ancestor of the decedent and the claimant, and then you count the steps down to the claimant from the common ancestor. The total number of steps is the degree of relationship. See the Table of Consanguinity on the facing page, where the degree of relationship to the decedent is printed above the upper left-hand corner of the box designating the relationship of the claimant.

Uniform Probate Code §2-103(4), supra page 77, is an example of a limited parentelic system. If there are no first-line collaterals, the intestate estate passes to grandparents and their descendants (second-line collaterals). The Uniform Probate Code does not permit inheritance by kin more remote than second-line collaterals. (The UPC also divides the intestate estate into equal shares between the maternal grandparents

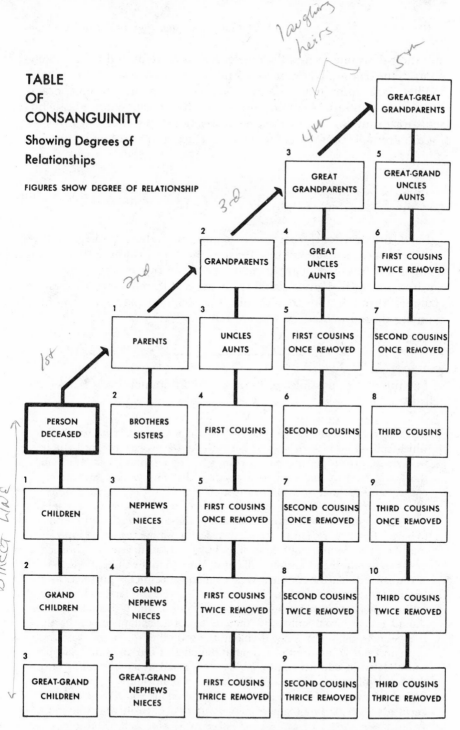

TABLE
OF
CONSANGUINITY

**Showing Degrees of
Relationships**

FIGURES SHOW DEGREE OF RELATIONSHIP

*laughing
heirs*

5th

4th

3rd

2nd

1st

DIRECT LINE

		3 GREAT GRANDPARENTS		5 GREAT-GRAND UNCLES AUNTS	GREAT-GREAT GRANDPARENTS

	2 GRANDPARENTS	4 GREAT UNCLES AUNTS	6 FIRST COUSINS TWICE REMOVED

1 PARENTS	3 UNCLES AUNTS	5 FIRST COUSINS ONCE REMOVED	7 SECOND COUSINS ONCE REMOVED

PERSON DECEASED	2 BROTHERS SISTERS	4 FIRST COUSINS	6 SECOND COUSINS	8 THIRD COUSINS

1 CHILDREN	3 NEPHEWS NIECES	5 FIRST COUSINS ONCE REMOVED	7 SECOND COUSINS ONCE REMOVED	9 THIRD COUSINS ONCE REMOVED

2 GRAND CHILDREN	4 GRAND NEPHEWS NIECES	6 FIRST COUSINS TWICE REMOVED	8 SECOND COUSINS TWICE REMOVED	10 THIRD COUSINS TWICE REMOVED

3 GREAT-GRAND CHILDREN	5 GREAT-GRAND NEPHEWS NIECES	7 FIRST COUSINS THRICE REMOVED	9 SECOND COUSINS THRICE REMOVED	11 THIRD COUSINS THRICE REMOVED

109

and their descendants and the paternal grandparents and their descendants. This division is not made in most states.)

There are numerous variations or mixtures of the parentelic and degree-of-relationship systems in force in the various states. Massachusetts, for example, follows a degree-of-relationship system but provides for a "parentelic preference" to break a tie between kin of equal degree.

Massachusetts General Laws Annotated
ch. 190, §3(6) (1981)

If he [the decedent] leaves no issue, and no father, mother, brother or sister, and no issue of any deceased brother or sister, then to his next of kin in equal degree; but if there are two or more collateral kindred in equal degree claiming through different ancestors, those claiming through the nearest ancestor shall be preferred to those claiming through an ancestor more remote.

———————

The number of possible collateral kindred is immense. As Blackstone tells us:

[A]s many ancestors as a man has, so many common stocks he has, from which collateral kinsmen may be derived. And as we are taught by holy writ, that there is one couple of ancestors belonging to us all, from whom the whole race of mankind is descended, the obvious and undeniable consequence is, that all men are in some degree related to each other. For indeed, if we only suppose each couple of our ancestors to have left, one with another, two children; and each of those children on an average to have left two more, (and, without such a supposition, the human species must be daily diminishing;) we shall find that all of us have now subsisting near two hundred and seventy millions of kindred in the fifteenth degree; at the same distance from the several common ancestors as ourselves are; besides those that are one or two descents nearer to or farther from the common stock, who may amount to as many more. And if this calculation should appear incompatible with the number of inhabitants on the earth, it is because, by intermarriages among the several descendants from the same ancestor, a hundred or a thousand modes of consanguinity may be consolidated in one person, or he may be related to us a hundred or a thousand different ways. [2 W. Blackstone, Commentaries *205. Blackstone also notes that if you go back 20 generations you have 1,048,576 ancestors (disregarding the possibility of intermarriage among relatives)!]

Should the law permit intestate succession by these remote collaterals, known to lawyers as "laughing heirs" (i.e., persons so distantly related to the decedent as to suffer no sense of bereavement)? This question was brought into sharp focus by three famous cases in this century, where hordes of fortune seekers appeared on death. These were the cases of Ella Wendel, Ida Wood, and Henrietta Garrett, all of whom died during the Great Depression.

Henrietta E. Garrett died intestate in Philadelphia in 1930, leaving an estate of over $17,000,000. Nearly 26,000 claims were filed by persons claiming to be her heirs. The testimony covered 390 volumes and over 115,000 pages. In addition, for 15 years the Attorney General of Pennsylvania vigorously contended that Henrietta died without heirs. Finally the attorney general entered into a compromise that recognized that the three persons found by the master to be first cousins of Henrietta were her heirs. In 1953 the Supreme Court of Pennsylvania finally ordered the Garrett estate closed. Estate of Garrett, 372 Pa. 438, 94 A.2d 357 (1953).

Ella Wendel, a recluse, died in 1931, leaving a will devising most of her $40,000,000 estate to charity. The only persons who may contest a will are those persons who would take if the will is held invalid. Some 2303 fortune hunters strove to establish they were her next of kin, so that they might contest her will. Reams of evidence were fabricated, birth and death certificates altered, and tales of bastardy and incest spun. One man was sent to jail for fabricating evidence, and Surrogate Foley referred the activities of six lawyers to the Grievance Committee of the Bar. Ultimately nine persons were established to be her cousins, and they settled out of court with the charities. In re Wendel, 143 Misc. 480, 257 N.Y.S. 87 (Sur. Ct. 1932); 146 Misc. 260, 262 N.Y.S. 41 (Sur. Ct. 1933); 159 Misc. 443, 287 N.Y.S. 893 (Sur. Ct. 1936). The late Justice Harlan's participation in the *Wendel* litigation is traced in Laporte, John M. Harlan Saves the Ella Wendel Estate, 59 A.B.A.J. 868 (1973).

Ida E. Mayfield Wood, the widow of a United States congressman from New York, died intestate in 1932. For more than 20 years she and her two sisters (who predeceased her) had barricaded themselves in a New York hotel room, into which no one was permitted to enter. During her life Ida had spun a web of deceit to hide who she really was. The evidence finally accepted by the court showed she had been born Ellen Walsh in Ireland, had moved with her parents to Boston, and had been her husband's mistress for ten years before he legalized her name. Once married and propelled into high society, Ida drew a curtain across her past. She made up vague stories of having been born a Mayfield and brought up in New Orleans. Her mother, and some other members of her family, took the name Mayfield, and Ida carved "Mayfield" on their tombstones. Fearful of a depression, Ida kept $500,000 in cash tied around her waist. When she died, some 1100 persons claimed to be her next of kin — including a great many persons named Mayfield from Louisiana. Ultimately the court established as

Ida's next of kin some first cousins once removed (none of whom Ida had seen since her marriage to Wood 65 years before). In re Wood, 164 Misc. 425, 299 N.Y.S. 195 (1937). The whole fascinating story is recounted in J. Cox, The Recluse of Herald Square (1964).[14]

With these cases in mind, Professor Cavers predicted in the 1930s that the rules of succession would be revised to abolish laughing heirs. Cavers, Change in the American Family and the "Laughing Heir," 20 Iowa L. Rev. 203, 208 (1935). However, only a few jurisdictions have done so. Uniform Probate Code §2-103 moves in this direction. It limits inheritance by intestate succession to lineal descendants of the decedent, parents and their lineal descendants, and grandparents and their lineal descendants. It eliminates inheritance by more remote relatives traced through great-grandparents and other more remote ancestors. The UPC rule has a number of advantages:

(1) It simplifies the administration of estates (and of trusts where there is a final gift to "heirs") by avoiding the delay and expense of attempting to find remote missing heirs and by minimizing the problems of notice.

(2) It eliminates the standing of remote heirs to bring will contests (or trust litigation) and thus minimizes the opportunity for unmeritorious litigation brought for the sole purpose of coercing a settlement (known as a "strike suit") — see the case of Ella Wendel above.

(3) It removes a significant source of uncertainty in land titles.

The UPC limitation, incorporated into the Michigan statute of descent, was held to bear a rational relationship to a permissible state objective and thus to be constitutional in Estate of Jurek, 170 Mich. App. 778, 428 N.W.2d 774 (1988).

The UPC limitation on inheritance has met with considerable resistance in legislatures and has not been adopted in all states enacting the UPC. Indeed, a few legislatures have moved in the opposite direction — permitting relatives of the decedent's spouse to inherit when the decedent leaves no blood relatives. See, e.g., Cal. Prob. Code §6402 (g) (1989); Va. Code §64.1-1 (1987). These legislatures seem determined to make escheat to the state a remote possibility.

If the intestate leaves no survivors entitled to take under the intestacy statute, the intestate's property escheats to the state in all jurisdictions. Escheats of substantial estates are rare. Relatives usually keep tabs on

---

14. M. Sussman, J. Cates & D. Smith, The Family and Inheritance 138-139 (1970), report that there are many professional heir-hunting firms who search the records and advise the uninformed heir that they will disclose the name of the estate in exchange for one-third of the inheritance.

kinfolk of obvious wealth, and thus the larger the estate, the more likely it is that there will be heirs claiming it.

NOTE: HALF-BLOODS

In England, which put great weight on whole-blood relations, the common law courts wholly excluded relatives of the half-blood from inheriting land through intestate succession. This rule has long been abolished in all the American states. In a large majority of states, a relative of the half-blood (e.g., a half-sister) is treated the same as a relative of the whole-blood. This is the position of Uniform Probate Code §2-107. In a few states a half-blood is given a half share; this was the Scottish rule and was introduced in this country in Virginia. Va. Code §64.1-2 (1987). In a few other states a half-blood takes only when there are no whole-blood relatives of the same degree. See Miss. Code §91-1-5 (1973).

PROBLEMS

1. The decedent is survived by his mother, his sister, and two nephews (children of a deceased brother). How is the decedent's estate distributed under the Uniform Probate Code? Under the intestacy statute of your state?

2. The decedent is survived by an uncle of his mother, *A*, two first cousins on his mother's side, *B* and *C*, and the daughter of his first cousin on his father's side, *D*. How is the decedent's estate distributed under the Uniform Probate Code? Under Mass. Gen. Laws ch. 190, §3(6) (1981), supra page 110? Under the intestacy statute of your state?

3. *M* has one child, *A*, by her first marriage and two children, *B* and *C*, by her second marriage. *M* and her second husband die. Then *C* dies intestate, unmarried, and without descendants. How is *C*'s property distributed under the Uniform Probate Code? Under Va. Code §64.1-2, supra? Under Miss. Code §91-1-5, supra?

4. Those interested in genealogy puzzles might like to try the one posed by the Rev. Charles L. Dodgson, an eminent mathematician better known as Lewis Carroll. The problem: The Governor of Kgovjni wants to give the very smallest dinner party possible and at the same time invite his father's brother-in-law, his brother's father-in-law, his father-in-law's brother, and his brother-in-law's father. To do this, how many guests is it absolute necessary to invite? The answer: One. If you cannot figure how this is done, using a genealogical tree of only fourteen

people, see L. Carroll, The Complete Works of Lewis Carroll 1031 (Mod. Lib. ed.).

If you want to pursue these teasers further, you may find the genealogical tree in the Egyptian royal family of the Eighteenth Dynasty worthy of exploration. For example, Princess Nefer-Neferu-aten's sister, Ankhesen-Paaten, was also her stepmother, her aunt, and her grandmother by marriage. See C. Desroches-Noblecourt, Tutankhamen 120, 290 (1969).

SECTION C.   BARS TO SUCCESSION

1. *Misconduct*

a. Killing Decedent

In re Estate of Mahoney
Supreme Court of Vermont, 1966
126 Vt. 31, 220 A.2d 475

SMITH, J.   The decedent, Howard Mahoney, died intestate on May 6, 1961, of gunshot wounds. His wife, Charlotte Mahoney, the appellant here, was tried for the murder of Howard Mahoney in the Addison County Court and was convicted by jury of the crime of manslaughter in March, 1962. She is presently serving a sentence of not less than 12 nor more than 15 years at the Women's Reformatory in Rutland.

Howard Mahoney left no issue, and was survived by his wife and his father and mother. His father, Mark Mahoney, was appointed administrator of his estate which at the present time amounts to $3,885.89. After due notice and hearing, the Probate Court for the District of Franklin entered a judgment order decreeing the residue of the Estate of Howard Mahoney, in equal shares, to the father and mother of the decedent. An appeal from the judgment order and decree has been taken here by the appellant widow. The question submitted is whether a widow convicted of manslaughter in connection with the death of her husband may inherit from his estate.

The general rules of descent provide that if a decedent is married and leaves no issue, his surviving spouse shall be entitled to the whole of decedent's estate if it does not exceed $8,000. 14 V.S.A. §551(2). Only if the decedent leaves no surviving spouse or issue does the estate descend in equal shares to the surviving father and mother. 14 V.S.A. §551(3). There is no statutory provision in Vermont regulating the descent and distribution of property from the decedent to the slayer. The question presented is one of first impression in this jurisdiction.

In a number of jurisdictions, statutes have been enacted which in certain instances, at least, prevent a person who has killed another from taking by descent or distribution from the person he has killed. A statute of this nature, carefully drawn, is considered by many authorities to be the best solution to the problems presented. See "Acquisition of property by wilfully killing another — a statutory solution," 49 Harvard Law Review 715 (1935-1936).

Courts in those states that have no statute preventing a slayer from taking by descent or distribution from the estate of his victim, have followed three separate and different lines of decision.

(1) The legal title passed to the slayer and may be retained by him in spite of his crime. The reasoning for so deciding is that devolution of the property of a decedent is controlled entirely by the statutes of descent and distribution; further, that denial of the inheritance to the slayer because of his crime would be imposing an additional punishment for his crime not provided by statute, and would violate the constitutional provision against corruption of blood. Carpenter's Estate, 170 Pa. 203, 32 A. 637, 29 L.R.A. 145; Wall v. Pfanschmidt, 265 Ill. 180, 106 N.E. 785, L.R.A. 1915C, 328; Bird v. Plunkett et al., 139 Conn. 491, 95 A.2d 71, 36 A.L.R.2d 951.

(2) The legal title will not pass to the slayer because of the equitable principle that no one should be permitted to profit by his own fraud, or take advantage and profit as a result of his own wrong or crime. Riggs v. Palmer, 115 N.Y. 506, 22 N.E. 188, 5 L.R.A. 340; Price v. Hitaffer, 164 Md. 505, 165 A. 470; Slocum v. Metropolitan Life Ins. Co., 245 Mass. 565, 139 N.E. 816, 27 A.L.R. 1517. Decisions so holding have been criticized as judicially engrafting an exception on the statute of descent and distribution and being "unwarranted judicial legislation." Wall v. Pfanschmidt, supra.

(3) The legal title passes to the slayer but equity holds him to be a constructive trustee for the heirs or next of kin of the decedent. This disposition of the question presented avoids a judicial engrafting on the statutory laws of descent and distribution, for title passes to the slayer. But because of the unconscionable mode by which the property is acquired by the slayer, equity treats him as a constructive trustee and compels him to convey the property to the heirs or next of kin of the deceased.

The reasoning behind the adoption of this doctrine was well expressed by Mr. Justice Cardozo in his lecture on "The Nature of the Judicial Process." "Consistency was preserved, logic received its tribute, by holding that the legal title passed, but it was subject to a constructive trust. A constructive trust is nothing but 'the formula through which the conscience of equity finds expression.' Property is acquired in such circumstances that the holder of legal title may not in good conscience retain the beneficial interest. Equity, to express its disapproval of his conduct, converts him into a trustee." See 4 Scott on Trusts (2d ed. 1956) §402; Bogert, Trusts and Trustees, (2d ed. 1960), §478. See Miller v. Belville, 98 Vt. 243, 126 A. 590.

The New Hampshire court was confronted with the same problem of the rights to the benefits of an estate by one who had slain the decedent, in the absence of a statute on the subject. Kelley v. State, 105 N.H. 240, 196 A.2d 68. Speaking for an unanimous court, Chief Justice Kenison said: "But, even in the absence of statute, a court applying common law techniques can reach a sensible solution by charging the spouse, heir or legatee as a constructive trustee of the property where equity and justice demand it." Kelley v. State, supra, pp. 69, 70. We approve of the doctrine so expressed.

However, the principle that one should not profit by his own wrong must not be extended to every case where a killer acquires property from his victim as a result of the killing. One who has killed while insane is not chargeable as a constructive trustee, or if the slayer had a vested interest in the property, it is property to which he would have been entitled if no slaying had occurred. The principle to be applied is that the slayer should not be permitted to improve his position by the killing, but should not be compelled to surrender property to which he would have been entitled if there had been no killing. The doctrine of constructive trust is involved to prevent the slayer from profiting from his crime, but not as an added criminal penalty. Kelley v. State, supra, p.70; Restatement of Restitution, §187(2), comment a.

The appellant here was, as we have noted, convicted of manslaughter and not of murder. She calls to our attention that while the Restatement of Restitution approves the application of the constructive trust doctrine where a devisee or legatee murders the testator, that such rules are not applicable where the slayer was guilty of manslaughter. Restatement of Restitution, §187, comment e.

The cases generally have not followed this limitation of the rule but hold that the line should not be drawn between murder and manslaughter, but between voluntary and involuntary manslaughter. Kelley v. State, supra; Chase v. Jennifer, 219 Md. 564, 150 A.2d 251, 254.

We think that this is the proper rule to follow. Voluntary manslaughter is an intentional and unlawful killing, with a real design and purpose to kill, even if such killing be the result of sudden passion or great provocation. Involuntary manslaughter is caused by an unlawful act, but not accompanied with any intention to take life. State v. McDonnell, 32 Vt. 491, 545. It is the intent to kill, which when accomplished, leads to the profit of the slayer that brings into play the constructive trust to prevent the unjust enrichment of the slayer by reason of his intentional killing.

In Vermont, an indictment for murder can result in a jury conviction on either voluntary or involuntary manslaughter. State v. Averill, 85 Vt. 115, 132, 81 A. 461. The legislature has provided the sentences that may be passed upon a person convicted of manslaughter, but provides no definition of that offense, nor any statutory distinction between voluntary and involuntary manslaughter. 13 V.S.A. §2304.

The cause now before us is here on a direct appeal from the probate court. Findings of fact were made below from which it appears that the judgment of the probate court decreeing the estate of Howard Mahoney to his parents, rather than to his widow, was based upon a finding of the felonious killing of her husband by Mrs. Mahoney. However, the appellees here have asked us to affirm the decree below by imposing a constructive trust on the estate in the hands of the widow.

But the Probate Court did not decree the estate to the widow, and then make her a constructive trustee of such estate for the benefit of the parents. The judgment below decreed the estate directly to the parents, which was in direct contravention of the statutes of descent and distribution. The Probate Court was bound to follow the statutes of descent and distribution and its decree was in error and must be reversed.

The Probate Court was without jurisdiction to impose a constructive trust on the estate in the hands of the appellant, even if it had attempted to do so. Probate courts are courts of special and limited jurisdiction given by statute and do not proceed according to common law. While probate courts possess a portion of equitable powers independent of statute, such powers do not extend to the establishment of purely equitable rights and claims. In re Estate of Prudenzano, 116 Vt. 55, 68 A.2d 704; Manley v. Brattleboro Trust Co., 116 Vt. 460, 464, 78 A.2d 488. The claim of the parents here to the Estate of Howard Mahoney is equitable in its origin, and in the extent of the rights in the estate claimed. The equity powers conferred upon the probate court do not extend to the establishment of purely equitable claims and equitable rights. Admr. of Leonard v. Executor of Leonard, 67 Vt. 318, 320, 31 A. 783.

However, the jurisdiction of the court of chancery may be invoked in probate matters in aid of the probate court when the powers of that court are inadequate, and it appears that the probate court cannot reasonably and adequately handle the question. The jurisdiction of the chancery court in so acting on probate matters is special and limited only to aiding the probate court. In re Will of Prudenzano, supra; Manley v. Brattleboro Trust Co., supra, 116 Vt. p.461, 78 A.2d 488.

The Probate Court, in making its decree, used the record of the conviction of the appellant for manslaughter for its determination that the appellant had feloniously killed her husband. If the jurisdiction of the court of chancery is invoked by the appellees here it will be for the determination of that court, upon proof, to determine whether the appellant wilfully killed her late husband, as it will upon all other equitable considerations that may be offered in evidence, upon charging the appellant with a constructive trust. "The fact that he is convicted of murder in a criminal case does not dispense with the necessity of proof of the murder in a proceedings in equity to charge him as a constructive trustee." Restatement of Restitution, §187, comment d.

The jurisdiction over charging the appellant with a constructive trust on the estate of Howard Mahoney lies in the court of chancery, and not in the probate court.

Decree reversed and cause remanded, with directions that the proceedings herein be stayed for sixty days to give the Administrator of the Estate of Howard Mahoney an opportunity to apply to the Franklin County Court of Chancery for relief. If application is so made, proceedings herein shall be stayed pending the final determination thereof. If application is not so made, the Probate Court for the District of Franklin shall assign to Charlotte Mahoney, surviving wife, the right and interest in and to the estate of her deceased husband which the Vermont Statutes confer.

NOTES AND PROBLEMS

1. In 1972 a statute was enacted in Vermont providing that an heir, devisee, or legatee who "stands convicted in any court . . . of intentionally and unlawfully killing the decedent" shall forfeit any share in the decedent's estate. Vt. Stat. Ann. tit. 14, §551(6) (1974).

The rights of a killer in the estate of a victim are usually covered by a state statute. These statutes vary in many details; there is by no means unanimous agreement as to what provisions are desirable. See Fellows, The Slayer Rule: Not Solely a Matter of Equity, 71 Iowa L. Rev. 489 (1986); McGovern, Homicide and Succession to Property, 68 Mich. L. Rev. 65 (1969); Annot., 25 A.L.R.4th 787 (1983). Some of the more debatable questions are raised in the problems that follow.

2. Suppose that *W* shoots *H* and is convicted of involuntary manslaughter. Is *W* barred as an heir under the Vermont statute above? Under Uniform Probate Code §2-803, infra? In Estate of Kramme, 30 Cal. 3d 567, 573 P.2d 1369, 143 Cal. Rptr. 542 (1978), the husband of the decedent pulled a gun on his wife's lover, engaged in a struggle, and accidentally shot his wife fatally. The court held that a statute that bars inheritance if the heir "unlawfully and intentionally caused the death of a decedent" refers to a death that was the intended consequence of the conduct, and concluded that the husband took as his wife's heir.

If a conviction of murder or voluntary manslaughter is conclusive, should an acquittal be conclusive? An acquittal in a criminal proceeding establishes that there was not proof beyond a reasonable doubt, but it does not establish that there was not proof by a preponderance of the evidence. If an acquittal is conclusive under the local statute, suppose that *W*, charged with murder, enters a negotiated plea of nolo contendere to involuntary manslaughter. Does *W* forfeit her inheritance rights? See Estate of McGowan, 35 Cal. App. 3d 611, 111 Cal. Rptr. 39 (1973); In re Estate of Safran, 102 Wis. 2d 79, 306 N.W.2d 27, 25 A.L.R.4th 766 (1981).

3.   Suppose that *A* and *B* own land as joint tenants with right of survivorship, and *A* murders *B*. What result? See In re Estate of Foster, 182 Kan. 315, 320 P.2d 855 (1958); In re Estate of King, 261 Wis. 266, 52 N.W.2d 885 (1952).

If one joint tenant murders another, and the court agrees to impose a constructive trust on the surviving joint tenant, what should be the terms of the trust? The Restatement of Restitution §188, Comment b, states that the murderer holds the entire property under a constructive trust for the dead tenant's estate except that the murderer is entitled to one-half the income therefrom for life. Uniform Probate Code §2-803 offers another solution. See also 5 A. Scott, Trusts §493.2 (W. Fratcher 4th ed. 1989).

Uniform Probate Code (1983)

§2-803   [Effect of Homicide on Intestate Succession, Wills, Joint Assets, Life Insurance and Beneficiary Designations]

(a)   A surviving spouse, heir or devisee who feloniously and intentionally kills the decedent is not entitled to any benefits under the will or under this Article, and the estate of decedent passes as if the killer had predeceased the decedent. Property appointed by the will of the decedent to or for the benefit of the killer passes as if the killer had predeceased the decedent.

(b)   Any joint tenant who feloniously and intentionally kills another joint tenant thereby effects a severance of the interest of the decedent so that the share of the decedent passes as his property and the killer has no rights by survivorship. This provision applies to joint tenancies [and tenancies by the entirety] in real and personal property, joint and multiple-party accounts in banks, savings and loan associations, credit unions and other institutions, and any other form of co-ownership with survivorship incidents.

(c)   A named beneficiary of a bond, life insurance policy, or other contractual arrangement who feloniously and intentionally kills the principal obligee or the person upon whose life the policy is issued is not entitled to any benefit under the bond, policy or other contractual arrangement, and it becomes payable as though the killer had predeceased the decedent.

(d) Any other acquisition of property or interest by the killer shall be treated in accordance with the principles of this section.

(e) A final judgment of conviction of felonious and intentional killing is conclusive for purposes of this section. In the absence of a conviction of felonious and intentional killing the Court may determine by a preponderance of evidence whether the killing was felonious and intentional for purposes of this section.

(f) This section does not affect the rights of any person who, before rights under this section have been adjudicated, purchases from the killer for value and without notice property which the killer would have acquired except for this section, but the killer is liable for the amount of the proceeds or the value of the property. Any insurance company, bank, or other obligor making payment according to the terms of its policy or obligation is not liable by reason of this section unless prior to payment it has received at its home office or principal address written notice of a claim under this section.

PROBLEMS

Observe that under UPC §2-803(a), the estate of decedent passes as if the killer had predeceased the decedent. Suppose that A has three children, B, C, and D, and four grandchildren, E, F, G, and H, and that C and D have predeceased A. Thus:

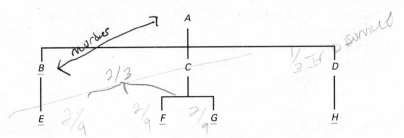

The survivors of the murder are underlined: all others are dead.

B murders A. Who takes A's property under a per capita with representation system of distribution as is provided in UPC §2-106, supra page 88? Suppose that B had three children rather than one. What result?

If D had survived A, what distribution would take place under a per capita at each generation representational scheme, supra page 90?

Would these changes in distributional shares follow from murder if the intestacy statute follows a strict per stirpes scheme?

See Fellows, The Slayer Rule: Not Solely a Matter of Equity, 71 Iowa L. Rev. 489, 524-527 (1986).

b.   Adultery and Desertion

In several states, parents and spouses are disqualified to take as heirs when they are deemed unworthy. Statutes may disqualify a parent as heir if the parent has failed or refused to support the child or has abandoned the child during his minority. See, e.g., N.Y. Est., Powers & Trusts Law §4-1.4 (1981). In a few states, statutes or case decisions disqualify a spouse from dower, inheritance, or an elective share if the spouse abandoned the decedent and committed adultery; sometimes abandonment alone is sufficient. See, e.g., Ky. Rev. Stat. §392.090 (1984); Va. Code §64.1-23 (1987).

2.   Transfer of Interest in Decedent's Estate

A person may be barred from succeeding to a decedent's estate because he has released, transferred, or disclaimed his interest.

a.   Release of Expectancy

The usual case of release of an expectancy arises when a child releases his expected inheritance to his parent. A child's release to his parent during the parent's lifetime is binding if given for fair consideration. Thus a child may accept a deed to Blackacre from a parent and execute a document saying that the land received is in satisfaction of the child's share of the parent's estate. The child is then barred from sharing in the parent's estate if other descendants survive the parent.

Since the child has no interest in his parent's property at the time he signs the release, the release cannot operate as a transfer of any interest. However, the release is usually treated as an advancement of the child's entire share, which is liquidated by agreement of the parties. See T. Atkinson, Wills 727 (2d ed. 1953).

b.   Transfer of Expectancy

In the eyes of the law no living person has heirs; to use the Latin phrase: *nemo est haeres viventis*. The persons who would be the heirs of

A, a living person, if *A* died within the next hour, are not the heirs of *A* but the *heirs apparent*. They have a mere *expectancy*. This expectancy can be destroyed by *A*'s deed or will. It is not a legal "interest" at all.[15] Not being an interest, an expectancy cannot be transferred at law. However, a purported transfer of an expectancy, for an adequate consideration, may be enforceable in equity as a contract to transfer if the court views it as fair under all the circumstances. Equity scrutinizes such transactions to protect prospective heirs from unfair bargains. See 3 American Law of Property §14.12 (1952).

c. Disclaimer

Under the common law, when a person dies *intestate*, title to real and personal property passes to the decedent's heirs by operation of law. An intestate successor cannot prevent title from passing to him or her. The original reason for this rule was that there must always be someone seised of the land — a reason once valid but of no importance today. Nonetheless, if the heir refuses to accept (or, more precisely, to keep) the inheritance, the common law treats the heir's renunciation as if title had passed to the heir and then from the heir to the next of kin.

On the other hand, if a person dies *testate*, a will beneficiary can refuse to accept a devise or bequest and thereby can prevent title from passing to him. Any gift, whether inter vivos or by will, requires acceptance by the donee. These different conceptions of how title passes at death formerly produced unexpectedly different tax results. If an heir renounced his inheritance and the common law rule applied, the situation was treated as though the heir had received the intestate share and then made a taxable gift to the persons who took by reason of the renunciation. Hardenburgh v. Commissioner, 198 F.2d 63 (8th Cir.), cert. denied, 344 U.S. 836 (1952). By contrast, if a legatee disclaimed a testamentary gift, there were no gift tax consequences. Brown v. Routzahn, 63 F.2d 914 (6th Cir.), cert denied, 290 U.S. 641 (1933).

In order to permit people to disclaim property without adverse tax

---

15. Why not? Suppose that *O* transfers property to *A* for life, remainder as *A* shall appoint by deed or will and in default of appointment to the heirs of *A*. Here the heirs of *A* are said to have an interest called a contingent remainder. Can you give any reasons for treating this case in a different manner than the case in which *A* has a fee simple and *A*'s heirs apparent have an expectancy?

Although the holder of an expectancy is protected against fraud, duress, or other tortious means calculated to induce the ancestor to disinherit the heir (see infra page 175), orthodox doctrine still declares that the heirs apparent do not have an "interest" in property. 3 Restatement of Property §315, Comment a (1940).

consequences, almost all states have enacted disclaimer[16] legislation that provides that the disclaimant is treated as having predeceased the decedent. Thus the decedent's property does not pass to the disclaimant, and the disclaimant makes no transfer of it. Uniform Probate Code §2-801 is typical.

Uniform Probate Code (1983)

§2-801 [RENUNCIATION OF SUCCESSION]

(a)   A person or the representative of an incapacitated or protected person, who is an heir, devisee, person succeeding to a renounced interest, beneficiary under a testamentary instrument, or appointee under a power of appointment exercised by a testamentary instrument, may renounce in whole or in part the right of succession to any property or interest therein, including a future interest, by filing a written renunciation under this Section. The right to renounce does not survive the death of the person having it. The instrument shall (1) describe the property or interest renounced, (2) declare the renunciation and extent thereof, and (3) be signed by the person renouncing.

(b)(1)   An instrument renouncing a present interest shall be filed not later than [9] months after the death of the decedent or the donee of the power.

(2) An instrument renouncing a future interest may be filed not later than [9] months after the event determining that the taker of the property or interest is finally ascertained and his interest is indefeasibly vested.

(3) The renunciation shall be filed in the [probate] court of the county in which proceedings have been commenced for the administration of the estate of the deceased owner or deceased donee of the power or, if they have not been commenced, in which they could be commenced. A copy of the renunciation shall be delivered in person or mailed by registered or certified mail to any personal representative, or other fiduciary of the decedent or donee of the power. If real property or an interest therein is renounced, a copy of the renunciation may be recorded in the office of the [Recorder of Deeds] of the county in which the real estate is situated.

(c)   Unless the decedent or donee of the power has otherwise provided, the property or interest renounced devolves as though the

---

16. By traditional usage, an heir *renounces;* a will beneficiary *disclaims.* Today the two words are used interchangeably; they are considered synonymous. The term disclaimer is the one more commonly used to describe the formal refusal to take by either an heir or a beneficiary.

person renouncing had predeceased the decedent or, if the person renouncing is designated to take under a power of appointment exercised by a testamentary instrument, as though the person renouncing had predeceased the donee of the power. A future interest that takes effect in possession or enjoyment after the termination of the estate or interest renounced takes effect as though the person renouncing had predeceased the decedent or the donee of the power. A renunciation relates back for all purposes to the date of the death of the decedent or the donee of the power.

(d)(1) The right to renounce property or an interest therein is barred by (i) an assignment, conveyance, encumbrance, pledge, or transfer of the property or interest, or a contract therefor, (ii) a written waiver of the right to renounce, (iii) an acceptance of the property or interest or benefit thereunder, or (iv) a sale of the property or interest under judicial sale made before the renunciation is effected.

(2) The right to renounce exists notwithstanding any limitation on the interest of the person renouncing in the nature of a spendthrift provision or similar restriction.

(3) A renunciation or a written waiver of the right to renounce is binding upon the person renouncing or person waiving and all persons claiming through or under him.

NOTES AND PROBLEMS

1. Disclaimers can be used to do "post-mortem estate planning." Suppose that *H* dies intestate, survived by *W* and one son, *S*, and no grandchildren. Under the state intestacy statute, *W* is entitled to one-half of *H*'s estate and *S* is entitled to one-half. If *S* disclaims, all of *H*'s property will pass to *W*. *S* may disclaim because *W* needs all the property or to qualify all the property for the federal estate tax marital deduction. If *S* has a child, however, *S*'s one-half of the estate will not pass to *W*, but to *S*'s child. Sometimes disclaimants have not been aware of who takes the disclaimed property, and the post-mortem estate planning has gone awry. See Webb v. Webb, 301 S.E.2d 570 (W. Va. 1983) (court refused to void disclaimer made under a mistaken belief that the disclaimed property would pass to the disclaimant's mother).

Observe that under the Uniform Probate Code "the right to renounce does not survive the death of the person having it." Under some disclaimer statutes, the personal representative of a beneficiary who dies soon after the decedent can disclaim with court approval. Under these statutes there may be a greater opportunity for tax savings than under the Uniform Probate Code.

2. *O* has two children, *A* and *B*. *B* dies, survived by one child, *C*.

Then *O*, a widow, dies intestate. *O*'s heirs are *A* and *C*. *A* has four
children. *A* disclaims. The jurisdiction has enacted UPC §2-103, supra
page 77. What distribution is made of *O*'s estate? Cf. Cal. Prob. Code
§282(b) (1989). Compare the result if *A* had murdered *O*; see supra
page 120.

Suppose that *A* had predeceased *O*, that *B* had survived *O*, and that
B had disclaimed. What result? See Welder v. Hitchcock, 617 S.W.2d
294 (Tex. Civ. App. 1981).

Assume the hypothetical facts in the first paragraph above, other
than *S*'s disclaimer. During his lifetime, *B* releases his expected inheritance to *O*, then predeceases *O*. What distribution is made of *O*'s estate?
See 3 American Law of Property §14.12 (1952):

> The courts generally hold that [*A*] takes the entire estate upon the ground
> that a child's release is binding upon the issue who take through the
> releasing child. However, it seems that if only grandchildren survive and
> if they take *per capita*, as they do in most jurisdictions, the release of the
> child will not exclude his issue in favor of the other grandchildren. The
> distinction here is between grandchildren who take as representatives of
> their predeceased parent and are hence bound by the latter's release, and
> those who take per capita or in their own right.

3. *T* dies leaving a will that devises his entire estate to his sister *S* if
she survives him, otherwise to *S*'s children. At the time of *T*'s death, *S*,
who is indigent, is in a nursing home, the cost of which is being paid
by Medicaid. *S* dies intestate four months after *T*, survived by two adult
sons; her sole asset is her interest in *T*'s estate, which *S* took no steps
to secure after *T*'s death. One of her sons has himself appointed
administrator of *S*'s estate and then files an instrument that purports
to disclaim all of *S*'s interest in *T*'s estate. The Medicaid authorities
contest the disclaimer, arguing that its sole purpose is to defeat
Medicaid's claim as a creditor of *S*'s estate, and that the disclaimer is
inconsistent with the administrator's fiduciary duties since he will
personally benefit from it. The jurisdiction has enacted UPC §2-801.
What result? Suppose the disclaimer statute authorizes the personal
representative to disclaim on behalf of a person who dies shortly after
the decedent. What result? See Estate of Schiffman, 105 Misc. 2d 1025,
430 N.Y.S.2d 229 (Sur. Ct. 1980); cf. Nielsen v. Cass County Social
Services Bd., 395 N.W.2d 157 (N.D. 1986). See Dobris, Medicaid Asset
Planning by the Elderly, 24 Real Prop., Prob. & Tr. J. 1, 17 (1989).

See generally W. McGovern, S. Kurtz & J. Rein, Wills, Trusts and
Estates §2.5 (1988); Hirsch, The Problem of the Insolvent Heir, 74
Cornell L. Rev. 587 (1989); Note, Renunciation of Testamentary Benefit
as Fraudulent Transfer, 37 Case W. Res. L. Rev. 148 (1987).

Because state disclaimer laws varied considerably, resulting in different tax treatment in different states, Congress in 1976 enacted a statute

providing that only certain "qualified disclaimers" will avoid transfer tax liability. If a person disclaims, and the disclaimer is not "qualified," gift tax liability results. Thus, if saving gift taxes is an important objective, Internal Revenue Code §2518 must be satisfied.

Internal Revenue Code of 1986

§2518 [DISCLAIMERS]

(a) *General Rule.* For purposes of this subtitle [imposing a gift tax], if a person makes a qualified disclaimer with respect to any interest in property, this subtitle shall apply with respect to such interest as if the interest had never been transferred to such person.

(b) *Qualified Disclaimer Defined.* For purposes of subsection (a), the term "qualified disclaimer" means an irrevocable and unqualified refusal by a person to accept an interest in property but only if —

(1) such refusal is in writing,

(2) such writing is received by the transferor of the interest, his legal representative, or the holder of the legal title to the property to which the interest relates no later than the date which is 9 months after the later of —

    (A) the day on which the transfer creating the interest in such person is made, or

    (B) the day on which such person attains age 21,

(3) such person has not accepted the interest or any of its benefits, and

(4) as a result of such refusal, the interest passes without any direction on the part of the person making the disclaimer and passes either —

    (A) to the spouse of the decedent, or

    (B) to a person other than the person making the disclaimer.

(c) *Other Rules.* For purposes of subsection (a) —

(1) *Disclaimer of undivided portion of interest.* A disclaimer with respect to an undivided portion of an interest which meets the requirements of the preceding sentence shall be treated as a qualified disclaimer of such portion of the interest.

(2) *Powers.* A power with respect to property shall be treated as an interest in such property.

(3) *Certain transfers treated as disclaimers.* A written transfer of the transferor's entire interest in the property —

    (A) which meets requirements similar to the requirements of paragraphs (2) and (3) of subsection (b), and

    (B) which is to a person or persons who would have received the property had the transferor made a qualified disclaimer (within the meaning of subsection (b)), shall be treated as a qualified disclaimer.

One very important thing to note about Section 2518 is that it requires the disclaimer to be made within nine months after the interest is created or after the donee reaches 21, whichever is later. Under state disclaimer laws, a future interest can be disclaimed within nine months after the interest becomes indefeasibly vested, an option not open under the Internal Revenue Code.

3

FORMALITIES OF WILLS: EXECUTION, REVOCATION, AND COMPONENT PARTS

SECTION A. MENTAL CAPACITY, UNDUE INFLUENCE, AND FRAUD

1. Mental Capacity

a. Why Require Mental Capacity?

It goes without saying that a person must be of sound mind to make a will.[1] But why should this be so? Why is not power of testation extended to all persons regardless of their mental capacity?

The requirement that the testator have mental capacity is an ancient one. It goes back at least as far as the Romans, who invented the will as we know it. Three explanations are usually given for the requirement, all owing something to how persons and property have been viewed in history. The *first* explanation is that a will should be given effect only if it represents the testator's true desires. In ancient times insane persons were viewed as possessed by an evil spirit or a devil. John tells us of the reaction of the Jews to Jesus' claim to be the good shepherd of the Twenty-third Psalm: "And many of them said, He hath a devil, and is mad; why hear ye him?" John 10:20. Equating madness with possession by an evil spirit came into English law through the ecclesiastical courts,

---

1. In almost all states a person must be age 18 to make a will. See W. McGovern, S. Kurtz & J. Rein, Wills, Trusts and Estates §7.2 (1988).

which had jurisdiction over succession to personal property and were much influenced by Roman law and the church's teachings about the power of the devil. In the late sixteenth century Swinburne, the author of the first English treatise on the law of wills, wrote:

> Madfolkes and Lunaticke persons, during the time of their furor or insanitie of minde, cannot make a testament, nor dispose anie thing by will, no not ad pias causas: the reason is most forcible, because they knowe not what they do. . . . And so strong is this impediment of insanitie of minde, that if the testator make his testament after this furor have overtaken him, and whiles as yet it doeth possesse his minde, albeit the furor afterwardes departing or ceasing, the testator recover his former understanding: yet doeth not the testament made during his former fit, recover any force or strength thereby. [H. Swinburne, Wills 36-37 (1590).]

Although demonological explanations of insanity are now out of favor, the notion that a will might not state the testator's real wishes still has currency. It draws some support from modern psychiatric concepts and discoveries about mental disorders. Freud, for example, held the view that a person might have and act upon unconscious desires of a destructive kind that overcome the conscious and rational self. Thus Freudian analytic theory might support the ancient notion that a will does not necessarily represent the testator's rational desires.

The *second* explanation for the mental capacity requirement is that a mentally incompetent man or woman is not defined as a "person." Since the post-renaissance, with its strong emphasis on the individual as the only recognized legal entity (as opposed to the family or clan), philosophers have sought to understand what it means to be a person. As Professor Radin recently wrote, "the concepts of sanity and personhood are intertwined: At some point we question whether the insane person is a person at all." Radin, Property and Personhood, 34 Stan. L. Rev. 957, 962-963, 969 (1982).

The *third* explanation is that the law requires mental capacity to protect the decedent's family. In primitive societies property was viewed as tribal property or family property, not owned by individuals. Although individual ownership in time developed, the notion persisted that the family was an economic unit and had some claim on the property. The Roman patriarch or pater familias might "own" the property, but he had moral and customary obligations to his children and kindred. See H. Maine, Ancient Law 183-198 (1861).

In medieval England — and indeed in twentieth-century England among the nobility, where land passes with a peerage — land was viewed as family property with the current primogenitary heir as present head of family. Today we do not look at property in the same way. We think of property as individually owned. Nonetheless, protection of the family remains a goal. Giving effect to the expectations of inheritance tends to preserve the family as a unit for mutual support. The institution of inheritance, through the principle of reciprocity, functions as a system for providing care and support for the aged.[2] Close family members — ordinarily those described as heirs in intestacy statutes — usually render services and give love and comfort to the aging relative. An inheritance is a delayed payment in reciprocity. By giving an economic incentive to heirs apparent, whose expectations cannot be defeated by insanity, society furthers its objective of caring for the aged in a humane manner. The principle of reciprocity is recognized when the court considers, sometimes sub silentio, the fairness of a disposition as a factor in mental capacity cases.

In addition to these three explanations deriving from history, several other possible justifications for mental capacity come to mind:

Fourth, to a large extent public acceptance of law rests upon a belief that legal institutions, including inheritance, are legitimate, and legitimacy cannot exist unless decisions are reasoned. Hence it is important that the succession to property be perceived as a responsible, reasoned act, according the survivors their just deserts.

Fifth, the requirement of mental capacity assures a sane person that the disposition he desires will be carried out even though he becomes insane and makes another will. This gives a person of sound mind the advantage of being able, while in a rational mind, to choose what will happen to his property in the future and to have confidence that his choices will be carried out.

Sixth, the requirement of mental capacity may protect society at large from irrational acts. This justification is dubious, however, because courts can and do strike down particular "anti-social" dispositions as against public policy. Then too, if society is not protected from a sane person acting irresponsibly, why is it protected against similar acts by an insane person?

Finally, requiring mental capacity may protect a senile or incompetent testator from "exploitation" by others. It must be kept in mind, however, that what may look like exploitation to the majority of persons may give the testator much pleasure. Also, exploitation may be adequately remedied by setting aside transfers because of undue influence.

For discussion of the reasons for, and theoretical underpinning of, the requirement of mental capacity, see Meiklejohn, Contractual and Donative Capacity, 39 Case W. Res L. Rev. 307 (1989); Epstein, Testamentary Capacity, Reasonableness and Family Maintenance: A

---

2. See C. Lévi-Strauss, The Principle of Reciprocity, *in* The Elementary Structures of Kinship 52-97 (rev. ed. 1969); J. Rosenfeld, The Legacy of Aging: Inheritance and Disinheritance in Social Perspective (1979).

Proposal for Meaningful Reform, 35 Temp. L.Q. 231 (1962); Green, Public Policies Underlying the Law of Mental Incompetency, 38 Mich. L. Rev. 1189 (1940).

b. Test of Mental Capacity

The specific requirements for mental capacity are minimal. The decedent only has to have the ability to know (1) the nature and extent of his property, (2) the persons who are the natural objects of his bounty, (3) the disposition that he is making, and (4) how these elements relate so as to form an orderly plan for the disposition of his property. The testator does not have to have average intelligence as this would incapacitate almost half the people making wills, but the testator must have mind and memory relevant to the four matters mentioned. He must understand the significance of his act.

Estate of Wright, 7 Cal. 2d 348, 60 P.2d 434 (1936), nicely illustrates the minimum requirements of mental capacity. The testator had numerous eccentricities and indulged in strange, even bizarre, behavior. Several witnesses expressed the view that the testator was of unsound mind. One witness gave as reasons that he lived in a little shack filled with dirt and junk, that he gave her a fish soaked in kerosene to eat, and that he insisted upon buying her household furniture, which was not for sale. Other witnesses testified that that testator was drunk much of the time, picked up articles from garbage cans and hid them around the house, put paper roses on rose bushes barren of blooms, claimed (falsely) to own a number of houses in Salt Lake City, held his breath and appeared to be dead in order to scare his neighbors, told persons he had sent them Christmas presents but had not done so, failed to speak to his granddaughter in the street, accepted invitations to dinner and then failed to appear or, appearing, left abruptly in the middle of dinner without explanation. The court reversed the order of the trial court denying admission of the will to probate. Said the court:

> Testamentary capacity cannot be destroyed by showing a few isolated acts, foibles, idiosyncrasies, moral or mental irregularities or departures from the normal unless they directly bear upon and have influenced the testamentary act. . . . [The testator] went alone to the scrivener's with a list of beneficiaries prepared by himself, giving his daughter one piece of improved real property and Charlotte Josephine Hindmarch, whom he designated as his friend, the other. To his granddaughter he bequeathed his undivided interest in an estate known as the Brazier Estate, and he named seven others to whom he made nominal bequests. There is no evidence that he did not appreciate his relations and obligations to others, or that he was not mindful of the property which he possessed. The

opinions or beliefs of those who testified that he was not of sound mind rest upon testimony of the most trivial character and do not establish testamentary incapacity at the time he executed his will. [Id. at 356-357, 60 P.2d at 438.]

And then the court added, significantly:

It does not appear that his daughter or members of her family were concerned as to his comfort or well-being, as the testimony of some of the witnesses shows that he lived a portion of his time in a condition of squalor and that he was cared for when ill by others. [Id.]

The fact that a person has been declared incompetent and put under a conservator does not necessarily mean the person has no capacity to execute a will thereafter. Capacity to make a will is governed by a different legal test and requires less competency than the power to make a contract or a gift. In the latter situation, the law has the objective of protecting the incompetent contractor or donor from suffering economic loss during lifetime, which might result in impoverishment. Protecting a dead person from economic loss is of course not a consideration. Thus in Lee v. Lee, 337 So. 2d 713 (Miss. 1976), the testator was placed under a conservatorship in 1968 because of age and physical incapacity. On May 9, 1970, testator executed a *will;* on that same date he executed and delivered a *deed* purporting to convey real property. The Mississippi Supreme Court held that the *deed* was void because one under a conservatorship is without the necessary contractual power to execute a deed but held the *will* valid. The court stated that one whose property is under a conservatorship may write a valid will if the trial court finds, as the trial court did here, that the will was written during a lucid interval. Other recent cases probating wills executed after the testator has been declared incompetent include In re Estate of Sorenson, 87 Wis. 2d 339, 274 N.W.2d 694 (1979) (testator declared incompetent and confined to Veterans Administration Hospital); In re Estate of Gentry, 32 Or. App. 45, 573 P.2d 322 (1978) (testator, diagnosed as a schizophrenic, institutionalized and declared incompetent); cf. In re Estate of Hastings, 479 Pa. 122, 387 A.2d 865 (1978) (testator adjudicated incompetent 11 days after executing will). See Note, Testamentary Capacity in a Nutshell: A Psychiatric Reevaluation, 18 Stan. L. Rev. 1119 (1966).

c. Insane Delusion

A person may have sufficient mental capacity to execute a will but may be suffering from an insane delusion so as to cause a particular provision in a will — or perhaps the entire will — to fail for lack of testamentary capacity. Only the part of the will caused by the insane delusion fails; if the entire will was caused by the insane delusion, the entire will fails.

An insane delusion is a legal, not a psychiatric, concept. A delusion is a false conception of reality. An example is a belief that all Irishmen have red hair. An insane delusion — which impairs testamentary capacity — is one to which the testator adheres against all evidence and reason to the contrary. Some courts have held that if there is any factual basis at all for the testator's delusion, it is not deemed insane. The majority view, however, is that a delusion is insane even if there is some factual basis for it if a rational person in the testator's situation could not have drawn the conclusion reached by the testator. Insane delusion cases often involve some false belief about a member of the testator's family.

In re Honigman

Court of Appeals of New York, 1960
8 N.Y.2d 244, 168 N.E.2d 676, 203 N.Y.S.2d 859

DYE, J. Frank Honigman died May 4, 1956, survived by his wife, Florence. By a purported last will and testament, executed April 3, 1956, just one month before his death, he gave $5,000 to each of three named grandnieces, and cut off his wife with a life use of her minimum statutory share plus $2,500, with direction to pay the principal upon her death to his surviving brothers and sisters and to the descendants of any predeceased brother or sister, per stirpes. The remaining one half of his estate was bequeathed in equal shares to his surviving brothers and sisters and to the descendants of any predeceased brother or sister, per stirpes, some of whom resided in Germany.

When the will was offered for probate in Surrogate's Court, Queens County, the widow Florence filed objections. A trial was had on framed issues, only one of which survived for determination by the jury, namely: "At the time of the execution of the paper offered for probate was the said Frank Honigman of sound and disposing mind and memory?" The jury answered in the negative, and the Surrogate then made a decree denying probate to the will.

Upon an appeal to the Appellate Division, Second Department, the Surrogate's decree was reversed upon the law and the facts, and probate was directed. Inconsistent findings of fact were reversed and new findings substituted.

We read this record as containing more than enough competent proof to warrant submitting to the jury the issue of decedent's testamentary capacity. By the same token the proof amply supports the jury findings, implicit in the verdict, that the testator, at the time he made his will, was suffering from an unwarranted and insane delusion that his wife was unfaithful to him, which condition affected the disposition made in the will. The record is replete with testimony, supplied by a large number of disinterested persons, that for quite some time before his death the testator had publicly and repeatedly told friends and strangers alike that he believed his wife was unfaithful, often using obscene and abusive language. Such manifestations of suspicion were quite unaccountable, coming as they did after nearly 40 years of a childless yet, to all outward appearances, a congenial and harmonious marriage, which had begun in 1916. During the intervening time they had worked together in the successful management, operation and ownership of various restaurants, bars and grills and, by their joint efforts of thrift and industry, had accumulated the substantial fortune now at stake.

The decedent and his wife retired from business in 1945 because of decedent's failing health. In the few years that followed he underwent a number of operations, including a prostatectomy in 1951, and an operation for cancer of the large bowel in 1954, when decedent was approximately 70 years of age.

From about this time, he began volubly to express his belief that Mrs. Honigman was unfaithful to him. This suspicion became an obsession with him, although all of the witnesses agreed that the deceased was normal and rational in other respects. Seemingly aware of his mental state, he once mentioned that he was "sick in the head" ("Mich krank gelassen in den Kopf"), and that "I know there is something wrong with me" in response to a light reference to his mental condition. In December, 1955 he went to Europe, a trip Mrs. Honigman learned of in a letter sent from Idlewild Airport after he had departed, and while there he visited a doctor. Upon his return he went to a psychiatrist who Mr. Honigman said "could not help" him. Finally, he went to a chiropractor with whom he was extremely satisfied.

On March 21, 1956, shortly after his return from Europe, Mr. Honigman instructed his attorney to prepare the will in question. He never again joined Mrs. Honigman in the marital home.

To offset and contradict this showing of irrational obsession the proponents adduced proof which, it is said, furnished a reasonable basis for decedent's belief, and which, when taken with other factors, made his testamentary disposition understandable. Briefly, this proof related to four incidents. One concerned an anniversary card sent by Mr. Krauss, a mutual acquaintance and friend of many years, bearing a printed message of congratulation in sweetly sentimental phraseology. Because it was addressed to the wife alone and not received on the anniversary date, Mr. Honigman viewed it as confirmatory of his suspicion. Then there was the reference to a letter which it is claimed contained prejudicial matter — but just what it was is not before us, because the letter was not produced in evidence and its contents were not established. There was also proof to show that whenever the house telephone rang Mrs. Honigman would answer it. From this Mr. Honigman drew added support for his suspicion that she was having an affair with Mr. Krauss. Mr. Honigman became so upset about it that for the last two years of their marriage he positively forbade her to answer the telephone. Another allegedly significant happening was an occasion when Mrs. Honigman asked the decedent as he was leaving the house what time she might expect him to return. This aroused his suspicion. He secreted himself at a vantage point in a nearby park and watched his home. He saw Mr. Krauss enter and, later, when he confronted his wife with knowledge of this incident, she allegedly asked him for a divorce. This incident was taken entirely from a statement made by Mr. Honigman to one of the witnesses. Mrs. Honigman flatly denied all of it. Their verdict shows that the jury evidently believed the objectant. Under the circumstances, we cannot say that this was wrong. The jury had the right to disregard the proponents' proof, or to go so far as to hold that such trivia afforded even additional grounds for decedent's irrational and unwarranted belief. The issue we must bear in mind is not whether Mrs. Honigman was unfaithful, but whether Mr. Honigman had any reasonable basis for believing that she was.

In a very early case we defined the applicable test as follows:

> If a person persistently believes supposed facts, which have no real existence except in his perverted imagination, and against all evidence and probability, and conducts himself, however logically, upon the assumption of their existence, he is, so far as they are concerned, under a morbid delusion; and delusion in that sense is insanity. Such a person is essentially mad or insane on those subjects, though on other subjects he may reason, act and speak like a sensible man. (American Seamen's Friend Soc. v. Hopper, 33 N.Y. 619, 624-625.)

It is true that the burden of proving testamentary incapacity is a difficult one to carry (Dobie v. Armstrong, 160 N.Y. 584), but when an objectant has gone forward, as Mrs. Honigman surely has, with evidence reflecting the operation of the testator's mind, it is the proponents' duty to provide a basis for the alleged delusion. We cannot conclude that as a matter of law they have performed this duty successfully. When, in the light of all the circumstances surrounding a long and happy marriage such as this, the husband publicly and repeatedly expresses suspicions of his wife's unfaithfulness; of misbehaving herself in a most unseemly fashion, by hiding male callers in the cellar of her own home, in various closets, and under the bed; of hauling men from the street up to her second-story bedroom by use of bed sheets; of making contacts over the household telephone; and of passing a clandestine note through the fence on her brother's property — and when he claims to have heard noises which he believed to be men running about his home, but which he had not investigated, and which he could not verify — the courts should have no hesitation in placing the issue of sanity in the jury's hands. To hold to the contrary would be to take from the jury its traditional function of passing on the facts.

. . . Mr. Honigman persisted over a long period of time in telling his suspicions to anyone who would listen to him, friends and strangers alike. That such belief was an obsession with him was clearly established by a preponderance of concededly competent evidence and, prima facie, there was presented a question of fact as to whether it affected the will he made shortly before his death.

The proponents argue that, even if decedent was indeed laboring under a delusion, the existence of other reasons for the disposition he chose is enough to support the validity of the instrument as a will. The other reasons are, first, the size of Mrs. Honigman's independent fortune, and, second, the financial need of his residuary legatees. These reasons, as well as his belief in his wife's infidelity, decedent expressed to his own attorney. We dispelled a similar contention in American Seamen's Friend Soc. v. Hopper (supra . . .) where we held that a will was bad when its "dispository provisions were or *might have been* caused or affected by the delusion" (emphasis supplied). . . .

We turn now to alleged errors committed by the Surrogate when he overruled objections based on section 347 of the Civil Practice Act.[3] Much of Mrs. Honigman's testimony, which should have been excluded as incompetent since it was evidence "concerning a personal transaction or communication between the witness [an interested party] and the deceased person," was admitted because the Surrogate believed that the proponents, by failing to object to such testimony at the earliest opportunity, irrevocably waived their right to protest on that ground.

---

3. New York Civil Practice Act §347, now N.Y. Civ. Prac. Law & R. §4519 (Supp. 1988), is New York's dead man statute. The statute excludes the testimony of a survivor "concerning a personal transaction or communication between the witness and the deceased person." In most states — but not in New York — the dead man's statute is not applicable to probate a will on the theory that the testator's will is not a "transaction or communication" between the testator and the legatees. The purpose of the statute is to protect estates of deceased persons from creditors and others making false claims respecting business transactions when testator's lips are sealed, and the statute excludes testimony only in suits upon claims between other persons and the deceased existing prior to his death. See Annot., 11 A.L.R. 1425 (1938). In New York, however, it was early held that the dead man's statute applied to probate of a will. In re Smith, 95 N.Y. 516 (1884).

Dead man statutes are highly unpopular with every evidence scholar and have been abolished in many states. Where they exist most courts construe them narrowly. See 2 J. Wigmore, Evidence §578 (J. Chadbourn rev. 1979). See also Slough, Testamentary Capacity: Evidentiary Aspects, 36 Tex. L. Rev. (1957). — Eds.

In de Laurent v. Townsend (243 N.Y. 130) this court was unanimous in holding that the rule as to waiver of objections under section 347 was to be found in that statute "and not elsewhere" (p.133). The statute provides an exception "where the executor, administrator, survivor, committee or person deriving title or interest is examined in his own behalf, or the testimony of the lunatic or deceased person is given in evidence, concerning the same transaction or communication." Since the exception is inapplicable to the circumstances here present, it was error not to exclude Mrs. Honigman's testimony whenever objections based on the prohibition of section 347 were appropriately raised.

Finally, since there is to be a new trial of the issues, the Surrogate's ruling with regard to the clergyman-penitent privilege deserves mention. Father Heitz, a Catholic priest, was called by the objectant, who sought to elicit from him a conversation he had had with the deceased at a time when the latter wanted advice concerning his marital problems. Although Father Heitz was willing, he was not permitted to testify to the conversation, "Specifically on the ground that any conversation with a priest, although not in the confessional, is privileged." There is nothing in the record to indicate the nature of the testimony sought. In this posture it cannot be determined whether such testimony falls within the privilege created by section 351 of the Civil Practice Act.

The order appealed from should be reversed and a new trial granted, with costs to abide the event.

FULD, J. (dissenting). I am willing to assume that the proof demonstrates that the testator's belief that his wife was unfaithful was completely groundless and unjust. However, that is not enough; it does not follow from this fact that the testator suffered from such a delusion as to stamp him mentally defective or as lacking in capacity to make a will. (See, e.g., Matter of Hargrove, 288 N.Y. 604, affg. 262 App. Div. 202; Dobie v. Armstrong, 160 N.Y. 584, 593-594; Matter of White, 121 N.Y. 406, 414; Clapp v. Fullerton, 34 N.Y. 190, 197.) "To sustain the allegation," this court wrote in the *Clapp* case (34 N.Y. 190, 197),

> it is not sufficient to show that his suspicion in this respect was not well founded. It is quite apparent, from the evidence, that his distrust of the fidelity of his wife was really groundless and unjust; but it does not follow that his doubts evince a condition of lunacy. The right of a testator to dispose of his estate, depends neither on the justice of his prejudices nor the soundness of his reasoning. He may do what he will with his own; and if there be no defect of testamentary capacity, and no undue influence or fraud, the law gives effect to his will, though its provisions are unreasonable and unjust.

As a matter of fact, in the case before us, a goodly portion of the widow's testimony bearing on her husband's alleged delusion should have been excluded, as the court itself notes, by reason of section 347 of the Civil Practice Act. And, of course, if such testimony had not been received in evidence, a number of items of proof upon which the widow relies would not have been available, with the consequence that the record would have contained even less basis for her claim of delusion.

Moreover, I share the Appellate Division's view that other and sound reasons, quite apart from the alleged decision, existed for the disposition made by the testator. Indeed, he himself had declared that his wife had enough money and he wanted to take care of his brothers and sisters living in Europe.

In short, the evidence adduced utterly failed to prove that the testator was suffering from an insane delusion or lacked testamentary capacity. The Appellate Division was eminently correct in concluding that there was no issue of fact for the jury's consideration and in directing the entry of a decree admitting the will to probate. Its order should be affirmed.

Chief Judge DESMOND and Judges FROESSEL and BURKE concur with Judge DYE; Judge FULD dissents in an opinion in which Judges VAN VOORHIS and FOSTER concur.

NOTES AND QUESTIONS

1. Under New York law applicable in 1956, when an intestate was survived by a spouse and brothers and sisters (as in the *Honigman* case), the spouse took one-half and the brothers and sisters the other half. Thus if Mr. Honigman's will was struck down because of an insane delusion, his estate would go by intestacy one-half to his wife and one-half to his brothers and sisters. In 1963 New York law was amended to give the surviving spouse the entire estate of an intestate if the intestate leaves no issue or parents. N.Y. Est., Powers & Trusts Law §4-1.1(a) (5) (1981). If Mr. Honigman had died after 1963, would the result of the case be the same?

Bear in mind that New York gives a surviving spouse a forced share in the estate of a spouse who dies testate. The surviving spouse can renounce the will and elect to take this share, which, in the case of a testate decedent without issue (as Mr. Honigman was), is one-half of the decedent's estate. However, New York has a special provision eliminating this election if the decedent gives his or her spouse $2,500 outright ($10,000 since 1966) and puts the rest of the surviving spouse's half in a trust to pay him or her income therefrom for life but giving the surviving spouse no control of the corpus of the trust at his or her death. Id. §5-1.1(a). This is what Mr. Honigman's will provided, which prevented Mrs. Honigman from electing to take 50 percent outright. For current New York law, see infra page 386. The consequence of the decision in *Honigman* (assuming the wife wins at the new trial) is that the wife receives one-half of her husband's property outright rather than an income interest in one-half. If the case arose today, the consequence would be that Mrs. Honigman would receive everything rather than an income interest in one-half of her husband's estate.

2. The law draws a distinction between an insane delusion and a mistake. An insane delusion is a belief not susceptible to correction by presenting the testator with evidence indicating the falsity of the belief. A mistake is susceptible to correction if the testator is told the truth. As a general rule, courts do not reform or invalidate wills because of mistake, whereas they do invalidate wills resulting from an insane delusion. Suppose, for example, that the testator falsely believes that her son has been killed and therefore executes a will leaving all her property to her daughter. In fact the son is alive. The testator is mistaken, not under an insane delusion, and the will is entitled to probate. See Bowerman v. Burris, 138 Tenn. 220, 197 S.W. 490 (1917). Compare Uniform Probate Code §2-302(b), infra page 428.

How do you tell the difference between a mistake and an insane delusion? To have an insane delusion must there be evidence that persons tried to talk the testator out of the belief and failed? See Dixon v. Webster, 551 S.W.2d 888 (Mo. App. 1977).

3. A study of California cases indicated that when mental capacity or undue influence was in issue, the jury found for the contestant in 77 percent of the cases, and over half of the verdicts for contestants were reversed by the supreme court upon appeal on grounds of insufficient evidence. Note, Will Contests on Trial, 6 Stan. L. Rev. 91, 92 (1953). Compare Note, Undue Influence — Judicial Implementation of Social Policy, 1968 Wis. L. Rev. 569, which finds that in Wisconsin, where the trial judge, not a jury, finds facts in will contests, appellate courts rarely reverse the trial judge's decision in undue influence cases.

The most recent empirical study is Schoenblum, Will Contests — An Empirical Study, 22 Real Prop., Prob. & Tr. J. 607 (1987). Professor Schoenblum studied contested wills over a nine-year period in Davidson County (Nashville), Tennessee, and came up with some interesting conclusions. (1) Wills disposing of large estates are almost never challenged, because — among other reasons — rich testators are more likely to have received sound estate planning advice. A large percentage of contests involved estates worth less than $50,000. (2) Undue influence and lack of mental capacity were the most common grounds for challenge. There was a disinclination to overturn a will when it favored one close relative over other close relatives, but the will was rarely sustained when it favored nonrelatives and friends over relatives. (3) Juries found for the contestant in about half of the cases. On the other hand, judges "are far more likely to hold for the proponent in a will contest than for the contestant, and are clearly more likely to do so than is a jury." Id. at 627.

The Schoenblum study confirms what the earlier studies cited above indicate: Juries are considerably more favorable to contestants than are judges. The Stanford Law Review note, supra, at 102, suggests that the jury serves a useful function in protecting against testamentary dispositions that do not "accord with the community's notions of justice." This suggestion is reminiscent of the practice in classical Greece whereby a jury could override a will thought unfair or in violation of custom. See Chroust, Estate Planning in Hellenic Antiquity: Aristotle's Last Will and Testament, 45 Notre Dame Law. 629 (1970). Do you think the jury should have this power?

4.   To prevent litigation of mental capacity after death, statutes in Arkansas, North Dakota, and Ohio permit probate of a will during the testator's life. These statutes authorize a person to institute during life an adversary proceeding to declare the validity of a will and the testamentary capacity and freedom from undue influence of the person executing the will. All beneficiaries named in the will and all testator's heirs apparent must be made parties to the action. Ark. Code Ann. §28-40-202 (1987); N.D. Cent. Code §30.1-08.1-01 (Supp. 1987); Ohio Rev. Code Ann. §2107.081 (1987). This procedure is known as "living probate" or "ante-mortem probate."

Langbein, Living Probate: The Conservatorship Model
77 Mich. L. Rev. 63, 64-66 (1978)

Discussion of living probate must begin with the problem of the will contest alleging testamentary incapacity. Although we do not have comparative data directly on point, the impression is widespread that such litigation occurs more frequently in the United States than on the Continent or in England. We may point to several factors that bear upon the differential:

(1)   In civil law countries, children as well as the spouse have a forced share entitlement in the estate of a parent. The disinherited child, who is the typical plaintiff in American testamentary capacity litigation, is unknown to European law. The European parent can leave his heir disgruntled with the statutory minimum, but that share will often be large enough by comparison with the potential winnings from litigation to deaden the incentive to contest.

(2)   Many American jurisdictions permit will contests on the question of capacity to be tried to a jury, which may be more disposed to work equity for the disinherited than to obey the directions of an eccentric decedent who is in any event beyond suffering. Civil jury trial has

disappeared from English estate law; it was never known on the Continent.

(3)   American law is unique among Western civil procedural systems in failing to charge a losing plaintiff with the attorney fees and other costs incurred by the defendant in the course of resisting the plaintiff's unjustified claim. In testamentary capacity litigation the American rule has the effect of requiring decedents' estates to subsidize the depredations of contestants. Put differently, the American rule diminishes the magnitude of a contestant's potential loss, which diminishes his disincentive to litigate an improbable claim.

(4)   Civil law systems provide for the so-called authenticated will, which is executed before a quasi-judicial officer called the notary. This is not the only means of making a valid will in European countries, and because it is costly it is not widely used. But the notarial procedure does permit a testator who fears a post-mortem contest to generate during his lifetime and have preserved with the will evidence of exceptional quality regarding, *inter alia*, his capacity. The notary before whom the testator executes his will is not a judge; he does not adjudicate capacity. But he is a legally qualified and experienced officer of the state who is obliged to satisfy himself of the testator's capacity as a precondition for receiving or transcribing the testament. The authenticated will is, therefore, extremely difficult for contestants to set aside for want of capacity in post-mortem proceedings. . . .

A major reason that the impact of capacity litigation in America is so difficult to measure is that most of it is directed towards provoking pretrial settlements, typically for a fraction of what the contestants would be entitled to receive if they were to defeat the will. Especially when such tactics succeed, they do not leave traces in the law reports. Thus, the odor of the strike suit hangs heavily over this field. The beneficiaries named in the will are likely to be either charitable organizations whom the testator preferred to his relatives, or else those of his relatives and friends whom he loved most and who are most likely to want to spare his reputation from a capacity suit. They are typically put to the choice of defending a lawsuit in which a skilled plaintiff's lawyer will present evidence to a jury at a public trial touching every eccentricity that might cast doubt upon the testator's condition, or compromising the suit, thereby overriding the disposition desired by the testator and rewarding the contestants for threatening to besmirch his name.

For more on ante-mortem probate, see Fink, Ante-Mortem Probate Revisited: Can an Idea Have a Life After Death?, 37 Ohio St. L.J. 264 (1976); Alexander, The Conservatorship Model: A Modification, 77

Mich. L. Rev. 86 (1978); Alexander & Pearson, Alternative Models of Ante-Mortem Probate and Procedural Due Process Limitations on Succession, 78 Mich. L. Rev. 89 (1979); Fellows, The Case Against Living Probate, 78 Mich. L. Rev. 1066 (1980) (finding many flaws in ante-mortem probate). Professor Fellows, like the other scholars cited, is troubled by the large number of lawsuits filed against estates of eccentric testators, alleging mental incapacity, with the purpose of extracting a pretrial settlement. She rejects ante-mortem probate as a remedy, however, and instead proposes abolishing the mental capacity requirement and providing a statutory election to those we most fear may suffer in the event of disinheritance. See Fellows, supra, at 1110-1112. Is this a good idea? Would you prefer a world where mental capacity is not required for a will to the existing world? Why or why not?

2. Undue Influence

Undue influence is one of the most bothersome concepts in all the law. It cannot be precisely defined. A hundred years ago Sir James Hannen gave the classic explanation of what kind of influence is undue in the eyes of the law:

> We are all familiar with the use of the word "influence"; we say that one person has an unbounded influence over another, and we speak of evil influences and good influences, but it is not because one person has unbounded influence over another that therefore when exercised, even though it may be very bad indeed, it is undue influence in the legal sense of the word. To give you some illustrations of what I mean, a young man may be caught in the toils of a harlot, who makes use of her influence to induce him to make a will in her favour, to the exclusion of his relatives. It is unfortunately quite natural that a man so entangled should yield to that influence and confer large bounties on the person with whom he has been brought into such relation; yet the law does not attempt to guard against those contingencies. A man may be the companion of another, and may encourage him in evil courses, and so obtain what is called an undue influence over him, and the consequence may be a will made in his favour. But that again, shocking as it is, perhaps even worse than the other, will not amount to undue influence.
>
> To be undue influence in the eye of the law there must be — to sum it up in a word — coercion. It must not be a case in which a person has been induced by means such as I have suggested to you to come to a conclusion that he or she will make a will in a particular person's favour, because if the testator has only been persuaded or induced by considerations which you may condemn, really and truly to intend to give his property to another, though you may disapprove of the act, yet it is

strictly legitimate in the sense of its being legal. It is only when the will of the person who becomes a testator is coerced into doing that which he or she does not desire to do, that it is undue influence.

The coercion may of course be of different kinds, it may be in the grossest form, such as actual confinement or violence, or a person in the last days or hours of life may have become so weak and feeble, that a very little pressure will be sufficient to bring about the desired result, and it may even be, that the mere talking to him at that stage of illness and pressing something upon him may so fatigue the brain, that the sick person may be induced, for quietness' sake, to do anything. This would equally be coercion, though not actual violence.

These illustrations will sufficiently bring home to your minds that even very immoral considerations either on the part of the testator, or of some one else offering them, do not amount to undue influence unless the testator is in such a condition, that if he could speak his wishes to the last, he would say, "this is not my wish, but I must do it."

If therefore the act is shewn to be the result of the wish and will of the testator at the time, then, however it has been brought about — for we are not dealing with a case of fraud — though you may condemn the testator for having such a wish, though you may condemn any person who has endeavoured to persuade and has succeeded in persuading the testator to adopt that view — still it is not undue influence.

There remains another general observation that I must make, and it is this, that it is not sufficient to establish that a person has the power unduly to overbear the will of the testator. It is necessary also to prove that in the particular case that power was exercised, and that it was by means of the exercise of that power, that the will such as it is, has been produced. [Wingrove v. Wingrove, 11 Prob. Div. 81 (1885).]

In more recent times judges have tried to cabin this unruly concept by saying that, to establish undue influence, it must be proved that the testator was susceptible to undue influence, that the influencer had the disposition and the opportunity to exercise undue influence, and that the disposition is the result of the influence. But this formulation begs the question because it does not tell us what influence is undue. Perhaps the only satisfactory way of acquiring a lawyer's feel about the contours of undue influence is to immerse yourself in the cases.

Although the cases that follow involve allegations of undue influence where there is a confidential relationship, a person may exercise undue influence where there is no such relationship.

Lipper v. Weslow
Texas Court of Civil Appeals, 1963
369 S.W.2d 698

McDONALD, C.J.   This is a contest of the will of Mrs. Sophie Block, on the ground of undue influence. Plaintiffs, Julian Weslow, Jr., Julia

Weslow Fortson and Alice Weslow Sale, are the 3 grandchildren of Mrs. Block by a deceased son; defendants are Mrs. Block's 2 surviving children, G. Frank Lipper and Irene Lipper Dover (half brother and half sister of plaintiffs' deceased father). (The will left the estate of testatrix to her 2 children, defendants herein; and left nothing to her grandchildren by the deceased son, plaintiffs herein.) Trial was to a jury, which found that Mrs. Block's will, signed by her on January 30, 1956, was procured by undue influence on the part of the proponent, Frank Lipper. The trial court entered judgment on the verdict, setting aside the will.

Defendants appeal, contending there is no evidence, or insufficient evidence, to support the finding that the will was procured by undue influence.

Testatrix was married 3 times. Of her first marriage she had one son, Julian Weslow (who died in 1949), who was father of plaintiffs herein. After the death of her first husband testatrix married a Mr. Lipper. Defendants are the 2 children of their marriage. After Mr. Lipper's death, testatrix married Max Block. There were no children born of this marriage. Max Block died several months after the death of testatrix.

On 30 January, 1956, Sophie Block executed the will in controversy. Such will was prepared by defendant, Frank Lipper, an attorney, one of the beneficiaries of the will, and Independent Executor of the will. The will was witnessed by 2 former business associates of Mr. Block. Pertinent provisions of the will are summarized as follows:

"That I, Mrs. Sophie Block, . . . do make, publish and declare this my last will and testament, hereby revoking all other wills by me heretofore made."

1, 2, 3 AND 4

(Provide for payment of debts; for burial in Beth Israel Cemetery; and for minor bequests to a servant, and to an old folks' home.)

5

(Devises the bulk of testatrix's estate to her 2 children, Mrs. Irene Lipper Dover and Frank Lipper (defendants herein), share and share alike.)

6

States that $7000. previously advanced to Mrs. Irene Lipper Dover, and $9300. previously advanced to Frank Lipper be taken into consideration in the final settlement of the estate; and cancels such amounts "that I gave or advanced to my deceased son, Julian."

7

Appoints G. Frank Lipper Independent Executor of the estate without bond.

8

Provides that if any legatee contests testatrix's will or the will of her husband, Max Block, that they forfeit all benefits under the will.

9

"‎:My son, Julian A. Weslow, died on August 6, 1949, and I want to explain why I have not provided anything under this will for my daughter-in-law, Bernice Weslow, widow of my deceased son, Julian, and her children, Julian A. Weslow, Jr., Alice Weslow Sale, and Julia Weslow Fortson, and I want to go into sufficient detail in explaining my relationship in past years with my said son's widow and his children, before mentioned, and it is my desire to record such relationship so that there will be no question as to my feelings in the matter or any thought or suggestion that my children, Irene Lipper Dover and G. Frank Lipper, or my husband, Max, may have influenced me in any manner in the execution of this will. During the time that my said son, Julian, was living, the attitude of his wife, Bernice, was at times, pleasant and friendly, but the majority of the years when my said son, Julian, was living, her attitude towards me and my husband, Max, was unfriendly and frequently months would pass when she was not in my home and I did not hear from her. When my said son, Julian, was living he was treated the same as I treated my other children; and, my husband, Max, and I gave to each of our children a home and various sums of money from time to time to help in taking care of medical expenses, other unusual expenses, as well as outright gifts. Since my said son Julian's death, his widow, Bernice, and all of her children have shown a most unfriendly and distant attitude towards me, my husband, Max, and my 2 children G. Frank Lipper and Irene Lipper Dover, which attitude I cannot reconcile as I have shown them many kindnesses since they have been members of my family, and their continued unfriendly attitude towards me, my husband, Max, and my said children has hurt me deeply in my declining years, for my life would have been much happier if they had shown a disposition to want to be a part of the family and enter into a normal family relationship that usually exists with a daughter-in-law and grandchildren and great grandchildren. I have not seen my grandson, Julian A. Weslow, Jr. in several years, neither have I heard from him. My granddaughter, Alice Weslow Sale, I have not seen in several years and I have not heard from her, but I heard a report some months ago that she was now living in California and has since married William G. Sale. My granddaughter, Julia Weslow Fortson, wife of Ben Fortson, I have not seen in several years and I was told that she had a child born to her sometime in December 1952, and I have not seen the child or heard from my said granddaughter, Julia, up to this writing, and was informed by a friend that Julia has had another child recently and is now living in Louisiana, having moved from Houston; and needless to say, my said daughter-in-law, Bernice, widow of my deceased son, Julian, I have not seen in several years as she has taken little or no interest in me or my husband, Max, since the death of my son, Julian, with the exception that Christmas a year ago, if I remember correctly, she sent some flowers, which I acknowledged, and I believe she had sent some greeting cards on some occasions prior to that time. My said daughter-in-law, Bernice Weslow, has expressed to me, on several occasions, an intense hatred for my son, G. Frank Lipper, and my daughter, Irene Lipper Dover, which I cannot understand, as my said children have always shown her and her children every consideration when possible, and have expressed a desire to be friendly with her, and them. My said children, G. Frank Lipper, and Irene Lipper Dover, have at all times been attentive to me and my husband, Max, especially during the past few years when we have not been well. I will be 82 years old in June of this year and my husband, Max, will be 80 years of age in October of this year, and we have both been in failing health for the past few years and rarely leave our home, and appreciate any attention that is given us, and my husband, Max, and I cannot understand the unfriendly and distant attitude of Bernice Weslow, widow of my said son, Julian, and his children, before mentioned."

10

(Concerns personal belongings already disposed of.)

"In Testimony Whereof, I have hereunto signed my name. . . .
"(S) *Sophie Block*"

(Here follows attestation clause and signature of the 2 witnesses.)

The record reflects that the will in question was executed 22 days before testatrix died at the age of 81 years. By its terms, it disinherits the children of testatrix's son, who died in 1949. Defendant, Frank Lipper, gets a larger share than would have been the case if the plaintiffs were not disinherited. Defendant Lipper is a lawyer, and is admittedly the scrivener of the will. There is evidence that defendant Lipper bore malice against his dead half brother. He lived next door to testatrix, and had a key to her house. The will was not read to testatrix prior to the time she signed same, and she had no discussion with anyone at the time she executed it. There is evidence that the recitations in the will that Bernice Weslow and her children were unfriendly, and never came about testatrix, were untrue. There is also evidence that the Weslows sent testatrix greeting cards and flowers from 1946 through 1954, more times than stated in the will.

Plaintiffs offered no direct evidence pertaining to the making and execution of the will on January 30, 1956, and admittedly rely wholly upon circumstantial evidence of undue influence to support the verdict.

All of the evidence is that testatrix was of sound mind at the time of the execution of the will; that she was a person of strong will; that she was in good physical health for her age; and that she was in fact physically active to the day of her death.

Mrs. Weslow's husband died in 1949; and after 1952 the Weslows came about testatrix less often than before.

The witness Lyda Friberg, who worked at the home of testatrix from 1949 to 1952, testified that in *1952* she had a conversation with Bernice Weslow in which Mrs. Weslow told her if her children didn't get their inheritance she would "sue them through every court in the Union"; that she told testatrix about this conversation, and that testatrix told her "she would have those wills fixed up so there would be no court business," and that she wasn't going to "leave them (the Weslows) a dime." The foregoing was prior to the execution of the will on January 30, 1956.

Subsequent to the execution of the will, testatrix had a conversation with her sister, Mrs. Levy. Mrs. Levy testified:

Q. Who did she say she was leaving her property to?
A. She was leaving it to her son and her daughter.
Q. What else did she say about the rest of her kin, if anything?
A. Well she said that Julian's children had been very ugly to her; that they never showed her any attention whatever; they married and she didn't know they were married; they had children and they didn't let her know. After Julian passed away, she never saw any of the family at all. They never came to see her.
Q. Did she make any statement?
A. Yes she did. When she passed away, she didn't want to leave them anything; that they did nothing for her when she was living.

Shortly before she passed away, testatrix told Mrs. Augusta Roos that she was going to leave her property to her 2 children, and further:

Q. Did she give any reason for it?

A. Yes. She said that Bernice had never been very nice to her and the children never were over.

Again, subsequent to the making of her will, testatrix talked with Effie Landry, her maid. Mrs. Landry testified:

Q. Did Mrs. Block on any occasion ever tell you anything about what was contained in her will?

A. Yes.

Q. What did she tell you about that?

A. She said she wasn't leaving the Weslow children anything.

The only question presented is whether there is any evidence of undue influence. The test of undue influence is whether such control was exercised over the mind of the testatrix as to overcome her free agency and free will and to substitute the will of another so as to cause the testatrix to do what she would not otherwise have done but for such control. Scott v. Townsend, 106 Tex. 322, 166 S.W. 1138; Curry v. Curry, 153 Tex. 421, 270 S.W.2d 208; Boyer v. Pool, 154 Tex. 586, 280 S.W.2d 564.

The evidence here establishes that testatrix was 81 years of age at the time of the execution of her will; that her son, defendant Lipper, who is a lawyer, wrote the will for her upon her instruction; that defendant Lipper bore malice against his deceased half brother (father of plaintiffs); that defendant Lipper lived next door to his mother and had a key to her home; that the will as written gave defendant Lipper a larger share of testatrix's estate than he would otherwise have received; that while testatrix had no discussion with anyone at the time she executed the will, she told the witness Friberg, prior to executing the will, that she was not going to leave anything to the Weslows; and subsequent to the execution of the will she told the witnesses Mrs. Levy, Mrs. Roos, and Mrs. Landry that she had not left the Weslows anything, and the reason why. The will likewise states the reasons for testatrix's action. The testatrix, although 81 years of age, was of sound mind and strong will; and in excellent physical health. There is evidence that the recitation in testatrix's will about the number of times the Weslows sent cards and flowers were incorrect, to the extent that cards and flowers were in fact sent oftener than such will recites.

The contestants established a confidential relationship, the opportunity, and perhaps a motive for undue influence by defendant Lipper. Proof of this type simply sets the stage. Contestants must go forward and prove in some fashion that the will as written resulted from the defendant Lipper substituting his mind and will for that of the testatrix. Here the will and the circumstances might raise suspicion, but it does not supply proof of the vital facts of undue influence — the substitution of a plan of testamentary disposition by another as the will of the testatrix. Boyer v. Pool, supra.

All of the evidence reflected that testatrix, although 81 years of age, was of sound mind; of strong will; and in excellent physical condition. Moreover, subsequent to the execution of the will she told 3 disinterested witnesses what she had done with her property in her will, and the reason therefor. A person of sound mind has the legal right to dispose of his property as he wishes, with the burden on those attacking the disposition to prove that it was the product of undue influence. Long v. Long, 133 Tex. 96, 125 S.W.2d 1034, 1035; Curry v. Curry, 153 Tex. 421, 270 S.W.2d 208.

Testatrix's will did make an unnatural disposition of her property in the sense that it preferred her 2 children over the grandchildren by a deceased son. However, the record contains an explanation from testatrix herself as to why she chose to do such. She had a right to do as she did, whether we think she was justified or not.

Plaintiffs contend that the record supports an inference that testatrix failed to receive the cards and flowers sent to her, or in the alternative that she failed to know she received same, due to conduct of defendant Lipper. Here again, defendant Lipper had the opportunity to prevent testatrix from receiving cards or flowers from the Weslows, but we think there is no evidence of probative force to support the conclusion that he in fact did such. Moreover, the will itself reflected that *some* cards and flowers were in fact received by the testatrix, the dispute in this particular area, going to the number of times that such were sent, rather than to the fact that any were sent. See also: Rothermel v. Duncan et al., Tex. Sup., 369 S.W.2d 917.

We conclude there is no evidence of probative force to support the verdict of the jury. The cause is reversed and rendered for defendants.

NOTES AND QUESTION

1. Mrs. Block's will included a statement setting forth the reasons why she was not making provision for Julian's children. When the possibility of a will contest is anticipated, is this a desirable practice to follow?

2. The rules about undue influence are complicated in most jurisdictions by nice questions about burdens of proof. A rule often applied is that where (1) a person in a confidential relationship (2) receives the bulk of the testator's property (3) from a testator of weakened intellect, the burden of proof shifts to the person occupying the confidential relation to prove affirmatively the absence of undue influence. In

several jurisdictions, however, there must be additional evidence that the beneficiary was active in procuring the execution of the will. See W. McGovern, S. Kurtz & J. Rein, Wills, Trusts and Estates 279-282 (1988).

3. If part of a will is the product of undue influence, those portions of the will that are the product of undue influence may be stricken and the remainder of the will allowed to stand if the invalid portions of the will can be separated without defeating the testator's intent or destroying the testamentary scheme. Williams v. Crickman, 81 Ill. 2d 105, 405 N.E.2d 799 (1980).

NOTE: BEQUESTS TO ATTORNEYS

The will in Lipper v. Weslow was drafted by Mrs. Block's son, an attorney and a principal beneficiary under the will. The general rule is that the mere existence of an attorney-client relationship does not by itself ordinarily raise a presumption of undue influence, but, if there is a suspicious circumstance (such as the exclusion of a natural object of the testator's bounty to the benefit of the attorney), a presumption of undue influence arises. In recent years, some courts, concerned with the appearance of impropriety, have held that a presumption of undue influence does arise when an attorney-drafter receives a legacy, which can be rebutted only by clear and convincing evidence provided by the attorney. See Franciscan Sisters Health Care Corp. v. Dean, 95 Ill. 2d 452, 448 N.E.2d 872 (1983).

Suppose that the attorney draws a will containing a bequest to another client of the attorney. What result? See Haynes v. First National Bank, 87 N.J. 163, 432 A.2d 890 (1981) (holding attorney was in position of irreconcilable conflict, which brought on a presumption of undue influence that will proponents must overcome by clear and convincing evidence).

In New York, upon probate, surrogates must investigate any bequest to the attorney who drafted the will. The attorney must submit an affidavit explaining the facts and circumstances of the gift, and if the surrogate is not satisfied with the explanation a hearing is held to determine whether the attorney's bequest was the result of undue influence. See Pace, Problem Areas in Will Drafting Under New York Law, 56 St. John's L. Rev. 459, 473-479 (1982).

Should an attorney who draws a will containing a bequest to himself or herself be subjected to disciplinary action? See In re Schuyler, 91 Ill. 2d 6, 434 N.E.2d 1137 (1982); deFuria, Testamentary Gifts from Client to the Attorney-Draftsman: From Probate Presumption to Ethical Prohibition, 66 Neb. L. Rev. 695 (1987); Johnston, An Ethical Analysis

"My goodness! Your dear old uncle seems to have left everything to <u>me</u>."

of Common Estate Planning Practices — Is Good Business Bad Ethics?, 45 Ohio St. L.J. 57, 60-86 (1984). See also A.B.A. Model Rules of Professional Conduct, Rule 1.8(c) (1983):

CONFLICT OF INTEREST: PROHIBITED TRANSACTIONS

A lawyer shall not prepare an instrument giving the lawyer or a person related to the lawyer as parent, child, sibling, or spouse any substantial gift from a client, including a testamentary gift, except where the client is related to the donee.

The comment to Rule 1.8 further advises:

A lawyer may accept a gift from a client, if the transaction meets general standards of fairness. For example, a simple gift such as a present given at a holiday or as a token of appreciation is permitted. If effectuation of a substantial gift requires preparing a legal instrument such as a will . . . , however, the client should have the detached advice that another lawyer can provide. Paragraph (c) recognizes an exception where the client is a relative of the donee or the gift is not substantial.

John D. Randall, president of the American Bar Association in 1959-1960, was disbarred by the Iowa Supreme Court in 1979 for naming himself the beneficiary of a client's $4.5 million estate. Committee on Professional Ethics v. Randall, 285 N.W.2d 161 (Iowa 1979), cert. denied, 446 U.S. 946 (1980).

In re Will of Moses
Supreme Court of Mississippi, 1969
227 So. 2d 829

[Fannie Taylor Moses was thrice married; each of her husbands died. During the second marriage she struck up a friendship with Clarence Holland, an attorney 15 years her junior. After the death of her third husband, Holland became Mrs. Moses' lover as well as attorney, and this relationship continued for several years until Mrs. Moses died at age 57. During the six or seven years preceding her death, Mrs. Moses suffered from serious heart trouble, had a breast removed because of cancer, and became an alcoholic. Three years before death she made a will devising almost all of her property to Holland. This will was drafted by a lawyer, Dan Shell, who had no connection with Holland, and who did not tell Holland of the will. Mrs. Moses' closest relative was an elder sister. The sister attacked the will on the ground of undue influence. The chancellor found undue influence and denied probate. Holland appealed.]

SMITH, J.   A number of grounds are assigned for reversal. However, appellant's chief argument is addressed to the proposition that even if Holland, as Mrs. Moses' attorney, occupied a continuing fiduciary relationship with respect to her on May 26, 1964, the date of the execution of the document under which he claimed her estate, the presumption of undue influence was overcome because, in making the will, Mrs. Moses had the independent advice and counsel of one entirely devoted to her interests. It is argued that, for this reason, a decree should be entered here reversing the chancellor and admitting the 1964 will to probate. . . .

The evidence supports the chancellor's finding that the confidential or fiduciary relationship which existed between Mrs. Moses and Holland, her attorney, was a subsisting and continuing relationship, having . . . ended only with Mrs. Moses' death. Moreover, its effect was enhanced by the fact that throughout this period, Holland was in almost daily attendance upon Mrs. Moses on terms of the utmost intimacy. There was strong evidence that this aging woman, seriously ill, disfigured by surgery, and hopelessly addicted to alcoholic excesses, was completely bemused by the constant and amorous attentions of Holland, a man 15 years her junior. There was testimony too indicating that she entertained the pathetic hope that he might marry her.[4] Although the evidence was not without conflict and was, in some of its aspects, circumstantial, it was sufficient to support the finding that the relationship existed on May 26, 1964, the date of the will tendered for probate by Holland.

The chancellor's factual finding of the existence of this relationship on that date is supported by evidence and is not manifestly wrong. Moreover, he was correct in his conclusion of law that such relationship gave rise to a presumption of undue influence which could be overcome only by evidence that, in making the 1964 will, Mrs. Moses had acted upon the independent advice and counsel of one entirely devoted to her interest.

Appellant takes the position that there was undisputed evidence that Mrs. Moses, in making the 1964 will did, in fact, have such advice and counsel. He relies upon the testimony of the attorney in whose office that document was prepared to support his assertion.

This attorney was and is a reputable and respected member of the bar, who had no prior connection with Holland and no knowledge of Mrs. Moses' relationship with him. He had never seen nor represented Mrs. Moses previously and never represented her afterward. He was acquainted with Holland and was aware that Holland was a lawyer.

---

4. The court perhaps has forgotten the wife of Bath in Chaucer's Canterbury Tales, who had five husbands, the last one 20 years younger than she. She craved another young and healthy husband who could satisfy her hearty sexual appetites, and no reader of Chaucer can doubt she got one. — Eds.

A brief summary of his testimony, with respect to the writing of the will, follows:

Mrs. Moses had telephoned him for an appointment and had come alone to his office on March 31, 1964. She was not intoxicated and in his opinion knew what she was doing. He asked her about her property and "marital background." He did this in order, he said, to advise her as to possible renunciation by a husband. She was also asked if she had children in order to determine whether she wished to "pretermit them." As she had neither husband nor children this subject was pursued no further. He asked as to the values of various items of property in order to consider possible tax problems. He told her it would be better if she had more accurate descriptions of the several items of real and personal property comprising her estate. No further "advice or counsel" was given her.

On some later date, Mrs. Moses sent in (the attorney did not think she came personally and in any event he did not see her), some tax receipts for purposes of supplying property descriptions. He prepared the will and mailed a draft to her. Upon receiving it, she telephoned that he had made a mistake in the devise of certain realty, in that he had provided that a relatively low valued property should go to Holland rather than a substantially more valuable property which she said she wanted Holland to have. He rewrote the will, making this change, and mailed it to her, as revised, on May 21, 1964. On the one occasion when he saw Mrs. Moses, there were no questions and no discussion of any kind as to Holland being preferred to the exclusion of her blood relatives. Nor was there any inquiry or discussion as to a possible client-attorney relationship with Holland. The attorney-draftsman wrote the will according to Mrs. Moses' instructions and said that he had "no interest in" how she disposed of her property. He testified "I try to draw the will to suit their purposes and if she (Mrs. Moses) wanted to leave him (Holland) everything she had, that was her business as far as I was concerned. I was trying to represent her in putting on paper in her will her desires, and it didn't matter to me to whom she left it . . . I couldn't have cared less."

When Mrs. Moses returned to the office to execute the will, the attorney was not there and it was witnessed by two secretaries. . . .

The attorney's testimony supports the chancellor's finding that no-where in the conversations with Mrs. Moses was there touched upon in any way the proposed testamentary disposition whereby preference was to be given a nonrelative to the exclusion of her blood relatives. There was no discussion of her relationship with Holland, nor as to who her legal heirs might be, nor as to their relationship to her, after it was discovered that she had neither a husband nor children.

It is clear from his own testimony that, in writing the will, the attorney-draftsman, did no more than write down, according to the forms of law, what Mrs. Moses told him. There was no meaningful independent advice or counsel touching upon the area in question and it is manifest that the role of the attorney in writing the will, as it relates to the present issue, was little more than that of scrivener. The chancellor was justified in holding that this did not meet the burden nor overcome the presumption.

The sexual morality of the personal relationship is not an issue. However, the intimate nature of this relationship is relevant to the present inquiry to the extent that its existence, under the circumstances, warranted an inference of undue influence, extending and augmenting that which flowed from the attorney-client relationship. Particularly is this true when viewed in the light of evidence indicating its employment for the personal aggrandizement of Holland.

. . . [T]he decree of the chancery court will be affirmed.

ROBERTSON, J. (dissenting).   . . . Mrs. Fannie T. Moses was the active manager of commercial property in the heart of Jackson, four apartment buildings containing ten rental units, and a 480-acre farm until the day of her death. All of the witnesses conceded that she was a good businesswoman, maintaining and repairing her properties with promptness and dispatch, and paying her bills promptly so that she would get the cash discount. She was a strong personality and pursued her own course, even though her manner of living did at times embarrass her sisters and estranged her from them.

It was not contended in this case that Holland was in any way actively concerned with the preparation or execution of the will. Appellees rely solely upon the finding of the chancellor that there were suspicious circumstances. However, the suspicious circumstances listed by the chancellor in his opinion had nothing whatsoever to do with the preparation or execution of the will. These were remote antecedent circumstances having to do with the meretricious relationship of the parties, and the fact that at times Mrs. Moses drank to excess and could be termed an alcoholic, but there is no proof in this long record that her use of alcohol affected her will power or her ability to look after her extensive real estate holdings. . . .

The majority was indeed hard put to find fault with . . . [the actions of Dan Shell, the attorney who drew the will,] on behalf of his client. . . . He ascertained that Mrs. Moses was competent to make a will; he satisfied himself that she was acting of her own free will and accord, and that she was disposing of her property exactly as she wished and intended. No more is required.

There is not one iota of testimony in the voluminous record that Clarence Holland even knew of this will, much less that he participated in the preparation or execution of it. The evidence is all to the contrary. The evidence is undisputed that she executed her last will after the fullest deliberation, with full knowledge of what she was doing, and with the independent consent and advice of an experienced and competent attorney whose sole purpose was to advise with her and prepare her will exactly as she wanted it.

In January 1967, about one month before her death and some two years and eight months after she had made her will, she called W.R. Patterson, an experienced, reliable and honorable attorney who was a friend of hers, and asked him to come by her home for a few minutes. Patterson testified:

> She said, "Well, the reason I called you out here is that I've got an envelope here with all of my important papers in it, and *that includes my last will and testament*," and says, "I would like to leave them with you if you've got a place to lock them up in your desk somewhere there in your office."
>
> ... [A]nd she said, *"Now, Dan Shell drew my will for me two or three years ago,"* and she says, *"It's exactly like I want it,"* and says, *"I had to go to his office two or three times to get it the way I wanted it, but this is the way I want it,* and if anything happens to me I want you to take all these papers and give them to Dan," and she says, "He'll know what to do with them." (Emphasis added).

What else could she have done? She met all the tests that this Court and other courts have carefully outlined and delineated. The majority opinion says that this still was not enough, that there were "suspicious circumstances" ..., but even these were not connected in any shape, form or fashion with the preparation or execution of her will. They had to do with her love life and her drinking habits and propensities. ...

If full knowledge, deliberate and voluntary action, and independent consent and advice have not been proved in this case, then they just cannot be proved. ...

I think that the judgment of the lower court should be reversed and the last will and testament of Fannie T. Moses executed on May 26, 1964, admitted to probate in solemn form.

QUESTIONS

1. Should Dan Shell, who drew Fannie Moses's will, be liable to Clarence Holland for malpractice?

2. Why is evidence of a sexual relationship outside of marriage admissible in undue influence cases? In In re Kelly's Estate, 150 Or. 598, 618, 46 P.2d 84, 92 (1935), the court suggested the reason was that a sexual relationship casts a suspicion of deceit and "cautions the court to examine the evidence with unusual care."

Inasmuch as a person ordinarily has a sustained sexual relationship only with a partner for whom there is considerable affection, perhaps even love, why does not evidence of such a relationship indicate that the partner is a natural object of the decedent's bounty? In view of changing mores of society in regard to sexual relationships without marriage (see Marvin v. Marvin, 18 Cal. 3d 660, 557 P.2d 106, 134 Cal. Rptr. 815 (1976)), why should sensual pleasures without benefit of clergy continue to be evidence of *undue* influence? See de Furia, Testamentary Gifts Resulting From Meretricious Relationships: Undue Influence or Natural Beneficence?, 64 Notre Dame L. Rev. 200 (1989).

For a collection of cases involving alleged undue influence by lovers, see Annot., 76 A.L.R.3d 743 (1977).

3. If in In re Will of Moses, Fannie Moses had been a man named Frank, and Clarence had been a woman named Clara, but otherwise the facts were essentially the same, would the result be the same? See In re Launius, 507 So. 2d 27 (Miss. 1987); A. Derenski & S. Landsberg, The Age Taboo: Older Women-Younger Men Relationships (1981).

Francine du Plessix Gray, The New "Older Woman"
N.Y. Times, §7 (Book Review), Jan. 15, 1978, at 3, col. 1

Americans' traditional unease with [Older Woman and Younger Man] alliances is not only based on a complex network of puritanical hangups but vastly reinforced by our literature. There is a remarkable dearth of these liaisons in British or American fiction; and novels, for better or for worse, have always fueled our most passionate romantic fantasies and erotic expectations. . . . [The] absence [of the Older Woman and Younger Man theme] from English language fiction since the birth of the novel two and a half centuries ago is most striking compared to its abundant presence on the Continent. The theme is central to . . . classics of European literature, . . . and most particularly the work of Colette. . . .

In any society tainted by Puritanism, I reflect, such a relationship is bound to remain taboo simply because it is too much fun, just as it is bound to flower in that Gallic world of Colette's, divinely untainted by any moral strictures that might curb that hedonism of the flesh.

. . . After centuries of calmly approving the myriad 70-year-old Dr. Spocks who take 24-year-old women to their marriage beds, and condoning vast networks of sugar daddies who heap trinkets on their molls, are we any readier for Colette's radically anti-Calvinist vision of the passive, unemployed younger man who ripens in the shelter of a powerful older woman? In the light of the new egalitarianism, in what sense is it more suspect to be a gigolo, or a man of modest employment living with a successful older woman, than to be a kept woman or a housewife? The taboos still hovering over such relationships may never be lifted until all present notions of traditional "masculinity" and of male dominance are radically demythologized.

IN RE KAUFMANN'S WILL, 20 A.D. 2d 464, 247 N.Y.S.2d 664 (1964), aff'd, 15 N.Y.2d 825, 257 N.Y.S.2d 941, 205 N.E.2d 864 (1965). In 1948, at the age of 34, Robert Kaufmann, a millionaire by inheritance, moved from Washington to New York City. There he began painting, underwent psychoanalysis, and met Walter Weiss, age 39. Within a year after their meeting, Walter moved into Robert's apartment, and in 1951 Robert bought a house into which they moved at 42 East 74th Street. Walter took full charge of the house, its furnishing, the employment of help, and the maintenance of the household. All mail and incoming telephone calls were routed to and through Walter. Robert spent a good deal of time painting in his studio. Over the next several years Robert and Walter travelled abroad extensively and entertained lavishly at home. They exhibited much love, affection, and mutual esteem. However, in business matters Robert became almost totally dependent upon Walter, who assumed control of Robert's bank accounts, safe-deposit box, household and other property as if it were his own. The two men lived together until 1959, when Robert died unexpectedly.[5]

Beginning in 1951, Robert made wills in successive years, each will increasing Walter's share of his estate. In 1958 Robert executed a will, drafted by a prominent New York law firm, which left substantially all his property to Walter. Accompanying it was a letter addressed to Robert's family signed by Robert in 1951 and passed along with each subsequent will. This letter might be described as a "coming out of the closet at death" letter. It stated that when Robert met Walter, Robert was "terribly unhappy, highly emotional and filled to the brim with a grandly variegated group of fears, guilt and assorted complexes." It stated that Walter encouraged Robert to submit to psychoanalysis, and went on to say:

> Walter gave me the courage to start, something which slowly but eventually permitted me to supply for myself everything my life had

---

5. A rather similar *ménage de vieux garçons* was The Pines, the celebrated villa occupied by Algernon Charles Swinburne, English poet, novelist, and sage, and Theodore Watts-Dunton, a county solicitor. In 1879, at the age of 42, Swinburne moved in with Watts-Dunton who had rescued him from delirium tremens and from a house of pleasure in St. John's Wood where a couple of blonde amazons flagellated the customers. Watts-Dunton laid down the rules, managed all of Swinburne's business affairs, ran the household, and doled out the pin money. Swinburne stayed at home and wrote. Watts-Dunton eventually married and his wife moved into The Pines with them. In 1909 Swinburne died, leaving everything to Watts-Dunton. Swinburne's family was hurt and indignant, but no one sued. M. Panter-Downes, At The Pines (1971).

heretofore lacked: an outlet for my long-latent but strong creative ability in painting . . . , a balanced, healthy sex life which before had been spotty, furtive and destructive; an ability to reorientate myself to actual life and to face it calmly and realistically. All of this adds up to Peace of Mind. . . . I am eternally grateful to my dearest friend — best pal, Walter A. Weiss. What could be more wonderful than a fruitful, contented life and who more deserving of gratitude now, in the form of an inheritance, than the person who helped most in securing that life? I cannot believe my family could be anything else but glad and happy for my own comfortable self-determination and contentment and equally grateful to the friend who made it possible.

Love to you all,
Bob

In 1952 Robert had also executed a document granting Walter exclusive power over Robert's corporeal remains and the authority to make all funeral arrangements; in addition, in the event Robert was incapacitated, Walter was granted the power to consent in Robert's behalf to the performance of any operation he deemed necessary after consultation with Robert's physicians. The instrument provided that Walter was to act as "though he were my nearest relative . . . and that his instructions and consents shall be controlling, regardless of who may object to them."

Robert's family in Washington deeply resented Walter's presence and his business advice about Kaufmann family corporations in which Robert was a shareholder. The 1951 letter appeared to confirm the family's suspicion that a homosexual relationship existed between Robert and Walter. Upon Robert's death his brother Joel sued to have the 1958 will set aside on the ground of undue influence. In his pretrial deposition Walter denied that a homosexual relationship existed between the two men, but the appellate judges, and probably the jury as well, suspected that this was a lie. Walter did not take the stand at the trial and, therefore, was not subject to cross-examination.

After two jury trials, both finding undue influence, the majority of the Appellate Division agreed that the evidence was sufficient "to find that the instrument of June 19, 1958 was the end result of an unnatural, insidious influence operating on a weak-willed, trusting, inexperienced Robert whose natural warm family attachment had been attenuated by false accusations against Joel, subtle flattery suggesting an independence he had not realized and which, in fact, Weiss had stultified, and planting in Robert's mind the conviction that Joel and other members of the family were resentful of and obstructing his drive for independence." Although the earlier wills were not directly in issue, the majority thought the undue influence began before 1951 and tainted all the prior wills and gifts to Walter; the letter signed by Robert, mentioned above, was deemed to be "cogent evidence of his complete domination by Weiss."

The Court of Appeals affirmed, saying:

> Where, as here, the record indicates that testator was pliable and easily taken advantage of, as proponent admitted, that there was a long and detailed history of dominance and subservience between them, that testator relied exclusively upon proponent's knowledge and judgment in the disposition of almost all of the material circumstances affecting the conduct of his life, and proponent is willed virtually the entire estate, we consider that a question of fact was presented concerning whether the instrument offered for probate was the free, untrammeled and intelligent expression of the wishes and intentions of testator or the product of the dominance of the beneficiary.

NOTES AND QUESTIONS

1. If, in In re Kaufmann's Will, Robert had been a woman named Roberta, would the result be the same? See Sherman, Undue Influence and the Homosexual Testator, 42 U. Pitt. L. Rev. 225, 239-248 (1981). Cf. T. Schaffer, Death, Property, and Lawyers 243-257 (1980) (analyzing the psychodynamics in *Kaufmann* and concluding the case was correctly decided).

2. The Los Angeles Daily Journal, Aug. 16, 1988, at 1, col. 5, carried a story entitled Legal Challenges to AIDS Patients' Wills Seen on Rise. The article reported:

> Attorneys in those cities [New York, San Francisco, and Los Angeles] are seeing a growing number of will contests and other fights between blood relatives of AIDS victims and the victims' friends and lovers.
>
> The challenges are usually based on the victims' competency when the will was made out, since loss of mental capacity is a common occurrence in AIDS cases. . . .
>
> San Francisco lawyer Gary J. Wood, who chairs the AIDS referral panel in the city, notes the emotional aspects of such contests. "In large estates, they're fighting over money. But other than that, there's also jealousy about this lover person that's involved in this guy's life, and the family feels that's wrong."
>
> [San Francisco lawyer Clint] Hockenberry says other factors enter into the conflict. "Sometimes it's a contest of cultures or family background. The family might come from the Midwest and, first of all, not know the son was gay; second, that the son had AIDS; and third, that the son had a lover. It's sort of a triple whammy.
>
> "They blame the lover for giving the son AIDS and bringing him out. So there's a lot of anger there — almost all of it misdirected," notes Hockenberry.

... "About 60 percent of AIDS victims will have central nervous system involvement by the time they die," according to AIDS expert Dr. Nelson Garcia of the University of California/Irvine Medical Center.

"And about 40 percent, by the time they die, will show some manifestations of AIDS dementia syndrome — intermittent episodes of confusion, forgetfulness or hallucinations," notes Garcia. . . .

[Boston attorney Denise] McWilliams and others also suggest videotaping the signing of the will, if the resources are available. But McWilliams adds, "There are two minds about that. I'm less of a fan of videotaping than others, because of the way a person looks in the advanced stages of the disease — when they've lost a lot of weight, look very gaunt and so forth."

See Johanson & Bay, Estate Planning for the Client with AIDS, 52 Texas B.J. 217 (1989).

3.   Wendy Brown's sister, Ruth Preston (see supra page 64), is your client. Ruth has been living with Terry Sikorski for 10 years in a condominium owned by Ruth, to which Terry contributes one-half the cost of maintenance. Terry is an architect. Ruth comes to you for advice about her will. She wants Terry to take all her property if Terry survives, and likewise Terry wants Ruth to take all if Ruth survives. What questions should you ask Ruth? What advice should you give her? Are there any inter vivos arrangements, such as a revocable trust, a durable power of attorney, or a cohabitation agreement that Ruth and Terry should consider? See Gutierrez, Estate Planning for the Unmarried Cohabitant, 13 U. Miami Inst. Est. Plan. ¶¶1600 et seq. (1979); Kramer, Estate Planning for the Stable and Not-So-Stable Marriage and Nonmarital Cohabitation, 39 N.Y.U. Inst. Fed. Tax. §56.07 (1981); Lovas, When Is a Family Not a Family? Inheritance and the Taxation of Inheritance Within the Non-Traditional Family, 24 Idaho L. Rev. 353 (1988); Wolk, Federal Tax Consequences of Wealth Transfer Between Unmarried Cohabitants, 27 UCLA L. Rev. 1240 (1980).

NOTE: SPECIAL PRECAUTIONS WHEN WILL CONTEST IS A POSSIBILITY

When the attorney senses that there is a possibility of a will contest, what special precautions should the attorney take? Consider the value of the following:

(1)   The attorney requests the client to write, in the client's handwriting, a letter to the attorney setting forth in detail the disposition the client wishes to make. Upon receipt of the letter, the attorney replies, detailing the consequences of the disposition on the client's heirs, and asks for a letter setting forth the reasons for the disposition.

After receipt of this letter, the will is drafted as the client wants. The letters are kept in the attorney's files to show any prospective contestant or to enter into evidence at trial, if necessary. See Jaworski, The Will Contest, 10 Baylor L. Rev. 87, 91-93 (1958). Compare the letter written by Robert Kaufmann, at his attorney's request, supra pages 159-160.

(2) The attorney videotapes or records a discussion between the testator and the witnesses wherein the testator explains why she wants to dispose of the property as she does. See Beyer, Videotaping the Will Execution Ceremony — Preventing Frustration of the Testator's Final Wishes, 15 St. Mary's L.J. 1 (1983); Buckley, Indiana's New Videotaped Wills Statute: Launching Probate Into the 21st Century, 20 Val. U.L. Rev. 83 (1985).

(3) The attorney obtains a psychiatric report on the mental condition of the testator at the time the will is executed. See Jaworski, supra, at 93.

NOTE: NO-CONTEST CLAUSES

A no-contest clause provides that a beneficiary who contests the will shall take nothing, or a token amount, in lieu of the provisions made for the beneficiary in the will. A no-contest clause is designed to discourage will contests. In dealing with these clauses courts have been pulled in several directions by conflicting policies. On the one hand, enforcement of a no-contest clause discourages unmeritorious litigation, family quarrels, and defaming the reputation of the testator. On the other hand, enforcement of a no-contest clause could inhibit a lawsuit proving forgery, fraud, or undue influence and nullify the safeguards built around the testamentary disposition of property.

Courts have often avoided a resolution of these conflicting policies by determining that a particular kind of litigation is "not a contest." Suits to construe wills are not contests; even an attack on certain provisions of the will as being illegal (e.g., in violation of the Rule against Perpetuities) has been held to be merely a suit for construction. A request by a beneficiary for a declaratory judgment as to whether a particular activity will violate a no-contest clause is not necessarily a contest. See Estate of Black, 160 Cal. App. 3d 582, 206 Cal. Rptr. 663 (1984) (holding filing of proposed petition claiming *Marvin*-type implied domestic partnership interest in cohabitant-testator's property would not violate no-contest clause).

If the lawsuit is determined to be a contest, the majority of courts enforce a no-contest clause unless there is probable cause for the contest. The probable cause rule is adopted by Uniform Probate Code §3-905 and by Restatement (Second) of Property, Donative Transfers §9.1

(1983). In a minority of jurisdictions courts enforce no-contest clauses unless the contestant alleges forgery or subsequent revocation by a later will or codicil, or the beneficiary is contesting a provision benefitting the drafter of the will or any witness thereto. These jurisdictions believe a probable cause rule encourages litigation and shifts the balance unduly in favor of contestants. The lawyer with a client who wishes to contest a will with a no-contest clause must investigate the local law carefully because there are subtle differences from state to state. See Restatement (Second), supra, Statutory Note to §9.1 and Reporter's Note to §9.1; Annot., 23 A.L.R.4th 369 (1983).

A PEARL OF GREAT PRICE[6]

In October 1966 a 95-year-old South Pasadena millionaire, Albert Otis Birch, with an estate estimated at $200,000,000, married his 59-year-old nurse, Pearl Choate. This was the climax of a wild 15-month chase across California, Mexico, and Texas — Birch and his first wife periodically disappearing with Pearl, only to be found by investigators hired by Birch's prospective legatees.

Pearl Choate was many times married. She had six husbands, one of whom she married twice. She also had a lengthy criminal record including an acquittal for murder in 1938 (she shot a ranch hand in the back, but was successful in her claim of self-defense). She spent 12 years in a Texas prison for murdering a carpenter who had obtained a civil judgment against her. Pearl had come to work for Birch and his 93-year-old wife, Estelle, in the summer of 1965. They procured her through a nurses' registry after Estelle developed cancer.

In April of 1966 Pearl moved the Birches from their 32-room South Pasadena mansion to her small home in Compton so she could better attend them. Two months later the Birches and Pearl disappeared. They were discovered in Mexico, where Otis Birch told investigators he had come of his own volition for his health. Not satisfied with this state of affairs, several distant relatives of the Birches (they had no close relatives) petitioned in Los Angeles to have a guardian of the persons and conservator of the property appointed for the couple. A cousin of Estelle, Martha Tulleys, was appointed guardian, and a bank was appointed conservator. Meanwhile the Birches and Pearl had disappeared again and were traced to Harlingen, Texas, where Birch fractured his hip in a fall. A local physician ordered Birch not to be moved for 30 days.

---

6. This phrase, from the King James Version (Matt. 13:46), is changed to "one pearl of great *value*" in the Revised Standard Version. The facts are taken from various issues of the Los Angeles Times during 1966-1970.

Dr. C. Adrian Heaton, president of California Baptist Theological Seminary, which had received large sums of money from Birch during his life and presumably would come in for a handsome gift at his death, flew to Harlingen only to find that Birch had been taken from the hospital and driven by Pearl 500 miles across Texas to Midland. There the trail was lost, and the whereabouts of the trio was not discovered until after Estelle died in Breckenridge, Texas, on October 7, 1966. Estelle's body was returned to Los Angeles and buried in Inglewood Park Cemetery.

After Estelle died, Harlan Moehn of Iowa, a relative of Estelle Birch, located Pearl and Otis Birch in Breckenridge, Texas, where one of Pearl's brothers ran a tavern. Moehn and Dr. Heaton discovered that Pearl had filed an adoption application to be named Birch's daughter. Moehn arranged to see Birch on October 25; the discussion became heated and Pearl attacked Moehn with a butcher knife, screaming, "I'll cut your heart out." He filed a complaint against Pearl, and she was arrested and booked on suspicion of assault with intent to commit murder. After posting bond in the case, Pearl put Otis Birch in a car and drove across the border to Altus, Oklahoma, where they were married in a flashy red sedan by a justice of the peace. Birch, recovering from hip surgery, was lying on a mattress in the back seat of the car when the ceremony was performed. "This was not a marriage of passion . . . he suggested it to protect my interests," Pearl told newsmen. She described the churchmen and relatives seeking to wrest Birch from her as "a bunch of vultures."

Harlan Moehn then sought a writ of habeas corpus in a Breckenridge court to release Birch from the control of his new wife. Pearl brought Birch to court, where he was the star witness. Almost totally deaf, he heard little of the proceedings. He had a new hearing aid, but Pearl had not yet obtained batteries for it. When handed questions in writing, Birch answered in a booming voice that he was not being restrained against his wishes and that he did not want to return to California where, he said, the "authorities" wanted to test him for insanity. The judge ruled that Birch was not being held against his will by his bride. Pearl put her arm around Otis Birch, and they both smiled broadly for photographers.

In the meantime the attorney general of California, overseer of charitable trusts, entered the case. His investigators turned up a very interesting bit of information: Pearl had married a Compton carwash worker in a proxy marriage in Tijuana, Mexico, on Sept. 2, 1965. Thus informed, the attorney general of California asked the county attorney in Oklahoma to prosecute Pearl for bigamy. But the information proved not wholly accurate. It was discovered that Mexican authorities had failed to record the marriage certificate, and under Mexican law this

Drawing by Handelsman.
Copyright © 1981 by The New Yorker Magazine, Inc.
Reproduced by permission.

final step is required for a valid proxy marriage. Hence the bigamy suit was called off.

In November 1966, Birch and his bride disappeared from Breckenridge. Her relatives refused to say where they had gone. They were spotted briefly in Wichita Falls. The Harlingen law firm Birch had hired during his one-month stay there — with an unpaid bill of $7,500 for legal services — discovered them in December occupying a house trailer in Odessa, Texas. From there they moved the trailer to Dallas, where Birch died on March 16, 1967. The next day Pearl had Birch's body entombed at the Laurel Land Mausoleum in Dallas.

By a handwritten will dated May 14, 1966, Birch devised all his property to Pearl. A prior will of September 7, 1965, had left his estate to sixteen charitable organizations, mainly Baptist institutions. The charitable organizations claimed Birch was mentally incompetent and unduly influenced by Pearl when he made the 1966 will, but, after an extended lawsuit, in 1970 the 1966 will was ordered probated by the district court in Dallas. Soon thereafter the Los Angeles Times reported that the Birch estate was vastly overestimated; it might not be worth more than $50,000. No one seemed to be able to find Otis's reputed assets.

After entombing her husband's body in Dallas, the widow Birch returned to her home in Compton, California, where she promptly had another run-in with the law. She quarreled with the tenant in her duplex, alleging the rent was overdue. When a neighbor called the police, she fired a .22 caliber rifle, barely missing a policeman and a bystander. On January 23, 1968, a jury found Pearl Choate Birch guilty of assault with a deadly weapon. She served 20 months in prison and was released in March 1970.

The Birch saga raises a whole complex of interesting issues. Let us approach them from the viewpoint of the lawyer giving advice. Suppose you are an attorney practicing in Breckenridge, Texas. Soon after Estelle died, Pearl Choate comes into your office and says Birch wants to leave her all his property and she wants to take care of him for the rest of his life. "He wants to protect me, and I want to look after him," she tells you. What do you advise Pearl Choate and Otis Birch to do? To draft a will for an incompetent person is a breach of professional ethics. Although it is by no means clear that Birch is incompetent and that you must ethically refuse to draft a will for him, under the circumstances of the case, a will might be attacked successfully on grounds of mental incompetency or undue influence. Hence consider the following alternatives.

1. You advise an adoption proceeding, and draw a petition for adoption, which Pearl and Otis Birch sign. The petition is approved by the court, which decrees that Pearl is the daughter of Otis. Birch's nearest relatives are not notified of the adoption proceeding. After Birch's death can his next-of-kin or his executor set aside the adoption? See In re Adoption of Sewall, 242 Cal. App. 2d 208, 51 Cal. Rptr. 367 (1966); In re Adoption of Russell, 166 Pa. Super. 590, 73 A.2d 794 (1950).

2. You advise Pearl and Otis to marry. They do. Under the laws of Texas and California, which have community property systems, Pearl would not be entitled to a forced share in Otis's estate. However, the surviving spouse does take a share if Otis dies intestate. Assume Otis dies intestate. Can the marriage be annulled by his next of kin? Before or after Otis's death? See McClure v. Donovan, 33 Cal. 2d 717, 205 P.2d 17 (1949); Greathouse v. Vosburgh, 19 Ill. 2d 555, 169 N.E.2d 97

(1960); In re Estate of Sadow, 356 So. 2d 845 (Fla. App. 1978). The two-year marriage of the former general manager of the Metropolitan Opera, Rudolf Bing, 87, suffering from Alzheimer's Disease, to a sometime patient in Bellevue Hospital's psychiatric division, was annulled in 1989, upon suit of his guardian. Bing's million-dollar estate was reported to have been reduced to $200,000 by the "bizarre behavior" of his wife. N.Y. Times, Sept. 7, 1989, §B, at 6, col. 3.

Estate of Park, [1953] 2 All E.R. 408, 411, is authority for the proposition that a person may have insufficient capacity to make a will on the same day as the person has sufficient capacity to marry. Does the concept of freedom to marry, classified for constitutional law as a fundamental right requiring strict scrutiny of limitations thereon, support the proposition that less mental capacity may be required for marriage than for a nonfundamental right, such as the right to make a will? See Note, The Right of the Mentally Disabled to Marry: A Statutory Evaluation, 15 J. Fam. L. 463 (1977).

Would you advise Pearl and Otis to marry and move to Florida, which gives the surviving spouse a forced share in the decedent's probate estate? In addition, Florida Stat. §732.301 (Supp. 1988), like Uniform Probate Code §2-301 and similar statutes in many states, provides that if a person marries after making a will, the will is revoked as to the new spouse, who takes her intestate share. See infra page 426. In Hoffman v. Kohns, 385 So. 2d 1064 (Fla. App. 1980), Herbert Kohns, 84 and childless, suffering from cerebral arteriosclerosis and senility and unable to handle his personal and financial affairs, hired a housekeeper named Eloise the last week of August 1975. On September 22 Eloise and Herbert were married by a notary public. The next day Herbert made a new will making Eloise sole beneficiary. Herbert died a year later. Upon suit by the testator's closest blood relative, a niece, the court found that Eloise had exercised undue influence and completely dominated Herbert. The court set aside the will but held that Herbert had competency to marry and that the marriage could not be set aside for undue influence after his death. Thus under Fla. Stat. §732.301 Eloise, a pretermitted spouse, received her intestate share, which was Herbert's entire probate estate because he had died without lineal descendants. See also Tarsagian v. Watt, 402 So. 2d 471 (Fla. App. 1981), setting aside a will because of undue influence of the nurse who became the second wife of an octogenarian but refusing to annul the marriage.

3.   You recommend an inter vivos trust. You draw a trust instrument, which Otis signs, transferring all his property to a bank as trustee to pay all the income to Otis for life and on the death of Otis to pay the principal to Pearl. Can either Otis's next of kin or the executor of his will set aside the trust on grounds of undue influence? See 4 A. Scott, Trusts §333.3 (W. Fratcher 4th ed. 1989); Rein, An Ounce of Prevention:

Grounds for Upsetting Wills and Will Substitutes, 20 Gonz. L. Rev. 1, 66-67 (1984).

4.   You recommend a contract to devise. The agreement, signed by Pearl and Otis, provides that Pearl promises to take care of Otis for the rest of his life and, in exchange therefor, Otis promises to devise all his property to Pearl. Pearl fulfills her promise and Otis either (1) dies intestate or (2) devises all his property to Pearl, which devise is set aside on grounds of undue influence. What are Pearl's rights on the contract? See infra pages 271-273.

3. *Fraud*

It is fairly easy to state the test for fraud but often difficult to apply it on particular facts. Fraud occurs where the testator is deceived by a misrepresentation and does that which the testator would not have done had the misrepresentation not been made. It is usually said that the misrepresentation must be made with both the *intent* to deceive the testator and the *purpose* of influencing the testamentary disposition. A provision in a will procured by fraud is invalid. The remaining portion of the will stands unless the fraud goes to the entire will or the portions invalidated by fraud are inseparable from the rest of the will.

The remedy usually granted for fraud is for a court to impose a constructive trust on the wrongdoer, compelling the wrongdoer to surrender the property acquired by the wrongful conduct.

If fraud occurs in the testamentary setting, it is usually either fraud in the inducement or fraud in the execution.

Fraud in the inducement occurs when a person misrepresents facts, thereby causing the testator to execute a will, to include particular provisions in the wrongdoer's favor, to refrain from revoking a will, or not to execute a will. Thus:

> *Case 1.* O's heir apparent, *H*, induces *O* not to execute a will in favor of *A* by promising *O* that *H* will convey the property to *A*. At the time *H* makes the promise, *H* has no intent to convey the property to *A*. This is fraud in the inducement. If, on the other hand, at the time of his promise *H* had intended to convey the property to *A*, but *H* had changed his mind after O's death and had refused to convey to *A*, no fraud is involved. However, *A* still may be able to recover from *H* on the theory of a secret trust. See infra page 487; 1A A. Scott, Trusts §55.3 (W. Fratcher 4th ed. 1987).

Questions of causation in fraud in the inducement are particularly tricky. The usual test is that a fraudulently procured inheritance or bequest is invalid if the testator would not have left the inheritance or made the bequest had he known the true facts. See T. Atkinson, Wills §56 (2d ed. 1953).

Fraud in the execution occurs when a person misrepresents the character or contents of the instrument signed by the testator, which does not in fact carry out the testator's intent. Thus:

> Case 2. *O*, with poor eyesight, asks her heir apparent, *H*, to bring her the document prepared for her as a will so that she can sign it. *H* brings *O* a document that is not *O*'s intended will, knowing it is not the document *O* wants. *O* signs it, believing it to be her will. This is fraud in the execution.

PROBLEM

T's first will devised everything to her favorite niece, Jean, who lived in a distant city. *T*'s second will, executed in the hospital two days before she died, revoked her prior will and devised everything to her friend, Carol. After *T*'s death a nurse in the hospital testifies that the day before the will was executed he heard Carol tell *T* that Jean had died. "In that case," *T* said, "I want you [Carol] to have everything." In fact, as Carol knew, Jean was alive. What result? See 5 A. Scott, Trusts §489 (W. Fratcher 4th ed. 1989).

Latham v. Father Divine
Court of Appeals of New York, 1949
299 N.Y. 22, 85 N.E.2d 168, 11 A.L.R.2d 802

DESMOND, J.   The amended complaint herein has, in response to a motion under rule 106 of the Rules of Civil Practice, been dismissed for insufficiency. Its principal allegations are these: plaintiffs are first cousins, but not distributees, of Mary Sheldon Lyon, who died in October, 1946, leaving a will, executed in 1943, which gave almost her whole estate to defendant Father Divine,[7] leader of a religious cult, and

---

7. Father Divine, a charismatic religious leader during the Depression who proclaimed his own divinity, attracted thousands of believers, mostly black but some, like Mary Sheldon Lyon, white. Whatever the merits of his claim, Father Divine was a master of theater. His inspirational sermons at a Harlem church roused his followers to spirited expression; his exuberant and melodious services were standing room only. Father Divine went beyond the spiritual; he preached racial equality and social action against segregation. He established communes ("heavens") and religious cooperatives around the country, often in white neighborhoods, where blacks from the ghetto could move to find work and food. Father Divine taught there was only one race, no "Negro" and "white"; people just had darker or lighter complexions. The press of the time disparaged Father Divine as a con man of the cloth. Yet, in the last decade, scholars searching for the roots of the

to two corporate defendants in some way connected with that cult, and to an individual defendant (Patience Budd) said to be one of Father Divine's active followers; that said will has been, after a contest instituted by distributees, probated under a compromise agreement with the distributees, by the terms of which agreement, to which plaintiffs were not parties, the defendants just above referred to will receive a large sum from the estate; that after the making of said will, decedent on several occasions expressed "a desire and a determination to revoke the said will, and to execute a new will by which the plaintiffs would receive a substantial portion of the estate," "that shortly prior to the death of the deceased she had certain attorneys draft a new will in which the plaintiffs were named as legatees for a very substantial amount, totalling approximately $350,000"; that "by reason of the said false representations, the said undue influence and the said physical force" certain of the defendants "prevented the deceased from executing the said new Will"; that, shortly before decedent's death, decedent again expressed her determination to execute the proposed new will which favored plaintiffs, and that defendants "thereupon conspired to kill, and did kill, the deceased by means of a surgical operation performed by a doctor engaged by the defendants without the consent or knowledge of any of the relatives of the deceased."

---

black churches' commitment to social action have come to reevaluate Father Divine. Many now view him as an influential and serious religious leader who gave his followers a feeling of goodness, who stuck his thumb in the eye of the white establishment (he rode around in a chauffeured Rolls-Royce, threw fabulous banquets, inhabited the fanciest houses, and claimed for blacks every perquisite of rich whites), and who crystallized the commitment of black churches to the struggle for racial justice. See R. Weisbrot, Father Divine and the Struggle for Racial Equality (1983); J. Watts, "Shout the Victory": History of Father Divine and the Peace Mission Movement 1879-1942 (Ph.D. dissertation U.C.L.A. 1989).

The turn in Father Divine's fortunes, which transformed him from a minor religious figure into an adored incarnation of God, came as a result of a brush with the law in 1932. Father Divine had bought a large house in Sayville on the south shore of Long Island. On Sundays flocks of the faithful from Harlem gathered there for some joyous prayer sessions. The white neighbors objected. Father Divine was arrested for disturbing the peace and conducting a public nuisance. This event was picked up by the national press. Father Divine was pictured as a martyr to racial prejudice. On trial, the jury found Father Divine guilty as charged. Some of Divine's partisans warned the judge that if he sent Divine to jail something terrible would happen to him. The judge, unheeding, gave Divine the maximum sentence of a year in jail. Three days later, perhaps by sheer coincidence, the judge keeled over and died. "When the warden and the guards found out about it in the middle of the night," writes Henry Louis Gates, Jr., "they raced to Father Divine's cell and woke him up. Father Divine, they said, your judge just dropped dead of a heart attack. Without missing a beat, Father Divine lifted his head and told them: 'I *hated* to do it.'" Gates, Whose Canon Is It Anyway?, N.Y. Times, Feb. 20, 1989, §7 (Book Review), at 1, col. 1. Although the story has been questioned, its repetition established Father Divine — among the believers — as an authentic voice of God.

Father Divine left New York in 1942 and retired to an estate in Philadelphia. His apparent powers of retribution faded. Judge Desmond, who wrote the opinion in *Latham*, died in 1987, at the age of 91. — Eds.

Nothing is better settled than that, on such a motion as this, all the averments of the attacked pleading are taken as true. For present purposes, then, we have a case where one possessed of a large property and having already made a will leaving it to certain persons, expressed an intent to make a new testament to contain legacies to other persons, attempted to carry out that intention by having a new will drawn which contained a large legacy to those others, but was, by means of misrepresentations, undue influence, force, and indeed, murder, prevented, by the beneficiaries named in the existing will, from signing the new one. Plaintiffs say that those facts, if proven, would entitle them to a judicial declaration, which their prayer for judgment demands, that defendants, taking under the already probated will, hold what they have so taken as constructive trustees for plaintiffs, whom decedent wished to, tried to, and was kept from, benefiting.

We find in New York no decision directly answering the question as to whether or not the allegations above summarized state a case for relief in equity. But reliable texts, and cases elsewhere, see 98 A.L.R. 477 et seq., answer it in the affirmative. Leading writers, 3 Scott on Trusts, pp. 2371-2376; 3 Bogert on Trusts and Trustees, part 1, §§473-474, 498, 499; 1 Perry on Trusts and Trustees [7th ed.], pp. 265, 371, in one form or another, state the law of the subject to be about as it is expressed in comment i under section 184 of the Restatement of the Law of Restitution: "*Preventing revocation of will and making new will.* Where a devisee or legatee under a will already executed prevents the testator by fraud, duress or undue influence from revoking the will and executing a new will in favor of another or from making a codicil, so that the testator dies leaving the original will in force, the devisee or legatee holds the property thus acquired upon a constructive trust for the intended devisee or legatee."

A frequently-cited case is Ransdel v. Moore, 153 Ind. 393, at pages 407-408, 53 N.E. 767, at page 771, 53 L.R.A. 753, where, with listing of many authorities, the rule is given thus: "when an heir or devisee in a will prevents the testator from providing for one for whom he would have provided but for the interference of the heir or devisee, such heir or devisee will be deemed a trustee, by operation of law, of the property, real or personal, received by him from the testator's estate, to the amount or extent that the defrauded party would have received had not the intention of the deceased been interfered with. This rule applies also when an heir prevents the making of a will or deed in favor of another, and thereby inherits the property that would otherwise have been given such other person." To the same effect, see 4 Page on Wills [3d ed.], p. 961.

While there is no New York case decreeing a constructive trust on the exact facts alleged here, there are several decisions in this court which, we think, suggest such a result and none which forbids it. Matter of O'Hara's Will, 95 N.Y. 403, 47 Am. Rep. 53; Trustees of Amherst College v. Ritch, 151 N.Y. 282, 45 N.E. 876, 37 L.R.A. 305; Edson v. Bartow, 154 N.Y. 199, 48 N.E. 541, and Ahrens v. Jones, 169 N.Y. 555, 62 N.E. 666, 88 Am. St. Rep. 620, which need not be closely analyzed here as to their facts, all announce, in one form or another, the rule that, where a legatee has taken property under a will, after agreeing outside the will, to devote that property to a purpose intended and declared by the testator, equity will enforce a constructive trust to effectuate that purpose, lest there be a fraud on the testator. In Williams v. Fitch, 18 N.Y. 546, a similar result was achieved in a suit for money had and received. In each of those four cases first above cited in this paragraph, the particular fraud consisted of the legatee's failure or refusal to carry out the testator's designs, after tacitly or expressly promising so to do. But we do not think that a breach of such an engagement is the only kind of fraud which will impel equity to action. A constructive trust will be erected whenever necessary to satisfy the demands of justice. Since a constructive trust is merely "the formula through which the conscience of equity finds expression," Beatty v. Guggenheim Exploration Co., 225 N.Y. 380, 386, 122 N.E. 378, 380 . . . , its applicability is limited only by the inventiveness of men who find new ways to enrich themselves unjustly by grasping what should not belong to them. Nothing short of true and complete justice satisfies equity, and always assuming these allegations to be true, there seems no way of achieving total justice except by the procedure used here. . . .

This is not a proceeding to probate or establish the will which plaintiffs say testatrix was prevented from signing. . . . The will Mary Sheldon Lyon did sign has been probated and plaintiffs are not contesting, but proceeding on, that probate, trying to reach property which has effectively passed thereunder. . . .

We do not agree with appellants that Riggs v. Palmer, 115 N.Y. 506, 22 N.E. 188, 5 L.R.A. 340, 12 Am. St. Rep. 819, completely controls our decision here. That was the famous case where a grandson, overeager to get the remainder interest set up for him in his grand-father's will, murdered his grandsire. After the will had been probated, two daughters of the testator who, under the will, would take if the grandson should predecease testator, sued and got judgment decreeing a constructive trust in their favor. It may be, as respondents assert, that the application of Riggs v. Palmer, supra, here would benefit not plaintiffs, but this testator's distributees. We need not pass on that now. But Riggs v. Palmer, supra, is generally helpful to appellants, since it forbade the grandson profiting by his own wrong in connection with a will; and, despite an already probated will and the Decedent Estate Law, Riggs v. Palmer, supra, used the device or formula of constructive trust to right the attempted wrong, and prevent unjust enrichment. . . .

This suit cannot be defeated by any argument that to give plaintiffs judgment would be to annul those provisions of the Statute of Wills requiring due execution by the testator. Such a contention, if valid, would have required the dismissal in a number of the suits herein cited. The answer is in Ahrens v. Jones, 169 N.Y. 555, 561, 62 N.E. 666, 668, 88 Am. St. Rep. 620, supra:

> The trust does not act directly upon the will by modifying the gift, for the law requires wills to be wholly in writing; but it acts upon the gift itself as it reaches the possession of the legatee, or as soon as he is entitled to receive it. The theory is that the will has full effect by passing an absolute legacy to the legatee, and that then equity, in order to defeat fraud, raises a trust in favor of those intended to be benefited by the testator, and compels the legatee, as a trustee ex maleficio, to turn over the gift to them.

The judgment of the Appellate Division, insofar as it dismissed the complaint herein, should be reversed, and the order of Special Term affirmed, with costs in this court and in the Appellate Division.[8]

NOTES

1. Another view of the contest of Mary Sheldon Lyon's will is presented by a biographer of Father Divine, S. Harris, Father Divine 278-281 (1953). Harris says that Mary Sheldon Lyon was a devotee of Father Divine from 1938 to 1946. She reports that after lower court rulings adverse to Father Divine, a settlement was reached giving Father Divine a small fraction of the amount bequeathed him. Harris suggests that the court rulings were motivated, at least in part, by racial prejudice against Father Divine and his followers.

2. A constructive trust is sometimes said to be a "fraud-rectifying" trust. But a constructive trust may be imposed where no fraud is involved but the court thinks that unjust enrichment would result if the person retained the property. As Judge Cardozo, speaking for the Court of Appeals of New York, said: "A constructive trust is the formula through which the conscience of equity finds expression. When property has been acquired in such circumstances that the holder of the legal title may not in good conscience retain the beneficial interest, equity converts him into a trustee." Beatty v. Guggenheim Exploration Co., 225 N.Y. 380, 386, 122 N.E. 378 (1919). On constructive trusts imposed where there is interference with willmaking, see 5 A. Scott, Trusts §§489-489.6 (W. Fratcher 4th ed. 1989).

3. Observe that if, in *Latham*, a constructive trust were to be imposed

---

8. Noted in 35 Cornell L.Q. 654; 63 Harv. L. Rev. 108; 48 Mich. L. Rev. 1048; 34 Minn. L. Rev. 90; 1 Syracuse L. Rev. 146. — Eds.

on Father Divine's churches, the court would — *in effect* — be distributing property according to a completely unexecuted will, a will that Mary Lyon might never have signed or, having signed, might later revoke. Keep this in mind as you consider the cases in the next section, where courts refuse to give effect to signed wills clearly intended as wills, but defectively executed for some reason. In these cases there is far more certainty than in *Latham* that the testator intended the document to be his or her will.

4. In the *Latham* case the plaintiffs asked for a constructive trust to be imposed upon the defendants to rectify alleged fraud or undue influence. Another theory that can be used is tortious interference with an expectancy. Restatement (Second) of Torts §744B (1979) includes intentional interference with an expected inheritance or gift as a valid cause of action. This theory extends to expected inheritances the protection courts have accorded commercial expectancies, such as the prospect of obtaining employment or customers. Under this theory, the plaintiff must prove that the interference involved conduct tortious in itself, such as fraud, duress, or undue influence. See Nemeth v. Banhalmi, 125 Ill. App. 3d 938, 466 N.E.2d 977 (1984).

Use of the tortious interference theory may be conditioned on exhausting probate remedies, such as challenging the will itself. It may prove a useful theory after the time for filing a contest has expired. The theory cannot be used when the challenge is based on testator's mental incapacity. See W. McGovern, S. Kurtz & J. Rein, Wills, Trusts and Estates §14.1 at 580 (1988).

In Estate of Legeas, 210 Cal. App. 3d 385, 258 Cal. Rptr. 858 (1989), the court held that where fraud on the testator was involved, plaintiffs who sued for tortious interference with their expected inheritance could recover punitive damages from the persons committing the fraud.

A suit for tortious interference with an expectancy, or a suit to impose a constructive trust because of fraud or undue influence, is not a will contest. Therefore a no-contest clause (see supra page 163) does not apply to it.

SECTION B.   EXECUTION OF WILLS

1.   *Attested Wills*

a.   **Requirements of Due Execution**

Gulliver & Tilson, Classification of Gratuitous Transfers
51 Yale L.J. 1, 2-5, 9-10 (1941)

One fundamental proposition is that, under a legal system recognizing the individualistic institution of private property and granting to the owner the power to determine his successors in ownership, the general philosophy of the courts should favor giving effect to an intentional exercise of that power. . . .

If this objective is primary, the requirements of execution, which concern only the form of the transfer — what the transferor or others must do to make it legally effective — seem justifiable only as implements for its accomplishment, and should be so interpreted by the courts in these cases. They surely should not be revered as ends in themselves, enthroning formality over frustrated intent. Why do these requirements exist and what functions may they usefully perform? . . .

In the first place, the court needs to be convinced that the statements of the transferor were deliberately intended to effectuate a transfer. People are often careless in conversation and in informal writings. Even if the witnesses are entirely truthful and accurate, what is a court to conclude from testimony showing only that a father once stated that he wanted to give certain bonds to his son John? Does this remark indicate *finality of intention to transfer*, or rambling meditation about some future disposition. . . . Or suppose the evidence shows, without more, that a writing containing dispositive language was found among papers of the deceased at the time of his death? Does this demonstrate a deliberate transfer, or was it merely a tentative draft of some contemplated instrument, or perhaps random scribbling? . . . Dispositive effect should not be given to statements which were not intended to have that effect. The formalities of transfer therefore generally require the performance of some ceremonial for the purpose of impressing the transferor with the significance of his statements and thus justifying the court in reaching the conclusion, if the ceremonial is performed, that they were deliberately intended to be operative. This purpose of the requirements of transfer may conveniently be termed their *ritual function.*

Secondly, the requirements of transfer may increase the reliability of the proof presented to the court. The extent to which the quantity and effect of available evidence should be restricted by qualitative standards is, of course, a controversial matter. Perhaps any and all evidence should be freely admitted in reliance on such safeguards as cross-examination, the oath, the proficiency of handwriting experts, and the discriminating judgment of courts and juries. On the other hand, the inaccuracies of oral testimony owing to lapse of memory, misinterpretation of the statements of others, and the more or less unconscious coloring of recollection in the light of the personal interest of the witness or of those with whom he is friendly, are very prevalent; and the possibilities of perjury and forgery cannot be disregarded. These difficulties are entitled to especially serious consideration in prescribing requirements for gratuitous transfers, because the issue of the validity of the transfer is almost always raised after the alleged transferor is dead, and therefore the main actor is usually unavailable to testify, or to clarify or contradict other evidence concerning his all-important intention. At any rate, whatever the ideal solution may be, it seems quite clear that the existing requirements of transfer emphasize the purpose of supplying satisfactory evidence to the court. This purpose may conveniently be termed their *evidentiary function*.

Thirdly, some of the requirements of the statutes of wills have the stated prophylactic purpose of safeguarding the testator, at the time of the execution of the will, against undue influence or other forms of imposition. . . . It may conveniently be termed the *protective function*. . . . This [protective function] is difficult to justify under modern conditions. . . . The protective provisions first appeared in the Statute of Frauds, from which they have been copied, perhaps sometimes blindly, by American legislatures. While there is little direct evidence, it is a reasonable assumption that, in the period prior to the Statute of Frauds, wills were usually executed on the death bed. A testator in this unfortunate situation may well need special protection against imposition. His powers of normal judgment and of resistance to improper influences may be seriously affected by a decrepit physical condition, a weakened mentality, or a morbid or unbalanced state of mind. Furthermore, in view of the propinquity of death, he would not have as much time or opportunity as would the usual inter vivos transferor to escape from the consequences of undue influence or other forms of imposition. Under modern conditions, however, wills are probably executed by most testators in the prime of life and in the presence of attorneys. [Emphasis added.]

Professor Langbein suggests that in addition to serving the ritual, evidentiary, and protective functions identified by Gulliver and Tilson, the formalities requirements of the Statute of Wills serve a channeling function. They create a safe harbor, which provides the testator with assurance that his wishes will be carried out.

> Compliance with the Wills Act formalities for executing witnessed wills results in considerable uniformity in the organization, language, and content of most wills. Courts are seldom left to puzzle whether the document was meant to be a will. . . .
>
> The standardization of testation achieved under the Wills Act also benefits the testator. He does not have to devise for himself a mode of communicating his testamentary wishes to the court, and to worry whether it will be effective. Instead, he has every inducement to comply with the Wills Act formalities. The court can process his estate routinely, because his testament is conventionally and unmistakably expressed and evidenced.

The lowered costs of routinized judicial administration benefit the estate and its ultimate distributees. [Langbein, Substantial Compliance with the Wills Act, 88 Harv. L. Rev. 489, 494 (1975).]

The formal requirements for execution of wills vary considerably in detail from state to state. Some of these variations result from the fact that England had two basic acts governing the execution of wills, the Statute of Frauds (1677) and the Wills Act (1837). Prior to enactment of the Statute of Frauds, personal property was transferable at death by either a written or oral will, perhaps given to the priest as part of the last confession.[9] Land was made devisable "by last will and testament in writing," by the Statute of Wills in 1540, but the statute required no signature or other formalities. The Statute of Frauds, coming 137 years later, required a written will signed by the testator in the presence of three witnesses for testamentary disposition of land. Less stringent formalities, which need not concern us here, applied to testamentary dispositions of personalty. Having different requirements for wills of realty and wills of personalty proved unsatisfactory, and in 1837 England passed a Wills Act requiring the same formalities for all wills.

The formalities required by the Wills Act of 1837 were stricter than those required by the Statute of Frauds. Under the Statute of Frauds the three witnesses did not have to be present at the same time; each could attest separately. And the testator did not have to sign at any particular place on the document. The Wills Act reduced the number of necessary witnesses to two, but it provided that the witnesses must both be present when the will is signed or acknowledged; in addition, the will must be signed "at the foot or end" of the will. (The exact language of the Wills Act is set out in the court's opinion in In re Groffman, *infra* page 183.) These two additional requirements of the Wills Act have given rise to much litigation.

Some states copied the English Statute of Frauds, others copied the Wills Act of 1837. In a few states the legislature added a requirement that the testator must "publish" the will by declaring before the witnesses

---

9. A few states permit nuncupative (oral) wills under very limited circumstances. Typically, these wills can be made only during a person's "last sickness" and can be used only to devise personal property of small value (say, up to $1,000); the will must be uttered before three persons, who must reduce the declaration to writing within a specified period. Military personnel and mariners at sea are, in some states, granted the privilege of making an oral will under limited circumstances. Oral wills admitted to probate are extremely rare. See Kay v. Sandler, 718 S.W.2d 872 (Tex. 1986), strictly construing nuncupative will statute. For a list of state nuncupative will statutes, see Restatement (Second) of Property, Donative Transfers §33.1, Statutory Note (Tent. Draft No. 12, 1989).

that the instrument is his will. The Uniform Probate Code generally adopts the less strict requirements of the Statute of Frauds but reduces the required number of witnesses to two.[10]

Uniform Probate Code (1983)

§2-502   [EXECUTION]

Except as provided for holographic wills, . . . every will shall be in writing signed by the testator or in the testator's name by some other person in the testator's presence and by his direction, and shall be signed by at least 2 persons each of whom witnessed either the signing or the testator's acknowledgment of the signature or of the will.

See supp
p. 27

In re Groffman
Probate, Divorce, and Admiralty Division
High Court of Justice, England, 1968
[1969] 1 W.L.R. 733, [1969] 2 All E.R. 108

SIMON, Pres.   In this case the executors of a will dated September 1, 1964, propound it in solemn form of law. The will is of the late Mr. Charles Groffman, who died on April 11, 1967. The first plaintiff, being the first executor named, is the son of the deceased testator. The second plaintiff, Mr. Block, is the second executor named and is the solicitor who prepared the will. The defendant, who claims that the will was not properly executed, is the widow of the deceased; and in the circumstances, the estate being of the region of £8,000 or £9,000 in total, she takes the whole of it in the event of an intestacy. The estate consists partly of what was the matrimonial home (as to just over half the total estate). That house belonged to the deceased. There was also a building society account held by the deceased; the defendant claims that that was held jointly with her, or that at least she has some interest in it.

property

The defendant was the second wife of the deceased. They married about 1948, the deceased being a widower and the defendant a widow. The marriage was childless; but the deceased had two children, the

facts

---

10. Formerly a number of states required three witnesses. Now only Vermont requires three witnesses rather than two. Vt. Stat. Ann. tit 14, §5 (1974). Louisiana requires two witnesses plus a notary. La. Rev. Stat. §9.2442 (Supp. 1989).

For a list of state witnessing requirements, see Restatement (Second) of Property, supra, §33.1, Statutory Note.

first plaintiff and a daughter who is in America. The defendant has a daughter by her first marriage, a Miss Berenson.

Most of the relevant events took place in 1964; and I do not think any witness can really be expected to remember the details, even Mr. Block the solicitor who prepared the will. Indeed, I think that many of the witnesses now think that they can remember more than they actually can. But the rough outline of events was this.

Sometime in the summer of 1964, the deceased went to Mr. Block, the solicitor. He was senior partner in the firm of Maxwell and Lawson. The deceased was not a regular client of his, but had been recommended to him by another client. He gave instructions for a will and the instructions were put into a draft, which is exhibit 1 to the plaintiffs' affidavit of scripts. That appointed the executors and trustees; it devises the house to the trustees on trust to allow the defendant to have the use and enjoyment of this during her lifetime. It also bequeaths all chattels to her for use during her life. Then the residue — what was not disposed by the dispositions I have referred to — was disposed of in this way. It was to be divided between the first plaintiff, the daughter in America, and the step-daughter, Miss Berenson. There was in that draft a clause dealing with the advancement of the residuary estate in the interest of the defendant, which subsequently disappeared. That draft was handed by the second plaintiff to the deceased, who took it away to discuss it with his son, the first plaintiff. As a result of that discussion, in which the first plaintiff made no comment as to the dispositions, the draft was brought back to the second plaintiff; some nine corrections were made and the advancement clause to which I have referred was cancelled. The document as amended was then typed out, engrossed ready for execution.

The second plaintiff told the deceased very generally what was the right method of execution; but realising that the deceased was an intelligent man relied in the main on the attestation clause to be a guide to the deceased. That was in the usual form, and it seems to me to have been a perfectly reasonable course for the second plaintiff to have taken.

The deceased and his wife were close family friends of a Mr. and Mrs. David Block and a Mr. and Mrs. Julius Leigh. They spent at least the summer holidays of 1964 together, and it was their custom to meet alternately at their respective houses, generally on a Tuesday night. This was because Mr. Leigh was a taxi driver and the Tuesday was his free evening. On a number of occasions after the engrossed document was handed to the deceased, he mentioned the matter to Mr. David Block, saying that he would like Mr. Block and Mr. Leigh to be witnesses to his will. Mr. Block, in a very usual reaction, said: "There's no hurry about that; there's plenty of time to be thinking about that sort of thing" — or words to that effect.

The parties met on a Tuesday evening in September, 1964. That may have been September 1, which is the date that the will bears. They met at the house of Mr. and Mrs. David Block, and the will purports to have been executed that evening in circumstances to which I shall have to refer. It is sufficient to say that, as I have already indicated, the attestation clause is the normal one, and Mr. Block and Mr. Leigh signed as attesting witnesses. The document also bears what is admittedly the signature of the deceased, and the date, September 1, 1964.

I am perfectly satisfied that the document was intended by the deceased to be executed as his will and that its contents represent his testamentary intentions.

After he had obtained the signatures of his friends, he took the will and handed it to his son, the first plaintiff. He appears to have referred to it to Mr. Block on a number of occasions thereafter; but nothing turns on that, since the only question that arises in this suit is as to the execution of the document.

The deceased died, as I have said, on April 11, 1967. The funeral was on April 13, and thereafter the widow and the first plaintiff observed a period of ritual mourning, during which there was no discussion of any testamentary instrument or disposition. At the end of that period, within a matter of a few days, the first plaintiff handed the document to the second plaintiff. At some time towards the end of April, and again within a month or two, there were meetings between the plaintiffs and the defendant; . . . the defendant showed considerable dissatisfaction with the dispositions in the purported will. She used the words, "My Charlie wouldn't have done that to me." . . .

As I have said, the only question that arises for the determination of the court is whether this will was duly executed. That takes me back to the occasion in September, 1964, which may have been September 1 — the episode at the house of Mr. and Mrs. David Block.

Mr. Leigh, the second purported attesting witness, has suffered a disabling ailment; and his evidence has been placed before me only in the form of a statement, dated August 22, 1967, which was obviously taken for the purposes of litigation. It has, therefore, not been cross-examined to. Since I am satisfied that the document propounded represents the deceased's testamentary dispositions and intentions and since the document is in regular form, a very strong presumption arises in its favour. If I merely had the statement of Mr. Leigh and the other witnesses, except for Mr. David Block and his son, Stewart, I should pronounce for the validity of this will. But that is not all I have.

Mr. David Block and his son, Stewart, seem to me to be credible and reliable witnesses. I have it in mind that the evidence they have given contradicts the statement in the attestation clause. I have it in mind that they are friends of the defendant and desire her to succeed in this action. I have it in mind that there is some discrepancy between the evidence that they respectively gave, though no more than I should expect in perfectly honest witnesses trying to recollect what happened over four years ago. I accept the evidence of Mr. David Block, borne out as it is by Stewart, and indeed by what Mr. Leigh says in his proferred statement.

I think that what happened on the evening in question was this. I have already said that the deceased had previously indicated to Mr. David Block that he would like him and Mr. Leigh to witness his will. On the evening in question, which was in all probability a Tuesday and possibly September 1, 1964, the deceased and the defendant, Mr. and Mrs. David Block and Mr. and Mrs. Julius Leigh, were all together in the lounge of the Blocks' house. Mr. Block's son, Stewart, was also in the house, though not in the lounge at the commencement of the transaction to which I refer.

During the course of the evening, when the coffee table, the only available table, was laden with coffee cups and cakes, the deceased said words to this effect, which he addressed to Mr. David Block and Mr. Julius Leigh: "I should like you now to witness my will." I think he may well have gestured towards his coat. The will in question as engrossed was of the usual double foolscap folded in two and then in four, so as to be a convenient size for putting in an inside pocket of a coat. That is where it was on this occasion. However, it was not taken out by the deceased in the lounge. At the most, he gestured towards the pocket where it was. There seems to me to be an overwhelming inference that his signature was on the document at that time. There being no convenient space for the execution in the lounge, Mr. Block led the deceased into the adjacent dining room. That was just across a small hall. There the deceased took the document from his pocket, unfolded it, and asked Mr. Block to sign, giving his occupation and address. The signature, as I have already said, was on the document at the time and was visible to Mr. Block at the time; indeed, he noted this. Mr. Leigh, who seems to have been somewhat cumbrous in his movements, was left behind. He was not there when Mr. Block signed his name. Mr. Block then returned to the lounge, leaving the deceased in the dining room. He said to Mr. Leigh words to this effect: "It is your turn now, don't keep him waiting, it's cold in there." Mr. Leigh then went into the dining room and, according to his statement, and as is indeed borne out by the form of the document that we now have, signed his name beneath that of Mr. David Block. In the meantime Mr. Block had remained in the lounge.

In other words, we are left with this situation — that the signature of the deceased was on the document before he asked either Mr. Block or Mr. Leigh to act as his witnesses; that Mr. Block signed his name in the presence of the deceased but not in the presence of Mr. Leigh; and that Mr. Leigh signed his name in the presence of the deceased but not in the presence of Mr. Block. The deceased did not sign in the presence of either of them; and the question is whether he acknowledged his signature in the presence of both of them.

As must appear from the fact that I have been satisfied that the document does represent the testamentary intentions of the deceased, I would very gladly find in its favour; but I am bound to apply the statute, which has been enacted by Parliament for good reason. The provision with which I am concerned is section 9 of the Wills Act, 1837. That reads:

> [N]o will shall be valid unless it shall be in writing and executed in manner hereinafter mentioned; (that is to say,) it shall be signed at the foot or end thereof by the testator, or by some other person in his presence and by his direction; and such signature shall be made or acknowledged by the testator in the presence of two or more witnesses present at the same time, and such witnesses shall attest and shall subscribe the will in the presence of the testator, but no form of attestation shall be necessary.

STATUTE

The question, as I have indicated, is whether the testator acknowledged his signature in the presence of Mr. Block and Mr. Leigh, those two witnesses being present at the same time. The matter has been considered by a number of eminent judges, starting with Dr. Lushington, and followed by the members of the Court of Appeal in Blake v. Blake (1882) 7 P.D. 102 and Daintree v. Butcher and Fasulo (1888) 13 P.D. 102. It seems presumptuous to say that I agree with their construction of the statute; but it appears to me to be clear. In any event I am bound by what was decided by the Court of Appeal, even if I were to disagree with it, which I do not. It seems to me that the authorities establish that the signature of the testator must be on the document at the time of acknowledgment (as I think it was), and that the witness saw or had an opportunity of seeing the signature at that time, in other words, at the time of acknowledgment.

In Blake v. Blake, 7 P.D. 102, Sir George Jessel M.R. gave a judgment in which he said, at p.107: "The question, then, arises whether the testatrix acknowledged her signature before the witnesses." That was a case where the testatrix had signed and had asked two attesting witnesses to add their signature, but had covered her own signature with blotting paper, so they could not see it. Sir George Jessel in those circumstances posed the question, at p.107-8:

"What is in law a sufficient acknowledgment under the statute?" — he answers — "What I take to be the law is correctly laid down in Jarman on Wills, 4th ed. p.108, in the following terms: 'There is no sufficient acknowledgment unless the witnesses either saw or might have seen the signature, not even though the testator should expressly declare that the paper to be attested by them is his will';" . . . He quotes Dr. Lushington in Hudson v. Parker (1844) 1 Rob. Eccl. 14, at p.25 "What do the words import but this? 'Here is my name written, I acknowledge that name so written to have been written by me; bear witness.'" . . .

In deference, however, to the interest and vigour of Mr. Craig's argument, I must deal with various alternative ways in which he puts his case. He says, first, that *Blake* is to be distinguished in that there was a deliberate concealment by the testatrix of her signature, which, he says, is the very negation of acknowledgment. But there is nothing at all in the judgments of Blake v. Blake, 7 P.D. 102, to indicate that that was the ratio decidendi, which was indeed afterwards explained in Daintree v. Butcher and Fasulo, 13 P.D. 102.

Second, he says, there is sufficient acknowledgment if the attesting witnesses had an opportunity to see the will or the signature or both if they had wished to. Opportunity to see, says Mr. Craig, does not mean physical opportunity: it means that they could have seen if they expressed the desire to see. If that were so, it seems to me that Blake v. Blake, 7 P.D. 102, could not have been decided in the way it was. The attesting witnesses could have asked the testatrix to remove the blotting paper, just as in the present case Mr. Block or Mr. Leigh could have asked the testator to remove the paper from his pocket and show it to them, or at least show them his signature.

There is, however, one final argument. Having submitted originally that there was a sufficient acknowledgment to satisfy the statute in what happened in the lounge, when admittedly both attesting witnesses were present, Mr. Craig puts his argument alternatively in this way. He says that what happened was all part of one res gestae — there was no break in the continuity of the transaction. Both attesting witnesses had an opportunity of seeing the signature at the time they signed the will, which was within a matter of seconds of each other and within a matter of seconds of being asked to witness it. On that argument the acknowledgment started in the lounge but ended in the dining room. Now, it seems to me that there is one fatal flow in that argument; namely, that if the acknowledgment was not completed until the dining room, then there was no completed acknowledgment in the presence of both attesting witnesses being present at the same time.

In the end, therefore, although I would gladly accede to the arguments for the plaintiffs if I could consistently with my judicial duty, in my view there was no acknowledgment or signature by the testator in the presence of two or more witnesses present at the same time; and I am bound to pronounce against this will. . . .

Order accordingly.[11]

---

11. Noted in 114 Sol. J. 198; 85 L.Q. Rev. 462. — Eds.

NOTES AND PROBLEMS

1. Specifically, why was Mr. Groffman's will denied probate? What formalities required by the Wills Act were not satisfied?

2. Were the ritual, evidentiary, and protective policies basing the Statute of Wills satisfied by the manner in which Groffman's will was executed and attested? If so, should Groffman's will have been denied probate? What policies were served by the court's decision denying probate of the will?

3. If Mr. Block, the solicitor who drew the will (to be distinguished from Mr. David Block, the witness), were sued by the beneficiaries named in the will, would he be liable? In Ross v. Caunters, [1980] 1 Ch. 297, a solicitor prepared a will and sent it to the testator with instructions for execution but did not warn the testator that it should not be witnessed by the spouse of a beneficiary. The will was witnessed by the spouse of the beneficiary, who, under English law, was deprived of her legacy. The court held that the solicitor was liable in malpractice to the beneficiary. Recent cases in the United States have held the lawyer supervising the will execution ceremony liable for faulty execution, though some states still retain the privity barrier. See Auric v. Continental Casualty Co., 111 Wis. 2d 507, 331 N.W.2d 325 (1983); Simon v. Zipperstein, 32 Ohio St. 3d 74, 512 N.E.2d 636 (1987); Johnston, Legal Malpractice in Estate Planning, 67 Iowa L. Rev. 629 (1982).

4. In England and in many American states the requirement that the witnesses sign in the "presence" of the testator is satisfied only if the testator is capable of seeing the witnesses in the act of signing. Under this *line of sight test,* the testator does not actually have to see the witnesses sign but must be able to see them were the testator to look. 1 T. Jarman, Wills 138 (8th ed. 1951). An exception is made for a blind person. In some states the line of sight rule has been rejected in favor of the *conscious presence test.* Under this test the witness is in the presence of the testator if the testator, through sight, hearing, or general consciousness of events, comprehends that the witness is in the act of signing. See Chaffin, Execution, Revocation, and Revalidation of Wills, 11 Ga. L. Rev. 297, 318-322 (1977).

Suppose that *T*'s attorney takes *T*'s will to *T*'s home, where *T* signs the will and the attorney attests as a witness. The attorney returns to her office with the will and has her secretary call *T* on the phone. By telephone, *T* requests the secretary to witness his will; the secretary then signs as an attesting witness. Can the will be probated? See In re Jefferson, 349 So. 2d 1032 (Miss. 1977); In re McGurrin, 113 Idaho 341, 743 P.2d 994 (Ida. App. 1987) (involving UPC §2-502).

5. A lawyer prepared a will for Patrick Mangeri, who was very ill. Underneath the signature line was typed "Patrick Mangeri." The will

was taken to Mangeri in his hospital room. Mangeri signed with an "X" because his hands were too shaky to write his name. The two attesting witnesses then signed. Can the will be probated? See Estate of Mangeri, 55 Cal. App. 3d 76, 127 Cal. Rptr. 438 (1976). But cf. Estate of Kajut, 2 Pa. Fiduc. 2d 197, 22 Pa. D. & C.3d 123 (Orphans' Ct. 1981); N.Y. Est., Powers & Trusts Law §3-2.1(a)(1)(c) (1981); Annots., 98 A.L.R.2d 824, 841 (1964). Suppose that Mangeri had written a shaky "Pat" rather than an "X." Same result? In re Young, 60 Ohio App. 2d 390, 397 N.E.2d 1223 (1978), held that the letter *J* subscribed by Joseph Young was sufficient when Joseph was partially paralyzed from a stroke.

6.   Statutes in several states have adopted the Wills Act requirement that the testator sign the will "at the foot or end thereof." Suppose that a typewritten will is found on which is written in testator's handwriting, below the testator's signature and above the witnesses' signatures, the following line: "I give Karen my diamond ring." Is the will entitled to probate? See N.Y. Est., Powers & Trusts Law §3-2.1(a)(1) (1981); Annot., 44 A.L.R.3d 701 (1972).

7.   Emma Amelia Beadle told two friends, Mr. and Mrs. Mayes, that she wanted them to help her make a will. She dictated her testamentary wishes to Mrs. Mayes, who copied them down on a single sheet of paper. Emma then signed the paper in the top right-hand corner and Mr. Mayes, but not Mrs. Mayes, signed as a witness. The paper was then placed in an envelope on which Emma wrote the words "My last will and testament, E.A. Beadle, to Charley and Maisy." Emma sealed it, and Mr. Mayes then wrote on the back of the envelope, "We certify that the contents of this letter was written in the presence of ourselves," and then Mr. and Mrs. Mayes signed the envelope. Emma kept the envelope, which was found among her papers at death. Is the will entitled to probate?

In Re Beadle, [1974] 1 All E.R. 493 (Ch.), the court held that (1) the signature in the top right-hand corner was not at the end, (2) the signature "E.A. Beadle" on the envelope was not intended to be a signature to the will but merely an identification of contents, and (3) in any case, the signatures of the two witnesses on the envelope were not a valid attestation since they merely intended to signify that, although the paper inside was signed by only one of them, both were present when the document had been written and signed by the testator. Hence the document was denied probate. Accord, In re Kretz' Estate, 410 Pa. 590, 189 A.2d 239 (1963).

8.   Suppose that the testator videotapes her will before witnesses. Does this comply with the requirement that the will be a "signed writing"? See Estate of Reed, 672 P.2d 829 (Wyo. 1983); Nash, A Videowill: Safe and Sure, 70 A.B.A.J. 70 (1984).

In re Estate of Peters
Supreme Court of New Jersey, 1987
107 N.J. 263, 526 A.2d 1005

HANDLER, J.

see p. 28 supp

I

Joseph Skrok commenced an action in the Middlesex County Surrogate's Court, seeking the admission to probate of a will executed by Conrad Peters, Skrok's step-father. The will designated Skrok as an executor. The Surrogate denied admission to probate of the proffered will for the reason that it did not bear the signature of two witnesses. This caused the intestacy of the decedent's estate, there apparently being no next-of-kin of the decedent. [Skrok then brought suit in Superior Court asking for an order requiring the Surrogate to probate the will.] Because the estate in intestacy would escheat to the State, the trial court directed the State to show cause why the proffered will should not be admitted to probate. The State then brought a motion for summary judgment to deny probate of the proffered will.

The testimony at the hearing on the motion disclosed that Conrad Peters, the testator, died on March 28, 1985. Prior to his death, Peters had been married to Marie Peters (formerly Gall); they had no children during their marriage. Marie Peters had been married once before, and had one son, Joseph Skrok, during her previous marriage. Marie Peters died on March 23, 1985, approximately 126 hours before the testator, so that at the time of his death Conrad Peters had no surviving relatives.

The circumstances surrounding the execution of the will are important. In December 1983, the testator was in the hospital for treatment following a stroke. While Peters was hospitalized, a will was prepared for his signature by Sophia M. Gall, Peters' sister-in-law. Ms. Gall had prepared an identical will for her sister, Marie Peters. The wills were drawn up at the request of Marie Peters, who apparently had discussed the need for these wills with her husband in mid-December, 1983. Although Conrad Peters was physically disabled as a result of the stroke, he suffered no mental disability; accordingly, his competency to make a will has not been questioned.

The dispositive provisions of the two wills complemented each other. Each provided for the distribution of the entire estate, after payment of debts and funeral expenses, to the surviving spouse. Both appointed the surviving spouse as executor. Additionally, both wills named Joseph Skrok, Marie Peters' son, as the alternate beneficiary and alternate executor.

On December 30, 1983, Sophia Gall came to the testator's hospital room with her husband and Marie Peters. Ms. Gall read the provisions of the will to Mr. Peters; he then assented to it, and signed it. Although Ms. Gall, her husband, and Mrs. Peters were present at the time, none of these individuals signed the will as witnesses. It was the apparent intention of Ms. Gall, who was an insurance agent and notary, to wait for the arrival of two employees from her office, who were to serve as witnesses.

When those two employees, Mary Elizabeth Gall and Kristen Spock, arrived at the hospital, Sophia Gall reviewed the will briefly with the testator, who, in the presence of the two women, again indicated his approval, and acknowledged his signature. Ms. Gall then signed the will as a notary, but neither of the two intended witnesses placed her signature on the will. Ms. Gall folded the will and handed it to Mrs. Peters. Conrad Peters died fifteen months later, on March 28, 1985. At the time of his death the will was still not signed by either of the witnesses.

At the Probate Court proceeding, Ms. Gall testified as to why the two intended witnesses never signed the will:

> As I say, just because of the emotional aspect of the whole situation, my sister-in-law was there, my husband, her brother was there, myself and the two girls. There were six of us. The other patients had visitors. It got to be kind of — I don't known how to explain it, just the situation, and the girls were in a hurry to get back to the office, because they had to leave the office.
>
> I honestly think in their minds, when they saw me sign the will, they thought that is why they were there. And we folded up the will, gave it [to] my sister-in-law. It was just that type of situation.

In an affidavit executed on June 28, 1985, Ms. Gall explained that her failure to obtain the signatures of the two witnesses was the result of her being "affected emotionally by [the testator's] appearance."

The trial court found that the proferred instrument "was properly executed" because . . . the notary could be considered a subscribing witness and . . . it had "equitable powers" to . . . order[] that the second witness, also present at the December 30, 1983, execution ceremony, be permitted to sign the document. Pursuant to this order, Skrok commenced an action in the Surrogate's Court, seeking to have the proferred will, now bearing the additional signature of a witness, admitted to probate in common form. Letters Testamentary were issued to Skrok.

The Appellate Division reversed the trial court and remanded the case for entry of judgment dismissing the action. In re Estate of Peters, 210 N.J. Super. 295 (1986). The court held that the Probate Court was

without power to cure a will's failure to comply with the statutory
formalities. . . .

II

The operative statute governing the validity of the execution of a will
is N.J.S.A. 3B:3-2. The statute prescribes the formalities necessary for
the proper execution of a will. It requires (1) that the will be in writing
and (2) that it be signed by the testator (or by someone in his presence
and at his direction). It also requires that a will be signed by at least
two persons who witnessed either (a) the signing or (b) the testator's
acknowledgement of his signature or of the will.

The narrow issue in this case is whether the statute authorizes a
person who has witnessed the testator's execution or acknowledgement
of the will to sign the will as a witness after the testator has died; the
broader issue is whether the statute places any limits on how long after
the testator's execution or acknowledgement of the will a witness may
affix his or her signature. These questions are necessarily determined
by what the Legislature intended by the formalities that are prescribed
in N.J.S.A. 3B:3-2, and by the extent to which the Legislature intended
that these formalities be strictly followed.

A

Wills are solely the creatures of positive law. "The right to make a
will . . . is derived from the statute." A. Clapp, 5 New Jersey Practice,
Wills and Administration §41, at 173 (3d ed. 1982). . . .

Historically, courts have held that, as statutory creations, wills must
adhere to the requirements prescribed by the statute. Failure to comply
with the statutory requirements has long resulted in a will being declared
invalid, no matter how accurately the document may have reflected the
wishes of the testator. See Murray v. Lewis, 94 N.J. Eq. 681, 684 (Ch.
Div. 1923).

This policy of construing the wills statute's formalities strictly came
to be criticized for producing inequitable results and for encouraging,
in effect, the circumvention of the wills statutes through such means as
conveyances in joint tenancy, revocable trusts, tentative or "Totten"
trusts, and cash value life insurance policies. See Langbein, "Substantial
Compliance With the Wills Acts," 88 Harv. L. Rev. 489, 503-09 (1975)
("the flexibility and comparative informality of the will substitutes . . .
is making the rule of literal compliance with Wills Act formalities ever
more incongruous and indefensible"); see also Langbein, "The Nonprobate Revolution and the Future of the Law of Succession," 97 Harv.
L. Rev. 1108 (1984) (describing will substitutes). The perception of
inequitable results, coupled with the decline of wills, relative to other
instruments, as means of devising property after death, led the National

Conference of Commissioners of Uniform State Laws and the American Bar Association, in August 1969, to propose adoption of the Uniform Probate Code. The Code's approach was not to encourage courts to abandon their strict construction of the formalities prescribed, but rather to reduce the number and refine the scope of those formalities so that, if strict construction were employed, "inequities" in individual cases would occur less frequently and would be justified by the importance of the interests protected by the formal requirements that were retained. See Love, "Imperfect Gifts as Declarations of Trust: An Unapologetic Anomaly," 67 Ky. L.J. 309, 329-31 (1978-79) ("The bare-bones formalities that remain [in the UPC] for a valid witnessed will are those that most laymen would associate with a will"). Thus, the General Comment to Part Five of the Code states:

> If the will is to be restored to its role as the major instrument for disposition of wealth at death, its execution must be kept simple. The basic intent of these sections is to validate the will whenever possible. To this end, . . . formalities for a written and attested will are kept to a minimum. . . .

A second approach to reform was proposed in 1975 by Professor John Langbein, in "Substantial Compliance With the Wills Act," supra, 88 Harv. L. Rev. 489. According to Professor Langbein, "[t]he finding of a formal defect should lead not to automatic invalidity, but to a further inquiry: does the noncomplying document express the decedent's testamentary intent, and does its form sufficiently approximate Wills Act formality to enable the court to conclude that it serves the purposes of the Wills Act?" Id. Thus, while addressing the same ills, the Uniform Probate Code and the substantial compliance doctrine endorse different remedies; the Uniform Probate Code reduces the number and refines the scope of formalities, whereas the "substantial compliance" approach relaxes the extent to which whatever formalities exist must be honored. One approach addresses the formalities themselves; the other addresses the formalism with which they are construed. As Professor Langbein put it,

> [w]hereas the argument [for substantial compliance] is for a rule of reduced formalism in enforcing whatever formalities the Wills Act requires, the UPC approach is to reduce the number of required formalities. Although both techniques work generally in the same direction, they will produce different results in many cases if the UPC's "minimal formalities" are to be enforced with the same literalism as before. [Id. at 512.]

This state's former statute, N.J.S.A. 3A:3-2 (repealed), was rife with the formal encrustations that had inspired the proposals for reform. It required that the testator sign his will (or acknowledge his signature) before two witnesses, both of whom were required to be present at the same time; that he declare the document to be his will; and that the witnesses subscribe the will in the presence of the testator. See In re Hale's Will, 21 N.J. 284, 295-97 (1956). The Legislature responded to the infirmities of the statute by enacting the Probate Reform Act of 1978, L. 1977, c. 412 (effective September 1, 1978), the current statute. . . .

B

It cannot be overemphasized that the Legislature, in reforming the Wills statute, did not dispense with the requirement that the execution of a will be witnessed. Indeed, it is arguable that as the number of formalities have been reduced, those retained by the Legislature have assumed even greater importance, and demand at least the degree of scrupulous adherence required under the former statute.

It is generally acknowledged that witnesses serve two functions, which can be characterized as "observatory" and "signatory." A. Clapp, 5 N.J. Practice, supra, §50 at 192. The current statute, N.J.S.A. 3B:3-2, clearly requires the fulfillment of both functions; a testamentary writing proffered as a will, in the statute's terms, "shall be *signed* by at least two persons each of whom *witnesses* either the signing or the testator's acknowledgement of the signature or of the will." Id. (emphasis added).

The observatory function consists of the actual witnessing — the direct and purposeful observation — of the testator's signature to or acknowledgement of the will. It entails more than physical presence or a casual or general awareness of the will's execution by the testator; the witnessing of a will is a concomitant condition and an integral part of the execution of the will.

The signatory function consists of the signing of the will by the persons who were witnesses. The signatory function may not have the same substantive significance as the observatory function, but it is not simply a ministerial or precatory requirement. While perhaps complementary to the observatory function, it is nonetheless a necessary element of the witnessing requirement. The witness' signature has significance as an evidentiary requirement or probative element, serving both to demonstrate and to confirm the fulfillment of the observatory function by the witnesses. There is nothing, therefore, to suggest that in retaining the requirement that a will's execution be witnessed, the Legislature meant to imply that either witnessing function is dispensable. The statutory policy to reduce the required formalities to a minimum should not, in our view, be construed to sanction relaxation of the formalities the statute retained.

Resolution of the issue of when the witnesses must sign the will in relation to their observations of the execution of the will by the testator follows from the purpose of the requirement that the will be signed. Because, as noted, the signatory function serves an evidentiary purpose, the signatures of the witnesses would lose probative worth and tend to fail of this purpose if the witnesses were permitted to sign at a time remote from their required observations as witnesses. Consequently, because the witnessing requirement of the statute consists of the dual acts of observation and signature, it is sensible to infer that both acts should occur either contemporaneously with or in close succession to one another.

We are thus satisfied that it would be unreasonable to construe the statute as placing no time limit on the requirement of obtaining two witnesses' signatures. By implication, the statute requires that the signatures of witnesses be affixed to a will within a reasonable period of time from the execution of the will. . . .

Given our conclusion that the witnesses must sign within a reasonable time from observation, the question is whether the time period involved here — in which the testator died with the will still unsigned by witnesses fifteen months after the will was witnessed — is reasonable. Two factors in this case affect our determination of reasonableness: (1) the fact that the witness signed after the testator's death; and (2) the fact that some eighteen months passed between the observatory and signatory functions of the witness. . . .

In this case, the Appellate Division declined to adopt a bright-line rule under N.J.S.A. 3B:3-2 requiring witnesses' signatures before the death of the testator. It expressly left open the question raised by In re Leo's Will, 12 Fla. Supp. 61 (Fla. Dade Co. Cir. Ct. 1958), concerning the validity of a will where a testator has died moments after execution, but before the witnesses have had an opportunity to sign. In re Estate of Peters, supra, 210 N.J. Super, at 305. We endorse this conclusion. There may indeed be cases in which the affixation of witnesses' signatures after the testator's death would be reasonable, particularly if the witnesses were somehow precluded from signing before the testator died. This case, however, does not present such a situation. Even if one accepts the testimony that the emotional trauma of the moment prevented the witnesses from signing the will while the testator was hospitalized, there is simply no adequate explanation of the failure to have obtained their signatures in the extended fifteen-month interval prior to his death. If the Legislature's retention of the signing requirement is to be at all effectual, signing must occur within a reasonable time of observation to assure that the signature attests to what was actually observed, and not to what is vaguely remembered. While this requirement does not necessarily entail subscription prior to the testator's death, the interval here between the observation and the testator's death was simply too long for subscription after death to have been reasonably within the contemplation of the statute.

C

Plaintiff argues in the alternative, however, that even if compliance with execution formalities was defective, this Court should validate the will in the absence of any allegation of fraud because it was in "substantial compliance" with the statute. Thus, given the historical trend toward liberalization of the wills statute described above, and the policy favoring validation of wills that "meet the minimal formalities of the statute," the ultimate question raised by this case is how courts should construe wills that fail to satisfy even the "minimal formalities" retained in the statute.

As Professor Langbein has explained, "[t]he substantial compliance doctrine would permit defective compliance with . . . ceremonials to be evaluated purposively. It would permit the proponents to prove that in the circumstances of the case the testator executed the will with finality and that the execution is adequately evidenced notwithstanding the defect." Langbein, "Substantial Compliance with the Wills Act," supra, 88 Harv. L. Rev. at 521. The doctrine has been criticized, however, because it reduces predictability of wills:

> The argument in favor of the implementation of the substantial compliance doctrine is that, while it lacks the predictability of the U.P.C., it does insist upon a higher degree of formality yet with the understanding that where the failure to comply with any formality is shown, proof may be received to demonstrate that the function of the formality has still been met. . . . The problem is that wills are unlike the world of contract where the demands of business often necessitate informality. . . . Wills are more often made without such demands of time pressure. The testator has every opportunity to comply with formality requirements. . . .
>
> A second problem is the ambiguity of "substantial compliance." . . . Does it mean that some formalities are more important than others and that substantial compliance involves completion of only the important formalities?
>
> [Nelson and Starck, "Formalities and Formalism: A Critical Look at the Execution of Wills," 6 Pepperdine L. Rev. 331, 355 (1979).]

It is undeniable that in liberalizing execution formalities in accordance with the Uniform Probate Code, the Legislature was responding to the perceived inequities resulting from strict construction of the former statute. The Legislature's response, as we have seen, was to reduce the number of formalities with which compliance is required, not necessarily to relax the extent to which the remaining "minimal formalities" must be honored; plaintiff now asks this Court to take this process of liberalization a step further by holding that, in the absence of fraud, even defective compliance with the remaining formalities may be sufficient.

To do so on the facts of this case would, in our view, effectively vitiate the statutory requirement that witnesses sign the will.[12] We continue to believe that, as a general proposition, strict, if not literal, adherence to statutory requirements is required in order to validate a will, and that the statutory requirements must be satisfied regardless of the possibility of fraud in any particular case.

IV

The prophylactic purpose of preventing fraud would be substantially undermined if "witnesses" to a will that contained no witnessing signatures could testify to their presence at execution, no matter how much time had elapsed between execution and the affixing of their signatures. As the Appellate Division pointed out, such an approach would have the effect of eliminating the signing requirement in its entirety. By acknowledging that there may be some cases where post-execution signatures may not be barred, the Appellate Division opinion indicates that witnesses' signatures may be obtained within a reasonable period after the will is executed. We agree; compliance in such cases need not necessarily be considered defective. We further concur in the Appellate Division's conclusion that a fifteen-month interval, without any extenuating circumstance, is too long to be reasonable, and may not be salvaged by resort to the doctrine of "substantial compliance."

Accordingly, for the reasons stated, the judgment below is affirmed.

NOTES AND QUESTIONS

1.   Professor Langbein first proposed that courts develop a substantial compliance doctrine in his article, Substantial Compliance With the Wills Act, 88 Harv. L. Rev. 489 (1975). Later in the same year that Langbein wrote, South Australia enacted a statute providing for the probate of a document that was not properly executed if the court "is satisfied that there can be no reasonable doubt that the deceased intended the document to constitute his will." S. Austl. Wills Act Amendment Act (No. 2), 1975, §9. This act excused noncompliance with the Statute of Wills. It gives the court what Langbein calls a "dispensing power" — the power to validate the will while acknowledg-

---

12. We are unwilling to foreclose consideration of the substantial compliance doctrine in a case where there is no question of fraud, and where, unlike this case, there has been a clear attempt to comply with a statutory formality but compliance is deficient. In this case, however, the statutory formalities contemplate at a minimum witnessing by *two* persons; the treatment of a notary's signature as that of a witness does not compensate for the absence of the signature of a second witness.

ing that the will does not comply. It differs from the substantial compliance doctrine in that substantial compliance requires the court to determine whether the formalities observed sufficiently approximated the formalities required by the Statute of Wills. After observing the South Australian experience and the experience of other foreign jurisdictions adopting a substantial compliance doctrine, Langbein, in 1987, reported that he had "come to prefer the dispensing power over substantial compliance as a legislative corrective." Langbein, Excusing Harmless Errors in the Execution of Wills: A Report on Australia's Tranquil Revolution in Probate Law, 87 Colum. L. Rev. 1, 7 (1987). The reason was that the "courts read into their substantial compliance doctrine a near-miss standard, ignoring the central issue of whether the testator's conduct evidenced testamentary intent." From 41 South Australian cases since 1975, Langbein concluded:

> Implicitly, this case law has produced a ranking of the Wills Act formalities. Of the three main formalities — writing, signature, and attestation — writing turns out to be indispensable. Because section 12(2) requires a "document," nobody has tried to use the dispensing power to enforce an oral will. Failure to give permanence to the terms of your will is not harmless. Signature ranks next in importance. If you leave your will unsigned, you raise a grievous doubt about the finality and genuineness of the instrument. An unsigned will is presumptively only a draft, . . . but that presumption is rightly overcome in compelling circumstances such as in the switched-wills cases. By contrast, attestation makes a more modest contribution, primarily of a protective character, to the Wills Act policies. But the truth is that most people do not need protecting, and there is usually strong evidence that want of attestation did not result in imposition. The South Australian courts have been quick to find such evidence and to excuse attestation defects under the dispensing power.
>
> In devaluing attestation while insisting on signature and writing, the South Australian legislation and case law has brought the South Australian law of wills into a kind of alignment with the American law of will substitutes, that is, with our nonprobate system, where business practice has settled the forms for transfer. In life insurance beneficiary designations; in bank transfer arrangements such as pay-on-death accounts, joint accounts, and Totten trusts; in pension accounts; and in revocable inter vivos trusts, writing is the indispensable formality of modern practice, and signature is nearly as universal. Attestation, however, is increasingly uncommon. . . .
>
> Americans should . . . shudder that we still inflict upon our citizens the injustice of the traditional law, and we should join in this movement to rid private law of relics so embarrassing. [Id. at 52-54.]

The Joint Editorial Board for the Uniform Probate Code has approved a new section providing that an improperly executed document will be "treated as if it had been executed in compliance with . . . [the

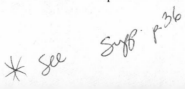

* see   Supp. p. 36

formalities requirements] if the proponent . . . establishes by clear and convincing evidence that the decedent intended the document" to constitute his will, a revocation or alteration of his will, or a revival of a formerly revoked will. The National Conference of Commissioners on Uniform State Laws is expected to consider this revision in 1990.

2. New York Est., Powers & Trusts Law §3-2.1(a)(4) (1981) requires the witnesses to sign their names within 30 days after the testator signs or acknowledges his signature to them. See Estate of Rimerman, 527 N.Y.S.2d 359 (Sur. Ct. 1988).

3. Most states require that a deed be notarized to be recorded in the county recorder's office; witnessing does not suffice. Why must deeds be *notarized* and wills *witnessed*? Would it be a good idea to permit a will to be either witnessed or notarized?

4. Justice Handler, who wrote the *Peters* decision rejecting substantial compliance, is known as a liberal on the New Jersey Supreme Court. Justice Grodin, who wrote the opinion in the next case in this book, Estate of Parsons, was in 1982 appointed to the California Supreme Court, where he became the intellectual leader of the liberal wing of the court. In fact, Grodin's opinions in areas other than the law of wills were so liberal that in 1986 the voters removed him—as well as Chief Justice Rose Bird—from the bench. Isn't it curious that when judges come to decide cases about effectuating donative transfers, any tendencies toward liberalism are usually restrained? The formalities requirements are scrupulously honored. Why is this so? Why is not "the conscience of equity" (see Note 2, supra page 174) moved?

Professor Baron believes the answer lies in the law's undervaluation of donative transfers. Judges, she says, think that donative transfers merely redistribute wealth and have no strong incentive to facilitate them. Baron compares the less strict requirements for contracts (basically, consideration) and finds that judges readily enforce contracts because market exchanges are viewed as creating wealth. Baron argues that donative transfers should be perceived as analogous to market exchanges, creating strong expectations about behavior and reciprocal benefits for donor and donee (though not necessarily measurable in economic terms). Society, she suggests, has as strong an interest in giving effect to the social and affective benefits resulting from donative transfers as it does in enforcing market exchanges. Baron, Gifts, Bargains, and Form, 64 Ind. L.J. 155 (1989).

b. Competency of Witnesses

Estate of Parsons

California Court of Appeal, First District, 1980
103 Cal. App. 3d 384, 163 Cal. Rptr. 70

GRODIN, J.   This case requires us to determine whether a subscribing witness to a will who is named in the will as a beneficiary becomes "disinterested" within the meaning of Probate Code section 51 by filing a disclaimer of her interest after the testatrix' death. While our own policy preferences tempt us to an affirmative answer, we feel constrained by existing law to hold that a disclaimer is ineffective for that purpose.

I

Geneve Parsons executed her will on May 3, 1976. Three persons signed the will as attesting witnesses: Evelyn Nielson, respondent Marie Gower, and Bob Warda, a notary public. Two of the witnesses, Nielson and Gower, were named in the will as beneficiaries. Nielson was given $100; Gower was given certain real property. Mrs. Parsons died on December 13, 1976, and her will was admitted to probate on the petition of her executors, respondents Gower and Lenice Haymond. On September 12, 1977, Nielson filed a disclaimer of her $100 bequest. Appellants [Mrs. Parsons's heirs] then claimed an interest in the estate on the ground that the devise to Gower was invalid. The trial court rejected their argument, which is now the sole contention on appeal.

Appellants base their claim on Probate Code section 51, which provides that a gift to a subscribing witness is void "unless there are two other and disinterested subscribing witnesses to the will."[13] Although Nielson disclaimed her bequest after subscribing the will, appellants submit that "a subsequent disclaimer is ineffective to transform an interested witness into a disinterested one." Appellants assert that because there was only one disinterested witness at the time of attestation, the devise to Gower is void by operation of law.

Respondents contend that appellants' argument is "purely technical" and "completely disregards the obvious and ascertainable intent" of the testatrix. They urge that the property should go to the person named as devisee rather than to distant relatives who, as the testatrix stated in her will, "have not been overlooked, but have been intentionally omitted." They stress that there has been no suggestion of any fraud or undue influence in this case, and they characterize Nielson's interest as a "token gift" which she relinquished pursuant to the disclaimer statute. (Prob. Code, §190 et seq.) Finally, respondents point to the following language of Probate Code section 190.6: "In every case, the disclaimer shall relate back for all purposes to the date of the creation of the interest." On the basis of that language, respondents conclude that Nielson "effectively became disinterested" by reason of her timely

---

13. Probate Code section 51 reads as follows: "All beneficial devises, bequests and legacies to a subscribing witness are void unless there are two other and disinterested subscribing witnesses to the will, except that if such interested witness would be entitled to any share of the estate of the testator in case the will were not established, he shall take such proportion of the devise or bequest made to him in the will as does not exceed the share of the estate which would be distributed to him if the will were not established."

disclaimer. According to respondents, the conditions of Probate Code section 51 have therefore been satisfied, and the devise to Gower should stand.

II

This appears to be a case of first impression in California, and our interpretation of Probate Code section 51 will determine its outcome. We are required to construe the statute "so as to effectuate the purpose of the law." (Select Base Materials v. Board of Equal. (1959) 51 Cal. 2d 640, 645, 335 P.2d 672.) To ascertain that purpose, we may consider its history.

At common law a party to an action, or one who had a direct interest in its outcome, was not competent to testify in court because it was thought that an interested witness would be tempted to perjure himself in favor of his interest. Centuries ago, this principle concerning the competence of witnesses in litigation was injected into the substantive law of wills. The statute of frauds of 1676 required that devises of land be attested and subscribed "by three or four credible witnesses, or else they shall be utterly void and of none effect." (29 Car. II, ch. 3, §5.) The word "credible" was construed to mean "competent" according to the common law principles then prevailing, and "competent" meant "disinterested" — so that persons having an interest under the will could not be "credible witnesses" within the meaning of the statute. The entire will would therefore fail if any one of the requisite number of attesting witnesses was also a beneficiary. In 1752 Parliament enacted a statute which saved the will by providing that the interest of an attesting witness was void. (25 Geo. II, ch. 6, §I.) Under such legislation, the competence of the witness is restored by invalidating his gift. The majority of American jurisdictions today have similar statutes; and California Probate Code section 51 falls into this category.

The common law disabilities to testify on account of interest have long been abolished. Having become a part of the substantive law of wills, Probate Code section 51, on the other hand, survives. Our task is to ascertain and effectuate its present purpose. When a court seeks to interpret legislation, "the various parts of a statutory enactment must be harmonized by considering the particular clause or section in the context of the statutory framework as a whole." (Moyer v. Workmen's Comp. Appeals Bd. (1973) 10 Cal. 3d 222, 230, 110 Cal. Rptr. 144, 514 P.2d 1224.) We therefore turn to the Probate Code.

In order to establish a will as genuine, it is not always necessary that each and every one of the subscribing witnesses testify in court. Moreover, Probate Code section 51 does not by its terms preclude any witness from testifying; nor does the section void the interest of a subscribing witness when "two other and disinterested" witnesses have also subscribed the will. It is therefore entirely conceivable and perfectly consistent with the statutory scheme that a will might be proved on the sole testimony of a subscribing witness who is named in the will as a beneficiary; and if the will had been attested by "two other and disinterested subscribing witnesses," the interested witness whose sole testimony established the will would also be permitted to take his gift, as provided in the instrument. If Probate Code section 51 serves any purpose under such circumstances, its purpose must necessarily have been accomplished before the will was offered for probate. Otherwise, in its statutory context, the provision would have no effect at all.

The quintessential function of a subscribing witness is performed when the will is executed. We believe that Probate Code section 51 looks in its operation solely to that time. The section operates to ensure that at least two of the subscribing witnesses are disinterested. Although disinterest may be a token of credibility, as at common law, it also connotes an absence of selfish motives. We conclude that the purpose of the statute is to protect the testator from fraud and undue influence at the very moment when he executes his will, by ensuring that at least two persons are present "who would not be financially motivated to join in a scheme to procure the execution of a spurious will by dishonest methods, and who therefore presumably might be led by human impulses of fairness to resist the efforts of others in that direction." (Gulliver & Tilson, Classification of Gratuitous Transfers (1941) 51 Yale L.J. 1, 11.) No other possible construction which has been brought to our attention squares so closely with the statutory framework.

III

Because we hold that Probate Code section 51 looks solely to the time of execution and attestation of the will, it follows that a subsequent disclaimer will be ineffective to transform an interested witness into a "disinterested" one within the meaning of that section. If the execution of a release or the filing of a disclaimer after the will has been attested could effect such a transformation, the purpose of the statute as we have defined it would be undermined.

Respondents' reliance on Probate Code section 190.6[14] is misplaced.

14. Probate Code section 190.6 provides:

Unless otherwise provided in the will, inter vivos trust, exercise of the power of appointment, or other written instrument creating or finally determining an interest, the interest disclaimed and any future interest which is to take effect in possession or enjoyment at or after the termination of the interest disclaimed, shall descend, go, be distributed or continue to be held as if the beneficiary disclaiming had predeceased the person creating the interest. In every case, the disclaimer shall relate back for all purposes to the date of the creation of the interest.

That section serves to equalize the tax consequences of disclaimers as between heirs at law and testamentary beneficiaries. Probate Code section 190, subdivision (a) defines "beneficiary" to mean "any person entitled, *but for his disclaimer*, to take an interest" by various means. (Italics added.) Even assuming that an "interest" arises within the meaning of the disclaimer statute from the execution of a will, Evelyn Nielson would *not* have been entitled to take under the will by reason of Probate Code section 51; and she was, therefore, not a "beneficiary" within the meaning of the disclaimer statute. The disclaimer statute therefore has no application here. In this case, when the will was executed and attested, only one of the subscribing witnesses was disinterested. The gifts to the other witnesses were therefore void, by operation of law. (Prob. Code, §51.) Nielson's disclaimer was a nullity, because she had no interest to disclaim.

Respondents' concern for the intentions of the testatrix is likewise misplaced. The construction of the will is not at issue here. We are faced instead with the operation of Probate Code section 51, which makes no reference to the intentions of the testatrix. Legislation voiding the interest of an attesting witness "often upsets genuine expressions of the testator's intent." (Chaffin, Execution, Revocation, and Revalidation of Wills: A Critique of Existing Statutory Formalities (1977) 11 Ga. L. Rev. 297, 317.) But that legislation controls the outcome of this case.

It has been said that statutes such as this are illsuited to guard against fraud and undue influence. "If the potential malefactor does not know of the rules, he will not be deterred. If he does know of them, which is unlikely, he will realize the impossibility of the financial gain supposed to be the motive of the legatee witness, and so will probably escape the operation of the remedy against himself." (Gulliver & Tilson, supra, 51 Yale L.J. at pp. 12-13.) Lord Mansfield observed over 200 years ago, "In all my experience at the Court of Delegates, I never knew a fraudulent will, but what was legally attested; and I have heard the same from many learned civilians." (Wyndham v. Chetwynd (K.B. 1757) 1 Black. W. 95, 100, 96 Eng. Rep. 53.) Yet Probate Code section 51 remains the law in California.

We are mindful that there has been no suggestion of any fraud or other misconduct in the case before us, and it may well be that "the vast majority of testators in modern society do not need the type of 'protection' that is afforded by our statute." (Chaffin, Improving Georgia's Probate Code (1970) 4 Ga. L. Rev. 505, 507.) "[T]he reported decisions give the impression that the remedies are employed more frequently against innocent parties who have accidentally transgressed the requirement than against deliberate wrongdoers, and this further confirms the imaginary character of the difficulty sought to be prevented." (Gulliver & Tilson, supra, 51 Yale L.J. at p.12.) But the

Legislature has spoken here, and in matters such as this, "the legislature has a wide discretion in determining the conditions to be imposed." (Estate of Mintaberry (1920) 183 Cal. 566, 568, 191 P. 909.)

Respondents note that a growing number of states have enacted statutes similar to Uniform Probate Code section 2-505, which dispenses with the rule contained in the California statute.[15] Perhaps statutes like California Probate Code section 51 represent a "mediaeval point of view" concerning the proper function of an attesting witness; and perhaps "the question whether he has abused his position should be made one of fact, like any other question having to do with the motives and conduct of parties who take part in the testamentary transaction." (Mechem, Why Not a Modern Wills Act? (1948) 33 Iowa L. Rev. 501, 506-507.) We cannot ignore what the statute commands, however, "merely because we do not agree that the statute as written is wise or beneficial legislation." (Estate of Carter (1935) 9 Cal. App. 2d 714, 718, 50 P.2d 1057.) Any remedial change must come from the Legislature.

That portion of the judgment from which this appeal is taken is therefore reversed.

NOTES AND PROBLEMS

1. In 1983 California adopted Uniform Probate Code §2-505, referred to in footnote 15 in the *Parsons* case, but adding that a devise to a witness "creates a presumption that the witness procured the devise by duress, menace, fraud, or undue influence." Cal. Prob. Code §6112 (1989). Since UPC §2-505 has been adopted in little more than one-third of the states, however, it is useful to probe further into the operation of purging statutes. California Probate Code §51, referred to in footnote 13 of the *Parsons* case, is substantially similar to purging statutes in many states, which purge the witness only of the benefit the witness receives that exceeds the benefit the witness would have received if the will had not been executed (that is, the "extra benefit"). For a list of state purging statutes, see Restatement (Second) of Property, Donative Transfers §33.1, Statutory Note (Tent. Draft No. 12, 1989.)

The Massachusetts purging statute, derived from the 1752 English statute referred to in the *Parsons* opinion, is different. It simply voids any devise to an attesting witness, who takes nothing under the will. Thus:

---

15. Uniform Probate Code section 2-505 provides: "(a) Any person generally competent to be a witness may act as a witness to a will. [¶] (b) A will or any provision thereof is not invalid because the will is signed by an interested witness."

Any person of sufficient understanding shall be deemed to be a competent witness to a will, notwithstanding any common law disqualification for interest or otherwise; but a beneficial devise or legacy to a subscribing witness or to the husband or wife of such witness shall be void unless there are two other subscribing witnesses to the will who are not similarly benefited thereunder. [Mass. Ann. Laws ch. 191, §2 (1981).]

Suppose that the real property devised to Marie Gower by Geneve Parsons was worth $50,000 and that under a previous will, not witnessed by Marie, Geneve had bequeathed Marie stock worth $70,000. Suppose also that the May 3, 1976, will contains a clause revoking all prior wills. What result under Cal. Prob. Code §51? Under Mass. Gen. Laws ch. 191, §2? Suppose that the prior will had bequeathed Marie stock worth $30,000. What result?

Suppose that the testator devised a house to the spouse of a witness. Is the devise void?

2. By will *T* left the bulk of his estate to the Union Church. One of the two witnesses was the minister of the Union Church, who receives a salary from the church. Is the bequest to the Union Church void? See Estate of Tkachuk, 73 Cal. App. 3d 14, 139 Cal. Rptr. 55 (1977).

Suppose that *T* is a resident of the Union Church Nursing Home, his will is witnessed by two employees of the home, and his will leaves his estate to the home. Is the bequest void?

3. An attorney unrelated to the testator draws a will nominating the attorney as executor. The attorney is one of the two attesting witnesses. Is the attorney entitled to be named executor? Courts have held that an attorney "earns" compensation as an executor, and, not receiving an unearned benefit, the attorney witness is not "purged" from the office of executor. However, the attorney does run some risk if he or she does not fully disclose to the testator the financial impact of naming the attorney as executor. In In re Estate of Weinstock, 40 N.Y.2d 1, 351 N.E.2d 647, 386 N.Y.S.2d 1 (1976), two attorneys (father and son) drafted a will for an 82-year-old man they had just met and named themselves executors. The court held the attorneys were guilty of "impropriety" and "overreaching" that constituted constructive fraud on the testator, precluding their appointment as executors. In State v. Gulbankian, 54 Wis. 2d 605, 196 N.W.2d 733 (1972), the court warned that a routine practice by an attorney to name the attorney as executor was suspicious and decided that it was unethical for the attorney-drafter to suggest, directly or indirectly, that the attorney be named as executor or lawyer for the executor. See Johnston, An Ethical Analysis of Common Estate Planning Practices — Is Good Business Bad Ethics?, 45 Ohio St. L.J. 57, 86-101 (1984).

Suppose that the will designates the attorney-drafter as the attorney for the executor. Is this designation enforceable by the attorney? Is it ethical? See Johnston, supra, at 101-114.

c. Recommended Method of Executing a Will

In executing a will, a lawyer should not rely on the formalities required by the statute in the client's home state. The client's will may be offered for probate in another state. The client may be domiciled elsewhere at death or may own real property in another state, or the will may exercise a power of appointment governed by the law of another state. Under the usual conflict of laws rules, the law of the decedent's domicile at death determines the validity of the will insofar as it disposes of personal property. The law of the state where real property is located determines the validity of a disposition of real property. If a person domiciled in Illinois executes a will, then moves to New Jersey and dies there, owning Florida real estate, some tangible personal property, and some stocks and bonds, the law of Illinois does not govern the validity of the will at all. New Jersey law determines the validity of the disposition of the tangible and intangible personalty, and Florida law governs the validity of the disposition of the real estate.[16] Most states have statutes recognizing as valid a will executed with the formalities required by (1) the state where the testator was domiciled at death, (2) the state where the will was executed, or (3) the state where the testator was domiciled when the will was executed. These statutes, where enacted, are not all uniform, however, and sometimes contain exceptions. See J. Schoenblum, Multistate and Multinational Estate Planning §14.02 (1982 and Supps.). A lawyer should draft wills so that there is no need to resort to such an act. Hence the careful lawyer in our highly mobile society draws a will and has it executed in a manner that satisfies the formal requirements in all states.

If the procedure set forth below[17] is followed, the instrument will be valid in all states, no matter in which state the testator is domiciled at the date of execution or at death or where the property is located.[18] If

---

16. If the client owns property in a foreign country or may die domiciled there, the law of the foreign country should be examined and the will executed in compliance with such law. See J. Schoenblum, Multistate and Multinational Estate Planning §§15.01-15.06 (1982 & Supps.). See also Uniform International Wills Act, found in Uniform Probate Code §§2-1001 to 2-1010 (1983) and adopted in many states, which sets out the procedure to be followed to comply with the 1973 Washington Convention on Wills. The procedure recommended in the text complies with the International Wills Act, except the self-proving affidavit at the end differs slightly from the affidavit required for an international will.

17. This procedure is an up-to-date version of the format recommended by Professor Leach in his Cases on Wills 44 (2d ed. 1949) and subsequently refined by Professor Casner in his work, 1 Estate Planning §3.1 (5th ed. 1984).

18. For Louisiana and Vermont law, see supra page 179, footnote 10. This procedure satisfies the Vermont requirement of three witnesses because the notary is the third witness; the notary is required in Louisiana. Both of these states have statutes providing that a will executed out of state is valid if valid either in the state where executed or in the state of the testator's domicile. La. Rev. Stat. §9.2401 (Supp. 1989); Vt. Stat. Ann. tit. 14, §112 (1974).

all these steps are not followed to the letter, in one or more states the will may be either invalid or extremely difficult to prove as a properly executed will.

(1)   If the will consists of more than one page, the pages are fastened together securely. The will specifies the exact number of pages of which it consists.

(2)   The lawyer should be certain that the testator has read the will and understands its contents.

(3)   The lawyer, the testator, two disinterested witnesses and a notary public are brought together in a room from which everyone else is excluded. (If the lawyer is a notary, an additional notary is unnecessary.) The door to the room is closed. No one enters or leaves the room until the ceremony is finished.

(4)   The lawyer asks the testator the following three questions:

> (a)"Is this your will?"[19]
> (b)"Have you read it and do you understand it?"
> (c)"Does it dispose of your property in accordance with your wishes?"

After each question the testator should answer "Yes" in a voice that can be heard by the two witnesses and the notary. It is neither necessary nor customary for the witnesses to know the terms of the will. If, however, the lawyer foresees a possible will contest, added precautions might be taken at this time. See supra page 162.

(5)   The lawyer asks the testator the following question. "Do you request _____ and _____ (the two witnesses) to witness the signing of your will?" The testator should answer "Yes" in a voice audible to the witnesses.

(6)   The witnesses should be standing or sitting so that all can see the testator sign. The testator signs on the margin of each page of the will. This is done for purposes of identification and to prevent subsequent substitution of pages. The testator then signs his or her name at the end of the will.

(7)   One of the witnesses reads aloud the *attestation clause*, which attests that the foregoing things were done. Here is an example: "On the _____ day of _____, 19_____, Wendy Brown declared to us, the

---

19. The purpose of publication is to assure that the testator is under no misapprehension as to the instrument testator is signing and to impress upon the witnesses the importance of the act and their consequent duties to vouch for the validity of the instrument. Nonetheless, the requirement of publication is rarely a bar to probate since the testator may indicate to the witnesses that the instrument is a will by words, signs, or conduct; even the words of another saying it is the testator's will are sufficient. It is only necessary that the evidence show that the testator and the witnesses understand that the instrument is a will.

undersigned, that the foregoing instrument was her last Will, and she requested us to act as witnesses to it and to her signature thereon. She then signed the Will in our presence, we being present at the same time. We now, at her request, in her presence, and in the presence of each other, hereunto subscribe our names as witnesses, and each of us declares that in his or her opinion this testator is of sound mind."[20]

(8) Each witness then signs and writes his or her address next to the signature. The first witness to sign writes, under the spaces provided for the witnesses' signatures, "The foregoing attestation clause has been read by us and is accurate," and places his or her initials immediately below this line, as does the other witness upon signing. The testator and the other witness watch each witness sign.

(9) A *self-proving affidavit,* typed at the end of the will, is then signed by the testator and the witnesses before the notary public, who in turn signs and attaches the required seal.[21] Why attach a self-proving

20. No state's statute requires the use of an attestation clause. The requirement of due execution can be satisfied merely by having the witnesses sign below the testator's signature as "witnesses." An attestation clause is very important, however. It makes out a prima facie case that the will was duly executed, and thus the will may be admitted to probate even though the witnesses predecease the testator or cannot recall the events of execution. See In re Estate of Collins, 60 N.Y.2d 466, 458 N.E.2d 797, 470 N.Y.S.2d 338 (1983). Moreover, if one of the attesting witnesses testifies that the steps for due execution were not satisfied, the attestation clause gives the will proponent's attorney ammunition for a vigorous cross-examination, and the will can be admitted to probate on the presumption of due execution despite such testimony.

In In re Estate of Koss, 84 Ill. App. 2d 59, 228 N.E.2d 510 (1967), one of the attesting witnesses, a nurse, testified that she did not know that the document was a will, that she was informed by the sole beneficiary that the document was a power of appointment so that the nurses could be paid, that she could not read any portion of the document she signed because her glasses were broken, and that the document she signed consisted of only one page instead of the three pages offered for probate. The court, in admitting the will to probate, said, "Where an attestation clause is in due form and the will bears the genuine signatures of the testatrix and of the witnesses this is prima facie evidence of the due execution of the will, which cannot usually be overcome by the testimony of a witness that there was not compliance with all of the statutory requisites. . . . The testimony of a subscribing witness which seeks to impeach a will is to be viewed with suspicion and received with caution." 84 Ill. App. 2d at 70, 228 N.E.2d at 515-516.

In Young v. Young, 20 Ill. App. 3d 242, 313 N.E.2d 593 (1974), a will executed some 27 years earlier without an attestation clause was denied probate because the witnesses could not remember whether the things necessary to proper execution were done.

21. Here is an example of a self-proving affidavit taken from Uniform Probate Code §2-504(b):

The State of _____
County of _____

We, _____, _____, and
_____, the testator and the witnesses, respectively, whose names are signed to the attached or foregoing instrument, being first duly sworn, do hereby declare to the undersigned authority that the testator signed and executed the instrument as his last will and that he signed willingly or directed another to sign for him, and

affidavit? Due execution of a will is usually proved after the testator's death by the witnesses testifying in court or executing affidavits. If the witnesses are dead or cannot be located or have moved far away, a self-proving affidavit reciting that all the requirements of due execution have been complied with permits the will to be probated. The will is valid without such an affidavit,[22] but the affidavit makes it easy to probate the will. The affidavit must be executed in front of a notary. The great majority of states recognize self-proving affidavits, an invention of the Uniform Probate Code that has proven very popular.[23]

---

that he executed it as his free and voluntary act for the purposes therein expressed; and that each of the witnesses, in the presence and hearing of the testator, signed the will as witness and that to the best of his knowledge the testator was at that time 18 or more years of age, of sound mind and under no constraint or undue influence.

_____
Testator

_____
Witness

_____
Witness

Subscribed, sworn to and acknowledged before me by _____
_____, the testator, and subscribed and sworn to before me by _____ and _____, witnesses, this _____ day of _____, _____.

(SEAL)   (Signed) _____

_____
(Official capacity of officer)

The Uniform Probate Code also authorizes combining the attestation clause and the self-proving affidavit so that the testator and witnesses sign once rather than twice.

Where the attestation and the self-proving affidavit are separate steps, make sure the testator and the witnesses sign *both* the will *and* the self-proving affidavit. If only the affidavit is signed, the will may not be entitled to probate. See Wich v. Fleming, 652 S.W.2d 353 (Tex. 1983).

22. But see supra page 179, footnote 10, for Louisiana law. Lawyers who do not attach self-proving affidavits may not have kept up with changes in the law and may not be familiar with the advantages of using self-proved wills. Professor Johnston suggests some lawyers may not do so in order to help ensure their retention as attorney for the estate; the executor will have to contact the witnesses in the lawyer's office to prove due execution. Johnston suggests that this is unethical and, to avoid the appearance of unethical conduct, lawyers should always use self-proving affidavits. Johnston, An Ethical Analysis of Common Estate Planning Practices — Is Good Business Bad Ethics?, 45 Ohio St. L.J. 57, 133-40 (1984).

23. Uniform Probate Code §3-406 provides that, if a will is self-proved, compliance with signature requirements for execution is conclusively presumed. In states adopting the UPC, a self-proved will cannot be attacked on grounds of failure to comply with signature requirements but may, of course, be attacked on other grounds such as undue

NOTE: SAFEGUARDING A WILL

What should be done with the client's will after it has been executed? A common practice is to give the will to the client together with instructions that it be kept in a safe place, such as in a safe-deposit box or among valuable papers at the client's home. This may not be the most desirable practice, however. The many reported cases involving notations, interlineations, or other markings on wills indicate that over the years a disturbing number of testators have attempted partial revocations or, perhaps, have used their wills as memo pads on which contemplated modifications have been noted. Also, an occasional testator has taken too seriously the lawyer's advice on safeguarding the will, with the result that the will cannot be located after death.[24] These potential difficulties have prompted some attorneys to follow the practice of retaining the client's will in their files. The client is given an unexecuted carbon copy of the will, on which the location of the original will is noted. However, keeping client's wills may have the appearance of soliciting business, an unethical practice. In State v.

---

influence or lack of capacity. In states that permit self-proved wills but have not otherwise adopted the UPC, a self-proved will may only give rise to a rebuttable presumption of due execution. See Mann, Self-Proving Affidavits and Formalism in Wills Adjudication, 63 Wash. U.L.Q. 39 (1985).

24.   Consider the case of Oscar P.'s will, a true story told in a letter to one of the editors from Mr. A.J. Robinson, an attorney in Amarillo, Texas. Mr. Robinson was counsel for one group of claimants under the will.

> Two men walked into our office in late August and told us that they were Mr. P.'s nephews. They were completely covered with chigger bites from the top of their shoes to their belts. Their legs were swollen and red all over. They told us that their uncle had died in East Texas on a 40-acre farm. They said that he was found dead in his old house that did not have any doors or windows and that the floor was about to fall in, that he kept his eggs in a bucket hanging from a tree limb by wire to keep the snakes from stealing them, that he hung his milk from a tree limb, dangling in a creek, that there was no stove in the house and that he had a wheel barrow with the wheel running at about a 45 degree angle that he pushed to and from town to carry all his supplies. They had been informed that their uncle had left a will, and the entire family had descended on the place over the weekend to hunt for it. They had spent two days digging in every place that they could think of on the entire 40 acres, hunting for the will that they assumed was buried somewhere. When they were about to quit, someone decided to dig up the floor of the chicken house. Underneath the chicken house floor they found a gallon jar, and in the gallon jar was a half-gallon jar, and in the half-gallon was a quart, and in the quart was a pint, and in the pint was a half-pint, and in the half-pint was a key which appeared to fit some safe-deposit box. Upon checking all the banks in the neighboring towns, they finally found a bank that had a safe-deposit box that the key would fit. Upon opening the safe-deposit box they found P.'s holographic will. The first sentence recited that this was Oscar P.'s last will. The second sentence read: "You will find the key to my safety deposit box in a jar under the floor in the chicken house."

Oscar P. left a substantial estate.

Gulbankian, 54 Wis. 2d 605, 196 N.W.2d 233 (1972), the Wisconsin court discussed the ethics of this practice and said:

> Nor do we approve of attorneys' "safekeeping" wills. In the old days this may have been explained on the ground many people did not have a safe place to keep valuable papers, but there is little justification today because most people do have safekeeping boxes, and if not, sec. 853.09, Stats., provides for the deposit of a will with the register in probate for safekeeping during the lifetime of the testator. The correct practice is that the original will should be delivered to the testator, and should only be kept by the attorney upon specific unsolicited request of the client. [54 Wis. 2d at 611-612, 196 N.W.2d at 736.]

Do you agree with the Wisconsin court? Can you think of a justification for the lawyer keeping the will not mentioned by the Wisconsin court? See Johnston, An Ethical Analysis of Common Estate Planning Practices — Is Good Business Bad Ethics?, 45 Ohio St. L.J. 57, 124-33 (1984); Report, Developments Regarding the Professional Responsibility of the Estate Planning Lawyer. The Effect of the Model Rules of Professional Conduct, 22 Real Prop., Prob. & Trust J. 1, 28 (1987).

Like Wisconsin, many states have statutes permitting deposit of wills with the clerk of the probate court. Uniform Probate Code §2-901 provides for the deposit of a will in court for safekeeping. Depositing a will with a probate court clerk is a rare practice, however. Most persons do not know such a depository is available.

d. Mistake in Execution of a Will

In re Pavlinko's Estate
Supreme Court of Pennsylvania, 1959
394 Pa. 564, 148 A.2d 528

BELL, J.   Vasil Pavlinko died February 8, 1957; his wife, Hellen, died October 15, 1951. A testamentary writing dated March 9, 1949, which purported to be the will of Hellen Pavlinko, was signed by Vasil Pavlinko, her husband. The residuary legatee named therein, a brother of Hellen, offered the writing for probate as the will of Vasil Pavlinko, but probate was refused. The Orphans' Court, after hearing and argument, affirmed the decision of the Register of Wills.

The facts are unusual and the result very unfortunate. Vasil Pavlinko and Hellen, his wife, retained a lawyer to draw their wills and wished to leave their property to each other. By mistake Hellen signed the will which was prepared for her husband, and Vasil signed the will which was prepared for his wife, each instrument being signed at the end thereof. The lawyer who drew the will and his secretary, Dorothy Zinkham, both signed as witnesses. Miss Zinkham admitted that she was unable to speak the language of Vasil and Hellen, and that no conversation took place between them. The wills were kept by Vasil and Hellen. For some undisclosed reason, Hellen's will was never offered for probate at her death; in this case it was offered merely as an exhibit.

The instrument which was offered for probate was short. It stated:

"I, *Hellen* Pavlinko, of . . . , do hereby make, publish and declare this to be *my* Last Will and Testament. . . ."

In the first paragraph she directed her executor to pay her debts and funeral expenses. In the second paragraph she gave her entire residuary estate to "my husband, Vasil Pavlinko . . . absolutely." She then provided:

> Third: If my aforesaid husband, Vasil Pavlinko, should predecease me, then and in that event, I give and bequeath:
> (a) To my brother-in-law, Mike Pavlinko, of McKees Rocks, Pennsylvania, the sum of Two Hundred ($200) Dollars.
> (b) To my sister-in-law, Maria Gerber, (nee Pavlinko), of Pittsburgh, Pennsylvania, the sum of Two Hundred ($200) Dollars.
> (c) The rest, residue and remainder of *my* estate, of whatsoever kind and nature and wheresoever situate, I give, devise and bequeath, absolutely, to *my brother*, Elias Martin, now residing at 520 Aidyl Avenue, Pittsburgh, Pennsylvania.
> I do hereby nominate, constitute and appoint my husband, Vasil Pavlinko, as Executor of this my Last Will and Testament."

It was then mistakenly signed "Vasil Pavlinko [Seal]".

While no attempt was made to probate, as Vasil's will, the writing which purported to be his will but was signed by Hellen, it could not have been probated as Vasil's will, because it was not signed by him at the end thereof.

The Wills Act of 1947 provides in clear, plain and unmistakable language in §2: "Every will, . . . shall be in writing and shall be signed *by the testator* at the end thereof," 20 P.S. §180.2, with certain exceptions not here relevant. The Court below correctly held that the paper which *recited* that it was the will of Hellen Pavlinko and intended and purported to give Hellen's estate to her husband, could not be probated as the will of Vasil and was a nullity.

In order to decide in favor of the residuary legatee, almost the entire will would have to be rewritten. The Court would have to substitute the words "Vasil Pavlinko" for "Hellen Pavlinko" and the words "my wife" wherever the words "my husband" appear in the will, and the relationship of the contingent residuary legatees would likewise have to be changed. To consider this paper — as written — as Vasil's will, it would give his entire residuary estate to "my husband, Vasil Pavlinko, absolutely" and "Third: If my husband, Vasil Pavlinko, should predecease me, then . . . I give and bequeath my residuary estate to my brother, Elias Martin." The language of this writing, which is signed at the end thereof by *Vasil* Pavlinko, is unambiguous, clear and unmistakable, and it is obvious that it is a meaningless nullity.

While no authority is needed to demonstate what is so obvious, there is a case which is directly in point and holds that such a writing cannot be probated as the will of Vasil Pavlinko. This exact situation arose in Alter's Appeal, 67 Pa. 341. The facts are recited in the unanimous opinion of the Court, speaking through Mr. Justice Agnew (at page 344):

> This is a hard case, but it seems to be without a remedy. An aged couple, husband and wife, having no lineal descendants, and each owning property, determined to make their wills in favor of each other, so that the survivor should have all they possessed. Their wills were drawn precisely alike, *mutatis mutandis*, and laid down on a table for execution. Each signed a paper, which was duly witnessed by three subscribing witnesses, and the papers were enclosed in separate envelopes, endorsed and sealed up. After the death of George A. Alter, the envelopes were opened and it was found that each had by mistake signed the will of the other. To remedy this error the legislature, by an Act approved the 23rd day of February 1870, conferred authority upon the Register's Court of this county to take proof of the mistake, and proceed as a court of chancery, to reform the will of George A. Alter and decree accordingly. . . . Was the paper signed by George A. Alter his will? Was it capable of being reformed by the Register's Court? The paper drawn up for his will was not a will in law, for it was not "signed by him at the end thereof," as the Wills Act requires. *The paper he signed was not his will, for it was drawn up for the will of his wife and gave the property to himself. It was insensible and absurd.* It is clear, therefore, that he had executed no will, and there was nothing to be reformed. There was a mistake, it is true, but that mistake was the same as if he had signed a blank sheet of paper. He had written his name, but not to his will. He had never signed his will, and the signature where it was, was the same as if he had not written it at all. He therefore died intestate, and his property descended as at law.

The Court further decided that the Legislative Act was void because it had no power to divest estates which were already vested at law on the death of George A. Alter without a will. . . .

Once a Court starts to ignore or alter or rewrite or make exceptions to clear, plain and unmistakable provisions of the Wills Act in order to accomplish equity and justice in that particular case, the Wills Act will become a meaningless, although well intentioned, scrap of paper, and the door will be opened wide to countless fraudulent claims which the Act successfully bars.

Decree affirmed. Each party shall pay their respective costs.

MUSMANNO, J. (dissenting)[25] Vasil Pavlinko and his wife, Hellen Pavlinko, being unlettered in English and unlearned in the ways of the law, wisely decided to have an attorney draw up their wills, since they were both approaching the age when reflecting persons must give thought to that voyage from which there is no return. They explained to the attorney, whose services they sought, that he should draw two wills which would state that when either of the partners had sailed

---

25. Justice Musmanno was a striking individualist, sometimes injudicious, always colorful. In dissenting from a majority holding that Henry Miller's Rabelaisian Tropic of Cancer was not obscene, Musmanno wrote:

> "Cancer" is not a book. It is a cesspool, an open sewer, a pit of putrefaction, a slimy gathering of all that is rotten in the debris of human depravity. And in the center of all this waste and stench, besmearing himself with its foulest defilement, splashes, leaps, cavorts and wallows a bifurcated specimen that responds to the name of Henry Miller. One wonders how the human species could have produced so lecherous, blasphemous, disgusting and amoral a human being as Henry Miller. One wonders why he is received in polite society. . . . From Pittsburgh to Philadelphia, from Dan to Beersheba, and from the ramparts of the Bible to Samuel Eliot Morison's Oxford History of the American People, I dissent. [Commonwealth v. Robin, 421 Pa. 70, 100, 218 A.2d 546, 561 (1966).]

In his first five years on the Pennsylvania Supreme Court, Musmanno filed more dissenting opinions than all the other members of that court had collectively filed in the preceding 50 years. One dissent got him into a lawsuit. Chief Justice Stern once ordered that Musmanno's dissent not be published in the official state reports because he had not circulated it among the court. Musmanno sought mandamus to compel the state reporter to publish his dissent. The supreme court denied the writ, Musmanno not sitting. Musmanno v. Eldredge, 382 Pa. 167, 114 A.2d 511 (1955). Justice Musmanno then moved his case to the court of last resort, the law reviews. His side of the controversy can be found in Musmanno, Dissenting Opinions, 60 Dick. L. Rev. 139 (1956). When asked whether he read Musmanno's dissents, Stern, C.J., replied that he was not "interested in current fiction." The New Republic, Feb. 3, 1968, at 14.

Musmanno's ancestors came from Italy, and he was a leading force in establishing Columbus Day as a special day for Italian-Americans. When Yale accepted the Vinland map as evidence that Norsemen and not an Italian, Christopher Columbus, had discovered America, Musmanno immediately rose to the attack. He dropped all his duties and went to Yale to dispute the archeologists, embarked on a six-month speaking tour attacking the authenticity of the Vinland Map, and wrote a book, Columbus Was Right! (In 1974 the Yale Library announced that the Vinland Map was a fake.)

Justice Musmanno's last opinion was a freewheeling dissent to a reversal of a rape conviction. The majority held that it was error for the judge to tell the jurors they would have to answer to God for their actions. Commonwealth v. Holton, 432 Pa. 11, 247 A.2d 228 (1968). Wrote Musmanno:

> God is not dead, and judges who criticize the invocation of Divine Assistance had better begin preparing a brief to use when they stand themselves at the Eternal Bar of Justice on Judgment Day. . . . I am perfectly willing to take my chances with [the trial judge] . . . at the gates of Saint Peter and answer on our voir dire that we were always willing to invoke the name of the Lord in seeking counsel. . . . Miserere nobis Omnipotens Deus!

Id. at 41, 43, 247 A.2d at 242-243. The next day, Columbus Day, 1968, Justice Musmanno dropped dead and presumably this voir dire took place. — Eds.

away, the one remaining ashore would become the owner of the property of the departing voyager. Vasil Pavlinko knew but little English. However, his lawyer, fortunately, was well versed in his clients' native language, known as Little Russian or Carpathian. The attorney thus discussed the whole matter with his two visitors in their language. He then dictated appropriate wills to his stenographer in English and then, after they had been transcribed, he translated the documents, paragraph by paragraph, to Mr. and Mrs. Pavlinko, who approved of all that he had written. The wills were laid before them and each signed the document purporting to be his or her will. The attorney gave Mrs. Pavlinko the paper she had signed and handed to her husband the paper he had signed. In accordance with customs they had brought with them from the old country, Mrs. Pavlinko turned her paper over to her husband. It did not matter, however, who held the papers since they were complementary of each other. Mrs. Pavlinko left her property to Mr. Pavlinko and Mr. Pavlinko left his property to Mrs. Pavlinko. They also agreed on a common residuary legatee, Elias Martin, the brother of Mrs. Pavlinko. . . .

We have also said time[s] without number that the intent of the testator must be gathered from the four corners of his will. Whether it be from the four corners of the will signed by Vasil Pavlinko or whether from the eight corners of the wills signed by Vasil and Hellen Pavlinko, all set out before the court below, the net result is always the same, namely that the residue of the property of the last surviving member of the Pavlinko couple was to go to Elias Martin. . . .

The Majority says that there is nothing we can do to effectuate the expressed intention of Vasil Pavlinko. But, I respectfully submit, the Majority does not make a serious effort to effectuate that expressed intent. The Majority contents itself with saying that "the facts are unusual and the result very unfortunate." But the results do not need to be unfortunate. . . . Elias Martin is being turned out of Court when there is no need for such a peremptory eviction. The Majority authorizes the eviction on the basis of a decision rendered by this Court in 1878 in the case of Alter's Appeal, 67 Pa. 341. There, wife and husband, also signed wrong papers and the Court in that Post-Civil War period, held nothing could be done to correct the error. But even if we say that the *Alter* decision makes impossible the transferring of the signature of Vasil Pavlinko to the will written in his name, I still do not see how it prevents this Court from enforcing the provision in the will which *was* signed by Vasil Pavlinko. In the *Alter* case an attempt was made to reform the will "by striking off the signature 'Catherine Alter,' and causing the name 'George A. Alter' to be signed thereto" so that the paper so signed could be "admitted to probate as the will of George A. Alter." But in our case here, no such substitution is being sought. What

Elias Martin seeks is admission to probate of a testamentary writing *actually signed by the testator Vasil Pavlinko*.

Moreover, in the *Alter* case, as distinguished from the Pavlinko will, George A. Alter left everything to himself. Even if we accept the Majority's conclusion, based on the *Alter* case, that all provisions in the Pavlinko will, which refer to himself, must be regarded as nullities, not correctible by parol evidence because they evince no latent ambiguities, it does not follow that the residuary clause must perish. The fact that some of the provisions in the Pavlinko will cannot be executed does not strike down the residuary clause, which is meaningful and stands on its own two feet. We know that one of the very purposes of a residuary clause is to provide a catch-all for undisposed-of or ineffectually disposed-of property. . . .

I see no insuperable obstacle to probating the will signed by Vasil Pavlinko. Even though it was originally prepared as the will of his wife, Hellen, he did adopt its testamentary provisions as his own. Some of its provisions are not effective but their ineffectuality in no way bars the legality and validity of the residuary clause which is complete in itself. I would, therefore, probate the paper signed by Vasil Pavlinko. . . .[26]

NOTES AND QUESTIONS

1.   In Guardian, Trust & Executors Co. of New Zealand v. Inwood, [1946] N.Z.L.R. 614, a will was prepared for Jane Remington that devised her property "to my sister Maude Lucy Remington" for life, remainder to *B*. A will was prepared for her sister Maude Lucy that devised her property "to my sister Jane Remington" for life, remainder to *B*. Both wills named the same executor and were in all other essential aspects the same. The sisters signed the wrong wills. Jane died. The court reasoned that there was testamentary intent with respect to the document signed. It granted probate of the will signed by Jane with the omission of the word "Jane" from the body of the will. The will as probated thus read, "to my sister _____ Remington for life." The *Inwood* case is followed in Re Brander, [1952] 4 D.L.R. 688, 6 W.W.R. (n.s.) 702 (B.C.).

The *Inwood* case rests on the principle of *falsa demonstratio non nocet*: A mere false description does not make the instrument inoperative. A false description of property or of the intended recipient may be stricken. The classic case of false description of property is Patch v. White, 117 U.S. 210 (1886). There the testator devised "lot number 6

---

26. Noted in 11 Mercer L. Rev. 229; 107 U. Pa. L. Rev. 1237. — Eds.

in square 403" to his brother. The testator owned no lot so numbered, but owned lot 3 in square 406. The court struck the misdescription and held that the lot owned by the testator passed to his brother.

Illustrative of misdescription of the person is Breckheimer v. Kraft, 133 Ill. App. 2d 410, 273 N.E.2d 468 (1971). There the testator bequeathed her residuary estate equally to her "nephew Raymond Schneikert and Mabel Schneikert his wife." Raymond's wife was named Evelyn. After hearing evidence that the testator intended Evelyn to be the legatee, the court struck the misdescription "Mabel Schneikert," leaving a bequest to "Raymond Schneikert and his wife."

Should *falsa demonstratio non nocet* have been applied in the *Pavlinko* case?

2. In In re Snide, 52 N.Y.2d 193, 418 N.E.2d 656, 437 N.Y.S.2d 63 (1981), a husband and wife mistakenly signed the will intended for the other; the issue was the same as in the *Pavlinko* case. The husband died first, and the court, 4-3, ordered the instrument signed by the husband admitted to probate.

> Of course it is essential to the validity of a will that the testator was possessed of testamentary intent; however, we decline the formalistic view that this intent attaches irrevocably to the document prepared, rather than the testamentary scheme it reflects. Certainly, had a carbon copy been substituted for the ribbon copy the testator intended to sign, it could not be seriously contended that the testator's intent should be frustrated. Here the situation is similar. Although Harvey mistakenly signed the will prepared for his wife, it is significant that the dispositive provisions in both wills, except for the names, were identical.
>
> Moreover, the significance of the only variance between the two instruments is fully explained by consideration of the documents together, as well as in the undisputed surrounding circumstances. Under such facts it would indeed be ironic — if not perverse — to state that because what has occurred is so obvious, and what was intended so clear, we must act to nullify rather than sustain this testamentary scheme. The instrument in question was undoubtedly genuine, and it was executed in the manner required by the statute. Under these circumstances it was properly admitted to probate.
>
> In reaching this conclusion we do not disregard settled principles, nor are we unmindful of the evils which the formalities of will execution are designed to avoid; namely, fraud and mistake. To be sure, full illumination of the nature of Harvey's testamentary scheme is dependent in part on proof outside of the will itself. However, this is a very unusual case, and the nature of the additional proof should not be ignored. Not only did the two instruments constitute reciprocal elements of a unified testamentary plan, they both were executed with statutory formality, including the same attesting witnesses, at a contemporaneous execution ceremony. There is absolutely no danger of fraud, and the refusal to read these wills together would serve merely to unnecessarily expand formalism,

without any corresponding benefit. On these narrow facts we decline this
unjust course. [52 N.Y.2d at 196-197, 418 N.E.2d at 657-658, 437 N.Y.S.2d
at 64-65.]

Is *Snide* an example of the "dispensing power," recommended by
Professor Langbein, supra page 194? See Comment, Mistakenly Signed
Reciprocal Wills: A Change in Tradition After In re Snide, 67 Iowa L.
Rev. 205 (1981).

3.   Inasmuch as a constructive trust may be imposed on an innocent
third party who takes property because of another's fraudulent wrongdoing, should a constructive trust be imposed upon Vasil Pavlinko's
heir in favor of Elias Martin? Should the policy of preventing unjust
enrichment of an innocent person be controlling when fraud in willmaking is involved and not controlling when mistake is involved? See
Henderson, Mistake and Fraud in Wills — Part I: A Comparative
Analysis of Existing Law, 47 B.U.L. Rev. 303, 386-388, 391-395 (1967).
Where there is mistake, is there any "wrong" upon which to predicate
a constructive trust? See Langbein & Waggoner, Reformation of Wills
on the Ground of Mistake: Change of Direction in American Law?, 130
U. Pa. L. Rev. 521, 576-577 (1982).

The *Pavlinko* case may be viewed as a case of innocent misrepresentation by the lawyer that the will presented to Vasil for his signature
was the will prepared for him. Should innocent misrepresentation be
treated like fraud (with a constructive trust imposed) or like mistake
(no relief)? Henderson, supra, at 406.

e.   Conditional Wills

A will may be written to say that it becomes operative if a stated event
occurs. Typically the stated event is a journey or a surgical operation
that the testator is about to undertake. The question is whether the
testator wants the will to be effective *only* if the event happens *or* to be
effective at the testator's death regardless of the occurrence of the
event.

In the famous case of Eaton v. Brown, 193 U.S. 411 (1904), Caroline
Holley executed the following instrument in Washington, D.C., on
August 31, 1901:

I am going on a Journey and may, not ever return. And if I do not, this
is my last request. The Mortgage on the King House, wich is in the
possession of Mr. H H Brown to go to the Methodist Church at
Bloomingburgh All the rest of my properday both real and personal to
My adopted Son L. B. Eaton of the life Saving Service, Treasury

Department Washington D.C, All I have is my one hard earnings and I propose to leave it to whome I please.

Caroline went on her journey, returned to Washington, resumed her work as a clerk in the Treasury Department, and died there on December 17, 1901. Caroline's will was offered for probate, and the question was whether the language, "And if I do not [return], this is my last request," was merely a statement of the inducement for execution of the will or stated a condition for probate of the will. The Supreme Court, per Holmes, J., ordered that the will be probated and given effect. "Obviously the first sentence, 'I am going on a journey and may not ever return,' expresses the fact which was on her mind as the occasion and inducement for writing it. . . . She was thinking of the possibility of death or she would not have made a will. But that possibility at that moment took the specific shape of not returning from her journey, and so she wrote 'if I do not return,' before giving her last commands." Id. at 414.

Most of the cases on conditional wills are in accord with Eaton v. Brown. They presume the will is not conditional, applying the standard presumption against intestacy. See Succession of Montero, 365 So. 2d 929 (La. 1978) (testator, about to go into surgery for a serious operation, wrote "in the event I do not come out of this OK" my estate is to go to three persons); Mason v. Mason, 268 S.E.2d 67 (W. Va. 1980) ("I am in the hospital for surgery, and in case I do not survive everything belongs to Mervin"). However, there are cases holding the will conditional when circumstances clearly indicate the testator so intended. See In re Pascal's Estate, 2 Misc. 2d 337, 152 N.Y.S.2d 185 (Sur. Ct. 1956).

See generally Annot., 1 A.L.R.3d 1048 (1965).

f. Statutory Wills

Perceiving a public demand for a legally valid will that can be written on a printed form available at stationery stores, several states have authorized simple "statutory wills." These are short wills, with the wording spelled out in a statute. The will provides spaces for the testator to fill in the names of the beneficiaries. A jurisdiction may have several forms of statutory wills — one to leave everything to a spouse; another to leave everything in trust for the spouse for life, remainder to the children; and still another to leave property in trust for children until they reach majority. See, e.g., Cal. Prob. Code §§6200-6248 (1989); Mich. Comp. Laws §§700.123(a)-(c) (Supp. 1989).

The purpose of authorizing simple statutory wills is to channel persons desirous of using a will form toward a well-drafted form. Statutory wills must be signed and attested in the same manner as any attested will.

The Uniform Statutory Will Act (1984) does not provide forms but operates on the principle of incorporation by reference. A testator may incorporate provisions of the uniform act (e.g., "I direct that my property be disposed of in accordance with the Uniform Statutory Will Act."). The uniform act provides only one scheme of disposition. If the testator leaves no surviving issue, the spouse takes everything. If the testator leaves issue and a surviving spouse, the spouse receives the house, tangible personal property, and the greater of $300,000 or one-half the estate. The income from the remaining portion of the estate is paid to the surviving spouse for life. If there is no surviving spouse (or, if there is one, upon the spouse's death), the estate is distributed to the testator's issue. If any issue are under the age of 23, property distributable to issue is held in trust. The uniform act provides a simple dispositive plan as an alternative to intestacy, but laypersons will probably not know of the uniform act and most lawyers will have their own forms that they prefer. See Note, The Statutory Will: A Simple Alternative to Intestacy, 35 Case W. Res. L. Rev. 307 (1984).

2. Holographic Wills

The Jolly Testator Who Makes His Own Will[27]

> Ye lawyers who live upon litigants' fees,
> And who need a good many to live at your ease,
> Grave or gay, wise or witty, whate'er your degree,
> Plain stuff or Queen's Counsel, take counsel of me:
> When a festive occasion your spirit unbends,
> You should never forget the profession's best friends;
> So we'll send round the wine, and a light bumper fill
> To the jolly testator who makes his own will.
>
> He premises his wish and his purpose to save
> All dispute among friends when he's laid in the grave;
> Then he straightway proceeds more disputes to create
> Than a long summer's day would give time to relate.
> He writes and erases, he blunders and blots,
> He produces such puzzles and Gordian knots,
> That a lawyer, intending to frame the thing ill,
> Couldn't match the testator who makes his own will.
>
>   LORD NEAVES

In about half of the states, primarily in the South and West, holo-

---

27. We reproduce only the first two stanzas of Lord Neaves' poem. For the entire poem, see W. Prosser, The Judicial Humorist 246 (1952). — Eds.

graphic wills are permitted.[28] A holographic will is a will written by the testator's hand and signed by the testator; attesting witnesses are not required. Holographic wills are of Roman origin and are recognized by the Code Napoleon and civil law countries. They were introduced into this country by a Virginia statute of 1751 and by the reception of the civil law into Louisiana.

Requirements for a valid holographic will vary. A majority of states allowing holographs have adopted the provisions of Uniform Probate Code §2-503: "A will . . . is valid as a holographic will, whether or not witnessed, if the signature and the material provisions are in the handwriting of the testator." Several states, however, require that a holographic will be "entirely" handwritten, a requirement that may cause problems if typed or printed matter is found on the holographic instrument. For example, in In re Estate of Dobson, 708 P.2d 422 (Wyo. 1985), the testator took her signed handwritten will to her local banker to discuss it with him. To make the will clearer, the banker penciled in certain numbers and parentheses and added to the devise of a tract of land, "including all mineral and oil rights," all with the consent of the testator. The court held the will could not be probated because not entirely in the handwriting of the decedent. See Annot., 37 A.L.R.4th 528 (1985).

A few states require that a holograph be dated, which means a full date of day, month, and year. A date is useful in determining which of two inconsistent testamentary instruments was written later; the last written instrument prevails. But of course the requirement of a date causes an undated instrument to fail even if there is no other inconsistent testamentary instrument.

In almost all states permitting holographs, a holograph may be signed at the end, at the beginning, or anywhere on the will, but if not signed at the end there may be doubt about whether the decedent intended his name to be a signature. See, for example, In re Estate of Fegley, 589 P.2d 80 (Colo. App. 1978), where the court denied probate to a handwritten instrument reading, "I, Henrietta Fegley, being of sound mind and disposing memory, declare this instrument to be my last will,"

---

28. The states are Alaska, Arizona, Arkansas, California, Colorado, Idaho, Kentucky, Louisiana, Maine, Michigan, Mississippi, Montana, Nebraska, Nevada, New Jersey, North Carolina, North Dakota, Oklahoma, Pennsylvania, South Dakota, Tennessee, Texas, Utah, Virginia, West Virginia, and Wyoming. In Maryland and New York holographic wills are permitted for soldiers and sailors. For a list of state statutes, see Restatement (Second) of Property, Donative Transfers §33.1, Statutory Note (Tent. Draft No. 12, 1989).

Suppose that the testator writes a holographic will in a state recognizing such a will, and then the testator moves to a state that does not recognize holographic wills and dies there. On this matter, the states that do not recognize holographs are split. Some permit probate of a holographic will if valid where executed; other states deny probate. See Black v. Seals, 474 So. 2d 696 (Ala. 1985), allowing holographic will of nonresident.

but not otherwise signed. Compare In re Estate of MacLeod, 206 Cal. App. 3d 1235, 254 Cal. Rptr. 156 (1988), reaching a contrary conclusion on virtually identical facts.

GULLIVER & TILSON, CLASSIFICATION OF GRATUITOUS TRANSFERS, 51 Yale L.J. 1, 13-14 (1941):   "The exemption of holographic wills from the usual statutory requirements seems almost exclusively justifiable in terms of the evidentiary function. The require-ment that a holographic will be entirely written in the handwriting of the testator furnishes more complete evidence for inspection by hand-writing experts than would exist if only the signature were available, and consequently tends to preclude the probate of a forged docu-ment. . . . While there is a certain ritual value in writing out the document, casual off-hand statements are frequently made in letters. The relative incompleteness of the performance of the functions of the regular statute of wills, and particularly the absence of any ritual value, may account for the fact that holographic wills are not recognized in the majority of the states, and for some decisions, in states recognizing them, requiring the most precise compliance with specified formalities."

In re Estate of Johnson
Arizona Court of Appeals, 1981
129 Ariz. 312, 630 P.2d 1044

WREN, C.J.   This appeal involves the question of whether the hand-written portions on a printed will form, submitted to the trial court as a holographic will, were sufficient to satisfy the requirements of A.R.S. §14-2503 that the material provisions of such a will must be entirely in the handwriting of the testator.

Arnold H. Johnson, the decedent, died on January 28, 1978 at the age of 79. One of his sons, John Mark Johnson, was appointed personal representative of the estate. In addition to John, the decedent was survived by five other children. Approximately three weeks following appointment of the personal representative, appellants, Barton Lee McLain and Marie Ganssle, petitioned for formal probate of an instru-ment dated March 22, 1977. The personal representative objected to the petition and filed a motion for summary judgment on the grounds that the instrument was invalid as a will, in that it was not attested by any witnesses as required by A.R.S. §14-2502, and did not qualify as a holographic will under A.R.S. §14-2503, since the material provisions thereof were not in the handwriting of the testator.

Appellants filed a cross-motion for summary judgment, urging that the document did constitute a holographic will. The trial court disagreed with appellants and granted the motion of the personal representative. We affirm.

The document claimed by appellants to be decedent's last will and testament was a printed will form available in various office supply and stationery stores. It bore certain printed provisions followed by blanks where the testator could insert any provisions he might desire. The entire contents of the instrument in question are set forth below, with the portions underscored which are in the decedent's handwriting.

THE LAST WILL AND TESTAMENT

I <u>Arnold H. Johnson</u> a resident of <u>Mesa Arizona</u> of <u>Maricopa</u> County, State of Arizona, being of sound and disposing mind and memory, do make, publish and declare this my last WILL AND TESTAMENT, hereby revoking and making null and void any and all other last Wills and Testaments heretofore by me made.

FIRST — My will is that all my just debts and funeral expenses and any Estate or Inheritance taxes shall be paid out of my Estate, as soon after my decease as shall be found convenient.

SECOND — I give devise and bequeath to <u>My six living children as follows</u>

<u>To John M. Johnson ⅛ of my Estate</u>	
<u>Helen Marchese</u>	⅛
<u>Sharon Clements</u>	⅛
<u>Mirriam Jennings</u>	⅛
<u>Mary D. Korman</u>	⅛
<u>A. David Johnson</u>	⅛
<u>To W. V. Grant, Souls Harbor Church</u>	
<u>3200 W. Davis Dallas Texas</u>	⅛
<u>To Barton Lee McLain</u>)	
<u>and Marie Gansels</u>)	
<u>Address 901 E. Broadway</u> ~~Phoenix~~)	⅛
<u>~~Az~~ Mesa</u>)	

I nominate and appoint <u>Mirriam Jennings my Daughter</u> of <u>Nashville Tenn.</u> as executress of this my Last Will and Testament <u>Address 1247 Saxon Drive Nashville Tenn.</u>

IN TESTIMONY WHEREOF, I have set my hand to this, My Last Will and Testament, at _____this <u>22</u> day of <u>March</u>, in the year of our Lord, One Thousand Nine Hundred <u>77</u>

The foregoing instrument was signed by said <u>Arnold H. Johnson</u> in our presence, and by _____ published and declared as and for _____ Last Will and Testament, and at _____ request, and in _____ presence, and in presence of each other, we hereunto subscribe our Names as

Attesting Witnesses, at ————————————— This <u>22</u> day of
<u>March</u>, 19<u>77</u>

My Commission expires   <u>Ann C. McGonagill</u>
Jan. 16, 1981   *(Notary public seal)*

Sections 14-101 to 14-134, Arizona Revised Statutes, 1956, and Amendments thereto

Initially it is to be noted that Arizona has adopted the Uniform Probate Code, the holographic will provisions being contained in §2-503, and found in A.R.S. §14-2503:

"A will which does not comply with §14-2502 is valid as a holographic will, whether or not witnessed, if the signature and the material provisions are in the handwriting of the testator."

The statutory requirement that the material provisions be drawn in the testator's own handwriting requires that the handwritten portion clearly express a *testamentary* intent. Estate of Morrison, 55 Ariz. 504, 103 P.2d 669 (1940). Appellants argue that the purported will here should thus be admitted to probate, since all the key dispositive provisions essential to its validity as a will are in the decedent's own handwriting; and further, when all the printed provisions are excised, the requisite intent to make a will is still evidenced. We do not agree. In our opinion, the only words which establish this requisite testamentary intent on the part of the decedent are found in the *printed* portion of the form.

The official comment to §2-503 of the Uniform Probate Code (ULA) sheds some light upon the situation where, as here, a printed will form is used: "By requiring only the 'material provisions' to be in the testator's handwriting (rather than requiring, as some existing statutes do, that the will be 'entirely' in the testator's handwriting) a holograph may be valid even though immaterial parts such as date or introductory wording be printed or stamped. A valid holograph might even be executed on some printed will forms if the printed portion could be eliminated and the handwritten portion could evidence the testator's will. For persons unable to obtain legal assistance, the holographic will may be adequate." . . .

This court, in In re Estate of Mulkins, 17 Ariz. App. 179, 180, 496 P.2d 605, 606 (1972) traced earlier Arizona decisions and determined that the "important thing is that the *testamentary* part of the will be wholly written by the testator and of course signed by him" (citing Estate of Morrison, supra) (emphasis in original). *Mulkins* also found that the printed words of the will, set forth below[29] were not essential to the meaning of the handwritten words and could not be held to defeat the intention of the deceased otherwise clearly expressed.

It is thus clear that, under the terminology of the statute and the comment thereto, an instrument may not be probated as a holographic will where it contains words not in the handwriting of the testator if such words are essential to the testamentary disposition. However, the mere fact that the testator used a blank form, whether of a will or some other document, does not invalidate what would otherwise be a valid will if the printed words may be entirely rejected as surplusage.

In support of their position appellants rely on Estate of Blake v. Benza, 120 Ariz. 552, 587 P.2d 271 (App. 1978). In *Blake* this court upheld the trial court's admission to probate, as a valid holograph the postscript to a personal letter:

"P.S. You can have my entire estate.

"/x/ Harry J. Blake (SAVE THIS)."

There having been no contention that the letter was not written and signed by the decedent, it was held that the postscript was more than a mere casual statement, and was deemed sufficient to demonstrate a testamentary intent. Analogizing to *Blake* which held that the use of the word "estate" by the decedent inferred that he was making a disposition of his property to take effect upon his death, appellants point to that portion of the document here which states: "TO (the name of the respective person) ⅛ of my estate." as being sufficient to likewise establish the requisite intent. Again, we do not agree.

Blake did not rely solely upon the use of the word "estate" to determine that the testator had a testamentary intent. The opinion focused upon the emphasized words "SAVE THIS" to support the position that the letter was to have a future significance. The fact that the formal signature following the dispositive clause bore the testator's name in full as opposed to simply "Your Uncle Harry," as in previous letters, was also supportive of a testamentary intent. Finally, the dispositive clause itself in *Blake* contained the phrase "you can have," which clearly imported a future connotation.

Contrasting the *Blake* will to the handwritten segments of the pur-

---

29. We have omitted the printed will form used in *Mulkins*. The dispositive language handwritten on the printed will form read:

> I hereby make my will to Lettie Smith as Sister now living in Flint Michigan at 2222 on Oklahoma Ave. and Betty Hart Elkins at Rt. 1. Box 267 36 St. Just North of Southern Ave Phoenix, Ariz. about a block. I have 10 acres on Rincon Road. The South 330 feet of the Northwest quarter of the Northeast quarter of Section Twenty six 26 of township eight 8 North range 5 West of the Gila and Salt River base and Meridian Yavapai County of Arizona this 8 day of April 1966.

This makes pretty good sense as a complete disposition. — Eds.

ported will before us, we find a marked difference. Though the decedent here used the word "estate," this word alone is insufficient to indicate an animus testandi.

In Webster's New Collegiate Dictionary, G & C Merriam & Company, Springfield, 1975 at 391, one of the definitions of the word, "estate" is, "the assets and liabilities left by a person at death." However, the same word is also defined as: "the degree, quality, nature, and extent of one's interest in land or other property. POSSESSIONS, PROPERTY *esp:* a person's property in land and tenements."

Judgment affirmed.

CONTRERAS, J., specially concurring. I find myself compelled to concur in this decision because established legal principles clearly indicate that the trial court did not err in refusing to admit the document to probate. Nonetheless, I feel similarly compelled to tender the observation that the intended simplification of our statutes regarding holographic wills has perhaps created more problems than it has solved.

The most basic purpose of the Uniform Probate Code is to "discover and make effective the intent of a decedent in distribution of his property." UPC §1-102(b)(2). With respect to the execution of wills, the purpose of the Code is to simplify the requirements of execution and validate the will whenever possible. The general comment to the Uniform Probate Code Part 5 relating to wills provides in part: "If the will is to be restored to its role as the major instrument for disposition of wealth at death, its execution must be kept simple. The basic intent of these sections is to validate the will whenever possible." The result in this case is contrary to all of these expressed purposes. The document before us is clearly denominated as "THE LAST WILL AND TES-TAMENT" and the first paragraph in which the decedent, in his own handwriting, placed his name and residence in the appropriate blanks, clearly and unequivocally establishes testamentary intent. However, when the printed portion of the first paragraph is excised, testamentary intent is not established and the document fails as a valid will. Based upon case law and the official comment relating to the holographic will section of the probate code, this is the legal result which must obtain. But it is an illogical result which defeats the intent of the decedent and fails to uphold the proferred will. In addition, it ignores the practical consideration of a lay person who desires to dispose of his small estate without the assistance of an attorney. Such a person would consider a form will to be a viable alternative to seeking the services of an attorney, but unless that document is witnessed, it will fail to dispose of the decedent's estate as he desired. See A.R.S. §14-2502. And since the material provisions are not in the testator's handwriting, the document fails to meet the requirements as set forth in A.R.S. §14-2503 in order to serve as a valid holographic will.

The result in this case defeats the purposes of effectuating the intent of the decedent and simplifying the execution of wills and, in my opinion, justifies a reappraisal of the statutorily expressed requirements of a holographic will in light of realistic and practical considerations.

Clearly then the word "estate" is not the sine qua non of an intent to draft a will. Likewise, the word "TO," by itself, has neither a present nor a future meaning. We are thus unable to determine from the handwritten portions of the will form whether it was meant by decedent to have a testamentary significance and thus hold that the trial court did not err in refusing to admit it to probate. . . .

NOTES AND PROBLEMS

1. In In re Estate of Muder, 159 Ariz. 173, 765 P.2d 997 (1988), the court had before it a will handwritten on a printed will form, signed and notarized but not witnessed. The relevant handwritten dispositive language, inserted in a printed paragraph saying "I give to," read:

> My wife Retha F. Muder, our home and property in Shumway, Navajo County, car — pick up, travel trailer, and all other earthly possessions belonging to me, livestock, cattle, sheep, etc. Tools, savings accounts, checking accounts, retirement benefits, etc.

The court, 3 to 2, upheld the will as a holograph. "Such handwritten provisions may draw testamentary context from both the printed and the handwritten language on the form. We see no need to ignore the preprinted words when the testator clearly did not, and the statute does not require us to do so." The majority opinion cited but did not discuss, approve, or disapprove of In re Estate of Johnson. Is this case consistent with the official comment to UPC §2-503, quoted in the *Johnson* case?

2. A few months after the death of her husband in March 1984, Esther Smith delivered to Harry Fass, her 84-year-old attorney, a writing which read:

> My entire estate is to be left *jointly* to my step-daughter, Roberta Crowley, and my step-son, David J. Smith.
>
> /s/ *Esther L. Smith*

According to the attorney's testimony, when Mrs. Smith handed him the writing, which was on a 5 × 7 piece of paper torn from a notebook, she said, "this is my will, this is the way I want my estate to go." The attorney, however, did not treat the paper as a will. He did not put the paper in his safe. He stapled the paper to the probate file of her husband. He wrote on the paper, "Extor-David," meaning David was to be the executor. In September 1984, the attorney wrote Mrs. Smith that he was retiring: "Your file and/or Last Will and Testament in my office is at your disposal if you do not care to retain [the attorney to whom he was transferring his practice]."

Mrs. Smith died in October 1984. Her heirs are her first cousins. Is the paper entitled to probate? In re Will of Smith, 108 N.J. 257, 528 A.2d 918 (1987).

3. The following letter was offered for probate by the deceased's sister, Nina.

> Los Angeles
> October 1, 1890

Nina:

I wrote you yesterday, hastily. Answer my letter at once. I want to know everything about mother, and all about you, — your children. I have reached the point of perfect independence, pecuniarily. My health is probably ruined, and I want to anticipate possibilities. You and your children get everything. Your boy I want given the best of educations. I would like him to go to Harvard. I would like to have him a lawyer. Don't bring him up a prejudiced southerner, but teach honor, — make it dearer than life, and he must, with the blood in his veins, be a man. Write me. As soon as I possibly can, I will be in Savannah.

> /s/ *Brother*

What result? In re Richardson's Estate, 94 Cal. 63, 29 P. 484 (1892).

Assuming the above letter was otherwise held to be a valid holographic will, would "Brother" satisfy the signature requirement? Would a testator's initials ("C.B.R.") satisfy the signature requirement? See Estate of Cook, [1960] 1 W.L.R. 353, 1 All E.R. 689, 75 A.L.R.2d 892; Annot., 98 A.L.R.2d 841 (1964).

4. Purported holographic wills have taken myriad forms — and shapes. Wills have been written on a nurse's petticoat, inscribed on an eggshell, and scratched on a tractor fender. If you are interested in this sort of thing, there is a lot of humor and human interest to be found in V. Harris, Ancient, Curious and Famous Wills (1911, reprint 1981); P. Menchin, The Last Caprice (1963); Million, Wills: Witty, Witless, and Wicked, 7 Wayne L. Rev. 335 (1960); Gest, Some Jolly Testators, 8 Temp. L.Q. 297 (1934). We offer a recent addition to the list, reported in the Austin (Texas) American-Statesman, October 15, 1968.

Unusual Will Names Dancer

PHILADELPHIA (AP) — A note to a belly dancer scribbled on a bedroom wall was offered Tuesday as a legal last will and testament.

An 18-inch square section of the plaster wall was sawed out under the supervision of Register of Wills John E. Walsh and submitted to Probate Court.

Aug 10 1948

NOTICE

Will-of-W.J. Burns-USN Vetern
Every-thing-I-posses-at-time-of-death
I will-to-my-son-T.E. Burns-615 S._____ Ave.
Yakima-Wn.

(s) W.J. Burns   [photograph]

***Holographic will to testator's son written on bot-
tom of chest of drawers, sawed out and admitted
to probate in Los Angeles County.***

The note, signed by Hermann Schmidt, 49, who died Sept. 15, said in part:

"Genevieve: You take care of all my belongings. This give's you authority. Love, Hermann, 8-14-1968."

Attorney Leio T. Connor said he believes this entitles Genevieve — Genevieve Decker, 42, a belly dancer and Schmidt's fiancee — to Schmidt's $12,000 estate and plans to file it for this purpose.

Would you be as confident as attorney Connor that the piece of plaster is entitled to probate? That Genevieve takes all of Hermann's estate if it is admitted to probate? Compare In re Estate of Gasparovich, 487 P.2d 1148 (Mont. 1971).

5. Under the dispensing power recommended by Professor Langbein (supra page 194), could a holographic will be probated in a state not authorizing holographic wills? If the witnesses can be dispensed

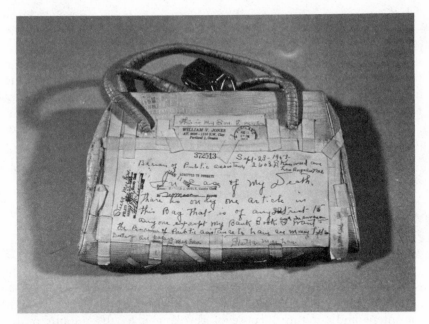

This is my Son S. Meehan
[printed name and address]

Sept-23-1953

Bureau of Public Assistance 2603 S. Kenwood Ave.
Los Angeles 7 Cal.
In case of my Death, there is only one article in this Bag that is of any Interest to anyone except my Bank Book and Insurance. I want the Bureau of Public Assistance to have any money Left. Destroy all papers.

(s) Stella Meehan.

Holographic will written on bag, admitted to probate in Los Angeles County.

---

with, what difference does it make whether the will is handwritten or typed?

SECTION C.   REVOCATION OF WILLS

1.   Revocation by Writing or Physical Act

A will is an ambulatory document, which means that it is subject to modification or revocation by the testator during his or her lifetime.

All states permit revocation of a will in one of two ways: (1) by a subsequent *writing* executed with testamentary formalities,[30] or (2) by a *physical act* such as destroying, obliterating, or burning the will. On the assumption that oral revocations would open the door wide for fraud, an oral declaration that a will is revoked, without more, is inoperative in all states. *If a duly executed will is not revoked in a manner permitted by statute, the will is admitted to probate.*

The Uniform Probate Code's revocation section is fairly representative of statutes setting forth methods of permissible revocation.

Uniform Probate Code (1983)

§2-507   [REVOCATION BY WRITING OR BY ACT]

A will or any part thereof is revoked

(1)   by a subsequent will which revokes the prior will or part expressly or by inconsistency; or

(2)   by being burned, torn, canceled, obliterated, or destroyed, with the intent and for the purpose of revoking it by the testator or by another person in his presence and by his direction.

PROBLEMS

1.   *Revocation by physical act.*   The testator writes the following note and has it delivered to Dr. O'Kennedy, who has custody of her will:

> Dr. O'Kennedy:
> Dear Friend. — Please destroy the Will I made in favor of Thomas Hart.
>
> /s/ *Margaret McGill*

Is the will revoked if Dr. O'Kennedy destroys the will? If he does not destroy it? In re McGill, 229 N.Y. 405, 128 N.E. 194 (1920).

Suppose that the testator calls Dr. O'Kennedy on the telephone and directs him to destroy the will. While she is on the other end of the line, Dr. O'Kennedy tears up the will and throws it in the wastebasket.

---

30. Uniform Probate Code §1-201(48) defines a *will* to include a "codicil and any testamentary instrument which merely appoints an executor or revokes or revises another will."

In states recognizing holographic wills, a holograph can revoke a typewritten, attested will.

Is the will revoked? See Estate of Kraus, 87 Misc. 2d 492, 385 N.Y.S.2d 933 (Sur. Ct. 1976).

Suppose that the testator lives for seven years after Dr. O'Kennedy destroys her will and never makes another will. Does the testator's failure to execute a new will give rise to a presumption of revocation? See In re Estate of McCaffrey, 453 Pa. 416, 309 A.2d 539, 61 A.L.R.3d 949 (1973).

2. *Will and codicil.* In 1985 *T* executes a will that gives all her property to *A*. In 1987 *T* executes a will that gives her diamond ring to *B* and her automobile to *C*. It contains no words of revocation. Even though the 1987 will makes no reference to the earlier will, the 1987 will is ordinarily called a codicil.

(a) In 1989 *T* destroys the codicil with the intention of revoking it; *T* dies in 1990. The 1985 will is offered for probate. Should it be admitted? See In re Estate of Hering, 108 Cal. App. 3d 88, 166 Cal. Rptr. 298 (1980); Annot., 7 A.L.R.3d 1143 (1966).

(b) Suppose, instead, that *T* destroys the 1985 will with the intention of revoking it. After *T*'s death the codicil is offered for probate. Should it be admitted? See Comment, Wills — Revocation by Act to the Document — Effect on Codicil, 60 Mich. L. Rev. 82 (1961).

NOTE: PROBATE OF LOST WILLS

In the absence of statute, a will that is lost, or is destroyed without the consent of the testator, or is destroyed with the consent of the testator but not in compliance with the revocation statute (see In re McGill, supra) can be admitted into probate if its contents are proved. A lost will can be proved by a copy in the lawyer-drafter's office or by a secretary who typed the will or by other clear and convincing evidence.

In some states, statutes dealing specifically with proof of lost wills might be barriers to probate. See Anderson v. Griggs, 402 So. 2d 904, 31 A.L.R.4th 297 (Ala. 1981). However, these statutes have usually been strictly interpreted by the courts. For example, in a few states statutes prohibit the probate of a lost or destroyed will unless the will was "in existence" at the testator's death (and destroyed thereafter) or was "fraudulently destroyed" during the testator's life. Theoretically, under such a statute a will accidentally tossed out by a housekeeper during the testator's life cannot be probated. Thus, on its face, such a statute is in conflict with the state's will revocation statute, since under it a will not legally revoked is nevertheless barred from probate. Courts have chosen to give effect to the will revocation statutes and have gutted the proof statutes by holding *either* that a will not lawfully revoked continues in "legal existence" until the testator's death (and the word "existence" in the statute means "legal existence") *or* that a will destroyed by a method not permitted by the will revocation statute has been "fraudulently destroyed." See Estate of Irvine v. Doyle, 710 P.2d 1366 (Nev. 1985).

With rare exceptions, the only proper way to revoke a will is by a subsequent will that unequivocally revokes "all wills and codicils heretofore made by me." Revocation by physical act, as by burning, tearing, or cancelling, is not a recommended method of revocation because the physical act is inherently ambiguous. To be legally effective, the act must be accompanied by an intention to revoke. The act, without *animus revocandi*, does not revoke the will. Proof of intent must be found in the words or conduct of the testator — as recalled by others, as the principal is never present to testify. In many cases there is no direct evidence of intent, and various presumptions are brought into play. Further, there may be no direct evidence that it was the testator who cancelled or obliterated the will, giving rise to a nagging suspicion that someone else may have wielded the scissors or the marking pencil.

At common law if it is shown that the will was in possession of the testator before death, and that the will cannot be found after death, a presumption arises that the testator destroyed the will with intent to revoke it. Board of Trustees of Univ. of Ala. v. Calhoun, 514 So. 2d 895 (Ala. 1987); In re Bonner, 17 N.Y.2d 9, 214 N.E.2d 154, 266 N.Y.S.2d 971, 28 A.L.R.3d 990 (1966). This presumption is not, however, a notably strong one. If the disinherited heir had an opportunity to destroy the will during the testator's last illness or before his death, the court may be persuaded — depending on other evidence — that the presumption is rebutted. Compare Stiles v. Brown, 380 So. 2d 792 (Ala. 1980), with Estate of Travers, 121 Ariz. 282, 589 P.2d 1314 (1978). See Annot., 70 A.L.R.4th 323 (1989).

PROBLEM

Although the practice has little to recommend it, testators sometimes execute duplicate original wills, usually upon the advice of a lawyer who keeps one duplicate in the lawyer's office safe and hands the other duplicate to the testator. (Why might a lawyer advise this?) Since both duplicates are properly executed, either is admissible into probate. In most states, if the testator destroys one of the duplicates with intent to revoke, both duplicate wills are revoked.

Suppose that *T* executes duplicate wills, leaving one for safekeeping with her attorney and taking the other home. At *T*'s death the duplicate will that *T* took home cannot be found. Can the duplicate in the attorney's possession be probated? See In re Estate of Millsap, 55 Ill. App. 3d 749, 371 N.E.2d 185 (1977). Suppose that *T* has one duplicate will in her safe-deposit box and one at home, and the copy kept at home in her desk cannot be found. What result? See Etgen v. Corboy, 230 Va. 413, 337 S.E.2d 286 (1985).

Thompson v. Royall
Supreme Court of Virginia, 1934
163 Va. 492, 175 S.E. 748

HUDGINS, J. The only question presented by this record is whether the will of Mrs. M. Lou Bowen Kroll had been revoked shortly before her death.

The uncontroverted facts are as follows: On the 4th day of September, 1932, Mrs. Kroll signed a will, typewritten on the five sheets of legal cap paper; the signature appeared on the last page duly attested by three subscribing witnesses. H.P. Brittain, the executor named in the will, was given possession of the instrument for safe-keeping. A codicil typed on the top third of one sheet of paper dated September 15, 1932, was signed by the testatrix in the presence of two subscribing witnesses. Possession of this instrument was given to Judge S.M.B. Coulling, the attorney who prepared both documents.

On September 19, 1932, at the request of Mrs. Kroll, Judge Coulling and Mr. Brittain took the will and the codicil to her home where she told her attorney, in the presence of Mr. Brittain and another, to destroy both. But, instead of destroying the papers, at the suggestion of Judge Coulling, she decided to retain them as memoranda, to be used as such in the event she decided to execute a new will. Upon the back of the manuscript cover, which was fastened to the five sheets by metal clasps, in the handwriting of Judge Coulling, signed by Mrs. Kroll, there is the following notation:

> This will null and void and to be only held by H.P. Brittain instead of being destroyed as a memorandum for another will if I desire to make same. This 19 Sept. 1932.
>
> *M. Lou Bowen Kroll.*

The same notation was made upon the back of the sheet on which the codicil was written, except that the name S.M.B. Coulling was substituted for H.P. Brittain; this was likewise signed by Mrs. Kroll.

Mrs. Kroll died October 2, 1932, leaving numerous nephews and nieces, some of whom were not mentioned in her will, and an estate valued at approximately $200,000. On motion of some of the beneficiaries, the will and codicil were offered for probate. All the interested parties including the heirs at law were convened, and on the issue devisavit vel non the jury found that the instruments dated September 4 and 15, 1932, were the last will and testament of Mrs. M. Lou Bowen Kroll. From an order sustaining the verdict and probating the will this writ of error was allowed.

For more than 100 years, the means by which a duly executed will may be revoked have been prescribed by statute. These requirements are found in section 5233 of the 1919 Code, the pertinent parts of which read thus: "No will or codicil, or any part thereof, shall be revoked, unless . . . by a subsequent will or codicil, or by some writing declaring an intention to revoke the same, and executed in the manner in which a will is required to be executed, or by the testator, or some person in his presence and by his direction, cutting, tearing, burning, obliterating, canceling, or destroying the same, or the signature thereto, with the intent to revoke."

The notations, dated September 19, 1932, are not wholly in the handwriting of the testatrix, nor are her signatures thereto attached attested by subscribing witnesses; hence under the statute they are ineffectual as "some writing declaring an intention to revoke." The faces of the two instruments bear no physical evidence of any cutting, tearing, burning, obliterating, canceling, or destroying. The only contention made by appellants is that the notation written in the presence, and with the approval, of Mrs. Kroll, on the back of the manuscript cover in the one instance, and on the back of the sheet containing the codicil in the other, constitute "canceling" within the meaning of the statute.

Both parties concede that to effect revocation of a duly executed will, in any of the methods prescribed by statute, two things are necessary: (1) The doing of one of the acts specified, (2) accompanied by the intent to revoke — the animo revocandi. Proof of either, without proof of the other, is insufficient. Malone v. Hobbs, 1 Rob. (40 Va.) 346, 39 Am. Dec. 263; 2 Minor Ins. 925.

The proof established the intention to revoke. The entire controversy is confined to the acts used in carrying out that purpose. The testatrix adopted the suggestion of her attorney to revoke her will by written memoranda, admittedly ineffectual as revocations by subsequent writings, but appellants contend the memoranda, in the handwriting of another, and testatrix' signatures, are sufficient to effect revocation by cancellation. To support this contention, appellants cite a number of authorities which hold that the modern definition of cancellation includes "any act which would destroy, revoke, recall, do away with, overrule, render null and void, the instrument."

Most of the authorities cited that approve the above or a similar meaning of the word were dealing with cancellation of simple contracts, or other instruments that require little or no formality in execution. However, there is one line of cases which apply this extended meaning of "canceling" to the revocation of wills. The leading case so holding is Warner v. Warner's Estate, 37 Vt. 356. In this case proof of the intent and the act were a notation on the same page with, and below the signature of, the testator, reading: "This will is hereby cancelled and annulled. In full this 15th day of March in the year 1859," and written lengthwise on the back of the fourth page of the foolscap paper, upon which no part of the written will appeared, were these words, "Cancelled and is null and void. (Signed) I. Warner." It was held this was sufficient to revoke the will under a statute similar to the one here under consideration.

In Evans' Appeal, 58 Pa. 238, the Pennsylvania court approved the reasoning of the Vermont court in Warner v. Warner's Estate, supra, but the force of the opinion is weakened when the facts are considered. It seems that there were lines drawn through two of the three signatures of the testator appearing in the Evans will, and the paper on which material parts of the will were written was torn in four places. It therefore appeared on the face of the instrument, when offered for probate, that there was a sufficient defacement to bring it within the meaning of both obliteration and cancellation.

The construction of the statute in Warner v. Warner's Estate, supra, has been criticized by eminent text-writers on wills, and the courts in the majority of the states in construing similar statutes have refused to follow the reasoning in that case. Jarman on Wills (6th Ed.) 147, note 1; Schouler on Wills (5th Ed.) §391; Redfield on the Law of Wills (4th Ed.) 323-325; 28 R.C.L. 180; 40 Cyc. 1173; Dowling v. Gilliland, 286 Ill. 530, 122 N.E. 70, 3 A.L.R. 839. . . .

The above, and other authorities that might be cited, hold that revocation of a will by cancellation within the meaning of the statute contemplates marks or lines across the written parts of the instrument or a physical defacement, or some mutilation of the writing itself, with the intent to revoke. If written words are used for the purpose, they must be so placed as to physically affect the written portion of the will, not merely on blank parts of the paper on which the will is written. If the writing intended to be the act of canceling does not mutilate, or erase, or deface, or otherwise physically come in contact with, any part of written words of the will, it cannot be given any greater weight than a similar writing on a separate sheet of paper, which identifies the will referred to, just as definitely as does the writing on the back. If a will may be revoked by writing on the back, separable from the will, it may be done by a writing not on the will. This the statute forbids. . . .

The attempted revocation is ineffectual, because testatrix intended to revoke her will by subsequent writings not executed as required by statute, and because it does not in any wise physically obliterate, mutilate, deface, or cancel any written parts of the will.

For the reasons stated, the judgment of the trial court is affirmed.

QUESTIONS AND PROBLEMS

1. If Judge Coulling had been sued for negligence by Mrs. Kroll's heirs, would he have been held liable?

2. What policy is served by the court's decision in the *Thompson* case? Given the clear and uncontroverted evidence of Mrs. Kroll's intention that her will be revoked, how can the court's decision be justified? Should a court have power to dispense with formalities when there is clear and convincing evidence that the testator intended to revoke the will? See supra pages 194-195.

3. Suppose that Mrs. Kroll had written, on the left-hand margin of each page of the will, "Cancelled. 19/9/32. M. Kroll." Would this be a valid revocation by physical act? See Kronauge v. Stoecklein, 33 Ohio App. 2d 229, 293 N.E.2d 320 (1972). Would this be a valid revocation in states permitting holographic wills? See McCarthy v. Bank of California, 64 Or. App. 473, 668 P.2d 481 (1983) (valid holographic revocation); but cf. In re Estate of Johnson, supra page 219, dealing with *execution* of holographic will.

4. Suppose that Mrs. Kroll had written "VOID" across the face of an unexecuted typewritten carbon copy of her will. Would this be a valid revocation by physical act? See In re D'Agostino's Will, 9 N.J. Super. 230, 75 A.2d 213 (1950); In re Wehr's Will, 247 Wis. 98, 18 N.W.2d 709 (1945).

5. In 1964 T executed a will devising his entire estate to A. In 1965 T informed his lawyer that he wanted to leave his property in equal shares to A and B. The lawyer thereupon, in the presence of T, removed the staples from the will and dictated to his secretary a new first page. The lawyer then directed the secretary to copy the remaining pages and instructed her to request another attorney in the same office to supervise the execution, as he had an appointment out of the office. The secretary typed the new page but, to save herself work, failed to carry out the other directions. She attached the new first page to the others, stapled them together, and had T initial all the pages. When the lawyer returned, she told him his instructions had been carried out. Is either the 1964 will or the 1965 will entitled to probate? In re Will

of Robinson, 26 A.D.2d 306, 273 N.Y.S.2d 985 (1966), held that the 1964 will was revoked by mutilation and the 1965 will was not validly executed. Is the lawyer liable for negligence? See Wade, Tort Liability of Paralegals and Lawyers Who Utilize Their Services, 24 Vand. L. Rev. 1133 (1971); cf. In re Peterson, 178 N.W.2d 738 (N.D. 1970), holding attorney responsible in disciplinary proceeding for improper acts of secretary that he should have discovered in the exercise of appropriate supervision.

Partial Revocation by Physical Act. Although UPC §2-507 and the statutes of a number of states authorize partial revocation by physical act, in several states a will cannot be revoked in part by an act of revocation; it can be revoked in part only by a subsequent instrument. The reasons for prohibiting partial revocation by physical act are two. First, cancelling a gift to one person necessarily results in someone else taking the gift, and this "new gift" — like all bequests — can be made only by an attested writing. Second, permitting partial revocation by physical act offers opportunity for fraud. The person who takes the "new gift" may be the one who made the cancelling marks. If partial revocation by act is not recognized, the will must be admitted to probate in the form in which it was originally executed if the original language can be ascertained.

PROBLEM

T executes a will that devises the residue of her estate to four named relatives. After *T*'s death some years later, her will is found in a stack of papers on her desk. One of the four names in the residuary clause has been lined out with a No. 3 lead pencil. There is no direct evidence that *T* marked out the name.

(a) What result in a state having a statute similar to Uniform Probate Code §2-507? See In re Byrne's Will, 223 Wis. 503, 271 N.W. 48 (1937); contra, Dodson v. Walton, 268 Ark. 431, 597 S.W.2d 814 (1980). See also Annots., 34 A.L.R.2d 619 (1954), 24 A.L.R.2d 514, 524 (1952).

(b) What result in a state that does not permit partial revocation by physical act? See McCray v. Reed, 358 So. 2d 432 (Ala. 1978); In re Estate of Haurin, 605 P.2d 65 (Colo. App. 1979).

(c) Suppose that *T*'s will is a holographic will in a jurisdiction permitting holographic wills. What result? See La Rue v. Lee, 63 W. Va. 388, 60 S.E. 388 (1908).

2. Dependent Relative Revocation and Revival

Simply put, the doctrine of dependent relative revocation is this: If the testator purports to revoke his will upon a mistaken assumption of law or fact, the revocation is ineffective if the testator would not have revoked his will had he known the truth. The usual case involves a situation where the testator destroys his will under a belief that a new will is valid but for some reason the new will is invalid. If the court finds that the testator would not have destroyed his will had he known the new will was ineffective, the court, applying the doctrine of dependent relative revocation, will cancel the revocation and probate the destroyed will. For example, suppose that T duly executes a will devising his property to "Peggy Martin." Thereafter T learns that the legal name of the intended devisee is "Margaret Martin," not "Peggy Martin," and T decides that this misdescription should be corrected. T therefore cancels his old will by writing "VOID" across it, and executes a new will devising his property to "Margaret Martin." Unfortunately Margaret Martin is one of the two witnesses to the new will, and the devise to her is ineffective. Since it is clear that T wants Martin to take his property, under the doctrine of dependent relative revocation the revocation of the first will is cancelled; the first will is probated and Margaret Martin (a.k.a. Peggy Martin) takes T's property under that will. The doctrine is applied to carry out the testator's presumed intent. On dependent relative revocation generally, see Palmer, Dependent Relative Revocation and Its Relation to Relief for Mistake, 69 Mich. L. Rev. 989 (1971); Warren, Dependent Relative Revocation, 33 Harv. L. Rev. 337 (1920).

PROBLEMS

1. Clause 5 of T's typewritten will provides: "I bequeath the sum of $1,000 to my nephew, Charles Blake." T crosses out the "$1,000" and substitutes therefore "$1,500." T then writes her initials and the date in the right-hand margin opposite this entry. After T's death some years later, her will is admitted to probate. Blake contends that he is entitled to $1,500 or, in the alternative, $1,000.

(a) What result in a state that recognizes holographic wills? See Estate of Phifer, 152 Cal. App. 3d 813, 200 Cal. Rptr. 319 (1984); but cf. McCarthy v. Bank of California, supra page 234; In re Estate of Muder, supra page 224.

(b) What result in a state that does not permit partial revocation by physical act?

(c) What result in a state that permits partial revocation by physical act? Should the doctrine of dependent relative revocation be applied? See Carpenter v. Wynn, 252 Ky. 543, 67 S.W.2d 688 (1934).

(d) Suppose that *T* had crossed out "$1,000" and substituted "$500." In a state that permits partial revocation by physical act, should the doctrine of dependent relative revocation be applied? See Ruel v. Hardy, 90 N.H. 240, 6 A.2d 753 (1939).

2. In his typewritten will, which contains a legacy of $5,000 to "John Boone," *T* crosses out "John" and writes in "Nancy." Nancy cannot take because the gift to her is not attested. In a state permitting partial revocation by physical act, should the legacy to John be given effect under the doctrine of dependent relative revocation? See In re Houghten's Estate, 310 Mich. 613, 17 N.W.2d 744 (1945); Annots., 24 A.L.R.2d 514, 556 (1952).

In a state that recognizes holographic wills, the change from John to Nancy is not a valid holograph even though *T* signs his name on the margin. Standing alone, the handwritten words are insufficient to constitute a will. Estate of Phifer, supra. On the other hand, if *T*'s will were entirely handwritten and a valid holograph, the change from John to Nancy would be permitted. See Stanley v. Henderson, 139 Tex. 160, 162 S.W.2d 95 (1942); Estate of Archer, 193 Cal. App. 3d 238, 239 Cal. Rptr. 137 (1987).

3. In Body Heat, a steamy 1981 *film noir* set in Florida, Matty Walker (Kathleen Turner), a silky sexpot bent on doing away with her rich older husband, entraps a not-so-smart, randy young lawyer, Ned Racine (William Hurt), to do the dirty work. The husband's existing will leaves half his fortune to Matty and half to his 10-year-old niece, Heather. After the husband is done in by Ned, Matty — a sometime legal secretary — produces a second will, written by Matty on stationery stolen from Ned's office, to which she has forged the signatures of her husband and — to his astonishment — Ned as a witness. (The second witness is — well, it takes too long to explain: you'll have to rent the videocassette.) This second will leaves half to Matty, but it puts Heather's half in a trust that violates the Rule against Perpetuities. At a family conference, the husband's lawyer, oozing unction at every pore, pronounces the second will void. As a result, the lawyer says, the husband died intestate, and under Florida law Matty takes her husband's entire estate. Little Heather and her mother meekly acquiesce and disappear from the movie. Matty ends up on an island paradise with all her husband's money and a new lover; the dupe Ned is left languishing in jail.

Before the movie was made, Florida had adopted wait-and-see for perpetuities violations (see infra page 816). Hence the husband's lawyer was too quick on the trigger; the trust for Heather might not turn out to be void. Apart from this oversight by the screenwriter, what other legal doctrine did the writer overlook that could have saved Heather's share? Though wills lawyers might grouse, these flaws seem not to have been noticed by the critics. The movie was boffo at the box office.

Estate of Alburn
Supreme Court of Wisconsin, 1963
18 Wis. 2d 340, 118 N.W.2d 919

FACTS

Ottilie L. Alburn, a resident of the city of Fort Atkinson, Jefferson county, died on November 13, 1960, at the age of eighty-five years. On December 5, 1960, Adele Ruedisili, a sister of deceased, filed a petition for appointment of an administrator of the estate, which petition alleged that deceased died intestate. Thereafter, Viola Henkey, a grandniece of the deceased, filed a petition for the probate of a will which deceased executed at Milwaukee, Wisconsin, in 1955 (hereinafter the "Milwaukee will"), in which Viola Henkey was named a legatee and also executrix. After the filing of these two petitions, Lulu Alburn and Doris Alburn filed a petition for the probate of a will which deceased executed at Kankakee, Illinois, in 1959 (hereinafter the "Kankakee will"). Neither of these last-named petitioners is a next-of-kin of the deceased but Lulu Alburn is a sister-in-law of deceased. Objections were filed to both the Milwaukee and Kankakee wills.

proc.

The county court held a joint hearing on all three petitions. . . . The court determined that the Kankakee will had been destroyed by deceased under the mistaken belief that by so doing she would revive the Milwaukee will which had been revoked by the revocation clause of the Kankakee will. The court applied the doctrine of dependent relative revocation and held that the Kankakee will was entitled to probate. By a judgment (denominated an "Order") entered December 28, 1961, the Kankakee will was admitted to probate. Adele Ruedisili has appealed this judgment. The proponents of the Milwaukee will have not appealed. Further facts will be stated in the opinion.

CURRIE, J.   This court is committed to the doctrine of dependent relative revocation. Estate of Eberhardt (1957), 1 Wis. 2d 439, 85 N.W.2d 483, and Estate of Callahan (1947), 251 Wis. 247, 29 N.W.2d 352. The usual situation for application of this doctrine arises where a testator executes one will and thereafter attempts to revoke it by making a later testamentary disposition which for some reason proves ineffective. In both the *Eberhardt* and *Callahan* Cases, however, the doctrine was applied to the unusual situation in which a testator revokes a later will under the mistaken belief that by so doing he is reinstating a prior will. In this unusual situation, the doctrine of dependent relative revocation is invoked to render the revocation ineffective. The basis of the doctrine is stated in Estate of Callahan, supra, as follows (251 Wis. at p.255, 29 N.W.2d at p.355):

The doctrine of dependent relative revocation is based upon the testator's inferred intention. It is held that as a matter of law the destruction of the later document is intended to be conditional where it is accompanied by the expressed intent of reinstating a former will and where there is no explanatory evidence. Of course if there is evidence that the testator intended the destruction to be absolute, there is no room for the application of the doctrine of dependent revocation.

The sole question raised by appellant on this appeal is whether the finding of the trial court that deceased revoked the Kankakee will under the mistaken belief that she was thereby reinstating the prior Milwaukee will is against the great weight and clear preponderance of the evidence. This requires that we review the pertinent evidence.

Testatrix was born in Wisconsin. For about thirty years she had resided in San Francisco, California, and later in Cleveland, Ohio. As a widow without children, she came to Milwaukee in the fall of 1954 and lived there with Viola Henkey, her grandniece. While so residing she executed the Milwaukee will on August 12, 1955. The original of this will was left with Attorney George R. Affeldt of Milwaukee, who had drafted it, where it remained until the death of testatrix. Sometime shortly prior to May 22, 1959, testatrix moved to Kankakee, Illinois, and resided there with her brother, Robert Lehmann. On May 22, 1959, she executed the Kankakee will.

On June 28, 1960, testatrix left Kankakee and came to Fort Atkinson, Wisconsin, and lived there with another brother, Edwin Lehmann, until her death in November of 1960. Testatrix was a patient at a hospital in Fort Atkinson during part of October and November of that year. Edwin testified that he had learned of the execution of the Kankakee will prior to the arrival of testatrix on June 28, 1960. On the evening of her arrival, he asked her what she had done with that will, and she replied, "What do you suppose, I got rid of it."[31] The next morning testatrix came downstairs with the torn pieces of the Kankakee will tied up in a handkerchief. Edwin provided her with a paper sack in which she deposited the pieces of the will. Edwin then took the sack with the garbage to the dump. There he opened the sack and let the pieces fly in the wind as testatrix had directed him to do.

Edwin was not questioned about any statement regarding the Milwaukee will which testatrix might have made in his presence at Fort

---

31. The trial court in its memorandum decision found that the attempted revocation of the Kankakee will took place in Illinois but held that Wisconsin law rather than Illinois law controlled the question of whether the doctrine of dependent relative revocation should be invoked. This ruling is in accord with Restatement, Conflicts, p.389, §307, which states: "Whether an act claimed to be a revocation of a will is effective to revoke it as a will of movables is determined by the law of the state in which the deceased was domiciled at the time of his death."

Atkinson. He did testify that after her death he searched through her effects for a will but failed to find one. In view of the following testimony given by Olga Lehmann, his wife, this gives rise to an inference that Edwin was searching for the Milwaukee will.

Olga Lehmann was called as a witness by counsel for proponents of the Kankakee will. . . . Olga Lehmann was then asked the following questions and gave the following answers thereto:

> Q. Did the deceased ever discuss in your presence the matter of the Milwaukee will at any other time other than the time we are just now referring to?
> A. Yes.
> Q. Who was present at that time?
> A. Just myself.
> Q. What did she tell you concerning the Milwaukee will?
> A. That was the one she wanted to stand.
> Q. Can you tell me in point of time when this might have been?
> A. No, we talked often.

We deem it significant that counsel for appellant did not cross-examine Olga Lehmann with respect to her testimony that testatrix said she wanted the Milwaukee will to stand. Therefore, Olga Lehmann's testimony was not qualified or limited in any way.

This statement by testatrix clearly occurred after her destruction of the Kankakee will. Appellant now attacks this statement on the ground that it was not made contemporaneously with such destruction. In Estate of Callahan, supra, however, the only evidence regarding the intent of testatrix when she destroyed her 1944 will was her husband's statement in her presence after the destruction and her silence indicating acquiescence. The husband stated that they both had destroyed their 1944 wills because they desired to put their son back in the position he occupied under their 1940 wills. Upon this evidence this court determined the doctrine of dependent relative revocation applied and affirmed the judgment of the county court which had admitted the 1944 will of testatrix to probate.

The plan of testamentary disposition under the two wills was in part as follows: The Milwaukee will contained specific bequests of jewelry and household furnishings to Viola Henkey, the grandniece of testatrix, and directed that any indebtedness owing deceased by Viola Henkey and her husband be deemed satisfied. The residuary clause bequeathed one fourth of the estate to her friend Olga Olson, one fourth to Doris Alburn, one fourth to Lulu Alburn, and one fourth to Viola Henkey. The Kankakee will included a bequest to Olga Olson of 38 shares of stock in the Bank of America National Trust & Savings Association and bequests of jewelry to Lulu and Addie Alburn. The remainder of the estate was bequeathed as follows: four tenths to Lulu Alburn, five tenths to Doris Alburn, and one tenth to Robert Lehmann, brother of testatrix. The Alburns are not related to testatrix but are relatives of her deceased husband. Viola Henkey, although a blood relative of testatrix, is not one of her next-of-kin who would inherit in the event testatrix had died intestate. The next-of-kin consist of four surviving brothers and one sister plus a large number of nieces and nephews of testatrix, the children of four deceased sisters and one deceased brother. Thus under the Milwaukee will, none of the next-of-kin were named as legatees, whereas under the Kankakee will, the only next-of-kin named a legatee was Robert, her brother. His share under the Kankakee will is somewhat less than the one-tenth share of the entire estate which he would receive if testatrix had died intestate. The bulk of the estate under both wills was bequeathed to the Alburns and Olga Olson. This plan of testamentary disposition extended as late as May, 1959.

There is no evidence of any change of circumstances occurring thereafter that would indicate any reason why testatrix should die intestate and nine tenths of her estate go to next-of-kin not named in either will. The one change in circumstance was her leaving the home of her brother Robert and moving in with her brother Edwin. This move might provide a reason for her desiring to revoke the Kankakee will, but certainly not for her wishing to die intestate. The learned trial judge, in the supplemental memorandum decision of December 26, 1961, stated, "I have a strong conviction that decedent did not want to die intestate." The evidence fully supports this conclusion despite the fact that testatrix took no steps between June 29, 1960, and her death nearly five months later to draft a new will. We deem that a reasonable inference, to be drawn from the competent evidence in this case, for her failure to make a new will is her evident belief that her Milwaukee will was still operative. Testatrix must have known that the original of the Milwaukee will was still in possession of Attorney Affeldt and believed that the only impediment to this will was the revocation clause of the Kankakee will. She also knew that the Kankakee will had been destroyed by tearing it in pieces and scattering the pieces so that they could not be found.[32]

We are constrained to conclude that the statement made to Olga Lehmann that testatrix wished her Milwaukee will to stand, the inference that she did not wish to die intestate, and the fact that she took no steps following the destruction of the Kankakee will to make a new will are sufficient evidence to support the finding that she destroyed the Kankakee will under the mistaken belief that the Milwaukee will would

---

32. The contents of the Kankakee will were proved by a carbon copy in the possession of the lawyer who had drafted it at Kankakee, Illinois.

control the disposition of her estate. Furthermore there is no evidence which controverts this finding. Therefore, it is not against the great weight and clear preponderance of the evidence.

Counsel for respondents Alburn request a review by this court of several rulings by the trial court which excluded certain evidence pursuant to objections made by counsel for appellant Ruedisili. This excluded evidence related to further statements made by testatrix, after destruction of the Kankakee will, that she then considered her Milwaukee will to be in effect or desired this result. In view of our conclusion that the trial court's determination may be sustained upon the evidence admitted, we find it unnecessary to review these rulings.

Judgment affirmed.

NOTE: REVIVAL

Under Wisconsin law the will executed by Ottilie Alburn in Milwaukee in 1955 could not be revived after it had been expressly revoked by the 1959 Kankakee will. Why not? The explanation requires a brief discussion of the doctrine of revival.

The question of revival typically arises under the following facts (which were present in Estate of Alburn): Testator executes will #1. Subsequently testator executes will #2, which revokes will #1 by an express clause or by inconsistency. Later testator revokes will #2. Is will #1 revived?

Although the law of revival contains many variations of view, the states generally fall within one of three groups. A few courts in the United States take the view of the English common law courts that will #1 is not revoked unless will #2 remains in effect until the testator's death. The theory is that, prior to the testator's death, neither will #1 nor will #2 is legally effective, and therefore will #1 is not "revoked" by will #2. Will #2 is viewed as merely "covering" will #1. When this "cover" is removed by the testator's act of revoking it, will #1 remains as testator's will. This theory rests upon a notion that a revocation is not "effective" until death. Technically it does not involve "revival" at all, because the first will has never been revoked.

The large majority of jurisdictions assume that will #2 legally revokes will #1 at the time will #2 is executed. But they divide into two groups. One group of states holds that upon revocation of will #2, will #1 is revived if the testator so intends. The testator's intent may be shown from the circumstances surrounding revocation of will #2 or from the testator's contemporaneous or subsequent oral declarations that will #1 is to take effect. This position is taken by Uniform Probate Code §2-509.

but "dep.- revoc.
rel. & rev."

UPC 2-509
supp. 41

The other group of states takes the view that a revoked will cannot be revived unless reexecuted with testamentary formalities or republished by being referred to in a later duly executed testamentary writing. Wisconsin is in this group of states. See In re Eberhardt's Estate, 1 Wis. 2d 439, 85 N.W.2d 483 (1957). See also Bird, Revocation of a Revoking Codicil: The Renaissance of Revival in California, 33 Hastings L.J. 357 (1981) (citing earlier studies in all jurisdictions).

———————

Courts do not ordinarily give relief for mistakes in the execution or revocation of wills. For example, no relief was given in *Pavlinko*, supra page 208, where the testator signed the wrong will, or in *McGill*, supra page 228, where the testator by mail directed Dr. O'Kennedy to destroy her will, or in Thompson v. Royall, supra page 231, where Mrs. Kroll signed an unattested revocation. Why then do courts remedy mistake when facts arise fitting the doctrine of dependent relative revocation? Professors Langbein and Waggoner give this answer:

> It is said that since cases of revocation by physical act are inherently ambiguous on the question of whether the act was accompanied by the requisite intent to revoke (i.e., was a will shredded by accident, or in order to revoke it?), extrinsic evidence must necessarily be received to resolve that point. However, the DRR rule extends beyond physical-act revocation to cases of revocation by subsequent instrument; and in any event, if the courts were consistent about the supposed virtues of excluding extrinsic evidence of mistake, they could easily limit their inquiry into a testator's intent in a revocation case by refusing to investigate whether a mistake of purpose vitiated a seemingly intended revocation. . . . The answer, we think, is that the "conditional intent" rubric of DRR facilitates a type of remedy that does not conflict with traditional notions of Wills Act compliance. The remedy is to deny effect to the revocation, hence to enforce the duly attested will that was attempted to be revoked. [Langbein & Waggoner, Reformation of Wills on the Ground of Mistake: Change of Direction in American Law?, 130 U. Pa. L. Rev. 521, 545 (1982).]

Courts have set limits on the dependent relative revocation doctrine. With rare exceptions, courts have held that DRR applies only (1) where there is an alternative plan of disposition or (2) where the mistake is recited in the terms of the revoking instrument. The alternative plan of disposition is usually in the form of another will, either duly or defectively executed, as in Estate of Alburn. Hence, the kind of extrinsic evidence that can be looked at is limited.

PROBLEMS

1. *T*'s will bequeaths $5,000 to his old friend, Judy, and the residue of his estate to his brother Mark. *T* later executes a codicil as follows:

"I revoke the legacy to Judy, since she is dead." In fact, Judy is still living and survives *T*. Does Judy take $5,000? In Campbell v. French, 3 Ves. Jr. 321, 30 Eng. Rep. 1033 (Ch. 1797), on similar facts, the court held that there was no revocation, "the cause being false."

Suppose that the codicil had read: "I revoke the legacy to Judy, since I have already given her $5,000." In fact, the testator did not give Judy $5,000 during life. What result? See Witt v. Rosen, 765 S.W.2d 956 (Ark. App. 1989).

Suppose that the codicil had read: "I revoke the legacy to Judy." Evidence is offered that shows that three weeks prior to execution of the codicil *T* was told by a friend that Judy had died, believing it to be true. In fact Judy survives *T*. What result? See In re Salmonski's Estate, 38 Cal. 2d 199, 238 P.2d 966 (1951).

2. *T*, a resident of Mississippi, executes a will that devises his residuary estate one-half to his wife and one-half to *X* charity. One year later *T* executes a new will *expressly revoking the earlier will*. The new will makes changes in specific bequests but devises his residuary estate in exactly the same manner as the prior will. *T* dies two months later. In Mississippi any charitable bequest in a will executed within 90 days of death is void.[33] Miss. Code Ann. §91-5-31 (Supp. 1988). Should dependent relative revocation be applied so that *X* charity takes one-half the residuary estate under the earlier will? See Crosby v. Alton Ochsner Medical Found., 276 So. 2d 661, 75 A.L.R.3d 853 (Miss. 1973) (holding that DRR does not apply where there is an express revocation clause). Cf. In re Kaufman's Estate, 25 Cal. 2d 854, 155 P.2d 831 (1945) (holding, in accordance with the majority view, that DRR applies where there is an express revocation clause). Which view is sounder?

3. Revocation by Operation of Law: Change in Family Circumstances

In all but a tiny handful of states, statutes provide that a divorce revokes any provision in the decedent's will for the divorced spouse. In a few states revocation occurs only if divorce is accompanied by a property settlement. Uniform Probate Code §2-508 is typical.

---

33. Three other states — Florida, Georgia, and Idaho — have similar statutes. Fla. Stat. Ann. §732.803 (Supp. 1988); Ga. Code Ann. §113-107 (Supp. 1988); Idaho Code §15-2-615 (1979). What is the purpose of these statutes?

Several other jurisdictions once had such statutes, but in recent years these have been either repealed or held in violation of the equal protection clause of the Constitution because not rationally related to a legitimate state objective. See Shriners' Hosp. for Crippled Children v. Hester, 23 Ohio St. 3d 198, 492 N.E.2d 153 (1986); Annot., 6 A.L.R.4th 603 (1981).

Uniform Probate Code (1983)

§2-508 [REVOCATION BY DIVORCE; NO REVOCATION BY OTHER CHANGES OF CIRCUMSTANCES]

If after executing a will the testator is divorced or his marriage annulled, the divorce or annulment revokes any disposition or appointment of property made by the will to the former spouse, any provision conferring a general or special power of appointment on the former spouse, and any nomination of the former spouse as executor, trustee, conservator, or guardian, unless the will expressly provides otherwise. Property prevented from passing to a former spouse because of revocation by divorce or annulment passes as if the former spouse failed to survive the decedent, and other provisions conferring some power or office on the former spouse are interpreted as if the spouse failed to survive the decedent. If provisions are revoked solely by this section, they are revived by testator's remarriage to the former spouse. For purposes of this section, divorce or annulment means any divorce or annulment which would exclude the spouse as a surviving spouse within the meaning of Section 2-802(b). A decree of separation which does not terminate the status of husband and wife is not a divorce for purposes of this section. No change of circumstances other than as described in this section revokes a will.

PROBLEMS

1. *T* executes a will devising all his property to his wife, Sena, and if Sena does not survive him to Sena's son, Wayne (*T*'s stepson). *T* divorces Sena and then dies. *T*'s heirs are his children by a prior marriage. Does Wayne take *T*'s property? See Porter v. Porter, 286 N.W.2d 649 (Iowa 1979); Bloom v. Selfon, 520 Pa. 519, 555 A.2d 75 (1989); Estate of Graef, 124 Wis. 2d 25, 368 N.W.2d 633 (1985).

2. In 1985 *T* takes out a $25,000 life insurance policy that names his wife, *W*, as beneficiary. In 1988 *W* divorces *T*. In 1991 *T* dies, survived by *W*. The state has a statute providing for revocation of wills by subsequent divorce, but it has no statute governing the disposition of life insurance proceeds in this situation. Is *W* entitled to the $25,000? See Stiles v. Stiles, 21 Mass. App. Ct. 514, 487 N.E.2d 874 (1986); Lewis v. Lewis, 693 S.W.2d 672 (Tex. Civ. App. 1985); Bersch v. Van Kleeck, 112 Wis. 2d 594, 334 N.W.2d 114 (1983).

Suppose that *T* had named *W* as beneficiary of the balance in his retirement fund. After the divorce *T* failed to change the beneficiary designation. Is *W* entitled to the amount in the retirement fund on *T*'s death? See Pepper v. Peacher, 742 P.2d 21 (Okla. 1987).

On the effect of divorce on will substitutes, see infra page 302.

Marriage. If the testator executes his will and subsequently marries, a large majority of states have statutes giving the spouse her intestate share, unless it appears from the will that the omission was intentional or the spouse is provided for in the will or by a will substitute with the intent that the transfer be in lieu of a testamentary provision. See Uniform Probate Code §2-301, infra page 426, which is a typical statute. In effect this kind of statute revokes the will to the extent of the spouse's intestate share. See Estate of Ganier, 418 So. 2d 256 (Fla. 1982), infra page 422.

In states where the spouse omitted from a premarital will does not take an intestate share, the spouse may nonetheless obtain an interest in the testator's estate. Most common law states give the surviving spouse an election to take a "forced share" of the decedent's estate. See infra page 377.

Birth of children. A small minority of states, either by statute or judicial decision, follow the common law rule that marriage followed by birth of issue revokes a will executed before marriage, but this rule has not been incorporated in the Uniform Probate Code and is rapidly disappearing. However, almost all states have pretermitted child statutes giving a child born after execution of the parent's will and not provided for in the will an intestate share in the parent's estate. See Uniform Probate Code §2-302 and infra page 428. The effect of such a statute is to produce a partial revocation of the parent's will.

SECTION D.   COMPONENTS OF A WILL

In Section B of this chapter we considered the formalities with which a will must be executed. We saw that if a state's wills statute is not complied with in all its particulars, a testamentary instrument is not entitled to probate, no matter how clearly it reflects the testator's intention that it be a will. Yet despite these formal requirements of transfer, it is possible for documents and acts not executed with testamentary formalities to have the effect of determining *who* takes *what* property belonging to the testator. In this section we are primarily concerned with two doctrines that can have this effect, two doctrines that permit extrinsic evidence to resolve the identity of persons or property. These are (1) the doctrine of incorporation by reference and

(2) the doctrine of acts of independent significance. Before we consider these doctrines, we must examine two others that are sometimes confused with them.

1. Integration of Wills

Wills are often written on more than one sheet of paper. Under the doctrine of integration, all papers present at the time of execution, intended to be part of the will, are integrated into the will. Hence the question may arise: Which sheets of paper, present at the time of execution, comprise the testator's duly executed will? Typically there is no problem, for the pages of the will are physically connected with a staple or ribbon or, failing this, there is a sufficient connection of language carrying over from page to page to show an internal coherence of the provisions. The attorney can prevent any problem from arising under the integration doctrine by seeing to it that the will is fastened together before the testator signs and by having the testator sign or initial each numbered page of the will for identification. The litigated cases involving integration arise when, for example, the pages are not physically connected and there is no internal coherence, or there is evidence that a staple has been removed or one page is typed with elite type whereas the rest of the will is in pica.

In re Estate of Beale, 15 Wis. 546, 113 N.W.2d 380 (1962), is illustrative of the integration cases. In that case the testator, a history professor at the University of Wisconsin, planning to take a trip to Russia, dictated his will to his secretary in Madison. He had three sons, 16, 15, and 10, and his earlier will treated the three sons equally. In this new will the testator left all his property to his wife and two older sons, disinheriting the youngest son. The will consisted of 14 pages, and the secretary gave the testator three carbon copies plus the original. The testator took all these sheets with him to New York on his way to Moscow. At a festive goodbye party in New York, given by a history professor at Columbia, the testator produced his will and asked three of his friends, all professors at eastern colleges, to witness his will. He laid "a pile" of papers on the table, declaring it was his will, and the testator and witnesses signed the last page. After the testator's death, none of the witnesses could identify any page except the signature page, but all pages of the will had the testator's initials on the margin. On the same day as the party, either before or after the execution ceremony, the testator wrote his secretary from New York asking her to retype pages 12 and 13, and make certain changes, including changing the executor from his wife to a friend. The letter to her enclosed pages 12 and 13. These pages were retyped by the secretary after the testator's death, and, as retyped, they too had the testator's initials on the margin! Noting that "the question is one of inference," the court upheld the trial court's decision to admit the will to probate as the will existed before any changes were made.

Keener v. Archibald
Indiana Court of Appeals, 1989
533 N.E.2d 1268

HOFFMAN, J.   Appellant Burl A. Keener, executor of the Edward S. Archibald estate, appeals a grant of summary judgment. The facts indicate that after Ed Archibald died January 16, 1987, Phyllis Felton found four sheets of paper stapled together underneath his television set. The first page was a preprinted form will titled "Last Will and Testament" — "Unmarried Individual with Two or More Beneficiaries." The first page was signed by Ed Archibald, three witnesses and dated February 21, 1986. The second page was a preprinted form will affidavit signed by three witnesses and notarized February 21, 1986.

The last two pages of the document consisted of a devisee list with names and addresses in the left column, phone numbers in the middle column and dollar amounts in the right column. The last page is signed by Edward Archibald and notarized October 17, 1985.

The four pages were offered for probate. On July 1, 1987, Ed Archibald's brothers filed a complaint to contest the pages submitted for probate. On a cross motion for summary judgment, the trial court found that the last two pages of the document were not incorporated by reference into the form will and the will was improperly executed. The trial court ruled that the decedent shall be considered as having died intestate. . . .

Appellant contends that the trial court erred in ruling that the preprinted form will and list of devisees were not integrated. Integration, as distinguished from incorporation by reference, occurs where there is no reference in the will to a distinctly extraneous document but it is clear that two or more separate writings are intended by the testator to be the will. 2A G. Henry, Probate and Practice 895 (7th Ed. 1979).

Appellant argues that the trial court should have integrated the form will and the devisee list. Appellant contends that the form will and the list of devisees were connected internally by the meaning of words and attached physically by staple. The form will has the words "equal shares" crossed out and leaves blank the line for an executor and the space for devisees. The last two pages name Burl Keener administrator and list devisees. Appellant claims that the decedent had the last two pages present when the form will was signed.

The trial court ruled that the four pages submitted to probate were improperly executed. The requirements for a properly executed will are stated at Ind. Code §29-1-5-1 et seq. (1982 Ed.). The trial court correctly ruled that the last two pages were not properly incorporated into the preprinted form will pursuant to Ind. Code §29-1-6-1(h) (1982 Ed.) which states:

> If a testator in his will refers to a writing of any kind, such writing, whether thereafter amended or revoked, as it existed at the time of execution of the will, shall be given the same effect as if set forth at length in the will, if such writing is clearly identified in the will and is in existence both at the time of the execution of the will and at the testator's death.

Indiana has not adopted the doctrine of integration by case law or statute. In Indiana, there is no such thing as a substantially correctly executed will. Either the will meets the legislative requirements or it is void. Scampmorte v. Scampmorte, Admr., et al. (1962), 133 Ind. App. 276, 281, 179 N.E.2d 302, 304. Since the last two pages were not incorporated, the preprinted form will devises nothing. The trial court correctly ruled that the decedent died intestate.

Affirmed.

2. Republication by Codicil

In its narrowest sense republication by codicil "means an implied restatement or rewriting of the language of a valid will as of the time of the republication." Evans, Testamentary Republication, 40 Harv. L. Rev. 71, 103 (1926). This may be accomplished by the execution of a valid codicil to a valid will. But courts have not so narrowly restricted the idea of republication. It has been used to revive an instrument that once had testamentary life but for some reason became void. (In this way the doctrine differs from incorporation by reference, infra page 250, which technically applies only when instruments that never had testamentary life are incorporated into a will and given testamentary effect.) For example, suppose that the testator revokes a first will by a second will and then executes a codicil to the first will. The first will is republished and thus the second will is revoked by implication ("squeezed out"). See In re Estate of Stormont, 34 Ohio App. 3d 92, 517 N.E.2d 259 (1986).

Republication by codicil has sometimes been used to validate a prior invalid will, though strictly speaking there cannot be a republication of a will that was never valid. One cannot restore life to that which never had life. Yet, used in this manner, the doctrine has enabled courts that do not permit incorporation of unattested documents by reference to give effect to instruments that are invalid for some reason other than faulty execution. In New York, for example, which does not in general permit incorporation by reference, a codicil can republish and thereby give testamentary effect to a will that was invalid because of mental incapacity or undue influence, but a codicil cannot republish an instrument never duly executed with the required formalities.

If a codicil republishes a will, the will is deemed to have been executed as of the date of the codicil. However, a codicil will not be deemed to have republished a will where updating the will would lead to a result contrary to the testator's intent. Application of the doctrine can arise in a number of contexts. Case 3 is illustrative.

> *Case 3.* The jurisdiction has an interested witness statute purging any gift to an attesting witness. In 1990 *T* executes a will devising all his property to *A*. *A* and *B* are witnesses to the will. In 1991 *T* executes a codicil bequeathing $5,000 to *C*. *C* and *D* are witnesses to the codicil. In 1992 *T* executes a second codicil bequeathing *C* a diamond ring. *D* and *E* are witnesses to the second codicil. Under the doctrine of republication by codicil, the will and first codicil are deemed to be re-executed in 1992 by the second codicil, which has two disinterested witnesses. *A* and *C* are not purged of their gifts. See King v. Smith, 123 N.J. Super. 179, 302 A.2d 144 (1973).

3. *Incorporation by Reference*

Simon v. Grayson
Supreme Court of California, 1940
15 Cal. 2d 531, 102 P.2d 1081

WASTE, C.J. The question presented for determination upon this appeal involves the construction and effect to be given a provision in a will purporting to incorporate a letter by reference. Respondent's claim to certain of the estate's funds is based upon the terms of the letter. The appellants, who are residuary legatees under the will, contend that the attempted incorporation by reference was ineffectual. The facts, which were presented to the trial court upon an agreed statement, are as follows:

S.M. Seeligsohn died in 1935. His safe deposit box was found to contain, among other things, a will and codicil and a letter addressed to his executors. The will, which was dated March 25, 1932, contained a provision in paragraph four, leaving $6,000 to his executors "to be paid by them in certain amounts to certain persons as shall be directed by me in a letter that will be found in my effects and which said letter will be addressed to Martin E. Simon and Arthur W. Green (the executors) and will be dated March 25, 1932." Paragraph four also provided that any one having an interest in the will "shall not inquire into the application of said moneys" and that the executors "shall not be accountable to any person whomsoever for the payment and/or application of said sum . . . this provision . . . is in no sense a trust."

The letter found in the testator's safe deposit box was dated July 3, 1933, and stated:

> In paragraph VIII of my will I have left you $6,000 — to be paid to the persons named in a letter and this letter is also mentioned in said paragraph. I direct that after my death you shall pay said $6,000 as follows: To Mrs. Esther Cohn, 1755 Van Ness Ave. San Francisco, Calif. the sum of $4,000 — . . . If any of the said persons cannot be found by you within six months after my death, or if any of the said persons shall predecease me, the sum directed to be paid to such persons . . . shall be paid by you to my heirs as described in paragraph IX of my said Will. . . .

This letter was written, dated and signed entirely in the handwriting of the testator. No letter dated March 25, 1932, was found among his effects.

The codicil to the will was executed November 25, 1933. It made no changes in paragraph IV of the will and contained no reference to the letter, but recited, "Except as expressly modified by this Codicil, my Will of March 25th 1932 shall remain in full force and effect."

Esther Cohn's whereabouts was known to the testator's executors immediately following his death, but she herself died a week later. Respondent, as her executrix, claimed the $4,000 mentioned in the letter. This claim was challenged by appellants, residuary legatees under Seeligsohn's will, and his executors brought suit interpleading the disputants. From the agreed facts the trial court drew conclusions of law and rendered judgment in favor of the respondent. The chief question is whether the letter was effectually incorporated by reference into the will.

It is settled law in this state that a testator may incorporate an extrinsic document into his will, provided the document is in existence at the time and provided, further, that the reference to it in the will clearly identifies it, or renders it capable of identification by extrinsic proof. (Estate of Plumel, 151 Cal. 77, 90 Pac. 192, 121 Am. St. Rep. 100; Garde v. Goldsmith, 204 Cal. 166, 267 Pac. 104; Estate of Martin, 31 Cal. App. (2d) 501, 88 Pac. (2d) 234; 16 Cal. L. Rev. 154.) An attempt to incorporate a future document is ineffectual, because a testator cannot be permitted to create for himself the power to dispose of his property without complying with the formalities required in making a will. (Keeler v. Merchant's Loan & Trust, 253 Ill. 528, 97 N.E. 1061.)

In the case at bar the letter presumably was not in existence when the will was executed, for the letter bore a date subsequent to the date of the will. (Code Civ. Proc., sec. 1963, subd. 23.) However, the letter was in existence at the time the codicil to the will was executed. The respondent points out that under the law the execution of a codicil has the effect of republishing the will which it modifies (Prob. Code, sec. 25), and argues from this that Seeligsohn's letter was an "existing document" within the incorporation rule. The only authorities cited by the parties on this point are several English decisions. These cases hold that although an informal document is not in existence when the will referring to it is executed, a later republication of the will by codicil will satisfy the "existing document" rule and will incorporate it by reference provided the testamentary instruments sufficiently identify it. (In re Goods of Lady Truro, (1866) L.R. 1 P. & D. 201; compare In re Goods of Smart, (1902) L.R. Prob. Div. 238; 4 Cal. L. Rev. 356.) The principle of republication thus applied is unquestionably sound. In revising his scheme of testamentary disposition by codicil a testator presumably reviews and reaffirms those portions of his will which remain unaffected. In substance, the will is reexecuted as of that time. Therefore, the testator's execution of the codicil in the present case must be taken as confirming the incorporation of the letter then in existence, provided the letter can be satisfactorily identified as the one referred to in the will. And this is true, notwithstanding the codicil made no reference to the letter and recited that the will should remain in full force "except as expressly modified by this codicil," for the letter, if properly incorporated, would be an integral part of the republished will.

We are also of the opinion that the trial court did not err in concluding that the letter found with the will was the letter referred to in the will. Conceding the contrary force of the discrepancy in dates, the evidence of identity was, nevertheless, sufficient to overcome the effect of that factor. The controlling authorities in this state do not require that the informal document be identified with exact precision; it is enough that the descriptive words and extrinsic circumstances combine to produce a reasonable certainty that the document in question is the one referred to by the testator in his will. (Estate of Miller, 128 Cal. App. 176, 17 Pac. (2d) 181; Estate of Martin, supra; Estate of Plumel, supra.) Here the letter was found in the safe deposit box with the will. It was addressed to the executors, as the will stated it would be. No other letter was found. Moreover, the letter is conceded to have been written by the testator, and its terms conform unmistakably to the letter described in the will. It identifies itself as the letter mentioned in the will and deals with the identical subject matter referred to in that portion of the will. All these circumstances leave no doubt that the letter of July 3, 1933, is the one that the testator intended to incorporate in paragraph four of his will.

Appellants also contend that the bequest to Esther Cohn lapsed upon her death seven days after the death of the testator. They would read the provisions of the will and letter as creating a contingent bequest payable only if the legatee should be alive at the time it became legally payable to her. Hence, it is said, the gift must fail because no distribution could have been made until at least four months after issuance of letters testamentary in the testator's estate. (Prob. Code, sec. 1000.) But such an interpretation is contradicted by the testator's own language. The letter creates only two contingencies upon which the legacies would lapse — the inability of the executors to find any of the legatees mentioned within six months after the testator's death, or the prior death of any of the legatees. As the stipulated facts show, neither of these contingencies occurred in the case of Esther Cohn. If it be conceded that the legacy to her would not vest until she was "found" by the executors, the facts show that they knew of her whereabouts within two days after the death of the testator. . . .

The conclusions we have reached make it unnecessary to pass upon the respondent's contention that the letter is sufficiently testamentary in character to stand as an independent testamentary instrument.

The judgment is affirmed.

Uniform Probate Code (1983)

§2-510 [INCORPORATION BY REFERENCE]

Any writing in existence when a will is executed may be incorporated by reference if the language of the will manifests this intent and describes the writing sufficiently to permit its identification.

Clark
supp 44

NOTES AND PROBLEMS

1. The doctrine of incorporation by reference is not recognized, as a general rule, in Connecticut,[34] Louisiana, and New York. However,

---

34. It was established in Hathaway v. Smith, 79 Conn. 506, 65 A. 1058 (1907), that the doctrine of incorporation by reference does not exist in Connecticut. An earlier, more interesting case suggested that ultimate result. In Bryan's Appeal, 77 Conn. 240, 58 A. 748 (1904), the testator, Philo S. Bennett, was a rich Connecticut friend and political ally of the Great Commoner and scourge of eastern capitalists, William Jennings Bryan, who thrice ran unsuccessfully for the Presidency on the Democratic ticket. ("You shall not press down upon the brow of labor this crown of thorns. You shall not crucify mankind on a cross of gold.") While on a visit to Bryan at Lincoln, Nebraska, Bennett, with Bryan's assistance, prepared his will. The will was duly executed on May 22, 1900. It provided: "I give and bequeath unto my wife, Grace Imogene Bennett, the sum of fifty thousand

the testator may refer in his will to a separate memorandum disposing of his tangible personal property, and if such memorandum is attached to the other pages of his will and was present at execution, such memorandum is entitled to probate under the doctrine of integration. In re Will of Hall, 59 Misc. 2d 881, 300 N.Y.S.2d 813 (Sur. Ct. 1969). Even though the memorandum is attached after the signature page, it will be deemed constructively inserted before the signature page so as to comply with the requirements that a will be signed at the end. In re Will of Powell, 90 Misc. 2d 635, 395 N.Y.S.2d 334 (Sur. Ct. 1977).

2.   Suppose that the 1933 codicil had never been executed in Simon v. Grayson. Under the dispensing power recommended by Professor Langbein (supra page 194), would Esther Cohn take $4,000?

3.   The testator executed a deed to his farm that named his niece as grantee. The deed was sealed in an envelope and placed by the testator in his safe-deposit box at a local bank, where it remained until his death. Sometime later, the testator executed a will containing the following provision: "Sixth: I have already deeded to my niece, Alta J. Pullman, the southeast quarter of section eight, township twenty-four, north, range four, east of the 6th P.M. in Cuming county, Nebraska, and for that reason I do not devise any real estate to her in this Will." After the testator's death it was held that the deed was not effective to convey title to the niece because it was not delivered by the grantor during his lifetime. The niece contends that the deed was incorporated by reference by the language of clause Sixth of the will. What result? See Estate of Dimmitt, 141 Neb. 413, 3 N.W.2d 752, 144 A.L.R. 704 (1942). Compare Werling v. Grosse, 76 Ill. App. 3d 834, 395 N.E.2d 629 (1979) (testator made an oral agreement to sell his farm to Werling; his will read: "Having by agreement sold my farm to Nelson Werling for $20,000, I give any balance due me from Nelson Werling to the Lighthouse for the Blind.").

---

dollars (50,000), in trust, however for the purposes set forth in a sealed letter which will be found with this will." Found with the will, at testator's death, was a letter dated "5/22/ 1900" addressed to "My Dear Wife", which referred to the $50,000 bequest in the will and stated that the $50,000 conveyed to her in trust was to be paid to William Jennings Bryan inasmuch "as his political work prevents the application of his time and talents to money making." Largely because Bennett left $20,000 to his mistress, Mrs. Bennett, angered by the will, refused to carry out Bennett's desires. Bryan sued and lost. The court held that even if incorporation by reference were recognized, the reference in the will was so vague as to be incapable of being applied to any particular instrument.

Bryan then sued Mrs. Bennett a second time, alleging that she held the $50,000 in a constructive trust for him (see infra page 487 on semisecret testamentary trusts). The court held that no trust arose because Mrs. Bennett had never been apprised of the terms of the will and had made no promise, an essential ingredient of a semisecret testamentary trust. Bryan v. Bigelow, 77 Conn. 604, 60 A. 266 (1905).

It may be that Bryan's Appeal is an example of the old adage that hard cases make bad law. Bryan, a lawyer, had acted indelicately — perhaps even unethically — in participating in this secret gift to himself, and the court was probably not disposed to rule in his favor.

4.   Wendy Brown's Aunt Fanny, an elderly widow without children, has a house full of furniture and objects, some valuable, all cherished by Aunt Fanny (see supra page 64). Her will, executed in 1986, contains the following clause: "All my wearing apparel, jewelry and all other articles of personal adornment, linen, silver, books, pictures, and household effects, I give and bequeath to my sister, Polly. She shall distribute them to the persons named in a memorandum of instructions I shall leave addressed to her." Suppose that after Aunt Fanny's death an envelope is found containing her will and a typewritten memorandum addressed to Polly. The memorandum, dated June 5, 1989, makes various bequests of these tangible items to 15 persons. It is signed by Aunt Fanny but it is not witnessed. Are the bequests valid? See Hastings v. Bridge, 86 N.H. 247, 166 A. 273 (1933); In re Salmon's Will, 24 A.D. 2d 962, 265 N.Y.S.2d 373 (1965). If not, how would you advise Aunt Fanny to obtain her objective?

Uniform Probate Code (1983)

§2-513   [Separate Writing Identifying Bequest of Tangible Property]

Whether or not the provisions relating to holographic wills apply, a will may refer to a written statement or list to dispose of items of tangible personal property not otherwise specifically disposed of by the will, other than money, evidences of indebtedness, documents of title, and securities, and property used in trade or business. To be admissible under this section as evidence of the intended disposition, the writing must either be in the handwriting of the testator or be signed by him and must describe the items and the devisees with reasonable certainty. The writing may be referred to as one to be in existence at the time of the testator's death; it may be prepared before or after the execution of the will; it may be altered by the testator after its preparation; and it may be a writing which has no significance apart from its effect upon the dispositions made by the will.

Johnson v. Johnson
Supreme Court of Oklahoma, 1954
279 P.2d 928

Per Curiam.   This is an appeal from a judgment of the District Court of Oklahoma County affirming the County Court of Oklahoma in denying probate to an instrument purporting to be the last will and testament of Dexter G. Johnson, who was sometimes known as D.G. Johnson.

The instrument in question was on a single sheet of paper and contained three typewritten paragraphs, started out with the words, "I, D.G. Johnson also known as Dexter G. Johnson, of Oklahoma City, Oklahoma County, State of Oklahoma do hereby make, publish and declare this to be my last Will and Testament . . ." and made numerous bequests and devises and concluded with recommending the employment of a certain attorney to probate the will. This typewritten portion was not dated nor did the testator sign his name at the conclusion thereof nor was it attested by two witnesses. At the end of the typewritten portion, at the bottom of [the] sheet of paper, appears the following, admitted to be in the handwriting of the deceased:

> To my brother James I give ten dollars only. This will shall be complete unless hereafter altered, changed or rewritten. Witness my hand this April 6, 1947. Easter Sunday, 2:30 P.M.
>
> > D.G. Johnson
> > Dexter G. Johnson

On trial de novo in the District Court the proponents of this purported will, plaintiffs in error here, introduced evidence over objections (which objections were never ruled on by the court) showing that Dexter G., or D.G. Johnson for many years was a practicing attorney in Oklahoma City; that during his practice he prepared many wills, all in proper form, for various clients; that in October, 1946, deceased told Jack G. Wiggins, his insurance counselor, that he had a will but it was out of date and needed changing; that in March, 1947, deceased told this insurance counselor that he was working on his will, making changes, and expected to complete it right away and told Mr. Wiggins in general the disposition he intended to make of his property; that in the latter part of 1946 Lowell M. Wickham, deceased's rental agent, was shown the instrument here in question at which time it had only the typewritten portions on it; that at that time deceased told him that was his will and he wanted Wickham to witness it, but he and deceased started discussing other business and neglected to do it at that time; that when Wickham left the paper was lying on deceased's desk; that some months later Wickham asked deceased about witnessing the will and deceased replied he had changed his will by codicil and did not need Wickham to sign it as witness; an offer by statement of counsel was made to show the intention of the testator in leaving his property to the persons he named as beneficiaries which was rejected by the court and is not helpful in deciding the questions raised here.

The above is a summary of all the testimony that appears in the record. None of the testimony presented to the County Court appears in the record; defendant below, contestant of the will and defendant in error here, offered no testimony.

Is this instrument one complete, integrated writing, partly typed and partly handwritten; or is it an unexecuted nonholographic will to which is appended a valid holographic codicil? If it be the former it cannot be admitted to probate because it was not signed in the presence of two subscribing witnesses as required by law.

Defendant in error urges that the instrument shows on its face that it is but one instrument and that it cannot be divided into two parts, one, the typewritten part to be called a will and the other, the handwritten part, to be called a codicil. In support of his contention he says that the typewritten portion standing alone is not a will because, though admittedly testamentary in character, it is not dated, signed, nor witnessed; that it takes the handwritten portion to complete the instrument; that by definition to have a codicil there must first be a will.

There is no question in this case that the typewritten instrument which was not signed, dated, nor attested was prepared by D.G. Johnson and that it is testamentary in character, or that he intended same as his will or that it effectively makes complete disposition of his estate. A will may be so defective, as here, that it is not entitled to probate but if testamentary in character it is a will, nonetheless. . . . Nor is there any question that the handwritten words were wholly in the handwriting of the testator.

The question next arises, do these words meet the requirements of a codicil? By definition a codicil is a supplement to, an addition to or qualification of, an existing will, made by the testator to alter, enlarge, or restrict the provisions of the will, to explain or republish it, or to revoke it, and it must be testamentary in character. In re Whittier's Estate, 26 Wash. 2d 833, 176 P.2d 281. A codicil need not be called a codicil, In re Carr's Estate, 93 Cal. App. 2d 750, 209 P.2d 956; In re Atkinson's Estate, 110 Cal. App. 499, 294 P. 425. The intention to add a codicil is controlling. Allgeier v. Brown, 199 Ky. 672, 251 S.W. 851; Stewart v. Stewart, 177 Mass. 493, 59 N.E. 116; In re Whittier's Estate, supra. The handwritten words are admittedly testamentary in character. It is clear that they made an addition to the provisions of the will theretofore existing. This codicil is on the same sheet of paper and the terms thereof, the circumstances surrounding it, as shown by the evidence indicate that the testator intended it as an addition to and republication of his will.

If it be a codicil, then, is it a valid one? It is written, dated, and signed by the testator. It meets all the requirements of a valid holographic codicil. The fact that the codicil was written on the same piece of paper as the typewritten will will not invalidate the codicil. In re Atkinson's Estate, supra.

It is admitted that a codicil republishes a previous will as modified by the codicil as of the date of the codicil. Can a valid, holographic codicil republish and validate a will which was theretofore inoperative because not dated, signed, or attested according to law?

The general principle of law is that a codicil validly executed operates as a republication of the will no matter what defects may have existed in the execution of the earlier document, that the instruments are incorporated as one, and that a proper execution of the codicil extends also to the will. Twenty-two states and England so hold. For citation of cases see Annotations 21 A.L.R.2d 823. That a properly executed codicil will give effect to a will which has never been signed has been specifically held in Kentucky, New Jersey, and England. See Beall v. Cunningham, 1843, 3 B. Mon. 390, 42 Ky. 390, in which it appeared that a paper wholly written by testator dated 1825 was denied probate, and thereafter there was offered for probate a typewritten will dated in 1827,[35] which was unsigned and unattested, together with a codicil dated 1832 on the same sheet of paper which was signed and attested; the opinion holds that the properly executed codicil had the effect of giving operation to the whole as one will. See also Hurley v. Blankinship, 1950, 313 Ky. 49, 229 S.W.2d 963, 21 A.L.R.2d 817, in which a holographic will which was not signed was held validated by properly executed holographic codicils; Doe v. Evans, 1832, 1 Cromp. & M. 42, 149 Eng. Reprint 307, in which an unsigned typewritten will was held validated by a properly executed codicil on the same sheet of paper; see also McCurdy v. Neall, 1886, 42 N.J. Eq. 333, 7 A. 466 and Smith v. Runkle, 1916, 86 N.J. Eq. 257, 98 A. 1086, in both of which the signatures to the wills were defective because not placed on the will in the presence of witnesses but it was held that valid codicils thereafter executed gave operation to the entire will and codicils; Rogers v. Agricola, 176 Ark. 287, 3 S.W.2d 26, in which an invalid typewritten will (due to only one witness) was held validated by a subsequent holographic codicil; In re Plumel's Estate, 151 Cal. 77, 90 P. 192, an invalid holographic will because of printing thereon was held validated by a subsequent holographic codicil written on the back of the will. . . .[36]

The only exception is New York which modifies the general rule by

---

35. Typewritten will in 1827? The first typewriters were placed on the market in 1874. Later in this paragraph the court refers to a typewritten will in Doe v. Evans, decided in 1832. In neither Beall v. Cunningham nor in Doe v. Evans was there mention of any typewriting.

This anachronism was called to our attention by John Cutcher, J.D. Vanderbilt 1987, whose sharp eyes spotted it while a student in Professor Jeffrey Schoenblum's wills course at Vanderbilt. — Eds.

36. Examine carefully the facts of the cases cited in this paragraph. Do you see why the cases cited are properly analyzed as applications of either incorporation by reference or integration and that republication by codicil is not involved? — Eds.

holding that a properly executed codicil validates a will originally invalid for want of testamentary capacity, undue influence, or revocation but does not validate a will defectively executed because of improper attestation. It will be noted, however, that Justice Cardozo in Re Fowles, 1918, 222 N.Y. 222, 118 N.E. 611, Ann. Cas. 1918D, 834, stated that the rule was malleable and uncertain and he anticipated that New York would abandon its limitations on the rule. . . .

We therefore hold that the valid holographic codicil incorporated the prior will by reference and republished and validated the prior will as of the date of the codicil, thus giving effect to the intention of the testator.

Reversed with directions to˙enter the will for probate.

JOHNSON, V.C.J. and WELCH, CORN, ARNOLD and BLACKBIRD, JJ., concur. HALLEY, C.J., WILLIAMS and DAVISON, JJ., dissent.

CORN, J. (concurring specially).[37]   I concur in the per curiam opinion.

---

37. In 1964 Justices Corn and Welch were convicted of federal income tax evasion and sentenced to prison terms of 18 months and 3 years respectively. New York Times, July 19, 1964, at 44, col. 1; id., Nov. 14, 1964, at 14, col. 6. Corn and Welch resigned their judicial positions. Subsequently Corn signed a statement in which Corn said Welch, Johnson, and he had accepted more than $150,000 in bribes for throwing cases. In 1965 Justice Johnson was convicted of corruption in office and removed from the court. Id., May 14, 1965, at 40, col. 1.

The newspaper accounts did not mention any evidence of bribery in the principal case of Johnson v. Johnson. Yet when a judge has been convicted of bribery in one case the public may suspect there was bribery in others. (Indeed, when Corn was asked if he could remember any year, in the 24 he served as Justice, when he did not take money for his votes, he replied: "Well, I don't know." Id., May 11, 1965, at 18, col. 6.) The votes of Corn, Welch, and Johnson were decisive in Johnson v. Johnson. Although there is no report of bribery in this case, *and none is to be inferred from this note*, does the mere appearance of possible impropriety require that the case now be reheard upon petition of the losing party?

In Johnson v. Johnson, 424 P.2d 414 (Okla. 1967), the executor of the losing party in the original case (who had since died) petitioned to have the 1954 decision vacated in view of Justice Corn's participation in that decision. Five of the supreme court justices who were on the court in 1954 disqualified themselves, and five special justices were appointed in their stead. In a unanimous decision, two justices specially concurring, the court denied the petition since there was no allegation of wrongdoing in the particular case. Among the reasons given were the practical consequences of a contrary decision:

It is apparent that if our holding were in the affirmative every decision from 1938 to January of 1959 in which Corn cast the deciding vote would have to be set aside. There are more than one thousand such cases. Rights of every kind have been settled by the decisions in such cases. Marriages have been contracted upon the basis of divorces granted, titles have been transferred and judgments paid. To now go back and reopen every such case for a possible new decision requiring new arguments and new hearings would cast intolerable and unjust burdens upon all the parties. Titles and status long thought put at rest would be thrown open to doubt. It would indeed create a "shambles" as Respondent contends. And this would be so in every case in which Corn cast the deciding vote even though no corruption occurred in such case.

To us this result seems unthinkable and contrary to the most elementary principles of justice. We think it more just that those cases in which no corruption can be found should be allowed to stand, at the same time giving full right to any person

In so doing I have in mind the purpose of our law-makers in enacting statutes regulating the making of a Will. They require certain steps to be taken in the execution of a Will solely for the purpose of permitting a person to dispose of his property by Will, to take effect after his death the way he desired, and to prevent someone, through fraud or by other means, from permitting this to be done. It was the purpose of our lawmakers, in passing the Act, to make it impossible for fraud or undue influence to be practiced in the execution of the Will, and in the disposition of the property disposed of by the Will.

It was not the intent of our law-makers, in enacting these statutes, if substantially complied with, to ever allow a miscarriage of justice by a wrongful disposition of the testator's property contrary to his intent. 84 O.S. 1951 §151 provides: "Intention of testator governs. — A will is to be construed according to the intention of the testator. . . ."

In Munger v. Elliott, 187 Okl. 19, 100 P.2d 876, 877, in syllabus 1, we held: "The cardinal rule for the construction of Wills is to ascertain the intent of the testator, and give effect thereto, if such intent does not attempt to effect that which the law forbids. All rules of construction are designed for this purpose, and all rules and presumptions are subordinate to the intent of the testator where that has been ascertained."

In the instant case, the intent expressed by the testator in the written instrument which he prepared, while of sound mind and disposing memory, is clear and beyond any question of doubt, free from fraud or undue influence of any kind. The only objection raised is that the statutes were not strictly complied with in the execution of the Will. I am of the opinion, when a person dies leaving a written instrument which he intended to be his last Will, and it is free from fraud or undue influence and in harmony with the purpose of our law-makers for enacting statutes regulating the execution of Wills, and also in accord with the laws of England and twenty-two of our states, it would be a miscarriage of justice to not admit the Will to probate, and thereby allow the property to be disposed of contrary to the testator's intent.

To hold otherwise would, in effect, permit a contrary disposition of testator's property against the purpose for which the statutory provisions were aimed.

---

who believes that any such decision has been corruptly obtained, to petition this Court for a hearing, in which, if corruption can be shown, the decision may be set aside.

Cf. Electric Auto-Lite Co. v. P. & D. Manufacturing Co., 109 F.2d 566 (2d Cir. 1940), where a rehearing was granted "because of the disqualification of one member of the original court [Judge Martin T. Manton, convicted of bribery in 1939], not known at the time."

For tales of other corrupt judges, including Sir Francis Bacon, see J. Borkin, The Corrupt Judge (1962). — Eds.

HALLEY, C.J., dissenting. . . . Counsel for the proponents of the purported will have come up with the ingenious idea that this instrument which is partly in typewriting and partly in handwriting is valid and should be admitted to probate for the fantastic reason that the handwriting is a codicil to the typewriting. It is my position that the typewritten part is not a will and the handwritten part is not a codicil. The handwritten part is only a continuation of the typewritten part and that combined, they constitute a will which was not attested and therefore cannot properly be admitted to probate.

. . . [T]here was nothing in the handwriting which referred to a previous will. It spoke of "this will" and not of a previous will. There is nothing about this handwriting to indicate that the testator intended it to be a codicil. He was completing his will with the handwriting.

I think he intended the typewritten portion to be a part of his will, not the completed will. A will is to be interpreted by what is found in its "four corners" and there is nothing to indicate that the testator intended it to be anything but one instrument. Parol or extrinsic evidence should not be admitted to show the contrary when the signed will is one instrument.

Under no circumstances should this be considered a codicil and I can never subscribe to the proposition that a holographic codicil will validate as a will an instrument that is typewritten, unfinished as to content, undated, unsigned and unattested. Not a case has been cited where a holographic codicil validates an instrument as a will which was not dated, signed or attested and no reference made in the purported codicil to the preceding will. . . .

Something is attempted to be made of the fact that the testator was a lawyer but that would prove nothing as many eminent lawyers have failed to properly prepare and execute their own wills. The will of Samuel J. Tilden is a notable example.

This will was one complete will unattested and therefore not admissible to probate and to give this will the construction that the majority has placed upon it is wholly unwarranted. Why make a mockery of the plain provision of our statutes? Property may only descend by will when the will is executed in conformity with the statutes.

I dissent.[38]

PROBLEM AND NOTE

1. In order to probate a holographic will it is necessary to eliminate typed matter on the face of a holographic will on the ground either

---

38. Noted in 8 Baylor L. Rev. 104; 7 Hastings L.J. 225; 44 Ky. L.J. 130; 30 N.Y.U.L. Rev. 1456; 9 Okla. L. Rev. 225; 34 Tex. L. Rev. 148; 23 U. Chi. L. Rev. 316; 17 U. Pitt. L. Rev. 312; 8 Vand. L. Rev. 924. — Eds.

that it is immaterial or that there is no intent to incorporate the typed matter. In view of this, can the handwritten part of Dexter G. Johnson's document be admitted as a holographic will, and then the typed part incorporated by reference?

Would the court have any problem probating Johnson's typed will if the handwritten portion had appeared on the back of the typed sheet rather than on the bottom? Could the handwritten portion incorporate the typed material by reference or are the front and back of a sheet integrated? See In re Estate of Plumel, 151 Cal. 77, 90 P. 192 (1907), referred to in the *Johnson* opinion at page 258.

2.   In Estate of Nielson, 105 Cal. App. 3d 796, 165 Cal. Rptr. 319 (1980), the testator drew lines through the dispositive provisions of his typewritten will and wrote between the lines: "Bulk of Estate — 1. — Shrine Hospital for Crippled Children — Los Angeles, $10,000 — 2. Society for Prevention of Cruelty to Animals." Near the margin of these cancellations and interlineations were the testator's initials and date. At the top and bottom of the will were the handwritten words, "Revised by Lloyd M. Nielson November 29, 1974." The court held the hand-written words constituted a holographic codicil, because they did not intend to incorporate the attested typed material. The holographic codicil republished the typewritten will, as modified.

4. Acts of Independent Significance

Now we turn to another doctrine permitting extrinsic evidence to identify the will beneficiaries or property passing under the will. If the beneficiary or property designations are identified by acts or events that have a lifetime motive and significance apart from their effect on the will, the gift will be upheld under the doctrine of acts of independent significance (also called the doctrine of nontestamentary acts). This is true even though the phrasing of the will leaves it in the testator's power to alter the beneficiaries or the property by a nontestamentary act. See Evans, Nontestamentary Acts and Incorporation by Reference, 16 U. Chi. L. Rev. 635 (1949).

Case 4 illustrates some common applications of the acts of independent significance doctrine.

Case 4.   *T*'s will devises "the automobile that I own at my death" to her nephew *N*, and gives $1,000 "to each person who shall be in my employ at my death." At the time the will is executed *T* owns a Volkswagen. Shortly before her death *T* trades the Volkswagen in on a new Cadillac, with the result that *T* dies owning a $30,000 automobile rather than one worth $3,000. In the year before her death *T* fires two long-time employees and hires three new ones. The gifts are valid. While *T*'s act in buying the

Cadillac had the practical effect of increasing the value of her gift to *N*, it is unlikely that this is what motivated her purchase. It is more probable that she bought the car because she wanted to drive a Cadillac. Similarly, *T*'s acts in hiring and firing various employees were doubtless prompted by business needs rather than a desire to make or unmake legatees under the will. Indeed, cases involving this form of devise typically assume the validity of the gift without discussion of the acts of independent significance doctrine.

Uniform Probate Code (1983)

§2-512 [Events of Independent Significance]

A will may dispose of property by reference to acts and events which have significance apart from their effect upon the dispositions made by the will, whether they occur before or after the execution of the will or before or after the testator's death. The execution or revocation of a will of another person is such an event.

PROBLEMS

1. *T* bequeaths the contents of the right-hand drawer of his desk to *A*. In the drawer at *T*'s death are a savings bank passbook in *T*'s name, a certificate for 100 shares of General Electric common stock, and a diamond ring. Does *A* take these items?

T bequeaths the contents of his safe-deposit box in Security Bank to *B* and the contents of his safe-deposit box in First National Bank to *C*. Do *B* and *C* take the items found in the respective boxes? See Annot., 5 A.L.R.3d 466 (1966).

T's will provides: "I have put in my safe-deposit box in Continental Bank shares of stock in several envelopes. Each envelope has on it the name of the person I desire to receive the stock contained in the envelope." At *T*'s death several envelopes are found in *T*'s safe-deposit box with the name of a person written on the envelope. Inside each is a stock certificate. For example, in one envelope is a certificate for 200 shares of Coca-Cola stock and on the envelope is written "For Ruth Moreno." Do Ruth Moreno and the other persons take the stock in the envelopes bearing their names? See Will of Le Collen, 190 Misc. 272, 72 N.Y.S.2d 467 (Sur. Ct. 1947); Smith v. Weitzel, 47 Tenn. App. 375, 338 S.W.2d 628 (Tenn. 1960).

2. In 1984 Sarah executes her will devising the residue of her estate to any charitable trust established by the last will and testament of her brother, Barney. In 1986 Barney executes his will, devising his property to the Barney Educational Trust, a charitable trust established by his

will. In 1987 Barney dies. In 1990 Sarah dies. Is the Barney Educational Trust entitled to the residue of Sarah's estate? See First National Bank v. Klein, 255 Ala. 505, 234 So. 2d 42 (1970). Suppose that Barney had survived Sarah. What result? See Restatement (Second) of Property, Donative Transfers §18.4, Comment f (1986).

SECTION E.   TERMINATION OF MEDICAL TREATMENT AND DISPOSITION OF THE BODY

1.   *Termination of Medical Treatment*

> Thou shalt not kill; but needst not strive
> Officiously to keep alive.
>
> A. H. CLOUGH
> *The Latest Decalogue (1863)*

In recent years a document has been created called, rather perversely it seems to us, a *living will*. It contains directives concerning termination of medical treatment, but it possibly could be viewed as an advance disposition of a person's life when competence is lost. The document provides that the signer's life shall not be artificially prolonged by extraordinary measures when there is no reasonable expectation of recovery from extreme physical or mental disability. About three-quarters of the states have living will legislation. These statutes vary in many particulars. Courts in a number of states have authorized living wills in the absence of statute. The lawyer advising a client to execute a living will document should consult local law. The local statute may prescribe the required form. The subject of living wills has generated a slew of law review articles about particular state law. For a general treatment, see Francis, The Evanescence of Living Wills, 14 J. Contemp. L. 27 (1988); Gelfand, Living Will Statutes: The First Decade, 1987 Wis. L. Rev. 737; Comment, Comparison of the Living Will Statutes of the Fifty States, 14 J. Contemp. L. 105 (1988); Note, Pregnancy Clauses in Living Will Statutes, 87 Colum. L. Rev 1280 (1987) (analyzing the validity of living will statutes voiding living wills of pregnant women). See also Uniform Rights of the Terminally Ill Act (1985).

Some state statutes have authorized a durable power of attorney for health care. A person can appoint an agent to make health care decisions in case of the person's incompetency. The power of the agent does not expire with the principal's incompetency (hence it is called "durable"); it expires only with the principal's death. A living will states the patient's wishes; a durable power puts decisions in the hands of a third person. The durable power enables the agent to respond flexibly to changing circumstances. The American Association of Retired Persons regularly advises people to have both a living will and a durable power, though in some circumstances they may conflict. See G. Alexander, Writing a Living Will: Using a Durable Power of Attorney (1987); Martyn & Jacobs, Legislating Advance Directives for the Terminally Ill: The Living Will and the Durable Power of Attorney, 63 Neb. L. Rev. 779 (1984); Note, Appointing an Agent to Make Medical Treatment Choice, 84 Colum. L. Rev. 985 (1984).

Cruzan supp. 50

2. Disposition of Decedent's Body

Historically, a person other than a monarch has had little say about what is done to his body after death. Until this century, burials were regarded as a matter of "sentiment and superstition" and were left to the jurisdiction of the church. With the rise of secularism, courts began to exercise a "benevolent discretion" to carry out the wishes of the deceased person, provided these wishes did not conflict unreasonably with the desires of the living. This power has been exercised in such a way that a person now has something more than a hope, but far less than an assurance, that his or her wishes will be carried out at death.[39]

39. In Holland v. Metalious, 105 N.H. 290, 198 A.2d 654, 7 A.L.R.3d 742 (1964), the will of Grace Metalious, author of the best-selling novel Peyton Place, forbade funeral services; the court refused to enjoin funeral services by the family. See Annot., 54 A.L.R.3d 1037 (1974).

In Meksrus Estate, 24 Pa. Fiduc. 249 (Orph. Ct. 1974), a testamentary direction to inter diamonds, jewelry, and paintings with the decedent's body was held to be against public policy and void. Such a provision, if enforced, the court thought, "is almost certain to tempt some people and invite others to overt action to procure the" buried treasure.

In March 1977, Sandra Ilene West of Beverly Hills died, devising her multimillion dollar estate to her brother-in-law upon the condition that she be buried in her 1964 baby-blue Ferrari dressed in a lace nightgown and with the seat slanted comfortably. Upon the brother-in-law's petition, the court ordered her buried, in the manner directed by her will, beside her husband in a cemetery in San Antonio, Texas. Los Angeles Times, May 20, 1977, pt.1, at 3.

Once buried, human remains cannot be exhumed except for compelling reasons and with consent of the next of kin. See Dougherty v. Mercantile-Safe Deposit & Trust Co., 282 Md. 617, 387 A.2d 244 (1978); Zablotower v. Mt. Zion Cemetery, 98 Misc. 2d 77, 413 N.Y.S.2d 106 (Sup. Ct. 1979) (by error Bessie Hoffenberg interred in grave reserved for Lena Hoffenberg (no relation), next to grave of Lena's husband; court refused to order Bessie's disinterment when Bessie's daughters objected on religious grounds). Cf. Alexander v. Alexander, 42 Ohio Misc. 2d 30, 537 N.E.2d 1310 (1988), where the court ordered disinterment of an alleged father of an illegitimate son so that the son might prove paternity by a genetic (DNA) test.

In addition, if a person dies by violence or in suspicious circumstances, statutes in all states require an autopsy regardless of the wishes of the deceased person or next of kin.

With the advent of cadaver organ transplantation, the first principle of law, medicine, and ethics — saving human life — became a relevant consideration in the disposition of the dead. To increase the quantity of cadaver organs for transplantation, all states have enacted the Uniform Anatomical Gift Act, either verbatim or in some modified version. This act permits a person to give his or her body to any hospital, physician, medical school, or body bank for research or transplantation. It also permits a gift of a body, or parts thereof, to any specified individual for therapy or transplantation needed by the individual. Under the original Uniform Anatomical Gift Act of 1968, the gift can be made by a duly executed will or by a card carried on the person if the card is "signed by the donor in the presence of two witnesses who must sign the document in his presence." Id. §4(a). In 1987 a new Uniform Anatomical Gift Act was promulgated, now adopted in a few states. The witnessing requirement was eliminated; only a signature on a card is required. In some states additional legislation has been enacted providing for an organ donation form to be affixed to the back of a driver's license. The Uniform Act provides that a surgeon who relies on the validity of the card or will "in good faith" is not civilly or criminally liable.[40]

The Uniform Anatomical Gift Act has had little effect on easing the shortage of organs. Only a small number of suitable organ donors (the best being healthy young persons who die from accidents) have signed instruments of gift. There are a number of reasons for this: (1) the difficulty of imagining one's death and others' using one's organs; (2) the fear that physicians might hasten a person's death in order to obtain organs; (3) unwillingness to be cut open after death, perhaps because of religious belief. In any case, throughout the 1970s and 1980s the waiting lists of people requiring kidneys, hearts, livers, and other organs grew rapidly. By the middle of the 1980s, it was conceded[41] that, however vigorous the campaign, not enough donors will sign donation forms to yield an adequate quantity of cadaver organs. See Weissman,

---

40. If the surgeon acts without the consent of the donor or the next-of-kin, the surgeon is liable in tort to the next-of-kin for unauthorized dissection.

41. Well, not by everyone. See Katz, Increasing the Supply of Human Organs for Transplantation: A Proposal for a System of Mandated Choice, 18 Bev. Hills B. Assn. J. 153 (1984) (advocating requiring a person to answer yes or no to cadaver organ donation before receiving a driver's license or enrolling in the social security system; declining to answer will prevent issuance of license or social security number).

See also Areen, A Scarcity of Organs, 38 J. Leg. Ed. 555 (1988), suggesting trying to increase donations by authorizing individuals to give a trusted person a durable power of attorney for organ donation at death.

Why the Uniform Anatomical Gift Act Has Failed, 116 Tr. & Est. 264 (1977).

A number of commentators, and some entrepreneurs ready to buy and sell organs, suggested that a market in human organs be established. A market, after all, is the traditional way of remedying inadequate supply. See Note, Sale of Human Body Parts, 72 Mich. L. Rev. 1182 (1974). In 1984, however, Congress forbade the sale of human organs. National Organ Transplant Act, Pub. L. No. 98-501, §301, 98 Stat. 2339, 42 U.S.C.A. §274(e) (1984). See Note, Regulating the Sale of Human Organs, 71 Va. L. Rev. 1015 (1985) (criticizing the federal statute). The British Parliament outlawed sale of human organs in 1989, after a public outcry over the sale of a kidney to a Londoner for £2000 by a Turkish peasant flown to London for the operation. N.Y. Times, Aug. 1, 1989, §B, at 5, col. 1. Suppose that the federal government paid the funeral expenses of any cadaver organ donor or gave a tax deduction of $10,000. Should that be prohibited as a sale? Suppose that health insurance companies, as a result of collective bargaining or govermental requirement, offered lower premiums to persons who agreed to donate their organs at death. Would this be a sale?

Sensing that seeking the decedent's prior consent would not produce the necessary organs, the federal government in 1986 took another tack. Hospitals should put pressure on the next of kin to consent. A government report urged states to adopt statutes requiring hospitals to request from families of prospective donors at the time of death permission to remove organs for transplantation. And a federal regulation of the same year made "routine request" a condition of hospital Medicare eligibility. See U.S. Dept. of Health & Human Services, Report of Task Force on Organ Transplantation (Apr. 1986). More than half the states have enacted "routine request" statutes. Yet, in view of difficulties families have in facing such requests in time of shock and grief, it is questionable whether the routine request approach will be successful. Requesting organs from next-of-kin also has come under sharp criticism by those who believe only the decedent, and not the next-of-kin, should have the right to consent to use of the decedent's organs. They base this on the principle of individual autonomy. See Quay, Utilizing the Bodies of the Dead, 28 St. Louis U.L.J. 889 (1984). See generally Cotton & Sandler, The Regulation of Organ Procurement and Transplantation in the United States, 7 J. Legal Med. 55 (1986); Statutory Regulation of Organ Donation in the United States (R. Manson ed. 1986).

A significant increase in the quantity of cadaver organs available for transplantation might result if usable organs were routinely removed from cadavers unless, before the time of removal, an objection has been entered, either by the deceased person during life or by the next-of-kin knowing of the decedent's objection immediately after decedent's death. This method presumes that the deceased person has consented, and thus it favors preserving life; the burden of objecting is put upon those who would deny life to another. A policy of presumed consent makes the donor the primary, and perhaps exclusive, decision maker in organ donation. Routine salvaging of cadaver organs for transplantation is practiced in many European countries. See Dukeminier, Supplying Organs for Transplantation, 68 Mich. L. Rev. 811 (1970); Matas, Arras, Muyskens, Tellis & Veith, A Proposal for Cadaver Organ Procurement: Routine Removal With Right of Informed Refusal, 10 J. Health Pol. Poly. & L. 231 (1985); Note, Refining the Law of Organ Donation: Lessons From the French Law of Presumed Consent, 19 N.Y.U.J. Intl. L. & Pol. 1013 (1987). Compare Silver, The Case for a Post-Mortem Organ Draft and a Proposed Model Organ Draft Act, 68 B.U.L. Rev. 681 (1988) (arguing for "conscription" of cadaver organs regardless of the wishes of decedent or next-of-kin, with an exemption only for religious objection).

In 1968 in the New England Journal of Medicine one of the editors, together with Dr. David Sanders, proposed routine salvaging of cadaver organs unless a prior objection is registered. This proposal brought the following delicious riposte.

Anthropophagy: Swift Reprisal
279 New Eng. J. Med. 890 (1968)

To the Editor:

As the author some time ago, of a certain modest proposal,[42] I find that the recent essay,[43] "Salvaging of Cadaver Organs," has presented, to my edification and delight, the prospect of an abundant annual harvest from (definably) dead bodies of gratifying numbers of "usable" kidneys, hearts and other viscera, no longer consigned to futile decay.

My enthusiasm is such that I have been moved to wonder whether the same arguments and approach might not, with a little imagination, be extended to the solution of a social and medical problem even more portentous than those of endstage uremia, congestive heart failure and so forth. I refer to the vast suffering and annual thousands of premature deaths occasioned by protein malnutrition.

Although I would not pretend that, either for sophistication or for enduring benefit, a kidney stew could successfully compete with the transplanted organ, nevertheless, when the problems of supply and demand are placed in perspective, I am sure that the following arguments will commend themselves to you.

---

42. Swift, J., Modest Proposal for Preventing the Children of the Poor People from Being a Burden to their Parents or the Country. 1729.

43. Dukeminier & Sanders, Organ Transplantation: Proposal for Routine Salvaging of Cadaver Organs. New Eng. J. Med. 279: 413-419, 1968.

Recently, the use for transplantation of kidneys, heart, lung and pancreas from a single cadaver was so impressive for its economy. "Waste not want not." In my proposal, not only could all these be salvaged, but also liver, intestines, spleen, bone marrow, muscles, even brain — indeed, almost the whole of the otherwise useless cadaver.

The problem of skilled personnel and equipment would be so much the less, able butchers and cooks being so much more numerous than surgeons, and cleavers and pots than equipped operating rooms. The advantage in undeveloped countries needs no emphasis.

With this form of introduction into living persons of the remnants of the dead the problem of immunologic rejection could be readily solved. By enzymatic attack upon the whole proteins, antigenicity could be removed. It should be possible, without elaborate equipment, to employ the in situ enzymatic apparatus of the digestive tracts of the recipients for this purpose. With the elimination of the need for immunologic matching, the number of potential donors would be vastly increased.

The exact definition of the moment of death would become less critical. Although I do not doubt that freshness would still be important, the urgency would be removed.

I am not insensible that the unthinking mob may cry, "Why this, Sir, is cannibalism!" Surely, we who believe in progress should not be dissuaded by appeals to outmoded legalisms and superstitions. We will keep in mind your authors' repeated assurances that the preservation of life is a primary good.

Recognizing that neither the route of introduction, nor the form of particular cadaver moieties is an ethically or scientifically important distinction, any objection could easily be met with such safeguards as those proposed by your authors — namely, a suitably limited right of objection by involved parties, acceptance of such salvage as routine, thereby sparing the bereaved needless participation in the process of decision. My friend Lemuel Gulliver, noted surgeon and world traveler,[44] assures me that the selection of donors and recipients could properly be left in the hands of the medical profession.

Religious authority, already being, we are told, not averse to one form of use of the dead, should not long withhold its approval from another.

> Your Obedient Servant,
> *Jonathan Swift*

Elysian Fields, Paradise 00000

Come to think of it, what *is* the difference between a starving person eating cadaver flesh to stay alive and a doctor inserting a cadaver heart or kidney in an otherwise dying patient? Is organ transplantation refined cannibalism?

44. Gulliver, L., Travels into Several Remote Nations of the World. 1726.

4

WILL SUBSTITUTES: AVOIDANCE OF PROBATE

SECTION A.   CONTRACTS RELATING TO WILLS

A person may enter into a contract *to make a will* or a contract *not to revoke a will*. Contract law, not the law of wills, applies. The contract beneficiary must sue under the law of contracts and prove a valid contract. If, after a contract becomes binding, a party dies leaving a will not complying with the contract, the will is probated but the contract beneficiary is entitled to enforce the contract by having a constructive trust impressed for his benefit upon the estate or devisees of the defaulting party.

1. Contracts to Make a Will

Questions respecting contracts to make a will may arise in a variety of fact situations, such as a claimed promise to make a will in exchange for an agreement to marry,[1] or to serve as nurse and housekeeper, or

---

1. In In re Estate of Lord, 93 N.M. 543, 602 P.2d 1030 (1979), there was an alleged oral antenuptial agreement whereby a 64-year-old woman, Bernice, afflicted with cancer, promised to devise her entire estate to Robert, if he would marry her and "take care of her like a husband would." Robert married Bernice and looked after her for over two years, but Bernice's will, executed the day after marriage, left only $10,000 to Robert and the bulk of her property to her sister. After Bernice's death Robert sued to enforce the contract. The court held that a contract whereby one person agrees to pay the other for care after marriage, which is part of the other's duty as a spouse, is invalid because against public policy. "It is the policy of this state to foster and protect the marriage institution. It is not the policy of the state to encourage spouses to marry for money." 93 N.M. at 544, 602 P.2d at 1031. Why should Robert win if he agrees to take care of Bernice but lose if he throws marriage into the bargain?

not to contest a will. In many states a contract to make a will must be in writing. In these states, if the promisee is not entitled to sue for specific performance, the promisee is entitled to receive the value to the decedent of services rendered (quantum meruit). The value the decedent put on the services in the oral agreement ("I promise to leave you half of my estate") is evidence of the reasonable value of those services. See Hastoupis v. Gargas, 9 Mass. App. Ct. 27, 398 N.E.2d 745 (1980). In some states an oral contract to make a will is specifically enforceable provided the terms are proved by clear and convincing evidence, the rendition of the services is wholly referable to the contract, and the services are of such peculiar value to the promisor as not to be estimated or compensable by any pecuniary standard. See Musselman v. Mitchell, 46 Or. App. 299, 611 P.2d 675 (1980). See generally Note, The Statute of Frauds' Lifetime and Testamentary Provisions: Safeguarding Decedents' Estates, 50 Fordham L. Rev. 239 (1981).

PROBLEMS AND NOTE

1. *T* makes a contract with *A* to leave everything to *A* at death if *A* will take care of *T* for life. *T* executes a will leaving her estate to *A*. Subsequently *A* changes her mind and decides not to care for *T*. *T* rescinds the contract. Upon *T*'s death is *A* entitled to take under *T*'s will? See Trotter v. Trotter, 490 So. 2d 827 (Miss. 1986).

2. *A* dies of AIDS. After *A*'s death, *A*'s roommate, *B*, claims half of *A*'s estate. *B* alleges that *A* promised to leave *B* half his estate if *B* cared for *A* for his life. *B* produces a document typed by *B* and signed by *A* and one witness devising one-half of his estate to *B*. The jurisdiction has enacted UPC §2-701, infra page 280, requiring that the contract be evidenced by a writing signed by the decedent. Is *B* entitled to one-half of *A*'s estate? See Estate of Fritz, 159 Mich. App. 69, 406 N.W.2d 475 (1987). Would it make any difference if *B* were *A*'s spouse?

3. In Marvin v. Marvin, 18 Cal. 3d 660, 557 P.2d 106, 134 Cal. Rptr. 815 (1976), the court held that when unmarried cohabitants separate, any implied contract to share all property accumulated during cohabitation is enforceable. Suppose that one of the cohabitants, Lee Marvin, dies. Should the surviving cohabitant, Michelle, be able to enforce an implied contract to share? If not, should the surviving cohabitant be entitled to recover for the value of services rendered or for support? See In re Estate of Lamb, 99 N.M. 157, 655 P.2d 1001 (1982); Poe v. Estate of Levy, 411 So. 2d 253 (Fla. App. 1982). If not, is Michelle better off splitting from Lee Marvin before he dies?

4. Property received by bequest or devise is not taxable as income under the federal income tax. On the other hand, a bequest made in

". . . And to my faithful valet, Sidney, who I promised to remember in my will — Hi there, Sidney!"

QUESTION

Does Sidney have an enforceable claim against his employer's estate?

---

consideration of caring for the testator is taxable compensation to the recipient. Wolder v. Commissioner, 58 T.C. 974 (1972), aff'd on this issue, 493 F.2d 608 (2d Cir. 1974); Jesse A. Miller, 53 T.C.M. (CCH) 962 (1987).

2. Contracts Not to Revoke a Will

Questions respecting contracts not to revoke a will typically arise where husband and wife have executed a joint will or mutual wills. A *joint will*

273

is one instrument executed by two or more persons as the will of both
(see the joint will executed in Rubenstein v. Mueller, infra). When one
testator dies, the instrument is probated as the testator's will; when the
other testator dies, the instrument is probated as the other testator's
will. *Mutual wills* are the separate wills of two or more persons that
contain similar or reciprocal provisions. A *joint and mutual will* is a term
commonly used by courts to describe a joint will that devises the
property in accordance with a contract. In this context mutuality refers
to the contract and not to reciprocal provisions of separate wills. See
Rauch v. Rauch, 112 Ill. App. 3d 198, 445 N.E.2d 77 (1983).

There are no legal consequences peculiar to joint or mutual wills
unless they are executed pursuant to a contract between the testators
not to revoke their wills. The initial problem is proof of the contract.
Most courts hold that a contract not to revoke is not enforceable unless
it is proved by clear and convincing evidence and that the mere execution
of a joint will or of mutual wills does not give rise to a presumption of
contract. See Estate of Kester, 477 Pa. 243, 383 A.2d 914 (1978). The
difficulty, however, is that the existence of a common dispositive scheme,
and, in the case of a joint will, the expression of the scheme in a jointly
executed instrument, strongly suggests an understanding or underlying
agreement and thus invites a claim of contract, the terms of which can
be inferred from the will or wills. The danger of litigation can be
reduced by inserting in every joint or mutual will a provision declaring
that the will was or was not executed pursuant to a contract, but the
lawyer who is astute enough to be aware of this problem will doubtless
also know that joint wills are notorious litigation-breeders that should
not be used at all.

Rubenstein v. Mueller
Court of Appeals of New York, 1967
19 N.Y.2d 228, 225 N.E.2d 540, 278 N.Y.S.2d 845

BURKE, J. On October 23, 1961, Bertha and Conrad Mueller, after
nearly a half century of marriage, executed a joint will providing that
the estate of the first to die should go to the survivor, and on the
survivor's death their property should go to certain named beneficiaries.
Nine months later in July of 1962, Bertha died and Conrad, pursuant
to the joint will, received her entire net estate. The following month
Mueller's cousin, Martha Louise Mueller, the defendant herein, came
to live with him, keeping house for him and after he became ill, nursing
him until his death in June, 1964. Conrad and Martha were married
on March 12, 1963, and a week later on March 20 Conrad executed a

new will naming his second wife sole beneficiary. This latter will has been admitted to probate.

On this appeal we are asked to determine the respective rights of the widow and the beneficiaries under the joint will to Mueller's property, consisting of a house and lot acquired by Bertha and Conrad as tenants by the entirety in 1919, and a joint bank account in Conrad and Martha's names, but funded with money received by Conrad as the surviving owner of joint bank accounts in the names of Bertha and himself. There is unanimity of opinion in this court that Conrad's final will was ineffective to alter the testamentary arrangement provided for in the joint will, but we are divided over the question of whether this decedent's earlier covenant with his first wife respecting the disposition to be made of their collective property on the death of the survivor should take precedence over the claim of the widow to a right of election to take against the earlier joint will.[2]

On the first issue raised herein, the revocability of the joint will, the language in the instrument clearly indicates the Muellers' intention that its provisions should be binding upon the survivor. It "imports the joint disposition of the collective property of both, not the independent disposition by each of his own." (Rastetter v. Hoenninger, 214 N.Y. 66, 72, 108 N.E. 210, 211.) The recently decided case of Matter of Zeh, 24 A.D.2d 983, 265 N.Y.S.2d 257, affd. 18 N.Y.2d 900, 276 N.Y.S.2d 635, 223 N.E.2d 43, wherein we held that the joint will in question was not binding upon the survivor, is distinguishable from the present case. In *Zeh* the survivor was given all the property, "meaning thereby that *the survivor of us shall be the absolute owner*, to him or to her to have and to hold, his or her heirs and assigns *absolutely and forever*, of all that both of us possess." (Emphasis added.) Under the rule that before the right to alter or revoke a will may be curtailed prior to the testator's death his intention to so bind himself must be manifested clearly and unambiguously (see Oursler v. Armstrong, 10 N.Y.2d 385, 389, 223 N.Y.S.2d 477, 478, 179 N.E.2d 489, 490), the use of language such as "absolutely" barred our finding that the survivor was bound to the testamentary plan found in that joint will. In the instant case, on the other hand, the

2. The widow does not actually assert a right of election, as provided in section 18 of the Decedent Estate Law, Consol. Laws, c. 13, since under the later will, properly admitted to probate as the last will and testament of her husband, she takes all, though subject to the claims of the beneficiaries named in the joint will. Her argument is, rather, that the public policy finding expression in section 18, seeking to guarantee the widow a distributive share in her husband's estate, constitutes a limitation upon the right of a party to a joint will to bind himself to a testamentary arrangement which would not provide a surviving spouse with such a share in his estate. Consequently, equity should decline to specifically enforce an otherwise binding obligation of the survivor under a joint will where such specific enforcement will frustrate this legislatively declared public policy.

Muellers' intention is clear and unambiguous.[3] The phrasing used in paragraph "Third," providing that "[u]pon the death of the second one of us to die, or in the event of our simultaneous deaths or deaths resulting from a common disaster, then the estate of the second decedent, or of both of us as the case may be, is hereby bequeathed, devised and disposed of as follows," is in the present tense, and thus implies a present joint intention to make a gift of the collective property to the named beneficiaries, effective upon the survivor's death, but binding as of the signing of the joint will. The entire context of the will is plural, the pronoun "we" is used instead of "I," "our" instead of "my" and "us" instead of "me." Moreover, this will contains an express revocation of a prior joint will and it *omits* the provision in that prior will describing the survivor's right to alter the disposition made of the signatories' property. The omission of this provision in the later joint will is persuasive evidence that the second joint will was intended to be irrevocable. . . .

On the other issue raised here, the effect of section 18 of the Decedent Estate Law on the right of the beneficiaries under the joint will to obtain specific enforcement of the covenant by Mueller contained in that will, we are of the opinion that the named beneficiaries under the joint will are entitled to prevail and a constructive trust in their favor was properly impressed upon the property received by the widow under the later will.

As to property received by Mueller under the joint will there can be no question but that upon his acceptance of such benefits under that instrument a trust was impressed in favor of the beneficiaries to the extent expressed in *Tutunjian*. As to such property Mueller really took but an interest during his life with a power to use or otherwise dispose

---

3. The exact language of the Muellers' will was:

WE, . . . do hereby make, publish and declare this to be the Last Will and Testament of each of us. . . .

Second: The first deceased hereby bequeaths and devises all real and personal property of whatever kind and wherever situated to the survivor of us outright.

Third: Upon the death of the second one of us to die, or in the event of our simultaneous deaths or deaths resulting from a common disaster, then the estate of said second decedent, or both of us as the case may be, is hereby bequeathed, devised and disposed of as follows: . . . .

Fourth: All the rest, residue and remainder of the estate or estates . . . we hereby give, devise and bequeath equally between Ruth Hanzlicsek and Wilma Rubenstein aforesaid.

Fifth: We purposely leave nothing to Anna Marie Davis, of Boston, Massachusetts, and Louise Stein, of New York City, New York, daughter and niece respectively of the testatrix herein, Bertha Mueller, because they have not shown any concern for us.

Rubenstein v. Mueller, 47 Misc. 2d 830, 832, 263 N.Y.S.2d 349, 351 (Sur. Ct. 1965). — Eds.

of principal, and the named beneficiaries took the interest which remained. Under such circumstances he had no property interest in these assets against which his widow's right of election could operate.

The bulk of the property involved did not come to Mueller under the joint will. His interest in the real property, for example, commenced as a tenant by the entirety, ripening into sole ownership through his surviving his first wife. Similarly, his formal title to most of the personalty, consisting of savings accounts, derived from his surviving Bertha, with whom he had these joint accounts. In addition, it is not clear from the stipulated facts whether any of this jointly held property represented the independent estate of Bertha Mueller or whether, as is typical, it represented the jointly held fruits of Conrad's labors outside the home aided by Bertha's efforts within the home for their lifetime together. In any event we do not attempt a segregation of assets of husband and wife after a marriage of this duration. For all practical purposes, equity may content itself with considering the assets as their collective property, as if their estates had merged.

As to this collective property we feel that, on the death of one party to the joint will, the survivor was bound by the mutual agreement that the named beneficiaries should receive the property remaining when the survivor died. (See Hermann v. Ludwig, 186 App. Div. 287, 297, 174 N.Y.S. 459, 474, affd. 229 N.Y. 544, 129 N.E. 908.) As we pointed out above, the agreement embodied in the joint will provides that "Upon the death of the second . . . the estate of the second . . . is hereby bequeathed, devised and disposed of as follows." The survivor's right to full ownership of the collective property is transformed and modified by this joint agreement, effective upon the other's death as stated above, into but an interest during the life of the survivor with power to use the principal. . . . After Bertha's death, then, the property received by Conrad was his but subject to an interest enforcible specifically as to so much of it as he did not consume during his lifetime.

Contrary to the result which we here reach, the defendant urges that the widow's right to election constitutes a limitation on the freedom of an individual to so incumber his estate. In support of this contention she directs our attention to a number of lower court cases involving marital separation agreements under which husbands covenanted to make a will leaving all or a portion of their property to the estranged wife or to their children and later remarried, leaving widows. In these cases the learned Surrogates correctly held that the former wife's right to specific enforcement of the agreement must give way to the widow's statutory right to a share in her husband's estate. (Matter of Lewis' Will, 4 Misc. 2d 937, 123 N.Y.S.2d 859; Matter of Erstein's Estate, 205 Misc. 924, 129 N.Y.S.2d 316; Matter of Hoyt's Estate, 174 Misc. 512, 21 N.Y.S.2d 107.) These cases are, however, distinguishable from the instant case and they present different equitable considerations. Separation agreements are usually attended by a present division of any jointly held property, and any provision for a future legacy is usually but an incident to the over-all settlement to be made with respect to the husband's individual property and his obligation of support. In the case of the joint will, however, this instrument typically represents the sole attempt by the signatories to effect a distribution of their collective property in a fashion agreeable to both. Most importantly, in those separation agreements there was no irrevocable obligation concerning the collective property. The husband did not, as Mueller did here, become sole owner of jointly owned property by virtue of surviving the former wife. As the divorced husband's property after the agreement remains his own individual property, to which he holds beneficial as well as legal title, his widow's right of election may be asserted against such assets.

Accordingly, the order of the Appellate Division affirming the judgment of Special Term should be affirmed, without costs.

[BERGAN, J., dissented in an opinion joined by FULD, C.J. The dissenters believed that, in an equitable action to impose a constructive trust, the equities of a surviving spouse were superior to those of the contract beneficiaries.]

NOTES AND PROBLEMS

1. After Bertha Mueller's death, what are Conrad's rights in the property during his lifetime? Since he has been given the property "outright," does he have the rights of a fee simple owner, with the gift on his death being only what he has not consumed, spent, or given away during his lifetime? See Flohr v. Walker, 520 P.2d 833 (Wyo. 1974) (survivor entitled to "income and reasonable portions of principal for his support and ordinary expenditures, . . . but cannot dissipate the estate or alienate by inter vivos transfers . . . to defeat the contract"); Estate of Chayka, 47 Wis. 2d 102, 176 N.W.2d 561 (1970) (inter vivos gifts by survivor can be set aside if not made in good faith). Suppose that Conrad thinks that a round-the-world cruise on the QE2 will be the perfect wedding present for his new bride. Is that permitted? Suppose he wants to buy Martha an emerald bracelet from Tiffany's. Okay?

If the contractual will is interpreted as causing Conrad's interest in Bertha's property, *as well as in his own property*, to be changed as of Bertha's death into a life estate with a power to invade corpus for his health, support, and maintenance (i.e., limited by an ascertainable standard of withdrawal, see infra page 724), Conrad has made, at Bertha's death, a taxable gift to the contract beneficiaries of a remainder interest in his property. See Pyle v. United States, 766 F.2d 1141 (7th Cir. 1985). On the other hand, if Conrad's power over the property is not limited by a standard but is limited only by a "good faith" or "prudent" obligation, Conrad has not made a taxable gift to the contract beneficiaries at the time of Bertha's death. See Estate of Lidbury v. Commissioner, 800 F.2d 649 (7th Cir. 1986). Both local law and the contract will have to be examined to decide what standard governs Conrad's dissipation of the principal. See Comment, The Contractual Will: Invitation to Litigation and Excess Taxation, 48 Tex. L. Rev. 909 (1970). Because of the uncertain tax consequences, a joint and mutual will should clearly be avoided by anyone who is concerned about federal transfer taxation.

2.   Does the contract apply only to Conrad's property owned at Bertha's death, or does it include property acquired by Conrad thereafter? Note that the Muellers' joint will (and thus the contract?) speaks of devising "the estate of the second decedent" on the survivor's death, which apparently means everything Conrad owns at death. Suppose that Conrad survives his second wife and receives property from her. Does the contract apply to this property? See Estate of Maloney v. Carsten, 381 N.E.2d 1263 (Ind. App. 1978); In re Estate of Wiggins, 45 A.D.2d 604, 360 N.Y.S.2d 129 (1974), aff'd on opinion below, 39 N.Y.2d 791, 385 N.Y.S.2d 287 (1976) (holding a joint will devising "all our property" on the survivor's death implied a contract with such a term; although through careful investment the surviving wife tripled her inheritance during the 21 years she survived her husband, the constructive trust imposed on all the wife's property prevented her from effectively bequeathing even a small legacy to persons other than contract beneficiaries).

3.   Suppose that a contract beneficiary does not survive Conrad. Is the beneficiary's estate entitled to enforce the contract against Conrad's estate? See Jones v. Jones, 692 S.W.2d 406 (Mo. App. 1985); Fiew v. Qualtrough, 624 S.W.2d 335 (Tex. Civ. App. 1981) (both cases holding that the contract beneficiary's rights vest upon the death of one of the contracting parties and imposing a constructive trust for the benefit of the beneficiary's estate). Suppose that Conrad does not make a new will in favor of his second wife and does not revoke his joint will. What result? See In re Estate of Arends, 311 N.W.2d 686 (Iowa 1981) (holding that contract beneficiary can sue on the contract only if the survivor revokes his will and breaches the contract; otherwise the will, which complies with the contract, controls, and a will beneficiary must survive the testator in order to take). Why should the beneficiary have an interest transmissible to her estate upon her prior death if a promisor breaches the contract but not if he dies in compliance?

See Comment, Contracts to Make Joint or Mutual Wills, 55 Marq. L. Rev. 103 (1972).

4. *H* and *W* have children by prior marriages. They want the survivor to have "everything" and "be comfortable," and they want all their property divided equally among their children upon the death of the survivor. But, knowing that the survivor will have closer ties to his or her own children, they feel uncomfortable leaving the disposition entirely in the survivor's hands. This is the basic dilemma suggested by many contractual wills. When you study trusts later in this course, you will find that *H* and *W*'s desires can be better realized, with fewer problems, by creating a trust rather than by using contractual wills.

5. For an annotation of cases on whether the language in a will is sufficient to establish a contract not to revoke, see Annot., 17 A.L.R.4th 167 (1982). Litigation is extensive and cases tend to be difficult to reconcile one with another. Should a lawyer insert in every reciprocal or joint will a statement that the will is (or is not) executed pursuant to a contract not to revoke? In an effort to reduce litigation, Uniform Probate Code §2-701 tightens the methods by which contracts relating to wills can be proved.

Uniform Probate Code (1983)

§2-701 [Contracts Concerning Succession]

A contract to make a will or devise, or not to revoke a will or devise, or to die intestate, if executed after the effective date of this Act, can be established only by (1) provisions of a will stating material provisions of the contract; (2) an express reference in a will to a contract and extrinsic evidence proving the terms of the contract; or (3) a writing signed by the decedent evidencing the contract. The execution of a joint will or mutual wills does not create a presumption of a contract not to revoke the will or wills.

For criticism of the drafting of UPC §2-701, noting many ambiguities, see Collins, Oral Contracts to Make a Will and the Uniform Probate Code: Boon or Boondoggle?, 20 Creighton L. Rev. 413 (1987).

SECTION B. CONTRACTS WITH PAYABLE-ON-DEATH PROVISIONS

Wilhoit v. Peoples Life Insurance Co.
United States Court of Appeals, Seventh Circuit, 1955
218 F.2d 887

Major, J.   The plaintiff, Robert Wilhoit, instituted this action against the defendants, Peoples Life Insurance Company (sometimes referred to as the company) and Thomas J. Owens, for the recovery of money held by the company. Roley Oscar Wilhoit was the insured and Sarah Louise Wilhoit, his wife, the beneficiary in a life insurance policy in the amount of $5,000, issued by Century Life Insurance Company and later reinsured in Peoples Life Insurance Company of Frankfort, Indiana. Mr. Wilhoit died prior to October 22, 1930 (the exact date not disclosed by the record), without having changed the beneficiary designated in the policy, and the proceeds thereof became due and payable to Mrs. Wilhoit. The amount due was paid to her and the policy surrendered, as is evidenced by the following receipt appearing on the back of the policy:

"$4,749.00   "Indianapolis, Ind.,
                                                       "Oct. 22-1930.

   "Received from Century Life Insurance Company Forty Seven hundred forty nine Dollars in full for all claims under the within policy, terminated by death of Roley O. Wilhoit.

                                        "Sarah Louise Wilhoit"

The main body of the policy contained a provision entitled "The Investment," as follows:

   Upon the maturity of this policy, the amount payable hereunder, or any portion thereof, not less than One Thousand Dollars, may be left on deposit with the Company, and the Company will pay interest annually in advance upon the amount so left on deposit at such rate as the Company may declare on such funds so held by it, but never at a rate less than three per cent, so long as the amount shall remain on deposit with the Company. The said deposit may be withdrawn at the end of any interest year; or upon the death of the payee the amount of said deposit will be paid to the executors, administrators or assigns of said payee.[4]

On November 14, 1930, Mrs. Wilhoit (twenty-three days after she had acknowledged receipt of the amount due her under the policy) from her home in Indiana signed and addressed a letter to the company in the same State, which in material parts reads as follows:

----

   4. Almost all life insurance policies give the beneficiary several options. The beneficiary may draw down the policy proceeds in a lump sum. Or the beneficiary may leave the proceeds with the company and draw interest. Or the beneficiary may elect an installment option. Installment options may include a life annuity, payments for a fixed period or for life whichever is longer, payments for a fixed period, or some other type of periodic payments. The option to which this footnote is appended is known as an *interest option.* — Eds.

I hereby acknowledge receipt of settlement in full under Policy No. C172 terminated by the death of Roley O. Wilhoit, the Insured, and I direct that the proceeds of $4,749.00 be held in trust by[5] the Peoples Life Insurance Company under the following conditions:

(1) Said amount or any part thereof (not less than $100.00) to be subject to withdrawal on demand of the undersigned.

(2) While on deposit, said amount or part thereof shall earn interest at the rate of 3½%, compounded annually, plus any excess interest authorized by the Board of Directors of the Company. Interest may be withdrawn at the end of each six months period or whenever the principal of the fund is withdrawn or may be allowed to accumulate compounded annually. Interest on this trust fund shall begin as of October 9th, 1930.

(3) In the event of my death, while any part of this trust fund is still in existence, the full amount, plus any accrued interest, shall be immediately payable to Robert G. Owens (Relationship) Brother.

The proposal contained in this letter was, on November 17, 1930, accepted by the company in the following form:

The above agreement creating a trust fund is hereby accepted and we acknowledge receipt of the deposit of $4,749.00 under the above specified conditions.

Robert G. Owens, a brother of Mrs. Wilhoit and the person mentioned in her November 14 letter to the company, died January 23, 1932, and Mrs. Wilhoit died April 12, 1951, each leaving a last will and testament. The will of the former by a general clause devised all his property to Thomas J. Owens, a defendant, and was admitted to probate in Marion County, Indiana. The will of Mrs. Wilhoit was admitted to probate in Edgar County, Illinois, and contained the following provision:

I now have the sum of Four Thousand Seven Hundred Forty Nine Dollars ($4,749.00), or approximately that amount, which is the proceeds of an insurance policy on the life of my deceased husband, Oscar Wilhoit, on deposit with the insurance company, the Peoples Life Insurance

---

5. Although Mrs. Wilhoit directed that the proceeds be held "in trust" and ordered that "this trust fund" be payable to Robert G. Owens upon her death, and the company accepted the agreement creating "a trust fund," no trust was created. A trust involves a duty to manage specific property. A debt involves merely a personal obligation to pay a sum of money. In this case a debt was created. The parties did not intend for the company to segregate $4,749 from its general assets and keep it as separate trust property; they intended the company to mix the money with its general assets. Moreover, the company was required to pay interest at a fixed rate of 3½ percent, not all the income it earned on $4,749. This shows that the parties intended the company to have the use of the money for its own purposes and to be under a personal liability to repay the sum to Mrs. Wilhoit. The company is thus a debtor, not a trustee. See 1 A. Scott, Trusts §12.2 (W. Fratcher 4th ed. 1987). — Eds.

Company of Frankfort, Indiana. This I give and bequeath to Robert Wilhoit, now of Seattle, Washington, who is another son of my said stepson, the same to be his property absolutely. . . .

The fund in controversy, deposited with the company by Mrs. Wilhoit on November 17, 1930, remained with the company continuously until the date of her death, April 12, 1951. The company refused to recognize the claim to the fund made by Robert Wilhoit, the legatee named in the will of Mrs. Wilhoit and the plaintiff in the instant action. . . . [The defendant] Thomas J. Owens claimed the fund as the legatee under the will of Robert G. Owens. . . . The district Court, on March 11, 1954, without opinion sustained the motion of the plaintiff for summary judgment. . . . Thereupon, judgment was entered in favor of the plaintiff in the sum of $4,749.00, together with interest and costs. . . .

Defendants . . . advance two theories in support of their argument for reversal, both of which are firmly grounded upon the premise that the agreement of November 17, 1930, between Mrs. Wilhoit and the company, was an insurance contract or a contract supplemental thereto. Thus premised, they argue (1) that the rights of the parties must be determined by the law of insurance and not by the statute of wills, and (2) that Mrs. Wilhoit as a primary beneficiary named Robert G. Owens as the successor beneficiary irrevocably, without right to revoke or change and without a "pre-decease of beneficiary" provision, and that as a result the rights of such successor beneficiary upon his death prior to the death of the primary beneficiary did not lapse but passed on to the heirs and assigns of such successor beneficiary.

On the other hand, plaintiff argues, in support of the judgment, that the disposition of the fund is not controlled by the law of insurance because the agreement between Mrs. Wilhoit and the company was not an insurance contract or a supplement thereto but was nothing more than a contract of deposit, and that the provision in the agreement by which Robert G. Owens was to take the funds in the event of her death was an invalid testamentary disposition. Further, it is argued that in any event any interest acquired by Robert G. Owens was extinguished upon his death, which occurred prior to that of Mrs. Wilhoit.

Defendants cite many cases from numerous jurisdictions which have held under a variety of circumstances that the proceeds of a life insurance policy are to be disposed of in accordance with its provisions, and that a beneficiary, if authorized by the policy, may designate a successor beneficiary to take on the death of the primary beneficiary.

. . . Obviously, defendants' contention is without merit and the cases cited in support thereof are without application unless we accept the premise upon which the contention is made, that is, that the agreement between Mrs. Wilhoit and the company was an insurance contract or an agreement supplemental thereto. While there may be room for differences of opinion, we have reached the conclusion that the premise is not sound, that the arrangement between the parties was the result of a separate and independent agreement, unrelated to the terms of the policy. . . .

The "investment" provision was an offer by the company by which Mrs. Wilhoit, on maturity of the policy, could have left the proceeds with the company on the terms and conditions therein stated. It is plain, however, that she did not take advantage of this offer. Instead, she accepted the proceeds, surrendered the policy and receipted the company in full "for all claims under the within policy," and presumably the proceeds were paid to her at that time. At any rate, it was not until twenty-three days later that she, by letter, made her own proposal to the company, which differed materially from that contained in the policy. The company proposed to pay interest annually in advance on the amount left on deposit, at a rate of interest not less than 3%. Her proposal provided for interest at the rate of 3½%, compounded annually, with a right to withdraw interest at the end of any six-month period. The company proposal provided that Mrs. Wilhoit could withdraw the deposit only at the end of any interest year, it made no provision for the withdrawal of any amount less than the total on deposit, while the offer of Mrs. Wilhoit provided for the right to withdraw, on demand, any amount or part thereof (not less than $100). Undoubtedly the company was obligated, upon request by Mrs. Wilhoit, to comply with the terms of the investment provision and, upon refusal, could have been forced by her to do so. On the other hand, it was under no obligation to accept the proposal made by her and, upon its refusal, she would have been without remedy.

. . . [We have] concluded that the agreement between Mrs. Wilhoit and the company was neither an insurance contract nor an agreement supplemental thereto. . . . Mrs. Wilhoit deposited her money with the company, which obligated itself to pay interest and return the principal to her on demand. Only "in the event of her death" was the deposit, if it still remained, payable to Robert G. Owens. If Mrs. Wilhoit had deposited her money with a bank rather than with the insurance company under the same form of agreement, we think it would have constituted an ineffectual disposition because of failure to comply with the Indiana statute of wills.

In conclusion, we think it not immaterial to take into consideration what appears to have been the intention of the parties. . . . As already shown, Robert G. Owens, through whom defendants claim, died in 1932, and in his will made no mention of the funds in controversy. . . . On the other hand, Mrs. Willhoit in her will specifically devised the fund in controversy to plaintiff, Robert Wilhoit. It thus appears plain that Mrs. Wilhoit did not intend that the fund go to the successors of Robert G. Owens but that after his death she thought she had a right to dispose of the fund as she saw fit, as is evidenced by the specific bequest contained in her will. We recognize that the intention of the parties or the belief which they entertained relative to the fund is not controlling, but under the circumstances presented, we think it is entitled to some consideration.

The judgment of the District Court is affirmed.

QUESTION AND NOTE

1. The court in *Wilhoit* strikes down a payable-on-death (P.O.D.) designation in a contract of deposit because it is a testamentary act not executed with the formalities required by the Statute of Wills. In Rubenstein v. Mueller, supra page 274, an implied contract not to revoke a will was enforced by imposing a constructive trust on the estate of the surviving spouse. If a court will not enforce a payable-on-death provision in a written contract, why will it enforce a contract not to revoke a will that is not attested, indeed may not even be in writing? Are not both types of contracts testamentary in the sense that they are designed to pass economic benefits at death? If Ruth Hanzlicsek and Wilma Rubenstein can enforce the contract between Bertha and Conrad Mueller as third party beneficiaries, why cannot Robert Owens enforce the contract between Sarah Wilhoit and the insurance company as a third party beneficiary? See In re Estate of Wright, 17 Ill. App. 3d 894, 308 N.E.2d 319 (1974).

2. The *Wilhoit* case applies the old rule, still followed in some states, that payable-on-death designations in contracts are invalid. Uniform Probate Code §6-201, below, authorizes such P.O.D. designations. This section has been adopted in about one-third of the states; some other states have similar legislation.

Uniform Probate Code (1983)

§6-201   [Provisions for Payment or Transfer at Death]

(a) Any of the following provisions in an insurance policy, contract of employment, bond, mortgage, promissory note, deposit agreement, pension plan, trust agreement, conveyance or any other written instrument effective as a contract, gift, conveyance, or trust is deemed to be nontestamentary, and this Code does not invalidate the instrument or any provision:

(1) that money or other benefits theretofore due to, controlled or owned by a decedent shall be paid after his death to a person designated by the decedent in either the instrument or a separate

writing, including a will, executed at the same time as the instrument or subsequently;

(2) that any money due or to become due under the instrument shall cease to be payable in event of the death of the promisee or the promissor before payment or demand; or

(3) that any property which is the subject of the instrument shall pass to a person designated by the decedent in either the instrument or a separate writing, including a will, executed at the same time as the instrument or subsequently.

(b)   Nothing in this section limits the rights of creditors under other laws of this state.

COMMENT

This section authorizes a variety of contractual arrangements which have in the past been treated as testamentary. For example most courts treat as testamentary a provision in a promissory note that if the payee dies before payment is made the note shall be paid to another named person, or a provision in a land contract that if the seller dies before payment is completed the balance shall be cancelled and the property shall belong to the vendee. These provisions often occur in family arrangements. The result of holding the provisions testamentary is usually to invalidate them because not executed in accordance with the statute of wills. On the other hand the same courts have for years upheld beneficiary designations in life insurance contracts. Similar kinds of problems are arising in regard to beneficiary designations in pension funds and under annuity contracts. The analogy of the power of appointment provides some historical base for solving some of these problems aside from a validating statute. However, there appear to be no policy reasons for continuing to treat these varied arrangements as testamentary. The revocable living trust and the multiple-party bank accounts, as well as the experience with United States government bonds payable on death to named beneficiaries, have demonstrated that the evils envisioned if the statute of wills is not rigidly enforced simply do not materialize. The fact that these provisions often are part of a business transaction and in any event are evidenced by a writing tends to eliminate the danger of "fraud."

Because the types of provisions described in the statute are characterized as nontestamentary, the instrument does not have to be executed in compliance with Section 2-502; nor does it have to be probated, nor does the personal representative have any power or duty with respect to the assets involved.

The sole purpose of this section is to eliminate the testamentary characterization from the arrangements falling within the terms of the section. It does not invalidate other arrangements by negative implication. Thus it is not intended by the section to embrace oral trusts to hold property at death for named persons; such arrangements are already generally enforceable under trust law.

QUESTIONS

1. Observe that UPC §6-201 is silent on whether a death beneficiary named in a contract must survive the contracting benefactor in order to take. How should the *Wilhoit* case be decided in a jurisdiction enacting UPC §6-201? Compare UPC §6-104, which provides that the death beneficiary of a P.O.D. *bank account* must survive the depositor in order to take. Also compare a contract not to revoke a will, where the third-party beneficiary's estate takes where the beneficiary does not survive the surviving contracting party (Problem 3, supra page 279). Should all will substitutes have the same survivorship rule for beneficiaries? Should it be the rule applied to wills — that the beneficiary must survive the testator in order to take? See Langbein, The Nonprobate Revolution and the Future of the Law of Succession, 97 Harv. L. Rev. 1108, 1136-1137 (1984): "Transferors use will substitutes to avoid probate, not to avoid the subsidiary law of wills. The subsidiary rules are the product of centuries of legal experience in attempting to discern transferors' wishes and suppress litigation. These rules should be treated as presumptively correct for will substitutes as well as for wills."

2. Should the *Wilhoit* case be decided in favor of Robert Wilhoit on the ground that Mrs. Wilhoit had the power to change a P.O.D. beneficiary by will? Consider the following case.

Changing ins. policy benef. by will

Cook v. Equitable Life Assurance Society
Indiana Court of Appeals, 1981
428 N.E.2d 110, 25 A.L.R.4th 1153

RATLIFF, J. Margaret A. Cook, Administratrix C.T.A. of the Estate of Douglas D. Cook (Douglas); Margaret A. Cook; and Daniel J. Cook (Margaret and Daniel) appeal from an entry of summary judgment granted by the trial court in favor of Doris J. Cook Combs (Doris) in an interpleader action brought by The Equitable Life Assurance Society of the United States (Equitable). We affirm.

FACTS

Douglas purchased a whole life insurance policy on March 13, 1953, from Equitable, naming his wife at that time, Doris, as the beneficiary. On March 5, 1965, Douglas and Doris were divorced. The divorce decree made no provision regarding the insurance policy, but did state the following: "It is further understood and agreed between the parties hereto that the provisions of this agreement shall be in full satisfaction of all claims by either of said parties against the other, including alimony, support and maintenance money."

After the divorce Douglas ceased paying the premiums on his life insurance policy, and Equitable notified him on July 2, 1965, that because the premium due on March 9, 1965, had not been paid, his whole life policy was automatically converted to a paid-up term policy with an expiration date of June 12, 1986. The policy contained the following provision with respect to beneficiaries:

BENEFICIARY. The Owner may change the beneficiary from time to time prior to the death of the Insured, by written notice to the Society, but any such change shall be effective only if it is endorsed on this policy by the Society, and, if there is a written assignment of this policy in force and on file with the Society (other than an assignment to the Society as security for an advance), such a change may be made only with the written consent of the assignee. The interest of a beneficiary shall be subject to the rights of any assignee of record with the Society.

On December 24, 1965, Douglas married Margaret, and a son Daniel, was born to them. On June 7, 1976, Douglas made a holographic will in which he bequeathed his insurance policy with Equitable Life to his wife and son, Margaret and Daniel:

Last Will & Testimint [sic]

I Douglas D. Cook

Being of sound mind do Hereby leave all my Worldly posessions [sic] to my Wife and son, Margaret A. Cook & Daniel Joseph Cook. being my Bank Accounts at Irwin Union Bank & trust to their Welfare [sic] my Insurance policys [sic] with Common Welth of Ky. and Equitable Life. all my machinecal [sic] tools to be left to my son if He is Interested in Working with them If not to be sold and money used for their welfair [sic] all my Gun Collection Kept as long as they, my Wife & Son [sic] and then sold and money used for their welfair [sic]

> I sighn [sic] this
> June 7 — 1976
> at Barth Conty
> Hospital Room
> 1114 Bed 2
> /s/ *Douglas D. Cook*
> /s/ *6-7-76 Margaret A. Cook wife*
> /s/ *Chas. W. Winkler*
> /s/ *Mary A. Winkler*

This will was admitted to probate in Bartholomew Superior Court after Douglas's death on June 9, 1979. On August 24, 1979, Margaret filed a claim with Equitable for the proceeds of Douglas's policy, but Equitable deposited the proceeds, along with its complaint in interpleader, with the Bartholomew Circuit Court on March 14, 1980. Discovery was made; interrogatories and affidavits were filed; and all parties moved for summary judgment. The trial court found that there was no genuine issue as to any material fact respecting Doris's claim to the proceeds of the policy and entered judgment in her favor as to the amount of the proceeds plus interest, a total of $3,154.09. Margaret and Daniel appeal from this award.

ISSUE

Is the trial court's entry of summary judgment in this case contrary to Indiana law because the court entered judgment in favor of the named beneficiary of an insurance policy rather than in compliance with the insured testator's intent as expressed in his will?

DISCUSSION AND DECISION

. . . Margaret and Daniel do not dispute the facts in this case, yet they contend that the court's entry of summary judgment was erroneous because Indiana law does not require strict compliance with the terms of an insurance policy relative to a change of beneficiary in all cases. They argue, therefore, that strict compliance with policy provisions is not required for the protection of either the insurer or the insured once the proceeds have been paid by the insurer into court in an action for interpleader and that the court should shape its relief in this case upon the equitable principle "that the insured's express and unambiguous intent should be given effect." . . .

Doris agrees that less than strict compliance with policy change requirements may be adequate to change a beneficiary where circumstances show the insured has done everything within his power to effect the change. Nevertheless, Doris asserts that Indiana adheres to the majority rule finding an attempt to change the beneficiary of a life insurance policy by will, without more, to be ineffectual. We agree with Doris.

Margaret and Daniel are correct in asserting that there are no Indiana cases involving precisely the same set of facts as occur in this case. Nevertheless, there is ample case law in this jurisdiction to support the trial court's determination. Almost one hundred years ago our supreme court in Holland v. Taylor, (1887) 111 Ind. 121, 12 N.E. 116, enunciated the general rule still followed in Indiana: an attempt to change the beneficiary of a life insurance contract by will and in disregard of the methods prescribed under the contract will be unsuccessful. . . .

Indiana courts have recognized exceptions to the general rule that strict compliance with policy requirements is necessary to effect a change of beneficiary. Three exceptions were noted by this court in Modern Brotherhood v. Matkovitch, (1914) 56 Ind. App. 8, 14, 104 N.E. 795, and reiterated in Heinzman v. Whiteman, (1923) 81 Ind. App. 29, 36, 139 N.E. 329, trans. denied:

1. If the society has waived a strict compliance with its own rules, and in pursuance of a request of the insured to change the beneficiary, has issued a new certificate to him, the original beneficiary will not be heard to complain that the course indicated by the regulations was not pursued. 2. If it be beyond the power of the insured to comply literally with the regulations, a court of equity will treat the change as having been legally made. 3. If the insured has pursued the course pointed out by the laws of the association, and has done all in his power to change the beneficiary; but before the new certificate is actually issued, he dies, a court of equity will decree that to be done which ought to be done, and act as though the certificate had been issued.

The public policy considerations undergirding this rule and its limited exceptions involve protection of the rights of all the parties concerned and should not be viewed, as appellants advocate, for the exclusive protection of the insurer. Indiana, in fact, has specifically rejected this position. In Stover v. Stover, (1965) 137 Ind. App. 578, 204 N.E.2d 374, 380, on rehearing 205 N.E.2d 178, trans. denied, the court recognized an insured's right to rely on the provisions of the policy in regard to change of beneficiary:

> We must reject appellant's contention that the provisions set forth in the certificate, as mentioned above, are for the exclusive benefit of the insurance company and may be waived at will. The deceased insured himself is entitled to rely upon such provisions that he may at all times know to whom the proceeds of the insurance shall be payable.

In *Holland* the court also recognized that the beneficiary had a right in the executed contract which was subject to defeat only by a change of beneficiary which had been executed in accord with the terms of the insurance contract: "In that contract Anna Laura, the beneficiary, had such an interest as that she had, and has, the right to insist that in order to cut her out, the change of beneficiary should be made in the manner provided in the contract." 111 Ind. 127, 12 N.E. 116. . . .

Clearly it is in the interest of insurance companies to require and to follow certain specified procedures in the change of beneficiaries of its policies so that they may pay over benefits to persons properly entitled to them without subjection to claims by others of whose rights they had no notice or knowledge. Certainly it is also in the interest of beneficiaries themselves to be entitled to prompt payment of benefits by insurance companies which do not withhold payment until the will has been probated in the fear of later litigation which might result from having paid the wrong party. . . . Finally, society's interest in the conservation of judicial energy and expense will be served where the rule and its limited exceptions are clearly stated and rigorously applied. . . .

Under the law of Indiana, therefore, in order for appellants to have defeated the motion for summary judgment in this case they must have made some showing that the insured had done all within his powers or all that reasonably could have been expected of him to comply with the policy provisions respecting a change of beneficiary, but that through no fault of his own he was unable to achieve his goal. Here there is no such indication or implication. Douglas was divorced in March of 1965 and remarried in December 1965. He was notified in July 1965 of the change in his policy, but took no action. A son was born of his second marriage. Eleven years after his divorce Douglas attempted to change the beneficiary of his insurance policy by a holographic will, but did not notify Equitable. He then lived three years after making that will. There is no indication that Douglas took any action in the fourteen years between his divorce from Doris and his death, other than the making of the will, to change the beneficiary of his life insurance policy from Doris to Margaret and Daniel. Surely, if Douglas had wanted to change the beneficiary he had ample time and opportunity to comply with the policy requirements. Nothing in the record suggests otherwise. . . .

We may be sympathetic to the cause of the decedent's widow and son, and it might seem that a departure from the general rule in an attempt to do equity under these facts would be noble. Nevertheless, such a course is fraught with the dangers of eroding a solidly paved pathway of the law and leaving in its stead only a gaping hole of uncertainty. Public policy requires that the insurer, insured, and beneficiary alike should be able to rely on the certainty that policy provisions pertaining to the naming and changing of beneficiaries will control except in extreme situations. We, therefore, invoke a maxim equally as venerable as the one upon which appellants rely in the determination of this cause: Equity aids the vigilant, not those who slumber on their rights.

Judgment affirmed.

NOTES AND PROBLEMS

1. UPC §6-201 does not contain any provision permitting or forbidding revocation of a P.O.D. designation by will. Compare UPC §6-

104(e), dealing with bank accounts, which provides that the beneficiary of a joint account, a savings account (Totten) trust, or a P.O.D. bank account may not be changed by will.

2.   Although the *Cook* case states the majority rule, there are a few cases permitting a will to change a life insurance beneficiary. See, e.g., Burkett v. Mott, 152 Ariz. 476, 733 P.2d 673 (App. 1986); Kane v. Union Mut. Life Ins. Co., 84 A.D.2d 148, 445 N.Y.S.2d 549 (1981) (dictum). Suppose that the rule is that a will can change a P.O.D. beneficiary. Is a change in the P.O.D. beneficiary *after* the will is executed allowed? Take this case. *O* designates *A* as P.O.D. beneficiary of *O*'s pension plan. Subsequently *O* executes a will providing that *B* is to take the pension benefits upon *O*'s death. Then *O* files a form in his employer's office changing the P.O.D. beneficiary from *A* to *C*. If *C* takes the pension benefits, is this a revocation of the will in a manner not permitted by the wills statute?

3.   Since the Uniform Probate Code was promulgated in the late 1960s, P.O.D. transfers have proliferated enormously. Today payable-on-death designations are found on IRA accounts, Keogh plans, and employee pension plans. The designation of a death beneficiary in these plans need not comply with the Statute of Wills because they are governed by contract or trust principles. See E.F. Hutton & Co. v. Wallace, 863 F.2d 472 (6th Cir. 1988). In states generally permitting P.O.D. designations, brokerage houses will put payable-on-death designations on customers' stock portfolios held in custodial accounts. Mutual funds permit payable-on-death designations. Some corporations offer to shareholders living in states that have enacted UPC §6-201 the option of registering securities with a P.O.D. designation. See Wellman, Transfer-on-Death Securities Registration: A New Title Form, 21 Ga. L. Rev. 789 (1987); Note, Uniform Probate Code Section 6-201: A Proposal to Include Stocks and Mutual Funds, 72 Cornell L. Rev. 397 (1987). A new Uniform Transfer-on-Death Registration Act was approved by the National Conference of Commissioners on Uniform State Laws in 1989. This act permits securities to be registered in a payable-on-death or other form. An enormous amount of property thus can pass, and is passing, outside the probate system. Do these types of transfers require formalities (evidentiary security and the likelihood of deliberation) that are substantial equivalents of those required by the Statute of Wills? See Langbein, The Nonprobate Revolution and the Future of the Law of Succession, 97 Harv. L. Rev. 1108 (1984).

Note that most will substitutes deal only with specific assets, not a person's entire estate. Compare Hibbler v. Knight, 738 S.W.2d 924 (Tex. Civ. App. 1987), holding that a written agreement between husband and wife that wife was to be entitled to husband's entire estate was not enforceable as a contract to devise, because it did not state that a contract existed, and was not enforceable under Texas's version of

UPC §6-201, which permits transfer of specific assets by contract but not a person's entire estate.

SECTION C.   MULTIPLE-PARTY BANK ACCOUNTS

Multiple-party bank accounts include a joint and survivor account, a payable-on-death account, an agency account, and a savings account trust.

The joint bank account gives rise to a number of difficulties because it is used for a variety of purposes. *A*, a bank depositor, may open a joint account with *B*, intending (1) that either *A* or *B* is to have power to draw on the account and the survivor owns the balance of the account (sometimes known as a "true joint tenancy account"), (2) that *B* is not to have power to withdraw on the account during life but is entitled to the balance upon *A*'s death (a P.O.D. account disguised as a joint account), or (3) that *B* is to have power to draw on the account during *A*'s life but is not entitled to the balance at *A*'s death (an agency account disguised as a joint account). Courts are often left with the problem of discerning which type of account is intended. If an agency account is intended, the survivor is not entitled to the proceeds in the account, which belong to the depositor's estate.

Franklin v. Anna National Bank of Anna
Illinois Appellate Court, 1986
140 Ill. App. 3d 533, 488 N.E.2d 1117

WELCH, J.   Plaintiff, Enola Stevens Franklin, as executor of the estate of Frank A. Whitehead, deceased, commenced this action in the circuit court of Union County against defendant Anna National Bank, alleging that the funds in a joint savings account were the property of the estate. The bank interpleaded Cora Goddard, who asserted her right to the money as the surviving joint owner. After a bench trial, the circuit court entered judgment for Mrs. Goddard. Mrs. Franklin appeals. We reverse.

This is the second time this case has been before the appellate court. In the prior appeal, Mrs. Franklin appealed from summary judgment in favor of Mrs. Goddard. This court reversed and remanded for trial. Franklin v. Anna National Bank (1983), 115 Ill. App. 3d 149, 450 N.E.2d 371.

Decedent died December 22, 1980. His wife Muriel Whitehead died in 1974. Mrs. Goddard was Muriel's sister. Decedent had eye surgery in May of 1978, and according to Mrs. Goddard was losing his eyesight in 1978. In April of 1978 Mrs. Goddard moved to Union County to help decedent and live with him. On April 17, 1978, Mrs. Goddard and decedent went to the bank, according to Mrs. Goddard to have his money put in both their names so she could get money when they needed it, "and he wanted me to have this money if I outlived him."

A bank employee prepared a signature card for savings account No. 3816 and Mrs. Goddard signed it. A copy of this card was in evidence at trial. The signatures of decedent and Mrs. Goddard appear on both sides of the card. It appears that Muriel Whitehead's signature was "whited out" and Mrs. Goddard's signature added. The front of the card states that one signature is required for withdrawals. The back of the card states that all funds deposited are owned by the signatories as joint tenants with right of survivorship.

Mrs. Goddard testified that she did not deposit any of the money in savings account No. 3816. She made no withdrawals, though she once took decedent to the bank so he could make a withdrawal. According to Mrs. Goddard, on the day she signed the signature card decedent "asked me if I needed my money because they had bought cemetery lots from me, and I told him, not at this time, that I didn't need it. He wanted to know if I needed any more money at that time and I said, no, and I said, just leave it in here and I will get it out whenever I need it." According to Mrs. Goddard, decedent promised to pay her $1,000 for the lots; she was never paid. Asked whether she ever had the passbook for savings account No. 3816 in her possession, Mrs. Goddard answered, "Only while I was at Frank's. It was there."

Later in 1978, Mrs. Franklin began to care for decedent. In January 1979, decedent telephoned the bank, then sent Mrs. Franklin to the bank to deliver a letter to Mrs. Kedron Boyer, a bank employee. The handwritten letter, dated January 13, 1979, and signed by decedent, stated: "I Frank Whitehead wish by Bank accounts be changed to Enola Stevens joint intendency [sic]. Nobody go in my lock box but me." According to Mrs. Franklin, Mrs. Boyer told her to tell decedent he would have to specify what type of account he was referring to. Decedent gave Mrs. Franklin a second letter which Mrs. Franklin delivered to Mrs. Carol Williams at the bank (Mrs. Boyer was absent). This handwritten letter, dated January 13, 1979, stated: "I Frank Whitehead want Enola Stevens and me only go in my lock box. Account type Saving and Checking. In case I can't see she is to take care of my bill or sick." According to Mrs. Franklin, Mrs. Williams said she would take care of it and give the letter to Mrs. Boyer. Mrs. Franklin testified that she signed the savings passbook in the presence of decedent and Mrs. Boyer. Mrs. Franklin took her present last name on May 8, 1979.

Mrs. Boyer, Mrs. Williams, and bank president Delano Mowery all testified at trial. These witnesses explained the usual procedures for account changes. None remembered much of the circumstances surrounding the bank's receipt of the January 13, 1979, letters. According to Mr. Mowery, the bank would not remove a signature from a signature card based on a letter; the most recent signature card the bank had for savings account No. 3816 was signed by decedent and Mrs. Goddard.

Mrs. Goddard's attorney's assertion at trial that there were no monthly statements on savings account No. 3816 was uncontradicted.

The trial court found that Mrs. Goddard was the sole owner of the funds in savings account No. 3816 by right of survivorship as surviving joint tenant, and that no part of the funds became part of decedent's estate.

Mrs. Franklin argues that decedent did not intend to make a gift of savings account No. 3816 to Mrs. Goddard.

The instrument creating a joint tenancy account presumably speaks the whole truth. In order to go behind the terms of the agreement, the one claiming adversely thereto has the burden of establishing by clear and convincing evidence that a gift was not intended. Each case involving a joint tenancy account must be evaluated on its own facts and circumstances. The form of the agreement is not conclusive regarding the intention of the depositors between themselves. (In re Estate of Schneider (1955), 6 Ill. 2d 180, 186, 127 N.E.2d 445, 449.) Evidence of lack of donative intent must relate back to the time of creation of the joint tenancy. The decision of the donor, made subsequent to the creation of the joint tenancy, that he did not want the proceeds to pass to the survivor, would not, in itself, be sufficient to sever the tenancy. However, it is proper to consider events occurring after creation of the joint account in determining whether the donor actually intended to transfer his interest in the account at his death to the surviving joint tenant. In re Estate of Guzak (1979), 69 Ill. App. 3d 552, 555, 388 N.E.2d 431, 433.

We examine the instant facts in light of the above principles: There appears no serious doubt that in January of 1979, just nine months after adding Mrs. Goddard's name to savings account No. 3816, decedent attempted to remove Mrs. Goddard's name and substitute Mrs. Franklin's. The second of decedent's handwritten letters to the bank in January of 1979 indicates decedent's concern that he might lose his sight and be unable to transact his own banking business. These facts show that decedent made Mrs. Goddard (and later Mrs. Franklin) a signatory for his own convenience, in case he could not get his money, and not with intent to effect a present gift. (See Dixon National Bank v. Morris (1965), 33 Ill. 2d 156, 159, 210 N.E.2d 505, 506; In re Estate of Guzak (1979), 69 Ill. App. 3d 552, 388 N.E.2d 431.) It does not appear that Mrs. Goddard ever exercised any authority or control over the joint account. While decedent's statement that he wanted Mrs.

Goddard to have the money in the account if she outlived him suggests decedent's donative intent, taken literally decedent's statement is inconsistent with intent to donate any interest during decedent's lifetime. (See Lipe v. Farmers State Bank (1970), 131 Ill. App. 2d 1024, 1026, 265 N.E.2d 204, 205.) Mrs. Goddard does not argue that there was a valid testamentary disposition in her favor, nor could we so find on the instant facts.

Of the many cases cited by the parties for comparison with the case at bar, the most persuasive is In re Estate of Schneider (1955), 6 Ill. 2d 180, 127 N.E.2d 445. In In re Estate of Schneider, the decedent's executor filed a petition alleging the funds in joint bank accounts belonged to the estate and not to Ralston, the surviving joint tenant. Ralston testified that all of the money in the account was deposited by the decedent, that the decedent at no time told Ralston he wanted Ralston to have any of the money, and that when Ralston's name was added to the accounts the decedent said, "I want your name on these bank accounts so that in case I am sick you can go and get the money for me." The trial court concluded that the decedent intended to retain actual ownership of the money. Our supreme court agreed. We reach the same conclusion here. In the case at bar, decedent's attempts to change the account show his consistent view of the account as his own. The surrounding circumstances show decedent's concern for his health and his relatively brief use of Mrs. Goddard (and later Mrs. Franklin) to assure his access to his funds. The money in account No. 3816 should have been found to be the property of the estate.

For the foregoing reasons, the judgment of the circuit court of Union County is reversed, and this cause is remanded for entry of judgment in favor of plaintiff.

Reversed.

NOTES AND PROBLEMS

1. Why did not the bank offer Frank Whitehead his choice of three accounts: a true joint tenancy account, an agency account, or a P.O.D. account? If banks did this, much of the litigation over the depositor's intention would disappear.

An agent's powers end upon the death or incompetency of the principal. Persons may use the joint account in an effort to avoid guardianship in the event of incapacity. A better way to avoid guardianship is to sign a *durable* power of attorney (called "durable" because it does not end upon incompetency but endures until the principal's death). See infra page 538. Durable powers are permitted in most states. See, e.g., Uniform Probate Code §§5-501 to 5-505. A bank offering an agency account should give the customer the choice of an account that ends upon incompetency or death *or* an account coupled with a durable power of attorney.

A payable-on-death account is invalid in some states for reasons given in the *Wilhoit* case, supra page 280. Professor Wellman lists 30 states permitting P.O.D. bank accounts. Wellman, Transfer-on-Death Securities Registration: A New Title Form, 21 Ga. L. Rev. 789, 806 n.50 (1987). Even in states permitting P.O.D. bank accounts, however, banks have resisted offering depositors clear choices. They continue to channel depositors into the joint bank account. Id. at 829 n.108.

2. Uniform Probate Code §6-104(a) provides that the surviving payee of a joint account is entitled to the balance "unless there is clear and convincing evidence of a different intention at the time the account is created."

In an attempt to limit litigation over whether a joint account was really intended as an agency account only, several states have statutes or decisions providing that the surviving joint tenant is entitled to the proceeds in a joint account unless mental incapacity, undue influence, fraud, or mistake is shown. See Hines v. Carr, 372 So. 2d 13 (Ala. 1979); In re Estate of La Garce, 487 S.W.2d 493 (Mo. 1972); Annot., 43 A.L.R.3d 971 (1972). In a few other states statutes provide that the presumption that survivorship rights were intended is conclusive. See In re Estate of Gainer, 466 So. 2d 1055 (Fla. 1985).

It has been held that a joint tenant who does not sign the signature card at the bank does not have rights of survivorship. Rynn v. Owens, 181 Ill. App. 3d 232, 536 N.E.2d 959 (1989). A P.O.D. beneficiary does not have to sign the card.

3. Uniform Probate Code §6-103(a) provides: "A joint account belongs, during the lifetime of all parties, to the parties in proportion to the net contributions by each to the sums on deposit, unless there is a clear and convincing evidence of a different intent." Thus the depositor to a joint tenancy account (unlike a joint tenant in land) can revoke the joint tenancy by withdrawing the funds and naming a new joint tenant.

4. Suppose that Frank Whitehead had made Enola Stevens Franklin a joint tenant of his safe-deposit box in order that Enola could enter it. The bank card (designated a "Lease of Safe-Deposit Box") signed by Frank and Enola provides: "The lessees are joint tenants with right of survivorship and all property of every kind at any time placed in said box is the joint property of both lessees and upon the death of either passes to the survivor." In the box are stock certificates, a diamond ring, and $2000 in cash, all placed there by Frank before the bank card was signed. Does Enola own all the items in the box at Frank's death? See In re Estate of Wilson, 404 Ill. 207, 88 N.E.2d 662 (1949);

Steinhauser v. Repko, 30 Ohio St. 2d 262, 285 N.E.2d 55 (1972);
Annots., 40 A.L.R.3d 462 (1971), 14 A.L.R.2d 948 (1950).

5. *The savings account trust (or Totten trust).* One type of multiple-
party bank account that functions as a P.O.D. account is the savings
account trust (not usually available at banks for checking accounts). In
the landmark case of In re Totten, 179 N.Y. 112, 71 N.E. 748 (1904),
O made deposits in a savings account in the name of "*O* as trustee for
A." *O* retained the right to revoke the trust by withdrawing the funds
at any time during his life. Since *A* is entitled only to the amount on
deposit at *O*'s death, in practical effect *A* is merely a payable-on-death
beneficiary of a "trust" of a savings account. The court upheld this
arrangement as not testamentary, declaring that a revocable trust had
been created at the time of the deposit. At *O*'s death any funds in the
account belong to *A*. Savings account trusts, often known at Totten
trusts, have now been accepted in a large majority of jurisdictions. The
savings account trust is sometimes known as "a poor man's will." See
Note, Totten Trust as Testamentary Substitute, 41 Alb. L. Rev. 605
(1977); Note, Savings Account Trusts: A Critical Examination, 49 Notre
Dame Law. 686 (1974).

Blanchette v. Blanchette
Supreme Judicial Court of Massachusetts, 1972
362 Mass. 518, 287 N.E.2d 459

BRAUCHER, J. This is a petition brought in connection with the
divorce of the parties by the petitioner Marie to determine her interest
in certain property including 168 shares (the stock) of the American
Telephone & Telegraph Company (the company). The petition was
referred to a master who heard the parties, filed a report, and made
general findings, among others, that the respondent Robert was the
sole owner of the stock and that there was no gift or attempted gift of
the stock to Marie.

Marie objected to that part of the report which related to the stock.
After a hearing, the judge issued a decree overruling Marie's exceptions,
confirming the report, declaring the stock to be the sole property of
Robert and ordering Marie to execute any documents necessary to give
effect to the ownership of the stock, as determined by the decree, upon
the records of the company. Marie appeals from the decree, contending
that the subsidiary facts reported by the master do not support his
general findings with respect to the ownership of the stock.

The master's report having been confirmed, his findings establish
the facts in the case. . . .

We summarize them. The parties were married on November 17,
1945. While married they both worked, with a few interruptions, at

steady jobs. In 1955 Robert was working for the company, and under a company plan began to buy shares of stock in the company at eighty-five per cent of market value through a weekly deduction from his pay.

Robert wanted to avoid the expense of probate and legal proceedings if he should die. When he expressed this desire in connection with the stock purchase plan to the people where he worked, he was told that the only way to achieve it was to have the stock issued to himself and Marie as joint tenants.[6] The stock could have been issued to the parties as tenants in common, but Robert purposely avoided that option.

When he started to acquire the stock, he told Marie he put them in both their names as joint tenants "in case something happened" to him and that they would then be hers "without probate or lawyer." The certificates were issued at his request to "Robert L. Blanchette & Mrs. Marie A. Blanchette, Joint Tenants." He executed assignments to himself and Marie "as Joint Tenants with rights of survivorship and not as Tenants in Common," and she also signed some of the documents in this form. The last certificate was issued on June 30, 1964.

Marie took no part in the purchase of the stock and did not know when the stock certificates were issued or how many shares were acquired. Her impression was that they would be hers only after Robert's death, and she did not think she had the right to sell any interest in them or to do anything with them without his signature. She signed dividend checks; on many occasions Robert signed her name to the checks. Robert never told her that she owned half of the stock. The certificates were kept in a wardrobe in their bedroom when they separated on February 7, 1965, and at that time Marie did demand one of two bankbooks usually kept in the same place, but she did not ask for any of the stock. She was content with the bankbook. There is no finding that she made any claim to the stock before the parties' divorce on May 14, 1969.

The master's general findings included the following: Robert "never at any time indicated by conduct or words that he intended to transfer any present interest in these stocks to his wife." The words "Joint Tenants" were used "only because this form of issuance was the only one authorized by Robert's employer which approximated his desire to make his wife 'his beneficiary' if he died. Robert did not in any way attempt to make a gift of these stocks to his wife and no gift of these stocks was in fact made."

1. The master's findings must stand unless they are inconsistent, contradictory or plainly wrong. . . . We have applied to share certificates

---

6. Why do you suppose Robert was told this? Would the company have any liability if it told Robert a payable-on-death designation was legally permissible if in fact it was not? See Robinson v. Colebrook Guaranty Savings Bank, 109 N.H. 382, 254 A.2d 837 (1969). — Eds.

in joint names the same principles we have applied to joint bank accounts. . . . In disputes arising while both parties to a joint bank account are still alive we have frequently upheld allegations or findings that there was no donative intent. . . . A finding as to the respective interests of the parties in joint deposits during their lives is a pure question of fact. . . .

Share certificates are less likely than bank accounts to be put in joint names merely for convenience, and in two cases we have disapproved findings that share certificates were placed in joint names without donative intent. MacLennan v. MacLennan, 316 Mass. 593, 597. Zambunos v. Zambunos, 324 Mass. 220, 223. Compare McPherson v. McPherson, 337 Mass. 611, 614 (real estate); Goldman v. Finkel, 341 Mass. 492, 494 (real estate). In both of those cases, as in this one, the intention was clear that the husband was to have sole control during his life and that whatever should remain at his death, if the wife survived, should ripen into full ownership by her. The finding that no present gift was intended would logically have the effect of frustrating the intention of the parties by rendering their arrangement testamentary and void. We avoided that result by substituting a finding of an intention to make a present gift of a joint interest, with the effect intended by the parties. In effect, there was a present gift of a future interest, subject to a reserved life estate in the husband and to his power to revoke his wife's interest. . . .

We think, however, that it is not necessary to modify the decree here, as was done in the *MacLennan* and *Zambunos* cases, to declare that the certificates are held in joint account, subject to the right of control reserved by the respondent. By contesting this suit the respondent has fully manifested his intention to exercise his right of control, and he has been prevented from doing so by the pendency of the suit. . . . The decree is to be affirmed without modification.

2. To avoid misunderstanding, we emphasize that nothing we say here is intended to impair the right of the survivor to joint bank accounts or to share certificates in joint names, where the donor has died without manifesting an intention to defeat the gift. If the owner of funds, with the assent of another, deposits the funds in an account in both their names, payable to either or the survivor, the deposit if so intended may take effect as a novation, creating contract rights against the bank in both parties in accordance with the deposit agreement. The statute of wills is not involved. As between the bank and the named depositors, the deposit agreement is binding. G.L. c. 167, §14. Sawyer v. National Shawmut Bank, 306 Mass. 313, 316.

The effect of such a deposit is a present and complete gift of the contract right intended, and it is not fatal that the original owner of the funds retains possession of the bankbook and a right to withdraw funds from the account and thus to defeat the gift. In numerous cases where the original owner had died, we have upheld the right of the survivor to the balance in the account. We have not regarded the form of the account as conclusive between the parties, but have allowed the representative of the estate of the decedent to show by attendant facts and circumstances that the decedent did not intend to make a present completed gift of a joint interest in the account. . . . Or the account may have been established merely for convenience in paying medical bills or the like. See Burns v. Paquin, 345 Mass. 329, 331; Astravas v. Petronis, 361 Mass. 366, 370. . . . In cases of conflicting evidence we have required that the question of donative intent be submitted to the trier of fact. . . . The burden of proof is on the person seeking to show that the transaction is not to be taken at face value. . . . Where as in the present case the intention has been clear that the donee's interest was to ripen into full ownership on the donor's death, we have overturned findings that there was no donative intent. Malone v. Walsh, 315 Mass. 484, 490-492. . . .

3. We recognize that under the cases cited the arrangement of the parties provides a substitute for a will. But we see no harm in that. "If an owner of property can find a means of disposing of it inter vivos that will render a will unnecessary for the accomplishment of his practical purposes, he has a right to employ it. The fact that the motive of a transfer is to obtain the practical advantages of a will without making one is immaterial." National Shawmut Bank v. Joy, 315 Mass. 457, 471-472, and cases cited. . . . An unattested testamentary document is ineffective. . . . But a trust is not rendered invalid by a testamentary motive. "The underlying purpose of the statute of wills against fraud is secured in the formalities attendant upon the execution of trusts and the solemnity of the actual transfer of property to trustees." Second Bank – State St. Trust Co. v. Pinion, 341 Mass. 366, 371. In cases of informal declarations of trust we have sought substitute safeguards in notice to and informal acceptance by the beneficiary. Aronian v. Asadoorian, 315 Mass. 274, 276-277, and cases cited. Contractual arrangements vary in their formality. In the present case, as in many cases of joint bank accounts, the parties were designated as joint tenants in formal documents embodying the rights in dispute, and there was notice to and implied acceptance by the donee.

Our law in this situation is in harmony with that in many other States. "The formal requisites of wills serve two main purposes: to insure that dispositions are carefully and seriously made, and to provide reliable evidence of the dispositions. Those purposes are adequately served by the institutional setting and the signed writing normally involved in taking out insurance, opening a bank account, buying United States Saving Bonds, or entering a government pension system." 1951 Rep. N.Y. Law Rev. Commn. 587, 597. In a very large number of cases joint bank accounts have been given effect as a "poor man's will." Estate of

Michaels, 26 Wis. 2d 382, 394-398. See Miles v. Hanten, 83 S.D. 635,
639; Scott, Trusts (3d ed.) §58.6; annotation, 43 A.L.R.3d 971. Similar
principles have been applied to share certificates in joint form. "The
revocable living trust and the multiple-party bank accounts, as well as
the experience with United States government bonds payable on death
to named beneficiaries, have demonstrated that the evils envisioned if
the statute of wills is not rigidly enforced simply do not materialize."
Comment, Uniform Probate Code, §6-201, promulgated in August,
1969. See also §§6-103(a), 6-104(a).

Decree affirmed.

NOTES AND QUESTIONS

1. The Uniform Probate Code treatment of multiple-party bank
accounts may, in one view, seem illogical. UPC §6-104 provides that if
a beneficiary of a savings account trust or a P.O.D. account dies before
the depositor, neither he nor his heirs or legatees take anything under
the account. In this respect the will substitutes are treated like a will (a
devisee under a will must survive in order to take). On the other hand,
UPC §6-104(e) provides that a will cannot change the survivorship
provision of a joint account, P.O.D. account, or savings account trust.
In this respect, the will substitutes are not treated like a prior will. Is
this sound? Compare the treatment of joint tenancies in land, discussed
infra page 304.

2. In addition to questions of survivorship and revocation by will,
will substitutes can raise several other issues that arise with regard to
wills. Consider these issues and whether the law of wills should apply.

(a) *Divorce.* If a property owner divorces a designated death beneficiary, should divorce revoke the designation? Compare law of wills,
supra page 244, and revocable trusts, infra page 520. See also Lynn,
Will Substitutes, Divorce, and Statutory Assistance for the Unthinking
Donor, 71 Marq. L. Rev. 1 (1987); Pepper v. Peacher, 742 P.2d 21
(Okla. 1987), holding divorce does not revoke designation of remarried
teacher's former husband as beneficiary of teacher's retirement fund.
The Joint Editorial Board for the Uniform Probate Code has approved
a new §2-508 of the code providing that divorce revokes dispositions
in favor of the divorced spouse in will substitutes such as life insurance
and pension plans, P.O.D. accounts, revocable inter vivos trusts, and
other revocable dispositions made before the divorce. It also converts
a joint tenancy between the divorcing spouses into a tenancy in common.
This revision, together with other proposed revisions noted below, is
expected to come before the National Conference of Commissioners
on Uniform State Laws for approval in 1990.

(b) *Adoption and illegitimates.* If the beneficiaries are described as "issue" or "children," are adopted or illegitimate children included? See infra pages 681-687. Is a child of the decedent adopted by another (adopted out of the class) included? See infra page 686.

(c) *Simultaneous death.* If the decedent and the beneficiary die in a common disaster, should the Simultaneous Death Act (supra page 79) apply? If the jurisdiction has the UPC rule that survivorship for 120 hours is required for intestate or testate succession (supra page 87), should this rule apply to will substitutes? The Joint Editorial Board for the Uniform Probate Code has approved a new §2-702 of the code applying the 120-hour rule to all will substitutes including joint tenancies.

(d) *Anti-lapse statutes.* Almost every state has an anti-lapse statute, providing in general that if a devisee does not survive the testator the devise goes to the issue of the devisee (see infra pages 340-343). Should the anti-lapse statute apply to one or more will substitutes? The Joint Editorial Board for the Uniform Probate Code has approved a new §2-706 of the code applying the anti-lapse statute to beneficiary designations in insurance policies, pension plans, and P.O.D. accounts.

(e) *Apportionment of death taxes.* Should death taxes be apportioned so that beneficiaries of will substitutes pay their share, or should the taxes be borne by the will beneficiaries? See infra page 939.

(f) *Creditors.* What rights should creditors of the decedent have against beneficiaries of will substitutes? Uniform Probate Code §6-201(b) preserves whatever rights creditors have to reach nonprobate assets, but life insurance, joint tenancies in land, and joint bank accounts are usually exempt from creditors of the decedent. Should these remain exempt, while P.O.D. accounts and savings account trusts are reachable by creditors? See Effland, Rights of Creditors in Nonprobate Assets, 48 Mo. L. Rev. 431 (1983). On the rights of creditors to reach a revocable inter vivos trust after the settlor's death, see State Street Bank & Trust Co. v. Reiser, infra page 504.

These issues are discussed in McGovern, The Payable-on-Death Account and Other Will Substitutes, 67 Nw. U.L. Rev. 7 (1972); W. McGovern, S. Kurtz & J. Rein, Wills, Trusts and Estates §§5.5, 6.4, 9.2, 9.3, 9.5 (1988).

3. In view of the many ways now available to pass property at death without going through probate (especially payable-on-death designations on contracts and bank accounts, Totten trusts, joint bank accounts, life insurance, and revocable trusts), would it be a good idea to permit a *blockbuster will*? A blockbuster will would annul the beneficiaries named in various nonprobate instruments and name a new beneficiary. Can you think of situations where a blockbuster will would be useful? What are the drawbacks? See Note, Should the Dead Hand Tighten Its Grasp? An Analysis of the Superwill, 1988 U. Ill. L. Rev. 1019; Note, The

Blockbuster Will: Effectuating the Testator's Intent to Change Will Substitute Beneficiaries, 21 Val. U.L. Rev. 719 (1987).

4. *Reprise.* The English developed their probate system largely to protect creditors of the decedent. An administrator or executor had to be appointed to oversee the payment of debts. On the European continent a different system emerged. The heirs or legatees succeeded to title and were personally liable for the decedent's debts to the extent of the property received. Probate was not necessary. The European system is known as universal succession (see supra page 48).

Today, as Professor Langbein has pointed out, *"creditors do not need or use probate."* Langbein, The Nonprobate Revolution and the Future of the Law of Succession, 97 Harv. L. Rev. 1108, 1120 (1984). Survivors ordinarily pay the decedent's debts, whether or not there is probate. And creditors have developed routine institutional procedures, including insurance against loss, which they rely on for debt collection or discharge. Langbein continues:

> In the late twentieth century, creditor protection and probate have largely parted company. Had this development been otherwise, the rise of the will substitutes could not have occurred. If creditors had continued to rely significantly upon probate for the payment of decedent's debts, creditors' interests would have constituted an impossible obstacle to the nonprobate revolution. . . . [T]he decentralized procedures of the nonprobate system materially disadvantage creditors. Whereas probate directs all assets and all claimants to a common pot, the nonprobate system disperses assets widely and facilitates transfer without creditors' knowledge. If modern creditors had needed to use probate very much, they would have applied their considerable political muscle to suppress the nonprobate system. Instead, they have acquiesced without struggle, as have the most powerful of creditor-like agencies, the federal and state revenue authorities. [Id. at 1124-1125.]

If probate is not necessary for the protection of creditors, why don't we abolish probate and adopt the continental system of universal succession? If we did, would the will regain its preeminence as a dispositive instrument and will substitutes decline greatly in importance? The development of so many avenues bypassing probate should bring into question the desirability of continuing the probate system itself.

SECTION D. JOINT TENANCIES IN LAND

A joint tenancy or a tenancy by the entirety in land is a common and popular method of avoiding the cost and delay of probate. Perhaps most family homes in this country are owned by husband and wife either in joint tenancy or tenancy by the entirety. See Hines, Real Property Joint Tenancies, 51 Iowa L. Rev. 582 (1966). Upon the death of one joint tenant or tenant by the entirety, the survivor owns the property absolutely, freed of any participation by the decedent. The common law theory is that the decedent's interest vanishes at death, and therefore no probate is necessary because no interest passes to the survivor at death. Joint tenancies and tenancies by the entireties are ordinarily covered in first-year courses in property. Only two features of joint tenancies need mention here.

First, a joint tenant cannot devise his or her share by will. If a joint tenant wants someone other than the co-tenant to take his share at death, he must sever the joint tenancy during life, converting it into a tenancy in common. Why is a will ineffective to change survivorship rights in a joint tenancy? The answer dictated by the vanishing theory of the common law is that since no property passes from the decedent joint tenant at death, there is no interest for the decedent's will to operate upon. But perhaps a more persuasive reason lies in policy. If a joint tenant could devise his share, the property would be subject to litigation to determine the validity of the will and, most importantly, whether the will made a disposition of the joint tenancy property. Does a residuary clause ("all the rest and residue of my property") dispose of joint tenancy property? Is a specific reference required? How specific? If joint tenants could devise their share, the mere existence of the testamentary power would give them less assurance that the survivor would take, unentangled by will construction, probate costs, and claims of third parties, because of the possibilities of inadvertent exercise of the power. The overwhelming number of joint tenants select the tenancy precisely because of the high degree of assurance of no entanglement with probate. To continue this assurance, the right of testamentary disposition must be denied, and the few attempts by ignorant testators to devise their joint tenancy property must fail.

If this reasoning is persuasive, does it apply to other will substitutes?

The second feature of joint tenancy to be noted relates to creditors' rights. A creditor of a joint tenant must seize the joint tenant's interest during life. At death the joint tenant's interest vanishes and there is nothing for the creditor to reach; it is too late. See Citizens Action League v. Kizer, 887 F.2d 1003 (9th Cir. 1989); Rembe v. Stewart, 387 N.W.2d 313 (Iowa 1986) (criticizing but upholding rule).

Apart from the vanishing theory of the common law, is there any reason why creditors of a decedent joint tenant cannot reach joint tenancy property if they can reach other will substitutes?

PROBLEM

In 1965 *H* buys a farm, taking title in *H* and *W* as joint tenants with right of survivorship. In 1990 *H* dies. Within nine months, *W* disclaims the interest she acquires by surviving *H*. Under the state law, upon disclaimer by *W*, *H*'s interest passes to *H*'s daughter. Is the disclaimer by *W* a taxable gift to *H*'s daughter? See Int. Rev. Code §2518 (1986), supra page 126, requiring disclaimers to be made within nine months after the interest is *created*; Kennedy v. Commissioner, 804 F.2d 1332 (7th Cir. 1986); Gladys L. McDonald, 89 T.C. 293 (1987). Would the result be different if *H* had taken title in himself for life, remainder to *W* if *W* survives *H*?

SECTION E.   REVOCABLE INTER VIVOS TRUSTS

Revocable inter vivos trusts have come into widespread use, particularly among the moderately and very wealthy. A revocable inter vivos trust is the most flexible of all will substitutes.

The reason why a revocable trust avoids probate is that it changes title to the trust property to the trustee while the settlor is alive. Hence probate — to change title — is not necessary. The following, if signed, would be a valid, bare-bones revocable inter vivos trust:

> I, *O*, hereby declare myself trustee of Blackacre, my 100 shares of General Motors, and my Rolex watch, for the benefit of myself for life, and upon my death the trust property is to belong to *A*. I retain the power to revoke this trust.

By signing this instrument, *O* has changed title to Blackacre, the stock, and the watch during *O*'s life. *O* now owns these items as trustee and must deal with them as trustee. At *O*'s death, *A* succeeds to the trust property by virtue of the trust instrument. *O* can revoke the trust at any time and declare a new trust for the benefit of *B* at *O*'s death.

Much more complicated forms of revocable inter vivos trusts can be constructed and, indeed, are usual. But this simple example is sufficient to show the essential reason revocable inter vivos trusts avoid probate.

The revocable inter vivos trust is discussed in detail in Chapter 7, dealing with trusts (see infra pages 495-538). It is mentioned here only to round out the list of will substitutes.

SECTION F.   DEEDS OF LAND

Wright v. Huskey
Tennessee Court of Appeals, 1979
592 S.W.2d 899

MATHERNE, J. The basic issue before the Court is whether an instrument, couched in terms normally associated with deeds, which purports to convey realty to named grantees but reserves in the grantor a life estate and the unlimited power to sell is testamentary in character.

The chancellor held that the instrument was a deed which conveyed a present vested remainder to the grantees with the reservation of the absolute power to revoke the conveyance of the remainder interest by sale during the life of the grantor. The chancellor held that the grantor holds a life estate in the realty with the absolute power to sell the property.

Sallie Wright, the grantor and the plaintiff in this lawsuit, executed an instrument which conveyed about 56 acres of land to her daughter Elva McNutt and her son-in-law Ernest Turnbow as equal tenants in common, subject to the following reservation:

> It is agreed, understood and made a part of the consideration of this transaction that the bargainor, Mrs. C.W. Wright, reserves a Life Estate in the said property, she to have full possession, rents and control thereof as long as she lives or desires to have same, and with the right to sell all or a part thereof without the bargainees, Elva McNutt and Ernest Turnbow signing the Deed, should she desire to sell name. The bargainor, Mrs. C.W. Wright, will pay the taxes on said property as long as she is in possession of same.

Shortly after the instrument was delivered the son-in-law Turnbow remarried and subsequently died leaving the defendant Sharon Turnbow Huskey as his only child and sole heir at law. It appears that the parties did not get along as well after the Turnbow remarriage as they did prior thereto. Sharon Turnbow Huskey learned that the plaintiff was planning to sell the farm whereupon she notified the real estate agent of her claim to the property and caused to be filed in the Register's Office of Lewis County, Tennessee, a Notice of Lis Pendens identifying the property. Thereupon, Sallie Wright, the grantor under the instrument, filed this lawsuit to clear title to the property and to cancel the Notice of Lis Pendens. The defendant Elva McNutt does not contest the right of the plaintiff to sell the property. . . .

This situation was dealt with in Ellis v. Pearson (1900) 104 Tenn. 591, 58 S.W. 318. In that lawsuit the instrument provided:

> Know all men by these presents: That I, J.H. Pearson, do give to my wife, after my death, the following described parcel of land [describing it]. I reserve the right in me, J.H. Pearson, to sell or dispose of the above described land till my death. When I sell or convey the above, this gift is of no effect. After my death, if my wife, L.M. Pearson, wants to sell, I give her the right to do so, for the love I have for her.

The Court reviewed other cases, namely, Walls v. Ward (1853) 32 Tenn. 648 and Swails v. Bushart (1859) 39 Tenn. 561, wherein the conveyances were not to take effect until the death of the grantor. The Court noted that in those prior cases there was a complete title in remainder in praesenti and the instruments were in fact deeds and not wills. The Court noted, however, that the situation in *Ellis* presented a "radical" departure from the other cases wherein the instrument reserved a life estate with "the power reserved to the donor to destroy what he had created, to defeat the ultimate enjoyment of the estate given, by a disposition thereof in any of the modes open under the law to accomplish that purpose." The court held the instrument to be testamentary in character and not a deed.

The chancellor relied upon the case of Stamper v. Venable (1906) 117 Tenn. 557, 97 S.W. 812. There the instrument provided that in consideration of $1.00 and the grantee's agreement to "deed back to the [grantor] when called for so to do, [the grantor] hath bargained and sold. . . ." Complete title was otherwise conveyed with usual warranties. Contemporaneously with the execution of this instrument, the grantee executed to the grantor a power of attorney authorizing the grantor to "collect and appropriate the rents of the property during [the grantor's] life." The grantor apparently never attempted to exercise the "deed back" provision of the instrument, and the *Stamper* lawsuit was brought by the grantor's heirs in an attempt to set the instrument aside on the ground that the "sell back" provision converted the instrument, which would otherwise be a deed, into one testamentary in character. The *Stamper* court first noted that grants may be revoked by virtue of a power expressly reserved in the deed. We must assume from the holding in *Stamper* that a deed conveying the fee with only a right of revocation reserved does pass an interest in praesenti to the grantee. The Court held that "the instrument is — what the parties intended that it should be — a grant in fee with a power of revocation alone reserved." The Court defined the estate thus conveyed as "a fee determinable only upon the grantor exercising the right of revocation reserved to her." In finding that the parties did not intend the instrument to be testamentary in character the Court reasoned:

> That the parties to this transaction did not so understand it is clear. Looking to the surrounding facts, as we may do, in its construction (Rice v. Rice, 68 Ala. 216; Tuttle v. Raish [116 Iowa 331,] 90 N.W. 66; Kiseckers Case, 190 Pa. 476, 42 A. 886), with a view of aiding in the ascertainment of the intent of the parties, it is evident they did not take this paper to be a will. For immediately upon its execution, believing that it passed the whole title to the grantee, in order that the grantor might have the usufruct of the property during her life, the power of attorney referred to was executed by the grantee.

It is of interest to note that the same Justice, Mr. Justice Beard, of the Supreme Court of Tennessee, wrote both the *Ellis* opinion and the

Stamper opinion. We hold that *Ellis* is clearly distinguishable from *Stamper* and that this lawsuit is governed by the rule announced in *Ellis*, supra.

In determining whether an instrument is testamentary in character or a deed, the intent of the grantor is controlling. Cockrell v. Tuell (1970) 61 Tenn. App. 423, 454 S.W.2d 713. In Ellis v. Pearson, supra, it is stated that:

> Whether a paper is to operate as a will or deed depends upon the intention of the maker, to be gathered from its language. In order that it be held a deed it must convey an interest to take effect *in praesenti*, though the enjoyment may rest *in futuro*. It is otherwise as to a will; it speaks as of the death of the testator.

The plaintiff-grantor testified by deposition that the purpose of the instrument was to defeat any claim her husband might assert against the property by divorce proceeding or as her survivor, and still reserve in herself the use of the property with the unlimited right to sell. That stated purpose shows within itself that she did not intend to grant a present interest. . . .

The decree of the chancellor is reversed and a judgment will be entered in this Court declaring the instrument recorded in Deed Book A-9, page 61, Register's Office of Lewis County, Tennessee, void and cancelling the Notice of Lis Pendens recorded in Lien Book 3, page 97, Register's Office of Lewis County, Tennessee. The cost in this Court is adjudged against the defendants-appellants.

NOTES AND PROBLEMS

1. Deeds on condition and revocable deeds have proved very troublesome to the courts and are dangerous will substitutes that should never be used. Typically these deeds have been used by persons of modest wealth who want to avoid probate and lawyers. Suppose that *O* executes a deed conveying Blackacre to *A* and his heirs. A provision of the deed reads: "This conveyance is made upon the following conditions: (1) this deed is not effective if *A* predeceases *O*; (2) this deed is not to take effect until *O*'s death; and (3) this deed is revocable by *O* at any time." The deed is delivered to *A*. Is the deed valid? The deed in Butler v. Sherwood, 196 App. Div. 603, 188 N.Y.S. 242 (1921), aff'd, 233 N.Y. 655, 135 N.E. 957 (1922), contained all three conditions set out in this hypothetical deed. The court held the deed void, but why should it be?

Courts traditionally have analyzed the problem as whether *O* intended to create a present interest in *A*. With respect to condition (1) there should be no problem. The condition is analogous to a springing executory interest, valid in law since 1536. An early use of the springing interest occurred in English marriage settlements. In order to give the intended groom, *G*, assurances that the bride, *B*, would come to the marriage endowed with property, the father of the bride would convey land, prior to the wedding ceremony, "to *B* and her heirs if she marries *G*." Condition (1) is analogous, but courts have often read the requirement of a present interest to mean a present *possessory* interest, forgetting that a future interest is a present interest in property. These courts have held that because the event upon which the grantee takes possession, if ever, is the grantor's death, the deed is testamentary and void. Others have held that a future interest passed to the grantee during the grantor's lifetime. See 1 W. Page, Wills §6.6 (W. Bowe-D. Parker rev. 1960).

Condition (2) also should be valid. Many courts have so held, construing "take effect on death" to mean that the grantor reserves a life estate and creates a remainder to take effect in possession on the grantor's death. A few courts, on the other hand, have construed the condition to mean that the deed was intended not to take effect at all until death; thus construed, the deed is void. See id., §6.5.

Condition (3) — the reservation of a power to revoke — was involved in Wright v. Huskey. On the validity of a deed with this condition, the cases are split. For a leading case contrary to Wright v. Huskey, upholding a deed where a life estate and power to revoke were reserved, see Tennant v. John Tennant Memorial Home, 167 Cal. 570, 140 P. 242 (1914).

See Garvey, Revocable Gifts of Legal Interests in Land, 54 Ky. L.J. 19 (1965); Browder, Giving or Leaving — What Is a Will?, 75 Mich. L. Rev. 845, 860-864 (1977).

If your client wants to use a revocable deed, talk the client out of it. Use a revocable trust instead. It is safe in all jurisdictions.

2.   Harold and Mildred Rosengrant, owners of a farm, ask their banker to prepare a deed naming Harold's nephew Jay as grantee. Harold and Mildred take Jay to the banker's office, sign the deed, and tell Jay that they want Jay to leave the deed with the banker. When they die Jay is to take the deed and record it and the farm will be his. Upon the advice of the banker, Harold hands the deed to Jay to "make this legal." Jay takes the deed, looks at it, and then hands it back to the banker who tells Jay he will put it in an envelope and keep it in his vault until Jay calls for it. The banker puts it in an envelope marked "Jay Rosengrant or Harold Rosengrant." Harold and Mildred stay in possession of the farm until their deaths. After they die the banker gives Jay the deed and he records it. Does Jay own the farm? See Rosengrant v. Rosengrant, 629 P.2d 800 (Okla. App. 1981), holding that Jay does not own the farm because the "writing on the envelope creates an inescapable conclusion that the deed was, in fact, retrievable

at any time by Harold before his death." A revocable escrow is void for want of delivery; the deed is not put beyond the grantor's dominion and control.

Why is not the banker a trustee? A revocable trust is valid. The stumbling block is the Statute of Frauds, which requires a writing where an express trust of land is created. An agency does not have to be created in writing. But the question remains: If a revocable trust is valid, why not a revocable escrow?

Suppose that Harold and Mildred had signed the deed in the banker's office, told Jay and the banker that the farm was now Jay's, and then Harold took the deed and put it in his safe-deposit box to which he and his wife alone had access. After the death of Harold and Mildred, who remained in possession of the farm, does Jay own the farm? See Bennion v. Hansen, 699 P.2d 757 (Utah 1985). Suppose that UPC §6-201, supra page 285, has been enacted. What result? See In re Estate of O'Brien, 109 Wash. 2d 913, 749 P.2d 154 (1988). See also Note, The Issue of Delivery Raised by "Dispositive" Conveyances, 18 Drake L. Rev. 67 (1968).

SECTION G.   GIFTS OF PERSONAL PROPERTY

To be effective a gift of personal property must be delivered. The requirement of delivery is separate and additional to the requirement that the donor intend to make a gift. Intention without delivery does not suffice for a gift. The donor, it is said, must feel the wrench of delivery.

The requirement of delivery serves ritual and evidentiary functions. It "makes vivid and concrete to the donor the significance of the act he is doing," and is strong evidence of the alleged gift. Mechem, The Requirement of Delivery in Gifts of Chattels, 21 Ill. L. Rev. 341, 348 (1926).

Delivery may be effectuated by handing over the object itself, or the object may be constructively or symbolically delivered when it would be difficult or impracticable to deliver the object manually because of its bulk or inaccessibility. Constructive delivery is the transfer of something that gives the donee physical access or control over the subject of the intended gift. The classic example is a key that opens a safe-deposit box or a heavy chest. Symbolic delivery is the transfer of something "symbolic" of the object. The typical example of symbolic delivery is handing over a written instrument of gift. Thus if *O* wishes to give *A* her grand piano, *O* can give *A* either a key that opens the keyboard or a signed instrument reading, "I give *A* my grand piano." But remember, constructive or symbolic delivery is not usually permitted when the object is easily delivered manually. See R. Brown, Personal Property §§7.5, 7.6, 7.10 (W. Raushenbush, 3d ed. 1975). See also Edinburg v. Edinburg, 22 Mass. App. Ct. 199, 492 N.E.2d 1164 (1986), where the court found symbolic delivery of valuable drawings on paper when the donor placed the donee's name on the container holding the drawings, kept them in her vault for security, and signed documents confirming that she had made the gift.

PROBLEMS

1. *O*, in New York, wants to give *A* a diamond ring and an antique secretary that are in *O*'s house in Boston. *O* hands the key to the house to *A* with the words, "The ring and secretary are yours. Go up to Boston and get them." *A* boards the train to Boston. Before *A* reaches Boston, *O* dies. Does *A* own the ring or the secretary?

2. An old man, ill and anticipating death, tells his daughter he wishes her to have $10,000 he has buried in various places on his property. He asks her, "If I get well, will you give it back to me?" The daughter replies, "Yes, papa, if you get well, you can have all of it. I will give it back to you if you get well." The next day the old man shows his daughter where the money is buried. The money remains there until the old man's death not much later. Has a valid gift been made? See Waite v. Grubbe, 43 Or. 406, 73 P. 206 (1903); Shankle v. Spahr, 121 Va. 598, 93 S.E. 605 (1917).

A gift causa mortis is a gift made when the donor is in apprehension of impending death or on his (apparent) death bed. If the grim reaper does not take the donor away, the gift is revoked. A gift causa mortis is one of the few instances where the law recognizes revocable gifts of personal property. See Garvey, Revocable Gifts of Personal Property: A Possible Will Substitute, 16 Cath. U.L. Rev. 119, 256 (1966) (arguing that revocable gifts should be recognized). Delivery is as essential to a gift causa mortis as it is to other gifts.

A gift causa mortis is a death-bed substitute for a will.

Scherer v. Hyland
Supreme Court of New Jersey, 1977
75 N.J. 127, 380 A.2d 698

PER CURIAM. Defendant, the Administrator ad litem of the Estate of Catherine Wagner, appeals from an Appellate Division decision, one judge dissenting, affirming a summary judgment by the trial court holding that Ms. Wagner had made a valid gift causa mortis of a check to plaintiff. We affirm.

The facts are not in dispute. Catherine Wagner and the plaintiff, Robert Scherer, lived together for approximately fifteen years prior to Ms. Wagner's death in January 1974. In 1970, the decedent and plaintiff were involved in an automobile accident in which decedent suffered facial wounds and a broken hip. Because of the hip injury, decedent's physical mobility was substantially impaired. She was forced to give up her job and to restrict her activities. After the accident, plaintiff cared for her and assumed the sole financial responsibility for maintaining their household. During the weeks preceding her death, Ms. Wagner was acutely depressed. On one occasion, she attempted suicide by slashing her wrists. On January 23, 1974, she committed suicide by jumping from the roof of the apartment building in which they lived.

On the morning of the day of her death. Ms. Wagner received a check for $17,400 drawn by a Pennsylvania attorney who had represented her in a claim arising out of the automobile accident. The check represented settlement of the claim. Plaintiff telephoned Ms. Wagner at around 11:30 A.M. that day and was told that the check had arrived. Plaintiff noticed nothing unusual in Ms. Wagner's voice. At about 3:20 P.M., decedent left the apartment building and jumped to her death. The police, as part of their investigation of the suicide, asked the building superintendent to admit them to the apartment. On the kitchen table they found the check, endorsed in blank, and two notes handwritten by the decedent. In one, she described her depression over her physical condition, expressed her love for Scherer, and asked him to forgive her "for taking the easy way out." In the other, she indicated that she "bequeathed" to plaintiff all of her possessions, including "the check for $17,400.00. . . ." The police took possession of the check, which was eventually placed in an interest-bearing account pending disposition of this action.

Under our wills statute it is clear that Ms. Wagner's note bequeathing all her possessions to Mr. Scherer cannot take effect as a testamentary disposition. N.J.S.A. 3A:3-2.[7] A *donatio causa mortis* has been traditionally defined as a gift of personal property made by a party in expectation of death, then imminent, subject to the condition that the donor die as anticipated. Establishment of the gift has uniformly called for proof of delivery.

The primary issue here is whether Ms. Wagner's acts of endorsing the settlement check, placing it on the kitchen table in the apartment she shared with Scherer, next to a writing clearly evidencing her intent

---

7. New Jersey did not permit holographic wills until 1981. — Eds.

to transfer the check to Scherer, and abandoning the apartment with a clear expectation of imminent death constituted delivery sufficient to sustain a gift causa mortis of the check. Defendant, relying on the principles established in Foster v. Reiss, 18 N.J. 41 (1955), argues that there was no delivery because the donor did not unequivocally relinquish control of the check before her death. Central to this argument is the contention that suicide, the perceived peril, was one which decedent herself created and one which was completely within her control. According to this contention, the donor at any time before she jumped from the apartment roof could have changed her mind, re-entered the apartment, and reclaimed the check. Defendant therefore reasons that decedent did not make an effective transfer of the check during her lifetime, as is required for a valid gift causa mortis. . . .

There is general agreement that the major purpose of the delivery requirement is evidentiary. Proof of delivery reduces the possibility that the evidence of intent has been fabricated or that a mere donative impulse, not consummated by action, has been mistaken for a completed gift. Since "these gifts come into question only after death has closed the lips of the donor," the delivery requirement provides a substantial safeguard against fraud and perjury. See Keepers v. Fidelity Title and Deposit Co., 56 N.J.L. 302, 308 (E. & A. 1893). In *Foster*, the majority concluded that these policies could best be fulfilled by a strict rule requiring actual manual tradition of the subject-matter of the gift except in a very narrow class of cases where "there can be no actual delivery" or where "the situation is incompatible with the performance of such ceremony." 18 N.J. at 50. Justice Jacobs, in his dissenting opinion (joined by Justices Brennan and Wachenfeld) questioned the reasonableness of requiring direct physical delivery in cases where donative intent is "freely and clearly expressed in a written instrument." Id. at 56. He observed that a more flexible approach to the delivery requirement had been taken by other jurisdictions and quoted approvingly from Devol v. Dye, 123 Ind. 321, 24 N.E. 246, 7 L.R.A. 439 (Sup. Ct. 1890). . . .

The balancing approach suggested in Devol v. Dye . . . takes into account the purposes served by the requirement of delivery in determining whether that requirement has been met. It would find a constructive delivery adequate to support the gift when the evidence of donative intent is concrete and undisputed, when there is every indication that the donor intended to make a present transfer of the subject-matter of the gift, and when the steps taken by the donor to effect such a transfer must have been deemed by the donor as sufficient to pass the donor's interest to the donee. We are persuaded that this approach, which does not minimize the need for evidentiary safeguards to prevent frauds upon the estates of the deceased, reflects the realities which attend transfers of this kind.

In this case, the evidence of decedent's intent to transfer the check to Robert Scherer is concrete, unequivocal, and undisputed. The circumstances definitely rule out any possibility of fraud. The sole question, then, is whether the steps taken by the decedent, independent of her writing of the suicide notes, were sufficient to support a finding that she effected a lifetime transfer of the check to Scherer. We think that they were. First, the act of endorsing a check represents, in common experience and understanding, the only act needed (short of actual delivery) to render a check negotiable. The significance of such an act is universally understood. Accordingly, we have no trouble in viewing Ms. Wagner's endorsement of the settlement check as a substantial step taken by her for the purpose of effecting a transfer to Scherer of her right to the check proceeds. Second, we note that the only person other than the decedent who had routine access to the apartment was Robert Scherer. Indeed, the apartment was leased in his name. It is clear that Ms. Wagner before leaving the apartment placed the check in a place where Scherer could not fail to see it and fully expected that he would take actual possession of the check when he entered. And, although Ms. Wagner's subsequent suicide does not itself constitute a component of the delivery of this gift, it does provide persuasive evidence that when Ms. Wagner locked the door of the apartment she did so with no expectation of returning. When we consider her state of mind as it must have been upon leaving the apartment, her surrender of possession at that moment was complete. We find, therefore, that when she left the apartment she completed a constructive delivery of the check to Robert Scherer. In light of her resolve to take her own life and of her obvious desire not to be deterred from that purpose, Ms. Wagner's failure manually to transfer the check to Scherer is understandable. She clearly did all that she could do or thought necessary to do to surrender the check. Her donative intent has been conclusively demonstrated by independent evidence. The law should effectuate that intent rather than indulge in nice distinctions which would thwart her purpose. Upon these facts, we find that the constructive delivery she made was adequate to support a gift causa mortis.

Defendant's assertion that suicide is not the sort of peril that will sustain a gift causa mortis finds some support in precedents from other jurisdictions. We are, however, not bound by those authorities nor do we find them persuasive. While it is true that a gift causa mortis is made by the donor with a view to impending death, death is no less impending because of a resolve to commit suicide. . . . And, the notion that one in a state of mental depression serious enough to lead to suicide is somehow "freer" to renounce the depression and thus the danger than one suffering from a physical illness, although it has a certain augustinian appeal, has long since been replaced by more enlightened views of human psychology. In re Van Wormer's Estate,

255 Mich. 399, 238 N.W. 210 (Sup. Ct. 1931) (melancholia ending in suicide sufficient to sustain a gift causa mortis). We also observe that an argument that the donor of a causa mortis gift might have changed his or her mind loses much of its force when one recalls that a causa mortis gift, by definition, can be revoked at any time before the donor dies and is automatically revoked if the donor recovers.

Judgment affirmed.

NOTES AND QUESTIONS

1. Suppose that Catherine did not have suicide in mind but had endorsed the check as a birthday present for Robert, had put it on a table in the apartment with a birthday card for Robert to find upon coming home, and then, upon going out to shop for dinner, had been struck by a car and killed. Would there be a valid gift?

2. In Faith Lutheran Retirement Home v. Veis, 156 Mont. 38, 473 P.2d 503 (1970), noted in 35 Mont. L. Rev. 132 (1974), the donor, an 81-year-old man, entered Faith Lutheran Retirement Home, signing the usual agreement that he would pay for room and board. He also signed and delivered to the home a writing that said:

> I made most of my money in Montana. The Church through Faith Lutheran Home has been doing a wonderful piece of work among my old friends. For the comfort, care, happiness I have while I am here be it short or long I wish to pay for these values the sum of $10,000 on demand. This may however be collectible against my estate if not demanded sooner, or paid by me.

Fourteen days later the donor left the home and moved to Minnesota where he died the following year. The home sued his estate for $10,000. The administrator of the home testified that the donor said he wanted to make a gift and did not want to make a will because he disliked lawyers. The court held that the note and testimony were sufficient evidence of an intent to make a gift and that there was an effective delivery because, "While a verbal gift is not valid unless there is actual or symbolical delivery to the donee of the thing given, this rule has no application when the gift is effected by an instrument in writing."

Should the writing in *Faith Lutheran Retirement Home* have been considered a promise to make a gift rather than a gift? The *Faith Lutheran* case may reflect the tendency of courts to strain to uphold promises to make gifts to charitable institutions even though consideration and reliance are lacking. Cf. Restatement (Second) of Contracts §90(2) (1981) stating that a charitable subscription is binding under principles of promissory estoppel without proof that the promise induced action or forbearance. The Montana court, however, applied straightforward gift analysis and did not mention promissory estoppel.

A gift by the donor of a check on his own account is an authorization to the bank to pay and is not a legal gift until the donor relinquishes control of the sum which the check represents. "To perfect the gift the check must be presented by the donee and accepted by the drawee, because the donor could stop payment, withdraw from his account the very funds which the check represents, or die before payment is made, any of which would revoke the gift." Malloy v. Smith, 265 Md. 460, 463, 290 A.2d 486, 487-488 (1972). Is *Faith Lutheran Retirement Home* consistent with this rule?

3.   Can a guardian or conservator of an incompetent person make gifts of the incompetent's property? See Fellows, In Search of Donative Intent, 73 Iowa L. Rev. 611, 622-630 (1988); Wormser, The Doctrine of Substitution of Judgment, 9 Inst. on Est. Plan. 15-1 (1975).

WILLS: CONSTRUCTION PROBLEMS

In speaking of the Sergeant of the Lawe, Chaucer wrote:

> Therto he koude endite and make a thyng,
> Ther koude no wight pynchen at his writying.[1]

Beginning in this chapter, almost every case in the rest of the book raises an issue that could have been — and should have been — solved by appropriate drafting. One of the objectives of this book is to help you acquire the ability of Chaucer's Sergeant at Law so that no one can fault your drafting. It is a skill that should stand you in good stead in drafting not only wills and trusts, but all kinds of instruments.

SECTION A. ADMISSION OF EXTRINSIC EVIDENCE: AMBIGUITY, MISTAKE, AND OMISSION

In construing wills, a majority of jurisdictions follow (or purport to follow) the plain meaning rule: A plain meaning in a will cannot be disturbed. The Kentucky court stated it thus:

---

1. G. Chaucer, Prologue to Canterbury Tales (line 325). Translated into modern English by F. Hill, The Canterbury Tales 9 (1946):

> And he could write, and pen a deed in law
> So in his writing none could pick a flaw.

If the language of a will, when all of it is considered together, is plain and unambiguous, there is nothing to do except to give it the meaning which its language clearly imports. If the language of a clause of a will is plain and is not clouded or made of uncertain meaning by other language of the will, it cannot be supposed that the testator meant or intended anything except what is said, and according to the ordinary meaning of the language used. The written language of a will is the best evidence of its meaning and the intention of the testator, and hence the intentions of the testator must be gathered from the language of the will itself, without the aid of extrinsic evidence, if it is unambiguous. [Carroll v. Cave Hill Cemetery Co., 172 Ky. 204, 211, 189 S.W.2d 186, 189 (1916).]

In some jurisdictions the plain meaning rule is not applied rigidly, but a plain meaning creates a strong presumption that can be overcome only by exceptionally strong evidence of another meaning. An example of such a strong presumption is presented by the facts of Re Herlichka, [1969] 3 D.L.R.3d 700, [1969] 1 Ont. 724. Stanley Herlichka deserted his wife Audrey and his two children in 1956. Shortly thereafter he moved in with Phyllis McKenna and three children were born to them. In 1965, Stanley executed his will. He gave "to my wife Phyllis Herlichka" all his tangible personal property, but did not refer by name to Phyllis again or to any other beneficiary. Stanley devised his residuary estate in trust, "[t]o hold whatever house and property I may own and be using as a home at the time of my death as a home for my wife during her lifetime, . . . and as a home for my children until" the youngest reaches 21, and to pay the net income to "my wife during her lifetime," and after her death to distribute the principal to his "children" when the youngest reached 21. The court held "that the testator intended to benefit exclusively his lawful wife and his legitimate children." The strong preference for the prima facie meaning of "wife" and "children" as referring to legitimate wife and children exclusively was not overcome by the circumstances surrounding the execution of the will nor by the reference in the will to "my wife Phyllis Herlichka."

The plain meaning rule has been criticized as fundamentally misdirected. Wigmore, the great authority on evidence, vigorously attacks the rule, saying, "The fallacy consists in assuming that there is or ever can be *some one real* or absolute meaning. In truth there can be only *some person's* meaning: and that person, whose meaning the law is seeking, is the writer of the document." 9 J. Wigmore, Evidence §2462 at 198 (J. Chadbourn rev. 1981) (emphasis in original). The plain meaning rule reflects a dream, a hope, of "that lawyer's Paradise, where all words have a fixed, precisely ascertained meaning, and where, if the writer has been careful, a lawyer having a document referred to him may sit in his chair, inspect the text, and answer all questions without raising his eyes." J. Thayer, Preliminary Treatise on Evidence

428 (1898).[2] But this is an illusion, for words always need interpretation. The process of interpretation invariably requires looking outside the text in order to identify persons and objects. For example, suppose that a man, having a wife and children, leaves a brief will: "I leave all to mother." No term could be plainer than "mother," for a man can have only one mother. Yet if the evidence shows that in the family circle the testator always called his wife "mother," such evidence should be and is admissible under the *personal usage exception*, and all the estate will go to the wife. See Moseley v. Goodman, 138 Tenn. 1, 195 S.W. 590 (1917). If evidence is admissible to show that the testator habitually used words to refer to persons not indicated by their common meaning, why is not evidence admissible in all cases to show what the testator meant by them?

Estate of Russell
Supreme Court of California, 1968
69 Cal. 2d 200, 444 P.2d 353, 70 Cal. Rptr. 561

SULLIVAN, J.   Georgia Nan Russell Hembree appeals from a judgment (Prob. Code, §1240[3]) entered in proceedings for the determination of heirship (§§1080-1082) decreeing inter alia that under the terms of the will of Thelma L. Russell, deceased, all of the residue of her estate should be distributed to Chester H. Quinn.

Thelma L. Russell died testate on September 8, 1965, leaving a validly executed holographic will written on a small card. The front of the card reads:

> Turn
> the card   March 18-1957
>   I leave everything
>   I own Real &
>   Personal to Chester
>   H. Quinn & Roxy Russell
>   Thelma L. Russell

The reverse side reads:

> My ($10.) Ten dollar gold
> Piece & diamonds I leave
> to Georgia Nan Russell.
> Alverata, Geogia [sic]

Chester H. Quinn was a close friend and companion of testatrix, who for over 25 years prior to her death had resided in one of the living

---

2. Another view of the plain meaning rule was expressed by A.P. Herbert's Lord Mildew: "If Parliament does not mean what it says it must say so." A.P. Herbert, Uncommon Law 313 (2d ed. 1936).

3. Hereafter unless otherwise indicated all section references are to the Probate Code.

units on her property and had stood in a relation of personal trust and confidence toward her. Roxy Russell was testatrix' pet dog which was alive on the date of the execution of testatrix' will but predeceased her.[4] Plaintiff is testatrix' niece and her only heir-at-law.

In her petition for determination of heirship plaintiff alleges, inter alia, that "Roxy Russell is an Airedale dog";[5] that section 27 enumerates those entitled to take by will; that "Dogs are not included among those listed in . . . Section 27. Not even Airedale dogs"; that the gift of one-half of the residue of testatrix' estate to Roxy Russell is invalid and void; and that plaintiff was entitled to such one-half as testatrix' sole heir-at-law.

At the hearing on the petition, plaintiff introduced without objection extrinsic evidence establishing that Roxy Russell was testatrix' Airedale dog which died on June 9, 1958. To this end plaintiff, in addition to an independent witness, called defendant pursuant to former Code of Civil Procedure section 2055 (now Evid. Code, §776). Upon redirect examination, counsel for Quinn then sought to introduce evidence of the latter's relationship with testatrix "in the event that your Honor feels that there is any necessity for further ascertainment of the intent above and beyond the document." Plaintiff's objections on the ground that it was inadmissible under the statute of wills and the parol evidence rule "because there is no ambiguity" and that it was inadmissible under section 105, were overruled. Over plaintiff's objection, counsel for Quinn also introduced certain documentary evidence consisting of testatrix' address book and a certain quitclaim deed "for the purpose of demonstrating the intention on the part of the deceased that she not die intestate." Of all this extrinsic evidence only the following infinitesimal portion of Quinn's testimony relates to care of the dog: "Q [Counsel for Quinn] Prior to the first Roxy's death did you ever discuss with Miss Russell taking care of Roxy if anything should ever happen to her? A Yes." Plaintiff carefully preserved an objection running to all of the above line of testimony and at the conclusion of the hearing moved to strike such evidence. Her motion was denied.

---

4. Actually the record indicates the existence of two Roxy Russells. The original Roxy was an Airedale dog which testatrix owned at the time she made her will, but which, according to Quinn, died after having had a fox tail removed from its nose, and which, according to the testimony of one Arthur Turner, owner of a pet cemetery, was buried on June 9, 1958. Roxy was replaced with another dog (breed not indicated in the record before us) which, although it answered to the name Roxy, was according to the record, in fact registered with the American Kennel Club as "Russel's [sic] Royal Kick Roxy."

5. In his "Petition for Probate of Holographic Will and for Letters of Administration with the Will Annexed," Quinn included under the names, ages and residences of the devisees and legatees of testatrix the following: "Roxy Russell, A 9 year old Airedale dog, [residing at] 4422 Palm Avenue, La Mesa, Calif." [Is this correct? Since the will was executed when the first Roxy was alive, isn't the second Roxy a pretermitted Airedale? — Eds.]

The trial court found, so far as is here material, that it was the intention of testatrix "that Chester H. Quinn was to receive her entire estate, excepting the gold coin and diamonds bequeathed to" plaintiff and that Quinn "was to care for the dog, Roxy Russell, in the event of Testatrix's death. The language contained in the Will, concerning the dog, Roxy Russell, was precatory in nature only, and merely indicative of the wish, desire and concern of Testatrix that Chester H. Quinn was to care for the dog, Roxy Russell, subsequent to Testatrix's death."[6] The court concluded that testatrix intended to and did make an absolute and outright gift to Mr. Quinn of all the residue of her estate, adding: "There occurred no lapse as to any portion of the residuary gift to Chester H. Quinn by reason of the language contained in the Will concerning the dog, Roxy Russell, such language not having the effect of being an attempted outright gift or gift in trust to the dog. The effect of such language is merely to indicate the intention of Testatrix that Chester H. Quinn was to take the entire residuary estate and to use whatever portion thereof as might be necessary to care for and maintain the dog, Roxy Russell." Judgment was entered accordingly. This appeal followed.

Plaintiff's position before us may be summarized thusly: That the gift of one-half of the residue of the estate to testatrix' dog was clear and unambiguous; that such gift was void and the property subject thereto passed to plaintiff under the laws of intestate succession; and that the court erred in admitting the extrinsic evidence offered by Quinn but that in any event the uncontradicted evidence in the record did not cure the invalidity of the gift. . . .

When the language of a will is ambiguous or uncertain resort may be had to extrinsic evidence in order to ascertain the intention of the testator. We have said that extrinsic evidence is admissible "to explain

---

6. The memorandum decision elaborates on this point, stating in part: "The obvious concern of the human who loves her pet is to see that it is properly cared for by someone who may be trusted to honor that concern and through resources the person may make available in the will to carry out this entreaty, desire, wish, recommendation or prayer. This, in other words, is a most logical example of a precatory provision. It is the only logical conclusion one can come to which would not do violence to the apparent intent of Mrs. Russell."

The trial court found further: "Testatrix intended that Georgia Nan Russell Hembree was not to have any other real or personal property belonging to Testatrix, other than the gold coin and diamonds." This finding also was elaborated on in the memorandum decision: "In making the will it is apparent she had Georgia on her mind. While there is other evidence in the case about Thelma Russell's frame of mind concerning her real property and her niece, which was admitted by the Court, over counsel's vigorous objection, because it concerned testatrix' frame of mind, a condition relevant to the material issue of intent, nevertheless this additional evidence was not necessary to this Court in reaching its conclusion." The additional evidence referred to included an address book of testatrix upon which she had written: "Chester, Don't let Augusta and Georgia have one penny of my place if it takes it all to fight it in Court. Thelma."

any ambiguity arising on the face of a will, or to resolve a latent ambiguity which does not so appear." (Estate of Torregano (1960) 54 Cal. 2d 234, 246, 5 Cal. Rptr. 137, 144, 352 P.2d 505, 512, 88 A.L.R.2d 597 citing §105.) A latent ambiguity is one which is not apparent on the face of the will but is disclosed by some fact collateral to it. . . .

Extrinsic evidence always may be introduced initially in order to show that under the circumstances of a particular case the seemingly clear language of a will describing either the subject of or the object of the gift actually embodies a latent ambiguity for it is only by the introduction of extrinsic evidence that the existence of such an ambiguity can be shown. Once shown, such ambiguity may be resolved by extrinsic evidence. . . .

A patent ambiguity is an uncertainty which appears on the face of the will. . . . "When an uncertainty arises upon the face of a will as to the meaning of any of its provisions, the testator's intent is to be ascertained from the words of the will, but the circumstances of the execution thereof may be taken into consideration, excluding the oral declarations of the testator as to his intentions." (Estate of Salmonski, . . . 38 Cal. 2d 199, 214, 238 P.2d 966, 975.) This is but a corollary derived from an older formalism. Long before *Salmonski* it was said in Estate of Wilson, . . . 171 Cal. 449, 456, 153 P. 927, 930: "The rule is well established that where the meaning of the will, on its face, taking the words in the ordinary sense, is entirely clear, and where no latent ambiguity is made to appear by extrinsic evidence, there can be no evidence of extrinsic circumstances to show that the testatrix intended or desired to do something not expressed in the will." However, this ancient touchstone has not necessarily uncovered judicial material of unquestioned purity.

In order to determine initially whether the terms of *any written instrument* are clear, definite and free from ambiguity the court must examine the instrument in the light of the circumstances surrounding its execution so as to ascertain what the parties meant by the words used. Only then can it be determined whether the seemingly clear language of the instrument is in fact ambiguous. "Words are used in an endless variety of contexts. Their meaning is not subsequently attached to them by the reader but is formulated by the writer and can only be found by interpretation in the light of all the circumstances that reveal the sense in which the writer used the words. The exclusion of parol evidence regarding such circumstances merely because the words do not appear ambiguous to the reader can easily lead to the attribution to a written instrument of a meaning that was never intended." (Universal Sales Corp. v. Cal., etc., Mfg. Co. (1942) 20 Cal. 2d 751, 776, 128 P.2d 665, 679 (Traynor, J., concurring).) "The court must determine the true meaning of the instrument in the light of the evidence available. It can neither exclude evidence relevant to that determination nor invoke such evidence to write a new or different instrument." (Laux v. Freed (1960) 53 Cal. 2d 512, 527, 2 Cal. Rptr. 265, 273, 348 P.2d 873, 881 (Traynor, J., concurring)); see also Corbin, The Interpretation of Words and the Parol Evidence Rule (1965) 50 Cornell L.Q. 161, 164: "[W]hen a judge refuses to consider relevant extrinsic evidence on the ground that the meaning of written words is to him plain and clear, his decision is formed by and wholly based upon the completely extrinsic evidence of his own personal education and experience"; Corbin, op. cit. supra, pp. 189-190. . . .

The foregoing reflects the modern development of rules governing interpretation, for in the words of Wigmore "The history of the law of Interpretation is the history of a progress from a stiff and superstitious formalism to a flexible rationalism." (9 Wigmore, [Evidence (3d ed. 1940)], §2461, p.187.) While "still surviving to us, in many Courts, from the old formalism . . . [is] the rule that you *cannot disturb a plain meaning*" (9 Wigmore, op. cit. supra, p.191, original emphasis) nevertheless decisions and authorities like those cited above bespeak the current tendency to abandon the "stiff formalism of earlier interpretation" and to show the meaning of words even though no ambiguity appears on the face of the document. . . .

Accordingly, we think it is self-evident that in the interpretation of a will, a court cannot determine whether the terms of the will are clear and definite in the first place until it considers the circumstances under which the will was made so that the judge may be placed in the position of the testator whose language he is interpreting. . . . Failure to enter upon such an inquiry is failure to recognize that the "ordinary standard or 'plain meaning,' is simply the meaning of the people who did *not* write the document." (9 Wigmore, op. cit. supra, §2462, p.191.)

. . . [E]xtrinsic evidence of the circumstances under which a will is made (except evidence expressly excluded by statute)[7] may be considered by the court in ascertaining what the testator meant by the words used in the will. If in the light of such extrinsic evidence, the provisions of the will are reasonably susceptible of two or more meanings claimed to have been intended by the testator, "an uncertainty arises upon the face of a will" (§105) and extrinsic evidence relevant to prove any of such meanings is admissible . . . subject to the restrictions imposed by statute (§105). If, on the other hand, in the light of such extrinsic evidence, the provisions of the will are not reasonably susceptible of two or more meanings, there is no uncertainty arising upon the face of the will . . . and any proffered evidence attempting to show an intention

---

7. As for example, under section 105 . . . which specifically excludes "the oral declarations of the testator as to his intentions." This opinion does not disturb the statutory proscription against the use of such evidence.

different from that expressed by the words therein, giving them the only meaning to which they are reasonably susceptible, is inadmissible. . . .

Examining testatrix' will in the light of the foregoing rules, we arrive at the following conclusions: Extrinsic evidence offered by plaintiff was admitted without objection and indeed would have been properly admitted over objection to raise and resolve the latent ambiguity as to Roxy Russell and ultimately to establish that Roxy Russell was a dog. Extrinsic evidence of the surrounding circumstances[8] was properly considered in order to ascertain what testatrix meant by the words of the will, including the words: "I leave everything I own Real & Personal to Chester H. Quinn & Roxy Russell" or as those words can now be read "to Chester H. Quinn and my dog Roxy Russell."

However, viewing the will in the light of the surrounding circumstances as are disclosed by the record, we conclude that the will cannot reasonably be construed as urged by Quinn and determined by the trial court as providing that testatrix intended to make an absolute and outright gift of the entire residue of her estate to Quinn who was "to use whatever portion thereof as might be necessary to care for and maintain the dog." No words of the will give the entire residuum to Quinn, much less indicate that the provision for the dog is merely precatory in nature. Such an interpretation is not consistent with a disposition which by its language leaves the residuum in equal shares to Quinn and the dog.[9] A disposition in equal shares to two beneficiaries cannot be equated with a disposition of the whole to one of them who may use "whatever portion thereof as might be necessary" on behalf of the other. . . . Neither can the bare language of a gift of one-half of the residue to the dog be so expanded as to mean a gift to Quinn in trust for the care of the dog, there being no words indicating an enforceable duty upon Quinn to do so or indicating to whom the trust property is to go upon termination of the trust. "While no particular form of expression is necessary for the creation of a trust, nevertheless some expression of intent to that end is requisite." (Estate of Doane, 190 Cal. 412, 415, 213 P. 53, 54. . . .)

Accordingly, since in the light of the extrinsic evidence introduced below, the terms of the will are not reasonably susceptible of the meaning claimed by Quinn to have been intended by testatrix, the extrinsic evidence offered to show such an intention should have been excluded by the trial court.[10] Upon an independent examination of the

---

8. Excluding however the oral declarations of testatrix as to her intentions. . . . It is to be noted that no such declarations are herein involved.

9. How's that again? — Eds.

10. Having concluded that the extrinsic evidence should have been stricken from the record, we need not reach plaintiff's second contention that, even considering such

"If you had an account here, it would be a different story."

QUESTION

Did Thelma Russell consider that her devisee tenants in common
might want to fix up the place?

---

will we conclude that the trial court's interpretation of the terms thereof
was erroneous. Interpreting the provisions relating to testatrix' residuary estate in accordance with the only meaning to which they are
reasonably susceptible, we conclude that testatrix intended to make a
disposition of all of the residue of the estate to Quinn and the dog in

---

extrinsic evidence, "There is neither jot nor tittle of evidence . . . which would support a
finding that Mrs. Russell intended to leave nothing to her dog." However, it is noteworthy
that, as we pointed out at the beginning of this opinion, the infinitesimal portion of the
extrinsic evidence actually referring to the care of the dog was devoid of all probative
value.

equal shares; therefore, as tenants in common. . . . As a dog cannot be the beneficiary under a will . . . the attempted gift to Roxy Russell is void. . . .[11]

There remains only the necessity of determining the effect of the void gift to the dog upon the disposition of the residuary estate. That portion of any residuary estate that is the subject of a lapsed gift to one of the residuary beneficiaries remains undisposed of by the will and passes to the heirs-at-law. . . . The rule is equally applicable with respect to a void gift to one of the residuary beneficiaries. . . . Therefore, notwithstanding testatrix' expressed intention to limit the extent of her gift by will to plaintiff . . . , one-half of the residuary estate passes to plaintiff as testatrix' only heir-at-law (§225). We conclude that the residue of testatrix' estate should be distributed in equal shares to Chester H. Quinn and Georgia Nan Russell Hembree, testatrix' niece.

The judgment is reversed.

NOTES AND QUESTIONS

1. What common law rule, not attacked by Chester's counsel or questioned by the court, causes the court to get involved in its elaborate discussion of the admission of extrinsic evidence? See the last paragraph of the court's opinion. Is such a rule sound? Had the court discarded that rule, the case would have been easy.

2. *Patent and Latent Ambiguities.* A latent ambiguity is an ambiguity that does not appear on the face of the will but appears when the terms of the will are applied to the testator's property or designated beneficiaries.[12] For example, in Ihl v. Oetting, 682 S.W.2d 865 (Mo. App. 1984), the testator devised his home to "Mr. and Mrs. Wendell Richard

---

11. As a consequence, the fact that Roxy Russell predeceased the testatrix is of no legal import. As appears, we have disposed of the issue raised by plaintiff's frontal attack on the eligibility of the dog to take a testamentary gift and therefore need not concern ourselves with the novel question as to whether the death of the dog during the lifetime of the testatrix resulted in a lapsed gift. (§92.)

12. Admission of evidence to clarify a latent ambiguity first began in cases of equivocation, where a description fits two or more external objects equally well (e.g., a devise "to my niece Alicia," when in fact testator has two nieces named Alicia). The courts reasoned that the extrinsic evidence did not add anything to the will, which would be forbidden; the evidence merely made the terms of the will more specific. Admission of evidence has since been extended to all latent ambiguities.

Where there is an equivocation, direct expressions of the testator's intent are admissible in evidence. Since a latent ambiguity is not easily distinguishable from an equivocation, courts today often admit the testator's direct declarations of intent in virtually all cases of latent ambiguity, while excluding such declarations where there is a patent ambiguity. Oral declarations of intent to the *scrivener* are admitted in most jurisdictions in case of any type of ambiguity.

Hess, or the survivor of them, presently residing at No. 17 Barbara Circle." When the will was executed in 1979, Wendell Hess and his wife Glenda resided at No. 17 Barbara Circle. Soon thereafter Wendell divorced Glenda, they sold No. 17 Barbara Circle, and Wendell married Verna. At the testator's death in 1983, Verna, relying on the rule that a will speaks as of the testator's death, claimed the "Mrs. Hess" share of the devise. She argued that no extrinsic evidence should be admitted since there was no ambiguity in the will — she alone met the description of "Mrs. Wendell Richard Hess." The court, however, found that a latent ambiguity arose from the description of the beneficiaries as "residing at No. 17 Barbara Circle." (Why was not this struck out as a misdescription? See supra page 213.) Verna Hess met the description of Mrs. Wendell Richard Hess at the time of the testator's death but she never resided at No. 17 Barbara Circle. Glenda met the description of the Mrs. Hess residing at No. 17 Barbara Circle when the will was executed but she no longer met that description at the time of the testator's death. The court admitted extrinsic evidence that, the court decided, showed an intent that Glenda — who shared a common interest in antiques with the testator — take.

Another recent latent ambiguity case involved a bequest by an Iowa testator to his "nieces and nephews." Although these terms are usually taken to refer only to those related by blood, the testator had but one niece and one nephew by blood. The plural reference created a latent ambiguity. Extrinsic evidence showed that the testator intended his 19 nieces and nephews by marriage to share. In re Estate of Anderson, 359 N.W.2d 479 (Iowa 1984).

A patent ambiguity is an ambiguity that appears on the face of the will. In some states evidence is not admissible to clarify the ambiguity, but courts often have disposed of the problem by simply construing the language of the will without the aid of extrinsic evidence. For example, in Estate of Akeley, 35 Cal. 2d 26, 215 P.2d 921 (1950), the testator, purporting to devise her entire estate, gave 25 percent to each of three charities. The court construed the clause to give one-third shares to each charity on the theory that the testator intended to devise her entire estate.[13] And in Smith v. Burt, 388 Ill. 162, 57 N.E.2d 493, 157 A.L.R. 1118 (1944), the testator, a distinguished judge, devised to

---

13. Devises of fractional shares that total less or more than one remind us of the old brainteaser about a man whose will specified that his 11 horses be divided so that his eldest son would get $\frac{1}{2}$, his middle son would get $\frac{1}{4}$, and his youngest son would get $\frac{1}{6}$. When he died, his executor could not figure out how to carry out these instructions. After all, horses are of little value when sliced into fractional parts. The executor went to a lawyer for advice. The lawyer solved the problem. How? The lawyer lent the executor his horse. The 12 animals were then easily divided according to the formula in the will, the eldest son getting six, the middle son three, and the youngest two. One horse was then left over, which was returned to the lawyer. That's horse sense for you!

A 80 acres out of the Station Street Farm and to *B* the remaining 140 acres of the same farm. The patent ambiguity is: Which 80 acres? The court held that *A* had no right of selection, which other courts might have given *A*, but that *A* and *B* were intended to be tenants in common in fractional shares in the farm. See Stephenson v. Rowe, 315 N.C. 330, 338 S.E.2d 301 (1986) (holding devisee has power to select 30 acres out of 164 and discussing other alternative constructions and cases from many states); Annot., 35 A.L.R.4th 788 (1985).

The distinction between patent and latent ambiguities is of diminishing importance. Many courts now admit extrinsic evidence where there is any ambiguity, latent or patent.

NOTE: LIABILITY FOR DRAFTING AMBIGUOUS WILL

When a lawyer has drafted an ambiguous will, should the lawyer be liable in malpractice for any costs and loss from litigation of the will? In Ventura County Humane Society v. Holloway, 40 Cal. App. 3d 897, 115 Cal. Rptr. 464 (1974), the court held that although an attorney is liable to testamentary beneficiaries if the beneficiaries clearly designated by the testator lose their legacy as a direct result of the attorney's negligence, the attorney is not liable for drafting an ambiguous document. "[T]he task of proving whether the claimed ambiguity was the result of negligence of the drafting attorney or whether it was the deliberate choice of the testator, would impose an insurmountable burden on the parties. . . . The duty thus created would amount to a requirement to draft litigation-proof legal documents . . . [and would be an] almost intolerable burden on the legal profession." The case is criticized in Comment, 24 UCLA L. Rev. 422 (1976). Compare St. Mary's Church of Schuyler v. Tomek, 212 Neb. 728, 325 N.W.2d 164 (1982), where the court avoided the question of liability for ambiguous drafting by holding that will beneficiaries cannot sue the lawyer because of a lack of privity of contract.

Connecticut Junior Republic v. Sharon Hospital
Supreme Court of Connecticut, 1982
188 Conn. 1, 448 A.2d 190

[The testator, Richard Emerson, executed a will on May 19, 1960, which created trusts for a designated person for life, remainder to seven named charities (the 1960 charities). In 1969, Emerson executed a codicil to his will deleting six of the seven 1960 charities and substituting for the six as remaindermen 11 different charities (the

1969 charities). Soon after this codicil was executed, the Internal Revenue Code was amended to deny the charitable deduction to bequests of remainders unless made in a certain specified form (see infra page 1018); the remainders in Emerson's 1969 codicil did not qualify. The executor and trustee of Emerson's will, Sager McDonald, called this point to the attention of Emerson in 1975, and Emerson instructed his attorney to amend the will and codicil in such a manner as to qualify the trusts as charitable bequests under the Tax Reform Act of 1969, so that the value of the remainders given to charity would be deductible on Emerson's federal estate tax return. The attorney drafted a second codicil, making the requested changes but also mistakenly reinstating the 1960 charities as remaindermen and deleting the 1969 charities. Emerson, who had never requested or authorized this change, signed the second codicil in 1975. Upon Emerson's death in 1979, the probate court admitted the second codicil to probate, refusing to permit introduction of extrinsic evidence as to the scrivener's mistake. The superior court affirmed. The plaintiffs (1969 charities) appeal.]

HEALEY, J. The plaintiffs claim that the lower court erred (1) in failing to find a distinction between a "will construction" proceeding and a proceeding to "admit a will to probate"; (2) in failing to hold that Connecticut cases support the admissibility of extrinsic evidence to prove that material has been mistakenly inserted into a testamentary instrument; (3) in holding that the second codicil contained no inconsistencies or ambiguities; and (4) in holding that the policy behind the statute of wills is inconsistent with the admissibility of extrinsic evidence to prove lack of testamentary intent for any valid reason including mistake.

I

The plaintiffs' first argument states that since the issue in this case is the validity of the second codicil and not its meaning, extrinsic evidence should be admissible to prove the scrivener's error. Specifically, they claim that courts which have considered the question have made a distinction between proceedings to admit a will to probate and will construction proceedings, holding or recognizing that extrinsic evidence showing a scrivener's error is admissible in the former but not in the latter proceeding, absent an ambiguity. See Annot., 90 A.L.R.2d 924, 931. Because of the scrivener's error, the plaintiffs claim that the mistake in reinstating the 1960 charities into the second codicil should have been allowed to have been proven by extrinsic evidence and should not have been admitted to probate. The lower court rejected this argument. . . .

In Connecticut, our cases have not, to this point, distinguished between the two types of proceedings. See Stearns v. Stearns, 103 Conn. 213, 130 A. 112 (1925) (will construction proceeding); Comstock v. Hadlyme Ecclesiastical Society, 8 Conn. 254 (1830) (proceeding to establish a will); Avery v. Chappel, 6 Conn. 270 (1826) (proceeding to establish a will). Neither the plaintiffs nor the defendants have presented us with any Connecticut authority which recognizes any distinction between the rules of evidence applicable to either of these two forms of proceedings. While it is obvious that the purpose behind each type of proceeding may be different, we are not inclined to establish a rule which would effectuate such a distinction. It would be unwise to maintain a separate rule regarding the admission of extrinsic evidence for each of these two proceedings. This is because a litigant, knowing that more favorable evidentiary rules await those with claims of mistake due to scrivener's error, will always strive to phrase his argument in a way so to state such a claim. . . .

This result would elevate the form over the substance of the argument and transform probate proceedings into mere semantic exercises. As an example, we point to the situation where a beneficiary under an unambiguous will, which also contains a scrivener's error, or words which effectuate a different result than that allegedly intended, knows that the extrinsic evidence demonstrating the mistake or a different intention than that expressed in the will is inadmissible in a will construction proceeding. To avoid this substantive barrier, he can merely rephrase his argument to allege that the scrivener did not follow instructions and, therefore, the will, even though otherwise validly executed, should not be admitted to probate since it does not represent the testator's true intention. See Stearns v. Stearns, supra, 103 Conn. 223, 130 A. 112; see also Travelers Bank & Trust Co. v. Birge, 136 Conn. 21, 27, 68, A.2d 138 (1949). Such a situation would expose many wills to litigation merely because a disappointed beneficiary did not receive exactly what he thought the testator would leave him. If a testator, during his lifetime, represented to a beneficiary that he would receive a certain bequest and, later, the testator changed the bequest in his will but neglected to inform the beneficiary, the beneficiary, knowing that extrinsic evidence is admissible in one but not the other proceeding, could certainly at least allege a scrivener's error and challenge the will's admission to probate on the basis that the testamentary document did not represent the true intent of the testator. This would tend to produce needless litigation by transforming a simple will construction proceeding into an admission to probate problem where no problem may have actually existed.

In order to avoid this, we believe that the better course is to recognize that the same evidentiary rules apply to both types of proceedings.

II

We now turn to the major issue presented by this case. The trial court held that

> parol evidence may not be admitted in the instant case to show that the scrivener erred in drafting the codicil or that the testator mistakenly signed it. Connecticut law does not allow extrinsic evidence of a testator's intent to be admitted in cases dealing with either will construction or cases challenging the probate of an instrument. While there is an exception to this rule when there is ambiguity on the face of the will or codicil itself, this exception is not applicable in the instant case.

We agree with the trial court.

There is no dispute that

> [w]hile extrinsic evidence may be admitted to identify the devisee or legatee named, or the property described in a will, also to make clear the doubtful meaning of language used in a will, it is never admissible, however clearly it may indicate the testator's intention, for the purpose of showing an intention not expressed in the will itself, nor for the purpose of proving a devise or bequest not contained in the will. It is "a settled principle, that the construction of a will must be derived from the words of it, and not from extrinsic averment." Greene v. Dennis, 6 Conn. 292, 299 [1826]. . . .

One annotator puts it this way:

> What the courts really mean when they say that parol evidence is not admissible to correct a mistake is that where the will as it stands is intelligible and is applicable with certainty to some person or thing in existence, such evidence is not competent to show the testator's intention to designate some other person or thing. In other words, the rule against admitting extrinsic evidence to correct mistakes or supply omissions in wills amounts to no more than a slightly different statement or application of the general rule against varying, contradicting, or adding to the terms of the will. Annot., 94 A.L.R. 26, 68-69.

A number of our cases shed light on the question of whether, in the absence of an ambiguity, extrinsic evidence may be admitted to show a scrivener's error. In an early "admission to probate" case, Comstock v. Hadlyme Ecclesiastical Society, 8 Conn. 254 (1830), the appellants argued that since the scrivener drafted the will contrary to the testatrix' instructions and since the testatrix executed the will without knowledge of the mistake, the instrument, as drawn, did not represent her will and should not have been admitted to probate. Id., 258. The appellants were the grandchildren and only heirs at law of the testatrix and claimed that the will was void because the scrivener failed to include a legacy of $100 to each of them as the testatrix had directed. The court held that such evidence of a scrivener's error was not admissible and stated:

> The statute, when it required all wills to be in writing, signed by the testator and attested by witnesses, certainly intended, that the evidence, and the whole evidence, of the disposition of property by will, should be the will itself; that the evidence of the intent of the devisor should be derived from the writing, signed by him and solemnly attested; otherwise, innumerable would be the cases where evidence of mistake would be claimed and proved. Id., 265-66.

[Discussion of other Connecticut cases, denying admission of extrinsic evidence to give relief from mistake in the process of construing wills, is omitted.]

There is no error.

PETERS, J. (dissenting).[14] . . . Must the true intent of the testator be thwarted when, because of the mistake of a scrivener, he has formally subscribed to a written bequest that substantially misstates his testamentary intention? For all practical purposes, this is a question of first impression in this state, certainly in this state in this century. I would permit extrinsic evidence of a scrivener's error to be introduced in litigation concerned with the admissibility of a disputed will to probate.

I take as a point of departure the established proposition that a will cannot validly be probated if it is executed by a testator in reliance on erroneous beliefs induced by fraud, duress, or undue influence. In all of these cases, the testamentary process is distorted by the interference of a third person who misleads the testator into making a testamentary disposition that would not otherwise have occurred. There is a similar distortion when a will is executed in reliance on erroneous beliefs induced by the innocent error, by the innocent misrepresentation, of the scrivener of a will. I can see no reason of logic or of policy to treat the mistake case differently from the fraud or undue influence case. In each instance, extrinsic evidence is required to demonstrate that a will, despite its formally proper execution, substantially misrepresents the true intent of the testator. . . .

Had the decedent's lawyer deliberately and fraudulently altered the second codicil, the relevant extrinsic evidence would unquestionably have been admitted. Under the modern law of misrepresentation,

---

14. Justice Ellen Ash Peters was a professor of contracts law at Yale prior to her appointment to the Connecticut Supreme Court in 1978. The first woman to sit on that court, Justice Peters was appointed Chief Justice in 1984. — Eds.

innocent misrepresentation is treated as generally equivalent to fraud in terms of its legal consequences. See Johnson v. Healy, 176 Conn. 97, 100, 405 A.2d 54 (1978). To allow the admissibility of extrinsic evidence to turn on the scrivener's fraudulent intent or lack thereof is to distort the purpose of a Probate Court. Its proper business is to determine what instrument, if any, the decedent properly executed as his will. Gray, "Striking Words Out of a Will," 26 Harv. L. Rev. 212, 217 (1913). The guilt or negligence of third parties is only incidentally relevant to such a determination, since the effect on the testator's mind of either fraud or mistake is subjectively the same. The Statute of Wills does not compel enforcement of testamentary dispositions that a testator never intended to make. . . .

Objection to the admission of extrinsic evidence . . . [rests on] a fear that allowing extrinsic evidence of mistake will give rise to a proliferation of groundless will contests. There is no doubt that our increasingly fact-based jurisprudence serves to expose many apparently final dispositions to the juridical risk of unjustified judicial intervention. In the law of contracts, where the parol evidence rule has undergone considerable erosion, this risk has not been found to be unmanageable. In the law of wills, the risk is limited by the narrowness of the exception that this case would warrant. I would today do no more than permit the opponent of a will to introduce extrinsic evidence of the error of a scrivener, and would require proof of such an extrinsic error to be established by clear and convincing evidence. See Lopinto v. Haines, 185 Conn. (43 C.L.J. 23, pp. 1, 4) 441 A.2d 551 (1981).

In sum, I see no greater risk of juridical error in the case of a scrivener's error than in the case of fraud or undue influence. I find it difficult to draw a clear line of demarcation between a scrivener's mistake and an innocent misrepresentation. I believe that the true interests of a testator are better protected by admitting rather than suppressing evidence of substantial third party interference with the formulation of a testamentary disposition. Wills that do not reflect the true intent of the testator should be refused probate.

NOTES

1. In Connecticut Junior Republic v. Doherty, 20 Mass. App. Ct. 107, 478 N.E.2d 735 (1985), the charities mentioned in Richard Emerson's 1969 will sued the lawyer who drafted the 1975 codicil (Doherty) for negligence. They claimed the negligence cost them $1,305,060 in lost bequests. The court held that the presumption that the testator who signs a will knows its contents was reinforced by the testimony of the testator's executor and trustee, Sager McDonald, that he had read

the contents of the will twice to the testator. Thus the change in beneficiaries, set in motion by Doherty's mistake, was ratified by the testator's knowledge of the will contents. The draftsman was not liable.

2. In some recent cases, courts have openly and directly remedied mistakes by the scrivener. In In re Estate of Ikuta, 639 P.2d 400 (Haw. 1981), the court substituted the word "youngest" for the word "oldst [oldest]" where extrinsic evidence showed that "oldst" did not make sense and was a scrivener's mistake. Where there has been an accidental omission by the scrivener or typist, courts have sometimes inserted the missing words when convinced from the face of the will and extrinsic evidence what missing words were intended. In Wilson v. First Florida Bank, 498 So. 2d 1289 (Fla. App. 1986), a will disposed of personal items, made pecuniary gifts, then said "To the University of Georgia" for a scholarship fund, but did not say what was given the university. The court admitted extrinsic evidence, including the embarrassed draftsman's testimony, and held that the will gave the residue to the university. Accord, McCauley v. Alexander, 543 S.W.2d 699 (Tex. Civ. App. 1976). But see Farmers & Merchants Bank of Keyser v. Farmers & Merchants Bank of Keyser, 216 S.E.2d 769 (W. Va. 1975) (refusing to admit lawyer's testimony that the testator intended to leave $35,000 to her church when amount accidentally omitted by the typist). In line with a growing trend to remedy scrivener's mistakes, perhaps pushed along by attorney liability for malpractice, English Administration of Justice Act 1982, Pt. IV, §20, provides for reformation of a will because of clerical error or failure to understand the testator's instructions.

3. In Estate of Taff, 63 Cal. App. 3d 319, 133 Cal. Rptr. 737 (1976), the testator devised the residue of her estate to her sister Margaret and if Margaret was not living at the testator's death "to my heirs in accordance with the laws of intestate succession, in effect at my death in the State of California." Under the laws of California, the testator's property would pass by intestate succession one-half to her natural heirs (some nieces and a nephew) and one-half to her predeceased husband's heirs. Extrinsic evidence, in the form of a written declaration by the testator to her sister and oral declarations by the testator to the attorney who drafted the will, was held admissible to show that the testator intended only her blood relatives to take as "my heirs." In *Taff* the extrinsic evidence was used to contradict the will. Was the evidence admitted in violation of the statement in *Russell*, supra page 325, that "any proferred evidence attempting to show an intention *different* from that expressed by the words therein, giving them only the meaning to which they are reasonably susceptible, is inadmissible"? See Langbein & Waggoner, Reformation of Wills on the Ground of Mistake: Change of Direction in American Law?, 130 U. Pa. L. Rev. 521, 557 (1982).

Compare Gustafson v. Svenson, 373 Mass. 273, 366 N.E.2d 761 (1977), where the will left part of the residuary estate to Enoch Anderson or "his heirs per stirpes," and Enoch predeceased the testator leaving a wife but no issue. Under Massachusetts law, Enoch's widow was his heir. The court held that testimony of the drafting attorney that the testator did not intend that Enoch's share go to his widow was inadmissible since the phrase "heirs per stirpes" was not ambiguous; hence Enoch's widow took his share.

NOTE: CORRECTING MISTAKES

A mistake in the inducement involves an error as to the facts outside the instrument itself. The testator may be mistaken about what property the testator owns, or about the conduct or status of the beneficiaries. When there has been a mistake in the inducement, courts ordinarily deny relief except possibly in the rare case where the will itself shows both the testator's mistaken belief and what the testator would have done had the mistake not occurred.

Three cases will suffice as illustrations. In In re Garrison's Estate, 374 S.W.2d 92 (Mo. 1964), Charles Garrison's father devised his 80-acre homeplace as follows: 40 acres to Charles in fee simple and 40 acres to Charles for life, remainder to Charles's daughter, Gladys, in fee simple. Although his father's will seems clear enough, Charles for some reason thought that Gladys would take the entire 80 acres upon his death. Charles's will provided: "I give and bequeath unto my daughter, Gladys Garrison, the sum of One Dollar ($1.00). This bequest is no indication of my love and affection for my daughter, Gladys Garrison, but inasmuch as she will receive at the time of my death 80 acres of land under the Last Will and Testament of my father, Robert Garrison, I have, therefore, reduced her gifts under this will." The court refused to give any relief for this mistake, and Gladys took only the 40 acres given her in remainder by her grandfather.

In Carpenter v. Tinney, 420 S.W.2d 241 (Tex. Civ. App. 1967), the testator's will made token bequests to two of her children and devised the residue of her estate to her other two children. Testimony was offered that tended to show that the testator believed her husband had a will devising all his estate to the two children given token bequests, that her will was motivated by a desire to equalize distribution of their property among the four children, and that had the testator not been mistaken as to the terms of her husband's will (he died intestate), she would have devised her estate to all four children in equal shares. The trial court's refusal to submit the issue of mistaken inducement to the jury was sustained on appeal.

Finally, in York v. Smith, 385 So. 2d 1110 (Fla. App. 1980), a will devising the testator's entire estate to his brother, and disinheriting his daughter Julie, was admitted into probate, even though the evidence showed that the will was written while the testator was under a mistaken belief that he was not Julie's father.

Standard doctrine says that the law does not cure mistakes in the law of wills because the court cannot give effect to unattested writing. No extrinsic evidence of a different intent is admissible. But there are numerous exceptions to this rule. Although courts say they cannot supply missing language, they can strike out a mistaken description (see supra page 213). Courts may remedy a mistaken belief about a member of the family by calling it an insane delusion (see supra page 134). Courts may also remedy mistake in the revocation of wills under the doctrine of dependent relative revocation (see supra page 236). Courts reform violations of the Rule against Perpetuities in some jurisdictions (see infra page 839). And, under the guise of construction, courts may remedy mistakes. The Uniform Probate Code remedies mistake in one context. Section 2-302(b), infra page 428, provides that if a testator fails to provide for a living child solely because he mistakenly believes the child to be dead, the child receives an intestate share in the testator's estate.

Finding the law of mistake a jumble that often results in unjust enrichment of the unintended donee at the expense of the intended donee, and pointing out that mistakes in contracts or trusts can be reformed, Professors Langbein and Waggoner propose a way to bring order and rationality to the law of mistake. They suggest correcting a mistake where the error is shown to have affected specific terms in the will and the mistake involves a fact or event of such particularity that it is susceptible of proof (thus not remedying a claim of "if Aunt Jane had known how much I loved her, she would have left me more"). Langbein and Waggoner believe that the essential safeguard in reforming nonprobate transfers is a requirement of clear and convincing evidence of mistake, more than just a preponderance of the evidence, and they would require that this high standard of proof be met to remedy mistakes in probate transfers. See Langbein & Waggoner, Reformation of Wills on the Ground of Mistake: Change of Direction in American Law?, 130 U. Pa. L. Rev. 521, 577-588 (1982).

Is it better to remedy mistakes by correcting them or by holding the lawyer liable for malpractice? See id. at 588-590.

NOTE: IMPLYING BEQUESTS TO FILL GAPS IN DISPOSITION

One of the recurring oversights in drafting is to leave a gap in the dispositive provisions. A particular contingency (which occurs) is not provided for. Here is an example that pops up with some frequency. *H*'s will leaves all to *W; W*'s will leaves all to *H*. Both wills provide that if *H* and *W* die in a common disaster, everything is to go to *A*. But neither will provides what happens if one spouse predeceases the other (except in a common disaster). What distribution is made of *W*'s property, when *H* predeceases her? Is there an implied gift to *A*? Did the testators intend a gift to *A* after this sequence of deaths, unintentionally overlooked by the drafter? The usual answer is that a gift to *A* will not be implied, but there are cases contrary. See Larison v. Record, 117 Ill. 2d 444, 512 N.E.2d 1251 (1987); In re Estate of Kronen, 67 N.Y.2d 587, 496 N.E.2d 670, 505 N.Y.S.2d 589 (1986); New Mexico Boys Ranch, Inc. v. Hanvey, 97 N.M. 771, 643 P.2d 857 (1982), noted 14 N.M.L. Rev. 419 (1983) (contra). On the drafter's liability for malpractice for this oversight, see Ogle v. Fuiten, 102 Ill. 2d 356, 466 N.E.2d 224 (1984), supra page 70.

To fill gaps in wills, New Jersey (apparently alone among the states) has developed a *doctrine of probable intent.* If a contingency for which no provision is made in the will occurs, the court studies the family circumstances and the plan of testamentary disposition set forth in the will. Then the court places itself in the position of the testator and decides how the testator probably would have responded to the contingency had he envisioned its occurrence. The court has even applied the doctrine to exclude the application of an anti-lapse statute when the court found the testator probably intended a result inconsistent with the anti-lapse statute. Engle v. Siegel, 74 N.J. 287, 377 A.2d 892 (1977).[15] No other jurisdiction so boldly reforms drafting oversights.

Although courts other than New Jersey's usually say they will not imply bequests, which would be adding words to the will, in fact bequests are implied in a number of circumstances where trusts are created by will. As we shall see later, an invasion power may be implied in the life tenant, infra page 568; a general gift to charity may be implied where the gift to a particular charity fails, infra page 591; a gift in default of appointment to the donee's children may be implied where the donee has a power to appoint among children and there is no gift in default, infra page 751; and a gift of principal may be implied when the income

---

15. In Engle v. Siegel, a husband and wife and their children died in a fire. The couple's assets derived almost entirely from the husband's earnings. The court imputed an intent to the husband to divide the assets equally between the husband's family and the wife's family. Here again, as in In re Honigman, supra page 134, we find a court manipulating doctrine to overcome consequences of a separate property regime for marital property and reaching results consistent with a community property system.

Although there is not enough evidence to call such manipulation a trend, we expect — with the widespread adoption of equitable division of spousal property upon divorce — that in will cases courts will more and more be persuaded to reach results consistent with equal sharing of spousal property, especially of a long marriage.

is given without limitation of time. Somehow or other, when a trust is involved a court feels freer to imply gifts, even though the trust was established by the will of the settlor and the court is implicitly adding words to the will.

Gifts may also be implied by the process of construction. For example, in Estate of Kime, 144 Cal. App. 3d 246, 193 Cal. Rptr. 718 (1983), the testator, using a printed form, filled in blanks as italicized here ("I appoint *Betty J. Hyde* as Execu*tris* of this Will"), but she failed to name a beneficiary. The court ordered the admission of evidence, including oral declarations, tending to show that the testator believed the printed word "appoint" designated a beneficiary and the word "executris" meant one to receive her estate.

Professor Mary Louise Fellows argues that the goal of the law in giving effect to distributive provisions of wills should be to accord all property owners the benefit of competent estate planning advice. Therefore the law should abandon the search for individual subjective intent when there is no objective evidence of intent. Instead, a court should remedy ambiguities, mistakes, and omissions by imputing that the testator intended what a competent estate planner would do, preferring traditional distribution schemes favoring equality within the family. Fellows, In Search of Donative Intent, 73 Iowa L. Rev. 611 (1988). Where the testator has atypical family relationships or wants a unique estate plan, neither traditional rules nor Fellows's theory of imputed intent of good estate planning may permit a court to salvage a botched-up job.

SECTION B.   DEATH OF BENEFICIARY BEFORE DEATH OF TESTATOR: LAPSE

The most common drafter's oversight is the failure to provide what disposition is to be made if a named beneficiary predeceases the testator. When this occurs, the gift lapses (i.e., fails). However, nearly all states have enacted anti-lapse statutes designed to provide a substitute beneficiary for the deceased devisee in certain situations.

Before turning to anti-lapse statutes, let us first note the common law rules regarding lapsed gifts. If a specific or general devise lapses, the devise falls into the residue. For example, if *T* bequeaths his watch (a specific bequest) and $10,000 (a general bequest) to *A*, and *A* predeceases *T*, the watch and the $10,000 go to the residuary devisee. See Uniform Probate Code §2-606(a), below. If the devise of the entire residue lapses, because the sole residuary devisee or all the residuary devisees predecease the testator, the heirs of the testator take. If a share of the residue lapses (such as happens when one of two residuary devisees predeceases testator), the common law rule is that a lapsed or void residuary share passes by intestacy to the testator's heirs rather than to the remaining residuary devisees. This rule was followed in Estate of Russell, supra page 321. This common law rule possibly arose because of the English courts' desire to pass property to the primogenitary heir, but in any case it does not carry out the average testator's intent and has been roundly criticized by courts and commentators alike. The rule has been overturned by statute or judicial decision in many states and is clearly on its way out. See Uniform Probate Code §2-606(b), below, providing that if the anti-lapse statute does not apply to the dead residuary devisee's share, the share goes to the other residuary devisees. These common law rules (and anti-lapse statutes) are default rules; they apply only if the will does not provide what happens when a beneficiary predeceases the testator.

Now let us turn to the effect of an anti-lapse statute upon a lapsed gift. The Uniform Probate Code lapse provisions are typical of anti-lapse statutes.

Uniform Probate Code (1983)

§2-601   [Requirement that Devisee Survive Testator by 120 Hours]

A devisee who does not survive the testator by 120 hours is treated as if he predeceased the testator, unless the will of decedent contains some language dealing explicitly with simultaneous deaths or deaths in a common disaster, or requiring that the devisee survive the testator or survive the testator for a stated period in order to take under the will.

§2-605   [Anti-lapse; Deceased Devisee; Class Gifts]

If a devisee who is a grandparent or a lineal descendant of a grandparent of the testator is dead at the time of execution of the will, fails to survive the testator, or is treated as if he predeceased the testator, the issue of the deceased devisee who survive the testator by 120 hours take in place of the deceased devisee and if they are all of the same degree of kinship to the devisee they take equally, but if of unequal degree then those of more remote degree take by representation. One who would have been a devisee under a class gift if he had survived the testator is treated as a devisee for purposes of this section whether his death occurred before or after the execution of the will.

§2-606 [FAILURE OF TESTAMENTARY PROVISION]

(a) Except as provided in Section 2-605 if a devise other than a residuary devise fails for any reason, it becomes a part of the residue.

(b) Except as provided in Section 2-605 if the residue is devised to two or more persons and the share of one of the residuary devisees fails for any reason, his share passes to the other residuary devisee, or to other residuary devisees in proportion to their interests in the residue.

Although the Uniform Probate Code is typical, in actuality state anti-lapse statutes differ in many details among themselves. Most of these differences can be noted in an examination of the UPC. First, the Uniform Probate Code requires a person to survive the testator by 120 hours in order to be a "survivor." This is a minority rule. The majority of statutes requires only that the beneficiary survive the testator in order to take — survival for any instant of time is sufficient.[16] Second, anti-lapse statutes apply only if the beneficiary comes within the relationship to the testator specified in the statute. Observe that UPC §2-605 applies only to devises to a person who is a grandparent or lineal descendant of a grandparent of the testator. It does not apply to devises to spouses, kindred of spouses, remote cousins, or friends. Some state statutes are narrower than UPC §2-605, applying only to devises to descendants of the testator or only to devises to parents of the testator and their descendants. Others are broader, applying to devises to all blood kindred, or to the spouse, or to relatives of spouses, or to all devisees. Third, under UPC §2-605 the deceased beneficiary's share goes to the beneficiary's surviving issue. This is true of almost all anti-lapse statutes, though one or two give the share to the deceased beneficiary's heirs or devisees. In the overwhelming majority of states, the gift lapses and is not saved by an anti-lapse statute if the beneficiary leaves no surviving issue. For an examination of anti-lapse statutes in all states, see French, Antilapse Statutes Are Blunt Instruments: A Blueprint for Reform, 37 Hast. L.J. 335 (1985) (discussing the inequit-

---

16. In Estate of Rowley, 257 Cal. App. 2d 324, 65 Cal. Rptr. 139 (1967), the jury found that the legatee survived the testator by 1/150,000th of a second and hence was entitled to the legacy. The decision was affirmed on appeal.

able results often reached through application or nonapplication of the anti-lapse statute); Roberts, Lapse Statutes: Recurring Construction Problems, 37 Emory L.J. 323 (1988).

Most anti-lapse statutes, like UPC §2-605, are too narrowly conceived. There is little empirical evidence to support the idea that the testator wants issue of blood relatives only to take a gift to a deceased beneficiary. The result is that, to carry out intent, courts struggle to find an alternative gift to issue in the will or, as we shall see, manipulate the concept of a "class" where there are two or more beneficiaries.

In re Estate of Ulrikson
Supreme Court of Minnesota, 1980
290 N.W.2d 757

YETKA, J.   In this contest over the construction of a residuary clause of a will, the Hennepin County Probate Court held the anti-lapse statute, Minn. Stat. §524.2-605 (1978), to be applicable. A three-judge panel appointed by the Chief Judge of the district court for the Fourth Judicial District affirmed. This court granted appellants' application for leave to appeal. We affirm.

The sole issue in this case is whether Minn. Stat. §524.2-605 (1978), the anti-lapse statute, applies where the residuary estate is given to a brother and sister, "and in the event that either one of them shall predecease me, then to the other surviving brother or sister," but in fact both brother and sister predecease the testatrix, the brother leaving issue.

This case is before the court on stipulated facts which can be summarized as follows: Bellida Ulrikson died testate in 1976 with a will drafted in 1971. The will made specific bequests of $1,000 each to nine nieces and nephews and two nieces by marriage; each respondent and appellant received one of these bequests. The residue is to be distributed as follows:

> SIXTH, All the rest, residue and remainder of my property of whatever kind or character, I give and bequeath to my brother MELVIN HOVLAND, and my sister, RODINE HELGER, share and share alike, and in the event that either one of them shall predecease me, then to the other surviving brother or sister.

Melvin Hovland and Rodine Helger were both alive when the will was drafted. Melvin Hovland died in 1974 and left surviving two children, Annabelle Erickson and Mavis Barth. Rodine Helger died in 1975 without issue. If the anti-lapse statute is applied to the residuary clause, the residue passes in equal shares to respondents Annabelle Erickson and Mavis Barth. Both lower courts so ordered.

In 1971, two other siblings of Bellida Ulrikson were deceased; namely, Sena Olson and Louis Hovland. These two siblings had seven surviving children in 1971, and the will gives $1,000 to each. Before 1976, three of these nieces and nephews died without issue, and one died leaving issue. Under the laws of intestacy, therefore, the residue would be divided into six shares among Tillman Olson, Leonard Olson, Guy Olson (appellants), Annabelle Erickson, Mavis Barth (respondents), and the issue of Eleanor Yankowiak[17] by right of representation. Minn. Stat. §525.16(4)(d) (1978).

The applicable Minnesota statutes, which incorporate portions of the Uniform Probate Code, contain the following provisions:

> 524.2-603 *Rules of construction and intention.* The intention of a testator as expressed in his will controls the legal effect of his dispositions. The rules of construction expressed in the succeeding sections of this part apply unless a contrary intention is indicated by the will.
>
> 524.2-604 *Construction that will passes all property; after acquired property.* A will is construed to pass all property which the testator owns at his death including property acquired after the execution of the will.
>
> 524.2-605 *Anti-lapse; deceased devisee; class gifts.* If a devisee who is a grandparent or a lineal descendant of a grandparent of the testator is dead at the time of execution of the will, or fails to survive the testator, the issue of the deceased devisee who survive the testator take in place of the deceased devisee and if they are all of the same degree of kinship to the devisee they take equally, but if of unequal degree then those of more remote degree take by representation. One who is a grandparent or a lineal descendant of a grandparent of the testator and who would have been a devisee under a class gift if he had survived the testator is treated as a devisee for purposes of this section whether his death occurred before or after the execution of the will.

Minn. Stat. §§524.2-603 to 524.2-605 (1978). Upon reading these statutes together, it is apparent that the law prefers testacy over intestacy and that the anti-lapse statute applies unless a contrary intention is indicated by the will.

The appellants argue that Bellida Ulrikson expressed an intention contrary to the application of the anti-lapse statute by the words "and in the event that either one of them shall predecease me, then to the other surviving brother or sister." They contend the testatrix intended to establish an absolute condition of survivorship to receive any residue.

---

17. The Eleanor Yankowiak sixth would be further divided with one-fifth going to each of Robert Yankowiak, Betty McCormick, Jerry Yankowiak and Allen Yankowiak and the last fifth in three equal shares to Daniel Brockmiller, David Brockmiller and Donald Brockmiller.

It is far more likely, however, as respondents contend, that Bellida Ulrikson simply did not contemplate that both her younger brother and sister would predecease her. The residuary clause in fact contains no instructions for the circumstances which occurred. In this case, we hold the words of survivorship to be effective only if there are survivors. Since there are no survivors in this case, the anti-lapse statute is free to operate.

The appellants further argue that by making a thousand-dollar bequest to each of her nieces and nephews, the testatrix expressed an intention to treat her legal heirs equally, and thus contrary to the anti-lapse statute. This argument loses sight of the fact that Melvin Hovland and Rodine Helger are preferred in the residuary clause of the will. The argument is further negated by the fact that two persons outside the testatrix's bloodline, the two "nieces by marriage," were also given thousand-dollar specific bequests.

In summary, this case appears to be precisely the type of case that our statutory scheme was designed to solve. Accordingly, the decision of the three-judge district court review panel is affirmed.

PROBLEMS

1. Suppose that Melvin Hovland had predeceased the testator but that Rodine Helger had survived. Would the anti-lapse statute apply to the devise to Melvin? Compare Estate of Kehler, 488 Pa. 165, 411 A.2d 749 (1980), where the testator devised his residuary estate to his brother and two sisters "and to the survivor or survivors of them." The brother predeceased the testator, leaving issue. The court held that the quoted language did not manifest a contrary intent; the anti-lapse statute applied, giving the brother's share to his issue.

2. Article 3 of *T*'s will devises Blackacre "to my son Sidney if he survives me." Article 4 devises "all the rest, residue and remainder of my estate to my wife Wanda." Sidney dies during *T*'s lifetime leaving two children. Then *T* dies; he is survived by his wife Wanda and by his two grandchildren. Who takes Blackacre? See Estate of Stroble, 6 Kan. App. 2d 955, 636 P.2d 236 (1981); Detzel v. Nieberding, 7 Ohio Misc. 262, 219 N.E.2d 327 (1966).

Suppose that Sidney dies one day after *T* and that UPC §2-601, supra page 341, is in effect. Suppose also that Sidney's will devised all his property to his wife. What result?

Jackson v. Schultz
Delaware Court of Chancery, 1959
38 Del. Ch. 332, 151 A.2d 284

MARVEL, V.C.   Plaintiffs, who are children of the late Bessie H. Bullock, have contracted to sell to defendant a house formerly owned by their stepfather the late Leonard S. Bullock, claiming to hold title to such property at 1012 Kirk Avenue in Wilmington under the terms of Mr. Bullock's will. Mr. Bullock, who had no children of his own, married plaintiffs' mother in 1918, caring for and supporting her three children during their minority, and continuing to support Beatrice after his wife's death some five years ago, a fact which is reflected in his income tax returns. He died on September 8, 1958.

Defendant has refused to perform the contract, claiming that plaintiffs' mother having predeceased the testator, plaintiffs took nothing under their stepfather's will of January 13, 1937, the controversial clause of which provides as follows:

"Second: I give, bequeath and devise unto my beloved wife, Bessie H. Bullock, all my property real, personal and mixed wheresoever situate and of whatever nature and kind, to her and her heirs and assigns forever."[18]

Defendant contends that when a devise is made to a named person, "his heirs and assigns forever," the heirs as such normally take nothing by way of substitution if the devisee predeceases the testator, such expression being deemed one of limitation defining the quantity of the estate devised. . . . In the absence of "something further" in the language used in a will the same rule has been applied in cases where the word "and" appears before the clause "heirs and assigns." . . . However, when "or" is used following a primary devise, the subsequent reference to "heirs" or the like has been deemed to designate those who will take by way of substitution in the event the primary devisee predeceased the testator, and a lapse is thereby avoided. . . .

It has also been held that the words "or" and "and" may be substituted for each other in arriving at a proper construction of a will, "and" having been read as "or" for the purpose of carrying out an obvious testamentary purpose in the cases of Kerrigan v. Tabb, N.J. Ch., 39 A. 701, and Huntress v. Place, 137 Mass. 409. . . .

According to the uncontroverted facts before me on plaintiffs' motion for summary judgment, the testator's father, a widower, died on January 7, 1936. He was survived by a brother, Harry, a step-son, Frederick, and his own son, Leonard. On January 18, 1936 these three survivors

---

18. At the time of this case, Delaware's anti-lapse statute applied only to devises and bequests to lineal descendants or brothers and sisters of the testator. In 1974 Delaware adopted §2-605 of the Uniform Probate Code, supra page 341, which applies to devises to the testator's grandparents and lineal descendants of grandparents. Del. Code Ann. tit. 12, §2313 (1987).

Should the anti-lapse statute be broadened to apply to devises to the testator's spouse? In a handful of states the anti-lapse statute applies to spouses. In Iowa the anti-lapse statute applies to all devisees *except* the spouse. Iowa Code Ann. §§633.273, 633.274 (1964). — Eds.

entered into an agreement which was designed to insure, inter alia, that in the event of Leonard's death during the settlement of his father's estate his share of such estate would go to his wife, Bessie, and not to his Uncle Harry, the latter agreeing to such an arrangement. Thus, while the legal theory of the agreement is dubious, it demonstrates Leonard S. Bullock's clear intent that his share of his father's estate should go to his wife and not to his only living blood relative. In his 1937 will, executed following settlement of his father's estate, he expressly directed that his entire estate should go to his wife, "to her and her heirs and assigns forever," and named her executrix.

In addition to this evidence of intent that his sole surviving blood relative should not share in his estate (Harry Bullock being the only one who would take in the absence of a will, there being no living brothers or sisters of either John, Harry or Leonard or descendants of any of them) there is the further fact that in 1939 Harry died. His wife having predeceased him and there being no known next of kin of the testator at the time of his death, his will should be read not only so as to carry out his intent but construed, if possible, so as to avoid not merely intestacy but a total escheat.

While the granting of a decree of specific performance is a matter requiring the exercise of judicial discretion, such decree should normally be granted in a land purchase case such as this unless to do so would require a buyer to accept a defective title subject to attack by an adverse interest not before the Court.... Here, however, their being no possibility of any adverse claim, according to the record before me, and being satisfied that there is a solid basis in law for sustaining plaintiffs' claim to a fee simple title in the lands here involved in the light of the uncontroverted facts, I am of the opinion that plaintiffs' motion should be granted.

There being a recognized rule of construction permitting "and" to be read as "or" when so to do will carry out the testator's intent in will construction cases such as this, I adopt such rule of construction in the light of the facts in the record before me. The language used by the draftsman of the will namely, ". . . to her and her heirs . . ." adapts readily to the rule which permits such a substitution, and were such rule not to be followed this is a case in which the total testamentary background calls for a finding of intent that a substitutionary gift over to the testator's stepchildren be made in the event of his wife's death prior to his own.

. . . Here the evidence sustains a ruling that the will be construed as making a substitutionary devise over to plaintiffs and their sister, persons whom the testator raised as his own, their mother having predeceased the testator.

Plaintiffs' motion for summary judgment is granted.

NOTES AND PROBLEMS

1. Hofing v. Willis, 31 Ill. 2d 365, 374, 201 N.E.2d 852, 856-857 (1964):

> While there is some support for the proposition that the phrase "and to their heirs" could be considered as words of purchase by reading the word "and" as "or," . . . the presence of the words "and assigns" makes such a construction unacceptable. If the word "and" is read "or," the language creates a substitutionary gift in favor of the "heirs and assigns" of George's sisters, who would take as purchasers. That a deceased sister's heirs should take as purchasers by way of substitution would be quite reasonable. But it is hardly reasonable to suppose that the grantor would create a substitutionary gift and at the same time designate the assigns of the named takers to take by way of substitution.

2. Nettie R. Robertson devised all the residue of her property "to Homer Shorts." Homer was a friend of Nettie's who predeceased her. Nettie died without known heirs. Homer's daughter, Carol, claimed the residue of Nettie's estate, contending that the devise meant "to Homer Shorts or his heirs." The court rejected Carol's claim, saying Carol's contention "is not resolution of ambiguity but a rewriting of the will. . . . [I]t is sought to establish the testatrix really meant something other than what she said clearly and concisely. There is no ambiguity asserted to be either established by or resolved by evidence extrinsic to the will." Boulger v. Evans, 54 Ohio St. 2d 371, 377 N.E.2d 753 (1978).

3. *H* devises ¾ of his estate to *W* and ¼ to charity. *H*'s two children are mentioned but not provided for in *H*'s will. *W* predeceases *H*. Who takes *H*'s estate?

4. Should the courts hold that if a beneficiary of a will substitute (such as life insurance, a contract not to revoke a will, a savings account trust, or a payable-on-death designation) does not survive the donor, the transfer lapses? See supra page 303. Should anti-lapse statutes be broadened to cover will substitutes? Should a court by analogy apply an anti-lapse statute to will substitutes?

———————

Class gifts. At common law, if there is a devise to a class, and one class member predeceases the testator, the surviving members of the class divide the gift. The share of the class member who predeceased does not lapse. Thus suppose that *T* bequeaths $10,000 to the children of her friend *A*, and that one child of *A*, named *B*, predeceases *T*, and that another child of *A*, named *C*, survives *T*. The $10,000 bequest goes to *C*.

The crucial question is: What is a class? A gift to persons described solely by a class label, such as "to *A*'s children," is a class gift. But a class label is not necessary for a class gift. If a group of persons described individually form a natural class, such as nieces and nephews, the gift may be determined to be a class gift. Thus in Sullivan v. Sullivan, 26 Mass. App. Ct. 502, 529 N.E.2d 890 (1988), where the testator devised property "to my nephews Marshall John McDonough, and David Condon McDonough, and to my niece Martha McDonough Sullivan, in equal shares, that is one-third each," and one nephew (Marshall) predeceased the testator without issue, the court held the devise was to a class and that the property was to be divided equally between the survivors David and Martha. Even a gift "to *H* and *W*" has been held to be a class gift (Eppes v. Locklin, 222 Ga. 86, 149 S.E.2d 148 (1966)), as has a devise "to Bessie and Louise," who happened to be the testator's close friends (Iozapavichus v. Fournier, 308 A.2d 573 (Me. 1973)).

In the final analysis, a court probably finds a class gift whenever it finds that the testator intended the consequences of a class gift or would have intended the consequences if the testator had thought about the matter. The exact language of the entire will and extrinsic evidence of the testator's intent are important in making this determination.

In re Moss

Court of Appeal, England, 1899
[1899] 2 Ch. 314, aff'd, [1901] A.C. 187 (H.L.)

Walter Moss by his will dated in 1876, after appointing his wife Elizabeth Moss and his niece Elizabeth Jane Fowler his executrixes, and making sundry devises and bequests, gave all his share or interest in the Daily Telegraph newspaper[19] unto the said E. Moss and E.J. Fowler "upon trust to pay the income thereof to my said wife for her life, and

---

19. The Daily Telegraph was organized as a partnership in 1855 by J.M. Levy. The Levy family held all but a one-eighth interest, which was sold to George Moss for £500. Moss is variously reported to have been the superintendent of Levy's printing plant or the owner of a public house nearby where the printers repaired for ale. The newspaper was an immediate success, selling for a penny a copy, featuring brilliant young writers on politics, and factually reporting titillating current court proceedings involving divorce, crime, and sex (a practice continuing to this day in most London newspapers). Levy invented the classified ad with a box number return to which persons could advertise for matrimonial or sexual partners. The Daily Telegraph, together with The New York Herald, sent Stanley to the rescue of Livingston. By the 1880s, the Daily Telegraph had the largest circulation in the world.

Moss's investment of £500 proved extremely profitable, soon returning £15,500 annually on Moss's capital investment. Walter Moss, the testator in the principal case, was the son of George Moss.

The Daily Telegraph remains today a leading London newspaper. See E. Burnham, Peterborough Court: The Story of the Daily Telegraph 1-3 (1955). — Eds.

after her decease, upon trust for the said E.J. Fowler and the child or children of my sister Emily Walter who shall attain the age of twenty-one years equally to be divided between them as tenants in common." And he gave the residue of his estate and effects to his wife. . . .

The testator died in 1893, and his will was proved by his widow, Elizabeth Moss, alone. At the date of his will there were living his niece Elizabeth Jane Fowler, who was then slightly under twenty-one, his sister Emily Walter, and five children of Emily Walter.

Elizabeth Jane Fowler died in 1891, in the testator's lifetime, a spinster. Emily Walter and her five children survived the testator.

The testator's widow, Elizabeth Moss, the tenant for life of his Daily Telegraph share and his residuary legatee, died in 1897, having by her will given her residuary estate . . . in trust for William George Kingsbury absolutely. . . .

At her death all the five children of Emily Walter were living and had attained twenty-one.

The question was whether, in consequence of the death of Elizabeth Jane Fowler in the lifetime of her uncle, the testator, the share bequeathed to her in his Daily Telegraph share had lapsed and fallen into his residuary estate, or whether the entirety passed to Emily Walter's five children: in other words, whether the gift by the testator of his Daily Telegraph share was a gift to a class, so that these five children, as the survivors of the class, took the whole.

To have this question decided, an originating summons was taken out by W.G. Kingsbury . . . to have it declared that the bequest of the testator's share in the Daily Telegraph newspaper upon trust, after the death of his wife, for Elizabeth Jane Fowler and the child or children of Emily Walter who should attain twenty-one equally, was not a gift to a class, but that the share bequeathed to Elizabeth Jane Fowler had lapsed by her death in the testator's lifetime and thus fell into the residue of the estate.

The summons was heard on December 14, 1898, by North J., who, after saying the cases upon the point were so irreconcilable that he should act independently of them, held that, as he could find nothing in the will to show that Elizabeth Jane Fowler was included in the class, the share given to her lapsed by reason of her death in the testator's lifetime, and so passed to the plaintiffs.

The defendants, the five children of Emily Walter, appealed.

LINDLEY, M.R. It is very difficult to construe this will by the light of the authorities. I entirely agree with North J. that the authorities do not help one much, because they are in inextricable confusion. I do not think there is any case which can be cited by either side which cannot be matched by a case on the other side more or less difficult to distinguish from it. The practical question which we have to decide on this will is, Who are the persons now entitled to the share of the testator in the Daily Telegraph newspaper? There are several rival views. One view is, and that is the one adopted by the learned judge below, that the share which Elizabeth Jane Fowler would have taken if she were alive — that is, one-sixth, as I understand it — has lapsed and has fallen into the residuary estate, so that, according to that view, one-sixth of that share has gone to persons who were certainly never intended to take it. That is obvious. That may be the legal result of the gift, but it is obvious it was never dreamt of by the testator. What he intended was that his share should go amongst the persons he has named and to no one else.

Now the difficulty lies in this. We hear about classes, and gifts to classes, and definitions of classes. You may define a class in a thousand ways: anybody may make any number of things or persons a class by setting out an attribute more or less common to them all and making that the definition of the class. . . . But after all, whether you call this a class or whether you call it a number of persons who are treated by the testator as if they were the class, appears to me to be merely a matter of language. One is very reluctant to frame definitions unless one can make a law to accord with the definitions, which judges cannot do. Now what is to be done with the share of this lady who has died? The testator says it is to be equally divided between her and the children of Emily Walter, to be equally divided between them all. If some of them are dead, are the shares of those who are dead to go to those who survive, or are they to go to someone else? That is the practical question; and whether you call the persons a class or "in effect" a class — as Mr. Theobald does in a passage of his work on wills, where he says (4th ed. p.645), "it is clear that a gift to *A.*, and the children of *B.*, may in effect be a gift to a class, if the testator treats the legatees as a class" — or whether you call them a number of persons who are to be treated as a class, is quite immaterial. The guiding question here is, What is to be done with this Daily Telegraph share which is to be divided amongst these legatees? It seems to me that it is to go to such of them as shall be living. That is the obvious intention. The alternative view takes the share away where it was never intended to go, and upon that ground it appears to me that we ought to differ from the learned judge. I confess, and I say so frankly, that if this case had come before me in the first instance I should have decided it as North J. did, but my brother Romer has convinced me that is not right. . . .

ROMER, L.J.[20] In the absence of any context negativing this view, I think that, when a testator gives property *X.* to *A.* and a class of persons

---

20. Lord Romer was a professor of mathematics before he took up the study of law. What assumption about the size of Elizabeth Jane Fowler's share does he make, which is essential to his argument? Would you make the same assumption if E.J. Fowler had been the testator's sister rather than his niece? — Eds.

— say the children of *B*. — in equal shares, he intends that the whole of *X*. shall pass by his gift if any one of the children of *B*. survive him, even although *A*. does not. Clearly, if *A*. survived and none of the children of *B*. survived so as to share, then *A*. would take the whole, for *A*. would either have to take the whole or nothing, unless indeed it could be said that you are to look at the number of children of *B*. living at the date of the will and say there is an intestacy as to the share of each child dying between the date of the will and the testator's death; but that to my mind is clearly an untenable proposition. If then the testator intended that *A*. should take the whole if none of the children of *B*. survived him to share, I think also he intended the children of *B*. to take the whole if *A*. did not survive so as to share. There is no satisfactory distinction, to my mind, between those two cases. I think that, in such a gift as I have mentioned, what the testator really means is that the property is to be shared equally by a body constituted of such of the following as should be existing at the date of the testator's death, that is to say, *A*. and the children of *B*. And generally, when the testator — there being nothing to negative the view in the rest of the will — gives property to be shared at a particular period equally between a class properly so called and an individual or individuals, I think that what the testator prima facie must be taken to mean is that you are to see which part of that aggregated body is to share in that property at the time it comes for distribution, and that such a gift is really a gift to a class; and though I am perfectly well aware of the danger there is in attempting to lay down general propositions — and few judges would more shrink from doing so than I, knowing as I do how a general proposition laid down often hampers judges in dealing with succeeding cases — yet I do think in the present case I may venture to make the following statement, especially as the cases are so complicated and there is no express decision of the Court of Appeal or of the House of Lords upon the point. In my opinion it is correct to say that a gift by will to a class properly so called and a named individual such as *A*. equally, so that the testator contemplates *A*. taking the same share that each member of the class will take, is primâ facie a gift to a class.

For those reasons, applying those principles to the case before us, I have no hesitation in saying that, in my opinion, the gift here was a gift to a class, and that Elizabeth Jane Fowler was only intended to share as one of a class; and that inasmuch as she did not survive so as to share, the rest of the class takes the whole of the property.

DAWSON v. YUCUS, 97 Ill. App. 2d 101, 239 N.E.2d 305 (1968). *T*'s will provided: "Through the Will of my late husband I received an undivided one-fifth interest in farm lands located in Sangamon

County, Illinois, and believing as I do that those farm lands should go back to my late husband's side of the house, I therefore give, devise and bequeath my one-fifth interest as follows: One-half of my interest therein to Stewart Wilson, a nephew, and one-half of my interest to Gene Burtle, a nephew." Stewart and Gene were her husband's nephews. Gene predeceased *T*, who died without issue. The court held that this was not a gift to a class and that the devise to Gene lapsed and passed under the residuary clause of the will. "In this case the testatrix named the individuals, Stewart Wilson and Gene Burtle, and gave them each a one-half portion of her interest in the farm, thus making certain the number of beneficiaries and the share each is to receive. The shares in no way depend upon the number who shall survive the death of the testatrix. There is nothing in the language of the will that indicates the testatrix intended to create a class or survivorship gift. The only other provision of the will, also contained in clause two, that has any bearing on the question is the statement, '. . . believing as I do that those farm lands should go back to my late husband's side of the house. . . .' While it is true that this language recites testatrix' desire that the one-fifth interest in the farm go back to her husband's side of the house, it does not indicate a survivorship gift was intended. Her intention to return the farm to her husband's side of the house was fulfilled when she named Stewart Wilson and Gene Burtle as the donees of the interest. . . .

"Further emphasis for the result we have reached is supplied by other factors found in the will and extrinsic evidence. First, . . . Restatement of Property, Future Interests, Sec. 280, Comment g., No. 1. Paragraph No. 2 of the same Restatement citation provides, 'The specification . . . of an exact proportion in the subject matter of the conveyance, which is to be received by each of the named and described persons, is strongly indicative of an intent to make a gift to individuals distributively whenever the [total of] . . . proportions so specified equals the entire subject matter given by the limitation in question.' Secondly, the common characteristic of the alleged class described by plaintiffs is that of relation to Dr. Stewart, or, in the words of clause two, the class is of 'my late husband's side of the house.' However, this characteristic is also shared by three other heirs of Dr. Stewart of the same degree of relationship to him as Stewart Wilson and Gene Burtle. It thus appears that Gene Burtle and Stewart Wilson do not constitute the alleged class but are individuals named from the class."

Application of Anti-Lapse Statutes to Class Gifts. Almost all states apply their anti-lapse statutes to class gifts. Many statutes expressly so provide, as does UPC §2-605, supra page 341. In states where the statute is unclear, courts reason that the anti-lapse statutes are designed to carry out the average testator's intent and that the average testator would prefer for the deceased beneficiary's share to go to the beneficiary's descendants rather than to the surviving members of the class.

PROBLEM

T, a widow, dies leaving a will that devises Blackacre "to my brothers and sisters in equal shares" and that devises her residuary estate to her son, *S*. At the time that *T* executed the will, she had two brothers, *A* and *B*, and two sisters, *C* and *D*, living. One sister, *E*, died before the will was executed, leaving children who survived *T*. *A* died during *T*'s lifetime leaving two children. *T* is survived by *A*'s children; by *B*, *C*, and *D*; by *E*'s children; and by *S*. Who takes Blackacre? See In re Stockbridge, 145 Mass. 517, 14 N.E. 928 (1888); In re Estate of Kalouse, 282 N.W.2d 98 (Iowa 1979).

SECTION C.   CHANGES IN PROPERTY AFTER EXECUTION OF WILL: THE DISTINCTION BETWEEN SPECIFIC AND GENERAL DEVISES

1. Ademption

Specific devises and bequests of real and personal property are subject to the doctrine of *ademption by extinction*. Suppose that the testator's will devises Blackacre to her son, John, and the residuary estate to her daughter, Mary. Some years later, the testator sells Blackacre and uses the sale proceeds to purchase Whiteacre, then dies without having changed her will. The gift of Blackacre is adeemed. Since Blackacre is not owned by the testator at her death, the devise fails. John has no claim to Whiteacre, for the will does not devise Whiteacre to him.

Ademption applies only to *specific* devises or bequests. Generally speaking, a specific devise or bequest is a disposition of a specific item of the testator's property. Gifts of Blackacre or of "my three-carat diamond ring given to me by my Aunt Jane" are examples. Ademption does not apply to *general* or *demonstrative* legacies. A legacy is general when the testator intends to confer a general benefit and not give a particular asset — for example, a legacy of $10,000 to *A*. If there is not $10,000 in cash in the testator's estate at death, the legacy is not adeemed; other assets must be sold to satisfy *A*'s general legacy. A demonstrative legacy is a hybrid: A general legacy payable from a specific source. Suppose that the testator's will gives *B* "the sum of $10,000, to be paid from the proceeds of sale of my General Motors stock." Most courts would hold this to be a demonstrative legacy. If the testator owns sufficient General Motors stock at death, in raising the $10,000 the executor must comply with the testamentary direction to sell the stock. But if the testator does not own any GM stock at death, the legacy is not adeemed. Other assets must be sold in order to raise the $10,000.

McGee v. McGee
Supreme Court of Rhode Island, 1980
413 A.2d 72

WEISBERGER, J. This is a complaint for declaratory judgment, in which the plaintiff administrator, Richard J. McGee (Richard), sought directions from the Superior Court in respect to the construction of certain provisions of the will of his mother, Claire E. McGee, and instructions relating to payment of debts and distribution of assets from the testatrix's estate. The sole issue presented by this appeal concerns the question of the ademption of an allegedly specific legacy to the grandchildren of the decedent and the consequent effect of such ademption upon payment of a bequest in the amount of $20,000 to Fedelma Hurd (Hurd), a friend of the testatrix. The provisions of the will pertinent to this appeal read as follows:

> Clause Eleventh:
> I give and bequeath to my good and faithful friend Fedelma Hurd, the sum of Twenty Thousand ($20,000.00) Dollars, as an expression to her of my appreciation for her many kindnesses.
> Clause Twelfth:
> I give and bequeath all of my shares of stock in the Texaco Company, and any and all monies standing in my name on deposit in any banking institution as follows:
> (a) My Executor shall divide the shares of stock, or the proceeds thereof from a sale of same, *with all of my monies, standing on deposit in my name, in any bank,* into three (3) equal parts and shall pay ⅓ over to the living children of my beloved son, Philip; ⅓ to the living children of my beloved son, Richard, and ⅓ over to the living children of my beloved son, Joseph. Each of my grandchildren shall share equally the ⅓ portion given to them. [Emphasis added.]

At the time of the execution of the will and up until a short time before the death of the testatrix, a substantial sum of money was on deposit in her name at the People's Savings Bank in Providence. About five weeks prior to his mother's death, Richard, proceeding pursuant to a written power of attorney as modified by an addendum executed the following month, withdrew approximately $50,000 from these savings accounts. Of this amount, he applied nearly $30,000 towards the purchase of four United States Treasury bonds, commonly denominated as "flower bonds," from the Federal Trust Company in Waterville, Maine (Richard then resided in that state). His objective in executing this transaction was to effect an advantageous method of satisfying potential federal estate tax liability.[21] The bonds, however, did not serve the intended purpose since at the time of Mrs. McGee's death her gross estate was such that apparently no federal estate tax liability was incurred. The remainder of the monies withdrawn from the savings accounts were deposited in Claire McGee's checking account to pay current bills and in a savings account in Richard's name to be transferred to his mother's account as the need might arise for the payment of her debts and future obligations. The sole sum that is now the subject of this appeal is the approximately $30,000 held in the form of United States Treasury bonds.

The complaint for declaratory judgment sought instructions concerning whether the administrator should first satisfy the specific legacy to the grandchildren from the proceeds of the sale of the flower bonds or whether he should first pay the $20,000 bequest to Fedelma Hurd, since the estate lacked assets sufficient to satisfy both bequests.

After hearing evidence and considering legal memoranda filed by the parties, the trial justice found that the bequest to the grandchildren contained in the twelfth clause of the will constituted a specific legacy. He held further, however, that Rhode Island regarded the concept of ademption with disfavor and he sought, therefore, to effectuate the intent of the testatrix. He proceeded to determine that since there is an assumption that one intends to leave his property to those who are the natural objects of his bounty, rather than to strangers, the administrator "should trace the funds used to purchase the Flower Bonds and should satisfy the specific legacy to the grandchildren" under the twelfth clause of the will. Consequently, the trial justice held that the legacy to Fedelma Hurd under the eleventh clause of the will must fail. This appeal ensued.

The McGee grandchildren suggest that the principal design of the testatrix's estate plan, ascertainable from a contemplation of the testamentary disposition of her property, was to benefit her family rather

---

21. Although not otherwise redeemable before maturity, flower bonds may be redeemed at par value, plus accrued interest, upon the owner's death for the purpose of paying the federal taxes on his estate. See Girard Trust Bank v. United States, 602 F.2d 938, 940 n.1 (Ct. Cl. 1979).

than "outsiders." They urge us to consider her intentions — which they assure us were concerned, in part, with protecting the family interests from an anticipated reduction of the estate's value by taxes — in determining whether the transfer of the funds in her accounts did in fact work an ademption. In addition, Richard points out that the decedent did not herself purchase these bonds. On the contrary, Richard acquired them in order to help discharge anticipated tax obligations of the estate and informed his mother of them only subsequently to the purchase. He argues, furthermore, not only that the funds with which he purchased the flower bonds originated in his mother's accounts, but also that since these bonds "are as liquid as cash" they are indeed monies standing in the decedent's name on deposit in a banking institution. He suggests that this description conforms in every respect to the formula drafted into the twelfth clause of her will. Merely the form of the legacy has changed, according to Richard, not its essential character, quality, or substance.

In response, appellant asserts that an ademption occurred by the voluntary act of the testatrix during her lifetime, since her son withdrew the funds as an authorized agent operating under a lawful power of attorney. There is evidence, moreover, that the testatrix subsequently ratified the purchase of the bonds when Richard afterwards told her of his actions and their intended effect upon estate taxes.[22] As a consequence, Hurd asserts that there was no longer any money standing on deposit in the name of the testatrix in any bank with which to discharge the specific legacy to the grandchildren. These transactions resulted in an extinction of the subject matter of the legacy. Hurd argues, in addition, that the intention of the testatrix, even if discernible, is irrelevant to the question of the ademption of the bequest. She therefore contends that her general legacy should be payable from the proceeds of the sale of the flower bonds.

At the outset, we recognize that the instant case concerns specifically the concept of ademption by extinction, a legal consequence that may attend a variety of circumstances occasioned either by operation of law or by the actions of a testator himself or through his guardian, conservator, or agent. Gardner v. McNeal, 117 Md. 27, 82 A. 988 (1911); In re Wright, 7 N.Y.2d 365, 165 N.E.2d 561, 197 N.Y.S.2d 711 (1960). In particular, a testamentary gift of specific real or personal property may be adeemed — fail completely to pass as prescribed in the testator's will — when the particular article devised or bequeathed no longer exists as part of the testator's estate at the moment of his death because of its prior consumption, loss, destruction, substantial

---

22. Richard testified his mother "was pleased that [he had] done this because there would be more money available for the children and grandchildren."

change, sale, or other alienation subsequent to the execution of the will. In consequence, neither the gift, its proceeds, nor similar substitute passes to the beneficiary, and this claim to the legacy is thereby barred. Atkinson, Handbook of the Law of Wills §134 at 741, 743-44 (2d ed. 1953); 6 Bowe & Parker, Page on the Law of Wills §54.1 at 242, §54.9 at 256-57 (1962); Note, Wills: Ademption of Specific Legacies and Devises, 43 Cal. L. Rev. 151 (1955).

The principle of ademption by extinction has reference only to specific devises and bequests and is thus inapplicable to demonstrative or general testamentary gifts. 6 Page, supra §54.3 at 245, §54.5 at 248. In Haslam v. de Alvarez, 70 R.I. 212, 38 A.2d 158 (1944), we prescribed the criteria for determining the character of a legacy, relying on the earlier case of Dean v. Rounds, 18 R.I. 436, 27 A. 515 (1893), wherein we held that "[a] specific legacy, as the term imports, is a gift or bequest of some definite specific thing, something which is capable of being designated and identified." Id. When the testator intends that the legatee shall receive the exact property bequeathed rather than its corresponding quantitative or ad valorem equivalent, the gift is a specific one, and when "the main intention is that the legacy be paid by the delivery of the identical thing, and that thing only, and in the event that at the time of the testator's death such thing is no longer in existence, the legacy will not be paid out of his general assets." Hanley v. Fernell, 54 R.I. 84, 86, 170 A. 88, 89 (1934). In particular, the designation and identification of the specific legacy in a testator's will describe the gift in a manner that serves to distinguish it from all other articles of the same general nature and prevents its distribution from the general assets of the testator's estate. 6 Page, supra §48.3 at 11-12.

In the case at bar, the trial justice construed the twelfth clause of Mrs. McGee's will as bequeathing a specific legacy to her grandchildren. . . .

Without a doubt, the trial justice properly interpreted the McGee grandchildren's bequest, primarily because of the tone of the other provisions, the tenor of the entire instrument, . . . and the specificity with which the testatrix described that portion of the twelfth clause relative to the Texaco stock. Additionally, money payable out of a fund — rather than out of the estate generally — described with sufficient accuracy and satisfiable only out of the payment of such fund, or a bequest of money deposited in a specific bank, . . . is, as a rule, a specific legacy. When a will bequeaths "the money owned by one which is on deposit" in a designated bank, although the amount remains unspecified, the gift is nevertheless identifiable and definite, apart from all other funds or property in the testator's estate; and the legacy is specific. Willis v. Barrow, 218 Ala. 549, 552, 119 So. 678, 680 (1929); Prendergast v. Walsh, 58 N.J. Eq. 149, 42 A. 1049 (Ch. 1899). Despite the fact that Mrs. McGee did not name any particular bank in the twelfth clause of her will, she bequeathed all the money in her name "in any bank." In view of the fact that she expected all of her money remaining at her death to go to her grandchildren and, further, the money to be payable from a particular source — that is, accounts in her name in banking institutions — we conclude that the legacy was sufficiently susceptible of identification to render it a specific one.

Accordingly, since the bequest to the grandchildren is specific, we must now determine whether or not it was adeemed by the purchase of the bonds. Note, Ademption and the Testator's Intent, 74 Harv. L. Rev. 741 (1961). In connection with the early theory of ademption, the courts looked to the intention of the testator as the basis of their decisions. 6 Page, supra §54.14 at 265. But ever since the landmark case of Ashburner v. MacGuire, 2 Bro. C.C. 108, 29 Eng. Rep. 62 (Ch. 1786), wherein Lord Thurlow enunciated the "modern theory," courts have utilized the identity doctrine or "in specie" test. This test focuses on two questions only: (1) whether the gift is a specific legacy and, if it is, (2) whether it is found in the estate at the time of the testator's death. Atkinson, supra §134 at 742; Note, 74 Harv. L. Rev. at 742; Comment, Ademption in Iowa — A Closer Look at the Testator's Intent, 57 Iowa L. Rev. 1211 (1972). The extinction of the property bequeathed works an ademption regardless of the testator's intent. . . .

The legatees of the twelfth clause argue that the subject matter of the specific bequest, although apparently now unidentifiable in its previous form, actually does exist in the estate of their grandmother but in another form as the result of an exchange or transfer of the original property. But there is a recognized distinction between a bequest of a particular item and a gift of its proceeds, see generally Annot., 45 A.L.R.3d 10 (1972); and the testatrix, in the instant case, did recognize the distinction in the twelfth clause of her will by bequeathing the Texaco stock "or the proceeds thereof from a sale of same" but omitting to include similar provisions regarding proceeds in connection with the language immediately following which described the bank-money legacy. It appears that the testatrix's intention, manifest on the face of her will, was that her grandchildren receive only the money in her bank accounts and not the money's proceeds or the investments that represent the conversion of that money into other holdings. . . .

In accordance with the generally accepted "form and substance rule," a substantial change in the nature or character of the subject matter of a bequest will operate as an ademption; but a merely nominal or formal change will not. In re Peirce, 25 R.I. 34, 54 A. 588 (1903) (no ademption since transfer of stock after consolidation of banks without formal liquidation was exchange and not sale); Willis v. Barrow, 218 Ala. 549, 119 So. 678 (1929) (no ademption by transfer of money from named bank to another since place of deposit was merely descriptive); In re

Hall, 60 N.J. Super. 597, 160 A.2d 49 (1960) (no ademption by transfer of the money from banks designated in will to another one since location was formal description only and did not affect substance of testamentary gift).

Since the money previously on deposit in Mrs. McGee's bank accounts no longer exists at the time of her death, the question arises whether the change was one of form only, rather than substance. We have determined that the change effected by Richard was not merely formal but was substantial. There is no language in the will that can be construed as reflecting an intention of the testatrix to bequeath a gift of bond investments to her grandchildren. The plain and explicit direction of the twelfth clause of the will is that they should receive whatever remained in her bank accounts at the time of her death. Since no sums of money were then on deposit, the specific legacy was adeemed. Clearly, this case is dissimilar to those in which the fund, at all times kept intact, is transferred to a different location, as in *Willis* and *Prendergast*, where the money merely "changed hands," not character. See also In re Tillinghast, 23 R.I. 121, 49 A. 634 (1901) (no ademption by mere act of transferring mortgages to own name since they were in specie at the time of testatrix's death). The fact that Mrs. McGee did not herself purchase the bonds is not significant. Disposal or distribution of the subject matter of a bequest by an agent of the testator or with the testator's authorization or ratification similarly operates to adeem the legacy. Gardner v. McNeal, 117 Md. 27, 82 A. 988 (1911); In re Wright, 7 N.Y.2d 365, 165 N.E.2d 561, 197 N.Y.S.2d 711 (1960); Glasscock v. Layle, 21 Ky. Law. Rep. 860, 53 S.W. 270 (Ky. 1899).

The petitioner improperly relies upon the case of Morse v. Converse, 80 N.H. 24, 113 A. 214 (1921). In that case the testatrix voluntarily placed her property into the hands of a conservator to care for and use for her support. The conservator purchased a Liberty bond out of bank deposits bequeathed in the testatrix's will, and the legacies were not adeemed thereby. But, contrary to the case at bar, the testatrix in *Morse* neither knew about nor consented to the conservator's acts; therefore, the court explained, the change "furnishes no evidence of an intentional revocation by her." Id. at 26, 113 A. at 215. But see In re Wright, citing Matter of Ireland's Estate, 257 N.Y. 155, 177 N.E. 405 (1931) (specifically bequeathed stock adeemed even though sold by conservator after testator had become incompetent).

Moreover, under the principles enunciated by Lord Thurlow in Ashburner v. MacGuire, and more fully expressed in the case of Humphreys v. Humphreys, 2 Cox Ch. 184, 30 Eng. Rep. 85 (Ch. 1789), only the fact of change or extinction, not the reason for the change or extinction, is truly relevant. The vast majority of jurisdictions adhere to this rule. See Atkinson, supra §134 at 741-42; 6 Page, supra §54.15 at 266-68. This "in specie" theory of ademption, although it may occasionally result in a failure to effectuate the actual intent of a testator, has many advantages. Significant among these advantages is simplicity of application, as opposed to ad hoc determination of intent from extrinsic evidence in each particular case. This theory further has the advantages of stability, uniformity, and predictability. The argument in support of Lord Thurlow's rule is well expressed in 6 Page, supra §54.15 at 266:

> If the sale or collection of the bequest works an ademption or not depending upon testator's intention as inferred from the surrounding circumstances, many cases will arise in which it is difficult or impossible to ascertain what testator's intention was; and probably, in many cases, testator did not think of the consequences which would follow from his conduct. If the sale or collection of the bequest operates as an ademption or not, depending upon his intentions, and such intention may be shown by his oral declarations, then the controlling evidence in the case will consist of the written will, executed in accordance with statute, together with testator's oral declarations. This violates both the letter and the spirit of state wills statutes, which insist on the formalities of writing and execution in order to avoid opportunities for perjury. For these reasons, it is now held that the sale, destruction, or collection, of the bequest or devise, adeems it without regard to the actual intention of the testator.

Accordingly, we hold that the trial justice erred in allowing the admission of extrinsic evidence regarding Mrs. McGee's intent. We further hold that the specific legacy in the twelfth clause of the testatrix's will is adeemed and the legatees' claim to this bequest is thereby barred. We direct the trial justice to order the petitioner to satisfy the general pecuniary legacy bequeathed in the eleventh clause of the will from the sale of the flower bonds, with the excess to pass under the residuary (fourteenth) clause of the will.

The respondent's appeal is sustained, the judgment below is reversed, and the cause is remanded to the Superior Court for proceedings consistent with this opinion.

NOTES AND PROBLEMS

1. Suppose that Claire McGee had bequeathed "my 100 shares of stock in the Texaco Company" to her grandchildren and, prior to death, had sold her Texaco stock. Would the bequest be adeemed? Suppose that the bequest had read, "100 shares of stock in the Texaco Company." Would the bequest be adeemed? See Paulus, Special and General Legacies of Securities — Whither Testator's Intent?, 43 Iowa L. Rev. 467, 478, 483 (1958).

Suppose that prior to Claire's death, Texaco Company had merged with Gulf Oil Company to form Giant Oil Corporation. Would the grandchildren be entitled to the shares Claire owned in Giant Oil? See In re Estate of Watkins, 284 So. 2d 679 (Fla. 1973); Uniform Probate Code §2-607(a)(3) (providing for no ademption of specific bequest of securities where the testator acquires new securities as the result of corporate merger or reorganization).

Suppose that Claire, owner of 100 shares of stock in Widget Corporation, a closely held corporation, had bequeathed "100 shares of Widget Corporation stock" to her grandchildren but had sold the stock before her death. Would the bequest be adeemed?

2. *T* has a pearl necklace consisting of two strings of pearls united by a jeweled clasp. *T* executes a will bequeathing "one string of my pearls" to *A* and "the second string of my pearls" to *B*. Subsequently *T* combines the pearls into one string. Are the bequests to *A* and *B* adeemed? See Elwyn v. DeGarmendia, 148 Md. 109, 128 A. 913 (1925).

3. The doctrine of ademption has been criticized as being merely a mechanical solution to the problem. See Paulus, Ademption by Extinction: Smiting Lord Thurlow's Ghost, 2 Tex. Tech. L. Rev. 195 (1971); Note, Ademption and Testator's Intent, 74 Harv. L. Rev. 741 (1961).

NOTE: ABATEMENT

The problem of abatement, like the problem of ademption, often turns on the classification of a bequest as general or specific. The problem of abatement arises when the estate has insufficient assets to pay debts and all the bequests; some bequests must be abated or reduced. In McGee v. McGee, for example, the testator bequeathed $20,000 (a general bequest) to her friend Fedelma and monies on deposit (approximately $50,000) to her grandchildren. The estate lacked assets to pay both the general bequest and the specific bequest to grandchildren; only $30,000 in flower bonds were available to satisfy bequests totaling $70,000. Had the court not held the specific bequest to grandchildren adeemed, the court would have had to abate the bequest to Fedelma. Bequests abate (are reduced) when the testator's estate is insufficient to pay all the bequests. In the absence of any indication in the will as to how bequests should abate or be reduced, bequests ordinarily abate in the following order: (1) residuary bequests are reduced first, (2) general legacies (such as given to Fedelma) are reduced second, and (3) specific and demonstrative legacies are the last to abate and are reduced pro rata. This plan is believed to follow the testator's intent that specific bequests be given effect before general bequests, and both be given effect before a residuary bequest. But the residuary legatee is often the most important legatee of the testator.

Uniform Probate Code (1983, as amended 1987)

§2-608 [NONADEMPTION OF SPECIFIC DEVISES IN CERTAIN CASES;
UNPAID PROCEEDS OF SALE, CONDEMNATION OR INSURANCE;
SALE BY CONSERVATOR]

(a) A specific devisee has the right to the remaining specifically devised property and:

(1) any balance of the purchase price (together with any security interest) owing from a purchaser to the testator at death by reason of sale of the property;

(2) any amount of a condemnation award for the taking of the property unpaid at death;

(3) any proceeds unpaid at death on fire or casualty insurance on the property; and

(4) property owned by testator at his death as a result of foreclosure, or obtained in lieu of foreclosure, of the security for a specifically devised obligation.

(b) If specifically devised property is sold by a conservator or an agent acting within the authority of a durable power of attorney for a principal who is under a disability, or if a condemnation award or insurance proceeds are paid to a conservator or an agent acting within the authority of a durable power of attorney for a principal who is under a disability as a result of condemnation, fire or casualty, the specific devisee has the right to a general pecuniary devise equal to the net sale price, the condemnation award, or the insurance proceeds. This subsection does not apply if subsequent to the sale, condemnation, or casualty, it is adjudicated that the disability of the testator has ceased and the testator survives the adjudication by one year. The right of the specific devisee under this subsection is reduced by any right he has under subsection (a).

PROBLEM

T executes a will devising Blackacre to *A*. Then *T* sells Blackacre to *B*, taking back a note and purchase money mortgage from *B*. At *T*'s death, $15,000 is still owed on the note and mortgage. Is *A* entitled to the note and mortgage? See Peacock v. Owens, 244 Ga. 203, 259 S.E.2d 458 (1979). Suppose that after the sale to *B*, *T* had executed a codicil to her will reading: "I devise the note and mortgage on Blackacre to *A*." Before *T* died, *B* paid the note and *T* deposited the amount in a savings account. Is *A* entitled to the amount paid on the note? See Effland, Will Construction Under the Uniform Probate Code, 63 Or. L. Rev. 337, 358-363 (1984).

NOTE: EXONERATION OF LIENS

Another problem that may arise with respect to a specific devise is whether land devised passes free and clear of any mortgage on the land. Suppose that the testator's will devises Blackacre to her daughter Maria. At the testator's death, Blackacre is subject to a mortgage that secures a note on which the testator was personally liable. Does Maria take Blackacre subject to the mortgage, or is she entitled to have the note paid out of residuary assets so that the title will pass to her free of the lien? In most states, Maria takes Blackacre free of the mortgage. Most jurisdictions apply the common law doctrine of "exoneration of liens." Under this doctrine, when a will makes a specific disposition of real or personal property that is subject to a mortgage to secure a note on which the testator is personally liable, it is presumed (absent contrary language in the will) that the testator wanted the debt, like other debts, to be paid out of the residuary estate. See Annot., 4 A.L.R.3d 1023 (1965).

Dissatisfaction with the exoneration doctrine has led to the enactment, in several states, of statutes reversing the common law rule. The real message, though, is that where a will makes a specific gift of encumbered property, the will should specify whether the lien is or is not to be exonerated. See Effland, supra, at 363-366.

Uniform Probate Code (1983)

§2-609   [NON-EXONERATION]

A specific devise passes subject to any security interest existing at the date of death, without right of exoneration, regardless of a general directive in the will to pay debts.

PROBLEM

H and W buy a home for $97,900, paying $10,000 down and signing as comakers a mortgage note for $87,900. The home is deeded to H and W as tenants in common. Subsequently H dies, devising all his property to his son, A. W claims H's estate is liable for the payment of one-half of the amount of the note. Is it? Pietro v. Leonetti, 30 Ohio St. 2d 178, 283 N.E.2d 172 (1972). If H's will had provided that W should take the home subject to the mortgage, what result?

2. Satisfaction

The doctrine of *satisfaction* (sometimes known as ademption by satisfaction) applies when the testator makes a transfer to a *beneficiary* after executing the will. If the testator is a parent of the beneficiary (or stands in loco parentis) and after execution of the will transfers to the beneficiary property of a similar nature to that given by the will, there is a rebuttable presumption that the gift is in satisfaction of the gift made by the will. Suppose that *T*'s will bequeaths $50,000 to his son, *S*, and his residuary estate to his daughter, *D*. After executing the will, *T* gives *S* $30,000. There is a presumption that the gift was in partial satisfaction of the legacy, so that *S* will take only $20,000 at *T*'s death.

This doctrine, which bears kinship to the doctrine of advancements under intestacy law (see supra page 105), applies to general pecuniary bequests, not to specific bequests. When specific property is given to the beneficiary during the testator's life there is ademption by extinction, not satisfaction. Satisfaction may also apply to residuary gifts and to demonstrative gifts, but the cases are not uniform in their holdings. In all states satisfaction depends upon the intention of the testator.

Because the intent of the testator is frequently so difficult to ascertain, some states have enacted statutes requiring that the intention of a testator to adeem by satisfaction must be shown in writing. Under such a statute, of course, there is no presumption of satisfaction by a gift to a child.

Uniform Probate Code (1983)

§2-612 [ADEMPTION BY SATISFACTION]

Property which a testator gave in his lifetime to a person is treated as a satisfaction of a devise to that person in whole or in part, only if the will provides for deduction of the lifetime gift, or the testator declares in a contemporaneous writing that the gift is to be deducted from the devise or is in satisfaction of the devise, or the devisee acknowledges in writing that the gift is in satisfaction. For purpose of partial satisfaction, property given during lifetime is valued as of the time the devisee came into possession or enjoyment of the property or as of the time of death of the testator, whichever occurs first.

PROBLEM

T's will devises $20,000 to her daughter *A*. Before *T*'s death *T*'s lawyer advised her that she ought to take advantage of the $10,000 annual exclusion per donee under the federal gift tax. *T* thereafter sent a check to *A* for $10,000 and a check to *A*'s husband for $10,000 with a covering letter saying these gifts were in lieu of the devise to *A* in the will. After *T*'s death, is *A* entitled to $10,000 under *T*'s will?

3. Stock Splits

Suppose that *T* executes a will devising 100 shares of stock of Tiger Corporation to *A*. Subsequently Tiger Corporation splits its stock three-for-one. At *T*'s death, *T* owns 300 shares of Tiger stock. Does *A* take 100 shares or 300 shares? The old-fashioned approach was to ask whether the bequest was specific or general. If the court found *T* intended to separate out and bequeath particular shares in *T*'s possession, the bequest was termed specific and *A* received the specified shares (100) as well as any accretions in a stock split (200). On the other hand, if the court found *T* did not have in mind particular property of his own but only desired to confer a general benefit, *A* received only 100 shares of stock. This mechanical approach does not recognize the basic nature of a stock split, which is a change in form, not substance. The shares held after the split represent the same proportional ownership of the corporation as the number of shares held before the split. The market value of the 300 shares of Tiger after the split should be approximately the same as 100 shares before the split. Therefore, many modern courts have discarded the old approach and have held that, absent a contrary showing of intent, a legatee of a bequest of stock is entitled to additional shares received by the testator as a result of a stock split. See Bostwick v. Hurstel, 364 Mass. 282, 304 N.E.2d 186 (1973); Shriners' Hosp. for Crippled Children v. Coltrane, 465 So. 2d 1073 (Miss. 1985).

Stock dividends are treated differently from stock splits by some courts. They analogize a stock dividend to a cash dividend and conclude that the legatee cannot logically be awarded the former when he is denied the latter. However, this analogy ignores the fact that after a stock dividend, as after a stock split, the testator's percentage of ownership remains the same. See Note, Rights to Stock Accretions Which Occur Prior to Testator's Death, 36 Alb. L. Rev. 182 (1971).

Uniform Probate Code §2-607 treats stock splits and stock dividends alike. But, in a questionable adherence to the old specific/general distinction, the code gives the additional stock (from split or dividend) to the legatee only if the testator "intended a specific devise of certain securities rather than the equivalent value thereof."

PROBLEM

T is a partner in Wolf Brothers. *T*'s will devises to her daughter "my partnership interest in Wolf Brothers." Subsequently *T* and her partners decide to incorporate. They change the name of Wolf Brothers to Fusion Technology, Inc. On *T*'s death does her daughter or the residuary legatee take the stock in Fusion Technology? See Effland, Will Construction Under the Uniform Probate Code, 63 Or. L. Rev. 337, 358 (1984).

6

RESTRICTIONS ON THE POWER OF DISPOSITION: PROTECTION OF THE FAMILY

SECTION A. RIGHTS OF THE SURVIVING SPOUSE

1. Introduction to Marital Property Systems

In the United States, two basic marital property systems exist — the system of separate property, originating in the common law of England, and the system of community property, originating on the continent of Europe and brought to this country by French and Spanish settlers. The fundamental difference between these systems is that under the common law system husband and wife own separately all property each acquires (except those items one spouse has agreed to put into joint ownership with the other), whereas under community property husband and wife own all acquisitions from earnings after marriage in equal undivided shares. There are, to be sure, many variations among the states adhering to one or another of these systems, and community property ideas have made noticeable inroads into the separate property system within the last fifty years. Nonetheless, separate property and community property are quite different ways of thinking about marital property ownership. The former stresses individual autonomy, the latter sharing between husband and wife.

Community property developed throughout the continent of Europe, allegedly spread by Germanic tribes after the fall of Rome. From these western countries it was taken by European settlers to parts of Africa, Central and South America, and Mexico. It is odd, then, that in England — separated from the continent by only a 21-mile-wide channel of

369

water — a separate property system, based on the husband's autonomy and effacement of the wife, grew. Why the English resisted so powerful an idea as the sharing principle of community property has intrigued scholars for generations. Adding to the puzzle is the fact that community property developed, and still flourishes, in Scotland. The most plausible explanations connect the separate property system with the highly centralized English feudal system, dominated by a powerful king, which required succession of power (land) from father to son and fealty between a (male) lord and a (male) tenant. Women were supported by their husbands, but they were denied an ownership share of, or power over, their husbands' acquests.[1] Whatever the reason for its existence, the English separate property system became well entrenched by the fourteenth century and was taken by the English settlers to the eastern seaboard of the United States, whence it spread westward.

Under the separate property system, whatever the worker earns is his — or hers. There is no sharing of earnings. If one spouse is the wage earner while the other spouse works in the home, the wage-earning spouse will own all the property acquired during marriage (other than gifts or inheritances from relatives or gifts by the wage earner to the homemaker). A crucial issue under a separate property system is: What protection against disinheritance should be given the surviving spouse who works in the home or works at a lower-paying job? Almost all of the separate property states answer this question by giving the surviving spouse, by statute, an elective share in the estate of the deceased spouse. The elective share is not limited to a share of property acquired with earnings, however. It is enforceable against all property owned by the decedent spouse at death.

In eight states (Arizona, California, Idaho, Louisiana, Nevada, New Mexico, Texas, and Washington) a community property system exists. The fundamental principle of community property is that all earnings of the spouses and property acquired from earnings are community property. Each spouse is the owner of an undivided one-half interest in the community property. The death of one spouse dissolves the community. The deceased spouse owns and has testamentary power only over his or her one-half community share.

The difference between the principles underlying the separate property and the community property systems can be seen by a simple illustration.

Case 1. H works outside the home, earning $50,000 a year. W works in the home, earning nothing. At the end of 20 years, H has through

---

1. See Donahue, What Causes Fundamental Legal Ideas? Marital Property in England and France in the Thirteenth Century, 78 Mich. L. Rev. 59 (1979).

savings of his salary bought a house in his name, a life insurance policy payable to his daughter, and $100,000 worth of stocks in his name. Under a separate property regime, during life *W* owns none of that property. At death, *W* has an elective share (usually one-third) of the house and the stocks but usually not the insurance policy because it is not in *H*'s probate estate. In a community property state, *W* owns half of *H*'s earnings during life, and thus at *H*'s death *W* owns one-half of the acquisitions from earnings (the house, the insurance proceeds, and the stocks). If *W* dies first, *W* can dispose of her half of the community property by will. In a separate property state, if *W* dies first, she has no property to dispose of.

Community property is based on the idea that husband and wife are an economic unit, that they decide together how to use the time of each so as to maximize their income, and that they should share equally acquests from economic activity of either. Property acquired before marriage and property acquired during marriage by gift, devise, or descent is the acquiring spouse's separate property.

In the late twentieth century, community property has come to be favored by many academics and some legislators. In 1983 the National Conference of Commissioners on Uniform State Laws promulgated a Uniform Marital Property Act. The act adopts community property principles, though the phrase "community property" is avoided and "marital property" used instead. Wisconsin adopted the Uniform Marital Property Act in 1984. Wis. Stat. Ann. §§766.001-766.97 (Supp. 1989). The Commissioner of Internal Revenue has ruled that under the provisions of the Wisconsin Marital Property Act the rights of the spouses are community property rights for purposes of federal income taxation. Rev. Rul. 87-13, 1987-1 Cum. Bull. 20. Hence Wisconsin must now be reckoned a community property state.

Whatever the prospects for widespread adoption of the Uniform Marital Property Act, the common law marital property system is under pressure to reform itself so that the results resemble those reached under community property systems. This has already happened with distribution of spousal property upon divorce. Equitable distribution of marital property (variously defined as property acquired from earnings after marriage or from any source after marriage or from any source before or after marriage) is now required in all separate property states. As we shall see, the community property idea of treating husband and wife as an economic unit is creeping into division of property upon death. In 1981, Congress established the marital economic unit idea in the federal estate and gift tax law by adopting a policy of not taxing any (qualifying) transfers between husband and wife (see infra page 997). See Comment, The Development of Sharing Principles in Common Law Marital Property States, 28 UCLA L. Rev. 1269 (1981). See also Rubenstein v. Mueller, supra page 274 at 277, where the New York court said, in relation to a contract not to revoke a will disposing of the couple's property, "[I]t is not clear . . . whether any of this jointly held property represented the independent estate of Bertha Mueller or whether, as is typical, it represented the jointly held fruits of Conrad's labors outside the home aided by Bertha's efforts within the home for their lifetime together. In any event, we do not attempt a segregation of assets of husband and wife after a marriage of this duration. For all practical purposes, equity may content itself with considering the assets as their collective property, as if their estates had merged."

In examining spousal rights, we turn first to rights of the surviving spouse to *support*, which (except for dower) are generally the same in both separate property and community property states. We next turn to the central topic — the right of the surviving spouse to a *share* in the decedent spouse's property or in the marital property. We examine this matter first in the separate property states, then in the community property states.

2.   *Rights of Surviving Spouse to Support*

a.   Social Security

In the 1930s Congress established the social security system, under which retirement benefits are paid to a worker and his or her surviving spouse. The social security system thus incorporates the principle of community property that the benefits of earnings should be shared by husband and wife. The worker has no right to shift the survivor's benefit to a person other than the spouse (though benefits may be paid to a deceased retired worker's dependents as well as to the worker's spouse).

Social security benefits are computed by a formula that takes into account the amount of quarters worked (it takes 40 quarters — ten years — to be fully insured), the amount of earnings taxed, and the age of retirement. Over 90 percent of all persons aged 65 or older receive social security benefits. For discussion, see T. Waterbury, Materials on Trusts and Estates 1-19 (1986). In 1986, the average monthly benefit for surviving spouses was $444. Statistical Abstract of the United States 342 (108th ed. 1988).

b.   Private Pension Plans

Private pension plans funded by employers or jointly funded by employer and employee contributions have mushroomed since the middle of this century. Billions of dollars are now held in private pension funds. Most of these plans are governed by the federal Employee Retirement Income Security Act of 1974 (ERISA), 29 U.S.C. §§1001 et seq. (1982 & Supp. 1989). The Retirement Equity Act of 1984, amending ERISA (29 U.S.C. §1055), requires that pensions paid under covered private plans must be paid as a joint and survivor annuity to the worker and his or her spouse, unless the nonworker spouse consents to some other form of payment of the retirement benefit. This act thus introduces the sharing principle of community property into private pension plans throughout the United States. The act will substantially increase the amount of income payable to workers' surviving spouses.

As with social security, the worker under a private pension plan cannot prevent the surviving spouse from sharing in the benefits under the plan.

PROBLEM

W designates *H* as the death beneficiary of her employer's pension plan. Subsequently *W* divorces *H*. Upon *W*'s death before retirement, is *H* entitled to the death benefits? What would be the result if *W* had remarried? What would be the result if *W* had changed the death beneficiary to her sister *S* after the divorce? Compare Problem 2(a), supra page 302.

c. Homestead

Nearly all states have homestead laws designed to secure the family home to the surviving spouse and minor children, free of the claims of creditors. Such a homestead is frequently called a *probate homestead*. Although the homestead laws vary in many details, generally the surviving spouse has the right to occupy the family home (or maybe the family farm) for his or her lifetime. In some states the homestead must be established by the decedent during his life, usually by filing a declaration of homestead in some public office; in other states the probate court has power to set aside real property as a homestead. The amount of the homestead exception is ridiculously small in some states (UPC §2-401 recommends $5,000!) and provides little protection to the surviving spouse. But in several states the homestead exemption is substantial and may even exempt the family home regardless of its value. The decedent has no power to dispose of a homestead so as to deprive the surviving spouse of statutory rights therein. The right to occupy the homestead is given in addition to any other rights the surviving spouse has in the decedent's estate. See Bratt, Family Protection Under Kentucky's Inheritance Laws: Is the Family Really Protected?, 76 Ky. L.J. 387 (1988) (criticizing homestead, personal property exemptions, and family allowances as being wholly inadequate to protect a decedent's family from hardship).

d.   Personal Property Set-Aside

Related to homestead is the right of the surviving spouse (and sometimes of minor children) to have set aside to her certain tangible personal property of the decedent enumerated in a statute. These items, which are also exempt from creditors' claims, usually include household furniture and clothing, but may also include a car and farm animals. The set-aside is usually subject to several conditions and limitations, but, if these are met, the decedent usually has no power to deprive the surviving spouse of the exempt items.

In a number of states, intangible personal property up to a fixed sum (say $20,000) may also be set aside to the surviving spouse under certain conditions. Usually this set-aside is available only in small estates, and it permits the surviving spouse to avoid probate administration.

e.   Family Allowance

Every state has a statute authorizing the probate court to award a family allowance for maintenance and support of the surviving spouse (and often of dependent children). The allowance may be limited by the statute to a fixed period (typically one year), or it may continue thereafter while the will is being contested or for the entire period of administration. The allowance, as with the homestead and personal property set-aside, is in addition to whatever other interests pass to the surviving spouse.

In some states, the maximum allowance that can be awarded is fixed by statute. In other states, a reasonable allowance tied to the spouse's standard of living is permitted. The reported decisions indicate that the courts tend to be generous in fixing these awards. See Moore v. Moore, 430 S.W.2d 247 (Tex. Civ. App. 1968); Annot., 90 A.L.R.2d 687 (1963).

Maintenance of the decedent's spouse and dependent children is not allowed after the estate is closed. It is not entirely clear that this should be so. In England, Australia, New Zealand, and Canada, the decedent's property continues to be used to support those who were dependent upon the decedent during lifetime. Any dependent who claims that the decedent's will failed to make proper provision for him may apply to the court for an order for adequate maintenance. The court, in its discretion, may order periodic payments or a lump-sum payment. Eligible dependents include the decedent's spouse, children, and parent, and — in England — *any* person who was being maintained by the decedent. If the estate is kept open to make payments, the personal representative is turned into a trustee who manages the estate and pays the income as directed by the court. See J. Martyn, Family Provision: Law and Practice (2d ed. 1985) (England); R. Wright, Testator's Family Maintenance in Australia and New Zealand (3d ed. 1974); Naresh, Dependants' Applications Under the Inheritance (Provision for Family and Dependants) Act 1975, 96 L.Q. Rev. 534 (1980). Although an occasional commentator has suggested that the English support system should be adopted here (see Note, Family Maintenance: An Inheritance Scheme for the Living, 8 Rut.-Cam. L.J. 673 (1977)), the weight of academic opinion in this country opposes it because of the vast discretion such a system gives to the probate judge. See Glendon, Fixed Rules and Discretion in Contemporary Family Law and Succession Law, 60 Tul. L. Rev. 1165 (1986); Langbein & Waggoner, Redesigning the Spouse's Forced Share, 22 Real Prop., Prob. & Tr. J. 303, 314 (1987). Cf. Oldham, Should the Surviving Spouse's Forced Share Be Retained?, 38 Case W. Res. L. Rev. 223, 235-243 (1987) (comparing support obligations at death and upon divorce and viewing favorably a lifetime support obligation after a long marriage).

QUESTION

H and *W* divorce. The divorce property settlement provides that *H* will provide spousal support and child support and that these obligations are to survive *H*'s death as a claim against *H*'s estate. (The general rule is that the duty to pay support closes at the obligor's death, unless an agreement provides otherwise.) Does it make sense for the spouse and children of a failed marriage to have greater rights, albeit created by contract, than the spouse and children of a marriage that has not failed? See W. McGovern, S. Kurtz & J. Rein, Wills, Trusts and Estates §§3.4, 3.5 (1988).

f. Dower

At common law, a widow had dower in all *land* of which her deceased husband had been seised during marriage and which was inheritable by the issue of husband and wife. Dower entitles the widow to a life estate in one-third of her husband's qualifying land. Thus:

> *Case 2.*   *H*, married to *W*, buys Blackacre, taking title in himself in fee simple. *H* subsequently dies. *W* is entitled to a life estate in one-third of Blackacre. (If *W* had predeceased *H*, her dower interest would be extinguished.)

In feudal times, when land was the chief form of wealth and provided the power base of the head of the family, dower provided generous support to the widow of a rich man. But today, when many people rent their homes and by far the greater part of wealth is in the form of intangible personal property (such as stocks and bonds), dower may give the surviving spouse no protection at all.

The right of dower attaches the moment the husband acquires title to land or upon marriage, whichever is later. Dower remains inchoate until the husband's death, when it becomes possessory. Once inchoate dower has attached, the husband cannot sell the land free and clear of the wife's dower interest. In Case 2, if *H*, after buying Blackacre, had conveyed it to *A*, *A* would take title subject to *W*'s dower, and if and when *W* survived *H*, *W* would be entitled to a life estate in one-third of Blackacre (now owned by *A*). No purchaser, bona fide or not, can cut off the wife's dower without her consent. To release her dower interest, the wife must sign the deed to the purchaser. Dower functions today primarily to make the signatures of both spouses a practical requirement to the sale of one spouse's land.

At common law, a husband had a support interest in his wife's lands, called curtesy. It was comparable to dower except (1) the husband did not acquire curtesy unless children were born of the marriage and (2) the husband was given a life estate in the entire parcel, not merely in one-third. Curtesy survives today in a few states only as a label given to the support interest of the husband, which in fact is identical with the wife's common law dower.

Dower has been abolished in the great majority of states. In only five jurisdictions does dower as it was known to the common law exist. Ark. Code Ann. §28-11-301 (1987); D.C. Code §19-102 (1981); Ky. Rev. Stat. §§392.020, 392.080 (1984); Mich. Comp. Laws §558.1 (1988); Ohio Rev. Code Ann. §2103.02 (Baldwin 1982). In all of these, except Michigan, dower has been extended to the husband as well as the wife. The Michigan statute, providing dower for a wife but not for a husband, is of doubtful constitutionality. Similar statutes were found violative of the equal protection clause in Stokes v. Stokes, 271 Ark. 300, 613 S.W.2d 372 (1981), and Boan v. Watson, 281 S.C. 516, 316 S.E.2d 401 (1984). In three other jurisdictions common law dower has been changed to give the surviving spouse a fractional fee simple interest, rather than a life estate, in the decedent's lands owned during marriage. Iowa Code

Ann. §633.212 (Supp. 1988) (one-half if decedent dies intestate; one-third if spouse elects against the will); Va. Code §64.1-19 (1987) (one-third); W. Va. Code §43-1-1 (1982) (one-third). In these three states dower is not a claim for support, as it was at common law, but a claim of ownership. A few states have abolished dower in fact but continue to use the term to refer to a surviving spouse's interest in land that the decedent owns at death (rather than during marriage); in this sense it does not differ from the elective share.

In most states retaining dower, the surviving spouse must elect to take dower, or to take a statutory share of the decedent's estate, or to take a share under the decedent's will. As the statutory elective share is almost always greater than dower, dower is rarely elected.

PROBLEMS

1. *H*, married to *W*, buys Blackacre, taking title in "*H* for life, remainder to *H*'s daughter *D*." Subsequently *H* buys Whiteacre, taking title in "*H* and *D* as joint tenants with right of survivorship." *H* dies. Does *W* have dower in Blackacre or Whiteacre? See Spears v. James, 319 Mich. 341, 29 N.W.2d 829 (1947); Jezo v. Jezo, 23 Wis. 2d 399, 129 N.W.2d 195 (1964). Suppose that *D* had died before *H*. Would *D*'s husband have dower in Blackacre?

2. *W*, a real estate developer, wants to be able to buy land and sell it without the consent or interference of her husband. The jurisdiction has common law dower for husbands and wives. *W* consults you. What do you recommend?

3. Rights of Surviving Spouse to a Share of Decedent's Property

a. The Elective Share and Its Rationale

All but one[2] of the separate property states give the surviving spouse, in addition to any support rights mentioned above, a share in the

---

2. Georgia is the only separate property state without an elective share statute. Professor Chaffin, a leading authority on Georgia wills law, approves of this on the ground that there is no evidence of widespread disinheritance of spouses or unfairness against them. Chaffin, A Reappraisal of the Wealth Transmission Process: The Surviving Spouse, Year's Support and Intestate Succession, 10 Ga. L. Rev. 447, 464-470 (1976). Not all Georgia students are convinced, however. A Note, Preventing Spousal Disinheritance in Georgia, 19 Ga. L. Rev. 427 (1985), argues for equitable distribution of a portion of the decedent's property to the surviving spouse. Observing that the Georgia Supreme Court adopted equitable distribution upon divorce on its own after the Georgia legislature failed to act, the note suggests that the court should atone for a supine legislature by extending equitable distribution to termination of marriage by death.

For other scholars who question the need for an elective share, see Clark, The Recapture of Testamentary Substitutes to Preserve the Spouse's Elective Share: An Appraisal of Recent Statutory Reforms, 2 Conn. L. Rev. 513 (1970); Plager, The Spouse's Nonbarrable Share: A Solution in Search of a Problem, 33 U. Chi. L. Rev. 681 (1966).

decedent's property. The underlying policy (at least in a long marriage) is that the surviving spouse contributed to the decedent's acquisition of wealth and deserves to have a portion of it. This policy is carried out by statutes giving the surviving spouse an *elective share* (sometimes called a *forced share*) of the decedent's property. These statutes provide the surviving spouse with an election: The spouse can take under the decedent's will or can renounce the will and take a fractional share of the decedent's estate. Uniform Probate Code §2-201 fixes the elective share at one-third, even though the spouse's intestate share is greater (see supra page 76). In some states the elective share is one-half or is increased to one-half if the decedent is not survived by children.

Although the policies underlying the elective share and community property are similar (rewarding the spouse's contribution to the economic success of the marriage), the implementing theory is quite different. With community property, a share of community property *belongs* to the nonworking spouse as soon as it is acquired. With an elective share, the surviving spouse has a share in the decedent's property owned at death, but the spouse must *elect to claim it*. The difference is between having something now and having in the future the power to obtain it.

In re Estate of Clarkson
Supreme Court of Nebraska, 1975
193 Neb. 201, 226 N.W.2d 334

SPENCER, J.   This is an action under section 30-108(2), R.R.S. 1943. It involves an election on behalf of an incompetent surviving spouse to either take under or against her husband's will. The District Court vacated an order of the county court electing on behalf of the widow to take the provision made for her in her husband's will. The executor prosecutes this appeal. We affirm.

Joseph D. Clarkson, deceased, married Evelyn Bell Clarkson April 16, 1953. Mr. Clarkson had two daughters from a prior marriage. Mrs. Clarkson had a son and a daughter by a prior marriage. No children were born of the second marriage. Mrs. Clarkson, who is 80 years of age, has been mentally incompetent since June 1965. The record indicates that her chances of recovery were and are nil. The will in question was executed November 18, 1969. The inventory filed in the estate indicates the value of the estate to be $1,229,263.56. The report of the guardian ad litem indicates the net value of the estate is $1,372,224. Only $62,000 is real estate, a Missouri farm valued at $40,000 and the residence property valued at $22,000.

The will makes the following provision for the incompetent: "If my wife, Evelyn Bell Clarkson, survives me, I give, devise and bequeath to the First National Bank of Omaha, as Trustee for my said wife, an amount equal to one-fourth ($\frac{1}{4}$) of the value of my net estate as finally determined for Federal Estate Tax purposes, unreduced by any taxes." The will directs the trustee to pay all income therefrom to Mrs. Clarkson and in addition provides for such amounts of principal to be paid to her from time to time as the trustee deems necessary or desirable to provide for her proper support and maintenance. The will further provides that upon Mrs. Clarkson's death the trust estate shall terminate and the assets remaining in the trust shall then be distributed and disposed of to such persons in such manner as Mrs. Clarkson by her last will and testament shall direct and appoint. If Mrs. Clarkson fails to exercise the general testamentary power of appointment upon her death, the will provides that the remaining assets shall be distributed as follows: "Twenty-five Thousand Dollars ($25,000) thereof shall be paid to each of my wife's children, Jerry W. Menck and Peggy Lou McVea, with the children of either of them who may be then deceased to take equally the share which the parent would have taken if then living; and the balance of said assets remaining shall be distributed to my daughters, Helen E. Clarkson, and Ruth C. Bollinger, share and share alike." The will was made at a time when Mrs. Clarkson was incompetent. There is no possibility of her exercising the power of appointment granted in the will because her condition cannot improve.

Pursuant to the provisions of section 30-108(2) R.R.S. 1943, the Douglas county court appointed Jack W. Marer as guardian ad litem to make such investigation as he deemed necessary and to report his recommendation to the court as to whether the court should elect on behalf of Mrs. Clarkson to take the provisions made for her under the last will and testament of Joseph D. Clarkson or to take by descent and distribution as provided by law. The guardian ad litem, after investigation, filed a report recommending that the court renounce the provision made for Evelyn Clarkson under the last will and testament of Joseph D. Clarkson and elect to take by descent and distribution as provided by law. The county judge declined to accept the recommendation. He determined her interests were not better served by renouncing the will but that the equities of the matter dictated that the testamentary plan of Joseph D. Clarkson should be adhered to.

The special guardian of the incompetent prosecuted an appeal to the District Court for Douglas County. The District Judge disagreed with the opinion of the county judge and followed the recommendation made by the guardian ad litem. He found an estate in fee title would be of greater value than a beneficial interest in a trust. He specifically determined that the best interests of the surviving spouse would require renouncing the provisions of the will and taking the estate in fee with full incidence of ownership, notwithstanding that title would vest in her guardian who would have fiduciary limitations on its disposal.

The incompetent, as the second wife of deceased, would receive one-fourth of the estate if she takes under the statute rather than the will. The parties are in agreement that there is no dollar difference between what Mr. Clarkson left his wife in trust and what she would take by an election. The difference comes about in that a fee title is of much greater value than a beneficial interest in the trust.

While this is a case of first impression in Nebraska, the question has arisen in many other jurisdictions. There is an exhaustive annotation on the subject at page 10 of 3 A.L.R.3d. As this annotation will illustrate, there is an irreconcilable conflict in the decisions. This conflict arises because of various theories used by the courts in interpreting and defining the meaning of the words "best interests" or similar words which are found in the several statutes under consideration. [Neb. Rev. Stat. §30-108(2) provides that upon hearing on the guardian ad litem's recommendation, the court "shall make such election as it deems the best interests of such surviving husband or wife shall require."] . . .

In the so-called minority view, all the decisions in one way or another indicate that the best interests of the incompetent will be served by electing the method which is the most valuable to the surviving spouse. This usually means the one having the greater pecuniary value is the one selected.

The majority view, as stated in Kinnett v. Hood (1962), 25 Ill. 2d 600, 185 N.E.2d 888, 3 A.L.R.3d 1, is that all the surrounding facts and circumstances should be taken into consideration by the court in order to make the election to take under the will or against it. In *Kinnett* the court says: "It is impractical to delineate the factors which would apply in every case or, in fact, the relative weight to be given each in order to determine what is to the best interest of the incompetent."

The majority rule emphasizes other considerations than monetary. It characterizes the minority cases as placing the election purely on monetary standards or what would result in the larger pecuniary value, to the detriment of other considerations. We concede that in some instances there may be other considerations than monetary which may promote the best interests of the incompetent. What, however, are those other considerations? It is impractical to delineate factors which could apply in every case or to specify the relative weight which should be given to such other possible considerations. If we follow our statutes, the best interests of an incompetent in most instances will require the election which will result in the larger pecuniary value. We cannot agree that the preservation of the decedent's estate plan is a major consideration as found by the county judge and as it appears to be in many cases espousing the majority view. Under our law the testator's testamentary desires have little or no importance in relation to the best interests of the surviving spouse.

In Nebraska we must start with the premise that the testator is presumed to know the law and that his surviving spouse may lawfully exercise her right to take against his will irrespective of his estate plan. In re Estate of Hunter (1935), 129 Neb. 529, 262 N.W. 41. In *Hunter* we said: "A testator is presumed to know that his widow may lawfully exercise her right under the statute to take against the will, and that such right is paramount to his will." We further held that such election did not render the will inoperative. As to other persons it will be enforced as nearly as may be in accordance with the intention of the testator.

Many of the majority view cases criticize the minority cases, suggesting that they tend to sanction: (1) The interests of the heirs of the incompetent as a consideration; and (2) give too much weight to what the surviving spouse would have done had she made her own election as a consideration. We are in full accord with the view that the interests of possible heirs of the incompetent should play no part in the decision. We would not, however, entirely ignore what the surviving spouse might have done had she made her own election.

We note that while the majority view would not permit a consideration of what the surviving spouse would have done in election, the cases seem to advance the notion that whether the surviving spouse would have wanted to abide by her husband's will should be considered. See Kinnett v. Hood, supra. No one can ever say exactly what the incompetent would have done if competent. If, however, we always assume that the surviving spouse would make the election which was in her best interests, there is no problem. If we follow that criteria, we are merely carrying out the intent of our statute.

It seems a little inconsistent under our law to say, as do some of the majority cases, that the election by the court to renounce the will should be made only if necessary to provide for the widow's needs. This would write a restriction into our statute. The statute requires the court to make the election which it deems is in the best interests of the incompetent spouse. This must be made without reference to whether she may be provided for otherwise. We observe that neither section 30-107 nor section 30-108, R.R.S. 1943, which create the right of election and provide the necessary procedural steps, make any mention of or suggest any restrictions under which an election might be made. While a competent surviving spouse may elect to take against the will, even if it would seem obviously against her best interests to do so, a court in making the choice for an incompetent does not have that privilege. It must consider only the best interests of the incompetent.

On the record we find no considerations other than the monetary value of the estate. We find that an estate in fee is of much greater value than a beneficial interest in a trust. We agree with the District

Judge that the best interests of the surviving spouse require taking the estate in fee with full incidents of ownership notwithstanding the title would vest in her guardian who would have fiduciary limitations on its disposal.

The judgment is affirmed.

McCown, J. (dissenting).   The testator's will here left to his wife, if she survived him, the exact amount and the specific share of his estate which she would receive if he had no will, but he left it in trust for her proper support and maintenance. The corporate trustee had the power to use all the income and all the principal for those purposes. The wife was given a full power of appointment of all remaining property on her death. At the time he executed the will his wife was incompetent and had been incompetent for some 4 years.

The majority opinion here determines that the best interests of the surviving spouse are better served by renouncing the will because "a fee title is of much greater value than a beneficial interest in the trust." That might well be so if the surviving spouse were competent, but she is not.

While technically an incompetent might be said to have a fee title, in literal practical fact an incompetent during his or her lifetime has no greater beneficial interest in property managed on his or her behalf by a guardian than in property managed by a trustee under the powers granted by the will here.

If there was any reasonable prospect that an incompetent might recover, the basis for the majority opinion might be at least arguably supportable. In this case, however, the evidence is simply undisputed that the surviving spouse is now and always will be incompetent. The entire foundation for the majority opinion here must, and does, therefore, rest on the wholly unsupported conclusion that $343,000 held and used for the maintenance and support of the incompetent surviving spouse during her lifetime has a greater value in the hands of a guardian that it does in the hands of a trustee under the will.

The majority opinion accepts the universal rule that the interests of possible heirs of an incompetent should play no part in the decision but states that the incompetent's estate must not be ignored. Under our Nebraska statute, the right of a surviving spouse to renounce the will and take a statutory share is personal to the surviving spouse and under no circumstances does it extend to an executor or administrator of the survivor's estate, or to heirs. If a surviving spouse dies before the expiration of the time for exercising the right, the right lapses altogether. The right of election is clearly for the benefit of the surviving spouse alone. Section 30-2315, R.S. Supp., 1974, which does not go into effect until January 1, 1977, makes it very clear that in the case of a protected person, such as the incompetent spouse here, the court shall exercise the election only "after finding that exercise is in the best interests of the protected person *during his probable life expectancy.*"[3] (Emphasis ours.)

The majority opinion here is not only too restrictive as applied in this case, but the impact of the holding upon other cases not presently before us has been largely ignored. It should be noted first that the trust provisions of the will here were obviously drawn to permit the share of the surviving spouse to qualify for the marital deduction under the federal estate tax laws. It must be noted too that thousands of Nebraska citizens have drawn wills which contain similar trust provisions which fully qualify for marital deduction treatment under federal laws. Because of the impact of estate and inheritance taxes, many husbands and wives have drawn and prepared separate wills to fit their joint estate tax plans. The majority opinion, if followed in the future, will now mean that the county court will be required to renounce a will on behalf of an incompetent surviving spouse whenever the will leaves the share of the surviving spouse in trust under marital deduction provisions similar to those here, even though the amount received by the incompetent's guardian will be identically the same. The holding necessarily poses a critical problem for estate tax planners where incompetence of a surviving spouse is involved. . . .

Where, as here, the trust provisions in a will for the welfare and comfort of an incompetent surviving spouse during her lifetime are at least equal to, or better than, the statutory provisions which regulate the providing of such welfare and comfort by a guardian, and the amount available is ample and exactly the same in either case, the testator's property should ordinarily be permitted to pass under the will.

NOTES

1. On the issues involved in *Clarkson,* see Note, The Incompetent Spouse's Election, 18 U. Mich. J.L. Ref. 1061 (1985).

2. *Federal estate tax marital deduction.* It is clear that Mr. Clarkson drafted his will so as to qualify his bequest to his wife for the federal estate tax marital deduction. The marital deduction was enacted in 1948 by Congress in an attempt to equalize the federal estate tax consequences between couples residing in community property states and couples residing in separate property states. Prior to 1948, community property couples paid substantially less estate taxes on their earned property than did couples in separate property states. Thus:

3. This provision is part of Uniform Probate Code §2-203, which became effective in Nebraska in 1977. — Eds.

Case 3. H and W are domiciled in a community property state. H is the wage earner. H dies leaving $500,000 in community property (from earnings). At H's death only half is taxable, because W owns the other half, which will be taxable at W's death. If H and W had been domiciled in a separate property state, the entire $500,000 would be taxable at H's death. Because of the graduated tax rates and exemptions (producing lower total taxes for two taxpayers than one) and because postponing taxation in community property states on half until W's death gave W the income during her life on the amount of tax not paid on her half, Congress felt the federal estate taxes fell inequitably upon the states.

Although gender-neutral terms are generally desirable, on occasion it clarifies matters to speak in genders. Talking about the marital deduction is one of these occasions. Men tend to earn more than women (considerably more in the 1940s when Congress first addressed the matter), and men, on average, die before women. Therefore we shall describe the marital deduction as if the (richer) husband dies first, though of course it is available to the wife if she dies first.

The essential problem facing Congress in 1948 was how to put the separate property wife, with no or lesser earnings of her own, into a tax position comparable with the community property wife, who owns half her husband's earnings. Congress solved the problem by giving the husband an estate tax marital deduction, up to 50 percent of the value of his estate, for property left to his surviving wife in a form comparable to the outright ownership the community property wife had. The word "comparable" is the rub. To equate the position of the separate property wife exactly with the community property wife, the former must end up with *outright ownership* of one-half her husband's earnings. Yet, for Congress to provide a powerful tax incentive for a husband to devise his widow outright ownership of half of his property was highly objectionable to (mostly male) estate planners and trust companies in New York and other rich separate property states; they thought the husband should have the right to put the widow's share in trust for her without suffering a tax disadvantage (see Note 5, infra). The objection was that a housewife, without business experience, might be incapable of managing her inherited wealth. (Never mind that widows in California, Texas, and other community property states had long been legally entrusted with managing their property after their husbands' deaths, with no noticeable adverse consequences to them.[4]) Congress effected a compromise: If a husband gave his wife a *life estate* (support) with the *power to appoint* the property to anyone she wished at her death (equivalent to complete ownership at her death), this arrangement would be deemed comparable to a fee simple and would

---

4. But cf. the "widow's election," infra page 416.

qualify for the marital deduction. This is what Mr. Clarkson gave his wife, though at the time he executed his will his wife was incompetent to exercise her testamentary power — which means that Clarkson, while benefitting from the marital deduction, thought he could in fact control the devolution of the property upon her death.

In 1982 the federal estate tax marital deduction was changed to incorporate a completely new principle: Interspousal transfers will not be taxed at all, provided the donor spouse gives the donee spouse at least a life estate in the property. A gift of a fee simple or its alleged equivalent (a life estate coupled with a general power of appointment) is no longer required for the marital deduction. Internal Revenue Code of 1986, §2056; see infra page 1009.

The 1948 version of the marital deduction provided a tax incentive to the donor spouse to give the surviving spouse support and an ownership share of the decedent spouse's property (even though complete control of that share could be postponed until the surviving spouse's death). The current marital deduction requires only that the donor spouse give his surviving spouse support for life to avoid transfer taxation. Thus, viewed through the precise eye of the marital deduction provisions only, the housewife (or the spouse with lower earnings) appears further now than before from being treated as well as her counterpart in community property states — as deserving a share of outright ownership in recognition of her contribution to the economic gains of a marriage. Yet this may be an illusion, for there remain other transfer tax incentives for equalizing the couple's estates to take advantage of credits and exemptions of both spouses and of graduated tax rates (see infra pages 1012-1014).

3. Observe that UPC §2-203, quoted in *Clarkson* at footnote 3, allows a guardian to elect only if this is necessary to support the spouse during her probable life expectancy. Why should a guardian not be able to elect to claim the spouse's full elective share? The restriction in the Uniform Probate Code may also mean that the guardian cannot elect against the will where not necessary for the spouse's support even though tax savings in the form of a larger marital deduction could be gained by an election. Thus if *H* makes no provision in his will for *W*, because she is rich in her own right and does not need support, under the Uniform Probate Code *W*'s guardian apparently cannot participate in postmortem estate planning (see infra page 1012) and save taxes.

4. The right of election is personal. If Mrs. Clarkson had survived her husband but had died before she (or her guardian) had made an election, the right of election could not be exercised. In re Estate of La Spina, 60 Ohio St. 2d 101, 397 N.E.2d 1196 (1979). Is this consistent with a support rationale of the elective share or with a contribution rationale?

5. Under the New York elective share statute, the elective share is

one-third if the decedent leaves issue, one-half if no issue. If the decedent bequeaths his spouse $10,000 and puts the rest of the capital value of the elective share in a trust for his spouse, giving the surviving spouse an indefeasible income for life, the spouse has no right of election. N.Y. Est., Powers & Trusts Law §5-1.1(c)(1)(1981). The provision that a decedent can satisfy his spouse's elective share by giving her a life income interest in trust attests the power of the New York estate planning bar and trust companies, which hold far more capital in private trusts than trust companies in any other state. The provision also reflects a view that the surviving spouse deserves only support, not ownership of a share of the economic gains during marriage. See also Mass. Ann. Laws ch. 191, §15 (1981) (similar to New York law); Annot., 48 A.L.R. 4th 972 (1986).

NOTE: WHO CONTRIBUTES TO THE ELECTIVE SHARE

In *Clarkson* the decedent's net estate was $1,372,224. The elective share, one-fourth, is $343,056.[5] Where is the $343,056 to come from? Should the ordinary rules of abatement (residuary abates first, then general legacies, then specific legacies, supra page 362) apply? Should the marital deduction trust corpus be set aside for the widow, wiping out the remainder interests in the trust? Should the elective share be paid out of the residuary estate, leaving the corpus of the trust intact but accelerating the remainder since Mrs. Clarkson, by electing, must relinquish the life income interest in the trust? In many states the disclaimer act provides that any interest disclaimed or renounced takes effect as if the disclaimant had predeceased the testator. See supra page 123. See generally In re Will of Rosenzweig, 19 N.Y.2d 92, 224 N.E.2d 705, 273 N.Y.S.2d 192 (1966).

Suppose that UPC §2-207 had been in force in Nebraska at the time of the decision. What result?

---

5. We say $343,056 because that is one-fourth of the size of the estate included in the guardian ad litem's report as available for the election. The report includes the Missouri farm, valued at $40,000. Under conflict of laws rules, Missouri law governs the disposition of Missouri land; however, the law of the situs (Missouri) usually applies the law of the domicile (Nebraska) to determine the rights of the surviving spouse to a statutory forced share in land located in the former state. The interest of the domiciliary state is generally deemed paramount in interspousal rights. See UPC §2-201; In re Clark, 21 N.Y.2d 478, 236 N.E.2d 152, 288 N.Y.S.2d 993 (1968), infra page 401; 1 J. Schoenblum, Multistate and Multinational Estate Planning §§10.03, 10.08, 10.10 (1982, Supp. 1988).

Uniform Probate Code (1983)

§2-207   [CHARGING SPOUSE WITH GIFTS RECEIVED; LIABILITY OF
OTHERS FOR BALANCE OF ELECTIVE SHARE]

(a)   In the proceeding for an elective share, values included in the augmented estate[6] which pass or have passed to the surviving spouse, or which would have passed to the spouse but were renounced, are applied first to satisfy the elective share and to reduce any contributions due from other recipients of transfers included in the augmented estate. For purposes of this subsection, the electing spouse's beneficial interest in any life estate or in any trust shall be computed as if worth one half of the total value of the property subject to the life estate, or of the trust estate, unless higher or lower values for these interests are established by proof.

(b)   Remaining property of the augmented estate is so applied that liability for the balance of the elective share of the surviving spouse is equitably apportioned among the recipients of the augmented estate in proportion to the value of their interests therein.

(c)   Only original transferees from, or appointees of, the decedent and their donees, to the extent the donees have the property or its proceeds, are subject to the contribution to make up the elective share of the surviving spouse. A person liable to contribution may choose to give up the property transferred to him or to pay its value as of the time it is considered in computing the augmented estate.

At the beginning of this section, we suggested that the policy underlying the elective share is to reward the spouse's contribution to the economic success of the marriage. But, of course, the elective share is not finely tuned to carry out that policy. First, the elective share gives the surviving spouse a fixed fractional share of the decedent's estate regardless of the length of marriage. The marriage may have lasted one hour[7] or fifty years; the elective share fraction is the same. Second, the elective share is of all the decedent's property, including inherited property and property acquired before marriage. It is not — as

---

6. *Augmented estate* is a term used in the Uniform Probate Code to refer to the probate estate and inter vivos transfers that are subject to the spouse's election. See infra page 389. — Eds.

7. Or less. In Estate of Neiderhiser, 2 Pa. D. & C.3d 202, 59 Westmoreland County L.J. 60 (1977), the groom dropped dead during the marriage ceremony, after he and the bride had each said "I will" (equal in other marriage ceremonies to "I do"). The court held that marriage occurs upon the exchange of vows, and the bride was entitled to an elective share in the groom's estate.

community property is — restricted to acquisitions from earnings during marriage.

Professors Langbein and Waggoner propose to remedy the first of these disparities by giving the surviving spouse a sliding-scale percentage of the elective share amount, based upon the duration of the marriage (10 percent upon marriage, with 5 percent annual accruals until 100 percent of the one-third or one-half elective share is reached after 18 years of marriage). Langbein & Waggoner, Redesigning the Spouse's Forced Share, 22 Real Prop., Prob. & Tr. J. 303 (1987). They believe this will approximate the results reached in most community property marriages, where the amount of savings from earnings (and hence community property) ordinarily increases with the duration of the marriage. A sliding-scale (or accrual) forced share also deals more equitably with second marriages among the elderly, which are not infrequent nowadays. Under current elective share law, the surviving second spouse (Mrs. Clarkson in the *Clarkson* case) is often pitted against the children of the first marriage, who regard one-third or one-half as too great a share of their parent's property.

The Joint Editorial Board of the Uniform Probate Code has approved the Langbein-Waggoner proposal. It will be incorporated in a revised Uniform Probate Code if approved by the National Conference of Commissioners on Uniform State Laws in 1990.

For more criticism of the elective share, see Oldham, Should the Surviving Spouse's Forced Share Be Retained?, 38 Case W. Res. L. Rev. 223 (1988). Professor Oldham believes the forced share should be 50 percent of acquisitions of the decedent during marriage (other than gifts and inheritances). His proposal makes the elective share more closely resemble community property than does the Langbein-Waggoner proposal, which gives an elective share in all property of the decedent, not just earned property. Langbein and Waggoner justify the inclusiveness of their proposal by saying that it eliminates tracing problems in determining what was acquired from earnings. Neither of these proposals gives a decedent spouse the power to dispose of half the surviving spouse's earned property, which is a feature of community property. In that respect, both proposals fall short of reaching community-like results.

b. Property Subject to the Elective Share

The early elective share statutes gave the surviving spouse a fractional share of the decedent's *probate estate*. With the proliferation of will substitutes (see Chapter 4), the question arises whether the elective share should be extended to some or all will substitutes.

Some states have statutes dealing with this matter. A statute may provide, for example, that the surviving spouse may reach any inter vivos conveyance over which the deceased spouse retained a power of appointment or revocation. Or a statute may be broader. New York Est., Powers & Trusts Law §5-1.1 (1981) provides that the surviving spouse can reach gifts causa mortis, Totten trust bank accounts, joint tenancies, and transfers over which the decedent retained "a power to revoke such disposition or a power to consume, invade or dispose of the principal thereof." Specifically excluded in New York are life insurance proceeds, pension plans, and United States savings bonds.

The Uniform Probate Code goes even further in broadening the types of will substitutes subject to the elective share. The enumerated inter vivos transfers, together with the probate estate, are part of the *augmented estate*. Section 2-202(1) of the code lists the inter vivos transfers that are subject to the spouse's election.

Uniform Probate Code (1983)

§2-201 [RIGHT TO ELECTIVE SHARE]

(a) If a married person domiciled in this state dies, the surviving spouse has a right of election to take an elective share of one-third of the augmented estate under the limitations and conditions hereinafter stated.

(b) If a married person not domiciled in this state dies, the right, if any, of the surviving spouse to take an elective share in property in this state is governed by the law of the decedent's domicile at death.

§2-202 [AUGMENTED ESTATE]

The augmented estate means the estate reduced by funeral and administration expenses, homestead allowance, family allowances and exemptions, and enforceable claims, to which is added the sum of the following amounts:

(1) The value of property transferred to anyone other than a bona fide purchaser by the decedent at any time during marriage, to or for the benefit of any person other than the surviving spouse, to the extent that the decedent did not receive adequate and full consideration in money or money's worth for the transfer, if the transfer is of any of the following types:

    (i) any transfer under which the decedent retained at the time of his death the possession or enjoyment of, or right to income from, the property;

    (ii) any transfer to the extent that the decedent retained at the time of his death a power, either alone or in conjunction with any other person, to revoke or to consume, invade or dispose of the principal for his own benefit;

    (iii)   any transfer whereby property is held at the time of decedent's death by decedent and another with right of survivorship;

    (iv)   any transfer made to a donee within two years of death of the decedent to the extent that the aggregate transfers to any one donee in either of the years exceed $3,000.00.

Any transfer is excluded if made with the written consent or joinder of the surviving spouse. Property is valued as of the decedent's death except that property given irrevocably to a donee during lifetime of the decedent is valued as of the date the donee came into possession or enjoyment if that occurs first. Nothing herein shall cause to be included in the augmented estate any life insurance, accident insurance, joint annuity, or pension payable to a person other than the surviving spouse.

(2)   The value of property owned by the surviving spouse at the decedent's death, plus the value of property transferred by the spouse at any time during marriage to any person other than the decedent which would have been includible in the spouse's augmented estate if the surviving spouse had predeceased the decedent to the extent the owned or transferred property is derived from the decedent by any means other than testate or intestate succession without a full consideration in money or money's worth. For purposes of this paragraph:

    (i)   Property derived from the decedent includes, but is not limited to, any beneficial interest of the surviving spouse in a trust created by the decedent during his lifetime, any property appointed to the spouse by the decedent's exercise of a general or special power of appointment also exercisable in favor of others than the spouse, any proceeds of insurance (including accidental death benefits) on the life of the decedent attributable to premiums paid by him, any lump sum immediately payable and the commuted value of the proceeds of annuity contracts under which the decedent was the primary annuitant attributable to premiums paid by him, the commuted value of amounts payable after the decedent's death under any public or private pension, disability compensation, death benefit or retirement plan, exclusive of the Federal Social Security system, by reason of service performed or disabilities incurred by the decedent, any property held at the time of decedent's death by decedent and the surviving spouse with right of survivorship, any property held by decedent and transferred by contract to the surviving spouse by reason of the decedent's death and the value of the share of the surviving spouse resulting from rights in community property in this or any other state formerly owned with the decedent. Premiums paid by the decedent's employer, his partner, a partnership of which he was a member, or his creditors, are deemed to have been paid by the decedent.

(ii) Property owned by the spouse at the decedent's death is valued as of the date of death. Property transferred by the spouse is valued at the time the transfer became irrevocable, or at the decedent's death, whichever occurred first. Income earned by included property prior to the decedent's death is not treated as property derived from the decedent.

(iii) Property owned by the surviving spouse as of the decedent's death, or previously transferred by the surviving spouse, is presumed to have been derived from the decedent except to the extent that the surviving spouse establishes that it was derived from another source.

(3) For purposes of this section a bona fide purchaser is a purchaser for value in good faith and without notice of any adverse claim. Any recorded instrument on which a state documentary fee is noted pursuant to [insert appropriate reference] is prima facie evidence that the transfer described therein was made to a bona fide purchaser.

———————

Observe that section 2-202(2) of the code includes in the augmented estate property given to the surviving spouse by the decedent during life. None of the other statutes do this, with the result that a spouse who has been well provided for by lifetime or nonprobate transfers can elect against the will and claim more than a "fair" share. Thus:

> *Case 4.* H, married to W, owns the family home in joint tenancy with W (the house is worth $80,000 at H's death). H owns insurance on his own life in the amount of $100,000, payable to W. During life H transfers $200,000 to a trust to pay H the income for life, then to pay W the income for life, then to pay the principal to H's children. H dies, leaving a probate estate of $100,000, which he devises to his children. In a state that has an elective share system but not the UPC system, W can elect to take a fractional share of H's probate estate; her elective share rights do not take into account the property she has received from H by nonprobate routes.

To be equitable, the UPC includes gifts to the spouse in the decedent's augmented estate, which gifts are credited against the elective share to which the surviving spouse is entitled.

Professors Langbein and Waggoner believe that the augmented estate concept falls short of approximating community property results, and they propose to change it to achieve results closer to those of a community property system. Langbein & Waggoner, Redesigning the

Spouse's Forced Share, 22 Real Prop., Prob. & Tr. J. 303, 318-319 (1987). They would do this by changing section 2-202(2) of the code so that the *survivor's augmented estate* (probate and nonprobate property), and not just the property the survivor received from the decedent, is set off against the surviving spouse's elective share. They would combine the decedent's property (his augmented estate) with the survivor's property (her augmented estate), then split it between the two in accordance with the applicable percentage, then charge the survivor with her property, thus determining the amount of the decedent's property to which the surviving spouse is entitled. At page 322 Langbein and Waggoner give this illustration (slightly changed).

> *Case 5.*   *H* and *W* have been married for 25 years, and *W* is entitled to an elective share of 50 percent. *H* owns $500,000 in assets (augmented estate). *W* owns $100,000 in assets (augmented estate). Combined, they own property worth $600,000. Upon *H*'s death, *W* has an elective share of $300,000. *W* is charged with the receipt of $100,000 (her assets). Hence she is entitled to an elective share of $200,000 in *H*'s augmented estate. Each spouse ends up controlling $300,000, if *H* dies first.

The essence of the Langbein-Waggoner proposal is to add up all the property of the spouses and split it between them according to a fixed percentage. It differs from community property, which splits only acquisitions from earnings and not gifts and inheritances and property acquired before marriage. The Joint Editorial Board of the Uniform Probate Code has approved this proposal, which, if adopted by the National Conference of Commissioners on Uniform State Laws, will be incorporated in a revised code.

On the UPC augmented estate, see Kurtz, The Augmented Estate Concept Under the Uniform Probate Code: In Search of an Equitable Elective Share, 62 Iowa L. Rev. 981 (1977) (also containing an examination of the elective share law in all jurisdictions). Determining the spouse's share in the augmented estate, particularly the surviving spouse's property derived from the decedent (includible in augmented estate under UPC §2-202(2)), can be as complicated as the tracing problems alleged to be a disadvantage of community property. See In re Estate of Smith, 718 P.2d 1069, 63 A.L.R. 4th 1159 (Colo. App. 1986).

NOTE AND QUESTION

1.   Under UPC §2-201, supra page 389, the surviving spouse may claim an elective share whether the decedent died intestate or testate. The amount of the elective share is the same in both instances. In some

states, if the surviving spouse elects against a will rather than against intestacy, her elective share is less. She may be entitled to a smaller fraction or to lifetime support only. In a few states, the surviving spouse has no right of election if the decedent spouse died intestate.

2. Why is insurance owned by the decedent exempt from the elective share? See Note, Probate Reform: The New Minnesota Elective Share Statutes, 70 Minn. L. Rev. 241, 257-260 (1985).

Sullivan v. Burkin
Supreme Judicial Court of Massachusetts, 1984
390 Mass. 864, 460 N.E.2d 571

WILKINS, J.[8] Mary A. Sullivan, the widow of Ernest G. Sullivan, has exercised her right, under G.L. c. 191, §15, to take a share of her husband's estate. By this action, she seeks a determination that assets held in an inter vivos trust created by her husband during the marriage should be considered as part of the estate in determining that share. A judge of the Probate Court for the county of Suffolk rejected the widow's claim and entered judgment dismissing the complaint. The widow appealed, and, on July 12, 1983, a panel of the Appeals Court reported the case to this court.

In September, 1973, Ernest G. Sullivan executed a deed of trust under which he transferred real estate to himself as sole trustee. The net income of the trust was payable to him during his life and the trustee was instructed to pay to him all or such part of the principal of the trust estate as he might request in writing from time to time. He retained the right to revoke the trust at any time. On his death, the successor trustee is directed to pay the principal and any undistributed income equally to the defendants, George F. Cronin, Sr., and Harold J. Cronin, if they should survive him, which they did. There were no witnesses to the execution of the deed of trust, but the husband acknowledged his signatures before a notary public, separately, as donor and as trustee.

The husband died on April 27, 1981, while still trustee of the inter vivos trust. He left a will in which he stated that he "intentionally neglected to make any provision for my wife, Mary A. Sullivan and my

---

8. In recent years the Massachusetts Supreme Judicial Court has reclaimed the eminent position among state courts it occupied during the nineteenth century. Justice Herbert Wilkins, one of the intellectual leaders of the Massachusetts court, appears to make a specialty of trust cases. He writes the opinions in Sullivan v. Burkin; Dewire v. Haveles, page 625; Beals v. State Street Bank & Trust Co., page 732; and Loring v. Marshall, page 746. For quality of judicial opinion writing, compare these opinions with others in this book. — Eds.

"Now read me the part again where I disinherit everybody."

Drawing by Peter Arno.
Copyright © 1940, 1968 by The New Yorker Magazine, Inc.
Reproduced by permission.

grandson, Mark Sullivan." He directed that, after the payment of debts, expenses, and all estate taxes levied by reason of his death, the residue of his estate should be paid over to the trustee of the inter vivos trust. The defendants George F. Cronin, Sr., and Harold J. Cronin were named coexecutors of the will. The defendant Burkin is successor trustee of the inter vivos trust. On October 21, 1981, the wife filed a claim, pursuant to G.L. c. 191, §15, for a portion [one-third] of the estate.

Although it does not appear in the record, the parties state in their briefs that Ernest G. Sullivan and Mary A. Sullivan had been separated for many years. We do know that in 1962 the wife obtained a court order providing for her temporary support. No final action was taken in that proceeding. The record provides no information about the value of any property owned by the husband at his death or about the value of any assets held in the inter vivos trust. At oral argument, we were advised that the husband owned personal property worth approximately $15,000 at his death and that the only asset in the trust was a house in Boston which was sold after the husband's death for approximately $85,000.

As presented in the complaint, and perhaps as presented to the motion judge, the wife's claim was simply that the inter vivos trust was an invalid testamentary disposition and that the trust assets "constitute assets of the estate" of Ernest G. Sullivan. There is no suggestion that the wife argued initially that, even if the trust were not testamentary, she had a special claim as a widow asserting her rights under G.L. c. 191, §15. If the wife is correct that the trust was an ineffective testamentary disposition, the trust assets would be part of the husband's probate estate. In that event, we would not have to consider any special consequences of the wife's election under G.L. c. 191, §15, or, in the words of the Appeals Court, "the present vitality" of Kerwin v. Donaghy, 317 Mass. 559, 572, 59 N.E.2d 299 (1945).

We conclude, however, that the trust was not testamentary in character and that the husband effectively created a valid inter vivos trust. Thus, whether the issue was initially involved in this case, we are now presented with the question (which the executors will have to resolve ultimately, in any event) whether the assets of the inter vivos trust are to be considered in determining the "portion of the estate of the deceased" (G.L. c. 191, §15) in which Mary A. Sullivan has rights. We conclude that, in this case, we should adhere to the principles expressed in Kerwin v. Donaghy, supra, that deny the surviving spouse any claim against the assets of a valid inter vivos trust created by the deceased spouse, even where the deceased spouse alone retained substantial rights and powers under the trust instrument. For the future, however, as to any inter vivos trust created or amended after the date of this opinion, we announce that the estate of a decedent, for the purposes of G.L. c. 191, §15, shall include the value of assets held in an inter vivos trust created by the deceased spouse as to which the deceased spouse alone retained the power during his or her life to direct the disposition of those trust assets for his or her benefit, as, for example, by the exercise of a power of appointment or by revocation of the trust. Such a power would be a general power of appointment for Federal estate tax purposes (I.R.C. §2041(b)(1) [1983]) and a "general power" as defined in the Restatement (Second) of Property §11.4(1) (Tent. Draft No. 5, 1982).

We consider first whether the inter vivos trust was invalid because it was testamentary. A trust with remainder interests given to others on the settlor's death is not invalid as a testamentary disposition simply because the settlor retained a broad power to modify or revoke the trust, the right to receive income, and the right to invade principal during his life. . . . We believe that the law of the Commonwealth is correctly represented by the statement in Restatement (Second) of Trusts §57, comment h (1959), that a trust is "not testamentary and invalid for failure to comply with the requirements of the Statute of Wills merely because the settlor-trustee reserves a beneficial life interest and power to revoke and modify the trust. The fact that as trustee he controls the administration of the trust does not invalidate it."

We come then to the question whether, even if the trust was not testamentary on general principles, the widow has special interests which should be recognized. Courts in this country have differed considerably in their reasoning and in their conclusions in passing on this question. See 1 A. Scott, Trusts §57.5 at 509-511 (3d ed. 1967 & 1983 Supp.); Restatement (Second) of Property — Donative Transfers, Supplement to Tent. Draft No. 5, reporter's note to §13.7 (1982); Annot., 39 A.L.R.3d 14 (1971), Validity of Inter Vivos Trust Established by One Spouse Which Impairs the Other Spouse's Distributive Share or Other Statutory Rights in Property. . . .

The rule of Kerwin v. Donaghy, supra 317 Mass. at 571, 59 N.E.2d 299, is that

[t]he right of a wife to waive her husband's will, and take, with certain limitations, "the same portion of the property of the deceased, real and personal, that . . . she would have taken if the deceased had died intestate" (G.L. [Ter. Ed.] c. 191, §15), does not extend to personal property that has been conveyed by the husband in his lifetime and does not form part of his estate at his death. Fiske v. Fiske, 173 Mass. 413, 419, 53 N.E. 916 [1899]. Shelton v. Sears, 187 Mass. 455, 73 N.E. 666 [1905]. In this Commonwealth a husband has an absolute right to dispose of any or all of his personal property in his lifetime, without the knowledge or consent of his wife, with the result that it will not form part of his estate for her to share under the statute of distributions (G.L. [Ter. Ed.] c. 190, §§1,

2), under his will, or by virtue of a waiver of his will. That is true even though his sole purpose was to disinherit her.

In the *Kerwin* case, we applied the rule to deny a surviving spouse the right to reach assets the deceased spouse had placed in an inter vivos trust of which the settlor's daughter by a previous marriage was trustee and over whose assets he had a general power of appointment. The rule of Kerwin v. Donaghy has been adhered to in this Commonwealth for almost forty years and was adumbrated even earlier. The bar has been entitled reasonably to rely on that rule in advising clients. In the area of property law, the retroactive invalidation of an established principle is to be undertaken with great caution. We conclude that, whether or not Ernest G. Sullivan established the inter vivos trust in order to defeat his wife's right to take her statutory share in the assets placed in the trust and even though he had a general power of appointment over the trust assets, Mary A. Sullivan obtained no right to share in the assets of that trust when she made her election under G.L. c. 191, §15.

We announce for the future that, as to any inter vivos trust created or amended after the date of this opinion, we shall no longer follow the rule announced in Kerwin v. Donaghy. There have been significant changes since 1945 in public policy considerations bearing on the right of one spouse to treat his or her property as he or she wishes during marriage. The interests of one spouse in the property of the other have been substantially increased upon the dissolution of a marriage by divorce.[9] We believe that, when a marriage is terminated by the death of one spouse, the rights of the surviving spouse should not be so restricted as they are by the rule in Kerwin v. Donaghy. It is neither equitable nor logical to extend to a divorced spouse greater rights in the assets of an inter vivos trust created and controlled by the other spouse than are extended to a spouse who remains married until the death of his or her spouse.

---

9. At the time of a divorce or at any subsequent time "the court may assign to either husband or wife all or any part of the estate of the other," on consideration of various factors, such as the length of the marriage, the conduct of the parties during marriage, their ages, their employability, their liabilities and needs, and opportunity for future acquisition of capital assets and income. G.L. c. 208, §34, as amended by St. 1982, c. 642, §1. The power to dispose completely of the property of the divorced litigants comes from a 1974 amendment to G.L. c. 208, §34. . . . It made a significant change in the respective rights of the husband and wife. . . . We have held that the "estate" subject to disposition on divorce includes not only property acquired during the marriage from the efforts of the husband and wife, but also all property of a spouse "whenever and however acquired." Rice v. Rice, 372 Mass. 398, 361 N.E.2d 1305 (1977). Without suggesting the outer limits of the meaning of the word "estate" under G.L. c. 208, §34, . . . after this decision there should be no doubt that the "estate" of . . . [a divorcing] spouse would include trust assets held in a trust created by the other spouse and having provisions such as the trust in the case before us.

The rule we now favor would treat as part of "the estate of the deceased" for the purposes of G.L. c. 191, §15, assets of an inter vivos trust created during the marriage by the deceased spouse over which he or she alone had a general power of appointment, exercisable by deed or by will. This objective test would involve no consideration of the motive or intention of the spouse in creating the trust. We would not need to engage in a determination of "whether the [spouse] has in good faith divested himself [or herself] of ownership of his [or her] property or has made an illusory transfer" (Newman v. Dore, 275 N.Y. 371, 379, 9 N.E.2d 966 [1937]) or with the factual question whether the spouse "intended to surrender complete dominion over the property" (Staples v. King, 433 A.2d 407, 411 [Me. 1981]). Nor would we have to participate in the rather unsatisfactory process of determining whether the inter vivos trust was, on some standard, "colorable," "fraudulent," or "illusory."

What we have announced as a rule for the future hardly resolves all the problems that may arise. There may be a different rule if some or all of the trust assets were conveyed to such a trust by a third person. Cf. Theodore v. Theodore, 356 Mass. 297, 249 N.E.2d 3 (1969). We have not, of course, dealt with a case in which the power of appointment is held jointly with another person. If the surviving spouse assented to the creation of the inter vivos trust, perhaps the rule we announce would not apply. We have not discussed which assets should be used to satisfy a surviving spouse's claim. We have not discussed the question whether a surviving spouse's interest in the intestate estate of a deceased spouse should reflect the value of assets held in an inter vivos trust created by the intestate spouse over which he or she had a general power of appointment. That situation and the one before us, however, do not seem readily distinguishable. See Schnakenberg v. Schnakenberg, 262 A.D. 234, 236-237, 28 N.Y.S.2d 841 (N.Y. 1941). A general power of appointment over assets in a trust created by a third person is said to present a different situation. Restatement (Second) of Property — Donative Transfers, Supplement to Tent. Draft No. 5, reporter's note to §13.7 at 29 (1982). Nor have we dealt with other assets not passing by will, such as a trust created before the marriage or insurance policies over which a deceased spouse had control. Id. at 30, 38.

The question of the rights of a surviving spouse in the estate of a deceased spouse, using the word "estate" in its broad sense, is one that can best be handled by legislation. See Uniform Probate Code, §§2-201, 2-202, 8 U.L.A. 74-75 (1983). See also Uniform Marital Property Act, §18 (Nat'l Conference of Comm'rs on Uniform State Laws, July, 1983), which adopts the concept of community property as to "marital property." But, until it is, the answers to these problems will "be determined in the usual way through the decisional process." Tucker

v. Badoian, 376 Mass. 907, 918-919, 384 N.E.2d 1195 (1978) (Kaplan, J., concurring).

We affirm the judgment of the Probate Court dismissing the plaintiff's complaint.

So ordered.

NOTES AND PROBLEM

1.   In Sullivan v. Burkin the court rejects tests applied in some other states to determine what inter vivos transfers are subject to the surviving spouse's election. The most famous of these is the *illusory transfer* test, laid down in Newman v. Dore, 275 N.Y. 371, 9 N.E.2d 966, 112 A.L.R. 643 (1937) (now replaced by statute in New York). A transfer over which the transferor retains a substantial quantum of ownership is deemed illusory and subject to the surviving spouse's election. Thus:

> *Case 6. H,* married to *W,* owns Blackacre, Whiteacre, stocks and bonds, a life insurance policy on his own life payable to *W,* and a savings account. *H,* angry with *W,* transfers Blackacre to his daughter *D* as a gift, takes title to Whiteacre with *D* in joint tenancy, transfers his stocks and bonds into a trust in which he retains the right to the income and the right to revoke, changes the beneficiary of the life insurance policy to *D,* and changes title to the savings account to *H* in trust for *D* (a Totten trust). *H* then dies. Under the illusory transfer test, *W* cannot reach Blackacre, which has been given absolutely, but *W* might be able to subject any of the other transfers to her elective share.

The test for "illusoriness" is difficult to define; cases tend to be resolved on a case-by-case basis. The key is the amount of control retained by the decedent spouse — but how much is too much? The illusory transfer test is itself illusory. Yet it is still followed in some states. See Falender, Protective Provisions for Surviving Spouses in Indiana: Considerations for a Legislative Response to *Leazenby,* 11 Ind. L. Rev. 755 (1978); Note, Estate Planning: Validity of Inter Vivos Transfers Which Reduce or Defeat the Surviving Spouse's Statutory Share in Decedent's Estate, 32 Okla. L. Rev. 837 (1979).

The second test rejected by the Massachusetts court is whether the decedent *intended to deprive* the surviving spouse of her elective share. Under this test, motive or intent is the controlling issue. Another test, slightly different from the intent-to-deprive test, is whether the transfer is in *fraud* of the marital rights of the surviving spouse. The fraud test weighs a wide variety of factors: The intent of the transferor, the completeness of the transfer, the amount of time between the transfer and death, and the degree to which the surviving spouse is left without an interest in the decedent's property or other means of support. See W. McGovern, S. Kurtz & J. Rein, Wills, Trusts and Estates §3.8 (1988).

In some states, nonprobate transfers are not subject to the spousal election under any of the above tests. See, e.g., Cherniack v. Home National Bank, 151 Conn. 367, 198 A.2d 58 (1964); In re Estate of Solnik, 401 So. 2d 896 (Fla. App. 1981).

The power of a court to subject inter vivos transfers to the elective share, applying one of these vague tests, is rather similar to the power of equitable distribution upon divorce. It is the exercise of a discretionary power, hard to predict. But if a court has the power of equitable distribution at divorce, should it not also have the power of equitable division of will substitutes at death if the legislature does not address the problem? See Kulzer, Law and the Housewife: Property, Divorce, and Death, 28 U. Fla. L. Rev. 1 (1975); Comment, Spousal Disinheritance: The New York Solution — A Critique of Forced Share Legislation, 7 W. New Eng. L. Rev. 881 (1985).

Restatement (Second) of Property, Donative Transfers §13.7 (1986), provides that assets in a funded revocable trust are treated as owned assets of a deceased spouse in determining the rights of the surviving spouse.

For a detailed argument that courts should by analogy treat, as subject to the elective share, all lifetime transfers includable in the decedent's federal gross estate under the federal estate tax, see Kwestel & Seplowitz, Testamentary Substitutes: Retained Interests, Custodial Accounts and Contractual Transactions — A New Approach, 38 Am. U.L. Rev. 1 (1988). Inter vivos transfers subject to estate taxation are discussed infra at pages 969-985.

2. If a state subjects inter vivos transfers to the surviving spouse's elective share, other problems may be encountered. If an inter vivos transfer is invalid with respect to the surviving spouse, is it entirely invalid or invalid only to the extent necessary to satisfy the statutory interest of the spouse? If the latter is the answer, a further question arises: Does the surviving spouse have a right to a fractional share of each item of property transferred inter vivos, or are the inter vivos transfers taken into consideration in fixing the amount of the spouse's share, which must be satisfied out of the probate estate before the property transferred inter vivos is reached? The cases are in some disagreement on these matters, though the clear trend seems to be in favor of the solution provided by Uniform Probate Code §2-207, supra page 387.

Under the Uniform Probate Code, the surviving spouse may claim an elective share without losing any benefits under the decedent's will unless the will makes express provision to the contrary. After the amount of the surviving spouse's elective share is determined, it is satisfied first by setting off to the spouse property included in the augmented estate that has passed to the spouse by inter vivos transfer from the decedent or that passes to the spouse by the decedent's will or by intestate succession. Then the elective share is satisfied from the remaining property of the augmented estate (some of which may be in the hands of third persons); it is charged against estate beneficiaries and inter vivos donees in proportion to the value of their interests. UPC §2-207. An inter vivos donee who is required to contribute to make up the elective share may either give up the specific property transferred or may pay its value into the estate. Id. If the third person refuses to pay, the personal representative may sue for contribution. See UPC §2-205(e).

If the decedent's will states that bequests to the surviving spouse are in lieu of all statutory rights in his estate, this does not necessarily bar the surviving spouse from taking under the will *and* claiming her share of any intestate property. "Statutory rights" have been defined to include dower, elective share, rights to support, and other rights, the assertion of which would disrupt the testamentary plan. See Waring v. Loring, 399 Mass. 419, 504 N.E.2d 644 (1987).

3. *H* and *W*, both 65 years of age, move to New York from Connecticut. They were married some 40 years before. *W* has little property of her own. *H* made a great deal of money in Connecticut during their marriage. After a fuss between *H* and *W*, *H* drives from New York to New Haven and sets up an inter vivos trust, retaining the right to the income, the power to appoint by will, and the power to revoke. He names a New Haven bank as trustee and transfers to the trustee title to practically all his assets. *H* dies domiciled in New York. Can *W* reach the assets in the New Haven trust by virtue of N.Y. Est. Powers & Trusts Law §5-1.1, supra page 389? How should she go about it? See National Shawmut Bank v. Cumming, 325 Mass. 457, 91 N.E.2d 337 (1950).

In this connection, compare two New York cases. In In re Clark, 21 N.Y.2d 478, 236 N.E.2d 152, 288 N.Y.S.2d 993 (1968), the court held that a Virginia domiciliary could not cut off his widow's right of election under Virginia law by providing in his will that the disposition of his personal property located in New York was to be governed by New York law. (New York permits the surviving spouse's elective share to be put in trust, with only a right to the income; Virginia gives it to the spouse outright.) The domiciliary state, Virginia, was deemed to have the paramount interest in enforcing marital property rights of its domiciliaries. In re Estate of Renard, 108 Misc. 2d 31, 437 N.Y.S.2d 860 (Sur. Ct. 1981), aff'd without opinion, 56 N.Y.2d 973, 439 N.E.2d 341 (1982), involved a forced share for a child rather than for a widow. The testator, domiciled in France but residing in New York, left a will providing that New York law would govern the disposition of her assets located in New York. The testator's son, who was entitled to a one-half share of her property under French law, sued to enforce his French forced share rights in the property located in New York. The court, holding that New York had a paramount interest in enforcing its policy of testamentary freedom against forced heirship for children, applied New York law and denied the son a one-half forced share. See Hendrickson, Choice-of-Law Directions for Disposing of Assets Situated Elsewhere than the Domicile of Their Owner — The Refractions of *Renard,* 18 Real. Prop., Prob. & Tr. J. 407 (1983).

Compare Uniform Probate Code §2-602, which provides: "The meaning and legal effect of a disposition in a will shall be determined by the local law of a particular state selected by the testator in his instrument unless the application of that law is contrary to the provisions relating to the elective share . . . of this State."

4.   *Contracts.*   Spouses may make a contract that the surviving spouse is entitled only to a specified amount of the decedent's property and will not claim an elective share. Such a contract may be made before or after marriage. A contract deemed unfair by the court or made without full disclosure of assets by the spouses may not be enforceable, however. The law on enforcing marital contracts is unsettled and changing. Such contracts are not yet reliable estate planning devices. See W. McGovern, S. Kurtz & J. Rein, Wills, Trusts and Estates §3.9 (1988).

4.   *Rights of Surviving Spouse in Community Property*

a.   Introduction

As explained earlier, eight states — containing more than one-fourth of the population of the United States — have a system of community property. These community property states, sweeping around the southwest border of the country from the Mississippi River to Canada, are Louisiana, Texas, New Mexico, Arizona, California, Nevada, Washington, and Idaho. In addition, Wisconsin must now be considered a community property state since it has adopted the Uniform Marital Property Act (providing for community property under the name of "marital property").

Community property in the United States is a community of acquests: Husband and wife own the earnings and acquisitions from earnings of both spouses during marriage in undivided equal shares. Whatever is bought with earnings is community property. All property that is not community property is the separate property of one spouse or the other or, in the case of a tenancy in common or joint tenancy, of both. Separate property includes property acquired before marriage and property acquired during marriage by gift or inheritance. In Idaho, Louisiana, and Texas, income from separate property is community property. (This rule is also adopted by the Uniform Marital Property Act.) In the other community property states, income from separate property retains its separate character. Where the characterization of the property is doubtful, there is a strong presumption that the property is community property. Where property has been commingled by the spouses, the party contending for separate property may have a difficult tracing burden.

Since one spouse cannot unilaterally appropriate the other spouse's property to himself, community property cannot be converted into the separate property of one spouse, or into any other kind of property, without the consent of both spouses. Because community property belongs to both, problems arise as to which spouse can manage the property and deal with third persons respecting the property. These problems may concern sale, leasing, mortgages, improving, or subjecting the property to creditors. Each community property state has statutes on this matter. Although these statutes differ in many details, we can indicate broadly the management roles. In Texas, the wife has sole management power over her earnings kept separate and the husband sole power over his. If the earnings are commingled, they are subject to the joint management of the spouses. In California and the other community property states, either the husband or wife, acting alone, has the power to manage community property. Statutes ordinarily require both spouses to join in transfers or mortgages of community real property, however. In most of these, gifts of community property to a third party can be set aside by the nondonor spouse, either entirely or in excess of a certain amount. We explore gifts of community property further at page 405 infra.

Upon the death of one spouse, the deceased spouse can dispose of his or her half of the community assets. The surviving spouse owns the other half, which is not, of course, subject to testamentary disposition by the deceased spouse. The one-half of the community property belonging to the deceased spouse may be devised to whomever the decedent pleases, the same as separate property.

Community property compared with the elective share.   The elective share available to a surviving spouse in a separate property state does not give the surviving spouse any rights in the property of the other spouse until the latter's death. Community property gives ownership rights to each spouse immediately upon acquisition. The problem of inter vivos transfers made by one spouse to defeat the elective share of the survivor does not arise with community property because the survivor owns one-half of the property from the time of acquisition. If the husband transfers community property into a revocable trust without the consent of his wife, after the husband's death the wife may be able to void the transfer to the extent of one-half (her interest in the community property).

The community property system does not protect the surviving spouse where there is no community property. This usually occurs in a marriage of short duration before any property can be accumulated from earnings, in a marriage of two retired persons, or in a marriage where an unemployed couple live off of inherited wealth. (Of course the surviving spouse in these situations may acquire some benefit as a result of a rule that income from separate property is community, or from the presumption that all property on hand at death is community property.) In these three situations, an elective share system, which gives the surviving spouse a share of all property of the deceased spouse, whether acquired from gift, inheritance, or earnings, is of more benefit to the surviving spouse.

b. Classification of Assets as Community or Separate Property

For the estate planner, a number of consequences turn on whether assets are classified as community or separate property. Community property states have different schemes of intestate distribution for separate and community property. As we have already indicated, each spouse's power of testamentary disposition extends only to an undivided one-half share of community assets but is unlimited with respect to separate assets. Thus it is important to know over which items of property each spouse has testamentary power.

How is it determined whether assets are separate or community property? In cases not readily resolved by the definitions given above, a state may have a particularized rule applicable to a certain type of property or to a certain situation. Here are some examples of common situations where separate and community property are mixed:

(1) *Asset acquired before marriage, with some payments made after marriage.* In some states an inception-of-title rule is applied. Under this rule, assets acquired before marriage remain separate property; the community is entitled to reimbursement for payments made after marriage with community funds. Take, for example, a life insurance policy taken out by the husband before marriage, with some premiums paid out of the husband's earnings after marriage. The policy remains the husband's separate property; the community is entitled to a return of premiums paid, with interest. McCurdy v. McCurdy, 372 S.W.2d 381 (Tex. Civ. App. 1963). Other states apply a pro-rata share rule in this situation. The assets (e.g., the proceeds of the life insurance policy) are characterized as separate or community property according to the proportion of payments made.

(2) *A business acquired before marriage, in which owner-spouse works after marriage.*   In this situation, some states treat any appreciation in value as separate property, provided the community was fairly compensated (by salary, dividends, or other payments) for the owner-spouse's work during marriage. California attempts to determine whether the appreciation was primarily due to the spouse's skills and activity, or to general market rise. If the former, the appreciation is community property. Beam v. Bank of America, 6 Cal. 3d 12, 490 P.2d 257, 98 Cal. Rptr. 137 (1971).

(3) *Asset acquired during marriage with both separate and community funds.*   Most states call for proportionate sharing in this situation, but there are often exceptions involving presumptions that one spouse is making a gift to the other.

These illustrations merely scratch the surface of many difficult problems of characterization. The details of this complicated matter must be left to a course in community property. See G. Blumberg, Community Property in California 133-402 (1987); W. Reppy & J. McKnight, Texas Marital Property Law 31-114 (1983); W. Reppy & C. Samuel, Community Property in the United States 51-164 (2d ed. 1982); H. Verrall & G. Bird, California Community Property, 41-111, 240-376 (5th ed. 1988).

Couples in community property states generally may make agreements regarding the character of their property. They may agree to "live separate in property," meaning their property rights will be determined as if they were not married. By agreement they may change separate property into community property, or they may change community property into a joint tenancy, a tenancy in common, or sole ownership by one spouse.[10] This change in characterization is called "transmutation." And, of course, one spouse may give his or her interest in community property to the other spouse. See W. Reppy & C. Samuel, supra, 23-49.

c.   Gifts of Community Property by One Spouse

Givens v. Girard Life Insurance Co.

Texas Court of Civil Appeals, 1972
480 S.W.2d 421

GUITTARD, J.   Girard Life Insurance Company filed this interpleader action to determine ownership of insurance proceeds on the life of

---

10. In Texas, it is unconstitutional(!) for spouses to convert separate property into community property. See W. Reppy & C. Samuel, supra, 378-381 (describing this result as "absurd"). Texas spouses can transmute community property into separate property by written agreement — but it took a constitutional amendment to permit such partitions.

Walter Morris, deceased. The petition names as defendants Weedoll Givens, the designated beneficiary, and Edna Morris, widow of the insured. The principal question is whether designation by the husband of an unrelated person as beneficiary of life insurance purchased with community funds is constructive fraud on the wife.

The case was tried on an agreed statement of facts, which includes the following information. Walter and Edna Morris were married in 1928, and had several children, some of whom survive, but when he died on June 22, 1970, he had not lived with Edna for more than ten years. He held a certificate of insurance under a group life insurance policy obtained from Girard Life by his employer, who paid all the premiums and made no deductions from his pay for that purpose. On June 27, 1967, Morris changed the beneficiary to Weedoll Givens, who was not related to him by blood or marriage and was described in the designation as a friend. She had been acquainted with him since 1963, and their friendship continued until his death.

The policy provided a death benefit of $4,000, which the insurance company paid into court. Other assets are described as follows: "The only known asset of the community estate of Walter Morris and Edna P. Morris, other than personal items, is approximately one acre of land near Fayetteville, Texas (and insurance policies, if same are considered assets of the community estate)."

No will was found. Community indebtedness consisted of $350 on a television and stereo purchased by Edna Morris, taxes due on the acre of land near Fayetteville, and unpaid funeral expenses of $215.

The trial court held that the insurance proceeds were community property and that the change of beneficiary from his wife Edna Morris to the unrelated friend "was an act of constructive fraud upon the rights of Edna P. Morris as to her half of the proceeds." Accordingly the judgment awarded one-half of the proceeds to the widow and the other half to the beneficiary, who appeals, contending that the stipulated facts fail to show any ground to defeat the prima facie case established by her designation as beneficiary. We hold that the facts support the judgment.

We agree with appellant that the rights of the insured husband under this contract were subject to his statutory power of management and disposition.[11]

Consequently, our question here is a particular aspect of the general question of the power of the managing spouse to make gifts of community property without consent of the other spouse. Reconciliation of the managerial power of one spouse with the interest of the other

---

11. Tex. Fam. Code §5.22 (1969) gives the husband management power over his earnings and the wife management power over her earnings. — Eds.

spouse as equal owner is a problem inherent in the concept of management by one spouse of marital property owned in common. This concept has come down to us from the laws of Spain and Mexico, and is carried forward in the statutes above mentioned without substantial change, except that the managerial powers of the husband have been restricted and those of the wife have been extended with respect to classes of property not now before us.

Our review of the authorities reveals that the husband's power to make gifts of community property has always been limited, though the limits have never been clearly defined. Early Spanish authorities expressed various opinions. Probably the prevailing Spanish view was stated by the commentator Escriche, as follows: ". . . the husband can, without the consent of the wife, make inter vivos conveyances [of their community property] and even moderate donations for just causes; but excessive or capricious gifts will be null, and alienations made with intent to defraud the wife, who will have action in all these cases against the properties of the husband and against the possessor of the things conveyed."[12]

In Stramler v. Coe, 15 Tex. 211 at 216 (1855), Chief Justice Hemphill, citing Escriche and other Spanish authorities, declares:

> The husband has the active control and administration of the ganancial property during the matrimony. No consent of the wife is necessary to a valid alienation of such property by the husband. But excessive or capricious donations and sales, made with the intent to defraud the wife, would be void; and she would be entitled to her action against the property of the husband and against third possessors.

Prof. Huie has pointed out that this is almost a literal translation of Escriche's language, and therefore the court must have intended to adopt the rule as laid down by Escriche, but that the court's statement is ambiguous as to whether a showing of fraudulent intent is required with respect to donations as well as sales, whereas Escriche made it clear that excessive or capricious gifts would be void without regard to whether the husband intended to defraud the wife. This distinction seems to have been overlooked in later cases in which Texas courts have said that the husband may use his managerial powers to give away community property so long as he does so without intent to defraud the wife. However, the Supreme Court has never held that proof of actual intent to defraud is required to avoid an "excessive or capricious" gift. Several courts of civil appeals have treated intent to defraud the

---

12. Translation quoted in Huie, [Community Property Laws as Applied to Life Insurance, 18 Tex. L. Rev. 121 (1940)] at 123, citing Escriche, Diccionario de Legislacion Anotado (1840) 71.

wife as a fact issue to be submitted to the jury. This approach has been criticized on the ground that making the validity of the gift depend on the subjective intent of the deceased husband leaves the wife's protection against excessive gifts inadequate and uncertain, and that the husband would never know in advance whether his gift would stand or fall, because its validity would depend upon a jury's speculation upon an issue of fact incapable of being accurately determined.

We are persuaded that the widow should not have the burden of establishing fraudulent intent in order to protect her interest in the community property from abuse of her husband's managerial powers. This view is sustained by Texas authority. In appropriate cases our courts have dispensed with proof of fraudulent intent on the theory of constructive fraud, a judicial convention employed to achieve a just result in cases where the wrong to the wife is so clear that intent is immaterial. Thus an "excessive or capricious donation" was held to be "presumptively fraudulent" in Hartman v. Crain, 398 S.W.2d 387 (Tex. Civ. App., Houston 1966, no writ). Also in Martin v. Moran, 11 Tex. Civ. App. 509, 32 S.W. 904 (Fort Worth 1895, no writ), the insured's designation of his own estate as beneficiary was held to be a fraud on the wife because he had no power to give her interest in the community property to himself. The constructive fraud concept has been applied in cases in which the beneficiary has been changed from the wife to a relative of the insured, and the community estate remaining was insolvent or its assets so meager that the value of the property left in the hands of the surviving spouse was less than the proceeds of the policy. Davis v. Prudential Ins. Co. of America, 331 F.2d 346 (5th Cir. 1964); Kemp v. Metropolitan Life Ins. Co., 205 F.2d 857 (5th Cir. 1953); . . . On the other hand, if adequate provision is made for the surviving spouse a gift to a relative, through life insurance or otherwise, is not considered fraudulent. Krueger v. Williams, 163 Tex. 545, 359 S.W.2d 48 (1962). . . .

All the cases above cited involved donees and beneficiaries related to the decedent. In such cases, as learned commentators have noted, the courts have considered objective factors in determining whether the situation was one in which the decedent might properly have made a gift of community funds, such as the relationship of the parties, whether special circumstances tended to justify the gift, and whether the community funds used for such purpose were reasonably in proportion to the community assets remaining.[13] Prof. Huie suggests that where life insurance is used as a means for distributing property at death to

13. Johanson, Revocable Trusts and Community Property, 47 Tex. L. Rev. 537, 568 (1969); 1 Oakes, Speer's Marital Rights in Texas, 4th Ed. §434 at 642 (1961); de Funiak, Principles of Community Property, §123 at 305 (1971).

nondependent relatives, the principles of testamentary disposition of community property should apply, so that the beneficiary designation should be upheld only when reimbursement can be had from the husband's part of the community estate, and that gifts to the wife should also be considered on the question of constructive fraud.

Although we have found no direct precedent dealing with application of the constructive fraud concept to an unrelated donee or beneficiary, the reasons for protecting the widow's interest against appropriation of community funds for relatives of the husband, such as a mother, sister or child of an earlier marriage, have even greater force when the beneficiary is entirely unrelated.[14] Persons outside the family do not ordinarily receive substantial gifts from donors in the modest circumstances of the deceased husband here. Neither are unrelated friends normally named as beneficiaries in life insurance contracts, which are designed primarily for protection of dependents on death of the insured by payment of debts and expenses and compensation for loss of support. Warthan v. Haynes, 155 Tex. 413, 288 S.W.2d 481 (1956). In our view, a husband's use of jointly owned funds to provide life insurance benefits to someone outside the family is so extraordinary as to raise a strong inference of misappropriation of the wife's interest in the community property. Consequently, we hold that purchase of life insurance with community funds for benefit of an unrelated person is constructively fraudulent in the absence of special justifying circumstances.

Under this holding the widow establishes constructive fraud prima facie by proof that life insurance was purchased with community funds for the benefit of an unrelated person, and the beneficiary then has the burden to justify such use of community funds. What special circumstances would justify designation of an unrelated beneficiary cannot properly be determined in this case. All we know from the agreed statement about the relationship of the beneficiary to the insured is that they had been acquainted since 1963 and their friendship continued until the insured's death. This relationship does not support a substantial benefit to the unrelated friend from funds owned in common by the husband and wife. Neither can the friend's recovery of the entire proceeds be justified as equivalent to testamentary disposition of the insured's half of the community. No compensating benefits were provided by will for the widow, and although the agreed statement mentions "insurance policies," it does not disclose the amount or beneficiary of any policy other than the certificate in question. In the absence of any proof of these matters, we hold that the trial court was

---

14. Johanson, supra note [13] at 568, citing cases in which gifts to mistresses have been declared fraudulent as against the wife. See Roberson v. Roberson, 420 S.W.2d 495 (Tex. Civ. App., Houston 14th Dist. 1967, writ ref'd n.r.e); Watson v. Harris, 61 Tex. Civ. App. 263, 130 S.W. 237 (Austin 1910, no writ).

correct in awarding to the widow half the insurance proceeds on the ground that the change of beneficiary from her to appellant Givens was an act of constructive fraud. . . .

Affirmed.

NOTES AND PROBLEMS

1. Since Land v. Marshall, 426 S.W.2d 841 (Tex. 1968), a gift of community property must not only be reasonable and not in fraud of the other spouse's right, it also must not be illusory. The Texas court invoked the illusory transfer doctrine of Newman v. Dore, supra page 399, in allowing a widow to reach community assets in a revocable trust created by her husband during his life. See Johanson, Revocable Trusts and Community Property: The Substantive Problems, 47 Tex. L. Rev. 537, 563-570 (1969).

2. California and Washington do not follow a reasonable gifts rule or a fraud rule. In these states a gift is not deemed to come within the management powers of the managing spouse. The nondonor spouse can set aside the entire gift if he or she acts during the donor spouse's lifetime. After the donor spouse's death, the nondonor spouse can set aside the transfer to the extent of one-half the transfer (or in Washington the entire transfer). If the property cannot be recovered from the donee, the nondonor spouse has a claim against the donor spouse or his estate for one-half the value of the assets transferred.

The other community property states vary considerably on how they treat gifts. In most of them under the old law, when the husband was the managing spouse, the manager could make reasonable gifts, but now that community property is subject to equal management of husband and wife, only time will clarify the extent to which one manager can give away community property without the consent of the other.

3. *H* is married to *W*, his second wife. *H* employs in his food brokerage business his son *S* by his first wife. *H* pays *S* a salary. Because *S* is hard-working, works Saturdays and Sundays, and is a most valuable employee, *H* opens a joint savings account with *S*. Each year, for 16 years, *H* deposits in the savings account funds withdrawn from his business account. *S* signs the savings account form card at the bank when the account is opened but does not know when deposits are made or in what amount. At *H*'s death, the joint savings account amounts to $75,000. *W* claims the account was created by use of community funds, without her consent and without valuable consideration. She therefore claims one-half as her share of community property. What result? Estate of Bray, 30 Cal. App. 2d 136, 40 Cal. Rptr. 750 (1964).

4. Almost all the community property states follow the theory that

H and *W* own equal shares in each item of community property at death. They do not own equal undivided shares in the aggregate of community property. Thus if *H* and *W* own Blackacre (worth $50,000) and Whiteacre (worth $50,000), each owns a half share in each tract. *W*'s will cannot devise Blackacre to *H* and Whiteacre to *D*, her daughter by a previous marriage, even though *H* would end up receiving property equal to the value of his community share. (Divorce is different. In most community property states, the divorce court may award Blackacre to *H* and Whiteacre to *W*; it may award specific items of community property to one spouse or the other, provided each spouse ends up with a share of the aggregate value of community property.)

Is the item theory, applicable at death, consistent with the reasonable gift approach of the Spanish law? Should will substitutes, such as life insurance, payable-on-death contracts, and joint tenancies, be treated as inter vivos transfers subject to a reasonable gifts rule or as testamentary transfers invoking the item theory? See G. Blumberg, Community Property in California 593-594 (1987).

d. Putting the Survivor to an Election

A spouse's will may attempt to dispose of the entire interest in community assets and put the other spouse to an election: "If you claim your share of the community property that I have devised by my will, you lose what I give you under my will." An essential element of the election doctrine is that the testator intends to dispose of property that is not in fact his own (that is, the spouse's share of community property) and is not within his power of disposition. The election may be made explicit (as above), or it may be implicit. A common kind of case where an election is implicit is when the testator is mistaken regarding the classification of particular property. Thus where the testator believes that all property on hand is his separate property (when in reality some of it is community property), so states in his will, and makes a devise to the surviving spouse, courts have found that an implicit election is required. The surviving spouse cannot claim both her share of the community property (contradicting the will) and her devise under the will. Estate of Wolfe, 48 Cal. 2d 570, 311 P.2d 476 (1957). On the other hand, where the testator does not characterize his property in his will and describes his property in general terms (e.g., "all my property"), the testator is presumed to intend to dispose only of his separate property and his one-half share of community property. In this situation, there is no inconsistency in permitting the surviving spouse to claim both her share of community property and her devise under the will.

Estate of Kennedy

California Court of Appeal, Second District, 1982
135 Cal. App. 3d 676, 185 Cal. Rptr. 540

ASHBY, J. The decedent Opal Corinne Kennedy (Decedent) died testate on December 23, 1977. Her will, which was admitted to probate May 12, 1978, made provisions for her husband, Bob C. Kennedy (Husband), and her daughter, Patricia Lou Kennedy, now Patricia Hoskin (Daughter). Husband thereafter died. The executor of Decedent's estate filed a petition to determine interest and entitlement to distribution pursuant to Probate Code section 1080, and statements of interest were filed by Daughter and by the executrix of Husband's estate, Christine McMahan. Pursuant to stipulation the matter was bifurcated so that the court could first determine legal issues, each side reserving the right to try any factual issues remaining after the court's resolution of legal issues.

The court determined that under the will Husband, and thereafter Husband's estate, was put to an election whether to take the property bequeathed by the will or to assert Husband's rights as surviving joint tenant to certain joint tenancy property which the will purported to bequeath to Daughter. Husband's executrix appeals, contending that the will did not force Husband to choose between taking the property left to him in the will and asserting his rights as surviving joint tenant. (Prob. Code, §1240, subd. (o).)

PROVISIONS OF THE WILL

The crucial provisions of Decedent's will are paragraphs third, fourth, fifth, and sixth as follows:

> Third: It should be known that all property standing in the name of my husband alone and all property standing in my name and my husband's name as joint tenants is our community property. It is my intention by this Will to dispose of all my separate property and my share of our community property (and quasi-community property, if any,) owned by me at the time of my death. In this regard it should also be known that the majority of the assets owned by my husband, Bob C. Kennedy, and myself, are held in the form of joint tenancy. Said titles held in the form of joint tenancy have at no time been intended to be truly vested in joint tenancy between my said husband and myself, and no right of survivorship is intended in connection with said assets. Said assets have been placed in the form of joint tenancy at the direction of my said husband, Bob C. Kennedy, as manager of our community estate. I am now and have at all times been convinced that any attempt that I may make to change the vesting of said property to its true nature of community property will result in unhappy differences existing between my said husband and

myself and may result in an injury to my health. However, for purposes of both my own estate and my husband's estate, whichever of us may be first to pass away, it must be known that community property is the true nature of all of our assets and said assets must be probated as if they were actually in the form of community property.

Fourth: Except as hereinafter provided, I give to my husband, Bob C. Kennedy, all interests that I may have in the goodwill of his accounting business and practice now conducted by him in his name and all of the personal property used by him directly in connection with said accounting business, and the balances in all commercial checking accounts that we may have and any interest that I may have in his clothing and similar personal effects, and in the personal automobile he may be using in connection with his business at the time of my death (which such automobile is now our 1972 Cadillac automobile), and I also give to my husband, Bob C. Kennedy, any interest that I may have in the older model Jeep vehicle and the 26 foot Stevens power boat, his guns, fishing equipment and tools, and our mooring in Avalon Harbor, Catalina, and all furniture, furnishings and household effects except for my china which is hand painted by my mother, all of my Wallace Grand Baroque silver, my silver tea set, and all oil paintings painted by my mother. In the event my husband, Bob C. Kennedy, fails to survive me, I then give all of the above described assets to my daughter, Patricia Lou Kennedy, or if she fails to survive me, I then give said assets equally to those of the children of my daughter, Patricia Lou Kennedy, who survive me.

Fifth: I give all of my community interest and my husband's community interest in our Wallace Grand Baroque silver, my silver tea set, and the oil paintings painted by my mother to my daughter, Patricia Lou Kennedy, providing she survives me, or in the event she fails to survive me, then equally to those of the children of my daughter, Patricia Lou Kennedy, who survive me. In the event my husband, Bob C. Kennedy, elects to take the rights given him by law in the assets described in this paragraph, all provisions in this Will shall be carried into effect as though my husband, Bob C. Kennedy, had predeceased me, and in such case I direct that no probate homestead, allowance, or other benefits be paid to or granted to my husband, Bob C. Kennedy, out of my estate.

Sixth: I give the entire residue of my estate, which shall include my undivided half interest in all community assets of my husband Bob C. Kennedy and myself, together with my entire separate estate, to my daughter, Patricia Lou Kennedy, providing she survives me, and in the event she fails to survive me, then equally to the living children of my daughter, Patricia Lou Kennedy, who survive me, and if she leaves no children who survive me, then to my husband, Bob C. Kennedy.

To summarize: Paragraph third declares that all property standing in the name of Husband alone or in the name of Decedent and Husband as joint tenants is in reality community property. Paragraph fourth bequeaths to Husband all of certain assets of Husband's business and certain items personal to him, Decedent relinquishing any community property rights she might have. Paragraph fifth bequeaths to Daughter all of the silver and oil paintings, including any community property interest Husband might have therein, and expressly requires Husband to waive all other benefits under the will if he asserts his community property interest in the silver and oil paintings. Paragraph sixth bequeaths the entire residue of the estate, including Decedent's "undivided half interest in all community assets of my husband Bob C. Kennedy and myself" to Daughter.

DISCUSSION

Decedent could not, of course, bequeath half of any joint tenancy property to Daughter, because upon Decedent's death Husband became sole owner of all joint tenancy property by right of survivorship. However, if decedent for whatever reason nevertheless believed she could make such disposition, and clearly intended to give half of the joint tenancy property to Daughter, she could force Husband to an election. In order to accept the benefits of the will, i.e., the property bequeathed to him in paragraph fourth, Husband must accept the will in its entirety, including the disposition of joint tenancy property. If, contrary to the testator's intention, he asserts his right to all the joint tenancy property by right of survivorship, he must give up the other benefits to him in the will. (Morrison v. Bowman (1865) 29 Cal. 337, 347-352; Estate of Cecala (1951) 104 Cal. App. 2d 526, 530, 232 P.2d 48; Estate of Waters (1972) 24 Cal. App. 3d 81, 85-86, 100 Cal. Rptr. 775.) The question presented is whether paragraph sixth did in fact bequeath half the joint tenancy property to Daughter and whether it would thwart Decedent's clearly manifested intent if Husband were allowed both to take the specific bequest in paragraph fourth and assert his right as survivor to all the joint tenancy property. (Morrison v. Bowman, supra, 29 Cal. at p.349; Estate of Wolfe (1957) 48 Cal. 2d 570, 574, 311 P.2d 476; Estate of Orwitz (1964) 229 Cal. App. 2d 767, 769, 40 Cal. Rptr. 545.)

Husband's executrix first argues that paragraph sixth did not in fact purport to give half the joint tenancy property to Daughter. The provision refers expressly to "the entire residue of my estate, which shall include my undivided half interest in all community assets of my husband Bob C. Kennedy and myself, . . ." Viewed in isolation, such provision could arguably be construed as indicating only an intent to dispose of Decedent's separate property and community property over which she had a rightful power of testamentary disposition. Such a construction is to be preferred, but it must give way when the other provisions of the will clearly show an intent to dispose of the joint tenancy property as well. (Estate of Wolfe, supra, 48 Cal. 2d at pp. 574-575.) In paragraph third Decedent unequivocally declared that "all property standing in the name of my husband alone and all property standing in my name and my husband's name as joint tenants is *our community property.*" (Italics added.) Paragraphs fourth and fifth dispose of Decedent's community property interests in various personal property. Therefore, when paragraph sixth referred to the entire residue of Decedent's estate including her half interest in all community assets, it necessarily included the joint tenancy property which Decedent had identified as community property in paragraph third. (See Estate of Vogt (1908) 154 Cal. 508, 511, 98 P. 265.)

Husband's executrix next argues that it was not Decedent's intent to put Husband to an election between the will and the joint tenancy property, because paragraph sixth did not *expressly* require such an election, in contrast to paragraph fifth, which did expressly require an election as to the silver and the oil paintings. This is a factor to be considered, but we do not find it controlling. An election may be required even though it is not expressed as such in the will. (Estate of Orwitz, supra, 229 Cal. App. 2d at p.769; Estate of Wolfe, supra, 48 Cal. 2d at p.574.) The court must determine from all the circumstances whether the intent of the testator would be thwarted by recognizing Husband's right of survivorship to all the joint tenancy property in addition to the bequests to him in the will. (Estate of Orwitz, supra; Estate of Wolfe, supra; Morrison v. Bowman, supra, 29 Cal. at p.349; Estate of Webb (1977) 76 Cal. App. 3d 169, 174, 142 Cal. Rptr. 642.) In this case the intent of Decedent is clear from paragraph third. She unequivocally declared, in considerable detail, that notwithstanding the form of title in joint tenancy, such property was in reality community property, that it was "my intention by this Will to dispose of all my separate property and my share of our community property," and that "said assets must be probated as if they were actually in the form of community property." With the exceptions of the personal property in paragraphs fourth and fifth, Decedent disposed of the entire residue of her estate including her half of community assets, to Daughter. Paragraph third obviously was intended to explain and justify giving half the joint tenancy property to Daughter notwithstanding the form of title. The "clear and manifest implication from the will" is that Husband's right of survivorship to all the joint tenancy property is inconsistent with the will. (Morrison v. Bowman, supra, 29 Cal. at p.349; Estate of Vogt, supra, 154 Cal. 508, 511-512; Estate of Emerson (1947) 82 Cal. App. 2d 510, 513, 514, 186 P.2d 734.) The trial court properly determined that an election was required.

The judgment is affirmed.

PROBLEM AND NOTES

1. When a will puts the surviving spouse to an election, the spouse is not required to make an election between her community property

rights and any interests passing to her by intestacy. She may elect to take her community property *and* her intestate share.

Suppose that Blackacre and Whiteacre are community property. *H* devises Blackacre to his daughter, *D*, and Whiteacre to *W*. *H* devises the residue of his property to *W*. Has *W* been put to an election? If she has, and she elects to take her share of community property in Blackacre and Whiteacre, who takes the rest of *H*'s property?

2. The surviving spouse is not required to elect between taking under the will and claiming her community property rights in lifetime transfers. To the extent the surviving spouse can set aside inter vivos transfers (see supra pages 405-410), she can claim her community share therein as well as the property devised to her by will.

3. *The "Widow's Election."* An estate planning device known as the *widow's election* developed in community property states in the days when the husband was the manager of community property and the wife was seen as a housewife without business experience. Through this device, the husband attempted to control the management of community property after his death by leaving a will that purported to devise all the community property in trust to pay the income to his wife for life, with remainder to others on the wife's death. Even after statutes gave the wife equal management power, after many wives went into business, and after gender-neutral terms were widely adopted, the name "widow's election" remains to describe a particular type of election plan with unusual tax consequences. As with the term "dower" in separate property states, which originally referred to widows' rights only, the "widow's election" describes rights which may be applicable to widowers as well as to widows. In explaining the widow's election, we shall assume the husband dies first, which is true in most cases.

The object of the widow's election is to create, at the death of the husband, a trust paying the widow for her life all the income from the community property — both the husband's half and the wife's half. In order to do this, the widow must consent to the transfer by electing to take "under" the will. If the widow so elects, the situation is treated as though the widow transferred her one-half community interest to the trust in exchange for receiving a life estate in her husband's one-half community interest. If, instead, the widow elects "against" the will, she takes the one-half interest to which she is entitled by law, but she forfeits the life estate devised to her by her husband's will. This is a *forced election:* If the widow wants to share in her husband's trust, she must surrender her community property. (The husband's will usually devises his interest in their home and tangible personal property to the widow free of any election; investment properties are the subject of a widow's election will.)

This arrangement may have tax advantages, which flow from the fact that the widow has made an exchange for consideration. Observe what happens to title if the widow elects to take under her husband's will. Two transfers are made, one by the husband and one by the wife. The husband's will makes a testamentary transfer of his property; by electing to take under her husband's will, the wife makes a transfer with a retained life estate of her community share. The wife has received a life estate in her husband's half of the community property *in exchange for* transferring a remainder interest in her half of the community property.

This exchange for consideration has federal gift, estate, and income tax consequences. By transferring a remainder interest in her half of the community property, the widow has made a gift of the remainder. This gift, however, is an exchange for partial consideration under §2512(b) (gift tax) and §2043(a) (estate tax) of the Internal Revenue Code of 1986. The widow can deduct from the value of the gift of the remainder the consideration received (the value of the life estate she receives in her husband's property). Thus:

> *Case 7.* H leaves a forced election will that devises his net share of community property, worth $900,000 after taxes and probate administration costs, to a widow's election trust, called the H trust. The decedent's 65-year-old widow, W, elects to take under the will and thereby is deemed to have transferred her share of the community property, worth $1,000,000, to an identical trust, called the W trust. W is entitled to receive the income for life from both trusts; at her death the principal is to be distributed to the issue of H and W. Assme that under §7520 of the Internal Revenue Code of 1986 (which governs the valuation of life estates and remainders), the interest rate to be used in valuing the interests is 10 percent. (The controlling interest rate changes from month to month.) At an assumed interest rate of 10 percent, the factor used to value a life estate in a 65-year-old person is .71213 times the principal amount, and the factor used to value the remainder following that life estate is .28787. Thus W transfers a remainder interest valued at $287,870 ($1,000,000 × .28787) in exchange for a life estate worth $640,917 ($900,000 × .71213). W has made no taxable gift.

At the widow's death, the property she transferred in trust must be included in her federal gross estate under §2036(a), as an inter vivos transfer with a retained life estate. It is included at the value of the trust corpus at the widow's death. However, a deduction (a "consideration offset") is allowed under §2043 for the consideration — the life estate — the widow received in exchange for making the transfer. Gradow v. United States, 11 Ct. Cl. 808, 1987-1 U.S. Tax Cas. (CCH) ¶13,711 (1987). (In Case 7, if the value of the W trust at W's death remains $1,000,000, W will make a taxable transfer at death of $1,000,000 *minus* $640,917, or $359,083.) The net result is that the widow's share of community property may be transferred to the couple's children at a saving in federal transfer (gift and estate) taxes.

The transfer-for-consideration theory may also offer income tax advantages. The widow may be entitled to amortize, against income received, the cost of the life interest she "purchased" in the husband's half of the community property. On the other hand, there may be income tax disadvantages, including the realization of capital gain when the widow elects to comply with her husband's will. The income tax consequences are not yet settled. The tax problems are discussed in J. Price, Contemporary Estate Planning §§9.24-9.30 (1983); Johanson, Revocable Trusts, Widow's Election Wills, and Community Property: The Tax Problems, 47 Texas L. Rev. 1247 (1969). Professor Price warns:

> A forced election plan is more complex than the ordinary plan for disposing of the community property. As a result it may be more difficult for clients to understand and more costly to implement. In addition, there is substantial risk that some of the tax advantages sought by the parties will be challenged. Overall, the forced widow's election is not suitable for most clients. A widow's election plan should be used only if it is understood by the husband and wife and is completely acceptable to them. Otherwise there is too great a risk that the widow will resent the plan and feel that she was not treated fairly by the husband or his planner.

An alternative to a forced widow's election is a *voluntary election.* A voluntary election will invites the widow to transfer her half of the community property into a trust similar to the husband's, but *she does not forfeit* her husband's bequest if she refuses to do so. A voluntary election provides none of the tax benefits of a forced election, because it is not an exchange of the widow's property for consideration. Nonetheless, the voluntary election plan may be attractive to couples who want unified trust management of the community property after the death of one of the spouses and assurances that the trust corpus will pass to their issue upon the death of the surviving spouse. See Kahn & Gallo, The Widow's Election: A Return to Fundamentals, 24 Stan. L. Rev. 531 (1972) (recommending voluntary elections).

The widow's election tax consequences are available in separate property states where the surviving spouse has property of her own that she can surrender in exchange for a life estate in her husband's property. See J. Price, supra, §9.22.

5. Migrating Couples and Multistate Property Holdings

The classic conflict-of-laws rules used to determine which state law governs marital property are:

(a) The law of the situs controls problems related to land.
(b) The law of the marital domicile at the time personal property is acquired controls the characterization of the property (that is, as separate or community).
(c) The law of the marital domicile at the death of one spouse controls the survivor's marital rights.

The application of these rules is to be examined in this subsection. See J. Schoenblum, Multistate and Multinational Estate Planning §§10.01-10.14 (1982).

It should be noted that although the state of the situs has the power to control its land, it may choose to apply the law of the marital domicile. Uniform Probate Code §2-201(b), for example, provides that the rights of a spouse to an elective share in land located in the state shall be governed by the law of the decedent's domicile at death.

a. Migration from Separate Property State to Community Property State

If a couple acquires property in a separate property state and moves to a community property state, serious problems of fairness to the surviving spouse may arise. The ownership of movable property is determined by the laws of the state where the couple is domiciled when the property is acquired. Thus if the husband is the wage earner, all of the property is the husband's in a separate property state. The wife is protected by the elective share scheme. When the couple moves to a community property state, the property remains the husband's and is now characterized as the husband's separate property. If the couple remains domiciled in the community property state until the husband dies, the law of the state of domicile at date of death governs the disposition of movable property. If neither spouse works in the community property state, there may be no community property for the surviving spouse. Hence, as a result of the move, the wife loses protection of the elective share system provided by the state where the movable property was acquired and is not protected by the system of community property (which she would have if the couple had been domiciled in the community property state when the husband was working). See Estate of Hanau v. Hanau, 730 S.W.2d 663 (Tex. 1987); Weintraub, Obstacles to Sensible Choice of Law for Determining Marital Property Rights on Divorce or in Probate: *Hanau* and the Situs Rule, 25 Hous. L. Rev. 1113 (1988).

Only two states, California and Idaho, give a remedy to the surviving spouse in this situation. These states have a concept of *quasi-community property.* Quasi-community property is property owned by the husband or the wife acquired while domiciled elsewhere, which would have been characterized as community property if the couple had been domiciled in California or Idaho when the property was acquired.[15] Real property situated outside the state is not treated as quasi-community property, because the spouse retains in it any forced share or dower given by the law of the situs.[16] During the continuance of the marriage, quasi-community property is for most purposes treated as the separate property of the acquiring spouse. However, upon the death of the acquiring spouse, one-half of the quasi-community property belongs to the surviving spouse; the other half is subject to testamentary disposition by the decedent. If the nonacquiring spouse dies first, the quasi-community property belongs absolutely to the acquiring spouse. Quasi-community property is analogous to an elective share in the deceased spouse's property acquired from earnings while domiciled in another state. Cal. Prob. Code §§66, 101 (1989); Idaho Code §15-2-201 (1979).

> *Case 8.*   H and W are domiciled in Illinois. H saves $500,000 from his earnings, which he invests in stocks and bonds. In Illinois this is his separate property. H and W then move to California. The stocks and bonds become quasi-community property in California. Upon H's death, W owns one-half of the stocks and bonds. If W dies first, she cannot dispose of any part of this wealth by will; H owns it all. If, instead, H and W had moved to Texas, on H's death W would have no interest in the assets brought from Illinois.

To prevent a spouse from attempting to defeat the survivor's quasi-community property rights by inter vivos transfers, California gives the surviving spouse the right to reach one-half of any gratuitous transfer where the decedent retained possession or enjoyment, or the right to income, or the power to revoke or consume, or a right of survivorship. Cal. Prob. Code §102 (1989). Cf. Idaho Code §15-2-202 (1979). These statutes are analogous to those enacted in separate property states to prevent avoidance of the elective share. See supra pages 388-401.

---

15. Arizona and Texas have adopted the quasi-community property concept for purposes of equitable division upon divorce. Quasi-community property is treated the same as community property in that situation. Ariz. Rev. Stat. §25-318 (1976); Tex. Fam. Code §3.63(b) (Supp. 1989). Neither state applies the quasi-community concept to dissolution of the marriage by death.

16. With respect to California land owned by a married couple domiciled outside California at all relevant times, Cal. Prob. Code §120 (1989) gives the surviving spouse the same elective share as given by the domiciliary state. To the same effect is Uniform Probate Code §2-201(b) (1983).

b. Migration from Community Property State to Separate Property State

Suppose that a husband and wife who have acquired community personal property move to a separate property state. What is the effect of this move on the community property? Generally speaking, a change in domicile from a community property state to a separate property state does not change the preexisting property rights of the husband or wife. Community property continues to be community property when the couple and the property move to a separate property state. In re Keisler's Estate, 177 Ohio St. 136, 203 N.E.2d 221 (1964). However, courts in a few separate property states, unfamiliar with community property concepts, have sometimes treated community property as analogous to a tenancy in common or, if title is in the name of one spouse, as the separate property of the titleholder subject to a constructive trust of one-half for the benefit of the other spouse. The Uniform Disposition of Community Property Rights at Death Act (1983), enacted in about a dozen separate property states, provides that community property brought into the state (and all property — including land in the state — traceable to community property) remains community property for purposes of testamentary disposition, unless the spouses have agreed to convert it into separate property. Each spouse has the right to dispose of one-half of the community property by will. Under the Uniform Act, community property brought into the state is not subject to the elective share.

Any couple moving community property into a separate property state should be careful to preserve its community nature, if such is desirable. If the community property is sold and the proceeds used to purchase other assets, title to the new property should be taken in the name of husband and wife as community property. If resistance from transfer agents, bankers, or title companies is met, the husband and wife should take title in the name of both spouses, at the same time executing a written agreement reciting their intention to retain the asset as community property.

Because of a general lack of understanding of the community property system among lawyers in separate property states, and because of the possible tax advantages of retaining the community character of the assets, lawyers often recommend to couples bringing community property into a separate property state that they change the title to joint tenancy or some other separate property form. If this is done, with the intent of changing community property into a common law concurrent interest, the tax advantages of community property are lost. An example:

Case 9. *H* and *W*, domiciled in Texas, buy property for $100,000. Since the property is paid for out of *H* and *W*'s earnings, it is community property. At *H*'s death several years later, the property is worth $300,000. Under the federal estate tax law one-half the value of the community property ($150,000) is subject to estate tax at *H*'s death (but it qualifies for the marital deduction if devised to *W*, thus incurring no estate taxation). *Note, however, the income tax consequences.* At the death of one spouse, the *entire* value of community property acquires a stepped-up basis for income tax purposes, i.e., its value at *H*'s death ($300,000). Internal Revenue Code of 1986, §§1014(a) and 1014(b)(6). If *W* sells the property after *H*'s death for $325,000, she will pay income tax only on $25,000 capital gain.

Suppose that before *H* dies, *H* and *W* move to Massachusetts. A Massachusetts lawyer advises them to change the title to the property to *H* and *W* as joint tenants. *H* and *W* do this. Then *H* dies, and the property is worth $300,000. The estate tax consequences of joint tenancy are the same as if the property had remained community property, but the income tax consequences are very different. Only one-half the value of joint tenancy property receives a stepped-up basis at *H*'s death. Rev. Rul. 68-80, 1968-1 C.B. 348. *W*'s new basis is $50,000 (her half of the old basis) plus $150,000 (stepped-up basis on *H*'s half) or $200,000. If *W* sells the property for $325,000, she will pay an income tax on $125,000 capital gain. Income tax on $100,000, which could have been avoided, is the result of advice by a lawyer unknowledgeable about community property.

See generally Johanson, The Migrating Client: Estate Planning for the Couple from a Community Property State, 9 U. Miami Inst. Est. Plan. ¶¶800 et seq. (1975); Note, Community Property in a Common Law Jurisdiction: A Seriously Neglected Area of the Law, 16 Washburn L.J. 77 (1976).

6.   *Spouse Omitted from Premarital Will*

Estate of Ganier
Supreme Court of Florida, 1982
418 So. 2d 256

OVERTON, J.   This is a petition to review the decision of the Fifth District Court of Appeal in Estate of Ganier v. Estate of Ganier, 402 So. 2d 418 (Fla. 5th DCA 1981). . . .

The issue concerns the rights of a surviving spouse in the estate of the decedent spouse whose will was executed prior to their marriage. It requires a construction and interpretation of Florida's pretermitted spouse statute, section 732.301, Florida Statutes (1979).

This case arose as the result of the marriage of two senior citizens, Emma Kennedy and Frederic Ganier. They met in 1973, when she was 79 years old and he was 76 years old, became close friends, and eventually shared a joint bank account from which they paid their living expenses. In January, 1977, Mrs. Kennedy executed a will which included a provision bequeathing two of her personal bank accounts to Fred Ganier. Mrs. Kennedy and Mr. Ganier were married approximately eighteen months after this will was executed, in July, 1978. Shortly after the marriage, Emma Ganier suffered a stroke; she was declared incompetent in November, 1978, and, on December 16, 1978, Mr. Ganier was appointed her guardian. In October, 1978, before she was found incompetent, Mrs. Ganier closed one of the bank accounts she had bequeathed to Mr. Ganier, and, after he became his wife's guardian, Mr. Ganier had the second account bequeathed to him transferred to Mrs. Ganier's guardianship account. Mr. Ganier expended almost all the funds from the guardianship account prior to Mrs. Ganier's death, which occurred January 7, 1979.

When Mrs. Ganier's 1977 will was admitted to probate, Mr. Ganier filed a petition in the trial court for a determination of beneficiaries. In this petition, Mr. Ganier asserted that he was entitled to an intestate share of his wife's estate because he was a pretermitted spouse within the meaning of section 732.301, Florida Statutes (1979), which provides:

> Pretermitted spouse. — When a person marries after making a will and the spouse survives the testator, the surviving spouse shall receive a share in the estate of the testator equal in value to that which the surviving spouse would have received if the testator had died intestate, unless:
>
> (1) Provision has been made for, or waived by, the spouse by prenuptial or postnuptial agreement;
>
> (2) The spouse is provided for in the will; or
>
> (3) The will discloses an intention not to make provision for the spouse. The share of the estate that is assigned to the pretermitted spouse shall be obtained in accordance with s. 733.805.

At the hearing, Mr. Ganier testified that he and Mrs. Ganier did not discuss marriage until long after the will in question was executed. No evidence was offered to refute this testimony.

The trial court determined that Mr. Ganier was a pretermitted spouse under the statute, finding that the two bank accounts Mrs. Ganier had left to Mr. Ganier in her will were not controlling, and stating:

> [S]aid provision in testatrix's Last Will and Testament did not constitute a provision for Frederic F. Ganier, also known as Fred Ganier, as testatrix's spouse, within the purview of Section 732.301(2), Florida Statutes. No testimony or evidence was offered in this cause to support the view that testatrix contemplated marriage to petitioner, Frederic F. Ganier, also known as Fred Ganier, at the time of the execution of her will. Said reference to petitioner was not made to him in the prospective status as husband of the testatrix; therefore, even though petitioner who was

designated by name as a beneficiary in testatrix's will, but who after will was executed, became testatrix's husband, was not "provided for in the will" within said statute limiting right of pretermitted surviving spouse to take a spouse's intestate share against decedent's will.

The trial court alternatively found that the two bank accounts devised to Mr. Ganier did not exist when Mrs. Ganier died so that there was no provision in the will for Mr. Ganier because the specific bequest had "lapsed."

The district court, in a split decision, reversed, finding that section 732.301(2) requires only that the surviving spouse be "provided for" in a will executed before marriage, and rejected the trial court's conclusion that this statutory provision would apply only if Mrs. Ganier had contemplated marriage to Mr. Ganier at the time she provided for him in her will. . . . We disagree.

Florida courts early recognized the rule of law which developed to prevent the inadvertent disinheritance of a spouse whom the testator had married after executing a will.[17] Our case law distinguished between a man's will and a woman's will and was expressed by this Court in two early cases. In Belton v. Summer, 31 Fla. 139, 12 So. 371 (1893), we held that a man's previously executed will was revoked by a subsequent marriage *and* the birth of a child, unless the will was executed in contemplation of marriage. In Colcord v. Conroy, 40 Fla. 97, 23 So. 561 (1898), we held that a woman's will was revoked by her marriage alone unless it was executed in contemplation of marriage. Other states had similar rules of law and many have codified these rules in statutes providing that, upon subsequent marriage, the will of either spouse is revoked unless the will provides for the surviving spouse or evidences the testator's intent not to so provide.[18] In some states, the statute itself requires that provision be made "in contemplation of marriage," while in other states, the courts have read the requirement into the statute.[19] The purpose of these statutes is the same as that of our case law: to avoid the inadvertent disinheritance of a spouse whom the testator married after executing a will.

This rule, with its total revocation provisions, solves one problem, that of protecting the surviving spouse's interest in the decedent spouse's estate by assuring that the surviving pretermitted spouse receives an intestate share of the estate. But, in doing so, it creates another problem

---

17. For a discussion of Florida law regarding revocation of wills upon subsequent marriage, see E. Simon, Redfearn Wills and Administration in Florida §8.10, at 106-109 (5th ed. 1977). For a general discussion of English common and canon law and American common and statutory law on this topic, see 2 W. Bowe & D. Parker, Page on the Law of Wills §§21.86-.103, at 496-526 (rev. treatise 1960).

18. See cases collected at Annot., 97 A.L.R.2d 1026 (1964).

19. Id.

by revoking the entire will. This results in all beneficiaries under the will who are not entitled to intestate distribution being foreclosed from receiving any bequest or devise.

To achieve a more equitable balance between the interests of the surviving spouse and the interests of the takers under the will, the Florida Legislature modified the revocation rule. . . . By these enactments, the legislature superseded prior case law in order to protect beneficiaries under the will from complete termination of their bequests. We find that the legislature, in modifying our judicially-established rule, had no intention of eliminating the "in contemplation of marriage" requirement in circumstances where the will provides for the surviving spouse, but was not made with the understanding that it was for the individual as a surviving spouse. . . .

Section 732.301(1)-(3) simply defines statutorily the "in contemplation of marriage" requirement. These three statutory provisions set forth the methods by which a will executed prior to marriage can be valid as to the surviving spouse, and they encompass all the situations in which a testator considers the effect of an upcoming marriage on the disposition of the estate and acts in contemplation of that marriage. A testator may evaluate an existing will and indicate the decision to leave the will untouched by executing a prenuptial or postnuptial agreement, section 732.301(1); a testator may change the will to provide for the intended spouse, section 732.301(2); or a testator can expressly disclose in the will a decision not to provide for the intended spouse, section 732.301(3). In each case, the testator must act "in contemplation of marriage" in order to avoid inadvertently failing to provide for an intended spouse *in the capacity of spouse.* . . .

The requirement that a will executed before marriage provide for a spouse *in the capacity* of spouse is consistent with the purposes of our prior case law and of Florida's Probate Code, chapters 731-735, Florida Statutes (1979). Marriage effects a profound change in a person's relationships and responsibilities. Substantially different considerations underlie a person's bequest to a friend or acquaintance and that person's testamentary provision for the well-being of a spouse. We hold that a spouse has not been "provided for," within the meaning of section 732.301(2), unless the testator both provided for a person named in the will executed before marriage and made such provision in contemplation of marriage to that named person.

In the instant factual situation, the question which must be resolved is whether Mrs. Ganier provided for Fred Ganier, in contemplation of her marriage to him, as her future spouse. . . . [W]hen a will executed before marriage contains a provision for a named individual who later becomes the testator's spouse, the surviving spouse has the burden of proving that the provision was *not* made in contemplation of marriage. Absent such proof, the surviving spouse will not be considered "pretermitted" and will, therefore, not be entitled to an intestate share of the estate. This proof need not be found in the will itself; evidence of the circumstances existing at the time of the will's execution is admissible in meeting this burden. Cf. Perkins v. Brown, 158 Fla. 21, 27 So. 2d 521 (1946) (evidence of surrounding circumstances admissible to prove that testator intended not to make provision for spouse).

The marriage of this elderly couple admittedly did not take place until eighteen months after the will's execution. The surviving spouse, Mr. Ganier, testified that he and the testatrix, Mrs. Ganier, did not discuss marriage until long after the will in question was executed. The record further reflects that no other evidence was offered to refute this testimony. The trial court found that "[n]o testimony or evidence was offered in this cause to support the view that testatrix contemplated marriage to . . . Fred Ganier, at the time of the execution of her will." We conclude that, on the basis of this record, the trial court could properly find that Mr. Ganier was a pretermitted spouse, entitled to an intestate share of Mrs. Ganier's estate.

The primary purpose of the pretermitted spouse rule is to assure that the decedent spouse considered the surviving spouse as a spouse when making his or her will. Eliminating the "in contemplation of marriage" requirement, as held by the district court, defeats the reason for the rule. For the reasons expressed, the decision of the district court below is quashed and this cause is remanded to reinstate the trial court's judgment.

It is so ordered.

PROBLEM AND NOTE

1. Suppose that after Emma Kennedy married Frederick Ganier, but before her stroke, Mrs. Ganier had occasion to visit her lawyer. In the course of her visit, the lawyer asked Mrs. Ganier about her will. She replied by saying that her January 1977 will was what she wanted and she didn't want to change it. Is Frederick Ganier entitled to an intestate share? See Comment, The Problem of the "Un-omitted Spouse" Under Section 2-301 of the Uniform Probate Code, 52 U. Chi. L. Rev. 481, 496 (1985).

2. Uniform Probate Code §2-301 (1983) gives an intestate share to a surviving spouse omitted in a premarital will "unless it appears from the will that the omission was intentional or the testator provided for the spouse by transfer outside the will and the intent that the transfer be in lieu of a testamentary provision is shown by statements of the testator or from the amount of the transfer or other evidence."

A revision of §2-301 has been approved by the Joint Editorial Board for the UPC and is scheduled to be presented for approval by the Commissioners on Uniform State Laws in 1990. This revision adds to the code a provision that the omitted spouse is entitled to an intestate share unless the will was made in contemplation of marriage, thus adopting the position of the *Ganier* court.

SECTION B.   RIGHTS OF ISSUE OMITTED FROM THE WILL

In all states except Louisiana, which has a legitime (forced share for issue) derived from civil law,[20] a child or other descendant has no statutory protection against disinheritance by a parent. There is no requirement that a testator leave any property to his child, not even the proverbial one dollar.[21] But while a parent has the power to disinherit children, he or she should think twice, or better, three times, before exercising the power. Although no statute or judicial decision flatly prohibits conscious disinheritance, the law does not favor cutting children out of the distributive plan when the testator leaves no spouse. A number of doctrines have been flexibly used to protect children, with the consequence that disinheritance is almost always a risky affair. A will disinheriting a child virtually invites a will contest. As we saw in Chapter 3, "lack of testamentary capacity," "undue influence," and "fraud" are subtle and elastic concepts that can be used by judges and juries to rewrite the testator's distributive plan in order to "do justice." In contests by disinherited children, judges and juries are frequently

---

20. For a debate on the merits of the Louisiana legitime, see Nathan, An Assault on the Citadel: A Rejection of Forced Heirship, 52 Tul. L. Rev. 5 (1977); Lemann, In Defense of Forced Heirship, id. at 20; LeVan, Alternatives to Forced Heirship, id. at 29.

In 1989 Louisiana limited the forced heirship law to apply only to children under the age of 23 and to handicapped adult children. The change has been criticized by Professors Cynthia Samuel and Mary Ann Glendon. Professor Samuel argues that the legitime guarantees that children don't get divorced from their inheritance when their parents get divorced from each other.

> Professor Glendon said that when a spouse remarries in other states, the children of the first marriage "are apt not to see property that was accumulated during that marriage," adding, "Louisiana enabled an older person to say to the second spouse 'the law requires me to leave a portion of my estate to my children.'"

N.Y. Times, Dec. 11, 1989, §B, at 10, col. 3.

21. At common law a child omitted from his parent's will had no remedy. It may have been thought that it was necessary to leave the heir a shilling to disinherit him effectively, but Blackstone says that this was an error. 2 W. Blackstone, Commentaries *502. Blackstone says "cutting the heir off with a shilling" is traceable to a Roman law notion that the testator had lost his memory or mind unless he gave some legacy to each child.

influenced by their sympathies for the children. This is well known to practicing lawyers, who will often advise the devisees to agree to an out-of-court settlement with a disinherited child.

We turn now to pretermission statutes, designed to prevent unintentional disinheritance of descendants. It was such a statute that induced Calvin Coolidge, noted for economy of language, to add an opening phrase to his will — the shortest will of any President of the United States. Coolidge's will read in its entirety:

"The White House"
Washington
Will of Calvin Coolidge of Northampton,
Hampshire County, Massachusetts

Not unmindful of my son John, I give all my estate both real and personal to my wife Grace Coolidge, in fee simple — Home at Washington, District of Columbia this twentieth day December, A.D. nineteen hundred and twenty six.

/s/ *Calvin Coolidge*

Signed by me on the date above in the presence of the testator and of each other as witnesses to said will and the signature thereof.

/s/ *Everett Sanders*
/s/ *Edward T. Clark*
/s/ *Erwin C. Geisser*

If Uniform Probate Code §2-302 had applied to President Coolidge's will, would the opening phrase have been necessary?

Uniform Probate Code (1983)

§2-302 [PRETERMITTED CHILDREN]

(a) If a testator fails to provide in his will for any of his children born or adopted after the execution of his will, the omitted child receives a share in the estate equal in value to that which he would have received if the testator had died intestate unless:

(1) it appears from the will that the omission was intentional;

(2) when the will was executed the testator had one or more children and devised substantially all his estate to the other parent of the omitted child;[22] or

(3) the testator provided for the child by transfer outside the will and the intent that the transfer be in lieu of a testamentary provision is shown by statements of the testator or from the amount of the transfer or other evidence.

(b) If at the time of execution of the will the testator fails to provide in his will for a living child solely because he believes the child to be dead, the child receives a share in the estate equal in value to that which he would have received if the testator had died intestate.

Crump's Estate v. Freeman
Supreme Court of Oklahoma, 1980
614 P.2d 1096

OPALA, J. The issue on appeal is whether it is apparent from the four corners of the will that testator's omission to provide for the daughter of his deceased son was intentional, and if not, would she be entitled to take her distributive share as an omitted heir within the meaning of 84 O.S. 1971 §132.[23] We hold there is no affirmative indication on the face of the will that testator intended to disinherit his granddaughter. Neither does the testamentary instrument reflect ambiguity of intention which would permit intentional exclusion to be shown by parol.

Several months after the will of W.E. Crump [decedent/testator] was admitted to probate, testator's granddaughter [contestant] sought her intestate share of the estate as a pretermitted heir under 84 O.S. 1971 §132. Contestant was one of three children of decedent's only child

---

22. In a revision of the UPC, to be submitted by the Joint Editorial Board to the National Conference of Commissioners on Uniform State Laws in 1990, §2-302(a)(2) is revised to read: "when the will was executed the testator devised all or substantially all his estate to the other parent of the omitted child." Why is the additional requirement that the decedent had one or more children when the will was executed dropped? — Eds.

23. 84 O.S. 1971 §132 provides:

When any testator omits to provide in his will for any of his children, or for the issue of any deceased child unless it appears that such omission was intentional, such child, or the issue of such child, must have the same share in the estate of the testator, as if he had died intestate, and succeeds thereto as provided in the preceding section.

who had predeceased him. Testator provided for the other two grand-children in his will but failed to include or mention the contestant. The will in controversy transfers substantially all of the testator's property to a testamentary trust to be used for the benefit of designated beneficiaries who include the two other grandchildren of decedent. The property not transferred in trust was the subject of a specific bequest. Nowhere in the will is decedent's granddaughter mentioned either by name or class. Nor is any provision made for her. The trial court ruled that contestant was a pretermitted heir entitled to inherit her distributive part of testator's estate. The co-executors of decedent's estate appeal from that decision.

Since 1928 this court has consistently interpreted and, for the most part, uniformly applied Oklahoma's pretermitted heir statute here under consideration. Intentional omission to provide for a testator's issue must appear from the four corners of the will. The purpose of the statute is to protect the issue's right to take unless the will itself gives clear expression of an intentional omission.

Two different approaches to the problem of an heir's omission from his ancestor's will are identified in national legal literature by reference to the Massachusetts and Missouri prototype statutes. The Missouri-type solution benefits children "not named or provided" for in the will, whereas Massachusetts makes superimposition of heirship status subject to the qualifying phrase "unless it shall appear that such omission was intentional *and not occasioned by any mistake or accident.*" Under a Massa-chusetts-type statute extrinsic evidence is admitted to show both pres-ence or absence of intention to disinherit, while under a Missouri-type solution any evidence offered to rebut the statutorily-created presump-tion of inadvertent omission must appear within the four corners of the will. Oklahoma's pretermitted-heir provision has been characterized as Massachusetts-derived although the quoted portion of that state's statute, italicized in this text, was never incorporated in our version. California's pretermitted-heir statute, with a version then similar to that of Oklahoma, was construed in the Matter of Estate of Garraud, 35 Cal. 336 [1868], as disallowing the use of parol proof to show testator's unexpressed intentional omission of children from the will. The court noted that the California statute made no reference to "accident or mistake" — the phrase used in the Massachusetts prototype. Utah, with a statute like ours, dealt with the very same problem settled earlier in California. Acting as a court of last resort for the then Territory of Utah, the U.S. Supreme Court reached in Coulam v. Doull, 133 U.S. 216, 231 [1889], the opposite conclusion from that in *Garraud*. In *Doull* the Court held that absence of reference to "accident or mistake" in the Utah statute did not preclude the use of parol evidence. In its analysis the Court treated the Utah Territory pretermitted-heir statute as an extraneous fact which, when interacting with the will's silence as to the testator's intent, resulted in latent ambiguity resolvable by parol. We cannot accept the *Doull* rationale. A latent ambiguity will arise from a fact or circumstance — extraneous to the text — which renders the meaning uncertain. Here there is *no* ambiguity but *only* silence for which the law's command has supplied its own answer. The pretermitted-heir statute superimposes itself upon the silent will to establish heirship in the protected person. The status once so created by force of law cannot be erased by parol.[24] The needed intent for the heir's omission cannot come *dehors* the will from sources not testamentary in character.

We cannot follow the so-called Massachusetts-type approach. Our pretermitted-heir statute, which makes no reference to "accident" or "mistake" appears to confine judicial inquiry to a search for the *expressed* testatorial intention to omit one's protected heir. The law in force in the state when the will is made forms part of that instrument. Testators must be assumed to have published their testamentary disposition with full knowledge of the applicable law.

Here the contestant was omitted from the will completely. There was no mention of her by name or class. The will contains no language which manifests this omission as an intentional act. The co-executors argue that because complete disposition of the testator's entire estate to the designated beneficiaries (of which the contestant was not one) was effected, this shows decedent's omission of his granddaughter was made by design. Testatorial disposition of the entire estate does not alone affirmatively evince an intent to omit to provide for a child or a deceased child's issue. Before "natural rights and expectations" of one's issue to share in the ancestor's wealth may be legally extinguished, the intent to disinherit must appear upon the face of the will in strong and convincing language. No requisite intent to disinherit the granddaughter appears in the will before us. . . .

Trial court's judgment is therefore affirmed.

NOTES AND PROBLEMS

1. Pretermitted child statutes, which have been enacted in almost all the states, follow one of two patterns. In about half the states, the statutes give protection only to children born (or adopted) after execution of the will. See Uniform Probate Code §2-302, supra page 428. In the remaining states, the statutes operate in favor of children alive when the will was executed as well as after-borns. In these jurisdictions,

---

24. The only exception to the parol evidence rule which seems to apply to wills is the one which admits parol evidence to resolve ambiguous expressions used in the text or created by the existence of facts extraneous to it.

the failure to name all of the testator's living children in the will invites a challenge under the pretermitted child statute.

Typically, statutes of both types give the pretermitted child an intestate share, but the will is operative with respect to the testator's remaining assets. The statutes vary considerably in detail, and many of them are inartfully drafted, leaving open subsidiary problems in statutory interpretation.

2.   *T* devises all his property to his wife *W* for life, remainder to *T*'s child *A*. *B*, born to *T* after the execution of the will, takes an intestate share under the applicable pretermission statute. How is *T*'s estate distributed?

3.   As with the Oklahoma statute, pretermission statutes in several states apply to grandchildren who are children of a deceased child of the testator. Suppose that *T*, a widower, devises $1 to his son, *S*, and all the rest of his property to his daughter, *D*. *S* predeceases *T*, leaving a child, *C*. If an anti-lapse statute applies, giving *C* the $1 bequest intended for *S*, is *C* entitled to a one-half share in *T*'s estate as a pretermitted grandchild? Suppose that *S* had not been given $1 but that *T*'s will had provided: "I intentionally make no provision for my son, *S*." Is *C* entitled to a one-half share in *T*'s estate? (Assume that the pretermission statute applies to children and grandchildren born before or after execution of the will.) On the distortions pretermission statutes cause in estate plans, see Rein, A More Rational System for the Protection of Family Members Against Disinheritance, 15 Gonz. L. Rev. 11 (1979). W. McGovern, S. Kurtz & J. Rein, Wills, Trusts and Estates §3.6 at 108 (1988), criticize the UPC for not extending pretermission protection to grandchildren. They say this "is hard to understand since the Code allows grandchildren of a decedent to take by representation if the decedent dies intestate."

4.   In a jurisdiction that includes within the pretermission statute children born before execution of the will, what provision would you recommend including in a will so as to cut out an illegitimate child without mentioning the child by name or suggesting his existence? Consider the following cases.

In Estate of Peterson, 74 Wash. 2d 91, 442 P.2d 980 (1968), the testator stated: "I declare that I have no children, no children of deceased children, and no adopted children." The court held that this did not disinherit a child of testator, whose paternity he denied. "[T]he mistaken denial that he has children seems to us a clear example of a situation in which the statute was intended to operate to protect a forgotten child from being disinherited. There is no indication in the will that the testator remembered the petitioner and intended to disinherit him." Id. at 95, 442 P.2d at 983.

In In re Estate of Padilla, 641 P.2d 539 (N.M. App. 1982), the testator's will declared: "I declare that I have no children whom I have omitted to name or provide for herein." The court held that this was not an intentional omission. "To disinherit Sanchez [the illegitimate child], an affirmative, not negative indication of intention must appear on the face of the Will." Id. at 544.

In Bridgeford v. Estate of Chamberlin, 573 P.2d 694 (Okla. 1977), the testator provided: "I fully understand who my heirs at law would be upon my death, and . . . I expressly provide that in the event any person whomsoever should contest the validity of this will and establish in a court of competent jurisdiction that he or she is an heir at law of mine, . . . then I hereby expressly give, devise and bequeath unto such person or persons, the sum of $5.00 and no more." The court held this showed an unambiguous intent to omit an illegitimate daughter of the testator. But cf. Estate of Torregano, 54 Cal. 2d 234, 352 P.2d 505, 5 Cal. Rptr. 137, 88 A.L.R.2d 597 (1960), holding a bequest of $1 to any person asserting any claim "by virtue of relationship or otherwise" insufficient to bar an omitted child; Estate of Gardner, 31 Cal. 3d 620, 580 P.2d 684, 147 Cal. Rptr. 184 (1978), holding clause, "I declare that I have intentionally failed to provide for any person not mentioned herein," insufficient to bar an omitted child.

NOTE: NEGATIVE DISINHERITANCE

An old rule of American wills law says that disinheritance is not possible by a simple declaration that "my son John shall receive none of my property." To disinherit, it is necessary that the entire estate be devised to other persons. If there is a partial intestacy for some reason, the child will take an intestate share notwithstanding such a provision in the will. A testator cannot alter the intestate distribution scheme without giving the property to others. See In re Estate of Cancik, 106 Ill. 2d 11, 476 N.E.2d 738 (1985).

This rule has come to be criticized in recent years as defeating the testator's intent and furthering no public policy. See Comment, The Intestate Claims of Heirs Excluded by Will: Should "Negative Wills" Be Enforced?, 52 U. Chi. L. Rev. 177 (1985) (arguing that express exclusion of an heir in a will should constitute an implied gift of his intestate share to the testator's other heirs). In New York by statute a "negative bequest" is permitted. The barred distributee is treated as having predeceased the testator and does not share in the estate. N.Y. Est., Powers & Trusts Law §1-2.18 (1981).

NOTE: TESTAMENTARY LIBEL

Would you advise a client who wants to disinherit a child to give the reason in the will? In Brown v. DuFrey, 1 N.Y.2d 190, 134 N.E.2d 469

(1956), the testator's will contained the following paragraph: "Fifth: I am mindful of the fact that I have made no provision for John H. Brown, my husband. I do so intentionally because of the fact that during my lifetime he abandoned me, made no provision for my support, treated me with complete indifference and did not display any affection or regard for me."[25] The testator died in 1951. She had married John H. Brown in 1901, and he had secured a divorce from her in 1917 on grounds of adultery. Brown had remarried in 1924 and was living with his second wife at the time of the testator's death. Brown sued the testator's estate for testamentary libel and recovered as damages a sum approximately equal to one-half the estate.

See Hudak, The Sleeping Tort: Testamentary Libel, 27 Mercer L. Rev. 1147 (1976), 12 Cal. W.L. Rev. 491 (1976); Reynolds, Defamation from the Grave: Testamentary Libel, 7 Cal. W.L. Rev. 91 (1971); Fuson, Testamentary Libel, The Case of the Vindictive Testator, 57 Ill. B.J. 840, 938 (1969); Annot., 21 A.L.R.3d 754 (1968).

---

25. Heinrich Heine, the German expatriate poet who died in France in 1856, also used his will to fire a parting shot at his wife. His will closed with these words: "I leave all my estate to my wife on the express condition that she remarry. I want at least one person to sincerely grieve my death." Reported in 74 Case & Comment 21 (Mar.-Apr. 1969).

7

TRUSTS: CREATION, TYPES, AND CHARACTERISTICS

> The trust . . . is a device for making dispositions
> of property. And no other system of law has for
> this purpose so flexible a tool. It is this that makes
> the trust unique. . . . The purposes for which trusts
> can be created are as unlimited as the
> imagination of lawyers.
>
> 1 A. Scott, Trusts 3, 4
> (W. Fratcher 4th ed. 1987)

SECTION A. INTRODUCTION

1. Background

Although a trust is, generally speaking, a device whereby a trustee
manages property for one or more beneficiaries, the theory of a trust
is somewhat complicated. It is not accurate to say that the trustee owns
the property but is under a duty to manage it for the beneficiary, who
has nothing more than a personal right to sue the trustee for breach
of duty. Nor is it accurate to say that the beneficiary owns the property,
but the trustee has full power to manage it. Neither trustee nor
beneficiary owns the property to the exclusion of the other, but each
owns a different interest in the property. The trustee owns the legal
interest, the beneficiary owns the equitable interest. It is this curious

435

bifurcation of ownership that sometimes baffles students beginning a study of the law of trusts.

The trust developed out of the historical circumstance that England had separate courts of law and equity. The ancestor of the modern trust is the medieval *use* (from a corruption of the Latin word *opus*, meaning benefit). Legal historians have traced the use back to the middle of the thirteenth century when the Franciscan friars came to England. Inasmuch as the friars were forbidden to own any sort of property, pious benefactors conveyed land to suitable persons in the neighborhood to hold to the use of the friars. Thus O, owner of Blackacre, would enfeoff A and his heirs to hold Blackacre *to the use of* the friars. By this transfer, the legal fee simple passed to the *feoffee to uses*, A, who held it for the benefit of the *cestui que use*, the mendicant order. The cestui que use went into possession of Blackacre, with the legal title being held by A.

Although there is some evidence that ecclesiastical courts enforced early uses,[1] in the beginning uses were not enforceable in the civil courts. Since no common law form of action existed whereby the cestui could bring an action against the feoffee, the law courts — paralyzed by the rigidity of their procedures — offered no relief. In time this state of affairs appeared to be unconscionable to the chancellor, and early in the fifteenth century the chancellor began to compel feoffees to uses to perform as they had promised. Once the chancellor enforced uses, thus removing the risk of faithless feoffees, uses grew rapidly. Landowners found that all sorts of benefits could be accomplished by putting legal title in a feoffee to uses.[2] For example, prior to the Statute of Wills in 1540, land could not be devised by will; it descended to the eldest son. Landowners seeking relief from forced primogeniture turned to the use and found the desired flexibility there. O could enfeoff A and his heirs to the use of O during O's lifetime and then to the use of such persons as O might appoint by will. The chancellor enforced the use in favor of O's devisees. Particularly because of its success in evading feudal death taxes (known as feudal incidents), the use became universally popular. It was the use of the use to avoid taxes that brought on the Statute of Uses.

Searching for a way to restore his feudal incidents and replenish his treasury, Henry VIII determined to abolish the use. Henry interested himself personally in a lawsuit in the courts, which resulted in a decision putting into doubt the legality of the use generally.[3] Fearing that uses might become unenforceable, with drastic consequences for the cestuis,

---

1. See Helmholz, The Early Enforcement of Uses, 79 Colum. L. Rev. 1503 (1979).
2. See Fratcher, Uses of Uses, 34 Mo. L. Rev. 39 (1969); 1 A. Scott, Trusts §1.4 (W. Fratcher 4th ed. 1987).
3. See Ives, The Genesis of the Statute of Uses, 82 Eng. Hist. Rev. 673, 691 (1967).

Parliament, on Henry's urging, reluctantly enacted the Statute of Uses in 1535, which became effective in 1536. By this statute, uses were not made illegal. On the contrary, legal title was taken away from the feoffee to uses and given to the cestui que use. In the words of the time, the use was executed, that is, converted into a legal interest. The former cestuis — now clothed with legal title — could breathe easy, but they had to pay the king his due upon death.

Although the purpose of the Statute of Uses was to abolish uses, imaginative lawyers and judges found holes in the statute. Within ten years after its enactment, courts held that the statute did not operate if the feoffee to uses (trustee in modern language) was given *active duties* to perform.[4] An active trust — imposing a duty on the trustee to deal with the property in a special manner — was regarded as quite different from the old use, where the feoffee merely held legal title and allowed the cestui que use himself to take the profits from the land. This reading of the statute permitted chancery to reassert its jurisdiction over uses under the name of trust and to develop the modern trust, wherein the trustee has legal title and the responsibilities of management and the beneficiaries have equitable title and the benefits flowing from the trustee's management.

As Professor Scott has noted, the trust can be used for purposes "as unlimited as the imagination of lawyers." These diverse purposes range from a simple estate plan to provide for a surviving spouse and children in accordance with their respective needs, to the running of vast business empires. The trust is a useful device for managing wealth held for charitable purposes or for pensions. It is also used for managing giant investment funds (e.g., common trust funds) or holding security for a loan (e.g., giving a mortgage in the form of a deed of trust). In the practice of law, you will find many other uses for the trust, particularly in situations where there are many beneficiaries or owners and it is desirable to avoid fragmented management of the property. Our present focus, however, is on the *private express trust* gratuitously created for the benefit of individual beneficiaries.

2. The Settlor

To create a trust, a property owner transfers assets to a trustee, with the trust instrument or will setting forth the terms of the trust. A

---

4. The courts also held that the Statute of Uses only executed one use. If *O* enfeoffed *A* and his heirs to the use of *B* and his heirs to the use of *C* and his heirs, the statute executed only the first use, giving *B* legal title, but it did not execute the second use. *B* held legal title for the use of *C*. Hence the statute could be evaded by the addition of a few words to the conveyance. See 1 A. Scott, Trusts §1.6 (W. Fratcher 4th ed. 1987).

Austin Wakeman Scott
Professor, Harvard Law School, 1909-1961

Reproduced by permission of Harvard Law School Art Collection.

Professor Scott, together with Professor George G. Bogert of the University of Chicago, molded the modern law of trusts in this country. Their influential treatises on the law of trusts, constantly cited by courts, are the starting point for analysis of questions of trust law.

properly drafted trust will set forth both the dispositive provisions fixing the beneficiaries' interests and the administrative provisions specifying the powers and duties of the trustee in managing the trust estate. A trust ordinarily involves at least three parties: The settlor, the trustee, and one or more beneficiaries. But three different persons are not necessary for a trust. One person can wear two, or even all three, hats.

The person who creates a trust is the *settlor* (sometimes called *trustor*). The trust may be created during the settlor's life, in which case it is an *inter vivos* (or *living*) trust. Or it may be created by will, in which case it is a *testamentary* trust. An inter vivos trust may be created either by a *declaration of trust* (in which the settlor declares that he holds certain property in trust) or by a *deed of trust* (in which the settlor transfers property to another person as trustee).

Under a declaration of trust, the settlor is the trustee. To make an outright gift of property, the donor must either deliver the property or execute a deed of gift. However, a declaration of trust of personal property requires neither delivery nor a deed of gift. It is therefore the simplest form of making a gift. All that is necessary is that the donor manifest an intention to hold the property in trust. Case 1 illustrates an oral declaration of trust of personal property.

> *Case 1. O* orally declares herself trustee of 100 shares of General Electric stock, with the duty to pay the income therefrom to *A* for life, and upon *A*'s death to deliver the stock to *B*. This is a valid declaration of trust. No delivery of the stock is necessary, and since the property is personal property, no written instrument is necessary.

If the trust property is real property, the Statute of Frauds requires a written instrument for a declaration of trust.

The settlor of the trust may be both trustee and a beneficiary. Thus:

> *Case 2. O* executes a written declaration of trust declaring herself trustee of Whiteacre, to pay the income therefrom to herself for life, and upon her death Whiteacre is to pass to *A*. This is a valid trust. *Note:* If *O* were the sole beneficiary and also the sole trustee, the trust would not be valid because no one could hold *O* accountable for performance of the trust duties. In order to have a valid trust, the trustee must owe equitable duties to someone other than herself.

If the settlor is not the trustee of an inter vivos trust, a deed of trust is necessary. In order to bring the trust into being, the deed of trust or the trust property must be delivered to the trustee. Thus in Case 2, if *O* wanted to make her lawyer, *C*, trustee, *O* would have to deliver a deed of trust to *C*.

If the trust is created by will, the settlor cannot, of course, be the trustee. The trustee will necessarily be someone other than the settlor.

3. The Trustee

There may be one trustee or several trustees. The trustee may be an individual or a corporation. Almost every large bank has a trust department set up to manage trusts and carry out the duties expected and required of a trustee.

The trustee may be the settlor or a third party, or the trustee may be a beneficiary. Thus:

> *Case 3.* By will, *H* devises property to *W* in trust to pay the income to *W* for life, and upon *W*'s death the property is to pass to *H*'s children free of trust. This is a valid trust. Although *W* is both trustee and beneficiary, *W* is not the sole beneficiary. *H*'s children have a remainder interest and can bring an action to enforce *W*'s duties as trustee. This trust arrangement has many advantages over a legal life estate in *W*, remainder in *H*'s children. *W* as trustee must keep the trust property separate from her own property and has broader powers of management, sale, and reinvestment than has a legal life tenant (see infra pages 444-447).

If the settlor intends to create a trust but fails to name a trustee, a court will appoint a trustee to carry out the trust. This rule is sometimes stated: *A trust will not fail for want of a trustee.* Thus:

> *Case 4.* *T* dies leaving a will that devises his residuary estate in trust, to pay the income to *A* for life, and on *A*'s death to distribute the trust property to *B*. However, the will does not name anyone as trustee. Since *T*'s will clearly manifests an intention to create a trust, the court will appoint a suitable person as trustee to carry out *T*'s trust purposes. (If the trust is created by a deed of trust and no trustee is named, the trust may fail for want of a transferee or for want of delivery.)

Similarly, if *T*'s will names someone as trustee but the named person refuses the appointment or dies while serving as trustee, and the will does not make provision for a successor trustee, the court will appoint a successor trustee.[5]

---

5. This rule does not apply if the court finds (or if the trust instrument specifies) that the trust powers were *personal to the named trustee.* If it is determined that the settlor intended the trust to continue only as long as the person designated as trustee continues to serve in that capacity, the trust terminates when the named person ceases to serve as trustee. This exception is rarely involved, however. In the usual case the court will determine that the primary purpose of the settlor was to have the trust continue for the indicated purposes and not that the particular person, and only that person, serve as trustee. See 2 A. Scott, Trusts §101.1 (W. Fratcher 4th ed. 1987).

The trustee holds legal title to the trust property; the beneficiaries have equitable interests. In managing the trust property, the trustee is held to a very high standard of conduct. The trustee is under a duty to administer the trust solely in the interest of the beneficiaries; self-dealing (wherein the trustee acts in the same transaction both in its fiduciary capacity and in an individual capacity) is sharply limited and for some transactions is prohibited altogether. The trustee must preserve the property, make it productive, and, where required by the trust instrument, pay the income to the beneficiary. In investment decisions the trustee owes a duty of fairness to both classes of beneficiaries: The income beneficiaries (who are interested in income and high yields) and the remaindermen (who are concerned about preservation of principal and appreciation in values). Other important duties of a trustee include the duty to keep the trust property separate from the trustee's own property, to keep accurate accounts, to invest prudently, and not to delegate trust powers. If the trustee improperly manages the trust estate, the trustee may be denied compensation, subjected to personal liability, and removed as trustee by a court. In Chapter 12 we give extended consideration to the duties and powers of trustees, to important problems in trust administration, and to the distinctive nature of the fiduciary office.

In order to have a trust, it is necessary for the trustee to have some duties to perform. If the trustee has no duties at all, there is no reason to have, or to recognize, a trust. The trust is then said to be "passive," or "dry," and the trust fails. When a trust fails because the trustee has no active duties, the beneficiaries acquire legal title to the trust property.

Because a trustee has onerous duties and liabilities, the law does not impose upon a person the office of trustee unless the person accepts. Once a person accepts the office of trustee, the person can be released from liability only with consent of the beneficiaries or by a court order.

PROBLEM

In January *O* executes a written instrument creating an irrevocable trust and naming *X* as trustee. The trust instrument provides that the income from the trust is to be paid to *A* for life, and upon *A*'s death the corpus is to be distributed to *B*. Shortly thereafter, *O* delivers a copy of the trust instrument and $100,000 in cash to *X* and tells *X* that this money is to be held by *X* under the trust. *X* immediately puts the money in his safe-deposit box.

O dies the following February. In November next, *X*, saying that he does not want to be trustee, divides the money between *D* and *E*, the residuary legatees of *O*'s estate, paying $50,000 to each. Has a trust been established? See 1 A. Scott, Trusts §35 (W. Fratcher 4th ed. 1987). Is *X* liable for $100,000? 2 id. §102.2. Can *A* and *B* recover the $100,000 from *D* and *E?* See 4 id. §292.

4. The Beneficiaries

The beneficiaries hold equitable interests. Generally speaking, this means that the beneficiaries have interests that originated in chancery and have different characteristics from legal interests. Of special importance are the remedies available to the beneficiaries for breach of trust. The beneficiaries have a personal claim against the trustee for breach of trust. However, this personal claim has no higher priority than the claim of other creditors of the trustee and thus might not protect the beneficiaries if it were their only remedy. Equity gives the beneficiaries additional remedies relating to the trust property itself. Other creditors of the trustee cannot reach the trust property. If the trustee goes bankrupt or wrongfully disposes of the trust property, the beneficiaries can recover the trust property unless it has come into the hands of a bona fide purchaser for value. If the trustee disposes of trust property and acquires other property with the proceeds of sale, the beneficiaries can enforce the trust on the newly acquired property. Largely because of these rights to reach the trust property, we say the beneficiaries have equitable title to the trust property.

Private trusts almost always create successive beneficial interests. Typically, trust income is payable to the beneficiary (or class of beneficiaries) for life, perhaps to be followed by life interests in another class of beneficiaries, with the trustee to distribute the trust corpus to yet another class of beneficiaries upon termination of the trust. Thus the creation of a trust involves the creation of one or more equitable future interests as well as a present interest in the income.

> *Case 5.* *O* transfers securities worth $100,000 to *X* in trust, to pay the income to *A* for life, then to *B* for life. On the death of the survivor of *A* and *B*, the trustee is to distribute the trust principal to *B*'s issue then living. *X* has legal title to the trust assets, and has a fiduciary duty to manage and invest the assets for the benefit of the indicated beneficiaries. *A* has an equitable life estate. *B* has an equitable remainder for life. *B*'s issue have an equitable contingent remainder in fee simple. *O* has an equitable reversion (often called a resulting trust). If on the death of the survivor of *A* and *B* there are no issue of *B* then living, the trust property will revert to *O* (or to *O*'s successors if *O* has died in the meantime).

Today most life estates and future interests are equitable rather than legal interests; they are created in trusts. Legal life estates and future interests in tangible or intangible personal property are rare and almost always inadvisable. Legal life estates and future interests in land are sometimes encountered. These too are almost always inadvisable. A trust with equitable interests is a much more flexible and useful means of giving property than a disposition that creates legal interests (see infra pages 444-447).

5. Use of Trusts in Estate Planning

The use of trusts has increased markedly over the past 50 years. Although there are many explanations for this, three reasons deserve special mention. First, many persons want to avoid the probate process at death, with its attendant costs, delays, and publicity. A person can avoid probate by transferring his property into a revocable inter vivos trust. Since World War II, the revocable trust has become a widely used device to avoid probate.[6]

Second, a trust can be used to secure income, gift, and estate tax savings that are not obtainable, or are not as readily obtainable, by any other form of disposition. For example, income (and income taxes) can be shifted to another, perhaps a child going through college, through the use of a trust. A discretionary trust — one in which the trustee has the power to decide who receives income or the power to pay out corpus — may be used to lessen the tax burden on family wealth by spraying income to various members of the family, or by accumulating or deferring income.[7] With respect to federal estate taxes, a trust under which the surviving spouse is entitled to receive all the income for life can be used to qualify for the marital deduction. Hence, a married person who does not want to give property outright to his spouse can get the benefits of the marital deduction through the use of a trust.[8] A person can create a trust for a child for life, with remainder to the child's descendants. Since the child's life income interest terminates at death, no estate tax is levied on the trust assets when the child dies.[9] Under the federal gift tax, there is an annual exclusion for gifts of up to $10,000 per donee per year. To qualify for the exclusion, the donee must be given a present interest, not a future interest. However, the Internal Revenue Code provides that a gift in trust for the benefit of a minor, with possession postponed until the minor reaches age 21,

6. The revocable inter vivos trust is treated infra at pages 495-538.
7. The discretionary trust is treated infra at pages 538-547.
8. A legal life estate also may qualify for the marital deduction but is seldom created for reasons given infra at pages 444-447. The marital deduction is treated infra at pages 997-1017.
9. A generation-skipping tax — somewhat comparable to an estate tax — may be imposed upon the death of the life tenant, however. See infra page 1024.

qualifies for the annual exclusion.[10] The foregoing are only a few illustrations of the many tax advantages available through the use of trusts.

Third, since World War II, there has been an enormous increase of private wealth in the United States. A great many more people have needs for property management that are best met through creation of a trust. A trust can be used to manage property transferred to a minor, an incompetent, or someone inexperienced in property management. A trust may serve to protect the settlor from his own indiscretions or his incompetence as he grows older or to protect his family against hazardous business ventures. Even persons of modest wealth may find the trust useful for various purposes, particularly where it is thought undesirable to give the donee possession and control of the property. "Thus," Professor Halbach has noted, "the trust plays a central role in modern estate planning and has utility in nearly every family situation. It is indeed a rare client who should not at least seriously consider the use of a trust for some circumstances, if only to cover certain contingencies that ought to be anticipated." Halbach, Trusts in Estate Planning, 2 Prob. Law. 1 (1975).

6.   *A Trust Compared with a Legal Life Estate*

A person who wants to give another a life estate may give the donee either a legal life estate or create a trust with the donee as life beneficiary. A legal life tenant has possession and control of the property, whereas a trustee controls trust property. Let us compare a legal life estate ("to A for life, remainder to A's children") with an equitable life estate ("to X in trust for A for life, remainder to A's children"). Is a legal life estate more or less desirable than a trust? This question is best answered by looking at problems that may arise during the legal life tenant's life and how proper drafting might solve them.

(1) *Sale.* The legal life tenant has no power to sell a fee simple unless such a power is granted in the instrument creating the life estate. If the life tenant is not granted a power of sale, it is possible for the tenant to go to court and obtain judicial approval of a sale. However, the law on this point is rather unclear. A lawsuit, even if successful, is expensive, and hence no legal life estate should be created without providing a mechanism for sale of the property should circumstances warrant it. (Exception: There may be no need for a power of sale if testator wants to pass grandfather's portrait, or some other item of family sentiment, from generation to generation.) Who is going to have the power of

10. See infra page 946.

sale? It could be given to the life tenant, but this may be undesirable for reasons noted below. The power of sale could be given to the life tenant and the adult remaindermen jointly, but it may prove difficult to get all interested parties to agree on sale and the opportunity for sale may be lost.

(2) *Reinvestment of proceeds of sale.* If the property is sold under a power of sale, what is to be done with the proceeds? If the life tenant is given a power of sale under which the proceeds go to the life tenant, the power of sale is in effect a general power of appointment — which means the property must be included in the life tenant's gross estate under the federal estate tax.[11] This may defeat the purpose of the life estate — to avoid death taxes on the life tenant's death. To get around this problem, the instrument could provide that the proceeds are to be held in trust (with the life tenant as trustee), to pay the income to the life tenant for life, then the proceeds to go to the remaindermen. However, the terms of this trust must be spelled out in the will; otherwise, litigation may ensue. See Annot., 47 A.L.R.3d 1078 (1973).

(3) *Borrowing money.* During the life tenant's lifetime, the real estate cannot be mortgaged by the life tenant. No banker is so foolish as to lend money with only a life estate as security. To put up the fee simple as security for a loan, it is necessary that the life tenant and *all* the remaindermen and reversioners sign the mortgage. It may be impossible to procure these signatures if the future takers are unascertained. It is ordinarily possible to give a mortgage on the property only when the remaindermen have an indefeasibly vested remainder, and for tax reasons indefeasibly vested remainders should almost never be created.[12] However, someone should be given the power to mortgage real estate. Without such a power the life tenant and remaindermen may be stuck with property that cannot be improved because it cannot be mortgaged. If the life tenant is given this power and can appropriate the loan to himself the power to mortgage is in effect a general power of appointment that may lead to tax problems in the life tenant's estate.

(4) *Leasing.* If rental property is involved, someone should be given the power to lease the property for a period extending beyond the life tenant's death. Otherwise it may be impossible to rent the premises. See Annot., 14 A.L.R.4th 1054 (1982). If the life tenant is given this power, and can accept a lump-sum payment in advance for the rent, the life tenant has the power to appropriate part of the remainder to himself. To the extent the life tenant can appoint the remainder to himself the life tenant has a general power of appointment.

(5) *Waste.* The life tenant may want to take oil out of the land, cut

11. See infra page 985.
12. See infra pages 646-649.

timber, or take down a still usable building. Each of these actions constitutes waste, and the remaindermen may be entitled to an injunction or damages. If the life tenant is given the power to drill for oil, open mines, or commit waste with impunity, the life tenant may be held to have a general power of appointment for tax purposes.

(6) *Expenses.* If land is involved, someone must pay taxes and maintain the property. The general rule is that the life tenant has the duty to pay taxes and keep the property in repair, but only to the extent the income from the property is adequate to cover those charges. The life tenant also has the duty to pay interest on, but not the principal of, the mortgage. However, the life tenant is under no duty to insure buildings on the land. If the life tenant does insure buildings, and the buildings are destroyed by fire, the life tenant has been held entitled to the whole proceeds and the remaindermen nothing. The instrument of gift may require the life tenant to insure the full value of the property or forfeit the life estate. But if this is done, and if the property is destroyed, what is to be done with the insurance proceeds? Similar problems arise as in the case of a sale; if the proceeds are to be held by the life tenant in trust, the trust must be spelled out in the testator's will. Since the life tenant may wish to use the proceeds to rebuild the premises, such a power should be granted the life tenant.

(7) *Creditors.* If the life tenant gets into debt, the creditor can seize the life estate and sell it. Of course, very little may be realized upon sale. Likely the creditor will buy it on judicial sale for a small amount, and if the life tenant lives a long time the creditor reaps a windfall. A forfeiture restraint against involuntary alienation could be put on the life estate, but its validity is questionable. If the debtor is a remainderman, the creditor may be able to seize the remainder and sell it. As with the life estate, the remainder may sell for very little, and the creditor usually will be the purchaser.

(8) *Miscellaneous.* Many other problems may arise. Trespassers may damage the property, the government may exercise eminent domain, a third party may be injured on the premises. The respective rights of the life tenant and the remaindermen must be covered in testator's will unless the law regarding the rights of a legal life tenant is clear and certain and satisfactory, and we can assure you that it isn't. If all these foreseeable problems are not covered in testator's will, they may end up being decided in expensive court proceedings.

When we consider all the problems that may arise in the future, we find that a trust is in most cases preferable to a legal life estate. If an independent trustee is not selected, the life tenant should be made a trustee rather than being given a legal life estate. Most of the above problems are administrative problems, and the law of trust administration is well established and extensive. If the trustee's powers are not spelled out in the trust instrument, the law will supply a charter of administration. Trust administration law is for the most part quite rational; in any case it is simpler and far more rational than the law respecting legal life estates and remainders. Look at the problems above.

(1) Standard administrative provisions from any form book almost always give the trustee a power of sale. The lawyer drafting the trust is unlikely to overlook this matter for it is natural to think of the trustee as a manager, whereas the life tenant may be thought of not as a manager but as a user. If the lawyer overlooks a power of sale, the courts are far more ready to find that a power of sale is conferred upon a trustee than upon a legal life tenant. (2) If the property is sold by a legal life tenant and the proceeds are to be put in trust, a trust must be created for the proceeds. This trust should be spelled out in the will, so the lawyer will not be saving words by creating a legal life estate. Why not have a trust from the beginning? (3, 4, 5, and 6.) As powers of sale are routinely put in any trust instrument, so are powers to mortgage, to lease, to give oil leases, and to pay taxes, insurance, and current charges. Where these powers are omitted in the trust instrument, the law often gives the trustee these powers. (7) A major difference between legal estates and equitable estates is that the latter can be put out of the reach of creditors. In most states a spendthrift trust, which disables creditors from reaching a beneficiary's interest, is permissible.[13]

A trustee is required to keep the trust property separate from the trustee's own property. A life tenant who is also trustee must keep separate books and account to the remaindermen. This requirement, plus the necessity for a separate tax return, tends to keep the book-keeping accurate and up-to-date and tends to eliminate litigation over the respective rights of the life tenant and the remaindermen. If a trustee mingles trust funds with the trustee's personal funds, the burden is on the trustee to show how much of the mingled fund is the trustee's own property. If the trustee cannot do this, the beneficiary may be entitled to the whole mingled fund.

NOTES

1. In view of the disadvantages of a legal life estate, why is not a legal life estate converted into a trust by statute? What purposes are served in having two bodies of law, one applicable to legal life estates and one applicable to life estates in trust?

By the English Law of Property Act of 1925, the legal life estate was abolished. Since that date only two kinds of legal estates can exist in England: the fee simple absolute in possession and the leasehold. Apart from leaseholds, all life estates and future interests of every kind (remainders, executory interests, reversions, possibilities of reverter, rights of entry) are equitable interests. The holder of the fee simple absolute in possession holds the property in trust for the other interested

---

13. See infra pages 547-568.

parties. The purpose of this legislation is to make land marketable by ensuring that a fee simple absolute owner is always available to sell the land. The result is to turn all family property settlements into trusts. See Bostick, Loosening the Grip of the Dead Hand: Shall We Abolish Legal Future Interests in Land, 32 Vand. L. Rev. 1061 (1979); Maudsley, Escaping the Tyranny of Common Law Estates, 42 Mo. L. Rev. 355 (1977).

2.   For an examination of the ideological role played by categories in legal consciousness, using trust law as a vehicle, see Alexander, The Transformation of Trusts as a Legal Category, 1800-1914, 5 Law & Hist. Rev. 303 (1987).

SECTION B.   CREATION OF A TRUST

1.   *Intent to Create a Trust*

No particular form of words is necessary to create a trust. The words trust or trustee need not be used. The sole question is whether the grantor manifested an intention to create a trust relationship.

Where the grantor conveys property to a grantee to hold "for the use and benefit" of another, this is a sufficient manifestation of an intention to create a trust. Thus in Fox v. Faulkner, 222 Ky. 584, 1 S.W.2d 1079 (1927), the grantor conveyed land "to Mary Pursiful for the use and benefit of Moses A. Cottrell, during his natural life — if said Moses A. Cottrell should leave children in lawful wedlock it shall go to them." The court held that a trust was created, saying:

> Though Mary Pursiful was designated as party of the second part in the deed, and the qualifying word "trustee" was not added after her name to indicate that she took merely in that capacity, the language of the granting clause is such as to exclude the conclusion that she took under it in any capacity other than as trustee for Moses A. Cottrell. The case is on a par with the celebrated bear case (Prewitt v. Clayton, 5 T.B. Mon. 5), where it was said: "A bear well painted and drawn to the life is yet a picture of a bear, although the painter may omit to write over it, 'This is the bear.'"

Jimenez v. Lee
Supreme Court of Oregon, 1976
274 Or. 457, 547 P.2d 126

O'CONNELL, C.J.   This is a suit brought by plaintiff against her father to compel him to account for assets which she alleges were held by defendant as trustee for her. Plaintiff appeals from a decree dismissing her complaint.

Plaintiff's claim against her father is based upon the theory that a trust arose in her favor when two separate gifts were made for her benefit. The first of these gifts was made in 1945, shortly after plaintiff's birth, when her paternal grandmother purchased a $1,000 face value U.S. Savings Bond which was registered in the names of defendant "and/or" plaintiff "and/or" Dorothy Lee, plaintiff's mother. It is uncontradicted that the bond was purchased to provide funds to be used for plaintiff's educational needs. A second gift in the amount of $500 was made in 1956 by Mrs. Adolph Diercks, one of defendant's clients. At the same time Mrs. Diercks made identical gifts for the benefit of defendant's two other children. The $1,500 was deposited by the donor in a savings account in the names of defendant and his three children.

In 1960 defendant cashed the savings bond and invested the proceeds in common stock of the Commercial Bank of Salem, Oregon. Ownership of the shares was registered as "Jason Lee, Custodian under the Laws of Oregon for Betsy Lee [plaintiff]." At the same time, the joint savings account containing the client's gifts to defendant's children was closed and $1,000 of the proceeds invested in Commercial Bank stock.[14] Defendant also took title to this stock as "custodian" for his children.

The trial court found that defendant did not hold either the savings bond or the savings account in trust for the benefit of plaintiff and that defendant held the shares of the Commercial Bank stock as custodian for plaintiff under the Uniform Gift to Minors Act (O.R.S. 126.805-126.880). Plaintiff contends that the gifts for her educational needs created trusts in each instance and that the trusts survived defendant's investment of the trust assets in the Commercial Bank stock.

It is undisputed that the gifts were made for the educational needs of plaintiff. The respective donors did not expressly direct defendant to hold the subject matter of the gift "in trust" but this is not essential to create a trust relationship. It is enough if the transfer of the property is made with the intent to vest the beneficial ownership in a third person. That was clearly shown in the present case. Even defendant's own testimony establishes such intent. When he was asked whether there was a stated purpose for the gift, he replied: ". . . Mother said that she felt that the children should all be treated equally and that she was going to supply a bond to help with Elizabeth's educational needs and that she was naming me and Dorothy, the ex-wife and mother of Elizabeth, to use the funds as may be most conducive to the educational needs of Elizabeth." Defendant also admitted that the gift from Mrs. Diercks was "for the educational needs of the children." There was nothing about either of the gifts which would suggest that the beneficial

---

14. The specific disposition of the balance of this account is not revealed in the record. Defendant testified that the portion of the gift not invested in the stock "was used for other unusual needs of the children." Defendant could not recall exactly how the money was used but thought some of it was spent for family vacations to Victoria, British Columbia and to satisfy his children's expensive taste in clothing.

ownership of the subject matter of the gift was to vest in defendant to use as he pleased with an obligation only to pay out of his own funds a similar amount for plaintiff's educational needs.

Defendant himself demonstrated that he knew that the savings bond was held by him in trust. In a letter to his mother, the donor, he wrote: "Dave and Bitsie [plaintiff] & Dorothy are aware of the fact that I hold $1,000 each for Dave & Bitsie in trust for them on account of your E-Bond gifts." It is fair to indulge in the presumption that defendant, as a lawyer, used the word "trust" in the ordinary legal sense of that term.

Defendant further contends that even if the respective donors intended to create trusts, the doctrine of merger defeated that intent because plaintiff acquired both legal and equitable title when the savings bond was registered in her name along with her parents names and when Mrs. Diercks' gift was deposited in the savings account in the name of plaintiff and her father, brother and sister. The answer to this contention is found in II Scott on Trusts §99.4, p. 811 (3d ed 1967):

> A trust may be created in which the trustees are *A* and *B* and the sole beneficiary is *A*. In such a case it might be argued that there is automatically a partial extinguishment of the trust, and that *A* holds an undivided half interest as joint tenant free of trust, although *B* holds a similar interest in trust for *A*. The better view is, however, that there is no such partial merger, and that *A* and *B* will hold the property as joint tenants in trust for *A*. . . .

Having decided that a trust was created for the benefit of plaintiff, it follows that defendant's purchase of the Commercial Bank stock as "custodian" for plaintiff under the Uniform Gift to Minors Act was ineffectual to expand defendant's powers over the trust property from that of trustee to that of custodian.[15]

Defendant's attempt to broaden his powers over the trust estate by investing the trust funds as custodian violated his duty to the beneficiary "to administer the trust solely in the interest of the beneficiary." Restatement (Second) of Trusts §170, p.364 (1959).

---

15. If defendant were "custodian" of the gifts, he would have the power under the Uniform Gift to Minors Act (O.R.S. 126.820) to use the property "as he may deem advisable for the support, maintenance, education and general use and benefit of the minor, in such manner, at such time or times, and to such extent as the custodian in his absolute discretion may deem advisable and proper, without court order or without regard to the duty of any person to support the minor, and without regard to any other funds which may be applicable or available for the purpose." As custodian defendant would not be required to account for his stewardship of the funds unless a petition for accounting were filed in circuit court no later than two years after the end of plaintiff's minority. O.R.S. 126.875. As the trustee of an educational trust, however, defendant has the power to use the trust funds for educational purposes only and has the duty to render clear and accurate accounts showing the funds have been used for trust purposes. See O.R.S. 128.010; Restatement (Second) of Trusts §172 (1959).

The money from the savings bond and savings account are clearly traceable into the bank stock. Therefore, plaintiff was entitled to impose a constructive trust or an equitable lien upon the stock so acquired. Plaintiff is also entitled to be credited for any dividends or increment in the value of that part of the stock representing plaintiff's proportional interest. Whether or not the assets of plaintiff's trust are traceable into a product, defendant is personally liable for that amount which would have accrued to plaintiff had there been no breach of trust. Defendant is, of course, entitled to deduct the amount which he expended out of the trust estate for plaintiff's educational needs. However, before he is entitled to be credited for such expenditures, he has the duty as trustee to identify them specifically and prove that they were made for trust purposes. A trustee's duty to maintain and render accurate accounts is a strict one. This strict standard is described in Bogert on Trusts and Trustees §962, pp. 10-13 (2d ed 1962):

> It is the duty of the trustees to keep full, accurate and orderly records of the statutes of the trust administration and of all acts thereunder. . . . "The general rule of law applicable to a trustee burdens him with the duty of showing that the account which he renders and the expenditures which he claims to have been made were correct, just and necessary. . . . He is bound to keep clear and accurate accounts, and if he does not the presumptions are all against him, obscurities and doubts being resolved adversely to him." [Quoting from White v. Rankin, 46 NYS 228, 18 App Div 293, 294, affirmed without opinion 162 NY 622, 57 NE 1128 (1897).] . . . He has the burden of showing on the accounting how much principal and income he has received and from whom, how much disbursed and to whom, and what is on hand at the time.

Defendant did not keep separate records of trust income and trust expenditures. He introduced into evidence a summary of various expenditures which he claimed were made for the benefit of plaintiff. It appears that the summary was prepared for the most part from cancelled checks gathered together for the purpose of defending the present suit. This obviously did not meet the requirement that a trustee "maintain records of his transactions so complete and accurate that he can show by them his faithfulness to his trust."[16]

In an even more general way defendant purported to account for the trust assets in a letter dated February 9, 1966, written to plaintiff shortly after her 21st birthday when she was in Europe where she had been receiving instruction and training in ballet. In that letter defendant revealed to plaintiff, apparently for the first time, that her grandmother had made a gift to her of a savings bond and that the proceeds of the

16.   Wood v. Honeyman, 178 Or. 484, 555-556, 169 P.2d 131, 162 (1946).

bond had been invested in stock. Without revealing the name of the stock, defendant represented that it had doubled in value of the bond from $750 to $1,500. The letter went on to suggest that plaintiff allocate $1,000 to defray the cost of additional ballet classes and that the remaining $500 be held in reserve to defray expenses in returning to the United States and in getting settled in a college or in a ballet company.

Defendant's letter was in no sense a trust accounting. In the first place, it was incomplete; it made no mention of Mrs. Diercks' gift. Moreover, it was inaccurate since it failed to reveal the true value attributable to the Commercial Bank stock. There was evidence which would put the value of plaintiff's interest in the stock at considerably more than $1,500.[17]

Defendant contends that even if a trust is found to exist and that the value of the trust assets is the amount claimed by plaintiff there is sufficient evidence to prove that the trust estate was exhausted by expenditures for legitimate trust purposes. Considering the character of the evidence presented by defendant, it is difficult to understand how such a result could be reached. As we noted above, the trust was for the educational needs of plaintiff. Some of the expenditures made by defendant would seem to fall clearly within the purposes of the trust. These would include the cost of ballet lessons, the cost of subscribing to a ballet magazine, and other items of expenditure related to plaintiff's education.[18] But many of the items defendant lists as trust expenditures are either questionable or clearly outside the purpose of an educational trust. For instance, defendant seeks credit against the trust for tickets to ballet performances on three different occasions while plaintiff was in high school. The cost of plaintiff's ticket to a ballet performance might be regarded as a part of plaintiff's educational program in learning the art of ballet, but defendant claims credit for expenditures made to purchase ballet tickets for himself and other members of the family, disbursements clearly beyond the purposes of the trust.

---

17. It appears that with the accumulation of cash and stock dividends the total value of plaintiff's interest at the time she received defendant's letter would amount to as much as $2,135. This figure is an approximation derived from the incomplete stock price information before us. It is important only to demonstrate that defendant did not render an adequate accounting. Our calculation does not include the value of plaintiff's interest in stock purchased with the proceeds of Mrs. Diercks' gift.

18. Defendant's failure to keep proper records makes it difficult, if not impossible, to determine whether some of these expenditures were made from the trust estate or from defendant's own funds. Moreover, it is unclear in some instances whether the expenditure was for educational purposes or simply for recreation. Thus defendant charges plaintiff with expenses incurred in connection with a European tour taken by plaintiff. It is not disclosed as to whether this was to provide an educational experience for plaintiff or for some other purpose.

Other expenditures claimed by defendant in his "accounting" are clearly not in furtherance of the purposes of the trust. Included in the cancelled checks introduced into evidence in support of defendant's claimed offset against the trust assets were: (1) checks made by defendant in payment of numerous medical bills dating from the time plaintiff was 15 years old (these were obligations which a parent owes to his minor children); (2) checks containing the notation "Happy Birthday" which plaintiff received from her parents on her 17th, 18th and 22nd birthdays; (3) a 1963 check with a notation "Honor Roll, Congratulations, Mom and Dad"; (4) defendant's check to a clothier which contains the notation "Betsy's Slacks and Sweater, Pat's Sweater, Dot's Sweater" (defendant attempted to charge the entire amount against the trust); (5) defendant's check to a Canadian Rotary Club for a meeting attended when he joined plaintiff in Banff after a summer ballet program; (6) $60 sent to plaintiff to enable her to travel from France, where she was studying ballet, to Austria to help care for her sister's newborn babies. There were also other items improperly claimed as expenditures for plaintiff's educational benefit, either because the purpose of the outlay could not be identified or because defendant claimed a double credit.[19]

It is apparent from the foregoing description of defendant's evidence that the trial court erred in finding that "Plaintiff in these proceedings has received the accounting which she sought and . . . is entitled to no further accounting." The trial court also erred in finding that "Defendant did not hold in trust for the benefit of Plaintiff" the product traceable to the two gifts.

The case must, therefore, be remanded for an accounting to be predicated upon a trustee's duty to account, and the trustee's burden to prove that the expenditures were made for trust purposes. There is a moral obligation and in proper cases a legal obligation for a parent to furnish his child with higher education. Where a parent is a trustee of an educational trust, as in the present case, and he makes expenditures out of his own funds, his intent on one hand may be to discharge his moral or legal obligation to educate his child or on the other hand to follow the directions of the trust.[20] It is a question of fact in each case

---

19. The double counting occurs where defendant claims credit for cashier's checks sent to plaintiff while she was staying in Europe and at the same time also claims credit for his personal checks used to purchase the cashier's checks.

20. The rule stated by Bogert indicates why defendant's intent is important:

> The trustee is entitled to be credited on the accounting with all sums paid or property transferred by him from trust funds, and with sums advanced by him from his own funds, when such payments or transfers were in the exercise of powers expressly or impliedly granted to him by the trust instrument, or powers given him by statute or court order, or reasonably incidental to the exercise of such powers.

Bogert on Trusts and Trustees §972(1) (2d ed 1962), pp. 218-220.

as to which of these two purposes the parent-trustee had in mind at the time of making the expenditures.[21] In determining whether defendant has met this strict burden of proof, the trial court must adhere to the rule that all doubts are resolved against a trustee who maintains an inadequate accounting system.

The decree of the trial court is reversed and the cause is remanded for further proceedings consistent with this opinion.[22]

NOTE: CUSTODIANSHIP UNDER UNIFORM TRANSFERS TO MINORS ACT

To provide a convenient procedure for making gifts to minors, who have no legal capacity to manage or sell property, every state has enacted either the Uniform Transfers to Minors Act (1983) or its earlier

---

If defendant made expenditures out of his own funds intending to discharge his obligation to educate his child, the payments were not "sums advanced by him from his own funds . . . in the exercise of [trust] powers." Such expenditures would be in his capacity as plaintiff's father and not as trustee.

21.   There is evidence that defendant considered expenditures made prior to February 9, 1966 (the date of defendant's letter to plaintiff which we previously described) as not being for trust purposes because at that date he regarded the proceeds from the savings bond still intact. The letter read:

I believe that it would be fair and realistic and I should henceforth offset against this $1500 such further funds as you may need to continue with your ballet instruction, or to travel to New York or elsewhere to commence your ballet career on an independent, self-supporting basis.

The situation is comparable to that of the mother bird that finally nudges the baby out of the nest so that it, too, may learn to fly.

22.   Jason Lee, the defendant in Jiminez v. Lee, was elected to the Oregon Court of Appeals in 1974, unseating an incumbent judge. As a result of the bitter campaign, a newspaper reporter sued the state bar under Oregon's open records law to reveal its disciplinary records on Jason Lee. In 1975, Lee filed for the Oregon Supreme Court seat of Chief Justice O'Connell, who was retiring in 1976. The decision in Jiminez v. Lee, written by Chief Justice O'Connell, was handed down on March 18, 1976. The next day, March 19, Jason Lee withdrew from the supreme court race. In June 1976, the supreme court decided the reporter's lawsuit and ordered the Jason Lee disciplinary records opened to the public. Lee's files weighed 15 pounds and revealed many complaints. A public letter of reprimand, for ambulance chasing and for directing his secretary as a notary to execute false acknowledgments, had been issued to Lee in 1965.

Judge Jason Lee did not resign from the court of appeals. Still sitting on that court, Lee died of a heart attack in 1980. Lee's will left all his property to his second wife, Merie. If Merie predeceased him (she didn't), his will devised his property in trust for his grandchildren: "I leave nothing but my love to my children."

The information in this footnote was furnished to the editors by Professor Valerie Vollmar of Willamette University College of Law. — Eds.

version, the Uniform Gifts to Minors Act (1956, revised 1966).[23] Under these acts, property may be transferred to a person (including the donor) as *custodian* for the benefit of the minor. A devise or gift may be made to *X* "as custodian for _____ (name of minor) under the _____ (name of state) Uniform Transfers to Minors Act." Thus creation of a custodianship is much simpler than creation of a trust.

Under Uniform Transfers to Minors Act §14(a) the custodian has discretionary power to expend

> for the minor's benefit so much or all the custodial property as the custodian deems advisable for the benefit of the minor, without court order and without regard to (i) the duty or ability of the custodian personally or of any other person to support the minor; or (ii) any other income or property of the minor which may be applicable or available for that purpose. . . .

To the extent that the custodial property is not so expended, the custodian is required to transfer the property to the minor on his attaining the age of 21 or, if the minor dies before attaining the age of 21, to the estate of the minor.

Uniform Transfers to Minors Act §14(a) provides that, "A delivery, payment, or expenditure under this section is in addition to, not in substitution for, and does not affect any obligation of a person to support the minor." This provision was inserted to prevent the income paid to the minor from being taxable to the minor's parent. If the income is used to discharge a legal obligation of support, it is taxable to the obligor.[24] The custodian has all the rights over custodial property that unmarried adult owners have over their own property. Id. §13. However, the custodian is a fiduciary and is subject to "the standard of care that would be observed by a prudent person dealing with property of another."[25] §12. A custodianship is useful for modest gifts to a

---

23.   The essential difference between these acts is that the original U.G.M.A. was more restricted in the types of property and the types of transfers covered. The U.G.M.A. was increasingly broadened by amendment in many jurisdictions until, finally, in 1983 the very broad U.T.M.A. was promulgated and enacted in a large majority of states. See Allison, The Uniform Transfers to Minors Act — New and Improved, but Shortcomings Still Exist, 10 U. Ark. Little Rock L.J. 339 (1988).

24.   A parent-custodian who uses the custodial assets to fulfill his support obligation is in breach of duty of loyalty and must restore the funds so used to the custodial account. Sutliff v. Sutliff, 515 Pa. 393, 528 A.2d 1318 (1987).

25.   A father who was custodian for his children under the Uniform Transfers to Minors Act invested half the funds in penny stocks and half in blue chips. The blue chip stocks sustained gains and losses reflecting general economic trends, while the speculative penny stocks suffered substantial losses. The father, sued by his ex-wife for breach of his fiduciary duties, was held liable for the losses in the penny stocks. Buder v. Sartore, 774 P.2d 1383 (Colo. 1989).

minor, but when a large amount of property is involved, a trust is usually preferable.

NOTE: PRECATORY LANGUAGE
AND EQUITABLE CHARGES

In a surprisingly large number of cases, the testator expresses a wish that the property devised should be disposed of by the devisee in some particular manner, but the language does not clearly indicate whether the testator intends to create a trust (with a legal duty so to dispose of the property) or merely a moral obligation unenforceable at law. If the language indicates the latter, it is called *precatory* language. (And sometimes courts speak of *precatory trusts*, meaning unenforceable dispositions of this sort.) Typical language raising this issue is a bequest "to A with the hope that A will care for B" or a devise of land "to C and it is my wish and desire that D should be able to live on the land during her life." To fathom the testator's intent, each will must be construed in accordance with the language used in each particular case in the light of all the circumstances. The result: much litigation. See 1 A. Scott, Trusts §25.2 (W. Fratcher 4th ed. 1987); Cickyj v. Sklepinska, 93 Ill. App. 3d 556, 417 N.E.2d 699 (1981). The problem can be avoided by clear drafting. If only a moral obligation is desired, say, "I wish, but do not legally require, that C permit D to live on the land."

Another distinction needs mention here: the difference between a trust and an equitable charge. If a testator devises property to a person, subject to the payment of a certain sum of money to another person, the testator creates an equitable charge, not a trust. The equitable charge is illustrated by Gadekar v. Phillips, 37 Md. App. 715, 375 A.2d 248 (Ct. Spec. App. 1977). In this case, S. Harold Phillips left the residue of his estate to his daughter Ruth "to do with whatsoever she shall deem fit and within her full and complete discretion, provided, however, that one-half of any rents and profits or proceeds of sale, or any other income from such property" was to be paid to his son Harold Hugh. In a suit for declaratory judgment, the court held that Phillips did not intend to create a trust with Ruth as trustee; the devise created a fee simple in Ruth with an "equitable charge" in favor of Harold Hugh. As a beneficiary of an equitable charge, Harold Hugh was a creditor of his sister with a security lien on the property devised.

> [T]he critical distinction between trusts and charges . . . is the absence of any fiduciary element in the chargee's duty toward the beneficiary of the charge. "The duty of a devisee subject to an equitable charge is a negative one; he must not so deal with the property as to destroy or interfere with the equitable lien of the encumbrances. . . ." Scott, Law of Trusts, at §10.

Other than this negative duty, the devisee of property subject to the charge has no special duties toward the beneficiary.

The court held also that Harold Hugh's interest would terminate upon his death, and that Ruth would have no obligation to make payments of income to his heirs.

2. Necessity of Trust Property

The usual definition of a trust includes three elements; a trustee, a beneficiary, and trust property. Since a trust is a method of disposing of, or managing, property, it is said that a trust cannot exist without trust property. When the meaning of property is examined, however, we find that it may refer to something other than a piece of land or a hefty chunk of money, such as $100,000. The trust property may be one dollar or one cent or it may be *any interest* in property that can be transferred. Contingent remainders, leasehold interests, choses in action, royalties, life insurance policies — anything that is called property — may be put in trust. The critical question is whether the particular claim will be called property by a court. When one ventures beyond what are historically conceded to be property interests, the circumstances that lead a court to classify a claim as property require a careful analysis of many variables.

Unthank v. Rippstein
Supreme Court of Texas, 1964
386 S.W.2d 134

STEAKLEY, J. Three days before his death C.P. Craft penned a lengthy personal letter to Mrs. Iva Rippstein. The letter was not written in terms of his anticipated early death; in fact, Craft spoke in the letter of his plans to go to the Mayo Clinic at a later date. The portion of the letter at issue reads as follows:

> Used most of yesterday and day before to "round up" my financial affairs, and to be sure I knew just where I stood before I made the statement that I would send you $200.00 cash the first week of each month for the next 5 years, provided I live that long, also to send you $200.00 cash for Sept. 1960 and thereafter send that amount in cash the first week of the following months of 1960, October, November and December. [opposite which in the margin there was written:]
> I have stricken out the words "provided I live that long" and hereby

and herewith bind my estate to make the $200.00 monthly payments provided for on this Page One of this letter of 9-17-60.

Mrs. Rippstein, Respondent here, first sought, unsuccessfully, to probate the writing as a [holographic] codicil to the will of Craft. The Court of Civil Appeals[26] held that the writing was not a testamentary instrument which was subject to probate. We refused the application of Mrs. Rippstein for writ of error with the notation "no reversible error." See Rule 483, Texas Rules of Civil Procedure.

The present suit was filed by Mrs. Rippstein against the executors of the estate of Craft, Petitioners here, for judgment in the amount of the monthly installments which had matured, and for declaratory judgment adjudicating the liability of the executors to pay future installments as they mature. The trial court granted the motion of the executors for summary judgment. The Court of Civil Appeals reversed and rendered judgment for Mrs. Rippstein, holding that the writing in question established a voluntary trust under which Craft bound his property to the extent of the promised payments; and that upon his death his legal heirs held the legal title for the benefit of Mrs. Rippstein to that portion of the estate required to make the promised monthly payments.

In her reply to the application for writ of error Mrs. Rippstein states that the sole question before us is whether the marginal notation constitutes "a declaration of trust whereby [Craft] agrees to thenceforth hold his estate in trust for the explicit purpose of making the payments." She argues that Craft imposed the obligation for the payment of the monies upon all of his property as if he had said "I henceforth hold my estate in trust for [such] purpose." She recognizes that under her position Craft became subject to the Texas Trust Act in the management of his property. Collaterally, however, Mrs. Rippstein takes the position that it being determinable by mathematical computation that less than ten per cent of the property owned by Craft at the time he wrote the letter would be required to discharge the monthly payments, the "remaining ninety per cent remained in Mr. Craft to do with as he would." Her theory is that that portion of Craft's property not exhausted in meeting his declared purpose would revert to him by way of a resulting trust eo instante with the legal and equitable title to such surplus merging in him.

These arguments in behalf of Mrs. Rippstein are indeed ingenious and resourceful, but in our opinion there is not sufficient certainty in the language of the marginal notation upon the basis of which a court of equity can declare a trust to exist which is subject to enforcement in such manner. The uncertainties with respect to the intention of Craft

_____

26.   In re Craft Estate, 358 S.W.2d 732 (C.C.A. 1962, writ ref. n.r.e.).

and with respect to the subject of the trust are apparent. The language of the notation cannot be expanded to show an intention on the part of Craft to place his property in trust with the result that his exercise of further dominion thereover would be wrongful except in a fiduciary capacity as trustee, and under which Craft would be subject to suit for conversion at the hands of Mrs. Rippstein if he spent or disposed of his property in a manner which would defeat his statement in the notation that a monthly payment of $200.00 in cash would be sent her the first week of each month. It is manifest that Craft did not expressly declare that all of his property, or any specific portion of the assets which he owned at such time, would constitute the corpus or res of a trust for the benefit of Mrs. Rippstein; and inferences may not be drawn from the language used sufficient for a holding to such effect to rest in implication. The conclusion is compelled that the most that Craft did was to express an intention to make monthly gifts to Mrs. Rippstein accompanied by an ineffectual attempt to bind his estate in futuro; the writing was no more than a promise to make similar gifts in the future and as such is unenforceable. The promise to give cannot be tortured into a trust declaration under which Craft while living, and as trustee, and his estate after his death, were under a legally enforceable obligation to pay Mrs. Rippstein the sum of $200.00 monthly for the five-year period. . . .

The judgment of the Court of Civil Appeals is reversed and that of the trial court is affirmed.

QUESTIONS

What policies are served by refusing to give effect to C.P. Craft's written intent? Where there is a written instrument making a gratuitous promise, which shows clearly that the donor intended to be legally bound, should the court give it effect as a declaration of trust? What would be the trust res? Would costs of so enforcing gratuitous promises exceed the gain from enforcement? See Baron, The Trust Res and Donative Intent, 61 Tul. L. Rev. 45 (1986) (arguing that the trust res requirement, supported by unconvincing rationales, defeats donative intent); Fellows, Donative Promises Redux, in Property Law and Legal Education 27 (P. Hay & M. Hoeflich eds. 1988); Love, Imperfect Gifts as Declarations of Trust: An Unapologetic Anomaly, 67 Ky. L.J. 309 (1979).

NOTE: RESULTING AND CONSTRUCTIVE TRUSTS

In *Unthank v. Rippstein*, Mrs. Rippstein argued that Craft, after transferring all his property into trust, had a resulting trust in the amount of his property not required to meet the payments to Mrs. Rippstein. What is a resulting trust?

A *resulting trust* is a trust that arises by operation of law in one of two situations: (a) where an express trust fails or makes an incomplete disposition or (b) where one person pays the purchase price for property, and causes title to the property to be taken in the name of another person who is not a natural object of the bounty of the purchaser. The relationship created by this latter situation is called a *purchase money resulting trust.* Thus:

> *Case 6. O* owns Blackacre. *A* pays *O* $10,000 for Blackacre; the deed conveying Blackacre names *B* as grantee. If *B* is not a natural object of *A*'s bounty, a presumption arises that *A* did not intend to make a gift of the property to *B* but had some other reason for causing *B* to be named as grantee. Unless the presumption is rebutted, *B* holds title on a resulting trust for *A.* The presumption can be rebutted by evidence, including oral testimony, showing that *A* did intend to make a gift to *B,* or that *A* made a loan to *B* of the purchase price. See 5 A. Scott, Trusts §441 (W. Fratcher 4th ed. 1989).
>
> *Case 6a.* Same facts as in Case 6, except that *B* is *A*'s son. Since *B* would be the likely object of a gift from *A,* a presumption arises that *A* intended to make a gift to *B.* The presumption of gift can be rebutted by evidence showing that *A* intended to retain beneficial enjoyment and had a reason for placing title in *B*'s name. See id. §442.

While some of the rules applicable to express trusts are applicable to resulting trusts, the Statute of Frauds is not. Even though the subject matter is real property, it is usually held that resulting trusts, as well as constructive trusts, arise by operation of law and hence are not subject to the Statute of Frauds. Moreover, a resulting trust does not contemplate an ongoing fiduciary relationship wherein the trustee holds and manages the property for the beneficiary. Once a resulting trust is found, the trustee must reconvey the property to the beneficial owner upon demand.

Another kind of fiduciary relationship, sometimes confused with a resulting trust, is the *constructive trust.* A constructive trust also arises by operation of law and not by the express terms of an instrument. Basically, the term constructive trust is the name given a flexible remedy imposed in a wide variety of situations to prevent unjust enrichment. When property has been acquired in such circumstances that the holder of the legal title may not in good conscience retain the beneficial interest, equity converts him into a trustee. A constructive trustee is under a duty to convey the property to another on the ground that retention of the property would be wrongful. The usual requirements for imposition of a constructive trust are: (1) a confidential or fiduciary relationship, (2) a promise, express or implied, (3) a transfer of property in reliance on the promise, and (4) unjust enrichment of the transferee. We have seen how a constructive trust may be imposed upon a person who procures an inheritance through fraud (supra pages 169-175) or upon the estate of a person who breaches a contract not to revoke a will (supra pages 273-280). Later in this chapter we shall see that a constructive trust may be imposed to enforce an oral trust of land which violates the Statute of Frauds (infra pages 479-485) or a secret testamentary trust (infra pages 485-488). In addition, a constructive trust may be imposed in situations where a confidential relationship or promise is not involved, but the court is moved simply by the desire to prevent unjust enrichment. Imposing a constructive trust upon a killer of the decedent to prevent him from profiting from his act (supra pages 114-121) is an example. On constructive trusts, see 5 A. Scott, Trusts §461-552 (W. Fratcher 4th ed. 1987).

NOTE: TRUST DISTINGUISHED FROM DEBT

The requirement of an identifiable trust res distinguishes a trust from a debt. A trust involves a duty to deal with some specific property, kept separate from the trustee's own funds. A debt involves an obligation to pay a sum of money to another. The crucial factor in distinguishing between a trust relationship and an ordinary debt is whether the recipient of the funds is entitled to use them as his own and commingle them with his own monies. For example, a life insurance company holding the proceeds of a matured policy under either an annuity option or an interest option is a debtor, not a trustee. The proceeds are not segregated and invested separately from the company's funds. The annuitant under the policy could, of course, transfer the annuity into a trust, and the annuity would then serve as a trust res. But an obligation to pay an annuity is not a res in the hands of the company. See Pierowich v. Metropolitan Life Insurance Co., 282 Mich. 118, 275 N.W. 789 (1937).

Similarly, money deposited in a bank ordinarily creates a debt, for the money is not segregated from the bank's general funds. However, the chose in action against the bank can serve as a res if the depositor transfers it in trust to another. What legal consequences might turn on the characterization of a relationship as a trust rather than a debt? See 1 A. Scott, Trusts §12 (W. Fratcher 4th ed. 1987).

A debt can be held in trust by the creditor but not by the debtor. Suppose that *A* owes *B* $5,000. *B* can hold the debt in trust for *C*, but *A* cannot hold the debt in trust for *C*. What is the reason for this rule? See 1A A. Scott, supra, §87.

Brainard v. Commissioner

United States Court of Appeals, Seventh Circuit, 1937
91 F.2d 880, cert. dismissed, 303 U.S. 665

SPARKS, J. This petition for review involves income taxes for the year 1928. The question presented is whether under the circumstances set forth in the findings of the Board of Tax Appeals, the taxpayer created a valid trust, the income of which was taxable to the beneficiaries under section 162 of the Revenue Act of 1928.

The facts as found by the Board of Tax Appeals are substantially as follows: In December, 1927, the taxpayer, having decided that conditions were favorable, contemplated trading in the stock market during 1928. He consulted a lawyer and was advised that it was possible for him to trade in trust for his children and other members of his family. Taxpayer thereupon discussed the matter with his wife and mother, and stated to them that he declared a trust of his stock trading during 1928 for the benefit of his family upon certain terms and conditions. Taxpayer agreed to assume personally any losses resulting from the venture, and to distribute the profits, if any, in equal shares to his wife, mother, and two minor children after deducting a reasonable compensation for his services. During 1928 taxpayer carried on the trading operations contemplated and at the end of the year determined his compensation at slightly less than $10,000, which he reported in his income tax return for that year. The profits remaining were then divided in approximately equal shares among the members of his family, and the amounts were reported in their respective tax returns for 1928. The amounts allocated to the beneficiaries were credited to them on taxpayer's books, but they did not receive the cash, except taxpayer's mother, to a small extent.

In addition to these findings the record discloses that taxpayer's two children were one and three years of age. Upon these facts the Board held that the income in controversy was taxable to the petitioner as a part of his gross income for 1928, and decided that there was a deficiency. It is here sought to review that decision.

In the determination of the questions here raised it is necessary to consider the nature of the trust, if any, that is said to have been created by the circumstances hereinbefore recited. It is clear that the taxpayer, at the time of his declaration, had no property interest in "profits in stock trading in 1928, if any," because there were none in existence at that time. Indeed it is not disclosed that the declarer at that time owned any stock. It is obvious, therefore, that the taxpayer based his declaration of trust upon an interest which at that time had not come into existence and in which no one had a present interest. In the Restatement of the Law of Trusts, vol. 1, §75, it is said that an interest which has not come

into existence or which has ceased to exist can not be held in trust. It
is there further said:

> A person can, it is true, make a contract binding himself to create a trust
> of an interest if he should thereafter acquire it; but such an agreement
> is not binding as a contract unless the requirements of the law of Contracts
> are complied with. . . .
>
> Thus, if a person gratuitously declares himself trustee of such shares
> as he may thereafter acquire in a corporation not yet organized, no trust
> is created. The result is the same where instead of declaring himself
> trustee, he purports to transfer to another as trustee such shares as he
> may thereafter acquire in a corporation not yet organized. In such a case
> there is at most a gratuitous undertaking to create a trust in the future,
> and such an undertaking is not binding as a contract for lack of
> consideration. . . .
>
> . . . If a person purports to declare himself trustee of an interest not in
> existence, or if he purports to transfer such an interest to another in
> trust, he is liable as upon a contract to create a trust if, but only if, the
> requirements of the law of Contracts are complied with.

See, also, Restatement, §30b; Bogert, Trusts and Trustees, vol. 1, §112.
In 42 Harvard Law Review 561, it is said: "With logical consistency, the
courts have uniformly held that an expectancy cannot be the subject
matter of a trust and that an attempted creation, being merely a promise
to transfer property in the future, is invalid unless supported by
consideration." Citing Lehigh Valley R.R. Co. v. Woodring, 116 Pa.
513, 9 A. 58. Hence, it is obvious under the facts here presented that
taxpayer's declaration amounted to nothing more than a promise to
create a trust in the future, and its binding force must be determined
by the requirements of the law of contracts.

It is elementary that an executory contract, in order to be enforceable,
must be based upon a valuable consideration. Here there was none.
The declaration was gratuitous. If we assume that it was based on love
and affection that would add nothing to its enforceability, for love and
affection, though a sufficient consideration for an executed conveyance,
is not a sufficient consideration for a promise. . . .

What has been said, however, does not mean that the taxpayer had
no right to carry out his declaration after the subject matter had come
into existence, even though there were no consideration. This he did
and the trust thereby became effective, after which it was enforceable
by the beneficiaries.

The questions with which we are concerned are at what times did
the respective earnings which constitute the trust fund come into
existence, and at what times did the trust attach to them. It is obvious
that the respective profits came into existence when and if such stocks
were sold at a profit in 1928. Did they come into existence impressed

with the trust, or was there any period of time intervening between the time they came into existence and the time the trust attached? If there were such intervening time, then during that time the taxpayer must be considered as the sole owner of the profits and they were properly taxed to him as a part of his income.

It is said in the Restatement of the Law of Trusts, §75c: "If a person purports to declare himself trustee of an interest not in existence or if he purports to transfer such an interest to another in trust, no trust arises even when the interest comes into existence in the absence of a manifestation of intention at that time." This we think is especially applicable where, as here, there was no consideration for the declaration. It is further stated, however, in the Restatement, §26k:

> If a person manifests an intention to become trustee at a subsequent time, his conduct at that subsequent time considered in connection with his original manifestation may be a sufficient manifestation of intention at that subsequent time to create a trust. . . . The act of acquiring the property coupled with the earlier declaration of trust *may be* a sufficient manifestation of an intention to create a trust at the time of the acquisition of the property. (Our italics, here and hereafter.)

In subsection 1 it is said ". . . Mere silence, however, ordinarily will not be such a manifestation. Whether silence is or is not such a manifestation is a question of interpretation." . . .

From what has been said we are convinced that appellant's profits in question were not impressed with a trust when they first came into existence. The Board was obviously of the impression that the trust first attached when appellant credited them to the beneficiaries on his books of account. This act, it seems to us, constituted his first subsequent expression of intention to become a trustee of the fund referred to in his original and gratuitous declaration. Prior to that time we think it is clear that the declaration could not have been enforced against him, and that his mere silence with respect thereto should not be considered as an expression of his intention to establish the trust at a time earlier than the credits. . . .

The order of the Board is affirmed.[27]

Speelman v. Pascal
Court of Appeals of New York, 1961
10 N.Y.2d 313, 178 N.E.2d 723, 222 N.Y.S.2d 324

DESMOND, C.J. Gabriel Pascal, defendant's intestate who died in 1954, had been for many years a theatrical producer. In 1952 an

---

27. Noted in 36 Mich. L. Rev. 1041. — Eds.

English corporation named Gabriel Pascal Enterprises, Ltd., of whose 100 shares Gabriel Pascal owned 98, made an agreement with the English Public Trustee who represented the estate of George Bernard Shaw. This agreement granted to Gabriel Pascal Enterprises, Ltd., the exclusive world rights to prepare and produce a musical play to be based on Shaw's play "Pygmalion" and a motion picture version of the musical play. The agreement recited, as was the fact, that the licensee owned a film scenario written by Pascal and based on "Pygmalion." In fact Pascal had, some time previously, produced a nonmusical movie version of "Pygmalion" under rights obtained by Pascal from George Bernard Shaw during the latter's lifetime. The 1952 agreement required the licensee corporation to pay the Shaw estate an initial advance and thereafter to pay the Shaw estate 3% of the gross receipts of the musical play and musical movie with a provision that the license was to terminate if within certain fixed periods the licensee did not arrange with Lerner[28] and Loewe or other similarly well-known composers to write the musical play and arrange to produce it. Before Pascal's death in July, 1954, he had made a number of unsuccessful efforts to get the musical written and produced and it was not until after his death that arrangements were made, through a New York bank as temporary administrator of his estate, for the writing and production of the highly successful "My Fair Lady." Meanwhile, on February 22, 1954, at a time when the license from the Shaw estate still had two years to run, Gabriel Pascal, who died four and a half months later, wrote, signed and delivered to plaintiff a document as follows:

Dear Miss Kingman

This is to confirm to you our understanding that I give you from my shares of profits of the Pygmalion Musical stage version five per cent (5%) in England, and two per cent (2%) of my shares of profits in the United States. From the film version, five per cent (5%) from my profit shares all over the world.

As soon as the contracts are signed, I will send a copy of this letter to my lawyer, Edwin Davies, in London, and he will confirm to you this arrangement in a legal form.

---

28. Alan Jay Lerner, dying in 1986, left what might be called a delicious bequest:

Third: I give and bequeath to Benjamin Welles, if he survives me, and Sydney Gruson, if he survives me, the sum of $1,000.00 each. The purpose of this modest remembrance is to defray the cost of one evening's merriment to be devoted to cheerful recollections of their departed friend.

The abstemious Bernard Shaw, vegetarian and teetotaler, who scathingly denounced the "artificial happiness, artificial courage, and artificial gaiety" provided by alcohol, would not have approved.—Eds.

> This participation in my shares of profits is a present to you in recognition for your loyal work for me as my Executive Secretary.[29]
>
> Very sincerely yours,
> *Gabriel Pascal*

The question in this lawsuit is: Did the delivery of this paper constitute a valid, complete, present gift to plaintiff by way of assignment of a share in future royalties when and if collected from the exhibition of the musical stage version and film version of "Pygmalion"? A consideration was, of course, unnecessary (Personal Property Law, §33, subd. 4)....

The only real question is as to whether the 1954 letter above quoted operated to transfer to plaintiff an enforcible right to the described percentages of the royalties to accrue to Pascal on the production of a stage or film version of a musical play based on "Pygmalion." We see no reason why this letter does not have that effect. It is true that at the time of the delivery of the letter there was no musical stage or film play in existence but Pascal, who owned and was conducting negotiations to realize on the stage and film rights, could grant to another a share of the moneys to accrue from the use of those rights by others. There are many instances of courts enforcing assignments of rights to sums which were expected thereafter to become due to the assignor. A typical case is Field v. Mayor of New York (6 N.Y. 179). One Bell, who had done much printing and similar work for the City of New York but had no present contract to do any more such work, gave an assignment in the amount of $1,500 of any moneys that might thereafter become due to Bell for such work. Bell did obtain such contracts or orders from the city and money became due to him therefor. This court held that while there was not at the time of the assignment any presently enforcible or even existing chose in action but merely a possibility that there would be such a chose of action, nevertheless there was a possibility of such which the parties expected to ripen into reality and which did afterwards ripen into reality and that, therefore, the assignment created an equitable title which the courts would enforce. A case similar to the

---

29. Pascal's loyal "Executive Secretary" is painted scarlet by Pascal's widow, Valerie, in her book, The Disciple and His Devil (1970). Marianne Speelman, also known as Zaya Kingman, was half Chinese and half Irish and the exotically beautiful widow of a Dutch banker who had made a fortune in China. She invited Gabriel Pascal to dinner in March of 1953 and that same night began a torrid love affair (id. at 252). As a result of her herb teas and food prepared with "life elixir," Pascal experienced "prodigious sexual powers" and felt as if he were flying. Marianne wrote that anybody who had ever made love to her could never again be satisfied with any other woman (id. at 255). Valerie states that soon after delivering the document in this case (id. at 297), Pascal attempted to break off his volcanic affair and, under the influence of an Indian mystic, renounced his fleshly desires forever (id. at 299). Spent, Pascal died some four months later. — Eds.

present one in general outline is Central Trust Co. v. West India Improvement Co. (169 N.Y. 314) where the assignor had a right or concession from the Colony of Jamaica to build a railroad on that island and the courts upheld a mortgage given by the concession owner on any property that would be acquired by the concession owner in consideration of building the railroad if and when the railroad should be built. The Court of Appeals pointed out in *Central Trust Co.*, at page 323, that the property as to which the mortgage was given had not yet come into existence at the time of the giving of the mortgage but that there was an expectation that such property, consisting of securities, would come into existence and accrue to the concession holder when and if the latter performed the underlying contract. This court held that the assignment would be recognized and enforced in equity. The cases cited by appellant (Young v. Young, 80 N.Y. 422; Vincent v. Rix, 248 N.Y. 76; Farmers' Loan & Trust Co. v. Winthrop, 207 App. Div. 356, mod. 238 N.Y. 477) are not to the contrary. In each of those instances the attempted gifts failed because there had not been such a completed and irrevocable delivery of the subject matter of the gift as to put the gift beyond cancellation by the donor. In every such case the question must be as to whether there was a completed delivery of a kind appropriate to the subject property. Ordinarily, if the property consists of existing stock certificates or corporate bonds, as in the *Young* and *Vincent* cases (supra), there must be a completed physical transfer of the stock certificates or bonds. In Farmers' Loan & Trust Co. v. Winthrop (supra) the dispute was as to the effect of a power of attorney but the maker of the power had used language which could not be construed as effectuating a present gift of the property which the donor expected to receive in the future from another estate.[30] The *Farmers' Loan & Trust Co.* case does not hold that property to be the subject of a valid gift must be in present physical existence and in the possession of the donor but it does hold that the language used in the particular document was not sufficient to show an irrevocable present intention to turn over to the donee securities which would come to the donor on the settlement of another estate. At page 485 of 238 New York this court held that all that need be established is "an intention that the title of the donor shall be presently divested and presently transferred" but that in the particular document under scrutiny in the *Farmer's Loan &*

---

30.   In Farmers' Loan & Trust Co. v. Winthrop, the settlor executed an inter vivos trust with Farmers' Loan as trustee of $5,000 "and all other property hereafter delivered." On the same day she gave a power of attorney to Farmers' Loan authorizing it to collect the assets she was entitled to receive from the estate of Jabez Bostwick, "and to transfer such securities and property to yourself as trustee." Before the executor of the Bostwick estate delivered the property to Farmers' Loan, the settlor died. The court held that the attempted transfer failed. — Eds.

Trust Co. case there was lacking any language to show an irrevocable intent of a gift to become operative at once. In our present case there was nothing left for Pascal to do in order to make an irrevocable transfer to plaintiff of part of Pascal's right to receive royalties from the productions. . . .

Judgment affirmed.[31]

NOTES AND PROBLEMS

1.   What doctrinal, factual, or other distinction justifies the different results reached in the *Brainard* case and the *Speelman* case? In terms of ritual and evidentiary policies, are the cases consistent?

2.   In which of the following cases has there been an effective transfer? Compare them with what happened in *Brainard* and *Speelman*.

(a)   *O* orally declares himself trustee for one year of all stocks he owns, with any profits from stock trading to go to *A*. See Barnette v. McNulty, 21 Ariz. App. 127, 516 P.2d 583 (1973).

(b)   In a notarized writing *O* declares himself trustee for the benefit of *A* of any profits *O* makes from stock trading during the next calendar year.

(c)   *O* orally declares himself trustee for the benefit of *A* of five percent of the profits, if there are any, of a musical play that *O* is writing, based upon Shaw's Pygmalion. See 1A A. Scott, Trusts §86.2 (W. Fratcher 4th ed. 1987).

(d)   *O* orally declares to *A:* "I give you 5 percent of the profits of a musical play based upon Shaw's Pygmalion, if I produce it and if there are any profits."

3.   The prevailing view is that a person can assign future earnings from an existing contract. The theory is that a person who has present ownership of the means of producing a thing has a present interest in the thing to be produced. In the *Speelman* case does it matter that Pascal has a license from the Shaw estate to produce a musical play based upon Pygmalion? Should it? Should it matter in *Brainard* that the taxpayer has the capital to produce the profits?

4.   On March 1, 1990, *H* executes a trust instrument naming *X* as trustee. The trust instrument provides that *X* is to pay the income from the trust property to *H*'s children until all reach 21 and then to distribute the property to *H*'s children. On the same day, *H* designates the beneficiaries on his life insurance policy thus: "payable on *H*'s death to *W* if *W* survives *H*, and, if *W* does not survive *H*, to *X* as trustee under a trust instrument executed by *H* on March 1, 1990." As owner of the

---

31.   Noted in 11 Catholic U.L. Rev. 115; 13 Syracuse L. Rev. 481. — Eds.

policy, *H* retains the right to change the beneficiaries. *H* delivers the trust instrument to *X*, and *X* signifies her acceptance by writing at the bottom of the trust instrument, "I accept this trust," and signing her name.

H dies intestate some time later, survived by three minor children. His wife, *W*, predeceased him. *G*, guardian of the children, claims that the proceeds of the life insurance policy are payable to him and not to *X*. *G* alleges that the trust did not arise during *H*'s lifetime because no property was transferred to the trust and the trustee has no active duties until *H*'s death. *G* further alleges that since the trust was not executed in accordance with the Statute of Wills, it fails as a testamentary trust. Is *G*'s position sound? See Gordon v. Portland Trust Bank, 201 Or. 648, 271 P.2d 653 (1954).

3.   Necessity of Trust Beneficiaries

It is said that a trust must have one or more beneficiaries. There must be someone to whom the trustee owes fiduciary duties, someone who can call the trustee to account.

There are exceptions, however, to this rule. The beneficiaries may be unborn or unascertained when the trust is created. Thus a trust created by *O*, who is childless, for the benefit of his future children would be a valid trust. The courts would protect the interests of the unborn children from improper acts of the trustee. On the other hand, if at the time the trust becomes effective the beneficiaries are too indefinite to be ascertained, the attempted trust may fail for want of ascertainable beneficiaries.

Clark v. Campbell
Supreme Court of New Hampshire, 1926
82 N.H. 281, 133 A. 166

Snow, J.   The ninth clause of the will of deceased reads:

My estate will comprise so many and such a variety of articles of personal property such as books, photographic albums, pictures, statuary, bronzes, bric-a-brac, hunting and fishing equipment, antiques, rugs, scrapbooks, canes and masonic jewels, that probably I shall not distribute all, and perhaps no great part thereof, during my life by gift among my friends. Each of my trustees is competent by reason of familiarity with the property, my wishes and friendships, to wisely distribute some portion at least of said property. I therefore give and bequeath to my trustees all my property embraced within the classification aforesaid in trust to make disposal by the way of a memento from myself, of such articles to such of my friends as they, my trustees, shall select. All of said property, not so disposed of by them, my trustees are directed to sell and the proceeds of such sale or sales to become and be disposed of as a part of the residue of my estate.

The question here reserved is whether or not the enumeration of chattels in this clause was intended to be restrictive or merely indicative of the variety of the personal property bequeathed. The question is immaterial if the bequest for the benefit of the testator's "friends" must fail for the want of certainty of the beneficiaries.

By the common law there cannot be a valid bequest to an indefinite person. There must be a beneficiary or a class of beneficiaries indicated in the will capable of coming into court and claiming the benefit of the bequest. Adve v. Smith, 44 Conn. 60. This principle applies to private but not to public trusts and charities. Harrington v. Pier, 105 Wis. 485; 28 R.C.L. 339, 340; Morice v. Bishop of Durham, 9 Ves. 399, 10 Ves. 521. The basis assigned for this distinction is the difference in the enforceability of the two classes of trusts. In the former there being no definite cestui que trust to assert his right, there is no one who can compel performance, with the consequent unjust enrichment of the trustee; while in the case of the latter, performance is considered to be sufficiently secured by the authority of the attorney-general to invoke the power of the courts. . . .

That the foregoing is the established doctrine seems to be conceded, but it is contended in argument that it was not the intention of the testator by the ninth clause to create a trust, at least as respects the selected articles, but to make an absolute gift thereof to the trustees individually. . . . It is a sufficient answer to this contention that the language of the ninth clause does not warrant the assumed construction. . . . When the clause is elided of unnecessary verbiage the testator is made to say: "I give to my trustees my property (of the described class) in trust to make disposal of to such of my friends as they shall select." It is difficult to conceive of language more clearly disclosing an intention to create a trust.

It is further sought to sustain the bequest as a power. The distinction apparently relied upon is that a power, unlike a trust (Goodale v. Mooney, 60 N.H. 528, 534), is not imperative and leaves the act to be done at the will of the donee of the power. 21 R.C.L. 773; 26 R.C.L. 1169. But the ninth clause by its terms imposes upon the trustees the imperative duty to dispose of the selected articles among the testator's friends. If, therefore, the authority bestowed by the testator by the use of a loose terminology may be called a power, it is not an optional power but a power coupled with a trust to which the principles incident to a trust so far as here involved clearly apply. . . .

We must, therefore, conclude that this clause presents the case of an attempt to create a private trust. . . .

The question presented, therefore, is whether or not the ninth clause provides for definite and ascertainable beneficiaries so that the bequest therein can be sustained as a private trust. . . .

Like the direct legatees in a will, the beneficiaries under a trust may be designated by class. But in such case the class must be capable of delimitation, as "brothers and sisters," "children," "issue," "nephews and nieces." A bequest giving the executor authority to distribute his property "among his relatives and for benevolent objects in such sums as in their judgment shall be for the best" was sustained upon evidence within the will that by "relatives" the testator intended such of his relatives within the statute of distributions as were needy, and thus brought the bequest within the line of charitable gifts and excluded all others as individuals. Goodale v. Mooney, 60 N.H. 528, 536. See Portsmouth v. Shackford, 46 N.H. 423, 425; Gafney v. Kenison, 64 N.H. 354, 356. Where a testator bequeathed his stocks to be apportioned to his "relations" according to the discretion of the trustee, to be enjoyed by them after his decease, it was held to be a power to appoint amongst his relations who were next of kin under the statute of distribution. . . .

In the case now under consideration the cestuis que trustent are designated as the "friends" of the testator. The word "friends" unlike "relations" has no accepted statutory or other controlling limitations, and in fact has no precise sense at all. Friendship is a word of broad and varied application. It is commonly used to describe the undefinable relationships which exist not only between those connected by ties of kinship or marriage, but as well between strangers in blood, and which vary in degree from the greatest intimacy to an acquaintance more or less casual. . . . There is no express evidence that the word is used in any restricted sense. The only implied limitation of the class is that fixed by the boundaries of the familiarity of the testator's trustees with his friendships. If such familiarity could be held to constitute such a line of demarcation as to define an ascertainable group, it is to be noted that the gift is not to such group as a class, the members of which are to take in some definite proportion (1 Jarman, Wills, 534; 1 Schouler, Wills, s. 1011) or according to their needs, but the disposition is to "such of my friends as they, my trustees, may select." No sufficient criterion is furnished to govern the selection of the individuals from the class. The assertion of the testator's confidence in the competency of his trustees "to wisely distribute some portion" of the enumerated articles "by reason of familiarity with the property, my wishes and friendships," does not furnish such a criterion. . . . Where an executor was given direction to distribute in a manner calculated to carry out "wishes which I have expressed to him or may express to him" and such wishes had been orally communicated to the executor by the testator, the devise could not be given effect as against the next of kin. Olliffe v. Wells, 130 Mass. 221, 224, 225. Much less can effect be given to the uncommunicated wishes of the testator here.

It was the evident purpose of the testator to invest his trustees with the power after his death to make disposition of the enumerated articles among an undefined class with practically the same freedom and irresponsibility that he himself would have exercised if living; that is, to substitute for the will of the testator the will and discretion of the trustees. Such a purpose is in contravention of the policy of the statute which provides that "no will shall be effectual to pass any real or personal estate . . . unless made by a person . . . in writing, signed by the testator or by some one in his presence and by his direction, and attested and subscribed in his presence by three or more credible witnesses." P.L., c. 297, s. 2.

Where a gift is impressed with a trust ineffectively declared and incapable of taking effect because of the indefiniteness of the cestui que trust, the donee will hold the property in trust for the next taker under the will, or for the next of kin by way of a resulting trust. . . . The trustees therefore hold title to the property enumerated in the paragraph under consideration, to be disposed of as a part of the residue, and the trustees are so advised. . . .

Case discharged.

All concurred.

NOTES

1.   Professor Scott argued that where there is a transfer in trust for members of an indefinite class of persons, no enforceable trust is created, but the transferee has a discretionary power to convey the property to such members of the class as he may select. 2 A. Scott, Trusts §122 (W. Fratcher 4th ed. 1987). In other words, the transferee has a power of appointment.

In trusts today, beneficiaries are often given powers of appointment, powers to choose among a designated class of persons. For example, *T* may devise his residuary estate in trust "for my wife *W* for life, and then to distribute the trust assets to such of my issue as my wife appoints." The power of appointment is discretionary; it is a nonfiduciary power. If *W* fails to exercise the power, the trust property passes to *T*'s heirs upon *W*'s death. Powers of appointment are treated in Chapter 10, beginning at page 705 infra.

In Clark v. Campbell the court says it cannot treat the will as creating a power of appointment because it is given to *trustees*. They hold it in a fiduciary capacity (unlike a nonfiduciary power given a beneficiary).

It is not an optional power but a "power coupled with a trust." Therefore trust principles apply. If the power of selection had been given "to my sister Polly and my friend Herbert" and not "to Polly and Herbert, *trustees* (or *executors*)" it would be a valid nonfiduciary power of appointment. (What is the drafting moral here?)

Restatement (Second) of Trusts §122 (1959) adopts Scott's position. Restatement (Second) of Property, Donative Transfers §12.1, Comment e (1986), agrees with the Restatement (Second) of Trusts:

> A provision in a will in relation to specified property may authorize the executors to make decisions as to the persons who will receive the property. . . . Rather than failing altogether, the provision should be construed to give the executors a power of appointment exercisable within a reasonable period of time after the appointment of the executors, with the specified property passing in default of appointment if the power is not exercised. Whether the power is general or non-general depends on the relationships and other circumstances involved.

Nonetheless, in spite of this academic condemnation, the rule applied in Clark v. Campbell ("indefinite beneficiaries") occasionally is applied to defeat a gift. See In re Kradwell's Estate, 44 Wis. 2d 40, 170 N.W.2d 773 (1969). Compare In re Estate of Reiman, 115 Ill. App. 3d 879, 450 N.E.2d 928 (1983), voiding devise to executor to distribute in accordance with "the verbal guide lines last given by me, and in accord with his best judgment." See generally Palmer, The Effect of Indefiniteness on the Validity of Trusts and Powers of Appointment, 10 UCLA L. Rev. 241 (1963).

2. A power in an executor or trustee to distribute property to the testator's "relatives" is usually upheld as having sufficiently definite beneficiaries. If the trustee fails to make a selection, the property passes to the relatives in accordance with the intestate succession statute. See W. McGovern, S. Kurtz & J. Rein, Wills, Trusts and Estates §8.5 (1988).

In re Searight's Estate
Ohio Court of Appeals, 1950
87 Ohio App. 417, 95 N.E.2d 779

HUNSICKER, J. George P. Searight, a resident of Wayne county, Ohio, died testate on November 27, 1948. Item "third" of his will provided:

> I give and bequeath my dog, Trixie, to Florence Hand of Wooster, Ohio, and I direct my executor to deposit in the Peoples Federal Savings and Loan Association, Wooster, Ohio, the sum of $1000.00 to be used by him to pay Florence Hand at the rate of 75 cents per day for the keep and

care of my dog as long as it shall live. If my dog shall die before the said
$1000.00 and the interest accruing therefrom shall have been used up, I
give and bequeath whatever remains of said $1000.00 to be divided
equally among those of the following persons who are living at that time,
to wit: Bessie Immler, Florence Hand, Reed Searight, Fern Olson and
Willis Horn.

At the time of his death, all of the persons, and his dog, Trixie, named
in such item third, were living.

Florence Hand accepted the bequest of Trixie, and the executor paid
to her from the $1000 fund, 75 cents a day for the keep and care of
the dog. The value of Trixie was agreed to be $5.

The Probate Court [held item third valid]. . . .

The questions presented by this appeal on questions of law are:

1. Is the testamentary bequest for the care of Trixie (a dog) valid
in Ohio —

(a)   as a proper subject of a so-called "honorary trust"?

(b)   as not being in violation of the rule against perpetuities? . . .

1(a).   The creation of a trust for the benefit of specific animals has
not been the subject of much litigation in the courts, and our research,
and that of able counsel in this case, have failed to disclose any reported
case on the subject in Ohio. The few reported cases in this country, in
England and in Ireland have been the subject of considerable comment
by the writers of text books and by the law reviews of leading law
schools. . . .

We do not have, in the instant case, the question of a trust established
for the care of dogs in general or of an indefinite number of dogs, but
we are here considering the validity of a testamentary bequest for the
benefit of a specific dog. This is not a charitable trust, nor is it a gift
of money to the Ohio Humane Society or a county humane society,
which societies are vested with broad statutory authority, Section 10062,
General Code, for the care of animals.

Text writers on the subject of trusts and many law professors designate
a bequest for the care of a specific animal as an "honorary trust"; that
is, one binding the conscience of the trustee, since there is no beneficiary
capable of enforcing the trust.

The rule in Ohio, that the absence of a beneficiary having a legal
standing in court and capable of demanding an accounting of the
trustee is fatal and the trust fails, was first announced in Mannix,
Assignee v. Purcell, 46 Ohio St. 102, 19 N.E. 572, 2 L.R.A. 753. . . .

In 1 Scott on the Law of Trusts, Section 124, the author says:

> There are certain classes of cases similar to those discussed in the preceding
> section in that there is no one who as beneficiary can enforce the purpose
> of the testator, but different in one respect, namely, that the purpose is
> definite. Such, for example, are bequests for the erection or maintenance

of tombstones or monuments or for the care of graves, and bequests for
the support of specific animals. It has been held in a number of cases
that such bequests as these do not necessarily fail. It is true that the
legatee cannot be compelled to carry out the intended purpose, since
there is no one to whom he owes a duty to carry out the purpose.

Even though the legatee cannot be compelled to apply the property to
the designated purpose, the courts have very generally held that he can
properly do so, and that no resulting trust arises so long as he is ready
and willing to carry it out. The legatee will not, however, be permitted
to retain the property for his own benefit; and if he refuses or neglects
to carry out the purpose, a resulting trust will arise in favor of the
testator's residuary legatee or next of kin. . . .

The object and purpose sought to be accomplished by the testator in
the instant case is not capricious or illegal. He sought to effect a worthy
purpose — the care of his pet dog.

Whether we designate the gift in this case as an "honorary trust" or
a gift with a power which is valid when exercised is not important, for
we do know that the one to whom the dog was given accepted the gift
and indicated her willingness to care for such dog, and the executor
proceeded to carry out the wishes of the testator.

Where the owner of property transfers it upon an intended trust for a
specific noncharitable purpose and there is no defintie or definitely
ascertainable beneficiary designated, no trust is created; but the transferee
has power to apply the property to the designated purpose, unless he is
authorized by the terms of the intended trust so to apply the property
beyond the period of the rule against perpetuities, or the purpose is
capricious. I Restatement of the Law of Trusts, Section 124.

To call this bequest for the care of the dog, Trixie, a trust in the
accepted sense in which that term is defined is, we know, an unjustified
conclusion. The modern authorities, as shown by the cases cited earlier
in this discussion, however, uphold the validity of a gift for the purpose
designated in the instant case, where the person to whom the power is
given is willing to carry out the testator's wishes. Whether called an
"honorary trust" or whatever terminology is used, we conclude that the
bequest for the care of the dog, Trixie, is not in and of itself unlawful.

1(b).   In Ohio, by statute, Section 10512-8, General Code, the rule
against perpetuities is specifically defined, and such statute further
says: "It is the intention by the adoption of this section to make effective
in Ohio what is generally known as the common law rule against
perpetuities."

It is to be noted, in every situation where the so-called "honorary
trust" is established for specific animals, that, unless the instrument
creating such trust limits the duration of the trust — that is, the time

during which the power is to be exercised — to human lives, we will have "honorary trusts" established for animals of great longevity, such as crocodiles, elephants and sea turtles. . . .

Restatement of the Law of Property . . . says, at Section 379:

> A limitation of property on an intended trust is invalid when, under the language and circumstances of such limitation, (a) the conveyee is to administer the property for the accomplishment of a specific noncharitable purpose and there is no definite or definitely ascertainable beneficiary designated; and (b) such administration can continue for longer than the maximum period [allowed by the rule against perpetuities]. . . .

If we then examine item third of testator's will, we discover that, although the bequest for his dog is for "as long as it shall live," the money given for this purpose is $1000 payable at the rate of 75¢ a day. By simple mathematical computation, this sum of money, expended at the rate determined by the testator, will be fully exhausted in three years and 238⅓ days. If we assume that this $1000 is deposited in a bank so that interest at the high rate of 6% per annum were earned thereon, the time needed to consume both principal and interest thereon (based on semiannual computation of such interest on the average unused balance during such six month period) would be four years, 57½ days.

It is thus very apparent that the testator provided a time limit for the exercise of the power given his executor, and that such time limit is much less than the maximum period allowed under the rule against perpetuities.

We therefore conclude that the bequest in the instant case for the care of the dog, Trixie, does not, by the terms of the creating instrument, violate the rule against perpetuities. . . .

The judgment of the Probate Court is affirmed.

NOTES

1. In *Searight's Estate* the Department of Taxation of Ohio argued that an inheritance tax was levied on the amount used for the care of Trixie. Ohio General Code §5332 levied a tax on all property passing to a "person, institution or corporation." In an omitted portion of the opinion, the court decided that a dog was none of these, and no inheritance tax was levied on the amount used for Trixie's care. A tax was levied, however, on the contingent amount passing to the five persons on the death of Trixie.

In the probate court proceedings, the Department also argued that a dog is personal property and a thing of value and should have been taxed as an inheritance of Florence Hand. The executor of the estate of George P. Searight testified:

> If the Court please: I am an innocent bystander of this situation and am not personally interested one way or the other except to be right. Let me say this to the Court, — I wrote this provision in the Will, and frankly, the question as to whether the dog was taxable or not was never considered. I had no idea we would have such a problem. When the time came to make the Will George was concerned that when something happened to him that the dog was not to go to the dog pound. In fact he had as much affection for his dog as for his relatives. He lived with the dog and lived down there like a recluse.
>
> So far as the tax matter is concerned, let me take Mr. Annat's last contention, so far as taxing the dog as a thing of value. The dog may have a value of two, three or five dollars. It has no value other than that of a mongrel fox-terrier dog. Frankly I would say it could be argued that the fair market value of the dog was zero. If Florence tried to sell the dog I don't think she could give it away. On the contention of whether or not it is a thing of value I am not disposed to argue. Whether it can be sold, I don't know. I do know this, — George had it and I know there was some question about Florence taking it, and only because he made that instruction in the Will she took it.

The parties settled the matter by agreeing that the dog had a value of $5 and Florence Hand owed a tax on that.

The executor's final accounting reported that $265.75 was distributed to Florence Hand for the care of Trixie, who died on October 30, 1949. The balance of the $1000 was divided among the five legatees.

Why did not the Ohio Court of Appeals, in deciding the perpetuities question, take into account the fact that Trixie had actually died before the court's decision was made?

2. An honorary trust is treated like a special power of appointment under the Rule against Perpetuities. A special power that can be exercised beyond lives in being plus 21 years is void ab initio. Similarly, an honorary trust (i.e., a trust for a definite but noncharitable purpose) is void if it can last beyond the perpetuities period. See J. Gray, The Rule Against Perpetuities §909.1 (4th ed. 1942); J. Morris & W. Leach, The Rule Against Perpetuities 324-327 (2d ed. 1962).

3. In In re Kelly, [1932] Ir. R. 255, the testator left £100 to his executors to spend £4 per year to support each of his dogs, with a gift over of the balance unexpended to the parish priest. The court held the gift over to the priest violated the Rule against Perpetuities, saying:

> "Lives" means human lives. It was suggested that the last of the dogs could in fact not outlive the testator by more than twenty-one years. I know nothing of that. The Court does not enter into the question of a

dog's expectation of life. In point of fact neighbor's dogs and cats are unpleasantly long-lived; but I have no knowledge of their precise expectation of life. Anyway the maximum period is exceeded by . . . the life of a single butterfly, . . . despite all the world of poetry that may be thereby destroyed. [Id. at 260-261.]

The court went on to hold that since the executors were to spend £4 *per year*, the executors had a series of successive annual powers, and it held that the annual powers exercisable during the first 21 years were valid, and the powers exercisable thereafter void. Hence the dogs could be supported for 21 years or until earlier death. After that, the court noted, "The dogs have to take their chance."

4.   For an argument that animals should have legal rights, see Comment, Rights for Nonhuman Animals: A Guardianship Model for Dogs and Cats, 14 San Diego L. Rev. 484 (1977). On whether animals can be ordered destroyed by will, see Carlisle, Destruction of Pets by Will Provision, 16 Real Prop., Prob. & Tr. J. 894 (1981).

NOTE: SHAW'S ALPHABET TRUSTS

George Bernard Shaw was long interested in reforming the English alphabet so that letters, singly and in combination, would have only one pronunciation. He pointed out that fish could be spelled "ghoti" if the "gh" were pronounced like the "gh" in "enough," "o" like the "o" in "women," and "ti" like "ti" in "notion." (He did not note that Shaw could be spelled "pshaw.") Shaw devised the residue of his estate (fattened by royalties from "My Fair Lady") to his executor, in trust for 21 years, to develop a new alphabet of 40 letters and to propagandize for its adoption. Upon the termination of the alphabet trusts "or if and so far as such trusts shall fail through judicial decision," the principal was to be distributed one-third to the British Museum "in acknowledgment of the incalculable value to me of my daily resort to the reading room of that institution at the beginning of my career," one-third to the National Gallery of Ireland, and one-third to the Royal Academy of Dramatic Art. The court held the alphabet trust was not for the advancement of education nor beneficial to the community, and therefore it was not a charitable trust. The court further held that the devise could not be treated as a private trust because it was not in favor of an ascertainable beneficiary. The court referred to the Restatement of Trusts §124 (quoted in In re Searight's Estate), which approves treating the gift as a power, and stated that it was

not at liberty to validate this trust by treating it as a power. . . . The result is that the alphabet trusts are, in my judgment, invalid, and must fail. It seems that their begetter suspected as much, hence his jibe about failure by judicial decision. I answer that it is not the fault of the law, but of the testator, who failed almost for the first time in his life to grasp the problem or to make up his mind what he wanted. [In re Shaw, [1957] 1 All E.R. 745, 759 (Ch.).]

Who would have thought that the figure of Nemesis would appear to Shaw in the guise of an alphabet trust?

The case was appealed, but while the appeal was pending a compromise was effected by which a sum was set aside to employ a phonetic expert to develop a phonetic alphabet, transliterate Shaw's play "Androcles and the Lion" into the new alphabet, and publish the transliterated play. How would you have drafted Shaw's will to carry out his desires? See Fratcher, Bequests for Purposes, 56 Iowa L. Rev. 773 (1971).

4. Oral Trusts

a. Oral Inter Vivos Trusts of Land

As we have seen, an inter vivos oral trust of personalty is enforceable. It is not within the Statute of Frauds. If the subject matter of an inter vivos trust is land, however, a written instrument is commonly required to make the trust effective. Section 7 of the English Statute of Frauds required "all declarations or creations of trusts . . . of any lands" to be in writing. Where O conveys land to X upon an oral trust to pay the income to A for life and upon A's death to convey the land to B, the Statute of Frauds prevents enforcement of the express trust. Is X permitted to keep the land? The cases go three ways: (1) X retains the land, because the Statute of Frauds forbids proof of the oral trust; (2) to prevent unjust enrichment of X, X holds on a constructive trust for the settlor; (3) to prevent unjust enrichment of X, X holds on a constructive trust for the beneficiaries. The older cases tended to favor solution (1). Yet, as the Statute of Frauds has been losing its bite in recent years, more and more courts now seem to reach solution (3), enforcing the trust for the intended beneficiaries. Professor Scott favored solution (2): "The policy of the Statute of Frauds, which does indeed forbid going forward with the transaction, does not forbid going back and putting the parties in statu quo." 1 A. Scott, Trusts §45 (W. Fratcher 4th ed. 1987). This restitutionary approach has not gained a large following, however. In any event, a constructive trust for the beneficiaries will be imposed where the transfer was wrongfully obtained by fraud or duress, where the transferee, X, was in a confidential relation to the transferor, or where the transfer was made in anticipation of the transferor's death. And most of the cases involve one of these situations.

More common than an oral trust for a third party is an oral trust for the benefit of the transferor. Indeed, judging by the cases, a surprising number of persons from time to time put title to land in another, relying upon the transferee's oral promise to reconvey. Some of the transferors are attempting to avoid their creditors or spouses or to achieve some tax benefit. Others transfer title to a member of the family for one reason or another. Of course, any lawyer knows these transferors are asking for trouble and, human nature being what it is, they usually, like King Lear, get it.

Evicted Couple Leave Pictures of Son Who Threw Them Out
Los Angeles Times, Dec. 10, 1977, pt. 1, at 24, col. 1

SEATTLE (UPI) — When Tom Rhodes and his wife were evicted, the only possessions they left behind in their $50,000 house were photographs of their son taped across the fireplace.

It was their son, Police Sgt. T.J. Rhodes, Jr., who had obtained the court order for their eviction.

"Now he is just Sgt. T.J. Rhodes," said Mrs. Rhodes, 58, who wept softly as a neighbor placed a comforting hand on her shoulder.

Tom Rhodes, Sr., 60, who had vowed he would have to be carried out of the house, gave in after a talk with Robert Lindquist, chief of the civil division of the King County Police, and walked out peacefully.

At the bottom of the stairs, Rhodes paused to remove an American flag. "That stands for justice," he said bitterly.

His son has steadfastly refused to answer questions about the eviction. His only public comments are in the cold legal language of court records.

"He has not talked to me in four years," the father said. "He will talk to his mother but not to me."

The couple said they had placed the home in their son's name to protect it when the elder Rhodes experienced financial troubles years ago. Monthly payments and taxes were paid by the father to the son, who forwarded them to the bank, the father said.

King County Superior Judge Robert Elston ruled in September that the younger Rhodes owned the house and was legally entitled to evict tenants, in this case his parents. Elston determined that loan papers and other documents showed that the elder Rhodeses had admitted they were "renting" from their son and that the parties had treated the house as rental property in their federal tax statements.

On the basis of the ruling, the younger Rhodes sent his parents a notice dated Sept. 30. "Please take notice," it began, "that the undersigned landlord, Thomas Rhodes, Jr., hereby gives you notice . . . to terminate your tenancy."

The parents went back to court to fight the eviction notice, but won nothing more than an extra 30 days to live in the house.

"I still think this is my house," the senior Rhodes said as he left it.

Hieble v. Hieble
Supreme Court of Connecticut, 1972
164 Conn. 56, 316 A.2d 777

SHAPIRO, J.   In this action the plaintiff sought a reconveyance of real property in the town of Killingworth which she had transferred to the defendant, claiming that he had agreed to reconvey the same to her, upon request, if she recovered from an illness. The trial court rendered judgment for the plaintiff and the defendant has appealed.

The trial court's finding of facts, which is not attacked, discloses that on May 9, 1959, the plaintiff, without consideration, transferred the title of her real estate by survivorship deed to her son, the defendant, and to her daughter. The plaintiff, who had that year undergone surgery for malignant cancer, feared a recurrence but believed that she would be out of danger if the cancer did not reappear within five years. She and the grantees orally agreed that the transfer would be a temporary arrangement; that she would remain in control of the property and pay all expenses and taxes; that once the danger of recrudescence had passed, the defendant and his sister would reconvey the property to the plaintiff on request. After the transfer, the plaintiff continued to reside on the property with her aged mother, whom she supported, her daughter and the defendant. In 1960, after the plaintiff expressed displeasure over the daughter's marriage, the daughter agreed to relinquish her interest in the property. A deed was prepared and the daughter and son, through a strawman, transferred title to the land to the plaintiff and her son in survivorship. In 1964, five years after the original conveyance, the plaintiff requested that the defendant reconvey his legal title to her, since she considered herself out of risk of a recurrence of cancer.

The plaintiff at that time needed money to make improvements on the land, particularly to install running water and indoor plumbing facilities as a convenience for her aged mother. The defendant procrastinated, feigning concern about the boundaries of an adjacent forty-acre parcel which the plaintiff had given him in 1956. Although the defendant refused to convey his interest in the jointly-owned premises, some friends of the plaintiff ultimately prevailed on him to sign a mortgage for an improvement loan in 1965. Thereafter, the defendant assured the plaintiff that he would never marry but would continue to live with her. These were his reasons for refusing reconveyance until his marriage plans were disclosed. Although the plaintiff proposed that her son could keep the property if he remained single, he did marry in 1967 and moved out of the house. After her attempts to obtain his voluntary reconveyance failed, the plaintiff brought suit in 1969. Throughout the entire period of time material to this litigation, the plaintiff has borne all expenses and costs of improvement to the property.

From these facts the trial court concluded that a constructive trust should be decreed on the basis of the oral agreement, the confidential relationship of the parties and their conduct with respect to the property. The defendant's appeal raises primarily the claim that the elements necessary to establish a confidential relationship, as the basis for a constructive trust, are lacking.

It hardly needs reciting that under our Statute of Frauds, General Statutes §52-550, oral agreements concerning interests in land are unenforceable. See Hanney v. Clark, 124 Conn. 140, 144-145, 198 A. 557. In this jurisdiction, however, the law is established that the Statute of Frauds does not apply to trusts arising by operation of law. Reynolds v. Reynolds, 121 Conn. 153, 158, 183 A. 394; Ward v. Ward, 59 Conn. 188, 196, 22 A. 149.

The case before us presents one of the most vexatious problems facing a court of equity in the area of constructive trusts, namely, whether equity should impose a constructive trust where a donee who by deed has received realty under an oral promise to hold and reconvey to the grantor has refused to perform his promise. See 3 Bogert, Trusts and Trustees (2d Ed.) §495; Costigan, "Trusts Based on Oral Promises," 12 Mich. L. Rev. 423, 515. Our task here, however, is considerably alleviated, since the defendant has not attacked the court's finding that the alleged agreement was in fact made, nor does he contest the receipt of parol evidence as having violated the Statute of Frauds. Although the deed recited that consideration was given for the 1959 transfer, the defendant does not attack the finding that there was no consideration for the conveyance. Indeed, in his brief the defendant abandons the claim that a recital of consideration suffices to rebut an allegation of a trust. . . .

Since the finding of facts is not challenged, the conclusion of the court that the parties stood in a confidential relationship must stand unless it is unreasonably drawn or unless it involves an erroneous application of law. The defendant's attack on this conclusion is without merit. He argues that because the plaintiff initiated the transfer and was a woman of mature years, and because he was an inexperienced young man, a court of equity should not recognize a relationship of confidentiality between them. We grant that the bond between parent and child is not per se a fiduciary one; it does generate, however, a natural inclination to repose great confidence and trust. See Suchy v. Hajicek, 364 Ill. 502, 509, 510, 4 N.E.2d 836; Wood v. Rabe, 96 N.Y. 414, 426. Coupled with the plaintiff's condition of weakness, her recent surgery, her anticipation of terminal illness, and the defendant's implicit reassurances of his faithfulness, this relationship becomes a classic example of the confidentiality to which equity will fasten consequences. See Restatement (Second), 1 Trusts §44, pp. 115-16; 3 Bogert, supra, §482. . . .

The defendant's next contention questions the sufficiency of the evidence to justify the imposition of a constructive trust. Since he does not attack the finding that there was an underlying oral agreement, he cannot question the sufficiency of evidence to support that finding. Brockett v. Jensen, 154 Conn. 328, 331, 225 A.2d 190; Davis v. Margolis, 107 Conn. 417, 422, 140 A. 823. Presumably, the defendant objects to the sufficiency of this 1959 oral agreement, standing by itself, to create a constructive trust. Here, three points are in order. First, the trial court reached its conclusion not only on the basis of that agreement but also on the conduct of the parties and the circumstances surrounding the conveyance, seen as a whole. As we have already noted, the defendant has failed to sustain his attack on the court's conclusion that a confidential relationship existed. Second, where a confidential relationship has been established, there is substantial authority that the burden of proof rests on the party denying the existence of a trust — and then, by clear and convincing evidence to negate such a trust. See Suchy v. Hajicek, supra, 364 Ill. 510, 4 N.E.2d 836; 89 C.J.S. Trusts §155. Our decision in Wilson v. Warner, 84 Conn. 560, 80 A. 718, is not contrary. There, in regard to an alleged resulting trust in a decedent's estate, the court said (pp. 564, 565, 80 A. p.719): "But in all cases where the claimed trust title to land is disputed, the facts from which such trust may be implied should be clearly and satisfactorily established." Third, as this court held in Dowd v. Tucker, 41 Conn. 197, 205, it is unnecessary to find fraudulent intent for the imposition of a constructive trust. Whether there be fraud at the inception or a repudiation afterward, the whole significance of such cases lies in the unjust enrichment of the grantee through his unconscionable retention of the trust res. . . .

The defendant's argument that the reconveyances in 1960 extinguished his obligation has no support in the finding. Rather, the court's finding of facts concerning his conduct subsequent to the 1960 transfers undermines his position. The court found that the defendant countered the plaintiff's request with delay, pretending concern about the boundaries of his adjacent forty-acre parcel; that he gave, as a reason for refusing to reconvey, assurances that he would never marry and that he would continue to reside with his mother. Of more weight to a court of equity, however, is the fact that the 1960 transfers effected no essential legal or equitable change in the defendant's initial undertaking. The finding reveals that his interest remained that of a joint tenant with right of survivorship upon the sister's surrender of her title to the plaintiff. Not only has the defendant failed to substantiate his contention, but his claim that the plaintiff's case must fail for lack of a concomitant renewal of the oral agreement in 1960 misconceives the nature of a constructive trust. See the discussion in Moses v. Moses, 140 N.J. Eq. 575, 580-581, 53 A.2d 805. Indeed, the defendant's assertion could amount to no more than a unilateral attempt to extinguish the original oral agreement. In short, the absence of an express renewal of the defendant's promise does not impair the soundness of the court's conclusion.

Finally, the defendant makes the claim that the plaintiff has unclean hands. There is nothing in the record to suggest that the 1959 transfer was an attempt to defraud creditors or to secrete assets from government agencies. Granted that the plaintiff offered to let her son keep the property in order to dissuade him from taking a wife, it cannot be said, as a matter of law, that her hands are tainted with an attempt to tamper with marriage, especially in view of the defendant's earlier assurances that he would never get married.

In light of the unattacked finding of the court that the defendant in fact had agreed to reconvey the property to the plaintiff upon request and the conclusion of the court, amply supported by the finding of fact, that a confidential relationship existed between the plaintiff and the defendant, the case comes squarely within the provisions of §44 of the Restatement (Second) of Trusts:

> Where the owner of an interest in land transfers it inter vivos to another in trust for the transferor, but no memorandum properly evidencing the intention to create a trust is signed, as required by the Statute of Frauds, and the transferee refuses to perform the trust, the transferee holds the interest upon a constructive trust for the transferor, if . . . (b) the transferee at the time of the transfer was in a confidential relation to the transferor.

There is no error.

NOTE

In Pappas v. Pappas, 164 Conn. 242, 320 A.2d 809 (1973), Andrew Pappas, age 67, married a 23-year-old woman while on a visit to Greece. On their return, marital difficulties arose, and just prior to the wife's suing for divorce, Andrew conveyed certain real estate to his son, George. George agreed to transfer the property back to Andrew once his marital difficulties were over. In the divorce action, Andrew testified that he made the conveyance for consideration in satisfaction of certain financial and other obligations. Immediately after the divorce action was concluded, with a lump sum alimony award to the wife of $25,000, Andrew demanded a reconveyance from George. George refused. The court held that a constructive trust could not be imposed upon George because Andrew, in misrepresenting the nature of the transfer in the divorce action, had perpetrated a fraud on the court and therefore did not have "clean hands."

b.   Oral Trusts for Disposition at Death

Olliffe v. Wells
Supreme Judicial Court of Massachusetts, 1881
130 Mass. 221

[Ellen Donovan died in 1877 leaving a will devising her residuary estate to the Rev. Eleazer M.P. Wells "to distribute the same in such manner as in his discretion shall appear best calculated to carry out wishes which I have expressed to him or may express to him." Wells was named executor. Ellen's heirs brought suit, claiming the residue should be distributed to them. In his answer, Wells stated that Ellen Donovan, before and after the execution of the will, had orally expressed to him her wish that her estate be used for charitable purposes, and especially for the poor, aged, infirm, and needy under the care of Saint Stephen's Mission of Boston.[32] Wells further stated that he desired and

---

32. Eleazer Mather Porter Wells, born in 1783, entered Brown University at the age of 22 but was dismissed as a result of a practical joke played on a professor by his  roommates. (O tempora! O mores!) Thereafter he was deeply affected by a profound religious experience, including voices in the night saying, "Go and do my work." At age 40, Wells entered the ministry, becoming an Episcopal priest. In 1843, at age 60, Wells opened St. Stephen's Mission. From here he provided food, nursing care, clothing, and shelter for the poor of the West End of Boston. On one occasion he was able to keep the fire at the mission going by burning 100 old volumes of Voltaire's writings, which had been given to the mission. These proved good kindling, and Wells is quoted as having said, "Well, even the worst of men are put to good uses for the benefit of others." The great Boston **The Rev. Wells** fire of 1872 destroyed St. Stephen's Mission, and for the remaining years of his life Wells worked to revitalize the mission to no avail.

Wells died in 1878 at age 95. A resolution adopted by the clergy of the Episcopal Diocese of Massachusetts paid tribute to Wells as,

A clergyman of stainless reputation and incorruptible integrity; an enthusiast in his sacred calling, especially in his self-selected mission to the destitute and afflicted, the outcast and the erring. . . . The work of Dr. Wells, continued so long a period at St. Stephen's Mission in Boston, and as the trusted almoner of very many of his

intended to distribute the residue for these purposes. The parties agreed that the facts alleged in the answer should be taken as true.]

GRAY, C.J.   Upon the face of this will the residuary bequest to the defendant gives him no beneficial interest. It expressly requires him to distribute all the property bequeathed to him, giving him no discretion upon the question whether he shall or shall not distribute it, or shall or shall not carry out the intentions of the testatrix, but allowing him a discretionary authority as to the manner only in which the property shall be distributed pursuant to her intentions. The will declares a trust too indefinite to be carried out, and the next of kin of the testatrix must take by way of resulting trust, unless the facts agreed show such a trust for the benefit of others as the court can execute. Nichols v. Allen, 130 Mass. 211. . . .

It has been held in England and in other States, although the question has never arisen in this Commonwealth, that, if a person procures an absolute devise or bequest to himself by orally promising the testator that he will convey the property to or hold it for the benefit of third persons, and afterwards refused to perform his promise, a trust arises out of the confidence reposed in him by the testator and of his own fraud, which a court of equity, upon clear and satisfactory proof of the facts, will enforce against him at the suit of such third persons. . . .

Upon like grounds, it has been held in England that, if a testator devises or bequeaths property to his executors upon trusts not defined in the will, but which, as he states in the will, he has communicated to them before its execution, such trusts, if for lawful purposes, may be proved by the admission of the executors, or by oral evidence, and enforced against them. . . . And in two or three comparatively recent cases it has been held that such trusts may be enforced against the heirs or next of kin of the testator, as well as against the devisee. . . . But these cases appear to us to have overlooked or disregarded a fundamental distinction.

Where a trust not declared in the will is established by a court of chancery against the devisee, it is by reason of the obligation resting upon the conscience of the devisee, and not as a valid testamentary disposition by the deceased. Cullen v. Attorney General, L.R. 1 H.L. 190. Where the bequest is outright upon its face, the setting up of a trust, while it diminishes the right of the devisee, does not impair any

---

fellow citizens, and withal his pure and consistent life as a man of God and of unremitting prayer, furnish a splendid commendation of religion.

Information supplied by Mark J. Duffy, Archivist of the Episcopal Diocese of Massachusetts, in a letter to Jesse Dukeminier dated April 13, 1982.

To what extent, if any, does the court's decision in Olliffe v. Wells turn on the facts that St. Stephen's Mission had been destroyed and the "trusted almoner" had died before the case reached the Supreme Judicial Court?

right of the heirs or next of kin, in any aspect of the case; for if the trust were not set up, the whole property would go to the devisee by force of the devise; if the trust set up is a lawful one, it enures to the benefit of the cestuis que trust; and if the trust setup is unlawful, the heirs or next of kin take by way of resulting trust.

Where the bequest is declared upon its face to be upon such trusts as the testator has otherwise signified to the devisee, it is equally clear that the devisee takes no beneficial interest; and, as between him and the beneficiaries intended, there is as much ground for establishing the trust as if the bequest to him were absolute on its face. But as between the devisee and the heirs or next of kin, the case stands differently. They are not excluded by the will itself. The will upon its face showing that the devisee takes the legal title only and not the beneficial interest, and the trust not being sufficiently defined by the will to take effect, the equitable interest goes, by way of resulting trust, to the heirs or next of kin, as property of the deceased, not disposed of by his will. Sears v. Hardy, 120 Mass. 524, 541, 542. They cannot be deprived of that equitable interest, which accrues to them directly from the deceased, by any conduct of the devisee; nor by any intention of the deceased, unless signified in those forms which the law makes essential to every testamentary disposition. A trust not sufficiently declared on the face of the will cannot therefore be set up by extrinsic evidence to defeat the rights of the heirs at law or next of kin. . . .

Decree for the plaintiffs.

NOTES AND PROBLEMS

1. Olliffe v. Wells is the origin of the distinction between a secret and semisecret trust followed in a considerable number of states in this country, although it is rejected in England and several states. The distinction is this: If Ellen Donovan had left a legacy to the Rev. Wells absolute on its face, without anything in the will indicating an intent to create a trust, a promise by the Rev. Wells to Ellen Donovan to use the legacy for St. Stephen's Mission would be enforceable by a constructive trust. This is called a secret trust because the will indicates no trust. Courts admit evidence of the promise for the purpose of preventing the Rev. Wells from unjustly enriching himself by pocketing the legacy. Having admitted proof of the promise, they proceed to enforce the promise by imposing a constructive trust on Wells for the benefit of St. Stephen's Mission.

On the other hand, if the will indicates that the Rev. Wells is to hold the legacy in trust but does not identify the beneficiary (as was true in Olliffe v. Wells), a semisecret trust is created. Since the will shows on its face an intent not to benefit Wells personally, it is not necessary to admit evidence of Wells' promise in order to prevent his unjust enrichment. Such evidence is excluded and the legacy to Wells fails.

Is the reasoning underlying this distinction sound? See 1A A. Scott, Trusts §§55.1, 55.8 (W. Fratcher 4th ed. 1987), who suggests that in both the secret and semisecret trust situations, a constructive trust should be imposed for testator's heirs, not for the intended beneficiaries. Scott argues that the policy of the Statute of Wills should prevent enforcing the trust for the intended beneficiaries, but to prevent unjust enrichment the property should be restored to testator's heirs. 1 Restatement (Second) of Trusts §§55, Comment h (1959), for which Scott was the reporter, does not adopt Scott's views but says instead that a constructive trust should be imposed in favor of the intended beneficiary in the semisecret, as well as secret, trust situation.

2.   Howard Brown's brother, Bruce, is your client (see supra page 64). Bruce has a long-time lover, another bank employee named Diane Robinson, to whom Bruce wishes to leave $10,000 at his death, without advertising the matter. Would you recommend that Bruce leave $10,000 in his will to his brother Howard and have a secret promise by Howard that he will give Diane the $10,000? Would this accomplish his objective of a secret gift? Would you recommend that Howard make the promise in a signed writing, which Bruce is to keep in his safe-deposit box? See Pfahl v. Pfahl, 10 Ohio Misc. 234, 225 N.E.2d 305 (1967). Would you recommend that Bruce leave the money to you and you promise to give it to Diane?

Refer back to Wendy Brown's Aunt Fanny d'Alessandro, an elderly lady with a house full of things and no descendants (Problem 4, supra page 255). Would a secret trust — an absolute devise by Aunt Fanny to her sister Polly, with a promise by Polly to distribute in accordance with a memorandum to be left — be enforceable? See 1A A. Scott, supra, §55.8 at 88. Suppose that Polly did not promise Aunt Fanny to hold the property in trust but that Aunt Fanny devised all her household contents to Polly and attached to the will by a paper clip a memorandum addressed to Polly telling her how to dispose of the household contents. What result?

SECTION C. TESTAMENTARY TRUSTS

A testamentary trust is a trust created by a will. It is sometimes called a court trust because it comes into being by an order of the probate court that supervises the administration of the estate, and in many states this court continues to supervise the administration of the testamentary trust after the estate is closed. An inter vivos trust, on the other hand, created by the settlor during lifetime, comes into being without any court order. It is not subject to any court supervision unless the beneficiary or the trustee comes into court to settle some trust matter.

Inasmuch as a testamentary trust is created by a court order, the trustee may have the duty to account to the court. Judicial approval of a trustee's accounts is often a time-consuming and expensive procedure. It may require the appointment of guardians ad litem to represent unborn and unascertained beneficiaries. To avoid this, the will may provide that certain beneficiaries (perhaps all adult, competent beneficiaries) have the power to approve the trustee's accounts without a court proceeding. Although such a provision would be effective in an inter vivos trust, whether it is effective in testamentary trusts varies from jurisdiction to jurisdiction. In some states, the probate court, having brought the testamentary trust into being, may refuse to be deprived of its authority to oversee the trustee's work. See W. McGovern, S. Kurtz & J. Rein, Wills, Trusts and Estates §14.10 at 702 (1988).

Uniform Probate Code §7-101 (1983) requires trustees to register trusts in the court in the principal place of administration. Registration consists of a statement identifying the settlor, trustee, and beneficiaries of the trust. The concept of trust registration is one of the UPC's most controversial provisions, and a majority of states adopting the UPC omit the registration provisions entirely. After a trust is registered, the Uniform Probate Code does not contemplate continuing judicial supervision of any trust. If the trustee or beneficiaries have problems that need judicial resolution, they may bring suit. Several states have moved away from continuing judicial supervision of testamentary trusts and provide for no court supervision unless the testator provides otherwise. See UPC §7-201(b).

Uniform Probate Code §7-307 also provides for informal accounting by the trustee to the trust beneficiaries. If the beneficiaries do not assert a claim within six months after receipt of the final account, they are barred.

To help you visualize what a testamentary trust instrument looks like, we reproduce below the will of Howard Brown that creates, if his wife does not survive and any child is under the age of 22, a testamentary trust for his children.

Will of Howard Brown

ARTICLE 1

I, Howard Brown, hereby make my will, and I revoke all other wills and codicils that I have previously made.

ARTICLE 2

I give all my jewelry, clothing, household furniture and furnishings, personal automobiles, books, and other tangible articles of a household or personal nature, or my interest in any such property, not otherwise specifically disposed of by this or in any other manner, together with any insurance on the property, to my wife, Wendy Brown, if she survives me; but if my wife does not survive me, then to my children who survive me, in substantially equal shares as they may select on the basis of valuation. These gifts shall be free of all death taxes.

The executor shall represent any child under age 18 in matters relating to any distribution of tangible personal property, including selecting the assets that shall constitute that child's share. In the executor's absolute discretion, the executor may (1) sell all or part of such child's share which the executor deems unsuitable for the child's use, (2) distribute the proceeds to the Children's Trust or share of such trust for the child's benefit, or (3) deliver the unsold property without bond to the minor if sufficiently mature or to any suitable person with whom the child resides or who has control or care of the child.

ARTICLE 3

I give the residue of my estate to my wife, Wendy Brown, if she survives me. If my wife does not survive me and all my children are 22 years of age or older at my death, I give the residue of my estate to my children and to the descendants of any then-deceased child by right of representation. If my wife does not survive me and any of my children are under the age of 22 at my death, I give the residue of my estate to the trustee of the Children's Trust set forth in Article 4.

ARTICLE 4

The trustee of the Children's Trust shall hold, administer, and distribute all property allocated to the Children's Trust for the benefit of my children as follows:

The trustee shall pay to or for any child as much of the income as is necessary for the child's health, education, support, or maintenance to maintain the child's accustomed manner of living. The trustee shall add to principal any net income not so distributed.

If the trustee considers the income insufficient, the trustee shall pay to or for a child as much of the principal as the trustee considers reasonably necessary for the child's health, education, support, maintenance, comfort, welfare, or happiness to maintain, at a minimum, the child's accustomed manner of living.

In making distributions, the trustee (1) may consider any other income or resources of the child, including the child's ability to obtain gainful employment and the obligation of others to support the child, known to the trustee and reasonably available for the purposes stated here, (2) may pay more to or apply more for some children than others and may make payments to or applications of benefits for one or more children to the exclusion of others, (3) may consider the value of the trust assets, the relative needs, both present and future, of each child, and the tax consequences to the trust and to any child, and (4) shall charge distributions of income and principal against the entire trust estate and not against the share of the child to whom or for whom the distribution was made.

The trustee, in the trustee's reasonable discretion, may from time to time make preliminary distributions of principal to any of my children who have attained the age of 22, if the trustee finds valid and productive reasons for making the distribution, such as the purchase of a residence or establishment of a business, and if the remaining principal and income will be adequate for the health, support, maintenance, and education of my other children. The trustee shall deduct such preliminary distributions without interest from the share ultimately distributed to such child or to such child's descendants. In the aggregate, the value of any preliminary distributions shall not exceed 50 percent of that child's putative share. The term putative share shall be that portion of the entire trust estate that would be distributable to a particular child, after considering all previous loans and advances, if the entire trust were divided into separate trusts on the date that the distribution to be measured against the putative share is made.

When every child of mine has reached the age of 22 or died before reaching that age, the trustee shall divide the trust into as many equal shares as there are children of mine then living and children of mine then deceased with descendants then living.

On the division of the Children's Trust into shares, the trustee shall distribute each living child's share outright to the child and each deceased child's share to the deceased child's then-living descendants by right of representation.

ARTICLE 5

I nominate as trustee of the Children's Trust Lucy Preston Lipman. If Lucy Preston Lipman fails to qualify or ceases to act, I nominate as successor trustee Bruce M. Brown.

The trustee may employ custodians, attorneys, accountants, investment advisers, corporate fiduciaries, or any other agents or advisers to assist the trustee in the administration of this trust, and the trustee may rely on the advice given by these agents. The trustee shall pay reasonable compensation for all services performed by these agents from the trust estate out of either income or principal as the trustee in the trustee's reasonable discretion shall determine. These payments shall not decrease the compensation of the trustee.

No trustee shall be liable to any person interested in this trust for any act or default unless it results from the trustee's bad faith, willful misconduct, or gross negligence.

The trustee shall have the power to continue to hold any property or to abandon any property that the trustee receives or acquires.

The trustee shall have the power to retain, purchase, or otherwise acquire unproductive property.

The trustee shall have the power to manage, control, grant options on, sell (for cash or on deferred payments with or without security), convey, exchange, partition, divide, improve, and repair trust property.

The trustee shall have the power to lease trust property for terms within or beyond the terms of the trust and for any purpose, including exploration for and removal of gas, oil, and other minerals, and to enter into oil leases, pooling, and utilization agreements.

The trustee shall have the power to invest and reinvest the trust estate in every kind of property, real, personal, or mixed, and every kind of investment, specifically including, but not by way of limitation, corporate obligations of every kind, preferred or common stocks, shares in investment trusts, investment companies, mutual funds, money market funds, index funds, and mortgage participations, which persons of prudence, discretion, and intelligence acquire for their own account, and any common trust fund administered by the trustee.

The trustee shall have all the rights, powers, and privileges of an owner of the securities held in trust, including, but not by way of limitation, the power to vote, give proxies, and pay assessments; the power to participate in voting trusts and pooling agreements (whether or not extending beyond the terms of the trust); the power to enter into shareholders' agreements; the power to consent to foreclosure, reorganizations, consolidations, merger liquidations, sales, and leases, and, incident to any such action, to deposit securities with and transfer title to any protective or other committee on such terms as the trustee may deem advisable; and the power to exercise or sell stock subscription or conversion rights.

The trustee shall have the power to hold securities or other property in the trustee's name as trustee under this trust, in the trustee's own name, in the name of a nominee, or in unregistered form so that ownership will pass by delivery.

The trustee shall have the power to carry, at the expense of the trust, insurance of such kinds and in such amounts as the trustee deems advisable to protect the trust estate against any damage or loss and to protect the trustee against liability with respect to third parties.

The trustee shall have the power to loan to any person, including a trust beneficiary or the estate of a trust beneficiary, at interest rates and with or without security as the trustee deems advisable.

Upon termination of the trust, the approval of the accounts of the trustee in an instrument signed by all the adult beneficiaries and guardians of any minor beneficiaries shall be a complete discharge and release of the trustee with respect to the administration of the trust property and shall be binding on all persons.

ARTICLE 6

If my wife, Wendy Brown, does not survive me and if at my death any of my children are minors, I nominate as guardian of the persons and the property of my minor children Lucy Preston Lipman. If for any reason she fails to qualify or ceases to serve in that capacity, I nominate Bruce M. Brown as guardian of the persons and the property of my minor children.

ARTICLE 7

The terms child and children as used in this will refer to my children David Adam, Susan Jane, and Barbara Carolyn and also to any child or children hereafter born to me.

ARTICLE 8

I nominate as executor of this will my wife, Wendy Brown. If for any reason she fails to qualify or ceases to act I nominate Lucy Preston Lipman to serve as executor.

My executor shall have the same powers granted the trustee under Article 5 to be exercised without court order, as well as any other powers that may be granted by law.

I direct that no bond or other security shall be required of any person, including nonresidents named in this will, acting as executor, trustee, or guardian.

———

I have signed this will, which is typewritten on _____ sheets of paper, on this _____ day of _____, 19_____, and, for the purposes of identification, I have also written my name on the margin of all pages before this signature page.

_____

Howard Brown

On the _____ day of _____, 19____, Howard Brown declared to us, the undersigned, that the foregoing instrument was his last will, and he requested us to act as witnesses to it and to his signature thereon. He then signed the will in our presence, we being present at the same time. We now, at his request, in his presence, and in the presence of each other, hereunto subscribe our names as witnesses, and each of us declares that in his or her opinion this testator is of sound and disposing mind and memory.

_____   _____

Name   *Address*

_____   _____

Name   *Address*

_____

Observe that the trust established for the Brown children is a single trust to be terminated when there is no child under the age of 22. Under this trust does the eldest child have an advantage over the younger children?

An alternative to a single trust is a separate trust for each child. This arrangement permits each child to receive the principal of his or her trust upon reaching a designated age, without waiting for the youngest child to do so.

QUESTION

If you, as Howard Brown's lawyer, draft the testamentary trust, is there anything unethical in naming yourself as trustee or as successor trustee? See de Furia, A Matter of Ethics Ignored: The Attorney-Draftsman as Testamentary Fiduciary, 36 Kan. L. Rev. 275 (1988).

SECTION D. REVOCABLE TRUSTS

1. Introduction

Under the typical revocable inter vivos trust involving a *deed of trust*, the settlor transfers assets to another person as trustee pursuant to a writing in which the settlor retains the power to revoke, alter, or amend the trust and the right to trust income during lifetime. On the settlor's death the assets are distributed to or held in further trust for other beneficiaries. While several early cases held these trusts invalid unless executed with testamentary formalities, all jurisdictions now recognize the validity of a trust in which the settlor reserves the power to revoke during life. The settlor may also reserve an income interest and a testamentary power of appointment.

The second context in which the question of validity arises is where there is a *revocable declaration of trust*, under which the settlor declares himself trustee for the benefit of himself during lifetime, with the remainder to pass to others at his death. During lifetime the "transferor" wears all three hats: Settlor, trustee, and beneficiary. Since there is little discernible change in the owner's relation to the property during lifetime, should the courts give effect to this arrangement to the extent that it causes assets to pass to others at the owner's death?

Farkas v. Williams
Supreme Court of Illinois, 1955
5 Ill. 2d 417, 125 N.E.2d 600

HERSHEY, J. . . . The plaintiffs asked the court to declare their legal rights, as co-administrators, in four stock certificates issued by Investors Mutual Inc. in the name of "Albert B. Farkas, as trustee for Richard J. Williams" and which were issued pursuant to written declarations of trust. The decree of the circuit court found that said declarations were testamentary in character, and not having been executed with the formalities of a will, were invalid, and directed that the stock be awarded to the plaintiffs as an asset of the estate of said Albert B. Farkas. Upon appeal to the Appellate Court, the decree was affirmed. See 3 Ill. App.

2d 248, 121 N.E.2d 344. We allowed defendants' petition for leave to appeal.

Albert B. Farkas died intestate at the age of sixty-seven years, a resident of Chicago, leaving as his only heirs-at-law brothers, sisters, a nephew and a niece. Although retired at the time of his death, he had for many years practiced veterinary medicine and operated a veterinarian establishment in Chicago. During a considerable portion of that time, he employed the defendant Williams, who was not related to him.

On four occasions (December 8, 1948; February 7, 1949; February 14, 1950; and March 1, 1950) Farkas purchased stock of Investors Mutual, Inc. At the time of each purchase he executed a written application to Investors Mutual, Inc., instructing them to issue the stock in his name "as trustee for Richard J. Williams." Investors Mutual, Inc., by its agent, accepted each of these applications in writing by signature on the face of the application. Coincident with the execution of these applications, Farkas signed separate declarations of trust, all of which were identical except as to dates. The terms of said trust instruments are as follows:

> Declaration of Trust — Revocable. I, the undersigned, having purchased or declared my intention to purchase certain shares of capital stock of Investors Mutual, Inc. (the Company), and having directed that the certificate for said stock be issued in my name as trustee for Richard J. Williams as beneficiary, whose address is 1704 W. North Ave. Chicago, Ill., under this Declaration of Trust Do Hereby Declare that the terms and conditions upon which I shall hold said stock in trust and any additional stock resulting from reinvestments of cash dividends upon such original or additional shares are as follows:
>
> (1) During my lifetime all cash dividends are to be paid to me individually for my own personal account and use; provided, however, that any such additional stock purchased under an authorized reinvestment of cash dividends shall become a part of and subject to this trust.
>
> (2) Upon my death the title to any stock subject hereto and the right to any subsequent payments or distributions shall be vested absolutely in the beneficiary.
>
> (3) During my lifetime I reserve the right, as trustee, to vote, sell, redeem, exchange or otherwise deal in or with the stock subject hereto, but upon any sale or redemption of said stock or any part thereof, the trust hereby declared shall terminate as to the stock sold or redeemed, and I shall be entitled to retain the proceeds of sale or redemption for my own personal account and use.
>
> (4) I reserve the right at any time to change the beneficiary or revoke this trust, but it is understood that no change of beneficiary and no revocation of this trust except by death of the beneficiary, shall be effective as to the Company for any purpose unless and until written notice thereof in such form as the Company shall prescribe is delivered to the Company

at Minneapolis, Minnesota. The decease of the beneficiary before my death shall operate as a revocation of this trust.

(5) In the event this trust shall be revoked or otherwise terminated, said stock and all rights and privileges thereunder shall belong to and be exercised by me in my individual capacity.

. . . The applications and declarations of trust were delivered to Investors Mutual, Inc., and held by the company until Farkas' death. The stock certificates were issued in the name of Farkas as "trustee for Richard J. Williams" and were discovered in a safety-deposit box of Farkas after his death, along with other securities, some of which were in the name of Williams alone. . . .

It is conceded that the instruments were not executed in such a way as to satisfy the requirements of the statute on wills; hence, our inquiry is limited to whether said trust instruments created valid inter vivos trusts effective to give the purported beneficiary, Williams, title to the stock in question after the death of the settlor-trustee, Farkas. To make this determination we must consider: (1) whether upon execution of the so-called trust instruments defendant Williams acquired an interest in the subject matter of the trusts, the stock of defendant Investors Mutual, Inc., (2) whether Farkas, as settlor-trustee, retained such control over the subject matter of the trusts as to render said trust instruments attempted testamentary dispositions.

First, upon execution of these trust instruments did defendant Williams presently acquire an interest in the subject matter of the intended trusts?

If no interest passed to Williams before the death of Farkas, the intended trusts are testamentary and hence invalid for failure to comply with the statute on wills. Oswald v. Caldwell, 225 Ill. 224, 80 N.E. 131; Troup v. Hunter, 300 Ill. 110, 133 N.E. 56; Restatement of the Law of Trusts, section 56. But considering the terms of these instruments we believe Farkas did intend to presently give Williams an interest in the property referred to. For it may be said, at the very least, that upon his executing one of these instruments, he showed an intention to presently part with some of the incidents of ownership in the stock. Immediately after the execution of each of these instruments, he could not deal with the stock therein referred to the same as if he owned the property absolutely, but only in accordance with the terms of the instrument. He purported to set himself up as trustee of the stock for the benefit of Williams, and the stock was registered in his name as trustee for Williams. Thus assuming to act as trustee, he is held to have intended to take on those obligations which are expressly set out in the instrument, as well as those fiduciary obligations implied by law. In addition, he manifested an intention to bind himself to having this property pass upon his death to Williams, unless he changed the beneficiary or revoked the trust, and then such change of beneficiary or revocation was not to be effective as to Investors Mutual, Inc., unless and until written notice thereof in such form as the company prescribed was delivered to them at Minneapolis, Minnesota. An absolute owner can dispose of his property, either in his lifetime or by will, in any way he sees fit without notifying or securing approval from anyone and without being held to the duties of a fiduciary in so doing.

It seems to follow that what incidents of ownership Farkas intended to relinquish, in a sense he intended Williams to acquire.... It is difficult to name this interest of Williams, nor is there any reason for so doing so long as it passed to him immediately upon the creation of the trust.[33] As stated in 4 Powell, The Law of Real Property, at page 87: "Interests of beneficiaries of private express trusts run the gamut from valuable substantialities to evanescent hopes. Such a beneficiary may have any one of an almost infinite variety of the possible aggregates of rights, privileges, powers and immunities."

An additional problem is presented here, however, for it is to be noted that the trust instruments provide: "The decease of the beneficiary before my death shall operate as a revocation of this trust." The plaintiffs argue that the presence of this provision removes the only possible distinction which might have been drawn between these instruments and a will. Being thus conditioned on his surviving, it is argued that the "interest" of Williams until the death of Farkas was a mere expectancy. Conversely, they assert, the interest of Farkas in the securities until his death was precisely the same as that of a testator who bequeaths securities by his will, since he had all the rights accruing to an absolute owner.

Admittedly, had this provision been absent the interest of Williams would have been greater, since he would then have had an inheritable interest in the lifetime of Farkas. But to say his interest would have been greater is not to say that he here did not have a beneficial interest, properly so-called, during the lifetime of Farkas. The provision purports to set up but another "contingency" which would serve to terminate the trust. The disposition is not testamentary and the intended trust is valid, even though the interest of the beneficiary is contingent upon the existence of a certain state of facts at the time of the settlor's death. (Restatement of the Law of Trusts, section 56, comment f.) In an

---

33. The idea of an interest smaller than any interest you can name, but nonetheless an interest, brings to mind the mathematical concept of the infinitesimal, developed by Isaac Newton and Gottfried Wilhelm von Leibnitz. Although scorned by Bishop Berkeley as "ghosts of departed quantities," infinitesimals proved very useful in differential calculus.

Would it be a good idea for the Illinois legislature to settle the matter by passing a statute providing that, if a settlor retained the powers Farkas retained, the beneficiary would be deemed to receive an infinitesimal interest? Should the legislature give the interest a name, such as a farkas, since the court finds naming so difficult? — Eds.

example contained in the previous reference, the authors of the Restatement have referred to the interest of a beneficiary under a trust who must survive the settlor (and where the settlor receives the income for life) as a contingent equitable interest in remainder. . . .

Second, did Farkas retain such control over the subject matter of the trust as to render said trust instruments attempted testamentary dispositions?

In each of these trust instruments, Farkas reserved to himself as settlor the following powers: (1) the right to receive during his lifetime all cash dividends; (2) the right at any time to change the beneficiary or revoke the trust; and (3) upon sale or redemption of any portion of the trust property, the right to retain the proceeds therefrom for his own use.

Additionally, Farkas reserved the right to act as sole trustee, and in such capacity, he was accorded the right to vote, sell, redeem, exchange or otherwise deal in the stock which formed the subject matter of the trust.

We shall consider first those enumerated powers which Farkas reserved to himself as settlor.

It is well established that the retention by the settlor of the power to revoke, even when coupled with the reservation of a life interest in the trust property, does not render the trust inoperative for want of execution as a will. . . .

A more difficult problem is posed, however, by the fact that Farkas is also trustee, and as such, is empowered to vote, sell, redeem, exchange and otherwise deal in and with the subject matter of the trusts. . . .

In the instant case the plaintiffs contend that Farkas, as settlor-trustee, retained complete control and dominion over the securities for his own benefit during his lifetime. It is argued that he had the power to deal with the property as he liked so long as he lived and owed no enforceable duties of any kind to Williams as beneficiary. . . .

That the retention of the power by Farkas as trustee to sell or redeem the stock and keep the proceeds for his own use should not render these trust instruments testamentary in character becomes more evident upon analyzing the real import and significance of the powers to revoke and to amend the trust, the reservation of which the courts uniformly hold does not invalidate an inter vivos trust.

It is obvious that a settlor with the power to revoke and to amend the trust at any time is, for all practical purpose, in a position to exert considerable control over the trustee regarding the administration of the trust. For anything believed to be inimicable to his best interest can be thwarted or prevented by simply revoking the trust or amending it in such a way as to conform to his wishes. Indeed, it seems that many of those powers which from time to time have been viewed as "additional powers" are already, in a sense, virtually contained within the overriding power of revocation or the power to amend the trust. Consider, for example, the following: (1) the power to consume the principal; (2) the power to sell or mortgage the trust property and appropriate the proceeds; (3) the power to appoint or remove trustees; (4) the power to supervise and direct investments; and (5) the power to otherwise direct and supervise the trustee in the administration of the trust. Actually, any of the above powers could readily be assumed by a settlor with the reserved power of revocation through the simple expedient of revoking the trust, and then, as absolute owner of the subject matter, doing with the property as he chooses. Even though no actual termination of the trust is effectuated, however, it could hardly be questioned but that the mere existence of this power in the settlor is sufficient to enable his influence to be felt in a practical way in the administration of the trust. . . .

In the case at bar, the power in Farkas to vote, sell, redeem, exchange or otherwise deal in the stock was reserved to him as trustee, and it was only upon sale or redemption that he was entitled to keep the proceeds for his own use. Thus, the control reserved is not as great as in those cases where said power is reserved to the owner as settlor. For as trustee he must so conduct himself in accordance with standards applicable to trustees generally. It is not a valid objection to this to say that Williams would never question Farkas' conduct, inasmuch as Farkas could then revoke the trust and destroy what interest Williams has. Such a possibility exists in any case where the settlor has the power of revocation. Still, Williams has rights the same as any beneficiary, although it may not be feasible for him to exercise them. Moreover, it is entirely possible that he might in certain situations have a right to hold Farkas' estate liable for breaches of trust committed by Farkas during his lifetime. In this regard, consider what would happen if, without having revoked the trust, Farkas as trustee had given the stock away without receiving any consideration therefor, had pledged the stock improperly for his own personal debt and allowed it to be lost by foreclosure or had exchanged the stock for another security or other worthless property in such manner as to constitute gross impropriety and gross negligence. In such instances, it would seem in accordance with the terms of these instruments that Williams would have had an enforceable claim against Farkas' estate for whatever damage had been suffered. Contrast this with the rights of a legatee or devisee under a will. The testator could waste the property or do anything with it he wished during his lifetime without incurring any liability to those designated by the will to inherit the property. . . .

Another factor often considered in determining whether an inter vivos trust is an attempted testamentary disposition is the formality of the transaction. Restatement of the Law of Trusts, section 57, comment g; Stouse v. First National Bank, Ky., 245 S.W.2d 914, 32 A.L.R.2d

1261; United Building and Loan Association v. Garrett, D.C. 64 F. Supp. 460; In re Sheasley's Trust, 366 Pa. 316, 77 A.2d 448. Historically, the purpose behind the enactment of the statute on wills was the prevention of fraud. The requirement as to witnesses was deemed necessary because a will is ordinarily an expression of the secret wish of the testator, signed out of the presence of all concerned. The possibility of forgery and fraud are ever present in such situations. Here, Farkas executed four separate applications for stock of Investors Mutual, Inc., in which he directed that the stock be issued in his name as trustee for Williams, and he executed four separate declarations of trust in which he declared he was holding said stock in trust for Williams. The stock certificates in question were issued in his name as trustee for Williams. He thus manifested his intention in a solemn and formal manner.

For the reasons stated, we conclude that these trust declarations executed by Farkas constituted valid inter vivos trusts and were not attempted testamentary dispositions. It must be conceded that they have, in the words of Mr. Justice Holmes in Bromley v. Mitchell, 155 Mass. 509, 30 N.E. 83, a "testamentary look." Moreover, it must be admitted that the line should be drawn somewhere, but after a study of this case we do not believe that point has been reached. . . .

Reversed and remanded, with directions.[34]

NOTES AND PROBLEMS

1. With the reasoning of the court in Farkas v. Williams, compare the reasoning of the Red Queen:

> "Try another subtraction sum. Take a bone from a dog; what remains?"
>
> Alice considered. "The bone wouldn't remain of course, if I took it — and the dog wouldn't remain; it would come to bite me — and I'm sure I shouldn't remain!"
>
> "Then you think nothing would remain?" said the Red Queen.
>
> "I think that's the answer."
>
> "Wrong, as usual," said the Red Queen. "The dog's temper would remain."
>
> "But I don't see how — "
>
> "Why, look here!" the Red Queen cried. "The dog would lose its temper, wouldn't it?"
>
> "Perhaps it would," Alice replied cautiously.
>
> "Then if the dog went away, its temper would remain!" the Queen exclaimed triumphantly.
>
> [L. Carroll, Through the Looking-Glass, ch. 9]

---

34. Noted in 5 De Paul L. Rev. 153; 23 U. Chi. L. Rev. 289, 303. — Eds.

What metaphor used by the court is similar to the metaphor of the Red Queen?

2.   Suppose that Farkas does not direct the company to issue new shares of stock in his name as trustee but executes a revocable declaration of trust of shares already owned by Farkas and staples to the declaration the share certificates previously issued in Farkas' sole name. Farkas gives no notice of the trust to anyone. At Farkas' death the declaration of trust with share certificates stapled to it are found in Farkas' safe-deposit box. What result? See In re Estate of Sanderson, 510 P.2d 452 (Colo. App. 1973).

Should Farkas have named a successor trustee — perhaps Williams — in the trust instrument?

3.   In Estate of Brenner, 547 P.2d 938 (Colo. App. 1976), R. Forrest Brenner executed a revocable declaration of trust (captioned "The R. Forrest Brenner Trust") of certain real property for the benefit of himself for life, remainder to his children by a prior marriage and a niece. On the date the trust instrument was executed, Brenner did not own the real property in question, but five days later this property was conveyed to "R. Forrest Brenner, Trustee for R. Forrest Brenner." On Brenner's death, the validity of the trust was challenged. The court held the trust valid, stating:

> . . . [W]e hold that the conveyance of the real property to Brenner as trustee five days after he executed the trust instrument effectively validated the trust. Where, as here, an individual manifests an intention to create a trust in property to be acquired in the future, and thereafter confirms this intent by taking the steps necessary to transfer the property to the trust, the property so transferred becomes subject to the terms of the trust. For reasons stated hereafter, we do not believe that the foregoing rule is inapplicable merely because Brenner was settlor, trustee, and lifetime beneficiary of the trust.
>
> Appellant contends, in effect, that the evidence failed to establish Brenner's intent to establish a trust. In support of this contention, appellant relies upon evidence, inter alia, that Brenner failed to prepare and file the requisite Colorado and federal tax forms relative to a trust, that he failed to keep separate books, records, and bank accounts relative to the trust property, that he reported income and expenses from trust property on an individual income tax form, and that he did not advise either [his wife] Evelyn or his accountant of the existence of the trust. However, other evidence established that Brenner took title to the property described in the "exhibit" as trustee, that he acquired additional real estate as trustee, and that he executed a contract as trustee relating to both properties. The evidence and inferences therefrom being in conflict, the trial court's determination that Brenner intended to create a trust and thereby provide for his children and niece, as natural objects of his bounty, may not be disturbed on review.
>
> Appellant next contends that the declaration of trust was invalid by

reason of the extensive control retained over the trust property by Brenner through his appointment as trustee, his reservation of all income during his lifetime, the right to revoke, alter, or amend the trust, and the sole power to invest, reinvest, manage, and control the trust property. We disagree. See Farkas v. Williams, 5 Ill. 2d 417, 125 N.E.2d 600.

4. The revocable declaration of trust is the key feature of Norman F. Dacey's book, How to Avoid Probate! (2d ed. 1983). Upon publication in 1965 the book became a runaway best-seller. Dacey, who is not a lawyer, opens his book with a slashing attack on lawyers who profit from the probate system. He charges:

> The probate system, conceived generations ago as a device for protecting heirs, has now become their greatest enemy. Almost universally corrupt, it is essentially a form of private taxation levied by the legal profession upon the rest of the population. All across the land, both large and small estates are being plundered by lawyers specializing in "probate practice." [Id. at 15.]

After denouncing the "extortionate legal fees" and delays of probate, Dacey offers a way to avoid probate: Declare yourself trustee of your property by using a revocable declaration of trust, with the trust property to pass to named beneficiaries upon your death. In other words, do what Albert Farkas did in Farkas v. Williams. Dacey's book contains all kinds of do-it-yourself trust and will forms designed for various kinds of assets and different family situations.

Neither the tone nor the content of Dacey's book was favorably received by the legal profession. After publication of the first edition, the New York County Lawyers' Association sought an injunction to ban sale of the book on the ground that Dacey (a nonlawyer) was giving legal advice. Successful in the lower courts, the Association lost in the New York Court of Appeals. New York County Lawyers' Association v. Dacey, 21 N.Y.2d 694, 234 N.E.2d 459, 287 N.Y.S.2d 422 (1967). How to Avoid Probate! was widely reviewed in legal periodicals. Almost all the reviews were negative. For a review by a lawyer of Dacey's 1980 revision, detailing specific defects in Dacey's forms, criticizing Dacey's failure to warn of possible tax problems, and concluding that "Dacey's trusts are bad. Very bad," see Zartman, How to Avoid Dacey — 1980, 69 Ill. B.J. 16 (1980).

Since Dacey first published his book there has been a groundswell of public demand for a simpler and less costly probate system. Reform has occurred in many states, often in the form of adoption of the Uniform Probate Code. It is fair to suggest that How to Avoid Probate!, and its astonishing reception by the public, served as a catalyst for probate reform. However, the reforms to date have not deprived the revocable trust of its advantage in bypassing probate. Probate remains costly. Only if states were to adopt universal succession, dispensing with administration entirely (see supra page 48), would the public not seek to bypass probate.

5. Refer back to the problem of Bruce Brown, who wants to give a legacy to Diane Robinson without advertising the matter (Problem 2, supra page 488). Would a revocable trust be useful in solving Brown's problem?

Refer back to Aunt Fanny d'Alessandro (Problem 2, supra page 488). Would a revocable trust be useful in handling Aunt Fanny's problem of disposing of her household goods? Remember: She wants to be able to change her mind about who gets what as friends and relatives indicate interest in particular items in her house.

6. In most states a trust, like any transfer, is irrevocable unless a power of revocation is expressly reserved or implied from language contained in the instrument. In a few states statutes reverse this rule and provide that a trust is revocable unless it is expressly made irrevocable. Cal. Prob. Code §15400 (1989); Okla. Stat. Ann. tit. 60, §175.41 (1971); Tex. Prop. Code §112.051 (1984). Which is the better rule? Compare the rules as to revocation of will substitutes, most of which permit the revocation of the death beneficiary by the owner during life. See supra pages 280-311.

State Street Bank & Trust Co. v. Reiser
Massachusetts Appeals Court, 1979
7 Mass. App. Ct. 633, 389 N.E.2d 768

KASS, J.   State Street Bank and Trust Company (the bank) seeks to reach the assets of an inter vivos trust in order to pay a debt to the bank owed by the estate of the settlor of the trust. We conclude that the bank can do so.

The probate judge found the material facts, and, although the evidence is reported, we accept his findings if not clearly erroneous. . . . We summarize those findings.

Wilfred A. Dunnebier created an inter vivos trust on September 30, 1971, with power to amend or revoke the trust and the right during his lifetime to direct the disposition of principal and income. He conveyed to the trust the capital stock of five closely held corporations. Immediately following execution of this trust, Dunnebier executed a will under which he left his residuary estate to the trust he had established.

About thirteen months later Dunnebier applied to the bank for a $75,000 working capital loan. A bank officer met with Dunnebier, examined a financial statement furnished by him and visited several single family home subdivisions which Dunnebier, or corporations he controlled, had built or were in the process of building. During their conversations, Dunnebier told the bank officer that he had controlling interests in the corporations which owned the most significant assets appearing on the financial statement. On the basis of what he saw of Dunnebier's work, recommendations from another bank, Dunnebier's borrowing history with the bank, and the general cut of Dunnebier's jib, the bank officer decided to make an unsecured loan to Dunnebier for the $75,000 he had asked for. To evidence this loan, Dunnebier, on November 1, 1972, signed a personal demand note to the order of the bank. The probate judge found that Dunnebier did not intend to defraud the bank or misrepresent his financial position by failing to call attention to the fact that he had placed the stock of his corporations in the trust.

Approximately four months after he borrowed this money Dunnebier died in an accident. His estate has insufficient assets to pay the entire indebtedness due the bank.

Under Article Fourteen of his inter vivos trust, Dunnebier's trustees ". . . may in their sole discretion pay from the principal and income of this Trust Estate any and all debts and expenses of administration of the Settlor's estate." The bank urges that, since the inter vivos trust was part of an estate plan in which the simultaneously executed will was an integrated document, the instruction in Dunnebier's will that his executor pay his debts[35] should be read into the trust instrument. This must have been Dunnebier's intent, goes the argument.

Leaving to one side whether the precatory language in the will could be read as mandatory, and whether the language of that separate, albeit related, instrument, constitutes a surrounding circumstance . . . which could guide us in interpreting the trust,[36] we find the trust agreement manifests no such intent by Dunnebier. Article Fourteen speaks of the sole discretion of the trustees. Subparagraphs A and B of Article Five, by contrast, direct the trustees unconditionally to pay two $15,000 legacies provided for in Dunnebier's will if his estate has insufficient funds to do so. It is apparent that when Dunnebier wanted his trustees unqualifiedly to discharge his estate's obligations, he knew how to direct them. As to those matters which Dunnebier, as settlor, left to the sole discretion of his trustees, we are not free to substitute our judgment for theirs as to what is wise or most to our taste. The court will substitute its discretion only on those relatively rare occasions when it is necessary to prevent an abuse of discretion. Here, the trustees could have

---

35. "It is my wish that all my just debts be fully paid."

36. As was said in First Natl. Bank v. Shawmut Bank, 378 Mass. 137, 143, 389 N.E.2d 1002, 1006 (1979), "In today's estate planning, it is not reasonable to conclude that a will is always of greater significance than an instrument creating an inter vivos trust."

considered preservation of the trust corpus for the benefit of the beneficiaries as most consistent with the trust purpose.

During the lifetime of the settlor, to be sure, the bank would have had access to the assets of the trust. When a person creates for his own benefit a trust for support or a discretionary trust, his creditors can reach the maximum amount which the trustee, under the terms of the trust, could pay to him or apply for his benefit. Ware v. Gulda, 331 Mass. 68, 70, 117 N.E.2d 137 (1954). Restatement (Second) of Trusts §156(2) (1959). This is so even if the trust contains spendthrift provisions. . . . Under the terms of Dunnebier's trust, all the income and principal were at his disposal while he lived.

We then face the question whether Dunnebier's death broke the vital chain. His powers to amend or revoke the trust, or to direct payments from it, obviously died with him, and the remainder interests of the beneficiaries of the trust became vested. The contingencies which might defeat those remainder interests could no longer occur. . . . In one jurisdiction, at least, it has been held that when the settlor of a revocable living trust dies, the property is no longer subject to his debts. Schofield v. Cleveland Trust Co., 135 Ohio St. 328, 334, 21 N.E.2d 119 (1939). See generally McGovern, The Payable on Death Account and Other Will Substitutes, 67 N.W.L. Rev. 7, 26-29 (1972). Cf. Griswold, Spendthrift Trusts §475 (2d ed. 1947). . . .

There has developed, however, another thread of decisions which takes cognizance of, and gives effect to, the power which a person exercises in life over property. When a person has a general power of appointment, exercisable by will or by deed, and exercises that power, any property so appointed is, in equity, considered part of his assets and becomes available to his creditors in preference to the claims of his voluntary appointees or legatees. Clapp v. Ingraham, 126 Mass. 200, 202 (1879); Shattuck v. Burrage, 229 Mass. 448, 452, 118 N.E. 889 (1918); State Street Trust Co. v. Kissel, 302 Mass. 328, 333, 19 N.E.2d 25 (1939). Compare Prescott v. Wordell, 319 Mass. 118, 120, 65 N.E.2d 19 (1946). These decisions rest on the theory that as to property which a person could appoint to himself or his executors, the property could have been devoted to the payment of debts and, therefore, creditors have an equitable right to reach that property. It taxes the imagination to invent reasons why the same analysis and policy should not apply to trust property over which the settlor retains dominion at least as great as a power of appointment. The Restatement of Property has, in fact, translated the doctrine applicable to powers of appointment to trusts:

> When a person transfers property in trust for himself for life and reserves a general power to appoint the remainder and creates no other beneficial interests which he cannot destroy by exercising the power, the property, though the power is unexercised, can be subjected to the payment of the

claims of creditors of such person and claims against his estate to whatever extent other available property is insufficient for that purpose.

Restatement of Property, §328 (1940). . . .

As an estate planning vehicle, the inter vivos trust has become common currency. See Second Bank – State St. Trust Co. v. Pinion, 341 Mass. 366, 371, 170 N.E.2d 350 (1960). Frequently, as Dunnebier did in the instant case, the settlor retains all the substantial incidents of ownership because access to the trust property is necessary or desirable as a matter of sound financial planning. Psychologically, the settlor thinks of the trust property as "his," as Dunnebier did when he took the bank's officer to visit the real estate owned by the corporation whose stock he had put in trust. . . . In other circumstances, persons place property in trust in order to obtain expert management of their assets, while retaining the power to invade principal and to amend and revoke the trust. It is excessive obeisance to the form in which property is held to prevent creditors from reaching property placed in trust under such terms. See Restatement of Property, §328, Comment a (1940).

This view was adopted in United States v. Ritter, 558 F.2d 1165, 1167 (4th Cir. 1977). In a concurring opinion in that case Judge Widener observed that it violates public policy for an individual to have an estate to live on, but not an estate to pay his debts with. Id. at 1168. The Internal Revenue Code institutionalizes the concept that a settlor of a trust who retains administrative powers, power to revoke or power to control beneficial enjoyment "owns" that trust property and provides that it shall be included in the settlor's personal estate. I.R.C. §§2038 and 2041.

We hold, therefore, that where a person places property in trust and reserves the right to amend and revoke, or to direct disposition of principal and income, the settlor's creditors may, following the death of the settlor, reach in satisfaction of the settlor's debts to them, to the extent not satisfied by the settlor's estate, those assets owned by the trust over which the settlor had such control at the time of his death as would have enabled the settlor to use the trust assets for his own benefit. Assets which pour over into such a trust as a consequence of the settlor's death or after the settlor's death, over which the settlor did not have control during his life, are not subject to the reach of creditors since, as to those assets, the equitable principles do not apply which place assets subject to creditors' disposal.[37]

The judgment is reversed, and a new judgment is to enter declaring

---

37. Suppose that the settlor had owned a life insurance policy on his own life, and the beneficiary under the policy was the trustee of the inter vivos trust created on September 30, 1971. Could creditors of the settlor reach the proceeds of the policy payable to the trustee? — Eds.

that the assets owned by the trust (Wilfred A. Dunnebier Trust, I) up to the time of Dunnebier's death can be reached and applied in satisfaction of a judgment entered in favor of the plaintiff against the estate of Dunnebier, to the extent assets of the estate are insufficient to satisfy such a judgment.

So ordered.

PROBLEMS

1.   Ann, age 76, and Mark, age 32, marry in September 1978. The following January, Ann creates a revocable trust with Florida National Bank as trustee. Under the terms of the trust she reserves the income for life and provides for the principal to pass on her death to others than her husband. Ann and Mark divorce in October 1979. In July 1980, Ann and Mark remarry. Five days later Ann writes a letter to the Florida National Bank, revoking her trust. The Bank refuses to accept it on the ground that Ann is under the undue influence of Mark. Must the Bank accept the revocation order? Florida National Bank of Palm Beach County v. Genova, 460 So. 2d 895 (Fla. 1984), held that the settlor of a revocable trust has an absolute right to revoke if she is competent; undue influence is irrelevant.

2.   On January 5, 1990, O creates a revocable trust. The trust provides that income is payable to O for life, and on O's death the trust property is to be distributed to A. O dies leaving a will that provides: "I revoke the trust created by me on January 5, 1990, and give the property held in trust to B." Who takes the trust property, A or B? Would it matter whether O or another person were the trustee, or whether the trust instrument provided that the trust could be amended or revoked only by an instrument in writing delivered to the trustee? See In re Estate of Lowry, 93 Ill. App. 3d 1077, 418 N.E.2d 10 (1981); Connecticut General Life Insurance Co. v. First National Bank of Minneapolis, 262 N.W.2d 403 (Minn. 1977).

2.   Testamentary "Pour-over" into an Inter Vivos Trust

Along with the increasing use of the revocable trust as an estate planning arrangement has come the development of the *pour-over will*. In concept it is simple. O sets up a revocable inter vivos trust naming X as trustee. O transfers to X, as trustee, his stocks and bonds. O then executes a will devising the residue of his estate to X, as trustee, to hold under the terms of the inter vivos trust. The pour-over is a useful device where O wants to establish an inter vivos trust of some of his assets and wants to merge after his death his testamentary estate, insurance proceeds, and other assets into a single receptacle subject to unified administration. As you will recall, the testator in the preceding case, State Street Bank & Trust Co. v. Reiser, executed a pour-over will to transfer his residuary estate to the inter vivos trust which held the stock of his five closely held corporations.

Prior to the 1960s, there was considerable uncertainty about the validity of pour-over provisions, particularly where the trust had been amended after the will had been executed. Some courts held that the amendments to a revocable trust could not be incorporated by reference, and the pour-over failed. Other courts permitted a pour-over into the trust to be disposed of in accordance with the terms of the trust deed as it stood at the time of execution of the will and not as subsequently amended. Still other courts, in the later cases, permitted the pour-over into a funded revocable trust as amended on the theory that the inter vivos trust had independent significance. Bowing to the demands of estate planners, legislatures in every state have enacted statutes permitting a will to pour over estate assets into an inter vivos trust as amended on the date of death. The Uniform Testamentary Additions to Trusts Act, reproduced below, has been adopted in 45 jurisdictions (with slight modifications in a few states); five states have statutes reaching the same results in most cases. The Uniform Act has been incorporated in the Uniform Probate Code as §2-511.

The Uniform Testamentary Additions to Trusts Act provides that when probate assets are poured over into an inter vivos trust, they become part of the inter vivos trust. A single trust simplifies administration and also may result in lower trustee's fees. An inter vivos trust has a number of advantages over a testamentary trust. Two are particularly pertinent here. First, a provision that certain beneficiaries can approve the trustee's accounts, thus avoiding a judicial accounting, is usually effective if the trust is an inter vivos trust. If the trust is testamentary, it may not be possible by a provision in the will to oust the court from jurisdiction to approve the trustee's accounts (see supra page 489). The second basic advantage of treating the poured-over assets as part of the inter vivos trust is the greater flexibility possible in the choice of law and of the trustee. For example, an out-of-state corporate trustee cannot act as testamentary trustee in many states. These restrictions can be avoided if the assets poured over are treated as poured into one inter vivos trust. Where the beneficiaries reside in another state, the testator may wish to avoid the retained jurisdiction of the probate court, especially if the trustee is domiciled elsewhere. A foreign trustee will usually be desirable where there are foreign beneficiaries and the trustee is given discretionary powers which can be soundly exercised only on the basis of personal contact with the beneficiaries. See Lynn, Problems with Pour-Over Wills, 47 Ohio St. L.J. 47 (1986).

Uniform Testamentary Additions to Trusts Act (1983)

§1

A devise or bequest, the validity of which is determinable by the law of this state, may be made by a will to the trustee or trustees of a trust established or to be established by the testator or by the testator and some other person or persons or by some other person or persons (including a funded or unfunded life insurance trust, although the trustor has reserved any or all rights of ownership of the insurance contracts) if the trust is identified in the testator's will and its terms are set forth in a written instrument (other than a will) executed before or concurrently with the execution of the testator's will or in the valid last will of a person who has predeceased the testator (regardless of the existence, size, or character of the corpus of the trust). The devise or bequest shall not be invalid because the trust is amendable or revocable, or both, or because the trust was amended after the execution of the will or after the death of the testator. Unless the testator's will provides otherwise, the property so devised or bequeathed (a) shall not be deemed to be held under a testamentary trust of the testator but shall become a part of the trust to which it is given and (b) shall be administered and disposed of in accordance with the provisions of the instrument or will setting forth the terms of the trust, including any amendments thereto made before the death of the testator (regardless of whether made before or after the execution of the testator's will) and, if the testator's will so provides, including any amendments to the trust made after the death of the testator.[38] A revocation or termination of the trust before the death of the testator shall cause the devise or bequest to lapse.

PROBLEM

Assume the Uniform Testamentary Additions to Trusts Act is the law in this jurisdiction. *O* executes a trust deed that names *X* as trustee

---

38. Compare N.Y. Est., Powers & Trusts Law §3-3.7 (1981), which requires that the trust and any amendments be executed with the formalities required for recording a deed in order to pour over into a trust as amended.

2 Restatement (Second) of Trusts §331, comment c (1959), says: "If the settlor reserves a power to modify the trust but does not specify any method of modification, the power may be exercised by any method which sufficiently manifests his intention to modify the trust." — Eds.

and provides that X shall pay the income to O's daughter, D, for life, remainder in fee to D's issue per stirpes. The trust deed provides that the trust can be revoked or amended at any time by a written or oral communication to X from O. O subsequently makes a will pouring over all his property into this trust. Then O invites X to come by his house for a drink one afternoon. O takes X on a tour of the house and tells X exactly what item he wants to go to whom. He also tells X he wants $1,000 each to go to M and N. A few days later O writes X a letter telling X that he wants M to have $2,000 rather than $1,000; he adds that with respect to the family silver, he is preparing a memorandum that will state who is to get which teapot, creamer, platter, etc., upon his death. Upon O's death, such a memorandum is found. What disposition is made of O's estate? Cf. Gabel v. Manetto, 177 N.J. Super. 460, 427 A.2d 71 (1981).

Tierce v. Macedonia United Methodist Church
Supreme Court of Alabama, 1987
519 So. 2d 451

Houston, J.   This declaratory judgment action was commenced by several plaintiffs, among them the Macedonia United Methodist Church of Northport (the "Church"), who sought the construction of the will of Octavia Hagler and of certain mortgages that she had accepted prior to her death, which occurred on April 6, 1983. The Church contended in its complaint that the will and the mortgages in question established a trust or trusts of the mortgage proceeds in its favor and the plaintiffs named as defendants Hagler's heirs and the executrix of her estate. . . .

After a hearing at which only documentary evidence was introduced, the trial court ruled in favor of the Church and the Church's fellow plaintiffs, entering a judgment establishing a trust in favor of the Church. Two of the defendants, Don Tierce and Festus Tierce, now appeal from that judgment, asserting that the trial court erred in establishing the trust in favor of the Church. We affirm in part, reverse in part, and remand.

Many of the operative facts in this case concern certain sales of real property by the decedent, Octavia Hagler. A few years prior to her death, she sold four parcels of this property to various purchasers, receiving in exchange four promissory notes providing for annual payments of portions of the purchase price. Each note was secured by a separate mortgage issued to the decedent as a consequence of each transaction. The first such sale was to Bobby C. Hagler, and this sale took place on December 11, 1980. The mortgage securing the debt resulting from this sale provided as follows:

> This mortgage is executed by the Mortgagor and accepted by the Mortgagee with the distinct understanding and agreement that the payments will be paid to the Mortgagee as long as she lives. After the death of the Mortgagee, the balance of the mortgage indebtedness will belong to Macedonia Methodist Church of Northport, Alabama, R.F.D. and the money will be invested by the Church in accounts guaranteed by the Federal Deposit Insurance Corporation and the income will be used for maintaining the Church. The amount paid to Macedonia Methodist Church will be deposited and become a part of the Trust fund administered by the Church and the income from said amount in said Trust Fund will be used for the upkeep of the Church.

Virtually identical language was also placed in the note given as a consequence of this sale.

The second sale took place one week later, on December 18, 1980. This sale was to Joe Hillary Shirley and Jean R. Shirley, and it was also consummated by the giving of a note and mortgage. Each of these documents contained language concerning the mortgage proceeds virtually identical to that contained in the documents issued in the previous sale to Bobby C. Hagler, and the mortgage, like the mortgage from Hagler, was recorded. Henceforth, we will refer to these two sales collectively as the "Hagler-Shirley Transfers."

The third transfer took place on January 29, 1981. In this sale, another parcel of land was conveyed to Ralph Harden and Louise T. Harden. This conveyance, henceforth referred to as the "Harden Transfer," was also consummated by the giving of a mortgage, and, presumably a note, although the note is not part of the record on this appeal. However, none of the language of the Hagler-Shirley Transfers concerning the Church's trust fund was contained in the mortgage relating to the Harden Transfer, nor was there any other indication of a transfer of the right to the mortgage proceeds arising from this sale.

The fourth sale was to Rogene S. Tierce and Sybil C. Tierce, and it took place on August 25, 1981. As with the previous sales, the decedent accepted a note and mortgage from the buyers. The mortgage given as a consequence of this sale contained the following language concerning a possible transfer in trust, language which differed significantly from that of the Hagler-Shirley Transfers:

> In the event of the death of Octavia T. Hagler, the balance of the payments are to be made to the Trustee of a Trust which will be set up for the benefit of Macedonia Methodist Church. However, the Mortgagee has the right to cancel this.

The note evidencing the debt resulting from this sale, however, contains no such language. We will subsequently refer to this conveyance as the "Tierce Transfer," bearing in mind that the Tierces who purchased this property are not the parties prosecuting this appeal.

In addition to a consideration of these notes and mortgages, our resolution of this case also depends upon a consideration of the will of the decedent. This will was executed March 24, 1981, subsequent to the Hagler-Shirley and Harden Transfers, but prior to the Tierce Transfer. The pertinent provision of this will provides as follows:

> Item Two:
> I now own three mortgages and one or more of them may not be paid in full before my death. Regardless of the statements contained in the said mortgages concerning the payment of balances to the Macedonia United Methodist Church located near Northport, Alabama, on Alabama State Highway 69, I now will to The First National Bank of Tuscaloosa, N.A., as Trustee acting under a certain Trust Agreement entered into and with The First National Bank of Tuscaloosa, N.A., for the purposes stated in said Trust Agreement.
> [The will then identified the three referenced mortgages as being the Hagler-Shirley and Harden Transfers noted above.]
> The Trust Agreement to be made and entered into by me with The First National Bank of Tuscaloosa, N.A., will be in memory of my beloved husband, John M. Hagler.[39]

A codicil revoking another section of the will was executed on October 20, 1981.

In addition to the above documents, we will also refer to a trust instrument that appears in the record, although the parties disagree as to whether this document was properly admitted into evidence. This document purports to establish an inter vivos trust with the Church as the beneficiary and the First National Bank of Tuscaloosa as trustee. Importantly, this trust instrument was never executed by the parties, and it is uncontradicted that the inter vivos trust described therein was never actually established by the decedent. We also note that the date of this instrument's drafting can only be narrowed to sometime within the year 1981, which is recited on several occasions in the language of the unexecuted trust instrument.

Construing the unexecuted trust instrument and the will together, the trial court concluded that a valid trust had been created in favor of the Church. The trial court apparently regarded the two documents as together creating a trust that conveyed all the disputed parcels to a trustee for the benefit of the Church. As the following analysis will show, the trial court was in error in reaching this conclusion. . . .

---

39. Although this provision of the will is poorly worded, the parties have treated the provision as an attempt to give the proceeds of the referenced mortgages, and we will do likewise, notwithstanding some ambiguity in the will's language.

I. THE WILL AND TRUST INSTRUMENT

We begin our analysis with the materials primarily relied upon by the trial court — the will and the trust instrument. . . .

[W]e think it beyond doubt that the testatrix tentatively intended by this will to devise the disputed mortgage proceeds to an inter vivos trust established by the testatrix. The will is unambiguously a "pour-over" will, and we may assume that the unexecuted trust instrument represents the contemplated inter vivos trust into which the proceeds noted in "Item Two" of the will were to be devised.

The trust instrument, however, was never executed, nor was the trust referenced therein ever otherwise established by the testatrix. Consequently, we think it clear that this attempted devise fails and that the devise in "Item Two" of the will therefore lapses.

The attempted devise fails in the first instance because it does not conform with Ala. Code (1975) §43-8-140, which sets forth the procedures for establishing pour-over gifts to an inter vivos trust. One requirement of that section is that the trust's "terms [be] set forth in a written instrument (other than a will) *executed before or concurrently with the execution of the testator's will.*" (Emphasis added.) The trust instrument clearly does not meet this requirement, as it was never executed.

The attempted devise fails in the second instance because it does not meet the requirements of certain other grounds that might be invoked to sustain it. We consider these grounds with some hesitation, because the legislature, in adopting §43-8-140, may have intended that the procedure set forth therein be the exclusive means of establishing testamentary additions to inter vivos trusts. Because we find, however, that the other grounds for upholding the devise in question cannot be properly invoked in this case, we need not decide the question of §43-8-140's exclusivity, and we expressly reserve that question for later decision.

The will states that the proceeds from three of the mortgages were to be devised "to the First National Bank of Tuscaloosa, N.A., as Trustee acting under a certain Trust Agreement entered into and with [the Trustee] for the purposes stated in said Trust Agreement," and notes that the "Trust Agreement to be made and entered into . . . will be in memory of my beloved husband."

It is well settled that documents not executed with the formalities required of wills can supplement the terms of a will in certain limited circumstances, including documents referencing or creating charitable trusts. See Baxley v. Birmingham Trust Nat. Bank, 334 So. 2d 848 (Ala. 1976); Restatement (Second) of Trusts §358 (1959). These circumstances exist where the terms of the trust can be gathered from a document or documents *incorporated by reference* into the will, and where the terms of the trust can be adduced from *a fact of independent significance. Baxley,* supra; Restatement (Second) of Trusts, supra.

Although Alabama adheres to the doctrine of incorporation by reference, see §43-8-139, the requirements of that doctrine are not met in the present case. "'The document which is to be incorporated *must have been in existence at the time the will was executed*, it must be referred to in the will, and it must be identified by clear and satisfactory proof as the paper referred to.'" Baxley v. Birmingham Trust Nat. Bank, 334 So. 2d at 852 (quoting Holt, Testate Succession in Alabama: Part I, 24 Ala. L. Rev. 221, 243-44 (1971) (emphasis added). There is insufficient proof in this case that the trust document in question was in existence at the time of the execution of the will.

As noted previously, the drafting of the trust document can be narrowed only to sometime within the year 1981, judging from the language of the document itself. Moreover, the testatrix died in 1983. Therefore, she could have asked her lawyer to draft this document at any time during the year 1981, and we note that her lawyer was apparently also dead at the time of this trial. Thus, no evidence was introduced that further narrows the date of the drafting of the trust document. Therefore, it would appear to be beyond dispute that this document could have come into existence at any time during the year 1981. The will, however, was clearly executed on March 24, 1981, and the codicil appended thereto was executed on October 20, 1981. Assuming that this codicil republished the will on October 20, there nevertheless would remain a period of nearly two and one-half months in 1981 during which the trust document could have been drafted subsequent to the republication of the will. Moreover, the will itself is ambiguous as to the existence of the trust document, as "Item Two," quoted at length above, refers to the trust both as being in existence and as yet "to be made and entered into." Thus, the proof that the trust document was in existence at the time of the will's execution is highly ambiguous at best, and it falls far short of the standard required to incorporate the document by reference into the will. An "incorporated" document *must* be in existence when the will is executed, Baxley v. Birmingham Trust Nat. Bank, supra; it is not enough to show that the document *might* have been in existence.

Likewise, the doctrine of "facts of independent significance," also adhered to in Alabama, see §43-8-141, is inapplicable to this case. "'The chief requirement [of the doctrine] is that the document referred to in the will have a separate legal identity and existence, and not be solely for the purpose of supplementing the will,'" Baxley v. Birmingham Trust Nat. Bank, 334 So. 2d, at 853 (quoting Holt, Testate Succession in Alabama: Part I, 24 Ala. L. Rev. 221, 244 (1971)). In the instant case, it is undisputed that the trust referred to in the trust document was never established. Hence, this "trust" never rose to the level of a "separate legal identity," and the doctrine of facts of independent significance is inapplicable. "It is not the trust instrument but the trust itself that has independent significance." 1A A. Scott & W. Fratcher, The Law of Trusts §54.3, at 12-13 (4th ed. 1987); see Restatement (Second) of Trusts, §54 comment f (1959). Thus, the doctrine of facts of independent significance, while it can sometimes serve as "an escape mechanism from the strict requirements of incorporation by reference," First Nat. Bank of Birmingham v. Klein, 285 Ala. 505, at 509, 234 So. 2d 42, at 46 (1970), cannot properly be invoked in the instant case.

Accordingly, no charitable trust was established by the will in this case. The attempted pour-over devise into the "trust" fails, because of a lack of compliance with the requirements of §43-8-140. Similarly, the trust instrument cannot be regarded as having been incorporated by reference, and the "trust" itself never achieved a "separate legal identity"; this fact foreclosed application of the doctrine of facts of independent significance. Therefore, even if we wished to assume that the testatrix's actual intention was to establish a trust by will, a trust similar to that evidenced by the trust instrument, we could not do so, because such a trust would be "prohibited by law." Mastin v. First Alabama Bank, 278 Ala. 251, 177 So. 2d 808 at 813 (1965).

We should note, however, that the evidence of the testatrix's intent in this case does not require such an assumption, and that, in fact, her actions could well indicate the opposite intent. As noted previously, the will is clearly a "pour-over will," and we must assume that the testatrix realized that such a testamentary scheme required a trust "receptacle" to render it operative. The testatrix lived more than two years after the will was executed and after she would have been made aware of the necessity of establishing a trust, yet she made no effort to consummate the pour-over scheme. We think that such inaction comports at least as well with an intention to allow the devise in the will to lapse as it does with an intention to make the devise. We note in this regard that §43-8-140 provides that the revocation of the inter vivos trust underlying a testator's pour-over scheme results in the lapse of any devise in the will to that trust. This is perhaps a legislative determination that a testator, by such a revocation, evidences an intent that the devise is to be distributed according to a residuary clause or by intestacy, rather than by the terms of the trust. A failure to create the underlying trust in the first place ought to be given a similar effect, at least in the circumstances in which this case arises. . . .

II.   The Notes and Mortgages

Although the trial court erred in upholding a trust on the basis of the will and the trust instrument, we must also consider the dispositions contained within the notes and mortgages referred to previously. If any of these documents created valid inter vivos trusts not subsequently revoked by the will, then the trial court's judgment is due to be upheld as to each such valid trust, in spite of the fact that the attempted devises in the will must be regarded as having lapsed.

A.   THE TIERCE TRANSFER

The language in the Tierce Transfer purporting to create a trust is unenforceable due to the lack of a *present intention* to create the trust. That language provides only that the balance of mortgage payments due the decedent at her death "are to be made to the Trustee of the Trust *which will be set up* for the benefit of [the Church]." "A manifestation of intention to create a trust inter vivos at some time subsequent to the time of manifestation does not create a trust." Restatement (Second) of Trusts §26 (1959); see 1 A. Scott & W. Fratcher, The Law of Trusts §26 (4th ed. 1987). Accordingly, no inter vivos trust was created by this language. In view of the fact that no valid testamentary trust was established with respect to this property, and that, indeed, these particular proceeds were not referenced in either the will or the trust document, the trial court was in error in including the proceeds from the Tierce Transfer in the trust it established in favor of the Church.

B.   THE HARDEN TRANSFER

The proceeds from the Harden Transfer were also improperly included in the trust established by the trial court. It is undisputed that the documents exchanged in the Harden Transfer contained no words indicating a gift in trust of those proceeds, and that no other manifestation of an intention to create an inter vivos trust was made by the decedent with respect to these proceeds. . . . There being no such manifestation in regard to these proceeds, no inter vivos trust was created, and, in of the fact that no valid testamentary trust was established by the testatrix's will, the trial court erred in including these proceeds in the trust it established in favor of the Church.

C.   THE HAGLER-SHIRLEY TRANSFERS

As noted previously, the Hagler-Shirley Transfers included documents containing language concerning an attempted gift in trust to the Church. Moreover, these transfers were irrevocable, because the settlor did not expressly reserve the right to revoke the transfers in trust for the benefit of the Church. See Underwood v. Bank of Huntsville, 494 So. 2d 619 (Ala. 1986); Restatement (Second) of Trusts §330 (1959); Comment, The Law of Trusts in Alabama, 25 Ala. L. Rev. 467, 523-27 (1973). Thus, the attempted revocation in "Item Two" of the will, quoted at length above, is of no effect in determining the validity of these gifts in trust. If these inter vivos transfers are valid, then the fact that the subsequent testamentary devise fails is of no import in sustaining the prior inter vivos transfers. As the following analysis will show, we hold that these two transfers resulted in valid inter vivos transfers in trust for the benefit of the Church, and that the trial court was correct in establishing a trust in favor of the Church as to these proceeds.

There is no doubt from the previously quoted language of these transfers that a transfer in trust was intended. The issues presented by these transfers concern the related matters of whether a present intent to convey an interest in the property was manifested by the language of the notes and mortgages, and whether such a transfer actually occurred.

The problem arises because the decedent expressly provided that she was to receive the mortgage proceeds during her life and that, upon her death, the proceeds were to go in trust to the Church for the specified purpose of building maintenance. The defendants argue that the language to this effect manifests an intent to establish a trust in the future, and is therefore invalid, as was the case with the Tierce Transfer. We disagree.

It is undisputed that mortgage proceeds may be held in trust, City Bank & Trust Co. v. Gardner, 225 Ala. 136, 142 So. 535 (1932); Hill v. Hill, 216 Ala. 435, 113 So. 306 (1927), and that such proceeds are considered to be personal property, *City Bank & Trust Co.,* supra; *Hill,* supra. Moreover, we have recognized that the reservation of a life estate in personalty does not serve to defeat a gift of the remainder interest in such personalty, so long as the gift of the remainder interest is reduced to a writing. Livingston v. Powell, 257 Ala. 38, 57 So. 2d 521 (1952). In addition, Hill v. Hill, supra, recognizes by implication that a remainder interest in mortgage proceeds is permissible, and we also note that

> [i]t is lawful to give a present vested right to future enjoyment. Thus there may be a present gift of a future interest in a fund or in the balance of the fund remaining when the time for enjoyment arrives; and, it has been held, such a gift is valid even though the donor reserves the power to draw out the fund. A conveyance to one as life tenant with power to dispose of or consume is not inconsistent with a present valid gift of the remainder.

38 C.J.S. Gifts §41, at 820-21 (1943).

The language in the documents exchanged as a result of the Hagler-Shirley Transfers is consistent with the construction that the decedent intended a present transfer in trust of a remainder interest in the mortgage proceeds for the benefit of the Church, retaining to herself a life estate in the proceeds. The transfer of this remainder interest was irrevocable and tied to no particular contingency; it was thus not ambulatory or testamentary in nature, but represented an attempt to make a present and absolute gift in trust of the balance of the mortgage proceeds existing at the time of the testatrix's death. Accordingly, we hold that this transfer in trust does not fail for lack of a present intent to create a trust. Unlike the Tierce Transfer, in which the proceeds were explicitly to go to a trust "which will be set-up" in the future, the Hagler-Shirley Transfers represent present transfers in trust of a future interest in the mortgage proceeds.[40]

The defendants also argue that the Hagler-Shirley Transfers failed because there was no effective delivery of the interest. We disagree.

These attempted trusts sprang from gratuitous transfers to the Church trust fund. Therefore, the question of whether an effective delivery occurred must be answered by reference to the general law of gifts. In this regard, we have recognized that the evidence in support of the gift must be clear and convincing. DeMouy v. Jepson, 255 Ala. 337, 51 So. 2d 506 (1951). We have also recognized, however, that "the rule [requiring delivery in the case of a gratuitous transfer] has been relaxed as to personal property not capable of manual delivery. In such a case a symbolic delivery is held sufficient. . . ." First Nat. Bank of Birmingham v. Hammel, 252 Ala. 624, 626, 42 So. 2d 459, 460 (1949). We are concerned here not just with intangible personal property — choses in action — but with a future interest in that property, further incorporealizing the interest conveyed. That such an interest is incapable of actual manual delivery would appear to be beyond dispute. We think, therefore, that the specification in the notes and mortgages of the interest to be conveyed and the subsequent recordation of those mortgages is a sufficient "symbolic" or "constructive" transfer to satisfy the delivery requirement in this case. We regard the recordation of the mortgages as particularly persuasive that "delivery" occurred in this case, in view of the rule, long recognized in this state, that the recording of a deed by a grantor can often constitute sufficient delivery of the instrument to convey title, if that is the intention of the grantor. . . .

III. CONCLUSION

For the foregoing reasons, the trial court incorrectly established the trusts allegedly created under the testatrix's will and the trust instrument. However, valid inter vivos transfers in trust were made as to the mortgage proceeds arising from the Hagler-Shirley Transfers. Accord-

---

40. We have noted that "Item Two" of the will attempts to revoke these transfers. Although this "revocation" constitutes some evidence that the grantor did not intend a present transfer of the interests conveyed in the notes and mortgages issued as a result of the Hagler-Shirley Transfers, we do not regard this attempted revocation as fatal to the transfer in this case. A gratuitous transfer, once made, is irrevocable, see Patterson v. Leonard, 240 Ala. 652, 200 So. 759 (1941), and our review of the evidence in this case convinces us that a valid inter vivos gift in trust was in fact made by the decedent. Consequently, this "revocation" has no legal effect on these transfers.

ingly, the trial court's establishment of a trust as regards these proceeds was entirely proper. . . .

Affirmed in part; reversed in part.

NOTE AND QUESTION

1. In Estate of Baer, 446 So. 2d 1129 (Fla. 1984), the testator executed a will pouring over his estate into a revocable trust. Subsequently he revoked the revocable trust. The court held that the trust instrument had been incorporated by reference into the will and continued to set forth the testator's distribution plan. Accordingly, the testator's estate was distributed under the terms of the trust instrument. The court referred to Fla. Stat. §732.512(1) (1981), adopting incorporation by reference. It did not refer to Fla. Stat. §732.513 (1981), which, similarly to the Uniform Testamentary Additions to Trusts Act, provides, "An entire revocation of the trust by an instrument in writing before the testator's death shall invalidate the devise or bequest."

2. Suppose that O creates a revocable trust and designates the trustee as the beneficiary of her life insurance policy. At the same time O executes a will pouring over her probate estate into the trust. Subsequently O cancels the life insurance policy, receiving the cash value of the policy. Thereafter the trust has no res. O then dies. Under the Uniform Testamentary Additions to Trusts Act, does the devise to the trust lapse because the trust has been revoked or terminated? See Estate of Garrison, 122 Cal. App. 3d 7, 175 Cal. Rptr. 809 (1981); Comment, Pour-Overs to a Non-Existent Trust, 1975 Ariz. St. L.J. 401.

Clymer v. Mayo
Supreme Judicial Court of Massachusetts, 1985
393 Mass. 754, 473 N.E.2d 1084

HENNESSEY, C.J.   This consolidated appeal arises out of the administration of the estate of Clara A. Mayo (decedent). We summarize the findings of the judge of the Probate and Family Court incorporating the parties' agreed statement of uncontested facts.

At the time of her death in November, 1981, the decedent, then fifty years of age, was employed by Boston University as a professor of psychology. She was married to James P. Mayo, Jr. (Mayo), from 1953 to 1978. The couple had no children. The decedent was an only child and her sole heirs at law are her parents, Joseph A. and Maria Weiss.

In 1963, the decedent executed a will designating Mayo as principal beneficiary. In 1964, she named Mayo as the beneficiary of her group annuity contract with John Hancock Mutual Life Insurance Company; and in 1965, made him the beneficiary of her Boston University retirement annuity contracts with Teachers Insurance and Annuity Association (TIAA) and College Retirement Equities Fund (CREF). As a consequence of a $300,000 gift to the couple from the Weisses in 1971, the decedent and Mayo executed new wills and indentures of trust on February 2, 1973, wherein each spouse was made the other's principal beneficiary. Under the terms of the decedent's will, Mayo was to receive her personal property. The residue of her estate was to "pour over" into the inter vivos trust she created that same day.

The decedent's trust instrument named herself and John P. Hill as trustees. As the donor, the decedent retained the right to amend or revoke the trust at any time by written instrument delivered to the trustees. In the event that Mayo survived the decedent, the trust estate was to be divided into two parts. Trust A, the marital deduction trust, was to be funded with an amount "equal to fifty (50%) percent of the value of the Donor's 'adjusted gross estate,'. . . for the purpose of the United States Tax Law, less an amount equal to the value of all interest in property, if any, allowable as 'marital deductions' for the purposes of such law. . . ." Mayo was the income beneficiary of Trust A and was entitled to reach the principal at his request or in the trustee's discretion. The trust instrument also gave Mayo a general power of appointment over the assets in Trust A.

The balance of the decedent's estate, excluding personal property passing to Mayo by will, or the entire estate if Mayo did not survive her, composed Trust B. Trust B provided for the payment of five initial specific bequests totalling $45,000. After those gifts were satisfied, the remaining trust assets were to be held for the benefit of Mayo for life. Upon Mayo's death, the assets in Trust B were to be held for "the benefit of the nephews and nieces of the Donor" living at the time of her death. The trustee was given discretion to spend so much of the income and principal as necessary for their comfort, support, and education. When all of these nephews and nieces reached the age of thirty, the trust was to terminate and its remaining assets were to be divided equally between Clark University and Boston University to assist in graduate education of women.

On the same day she established her trust, the decedent changed the beneficiary of her Boston University group life insurance policy from Mayo to the trustees. One month later, in March, 1973, she also executed a change in her retirement annuity contracts to designate the trustees as beneficiaries. At the time of its creation in 1973, the trust was not funded. Its future assets were to consist solely of the proceeds of these policies and the property which would pour over under the will's residuary clause. The judge found that the remaining trustee has never received any property or held any funds subsequent to the execution of the trust nor has he paid any trust taxes or filed any trust tax returns.

Mayo moved out of the marital home in 1975. In June, 1977, the decedent changed the designation of beneficiary on her Boston University life insurance policy for a second time, substituting Marianne LaFrance for the trustees.[41] LaFrance had lived with the Mayos since 1972, and shared a close friendship with the decedent up until her death. Mayo filed for divorce on September 9, 1977, in New Hampshire. The divorce was decreed on January 3, 1978, and the court incorporated into the decree a permanent stipulation of the parties' property settlement. Under the terms of that settlement, Mayo waived any "right, title or interest" in the decedent's "securities, savings accounts, savings certificates, and retirement fund," as well as her "furniture, furnishings and art." Mayo remarried on August 28, 1978, and later executed a new will in favor of his new wife. The decedent died on November 21, 1981. Her will was allowed on November 18, 1982, and the court appointed John H. Clymer as administrator with the will annexed.

What is primarily at issue in these actions is the effect of the Mayos' divorce upon dispositions provided in the decedent's will and indenture of trust. . . . [T]he court-appointed administrator of the decedent's estate petitioned for instructions with respect to the impact of the divorce on the estate's administration. Named as defendants were Mayo, the decedent's parents (the Weisses), and the trustee under the indenture of trust (John P. Hill).

1. THE JUDGE'S CONCLUSIONS.

On November 1, 1983, the judge issued his rulings of law. . . . The rulings that have been challenged by one or more parties on appeal are as follows: (1) the decedent's inter vivos trust, executed contemporaneously with her will, is valid under G.L. c. 203, §3B, despite the fact that the trust did not receive funding until the decedent's death; (2) Mayo does not take under Trust A because that transfer was intended to qualify for a marital deduction for Federal estate tax purposes and this objective became impossible after the Mayos' divorce; (3) Mayo is entitled to take under Trust B because the purpose of that trust was to create a life interest in him, the decedent failed to revoke the trust provisions benefiting Mayo, and G.L. c. 191, §9, operates to revoke only testamentary dispositions in favor of a former spouse; (4) J. Chamberlain, A. Chamberlain, and Hinman, the decedent's nephews and niece by marriage at the time of the trust's creation, are entitled to take under Trust B as the decedent's intended beneficiaries. . . .

---

41. Upon the decedent's death the benefits under said policy were paid to LaFrance.

For the reasons to follow we affirm the judge's conclusions that: (1) the decedent established a valid trust under G.L. c. 203, §3B; (2) Mayo's interest in Trust A was terminated as a result of the divorce; (3) the Chamberlains and Hinman are entitled to take as intended beneficiaries under Trust B, with the remainder interest to be divided equally between Clark University and Boston University. . . . However, we reverse the judge's ruling that Mayo is to take under Trust B, and we remand the question of attorneys' fees for reconsideration.

2. VALIDITY OF "POUR-OVER" TRUST.

The Weisses claim that the judge erred in ruling that the decedent's trust was validly created despite the fact that it was not funded until her death. They rely on the common law rule that a trust can be created only when a trust res exists. New England Trust Co. v. Sanger, 337 Mass. 342, 348 (1958). Arguing that the trust never came into existence, the Weisses claim they are entitled to the decedent's entire estate as her sole heirs at law.

In upholding the validity of the decedent's pour-over trust, the judge cited the relevant provisions of G.L. c. 203, §3B, inserted by St. 1963, c. 418, §1, the Commonwealth's version of the Uniform Testamentary Additions to Trusts Act.

> A devise or bequest, the validity of which is determinable by the laws of the commonwealth, may be made to the trustee or trustees of a trust established or to be established by the testator . . . including a funded or unfunded life insurance trust, although the trustor has reserved any or all rights of ownership of the insurance contracts, if the trust is identified in the will and the terms of the trust are set forth in a written instrument executed before or concurrently with the execution of the testator's will . . . *regardless of the existence, size or character of the corpus of the trust* (emphasis added).

The decedent's trust instrument, which was executed in Massachusetts and states that it is to be governed by the laws of the Commonwealth, satisfies these statutory conditions. The trust is identified in the residuary clause of her will and the terms of the trust are set out in a written instrument executed contemporaneously with the will. However, the Weisses claim that G.L. c. 203, §3B, was not intended to change the common law with respect to the necessity for a trust corpus despite the clear language validating pour-over trusts, "regardless of the existence, size or character of the corpus." The Weisses make no showing of legislative intent that would contradict the plain meaning of these words. It is well established that "the statutory language is the principal source of insight into legislative purpose." Bronstein v. Prudential Ins.

Co. of Am., 390 Mass. 701, 704 (1984). Moreover, the development of the common law of this Commonwealth with regard to pour-over trusts demonstrates that G.L. c. 203, §3B, takes on practical meaning only if the Legislature meant exactly what the statute says concerning the need for a trust corpus.

This court was one of the first courts to validate pour-over devises to a living trust. In Second Bank-State St. Trust Co. v. Pinion, 341 Mass. 366, 371 (1960), decided prior to the adoption of G.L. c. 203, §3B, we upheld a testamentary gift to a revocable and amendable inter vivos trust established by the testator before the execution of his will and which he amended after the will's execution. Recognizing the importance of the pour-over devise in modern estate planning, we explained that such transfers do not violate the statute of wills despite the testator's ability to amend the trust and thereby change the disposition of property at his death without complying with the statute's formalities. "We agree with modern legal thought that a subsequent amendment is effective because of the applicability of the established equitable doctrine that subsequent acts of independent significance do not require attestation under the statute of wills." Id. at 369.

At that time we noted that "[t]he long established recognition in Massachusetts of the doctrine of independent significance makes unnecessary statutory affirmance of its application to pour-over trusts." Id. at 371. It is evident from *Pinion* that there was no need for the Legislature to enact G.L. c. 203, §3B, simply to validate pour-over devises from wills to funded revocable trusts.

However, in *Pinion*, we were not presented with an unfunded pour-over trust. Nor, prior to G.L. c. 203, §3B, did other authority exist in this Commonwealth for recognizing testamentary transfers to unfunded trusts. The doctrine of independent significance, upon which we relied in *Pinion*, assumes that "property was included in the purported inter vivos trust, prior to the testator's death." Restatement (Second) of Trusts §54 comment f (1959). That is why commentators have recognized that G.L. c. 203, §3B, "[m]akes some . . . modification of the *Pinion* doctrine. The act does not require that the trust res be more than nominal or even existent." E. Slizewski, Legislation: Uniform Testamentary Additions to Trusts Act, 1963 Ann. Survey Mass. Law §2.7, 39. See Osgood, Pour Over Will: Appraisal of Uniform Testamentary Additions to Trusts Act, 104 Trusts 768, 769 (1965) ("The Act . . . eliminates the necessity that there be a trust corpus").

For the foregoing reasons we conclude, in accordance with G.L. c. 203, §3B, that the decedent established a valid inter vivos trust in 1973 and that its trustee may properly receive the residue of her estate. We affirm the judge's ruling on this issue. . . .

4.   Termination of Trust A.

The judge terminated Trust A upon finding that its purpose — to qualify the trust for an estate tax marital deduction — became impossible to achieve after the Mayos' divorce. Mayo appeals this ruling. It is well established that the Probate Courts are empowered to terminate or reform a trust in whole or in part where its purposes have become impossible to achieve and the settlor did not contemplate continuation of the trust under the new circumstances. Gordon v. Gordon, 332 Mass. 193, 197 (1955). Ames v. Hall, 313 Mass. 33, 37 (1943).

The language the decedent employed in her indenture of trust makes it clear that by setting off Trusts A and B she intended to reduce estate tax liability in compliance with then existing provisions of the Internal Revenue Code. Therefore we have no disagreement with the judge's reasoning. See Putnam v. Putnam, 366 Mass. 261, 267 (1974). However, we add that our reasoning below — that by operation of G.L. c. 191, §9, Mayo has no beneficial interest in the trust — clearly disposes of Mayo's claim to Trust A.

5.   Mayo's Interest in Trust B.

The judge's decision to uphold Mayo's beneficial interest in Trust B was appealed by the Weisses, as well as by Boston University and Clark University. The judge reasoned that the decedent intended to create a life interest in Mayo when she established Trust B and failed either to revoke or to amend the trust after the couple's divorce. The appellants argue that we should extend the reach of G.L. c. 191, §9, to revoke all Mayo's interests under the trust. General Laws c. 191, §9, as amended through St. 1977, c. 76, §2, provides in relevant part:

> If, after executing a will, the testator shall be divorced or his marriage shall be annulled, the divorce or annulment shall revoke any disposition or appointment of property made by the will to the former spouse, any provision conferring a general or special power of appointment on the former spouse, and any nomination of the former spouse, as executor, trustee, conservator or guardian, unless the will shall expressly provide otherwise. Property prevented from passing to a former spouse because of a revocation by divorce shall pass as if a former spouse had failed to survive the decedent, and other provisions conferring a power of office on the former spouse shall be interpreted as if the spouse had failed to survive the decedent.

The judge ruled that Mayo's interest in Trust B is unaffected by G.L. c. 191, §9, because his interest in that trust is not derived from a "disposition . . . made by the will" but rather from the execution of an inter vivos trust with independent legal significance. We disagree, but in fairness we add that the judge here confronted a question of first impression in this Commonwealth.

. . . In this case we must determine what effect, if any, G.L. c. 191, §9, has on the former spouse's interest in the testator's pour-over trust.

While, by virtue of G.L. c. 203, §3B, the decedent's trust bore independent significance at the time of its creation in 1973, the trust had no practical significance until her death in 1981. The decedent executed both her will and indenture of trust on February 2, 1973. She transferred no property or funds to the trust at that time. The trust was to receive its funding at the decedent's death, in part through her life insurance policy and retirement benefits, and in part through a pour-over from the will's residuary clause. Mayo, the proposed executor and sole legatee under the will, was also made the primary beneficiary of the trust with power, as to Trust A only, to reach both income and principal.

During her lifetime, the decedent retained power to amend or revoke the trust. Since the trust was unfunded, her cotrustee was subject to no duties or obligations until her death. Similarly, it was only as a result of the decedent's death that Mayo could claim any right to the trust assets. It is evident from the time and manner in which the trust was created and funded, that the decedent's will and trust were integrally related components of a single testamentary scheme. For all practical purposes the trust, like the will, "spoke" only at the decedent's death. For this reason Mayo's interest in the trust was revoked by operation of G.L. c. 191, §9, at the same time his interest under the decedent's will was revoked.

It has reasonably been contended that in enacting G.L. c. 191, §9, the Legislature "intended to bring the law into line with the expectations of most people. . . . Divorce usually represents a stormy parting, where the last thing one of the parties wishes is to have an earlier will carried out giving everything to the former spouse." Young, Probate Reform, 18 B.B.J. 7, 11 (1974). To carry out the testator's implied intent, the law revokes "any disposition or appointment of property made by the will to the former spouse." It is indisputable that if the decedent's trust was either testamentary or incorporated by reference into her will, Mayo's beneficial interest in the trust would be revoked by operation of the statute. However, the judge stopped short of mandating the same result in this case because here the trust had "independent significance" by virtue of c. 203, §3B. While correct, this characterization of the trust does not end our analysis. For example, in Sullivan v. Burkin, 390 Mass. 864, 867 (1984), we ruled prospectively that the assets of a revocable trust will be considered part of the "estate of the decedent" in determining the surviving spouse's statutory share.

Treating the components of the decedent's estate plan separately, and not as parts of an interrelated whole, brings about inconsistent results. Applying c. 191, §9, the judge correctly revoked the will provisions benefiting Mayo. As a result, the decedent's personal property — originally left to Mayo — fell into the will's residuary clause and passed to the trust. The judge then appropriately terminated Trust A for impossibility of purpose thereby denying Mayo his beneficial interest under Trust A. Yet, by upholding Mayo's interest under Trust B, the judge returned to Mayo a life interest in the same assets that composed the corpus of Trust A — both property passing by way of the decedent's will and the proceeds of her TIAA/CREF annuity contracts.

We are aware of only one case concerning the impact of a statute similar to G.L. c. 191, §9, on trust provisions benefiting a former spouse. In Miller v. First Nat'l Bank & Trust Co., 637 P.2d 75 (Okla. 1981), the testator also simultaneously executed an indenture of trust and will naming his spouse as primary beneficiary. As in this case, the trust was to be funded at the testator's death by insurance proceeds and a will pour-over. Subsequently, the testator divorced his wife but failed to change the terms of his will and trust. The District Court revoked the will provisions favoring the testator's former wife by applying a statute similar to G.L. c. 191, §9. Recognizing that "[t]he will without the trust has no meaning or value to the decedent's estate plan," the Oklahoma Supreme Court revoked the trust benefits as well. Id. at 77. However, we do not agree with the court's reasoning. Because the Oklahoma statute, like G.L. c. 191, §9, revokes dispositions of property made by will, the court stretched the doctrine of incorporation by reference to render the decedent's trust testamentary. We do not agree that reference to an existing trust in a will's pour-over clause is sufficient to incorporate that trust by reference without evidence that the testator intended such a result. See Second Bank-State St. Trust Co. v. Pinion, 341 Mass. 366, 367 (1960). However, it is not necessary for us to indulge in such reasoning, because we have concluded that the legislative intent under G.L. c. 191, §9, is that a divorced spouse should not take under a trust executed in these circumstances. In the absence of an expressed contrary intent, that statute implies an intent on the part of a testator to revoke will provisions favoring a former spouse. It is incongruous then to ignore that same intent with regard to a trust funded in part through her will's pour-over at the decedent's death. As one law review commentator has noted, "[t]ransferors use will substitutes to avoid probate, not to avoid the subsidiary law of wills. The subsidiary rules are the product of centuries of legal experience in attempting to discern transferors' wishes and suppress litigation. These rules should be treated as presumptively correct for will substitutes as well as for wills." Langbein, The Nonprobate Revolution and the Future of the Law of Succession, 97 Harv. L. Rev. 1108, 1136-1137 (1984).

Restricting our holding to the particular facts of this case — specifically the existence of a revocable pour-over trust funded entirely at the time of the decedent's death — we conclude that G.L. c. 191, §9, revokes Mayo's interest under Trust B.[42]

6.   NEPHEWS AND NIECES OF DONOR.

According to the terms of G.L. c. 191, §9, "[p]roperty prevented from passing to a former spouse because of revocation by divorce shall pass as if a former spouse had failed to survive the decedent. . . ." In this case, the decedent's indenture of trust provides that if Mayo failed to survive her, "the balance of 'Trust B' shall be held . . . for the benefit of the nephews and nieces of the Donor living at the time of the death of the Donor." The trustee is directed to expend as much of the net income and principal as he deems "advisable for [their] reasonable comfort, support and education" until all living nephews and nieces have attained the age of thirty. At that time, the trust is to terminate and Boston University and Clark University are each to receive fifty percent of the trust property to assit women students in their graduate programs.

The decedent had no siblings and therefore no nephews and nieces who were blood relations.[43] However, when she executed her trust in 1973, her husband, James P. Mayo, Jr., had two nephews and one niece — John and Allan Chamberlain and Mira Hinman. Before her divorce, the decedent maintained friendly relations with these young people and, along with her former husband, contributed toward their educational expenses. The three have survived the decedent.

The Weisses, Boston University, and Clark University appeal the decision of the judge upholding the decedent's gift to these three individuals. They argue that at the time the decedent created her trust she had no "nephews and nieces" by blood and that, at her death, her marital ties to Mayo's nephews and niece had been severed by divorce. Therefore, they contend that the class gift to the donor's "nephews and nieces" lapses for lack of identifiable beneficiaries.

The judge concluded that the trust language created an ambiguity, and thus he considered extrinsic evidence of the decedent's meaning and intent. Based upon that evidence, he decided that the decedent

---

42. As an alternative ground the appellants argue that the terms of the Mayos' divorce settlement, in which Mayo waived "any right, title or interest" in the assets that later funded the decedent's trust, amount to a disclaimer of his trust interest. We decline to base our holding on such reasoning because a disclaimer of rights "must be clear and unequivocal," Second Bank-State St. Trust Co. v. Yale Univ. Alumni Fund, 338 Mass. 520, 524 (1959), and we find no such disclaimer in the Mayos' divorce agreement.

43. Considering the ages of all concerned, it could not reasonably be argued that the decedent might have contemplated the possibility of siblings to be born after the trust was executed.

intended to provide for her nieces and nephews by marriage when she created the trust. Because the decedent never revoked this gift, he found that the Chamberlains and Hinman are entitled to their beneficial interests under the trust. We agree.

The appellants . . . [argue] that the Mayos' divorce left the decedent without *any* nephews and nieces — by blood or marriage — at the time of her death. They argue that even if the decedent had intended to provide for the Chamberlains and Hinman when she executed her indenture of trust, we should rule that the Mayos' divorce somehow "revoked" this gift. According to Boston University, since the beneficiaries are identified by their relationship to the decedent through her marriage and not by name, we should presume that the decedent no longer intended to benefit her former relatives once her marriage ended. General Laws c. 191, §9, does not provide the authority for revoking gifts to the blood relatives of a former spouse. The law implies an intent to revoke testamentary gifts between the divorcing parties because of the profound emotional and financial changes divorce normally engenders. There is no indication in the statutory language that the Legislature presumed to know how these changes affect a testator's relations with more distant family members. We therefore conclude that the Chamberlains and Hinman are entitled to take as the decedent's "nephews and nieces" under Trust B. . . .

In sum, we conclude that the decedent established a valid trust under G.L. c. 203, §3B; Mayo's beneficial interest in Trust A and Trust B is revoked by operation of G.L. c. 191, §9; [and] the Chamberlains and Hinman are entitled to take the interest given to the decedent's "nephews and nieces" under Trust B, leaving the remainder to Clark University and Boston University. . . .

So ordered.

NOTES AND PROBLEMS

1. Recent statutes in some states provide that divorce revokes any provision in a revocable trust for the spouse, who is deemed to have predeceased the settlor. See, e.g., Ohio Rev. Code §1339.62 (1988); Okla. Stat. Ann. ch. 60, §175 (Supp. 1989).

2. Suppose that in Clymer v. Mayo Clara Mayo's pour-over Trust B had given $10,000 to her cousin Sarah, and that Sarah had predeceased the settlor, leaving issue. Would the anti-lapse statute make Sarah's issue beneficiaries of the trust? Dollar Savings & Trust Co. v. Turner, 39 Ohio St. 3d 182, 529 N.E.2d 1261 (1988), held that an anti-lapse statute, which by its terms applied only to devises by will, applied equally to revocable trusts.

3. Suppose that Clara and James Mayo had not gotten a divorce. Suppose further that at Clara's death James elected against Clara's will to take a surviving spouse's share of Clara's estate (which we will assume is one-third in fee simple). Would James also be entitled to receive income as the life beneficiary of the pour-over trust? See Carnahan v. Stallman, 29 Ohio App. 3d 293, 504 N.E.2d 1218 (1986), holding that the electing spouse did not lose her income interest in a nonfunded pour-over trust because the spouse's trust interest in the poured-over residuary assets did not arise until after the assets were transferred to the trustee, when they were no longer part of the decedent's estate, which she had renounced; Ohio Rev. Code Ann. §2107.39 (Page Supp. 1988), reversing *Carnahan* holding. See also Estate of Harper, 93 T.C. No. 32 (1989), following *Carnahan* as a correct interpretation of a similar Kentucky election statute and further holding that the residuary estate bequeathed to a pour-over trust "passed from the decedent" to the surviving spouse so as to qualify for the QTIP marital deduction (infra page 1009)!

4. Pablo Olmos executes an unfunded inter vivos trust naming Eduardo Guillen as beneficiary. Olmos also executes a will pouring over all his assets into the trust. The will contains a no-contest clause, providing that any person contesting the will shall forfeit any interest given by the will. Subsequently Olmos amends his trust to name Peregrina Meza as a 50-percent beneficiary of the trust. Upon Olmos's death, Guillen contests the trust amendment on the ground that Olmos lacked mental capacity when the trust was amended. The court holds there is no probable cause for Guillen's lawsuit. (On no-contest clauses, see supra page 163.) Does Guillen forfeit his beneficial interest under the trust instrument? See In re Lindstrom, 191 Cal. App. 3d 375, 236 Cal. Rptr. 376 (1987).

NOTE: DESIGNATION OF TESTAMENTARY TRUSTEE AS RECIPIENT OF LIFE INSURANCE

The unfunded revocable life insurance trust coupled with a will pour-over is one means of making a unified trust disposition of life insurance proceeds and testamentary assets. Another method works in the opposite direction. The will contains trust provisions, and the testator's life insurance policies are made payable "to the trustee named in my will." In recent years a number of states have enacted statutes authorizing such beneficiary designations. These statutes have in effect waived any Statute of Wills requirements that might otherwise be applicable to designation of a testamentary trustee as beneficiary of an insurance policy. However, the testamentary trust ordinarily remains a court trust, subject to the jurisdiction of the probate court. The statutes have also exempted the proceeds so payable from the claims of creditors and from inheritance tax (to the extent life insurance proceeds payable to a named beneficiary are exempt from taxation). The statutes often authorize a testamentary trustee to receive pension benefits as well as life insurance proceeds. For illustrative statutes see Cal. Prob. Code §§6320-6330 (1989); N.Y. Est., Powers & Trusts Law §13-3.3 (Supp. 1989).

What problems are encountered if the jurisdiction does not have a statute authorizing designation of a testamentary trustee as the beneficiary of insurance proceeds? See Haskell, Testamentary Trustee as Insurance Beneficiary: An Estate Planning Gimmick, 41 N.Y.U.L. Rev. 566 (1966); Note, The Testamentary Life Insurance Trust, 51 Minn. L. Rev. 118 (1967).

ESTATE PLANNING PROBLEM

Howard Brown is married to Wendy Brown, and they have three minor children (see supra pages 59-69). Howard's life insurance policies name Wendy as primary beneficiary. If Wendy predeceases him, Howard wants the proceeds to go to his sister-in-law, Lucy Lipman, to be held in trust for the benefit of Howard's three minor children, with the children receiving the principal when the youngest child reaches 22 (see testamentary trust set forth on pages 489-494). Which of the following plans do you recommend to carry out Howard's wishes?

Plan A (payable to testamentary trust).   The proceeds of the policies are made payable to Wendy if she survives Howard. If Wendy does not survive Howard, the proceeds are made payable to a testamentary trustee. Thus the secondary beneficiary will be designated on the policies as "the trustee named in the Will of Howard Brown." Howard then executes a will devising his residuary estate to Wendy if she survives Howard; otherwise to his sister-in-law, Lucy, in trust for the Brown children (see will on pages 489-494).

Plan B (payable to inter vivos trust).   The proceeds of the policies are made payable to Wendy if she survives Howard. If Wendy does not survive Howard, the proceeds are payable to "Lucy Preston Lipman, trustee under the Howard Brown Revocable Trust, executed on (date)." Contemporaneously, Howard executes an unfunded revocable trust for the benefit of the Brown children, naming Lucy as trustee. Howard then executes a will devising his residuary estate to Wendy if she survives him; otherwise to "Lucy Preston Lipman, trustee under the Howard Brown Revocable Trust, executed on (date)."

3. Use of Revocable Trusts in Estate Planning

a. Introduction

A revocable trust can be created by a declaration of trust, whereby the settlor becomes the trustee of the trust property. In the trust instrument, the settlor should name a successor trustee to take over the trusteeship upon the settlor's death or incompetency. Where the trust is to end on the settlor's death, and the trust is merely a means of avoiding probate, the death beneficiary should ordinarily be named successor trustee. At the settlor's death, the successor trustee automatically takes over and distributes the property to the trust beneficiaries. A revocable declaration of trust was involved in Farkas v. Williams, supra page 495.

A revocable trust can also be created by a deed of trust, naming a third party as trustee. The settlor can be co-trustee, if desired. A revocable trust can be funded, as in State Street Bank & Trust Co. v. Reiser, supra page 504, where the settlor transferred his stock to the trust; or the trust can be unfunded, as in Clymer v. Mayo, supra page 520.

The terms of a revocable trust may call for distribution of the trust assets at the settlor's death. Or they may direct that the assets are to be poured over at the settlor's death to some preexisting trust (such as an irrevocable or testamentary trust created by the settlor or by someone else). Or the revocable trust may provide the "main vehicle" for the disposition of the settlor's estate, either outright or in further trust after his death; assets in the settlor's probate estate can be poured over into the revocable trust to bring about a uniform disposition of the settlor's assets. In fact, if unified control of assets is desired during life, the settlor can change all the beneficiary designations on the settlor's nonprobate assets to make them payable to the revocable trust and also execute a will pouring over all probate assets to the revocable trust. After doing this, the settlor has consolidated under one document his dispositive plan for all his assets. He can later amend it as he could amend a will. Under this scheme, the revocable trust, with amendments, functions as a will did in the days before the proliferation of will substitutes.

It is rather ironic that a generation after the will began to lose its dominance because of the public's desire to avoid probate, the revocable trust has replaced it as a document with almost all the same attributes of a will, but without probate. Because we were unwilling to abolish probate or make it optional (see supra page 48), in giving people what they demanded, we paid a substantial cost in complexity. Perhaps we should think anew about a system of universal succession.

Now let us take a closer look at the advantages and disadvantages of revocable trusts. While the revocable trust may have advantages for many clients, for some it will be unsuitable.

b.   Consequences During Life of Settlor

(1)   Property Management by Fiduciary

A third-party trustee may be selected to manage a funded revocable trust. The settlor may want to be relieved of the burdens of financial management. Although a custodianship account for securities or other assets might be used for this purpose, a custodianship is an agency relationship and terminates on the disability or death of the principal. By contrast, a revocable trust continues during the settlor's incapacity and can provide for disposition of the trust assets at the settlor's death. The settlor can evaluate the trustee's performance and name a new trustee if not satisfied — an opportunity not available to the settlor's executor.

On the other hand, when property is put in trust, some inconveniences may arise upon sale or mortgage of the property. Third parties such as banks and transfer agents may require copies of the trust to determine whether the trustee has power to engage in the transaction. It is not as easy to conduct some transactions when title to the property is in a trustee as it is when title is in a private individual.

(2)   Dealing with Incompetency

Increased longevity has brought with it an increased chance that a person's last days (or perhaps months or years) may be spent in a state of mental or physical disability, requiring some form of fiduciary administration of the person's assets. Many persons are reluctant to have a spouse or parent formally adjudicated an incompetent. Moreover, in many states guardianship or conservatorship proceedings are cumbersome and expensive and invite unwanted publicity. When Groucho Marx was in his 80s, he was declared incompetent by a court, against his wishes. At the time he was living with a woman named Erin Fleming, who said he preferred her as his guardian if he had to have one. After a messy court fight, with the newspapers titillating readers with intimate family details, a relative of Marx was appointed guardian.

A revocable trust can be used in planning for the contingency of incapacity. The settlor may be co-trustee, with the trust instrument providing that either trustee alone may act on behalf of the trust. Or the trust instrument may provide that the other co-trustee shall act as sole trustee if the settlor becomes incompetent. An alternative to a revocable trust is a durable power of attorney, described infra page 538.

(3) Clarification of Title

A revocable trust is useful in keeping separate and apart property that a husband or wife or both want not to be commingled with their other assets. A husband and wife, for example, may want to establish separate revocable trusts of property each brings to the marriage or acquires by inheritance. This may prevent ambiguities of ownership from developing later, with consequent problems upon divorce or death.

(4) Income and Gift Taxes

Under the federal income, gift, and estate taxes, assets in a revocable trust are treated as still owned by the settlor. When the revocable trust is created, it is not treated as a completed gift to the beneficiaries under the federal gift tax (see infra page 940). Because of the retained power to revoke, trust income is taxable to the settlor regardless of to whom it is paid. Internal Revenue Code of 1986 §676(a). There are no federal tax advantages in creating a revocable trust.

c. Consequences at Death of Settlor: Avoidance of Probate

(1) Costs

Assets transferred during life to a revocable trust avoid probate because legal title to the assets passes to the trustee, and there is no need to change the title to the trust assets by probate administration on the settlor's death. Although trustee's fees may be payable if a third-party trustee is named, these fees will be considerably smaller than court costs, attorney's fees, and executor's commissions incurred in probate.

Against the savings in probate fees, certain other costs must be offset. Lawyers charge more to draft a revocable trust than a will, particularly when there are related pour-over documents. These documents are more complicated than a will. In addition, transferring title of assets to the trustee may entail certain costs, for example, stock transfer fees.

(2) Delays

In an estate administration, the assets may be in the executor's possession and control for several months or years; under a revocable trust continuing after the settlor's death, income and even principal can be disbursed to the beneficiaries relatively promptly. In some states, executors (viewed as temporary "caretakers") are restricted to purchasing very safe investments. On the other hand, trustees are viewed as managers governed only by the prudent investor rule. Because rules governing trustees are more liberal than rules applicable to executors, it is usually simpler for a trustee rather than an executor to deal with an ongoing business in the form of a partnership or sole proprietorship, and for a trustee to exercise options, borrow money, and participate in reorganizations.

(3)   Creditors

In probate a short-term statute of limitations is applicable to creditors (see supra pages 39-47). If creditors do not file claims within (usually) four months of the issuance of letters testamentary, the creditors are forever barred. There is no short-term statute of limitations applicable to revocable trusts; the limitations period is the normal one applicable to the particular claim. Where it is important to cut off the rights of creditors — as might be true with professionals such as doctors or lawyers where the statute of limitations on malpractice runs from discovery — probate holds an advantage over the revocable trust. On creditors' rights against revocable trusts, see State Street Bank & Trust Co. v. Reiser, supra page 504.

(4)   Publicity

A will is a public record, open to disappointed heirs, newspaper reporters, and the just plain curious. Any inventory of property and the named beneficiaries are there for all the world to see. An inter vivos trust is not recorded in a public place. The identity and amount of the settlor's property and the names of the beneficiaries need not be disclosed to any public officials except the tax authorities (whose records are private). Hence, revocable trusts are especially attractive to persons desiring secrecy. Such persons include personalities trying to keep out of the tabloids and persons of great wealth who fear kidnapping or other victimization of their beneficiaries or theft of their art collections, jewels, or other property. For example, in In re Estate of Hearst, 67 Cal. App. 3d 777, 136 Cal. Rptr. 821 (1977), William Randolph Hearst had created a testamentary trust to care for his descendants and relatives. After Patty Hearst was kidnapped by the Symbionese Liberation Army, the trustees asked the court to cut off public access to the probate files in Hearst's estate, fearing that radicals would find hitherto unnoticed members of the family and the location of their homes and properties. The court agreed to restrict public access while the Hearst family was in danger of attack. If W.R. Hearst had created a funded revocable trust, the family records would have been kept private.

(5)   Ancillary Probate

If the settlor owns real property located outside the domiciliary state, any will passing title to that property must be probated in the state where the land is located. To avoid ancillary probate, which may be cumbersome and expensive, land in another state can be transferred to a revocable inter vivos trust. Through this device, title to the land is changed to the trustee during the owner's life.

(6)   Avoiding Restrictions Protecting Family Members

In many states the surviving spouse is given by statute an elective share in the decedent's probate estate only. The elective share does not extend — as it does under the augmented estate concept of the Uniform Probate Code — to revocable trusts created by the decedent spouse. Courts in most of these jurisdictions, however, have permitted the surviving spouse to reach the assets in a revocable trust under varying circumstances. See supra pages 393-402. In a particular jurisdiction the law might permit a funded revocable trust to defeat a spouse's elective share in certain circumstances.

A funded revocable trust may be used to put assets beyond the reach of an illegitimate child, protected by a pretermission statute, whom the client does not wish to mention in his will. Pretermission statutes apply only to probate property. See supra page 428.

A funded revocable trust may be used to avoid the need to pay a family allowance (supra page 374). The family allowance during probate administration is not available from a revocable trust.

(7)   Avoiding Restrictions on Testamentary Trusts

As a general rule, the settlor of an inter vivos trust of personal property may choose the state law that is to govern the trust. (If a trust asset is land, the law of the state where the land is located governs.) The settlor may choose the law of the domicile of the settlor or of the beneficiaries, or the law of the state where the trust is administered. A testator may not have this freedom of choice. Many states apply the law of the settlor's domicile to a testamentary trust, because it was created by a will probated in that state, regardless of the testator's intent that the law of another state apply. In many states a nondomiciliary bank cannot serve as testamentary trustee under the will of a testator who was a domiciliary of the state. By contrast, the settlor of an inter vivos trust can name as trustee a bank in another state, perhaps the state where the beneficiaries live. The settlor of an inter vivos trust can create the trust in a state that has the most permissive period of perpetuities[44] or that permits spendthrift trusts if the domiciliary state does not.

---

44. Delaware, South Dakota, and Wisconsin have abolished the application of the common law Rule against Perpetuities to trusts. In South Dakota and Wisconsin a trust can endure indefinitely if the trustee has a power of sale. See infra page 835. In Delaware a trust must terminate after 110 years. See infra page 836. For the generation-skipping transfer tax advantages of creating a trust to endure as long as perpetuities law allows, see infra page 1029.

Uniform Probate Code §2-602 changes the old law and provides that the testator may select the state law to govern the meaning and legal effect of his will, unless that law is contrary to the domiciliary state's law protecting the surviving spouse or any other public policy of the domiciliary state. This provision aligns testamentary choice of law rules with those generally used for inter vivos trusts, and, where adopted, it lessens the need to create an inter vivos trust to achieve some benefit available in some other state. For a comprehensive discussion of choice-of-law rules applicable to trusts, see Report, Legal Problems in Controlling Devolution of Property Under Multi-State Trusts and Relevant Varying Situs Rules of Multiple Jurisdictions, 18 Real Prop., Prob. & Tr. J. 331 (1983).

(8) Lack of Certainty in the Law

Where a revocable trust is used as a substitute for a will, the law may be more uncertain in solving a problem that arises than it would be in case of a will. Wills rules developed over the centuries — for dealing with divorce, adoption, lapse, ademption, simultaneous death, apportionment of death taxes, and creditor's rights — may or may not be applicable to revocable trusts. Most of these issues can be solved by appropriate drafting if the drafter is awake to the problems. See supra pages 302-304.

(9) Avoiding Will Contests

A revocable trust, like a will, can be contested for lack of mental capacity and undue influence. In practice, however, it is more difficult to set aside a revocable trust than a will on these grounds. (Can you see why?) If a will contest is foreseen, creating a revocable trust of the client's assets may be advisable.

(10) Estate Taxation

As mentioned above, there are no federal tax advantages to a revocable trust. The assets of a revocable trust are included in the gross estate of the settlor under §2038 of the Internal Revenue Code of 1986. See infra page 979.

(11) Controlling Surviving Spouse's Disposition

When one spouse wants some assurance that the surviving spouse's property will be disposed of in accordance with a mutual estate plan, both spouses can create a revocable trust of their property — to become irrevocable upon the death of one spouse. The trust may provide, for example, that all the income shall be payable to the surviving spouse, and upon the surviving spouse's death the trust principal shall be divided equally between the husband's son and the wife's daughter by prior marriages. This use of the revocable trust may be especially attractive in second marriages. But — since the surviving spouse may make a gift of the remainder interest in her property upon the death of the first spouse — the tax consequences of a co-settled revocable trust must be carefully examined. See supra pages 416-418; Johanson, Revocable Trusts and Community Property: The Substantive Problems, 47 Tex. L. Rev. 537 (1969); Johanson, Revocable Trusts, Widow's Election Wills, and Community Property: The Tax Problems, 47 Tex. L. Rev. 1247 (1969).

NOTE: DURABLE POWER OF ATTORNEY

The durable power of attorney, like the revocable trust, is useful in planning for incapacity. Unlike an ordinary power of attorney, which terminates on the incapacity of the principal, a durable power continues throughout the incapacity of the principal until the principal dies. A durable power is permitted by Uniform Probate Code §§5-501 to 5-505 and by statutes in a large majority of states. See also Uniform Durable Power of Attorney Act (1983). Some specific language is required in the instrument creating the durable power expressing the intent of the principal that the power not terminate upon incapacity. The Uniform Probate Code permits the durable power to arise upon incapacity (a "springing" power). The durable power is a useful alternative to a trust for persons of modest means, but persons with substantial estates will find the trust much more flexible and useful.

A person may create a durable power authorizing the *agent* to create a revocable trust for the client upon the client's incompetency. For example, O may execute a durable power of attorney authorizing A, upon O's incompetency, to execute, on behalf of O, a trust for O's benefit, revocable by O, and also authorizing A to transfer O's assets to the trustee of the trust. The revocable trust may be drafted at the same time the power is executed and attached to the power.

See California Continuing Education of the Bar, Durable Power of Attorney Handbook (1989). See also durable powers for health care, supra page 264.

SECTION E. DISCRETIONARY TRUSTS

Trusts can be divided into mandatory trusts and discretionary trusts. In a *mandatory* trust, the trustee must distribute all the income. Thus:

Case 7.   O transfers property to X in trust to distribute all the income to A. This is a mandatory trust. The trustee has no discretion to choose either the persons who will receive the income or the amount to be distributed.

In a *discretionary* trust, the trustee has discretion over payment of either the income or the principal or both. Discretionary powers of a trustee may be drafted in limitless variety. The following hypothetical case illustrates discretionary powers over income:

Case 8.   O transfers property to X in trust to distribute all the income to one or more members of a group consisting of A, A's spouse, and A's children in such amounts as the trustee determines. This is a kind of discretionary trust known as a *spray* or *sprinkle* trust. The trustee must distribute all the income currently, but has discretion to determine who gets it and in what amount. If desired, the trustee could be given discretionary power to accumulate income and add it to principal.

With respect to the principal of the trust, the trust instrument may specify that the trustee has discretionary power to distribute principal to the income beneficiary. Such a power may be limited by a standard ("such amounts as are necessary to support my wife in the style of living to which she has become accustomed"), or the trustee may be given wide discretion.

Old Colony Trust Co. v. Rodd
Supreme Judicial Court of Massachusetts, 1970
356 Mass. 584, 254 N.E.2d 886

KIRK, J.   The respondent, a life beneficiary of a trust created by the will of George A. Sanderson, filed specifications of objection to the allowance of the fortieth and forty-first accounts of the petitioner as trustee under the will. After a hearing, the probate judge entered two decrees allowing the accounts. The respondent appeals, challenging the adequacy of the amounts paid to her by the trustee, the reasonableness of the trustee's accounting procedure, and the amount of its fees. Her attorney appeals from the denial of his petition to be allowed counsel fees from the trust assets.

Item 8 of Sanderson's will directed the trustee to pay over during the lives of designated beneficiaries

such part of the income or principal as may be necessary in its judgment for the comfortable support of any one or more of said persons, provided that in the judgment of said trustee any one or more of said persons shall need assistance and shall be worthy of the same, it being my intention

hereby to carry out as far as possible the wishes of my wife's father . . .
as expressed to me on many occasions, namely, that he wished to see to
the comfortable support and maintenance of his descendants.

The life beneficiaries of the fund were named persons (descendants of
the testator's wife's father) "and the children or grandchildren of any
of the above named persons who may be living at the time of my
decease and born prior to my decease" with one named exception, not
here material. Item 8 further directed the trustee, at the death of the
last survivor of the life beneficiaries, to transfer free of all trusts
whatever remained of the fund "in such proportions as said trustee will
decide will accomplish the most good, unto such charities in said Boston,
said Berlin [in Massachusetts] . . . and Kingston [in Rhode Island] . . .
as said trustee shall select."

We summarize the report of material facts made by the judge. The
periods covered by the contested accounts are from November, 1963,
through November, 1965. The book value of the trust, comprised of
securities, is approximately $220,000, plus $30,000 in accumulated
income to which a further accumulation of $3,500 in unexpended
income was added during the accounting periods under consideration.
The market value of the securities is approximately $423,000. During
the accounting periods there were fifteen potential beneficiaries of the
trust, three of whom were over eighty years of age, two between seventy-
five and eighty, five between sixty and seventy-five, and the remaining
five between forty and sixty. The trustee each year sent a questionnaire
to each potential beneficiary in order to determine which if any of
them required assistance. In instances where answers to the questionnaire were incomplete, the trustee made no further inquiry of the
applicant in order to make an accurate determination of his net worth.
The total paid to ten beneficiaries who requested assistance was $7,836
for the fortieth accounting period and $10,850 for the next period.
One of the beneficiaries, who died during the accounting periods, who
owned a home without a mortgage and had no other assets, was paid
$100 a month, and $1,100 for hospital and medical expenses. Two
other elderly beneficiaries, with incomes of $2,540 and $3,000, received
monthly payments of from $35 to $50. Another elderly beneficiary,
with an annual income of $1,985, received $50 a month plus $752.70
for the payment of medical bills. Two other beneficiaries had medical
and dental bills paid. An army colonel, fifty years of age, married, and
stationed in Europe, with an annual salary of $13,800, exclusive of
allowances, received two payments of $500 toward the educational
expenses of one of his two daughters. A married woman, age forty-six,
whose husband's salary was $10,000 a year, received $500 and $1,500,
in the fortieth and forty-first accounting periods, respectively, toward
the educational expenses of her two children, seventeen and eighteen

years of age. Another married woman, age forty-five, whose husband, a college professor, earned an annual salary of $16,500, received $500 and $1,250 in the fortieth and forty-first accounting periods, respectively, for educational expenses of her two children sixteen and eighteen years of age.

The respondent, age forty-seven, is single, with no dependents. She has no resources other than her salary. During the fortieth accounting period she was employed full time, and earned a gross salary of $4,625. The trustee paid her Federal income taxes, various personal bills, and an allowance of $65 a month, for a total of $2,074. In the forty-first accounting period she earned $5,292. The trustee again paid her Federal income taxes and various personal bills. For the last seven months of the period, her allowance was raised to $115 a month; the total disbursement to her for the year was $2,131.

The trustee charged a fee of five percent of the income of the trust, and three-tenths of one percent of the principal.

1. The judge found no facts to support the respondent's objections to the trustee's accounting procedure, investment practice, or the amount of its fees. We agree. The trustee was not obliged to adhere strictly to the accounting form supplied by the Probate Court. General Laws c. 206, §2, requires only a reasonable and orderly statement of the account, and does not require rigid adherence to any method of accounting. Hutchinson v. King, 339 Mass. 41, 157 N.E.2d 525. The respondent also argues that the trustee's filing of the two accounts at the same time, some five months after the close of the forty-first accounting period, violated G.L. c. 206, §1. That section provides that a trustee "shall render an account . . . at least once a year . . . until his trust is fulfilled; but the court may at his request excuse him from rendering an account in any year, if satisfied that it is not necessary or expedient that it should be rendered." In allowing the accounts, the probate judge impliedly found that it was not "necessary or expedient" for the accounts to be filed separately each year. At the most, the failure to file timely was a "mere technical breach" (Attorney Gen. v. Olson, 346 Mass. 190, 195, 191 N.E.2d 132) and done without objection at the time by any beneficiary. See Newhall, Settlement of Estates (4th ed.) §435. Finally, the fees allowed the trustee cannot be said to be unreasonable merely because they are apportioned between income and principal. Such apportionment is expressly permitted by G.L. c. 206, §16. See Old Colony Trust Co. v. Townsend, 324 Mass. 298, 85 N.E.2d 784.

2. The judge found that the "method employed by the trustee in determining the amount of assistance required in each case to attain 'comfortable support and maintenance' was superficial. And having in mind the intent of the settlor, the amounts allocated not only to the respondent but to others of the beneficiaries were parsimonious." With

these observations we emphatically agree. The ultimate conclusion of the judge was, "However, the trustee was here given broad discretion and I do not quite find that it has been abused."

This court recently said that in exercising a power of this sort a trustee is "unquestionably under an obligation to give serious and responsible consideration both as to the propriety of the amounts and as to their consistency with the terms and purposes of the trust." Holyoke Natl. Bank v. Wilson, 350 Mass. 223, 227, 214 N.E.2d 42, 45. A court of equity may control a trustee in the exercise of a fiduciary discretion if it fails to observe standards of judgment apparent from the applicable instrument. Copp v. Worcester County Natl. Bank, 347 Mass. 548, 551, 199 N.E.2d 200. Old Colony Trust Co. v. Silliman, 352 Mass. 6, 223 N.E.2d 504. It is our view that, whether due to misuse of discretion or to misconception of the purpose of the trust on the part of the trustee, several of the intended primary beneficiaries of the trust are not receiving that which the settlor intended they should receive and which the trustee has the means to provide: "comfortable support and maintenance." The settlor by will expressed his intention in terms that imported a deep sense of personal obligation to fulfill the wishes of another. By providing for access to principal he provided means "to carry out as far as possible" those wishes. It is inferable that the persons who could be benefited have long since been identified and that with the passing years their number has diminished and henceforth will diminish rapidly. At the same time it is obvious that the corpus of the trust has grown. Inevitably the remainder will go to charities unspecified and unknown to anyone, except, possibly, the trustee. It is clear from the will that the gift of the remainder was of minor significance. And yet it would appear that the trustee regards the disposition of the remainder as the dominant purpose of the trust. The trustee has not only kept the principal inviolate but has accumulated and retained over $30,000 in income. The trustee justifies this course as reasonable and prudent in light of rising medical costs and the advancing age of the beneficiaries. However that may be, the fact remains that the book value of the trust is $220,000 and the market value, at the time of the judge's findings, double that amount. The prospect of illness in old age does not warrant a persistent policy of niggardliness toward individuals for whose comfortable support in life the trust has been established. The payments made to the respondent and several other beneficiaries, viewed in light of their assets and needs, when measured against the assets of the trust show that little consideration has been given to the "comfortable support" of the beneficiaries. Compare Holyoke Natl. Bank v. Wilson, 350 Mass. 223, 214 N.E.2d 42.

Another manifestation of the trustee's indifference to its "obligation to give serious and responsible consideration both as to the propriety of the amounts and as to their consistency with the terms and purposes of the trust" is the payment, noted above, of sums to beneficiaries to assist in the education of their children. In each of the three cases the family income was in excess of $10,000. In each case, laudable though the purpose may have been, the contribution, strictly speaking, was not for "comfortable support" nor was the actual beneficiary a designated beneficiary. Homans v. Foster, 232 Mass. 4, 6, 121 N.E. 417; Parker v. Lloyd, 321 Mass. 126, 134, 71 N.E.2d 889. See Boston Safe Deposit & Trust Co. v. Stebbins, 309 Mass. 282, 287, 34 N.E.2d 616, 148 A.L.R. 1036. In two of the three cases referred to, the amounts given for the education of nonbeneficiaries was greater than one half of the amount granted to the respondent for "comfortable support." The respondent asked that the payments made to her as noted in the fortieth and forty-first accounts be increased by at least fifteen percent. We think that the request is a modest one.

3. We do not reverse the decrees. Comfort cannot be retroactively given. Our order is that all accounts of the trustee, subsequent to the forty-first account under Item 8 of the will of George A. Sanderson, be so prepared or, if already prepared, be so modified to reflect a trusteeship that is neither superficial in its administration nor parsimonious in its spirit.

4. We think that the probate judge, upon further proceedings, might with complete propriety allow reasonable counsel fees for the respondent's attorney payable from the trust principal. We leave the matter entirely to his discretion.

5. The decrees are affirmed. The case is remanded to the Probate Court for further proceedings consistent with this opinion.

So ordered.

NOTES AND QUESTIONS

1. Several of the directors of the Old Colony Trust Co. in 1964 were also directors or trustees of various charities in Boston and New England. Did Old Colony have a conflict of interest in administering the Sanderson trust? If so, what should have been done about it?

Why is the trustee's natural tendency to favor the remaindermen over the life tenant, to be conservative in paying out income or principal?

2. If the trustee has simple discretion unqualified by the adjective "sole" or the like, the courts will not substitute their judgment for that of the trustee as long as the trustee "acts not only in good faith and from proper motives, but also within the bounds of a reasonable judgment." 3 A. Scott, Trusts, §187 (W. Fratcher 4th ed. 1988). When the instrument purports to free the trustee from some or all of these limitations, problems in construction arise. At one extreme are instru-

ments that purport to give unlimited discretionary power to the trustee. But a discretionary power to be exercised "in the trustee's absolute and uncontrolled discretion" is not in fact absolute. As Judge Learned Hand remarked, "[N]o language, however strong, will entirely remove any power held in trust from the reach of a court of equity. After allowance has been made for every possible factor which could rationally enter into the trustee's decision, if it appears that he has utterly disregarded the interests of the beneficiary, the Court will intervene. Indeed were that not true, the power would not be held in trust at all; the language would be no more than a precatory admonition." Stix v. Commissioner, 152 F.2d 562, 563 (2d Cir. 1945).

What, then, are the limitations on the trustee's freedom when the trustee has "absolute and uncontrolled discretion"? All agree that the trustee cannot refuse to exercise discretion; the trustee must decide, even though the decision may be to do nothing. Beyond that limitation, there is disagreement. Professor Scott argued for a subjective standard, emphasizing the trustee's "good faith" and proper motives and dispensing with the requirement of reasonableness. He suggested, and the Restatement for which he was the chief reporter adopted, a standard of whether the trustee has acted "in that state of mind in which it was contemplated by the settlor that he should act." 3 A. Scott, supra; 1 Restatement (Second) of Trusts §187, Comment j (1959). Professor Halbach has argued that there is little authority to support the Restatement position that reasonableness is not required. "It is extremely doubtful," he wrote, "that a court would refrain from interfering with an unreasonable exercise of an 'absolute discretion' especially when the settlor has provided a standard, such as support, against which reasonableness may readily be measured." Halbach, Problems of Discretion in Discretionary Trusts, 61 Colum. L. Rev. 1425, 1432 (1961). Some courts, relying on the Restatement good faith standard, declare that the trustee must not act arbitrarily or capriciously, seemingly bringing in a reasonableness test under the guise of other words. Other courts apply a reasonableness test even when the discretion is "absolute." In the final analysis it appears that the difference between simple discretion and "absolute" discretion is one of degree and that the trustee's action must not only be in good faith but also to some extent reasonable, with more elasticity in the concept of reasonableness the greater the discretion given.

3. In his study of discretionary trusts, Professor Halbach found that the most troublesome source of litigation was the question of whether the trustee may consider the other resources of the beneficiary in determining whether to pay income or principal. This should be covered in the trust instrument, of course; if it is not, litigation may result. 1 Restatement (Second) of Trusts §128, Comment e (1959), provides:

By the terms of the trust it may be provided that the trustee shall pay or apply only so much of the income and principal or either as is necessary for the education or support of a beneficiary. In such a case the beneficiary cannot compel the trustee to pay to him or to apply for his benefit more than the trustee in the exercise of a sound discretion deems necessary for his education or support.

It is a question of interpretation whether the beneficiary is entitled to support out of the trust fund even though he has other resources. The inference is that he is so entitled. It is a question of interpretation whether the trustee is authorized to pay the funeral expenses of the beneficiary. The inference is that he is so authorized.

The Restatement position seems to be followed by a majority of courts, but the presumption that the settlor did not want the trustee to consider the beneficiary's other financial resources can be rebutted by rather slight evidence. These cases tend to be resolved on their own facts. See, e.g., In re Will of Flyer, 23 N.Y. 2d 579, 245 N.E.2d 718, 297 N.Y.S.2d 956, 41 A.L.R.3d 243 (1969).

4. Under the common law, income can be accumulated during the perpetuities period. A direction to accumulate income for a period in excess of lives in being plus 21 years is wholly void. In some states, statutes provide that only the excessive period of accumulation is void. See Restatement (Second) of Property, Donative Transfers §2.2 (1983).

NOTE: TAXATION OF GRANTOR TRUSTS

Where the settlor retains any interest in, or discretionary power over, the trust, care must be taken to avoid §§671-677 of the Internal Revenue Code of 1986. These sections define what are called *grantor trusts* — trusts in which the income is taxable to the settlor (grantor) because the settlor has retained substantial control and is deemed by the Code still to be the owner of the trust assets. We have noted earlier, at page 534, that trust income of a revocable trust is taxable to the settlor. A revocable trust is an example of a grantor trust. IRC §676. Now we treat grantor trusts where the settlor retains not a right to revoke the trust but some lesser power.

Under these sections of the Code there is a spousal attribution rule: A settlor is treated as holding any power or interest that is held by the settlor's spouse if the spouse is living with the settlor at the time the property is transferred into trust.

Where the grantor has a *reversionary interest* in either the corpus (or the income), and the reversionary interest at the inception of the trust exceeds 5 percent of the value of the corpus (or the income), the trust is a grantor trust. The income from the trust is taxable to the settlor. IRC §673. There is one important exception. The settlor is exempt from this rule if he or she creates a trust for a minor lineal descendant, who has the entire present interest, and the settlor retains a reversionary interest that will take effect only upon the death of the lineal descendant under the age of 21. IRC §673(b). The drafting moral here is clear: Except in the one case mentioned, do not leave a reversionary interest of any value in the settlor. (On how to avoid reversionary interests in the settlor, see Chapter 9 on Future Interests, particularly pages 648-649.)

Where the *settlor* or a *nonadverse party* — either as trustee or in any individual capacity — is given discretionary power over income or principal exercisable without the consent of an adverse party, the trust is a grantor trust. The income is taxable to the settlor. Internal Revenue Code §674. Thus:

> *Case 9.* O creates a trust, with herself and the First National Bank as co-trustees, to pay the income to O's two children in such amounts as the trustees shall determine or to accumulate it and, upon the death of O's two children, to distribute the principal to O's grandchildren then living. The trustees earn $70,000 income the first year, which the trustees distribute equally to O's two children. The $70,000 income is taxable to O, the settlor of a grantor trust, *and* O has made a gift to each child of $35,000. Each gift qualifies for a $10,000 annual gift tax exclusion, so O has made a net taxable gift to each child of $25,000. (On the gift tax exclusion, see infra page 946.) The amount received by O's children is not income to them because it is a gift from O.

There are two major exceptions to §674. The first is that a discretionary power to distribute, apportion, or accumulate income or to pay out corpus can be given to an *independent* trustee without adverse tax consequences to the settlor. Id. §674(c). If in Case 9 the First National Bank had been named sole trustee, the income would not be taxable to O. It is important to distinguish between an independent trustee and a nonadverse party. An independent trustee is one who is not related or subordinate to the settlor nor subservient to her wishes, whereas a nonadverse party is a person who is related, subordinate, or subservient to the settlor (e.g., the settlor's brother).

The second major exception to §674 permits (a) a power to be given the settlor or any trustee to distribute *corpus* pursuant to a "reasonably definite standard which is set forth in the trust instrument" or (b) a power to be given any trustee other than the settlor or the settlor's spouse to distribute *income* pursuant to a "reasonably definite external standard which is set forth in the trust instrument." Id. §§674(b)(5)(A), 674(d).

Another type of grantor trust is one where certain administrative powers can be exercised for the benefit of the settlor rather than for the beneficiaries of the trust. Generally, the settlor will be taxable on the income if there is a power exercisable by the settlor or a nonadverse party (1) to purchase trust assets for less than an adequate consideration, (2) to borrow trust assets without adequate security, (3) to vote or acquire stock in a corporation in which the settlor has a significant voting interest, or (4) to reacquire the trust corpus. Any of these indicia of dominion and control may be sufficient to tax the settlor on the trust income. See Internal Revenue Code §675.

The category of grantor trusts also includes a trust where the settlor, a nonadverse party, or an independent trustee has the power to distribute trust income to the settlor or the settlor's spouse. Id. §677(a). Under §677, income is not taxable to the settlor merely because the trustee may distribute it for the support of a beneficiary (other than the settlor's spouse) whom the settlor is legally obligated to support. If the trust property is in fact used to discharge the settlor's legal obligation, however, the settlor is taxable on the income to the extent income is actually so used. Id. §677(b). Thus:

> *Case 10.* *O* transfers property to the First National Bank in trust to pay the income in its discretion for the support of *O*'s children. Even though the trustee has discretion to use the income for the support of *O*'s minor children (thereby discharging *O*'s legal obligation of support), *O* is taxable on the income only to the extent it is actually so applied. If the income used for the support of *O*'s children is in excess of the amount *O* is legally obligated to provide, the excess income is not taxable to *O*.

In Case 10, a provision could be inserted in the trust instrument providing that any distributions by the trustee would not discharge the settlor's legal obligation of support. Such a provision would prevent taxation of the income to the settlor and would not, as a practical matter, interfere with any trust distribution by the trustee.

Any lawyer creating an inter vivos trust should pay close attention to §§671-677 of the Internal Revenue Code and the relevant regulations if the settlor desires to escape taxation on the income. Also it should be kept in mind that although the income and estate and gift taxes are not exactly parallel, if the settlor is treated as owner and taxable on the income of the trust assets there is a good chance that the trust assets will be subject to estate taxation at the settlor's death. See discussion of §§2036 and 2038 at pages 968-981 infra. For a client who wants to avoid income and estate taxation, the lawyer will want to draft a trust that skirts the reach of both the income and estate tax sections of the Code and leaves the client in a safe harbor.

SECTION F. SPENDTHRIFT TRUSTS

> The law, in its majestic equality,
> forbids the rich as well as the poor
> to sleep under bridges, to beg
> in the streets, and to steal bread.
>
> ANATOLE FRANCE
> *Le Lys Rouge, ch. 7 (1894)*

The rich have — at least in Anglo-American history — continually sought ways to secure their property to their children and grandchildren so that it remains in the family safe from the accidents of fortune and bad management. The fee tail and later the strict settlement were the standard devices used in England to keep land in the family. The fee tail was early abolished in this country and the strict settlement never took hold here. The spendthrift trust, an American invention not recognized in England, is their ideological descendant.

In a spendthrift trust, the beneficiaries cannot voluntarily alienate their interests nor can their creditors reach their interests. It is created by imposing a *disabling restraint* upon the beneficiaries and their creditors. Thus:

> *Case 11.* *T* devises property to *X* in trust to pay the income to *A* for life and upon *A*'s death to distribute the property to *A*'s children. A clause in the trust provides that *A* may not transfer his life estate, and it may not be reached by *A*'s creditors (see the spendthrift clause, numbered (8), in Shelley v. Shelley, *infra*, at page 550). By this trust *A* is given a stream of income that *A* cannot alienate and his creditors cannot reach.

The two decisions largely responsible for the spendthrift trust doctrine are Nichols v. Eaton, 91 U.S. 716 (1875), and Broadway National Bank v. Adams, 133 Mass. 170 (1882). In Nichols v. Eaton, Justice Miller inserted an elaborate dictum upholding spendthrift trusts. Reflecting the spirit "of individualism, at least of individualism for the man of property,"[45] so attractive to judges who grew up in America's pioneer period, Justice Miller reasoned: "Why a parent, or one who loves another, and wishes to use his own property in securing the object of his affection, as far as property can do it, from the ills of life, the vicissitudes of fortune, and even his own improvidence, or incapacity for self-protection, should not be permitted to do so, is not readily perceived." 91 U.S. at 727. In Broadway National Bank v. Adams, the Massachusetts court upheld the spendthrift trust.

John Chipman Gray was so outraged at the introduction of spendthrift trusts that he was moved to write his Restraints on Alienation, first

---

45. E. Griswold, Spendthrift Trusts §29(3), at 26 (2d ed. 1947).

published in 1883, in refutation of Nichols v. Eaton. He said, "If there is one sentiment, therefore, which it would seem to be the part of all authority, and particularly of all judges, to fortify, it is the duty of keeping one's promises and paying one's debts." J. Gray, Restraints on the Alienation of Property iii (2d ed. 1895). He also suggested that the judges who aided in the introduction of spendthrift trusts were influenced, unconsciously perhaps, "by that spirit, in short, of paternalism, which is the fundamental essence alike of spendthrift trusts and of socialism." Id. at ix. In spite of Gray's strictures, by the time the second edition of his book was published, the battle was lost. "State after State has given in its adhesion to the new doctrine . . . and yet I cannot recant." Id. at iv-v. The spendthrift trust has today been recognized in almost all jurisdictions.

On the rise of the spendthrift trust in the United States, see Friedman, The Dynastic Trust, 73 Yale L.J. 547, 578-583 (1964).

QUESTIONS

1. A disabling restraint upon a legal life estate is void. Restatement (Second) of Property, Donative Transfers §4.1, Illustration 7 (1983). Thus in Case 11, if *O* had transferred property directly to *A* for life, with a clause that *A* may not alienate his life estate and his creditors may not reach it, the clause would be invalid as an unlawful restraint on alienation. Why, then, is a disabling restraint upon an equitable life estate *in trust* valid? Is it because a restraint on an equitable life estate does not make the specific assets held in trust inalienable (the trustee may transfer the fee simple title to them), whereas a disabling restraint on a legal life estate makes inalienable the specific asset in which the life estate is held? See Bushman, The (In)Validity of Spendthrift Trusts, 47 Or. L. Rev. 304 (1968); Wicker, Spendthrift Trusts, 10 Gonz. L. Rev. 1 (1974); Note, A Rationale for the Spendthrift Trust, 64 Colum. L. Rev. 1323 (1964).

2. What is the impact of the symbolism of the spendthrift trust upon a wage earner's sense of equal protection of the laws? Should judges have a special sensitivity to the symbolic impact of the spendthrift trust on a wage-earner's sense of first-class citizenship? See Karst, "A Discrimination so Trivial": A Note on Law and the Symbolism of Women's Dependency, 35 Ohio St. L.J. 546, 549-554 (1974).

Shelley v. Shelley
Supreme Court of Oregon, 1960
223 Or. 328, 354 P.2d 282

O'CONNELL, J.   This is an appeal from a decree of the circuit court for Multnomah county establishing the rights of the parties to the income and corpus of a trust of which the defendant, the United States National Bank of Portland (Oregon) is trustee.

The assignments of error are directed at the trial court's interpretation of the trust. The trust involved in this suit was created by Hugh T. Shelley. The pertinent parts of the trust are as follows:

> Ninth: All of the rest, residue, and remainder of my said estate, . . . I give, devise, and bequeath to the United States National Bank of Portland (Oregon), in trust, . . . upon the following trust: . . .
>
> (2) I direct that, all income derived from my trust estate be paid to my wife, Gertrude R. Shelley, as long as she lives, said income to be paid to her at intervals of not less than three (3) months apart; . . .
>
> (4) If my said wife, Gertrude R. Shelley, shall predecease me, and my said son is then alive, or upon my wife's death after my death and my son being alive, it is my desire, and I direct, that, the United States National Bank of Portland (Oregon), as trustee, shall continue this estate in trust and pay all income derived therefrom to my son, Grant R. Shelley, as long as he lives, said income to be paid to him at intervals not less than three (3) months apart; Provided, Further, That when my son, Grant R. Shelley, arrives at the age of thirty (30) years, my trustee may then, or at any time thereafter, and from time to time, distribute to my son absolutely and as his own all or any part of the principal of said trust fund that it may then or from time to time thereafter deem him capable of successfully investing without the restraints of this trust; Provided, However, That such disbursements of principal of said trust so made to my son after he attains the age of thirty (30) years shall be first approved in writing by either one of my brothers-in-law, that is: Dr. Frank L. Ralston, now of Walla Walla, Washington, or Russell C. Ralston, now of Palo Alto, California, if either of them is then living, but if neither of them is then living, then my trustee is authorized to make said disbursements of principal to my son in the exercise of its sole and absolute judgment and discretion; Provided, Further, That, said trust shall continue as to all or any part of the undistributed portion of the principal thereof to and until the death of my said son.
>
> (5) I further direct and authorize my trustee, from time to time (but only upon the written approval of my said wife if she be then living, otherwise in the exercise of my trustee's sole discretion) to make disbursements for the use and benefit of my son, Grant R. Shelley, or his children, in case of any emergency arising whereby unusual and extraordinary expenses are necessary for the proper support and care of my said son, or said children.
>
> (8) Each beneficiary hereunder is hereby restrained from alienating, anticipating, encumbering, or in any manner assigning his or her interest or estate, either in principal or income, and is without power so to do, nor shall such interest or estate be subject to his or her liabilities or obligations nor to judgment or other legal process, bankruptcy proceedings or claims of creditors or others.

The principal question on appeal is whether the income and corpus of the Shelley trust can be reached by Grant Shelley's former wives and his children.

Grant Shelley was first married to defendant, Patricia C. Shelley. Two children were born of this marriage. Patricia divorced Grant in 1951. The decree required Grant to pay support money for the children; the decree did not call for the payment of alimony. Thereafter, Grant married the plaintiff, Betty Shelley. Two children were born of this marriage. The plaintiff obtained a divorce from Grant in August, 1958. The decree in this latter suit required the payment of both alimony and a designated monthly amount for the support of the children of that marriage.

Some time after his marriage to the plaintiff, Grant disappeared and his whereabouts was not known at the time of this suit. The defendant bank, as trustee, invested the trust assets in securities which are now held by it, together with undisbursed income from the trust estate. The plaintiff obtained an injunction restraining the defendant trustee from disbursing any of the trust assets. Patricia Shelley brought a garnishment proceeding against the trustee, by which she sought to subject the trust to the claim for support money provided for in the 1951 decree of divorce. . . .

The defendant bank finally brought a bill of interpleader tendering to the court for disbursement all of the funds held in trust, praying for an order establishing the respective rights of the interpleaded parties to the trust assets.

The trial court entered a decree subjecting the accrued income of the trust to the existing claims of the plaintiff and Patricia Shelley; subjecting future income of the trust to the periodic obligations subsequently accruing by the terms of the decrees in the divorce proceedings brought by plaintiff and Patricia Shelley; and further providing that in the event that the trust income was insufficient to satisfy such claims, the corpus of the trust was subject to invasion.

We shall first consider that part of the decree which subjects the income of the trust to the claims of plaintiff and of defendant, Patricia Shelley. The trust places no conditions upon the right of Grant Shelley to receive the trust income during his lifetime. Therefore, plaintiff and Patricia Shelley may reach such income unless the spendthrift provision of the trust precludes them from doing so.

The validity of spendthrift trusts has been established by our former cases. . . . The question on this appeal is whether the spendthrift provision will be given effect to bar the claims of the beneficiary's children for support and the plaintiff's claim for alimony.

In Cogswell v. Cogswell et al., 1946, 178 Or. 417, 167 P.2d 324, 335, we held that the spendthrift provision of a trust is not effective against the claims of the beneficiary's former wife for alimony and for support of the beneficiary's child. In that case the court adopted the rule stated in 1 Restatement, Trusts, §157, which reads in part as follows:

§157. Particular Classes of Claimants.

Although a trust is a spendthrift trust or trust for support, the interest of the beneficiary can be reached in satisfaction of an enforceable claim against the beneficiary,

(a) by the wife or child of the beneficiary for support, or by the wife for alimony.

The defendant bank concedes that the *Cogswell* case is controlling in the case at bar, but asks us to overrule it on the ground that it is inconsistent with our own cases recognizing the testator's privilege to dispose of his property as he pleases and, further, that it is inconsistent with various Oregon statutes expressing the same policy of free alienation. If we should accept the premise urged by the defendant bank, that a testator has an inviolable right to dispose of his property as he pleases subject only to legislative restriction, the conclusion is inevitable that the testator may create in a beneficiary an interest free from all claims, including those for support and alimony.

But the premise is not sound. The privilege of disposing of property is not absolute; it is hedged with various restrictions where there are policy considerations warranting the limitation. . . . Not all of these restrictions are imposed by statute. The rule against perpetuities, the rule against restraints on alienation, the refusal to recognize trusts for capricious purposes or for illegal purposes, or for any purpose contrary to public policy, are all instances of judge-made rules limiting the privilege of alienation. Many others could be recited. Griswold, Spendthrift Trusts (2d ed.) §553; Simes, Public Policy and the Dead Hand, passim; Scott, Control of Property by the Dead, 65 U. Pa. L. Rev. 527, 632 (1917). See also Nussbaum, Liberty of Testation, 23 A.B.A.J. 183 (1937); McMurray, Liberty of Testation and Some Modern Limitations Thereon, 14 Ill. L. Rev. 96 (1919); Keeton & Gower, Freedom of Testation in English Law, 20 Iowa L. Rev. 326 (1935). It is within the court's power to impose upon the privilege of disposing of property such restrictions as are consistent with its view of sound public policy, unless, of course, the legislature has expressed a contrary view. Our own statutes do not purport to deal with the specific question before us, that is as to whether there should be limitations on the owner's privilege to create a spendthrift trust. . . .

In holding that a spendthrift trust is subject to claims for alimony and support the court, in Cogswell v. Cogswell et al., supra, did not disclose the reasoning by which it reached its conclusion. This failure to examine the question of public policy in the area of spendthrift trusts is not unusual, for as Griswold, Spendthrift Trusts (2d ed.), p.634

points out in discussing the validity of spendthrift trusts, "examination [of public policy] has rarely, if ever, been attempted by the courts," which he admits that "it is obviously a matter difficult to approach and one about which dogmatic conclusions cannot be reached." But once having recognized the validity of spendthrift trusts, which we have and which conclusion defendant bank endorses, the more specific question of the validity of the restraint of such a trust as against the claims of children for support and of the beneficiary's former wife for alimony presents a narrower question of policy which, we believe, is easier to answer. The question is whether a person should be entitled to enjoy the benefits of a trust and at the same time refuse to pay the obligations arising out of his marriage.

We have no hesitation in declaring that public policy requires that the interest of the beneficiary of a trust should be subject to the claims for support of his children. . . . Certainly the defendant will accept the societal postulate that parents have the obligation to support their children. If we give effect to the spendthrift provision to bar the claims for support, we have the spectacle of a man enjoying the benefits of a trust immune from claims which are justly due, while the community pays for the support of his children. Wetmore v. Wetmore, 1896, 149 N.Y. 520, 44 N.E. 169, 33 L.R.A. 708. We do not believe that it is sound policy to use the welfare funds of this state in support of the beneficiary's children, while he stands behind the shield of immunity created by a spendthrift trust provision. To endorse such a policy and to permit the spectacle which we have described above would be to invite disrespect for the administration of justice. . . .

The justification for permitting a claim for alimony is, perhaps, not as clear. The adjustment of the economic interests of the parties to a divorce may depend upon a variety of factors, including the respective fault of the parties, the ability of the wife to support herself, the duration of the marriage, and other considerations. Whether alimony is to be granted and its amount are questions which are determined in light of these various interests. It is probably fair to say that the duties created by the marriage relation, at least as they are evaluated upon the termination of the marriage, are conceived of as more qualified than those arising out of the paternal relationship. On the theory that divorce terminates the husband's duty to support his former wife and that she stands in no better position than other creditors, some courts have held that the spendthrift provision insulates the beneficiary's interest in the trust from her claim. Lippincott v. Lippincott, 1944, 349 Pa. 501, 37 A.2d 741. Recognizing the difference in marital and parental duties suggested above, it has been held that a spendthrift trust is subject to the claims for the support of children but free from the claims of the former wife. Eaton v. Eaton, 1926, 82 N.H. 216, 132 A. 10, commented upon in 35 Yale L.J. 1025 (1926). . . . A majority of the cases, however, hold that a spendthrift provision will not bar a claim for alimony. . . .

As we have already mentioned, the case of Cogswell v. Cogswell, supra, is in accord with this latter view. We are of the opinion that the conclusion there reached should be affirmed. The duty of the husband to support his former wife should override the restriction called for by the spendthrift provision. The same reason advanced above for requiring the support of the beneficiary's children will, in many cases, be applicable to the claim of a divorced wife; if the beneficiary's interest cannot be reached, the state may be called upon to support her. . . .

We hold that the beneficiaries' interest in the income of the Shelley Trust is subject to the claims of the plaintiff for alimony and to the claims for the support of Grant Shelley's children as provided for under both decrees for divorce. These claims are not without limit. We adopt the view that such claimants may reach only that much of the income which the trial court deems reasonable under the circumstances, having in mind the respective needs of the husband and wife, the needs of the children, the amount of the trust income, the availability of the corpus for the various needs, and any other factors which are relevant in adjusting equitably the interests of the claimants and the beneficiary. Griswold, Spendthrift Trusts (2d Ed.) §339; 2 Scott on Trusts, §157.1; Note, 28 Va. L. Rev. 527 (1942). . . .

The question of the claimants' rights to reach the corpus of the trust involves other considerations. For the reasons heretofore stated, the beneficiary's interest in the corpus is not made immune from these claims. But, by the terms of the trust, the disbursement of the corpus is within the discretion of the trustee (or, in some instances subject to the approval of others), and, therefore, Grant Shelley's right to receive any part of the corpus does not arise until the trustee has exercised his discretion and has decided to invade the corpus. Until that time, the plaintiff and Patricia Shelley cannot reach the corpus of the trust because the beneficiary has no realizable interest in it. Mattison v. Mattison, 1909, 53 Or. 254, 100 P. 4, 133 Am. St. Rep. 829. It has been held that a discretionary trust for the "sole benefit" of the testator's son was enforceable by the son's destitute wife and children on the ground that the support of the son's family fell within the terms of the trust. Gardner v. O'Loughlin, 1912, 76 N.H. 481, 84 A. 935, 936. But, assuming without deciding that such an interpretation is reasonable, it has not been extended to a case where there has been a divorce and the wife has ceased to be a member of the family and, therefore, has ceased to be a beneficiary of the trust. Eaton v. Eaton, supra. There is nothing in the trust before us which would indicate the testator's intent to make the plaintiff, either directly or indirectly, the beneficiary of the trust. Patricia Shelley could not be regarded as a beneficiary because the decree under which she claims called only for the payment of support money for the children and not alimony. In some jurisdictions a creditor of the beneficiary of a discretionary trust may attach the potential interest of the beneficiary. Sand v. Beach, 1936, 270 N.Y. 281, 200 N.E. 821; Hamilton v. Drogo, 1926, 241 N.Y. 401, 150 N.E. 496; 214 App. Div. 819, 210 N.Y.S. 859, commented upon in 26 Colum. L. Rev. 776 (1926). See Griswold, Spendthrift Trusts (2d ed.), §§367, 368, 357, 2 Scott on Trusts, §155.1. There is no such procedure in Oregon available to the creditor. And at least with respect to the corpus, O.R.S. 29.175(2) makes the interest constituting the subject matter of the trust free from attachment. It follows that the decree of the lower court in making the corpus of the Shelley Trust subject to the plaintiff's claim for alimony was erroneous.

The claims for the support of Grant Shelley's children, provided for in the two divorce decrees, involve a different problem. The trust directed and authorized the trustee, in the exercise of its sole discretion upon the death of the settlor's wife, to make disbursements for the use and benefit not only of Grant Shelley, but also for his children. The disbursements were to be made "in case of any emergency arising whereby unusual and extraordinary expenses are necessary for the proper support and care of my said son, or said children." Here the children are named as beneficiaries of the trust and need not claim derivatively through their father. However, they are entitled to a share of the corpus only if, in the trustee's discretion, it is determined that an emergency exists. The defendant bank contends that the expenses of supporting Grant Shelley's children claimed in this case were for the usual and ordinary costs of support and do not, therefore, constitute "unusual and extraordinary expenses" within the meaning of the trust provision. It is contended that there was no "emergency" calling for "unusual and extraordinary expenses" because there was no proof of an unexpected occurrence or of an unexpected situation requiring immediate action. We disagree with defendant's interpretation. We construe the clause to include the circumstances involved here, i.e., where the children are deserted by their father and are in need of support. We think that the testator intended to provide that in the event that the income from the trust was not sufficient to cover disbursements for the support and care of either the son or his children an "emergency" had arisen and the corpus could then be invaded. The decree of the lower court would permit the corpus to be employed if the "assets in the hands of the Executor [trustee] and the income cash from said trust shall be insufficient to pay the obligations of Defendant Grant R. Shelley" to plaintiff and Patricia Shelley. The decree is too broad; first because, as we have already indicated, it improperly includes the plaintiff's claim for alimony; second, because it permits encroachment upon the corpus without reference to whether the trustee has exercised his discretion or whether there has been an emergency as contemplated by the testator.

It is to be noted that the children of Grant Shelley are not beneficiaries of the income of the trust; they may reach it only as persons having claims against the beneficiary, Grant Shelley. If, for example, Grant Shelley should decide to support his children out of assets other than income of the trust, the children would have no claim whatsoever against his interest in the trust. The decree, therefore, should have permitted an invasion of the corpus only if it was necessary to first reach the income under the circumstances just mentioned and such income was insufficient. And further, the decree should have made such corpus available only in the event of the trustee's exercise of discretion authorizing the disbursement for the support of the children under the emergency circumstances provided for in the trust. After the entry of such a decree, if the trustee should refuse to exercise his discretion, or if it is claimed that he exercised it unreasonably, relief may be sought in a court of equity by the children.

The decree of the lower court is affirmed and the cause remanded with directions to modify the decree in accordance with the views expressed in this opinion.

NOTES

1. The position taken in Shelley v. Shelley regarding the enforcement of judgments for child support and alimony represents the majority rule. See Restatement of Trusts (Second) §157 (1959); Baccardi v. White, 463 So. 2d 218 (Fla. 1985). Nonetheless, a substantial minority refuses to permit a spouse or children to reach a spendthrift trust to satisfy alimony or child support judgments. See In re Campbell's Trusts, 258 N.W.2d 856 (Minn. 1977); Martin v. Martin, 54 Ohio St. 2d 101, 374 N.E.2d 1384 (1978) (alimony); Note, Garnishment of Spendthrift Trusts for the Enforcement of Court Ordered Alimony or Child Support: A Public Policy Decision, 13 Fla. St. U.L. Rev. 433 (1985).

Besides spouses and children, a few other classes of claimants have usually been permitted to enforce a claim against the beneficiary of a spendthrift trust. For example, a person who has furnished necessary services or supplies can reach the trust interest. See In re Estate of Dodge, 281 N.W.2d 447 (Iowa 1979); 2A A. Scott, Trusts §157.2 (W. Fratcher 4th ed. 1987).

The United States or a state can reach the beneficiary's interest to satisfy a tax claim against the beneficiary. La Salle National Bank v. United States, 636 F. Supp. 874 (N.D. Ill. 1986); United States v. Riggs National Bank, 636 F. Supp. 172 (D.D.C. 1986) (upholding government levy in spite of a clause providing for forfeiture of the beneficiary's interest in case of any levy of execution).

2. In New York by statute all trusts are spendthrift trusts unless the settlor expressly makes the beneficiary's interest transferable. N.Y. Est., Powers & Trusts Law §7.1-5 (Supp. 1989).

New York also has a statute, originally adopted in 1830, providing that the beneficiary's creditors can reach that part of spendthrift trust income in excess of the amount needed for the support and education of the beneficiary. See N.Y. Est., Powers & Trusts Law §7-3.4 (1967). Several states copied this New York statute. In determining what is necessary for the support of the beneficiary and what is excess (reachable by creditors), courts developed a *station-in-life rule.* Creditors can reach only the amount in excess of what is needed to maintain the beneficiary in his station in life. The station-in-life rule rendered these excess-income statutes relatively useless to creditors. Spendthrift trusts are usually created only by persons of considerable wealth who have raised their children in substantial luxury. The accustomed manner of living of the child-beneficiary is likely to require the full income from the trust.[46]

In a few states a creditor is permitted to reach a certain percentage (usually between 10 and 30 percent) of the income of the spendthrift trust beneficiary in a garnishment proceeding ordinarily applicable to wage earners. See Cal. Code Civ. Proc. §709.010 (1989); 2A A. Scott, *supra,* §152.1. In several states dollar limits are placed on the amount that can be shielded in a spendthrift trust.

3. A beneficial interest in a spendthrift trust cannot be reached by creditors in bankruptcy. The Bankruptcy Act of 1978 provides that an

---

46. John Chipman Gray was even more scornful of the New York scheme than of spendthrift trusts.

> It may be said that, if the Courts have been wrong in tolerating spendthrift trusts, a remedy is to be found in the legislatures. If the remedy is like that applied in New York, it is, if not worse, more disgusting than the disease. . . . The Statutes of New York, as interpreted by the Courts, provide that the surplus of income given in trust beyond what is necessary for the education and support of the beneficiary shall be liable for his debts. . . . The Court takes into account that the debtor is "a gentleman of high social standing, whose associations are chiefly with men of leisure, and who is connected with a number of clubs," and that his income is not more than sufficient to maintain his position according to his education, habits, and associations.
>
> To say that whatever money is given to a man cannot be taken by his creditors is bad enough; at any rate, however, it is law for rich and poor alike; but to say that from a sum which creditors can reach one man, who has lived simply and plainly, can deduct but a small sum, while a large sum may be deducted by another man because he is "of high social standing" . . . is to descend to a depth of as shameless snobbishness as any into which the justice of a country was ever plunged.
> [J. Gray, Restraints on the Alienation of Property x-xi (2d ed. 1895).]

interest in a trust which is not alienable under local law does not pass to the trustee in bankruptcy. 11 U.S.C.A. §541(c)(2) (1982).

4. In a majority of jurisdictions, a disabling restraint may be imposed upon a remainder interest as well as an income interest in trust. If a disabling restraint is attached to the remainder in trust, the remainderman cannot transfer his interest by sale, gift, or devise. In re Estate of Vought, 25 N.Y.2d 163, 250 N.E.2d 343, 303 N.Y.S.2d 61 (1969).

In England, which does not permit restraints upon equitable interests, there is a lively auction market in remainders and reversions, put up for sale by persons who would rather have cash now than wait until the life beneficiary dies. See The New York Times, Mar. 6, 1978, §D, at 1, col. 2. Because spendthrift clauses are enforceable in the United States, no auction market for remainders or reversions has developed in this country.

5. A spendthrift trust cannot be set up by the settlor for the settlor's own benefit. The Restatement (Second) of Trusts §156 (1959) states the rule thus:

> (1) Where a person creates for his own benefit a trust with a provision restraining the voluntary or involuntary transfer of his interest, his transferee or creditors can reach his interest.
>
> (2) Where a person creates for his own benefit a trust for support or a discretionary trust, his transferee or creditors can reach the maximum amount which the trustee under the terms of the trust could pay to him or apply for his benefit.

Pension trusts of many types are rapidly increasing. The federal Employee Retirement Income Security Act (ERISA), 29 U.S.C.A. §1056(d)(1) (1982 & 1989 Supp.), requires that every plan covered by the act contain a spendthrift clause providing that "benefits provided under the plan may not be assigned or alienated." ERISA also provides that such benefits may be reached for child support, alimony, or marital property rights. Id. §1056(d)(3). The rights of creditors other than spouses and children are thus to be determined by the state law applicable to spendthrift trusts. If a pension trust is funded by the employer, a pension trust with a spendthrift clause is presumably treated the same as an ordinary spendthrift trust. On the other hand, if the employee makes all the contributions, as in a Keogh or I.R.A. plan, the trust is not normally protected by a spendthrift clause (see rule stated in first sentence of this Note). Nonetheless, some states have statutes specifically exempting private pension plans from contract creditors, regardless of whether they are funded by the employee, the employer, or both jointly. See Cal. Code Civ. Proc. §704.115(b) (1989); Sherman, Spendthrift Trusts and Employee Pensions: The Problem of Creditors' Rights, 55 Ind. L. Rev. 247 (1980); 2A A. Scott, supra, §157.1 at 200.

6.   A spendthrift clause should not be routinely inserted in every trust; it may have undesirable consequences. It may prevent the beneficiaries from later terminating the trust if they all desire to do so (see infra page 574). Also, if at some later date an income beneficiary desires to release the income, the beneficiary cannot do so. Howard v. Chapman, 101 Ill. App. 2d 135, 241 N.E.2d 492 (1968), is an illustration. In this case Levi Z. Leiter, the co-founder of the Marshall Field empire, created a spendthrift trust in 1904 for the benefit of his children and grandchildren. One of his children, Lady Suffolk, in the 1960s paid income taxes on a very large income. To reduce taxes, she executed assignments of her right to the income to members of her family. The assignments were held void.

In most states a restraint on involuntary alienation alone is invalid. A valid spendthrift trust must restrain both voluntary and involuntary alienation. In a few states courts have recognized a restraint that only prevents creditors from reaching the beneficiaries' interest. See Bank of New England v. Strandlund, 402 Mass. 707, 529 N.E.2d 394 (1988). In these states, if the restraint is only against voluntary alienation, a voluntary assignment to reduce taxes is possible.

NOTE: CREDITORS' RIGHTS IN SUPPORT TRUSTS AND DISCRETIONARY TRUSTS

A *support trust* is a trust that requires the trustee to make payments of income (or, if so specified, of principal too) to the beneficiary in an amount necessary for the education or support of the beneficiary in accordance with an ascertainable standard. A support trust is a gift of support to the beneficiary — whatever is required to support the beneficiary, no more, no less. Creditors of the beneficiary of a support trust cannot reach the beneficiary's interest, except suppliers of necessaries may recover through the beneficiary's right to support.

A *discretionary trust* gives the trustee discretion to pay over income (or principal) or to withhold it completely. The standard rule, followed in Shelley v. Shelley, is that courts cannot compel the trustee to exercise discretion (absent an improper motive or, perhaps, an unreasonable judgment). See Note 2, supra page 543.

Although a creditor cannot, by judicial order, compel the trustee of a discretionary trust to pay him, in some states the creditor can, by serving an order of execution on the trustee, prevent the trustee from paying the beneficiary before paying the creditor. The creditor thus can cut off the beneficiary's income from the trust fund even though the creditor does not benefit.

This principle was established in New York in Hamilton v. Drogo,

241 N.Y. 401, 150 N.E. 496 (1926), referred to in Shelley v. Shelley at page 555. Hamilton v. Drogo involved a discretionary trust established by the will of the dowager Duchess of Manchester to provide her spendthrift son, the ninth duke,[47] freedom from the travails of penury. Andrews, J., explained how the rule worked:

> We may not interfere with the discretion which the testatrix has vested in the trustee any more than her son may do so. Its judgment is final. But at least annually this judgment must be exercised. And if it is exercised in favor of the duke [the beneficiary], then there is due him the whole or such part of the income as the trustee may allot to him. After such allotment, he may compel its payment. At least for some appreciable time, however brief, the award must precede the delivery of the income he is to receive, and during that time the lien of the execution attaches.

Since the trustee is said to exercise discretion to pay the beneficiary at a moment in time before the property is transferred to the beneficiary, what acts constitute exercise of discretion? Crediting the beneficiary's account on the trustee's books or an oral or written declaration to the beneficiary may be sufficient acts to indicate the power has been exercised. After such exercise by the trustee, the creditor may seize the property awarded to the beneficiary while it remains in the hands of the trustee. See Canfield v. Security-First National Bank, 13 Cal. 2d 1, 87 P.2d 830 (1939); Note, What Amounts to an Exercise of Discretion in a Discretionary Trust?, 43 Iowa L. Rev. 626 (1958). It appears, however, that even this limited amount of protection given creditors can be circumvented by a provision in the trust instrument permitting the trustee in his discretion to pay money to third parties for the benefit of the beneficiary.

PROBLEMS

1.   *O* transfers property to *X* in trust to pay the income annually during *A*'s lifetime "to *A* personally, to be for *A*'s support," and on *A*'s death, to pay the principal to *B*. One year later *A* gratuitously writes, signs, and delivers to his cousin, *C*, the following memorandum: "I hereby assign to my cousin *C* all my right to receive future income for

47. William Angus Drogo Montagu, ninth Duke of Manchester, was dubbed "spendthrift extraordinary and bankrupt plenipotentiary" by Time, June 17, 1935, at 19, in a story about the duke. Manchester once owed $5,000 for tennis balls alone, probably a record. "Going bankrupt isn't so bad as it sounds," he has said, adding reminiscently, "I remember my first bankruptcy. I was only 16 and went broke for a couple of thousand pounds. My trouble is that I have always been a mug — too trustful and willing to help others."

my lifetime from the trust," identifying the above trust in the memorandum. *X*, who has no notice of the assignment, pays the next annual installment of income, $5,000, to *A*, who, having meanwhile become angry with *C*, refuses to pay this sum over to *C*. Instead *A* uses it to buy stock for himself. The stock is now worth $10,000. Does *C* have any claim against *A*? See 2A A. Scott, supra, §154.

2. Carla and Margaret have a controlling mother. Concerned about their mother's attempts to play off one daughter against the other, Carla and Margaret sign an agreement to share equally whatever mother leaves them. Mother dies, leaving the bulk of her estate in a spendthrift trust to pay all the income to Carla, with discretion in the trustee to invade the trust principal "up to the whole thereof," for Carla's maintenance and support. What are the rights of Margaret against Carla? See DeMille v. Ramsey, 207 Cal. App. 3d 116, 254 Cal. Rptr. 573 (1989); Moffat v. Lynch, 642 S.W.2d 624 (Mo. 1982); Note, Spendthrift Trusts: Enforceability of Agreements to Pay Over Income on Receipt, 52 UMKC L. Rev. 114 (1983).

First National Bank of Maryland v. Department of Health & Mental Hygiene
Court of Appeals of Maryland, 1979
284 Md. 720, 399 A.2d 821

DIGGES, J. The event that precipitated this case occurred in mid-1975 when the petitioners, the trustees of a trust created by the will of Annesley Bond Baugh, were notified by respondent Maryland Department of Health and Mental Hygiene that as of July 1, 1975, the charge to the trust for the care of the testatrix's daughter at Spring Grove State Hospital was being increased. The daughter, also named Annesley Bond Baugh, is now approximately sixty-eight years old and has resided at this mental hospital since 1944. The facts, none of which are here in dispute, show that from 1968, when the mother died, until July 1975 all costs for her daugher's care were paid out of the trust created by Mrs. Baugh's will. The will, executed in 1957 and amended to a minor degree by codicils in 1961 and 1963, provides in pertinent part:

Fifth: I give, devise and bequeath all of the rest and residue of my estate, including all property over which I have a power of testamentary disposition under any will of my husband, Frederick H. Baugh, unto my son, Frederick H. Baugh, Jr., and First National Bank of Baltimore, the survivor of them and their successors, as Trustees, IN TRUST AND CONFIDENCE, NEVERTHELESS, for the following uses and purposes:

A. My Trustees shall collect the rents, revenues, income and profits from my trust estate and after paying or providing for the payment of all taxes, dues, charges and expenses, shall dispose of the income and principal as follows:

1. My Trustees, accounting from the date of my death, shall pay from time to time the net income and so much of the principal as they, in their absolute and uncontrolled discretion, may determine, to my daughter, Annesley Bond Baugh, or, in their absolute and uncontrolled discretion, may apply the same for her maintenance, comfort and support.

2. Upon the death of my daughter my Trustees shall pay her funeral expenses unless her individual estate is sufficient to pay such expenses and shall transfer and deliver the balance of my trust estate then in their hands unto my son, Frederick H. Baugh, Jr., if he be then living. If my son should not be then living, my surviving Trustee shall retain the trust estate and pay the net income therefrom for the maintenance, education, comfort and support of his children living from time to time. When the youngest child of my son reaches the age of twenty-one (21) years, this trust shall terminate and cease and the surviving Trustee shall transfer and deliver the principal of the trust estate and all accumulated income thereon to the then living children and descendants of my son, per stirpes.

From 1968 until 1973, the income generated by the trust corpus proved to be sufficient to pay all costs of the daughter's care at the hospital and the trustees applied it to that cause. The income, however, became insufficient in 1973 to discharge this obligation and from then until 1975 the trustees exercised the discretion granted them by the will and invaded the principal in order to pay the difference between the trust income and the hospital charges. Upon receipt in mid-July 1975 of a notice from the hospital of an additional increase in costs, the trustees decided that further invasion of the principal would not advance the testatrix's purposes in creating the trust and, as a consequence, notified the respondent that future payments would be limited to the trust income.[48] The Department of Health and Mental Hygiene, in contesting the trustees' construction of their responsibilities to Miss Baugh under the will, maintained the position that both the trust income and the principal, if need be, could be used in an appropriate amount to help defray the total cost of the daughter's care.

As a result of this conflict, a series of administrative appeals followed. When each resulted in a ruling adverse to the trustees, they sought judicial review by appealing to the Baltimore City Court. . . . That court held that after all the income of Mrs. Baugh's trust had been utilized on her daughter's behalf, the corpus was, as an asset of the patient, then legally chargeable for the unpaid portion of the cost of the daughter's care assessed under Md. Code (1957, 1972 Repl. Vol., 1975

---

48. It is undisputed that as of July 1975 the principal of the trust, having a value of approximately $100,000, generated an annual income of about $5200, while the yearly cost of care for Miss Baugh at the hospital was about $14,400.

Cum. Supp.), Art. 59, §40 (currently codified at Md. Code (1957, 1971 Repl. Vol., 1978 Cum. Supp.), Art, 43, §601). From this order a timely appeal was taken by the trustees to the Court of Special Appeals and we granted certiorari prior to that court's consideration of the matter. Having concluded that the trustees acted within the authority granted them by the provisions of the trust in refusing to further deplete its principal, we will reverse.

The paramount issue now before us is whether the trust principal may be charged with the costs of the care of Annesley Bond Baugh. The answer to this question, in turn, depends on which of two commonly recognized types of trusts the testatrix intended to create, that is, whether by the fifth item of her will she intended to establish a support trust or a discretionary trust.

A support trust, it is generally recognized, is one that provides that "the trustee shall pay or apply only so much of the income and principal or either as is necessary for the education or support of the beneficiary," thereby barring the beneficiary from transferring his interest and precluding his creditors from reaching it. Restatement (Second) of Trusts §154 (1957); accord, G.G. Bogert & G.T. Bogert, The Law of Trusts and Trustees §229, at 726 (2d ed. 1965); 2 A. Scott, The Law of Trusts §154, at 1176 (3d ed. 1967). If this trust were entirely for the support of Miss Baugh, however, she could, by showing the trustees have abused their discretion, compel them to make any payment reasonably necessary for that purpose, Offutt v. Offutt, 204 Md. 101, 110, 102 A.2d 554, 559 (1954) (quoting Restatement of Trusts §128, Comment e (1935)); likewise, this Court has recognized that when a supplier of necessaries — the State in this case — has a claim against the beneficiary of a support trust, the interest of the beneficiary in the trust can be reached to compel payment for the required items or services. Safe Deposit & Tr. Co. v. Robertson, 192 Md. 653, 660, 65 A.2d 292, 295 (1949) (quoting Restatement of Trusts §157 (1935)); see Pole v. Pietsch, 61 Md. 570, 573-74 (1884).[49]

In contrast, if, by direction of the settlor, all or any part of the trust assets can be totally withheld from the beneficiary by the trustees then, to the extent it can be so retained, a discretionary trust would be created. The Restatement of Trusts, Second, sets forth the definition and incidents of a discretionary trust as follows:

[I]f by the terms of a trust it is provided that the trustee shall pay to or

---

49. Even though the State provides the beneficiary here with the necessities of life, because such care and support is not gratuitous, Whitworth, Adm'r v. Department, 222 Md. 98, 105, 158 A.2d 765, 769 (1960), it cannot be considered an independent source of income to the beneficiary so as to relieve the trustees of any duty they may otherwise have to pay. See In re Gruber's Will, 122 N.Y.S.2d 654, 656-57 (Sur. Ct. 1953).

> apply for a beneficiary only so much of the income and principal
> or either as the trustee in his uncontrolled discretion shall see fit to
> pay or apply, a transferee or creditor of the beneficiary cannot compel the
> trustee to pay any part of the income or principal. [Restatement
> (Second) of Trusts §155(1) (1957).]

Accord, G.G. Bogert & G.T. Bogert, supra, §228, at 717, 720-21; 2 A.
Scott, supra, §155, at 1180. Thus, payment cannot be compelled out of
a discretionary trust unless it is shown that the trustees have acted
arbitrarily, dishonestly, or from an improper motive in denying the
beneficiary the funds sought. . . .

Bearing in mind these trust classifications, we proceed to the task of
ascertaining, from the four corners of the will, which form of trust the
testatrix-settlor intended to create. . . . After reviewing the will and its
codicils to determine Mrs. Baugh's intent, we think the critical passage
indicating her desires and directions is found in paragraph one of the
fifth clause which, because of its importance, we here set out again:

> 1.   My Trustees, accounting from the date of my death, shall pay from
> time to time the net income and so much of the principal as they, in their
> absolute and uncontrolled discretion, may determine, to my daughter,
> Annesley Bond Baugh, or, in their absolute and uncontrolled discretion,
> may apply the same for her maintenance, comfort and support.

The respondent contends that the testatrix, by the use of these words,
exhibited an intention to devote the principal of the trust fund to the
maintenance, comfort, and support of her daughter, while the petitioners have consistently declared that the principal, as distinguished from
the income, was not unreservedly devoted to the support of Annesley
Bond Baugh but is to be dispensed only as the trustees, in their absolute
discretion, see fit.[50]

In examining the language of this paragraph as it deals with the trust
corpus, we observe that it speaks of the distribution of the principal in
two different contexts. It first declares: "My trustees . . . shall pay . . .
so much of the principal as they, in their absolute and uncontrolled
discretion, may determine, to my daughter Annesley Bond Baugh. . . ."
Although this provision allows the trustees to pay any part of the
principal to Miss Baugh for any reason, it also forecloses her right to
compel such payments because any distribution rests solely within the

---

50. The disposition of the Baugh trust's income is not at issue here as the trustees have
indicated that pursuant to the language of the above quoted paragraph directing them
to "pay from time to time the net income . . . to my daughter," they will remit the income
derived from the trust to the State for Miss Baugh's care. There is, of course, nothing to
prevent a settlor from designating that his trustees exercise one measure of control over
a trust's income and another type over the principal.

trustees' discretion, if that discretion is honestly exercised. Thus, when considered alone, this language indicates the testatrix desired that the distribution of the principal be handled by the trustees under the rules and incidents applying to discretionary trusts. The application of this seemingly clearcut provision is somewhat muddled, however, by the textatrix's additional direction that her trustees "in their absolute and uncontrolled discretion, may apply the same for [my daughter's] maintenance, comfort and support." Respondent argues that by mixing language that traditionally connotes a discretionary trust with that often used to establish a support trust, the testatrix in this instance was qualifying her earlier grant of absolute discretion to her trustees and mandating that they act consistent with the more limited discretion connected with a trust for support when dealing with matters involving her daughter's maintenance.

Usually, if the purpose of the trust is to provide support, words to that effect are included in the clause directing the trustees to pay. For example, "the trustees shall pay to the beneficiary of this trust so much of the income or principal as they deem necessary for his maintenance, comfort, and support," is a fairly typical clause that clearly shows the testator's intent to create a support trust. Indeed, the testatrix in this instance included within part A of the fifth item a paragraph designated as "2," quoted earlier, that provides that after her daughter's death, if her son were also dead, "my surviving Trustee shall retain the trust estate and pay the net income therefrom for the maintenance, education, comfort and support of his children living from time to time." This is clearly a support clause for her grandchildren and, had the testatrix so desired, she could have provided for Miss Baugh's support with similar language. She did not do so, however, but instead qualified the language of support by adding words describing the discretion her trustees were to exercise as being "absolute and uncontrolled," an addition negating any suggestion that the testatrix wished to limit her trustees' power to deal with the principal in matters concerning her daughter's support and maintenance to the somewhat more restricted authority that is associated with a support trust. . . . Our conclusion, therefore, is that the trust, as it related to the principal, was not unqualifiedly for the support of Miss Baugh, but rather could be used for such a purpose at the sole discretion of the trustees.

In so stating, we are aware that this interpretation of paragraph one's language appears to deprive the second half of that paragraph of any independent meaning, because it does not seem to change or add to the trustees' power, thereby contravening the constructional rule that "[a]ll of the language in [a trust instrument] should be given effect where possible." Vickery v. Maryland Trust Co., 188 Md. 178, 188, 52 A.2d 100, 105 (1947). Upon closer scrutiny, however, we think this is not the case. With regard to discretionary trusts, the Restatement, Second, points out:

> Unless a valid restraint on alienation has been imposed . . . , if the trustee pays to or applies for the beneficiary any part of the income or principal with knowledge of the transfer or after he has been served with process in a proceeding by a creditor to reach it, he is liable to such transferee or creditor.

Restatement (Second) of Trusts §155(2) (1957). In this case, the testatrix imposed a restraint on alienation, of the kind denoted above, in the fifth item of her will by stating that "[e]xcept as otherwise provided in this will, my Trustee shall pay all amounts of income and principal payable hereunder to any person into the hands of such person and not unto any other person or corporation whatsoever, . . . nor can any of said payments be anticipated." The effect of this spendthrift provision upon any discretionary payment of the principal, whether for support or some other purpose, would be to require that it be given directly to Miss Baugh and not to her creditors or assigns. By adding the latter provision of the first paragraph, however, we think testatrix was expressing her intention that the trustees could make discretionary payments for support from the principal directly to a creditor despite the spendthrift provision. Thus, our conclusion is that Mrs. Baugh, taking into account her daughter's mental condition, sought to insure her well-being by giving her the income from the trust and, in addition, sought to clothe her trustees with maximum flexibility to deal with the trust corpus so that they, in their absolute discretion, might make payments directly into the hands of her daughter or directly to creditors providing her daughter with necessary items or services.[51]

Our determination that the testatrix created a discretionary trust, of course, precludes any argument that the trustees can be compelled to pay the principal of the trust for Miss Baugh's care at Spring Grove unless it can be shown that they acted "dishonestly or arbitrarily or from an improper motive." Restatement (Second) of Trusts §128, Comment d (1957); see Town of Randolph v. Roberts, supra, 195 N.E.2d at 73 ("arbitrarily, capriciously, or in bad faith"). No such showing was made or even attempted to be made here. In a memorandum filed in the course of the trustees' appeal to the Baltimore City Court they declared: "In declining to consume the corpus of the trust

---

51. Likewise, we think that the testatrix's reference to the application of the "same" for her daughter's support gives the trustees license to ignore the spendthrift clause and, as they have heretofore done in paying the State for Miss Baugh's care at the hospital, deliver the income, not into the hands of Miss Baugh, but to those providing her with necessaries.

to meet the escalating costs for Miss Baugh's care at Spring Grove, the Trustees have given thoughtful consideration to Miss Baugh's age, her continuing and future needs in relation to the size of the trust estate, and the fact that the Trustees have been notified that Miss Baugh may be discharged from Spring Grove in the near future and require maintenance and support independent of a state facility." We cannot say that they have misstated their reasons or that their decision was in any way capricious, dishonest, or improperly motivated. As such, the trust principal is not chargeable for the costs of Miss Baugh's care and the trustees cannot be compelled to invade it to defray those costs. . . .

Judgment of the Baltimore City Court reversed. Costs to be paid by respondent.[52]

NOTES AND PROBLEM

1.   The right of the state to be reimbursed from a trust for care given an institutionalized beneficiary of the trust has been much litigated in recent years. According to most courts, the controlling question is whether the settlor intended to provide only benefits that the state is unwilling or unable to provide or intended the trust to pay for the beneficiary's support regardless of whether he is in a public institution. If the former, the court will not interfere with the trustee's decision, and the state cannot reach the trust assets. If the latter, the state may reach the assets. See Button v. Elmhurst National Bank, 169 Ill. App. 3d 28, 522 N.E.2d 1368 (1988); Miller v. Department of Mental Health, 432 Mich. 426, 442 N.W.2d 617 (1989); Third National Bank in Nashville v. Brown, 691 S.W.2d 557 (Tenn. 1985).

2.   Massey, Protecting the Mentally Incompetent Child's Trust Interest from State Reimbursement Claims, 58 Den. L.J. 557, 563-564 (1981):

> The parent who wants to establish a testamentary trust for a mentally incompetent child, secure from public reimbursement claims for institutional care, may do so by drafting a discretionary trust carefully limited to *exclude any provisions for support, care, or maintenance.* The parent-testator should make clear his intent to *limit application of the trust assets to supplementing benefits provided at public expense.* Such a trust clearly withdraws whatever interest the child may possess from the property classification essential to a public reimbursement claim. This trust construction rule is in accord with accepted testamentary and trust provisions applied in cases dealing with reimbursement statutes.

---

52. Commented on in Abravanel, Discretionary Support Trusts, 68 Iowa L. Rev. 273, 283-287 (1983). — Eds.

See also Mooney, Discretionary Trusts: An Estate Plan to Supplement Public Assistance for Disabled Persons, 25 Ariz. L. Rev. 939 (1983); Frolik, Discretionary Trusts for a Disabled Beneficiary: A Solution or a Trap for the Unwary?, 46 U. Pitt. L. Rev. 335 (1985).

3. When a person applies for public welfare, a support trust is counted as an asset of the beneficiary, which may deprive the beneficiary of entitlement to public assistance. Suppose that the trust is a discretionary trust for the beneficiary's support. Is this counted as an asset? See Lang v. Commonwealth Dept. of Public Welfare, 515 Pa. 428, 528 A.2d 1335 (1987) (holding not an asset when the beneficiary cannot force the trustee to pay).

SECTION G. MODIFICATION AND TERMINATION OF TRUSTS

1. Modification of Distributive Provisions

In re Wolcott
Supreme Court of New Hampshire, 1948
95 N.H. 23, 56 A.2d 641, 1 A.L.R.2d 1323

Petition for instructions brought by trustees under the will of Francis E. Getty, late of North Conway, seeking authority to make payments out of principal to the life beneficiary of a trust established under the will. Certain facts were found by the Court (Grimes, J.), who transferred without ruling the question of law presented by the petition.

The testator died on September 23, 1944. By his will made in 1932, he bequeathed to his widow, Ada C. Getty, the sum of $2,500, and all of his personal and household goods, supplies and furniture, of every kind and nature. To each of his two sons, he bequeathed the sum of $5,000. The residue of his estate, he devised and bequeathed to the trustees "to pay over the net income thereof to my wife so long as she lives," and upon her death to pay the principal and any accumulated income "to my then living issue in equal shares by right of representation, and, in default of such issue, to the persons to whom and in the proportions in which the same would be distributable if I had then died intestate and owning such property absolutely." In the event of the wife's decease prior to the testator's, the residue was disposed of by provisions identical with those disposing of the remainder after the life estate.

The will conferred upon the trustees broad powers with respect to investments and management of the trust, including the right to determine what receipts should be "credited to income and what to principal, notwithstanding any determination by the courts," and the power "generally to do all things in relation to the trust fund which the testator could have done if living."

According to the allegations of the petition, the annual income from the trust fund is now slightly in excess of $2,300, and the principal approximates $107,000. The Court has found that the widow is eighty-two years of age, and that she "is ill and infirm and the income of the trust is insufficient to afford her adequate subsistence." It is alleged that her "reasonable and necessary expenses" including those of constant attendance of a nurse and frequent visits of her physician, exceed $5,800. The trustees accordingly ask that they may be authorized and instructed to invade the principal of the fund for the purpose of providing her with reasonable support, the invasion not to exceed $4,000 a year.

In this petition the trustees are joined by the testator's sons, both of whom survived him, and by the eighteen year old son of one of them. The latter is represented by a guardian ad litem, also appointed to represent the possible interests of persons as yet unborn. Because of provisions against alienation by anticipation, the sons may not utilize their interests to benefit their mother; but by joining with the trustees in their petition, they seek to bring to realization their expressed belief that "it could not have been their father's intention that their mother should be deprived of proper support in order that remote future interests might be protected."

DUNCAN, J. Although not expressly stated, the testator's purpose that during her life, his wife should have the beneficial use of his entire estate, except for $10,000 bequeathed to his sons, is readily apparent. Apart from these legatees, the only others who might share in the estate are designated not by name, but as members of a class, or as heirs or next of kin, and would take only in the event that the widow survived one or both of the sons. The residue, at the widow's death, is to be distributed among the testator's "then living issue in equal shares by right of representation," a phrase plainly descriptive of the testator's lineal descendants. Kimball v. Penhallow, 60 N.H. 448. See R.L., c. 7, 20. The widow's death before that of her sons would result in a division between them. The only other living issue, whose interest is purely contingent, is the grandson petitioner.

Despite broad discretionary powers conferred upon the trustees, the will contains no provision for the use of principal for the benefit of the widow. On the other hand, such use is not specifically forbidden. It may fairly be assumed that the beneficiary's need of the principal was not anticipated because of a failure to foresee changes which have occurred since the testator's death, including shrinkage in investment returns, decline in purchasing power, and the expense occasioned by the widow's extreme infirmity. The powers conferred upon the trustees as to investments and the allocation of receipts to income are indicative of a purpose to provide the widow with a liberal income, unrestricted by technical rules. No purpose to transmit any specific residuary amount to the sons or to any other issue is disclosed. Fairly construed, the will evidences as its primary purpose "ample and certain provision" for the testator's wife. Cf. Smith v. Fellows, 131 Mass. 20, 22; Trust Co. v. Glunz, 119 N.J. Eq 73, 77, 181 A. 27.

What is sought by the petition is not construction of any particular provision of the will but rather authority to deviate from the provisions by which principal would be retained intact during the widow's lifetime. No reliance is placed by the trustees upon their general power "to do all things in relation to the trust which the testator could have done if living." The power is at best obscure in meaning, and if construed independently of other provisions, would have doubtful validity. Clark v. Campbell, 82 N.H. 281, 133 A. 166, 45 A.L.R. 1433. Because of the emergency confronting the life beneficiary, the trustees seek authority to do what the testator presumably would have authorized had he foreseen the emergency.

Where a remainder succeeding a life estate may ultimately vest in persons as yet undetermined and perhaps unborn, courts of equity have at times hesitated or refused to sanction an invasion of principal for the benefit of the life tenant. See Annotations, 39 A.L.R. 40; 46 L.R.A., N.S., 43, and cases cited. In one view, permission is sought to appropriate to the use of one beneficiary the property of others without the consent of all. See In re Van Deusen's Estate, Cal. Sup., 182 P.2d 565; Marshall v. Holloway, 2 Swanst. 432; Errat v. Barlow, 14 Ves. Jr. 202. But this view, in our opinion, may be deemed applicable only to the extent that the testator's disclosed intention affords it a foundation. Strictly applied, it may prevent accomplishment of the testator's primary purpose. As is said in 2 Scott, Trusts, §168, p.855: "As a matter of strict logic it may be necessary to permit a child to suffer in order to protect the possible children which he may ultimately have, but it is difficult to believe that the settlor would ever desire such a result." Where the testator's desire may be gathered from the will, "strict logic" need not to be controlling.

Traditionally, the courts of this jurisdiction have shown a signal regard for the intent of the testator (see Clark v. Campbell, supra), at times at the expense of other recognized principles deemed less cogent in their application. Cf. Edgerly v. Barker, 66 N.H. 434, 31 A. 900, 28 L.R.A. 328. In order to prevent impairment of a testator's primary purpose, authority to deviate from the express terms of a gift has been granted in cases of emergency unforeseen by him, even though contingent remainder interests were incidentally affected.

In Brown v. Berry, 71 N.H. 241, 52 A. 870, 872, trustees under a will sought advice as to whether, when income proved insufficient, principal might be used for the support of the testator's children, and the support and education of his grandchildren. The will directed payment "out of the net income" of sums sufficient for the purposes named, and bequeathed the residue to the grandchildren when the youngest should reach a specified age. In advising the trustees that principal might be used, this court said,

> the reading of the testator's will . . . leaves no room for doubt that his primary and controlling purpose was to provide for the proper and reasonable support of his children and grandchildren. . . . For these objects he designated the net income of his large estate as the source of payment, and doubtless supposed, as he reasonably might, that it would be amply sufficient. . . . That this purpose cannot be executed in the particular manner he intended affords no valid reason why it should not be executed at all.

In McGill v. Young, 75 N.H. 133, 71 A. 637, the use of principal for the support of the testator's son was authorized, although the will directed the trustee "to pay out of and from said net income . . . the money . . . necessary" for his support. (Demeritt v. Young, 72 N.H. 202, 203, 55 A. 1047, 1048.) The court considered it "highly improbable it was intended to limit the trustee to that fund and to forbid him to use the principal if at any time the income should be insufficient for the purpose. . . ." [75 N.H. 133, 71 A. 637.]

In the will before us, the testator's purpose to furnish reasonable support for his wife is not expressed in words, but it is nevertheless implicit in the disposition made of his estate. His direction that his wife should have the income was a means of executing his purpose, and is "properly to be read as subordinate to (his) paramount intention." In re Walker, (1901) 1 Ch. 879, 885. His intent to provide reasonable support to the widow being evident from the will, those whose interests are secondary to hers take subject to the execution of that intent. The remaindermen are deprived of no rights so long as rights which the life tenant was intended to have are not exceeded.

Because of circumstances not provided for by the will and obviously not anticipated by the testator, an emergency threatens accomplishment of his purpose by the means which he provided. Those whose interests are most immediate consent to the authorization sought by the trustees, and there is no objection by the guardian ad litem. If the consent or acquiescence of the parties is not binding upon unborn contingent remaindermen, still they are sufficiently represented by those having like interests to be bound by a decree. 3 Simes, Future Interests, §676; 33 Am. Jur. 650, §§182, 183. Cf. Longworth v. Duff, 297 Ill. 479, 130

N.E. 690. In this situation a court of equity need not hesitate to exercise its undoubted power to permit a deviation from the literal provisions of the will. A means of accomplishing the testator's purpose is thereby furnished, which it may reasonably be inferred that he himself would have provided, had he been able to foresee the exigency. Trust Co. v. Glunz, supra; Pennington v. Metropolitan Museum of Art, 65 N.J. Eq. 11, 55 A. 468; Curtiss v. Brown, 29 Ill. 201. Cf. Citizens' Nat. Bank v. Morgan, 94 N.H. 284, 51 A.2d 841, and cases cited. This conclusion is in harmony with our own decisions and not without support in other authorities. Longwith v. Riggs, 123 Ill. 258, 14 N.E. 840; McAfee v. Thomas, 121 Or. 351, 255 P. 333.

The trustees are advised that principal not in excess of $4,000 a year may be used to supplement the income of the trust, for the purpose of providing the widow with reasonable support, if the trial court shall find in accordance with the uncontroverted allegations of the petition, and it shall appear that the widow has no other income. In view of the discretion vested in the trustees by the testator, there is no reason why they may not safely be left to determine the amount of principal necessary within the limit specified, due regard being given to considerations of what is prudent and reasonable, and best calculated to accomplish the testator's purposes as a whole. Woodward v. Jolbert, 94 N.H. 324, 52 A.2d 641.

If the requisite findings are made, a decree in accordance with this opinion may be entered by the Superior Court.

Case discharged.

All concurred.[53]

NOTES

1. Where a destitute income beneficiary petitions for power to invade principal for support, and all the beneficiaries do not consent, relief is ordinarily denied unless the trust instrument is construed to contain a power to invade, express or implied. See In re Van Deusen's Estate, 30 Cal. 2d 285, 182 P.2d 565 (1947); 2A A. Scott, Trusts §168 (W. Fratcher 4th ed. 1987). There is, however, a good deal of unhappiness with the state of the law. See Haskell, Justifying the Principle of Distributive Deviation in the Law of Trusts, 18 Hastings L.J. 267 (1967); Report, Modification of Terms Regarding Amount or Time of Payments to Income Beneficiaries, 4 Real Prop., Prob. & Tr. J. 359 (1969). Statutes in some states provide that a court may direct principal to be paid to an income beneficiary for support if the court finds such effectuates

---

53. Noted in 28 B.U.L. Rev. 387; 47 Mich. L. Rev. 422. — Eds.

the intention of the settlor. See, e.g., New York Est., Powers & Trusts Law §7-1.6 (1967).

2. In the *Wolcott* case, the remainder is given, after the widow's death, to the testator's living issue, and if none, to the testator's heirs. To bind any unborn remainderman to the decree, the court uses the doctrine of *virtual representation* (see page 571 of the opinion). Under virtual representation, an owner of a future interest is bound by a judgment in a lawsuit, although not made a party thereto, when a party to the lawsuit has an interest in the property that will be affected by the judgment in the same way as the party represented (an "identity of interest"). The relationship between the representative and the person represented must be such "that an adequate presentation of the legal position of the . . . [representative] would be an adequate presentation of the legal position of the unborn person." Restatement of Property §183(a) (1936). The doctrine rests upon the necessity of effectively adjudicating title when not all interested parties are available.

The doctrine of virtual representation applies to a class gift. One living member of the class may represent unborn members of the class. Mabry v. Scott, 51 Cal. App. 2d 245, 124 P.2d 659 (1942).

3. In 1911 Joseph Pulitzer's will created a trust for the benefit of his descendants. Pulitzer bequeathed to the trustees shares of stock in a corporation publishing the World newspapers, and his will provided that the sale of these shares was not authorized under any circumstances. After several years of large and increasing losses from the publication of the World, the trustees in 1931 petitioned the court to approve sale of the shares. The court held that, even though sale was prohibited by Pulitzer, it had power to authorize sale in circumstances where the trust estate was in jeopardy, and it approved the sale. In re Pulitzer, 139 Misc. 575, 249 N.Y.S. 87 (Sur. Ct. 1931). See also American State Bank v. Kupfer, 114 Ill. App. 3d 760, 449 N.E.2d 1024 (1983).

2. Termination of Trusts

If the *settlor* and *all the beneficiaries* consent, a trust may be terminated. No one else has any beneficial interest in the trust. The trustee has no beneficial interest and cannot object. Such a right to terminate exists even if the trust contains a spendthrift clause. See Woodruff v. Trust Company of Georgia, 233 Ga. 135, 210 S.E.2d 321 (1974) (settlor can revoke trust where settlor is sole beneficiary even though trust instrument provided consent of trustee to revocation is required); Johnson v. First National Bank of Jackson, 386 So. 2d 1112 (Miss. 1980).

If, however, the settlor is dead or does not consent to the termination of the trust, the question arises whether the beneficiaries can terminate the trust if they all agree to. Let us first look at the law in England. In Saunders v. Vautier, 49 Eng. Rep. 282, 4 Beav. 115 (1841), the English court held that a trust can be terminated at any time if all the beneficiaries are adult and sui juris and all consent. In the 1950s, the English Variation of Trusts Act of 1958, 6 & 7 Eliz. 2, ch. 53, §1, greatly expanded the power of courts to terminate trusts. It provided that a court may consent to modification or termination of the trust on behalf of incompetent, minor, or unborn beneficiaries whenever the court finds it beneficial to the beneficiaries. Similar statutes have been enacted in Canada and Australia. Professor Waters tells us, "It is sometimes not realized how considerable is the scope of this power. It means that revocation on any terms is possible and that variation of any degree is also possible." D. Waters, The Law of Trusts in Canada 1074 (2d ed. 1984). The end result is to permit beneficiaries "to make vast inroads upon the schemes of beneficial interests as contrived by settlors and testators." Id. at 287. What has happened in England and some of the Commonwealth countries is that, after the settlor's death, the trust is regarded as the beneficiaries' property, not as the settlor's property — and the dead hand continues to rule only by the sufferance of the beneficiaries.

Variation or termination of trusts in England is strikingly different from the practice in this country, where the settlor's intent cannot be set aside after his death. In the United States, the great weight of authority holds that a trust cannot be terminated prior to the time fixed for termination, even though all the beneficiaries consent, *if termination would be contrary to a material purpose of the settlor*. The leading case establishing this rule is Claflin v. Claflin, 149 Mass. 19, 20 N.E. 545 (1889), and the rule is often referred to as the Claflin doctrine. In that case a trust was established for testator's son, with principal to be paid to the son at age 30. After age 21 the son sued to terminate the trust, pointing out that he was the sole beneficiary. The court refused to permit termination as this would violate the intent of the testator.

> [A] testator has a right to dispose of his own property with such restrictions and limitations, not repugnant to law, as he sees fit, and . . . his intentions ought to be carried out, unless they contravene some positive rule of law, or are against public policy. . . . It cannot be said that these restrictions upon the plaintiff's possession and control of the property are altogether useless, for there is not the same danger that he will spend the property while it is in the hands of the trustees as there would be if it were in his own. [149 Mass. at 23, 20 N.E. at 456.]

Although the Claflin doctrine is easy to state, there is considerable disagreement as to the circumstances under which termination would be contrary to the purpose of the settlor. Generally, a trust cannot be terminated if it is a spendthrift trust, if the beneficiary is not to receive the principal until attaining a specified age, if it is a discretionary trust, or if it is a trust for support of the beneficiary. Such provisions are usually deemed to state a material purpose of the settlor. The cases are collected in G. Bogert & G. Bogert, Trusts and Trustees §§1007-1008 (rev. 2d ed. 1983); 4 A. Scott, Trusts §§337-337.8 (W. Fratcher 4th ed. 1987).

In re Estate of Brown
Supreme Court of Vermont, 1987
148 Vt. 94, 528 A.2d 752

GIBSON, J.   The trustee of a testamentary trust appeals an order of the Washington Superior Court granting the petition of the lifetime and residual beneficiaries of the trust to terminate it and to distribute the proceeds to the life tenants. We reverse.

The primary issue raised on appeal is whether any material purpose of the trust remains to be accomplished, thus barring its termination. The appellant/trustee also raises the closely related issue of whether all beneficiaries are before the court, i.e., whether the class of beneficiaries has closed.

Andrew J. Brown died in 1977, settling his entire estate in a trust, all of which is held by the trustee under terms and conditions that are the subject of this appeal. The relevant portion of the trust instrument provides:

(3)   The . . . trust . . . shall be used to provide an education, particularly a college education, for the children of my nephew, Woolson S. Brown. My Trustee is hereby directed to use the income from said trust and such part of the principal as may be necessary to accomplish this purpose. Said trust to continue for said purpose until the last child has received his or her education and the Trustee, in its discretion, has determined that the purpose hereof has been accomplished.

At such time as this purpose has been accomplished and the Trustee has so determined, *the income from said trust and such part of the principal as may be necessary shall be used by said Trustee for the care, maintenance and welfare of my nephew, Woolson S. Brown and his wife, Rosemary Brown, so that they may live in the style and manner to which they are accustomed, for and during the remainder of their natural lives.* Upon their demise, any remainder of said trust, together with any accumulation thereon, shall be paid to their then living children in equal shares, share and share alike. (Emphasis added.)

The trustee complied with the terms of the trust by using the proceeds to pay for the education of the children of Woolson and Rosemary Brown. After he determined that the education of these children was completed, the trustee began distribution of trust income to the lifetime beneficiaries, Woolson and Rosemary.

On June 17, 1983, the lifetime beneficiaries petitioned the probate court for termination of the trust, arguing that the sole remaining purpose of the trust was to maintain their lifestyle and that distribution of the remaining assets was necessary to accomplish this purpose. The remaindermen, the children of the lifetime beneficiaries, filed consents to the proposed termination. The probate court denied the petition to terminate, and the petitioners appealed to the Washington Superior Court. The superior court reversed, concluding that continuation of the trust was no longer necessary because the only material purpose, the education of the children, had been accomplished. This appeal by the trustee followed.

Ordinarily, a trial court's conclusions will be upheld where they are supported by its findings. Dartmouth Savings Bank v. F.O.S. Associates, 145 Vt. 62, 66, 486 A.2d 623, 625 (1984). Here, the superior court's conclusion that the trust could be terminated because the material purpose of the trust had been accomplished has an insufficient basis in its findings, and this conclusion cannot stand.

An active trust may not be terminated, even with the consent of all the beneficiaries, if a material purpose of the settlor remains to be accomplished. See, e.g., Ambrose v. First National Bank, 87 Nev. 114, 117, 482 P.2d 828, 829 (1971); Sundquist v. Sundquist, 639 P.2d 181, 187 (Utah 1981); Restatement (Second) of Trusts §337 (1959); 4 A. Scott, Scott on Trusts §337, at 2655 (3d ed. 1967). This Court has invoked a corollary of this rule in a case where partial termination of a trust was at issue. In re Bayley Trust, 127 Vt. 380, 385, 250 A.2d 516, 519 (1969).

As a threshold matter, we reject the trustee's argument that the trust cannot be terminated because it is both a support trust and a spendthrift trust. It is true that, were either of these forms of trust involved, termination could not be compelled by the beneficiaries because a material purpose of the settlor would remain unsatisfied. See Restatement (Second) of Trusts §337.

The trust at issue does not qualify as a support trust. A support trust is created where the trustee is directed to use trust income or principal for the benefit of an individual, but only to the extent necessary to support the individual. 2 A. Scott, Scott on Trusts §154, at 1176; G. Bogert, Trusts and Trustees §229, at 519 (2d ed. rev. 1979). Here, the terms of the trust provide that, when the educational purpose of the trust has been accomplished and the trustee, in his discretion, has so determined, "the income . . . and such part of the principal as may be necessary shall be used by said Trustee for the care, maintenance and welfare of . . . [Rosemary and Woolson Brown] so that they may live in the style and manner to which they are accustomed. . . ." The trustee has, in fact, made the determination that the educational purpose has been accomplished and has begun to transfer the income of the trust to the lifetime beneficiaries. Because the trustee must, at the very least, pay all of the trust income to beneficiaries Rosemary and Woolson Brown, the trust cannot be characterized as a support trust.

Nor is this a spendthrift trust. "A trust in which by the terms of the trust or by statute a *valid restraint on the voluntary and involuntary transfer of the interest* of the beneficiary is imposed is a spendthrift trust." Restatement (Second) of Trusts §152(2). (Emphasis added.) While no specific language is needed to create a spendthrift trust, id. at comment c, here the terms of the trust instrument do not manifest Andrew J. Brown's intention to create such a trust. See Huestis v. Manley, 110 Vt. 413, 419, 8 A.2d 644, 646 (1939).

The trustee cites Barnes v. Dow, 59 Vt. 530, 10 A. 258 (1887), for the proposition that a gift of support for life must be deemed a spendthrift trust. In fact, in *Barnes*, the terms of the will gave the testator's sister "support during her natural lifetime out of my estate." Id. at 541, 10 A. at 261. This Court construed the will as establishing a trust for support and held that an interest arising under such a trust is inalienable. Id. The mere fact that an interest in a trust is not transferable does not make the trust a spendthrift trust. See Restatement (Second) of Trusts §154 comment b. In any event, *Barnes* is inapplicable here because a support trust is not at issue.

Although the issue as to whether a material purpose of the trust remains cannot be answered through resort to the foregoing formal categories traditionally imposed upon trust instruments, we hold that termination cannot be compelled here because a material purpose of the settlor remains unaccomplished. In the interpretation of trusts, the intent of the settlor, as revealed by the language of the instrument, is determinative. In re Jones, 138 Vt. 223, 228, 415 A.2d 202, 205 (1980) (citing Destitute of Bennington County v. Putnam Memorial Hospital, 125 Vt. 289, 293, 215 A.2d 134, 137 (1965)).

We find that the trust instrument at hand has two purposes. First, the trust provides for the education of the children of Woolson and Rosemary Brown. The Washington Superior Court found that Rosemary Brown was incapable of having more children and that the chance of Woolson Brown fathering more children was remote; on this basis, the court concluded that the educational purpose of the trust had been achieved.

The settlor also intended a second purpose, however: the assurance of a life-long income for the beneficiaries through the management and discretion of the trustee. We recognize that, had the trust merely provided for successive beneficiaries, no inference could be drawn that the settlor intended to deprive the beneficiaries of the right to manage the trust property during the period of the trust. Estate of Weeks, 485

Pa. 329, 332, 402 A.2d 657, 658 (1979) (quoting Restatement (Second) of Trusts §337 comment f). Here, however, the language of the instrument does more than create successive gifts. The settlor provided that the trustee must provide for the "care, maintenance and welfare" of the lifetime beneficiaries "so that they may live in the style and manner to which they are accustomed, *for and during the remainder of their natural lives."* (Emphasis added.) The trustee must use all of the income and such part of the principal as is necessary for this purpose. We believe that the settlor's intention to assure a life-long income to Woolson and Rosemary Brown would be defeated if termination of the trust were allowed. See 4 Scott, Scott on Trusts §337.1, at 2261-64; see also Will of Hamburger, 185 Wis. 270, 282, 201 N.W. 267, 271 (1924) (court refused to terminate trust since testator desired it to continue during life of his wife).

Because of our holding regarding the second and continuing material purpose of the trust, we do not reach the question of whether the trial court erred in holding that the educational purpose of the trust has been accomplished.

Reversed; judgment for petitioners vacated and judgment for appellant entered.

NOTES AND QUESTIONS

1. Suppose that Woolson and Rosemary transferred all their interest in Uncle Andrew's trust to their living children. Could the children then demand termination of the trust? See In re Bassett's Estate, 104 N.H. 504, 190 A.2d 415 (1963).

2. Isn't it odd that Americans permit more extensive dead-hand control through trusts than do the English — a people whose whole history since the Conquest has been marked by inventions of lawyers to assist their rich clients in controlling their descendants' fortunes after their deaths? The English do not permit a spendthrift trust. The beneficiaries can voluntarily transfer their interests, and their creditors can reach them. If dissatisfied with a trust, the beneficiaries can terminate a trust at will if all are adult. If there are minors or unborn beneficiaries, a court can agree on their behalf to termination if it is in the best interests of the *beneficiaries*. The desire of a dead settlor to continue a trust is of no importance.

Is it time for a change in American trust termination law? See Bird, Trust Termination: Unborn, Living, and Dead Hands — Too Many Fingers in the Trust Pie, 36 Hastings L.J. 563 (1985).

3. It may be possible to terminate a testamentary trust by a compromise agreement between the beneficiaries and heirs entered into

soon after the testator's death. In Massachusetts, as in many states, courts will approve compromise agreements that deliberately eliminate trusts, even spendthrift trusts, which the Massachusetts court has gone to such lengths to uphold. In Budin v. Levy, 343 Mass. 644, 180 N.E.2d 74 (1962), the court decided that a compromise agreement was effective without regard to whether a material purpose of the testator was defeated thereby.

> Such an agreement of compromise as to interests which might be received from an estate is apart from the provisions of the will. Rights under the agreement are wholly contractual and in no sense testamentary.... Indeed, the result may be quite contrary to the testator's intent. This means that before the allowance of a will a trust may be changed or even eliminated by a compromise otherwise valid and approved by the court. [Id. at 649, 180 N.E.2d at 77.]

Some courts, however, refuse to approve a will compromise where the compromise destroys a trust that is essential to a material purpose of the settlor. See Adams v. Link, 145 Conn. 634, 145 A.2d 753 (1958). See also Annot., 29 A.L.R.3d 8 (1970).

Ohio Rev. Code (Supp. 1989)

§1339.66

(A)(1) Upon the filing of a motion by a trustee with the court that has jurisdiction over the trust, upon the provision of reasonable notice to all beneficiaries who are known and in being and who have vested or contingent interests in the trust, and after holding a hearing, the court may terminate the trust, in whole or in part, if it determines that all of the following apply:

(a) It is no longer economically feasible to continue the trust;

(b) The termination of the trust is for the benefit of the beneficiaries;

(c) The termination of the trust is equitable and practical;

(d) The current value of the trust is less than fifty thousand dollars.

(2) The existence of a spendthrift or similar provision in a trust instrument or will does not preclude the termination of a trust pursuant to this section.

(B) If property is to be distributed from an estate being probated to a trust and the termination of the trust pursuant to this section does not clearly defeat the intent of the testator, the probate court has jurisdiction to order the outright distribution of the property or to make the property custodial property under sections 1339.31 to 1339.39

of the revised code. A probate court may so order whether the application for the order is made by an inter vivos trustee named in the will of the decedent or by a testamentary trustee.

Why not eliminate the $50,000 limitation in the Ohio statute? Should a trust of any size be terminated when "it is no longer economically feasible to continue the trust" and the other requirements of the statute are met? Compare In re Wolcott, supra page 568, where the trust principal was $107,000.

NOTE: TRUSTS REMAINING INDESTRUCTIBLE BEYOND THE PERPETUITIES PERIOD

A trust is not void merely because it can extend beyond the perpetuities period. The Rule against Perpetuities indirectly limits the duration of a trust by requiring that equitable interests in trust must be certain to vest or fail within 21 years after the death of all persons who can affect vesting of the interests (known as the perpetuities period), but the Rule does not directly limit the duration of a trust. Nonetheless, a settlor cannot prevent termination of a trust when the perpetuities period is exceeded. This is a limitation upon the Claflin doctrine.

It is not entirely clear whether a restraint on termination is void from the beginning if it can endure beyond the perpetuities period or whether, after the relevant lives-in-being-plus-21-years have expired, the beneficiaries can terminate the trust regardless of the intent of the settlor. Suppose that a testator devises property in trust for A for life, remainder to A's children to be paid when the youngest child reaches age 30. At testator's death, A has no children. The gift to A's children is valid under the Rule against Perpetuities because it will vest on A's death with possession postponed. The trust is not invalid even though it may last for more than 21 years after A's death. Nonetheless, *either* the trust can be terminated after A's death when all of A's children reach majority (because the limitation is void ab initio) *or* the trust can be terminated 21 years after A's death (a wait-and-see approach incorporated in the Restatement (Second) of Property, Donative Transfers §2.1 (1983)). See also May v. Hunt, 404 So. 2d 1373 (Miss. 1981), reforming trust so as to terminate it at expiration of relevant lives in being; 1A A. Scott, Trusts §62.10 (W. Fratcher 4th ed. 1987).

8

CHARITABLE TRUSTS

SECTION A.   NATURE OF CHARITABLE PURPOSES

Shenandoah Valley National Bank v. Taylor
Supreme Court of Appeals of Virginia, 1951
192 Va. 135, 63 S.E.2d 786

MILLER, J.   Charles B. Henry,[1] a resident of Winchester, Virginia, died testate on the 23rd day of April, 1949. His will dated April 21, 1949, was duly admitted to probate and the Shenandoah Valley National

---

1. The testator, Charles B. Henry, operated a fruit and vegetable stand until shortly before his death. In earlier years in addition to the stand, he hawked fruits and vegetables through the town from a horse-drawn wagon.

A number of years before his death he lost his only child, a very pretty little daughter. This, so I am told, profoundly affected him, causing him to become more and more a recluse and this became even more pronounced after the death of his wife, who predeceased him by some years. Along with this increasing withdrawal from general social intercourse, there seems to have developed an increasing tendency to become miserly. This was indicated by such things as avoidance of use of electric lights except when absolutely necessary and making the produce which was no longer salable a substantial part of his diet.

Nonetheless, perhaps because of memory of his own deceased child, he seems to have maintained a strong affection for children generally. As a fruit vendor, he was widely known among the older generation of local citizens.

He saved and hoarded his money and made some investments, and I recollected being told by someone, possibly an official of the Shenandoah Valley Bank that when the Great Depression struck, he was frantic to the point of unnatural frenzy at the depreciation of his investments.

My firm received the case as a result of the complainant being the babysitter for

Bank of Winchester, the designated executor and trustee, qualified thereunder.

Subject to two inconsequential provisions not material to this litigation, the testator's entire estate valued at $86,000, was left as follows:

> Second: All the rest, residue and remainder of my estate, real, personal, intangible and mixed, of whatsoever kind and wherever situate, . . . , I give, bequeath and devise to the Shenandoah Valley National Bank of Winchester, Virginia, in trust, to be known as the "Charles B. Henry and Fannie Belle Henry Fund," for the following uses and purposes:
>
> (a) My Trustee shall invest and reinvest my trust estate, shall collect the income therefrom and shall pay the net income as follows:
>
> (1) On the last school day of each calendar year before Easter my Trustee shall divide the net income into as many equal parts as there are children in the first, second and third grades of the John Kerr School of the City of Winchester, and shall pay one of such equal parts to each child in such grades, to be used by such child in the furtherance of his or her obtainment of an education.
>
> (2) On the last school day of each calendar year before Christmas my trustee shall divide the net income into as many equal parts as there are children in the first, second and third grades of the John Kerr School of the City of Winchester, and shall pay one of such equal parts to each child in such grades, to be used by such child in the furtherance of his or her obtainment of an education.

By paragraphs (3) and (4) it is provided that the names of the children in the three grades shall be determined each year from the school records, and payment of the income to them "shall be as nearly equal in amounts as it is practicable" to arrange.

Paragraph (5) provides that if the John Kerr School is ever discontinued for any reason the payments shall be made to the children of the same grades of the school or schools that take its place, and the School Board of Winchester is to determine what school or schools are substituted for it.

Under clause "Third" the trustee is given authority, power, and discretion to retain or from time to time sell and invest and reinvest

---

my partner's sister and brother-in-law and was the second or third cousin to Charlie Henry. For some time she had been helping to look after him and bringing him food, undoubtedly with that expectation so often disappointed that he would remember her in his will; in fact, I recollect that she claimed that he had flatly promised to do so or by artful insinuation had convinced her that he would. Her disappointment and resulting ire prompted her to seek counsel.

Letter to the editors, dated July 7, 1975, from the Hon. Robert K. Waltz, winning counsel in the Taylor case and later circuit court judge in Virginia. — Eds.

the estate, or any part thereof, as it shall deem to be the best interest of the trust.

The John Kerr School is a public school used by the local school board for primary grades and had an enrollment of 458 boys and girls so there will be that number of pupils or thereabouts who would share in the distribution of the income.

The testator left no children or near relatives. Those who would be his heirs and distributees in case of intestacy were first cousins and others more remotely related. One of these next of kin filed a suit against the executor and trustee, and others challenging the validity of the provisions of the will which undertook to create a charitable trust. . . .

The sole question presented is: does the will create a valid charitable trust?

Construction of the challenged provisions is required and in this undertaking the testator's intent as disclosed by the words used in the will must be ascertained. If his dominant intent as expressed was charitable, the trust should be accorded efficacy and sustained.

But on the other hand, if the testator's intent as expressed is merely benevolent, though the disposition of his property be meritorious and evince traits of generosity, the trust must nevertheless be declared invalid because it violates the rule against perpetuities. . . .[2]

Authoritative definitions of charitable trusts may be found in 4 Pomeroy's Equity Jurisprudence, 5th Ed., sec. 1020, and Restatement of the Law of Trusts, sec. 368, p.1140. The latter gives a comprehensive classification definition. It is:

Charitable purposes include:
(a) the relief of poverty;
(b) the advancement of education;
(c) the advancement of religion;
(d) the promotion of health;
(e) governmental or municipal purposes; and
(f) other purposes the accomplishment of which is beneficial to the community.

In the recent decision of Allaun v. First, etc., National Bank, 190 Va. 104, 56 S.E.2d 83, the definition that appears in 3 M.J., Charitable Trust, sec. 2, p.872, was approved and adopted. It reads:

"A charity," in a legal sense, may be described as a gift to be applied, consistently with existing laws, for the benefit of an indefinite number of

---

2. In general, a charitable trust is exempt from the Rule against Perpetuities and may endure forever. See infra page 786. A noncharitable purpose trust is void if it can endure longer than the perpetuities period (lives in being plus 21 years). See supra page 477.

persons, either by bringing their hearts under the influence of education or religion, by relieving their bodies from disease, suffering or constraint, by assisting them to establish themselves for life, or by erecting or maintaining public building or works, or otherwise lessening the burdens of government. It is immaterial whether the purpose is called charitable in the gift itself, if it is so described as to show that it is charitable. Generally speaking, any gift not inconsistent with existing laws which is promotive of science or tends to the education, enlightening, benefit or amelioration of the condition of mankind or the diffusion of useful knowledge, or is for the public convenience is a charity. It is essential that a charity be for the benefit of an indefinite number of persons; for if all the beneficiaries are personally designated, the trust lacks the essential element of indefiniteness, which is one characteristic of a legal charity. (190 Va. p.108.) . . .

In the law of trusts there is a real and fundamental distinction between a charitable trust and one that is devoted to mere benevolence. The former is public in nature and valid; the latter is private and if it offends the rule against perpetuities, it is void. "It is quite clear that trusts which are devoted to mere benevolence or liberality, or generosity, cannot be upheld as charities. Benevolent objects include acts dictated by mere kindness, good will, or a disposition to do good. . . . Charity in a legal sense must be distinguished from acts of liberality or benevolence. To constitute a charity the use must be public in its nature." Zollman on Charities, sec. 398, p.268.

We are, however, reminded that charitable trusts are favored creatures of the law enjoying the especial solicitude of courts of equity and a liberal interpretation is employed to uphold them. Zollman on Charities, sec. 570, p.391; 2 Bogert on Trusts, sec. 369, p.1129. . . .

Appellant contends that the gift . . . not only meets the requirements of a charitable trust as defined in Restatement of the Law of Trusts, supra, but specifically fits two of those classifications, viz.:

> (b) trusts for the advancement of education;
> (f) other purposes the accomplishment of which is beneficial to the community.

We now turn to the language of the will for from its context the testator's intent is to be derived. Sheridan v. Krause, 161 Va. 873, 172 S.E. 508, 91 A.L.R. 1067. Its interpretation must be free from and uninfluenced by the unyielding rule against perpetuities. Yet, when the testator's intent is ascertained, if it is found to be in contravention of the rule, the will, in that particular, must be declared invalid. . . .

In paragraphs (1) and (2), respectively, of clause "Second" in clear and definite language the discretion, power and authority of the trustee in its disposition and application of the income are specified and limited.

Yearly on the last school day before Easter and Christmas each youthful beneficiary of the testator's generosity is to be paid an equal share of the income. In mandatory language the duty and the duty alone to make cash payments to each individual child just before Easter and Christmas is enjoined upon the trustee by the certain and explicit words that it "shall divide the net income . . . and shall pay one of such equal shares to each child in such grades."

Without more, that language, and the occasions specified for payment of the funds to the children being when their minds and interests would be far removed from studies or other school activities definitely indicate that no educational purpose was in the testator's mind. It is manifest that there was no intent or belief that the funds would be put to any use other than such as youthful impulse and desire might dictate. But in each instance immediately following the above-quoted language the sentence concludes with the words or phrase "to be used by such child in the furtherance of his or her obtainment of an education." It is significant that by this latter phrase the trustee is given no power, control or discretion over the funds so received by the child. Full and complete execution of the mandate and trust imposed upon the trustee accomplishes no educational purpose. Nothing toward the advancement of education is attained by the ultimate performance by the trustee of its full duty. It merely places the income irretrievably and forever beyond the range of the trust.

Appellant says that the latter phrase, "to be used by such child in furtherance of his or her obtainment of an education," evinces the testator's dominant purpose and intent. Yet it is not denied that the preceding provision "shall divide the net income into as many equal parts . . . and shall pay one of each equal parts to such child" is at odds with the phrase it relies upon. The appended qualification, it says, however, discloses a controlling intent that the 450 or more shares are to be used in the furtherance of education, and it was not really intended that a share be paid to each child so that he or she could during the Christmas and Easter holdays, or at any other time, use it "without let or hindrance, encumbrance or care." With that contruction we cannot agree. In our opinion, the words of the will import an intent to have the trustee pay to each child his allotted share. If that be true, — and it is directed to be done in no uncertain language — we know that the admonition to the children would be wholly impotent and of no avail.

In construing wills, we may not forget or disregard the experiences of life and the realities of the occasion. Nor may we assume or indulge in the belief that the testator by his injunction to the donees intended or thought that he could change childhood nature and set at naught childhood impulses and desires.

Appellant asserts that literal performance of the duty imposed upon it — pay to each child his share — would be impracticable and should not be done. Its position in that respect is stated thus: "We do not understand that under the law of Virginia a court would pay money for education into the hands of children who are incapable of handling it." It then says that the funds could be administered by a guardian or under sec. 8-751, Code, 1950 (where the amounts are under $500), a court could direct payment to be made to the recipient's parents.

With these statements, we agree. But because the funds could be administered under applicable statutes has no bearing upon nor may that device be resorted to as an aid to prove or establish the testator's intent. We are of opinion that the testator's dominant intent appears from and is expressed in his unequivocal direction to the trustee to divide the income into as many equal parts as there are children beneficiaries and pay one share to each. This expressed purpose and intent is inconsistent with the appended direction to each child as to the use of his respective share and the latter phrase is thus ineffectual to create an educational trust. The testator's purpose and intent were, we think, to bestow upon the children gifts that would bring to them happiness on the two holidays, but that falls short of an educational trust.

If it be determined that the will fails to create a charitable trust for *educational purposes* (and our conclusion is that it is inoperative to create such a trust), it is earnestly insisted that the trust provided for is nevertheless charitable and valid. In this respect it is claimed that the two yearly payments to be made to the children just before Christmas and Easter produce "a desirable social effect" and are "promotive of public convenience and needs, and happiness and contentment" and thus the fund set up in the will consititutes a charitable trust. 2 Bogert on Trusts, sec. 361, p.1090, and 3 Scott on Trusts, sec. 368, p.1972. . . .

Numerous cases that deal with and construe specific provisions of wills or other instruments are cited by appellant to uphold the contention that the provisions of this will, without reference to and deleting the phrase "to be used by such child in the furtherance of his or her obtainment of an education" meet the requirements of a charitable trust.

Upon examination of these decisions, it will be found that where a gift results in mere financial enrichment, a trust was sustained only when the court found and concluded from the entire context of the will that the ultimate intended recipients were poor or in necessitous circumstances.

A trust from which the income is to be paid at stated intervals to each member of a designated segment of the public, without regard to whether or not the recipients are poor or in need, is not for the relief of poverty, nor is it a social benefit to the community. It is a mere benevolence — a private trust — and may not be upheld as a charitable trust. Restatement of the Law of Trusts, sec. 374, p.1156: ". . . if a large sum of money is given in trust to apply the income each year in paying a certain sum to every inhabitant of a city, whether rich or poor, the trust is not charitable, since although each inhabitant may receive a benefit, the social interest of the community as such is not thereby promoted."

In 2 Bogert on Trusts, sec. 380, we find:

> As previously stated, gifts which are mere exhibitions of liberality and generosity, without regard to their effect upon the donees, are not charitable. There must be an amelioration of the condition of the donees as a result of the gift, and this improvement must be of a mental, physical, or spiritual nature and not merely financial. Thus, trusts to provide gifts to children, regardless of their need, or to make Christmas gifts to members of a certain class, without consideration of need or effect, are not charitable. . . . (p. 1218.)
>
> Gifts which are made out of mere sentiment, and will have no practical result except the satisfying of a whim of the donor, are obviously lacking in the widespread social effect necessary to a charity. (p. 1219.) . . .

Nor do we find any language in this will that permits the trustee to limit the recipients of the donations to the school children in the designated grades who are in necessitous circumstances, and thus bring the trust under the influence of the case styled Appeal of Eliot, 74 Conn. 586, 51 A. 558.

The conclusion there reached was that where a trust is set up and a class is designated as beneficiary which generally contains needy persons, the testator will be presumed to have intended as recipients those members of the class who are in necessitous circumstances.

Payment to the children of their cash bequests on the two occasions specified would bring to them pleasure and happiness and no doubt cause them to remember or think of their benefactor with gratitude and thanksgiving. That was, we think, Charles B. Henry's intent. Laudable, generous and praiseworthy though it may be, it is not for the relief of the poor or needy, nor does it otherwise so benefit or advance the social interest of the community as to justify its continuance in perpetuity as a charitable trust. . . .

No error is found in the decrees appealed from and they are affirmed. Affirmed.[3]

NOTES AND QUESTIONS

1. To be classified as charitable, a trust that is for the benefit of a class of persons and not for the benefit of the community at large must

---

3. Noted in 23 Miss. L.J. 62; 20 U. Cin. L. Rev. 505; 37 Va. L. Rev. 642; 9 Wash. & Lee L. Rev. 310. — Eds.

be for the relief of poverty or for the advancement of education, religion, health, or other charitable purpose. A trust is not charitable merely because it is for the benefit of a class of persons. Thus a trust for the benefit of needy sailors is charitable, but a trust for the general benefit of sailors is not. Likewise, a trust to pay the salary of a law professor is charitable because it promotes education, but a trust for the general benefit of lawyers is not. 4A A. Scott, Trusts §375 (W. Fratcher 4th ed. 1989).

A trust may be a valid charitable trust although the persons who directly benefit are limited in number. A trust awarding scholarships or prizes for educational achievement is charitable. Annot., 7 A.L.R.3d 1281 (1966).

A trust to educate a particular person or named persons is not charitable. But a trust for the education of one person is charitable if the purpose is to benefit the community. Thus a trust to send a young person through medical school upon his promise that he will return to the testator's hometown to practice has been held charitable. Estate of Carlson, 187 Kan. 543, 358 P.2d 669 (1961).

For analysis of the factors that courts should consider in determining what is charitable, see Lynn, The Questionable Testamentary Gift to Charity: A Suggested Approach to Judicial Decision, 30 U. Chi. L. Rev. 450 (1963).

2.   *Trusts to benefit a political party.*   It is against public policy to endow perpetually a political party; hence a trust to promote the success of a particular political party is not charitable. See Note, Charitable Trusts for Political Purposes, 37 Va. L. Rev. 988 (1951). However, some rather subtle distinctions have been drawn between a trust for a political party and a trust for the improvement of the structure and methods of government, which is charitable. For example, a trust to advance "the principles of socialism and those causes related to socialism," including supporting candidates for public office, has been held charitable. In re Estate of Breeden, 208 Cal. App. 3d 981, 256 Cal. Rptr. 813 (1989). Having been given this distinction, do you think a trust for the advancement of adult education especially for the purpose of indoctrinating persons in the theories and ambitions of the Labor party is charitable? See Re Hopkinson, [1949] 1 All E.R. 346 (Ch.).

A trust with the purpose of bringing about a change in the law may be charitable, provided the purpose is not to bring about changes in the law by illegal means, such as revolution or illegal lobbying. See 2 Restatement (Second) of Trusts §374, Comment j (1959).

3.   *Illegal purposes.*   A trust cannot be created for an illegal purpose. Some purposes formerly found illegal, such as the promotion of atheism, probably would not be found illegal today. Sometimes it is difficult to draw the line. In Estate of Robbins, 57 Cal. 2d 718, 37 P.2d 573, 21 Cal. Rptr. 797 (1962), the testator devised property in trust to use for

the support and education "of such minor Negro child or children, whose father or mother, or both, have been ... imprisoned ... as a result of the conviction of a crime or misdemeanor of a political nature." The next-of-kin contended that the trust encouraged the commission of crime and was therefore illegal. The court held the trust to be charitable on the ground that support of children whose parents were imprisoned was unquestionably of social value and the risk that a parent might be induced to commit a crime so that his or her child might become a trust beneficiary was remote. The court stated that testator's motive, which might have been to encourage unlawful dissent, was not relevant.

4. Community Funds, Inc., an affiliate of the New York Community Trust, administers charitable funds received from thousands of donors. These funds are administered in accordance with the wishes of the individual donors. One fund administered by Community Funds is the Golda and Mollie Fine Fund. In accordance with the donor's will, the fund is used for the following purposes.

PURPOSES OF THE GOLDA AND MOLLIE FINE FUND

Except in instances where it is known that such purpose or purposes have already been adequately provided for in other trust funds or foundations, direct grants are to be made under the above title to promote by word of mouth, for example, in lectures, talks, college courses, meetings and seminars, and by written word, for example, in magazines and newspaper articles and books, the following objectives:

1. *Promotion of a More Effective Control of Noise*

A more efficient control of noise both indoors and outdoors, especially noise from televisions, radios, records and tapes, and the elimination of unnecessary noises and their causes.

2. *Continuity and Avoidance of Duplication*

An effort should be made to do away with the present "hand to mouth" and "pushcart" type procedures in all human endeavor including the rendering of services, by means of the following:

    a. the promotion of continuity;
    b. the avoidance of duplication;
    c. better utilization by professionals of patients' histories.

At present every time someone gets a "brainstorm" in the social, economic or political fields, lo and behold a new agency, a new location, new officers, new stationery and a new publication are created without first an investigation being made of the existing facilities in that field. The curtailing of the present tendency toward the lack of continuity and duplication should also produce such things as shorter and more easily readable medical and dental histories, which will actually be read by doctors and dentists, who will then be better informed about their patients and thus will be better able to treat them.

3. *Preventive Measures*

Preventive medicine, dentistry and law enforcement, fire and accident prevention. Also to be emphasized is the prevention of abuses in the political and law making aspects of our governmental system. Preventive measures should be instituted before a tragedy or abuse occurs and not afterwards.

4. *Standard of Expression*

The promotion of completeness, exactness and accuracy in expression and in performance. Support should be given to any tendency to minimize the use of acronyms and other abbreviations in print and in all communications media. Where there are students who can demonstrate their commitment to a career promoting such improvement in standards of expression and performance they should be assisted in the furtherance of such a career.

5. *Gadgetry*

The promotion of a decrease in the present tendency toward gadgetry for gadgetry's sake.

6. *Fund-Raising Agencies*

The promotion of full disclosure by fund-raising agencies and groups to prospective contributors with respect to other organizations with the same or similar causes. Such fund-raising agencies and groups are not to be permitted to give the impression that they are the only agencies with a particular cause when that is not, in fact, the case.

7. *Commercials*

The promotion of a campaign against excessive and indiscriminate use of musical accompaniment in radio and television commercials. These accompaniments actually defeat the purpose of such commercials by drowning out the words spoken. Another practice that should be eliminated is the inevitable announcement "I am _____" or "This is _____ reporting" at the end of a bit of news from some distant location by an obscure, unknown correspondent whose self-identification is of no interest whatsoever to the listener.

The above numbered purposes are listed in order of importance to me and grants are to be made from the net income of the fund with this in mind. However, upon investigation if it is the opinion of a majority of the Board of Directors of the Community Funds Inc. that all of the above purposes have already been provided for in other trusts or foundations, then the net income from the Golda and Mollie Fine Fund shall be available for the "Special Projects" of the Community Funds Inc.

5.   In Estate of Kidd, 106 Ariz. 554, 479 P.2d 697 (1971), James Kidd, a bachelor of frugal nature, wrote a holographic will in 1946 leaving his estate for "reserach [sic] or some scientific proof of a soul of the human body which leaves at death I think in time their [sic] can be a Photograph of soul leaving the human at death." Shortly thereafter Kidd disappeared without a trace. In 1964, Kidd's will was discovered and offered for probate. His estate amounted to $175,000. More than a hundred claimants stepped forth. Some of the claimants argued that there was no intent to create a charitable trust but an outright bequest to any person who had scientific proof of a soul that leaves the body at death; one of these claimed to have seen her soul leave her body and another claimed that scientific proof included inductive logical arguments based upon the Bible. The court held, however, that a charitable trust was intended. Upon remand, the trial court awarded the bequest to the American Society for Psychical Research in New York City. 110 Trusts & Estates 1058 (1971). In 1975, the society filed a report in the Arizona probate court, stating that it had spent the money from the Kidd estate but had failed to prove the existence of the human soul. N.Y. Times, June 16, 1975, at 30, col. 3.

6.   The lawyer drawing a will making a gift to charity should make sure (a) of the exact legal name of the charity and (b), if there is any doubt, whether the charity is tax-exempt under the Internal Revenue Code. The lawyer drafting a trust giving the trustees discretion to spray the income among charitable organizations should draft the trust so as to restrict the recipient charities to those qualifying as such under the Internal Revenue Code. Trusts for "benevolent" or "philanthropic" purposes should be avoided. Some English cases held that these words are broader than "charitable," and, if so, the trust may fail as a charitable trust because the income can be used for noncharitable purposes. Modern American cases tend to construe these words as synonymous with "charitable," but, out of caution, they should be avoided. See Wilson v. Flowers, 58 N.J. 250, 277 A.2d 199 (1971).

SECTION B.   MODIFICATION OF CHARITABLE TRUSTS: CY PRES

In England, at common law, there was a prerogative power of cy pres as well as a judicial doctrine of cy pres. Under the prerogative doctrine, charitable gifts were expected to comply with public policy as established by the king. Any deviations were corrected by the crown, regardless of the testator's intent. For example, in Da Costa v. De Pas, 1 Amb. 228, 27 Eng. Rep. 150 (Ch. 1754), a Jewish testator left money in trust to form an assembly for the purpose of teaching Jewish law and religion. The trust encouraged a religion other than the state religion and was referred to the king by the chancellor for instructions. Applying prerogative cy pres, the king allotted the money to instruct foundlings in the Christian religion.

Largely as a reaction to the abuse of prerogative cy pres by the crown, disregarding entirely the probable wishes of the testator, courts in this country were reluctant to adopt judicial cy pres. It, too, could be abused. Courts seldom altered an instrument creating a charitable trust until the twentieth century. As the nineteenth century receded into history, however, various changes in circumstances made it difficult or impractical to administer charitable trusts as specifically intended by the donors. A nineteenth-century trust to care for old horses retired from pulling fire wagons and street-cars could not be administered for these purposes in the twentieth century. Hence, American courts finally came to accept a judicial doctrine of cy pres, set forth in the Restatement (Second) of Trusts, below.

Restatement (Second) of Trusts §399 (1959)

If property is given in trust to be applied to a particular charitable purpose, and it is or becomes impossible or impracticable or illegal to carry out the particular purpose, and if the settlor manifested a more general intention to devote the property to charitable purposes, the trust will not fail but the court will direct the application of the property to some charitable purpose which falls within the general charitable intention of the settlor.

R. Posner, Economic Analysis of Law 482-483 (3d ed. 1986)

A policy of rigid adherence to the letter of the donative instrument is likely to frustrate both the donor's purposes and the efficient use of resources. . . .

Where the continued enforcement of conditions in a charitable gift is no longer economically feasible, because of illegality . . . or opportunity costs. . . , the court, rather than declaring the gift void and transferring the property to the residuary legatees (if any can be identified), will authorize the administrators of the charitable trust to apply the assets of the trust to a related (*cy pres*) purpose within the general scope of the donor's intent.

In re Estate of Buck

California Superior Court, Marin County, 1986
Opinion Reprinted from 21 U.S.F.L. Rev. 691 (1987)

[In 1975, Beryl Buck, a childless widow, died, a resident of Marin County, California.[4] Marin County, lying across the bay northward from San Francisco, at the north end of the Golden Gate Bridge, is the most affluent of the counties in the Bay Area. Known as the "hot-tub capital of the world," Marin is the nation's second-wealthiest county of more than 50,000 residents.

Mrs. Buck's will left the residue of her estate to the San Francisco Foundation, a community trust administering charitable funds in five counties in the San Francisco Bay Area (Alameda, Contra Costa, Marin, San Francisco, and San Mateo). Mrs. Buck's will directed that the residue of her estate, to be known and administered as the Leonard and Beryl Buck Foundation,

> shall always be held and used for exclusively non-profit charitable, religious or educational purposes in providing care for the needy in Marin County, California, and for other non-profit charitable, religious, or educational purposes in that county.

At the time of Mrs. Buck's death, the largest asset in her estate consisted of a block of stock in Beldridge Oil Company, a privately held company with rich oil reserves in Southern California, founded by her father-in-law. In 1975 this stock was worth about $9 million, but soon thereafter, in 1979, Shell Oil won a bidding war and bought the stock in the Buck Trust for $260 million. This sudden embarrassment of riches, which increased to well over $300 million by 1984, and all of which was directed by Mrs. Buck's will to be spent on 7 percent of the Bay Area's residents in rich Marin County, seemed to threaten the integrity of the San Francisco Foundation in equitably administering charitable dollars in the Bay Area. In 1984, the Foundation brought suit seeking judicial authorization to spend some portion of Buck Trust income in the other four counties of the Bay Area.

The Foundation's petition for cy pres rested upon the following theory: The enormous increase in the value of principal was a post-

---

4. This statement of facts comes from the trial court's opinion and from Malone, McEachron & Cutler, The Buck Trust Trial — A Litigator's Perspective, 21 U.S.F.L. Rev. 585 (1987).

Beryl H. Buck

594

humous "surprise," a change in circumstances raising substantial doubt whether Mrs. Buck, had she anticipated such an event, would have limited her beneficence to Marin County. This "surprise" warranted inquiry into what Mrs. Buck would have done had she known of this bonanza. The Foundation argued that she would not have limited her beneficence to Marin County because (a) she selected as trustee a foundation administering funds for the benefit of five counties; (b) other philanthropists, as shown by the 50 largest American charitable foundations (with the sole exception of the Buck Trust), reach out beyond their parochial origins as their resources grow and seek to serve a more populous and diverse slice of humanity, following a principle of proportionality; and (c), in the face of such an increase in wealth, the donor would be less interested in a small geographical area and more interested in the efficiency of the charitable dollar. This, the Foundation argued, was the philanthropic standard followed by almost all the great philanthropists of wealth equal to Mrs. Buck's posthumous fortune. It was the way other extremely rich philanthropists behave.

The Foundation's action proved to be throwing fat into a fire. Marin County officials were outraged. One called the Foundation "grave-robbing bastards," and characterized the cy pres petition as a "criminal attack upon the sanctity of wills." Marin officials were joined by the Marin Council of Agencies (a consortium of Marin County nonprofit agencies) in opposing the petition. Forty-six individuals and charitable organizations in the other four counties (called "Objector-Beneficiaries") were allowed to intervene to object to the Marin-only limitation. The Attorney General of California (John Van de Kamp, a leading Democratic politician), as supervisor of charitable trusts, also intervened, arguing against cy pres and asking whether the Foundation was in violation of its fiduciary duties for bringing such a suit and ought to be removed as trustee.

The case caused an uproar in San Francisco, with the local newspaper columnists opening all the stops. At first the commentators were incensed at all that money being spent in rich Marin, but then — on second thought — public opinion began to coalesce behind the idea that Mrs. Buck had the right to do with her property as she wished and the San Francisco Foundation became an object of calumny.

At trial the Foundation proposed to offer expert testimony from Professor John O. Simon of the Yale Law School, one of the country's leading authorities on charitable foundations. Professor Simon proposed to testify that the surprise increase in the Buck endowment, coupled with a finding that charitable dollars were being spent inefficiently, justified application of cy pres.[5] Expert testimony in favor of cy pres

---

5. Professor Simon's theory of cy pres is spelled out in Simon, American Philanthropy and the Buck Trust, 21 U.S.F.L. Rev. 641 (1987).

was also offered by Professor Mitchell Polinsky of Stanford Law School, who proposed to testify that a primary purpose of the cy pres doctrine was to promote efficiency in the use of charitable resources under changed circumstances. The trial court ruled that Simon's and Polinsky's proposed testimony was inadmissible as evidence of the testator's intent.

Near the close of the respondent's case, after nearly six months of trial, the Foundation — pilloried by the Marin County authorities, the press, and the state Attorney General — offered to resign as trustee. All the parties except the 46 Objector-Beneficiaries agreed to a settlement, with the trust to be administered by a new Marin-based community foundation. The 46 Objector-Beneficiaries refused to join in the settlement on the ground that it was a sell-out of the needy in the Bay Area. On July 31, 1986, the Foundation was permitted to resign, and the court dismissed its cy pres petition.

The 46 Objector-Beneficiaries, intervenors, continued to urge the court to apply cy pres to allow Buck Trust money to be spent outside Marin County. On August 15, 1986, the trial court rendered judgment against the 46 Objector-Beneficiaries. After a lengthy statement of the facts and a recitation of how the Foundation had thwarted Mrs. Buck's intentions (e.g., the Foundation's policy was to make grants to religious organizations only when a "substantial secular benefit" was involved, whereas Mrs. Buck explicitly provided for "religious purposes"), the trial court's opinion turned to the application of cy pres.]

THOMPSON, J.

THE DOCTRINE OF CY PRES

    A.   CY PRES APPLIES ONLY WHERE THE PURPOSE OF A TRUST HAS BECOME
       ILLEGAL, IMPOSSIBLE OR PERMANENTLY IMPRACTICABLE OF
       PERFORMANCE

The purpose of the cy pres doctrine "is to prevent the failure of valid charitable trust gifts." Estate of Zahn (1971) 16 Cal. App. 3d 106, 114, cert. denied sub nom. Zahn v. Security Pacific Nat. Bank, 404 U.S. 938. As explained by Professor Scott:

> Where property is given in trust for a particular charitable purpose, the trust will not ordinarily fail even though it is impossible to carry out the particular purpose. In such a case the court will ordinarily direct that the property be applied to a similar charitable purpose. 4 Scott on Trusts (3d ed. 1967), Charitable Trusts, §399 at 3084.

The words "cy pres" mean "as near." The full phrase in Norman French was "cy pres comme possible," meaning "as near as possible." Bogert, Trusts and Trustees (2d ed. 1964) §431 at 490. Thus, cy pres is a rule "of construction, the object of which is 'to permit the main purpose of the donor of a charitable trust to be carried out as nearly as may be where it cannot be done to the letter.'" Society of California Pioneers v. McElroy (1944) 63 Cal. App. 2d 332, 337.

The Restatement (Second) of Trusts, section 399 at 297, describes the cy pres doctrine as follows:

> If property is given in trust to be applied to a particular charitable purpose and *it is or becomes impossible or impracticable or illegal to carry out the particular purpose,* and if the settlor manifested a more general intention to devote the property to charitable purposes, the trust will not fail but the court will direct the application of the property to some charitable purpose which falls within the general charitable intention of the settlor. (Emphasis added).

These eminent authorities, followed by statutory and/or case law in many states, provide that where a purpose of a charitable trust becomes *illegal, impossible or impracticable* of fulfillment, and the testator manifested a general charitable intention, the court may direct that the property be applied to a similar charitable purpose.[6]

Courts in California, as in other states, exercise extreme caution before they will vary the terms of a charitable trust:

> Basically, "charitable contributions must be used only for the purposes for which they were received in trust." (Holt v. College of Osteopathic Physicians & Surgeons (1964) 61 Cal. 2d 750, 754 [40 Cal. Rptr. 244, 394 P.2d 932]). "The policy of the law in favor of charitable gifts requires a court to carry out the dominant purpose of the donor to make a charitable gift for the purposes expressed in the articles of the original corporate donee." (In re Los Angeles County Pioneer Soc. (1953) 40 Cal. 2d 852, 865-66). Only when compliance with these foregoing rules becomes impossible does the application of cy pres come into play. In re Veterans' Industries, Inc., (1970) 8 Cal. App. 3d 902, 919; In re Metropolitan Baptist Church of Richmond, Inc. (1975) 48 Cal. App. 3d 850, 860.

California courts have often quoted the language of the Restatement

---

6. Bogert includes "inexpedient" as a possible prerequisite for the application of cy pres. He describes the doctrine as follows:

> Roughly speaking, it is the doctrine that equity will, when a charity is originally or later becomes impossible, inexpedient, or impracticable of fulfillment, substitute another charitable object which is believed to approach the original purpose as closely as possible. Bogert, Trusts and Trustees, supra, §431 at 490.

Although a few California courts have quoted Bogert in dicta (In re Veteran's Industries, Inc. (1970) 8 Cal. App. 3d 902, 917, n.12, Estate of Jackson (1979) 92 Cal. App. 3d 486, 489), no California court has ever applied cy pres upon finding "inexpediency," or ever applied an "inexpediency" standard for cy pres.

of Trusts setting forth the cy pres standard of illegality, impossibility, or impracticability. The impossibility or impracticability prerequisite, however, has been interpreted in California to require a "*permanency* of the impossibility or impracticability of carrying out the specific charitable purpose or purposes of the creator of the trust." Estate of Mabury (1976) 54 Cal. App. 3d 969, 985 (emphasis in original).

Other California courts have stated that cy pres applies where "the testator has expressed a general charitable intent, and for some reason his purpose cannot be accomplished in the manner specified. . . ." Estate of Gatlin (1971) 16 Cal. App. 3d 644, 648; Estate of Klinkner (1978) 85 Cal. App. 3d 942, 951.

In practice, cy pres has most often been applied in California in such cases — where the charitable trust purpose is or has become literally impossible to fulfill (it "cannot be accomplished") — or in cases where it has become "reasonably impossible of performance." E.g., Society of California Pioneers v. McElroy, supra, 63 Cal. App. 2d 332, 334-35 ("no longer reasonably possible to carry out the testator's intention"), O'Hara v. Grand Lodge of I.O.G.T. (1931) 213 Cal. 131, 140 (method of carrying out the general charitable purpose "has become reasonably impossible of performance").

B.   NEITHER INEFFICIENCY NOR INEFFECTIVE PHILANTHROPY CONSTITUTES IMPRACTICABILITY

"Impracticability" has been defined as "impossible" as early as 1850 in Dr. Johnson's famous dictionary (A Dictionary of the English Language (Henry G. Bohn: London, 1850), p.616). Other prestigious dictionaries have defined impracticability in the same sense, e.g., "incapable of being done or carried out," "a practical impossibility" (Oxford English Dictionary Vol. V. (Oxford University Press: England, 1933), p.106); "incapable of accomplishment" (The Century Dictionary (The Century Co.: New York, 1897), p.3014); "incapable of being performed or carried out" (Webster's Third International Dictionary (G. & C. Merriam Co.: Springfield, Massachusetts, 1967), p.1136); "practically impossible" (The Dictionary of Hard Words (Dodd Mead: New York, 1910), p.275).

California courts have never adopted a broad interpretation of the term "impracticable" in charitable trust cases. One California court, in Estate of Butin (1947) 81 Cal. App. 2d 76, found the trust purpose to be impractical to fulfill. Estate of Butin involved a situation where there was insufficient funds to fulfill the trust purpose. The testatrix had directed the executors of her will to erect in the courthouse park at Madera, California, "a granite tower . . . to contain a carillon of eighteen bells" to be placed in the park at a reasonable cost and with a certain inscription. The testatrix' will also stated that:

I realize that future conditions are very uncertain and if, for any good reason, it is impractical to erect this type of memorial, my executors are then authorized to use their own discretion as to the type of memorial to be erected and the cost thereof. Id. at 79.

The court indicated that "it appeared impractical to construct the memorial . . ." for the following reasons:

that a site for the tower to be located on county property could not be procured, that it would interfere with the public business conducted in the courthouse, and that it would cost more than $100,000, which is in excess of the value of the entire estate. Id. at 81.

The court, then, actually applied the standard — i.e., impractical — set forth by the testatrix in her will. The fact situation itself, given the insufficient funds to construct the tower, essentially involved an impossibility.

In an early case where reversion of the charitable trust, rather than cy pres, was sought, the court rejected a claim that the trust had become "impracticable." In People v. Cogswell (1896) 113 Cal. 129, it was asserted, inter alia, that the trustees had abandoned and violated the trust, and that the trust had become impracticable; therefore, the property should revert to the founders. The California Supreme Court held that:

A trust in this state is not extinguished, nor does the property revert, for any of these reasons. If the trustees abandon or in any way abuse their trust, equity will correct the abuses and remove the offenders. A trust is extinguished by the *entire fulfillment of its object, by its object becoming impossible,* or by its *object becoming unlawful.* (Civ. Code, sec. 2279.) *No one of these contingencies has arisen, and the court was right in finding that the object of the trust had not become impracticable.* The founders had reserved no power of revocation (Civ. Code, sec. 2280), and the acts complained of were mere abuses which, in the absence of an express condition to that effect, did not work a reversion, but merely warranted the interposition of equity for their correction. Id. at 141-42 (emphasis added).

Like California courts, courts from other states often describe the standard for cy pres as one of "illegality, impossibility or impracticability." In many of those jurisdictions, however, "impracticability" is equated with "impossibility." Dunbar v. Board of Trustees (1969) 170 Colo. 327, 461 P.2d 28, 32 (dicta).

The Restatement (Second) of Trusts, (1959) section 399, comment q at 306, does not require a literal impossibility. Rather, it defines "impracticability" as follows:

The doctrine of cy pres is applicable even though it is possible to carry out the particular purpose of the settlor, if to carry it out would *fail to accomplish the general charitable intention* of the settlor. In such case it is "impracticable" to carry out the particular purpose. . . . (Emphasis added).

Ineffective philanthropy, inefficiency and relative inefficiency, that is, inefficiency of trust expenditures in one location given greater relative needs or benefits elsewhere, do not constitute impracticability under either view. Such situation is not the equivalent of impossibility; nor is there any threat that the operation of the trust will fail to fulfill the general charitable intention of the settlor.[7] As stated by one court, "the court's power over the disposition of other people's assets is limited to removing restrictions only if they are incompatible with the testator's dominant purpose." Estate of Wilson (1982) 451 N.Y.S.2d 891, 894 aff'd (1983) 465 N.Y.S.2d 900, 452 N.E.2d 1228. In *Wilson*, although the alternative scheme proposed a gender neutral educational trust, which would have been preferable on public policy grounds, the court stated that:

there is another competing public policy consideration, namely, preserving the right of the testator to dispose of his property as he wishes. (Citation omitted). This rule becomes even more compelling when applied to the area of private charitable trusts, for òne of the very reasons for the rule is to encourage bequests for charitable purposes. Id.

The foregoing policy considerations fully justify the dominant ten-

---

7. To the extent that concepts of effective philanthropy or efficiency relate to achieving the greatest benefit for the cost incurred they should not form the basis for modifying a donor's wishes. No law requires a testator to make a gift which the trustees deem efficient or to constitute effective philanthropy. Moreover, calculating "benefit" involves inherently subjective determinations; thus, what is "effective" or "efficient" will vary, depending on the interests and concerns of the person or persons making the determination. Cy pres does not authorize a court to vary the terms of the bequest merely because the variation will accommodate the desire of the trustee. Connecticut College v. United States (D.C. Cir. 1960) 276 F.2d 491, 493; In re Hawley's Estate (1961) 223 N.Y.S. 803, 805.

To the extent that the term efficiency embraces the concept of relative need, it is not an appropriate basis for modifying the terms of a testamentary trust. (The Foundation itself has acknowledged this, and indicated that such a concept "is neither what Mrs. Buck's will contemplates, nor a term which has any readily ascertainable meaning." (San Francisco Foundation's Statement Regarding Attorney General's Supplemental Response to Second Annual Report, judicially noticed on February 6, 1986.)) If it were otherwise, all charitable gifts, and the fundamental basis of philanthropy would be threatened, as there may always be more compelling "needs" to fill than the gift chosen by the testator. Gifts to Harvard or Stanford University, for example, could fail simply because institutions elsewhere are more needy. Similarly, needs in the Bay Area cannot be equated with the grueling poverty of India or the soul-wrenching famine in Ethiopia. Moreover, a standard of relative need would interpose governmental regulation on philanthropy because courts would be required to consider questions of comparative equity, social utility, or benefit, perhaps even wisdom, and ultimately substitute their judgments or those of the trustees for those of the donors.

dency of courts to require a situation of illegality, impossibility or strict impracticability before they will vary the terms of a charitable trust through an application of cy pres.

The present and well-tested law that cy pres will be invoked to save a charitable bequest that has become impossible or impracticable of fulfillment where the testator has a general charitable intent provides an intermediate concept "between the well established rules of construction that a will is to be construed so as to effectuate the intent of the testator, and that a gift to charity should be effectuated whenever possible." Estate of Klinkner, supra, 85 Cal. App. 3d 942, 951. Where both the testator's intent and the charitable gift can, in fact, be effectuated, i.e., the specified trust purpose has not become impossible or impracticable of performance, there is no justification for cy pres.

The cy pres doctrine should not be so distorted by the adoption of subjective, relative, and nebulous standards such as "inefficiency" or "ineffective philanthropy" to the extent that it becomes a facile vehicle for charitable trustees to vary the terms of a trust simply because they believe that they can spend the trust income better or more wisely elsewhere, or as in this case, prefer to do so. There is no basis in law for the application of standards such as "efficiency" or "effectiveness" to modify a trust, nor is there any authority that would elevate these standards to the level of impracticability.

C. CY PRES MAY NOT BE INVOKED UPON THE BELIEF THAT THE MODIFIED SCHEME WOULD BE MORE DESIRABLE OR WOULD CONSTITUTE A BETTER USE OF THE INCOME

Where the income of a charitable trust can be used for the purpose specified by the testator, cy pres may not be invoked on the grounds that a different use of the income would be more useful or desirable. Several cases from other states elaborate on this principle.

The trustees in In re Oshkosh Foundation (1973) 61 Wis. 2d 432, 213 N.W.2d 54, for example, sought to expand the geographical limits of the trust from the City of Oshkosh to that city plus the various townships which comprised the Oshkosh area school district. The trustees claimed that it was "impractical" to confine disbursements of trust funds to the city limits, as the city's influence extends far beyond its boundaries, and "[t]o treat [the inhabitants of the City of Oshkosh and those of the surrounding area] differently would be unfair to each group." 213 N.W.2d at 56. The court held that cy pres did not apply. Indicating that an application of cy pres requires a finding that compliance with the trust's stated purpose has become impossible, unlawful or impracticable, the court stated that:

> No argument is here made that the purpose of the trust has become either impossible or illegal. Rather it is claimed that compliance with the

trust has become "impracticable" because it has become "unfair." The underlined words are not synonyms. The trustee, in substance, claims only that the use of school district limits would be more useful and desirable than the use of city limits as prescribed in the trust. But *cy pres does not warrant a court substituting a different plan for that set forth in the trust solely because trustee or court, or both, believe the substituted plan to be a better plan.* Where it was neither claimed nor established that there was a lack of qualified scholarship recipients or charitable requests within the limits set by the trust, there is no basis for holding that it has become, in the words of the statute, "impracticable, impossible or unlawful" to comply with the express terms and limits of the trust. Id. at 57 (footnotes omitted) (emphasis added).

Similarly, in In re Petition of Downer Home (1975) 67 Wis. 2d 55, 226 N.W.2d 444, the court admonished that a belief that a substituted use "would be a better use of the income" than the designated use "is not the test" for the application of cy pres. 226 N.W.2d at 450.

Courts have also held that terms of a charitable trust may not be modified on the grounds that a different use would be more beneficial to the community or advantageous to the charity. The trial court in Crow v. Clay County (1906) 196 Mo. 234, 95 S.W. 369 upheld the age and location restriction of a trust "to pay the tuition or education of orphans or poor children under the age of sixteen years, at or within two miles of the county seat of said Clay County." 95 S.W. at 370. Petitioners alleged that because of changed circumstances, i.e., the development of a public school system as opposed to the voluntary system of education operating at the time testator died, the testator's charitable intent could not be carried out. They requested the court to invoke the cy pres doctrine to remove the restrictions and apply the funds toward students' tuition and education in colleges, universities and high technical institutes whether located in the City of Liberty, or elsewhere. Declining to apply the cy pres doctrine, the court quoted several cases to the effect that the trust terms may not be varied on grounds of expediency to the community, policy or convenience. A court

has no right and is not at liberty to speculate on whether it would have been more expedient or beneficial to the community that a different mode of application of funds in charity should have occurred to the mind of the testator. . . . Id. at 376 (quoting Philpott v. St. George's Hospital, 27 Beav. 107).

Similarly,

"there is no just principal which confers a permission to [modify an express provision] at the mere discretion of the court, or upon the sole ground that it appears to be advantageous to the charity. The question is not one of expediency, but of existing exigency." Id. at 377 (quoting Cary Library v. Bliss (1980) 151 Mass. 364-75, 25 N.E.2d 92).

Moreover,

"The intention of the testator is the guide, or in the language of Lord Coke, the lodestone of the court and, therefore, whenever a charitable gift can be administered according to the express directions, the court, like the court of chancery in England, is not at liberty to modify it upon considerations of policy or convenience." Id. at 379 (quoting Jackson v. Phillips, 14 Allen (Mass.) 591-93).

Rejecting contentions that the charity fund would be wasted and misappropriated, the Supreme Court of Missouri affirmed the trial court's decree upholding the trust restrictions as to age and territorial limits.

Thus, cy pres may not be invoked on the grounds that it would be more "fair," "equitable" or "efficient" to spend the Trust funds in a manner different from that specified by the testator.

D. CY PRES DOES NOT AUTHORIZE THE COURT TO VARY THE TERMS OF A
    TRUST MERELY BECAUSE THE VARIATION WILL MEET THE DESIRE AND
    SUIT THE CONVENIENCE OF THE TRUSTEE

Nor is cy pres warranted to alleviate the strain or burden a trust has placed on a trustee organization and as stated by Martin Paley [Director of the San Francisco Foundation], to "modify the nature of the Buck Trust to conform to and become compatible with the values and procedures of the Foundation as a whole."

"[T]he cy pres doctrine does not authorize or permit a court to vary the terms of a bequest and to that extent defeat the intention of the testator merely because the *variation will meet the desire and suit the convenience of the trustee.*" Connecticut College v. United States (1960) 276 F.2d 491, 497. (Emphasis added).

Rather, "[e]ither impossibility or impracticability of literal compliance with the donor's plan is indispensibly necessary if cy pres is applied." Id.[8] . . . See also In re Hawley's Estate (1961) 223 N.Y.S.2d 803, 805 (before relief may be afforded the court must be satisfied that, *inter alia*, "the variation from the terms of the will is not merely a matter of satisfying the desires and suiting the convenience of the trustee").

---

8. In Connecticut College v. United States, the testator left funds for the construction of a memorial building in a particular location at the United States Military Academy. The Academy declined to erect the building at the proposed site because the location did not accord with its building expansion program. The court refused to apply cy pres to permit the Academy to use the funds to construct a wing on an existing building. — Eds.

The Foundation accepted the Buck Trust fully cognizant of the . . . administrative burden. . . . That, in fact, it has caused an administrative burden on the Foundation and is perceived to be a threat to the integrity of the Foundation as a whole does not warrant varying the terms of Mrs. Buck's bequest. . . .

Cy pres may not be applied to modify the terms of the Buck Trust.

CONCLUSIONS

The residents of Marin County have substantial unmet needs which are within the scope of the purposes of the Buck Trust. In addition, there are significant opportunities to spend Buck Trust funds on non-profit charitable, religious or educational purposes in Marin County which could benefit Marin County, and, if appropriate, all of human-kind. The entire income of the Buck Trust is presently insufficient, and will remain insufficient in the future, to address all of these needs and opportunities.

A Judgment pursuant to this Statement of Decision should be entered denying the Petition for Modification.

NOTES AND QUESTIONS

1. No appeal was taken from the superior court decision in *Buck*. The superior court ordered the creation of the Marin Community Foundation to administer the Buck Trust. The new foundation is to be governed by seven trustees, two appointed by the Marin County Board of Supervisors, one by the Marin Council of Agencies, one by the President of the University of California, one by the Interfaith Council of Marin, one by the Buck family, and one by the M.C.F. board. The superior court appointed a special full-time master to supervise the M.C.F., with authority to approve, item by item, M.C.F.'s budget. The master was required to make regular reports to the court. The court order required 20 percent of Buck money to be spent annually on major projects "located in Marin County, the benefits from which will inure not only to Marin County but all of humankind." The special master invited proposals, and the trial judge chose three Marin-based research institutes to divide approximately $6 million annually: The Buck Center on Aging, The Institute on Alcohol and Other Drug Problems, and The Marin Educational Institute. The superior court reserved the right in the special master and court to monitor the financial needs of these institutions. See Maloney, The Aftermath, 21 U.S.F.L. Rev. 681 (1987).

Professor Simon commented on the supervisory role assumed by the trial court over the Buck Trust at the end:

The extraordinary command role the court reserved for itself over the decision-making process . . . violates the basic concept of private philanthropy and disregards the role assigned to charitable trustees in the nonprofit sector. . . .

[I]t is not obvious that these programs would have been *preferred* by the donor over distributions to neighboring Bay Area counties served by the Foundation. As noted above, the fact that she picked a community foundation focused on the Bay Area as the instrument of her charity cannot be ignored when shaping a cy pres solution. [Simon, American Philanthropy and the Buck Trust, 21 U.S.F.L. Rev. 641, 666-668 (1987).]

For other comments on the *Buck* case, see Note, Phantom Selves: The Search for a General Charitable Intent in the Application of the Cy Pres Doctrine, 40 Stan. L. Rev. 973 (1988); Note, Relaxing the Dead Hand's Grip: Charitable Efficiency and the Doctrine of Cy Pres, 74 Va. L. Rev. 635 (1988); Comment, Cy Pres Inexpediency and the Buck Trust, 20 U.S.F.L. Rev. 577 (1986).

2. Modern academic commentators favor expanding the use of judicial cy pres to change charitable trust provisions to maximize community benefits as required by changing community needs. See Johnson & Taylor, Revolutionizing Judicial Interpretation of Charitable Trusts: Applying Relational Contracts and Dynamic Interpretation to Cy Pres and America's Cup Litigation, 74 Iowa L. Rev. 545 (1989); Chester, Cy Pres: A Promise Unfulfilled, 54 Ind. L.J. 407 (1979); DiClerico, Cy Pres: A Proposal for Change, 47 B.U.L. Rev. 153 (1967). But cf. Macey, Private Trusts for the Provision of Private Goods, 37 Emory L.J. 295 (1988) (arguing that cy pres should be severely limited because the attempt to discern the testator's intent creates increased error costs and transaction costs).

In his thoughtful book, Public Policy and the Dead Hand, Professor Lewis Simes argued that after 30 years courts should have enlarged cy pres power to modify charitable trusts "not only if the original purpose was found impracticable but also if . . . the amount to be expended is out of all proportion to its value to society." L. Simes, Public Policy and the Dead Hand 139 (1955). Is this a good idea? See also Luxton, Cy-Pres and the Ghost of Things That Might Have Been, 1983 Convey. 107, suggesting giving importance to the testator's intention in the early years of the trust but, at the end of the perpetuities period, treating the property as dedicated to charity.

3. Courts have used cy pres when money has been left to an entity that does not exist. Thus a gift to the Cancer Research Fund, a nonexistent entity, has been given to the American Cancer Society, which sponsors cancer research. In re Tomlinson's Estate, 65 Ill. 2d 382, 359 N.E.2d 109 (1976).

4. Cy pres should be contrasted with *administrative deviation*. A court will permit deviation in the administrative terms of a trust when

compliance would defeat or substantially impair the accomplishment of the purposes of the trust. It is not always clear what is an administrative term and what is a central purpose, however, and courts have been known to interpret "administrative" broadly on appealing facts. In Dartmouth College v. City of Quincy, 357 Mass. 521, 258 N.E.2d 745 (1970), for example, the testator in 1870 established a trust to build and support the Woodward School for the education of females born in Quincy, Massachusetts. In 1968, the fund provided only $13,000 toward the school's total $53,000 operating costs, and to generate additional income the trustees proposed to admit non-Quincy-born girls, charging them a higher tuition than Quincy-born girls. The court held that it would permit deviation in the administrative terms of the trust and approved the trustees' plan.

See also Grant Home v. Medlock, 349 S.E.2d 655 (S.C. App. 1986) (permitting trustees operating home for needy white Presbyterians in deteriorating neighborhood to sell home and use proceeds to establish housing subsidy funds for needy Presbyterians of all races residing in Charleston).

5. It is sometimes said that the presence of a gift over precludes the exercise of cy pres to save the gift. The gift over is thought to be inconsistent with the general charitable intent requirement of cy pres. However, careful analysis shows that the gift over is only one factor to be weighed in ascertaining the donor's intent. See Chester, Cy Pres or Gift Over?: The Search for Coherence in Judicial Reform of Failed Charitable Trusts, 23 Suffolk U.L. Rev. 41 (1989).

In re Wilson
Court of Appeals of New York, 1983
59 N.Y.2d 461, 452 N.E.2d 1228, 465 N.Y.S.2d 900

COOKE, C.J.   These appeals present the question whether the equal protection clause of the Fourteenth Amendment is violated when a court permits the administration of private charitable trusts according to the testators' intent to finance the education of male students and not female students. When a court applies trust law that neither encourages, nor affirmatively promotes, nor compels private discrimination but allows parties to engage in private selection in the devise or bequest of their property, that choice will not be attributable to the State and subjected to the Fourteenth Amendment's strictures.

I

The factual patterns in each of these matters are different, but the underlying legal issues are the same. In each there is imposed a decedent's intention to create a testamentary trust under which the class of beneficiaries are members of one sex.

In Matter of Wilson, Article Eleventh of Clark W. Wilson's will provided that the residuary of his estate be held in trust (Wilson Trust) and that the income "be applied to defraying the education and other expenses of the first year at college of five (5) young men who shall have graduated from the Canastota High School, three (3) of whom shall have attained the highest grades in the study of science and two (2) of whom shall have attained the highest grades in the study of chemistry, as may be certified to by the then superintendent for the Canastota Central School District." Wilson died in June 1969 and for the next 11 years the Wilson Trust was administered according to its terms.

In early 1981, the Civil Rights Office of the United States Department of Education received a complaint alleging that the Superintendent's acts in connection with the Wilson Trust violated Title IX of the Education Amendments of 1972 (U.S. Code, tit. 20, section 1681, et seq.), which prohibits gender discrimination in federally financed education programs. The Department of Education informed the Canastota Central School District that the complaint would be investigated. Before the investigation was completed, the School District agreed to refrain from again providing names of students to the trustee. The trustee, Key Bank of Central New York, initiated this proceeding for a determination of the effect and validity of the trust provision of the will.

The Surrogate's Court held that the School Superintendent's cooperation with the trustee violated no federal statute or regulation prohibiting sexual discrimination, nor did it implicate the equal protection clause of the Fourteenth Amendment. The Court ordered the trustee to continue administering the trust.

A unanimous Appellate Division, Third Department, modified the Surrogate's decree. The court affirmed the Surrogate's finding that the testator intended the trust to benefit male students only and, noting that the school was under no legal obligation to provide the names of qualified male candidates, found "administration of the trust according to its literal terms impossible." The Court then exercised its cy pres power to reform the trust by striking the clause in the will providing for the School Superintendent's certification of the names of qualified candidates for the scholarships. The candidates were permitted to apply directly to the trustee.

Matter of Johnson also involves a call for judicial construction of a testamentary trust created for the exclusive benefit of male students. By a will dated December 13, 1975, Edwin Irving Johnson left his residuary estate in trust (Johnson Trust). Article Sixth of the will provided that the income of the trust was to "be used and applied, each year to the extent available, for scholarships or grants for bright and deserving young men who have graduated from the High School of [the Croton-Harmon Union Free] School District, and whose parents are financially unable to send them to college, and who shall be selected by the Board of Education of such School District with the assistance of the principal of such High School."

Johnson died in 1978. In accordance with the terms of the trust, the Board of Education, acting as trustee, announced that applications from male students would be accepted on or before May 1, 1979. Before any scholarships were awarded, however, the National Organization for Women filed a complaint with the Civil Rights Office of the United States Department of Education. This complaint alleged that the School District's involvement in the Johnson Trust constituted illegal gender-based discrimination.

During the pendency of the Department of Education's investigation, a stipulation was entered into between the executrix of the will, the President of the Board of Education, and the Attorney General. The parties sought "to avoid administering the educational bequest set forth in Article Sixth in a manner which is in conflict with the law and public policy prohibiting discrimination based on sex." The stipulation provided that "all interested parties agree to the deletion of the word 'men' in Article Sixth of the Will and the insertion of the word 'persons' in its place." The Attorney General then brought this proceeding by petition to the Surrogate's Court to construe Article Sixth of the will.

The Surrogate found that the trustee's unwillingness to administer the trust according to its terms rendered administration of the trust impossible. The court, however, declined to reform the trust by giving effect to the stipulation. Rather, it reasoned that the testator's primary intent to benefit "deserving young men" would be most closely effected by replacing the School District with a private trustee.

A divided Appellate Division, Second Department, reversed, holding that under the equal protection clause of the Fourteenth Amendment, a court cannot reform a trust that, by its own terms, would deny equal protection of law. The court reasoned that inasmuch as an agent of the State had been appointed trustee, the trust, if administered, would violate the equal protection clause. Judicial reformation of the trust by substituting trustees would, in that court's view, itself constitute state action in violation of the Fourteenth Amendment. The court determined that administration of the trust was impossible and, in an exercise of its cy pres power, reformed the trust by eliminating the gender restriction.

II

On these appeals, this court is called upon to consider the testators' intent in establishing these trusts, evaluate the public policy implications of gender restrictive trusts generally, and determine whether the judicial reformation of these trusts violates the equal protection clause of the Fourteenth Amendment.

There can be no question that these trusts, established for the promotion of education, are for a charitable purpose within the meaning of the law. . . .

When a court determines that changed circumstances have rendered the administration of a charitable trust according to its literal terms either "impracticable or impossible," the court may exercise its cy pres power to reform the trust in a manner that "will most effectively accomplish its general purposes" (E.P.T.L. §8-1.1, subd.(c)). In reforming trusts pursuant to this power, care must be taken to evaluate the precise purpose or direction of the testator, so that when the court directs the trust towards another charitable end, it will "give effect insofar as practicable to the full design of the testator as manifested by his will and codicil" (Matter of Scott, 8 N.Y.2d 419, 427; see Bogert, Trusts and Trustees §442 (Rev. 2d ed.)).

The court, of course, cannot invoke its cy pres power without first determining that the testator's specific charitable purpose is no longer capable of being performed by the trust (see, e.g., matter of Scott, supra; Matter of Swan, 237 App. Div. 454, aff'd sub nom. Matter of St. Johns Church of Mt. Morris, 263 N.Y. 638; Matter of Fairchild, 15 Misc. 2d 272). In establishing these trusts, the testators expressly and unequivocally intended that they provide for the educational expenses of male students. It cannot be said that the accomplishment of the testators' specific expression of charitable intent is "impossible or impracticable." So long as the subject high schools graduate boys with the requisite qualifications, the testators' specific charitable intent can be fulfilled.

Nor are the trusts' particular limitation of beneficiaries by gender invalid and incapable of being accomplished as violative of public policy. It is true that the eradication in this state of gender-based discrimination is an important public policy. Indeed, the Legislature has barred gender-based discrimination in education (see Education Law, §3201-a), employment (see Labor Law, §§194, 197, 220-e; General Business Law, §187), housing, credit, and many other areas (see Executive Law, §296). As a result, women, once viewed as able to assume only restricted roles in our society (see Bradwell v. State, 83 U.S. 130, 141), now project significant numbers "in business, in the professions, in government and, indeed, in all walks of life where education is a desirable, if not always a necessary antecedent" (Stanton v. Stanton, 421 U.S. 7, 15). The restrictions in these trusts run contrary to this policy favoring equal opportunity and treatment of men and women. A provision in a charitable trust, however, that is central to the testator's or settlor's charitable purpose, and is not illegal, should not be invalidated on public policy grounds unless that provision, if given effect, would substantially mitigate the general charitable effect of the gift (see IV Scott on Trusts, §399.4 (3d ed.)).

Proscribing the enforcement of gender restrictions in private charitable trusts would operate with equal force towards trusts whose benefits are bestowed exclusively on women. "Reduction of disparity in economic condition between men and women caused by the long history of discrimination against women has been recognized as . . . an important governmental objective" (Califano v. Webster, 430 U.S. 313, 317). There can be little doubt that important efforts in effecting this type of social change can be and are performed through private philanthropy (see, generally, Commission on Private Philanthropy and Public Needs, Giving in America: Toward a Stronger Voluntary Section (1975)). And, the private funding of programs for the advancement of women is substantial and growing (see Bernstein, Funding for Women's Higher Education: Looking Backward and Ahead, Grant Magazine Vol. 4, No. 4 pp. 225-229; Ford Foundation, Financial Support of Women's Programs in the 1970's (1979); Yarrow, Feminist Philanthropy Comes Into Its Own, N.Y. Times, May 21, 1983, at p.7, col. 2). Indeed, one compilation of financial assistance offered primarily or exclusively to women lists 854 sources of funding (see Schlacter, Directory of Financial Aids for Women (2d ed. 1981); see, also, Note, Sex Restricted Scholarships and the Charitable Trust, 59 Iowa L. Rev. 1000, 1000-1001 & nn. 10, 11). Current thinking in private philanthropic institutions advocates that funding offered by such institutions and the opportunities within the institutions themselves be directly responsive to the needs of particular groups (see Ford Foundation, supra at pp. 41-44; Fleming, Foundations and Affirmative Action, 4 Foundation News No. 4 at pp. 14-17; Griffen, Funding for Women's Programs, 6 Grantsmanship Center News, No. 2 at pp. 34-45). It is evident, therefore, that the focusing of private philanthropy on certain classes within society may be consistent with public policy. Consequently, that the restrictions in the trusts before this court may run contrary to public efforts promoting equality of opportunity for women does not justify imposing a per se rule that gender restrictions in private charitable trusts violate public policy.

Finally, this is not an instance in which the restriction of the trusts serves to frustrate a paramount charitable purpose. In Howard Savings Institution v. Peep (34 N.J. 494), for example, the testator made a charitable bequest to Amherst College to be placed in trust and to provide scholarships for "deserving American born, Protestant, Gentile boys of good moral repute, not given to gambling, smoking, drinking or similar acts." Due to the religious restrictions, the college declined to accept the bequest as contrary to its charter. The court found that the college was the principal beneficiary of the trust, so that removing the religious restriction and thereby allowing the college to accept the gift would permit administration of the trust in a manner most closely effectuating the testator's intent (see, also, Matter of Hawley, 32 Misc. 2d 624; Coffee v. William Marsh Rice University, 408 S.W.2d 269).

In contrast, the trusts subject to these appeals were not intended to directly benefit the school districts. Although the testators sought the school districts' participation, this was incidental to their primary intent of financing part of the college education of boys who attended the schools. Consequently, severance of the school districts' role in the trusts' administration will not frustrate any part of the testators' charitable purposes. Inasmuch as the specific charitable intent of the testators is not inherently "impossible or impracticable" of being achieved by the trusts, there is no occasion to exercise cy pres power.

Although not inherently so, these trusts are currently incapable of being administered as originally intended because of the school districts' unwillingness to cooperate. These impediments, however, may be remedied by an exercise of a court's general equitable power over all trusts to permit a deviation from the administrative terms of a trust and to appoint a successor trustee.

A testamentary trust will not fail for want of a trustee and, in the event a trustee is unwilling or unable to act, a court may replace the trustee with another. Accordingly, the proper means of continuing the Johnson Trust would be to replace the School District with someone able and willing to administer the trust according to its terms.

When an impasse is reached in the administration of a trust due to an incidental requirement of its terms, a court may effect, or permit the trustee to effect, a deviation from the trust's literal terms. This power differs from a court's cy pres power in that "[t]hrough exercise of its deviation power the court alters or amends administrative provisions in the trust instrument but does not alter the purpose of the charitable trust or change its dispositive provisions" (Bogert, Trusts and Trustees, §394 p. 249 (Rev. 2d ed.); see, e.g., Trustees of Sailors' Snug Harbor v. Carmody, 221 N.Y. 286; Matter of Bruen, 83 N.Y.S.2d 197; Matter of Godfrey, 36 N.Y.S.2d 414, aff'd no opn. 264 App. Div. 885). The Wilson Trust provision that the School District certify a list of students is an incidental part of the trust's administrative requirements, which no longer can be satisfied in light of the District's refusal to cooperate. The same result intended by the testator may be accomplished by permitting the students to apply directly to the trustee. Therefore, a deviation from the Wilson Trust's administrative terms by eliminating the certification requirement would be the appropriate method of continuing that trust's administration.

III

It is argued before this court that the judicial facilitation of the continued administration of gender-restrictive charitable trusts violates the equal protection clause of the Fourteenth Amendment (see U.S. Const., 14th Amdt., §1). The strictures of the equal protection clause are invoked when the State engages in invidious discrimination (see Moose Lodge No. 107 v. Irvis, 407 U.S. 163, 173, 176-177; Burton v. Wilmington Parking Auth., 365 U.S. 715, 721; The Civil Rights Cases, 109 U.S. 3). Indeed, the State itself cannot, consistent with the Fourteenth Amendment, award scholarships that are gender restrictive (see Mississippi University for Women v. Hogan, 458 U.S. 962; Kirchberg v. Feenstra, 450 U.S. 455; Stanton v. Stanton, 421 U.S. 7, supra).

The Fourteenth Amendment, however, "erects no shield against merely private conduct, however discriminatory or wrongful." (Shelley v. Kraemer, 334 U.S. 1, 13; see Blum v. Yaretski, 457 U.S. 991; Jackson v. Metropolitan Edison Co., 419 U.S. 345, 349; Moose Lodge No. 107 v. Irvis, 407 U.S. 163, 171-179, supra; Evans v. Abney, 396 U.S. 435, 445. . . .) Private discrimination may violate equal protection of the law when accompanied by state participation in, facilitation of, and, in some cases, acquiescence in the discrimination. Although there is no conclusive test to determine when state involvement in private discrimination will violate the Fourteenth Amendment, the general standard that has evolved is whether "the conduct allegedly causing the deprivation of a federal right [is] fairly attributable to the State" (Lugar v. Edmondson Oil Co., 457 U.S. 922). Therefore, it is a question of "state responsibility" and "[o]nly by sifting facts and weighing circumstances can the . . . involvement of the State in private conduct be attributed its true significance" (Burton v. Wilmington Parking Auth., 365 U.S. 715, 722, supra). . . .

In Shelley v. Kraemer, for example, the Supreme Court held that the equal protection clause was violated by judicial enforcement of a private covenant that prohibited the sale of affected properties to "people of Negro or Mongolian Race." When one of the properties was sold to a black family, the other property owners sought to enforce the covenant in state court and the family was ordered to move from the property. The Supreme Court noted

> that the restrictive agreements standing alone cannot be regarded as violative of any rights guaranteed to petitioners by the Fourteenth Amendment. So long as the purposes of those agreements are effectuated by voluntary adherence to their terms, it would appear clear that there has been no action by the State and the provisions of the Amendment have not been violated (334 U.S. at p.13).

The court held, however, that it did not have before it cases in which the States have merely abstained from action, leaving private individuals free to impose such discriminations as they see fit. Rather, these are cases in which the States have made available to such individuals the full coercive power of the government to deny petitioners, on the grounds of race or color, the enjoyment of property rights (id. at p.19).

It was not the neutral regulation of contracts permitting parties to enter discriminatory agreements that caused the discrimination to be attributable to the State. Instead, it was that the State court's exercise of its judicial power directly effected a discriminatory act.

In Barrows v. Jackson (346 U.S. 249), the Court applied the same reasoning when it held that a court's awarding damages against a party who has breached a racially restrictive covenant also violates the equal protection clause. The Court reiterated that "voluntary adherence [to the covenant] would constitute individual action only" (id. at p.253). But, "[t]o compel respondent to respond in damages would be for the State to punish her for her failure to perform her covenant to continue to discriminate against non-Caucasians in the use of her property. . . . Thus, it becomes not respondent's voluntary choice but the State's choice that she observe her covenant or suffer damages" (id. at p.254). . . .

A court's application of its equitable power to permit the continued administration of the trusts involved in these appeals falls outside the ambit of the Fourteenth Amendment. Although the field of trusts is regulated by the state, the Legislature's failure to forbid private discriminatory trusts does not cause such trusts, when they arise, to be attributable to the State (see Flagg Bros., Inc. v. Brooks, 436 U.S. 149, 165; see, also, Evans v. Abney, 396 U.S. 435, 458 (Brennan, J., dissenting), supra). It naturally follows that, when a court applies this trust law and determines that it permits the continued existence of private discriminatory trusts, the Fourteenth Amendment is not implicated.

In the present appeals, the coercive power of the State has never been enlisted to enforce private discrimination. Upon finding that requisite formalities of creating a trust had been met, the courts below determined the testator's intent, and applied the relevant law permitting those intentions to be privately carried out. The court's power compelled no discrimination. That discrimination had been sealed in the private execution of the wills. Recourse to the courts was had here only for the purpose of facilitating the administration of the trusts, not for enforcement of their discriminatory dispositive provisions.

This is not to say that a court's exercise of its power over trusts can never invoke the scrutiny of the Fourteenth Amendment. This court holds only that a trust's discriminatory terms are not fairly attributable to the State when a court applies trust principles that permit private discrimination but do not encourage, affirmatively promote, or compel it.

The testators' intention to involve the State in the administration of these trusts does not alter this result, notwithstanding that the effect of the courts' action respecting the trusts was to eliminate this involvement. The courts' power to replace a trustee who is unwilling to act as in *Johnson* or to permit a deviation from an incidental administrative term in the trust as in *Wilson* is a part of the law permitting this private conduct and extends to all trusts regardless of their purposes. It compels no discrimination. Moreover, the minimal State participation in the trusts' administration prior to the time that they reached the courts for the constructions under review did not cause the trusts to take on an indelible public character (see Evans v. Newton, 382 U.S. 296, 301; Pennsylvania v. Brown, 392 F.2d 120).

In sum, the Fourteenth Amendment does not require the State to exercise the full extent of its power to eradicate private discrimination. It is only when the State itself discriminates, compels another to discriminate, or allows another to assume one of its functions and discriminate that such discrimination will implicate the Amendment.

Accordingly, in Matter of Wilson, the order of the Appellate Division should be affirmed, with costs payable out of the estate to all parties appearing separately and filing separate briefs.

In Matter of Johnson, the order of the Appellate Division should be reversed, with costs payable out of the estate to all parties appearing separately and filing separate briefs and the decree of the Surrogate's Court, Westchester County, reinstated.[9]

NOTES AND PROBLEMS

1. In Evans v. Newton, 382 U.S. 296 (1966), the court held that a public park given in 1911 by Senator Bacon to Macon, Georgia, in trust, as long as it was used by white persons only, could not continue to be operated on a racially discriminatory basis. Upon remand, the Supreme Court of Georgia ruled that since Senator Bacon's intention to provide a park for whites only had become impossible to fulfill, the trust failed and the land reverted to the heirs of the senator. The United States Supreme Court affirmed. Evans v. Abney, 396 U.S. 435 (1970). The Supreme Court found the decision by the Georgia court not to apply cy pres was not unconstitutional state action. Said the Court:

Surely the Fourteenth Amendment is not violated where, as here, a state

---

9. Noted in 12 Hastings Const. L.Q. 127; 5 Pace L. Rev. 433; 53 U. Cin. L. Rev. 297.

court operating in its judicial capacity fairly applies its normal principles of construction to determine the testator's true intent in establishing a charitable trust and then reaches a conclusion with regard to that intent which, because of the operation of neutral and non-discriminatory state trust laws, effectively denies everyone, whites as well as Negroes, the benefits of the trust. [Id. at 446.]

2. In Trustees of University of Delaware v. Gebelein, 420 A.2d 1191 (Del. Ch. 1980), the court dealt with a scholarship fund for women only administered by the University of Delaware. The court held that the administration of the trust by trustees at a state university must be deemed state action but that sex discrimination in favor of women was permissible because its purpose was to compensate women for past acts of discrimination. In Ebitz v. Pioneer National Bank, 372 Mass. 207, 361 N.E.2d 225 (1977), a scholarship fund established to aid "young men to acquire a legal education" was construed to include women on the theory that testator used "men" in its generic sense, meaning persons.

3. Testator's will provides: "I do give one dollar each to my brothers & sisters and the rest to some Protestant school that is all white of Engineering training, I care not which." What should the court do? See In re Estate of Vanderhoofven, 18 Cal. App. 3d 940, 96 Cal. Rptr. 260 (1971); cf. In re Estate of Zahn, 16 Cal. App. 3d 106, 93 Cal. Rptr. 810 (1971). Suppose that the testator bequeaths a sum of money to the First National Bank in trust to provide college scholarships for white Protestant persons only. Would enforcement of the trust be unconstitutional? See Lockwood v. Killian, 172 Conn. 496, 375 A.2d 998 (1977), 179 Conn. 62, 425 A.2d 909 (1979). Cf. Tinnin v. First United Bank of Mississippi, 50 So. 2d 659 (Miss. 1987).

See Luria, Prying Loose the Dead Hand of the Past: How Courts Apply Cy Pres to Race, Gender, and Religiously Restricted Trusts, 21 U.S.F.L. Rev. 41 (1987); Swanson, Discriminatory Charitable Trusts: Time For a Legislative Solution, 48 U. Pitt. L. Rev. 153 (1986); Leacock, Racial Preferences in Educational Trusts: An Overview of the United States Experience, 28 How. L.J. 715 (1985); Adams, Racial and Religious Discrimination in Charitable Trusts: A Current Analysis of Constitutional and Trust Law Solutions, 25 Clev. St. L. Rev. 1 (1976).

SECTION C. SUPERVISION OF CHARITABLE TRUSTS

R. Posner, Economic Analysis of Law
484 (3d ed. 1986)

Even where no unforeseen contingencies occur, perpetual charitable gifts raise an economic issue that echoes the concern with the separation of ownership and control in the modern business corporation. A charitable foundation that enjoys a substantial income, in perpetuity, from its original endowment is an institution that does not compete in any product market or in the capital markets and that has no stockholders. Its board of trustees is self-perpetuating and is accountable to no one (except itself) for the performance of the enterprise. (Although state attorneys general have legal authority over the administration of charitable trusts, it is largely formal.) At the same time, neither the trustees nor the staff have the kind of property right in the foundation's assets or income that would generate a strong incentive for them to maximize value. Neither the carrot nor the stick is in play.

The incentives to efficient management of foundation assets could be strengthened by a rule requiring charitable foundations to distribute every gift received, principal and interest, including the original endowment, within a specified period of years. The foundation would not be required to wind up its operations within the period; it could continue indefinitely. But it would have to receive new gifts from time to time in order to avoid exhausting all of its funds. Since donors are unlikely to give money to an enterprise known to be slack, the necessity of returning periodically to the market for charitable donations would give trustees and managers of charitable foundations an incentive they now lack to conduct a tight operation. Foundations — mostly religious and educational — that market their services or depend on continuing charitable support, and are therefore already subject to some competitive constraints, could be exempted from the exhaustion rule.

The objections to the suggested rule are that it is unnecessary — donors are already free to limit the duration of their charitable bequests — and that it might therefore (why therefore?) reduce the incentives to make charitable gifts. A counterargument is that many perpetual foundations were established at a time when the foundation was a novel institution; a person creating one at that time simply could not have foreseen the problem of inefficient and unresponsive management that might plague a perpetual foundation as a result of the peculiar set of constraints (or rather lack of constraints) under which they operate.

Since 1940 the amount of private wealth devoted to charitable purposes in the United States has increased spectacularly. This is largely the result of various income and estate tax savings that can be achieved by gifts to charity. Founders of new charitable enterprises can choose to organize either as a corporation or as a trust. In both cases the governing trustees are fiduciaries performing trust duties. Rules governing charitable trusts ordinarily apply to charitable corporations as well.

The Foundation Directory (11th ed., 1987) reported that in 1986 there were approximately 24,859 active grant-making foundations in the United States. These foundations held around $93 billion in assets and awarded about $6 billion annually in grants. About 97 percent of the assets were owned by 5,148 foundations, each with more than $1 million in assets. Id. at xiv. The 11 largest foundations, each with over a billion dollars in assets, were (id. at xv):

	Assets *(Millions)*	*Grants* *(Millions)*
Ford Foundation	$4,759	$170
J. Paul Getty Trust	3,691	159
W.K. Kellogg Foundation	3,108	75
John D. & Catherine T. MacArthur Foundation	2,271	105
Lilly Endowment	1,914	57
Robert Wood Johnson Foundation	1,804	95
Rockefeller Foundation	1,606	45
Pew Memorial Trust	1,550	59
Andrew W. Mellon Foundation	1,477	67
Kresge Foundation	1,147	42

The Marin Community Foundation, created as a result of the court order in In re Estate of Buck, is listed as having $430 million in assets. The San Francisco Foundation, without the Buck Trust, has assets of $177 million. Among community foundations, the Marin Community Foundation is exceeded in assets only by the New York Community Trust, which has $527 million.

Grants were dispersed in 1986 by 5,148 charitable foundations for the following purposes (id. at xxxv):

	Millions	*Percent*
Welfare	$ 586	26
Education	485	22
Health	454	21
Cultural Activities	327	15
Social Science	194	9
Science	142	6
Religion	27	1
	$2,215	100

The government has two basic interests in the administration of charitable foundations: (1) preventing the abuse of tax privileges granted by the state and (2) as representative of the public, which is the ultimate beneficiary of these funds, assuring their proper administration. The federal government has the primary responsibility of protecting the first interest, and the state governments — through their respective attorneys general — have authority to supervise charitable foundations.

The common law confers power on the state attorney general to enforce charitable trusts. As Judge Posner points out, this is largely a formal supervision. Unless newspaper publicity is given to some alleged irregularity, the attorneys general rarely investigate the internal workings of charitable foundations. See Karst, The Efficiency of the Charitable Dollar: An Unfulfilled State Responsibility, 73 Harv. L. Rev. 433 (1960); Symposium, Foundations, Charities and the Law: The Interaction of External Controls and Internal Policies, 13 UCLA L. Rev. 933-1133 (1966).

The only person other than the attorney general who can enforce a charitable trust is a person with a special interest as a beneficiary. The person must show that he or she is entitled to receive a benefit under the trust that is not available to the public at large or to an average beneficiary. Thus, for example, a parishioner can sue to enforce a trust for the benefit of his church. Gray v. St. Matthews Cathedral, 544 S.W.2d 488, 94 A.L.R.3d 1197 (Tex. Civ. App. 1976). In recent years, the courts have broadened the definition of what constitutes a special interest. A taxpayer has been permitted to sue to prevent the transfer of a library held in trust from Peabody Institute in Baltimore to the Pratt Library in that city. Gordon v. City of Baltimore, 258 Md. 682, 267 A.2d 98 (1970). A citizen has been permitted to sue to enjoin deviation where a gift of land was made to the University of Illinois for a park. Parsons v. Walker, 28 Ill. App. 3d 517, 328 N.E.2d 920 (1975). Whether students have special standing to sue college trustees is not settled. See Miller v. Aderhold, 228 Ga. 65, 184 S.E.2d 172 (1971) (denying standing); Jones v. Grant, 344 So. 2d 1210 (Ala. 1977) (granting standing); Berry & Buchwald, Enforcement of College Trustees' Fiduciary Duties: Students and the Problems of Standing, 9 U.S.F.L. Rev. 1 (1974).

QUESTIONS AND NOTE

1.   In the case of a private corporation, stockholders and creditors can bring suit against the directors. What are the objections to suits by potential beneficiaries to enforce a charitable trust? A charitable gift deducted from the donor's income tax is in effect a subsidy of the charity by the government. Assuming a taxpayer's suit against the government is allowed under local procedure, should such a suit be allowed against a charity for breach of trust?

2.   Most charitable trusts have self-perpetuating boards. The trustees select their successors, who usually look pretty much like their predecessors. In view of the income, estate, and gift tax deduction for charitable gifts, should there be some public input in the selection of trustees? See Lipton, Significant Private Foundations and the Need for Public Selection of Their Trustees, 64 Va. L. Rev. 779 (1978).

3.   Internal Revenue Code §4942 imposes substantial tax penalties on private charitable foundations (but not on publicly supported charities) that do not distribute annually income in an amount equal to 5 percent of the value of the endowment. If the foundation has a return on its endowment of more than 5 percent and wishes to avoid taxation, it must distribute 5 percent; it can accumulate only the amount in excess of 5 percent. If the foundation has a return of less than 5 percent, to avoid taxation it must distribute principal in an amount equal to the difference between the income distributed and 5 percent of the value of the foundation's assets. The purpose of this legislation is to make investing more efficient and to penalize trusts with high expenses and little income. Compare R. Posner, Economic Analysis of Law, supra.

9

FUTURE INTERESTS: DISPOSITIVE PROVISIONS OF THE TRUST INSTRUMENT

I am quite aware that this is all largely matter of words, but so is much of the law of property; and unless we treat such distinctions as real, the law will melt away and leave not a rack behind.

LEARNED HAND, J.
in Commissioner v. City Bank
Farmers' Trust Co.
74 F.2d 242, 247 (2d Cir. 1934)

SECTION A. INTRODUCTION

Today future interests ordinarily arise in the context of trust settlements. Whenever a life estate is given, a future interest is also created: Someone is going to take the property upon termination of the life estate. Hence the attorney drafting trusts must be familiar with the types of future interests that can be employed and with constructional and other problems attendant to their use.

The law of future interests has its roots deep in history and grew out of the great and continuing conflict in England between the heads of rich families, who wanted to tie up land for future generations of the family, and the judges, who wanted to make land alienable. In dealing with these dynastic plans, English judges gradually developed the law of future interests — a highly artificial system of terminology and doctrines. The basic conceptual idea underlying the law of future interests is that future interests are thought of as "things." The medieval mind reified (made things of) its abstractions, in much the same way as the primitive mind thought of a golden calf or of the sun when it thought of God. As Digby wrote, "The tendency of philosophical thought prevailing at the period in question was to invest all abstract ideas with a real and substantial existence, . . . and possessing definite attributes or properties necessarily inherent in their essence." K. Digby, History of the Law of Real Property 266 (1875). Many paradoxes arise from our continued adherence to this "fallacy of misplaced concreteness," to borrow a phrase from Alfred North Whitehead.[1]

In your course in property you were introduced to the reification of abstractions, particularly the fee simple. Now, when you think of a fee simple, your mind's eye undoubtedly sees it as a thing, and you probably speak of a fee simple as a *bundle* of rights. Indeed, once you have been introduced to property law, it is hard not to think of a fee simple in any way but as a thing: The owner may transfer *it*, creditors may seize *it, it* passes on death, and so forth. Therefore the reification of future interests should not prove difficult to grasp, and you will soon picture these interests accelerating, merging, divesting, and failing — all in accordance with certain rules.

Another important intellectual characteristic of the law of future interests is that the concepts, defined precisely, fit together in a logical way. In a surprising number of problems you can come to one, and only one, answer. The law of future interests hence has a mathematical quality. And, as in all mathematics, symbols (words) must be used precisely and not approximately. This will take some practice, some adjustment — particularly when you come to the Rule against Perpetuities — in what you think the mind is capable of,[2] and more precision in verbal analysis and in the use of words than you are accustomed to.

1. Compare the White King speaking to Alice about the two Messengers:

". . . And I haven't sent the two Messengers, either. They're both gone to the town. Just look along the road and tell me if you see either of them."

"I see nobody on the road," said Alice.

"I only wish *I* had such eyes," the King remarked in a fretful tone. "To be able to see Nobody! And at that distance too! Why, it's as much as *I* can do to see real people, by this light!"

L. Carroll, Through the Looking-Glass, ch. 7.

2. You may find the advice of the White Queen sound:

"Now I'll give *you* something to believe. I'm just one hundred and one, five months and a day."

"I can't believe *that!*" said Alice.

"Can't you?" the queen said in a pitying tone. "Try again: draw a long breath, and shut your eyes."

Alice laughed. "There's no use trying," she said: "one *can't* believe impossible things."

"I daresay you haven't had much practice," said the Queen. "When I was your

So now we take a look at the law of future interests — not because we professors find any unusual enchantment in the antiquarian base of the subject or because we get some kind of perverse satisfaction in pushing students through the quirks and quiddities and sometimes infuriating distinctions that make up this area of the law. Rather, we study future interests because we must, for they are the stuff of which the dispositive provisions of trusts are made. On the positive side, we shall seek to gain an understanding of those facets of future interests law that are relevant and useful to the drafter. On the negative side we must be able to identify, so that we can avoid, (a) the intent-defeating technical rules of future interests law still with us, and (b) some commonly encountered problems of construction.

If you want to do some outside reading on the historical development of future interests, which is a considerable aid to understanding, we recommend T. Bergin & P. Haskell, Preface to Estates in Land and Future Interests (2d ed. 1984).

SECTION B.   POSSESSORY ESTATES

The possessory estates permitted by modern law that are of primary concern to us are the fee simple and the life estate. In a few states a fee tail may be created, but where encountered it is merely an obsolescent survivor of feudalism. A term of years may be used in an estate plan, but it is uncommon.

1.   *The Fee Simple*

A fee simple is an estate of infinite duration. It is absolute ownership, as far as absolute ownership is known to our law. At common law, a deed could create a fee simple only by using words indicating that the estate was inheritable. In a conveyance *O* had to say "to *A* and his heirs" in order to create a fee simple in *A*. The words "and his heirs" were the necessary words of inheritance indicating the estate was inheritable. These words did not (and do not today) give *A*'s heirs any interest in the property; they were (and are) words describing *A*'s estate as a fee simple. Although the words "and his heirs" were necessary in a deed,

---

age, I always did it for half-an-hour a day. Why sometimes I've believed as many as six impossible things before breakfast."

L. Carroll, Through the Looking-Glass, ch. 5.

they were not necessary in a will. It was presumed that the testator intended to dispose of as large an estate as the testator had. The common law requirement that "and his heirs" be used in a deed in order to create a fee simple has been abolished in almost all states. It is today presumed that a transferor intends to transfer as large an estate as the transferor has. Notwithstanding that the phrase "and his heirs" is no longer required for a fee simple, lawyers, being creatures of habit, continue to insert it.

Fee simple comes from the feudal "fief," and because of this origin there is a fee simple only in land, not in personal property. The analogue to fee simple ownership of land is absolute ownership of personalty. You will observe, though, that an occasional court, commentator, or law professor will refer to fee simple ownership of personalty. While technically imprecise, as far as we can tell there is no harm in the use of this colloquialism. (Although the law of estates and the law of future interests grew out of dispositions of land, courts generally permitted the same kinds of estates and future interests to be created in personal property.)

A fee simple may be *absolute* or *defeasible*. If it is absolute, there is no future interest in the property. If it is defeasible, the fee simple may terminate or be cut short in the future. There are two basic kinds of defeasible fees: The fee simple determinable, which terminates automatically upon the happening of a stated event, and the fee simple subject to condition subsequent, which is subject to an optional right of entry in the grantor to retake the property. We give little attention to possessory defeasible fees in this book because they are rarely used in family wealth transmission. They are almost always used as devices for controlling the use of land. See J. Dukeminier & J. Krier, Property 185-201 (2d ed. 1988).

Fee tail. Where it still exists, a fee tail is an estate created by a conveyance "to A and the heirs of his body." It has two distinctive features: (1) the estate lasts only so long as there are descendants of the original tenant in fee tail, A, and (2) the estate can be inherited only by descendants of A. The fee tail estate was authorized by the Statute de Donis, enacted by Parliament in 1285 at the behest of the landed aristocracy. Its purpose was to keep land within the family. After the fifteenth century, it became possible for the fee tail tenant to disentail and convert the fee tail into a fee simple. Today, wherever the fee tail exists, a fee tail tenant can convey a fee simple absolute by deed, cutting off all rights of issue as well as the reversioner.

A fee tail can be created only in Delaware, Maine, Massachusetts, and Rhode Island (by deed only, not by will). In other states, the fee tail is abolished and a limitation formerly effective to create a fee tail ("to A and the heirs of his body") now creates by statute some other kind of estate, usually a fee simple. In a few states a grant "to A and the heirs of his body" gives *A* a life estate, with remainder in fee simple to *A*'s issue. See 2 R. Powell, Real Property §198 (P. Rohan rev. ed. 1988). But see Orth, Does the Fee Tail Exist in North Carolina?, 23 Wake Forest L. Rev. 767 (1988), arguing that a fee tail can exist as a future interest but not as a possessory estate in North Carolina.

2. The Life Estate

A life estate is an estate that endures only for the life of a person. A life estate may be measured by the life span of the owner of the life estate (e.g., "to *A* for life") or by the life span of another (e.g., "to *A* for the life of *B*"). The latter is called a life estate pur autre vie.

A life estate may be a legal estate or an equitable estate (in trust). A life estate may be created so as to be defeasible in the same ways as a fee simple is defeasible. It may be determinable (e.g., "to my wife for life or until her remarriage") or it may be subject to condition subsequent (e.g., "to my wife for life, but if my wife remarries, to *A*").

Dewire v. Haveles
Supreme Judicial Court of Massachusetts, 1989
404 Mass. 274, 534 N.E.2d 782

WILKINS, J. This petition for a declaration of rights seeks answers to questions arising from an artlessly drafted will that, among its many inadequacies, includes a blatant violation of the rule against perpetuities. The case is before us on a reservation and report by a judge of the Probate and Family court on a statement of agreed facts. The judge listed a large number of issues, but we shall deal with them only to the extent necessary to permit a declaration of the present rights of the parties. We transferred the case here on our own motion.

Thomas A. Dewire died in January, 1941, survived by his widow, his son Thomas, Jr., and three grandchildren (Thomas, III, Paula, and Deborah, all children of Thomas, Jr.). His will placed substantially all his estate in a residuary trust. The income of the trust was payable to his widow for life and, on her death, the income was payable to his son Thomas, Jr., the widow of Thomas, Jr., and Thomas Jr.'s children.[3]

---

3. The language of the will directing this distribution appears in article third of the will and reads as follows:

> Third: To my wife, Mabel G. Dewire, I give, devise and bequeath all the rest, residue and remainder of all the estate of which I shall die seized, for and during the term of her natural life, and upon her decease to my son, Thomas A. Dewire, Jr., and his heirs and assigns, but in trust nevertheless upon the following trusts and for the following purposes:

After the testator's death, Thomas, Jr., had three more children by a second wife. Thomas, Jr., died on May 28, 1978, a widower, survived by all six of his children. Thomas, III, who had served as trustee since 1978, died on March 19, 1987, leaving a widow and one child, Jennifer. Among the questions presented, and the most important one for present purposes, is to whom the one-sixth share of the trust income, once payable to Thomas, III, is now payable.

In his will, the testator stated: "It is my will, except as hereinabove provided, that my grandchildren, under guidance and discretion of my Trustee, shall share equally in the net income of my said estate." At another point, he referred to the trust income being "divided equally amongst my grandchildren." The rule against perpetuities violation occurred because the will provided for the trust's termination "twenty-one years after the death of the last surviving child of my said son, Thomas A. Dewire, Jr., when the property of the trust shall be equally divided amongst the lineal descendants of my grandchildren."[4]

There is no explicit provision in the will concerning the distribution of income on the death of a grandchild while the gift of income to grandchildren continues, nor is there any statement as to what the trustee should do with trust income between the death of the last grandchild and the date assigned for termination of the trust twenty-one years later.

Our task is to discern the testator's intention concerning the distribution of a grandchild's share of the trust income on his death. As a practical matter, in cases of this sort, where there is no express intention, we must resort to reasonable inferences in the particular circumstances which on occasion shade into rules of construction that are applied when no intention at all can be inferred on the issue. In this case, the reasonable inference as to the testator's intention is that Jennifer should take her father's share in the income.

Certain points are not in serious controversy and are relatively easy to resolve. The gift of net income to the testator's grandchildren, divided equally or to be shared equally, is a class gift. See Smith v. Haynes, 202 Mass. 531, 533, 89 N.E. 158 (1909). The class includes all

---

A. To hold, direct, manage and conserve the trust estate, so given, for the benefit of himself, his wife and children in the manner following, that is to say:

To expend out of the net income so much as may be necessary for the proper care, maintenance of himself and wife conformable to their station in life, and for the care, maintenance and education of his children born to him in his lifetime, in such manner as in his judgment and discretion shall seem proper, and his judgment and discretion shall be final.

4. As we shall explain, the possibility that Thomas, Jr., would have a child born after the testator's death was sufficient to cause the violation of the rule against perpetuities. The fact that Thomas, Jr., had children born after the testator's death makes possible a violation of the rule in actual fact.

six grandchildren, three of whom were born before and three of whom were born after the testator's death. B.M.C. Durfee Trust Co. v. Taylor, 325 Mass. 201, 204, 89 N.E.2d 777 (1950). Hall v. Hall, 123 Mass. 120, 122 (1877). See Casner, Class Gifts to Others than to "Heirs" or "Next of Kin": Increase in the Class Membership, 51 Harv. L. Rev. 254, 260 (1937). Because there is a gift over at the end of the class gift, the testator intended the class gift to his grandchildren only to be a gift of a life interest in the income of the trust. Rolland v. Hamilton, 314 Mass. 56, 57-59, 49 N.E.2d 436 (1943), and cases cited. The general rule is that, in the absence of a contrary intent expressed in the will or a controlling statute stating otherwise, members of a class are joint tenants with rights of survivorship. Old Colony Trust Co. v. Treadwell, 312 Mass. 214, 218, 43 N.E.2d 777 (1942). Meserve v. Haak, 191 Mass. 220, 223, 77 N.E. 377 (1906). See G.L. c. 191, §22 (1986 ed.) (antilapse statute).

This last stated principle becomes important in deciding whether Jennifer, the child of the deceased grandson, takes her deceased father's share in the trust income or whether the remaining class members, the other five grandchildren, take that income share equally by right of survivorship. Jennifer argues, under the general rule, that the will manifests an intent contrary to a class gift with rights of survivorship. We agree with this conclusion. Thus we need not decide, as Jennifer further argues, whether the rule of construction presuming a right of survivorship in class members should be rejected in the circumstances and replaced by a rule based on principles similar to those expressed in the antilapse statute.[5]

Before we explain why the will expresses an intention that, during the term of the class gift, Jennifer, while living, should take her father's

---

5. The Massachusetts antilapse statute applies only to testamentary gifts to a child or other relation of a testator who predeceased the testator leaving issue surviving the testator and to class gifts to children or other relations where one or more class member predeceased the testator (even if the class member had died before the will was executed). G.L. c. 191, §22. The rule of construction of §22 is that the issue of a deceased relation take his share by right of representation "unless a different disposition is made or required by the will."

In this case, no class member predeceased the testator and, therefore, §22 does not explicitly aid Jennifer. The policy underlying §22 might fairly be seen as supporting, as a rule of construction (absent a contrary intent), the substitution of a class member's surviving issue for a deceased class member if the class is made up of children or other relations of the testator. See Bigelow v. Clap, 166 Mass. 88, 91, 43 N.E. 1037 (1896). It has been suggested that "[t]he policy of [antilapse] statutes [dealing with the death of a class member after the testator's death] commends itself to decisional law." Restatement (Second) of Property, Donative Transfers §27.3 comment i (Tent. Draft No. 9, 1986). If the antilapse statute protects the interests of the issue of a relation who predeceases a testator, there is good reason why we should adopt, as a rule of construction, the same principle as to a relation of a testator who survives the testator but dies before an interest comes into possession. In the case of a class gift of income from a trust, the interest could be viewed as coming into possession on each income distribution date.

share in the income, we discuss the rule against perpetuities problem.[6] The prospect that interests under this will may vest beyond the permissible limit of the rule against perpetuities is not only theoretically possible, it is actuarially likely. The interests of the grandchildren in the trust income vested at their father's death (if not sooner) and, because he was a life in being at the testator's death, those interests vested within the period of the rule. The gift over at the end of the class gift of income to the grandchildren, however, might not vest seasonably because another grandchild could have been born after the testator's death and could be the surviving grandchild. In this case, in fact, the three youngest grandchildren were born after the death of the testator but they are measuring lives for the term of the class gift. The parties agree that the purported gift of the remainder to the lineal descendants of the testator's grandchildren "twenty-one years after the death of the last surviving" grandchild violates the rule against perpetuities in its traditional form and would be void. See Second Bank-State St. Trust Co. v. Second Bank-State St. Trust Co., 335 Mass. 407, 410-411, 140 N.E.2d 201 (1957). There is no need at this time to decide the question of the proper distribution of trust income or assets at the death of the last grandchild. The question will be acute at the death of the last grandchild, when the class gift of income from the trust will terminate.[7]

The rule against perpetuities problem need not be resolved at this time. It has some bearing, however, on what should be done during the term of the class gift with the one-sixth share of the trust income that is in dispute. We reject the argument that, because of the violation of the rule against perpetuities, the income interests should be treated as being more than life interests. There is no authority for such a

---

6. In its classic formulation, the rule against perpetuities declares that: "No interest is good unless it must vest, if at all, not later than twenty-one years after some life in being at the creation of the interest." J.C. Gray, The Rule Against Perpetuities §201, at 191 (4th ed. 1942). See Eastman Marble Co. v. Vermont Marble Co., 236 Mass. 138, 152, 128 N.E. 177 (1920).

7. The common law rule against perpetuities has been modified by statute. See G.L. c. 184A, §1 (1986 ed.), applicable to wills of persons dying after January 1, 1955 (St. 1954, c. 641, §2) and thus not directly applicable in this case. The second look or wait-and-see principle of G.L. c. 184A, §1, has been applied as a matter of decisional law to an instrument to which §1 did not apply. See Warner v. Whitman, 353 Mass. 468, 472, 233 N.E.2d 14 (1968). If a wait-and-see approach is applicable here, and if the last surviving grandchild were to be one of the grandchildren alive at the death of the testator, there would be no violation of the rule against perpetuities. We might even decide that there was no violation of the rule if all the grandchildren were to die within twenty-one years of the death of the last grandchild who was living at the testator's death. See Restatement (Second) of Property, Donative Transfers §1.4 (1983).

proposition.[8] Although the gift over violates the rule against perpetuities in its traditional form and in time may prove to violate it in actual fact, the language providing for such a distribution may properly be considered in determining a testator's intention with respect to other aspects of his will. See J.C. Gray, The Rule Against Perpetuities §§629-631, at 599-600 (4th ed. 1942) ("a provision void for remoteness is still to be resorted to for construing the rest of the will"). For the purposes of distribution of assets, a will is to be construed as if a provision violating the rule against perpetuities is not contained in it (Fosdick v. Fosdick, 6 Allen 41, 43 [1863]), but we have never said that the language of a void clause cannot be used to determine the testator's intention as to dispositions that do not violate the rule.

We are now in a position to discuss the question whether the class gift of income to grandchildren calls for the payment of income equally to those grandchildren living from time to time (as joint tenants with rights of survivorship) or whether the issue of any deceased grandchild succeeds by right of representation to his income interest. The latter result better conforms with the testator's intentions.

The testator provided that the trust should terminate twenty-one years after the death of his last grandchild. It is unlikely that the testator intended that trust income should be accumulated for twenty-one years, and we would tend to avoid such a construction. See Meserve v. Haak, 191 Mass. 220, 222, 77 N.E. 377 (1906). Certainly, we should not presume that he intended an intestacy as to that twenty-one year period. See Anderson v. Harris, 320 Mass. 101, 104-105, 67 N.E.2d 670 (1946). He must have expected that someone would receive distributions of income during those years.[9] The only logical recipients of that income would be the issue (by right of representation) of deceased grandchildren, the same group of people who would take the trust assets on termination of the trust (assuming no violation of the rule against perpetuities).[10] If these people were intended to receive income during the last twenty-one years of the trust as well as the trust assets on its

---

8. We also reject the contention that the trust beneficiaries can properly compel termination of the trust and a distribution of the trust assets at this time. They are not all now ascertained or ascertainable, and there is no reason to invalidate the class gift of income. See Allen v. First Nat'l Bank & Trust Co., 319 Mass. 693, 697, 67 N.E.2d 472 (1946).

9. At one point in his will, the testator says that the trust income is payable "to [Thomas, Jr.] and his children and their heirs at law."

10. "[T]he property of the trust shall be equally divided amongst the lineal descendants of my grandchildren." "Equally," referring to a multigenerational class, normally means per stirpes. New England Trust Co. v. McAleer, 344 Mass. 107, 112, 181 N.E.2d 569 (1962). Dexter v. Inches, 147 Mass. 324, 326, 17 N.E. 551 (1888). In such a case, the stirpes are normally placed at one generation before the takers. See Bradlee v. Converse, 318 Mass. 117, 120, 60 N.E.2d 345 (1945).

termination, it is logical that they should also receive income during the term of the class gift if their ancestor (one of the grandchildren) should die. Such a pattern treats each grandchild and his issue equally throughout the intended term of the trust. Where, among other things, every other provision in the will concerning the distribution of trust income and principal (after the death of the testator and his wife) points to equal treatment of the testator's issue per stirpes, there is a sufficient contrary intent shown to overcome the rule of construction that the class gift of income to grandchildren is given to them as joint tenants with the right of survivorship.

We deal briefly with one other point. No language in the will gives discretion to the trustee to distribute principal during the term of the class gift of income. The fact that the trustee has discretion on termination to distribute trust real estate in kind does not authorize a distribution of principal during the term of the trust. If the will should be read to mandate the retention of that real estate in the trust, that mandate will not survive the trust's lawful term, and it is, therefore, not an unlawful restraint on alienation.

Judgment shall be entered declaring that (1) Jennifer Ann Dewire in her lifetime is entitled to one-sixth of the net income of the trust during the period of the class gift of income, that is, until the death of the last grandchild (and a proportionate share of the income of any grandchild who dies leaving no issue), (2) no declaration shall be made at this time concerning the disposition of trust income or principal on the death of the last grandchild of Thomas A. Dewire, (3) no provision in the will is an illegal restraint on alienation during the lawful term of the trust, and (4) the trustee has no authority to distribute trust principal during the term of the class gift of income.

So ordered.

PROBLEM

T bequeaths a fund in trust to pay the income "to each of my children Gertrude, Charlotte, and John in equal amounts during their lives, and upon the death of the last survivor, to distribute the principal to their issue per stirpes then living." Gertrude dies. What distribution of income is made? Cf. Svenson v. First National Bank of Boston, 5 Mass. App. Ct. 440, 363 N.E.2d 1129 (1977) (devise of income substantially identical except made to testator's servants rather than her children; court held gift of income was a class gift, to be divided by surviving servants). If Charlotte and John receive Gertrude's share, Gertrude's spouse and children are cut off from any benefits they have been receiving from Gertrude's share and the surviving children get richer.

Is this what the average testator intends? How would you draft the will
to avoid this problem?

NOTE: CONSUMABLE PROPERTY

Consumable property is something that is necessarily destroyed or
used up in its normal use. The courts have laid down a rule limiting
life estates and future interests in consumable personal property. The
rule is: A gift of a consumable to *A* for life is in law a gift to *A* of
absolute ownership, and any future interest is void, unless *A* is also
given an express or implied power to sell the consumable. If *A* is given
such power, and exercises it, any future interests attach to the proceeds
of sale. The reason for this rule is probably that consumables are usually
of little value, and to permit a life estate in consumables, with the
attendant problems about what rights the life tenant has when the life
tenant cannot sell the consumable, would be wasteful of judicial time.

PROBLEM

Cases involving consumables usually arise from a devise of a farm
and all objects on the farm. Thus: *T* devises his farm to *A* for life
together with 7 horses, 27 sheep, 1 cow, 40 fat hogs, 5 bushels of corn,
a tractor, and all the farming implements. Can *A* sell or slaughter the
hogs or the sheep? See Davison's Administrator v. Davison's Administratrix, 149 Ky. 571, 149 S.W. 982 (1912). Might the tractor be
considered a consumable? Cf. Seabrook v. Grimes, 107 Md. 410, 68 A.
883 (1908). How would you draft *T*'s will?

SECTION C. CLASSIFICATION OF FUTURE
INTERESTS

1. Types of Future Interests

Future interests recognized by our legal system are:

1. Interests in the transferor known as:
    a. Reversion

  b. Possibility of reverter
  c. Right of entry (also known as power of termination)
2. Interests in a transferee known as:
  a. Vested remainder
  b. Contingent remainder
  c. Executory interest

These interests are called *future interests* because the person who holds one of them is not entitled to present possession or enjoyment of the property but may or will become entitled to possession in the future. All future interests in property must be placed in one of the above categories.

Future interests are presently existing interests. A person who has a future interest has present rights and liabilities. Take this case: *O* conveys "to *A* for life, then to *B*." *B* has a remainder, which *B* can sell or give away. *B*'s creditors can reach it. *B* can enjoin *A* from committing waste or doing other acts that impair the value of *B*'s right to future possession. If *B* dies before *A*, the value of *B*'s remainder is subject to federal estate taxation. A person who has a future interest has a complex of present rights, privileges, duties, liabilities, and immunities, and in that sense presently owns an interest. But the holder of the interest does not have perhaps the most important right in the bundle — the right to present possession — and it is because of the absence of this right that we call the interest "future."

Any estate that may be created in possession, such as a fee simple or a life estate, may be created as a future interest. Hence *O* may convey "to *A* for life, then to *B* for life, then to *C*." *B* has a remainder for life, and *C* has a remainder in fee simple. By saying that *C* has a remainder in fee simple we mean that when *C*'s remainder becomes possessory it will be a fee simple.

NOTE: THE PLANE OF TIME

In describing the "wonderful calculus of estates," Sir Frederic Maitland wrote that proprietary rights are "projected upon the plane of time." 2 F. Pollock & F. Maitland, History of English Law 10 (2d ed. 1911). This metaphorical way of looking at future interests has proven very useful in helping students to *see* (reify) future interests and classify them appropriately. Consider first, a plane of time running through space toward infinity, like this:

_____ ∞

We shall divide this plane sequentially according to who has the right to possession. If one person has the right to possession to infinity, he has a fee simple (which by definition, is of infinite duration). We can show this on the plane of time, in this manner:

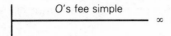

The fee simple owner can convey a "lesser" estate of shorter duration and thereby carve the fee into sequential interests that follow each other on the plane of time. Suppose *O* conveys to *A* the right to possession of Blackacre during *A*'s lifetime. We take this right, call it a life estate, and reify it. In this case we can cut up the plane of time and designate on it who has the right of possession, thus:

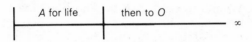

A has a life estate. *O* has a reversion in fee simple. When *A* dies and the life estate terminates, *O* will again have a present possessory estate in fee simple absolute.

As we go through the types of future interests, we shall diagram them on the plane of time. For more diagrams of future interests on the plane of time, together with extensive problems and answers, see R. Laurence and P. Minzner, A Student's Guide to Estates in Land and Future Interests (1981).

2.   *Future Interests in the Transferor*

a.   **Reversion**

There are three types of future interests that may be retained by the transferor: reversion, possibility of reverter, and right of entry for condition broken. By far the most important of these is the reversion. "A reversion is," in the words of Professor Lewis Simes, "the interest remaining in the grantor, or in the successor in interest of a testator, who transfers a vested estate of a lesser quantum than that of the vested estate which he has." 1 American Law of Property §4.16 (1952). A reversion is never created; it is a retained interest that always arises by operation of law because the transferor has conveyed away a lesser estate than the transferor had. If a reversion is retained in an inter vivos conveyance, it is always retained by the grantor. If a reversion is retained by a will, it is retained in the testator's heirs who are substituted by law for the dead transferor.

A reversion cannot be created in a transferee. If by deed or will a future interest is created in a transferee, the future interest must be given one of the labels that we give to future interests in transferees: It is either a remainder or an executory interest.

PROBLEMS

1.   *O* desires to transfer Whiteacre to *A* for life, then to *B*. If *O* conveys by a deed reading "to *A* for life, then to *B*," *B* takes a remainder. For some reason *O* wants *B* to have a reversion, not a remainder. How can *O* arrange the transaction so that *B* receives a reversion?

2.   *T*'s will devises Blackacre to *A* for life, and the residue of *T*'s property to *B*. What interest does *B* have in Blackacre?

Reversions are thought of as part of the transferor's old estate: what the transferor retained when he conveyed away less than he had. Hence all reversions are vested interests. The fact that all reversions are vested does not mean, however, that all reversions will become possessory. Some may not. Thus:

> Case 1.   *O* conveys "to *A* for life, then to *A*'s children who survive *A*." *A*'s children have a contingent remainder. *O* has a *vested reversion*, which will be divested if *A* leaves surviving children. (*Warning:* Do not call *O*'s interest a "contingent reversion" or a "possibility of reversion" as there are no such interests known to law. If you use the latter term, you may end up confusing a reversion with a possibility of reverter, an entirely different interest. Call the interest by its correct name.)

Case 1 illustrates that the concept of "vesting in interest" — so important in future interests law — has very little to do with the certainty that a future interest will become possessory. The reversion in Case 1, vested in interest, may not become possessory. Future interests are deemed vested or not by arbitrary rules of the common law, not by the certainty or uncertainty of future possession.

To determine when a transferor has a reversion, you can save yourself much trouble if you will memorize this simple Rule of Reversions: *O, owner of a fee simple, will not have a reversion in fee simple if O transfers a possessory fee simple or a vested remainder in fee simple; in all other cases where O transfers a present possessory interest, O will have a reversion in fee simple.* Hence, whenever *O* transfers a life estate, not followed by a vested remainder in fee, *O* has a reversion. If *O* transfers a life estate followed by 100 contingent remainders in fee, but no vested remainder in fee, *O* retains a reversion.

You will see why this rule operates if you consider a reversion a shorthand way of saying that when a vested estate of the same duration is not transferred, "there is either a certainty or a possibility that the right to posssession will return to the grantor." Thus when the owner of an estate in Blackacre carves out a lesser estate and does not add a vested remainder of the same duration as the owner's estate, there is a possibility that Blackacre will be his again.

PROBLEMS

1. *O* conveys Blackacre "to *A* for life, then to *B* if *B* survives *A*, and if *B* does not survive *A*, to *C*." Does *O* have a reversion? Yes. But how is it possible for Blackacre to return to *O*? At common law the answer was easy: A life estate could terminate prior to the death of the life tenant if the life tenant were convicted of a felony or committed a tortious feoffment. But in the United States forfeiture on these grounds has been abolished. Can you think of any way for Blackacre to return to *O*? Suppose that Blackacre were conveyed in trust "to *A* for life, etc." Might the income from Blackacre ever be payable to *O*? See Dukeminier, Perpetuities: The Measuring Lives, 85 Colum. L. Rev. 1648, 1690-1692 (1985).

2. *O* conveys Whiteacre "to *A* for life, then to *B*, but if *B* dies before *A* without issue surviving *B*, then to *C* at *A*'s death." Does *O* have a reversion? Suppose that *B* dies leaving surviving a child, *D*; *B*'s will devises all her property to her husband, *H*. Then *D* dies. Then *A* dies. Who owns Whiteacre?

3. *T* devises Greenacre "to *A* for life, then to *B*, but if *C* returns from Rome to *C*." Suppose that *B* survives *A* and, two months after *A* dies, while *C* remains in Rome, *B* disclaims. The jurisdiction has adopted the disclaimer provisions of Uniform Probate Code §2-801, supra page 123. This disclaimer statute, like most, provides that a future interest can be disclaimed within nine months "after the event determining that the taker of the property or interest is finally ascertained and his interest is indefeasibly vested." Who owns Greenacre? If you answer, "there is a reversion in *O*," how do you reconcile your answer with the Rule of Reversions? See Dukeminier, supra, at 1692.

4. Section 673 of the Internal Revenue Code of 1986 taxes the income of a trust to the settlor if the settlor retains a reversion worth more than 5 percent (see supra page 545). In view of the Rule of Reversions, how do you draft a trust so as to avoid leaving a reversion in the settlor worth more than 5 percent of the corpus?

b. Possibility of Reverter; Right of Entry

A *possibility of reverter* is the future interest that remains in the grantor who conveys a fee simple determinable. For example, O conveys "to School Board so long as used for a school." The School Board has a fee simple determinable; O has a possibility of reverter, which becomes possessory automatically upon expiration of the determinable fee.

A *right of entry* for condition broken is the future interest that is retained by the grantor who conveys a fee simple subject to a condition subsequent. For example, O conveys "to School Board, but if the land ceases to be used for school purposes, O has a right to reenter." The School Board has a fee simple subject to condition subsequent; O has a right of entry, which O has the option to exercise or not.

Possibilities of reverter and rights of entry are almost never encountered in a trust. They are typically retained to control the use of land and are covered in the basic course in Property. See J. Dukeminier & J. Krier, Property 185-211, 265-273 (2d ed. 1988).

3. *Future Interests in Transferees*

There are three types of future interests in transferees: vested remainders, contingent remainders, and executory interests. Vested remainders may be further divided into remainders indefeasibly vested, vested subject to open, and vested subject to total divestment.

a. Remainders

A remainder is a future interest in a transferee that can become possessory upon the expiration of all prior interests simultaneously created. A remainder cannot divest any prior interest in a transferee; it patiently waits until the preceding interests expire. Thus:

> *Case 2.* O conveys "to A for life, then to B." B's future interest is a remainder. It can become a present interest (here it *will* become a present interest) on the expiration of A's life estate. When B's future interest becomes possessory, it will not divest A's life estate; it will follow immediately upon the termination of the life estate. B's remainder can be portrayed on the plane of time thus:

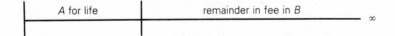

For a future interest to be a remainder, it must only be possible, not necessarily certain, that the future interest will become possessory upon the termination of the preceding estate. The following case illustrates a remainder that may, but is not certain to, become possessory upon the expiration of the preceding life estate.

> *Case 3.* *O* conveys "to *A* for life, then to *B* if *B* lives to attain the age of 25 years." *B* is 15 years old at the time of the conveyance. Here *B*'s interest is subject to a condition precedent that *B* attain the age of 25 years. *B*'s interest is a remainder, for it is possible for *B* to take immediately on the expiration of the preceding estate if *B* attains age 25 during *A*'s lifetime.[11] We can diagram this on the plane of time thus:

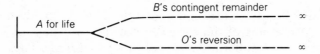

Remainders are either vested or contingent. In general, a remainder is vested when it is given to an ascertained person and it is not subject to a condition precedent (other than the termination of the preceding estate or estates). A contingent remainder is a remainder created in an unascertained person or subject to a condition precedent. There are different types of vested remainders.

(1)   Indefeasibly Vested Remainder

An indefeasibly vested remainder is a remainder certain to become possessory permanently. The classic example of an indefeasibly vested remainder is Case 2 supra. In that case *B* or *B*'s successor in interest is certain to take on *A*'s death; there is no condition precedent to *B*'s taking other than the termination of *A*'s life estate. Similarly, in Case 3, if *B* attains the age of 25 during *A*'s lifetime, *B*'s contingent remainder indefeasibly vests and the reversion in *O* is divested. *B* or *B*'s successor in interest is thereafter certain to take possession.

(2)   Vested Remainder Subject to Open

A vested remainder subject to open is a vested remainder in a class that has not closed. Thus:

> *Case 4.* *O* conveys "to *A* for life, then to *A*'s children." *A* has a child, *C*, alive at the time of the conveyance. *C* has a vested remainder subject to open. As with an indefeasibly vested remainder, *C* or *C*'s successor is

---

11. If *B* does not attain 25 before *A* dies, *O*'s reversion becomes possessory at *A*'s death. *B*'s remainder is not destroyed but *B* takes the property from *O* when and if *B* reaches 25. Under the common law doctrine of destructibility of contingent remainders (see infra page 643), if *B*'s remainder was a *legal* remainder in *land*, it was destroyed if it did not vest at or prior to the termination of the preceding life estate. This doctrine has been abolished in almost all — perhaps all — states.

certain to acquire a present interest at some time in the future, but C's share of the remainder will be diminished if A has any more children. The amount of C's share will depend on how many children, if any, are subsequently born to A. If at some time in the future A has another child — let's call her D — the class of remaindermen "opens," and C and D will have vested remainders subject to open. The class will remain "open" until A is no longer capable of having more children (which means until A's death).

PROBLEM

O conveys "to A for life, and on A's death to A's children in equal shares." At the time of the conveyance A has two children, B and C. Two years later D is born to A. A year after that B dies intestate, then A dies. What is the state of the title?

---

(3)   Vested Remainder Subject to Divestment

A vested remainder subject to divestment is exactly what its name implies. It is held by an ascertained person and is subject to no condition precedent, *but it is subject to a condition subsequent.* Thus:

> Case 5.   O conveys "to A for life, then to B, but if B does not leave any surviving children, to C." B has a vested remainder in fee simple subject to being divested by an executory interest in C.

(4)   Contingent Remainder

As stated above, a contingent remainder is a remainder either (1) given to an unascertained person or persons *or* (2) subject to a condition precedent. Case 6 illustrates a remainder contingent because the takers are unascertained.

> Case 6.   O conveys "to A for life, then to A's children." A has no children at the time of the conveyance. The remainder is contingent because the takers are not ascertained.[12]

---

12. Contingent remainder in whom? A remainder is a concept standing for legal relations between persons. Can unborn persons have legal relations? 2 Restatement of Property §153, Comment a (1936), says we cannot accurately say that an unborn person has a future interest. Yet it is quite clear that the law treats the limitation as if a future interest has been created. Some say the correct terminology is, "*There is* a contingent remainder in the unborn children of A," rather than, "The unborn children of A have a contingent remainder," and if that helps you get the idea, fine.

Some 500 years ago, the common law courts got around a similar conceptual impasse by simply declaring that the remainder was *in nubibus* (in the clouds) or *in gremio legis* (in the bosom of the law). R. Megarry & H. Wade, Real Property 1177 (5th ed. 1984). In this course, the sky is the limit for a truly imaginative mind!

Case 3, supra, illustrates a remainder that is contingent because subject to a condition precedent.

PROBLEMS

1. *O* conveys land "to *A* for life, then to the first child of *A* who attains the age of 21." *A* has a son, *C* (age 18), and a son, *D* (age 12). What interests are created? What would be created if the remainder were limited "to the first son of *A* if he attains the age of 21"?

2. *O* conveys "to *A* for life, then to *B* for life, then to *C*." Two years later *B* dies, survived by *A* and *C*. Did *B* ever own anything? If the answer is yes, what did he own and was it worth anything?

3. In 1984 *O* conveys land "to *A* for life, and on *A*'s death to the heirs of *B*." At the time of the conveyance *A* and *B* are both alive and *B* has two children, *C* and *D*. If *B* were to die intestate immediately after the conveyance, *C* and *D* would be *B*'s heirs. In 1986 *D* dies, leaving a minor son, *E*, and a will devising all his property to his wife, *W*. In 1988 *B* dies leaving a will that devises *B*'s entire estate to the American Red Cross. *A* dies in 1990; *A* is survived by *C*, *E*, and *W*. Who owns the land? What would be the result if *B* had died before *D*?

If the taker of the remainder is ascertained, but the remainder will be defeated if a specified event occurs, whether the remainder is vested subject to divestment or is contingent depends upon whether the conditional event is expressed as a condition subsequent or a condition precedent. Whether a condition is precedent or subsequent depends, with few exceptions, on *the sequence of words in the instrument*. Interests are classified in sequence. If the condition is incorporated into the gift of the remainder, if it comes — so to speak — between the commas setting apart the remainder, the condition is precedent. But if the remainder is given, and then words of divestment are added, the condition is subsequent. This distinction is best seen by examples.

Case 7. *O* conveys "to *A* for life, then to *B* if *B* survives *A*, and if *B* does not survive *A*, to *C*." *B* has a contingent remainder because the words "if *B* survives *A*" are incorporated into *B*'s gift; they come between the commas. (Of course, if the commas were not there, you would have to decide where the court would mentally insert the commas. The essential idea to grasp is that the words "if *B* survives *A*" are part of the gift to *B*.) *C* has an alternative contingent remainder. Here are alternative contingent remainders on the plane of time:

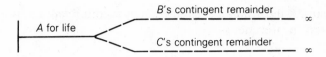

Case 8. O conveys "to A for life, then to B, but if B does not survive A, to C." B has a vested remainder subject to divestment by C's executory interest. Between the commas setting off B's gift there are no words of condition. There is a condition subsequent introducing the gift over to C. B's and C's interests diagrammed on the plane of time look like this:

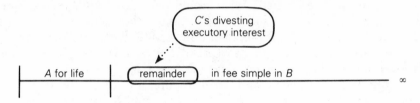

Note that B's vested remainder in fee simple occupies the entire plane of time after A's life estate. C's executory interest "hovers over" the plane of time, waiting to divest B's remainder if B dies during A's life.

As Cases 7 and 8 illustrate, you must look very carefully at the exact language used and classify the interests in sequence. O's intent may be identical in those two cases, but it has been expressed in different ways, resulting in different interests being created. As you can see, much turns on careful drafting.

b. Executory Interests

An executory interest is a future interest in a transferee that must, in order to become possessory,

(1)   divest or cut short some interest in another transferee (this is a shifting executory interest),[13] or

(2)   divest the transferor following a certain period of time during which no transferee is entitled to possession (this is a springing executory interest).

Although we differentiate here between a shifting executory interest

---

13. If a future interest is created in a transferee following a fee simple determinable, this is called an executory interest even though it does not cut short the determinable fee. It patiently waits until the determinable fee automatically ends. But because of the rule that a remainder cannot follow a fee simple, the courts decided to call the future interest an executory interest even though it is not a shifting interest.

and a springing executory interest because we think it helps you understand more easily what are executory interests, shifting and springing interests are treated alike by the law.

Executory interests are interests that would have been void at law prior to the Statute of Uses in 1536 but were made legal interests by that statute. Prior to the Statute of Uses, shifting and springing interests were valid only in chancery. They gave a rich father needed flexibility in shifting land from one son to another upon the happening of some event and in settling land upon his daughter upon her future marriage. The rise of uses in chancery and the Statute of Uses have been discussed supra at pages 436-437. For a more extended treatment of the development of executory interests, see J. Dukeminier & J. Krier, Property 224-233 (2d ed. 1988).

Executory interests are almost always created in one of two basic forms. These are illustrated by Cases 9 and 10, below.

> *Case 9. Executory interest divesting a possessory fee simple upon an uncertain event.* O conveys "to A, but if A dies at any time without children him surviving, to B." A has a fee simple subject to divestment by B's executory interest. B's executory interest is subject to a condition precedent (A's death without surviving children) and is not certain to become possessory.

B's executory interest is analogous to a contingent remainder but is not called a contingent remainder because it is a divesting interest. A variation of Case 9 is a conveyance by O "to B if B returns from Rome," which gives B a springing executory interest divesting the transferor, O, rather than a transferee.

> *Case 10. Executory interest divesting a vested remainder.* O conveys "to A for life, and on A's death to B, but if B is not then living to C." B has a vested remainder in fee simple subject to divestment by C's executory interest. C's executory interest is subject to a condition precedent (B dying before A dies) and is not certain to become possessory.

C's executory interest is analogous to a contingent remainder but is not called a contingent remainder because it is a divesting interest.

PROBLEMS

1. (a) O conveys "to A for life, then to A's children, but if at A's death A is not survived by any children, then to B." At the time of the conveyance, A has no children. What interests are created?

(b) Consider the same facts as in Problem 1(a). A few years later, two children, *C* and *D*, are born to *A*. *C* dies, devising his property to his wife, *W*. *A* dies. What is the state of the title?

(c) *O* conveys "to *A* for life, then to such of *A*'s children as survive *A*, but if none of *A*'s children survive *A*, then to *B*." At the time of the conveyance, *A* has two children, *C* and *D*. *C* dies, devising his property to his wife, *W*. *A* dies. What is the state of the title?

2. *O* conveys Blackacre "to *A* 30 years from now." *A* has a springing executory interest that divests *O*'s fee simple upon an event certain to happen. *O*'s fee simple is certain to end. But how can this be? How can *O* have a fee simple when *O*'s estate is certain to end in 30 years? The essence of a fee simple is that it is an estate with a potentially infinite duration, and *O*'s fee simple does not have this potential.[14] Hint: The Statute of Uses permitted new springing and shifting interests to be created (which were formerly void at law). It did not change the names of estates theretofore valid. What does *O* have if *A*'s interest is invalid?

3. *T* devises Blackacre to *A* for life, then to *A*'s children who survive her. The residuary clause of *T*'s will devises to *B* "all of the rest and residue of my property of whatever kind and wherever located that I own at my death, including any of the foregoing gifts in this will that for any reason fail to take effect." What is the state of the title? Egerton v. Massey, 3 C.B. (N.S.) 338, 140 Eng. Rep. 771 (C.P. 1857), and J. Gray, The Rule Against Perpetuities §113.1 (4th ed. 1942), say *A*'s children have a contingent remainder and *B* has a reversion. Do you see how this classification assumes that *C* can die twice? 2 H. Tiffany, Real Property §333 (3d ed. 1939), says *A*'s children have a contingent remainder in fee, and *B* has a vested remainder in fee, but this classification runs into this difficulty: If the contingent remainder vests, it divests a vested remainder, and by definition a contingent remainder can, by vesting, divest only a reversion. Of future interests in transferees, only executory interests can divest a vested remainder. A. Kales, Estates, Future Interests and Illegal Conditions and Restraints in Illinois §95 (2d ed. 1920), says we should read the clauses in reverse order, giving *B* a vested remainder and *A*'s children an executory interest. 3 Restatement of Property §278, Comment d (1940), says *A*'s children and *B* have alternative contingent remainders. Which of the above answers is correct? See Holt, The Testator Who Gave Away Less Than All He or She Had: Perversions in the Law of Future Interests, 32 Ala. L. Rev. 69 (1980).

---

14. The inconsistency here brings to mind the self-contradictory epigrams, called "Irish bulls," of J.P. Mahaffy, the Irish wit and classicist. Mahaffy's best example: "An Irish bull is always pregnant." Another example: "If she'd wanted a family, she shouldn't have married him; he comes from a long line of childless couples." W. Stanford & R. McDowell, Mahaffy: A Biography of an Anglo-Irishman 79 (1971).

What difference in legal consequences does it make whether an interest is classified as an executory interest rather than as a remainder? At common law, there were differences between these interests, but it is very difficult, if not impossible, to prove that there is any difference in the treatment of these two interests today. The great historic difference between remainders and executory interests was this: A legal contingent remainder in land was destroyed if it did not vest at or before the termination of the preceding freehold estate, whereas an executory interest was not subject to destruction (see Note below). This rule has been abolished in almost all jurisdictions, and, where abolished, it is doubtful that any significant differences in legal consequences between executory interests and remainders can be found. Although there may be some theoretical differences, modern cases treating executory interests differently from remainders are about as scarce as hen's teeth. See Dukeminier, Contingent Remainders and Executory Interests: A Requiem for the Distinction, 43 Minn. L. Rev. 13 (1958); 2A R. Powell, Real Property ¶291 [4] (P. Rohan rev. ed. 1988).

In New York, by statute, all future interests in transferees, including what are called executory interests at common law, are called remainders. N.Y. Est., Powers & Trusts Law §6-4.3 (1967). This statute recognizes the functional equivalence of these interests and simplifies the law by discarding the executory interest as superfluous.

NOTE: DESTRUCTIBILITY OF CONTINGENT REMAINDERS

One great historical difference between contingent remainders and other future interests in transferees was that a *legal* contingent remainder in *land* was destroyed if it did not vest at the termination of the preceding life estate. Vested remainders and executory interests were not so destructible. The doctrine of destructibility of contingent remainders is this: *If a legal contingent remainder in land does not vest before or at the termination of the preceding freehold estate, the remainder is destroyed.*[15] Thus:

Case 11. *O* conveys Blackacre "to *A* for life, then to *B* if *B* attains the age of 25." *B* is 15 years old at the time of the conveyance. If *B* attains

---

15. The destructibility doctrine, which is based on the necessity of continuity of seisin, has no application to personal property (in which there is no seisin) nor to equitable interests. Thus it has no application to trusts.

the age of 25 during *A*'s lifetime, *B*'s remainder will become indefeasibly vested, and *B* will take on the termination of *A*'s life estate. If, however, *A*'s life estate comes to an end before *B* reaches 25, *B*'s contingent remainder is destroyed. The land reverts to *O*. (Why was not *B*'s interest given effect when *B* reached 25 *after A*'s death? Because to do so it would have to divest *O*, and divesting interests were not permitted at law when the doctrine of destructibility was laid down.)[16]

The destructibility rule does not apply to executory interests, which do not take effect upon the termination of the life estate but are divesting interests.

Modern status of the destructibility doctrine.   After the development of the Rule against Perpetuities to curb executory interests and contingent remainders in trust that might not vest within lives in being plus 21 years, it appeared a good idea to have one time period governing the creation and existence of all contingent interests and to abolish the destructibility doctrine, which applied only to legal contingent remainders in land. In fact, because the doctrine was easily avoided, by creating a trust rather than a legal interest, the destructibility doctrine only penalized persons who did not have competent lawyers draft their deeds or wills. In England, destructibility of contingent remainders was abolished in 1877. In about three-fourths of the states, the destructibility rule has been abolished by statute or judicial decision. What of the other jurisdictions? It is not easy to say. In 1982 Powell said, "Florida, Oregon, Pennsylvania, and Tennessee are reasonably certain to have the doctrine. Arkansas, North Carolina, and South Carolina have dicta, but no decisions, that the doctrine exists in those states." 2A R. Powell, Real Property ¶314 (P. Rohan rev. ed. 1982). In the most recent edition of Powell's treatise, the subject of destructibility has been dropped entirely, suggesting perhaps that it has disappeared from lack of use.

Other commentators have appraised the situation differently. Dukeminier, Contingent Remainders and Executory Interests: A Requiem for the Distinction, 43 Minn. L. Rev. 13, 34-36 (1958), argues that the doctrine has died off in all states. On the other hand, Fetters, Destructibility of Contingent Remainders, 21 Ark. L. Rev. 145 (1967), and Jones & Heck, Destructibility of Contingent Remainders in Tennessee, 42 Tenn. L. Rev. 761 (1975), suggest that the doctrine exists in Arkansas and Tennessee respectively.

Almost all cases noticing destructibility are more than three genera-

---

16. Case 11 illustrates how a contingent remainder could be destroyed at the *natural* termination of the life estate. A contingent remainder could also be destroyed by *merger*. Suppose that in Case 11, before *B* attains 25, *A* conveys the life estate to *O*, the reversioner. The common law courts held that *A*'s life estate merged into the reversion in fee simple, thereby giving *O* a fee simple absolute — and destroying *B*'s contingent remainder in the process.

tions old. In the only case raising the issue in recent years, Abo Petroleum Corp. v. Amstutz, 93 N.M. 332, 600 P.2d 278 (1979), the court flatly rejected the destructibility doctrine as having no justification or support in modern society.[17]

PROBLEM

In a jurisdiction in which the destructibility rule has been abolished by statute, *O* conveys land "to *A* for life, then to such of *A*'s children as attain the age of 21." Two years later *A* dies leaving two children: *C*, age 8, and *D*, age 4. What is the state of title? If *C* reaches age 21, will *C* take any interest in Blackacre? If so, what will be the name of *C*'s interest and, if *D* is still alive, *D*'s interest?

SECTION D.   CONSTRUCTION AND DRAFTING PROBLEMS

The cases and materials in this section have two purposes. One is to teach the techniques and rules courts have developed in construing instruments. The second, and more important, is to explore the ambiguities lying hidden in common provisions in wills and trusts. The second is more important because only by training in spotting ambiguities, and in foreseeing everything that may happen to the people involved, can you develop the ability to draft an air-tight instrument.

It is written in Psalms 39:6: "Surely every man walketh in a vain shew: . . . he heapeth up riches and knoweth not who shall gather them." When you are admitted to the bar, let not these words of David be said of your clients.

1.   Preference for Vested Interests

The common law had a strong preference for construing ambiguous instruments as creating a vested rather than a contingent remainder. As Sir Edward Coke said, "the law always delights in vesting of estates,

---

17. Statutes abolishing the destructibility doctrine are not retroactive, and sometimes an old deed or will is litigated in modern times. Illinois has been especially plagued by litigation of old instruments. See Belleville National Bank v. Trauernicht, 112 Ill. App. 3d 756, 445 N.E.2d 958 (1983) (attempted destruction by merger in 1919).

and contingencies are odious in the law, and are the causes of troubles, and vesting and settling of estates, the cause of repose and certainty." Roberts v. Roberts, 2 Bulst. 123, 131, 80 Eng. Rep. 1002, 1009 (K.B. 1613). This preference arose in feudal England at a time when contingent interests were barely recognized as interests, and it continued to modern times because of the allegedly desirable consequences of a vested construction. These consequences were:

(1)   a vested remainder was not subject to the capricious destructibility doctrine that defeated the grantor's intent (see supra page 643),

(2)   a vested remainder was transferable inter vivos, making land more alienable (see below),

(3)   a vested remainder accelerated into possession upon termination of the life estate, thus solving vexing problems of possession and undisposed income (see infra page 653 n.20), and

(4)   a vested remainder was not subject to the Rule against Perpetuities, a dread rule that defeats the grantor's intent (see Chapter 11).

To implement the preference for a vested interest, courts invented a number of constructional techniques illustrated in this section.

a.   Transferability and Taxation

At common law, vested remainders, including defeasibly vested ones, were transferable inter vivos. A contingent remainder or an executory interest, which in early law was thought of not as an interest but as a mere chance of ownership, was not transferable. There were three exceptions to this rule of inalienability. Contingent interests were transferable (1) if released to the holder of the possessory estate, (2) in equity as a contract to convey if made for a valuable consideration, or (3) through application of estoppel by deed. In the United States, over 40 states have by statute or judicial decision made contingent interests transferable. In the handful of states remaining, the common law position on alienability is apparently still maintained, although modern cases on the issue are exceedingly few. See 1 American Law of Property §4.67 (1952). Future interests in trust may, of course, be made inalienable during life by a spendthrift clause.

Reversions, remainders, and executory interests are descendible and devisable at death in the same manner as possessory interests. The future interest passes to the heirs or devisees of its owner. Thus:

Case 12.   O conveys Blackacre "to *A* for life, then to *B*." *B* dies during

A's lifetime. *B*'s remainder passes to *B*'s devisees if *B* leaves a will or to *B*'s heirs if *B* dies intestate.

A future interest contingent upon surviving to the time of possession is not transmissible at death. Thus, if in Case 12 *O* had conveyed a remainder "to *B* if *B* survives *A*," *B* could not transmit the remainder to another person if *B* died during *A*'s lifetime.

The federal government subjects to gift or estate taxation any gratuitous transfer of a property interest. IRC §2033 (estate tax), 2501(a) (gift tax). A future interest, like a possessory estate, is an interest in property and is subject to federal gift and estate taxation. If, in Case 12, *B* dies during *A*'s lifetime, the value of *B*'s remainder is subject to estate taxation because it is *transmitted* at death. Federal estate and gift taxation turns upon whether a future interest is transmissible, not upon whether it is vested or contingent. If it is transmissible, it is subject to taxation.

PROBLEMS AND NOTES

1.   *T*'s will devises Blackacre "to *A* for life, then to *B* if *B* survives *A*, and if *B* does not survive *A* to *C*." If *B* dies during *A*'s lifetime, is any portion of Blackacre's value includible in *B*'s federal gross estate? If *C* dies before *A* and *B*, is any portion of Blackacre's value includible in *C*'s federal gross estate? Would your answers be different had "if *B* survives *A*" been omitted from the will?

2.   *T*'s will bequeaths a sum in trust, to pay the income to *A* for life, and giving *A* the power to invade trust principal if necessary for *A*'s comfort and support. On *A*'s death, the trustee is to pay the trust principal to *B*. *B* dies during *A*'s lifetime. Is the value of the remainder interest taxable in *B*'s estate? If so, how is it valued? See Karlson v. Commissioner, 74-2 U.S. Tax Cas. (CCH) ¶13,014 (E.D.N.Y. 1974).

3.   *Valuation of a future interest.*   If a future interest is subject to gift or estate taxation, the interest must be valued. How is this done? Consider the following excerpt:

> To value a remainder we must ascertain the present value of a sum of money to be received on the life tenant's death. The right to $1 one year from now is not worth $1 now, but only $1 less the amount of interest that could be earned on it. Assuming a 6 percent rate of interest, 94 cents today will grow to $1 a year from today. Hence, assuming a 6 percent interest rate, the right to $1 a year from now is now worth 94 cents. The more distant the right to receive the sum, the lower its present value. A dollar due in two years is worth 89 cents today (at 6 percent interest); by reinvesting interest, 89 cents today will grow into 94 cents one year from

now, which will grow into $1 two years from now. The present value of the right to receive $1 at the end of three years is 84 cents. Proof:

84 × .06 = 5.04 (added to 84 = 89.04 at end of first
    year)
89.04 × .06 = 5.34 (added to 89.04 = 94.38 at end
    of second year)
94.38 × .06 = 5.66 (added to 94.38 = 100.04 at end
    of third year)

To put it another way, 84 cents invested at 6 percent with interest compounded annually will be worth $1 at the end of three years.

In order to value a remainder we must know the number of years the right to receive the sum will be deferred. Since we do not know how long the life tenant will actually live, we assume the life tenant will die at the time predicted by a life expectancy (mortality) table.

The present value of a life estate and of a remainder together equal the present value of the whole property. Let us assume that we have property worth $100,000 today, an interest rate of 6 percent, a life estate in A, a remainder in B. How do we apportion this $100,000 present value between A's and B's interests? First, as for A, what is the present value of the right to receive $6,000 annually (6 percent of $100,000) for the life tenant's life expectancy? We seek a sum which, invested for the life tenant's life expectancy at 6 percent, will pay $6,000 for the given number of years and exhaust itself on final payment — in short, the price of an annuity. To simplify the problem let us assume A has a life expectancy of only three years. As shown above the present value of $1 due at the end of one year is 94 cents; the present value of $1 due at the end of two years is 89 cents; and the present value of the right to receive $1 at the end of three years is 84 cents. The present value of the right to receive $1 for each of the three years is the sum of 94 cents and 89 cents and 84 cents, which is $2.67. Now what is the present value of the right to receive $6,000 for three years? $6,000 × 2.67 = $16,020, which is the present value of the life estate. The remainder has a present worth of $83,980. [J. Dukeminier & J. Krier, Property 223–224 (2d ed. 1988).]

Section 7520 of the Internal Revenue Code of 1986 governs the valuation of life estates and remainders for federal tax purposes. Under this section the interest rate changes monthly with market rates of interest.

When a future interest cannot be valued by resort to mortality tables, the interest is valued with reference to all relevant facts, including the likelihood of the contingent events happening. Cases posing difficult evaluation problems are usually solved by the commissioner and the taxpayer coming to some agreement without resort to a lawsuit.

4. In view of the federal gift and estate tax consequences of creating transmissible future interests, how should you draft an instrument to avoid the potential taxation of a future interest at the death of its owner

prior to the death of the life tenant? The correct drafting precept is *not*, as is sometimes said, "Do not create a vested remainder." Taxation does not turn on whether a remainder is vested or contingent. Transmissible contingent remainders are subject to estate taxation, for example, whereas vested remainders subject to divestment upon death before the life tenant's death are not. The correct precept is, "Do not create a *transmissible* future interest." *If you want to give the remainderman power to transmit the future interest at death, give him a remainder contingent upon surviving* plus *a special power of appointment over the remainder.* A special power is not subject to estate taxation. Special powers are explained infra at pages 706-708.

If you don't believe that taxation can be devastating, see Estate of Benson, 447 Pa. 62, 285 A.2d 101 (1971), where the inclusion of a transmissible remainder in the decedent's estate resulted in additional federal estate taxes of $1,244,000! The court refused to construe the instrument, which was ambiguous, so as to avoid taxation. It regarded avoidance of taxation as irrelevant to the testator's intent. See also Estate of Houston, 414 Pa. 579, 201 A.2d (1964), where the court noted that if the remainder had been contingent on surviving to the time of possession there would have been a "colossal" tax saving in the remainderman's estate but construed it to be transmissible and taxable.

b. Acceleration into Possession

Ohio National Bank of Columbus v. Adair
Supreme Court of Ohio, 1978
54 Ohio St. 2d 26, 374 N.E.2d 415, 7 A.L.R.4th 1084

Samuel B. Hartman (testator) died on February 4, 1918, and his will was admitted to probate on February 7, 1918. Surviving at his death were his wife, Sara H. Hartman; his daughter, Maribel Schumacher; and his three granddaughters, Kathleen Hughston Cunningham, Virginia Hughston Jones, and Maribel H. Finnell (Maribel). The wife and daughter are both now deceased. Maribel is the only living child of the daughter. The two other children, Kathleen and Virginia, died without issue.

Maribel, at age 81, is the sole surviving grandchild of the testator. As such, Maribel is the last income beneficiary under the testamentary trust created in item five of the testator's will. By the terms of the trust, the next beneficiaries will receive the trust corpus, thus terminating the trust. Paragraphs 14 and 15 of item five provide for the distribution of the remainder in alternative fashions. Paragraph 14 distributes the remainder to Maribel's issue surviving her. Paragraph 15 provides for a distribution of one-third of the corpus to the heirs of the testator's wife and two-thirds to the testator's heirs if Maribel, the last life tenant, ". . . shall die without issue surviving [her]. . . ."

At the present, Maribel has two children, Patricia Kulha and Michael H. Finnell. They are the great-grandchildren of the testator. Additionally, there are three great-great-grandchildren of the testator, Lesley H. Finnell, Carter H. Finnell and Hunter V. Finnell, through Michael. Patricia is at this time without issue.

Pursuant to a complaint for declaratory judgment filed by The Ohio National Bank of Columbus, as successor trustee, in the Probate Division of the Court of Common Pleas of Franklin County, the trial court found, after a hearing and upon consideration of the arguments of the parties, that the testamentary trust will terminate upon a renunciation and a relinquishment of all interests in the income of the trust by Maribel, the sole remaining income beneficiary, and that the distribution of the trust corpus shall thereby be accelerated and distributed in conformity with the provisions of said trust to Patricia and Michael, per stirpes.

The Court of Appeals, in a majority opinion, affirmed the judgment of the Probate Court, finding that a renunciation of the life interest would accelerate the distribution of the corpus.

LOCHER, J.   The cardinal question presented is whether the trust will terminate upon the renunciation and the relinquishment of the income received by the sole remaining income beneficiary, Maribel, and the distribution of the trust corpus shall thereby be accelerated and distributed to her children, Michael and Patricia.

The doctrine of acceleration, as applied to the law of property, refers to the hastening of the owner of a future interest towards a status of present possession or enjoyment by reason of the failure of the preceding estate. 2 Simes & Smith, Law of Future Interests (2 Ed.) 263, What is Acceleration, Section 791. The doctrine of acceleration is generally used when the temporary interest, preceding the remainder, fails to come into existence, or, as in the case sub judice, coming into existence, terminates in some manner for which the testator did not provide. 2 Texas Tech. L. Rev. 132 (1970). It is apparent that, in Ohio, the acceleration principle in renunciation cases has been adopted, at least where the remainder is vested. . . . The rationale given for this rule in 2 Restatement of Property 962, Comment a, Section 231 (1936), is that acceleration is in accordance with what is normally to be inferred as the intent of the "conveyor" (herein testator), namely that as each successive interest sought to be created by him ends or becomes impossible, the next interest in order should move up. However, the application of the doctrine of acceleration must be in furtherance of the intention of the testator, and never in contravention thereof. . . .

Acceleration of the remainder interest in the present cause must be based upon the testator's general intent as found from a reconstruction of the trust instrument in view of this unanticipated renunciation. . . .

Item five of the will establishes a testamentary trust of the residue of the estate and, as herein pertinent, provides:

14.   If any of my said grandchildren or great grandchildren, who shall have been born before my death, . . . shall die leaving issue surviving them, or any of them, I hereby give, devise, and bequeath to such issue or to the issue of the survivor or survivors of them in equal shares, per stirpes, . . . absolutely and in fee simple, all of my estate, real, personal, and mixed. . . .

It is evident from reading the preceding provisions and other provisions within item five that the testator has clearly manifested his intentions. His plan, as noted by Judge Whiteside's dissent in the Court of Appeals, was to hold the corpus in trust and to delay the determination of the ultimate beneficiary as long as permitted to assure that his estate would pass to his issue, with a contingency plan specifying the heirs of his wife and himself if there were no surviving issue. This intent to delay distribution is further evinced by an examination of the nonmaterialized estates provided for in item five. Under paragraphs 12[18] and 14, had any of the grandchildren predeceased the testator leaving issue (great-grandchildren) surviving his death, the trust would have continued another generation beyond Maribel's life estate. The complexity and the detailed alternatives demonstrate that the trust was the product of a skilled draftsman in the law,[19] attempting to delay the vesting of the estate by meticulously avoiding the oscillating grasp of the rule of perpetuities. We can not agree with the trial court's finding that there was no support for the conclusion that the testator would not want acceleration upon the renunciation of the life estate. Acceleration would clearly seem to vitiate the expressed intentions of the testator. As an example, if acceleration presently would occur, one-half of the estate

---

18. Paragraph 12 of item five reads as follows:

Subject to the foregoing bequests, I give and bequeath all of the net income of my estate to the child or children of my daughter, Maribel Schumacher, and to the issue of the deceased child or children of my said daughter, who shall survive me, if any there be, and direct my executor and trustee to pay the same to them, or to the survivor or survivors of them, share and share alike, per stirpes and not per capita, during their natural lives. . . .

19. How skilled? A knowledgeable and experienced estate planner should think through what might happen during a long-term trust and try to structure it so that living persons can deal intelligently with changing circumstances. Should Maribel have been given a special power to appoint the trust principal to her issue, exercisable by deed or will, thus permitting her to terminate the trust? No small part of the job of an experienced attorney is to point out to the client the nonwisdom of a rigid long-term trust, such as Samuel Hartman created. — Eds.

will pass to Patricia, who has no issue. If she then predeceases Maribel, remains of one-half of the testator's estate would not go to the surviving issue of Maribel as directed by item five, paragraph 14, but would descend to the heirs of Patricia.

We are not, in this case, confronted with the usual situation involving acceleration, where the testator leaves the property to his wife for life with a remainder upon her death and she renounces the will. But, here we are involved with the termination of the third of four once possible life estates provided under this instrument, not for the wife, but for the surviving granddaughter. In this situation, the granddaughter possessed no alternative to taking under the trust. Although the trial court found no impediment to her renunciation of her life interest, this does not give her a right to terminate the trust merely because the testator did not expressly negate acceleration upon such an occurrence. To view this life estate as merely a burden upon the remainder and an impediment to the remainder's vesting as urged by appellees is to ignore its viable role in keeping the estate in the testator's family, i.e., lineal descendants. . . .

Furthermore, acceleration in the instant cause is not only inconsistent with the testator's intentions as inferred from a careful exegesis of the entire instrument, but is antithetical to the precise wording of the residuary bequest and its meaning as described in the case law of Ohio. Townsend's Executors v. Townsend (1874) 25 Ohio St. 477. In reiteration, paragraph 14 of item five states, in relevant part: "If any of my said grandchildren . . . shall die *leaving issue surviving them*, or any of them, I hereby give, devise and bequeath to such issue . . . in equal shares, *per stirpes* . . . all of my estate. . . ." (Emphasis added.)

In Stevens v. Stevens (1929), 121 Ohio St. 490, where a legacy was payable upon death of a life tenant to a named legatee "should he then be living," this court refused to accelerate. Judge Matthias, explaining in *Stevens*, stated, at page 493:

> The express condition in the bequest to Buck and in the bequest to Stevens, "*should he then be living*," referring to the time of the death of testator's wife, cannot be ignored. Under the very terms of this will these two legatees cannot take the bequest prior to the time designated, and, if not then living, the legacy would lapse. The intention of the testator is plain and cannot be thwarted or defeated by the action of another. . . . (Emphasis added.) . . .

Clearly, Judge Matthias' statement in Stevens v. Stevens, supra (121 Ohio St. 490), that an expressed condition of survival can not be ignored is in accordance with this court's interpretation of similar conditions of survival in its other decisions. Applying the rationale of *Stevens* to the case sub judice, the testator's expressed condition in the bequest to the "issue surviving," referring to the time of death of the testator's granddaughter, can not be ignored. Under the provisions of paragraph 14 of item five, the surviving issue of Maribel can not take the bequest prior to the time designated, i.e., the death of Maribel. If there are no surviving issue, the estate is distributed according to paragraph 15 of item five. The intention of the testator is plainly manifested by his usage of words of survivorship. The persons entitled to the enjoyment of the fund can not be determined until the death of Maribel. To ignore the expressed condition of survival and to allow acceleration would be an utter disregard of the instructions in Townsend's Executors v. Townsend, supra (25 Ohio St. 577), that effect be given to every word of the instrument and the words, if technical, must be given their technical sense.

We, therefore, find the testator has exhibited through the instrument a discernible intent that the trust instrument terminate upon the death of Maribel. Only at that time may it be determined which, if any, of her issue are living. Maribel is still living, so that a determination of who will take pursuant to the trust instrument must await her death. It is impossible to ascertain which, if any or if all, of her issue will predecease her. Furthermore, acceleration at this time will exclude the remote possibility of an unborn grandchild's right to enjoyment. A person is presumed to be able to have issue as long as he or she is alive. 2 Simes & Smith, Law of Future Interests, supra, at page 256, Presumption of Possibility of Issue, Section 777. Accordingly, we hold that an acceleration of the succeeding interest upon the renunciation and relinquishment of the income received by the sole remaining life beneficiary, Maribel, prior to her death will defeat the intent of the testator and will be denied.[20]

---

20. A substantial portion of the briefs of both parties was addressed to the nature and technical classification of the remainders. Apparently, whether the remainder is vested, subject to defeasance or subject to a condition precedent, is, according to legal authorities, still of importance in determining whether the remainder will be accelerated. 2A Powell on Real Property, ¶¶309 & 310. Generally, it is stated that acceleration is not possible for a remainder, subject to a condition precedent, in which the condition precedent is one of survival and is construed as indicating an intention that the persons are to be ascertained at the time of death of the life tenant. Powell, supra ¶¶309 & 310; 5 Scott on Trusts (3 Ed. 1967), §412.1; 2 Restatement of Property, §233 and Comment e; 2 L. Simes and A. Smith, The Law of Future Interests (2d ed. 1936), §796.

In Ohio, every will construction is sui generis in the sense that the intent of the testator is to be determined from the will under construction and technical rules of interpretation can be resorted to as an aid in construction, but may not control contrary to the testator's intent. . . . In the present case, we determined without resorting to the well-settled, technical rules of interpretation that acceleration would not be allowed, based upon a study of the trust instrument. It does appear, since the remainder sought to be accelerated in the case sub judice is subject to a condition precedent (see 3 Restatement of Property, supra, §250(d) and Comments i and j; Powell, supra, ¶328; Bergin & Haskell, Preface to Estates in Land and Future Interests, p.75, and, generally, pp. 69-85 [1966]), that if the technical rule would have been applied, . . . the result would still be to deny acceleration.

The judgment of the Court of Appeals is reversed.

Judgment reversed.

NOTES

1. Under Uniform Probate Code §2-801, dealing with disclaimer (see supra page 123), a disclaimant is treated as predeceasing the testator. The Ohio disclaimer statute, enacted in 1976, provides the same thing. Ohio Rev. Code §1339.60(G) (Baldwin 1988). Disclaimer or renunciation must occur before the beneficiary accepts the interest. In the *Adair* case, despite the court's reference to a renunciation by Maribel, Maribel Finnell is not disclaiming or renouncing her interest, because she has been receiving income from the trust for many years. Maribel is proposing to *release* her interest. If Maribel can lawfully release her interest (this is apparently not a spendthrift trust), why does not the court apply the disclaimer statute by analogy? Why should Maribel be treated as dead if she disclaims, but not if she releases the income?

2. Under Uniform Probate Code §2-801 and similar uniform disclaimer acts, the donee of a contingent or defeasibly vested interest may wait until nine months after the interest becomes indefeasibly vested to disclaim. This permits the contingent remainderman to decide at the life tenant's death whether to accept the property or not. Thus:

> *Case 13.* *T* devises property in trust for *A* for life, then to *B* if *B* survives *A*, and if *B* does not survive *A*, to *B*'s issue. At *A*'s death, *B* can decide whether to disclaim and let the property then pass to *B*'s issue. If *B* disclaimed, no federal estate taxes would be payable at *B*'s death.

Why do you suppose the uniform acts permit contingent and defeasibly vested future interests to be disclaimed within nine months of the life tenant's death whereas indefeasibly vested interests must be disclaimed within nine months of the testator's death?

Because disclaimers could be used to avoid estate taxes, as in Case 13, Congress has provided that a disclaimer of a property interest is subject to federal gift tax liability unless the disclaimer occurs within nine months after the interest is created or nine months after the donee attains 21, whichever is later. IRC §2518(b)(2). Thus tax savings by disclaiming a future interest when it becomes possessory are no longer possible. In Case 13, if *B* disclaimed at *A*'s death, a gift tax would be payable by *B* at that time. See Schwartz, Effective Use of Disclaimers, 19 B.C.L. Rev. 551 (1978); Wenig, Recent Developments in Estate and Gift Taxes: Disclaimer, 15 Real Prop., Prob. & Tr. J. 743 (1980).

As a foundation for the next case, Edwards v. Hammond, observe that in a few situations, courts have treated words that might appear to state a condition precedent as mere surplusage. The courts say that the instrument means the same thing with or without the "surplus" words, and by eliminating the surplus words the courts manage to vest the remainder. For example, suppose that *O* conveys "to *A* for life, and then after *A*'s death to *B*." The words "after *A*'s death" do not state a condition precedent. They are surplusage. *B*'s remainder is vested, and if *A*'s life estate ends prior to *A*'s death (by disclaimer, release, forfeiture, or whatever), *B* is entitled to possession.

PROBLEM

O conveys "to *A* for life, then to *B* for life if *B* is then living, then to *C*." What interests are created? See Webb v. Hearing, Cro. Jac. 415, 79 Eng. Rep. 355 (K.B. 1617); L. Simes, Future Interests 23 n.11 (2d ed. 1966).

Edwards v. Hammond
Court of Common Pleas, England, 1683
3 Lev. 132, 83 Eng. Rep. 614

Ejectment upon not guilty, and special verdict, the case was. A copyholder of land,[21] burrough English,[22] surrendered to the use of himself for life, and after to the use of his eldest son and his heirs, if he lived to the age of 21 years; provided, and upon condition, that if he die before 21, that then it shall remain to the surrenderer and his heirs. The surrenderer died, the youngest son entered; and the eldest son being 17 brought an ejectment; and the sole question was, whether the devise to the eldest son be upon condition precedent, or if the condition be subsequent; *scil.* that the estate in fee shall vest immediately upon the death of the father, to be divested if he die before 21. For

---

21. The land involved was copyhold, not freehold. Copyhold began as a servile type of tenure held from the lord of the manor, and because of its inferior origin, the lord, and not the tenant, held seisin. A contingent remainder in copyhold land was not destroyed if it did not vest at the termination of the preceding life estate. — Eds.

22. In some parts of England it was common for copyhold land to descend to the youngest son, rather than the eldest, under the custom known as "borough English." Forced to choose one child as heir, why would many of the lower class prefer the youngest son? Some have imagined it associated with the *droit de seigneur*. See 2 W. Blackstone, Commentaries *82; Cairns, The Explanatory Process in the Field of Inheritance, 20 Iowa L. Rev. 266, 277 (1935). — Eds.

the defendant it was argued, that the condition was precedent, and that the estate should descend to the youngest son in the mean time, or at least shall be in contingency and in abeyance til the first son shall attain to one and twenty; and so the eldest son has no title now, being no more than 17. On the other side it was argued, and so agreed by the Court; that though by the first words this may seem to be a condition precedent, yet, taking all the words together, this was not a condition precedent, but a present devise to the eldest son, subject to and defeasible by this condition subsequent, *scil.* his not attaining the age of 21. . . . Accordingly this case was adjudged in Mich. term next following.

NOTES

1. In Edwards v. Hammond a father wanted to give possession of land at his death to his eldest son, who was not his heir. Inasmuch as a copyhold could be transferred only by a surrender and admittance made in the lord's court, the father surrendered his land to his lord, who then admitted as tenant the person or persons nominated by the father. For ease of discussion, the conveyance in Edwards v. Hammond can be paraphrased as follows: O conveys "to O for life, then to O's eldest son A and his heirs if A attains the age of 21, but if A dies under 21, to O and his heirs." O died when A was 17. B, O's youngest son, was the heir of O.

(a) Exactly what was the practical problem facing the court? What policies support the court's decision to put A into possession rather than B?

(b) Assuming that it makes more sense to put A into possession, why could the court not put a contingent remainderman in possession?

2. The rule of Edwards v. Hammond is that if an age condition is stated both as a condition precedent and as a divesting contingency, the first statement (as a condition precedent) can be ignored as surplusage.

The English courts limited the rule of Edwards v. Hammond in two ways. First, they restricted it to *age contingencies*, although, as Jarman says, "the rule of construction appears to be as reasonably applicable where the contingency is that of the devisee being alive when the remainder naturally falls into possession, as where it is the attainment by him of the age which presumably in the testator's mind qualifies him for the possession and legal control." T. Jarman, Wills 1367 (8th ed. 1951). Second, they limited its application by refusing to apply it to class gifts, for the reason given in the following case, Festing v. Allen. See H. Theobald, Wills 563 (14th ed. 1982).

Why do you suppose the courts were so hostile to the rule of Edwards v. Hammond, especially in view of the stated preference for a vested construction? If left to expand to the limits of the surplusage theory,

Edwards v. Hammond would have vested a lot of remainders. Many instruments are drafted so as to state both a condition precedent and a gift over for failure to meet the condition. Did the English judges find some virtues in contingent remainders after all?

Festing v. Allen
Court of Exchequer, England, 1843
12 Mees. & Wels. 279, 152 Eng. Rep. 1204

[Roger Belk died devising land by a testamentary clause that went on for more than 550 words without a stop. Simplified, the devise was "to my wife for life, and after her death to my grand-daughter Martha Hannah Johnson for life, and after her death to the children of Martha Hannah who shall attain the age of 21, and for want of any such issue to [Ann Johnson and others]." Testator's widow died. Then Martha, who had married Maurice Festing a year after the testator's death, died survived by three minor children. If Martha's children had a contingent remainder, it was destroyed at Martha's death by failure to vest prior to the termination of the life estate. See supra page 643, on destructibility of contingent remainders.]

ROLFE, B. . . . [T]he main question is, whether those children took on her death any interest in the devised estates.

We think that they did not. It was contended on their behalf that they took vested estates in fee immediately on the death of their mother, subject only to be devested in the event of their dying under twenty-one, and the case, it was said, must be treated as coming within the principle of . . . [Edwards v. Hammond]. To this, however, we cannot accede. In all those cases there was an absolute gift to some ascertained person or persons, and the Courts held, that words accompanying the gift, though apparently importing a contingency or contingencies, did in reality only indicate certain circumstances on the happening or not happening of which the estate previously devised should be devested, and pass from the first devisee into some other channel. The clear distinction in the present case is, that here there is no gift to any one who does not answer the whole of the requisite description. The gift is not to the children of Mrs. Festing, but to the children who shall attain twenty-one, and no one who has not attained his age of twenty-one years is an object of the testator's bounty, any more than a person who is not a child of Mrs. Festing. . . . We think that Mrs. Festing was tenant for life, with contingent remainders in fee to such of her children as should attain twenty-one; and as no child had attained twenty-one when the particular estate determined by her death, the remainder was necessarily defeated. It is equally clear that all the other limitations were defeated by the same event, namely, the death of Mrs. Festing leaving several infant children, but no child who had then attained the age of twenty-one years. For the limitations to take effect at her decease were all of them contingent remaidners in fee, one or other of which was to take effect according to the events pointed out. . . . If . . . there had at her decease been a failure of her child or children who should attain twenty-one, then the alternative limitations would have taken effect; but this did not happen, for though she left no child the age of twenty-one years, and therefore capable of taking under the devise in favour of her children, yet neither is it possible to say that there was at her decease a failure of her issue who should attain the age of twenty-one years, for she left three children, all or any of whom might and still may attain the prescribed age; so that the contingency on which alone the alternative limitations were to take effect had not happened when the particular estate determined, and those alternative limitations, all of which were clearly contingent remainders, were therefore defeated. On these short grounds, we think it clear, that neither the infant children of Mrs. Festing, nor the parties who were to take the estate in case of her leaving no child who should attain twenty-one, take any interest whatever, but that on her death the whole estate and interest vested in the heir-at-law [of Roger Belk].

PROBLEM

Apply the principles of Edwards v. Hammond and Festing v. Allen to the following cases. At the time of the conveyance *A* and *B* are alive, and *A* has a son, *C*, age 5, and a second son, *D*, age 3. When is the age condition an essential part of the description of the beneficiaries?

(a) To *A* for life, then to *B* if *B* reaches 21, but if *B* does not reach 21, to *C*.

(b) To *A* for life, then to the first son of *A* *if* he reaches 21, and if he does not reach 21, to *B*.

(c) To *A* for life, then the first son of *A* *who* reaches 21, and if no son of *A* reaches 21, to *B*. (See Re Astor, [1922] 1 Ch. 364.)

(d) To *A* for life, then to *such* children of *A* *as* reach 21, but if none reach 21, to *B*.

c. Requiring Survival to Time of Possession

As a general rule, there is no requirement that a remainderman live to the time of possession. If the remainderman dies before the life tenant, the remainder passes to the remainderman's estate. Of course, the testator may expressly require survival, and in a few situations, hereafter noted, courts will imply a requirement of survival.

If a vested remainder subject to divestment is created, courts ordinarily read the divesting language strictly as written and do not expand it to cause divestment in events other than those stated.

Security Trust Co. v. Irvine
Delaware Court of Chancery, 1953
33 Del. Ch. 375, 93 A.2d 528

BRAMHALL, V.C. In this case this court is asked to determine two issues: (1) whether or not the residuary estate left to brothers and sisters of the testator vested as of the date of his death or at the time of the death of the last life tenant; (2) if it should be decided that the residuary estate vested as of the time of the death of the testator, do the life tenants take as members of the class of brothers and sisters receiving the residuary estate?

Plaintiff is trustee under the last will and testament of James Wilson, deceased, who died on July 29, 1918, leaving a last will and testament dated October 25, 1915. After providing for certain specific bequests, testator gave and devised all his "real and mixed estate" to the Security Trust and Safe Deposit Company, — now the Security Trust Company, — to two sisters, Martha B. Wilson and Mary E. Wilson, during their joint lives and during the lifetime of the survivor of them. Testator further provided that in the event that his sister, Margaret W. Irvine, should be left a widow, she should share equally with the two sisters above named in the benefits of the trust so provided. As to the remainder, testator provided as follows:

> Upon the death of two sisters, Martha B. Wilson and Mary E. Wilson, and the survivor of them, then it is my will that all of my real and mixed estate and any proceeds that may have arisen from the sale of any part thereof, together with any unexpended income there may be, shall be equally divided among my brothers and sisters, share and share alike, their heirs and assigns forever, the issue of any deceased brother or sister to take his or her parent's share.

Testator was survived by his five brothers and sisters: Samuel H. Wilson, Margaret W. Irvine, Martha B. Wilson, Mary E. Wilson, and Henry Wilson. At the time of the execution of the will the ages of the brothers and sisters ranged from 39 to 52 years. Martha B. Wilson and Mary E. Wilson, the two life tenants, died respectively on June 9, 1928, and August 18, 1951, unmarried and without issue, the trust therefore terminating on the latter date. The other devisees all predeceased Mary E. Wilson, the surviving life tenant. Samuel H. Wilson died on October 26, 1925, leaving to survive him three children, Frazer Wilson, Jeannette A. Wilson, and Samuel H. Wilson, Jr., and Grace Wilson Gearhart, daughter of a deceased son, Francis Paul Wilson. Samuel H. Wilson, Jr., died in 1924, unmarried and without issue.

Samuel Irvine, one of the defendants, is the sole residuary legatee under the will of Margaret W. Irvine, deceased. Martha B. Wilson died

SECURITY TRUST CO. v. IRVINE

James Wilson devises his residuary estate in trust to pay the income to his sisters
Martha and Mary for their joint lives and the life of the survivor, and upon the death
of the survivor of them the trust corpus "shall be equally divided among my brothers
and sisters, share and share alike, their heirs and assigns forever, the issue of any
deceased brother or sister to take his or her parent's share."

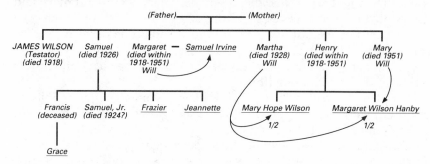

Survivors are underlined.

Do you see that the big fight is between Samuel's descendants and Henry's descendants, and that the latter end up with 3/5 of the trust property and the former with only
1/5?

testate on June 9, 1928, leaving her residuary estate to her two nieces,
Margaret Gregg Wilson, now Margaret W. Hanby, and Mary Hope
Wilson, each an undivided one-half interest therein.

Mary E. Wilson died testate on August 18, 1951, leaving her entire
residuary estate to Margaret W. Hanby, after providing for the payment
of her debts and a legacy to Mary Hope Wilson in the sum of $100.

The estate of Martha B. Wilson has been closed, the final account
having been passed on February 9, 1935; the estate of Mary E. Wilson
has also been closed, the final account in that estate having been passed
on September 15, 1952.

I must first determine whether or not the remainder interest of the
testator became vested at the time of his death or at the time of the
death of the last life tenant, Mary E. Wilson, on August 18, 1951. In
order to resolve this question the intention of the testator at the time
of the drafting of the will must first be ascertained. If it should be clear
that testator intended this provision of the will to take effect at some
future date, then the intention of the testator, so far as it may be legally
carried out, will prevail. However, in reaching my conclusion, I must
accept certain well recognized rules of construction.

The law favors the early vesting of devised estates and will presume
that words of survivorship relate to the death of the testator, if fairly
capable of that construction. In the absence of a clear and unambiguous
indication of an intention to the contrary, the heirs will be determined
as of the date of the death of the testator and not at some future date.

When the language employed by the testator annexes futurity, clearly indicating his intention to limit his estate to take effect upon a dubious and uncertain event, the vesting is suspended until the time of the occurrence of the event. See Delaware Trust Company v. Delaware Trust Company, 33 Del. Ch. 135, 91 A.2d 44, and cases therein cited.

The assertion that it is indicated in the will that the testator intended the residuary estate to be vested as of the date of the death of the last life tenant is based upon the contentions: (1) the fact that testator left a life estate to two of his sisters and then gave the residuary estate to his brothers and sisters indicates that testator did not intend the two sisters to share in his residuary estate and therefore the residuary estate did not vest until the date of the death of the last life tenant; (2) the use of the words "upon the death of two sisters" and the provision in the will of testator that his estate "should be equally divided among my brothers and sisters" indicates an intention that testator intended a future vesting of his residuary estate.

Whatever may be the law in other states it is well settled in this state that the fact that a life tenant is a member of a class, in the absence of any clear indication in the will to the contrary, does not prevent the life tenant from participating in the remainder of testator's estate as a part of the class. . . .

As to the use of the word "upon," it is equally clear under the decisions in this state and elsewhere, that this word and other words of this nature refer only to the time of payment and not to the substance of the devise. Cann v. Van Sant, 24 Del. Ch. 300, 11 A.2d 388; In re Nelson's Estate, 9 Del. Ch. 1, 74 A. 851. Other Delaware cases are to the same effect. In any event, the use of this word, and the provision for dividing its remainder, under the circumstances of this case would not alone be sufficient to overcome the presumption of immediate vesting.

It is contended on behalf of certain defendants that even though it should be determined that the gift to the brothers and sisters vested as of the date of the death of testator, the life tenants should be excluded from membership in the class of brothers and sisters. They base their contention upon the fact that testator in another item of his will gave them a life interest in his residuary estate.

In endeavoring to ascertain the intention of testator, it is uniformly held that such a provision is not of itself sufficient to prevent the life tenant from participating in the remainder as part of the class. See cases cited in 13 A.L.R. 620. It is not sufficient to show the absence of an intention to include the life tenants; there must be some indication of a clear and unambiguous nature to exclude them. Dillman v. Dillman, 409 Ill. 494, 499, 100 N.E.2d 567; Carver v. Wright, 119 Me. 185, 109 A. 896. I can find no incongruity in the mere fact that testator provided a life estate for his two sisters and later gave the remainder to his brothers and sisters, of which the two sisters were part of the class.

They were unmarried. They were no longer young. It seems to be clear from the several provisions in the will of the testator that it was his purpose to provide for them. Such provision does not indicate to me that testator did not intend that they should participate further in his estate. Certainly there is no legal inconsistency in life tenants participating in the remainder. The theory that the testator particularly desired to see that his sisters were provided for is at least as strong as the supposition that he intended to exclude them from participating in the remainder.

I conclude that the life tenants should participate in the remainder devised by testator to his brothers and sisters.

Having determined that the life tenants should participate in the provision for the brothers and sisters, I must next consider the effect of the provision that the "issue of any deceased brothers or sisters to take his or her parent's share."

As to the brothers and sisters who died leaving issue, it was specifically provided that such issue should take the interest of such brother or sister leaving issue. Their interest was thereby divested, their issue being substituted in their place. In such case, the brother or sister dying leaving issue would have no power of disposition of his or her interest in the estate. In re Nelson's Estate, supra.

The will of testator is silent as to any provision relative to any of the brothers and sisters dying without leaving issue. Martha B. Wilson, Mary E. Wilson and Margaret W. Irvine, three sisters of testator, left no issue at the time of their death. Was their interest divested by their death, even though they left no issue, or did their estates receive an absolute interest, free and clear of any conditions subsequent?

Under the will of testator, the death of the life tenants leaving issue caused their interest to be divested. I have determined that the brothers and sisters received an absolute estate, subject to the provision that the interest of any brother or sister dying prior to the death of the life tenant should go by substitution to the issue of such brother or sister. However, this provision of the will does not apply where there is no issue, since there would then be no limitation upon their estate. The decisions in this state are silent as to what would happen under such circumstances. However, the weight of authority in other states is to the effect that in the event of the death of the devisees leaving no issue, the interest of such devisees is not divested by their death. McArthur v. Scott, 113 U.S. 340; Plitt v. Plitt, 167 Md. 252, 173 A. 35, 109 A.L.R. 1; Jacobs v. Whitney, 205 Mass. 477, 91 N.E. 1009; Rutledge v. Fishburne, 66 S.C. 155, 44 S.E. 564; Gardner v. Vanlandingham, 334 Mo. 1054, 69 S.W.2d 947. Since the estates created were absolute except for the condition subsequent, and since the subsequent condition has been removed, the estates of the sisters dying without issue would have an absolute interest unrestricted by any condition.

I believe that such a determination would be in accord with the plain intention of the testator. He apparently desired to provide for his own brothers and sisters and their issue. If he had desired to provide that the interest of any brother or sister dying without issue should go to the surviving brothers or sisters or had intended to make some other similar provision, it would have been easy for him to do so. The fact that he did not, indicates that he had so such intention. I conclude that the interests of Martha B. Wilson, Mary E. Wilson and Margaret W. Irvine, were not divested by their death without issue and that their interests in the estate of the testator under the residuary clause of the will should go to their respective estates.

The estates of Martha B. Wilson and Mary E. Wilson have been closed. In accordance with the opinion of this court in Cooling v. Security Trust Co., 29 Del. Ch. 286, 76 A.2d 1, their shares may be distributed by the trustee directly to the persons entitled to receive the same, the trustees first seeing that any taxes which may be due or any costs which may be incurred by reason thereof are paid.

NOTES AND PROBLEMS

1. A transmissible future interest has several disadvantages today. First, it is subject to the federal estate tax upon the death of the remainderman (see supra page 647). What are the federal estate tax consequences of construing the remainders in the James Wilson trust to be vested subject to divestment only if the remainderman died with issue during the life tenant's life?

Second, a transmissible future interest goes through the probate estate of the transferor-remainderman. There it is subject to probate costs and to creditors. The ruling of the court in the *Irvine* case, directing the trustee to bypass closed estates and distribute the property directly to persons entitled to receive it, may make good sense but is unusual. See Will of Woodcock, 19 Misc. 2d 268, 186 N.Y.S.2d 447 (1959), rejecting such a suggestion.

2. The result in *Irvine* is the orthodox one. As Professor French says, "If the instrument names a substitute taker to take property under some circumstances, but not others, the survival condition operates only under the circumstance when the instrument names a substitute taker." French, Imposing a General Survival Requirement on Beneficiaries of Future Interests: Solving the Problems Caused by the Death of a Beneficiary Before the Time Set for Distribution, 27 Ariz. L. Rev. 801, 809 & n.40 (1985).

There is, nonetheless, a feeling among some commentators that the result in *Irvine* does not carry out the ordinary testator's intent. See

Halbach, Future Interests: Express and Implied Conditions of Survival (pts. 1 & 2), 49 Calif. L. Rev. 297, 431, at 460 (1961).

Restatement (Second) of Property, Donative Transfers §27.3, Illustration 3 (Tent. Draft No. 9, 1986), is contrary to the result reached in the *Irvine* case. Comment e of that section states:

> Because of the undesirability of having the gift pass through the deceased member's estate and because the provision for substitution of issue is a sufficient indication of the donor's intent that he did not wish such a result, it should be presumed, in the absence of contrary indication, that the donor who provides for substitution of issue intends that the share of the other class members be enlarged if a class member fails to survive to the date of distribution and leaves no issue who so survive.

3.   Although courts do not imply survival requirements in gifts to single-generational classes, such as "children" or "brothers and sisters," they do imply survival requirements in gifts to multi-generational classes, such as "issue" or "descendants." See Halbach, supra, at 314-315; 5 American Law of Property §21.13 (1952). Thus suppose that *T*'s will devises property "to *A* for life, then to *A*'s issue." *A* has a son, *B*, and a daughter, *C*. *B* predeceases *A*, devising all his property to his wife. *B* is also survived by a daughter, *D*. *D*, and not *B*'s wife, succeeds to *B*'s share on *A*'s death.

Similarly, where there is a gift to the "heirs" of *A*, a survival requirement to the death of *A* is implied.

4.   If there is a gift "to *A* for life, remainder to *B* or *C*," the little word "or" is read as imposing a survival requirement on *B*. The remainder is hence read as "to *B*, if *B* is then living, and if not, to *C*." Note there is no survival requirement on *C*'s interest. See 5 American Law of Property, supra, §21.16.

5.   *T* devises property "to my husband *H* for life, then to my *surviving* children." *T* is survived by two children, *A* and *B*. *A* dies intestate before *H*, survived by a child *C*. *H* dies. Is *C* entitled to a share in the property? Does "surviving" refer to "surviving *T*" or "surviving *H*"? See 2 L. Simes & A. Smith, The Law of Future Interests §577 (2d ed. 1956).

6.   For critical analyses of a number of the rules studied in this chapter, see Fellows, In Search of Donative Intent, 73 Iowa L. Rev. 611 (1988); McGovern, Facts and Rules in the Construction of Wills, 26 UCLA L. Rev. 285 (1978).

Lawson v. Lawson
Supreme Court of North Carolina, 1966
267 N.C. 643, 148 S.E.2d 546

Petition for partition. Petitioners, J. Roscoe Lawson, Ina Rose Lawson Denning, J. Alva Lawson, and Sadie Lawson Long allege that each of them owns a one-fourth undivided interest in the land described in the petition and that respondents have no interest in it. Respondent William Lawson alleges that he owns a one-sixth undivided interest in the property; respondents Leo Harold Lawson, Kenneth Bryan Lawson, Bonnie Jewel Lawson and Barbara Ann Lawson West allege that together they own a one-sixth undivided interest. The facts are admitted in the pleadings.

J. Rad Lawson, the father of petitioners and the grandfather of respondents, died testate in March 1950. He devised the land in suit to his daughter, Opal Lawson Long, with the following provision:

> To be hers for and during the term of her natural life, and at her death to her children, if any, in fee simple; if none, to the whole brothers and sisters of my daughter, Opal Lawson Long, in fee simple. Should my daughter, Opal Lawson Long predecease me, then the lands herein devised shall go to her children, if any, in fee simple; if none, to the whole brothers and sisters of my said daughter, in fee simple.

Opal Lawson Long died in November 1965. She left no children or descendants of children. The whole brothers and sisters who survived her are the petitioners named above. Respondent William Lawson is the only child and descendant of Earl Lawson, a whole brother who died in 1950. The other respondents are the only children and descendants of Leo Lawson, a whole brother who died in 1953.

Upon these facts, Judge Johnson entered judgment decreeing that petitioners own the described property in fee simple and that respondents have no interests in the land. He ordered that it be sold for partition among petitioners. Respondents excepted to this judgment and appealed.

SHARP, J.[23]   Respondents contend that at the death of the testator,

---

23. Justice Susie Sharp (known as "Judge Susie" to North Carolinians) was appointed to the court in 1962 and elected Chief Justice in 1974, the first woman chief justice of any state. Time Magazine called her one of the ten most important women in America.

Justice Sharp

In the 1980s, terrible tragedy erupted in Justice Sharp's family. Her favorite niece and namesake, Susie Sharp Lynch, divorced her husband Tom and, with their two young boys, moved back to North Carolina from Albuquerque two weeks before Justice Sharp retired as Chief Justice. Susie took up with her first cousin (and Justice Sharp's nephew), Fritz Klenner, a man with a taste for guns and more than a touch of paranoia. Fritz moved in with Susie, and they began calling themselves husband and wife, shocking the family. (Marriage between first cousins is prohibited in North Carolina.) Bitter toward her former husband, Susie — like Medea of old — set about to destroy him. Her former mother-in-law had once called Susie — with unrealizing fatefulness — a witch. So, on a fast, secret weekend trip to Kentucky in July 1984, Susie and Fritz waited outside Tom's mother's house until she returned from church, then shot her to death. They shot Tom's sister in the head too, just because she happened to be in the house.

Susie threw up obstacle after obstacle to the boys visiting their father in Albuquerque.

J. Rad Lawson, the six whole brothers and sisters of the life tenant, all of whom were then living, took a vested remainder in the land, and that they, as children of the two whole brothers who predeceased Opal Lawson Long, inherited their interest. The law, however, is otherwise.

This case presents a typical example of a contingent remainder. . . .

Clearly the interests of the whole brothers and sisters were contingent and could not vest before the death of the life tenant, for not until then could it be determined that she would leave no issue surviving. Priddy & Co. v. Sanderford, 221 N.C. 422, 20 S.E.2d 341. "Where those who are to take in remainder cannot be determined until the happening of a stated event, the remainder is contingent. Only those who can answer the roll immediately upon the happening of the event acquire any estate in the properties granted." Strickland v. Jackson, 259 N.C. 81, 84, 130 S.E.2d 22, 25. Respondents' parents, having predeceased the life tenant, could not answer the roll call at her death.

The judgment of the court below is

Affirmed.[24]

NOTES

1. In accord with Lawson v. Lawson are Fletcher v. Hurdle, 259 Ark. 640, 536 S.W.2d 109 (1976), criticized in 31 Ark. L. Rev. 134

In the spring of 1985, Tom asked the North Carolina court to allow a two-weeks-longer visit by his boys the next summer. Susie's father, who liked Tom, approved of an extended visit and prepared to go to court to testify in Tom's favor. A family row ensued. Susie's mother loudly objected to Susie's misalliance with Fritz. Susie and Fritz left, swearing they would not come back. But they did. One evening, shortly thereafter, Fritz returned and shot to death Susie's father, her mother, and her grandmother — and, for good measure, he slit Susie's mother's throat.

Connecting the Kentucky and North Carolina murders, the North Carolina police put Fritz and Susie under surveillance. Growing suspicious, Fritz and Susie packed their Chevrolet Blazer with an arsenal of weapons, put the two boys and their two dogs in the back seat, and drove away. The police followed. Fritz stepped out and fired a submachine gun at them, then got back in and calmly drove on. As the police kept a safe distance, Fritz brought the car to a halt. The police observed something going on in the Blazer; it turned out to be monstrous. The two boys were given cyanide capsules. Then, to make sure their father didn't get them, either Susie or Fritz shot each boy in the head. Unlike Medea, having no chariot drawn by dragons to escape, Susie and Fritz blew themselves up, a second or so later, with dynamite. This tragic tale of vengeance and madness is told by J. Bledsoe, Bitter Blood (1988).

Subsequently Tom Lynch sued, claiming (as heir of his sons) a share in the estates of Susie, her parents, and her grandmother. Tom claimed that either (1) the boys survived Susie or (2) Susie either intentionally killed or was culpably negligent in causing the deaths of the boys and her estate cannot profit from her wrong. In reversing a dismissal of Tom's lawsuit, the North Carolina appellate court held that it stated a cause of action. The court held that the North Carolina slayer statute "did not abrogate any of the many procedures devised by the common law to prevent one from profiting by his own wrong." Lynch v. Newsom, 384 S.E.2d 284 (N.C. App. 1989). But cf. Fellows, The Slayer Rule: Not Solely a Matter of Equity, 71 Iowa L. Rev. 489, 512 n.67 (1986), suggesting that the victim ought not to inherit as the heir of the slayer. — Eds.

24. Noted in 45 N.C.L. Rev. 264. — Eds.

(1977), and Schau v. Cecil, 257 Iowa 1296, 136 N.W.2d 515 (1965), criticized in 65 Mich. L. Rev. 203 (1966). The difficulties caused by Schau v. Cecil are discussed in Note, 63 Iowa L. Rev. 924 (1978). See also Roberts, Class Gifts in North Carolina — When Do We "Call the Roll?," 21 Wake Forest L. Rev. 1, 11-14 (1985).

By far the majority of states take a contrary view: A future interest that is subject to some express condition precedent other than survival is not subject to an implied condition of survival. The interest is defeated only if the stated contingency fails to occur. See 5 American Law of Property §21.25 (1952); 2 L. Simes & A. Smith, The Law of Future Interests §594 (2d ed. 1956).

2.   Why did not an anti-lapse statute apply in Lawson v. Lawson? Because an anti-lapse statute applies only when a will beneficiary *predeceases the testator*. In *Lawson*, Earl and Leo survived the testator but predeceased the life tenant. Professor Rabin has argued that the only persuasive reason for preferring a vested construction is to "prevent disinheritance of issue of deceased remaindermen." Rabin, The Law Favors the Vesting of Estates. Why?, 65 Colum. L. Rev. 467, 483-484 (1965). Construing an ambiguous remainder as transmissible tends to substitute issue for the deceased taker, thus achieving the same result that is prescribed by most anti-lapse statutes. Take this case: *T* devises property "to my daughter Opal for life, and then to Opal's children." Opal has two children, *A* and *B*. During Opal's life, *A* dies intestate and unmarried, leaving a child, *C*, surviving. The remainder to Opal's children is vested, and at Opal's death the property is divided equally between child *B* and grandchild *C*. The same result would be reached if an anti-lapse statute applied, i.e., if *A* had predeceased the testator rather than Opal.

Of course, construing a remainder as transmissible does not necessarily pass the remainder to the remainderman's issue. The remainderman's heirs may include a spouse as well as issue, or the remainderman may devise the remainder to another, say a spouse. In the example above, if *A* had died married, leaving a will devising all his property to his wife *W*, *W* and not *C* would take *A*'s share of the remainder. On the other hand, if *W* were the mother of *C*, *C* might later inherit *A*'s original share from his mother. Thus it can be said that construing a remainder as transmissible tends to preserve a remainderman's share for his issue, although it does not guarantee it.

NOTE: SHOULD THE PREFERENCE FOR VESTED INTERESTS BE ABANDONED?

In a comprehensive study, Professor Susan French suggests abandoning the preference for vested future interests. French, Imposing a

General Survival Requirement on Beneficiaries of Future Interests: Solving the Problems Caused by the Death of a Beneficiary Before the Time Set for Distribution, 27 Ariz. L. Rev. 801 (1985). Professor French recognizes that the preference for vesting serves several useful functions, such as promoting transferability and termination of trusts, avoiding violations of the Rule against Perpetuities, and carrying out the donor's presumed intent that the future interest pass to the donee's heirs. The presumption of vesting also avoids the need to determine who are the substitute takers where the beneficiary does not survive until distribution.

On the other hand, the preference for vesting has several serious disadvantages, mentioned earlier. Distribution to the beneficiary's estate, perhaps years after the life tenant's death when the existence of the future interest is discovered, requires probate to pass the interest and may bring federal estate tax liability for the value of the transmissible future interest.

Professor French suggests that, on balance, it is a good idea for the law to require beneficiaries to survive until the time of distribution. However, she warns that if this is done, an appropriate substitute disposition must be provided by law in case the beneficiary does not survive. After examining several possible approaches to the substitute disposition problem, Professor French concludes that the best solution is to give the dying beneficiary a special power of appointment over the future interest. Id. at 812-820. The advantages of this approach are that it would avoid subjecting the property to taxation and probate expenses in the donee's estate and to the donee's creditors. (On powers of appointment, see infra pages 985-997.) French also discusses who should take in default of exercise of the power of appointment. To illustrate French's proposal, take this case:

> *Case 14.* T devises property "to A for life, remainder to B." Under present law, B's remainder is vested and transmissible at B's death during A's life. Under French's proposal, B's remainder is contingent on surviving A. If B predeceases A, B may appoint the remainder to anyone B wishes except B, B's estate, B's creditors, or the creditors of B's estate (the power is so defined to avoid federal estate taxation in B's estate, see infra page 985). If B does not appoint the remainder, at A's death after B's death the remainder passes to B's issue (or B's heirs).

The Joint Editorial Board for the Uniform Probate Code agrees with Professor French that a requirement of survival to the time of possession should be imposed on all future interests. But it does not agree with her that the donee should have a special power of appointment. The Board prefers an anti-lapse statute approach and would substitute the issue of the predeceasing beneficiary for the beneficiary. The chief disadvantage of this approach is that it does not permit *B* in Case 14 to devise the remainder to *B*'s spouse. In that respect it seems inconsistent with the other provisions of the code that favor the spouse more than does the existing law in most states. The Joint Editorial Board has drafted a new (and quite complex) UPC §2-707, incorporating its ideas. This new section is scheduled to come before the National Conference of Commissioners on Uniform State Laws for approval in 1990.

The Board's proposed statute has limited antecedents existing in a few states. Illinois, Pennsylvania, and Tennessee have anti-lapse statutes that apply, at the life tenant's death, to future interests given to a class. Although the statutes differ in details, generally they require survivorship of class members to the time of possession, and they give the issue of any then-deceased class member his or her share by representation. Ill. Ann. Stat. ch. 110½, ¶4-11 (1978); Pa. Cons. Stat Ann. tit. 20, §2514(5) (1975); Tenn. Code Ann. §32-3-104 (1984). See Waggoner, Future Interests Legislation: Implied Conditions of Survivorship and Substitutionary Gifts Under the New Illinois "Anti-Lapse" Provision, 1969 U. Ill. L.F. 423; Note, Testamentary Gifts of Future Interests: Is There an "Immediate" Problem with the Tennessee Antilapse Statute?, 17 Mem. St. U.L. Rev. 263 (1987).

The California anti-lapse statute applies to a gift to a devisee who "fails to survive . . . until a future time required by the will." The issue of the devisee are substituted in his place, unless the will expresses a contrary intention or a substitute disposition. Cal. Prob. Code §6147 (1989). Thus in California if *T* devises property "to *A* for life, then to my daugher *B* if *B* survives *A*," and *T*'s will contains no residuary clause, *B*'s issue take the remainder if *B* dies before *A*.

Clobberie's Case

Court of Chancery, England, 1677
2 Vent. 342, 86 Eng. Rep. 476

In one Clobberie's case it was held, that where one bequeathed a sum of money to a woman, at her age of twenty-one years, or day of marriage, to be paid unto her with interest, and she died before either, that the money should go to her executor; and was so decreed by my Lord Chancellor Finch [later Lord Nottingham].

But he said, if money were bequeathed to one at his age of twenty-one years, if he dies before that age, the money is lost.

On the other side, if money be given to one, to be paid at the age of twenty-one years; there, if the party dies before, it shall go to the executors.

NOTE AND PROBLEM

1. The first and third rules of construction laid down in Clobberie's Case are widely followed today. See 5 American Law of Property, supra, §21.20 (gift of *entire income*, with principal paid at designated age, indicates no survival required), and §21.18 (gift "payable" at designated age indicates no survival required). The American cases are split over whether to follow the second rule (gift "at" designated age implies survival required). See id. §21.17. The distinction between a legacy "at 21" and a legacy "to be paid at 21" has been criticized by most commentators as a distinction without a difference.

2. *T* bequeaths $10,000 "to *A* when *A* attains 21." *A* is age 15 at *T*'s death. Who is entitled to income from the $10,000 before *A* reaches 21? If *A* dies at age 16, does the legacy fail or is *A*'s administrator entitled to demand payment of $10,000 at *A*'s death or when *A* would have reached 21 had *A* lived? See Annot., 57 A.L.R.2d 103 (1958); Halbach, supra, at 299-302.

2. Gifts to Classes

a. Limiting Increase in Class Membership: The Rule of Convenience

(1) Introduction

A central characteristic of a gift to a class of persons, such as "to the children of *B*," is that if *B* is alive and capable of having more children, the persons to whom the class description applies can increase in number. The problem we now deal with is: How long can the class increase in membership? In a gift "to *B* for life, then to *B*'s children," all of *B*'s children will be alive (or in gestation) when the class is physiologically closed at *B*'s death. No difficulties will be encountered on distributing the property upon *B*'s death among all *B*'s children or their estates. But suppose the disposition is "to *A* for life, then to *B*'s children." Here we may have a different kettle of fish. If *A* dies during *B*'s lifetime, what should be done with the property, given that *B* may have more children?

There are several alternative solutions possible when the class is not closed physiologically, but one or more members of the class stand ready to take their shares. Distribution could be postponed until all possible class members are on the scene. Or a partial distribution could be made to *B*'s present children and a "reasonable" portion withheld (until *B*'s death) for possible future distribution to later-born children. Or full distribution could be made to the children now at hand, subject to a requirement that they rebate a portion of each share as *B* has more children. Or the class could be "closed" at *A*'s death, with full distribution to the present children and the exclusion of all children later born to *B*.

The practical problems that would be raised by postponing distribution, or by making a partial or defeasible distribution to existing class members, have led the courts to adopt the last alternative. This is called the *rule of convenience*. It is a rule of construction, giving way to sufficient evidence of the testator's contrary intent, but it is adhered to more closely than any other rule of construction — so closely, in fact, that it has sometimes been referred to erroneously as a rule of law. See Re Wernher's Settlement Trusts, [1961] 1 All E.R. 184.

Under the rule of convenience, *a class will close whenever any member of the class is entitled to possession and enjoyment of his or her share.* The key point in time is when one member is *entitled* to demand payment. The fact that actual payment may be delayed because of administrative problems does not keep the class open; it closes when the right to payment arises.

When a class is open, persons not yet born can come into the class. When a class is closed, no more members can be added to the class. Note well that this is all we mean when we say that a class is closed: *No person born after this date can share in the property.*[25] The fact that a class is closed does not mean that all members of the class will share in the property. No one can come in, but present class members can drop out by failing to meet some condition precedent.

(2)   Immediate Gifts

The rule of convenience can best be understood by a series of illustrative cases. In all these cases where we have gifts to the children of *B*, it is assumed that *B* is alive at the testator's death. Otherwise the class would be physiologically closed.

Where there is an immediate gift to a class, the class closes as soon as any member can demand possession, either at the testator's death or later. Thus:

Case 15.   *T* bequeaths $10,000 "to the children of *B*." *B* is alive and

---

25. More accurately, we would say that no person conceived after this date can share, for here as elsewhere in property law a child is treated as in being from the time of conception if he is later born alive. We speak of birth, but we mean conception.

Even more accurately, when children are adopted, the time of adoption, not birth, is controlling. In re Silberman's Will, 23 N.Y.2d 98, 243 N.E.2d 736 (1968). The adopted child must be adopted into the class before the class closes. A child in being when the class closes, but subsequently adopted, does not share. Do you see the reason for this? See Fetters, The Determination of Maximum Membership in Class Gifts in Relation to Adopted Children: In Re Silberman's Will Examined, 21 Syracuse L. Rev. 1 (1969).

has two children, *C* and *D*. *C* and *D* can demand immediate possession of their shares. The class closes. $5,000 is paid to *C* and $5,000 to *D*. A year later *E* is born to *B*. *E* does not share in the bequest.

There is an exception to this rule if no members of the class have been born before the testator's death. Since the testator must have known there were no class members alive at his death, it is assumed the testator intended all class members, whenever born, to share. Hence, in this case, the class does not close until the death of the designated ancestor of the class. In Case 15, if *B* had no children born before the testator's death, the class would not close until *B*'s death. See Restatement (Second) of Property, Donative Transfers §26.1 (2) (Tent. Draft No. 9, 1986).

> *Case 16.* *T* bequeaths $10,000 "to the children of *B* who reach 21." *B* has children alive, but no child is 21 at *T*'s death. The class will close when a child of *B* reaches 21.

> *Case 17.* *T* bequeaths $10,000 "to the children of *B*, to be paid to them in equal shares as they respectively reach 21." *B* has children alive, but all are under 21. The gift is vested with payment postponed. The class will close when the eldest child of *B* reaches 21 or, if the eldest child dies under that age, when the eldest child would have reached 21 had he lived.

PROBLEM

T bequeaths $15,000 "to the children of *B* who reach 21." At *T*'s death, *B* has two children, *C* (age 7) and *D* (age 4). Three years later *E* is born to *B*. Thereafter *C* reaches 21. What distribution is made to *C*? One year thereafter *F* is born to *B*. *D* dies at age 20. Is any distribution made? *E* then reaches 21. Is any distribution made? *F* then reaches 21. Is any distribution made?

Gifts of specific sums. If a specific sum is given to each member of the class, the class closes at the death of the testator regardless of whether any members of the class are then alive. Thus:

> *Case 18.* *T* bequeaths £500 apiece to each child of *A*. *A* has no children living at *T*'s death. The class closes at *T*'s death, and no child of *A* ever takes anything. Rogers v. Mutch, 10 Ch. Div. 25 (1878).

> > Life looked rosy to *A* as he sat
> > By the crepe-draped casket of *T*.

Five hundred pounds for each child he begat
Would soon make him wealthy mused he.
So he married at once, and began procreating
At five hundred per, he supposed;
But you know and I know (what hardly needs stating)
That the class had already closed.
Mistakes of this sort are bound to arise
When a client takes actions like these
Without seeing his lawyer as soon as *T* dies,
And paying the usual fees.

FRANK L. DEWEY[26]

What is the reason for closing the class at the death of the testator when the gift is of a fixed sum to each member of a class?

(3)   Postponed Gifts

If the gift is postponed in possession after a life estate, the class will not close under the rule of convenience until the time for taking possession. Thus a gift to a class of remaindermen will not close until the life tenant is dead, and it will not then close unless one remainderman is entitled to possession.

> *Case 19.*   *T* bequeaths $10,000 "to *A* for life, then to the children of my daughter *B*." The class will not close under the rule of convenience until the death of *A*. *B* survives *A*. The class will close at *A*'s death if (a) a child of *B* is then alive, (b) a child of *B* predeceased *T* and the gift did not lapse but went to such child's issue under an anti-lapse statute,[27] or (c) a child of *B* was alive at *T*'s death or was born after *T*'s death and such child predeceased *A*. In each of those cases, a child or the child's representative can demand payment at *A*'s death.

Suppose that in Case 19, at the death of *A, B* has not yet had any children born to her. Will the class be left open until the death of *B*, as in the case of an immediate gift to a class where no one has yet been born at the time of taking possession? Restatement (Second) of Property, supra, §26.2 (2) says yes, but there are few cases on the matter.

The rule of convenience applies only to gifts of principal, not to gifts of income. Suppose there is a trust to pay income to *A* for life, then to pay income to the children of *B*. There is no need to close the class at the death of *A*. The class closes for the gift of income periodically as the income is accrued.

---

26. Reproduced from W. Leach, Langdell Lyrics of 1938 (1938).

27. Suppose this were an inter vivos trust created by *T* during *T*'s lifetime. If at *A*'s death, a child of *B* had predeceased *T* with issue, could the issue demand payment and close the class at *A*'s death? Would an anti-lapse statute apply? Does it matter whether it is a revocable trust or not? See Dollar Savings & Trust Co. v. Turner, 39 Ohio St. 3d 182, 529 N.E.2d 1261 (1988), holding anti-lapse statute applied to gifts under a revocable trust.

PROBLEMS

1. *T* bequeaths a fund in trust "to pay the income to *A* for life, then to distribute the principal to the children of *B* who reach 21, and in the meantime the children of *B* who are eligible to receive, but have not yet received, a share of the principal are to receive the income." At *A*'s death, *B* is alive and has one child, *C* (age 5). After *A* dies, the following events occur: *D* is born to *B*; *C* reaches 21; one year later *E* is born to *B*; *D* and, later, *E* reach 21.

(a) After *A*'s death, who is entitled to the income?

(b) When is the first distribution of principal made, to whom, and how much?

(c) How is the principal ultimately divided?

2. *T* bequeaths a fund in trust "to divide the fund among the children of *B*, payable to each at age 21, and in the meantime they are to receive the income." At *T*'s death, *B* is alive and has one child, *C* (age 5). One year later, *C* dies, Is *C*'s administrator entitled to demand immediate distribution of *C*'s share? Would your answer be different if *B* *predeceased T*?

3. *T* devises property in trust "for *A* for life, then on *A*'s death to *A*'s children." *A* disclaims. *A* has a child 5 years of age. When does the class close? See Uniform Probate Code §2-801(c), *supra* page 123; Pate v. Ford, 360 S.E.2d 145 (S.C. App. 1987).

Lux v. Lux

Supreme Court of Rhode Island, 1972
109 R.I. 592, 288 A.2d 701

KELLEHER, J. The artless efforts of a draftsman have precipitated this suit which seeks the construction of and instructions relating to the will of Philomena Lux who died a resident of Cumberland on August 15, 1968. We hasten to add that the will was drawn by someone other than counsel of record. . . .

Philomena Lux executed her will on May 9, 1966. She left her residuary estate to her husband, Anthony John Lux, and nominated him as the executor. Anthony predeceased his wife. His death triggered the following pertinent provisions of Philomena's will:

> Fourth: In the event that my said husband, Anthony John Lux, shall predecease me, then I make the following disposition of my estate:
>
> 1. . . .
>
> 2. All the rest, residue and remainder of my estate, real and personal, of whatsoever kind and nature, and wherever situated, of which I shall die seized and possessed, or over which I may have power of appointment,

or to which I may be in any manner entitled at my death, I give, devise and bequeath to my grandchildren, share and share alike.

3. Any real estate included in said residue shall be maintained for the benefit of said grandchildren and shall not be sold until the youngest of said grandchildren has reached twenty-one years of age.

4. Should it become necessary to sell any of said real estate to pay my debts, costs of administration, or to make distribution of my estate or for any other lawful reason, then, in that event, it is my express desire that said real estate be sold to a member of my family.

Philomena was survived by one son, Anthony John Lux, Jr., and five grandchildren whose ages range from two to eight. All the grandchildren were children of Anthony. The youngest grandchild was born after the execution of the will but before Philomena's death. The son is named in the will as the alternate executor. He informed the trial court that he and his wife plan to have more children. At the time of the hearing, Anthony was 30. The Superior Court appointed a guardian ad litem to represent the interests of the grandchildren. It also designated an attorney to represent the rights of the individuals who may have an interest under the will but who are at this time unknown, unascertained or not in being. . . .

At the time of her death, the testatrix owned real estate valued at approximately $35,000 and tangible and intangible personal property, including bank accounts, that totaled some $7,400. The real estate, which consists of two large tenement houses, is located in Cumberland. The sole dispute is as to the nature of the devise of the real estate. Did Philomena make an absolute gift of it to the grandchildren or did she place it in trust for their benefit? The guardian takes the view that the grandchildren hold the real estate in fee simple. All the other parties take a contrary position.

From the record before us, we believe that Philomena intended that her real estate be held in trust for the benefit of her grandchildren. In reaching this conclusion, we must emphasize that there is no fixed formula as to when a testamentary disposition should be classified as an outright gift or a trust. The result reached depends on the circumstances of each particular case.

We are not unmindful of the formal requirements necessary for the creation of a testamentary trust. It is an elementary proposition of law that a trust is created when legal title to property is held by one person for the benefit of another. . . . However, no particular words are required to create a testamentary trust. The absence of such words as "trust" or "trustee" is immaterial where the requisite intent of the testator can be found. . . . A trust never fails for lack of a trustee. . . .

When the residuary clause in the instant case is viewed in its entirety, it is clear that Philomena did not give her grandchildren a fee simple title to the realty. It appears that she, realizing the nature of this bequest and the age of the beneficiaries, intended that someone would hold and manage the property until they were of sufficient age to do so themselves. The property is income-producing and apparently she felt that the ultimate interest of her grandchildren would be protected if the realty was left intact until the designated time for distribution. The use of the terms "shall be maintained" and "shall not be sold" is a strong indication of Philomena's intent that the property was to be retained and managed by some person for some considerable time in the future for the benefit of her son's children. This is a duty usually associated with a trustee. We therefore hold that Philomena's will does create a trust on her real estate.

Having found the trust, the question of who shall serve as trustee is easily answered. The general rule is that, unless a contrary intention appears in the will or such an appointment is deemed improper or undesirable, the executor would be named to the position of trustee. . . .

The ascertainment of time within which a person who answers a class description such as "children" or "grandchildren" must be born in order to be entitled to share in a testator's bounty is not an easy matter. In seeking a solution, the court must seek to effectuate the testator's intent. . . .

The rationale for permitting a class to increase in size until the time for distribution stems from a judicial recognition that generally, when a testator describes the beneficiaries of his bounty by some group designation, he has in mind all those persons whenever born who come within the definition of the term used to describe the group. Normally, if he had in mind the individual members of the designated group, he would have described them by name. This recognition is tempered by the presumption that testators usually would not intend to keep the class open at the expense of an indefinite delay in the distribution of the estate. Since there is no good reason to exclude any person who is born before the period of distribution, all such persons are, in the absence of a contrary testamentary intent, deemed to be members of the class. Casner, Class Gifts to Others than to "Heirs" or "Next of Kin": Increase in the Class Membership, 51 Harv. L. Rev. 254 (1938); 5 American Law of Property §§22.40, 22.41 (1952); see concurring opinion, Frost and Roberts, JJ., Rhode Island Hospital Trust Co. v. Bateman, 93 R.I. 116, 172 A.2d 84 (1961).

Despite our invocation of the rule requiring the class to remain open until the corpus is distributed, we still must determine what Philomena intended when she said that the corpus has to be preserved until the "youngest grandchild" becomes twenty-one.

There are four possible distribution dates depending on the meaning of "youngest." Distribution might be made when the youngest member of the class in being when the will was executed attains twenty-one; or when the youngest in being when the will takes effect becomes twenty-one; or when the youngest of all living class members in being at any one time attains twenty-one even though it is physically possible for others to be born; or when the youngest whenever it is born attains twenty-one. This last alternative poses a question. Should we delay distribution here and keep the class open until the possibility that Philomena's son can become a father becomes extinct? We think not.

We are conscious of the presumption in the law that a man or a woman is capable of having children so long as life lasts. A construction suit, however, has for its ultimate goal the ascertainment of the average testator's probable intent if he was aware of the problems that lead to this type of litigation. Manufacturers National Bank v. McCoy, 100 R.I. 154, 212 A.2d 53 (1965). It is our belief that the average testator, when faced with the problem presented by the record before us, would endorse the view expressed in 3 Restatement, Property §295, comment k at 1594 (1940), where in urging the adoption of the rule that calls for the closing of the class when the youngest living member reaches the age when distribution could be made, states:

> When all existent members of the class have attained the stated age, considerations of convenience . . . require that distribution shall then be made and that the property shall not be further kept from full utilization to await the uncertain and often highly improbable conception of further members of the group. The infrequency with which a parent has further children after all of his living children have attained maturity, makes this application of the rule of convenience justifiable and causes it to frustrate the unexpressed desires of a conveyor in few, if any, cases.

We hold, therefore, that distribution of the trust corpus shall be made at any time when the youngest of the then living grandchildren has attained the age of twenty-one. When this milestone is reached, there is no longer any necessity to maintain the trust to await the possible conception of additional members of the class.

Although Philomena declared that the real estate was not to be sold until the youngest grandchildren became twenty-one, her later statements about the necessity of its sale amounted to her awareness that future circumstances might require the liquidation of her real estate sometime prior to the time her youngest grandchild becomes twenty-one. The Superior Court was informed and documentary evidence was introduced which showed such a precipitous drop in the rental income as would warrant a trustee to seek a better investment.

Section 18-4-2(b) provides that, in the absence of any provision to the contrary, every trust shall be deemed to have conferred upon the trustee a discretionary power to sell the trust estate, be it real or personal property. Section 18-4-10 specifically authorizes a trustee, whenever he believes it desirable to sell trust property, to seek the Superior Court's approval for such a transaction.

When the real estate is sold, the proceeds from such sale shall, because of the doctrine of the substitute res, replace the realty as the trust corpus. Industrial National Bank v. Colt, 102 R.I. 672, 233 A.2d 112 (1957); Dresser v. Booker, 76 R.I. 238, 69 A.2d 45 (1949).

The impending sale brings into focus the testatrix's "express *desire* that said real estate be sold to a member of my family." (emphasis added) The words "express desire" are purely precatory. We have said that precatory language will be construed as words of command only if it is clear that the testator intended to impose on the individual concerned a legal obligation to make the desired disposition. Young v. Exum, 94 R.I. 143, 179 A.2d 107 (1962). We think it clear that since Philomena's primary goal was to benefit her grandchildren, we see nothing in the record that would justify a conclusion that she intended that the potential purchasers of her real estate be limited to the members of her family.

Finally, we come to the allocation of income. The will is silent as to this item. Over a half-century ago, we said that if the will shows no intention on the part of the testator that income be accumulated, income is payable to the beneficiary as it accrues. Butler v. Butler, 40 R.I. 425, 101 A. 115 (1917). This rule has been reaffirmed on many occasions. Should Philomena's son's hope for additional progeny become a reality, the quantum of each share of income received by a grandchild would be reduced as each new member of the class joins his brothers and sisters.

The parties may present to this court for approval a form of judgment in accordance with this opinion, which will be entered in the Superior Court.

b.   Gifts to Children or Issue

(1)   Per Stirpes Distributions

The law presumes that the word *children* means only the immediate offspring of the parent and does not include grandchildren. The words *descendants* and *issue* include children, grandchildren, and more remote descendants. However, words are not always carefully chosen, and there are many cases, often involving homemade wills, litigating the question of whether the testator meant by children persons other than immediate offspring. Other language in the will, or extrinsic circumstances, may indicate that testator in fact meant descendants. See Restatement (Second) of Property, Donative Transfers §25.1 (Tent. Draft No. 8, 1985); Annot., 30 A.L.R.4th 319 (1984).

Where there is a gift "to the issue of *A*," the question arises whether the issue take per capita or per stirpes. If the issue take *per capita*, all issue who are born before the period of distribution take an equal share. Descendants with living parents share equally with their parents. Thus if *A* has three children and one of these children has two children, the property is divided into five shares. If the issue take *per stirpes*, the children of a child of the designated ancestor can take nothing if their parent is alive, and if the parent is dead, the children usually take only what the parent would have taken if living. Thus if *A* has three children and one of these three predeceases *A*, leaving two children surviving *A*, the property is divided into three shares and the children of the predeceased child divide that child's one-third share. A devise to the issue of *A* is presumptively distributed per stirpes.[28]

What does a per stirpes distribution mean? In England the intestacy statute provided a straight per stirpes distribution, dividing the decedent's property into as many shares as there were living children and predeceased children leaving issue alive. See supra page 88. The English courts interpreted the words *per stirpes* in a will to call for a similar distribution. Thus distribution of a bequest to the issue per stirpes of a named person mirrored intestate distribution to the issue of a decedent.

In this country, the first Restatement of Property §303 (1940) took the position — as did the English courts — that the phrases *per stirpes* or *by right of representation*, used in a will, are to be given the same meaning as representation has under the intestacy statutes of the particular jurisdiction. Hence the presumed intent of a testator making a gift to issue is the same as that of an intestate decedent leaving property to issue. The first Restatement's position appears to accord with that taken by a majority of courts.

The second Restatement of Property, Donative Transfers §28.12 (Tent. Draft No. 10. 1987), abandons the position of the first Restatement. It provides that a gift to issue or to issue per stirpes will not be referred to the intestacy law for meaning but will be divided into as many shares as there are children, whether living or not, of the designated ancestor (a straight per stirpes distribution). Professor Casner, the Reporter, took the position that looking to the intestacy law brings a lot of ambiguity to interpretation of wills. How a gift to issue is to be divided would depend on what state a person dies in and whether the intestate statute in effect at the testator's death or the statute in effect at the time of possession applies.

The Joint Editorial Board for the Uniform Probate Code has rejected the second Restatement in favor of the position of the first Restatement.

---

28. But not everywhere. The English took the word *issue* literally and distributed among issue per capita. So too in South Carolina. If the words "per stirpes" are not added to a gift to issue in that state, all issue take per capita, with grandchildren sharing equally with children. Bonney v. Granger, 356 S.E.2d 138 (S.C. App. 1987).

It has proposed a new UPC §2-707, expressly referring the question of construction of a gift to issue or descendants to the applicable intestacy statutes. Under Uniform Probate Code §2-106, the division of intestate shares of descendants is made at the level where issue are alive. To see the difference between the second Restatement and the UPC, look at Case 20.

> *Case 20.* *T* devises property "to *A* for life, then to *A*'s issue per stirpes." At *T*'s death, *A* has two children, *B* and *C*, living. Thereafter *B* dies, survived by one child, *D*. Then *C* dies, survived by two children, *E* and *F*. Then *E* dies, survived by two children, *G* and *H*. Then *A* dies. Who takes the property? Here is a diagram of the family tree.

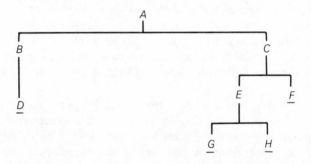

The second Restatement divides the property at *A*'s death as follows: ½ to *D*, ¼ to *F*, and ⅛ each to *G* and *H*. The UPC group would divide the property at *A*'s death as follows: ⅓ to *D*, ⅓ to *F*, and ⅙ each to *G* and *H*.

A study of client preferences, Young, Meaning of "Issue" and "Descendants," 13 Prob. Notes 227 (1988), indicates that 85 percent of lawyers believe their clients want a straight per stirpes distribution, but that 71 percent of the clients themselves, when polled, want distribution per capita at each generation (for explanation, see supra page 89).[29] Perhaps this striking difference between what clients want and what lawyers think they want is the result of law schools' continued teaching, as background for American law, the old English system of primogeniture, succession down the bloodlines, and straight per stirpes repre-

---

29. The latter finding is questionable. It conflicts with the comprehensive, detailed studies by Fellows and others indicating that an overwhelming majority of persons prefer per capita with representation, dividing the stocks at the level where issue are alive. See supra page 89. The Young questionnaire was too crudely designed to present clients a clear choice between per capita with representation and per capita at each generation. But all the studies agree that the majority of clients do not want a straight per stirpes distribution.

sentation. The ghost of the past is in the lawyer's minds; their clients have never beheld it.[30]

The problem of what distributional scheme is to be applied to gifts to issue can be taken care of by inserting in the instrument a definition of per stirpes: "When a distribution is directed to be made to any person's issue per stirpes, distribution shall be made to such issue in such shares as they would receive under the _____(state) law of intestate succession if such person had died intestate on the date of the final ascertainment of the membership in the class, owning the subject matter of the gift." If the distribution called for by the state intestate succession law is not what the client wants, say so by providing at what level the initial division into shares is to take place.

(2) Adopted Children

No coast-to-coast statement is possible as to whether a child adopted by *A* is entitled to share in a gift by *T* to the "children," "issue," "descendants," or "heirs" of *A*. Adoption was unknown to the common law and "children" and "issue" necessarily connoted a blood relationship. When adoption laws were enacted in the second half of the nineteenth century, courts were faced with the question of whether an adopted child took under the will of a person who was not the adoptive parent. The early cases were heavily influenced by the inherited reverence for blood relationships; they held an adopted child could not take. These cases gave rise to the stranger-to-the-adoption rule: The adopted child is presumptively barred, whatever generic word is used, except when the donor is the adoptive parent. As adoption became more common and more socially acceptable, courts began to carve exceptions in the stranger-to-the-adoption rule. For example, an adopted child might be permitted to take if adopted before, and not after, the testator's death. Some courts also drew distinctions between a gift to "*A*'s children" and a gift to "*A*'s issue" or the "the heirs of *A*'s body." Unlike the latter terms, which were thought to have a biological connotation, a gift to "*A*'s children" presumptively included *A*'s adopted children. Where judicial decisions were found unsatisfactory, legislatures began to inter-

---

30. California effected a compromise between the California Law Revision Commission, which thought the average person wanted the UPC scheme, and the lawyers, who strongly believed their will clients preferred straight per stirpes. Cal. Prob. Code §245 (1989) provides that a gift to "issue" will be distributed in accordance with the intestacy law (which adopts the current UPC scheme). Cal. Prob. Code §246 (1989) provides that a gift to "issue per stirpes" will be distributed on a straight per stirpes basis. Cal. Prob. Code §247 (1989) provides that a gift to "issue per capita at each generation" will be distributed on that basis. Is this a good idea?

In Bank of New England v. McKennan, 19 Mass. App. Ct. 686, 477 N.E.2d 170 (1985), the court held that a devise to "my issue according to the stocks" called for a straight per stirpes distribution, whereas a devise to "my issue" would have passed in accordance with the Massachusetts statute of descent (the current UPC scheme).

vene in favor of the adopted child. The legislation was seldom retroactive and was sometimes ambiguous. Today in most states adopted children are presumptively included in gifts by T to the "children," "issue," "descendants," and "heirs" of A. But the law of many of these states is likely to have been developed by changing judicial decisions and statutes over the last half century, and, since the change may not be retroactive, whether the adopted child is included may depend on what the law was at testator's death in, say, 1955. See Fischer v. La Fave, 188 Ill. App. 3d 16, 544 N.E.2d 55 (1989); Elliott v. Hiddleson, 303 N.W.2d 140 (Iowa 1981); New England Merchants National Bank v. Groswold, 387 Mass. 822, 444 N.E.2d 359 (1983) (setting forth the complicated history of this issue in Massachusetts); Hyman v. Glover, 232 Va. 140, 348 S.E.2d 269 (1986) (overruled by Va. Code §64.1-71.1 (1987)). See Halbach, Issues About Issue: Some Recurrent Class Gift Problems, 48 Mo. L. Rev. 333, 336-340 (1983); Annot., 71 A.L.R.4th 374 (1989).

Uniform Probate Code (1983)

§2-611 [CONSTRUCTION OF GENERIC TERMS TO ACCORD WITH RELATIONSHIPS AS DEFINED FOR INTESTATE SUCCESSION]

Halfbloods, adopted persons and persons born out of wedlock are included in class gift terminology and terms of relationship in accordance with rules for determining relationships for purposes of intestate succession, but a person born out of wedlock is not treated as the child of the father unless the person is openly and notoriously so treated by the father.

Minary v. Citizens Fidelity Bank & Trust Co.
Court of Appeals of Kentucky, 1967
419 S.W.2d 340

OSBORNE, J. [Amelia S. Minary died in 1932, leaving a will devising her residuary estate in trust, to pay the income to her husband and three sons, James, Thomas, and Alfred, for their respective lives. The trust was to terminate upon the death of the last surviving beneficiary, at which time the corpus was to be distributed as follows:

> After the Trust terminates, the remaining portion of the Trust Fund shall be distributed to my then surviving heirs, according to the laws of descent and distribution then in force in Kentucky, and, if no such heirs, then to the First Christian Church, Louisville, Kentucky.

The husband died, then James died without issue, then Thomas died leaving two children: Thomas Jr. and Amelia Minary Gant. In 1934, Alfred married Myra, and in 1959 he adopted her as his child. The trust terminated upon Alfred's death without natural issue in 1963.]

The question herein presented is, "Did Alfred's adoption of his wife Myra make her eligible to inherit under the provisions of his mother's will?" More specifically, the question is, "Is Myra included in the term 'my then surviving heirs according to the laws of descent and distribution in force in Kentucky'?"

This has revived a lively question in the jurisprudence of this state and presents two rather difficult legal problems. The first being under what conditions, if any, should an adopted child inherit from or through its adoptive parent? We have encountered little difficulty with the problem of inheriting from an adoptive parent but the question of when will an adoptive child inherit through an adoptive parent has given us considerable trouble. As late as 1945 in Copeland et al. v. State Bank and Trust Company et al., 300 Ky. 432, 188 S.W.2d 1017, we held without hesitation or equivocation that the words "heirs" and "issue" as well as "children" and all other words of similar import as used in a will referred only to the natural blood relations and did not include an adopted child.

In 1950, in Isaacs v. Manning et al., 312 Ky. 326, 227 S.W.2d 418, we adopted the contrary position and held that an adopted child was included in the phrase "heirs at law" wherein a will devised property to designated children and then upon their death to their heirs at law. In the course of the opinion, we said, "where no language [shows] a contrary intent . . . an adopted daughter clearly falls within the class designated." In this case we distinguish the *Copeland* case, supra.

In 1953, in Major v. Kammer et al., 258 S.W.2d 506, we again held that an adopted child was included in the term "heirs at law," basing our decision upon the legislative changes made in the adoption laws and overruling Copeland v. State Bank and Trust Company, supra. In Edmands v. Tice, Ky., 324 S.W.2d 491, which was decided in 1959, we held that where testator used the word children, an adopted child could inherit through an adopted parent the same as if heirs at law or issue had been used. . . .

From the foregoing we conclude that when Amelia S. Minary used the phrase, "my then surviving heirs according to the laws of descent and distribution then in force in Kentucky," she included the adoptive children of her sons. This leaves us with the extremely bothersome question of: "Does the fact that Myra Minary was an adult and the wife of Alfred at the time she was adopted affect her status as an 'heir' under the will?" KRS 405.390 provides: "An adult person . . . may be adopted in the same manner as provided by law for the adoption of a child and with the same legal effect. . . .

KRS 199.520 provides: "From and after the date of the judgment the child shall be deemed the child of petitioners and shall be considered for purposes of inheritance and succession and for all other legal considerations, the natural, legitimate child of the parents adopting it the same as if born of their bodies."

It would appear from examination of the authorities that the adoption of an adult for the purpose of making him an heir has been an accepted practice in our law for many years. However, here it should be pointed out that the practice in its ancient form made the person so adopted the legal heir of the adopting party only. This court has dealt with the problem of adopting adults for the purpose of making them heirs on several occasions . . .

In 1957, in Bedinger v. Graybill's Executors, Ky., 302 S.W.2d 594, we had before us a case almost identical to the one here under consideration. In that case Mrs. Lulu Graybill, in 1914, set up a trust for her son Robert by will. She then provided after the death of the son that the trust "be paid over and distributed by the Trustee to the heirs at law of my said son according to the laws of descent and distribution in force in Kentucky at the time of his death." There was a devise over to others in the event that Robert died without heirs. Robert having no issue adopted his wife long after his mother's death. We held that the wife should inherit the same as an adopted child, there being no public policy against the adoption of a wife. However, it will be noted that in the course of the opinion it is carefully pointed out that the will directed the estate be paid to the "heirs at law of Robert" and did not provide that the estate should go to "my heirs," "his children" or to "his issue," indicating by this language that if the phrase had been one of the others set out the results might have been different. . . .

This case could properly be distinguished from Bedinger v. Graybill's Executors, supra, on the basis of the difference in language used in the two wills[;] however, no useful purpose could be served by so distinguishing them. The time has come to face again this problem which has persistently perplexed the court when an adult is adopted for the sole purpose of making him or her an heir and claimant to the estate of an ancestor under the terms of a testamentary instrument known and in existence at the time of the adoption. Even though the statute permits such adoption and even though it expressly provides that it shall be "with the same legal effect as the adoption of a child," we, nevertheless, are constrained to view this practice to be an act of subterfuge which in effect thwarts the intent of the ancestor whose property is being distributed and cheats the rightful heirs. We are faced with a situation wherein we must choose between carrying out the intent of deceased testators or giving a strict and rigid construction to a statute which thwarts that intent. In the *Bedinger* case there is no doubt but what the intent of the testatrix, as to the disposition of her property, was circumvented. It is our opinion that by giving a strict and literal construction to the adoption statutes, we thwarted the efforts of the deceased to dispose of her property as she saw fit.

When one rule of law does violence to another it becomes inevitable that one must then give way to the other. It is of paramount importance that a man be permitted to pass on his property at his death to those who represent the natural objects of his bounty. This is an ancient and precious right running from the dawn of civilization in an unbroken line down to the present day. Our adoption statutes are humanitarian in nature and of great importance to the welfare of the public. However, these statutes should not be given a construction that does violence to the above rule and to the extent that they violate the rule and prevent one from passing on his property in accord with his wishes, they must give way. Adoption of an adult for the purpose of bringing that person under the provisions of a preexisting testamentary instrument when he clearly was not intended to be so covered should not be permitted and we do not view this as doing any great violence to the intent and purpose of our adoption laws.

For the foregoing reasons the action of the trial court in declaring Myra Galvin Minary an heir of Amelia S. Minary is reversed.

The judgment is reversed.

All concur.[31]

NOTES AND PROBLEMS

1. Adoption may be used for a number of purposes other than creating an ordinary parent-child relationship. *A* may adopt *B* in order to prevent *A*'s parents or more remote relatives from contesting *A*'s will or to qualify *B* as a member of a class given a future interest in a trust as in the *Minary* case, or, when *A* and *B* live together, to prevent eviction by a landlord for violating a lease clause restricting occupancy of an apartment to members of the tenant's immediate family only. In the large majority of states, an adult person, married or unmarried, may adopt any other person, minor or adult. See supra page 95.

Most of the recent cases hold, contrary to the *Minary* case, that adult adoptees are included within class gift terminology for purposes of will and trust dispositions. See Evans v. McCoy, 291 Md. 562, 436 A.2d 436 (1981) (76-year-old woman adopts 21-year-old neighbor and 53-year-old cousin in order to defeat executory interest of her cousins); In re

---

31. Discussed in Note, The Dilemma of Adoptees in the Class Gift Structure — The Kentucky Approach: A Rule Without Reason, 59 Ky. L.J. 921 (1971). — Eds.

Estate of Fortnoy, 5 Kan. App. 2d 14, 611 P.2d 599 (1980) (90-year-old man adopts 65-year-old nephew of wife); Chichester v. Wilmington Trust Co., 377 A.2d 11 (Del. 1977); but see Cross v. Cross, 177 Ill. App. 3d 588, 532 N.E.2d 486 (1988), agreeing with *Minary*. If adult adoptees are included within class gifts in will and trust dispositions, is there any reason for excluding a spouse-adopted-as-a-child from such a gift?

Oregon Rev. Stat. §112.195 (1981) provides that adopted children are included in class gift terminology only if adopted as a minor or "after having been a member of the household of the adoptive parent while a minor." California Prob. Code §6152(a)(1985) is similar. Restatement (Second) of Property, Donative Transfers §25.4 (Tent. Draft No. 8, 1985), includes an adopted child in a gift to the children of *A* if *A* has "raised" the adopted child.

2. *Children "adopted out."* *T* bequeaths a fund in trust "for my wife for life, then to my issue then living per stirpes." After *T*'s death, his son *A* dies, leaving a wife and a minor child, *B*. *A*'s wife remarries, and her second husband adopts *B*. *T*'s wife then dies. Is *B* entitled to share in the trust fund? See In re McLaughlin Trust, 361 N.W.2d 43 (Minn. 1985); Estate of Leonard, 128 N.H. 407, 514 A.2d 822 (1986); Monroney v. Mercantile-Safe Deposit & Trust Co., 291 Md. 546, 435 A.2d 788 (1981); Note, When Blood Isn't Thicker Than Water: The Inheritance Rights of Adopted-out Children in New York, 53 Brooklyn L. Rev. 1007 (1988). Restatement (Second) of Property, supra, §25.5 provides that a gift to "children" of *A* does not include a child of *A* adopted by another, "if such adoption removes the child from the broader family circle of the designated person."

3. Absent expression of a contrary intent by the testator, the term "children" is presumed not to include stepchildren or persons related only by affinity. See Restatement (Second) of Property, supra, §25.6; Mahoney, Stepfamilies in the Law of Intestate Succession and Wills, 22 U.C. Davis L. Rev. 917 (1989).

4. In Estate of Walker, 64 N.Y.2d 354, 476 N.E.2d 298, 486 N.Y.S.2d 899 (1985), the former mayor of New York, Jimmy Walker, bequeathed all his personal property to his adopted son and adopted daughter. Copies of the sealed adoption decrees were held by Walker's lawyer. The lawyer refused to turn the decrees over to the adopted children, who were searching for their natural parents. The court held that even though the decrees were personal property, the legacy could not be given effect because to do so would violate the public policy of the state to preserve the natural parents' confidentiality.

(3) Illegitimate Children

At common law the word children in a will or trust presumptively referred to legitimate children only. With the recent changes in the treatment of illegitimate children in intestacy laws and elsewhere, this presumption has become increasingly unreliable. In a reversal of precedents on the question, In re Hoffman, 53 A.D.2d 55, 385 N.Y.S.2d 49 (1976), noted in 5 Hofstra L. Rev. 697 (1977), held that absent an express intent to the contrary the word issue, where it appears unqualified in a will, refers to illegitimate as well as legitimate descendants. See also Walton v. Lindsey, 349 So. 2d 41 (Ala. 1977), holding that the existence of an illegitimate child created a latent ambiguity and evidence was admissible to determine whether the testator intended to include the illegitimate child as a member of the class of children to which he was leaving his estate.

In Estate of Dulles, 494 Pa. 180, 431 A.2d 208, 17 A.L.R.4th 1279 (1981), it was held that a statutory canon of construction that illegitimates not be considered children of their father violated the equal protection clause of the Constitution. In Powers v. Wilkinson, 399 Mass. 650, 506 N.E.2d 842 (1987), the court held — contrary to the *Dulles* case — that the presumption excluding illegitimates in a gift to issue did not violate the equal protection clause of the Constitution. "Thus we hold that state action is not involved, nor is the equal protection clause of the Fourteenth Amendment implicated, when courts apply rules of construction to wills and trust instruments." However, the Massachusetts court announced it would thereafter presume, as to all instruments executed after the date of the case, that the word *issue* includes illegitimates.

See Restatement (Second) of Property, supra, §25.2.

Lawyers drafting wills often define words in order to avoid ambiguity. The Sisyphus Prize for Heroic Attempts must go to a prominent Detroit law firm that drafted the will of Clyde H. Giltner, late of Tecumseh, Michigan. The will reads:

(1) The word "descendant" shall mean and include a child, grandchild, great grandchild, great-great grandchild, great-great-great grandchild, and great-great-great-great grandchild, whether by blood, by adoption, or otherwise, of the person whose descendant is referred to, and also any adopted child of any child, grandchild, great grandchild, great-great grandchild or great-great-great grandchild of such person.

(2) The words "child" and "children" shall mean and include, respectively, any child and any children of the person whose child or children is or are referred to by blood, by adoption, or otherwise.

(3) The words "grandchild," "great grandchild," "great-great grandchild," "great-great-great grandchild," or "great-great-great-great grandchild" shall mean and include, respectively, a grandchild, great grandchild, great-great grandchild, great-great-great grandchild, and great-great-

great-great grandchild of the person whose grandchild, great grandchild, great-great grandchild, great-great-great grandchild or great-great-great-great grandchild is referred to, whether by blood, by adoption, or otherwise, and also any adopted child of any child, any adopted child of any child of any child, any adopted child of any child of any child of any child and any adopted child of any child of any child of any child of such person.

Suppose that Mr. Giltner bequeaths property "to A for life, then to A's children." (1) A has an illegitimate child, B. (2) A adopts his wife, C. (3) A's wife has a baby D during marriage; D is surrendered for adoption and is adopted by Mr. and Mrs. X. (4) A's wife had a previous husband, and their divorce is invalid; A has child E by his wife. (5) A's wife has a child F by artificial insemination by a third-party donor. (6) A gives his twin brother Y one of his testicles for transplantation (Y's testicles were removed earlier because of cancer); 10 months later Y's wife gives birth to G. (7) A takes into his home his niece, H, age 2, when her parents are killed in an auto wreck; H is reared by A and treated as A's child but never formally adopted. On A's death do B, C, D, E, F, G, and H share in the bequest of Mr. Giltner? How would you draft a will to take care of these possible problems?

NOTE: GIFTS OVER ON DEATH WITHOUT ISSUE

Suppose that the testator devises property to a person, with a gift over to another if the person dies without issue. What is the meaning of the phrase "dies without issue"? This can best be explored by taking two hypothetical cases.

Case 21.   T devises property "to B, but if B dies without issue surviving her, to C."

Case 22.   T devises property "to A for life, then to B, but if B dies without issue surviving her, to C."

In Case 21, C's interest may divest a possessory fee simple. In Case 22, C's interest may divest a remainder. In both cases there is an ambiguity. In Case 21, does T intend C to take only if B dies *before* T without surviving issue? If so, then the gift over is a substitute for a lapsed gift. If B survives T, C's interest fails. Or does T intend C to take if B dies *before or after* T without surviving issue? If so, then C can succeed B in possession if B leaves no issue at B's death. In Case 21, the majority of courts favor the second — or "successive" — construction. See 5 American Law of Property §§21.51, 21.52 (1952).

In Case 22, a similar ambiguity is present. Does *T* intend *C* to take only if *B* dies *before A* without issue? Or does *T* intend *C* to take if *B* dies *at any time* without issue? The majority of courts favor the first construction here, where a remainder rather than a possessory fee simple is to be divested. Accordingly, if *B* survives *A*, *B* has a fee simple absolute and can never be divested by *C*. See 5 American Law of Property, supra, §21.53; Annot., 26 A.L.R.3d 407 (1969).

The ambiguities in these cases can be avoided if the drafter inserts in the instrument the italicized words above that fit the client's intent.

Historical Note: Indefinite failure of issue.   In England, when *T* devised land "to *A* and the heirs of his body, and if *A* dies without issue to *B* and her heirs," the courts construed the phrase "if *A* dies without issue" to mean "when *A*'s descendants become extinct." In the context of a conveyance of a fee tail, this construction was understandable, referring to the expiration of the fee tail. But English judges, who liked to give fixed meanings to words regardless of the context, extended this construction to cases where "if *A* dies without issue" did not follow a fee tail. For example, where there was a devise "to *A* and his heirs, but if *A* dies without issue to *B* and her heirs," the courts assumed that testator wanted *B* to take the property whenever *A* had no descendants alive on the face of the earth. This construction did not prove congenial to the American mind, which had little use for the fee tail from which this construction originated. The indefinite failure construction was discarded, and today it exists as a preferred construction in few, if any, states.

c. Gifts to "*A* and Her Children": The Rule in Wild's Case

In re Parant's Will

New York Surrogate's Court, Washington County, 1963
39 Misc. 2d 285, 240 N.Y.S.2d 558

BASCOM, S.   Clause Fifth of the will of Helen C. Parant, which was executed August 17, 1960 and admitted to probate May 29, 1962, reads as follows:

> I give, devise and bequeath all of my real property located on the Vaughn Corners Road in the Town of Kingsbury, New York and the contents of the house and barn, excepting the above bequeathed articles mentioned in the Fourth clause of this will, to my niece Mary Esther Cronkhite Woodward and to her children.

Both on the date of the execution of the will and on the date of death of the testatrix, Mrs. Woodward had two living children.

A determination is sought as to whether the quoted clause vested a fee simple absolute in the named legatee or whether any interest was vested in her children, and if so, the nature of the respective estates and the respective proportions in which Mrs. Woodward and her children share. There appears to be a paucity of law on the subject in this jurisdiction and the precise question, as far as the interpretation of a devise and bequest to a named person and her children is concerned, seems not to have been entertained by the courts of this state for a hundred twenty years.

Three possible interpretations of this particular language are suggested, namely (a) that Mary Esther Cronkhite Woodward takes a fee simple absolute to the exclusion of her children, either on the theory that the words "and to her children" are words of limitation, or that the word "or" was intended for the word "and" and that the gift to the children was substitutional; (b) that Mrs. Woodward takes a life estate with remainder on her death to her children, as similar devises or grants have been interpreted in other jurisdictions, notably Pennsylvania; and (c) that Mrs. Woodward and her two children are tenants in common, each having an undivided one-third interest in the property. . . .

In support of her contention that she takes an absolute fee, to the exclusion of her children, petitioner contends that the word "and" was intended to be "or" and was inadvertently used by the draftsman, with the result that the gift to the children was meant to be substitutional in the event of Mrs. Woodward's predeceasing testatrix. To bolster her contention of inadvertence, she points to the residuary clause which follows the one in question, where the residue is given to Mrs. Woodward and to two other named persons, in equal shares, and provides that in the event of Mrs. Woodward's prior death, her share is given and bequeathed to her children in equal shares; that having demonstrated her ability to create a substitutional gift of the residue, it is improbable the testatrix intended other than that in devising real estate in such a manner that it would be held by an unknown number of infant co-owners, thereby rendering the title inalienable except by order of court. The argument, though plausible, is not elevated to the plane of conviction. To conclude that simply because testatrix made a substitutional or alternative gift in the residuary clause, she must have intended a like gift in another clause, is purely speculative and capricious. When a testator in one part of his will demonstrates his ability to make a certain variety of gift by apt terms, the use of a different mode of expression in another direction raises the inference that he had a diverse disposition in mind (Matter of Corlie's Will, 150 Misc. 596, 599, 269 N.Y.S. 890, 894).

There being nothing else in the will from which to glean an indication of testatrix' intent, and the will having been prepared by an experienced draftsman, we must take the words "and to her children" as we find them and give to them "their usual and accepted meanings without enlargement and without restriction . . . and when particular or technical terms are used, particular or technical interpretation or construction follows as of course, in the absence of all clear intent to the contrary" (Matter of Barrett's Estate, 141 Misc. 637, 638-639, 253 N.Y.S. 658, 660, 661; Graves v. Deterling, 120 N.Y. 447, 457, 24 N.E. 655, 657).

In its usual and commonly accepted meaning "and" is a connective, while "or" is a disjunctive. "And" is not correctly or generally used to express an alternative, unless followed by words which clearly indicate that intent. "Or" is correctly and generally used for that purpose (Matter of Barrett's Estate, supra, 141 Misc. p.640, 253 N.Y.S. p.663). As the court said in the last cited case (p.641):

> It seems to me that it must be assumed that an experienced lawyer would have used the word "or" rather than the word "and" to express a gift intended to be in the alternative, and that, having made use of the word "and," he would have added thereto words clearly indicating that it was intended to be used in the alternative sense if that was the testator's intention. There were no such words added here.

We must therefore reject the theory that an alternative or substitutional gift to the children was intended.

The word "children" in its primary and natural sense is always a word of purchase and not of limitation (Chrystie v. Phyfe, 19 N.Y. 311; . . .). As was said by the Court of Appeals in Chrystie v. Phyfe (p.354):

> There is one class of cases, and one only, in which the term "children" is considered as a word of limitation; that is, where there is a present devise to one and his children, when he has no children at the time. There if the word "children" should be interpreted as words of purchase, future children could not take at all, and in order that the will of the testator may operate favorably to them and not confine the gift to the parent for life, "children" is then deemed a word of limitation.

We conclude, therefore, that Mrs. Woodward and her children living at the death of testatrix (Campbell v. Rawdon, 18 N.Y. 412) all took some interest in the real and personal property devised and bequeathed by the clause of the will in question. It remains to determine their respective interests. . . .

Wild's Case, decided in 1599, expresses the common-law on the subject and from it evolved the so-called Rule in Wild's Case. This was in the form of two "resolutions," both of which were dicta. Under the first, if *A* devises his lands to *B* and to his (*B*'s) children or issue, and he (*B*) has not any issue at the time of the devise, the same is an estate-tail. (This of course would be a fee simple absolute today.) Under the second "resolution," with which we are here concerned, if A devises his lands to B and to his children, and B has children at the death of A, the parent and children take equal and concurrent estates. The rule has been subject to some criticism and although generally accepted, has not been uniformly adopted. In Pennsylvania, for example, a life estate is found in the named devisee, with remainder to the children, as witness Crawford v. Forest Oil Co., 77 F. 534, affd. 77 F. 106, . . . where there was a devise to son Matthew and his children. Matthew had six children living when the will was made, and seven at testator's death, and the court found that by the use of the term "children" the testator vested an estate in remainder in a specified class of persons and a precedent life estate in Matthew the father. In Hague v. Hague, 161 Pa. 643, 29 A. 261, a grant by deed was to Sarah Hague and her children, and the court said that if they were strangers it would constitute them all tenants in common, but the weight of authority holds the mother to be only a tenant for life. . . .

In re McCullough's Estate, 272 Pa. 509, 116 A. 477 is in the same vein, but on the other hand, In re McIntosh's Estate, 158 Pa. 528, 527 A. 1044 holds to the contrary, as there a devise to James and his children was held to give the children equal distributive rights with their father.

Kentucky seems to follow the majority of the Pennsylvania cases, as witness Smith v. Smith, 119 Ky. 899, 902, 85 S.W. 169, 170, where there was a devise "to my son and his children" and it was held that the son took a life estate, with remainder to the children. See also Bowe v. Richmond, 33 Ky. L. Rep. 173, 109 S.W. 359. Indiana is in the same category (Edwards v. Bates, 79 Ind. App. 578, 139 N.E. 192).

Virginia, on the other hand, interprets such a devise as giving the parent a fee simple on the theory that the words "and his children" like the words "and his heirs," are words of limitation and not of purchase (Wallace v. Dold's Ex'rs., 3 Leigh, [30 Va.] 258).

Other jurisdictions, however, follow the Rule in Wild's Case. A sampling of such decisions would include In re Utz's Estate, 43 Cal. 200, where a devise to testator's daughter and her children, entitled the children to share in the devise, and it passed to the daughter and her children as tenants in common. Also Jones' Executors v. Jones, 13 N.J. Eq. 236, wherein a devise to a woman and her children, she having children living at the time of the devise, the word "children" was said to be a word of purchase to be taken according to its natural import, and the children took a joint estate with the mother in the land devised. Moore v. Ennis, 10 Del. Ch. 170, 87 A. 1009, where the testator gave two of his sons and their children bequests of money, is to the same effect, and it was held that the children took jointly and in equal shares with the parents. In Davis v. Sanders, 123 Ga. 177, 51 S.E. 298, testator directed his property be divided "equally between my wife . . . my daughter-in-law . . . and her children, my daughter . . . and her children . . . now or hereafter born," and it was held that the children took equally with the parents.

North Carolina takes the same position, for there it is held that in a deed to A and his children, if A has children when the deed is executed, he and his children will take as tenants in common (Boyd v. Campbell, 192 N.C. 398, 135 S.E. 121; Cullens v. Cullens, 161 N.C. 344, 77 S.E. 228, 5 L.R.A. 1917B, 74).

Thus it appears that Wild's Case is followed more often than rejected and we apprehend it is the law in this state, insofar as the factual situation now before us is concerned.

There is, however, another basis upon which to rest our determination, and that is, absent a showing of a contrary intent, the devise and bequest here involved is a class gift and the named parent is treated as a member of the class composed of herself and her children. If Mrs. Woodward had predeceased testatrix, or if the gift to her had been revoked by codicil, the gift would have gone to those who were members of the class at the time for distribution, namely her children. In the absence of facts showing a different intent of the testatrix, the members of the class receive undivided interests as tenants in common in an estate in fee simple absolute as to the realty, and fractional shares in undivided complete ownership as tenants in common of the personalty (3 Restatement, Property, Ch. 22, §283). Clause Fifth of Helen C. Parant's will is construed accordingly.

NOTE

The first resolution in Wild's Case, adverted to by Surrogate Bascom, is that if testator devises land to A and his children (or to A and his issue) and A has no children (or issue) at the time of the devise, A takes a fee tail. This construction may have been justified on the ground that it approximated testator's intent more closely than any other alternatives existing in 1599; the fee tail would descend to A's children on A's death unless A barred the entail in some way. Inasmuch as the fee tail has been abolished in almost all states, this resolution has been repudiated almost everywhere. See 5 American Law of Property §22.20 (1952).

Restatement (Second) of Property, Donative Transfers §28.3 (Tent. Draft No. 10, 1987), repudiates both resolutions in Wild's Case. It provides that a gift "to A and her children" creates a life estate in A with a remainder in her children. But suppose that A never has any children. Would a better construction be "to A in fee simple, but if A has children, to A's children at A's death"?

For a comprehensive examination of all the ins and outs of Wild's Case in one jurisdiction, and its condemnation, see Link, The Rule in Wild's Case in North Carolina, 55 N.C.L. Rev. 751 (1977).

d. Gifts to Heirs

Warren-Boynton State Bank v. Wallbaum
Supreme Court of Illinois, 1988
123 Ill. 2d 429, 528 N.E.2d 640

CLARK, J.   The following issues are presented for review in what originated at the trial court level as a partition action requiring construction of language in a 1903 deed: (1) whether alternate contingent remainders created in the 1903 deed are subject to an implied condition of survival to the date of distribution, that is, the time of the death of the life tenant, or whether the remaindermen are instead to be determined at the death of the grantor; (2) whether the Doctrine of Worthier Title is applicable to the deed in question; and (3) whether the Rule in Shelley's Case is applicable to the deed.

Appellants are the executor of the estate of Emma Mae Wallbaum, the daughter of the grantor of the deed in question, and the executor of the estate of Elaine B. Stillwell, a beneficiary under the will of Emma Mae Wallbaum. Appellees are certain descendants of William Wallbaum's three sons.

In 1903 William Wallbaum executed a deed by which he conveyed 400 acres of property in Sangamon County to his daughter Emma Mae by creating a life estate. Emma Mae's life estate would become possessory at the termination of the life estate which he reserved for himself. The exact language of the deed is as follows:

> The Grantor, William Wallbaum (widower) of the County of Sangamon and State of Illinois for and in consideration of One Dollar and other good and valuable considerations in hand paid, conveys and warrants to Emma May Wallbaum of the County of Sangamon and State of Illinois. A life estate in the following described real estate, to-wit: [legal description omitted.] Hereby releasing and waiving all rights under and by virtue of the Homestead Exemptions Laws of this State. The said William Wallbaum hereby reserves a life estate in the above described land to-wit: He shall have the right to the use and occupancy of said land and to all the rents, issues and profits thereof during his natural life. And upon the death to said Emma May Wallbaum leaving children of her body her surviving, the above described real estate shall descend to such children share and share alike. The children of any deceased child, taking only the share which their parent would inherit if living. Upon the death of said Emma May Wallbaum leaving no such children her surviving the above described

real estate shall descend to the heirs of said William Wallbaum share and share alike. The children of any deceased child taking only the share which their parent would inherit if living.

At the time of the transfer William was 65 years old and Emma Mae was 5. Her mother, William's second wife, had died the previous year. Emma Mae had two half-brothers who were in their thirties, children of William's first marriage. Several months after executing the deed here in question, William married a third time. He had a fourth child, a son, during this marriage. William died, however, in 1905 before his youngest son was six months old.

William Wallbaum's will devised all of his property to his four children and to Martha, his third wife. The will contained no residuary clause and no mention was made of the 400 acres involved here. . . .

Emma Mae died in 1984, the last of William Wallbaum's children to survive. Her older brothers, Ernest and Frederick, had died in 1928 and 1926, respectively. Each was survived by children. Her younger brother, W. Conway, died in 1941, also survived by a child. Emma Mae never married and had no children.

All parties agree that by the 1903 deed the following estates existed: (1) reserved life estate in William Wallbaum, (2) life estate in Emma Mae Wallbaum, (3) contingent remainder in the children of Emma Mae, (4) alternate contingent remainder in the "heirs of William Wallbaum." Both life estates are extinguished and there is no disagreement that the contingent remainder to Emma Mae's children failed, as she died without children. At issue is the interpretation of the alternate contingent remainder: "Upon the death of said Emma May [sic] Wallbaum leaving no such children her surviving the above described real estate shall descend to the heirs of said William Wallbaum share and share alike. The children of any deceased child taking only the share which their parent would inherit if living." The interpretation depends on what is meant by the phrase "heirs of said William Wallbaum."

The trial court, in a memorandum of opinion, held that the "heirs of said William Wallbaum" in the alternate contingent remainder meant "heirs" in the technical sense of the word, i.e. those taking his property by will or intestacy. "Heirs" in this technical sense are always determined at the time of the grantor's death. At William Wallbaum's death he had as his heirs his four children: Ernest, Frederick, Emma Mae and W. Conway. Emma Mae was a member of that class of heirs. Since the deed contained no language creating a condition that the heirs must survive the life tenant, and the court would not imply such a condition, Emma Mae received a one-fourth vested interest in the property at her death. This one-fourth interest was to pass according to the terms of Emma Mae's will. The remaining three-fourths was to be distributed one-fourth to the heirs of each deceased brother. The diagram attached as Appendix I illustrates this distribution.

The appellate court, reversing the trial court, held that the word "heirs" was used in its nontechnical sense to mean "children." Having equated "heirs" with "children," the appellate court determined that there was an implied condition of survival, that is, that William's children must survive the life tenant in order to take as remaindermen. Since Emma Mae could not survive herself she took nothing. The remainder to each of William Wallbaum's other children, the court indicated, was extinguished at each one's death, but the gift over to the "children of any deceased child" vested that particular portion at the time of the child's death with a child or children surviving subject to subsequent increase or decrease. Although the appellate court gave no directions on remand, a careful reading and analysis of the court's opinion indicates that it would order distribution of the 400 acres here in question as follows: one-third to the descendants of each son of William Wallbaum. (143 Ill. App. 3d 628, 97 Ill. Dec. 539, 493 N.E.2d 21.) A diagram of that distribution is attached as Appendix II.

The entirely different results reached by the two lower courts is illustrative of the confusion which prevails in the law of future interests. There is a pervasive cloud of uncertainty which surrounds this field of law. This obscurity and uncertainty has had its uses. Often it seems as if a particular court will first determine an equitable distribution and thereafter fill in the blanks with appropriate bits and pieces of the law of future interests in order to reach the desired result. This is by no means an indictment of any court but merely an indication of the quagmire that confronts a court in reaching its opinion.

Central to our discussion here is a determination of the meaning of "heir" in the alternate contingent remainder. The question is not one of what we might determine to be fair in light of our modern day understandings, but one of what the grantor meant by his use of the word in the deed. (Hull v. Adams (1948), 399 Ill. 347, 77 N.E.2d 706.) What was William Wallbaum's intent? . . .

The term "heir" may be used as a technical legal word to designate those persons who would take property, whether real or personal, in case of intestacy. (Harris Trust & Savings Bank v. Jackson (1952), 412 Ill. 261, 269, 106 N.E.2d 188.) When used in this purely technical sense, heirs are determined at the time of the testator's or grantor's death unless the instrument in question provides clear evidence to the contrary. (Stites v. Gray (1954), 4 Ill. 2d 510, 513, 123 N.E.2d 483; Hull v. Adams (1948), 399 Ill. 347, 352, 77 N.E.2d 706.) As we noted in Harris Trust & Savings Bank v. Beach (1987), 118 Ill. 2d 1, 112 Ill. Dec. 224, 513 N.E.2d 833, however, our court has not adopted the technical meaning of the word "heir" as a rule of law. (118 Ill. 2d at

10, 112 Ill. Dec. 224, 513 N.E.2d 833.) The determination of "heirs" is governed by the transferor's intent.

. . . [T]he term "heirs" can be used nontechnically in two different instances. We need to distinguish and clearly clarify these different instances because one of these meanings was relied upon erroneously by the appellate court and was also urged as an interpretation by both the appellants and appellees. In its nontechnical use, "heirs" may be used as a synonym for the words "children" or "grandchildren." (Stites v. Gray (1954), 4 Ill. 2d 510, 513, 123 N.E.2d 483.) It may also, however, be used to mean "heirs" of the testator or grantor to be determined at a time other than his or her own death. Harris Trust & Savings Bank v. Beach (1987), 118 Ill. 2d 1, 10, 112 Ill.Dec. 224, 513 N.E.2d 833.

While we agree with the appellate court that William Wallbaum used the term "heir" in a nontechnical sense, we do not agree with its conclusion that the term was used as a synonym for the word "children." Rather, we believe that the language of the deed indicates that he meant that the time for determination of the heirs should be different than the time of his own death. More precisely, we believe that he meant that the heirs should be determined at Emma Mae's death. Several factors support this conclusion. We look first to the deed itself and the language used in the entire document. William Wallbaum intended that his daughter have a life estate only. Any fee interest would vest either in her children or her children's children should they come into being (the contingent remainder) or alternatively in the heirs of William Wallbaum (the alternate contingent remainder). These prior references to "children" suggest that when William Wallbaum meant "children" he said "children." Indeed, he could have referred to Emma Mae's children as her heirs for the sake of continuity, but he did not. While the use of the word "heirs" in the alternate contingent remainder does not alone determine intent, the use of that word in a document where the word "children" was used previously strongly suggests that William Wallbaum used the word he meant. We see no reason to doubt that Mr. Wallbaum used the word in the alternate contingent remainder that he intended.

In conjunction with the language in the deed, we also looked to the circumstances surrounding the creation of the deed. These circumstances also suggest that William Wallbaum was thinking of his heirs at the time of Emma Mae's death and not of his own children. Mr. Wallbaum, as we already noted, was 65 years old when he conveyed the life estate to his five-year-old daughter. He had two sons who were already in their thirties. Mr. Wallbaum was well versed in the turns, changes and evolutions of family life; he had himself recently lost his second wife, who was herself a young woman at the time of her death. With some 60 years difference in age between him and his young daughter and approximately 30 years difference between his sons and his daughter, it seems logical that he would be very much aware of the possibility that both he and his sons would die before Emma Mae. . . .

William was not looking towards a future where his sons, nor perhaps even his grandchildren, would take the property he was transferring to Emma Mae. It made sense to provide an alternate contingent remainder that would, if it were used, leave the property to descendants alive at the death of Emma Mae rather than to his own children or grandchildren who were likely to die before Emma Mae. . . .

Appellants' arguments to construe heirs as those of William Wallbaum at his death are not persuasive. We have already noted the great age disparities among members of the family alive at the creation of the deed in 1903. William had every reason to believe that Emma would outlive all of them — her life interest was the focus of the deed. Takers under the alternate contingent remainder could not take until the death of Emma Mae without children or grandchildren. . . .

Therefore, under the "preponderance of evidence" test enunciated in Harris Trust & Savings Bank v. Beach, determination of the heirs of William Wallbaum to take at the termination of the life estate shall be at the death of the life tenant, Emma Mae Wallbaum.

Because the heirs of William Wallbaum are to be determined at the death of Emma Mae, we need not here deal with the concept of implied condition of survival. We note, however, that the language in the last sentence of the alternate contingent remainder serves as a limitation on the distribution to the heirs. We construe the language to mean that each surviving familial line of descent is to share the property equally. Surviving descendants are found in Ernest's line of descendants and in W. Conway's line of descendants. Emma Mae died without issue and the last survivor of Frederick's line died in 1965, 19 years prior to the

APPENDIX I - TRIAL COURT DIAGRAM

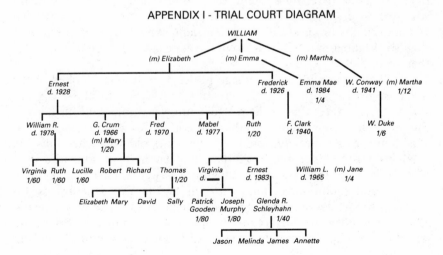

APPENDIX II - APPELLATE COURT DIAGRAM

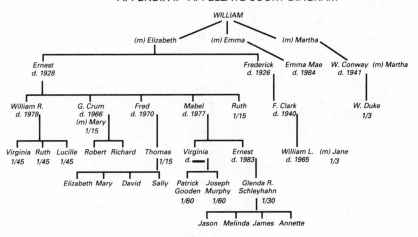

APPENDIX III - REMAND DIAGRAM

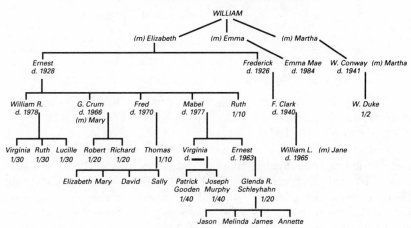

death of the life tenant. Therefore, distribution among the heirs is as shown in the diagram attached as Appendix III.

Because the appellants presented the issues of the applicability of the Doctrine of Worthier Title and the Rule in Shelley's Case, we will briefly address them, but note that they are not necessary to a determination of this case. Determination of the heirs at a time different than the grantor's death precludes application of the Doctrine of Worthier Title. Our court fully addressed that issue in Harris Trust & Savings Bank v. Beach, 118 Ill. 2d at 20, 112 Ill. Dec. 224, 513 N.E.2d 833. Additionally, the Rule in Shelley's Case is inapplicable because the deed did not create the life estate in William Wallbaum, whose heirs were the remaindermen; it merely reserved the life estate in property he owned in fee prior to the transfer. A remainder in the grantor's heirs does not trigger the rule. Cahill v. Cahill (1949), 402 Ill. 416, 84 N.E.2d 380.

We conclude that the remainder in the heirs be distributed one-half to W. Conway's line of descendants and one-half to Ernest's line of descendants. The judgments of both the circuit court and appellate courts are reversed, and the case is remanded to the circuit court of Sangamon County for entry of an order of partition in a manner consistent with this opinon.

Judgments reversed; cause remanded.

> . . . words strain,
> Crack and sometimes break, under the burden,
> Under the tension, slip, slide, perish,
> Decay with imprecision, will not stay in place,
> Will not stay still.
>
> T. S. ELIOT
> *"Burnt Norton" In Four Quartets*

NOTES

1. The many problems arising from gifts to "heirs" are catalogued in Restatement (Second) of Property, Donative Transfers §§29.1-29.8 (Tent. Draft No. 10, 1987).

The court in *Wallbaum* applies a straight per stirpes division to the land deeded in 1903. Such a division is provided by the Illinois intestacy statute. Ill. Rev. Stat. ch. 110½, ¶2-1 (1978). Suppose that in 1903 the Illinois intestacy statute had provided for representation in the manner of Uniform Probate Code §2-106, supra page 77. Would the statute in effect in 1903 or in 1984 (at Emma Mae's death) be applicable in determining William Wallbaum's heirs? See Restatement (Second) of Property, supra, §29.3, providing that the relevant statute is that in force when the designated person (William Wallbaum) dies. But a number of cases are contra.

2. Because a transmissible remainder is subject to the federal estate tax, estate planners in several states have successfully urged legislatures to enact a statute providing that where a remainder is given to a person's heirs, the heirs will not be ascertained until the remainder becomes possessory. Under such a statute, no remainderman has a transmissible interest because if he dies before the remainder becomes possessory, he will not be alive when heirs are ascertained and, therefore, cannot be an heir. The Pennsylvania statute reproduced below is illustrative of such statutes.

Pennsylvania Consolidated Statutes Annotated
tit. 20, §2514 (1975)

In the absence of a contrary intent appearing therein, wills shall be construed as to real and personal estate in accordance with the following rules: . . .

(4) *Meaning of "heirs" and "next of kin," etc.; time of ascertaining class.* A devise or bequest of real or personal estate, whether directly or in trust, to the testator's or another designated person's "heirs" or "next of kin" or "relatives" or "family" or to "the persons thereunto entitled under the intestate laws" or to persons described by words of similar import, shall mean those persons, including the spouse, who would take under the intestate laws if the testator or other designated person were to die intestate at the time when such class is to be ascertained, a resident of the Commonwealth, and owning the estate so devised or bequeathed: Provided, however, that the share of a spouse, other than the spouse of the testator, shall not include the allowance under the intestate laws. The time when such class is to be ascertained shall be the time when the devise or bequest is to take effect in enjoyment.

NOTE: THE DOCTRINE OF WORTHIER TITLE

The doctrine of worthier title, referred to by the court in *Wallbaum*, apparently still exists in some states. It was abolished in Illinois in 1955, but still maintains a ghostly presence over pre-1955 instruments. Simply put, the doctrine provides that when a settlor transfers property in trust, with a life estate in the settlor or in another, and purports to create a remainder in the *settlor's heirs*, it is presumed that the settlor intended to retain a reversion in himself and not create a remainder in his heirs. Thus the remainder is presumptively not created. The doctrine is a rule of presumed intent, which can be rebutted by evidence that the settlor did intend to create a remainder in his heirs. See J. Dukeminier & J. Krier, Property 244-246 (2d ed. 1988).

The doctrine was roused from a sleep of several centuries by Judge Cardozo in Doctor v. Hughes, 225 N.Y 305, 122 N.E. 221 (1919), in order to do equity on some particular facts. But the states that followed Cardozo's lead and adopted the doctrine found that it produced a passel of lawsuits involving the most speculative evidence about whether the settlor intended to create a remainder rather than retain a reversion.[32] As a result of this experience, Arkansas, California, Illinois,

---

32. See R. Powell, Cases on Future Interests 88 n.14 (3d ed. 1961): "[T]here were literally scores of [New York] cases, many of which reached the Appellate Division, and no case involving a substantial sum could be fairly regarded as closed until its language and circumstances had been passed upon by the Court of Appeals."

Massachusetts, Minnesota, Nebraska, New York, North Carolina, Texas, and West Virginia abolished the doctrine of worthier title. The Restatement of Property (Second), Donative Transfers §30.2(1) (Tent. Draft No. 10, 1987), says the doctrine exists in states where not specifically abolished, but this is hard to verify with actual cases. The Joint Editorial Board for the Uniform Probate Code has proposed a new §2-710 abolishing the doctrine of worthier title.

Although rejection of the doctrine of worthier title seems sound, it does leave us with the problem of securing consent of the unascertained heirs of a living settlor to modification or termination of a trust. Statutes in some states abolishing worthier title have dealt with this problem by providing that a trust may be revoked by the settlor alone when the only other interested persons are the settlor's heirs. See, e.g., N.Y. Est., Powers & Trusts Law §7-1.9(b) (1967).

NOTE: THE RULE IN SHELLEY'S CASE

At common law, if land were conveyed to a grantee for life, then to the *grantee's heirs*, the attempted creation of a contingent remainder in the heirs was not recognized. Instead, the grantee took the remainder. The life estate then merged into the remainder, giving the grantee a possessory fee simple absolute. Although this rule was recognized more than two centuries earlier, it was not given form until Shelley's Case, 1 Co. Rep. 93b, 76 Eng. Rep 206 (C.B. 1579), which also gave the rule its name.

Here is a simplified[33] statement of the rule: If

(1)   one instrument (deed, will, or trust)
(2)   creates a life estate in land in A, and
(3)   purports to create a remainder in A's heirs (or the heirs of A's body), and
(4)   the estates are both legal or both equitable,

the remainder becomes a remainder in fee simple (or fee tail) in A. If there is no intervening estate, the life estate merges into the remainder, giving A a fee simple (or fee tail). The rule in Shelley's Case is not a rule of construction. It is a rule of law, and it applies regardless of the intent of the transferor.

---

33. In Van Grutten v. Foxwell, [1879] A.C. 658, 671, Lord Macnaghten said, "It is one thing to put a case like *Shelley*'s in a nutshell and another thing to keep it there." If you doubt the intricacies of the rule, take a look at the 205-page note on the rule at 29 L.R.A. 965 (1911), where it is said of Shelley's Case, as "of Goldsmith's village parson, that those who came to scoff remain to pray."

Although there may have been various original reasons for the rule in Shelley's Case, there can be only one reason today to justify it. The rule makes the property alienable earlier by destroying a purported remainder in unascertained persons. See Ziff & Litman, Shelley's Rule in a Modern Context: Clearing the "Heir," 34 U. Toronto L.J. 170 (1984). On the other hand, it defeats the intent of the testator and is a malpractice trap for lawyers.

PROBLEMS

1. State the effect of the rule in Shelley's Case upon each of the following transfers of land:
   (a)   *O* conveys "to *A* for life, then to *A*'s children and their heirs."
   (b)   *O* conveys "to *A* for life, then to *A*'s heirs if *A* survives *B*."
   (c)   *O* conveys "to *A* for 100 years if *A* so long live, then to *A*'s heirs."
   (d)   *O* conveys "to *A* for life." *O* subsequently devises the reversion to *A*'s heirs.
2. *O* conveys to *A* for life, remainder to *A*'s heirs. The conveyance further provides: "I intend that *A* shall take a life estate only and that the rule in Shelley's Case shall not apply." What result? See Bishop v. Williams, 221 Ark. 617, 255 S.W.2d 171 (1953). How should *O*'s lawyer have drafted the conveyance? Is a lawyer who does not avoid the rule in Shelley's Case liable for malpractice?

———————

Modern status of the rule in Shelley's Case.   The rule in Shelley's Case has been abolished in practically all states and the District of Columbia, as well as in England. See Restatement (Second) of Property, Donative Transfers §30.1, Statutory Note (Tent. Draft No. 10, 1987). In some states, however, the abolition by statute is fairly recent and does not apply retroactively. In these states, cases involving the rule continue to crop up from time to time. Illinois abolished the rule in Shelley's Case in 1953; North Carolina abolished the rule in Shelley's Case in 1987. See Orth, Requiem for the Rule in Shelley's Case, 67 N.C.L. Rev. 681 (1989).

10

POWERS OF APPOINTMENT: BUILDING FLEXIBILITY INTO THE ESTATE PLAN

SECTION A. INTRODUCTION

1. Types of Powers

We now turn to powers of appointment in trust *beneficiaries*, powers that give the beneficiaries the ability to deal flexibly with changing circumstances in the future — with births, deaths, and marriages in the family; with the ability of children to manage property; with changes in the economy and investment returns; and with changes in the laws. There are few trusts where the skillful drafter does not give some thought to whether one or more beneficiaries should have a power of appointment.

In studying the law of powers, the first thing to do is to get the terminology and relationships straight. The person who creates the power of appointment is the *donor* of the power; the person who holds the power is the *donee*. The persons in whose favor the power may be exercised are the *objects* of the power. When a power is exercised in favor of a person, such person becomes an *appointee*. The instrument creating the power may provide for *takers in default of appointment* if the donee fails to exercise the power.

All powers can be divided into general powers and special powers. A *general power* is, in the language of the Internal Revenue Code, "a power which is exercisable in favor of the decedent [donee], his estate, his creditors, or the creditors of his estate."[1] Under the federal estate and

---

1. Int. Rev. Code of 1986, §2041(b) (estate tax); the comparable definition under the

gift tax laws, any power that is not a general power is classified as a special power. Thus a *special power* is a power not exercisable in favor of the donee, his estate, his creditors, or the creditors of his estate. Prevailing professional usage of these terms is in accord with the definitions contained in the tax laws.[2]

A general power of appointment may permit the donee to do most of the things an owner of the fee simple could do. This is true of a general power presently exercisable. Thus:

> *Case 1.* *T* devises property to *X* in trust to pay the income to *A* for life or until such time as *A* appoints and to distribute the principal to such person or persons as *A* shall appoint either by deed during *A*'s lifetime or by will; if *A* does not exercise the power of appointment, at *A*'s death *X* is to distribute the principal to *B*. *T* is the donor. *A* is the donee of a general power of appointment exercisable by deed or will. *B* is the taker in default of appointment.

In Case 1, *A* is very close to being absolute owner of the property since the only thing that stands between *A* and absolute ownership is a piece of paper *A* can sign at any time. To acquire title, *A* has merely to write, "I hereby appoint to myself." Even though *A* can acquire absolute ownership at any time, however, *A* does not have it until the power is exercised in *A*'s favor. If *A* does not exercise the power, the property will pass to the taker in default, *B*, and not to *A*'s heirs. If the creating instrument does not name a taker in default, the property passes back to the donor or the donor's estate if the power is not exercised.

The objects of a general power of appointment are necessarily broader than the objects of a special power. The most common kind of special power is the power to appoint among the issue of the donee. Thus:

> *Case 2.* *T* devises property to *X* in trust to pay the income to *A* for life, and on *A*'s death to distribute the principal to such one or more of *A*'s issue as *A* shall appoint by will; if *A* does not exercise the power of appointment, at *A*'s death *X* is to distribute the principal to *A*'s then living issue, such issue to take per stirpes.

There is a profound difference between the general power presently exercisable in Case 1 and the special power in Case 2. In Case 2, *A*

---

federal gift tax is in §2514(c). The Code goes on to exclude from the definition of a general power a power to consume principal "limited by an ascertainable standard relating to the health, education, support, or maintenance" of the donee, a power held with an adverse party, and certain powers created prior to 1942. §§2041(b)(1)(A)-2041(b)(1)(C) and §§2514(c)(1)-2514(c)(3). See infra pages 986-987.

2. Restatement (Second) of Property, Donative Transfers §11.4 (1984), prefers the term "non-general" to special.

occupies a position similar to that of *T*'s agent. *A* can exercise the power to benefit *A*'s issue, but *A* cannot appoint the property in such a way as to benefit *A* or *A*'s estate.[3]

Powers of appointment may be capable of being exercised by either deed or will as in Case 1, by deed[4] alone, or by will alone as in Case 2. When exercisable only by will, the power is called a *testamentary* power.

To be absolutely accurate, we should point out that a power of appointment may be created in a trustee, a beneficiary of a trust, a person with a legal interest not held in trust, or in a person who has no other interest in the property. In other words, a power may be created in anyone.[5] Almost all powers of appointment are created in trustees or in beneficiaries of trusts, however. A trustee who has discretion to pay income or principal to a named beneficiary, or discretion to spray income among a group of beneficiaries, has a special power of appointment. Special powers in trustees were treated in the section on Discretionary Trusts in Chapter 7 at pages 538-547. In this chapter we are primarily concerned with powers of appointment given to beneficiaries of trusts.

2. Does the Appointive Property Belong to the Donor or the Donee?

Under the common law, property subject to a power of appointment was viewed as owned by the donor, and the power was conceived as merely authority of the donee to do an act for the donor. The donee

---

3. The existence of the power can, of course, benefit *A* by assuring filial devotion.

> It doubtless occurred to the testator that by restraining a disposition of his property except by will, which is in its nature revocable, [his widow] would, to the end of her life, retain the influence over, and secure the respect of, the several objects of his bounty, which he intended her to have — a result less likely to be accomplished if power were given her to dispose of the property by deed or other irrevocable act to take effect in her lifetime. [Hood v. Haden, 82 Va. 588, 591 (1886).]

As someone once said, a special power over a hundred thousand dollars never hurt an old lady — or an old man.

4. Restatement (Second) of Property, Donative Transfers §18.2, Comment d (1986), says that when the donor prescribes exercise "by deed," the power cannot be exercised by will. Statutes in some states incorporate the opposite rule: Powers expressly stated to be exercisable by deed can also be exercised by will unless this is expressly forbidden by the instrument creating the power. See, e.g., Cal. Civ. Code §1385.1 (1989); N.Y. Est., Powers & Trusts Law §10-6.2 (1967).

5. With one exception: A power may not be created in a donee over property owned by the donee. For example, if *T* devises Blackacre "to *A* in fee simple and to such person as *A* appoints," *A* has a fee simple and the power is void. This type of power, known as a power appendant, was valid in England but is not recognized in the United States. See Restatement (Second) of Property, Donative Transfers §12.3 (1986).

was thought of as having a power to fill in a blank in the donor's will. This was known as the *relation-back doctrine*. This doctrine pretty much describes how the law treats special powers of appointment, where the donee can reap no personal pecuniary benefit, but it has never been consistently applied to general powers of appointment.

In some situations, the donee of a general power of appointment is treated as owner of the property. The primary example is under the federal tax laws. The donee of a general power is treated as owner of the appointive property for income, estate, and gift tax purposes. Congress pays no mind to the technicalities of property law here but makes taxation turn upon the fact that the donee, if he chooses, can receive economic benefit by exercising the power.

Irwin Union Bank & Trust Co. v. Long
Indiana Court of Appeals, 1974
160 Ind. App. 509, 312 N.E.2d 908

LOWDERMILK, J. On February 3, 1957, Victoria Long, appellee herein, obtained a judgment in the amount of $15,000 against Philip W. Long, which judgment emanated from a divorce decree. This action is the result of the filing by appellee of a petition in proceedings supplemental to execution on the prior judgment. Appellee sought satisfaction of that judgment by pursuing funds allegedly owed to Philip W. Long as a result of a trust set up by Laura Long, his mother.

Appellee alleged that the Irwin Union Bank and Trust Company (Union Bank) was indebted to Philip W. Long as the result of its position as trustee of the trust created by Laura Long. On April 24, 1969, the trial court ordered that any income, property, or profits, which were owed to Philip Long and not exempt from execution should be applied to the divorce judgment. Thereafter, on February 13, 1973, the trial court ordered that four percent (4%) of the trust corpus of the trust created by Laura Long which benefited Philip Long was not exempt from execution and could be levied upon by appellee and ordered a writ of execution. . . .

The pertinent portion of the trust created by Laura Long is as follows, to-wit:

ITEM V C

Withdrawal of Principal.
When Philip W. Long, Jr. has attained the age of twenty-one (21) years and is not a full-time student at an educational institution as a candidate for a Bachelor of Arts or Bachelor of Sciences degree, Philip W. Long shall have the right to withdraw from principal once in any calendar year upon thirty (30) days written notice to the Trustee up to four percent

(4%) of the market value of the entire trust principal on the date of such notice, which right shall not be cumulative; provided, however, that the amount distributable hereunder shall not be in excess of the market value of the assets of the trust on the date of such notice other than interests in real estate.

The primary issue raised on this appeal is whether the trial court erred in allowing execution on the 4% of the trust corpus.

Appellant contends that Philip Long's right to withdraw 4% of the trust corpus is, in fact, a general power of appointment. Union Bank further contends that since Philip Long has never exercised his right of withdrawal, pursuant to the provisions of the trust instrument, no creditors of Philip Long can reach the trust corpus. Appellant points out that if the power of appointment is unexercised, the creditors cannot force the exercise of said power and cannot reach the trust corpus in this case. . . .

Appellee . . . argues that Philip has absolute control and use of the 4% of the corpus and that the bank does not have control over that portion of the corpus if Philip decides to exercise his right of withdrawal. Appellee argues that the intention of Laura Long was to give Philip not only an income interest in the trust but a fixed amount of corpus which he could use as he saw fit. Thus, Philip Long would have a right to the present enjoyment of 4% of the trust corpus. A summation of appellee's argument, as stated in her brief, is as follows: "So it is with Philip — he can get it if he desires it, so why cannot Victoria get it even if Philip does not desire it?"

We have had no Indiana authority directly in point cited to us by either of the parties and a thorough research of this issue does not reveal any Indiana authority on point. Thus, this issue so far as we can determine is one of first impression in Indiana. . . .

The leading case on this issue is Gilman v. Bell (1881), 99 Ill. 144, 150, 151, wherein the Illinois Supreme Court discussed powers of appointment and vesting as follows:

> . . . No title or interest in the thing vests in the donee of the power until he exercises the power. It is virtually an offer to him of the estate or fund, that he may receive or reject at will, and like any other offer to donate property to a person, no title can vest until he accepts the offer, nor can a court of equity compel him to accept the property or fund against his will, even for the benefit of creditors. If it should, it would be to convert the property of the person offering to make the donation to the payment of the debts of another person. Until accepted, the person to whom the offer is made has not, nor can he have, the slightest interest or title to the property. So the donee of the power only receives the naked power to make the property or fund his own. And when he exercises the power, he thereby consents to receive it, and the title thereby

vests in him, although it may pass out of him *eo instanti*, to the appointee. . . .

See, also, 59 A.L.R. 1510. . . .

Contrary to the contention of appellee, it is our opinion that Philip Long has no control over the trust corpus until he exercises his power of appointment and gives notice to the trustee that he wishes to receive his 4% of the trust corpus. Until such an exercise is made, the trustee has the absolute control and benefit of the trust corpus within the terms of the trust instrument.

While not controlling as precedent, we find that the Federal Estate Tax laws are quite analogous to the case at bar. Under §2041, Powers of Appointment, of the Internal Revenue Code, it is clear that the interest given to Philip Long under Item V C would be considered a power of appointment for estate tax purposes. A general power of appointment is defined in §2041(b)(1) as follows:

> (1) General power of appointment. — The term "general power of appointment" means a power which is exercisable in favor of the decedent, his estate, his creditors, or the creditors of his estate; . . .

The regulations pertinent to this issue discuss a power of appointment as it is used for estate tax purposes as follows:

> (b) Definition of "power of appointment" (1) In general. The term "power of appointment" includes all powers which are in substance and effect powers of appointment regardless of the nomenclature used in creating the power and regardless of local property law connotations. For example, if a trust instrument provides that the beneficiary may appropriate or consume the principal of the trust, the power to consume or appropriate is a power of appointment. . . . 20.2041-1(b)(1)

For estate tax purposes even the failure to exercise a power of appointment may lead to tax consequences. Under §2041(b)(2) the lapse of a power of appointment will be considered a release of such power during the calendar year to the extent of the value of the power in question. However, the lapsed power will only be considered a release and includable in the gross estate of a decedent if the value of the lapsed power is greater than $5,000 or 5% of the aggregate value of the assets out of which the lapsed power could have been satisfied.

The trust instrument was obviously carefully drawn with the tax consequences bearing an important place in the overall intent of the testator. The trust as a whole is set up to give the grandchildren of Laura Long the substantial portion of the assets involved. We note with interest that the percentage of corpus which Philip Long may receive is carefully limited to a percentage less than that which would be includable in the gross estate of Philip Long should he die within a year in which he had allowed his power of appointment to lapse.

. . . The trust created in the will of Laura Long, in our opinion, has the legal effect of creating a [general] power of appointment in Philip Long under Item V C of the trust.

Philip Long has never exercised his power of appointment under the trust. Such a situation is discussed in II Scott on Trusts, §147.3 as follows:

> . . . Where the power is a special power, a power to appoint only among a group of persons, the power is not beneficial to the donee and cannot, of course, be reached by his creditors. Where the power is a general power, that is, a power to appoint to anyone including the donee himself or his estate, the power is beneficial to the donee. If the donee exercises the power by appointing to a volunteer, the property appointed can be reached by his creditors if his other assets are insufficient for the payment of his debts. But where the donee of a general power created by some person other than himself fails to exercise the power, his creditors cannot acquire the power or compel its exercise, nor can they reach the property covered by the power, unless it is otherwise provided by statute. . . .

Indiana has no statute which would authorize a creditor to reach property covered by a power of appointment which is unexercised.

In Gilman v. Bell, supra, the court analyzed the situation where a general power of appointment was unexercised and discussed the position of creditors of the donee of the power as follows:

> But it is insisted, that, conceding it to be a mere naked power of appointment in favor of himself, in favor of creditors he should be compelled by a court of equity to so appoint, or be treated as the owner, and the property subjected to the payment of his debts. The doctrine has been long established in the English courts, that the courts of equity will not aid creditors in case there is a non-execution of the power. . . .

Appellee concedes that if we find that Philip Long had merely an unexercised power of appointment then creditors are in no position to either force the exercise of the power or to reach the trust corpus. Thus, it is clear that the trial court erred. . . .

Reversed and remanded.

NOTES AND QUESTIONS

1. Restatement (Second) of Property, Donative Transfers §13.2 (1986), agrees with the *Long* case. Is this sound? The courts following the rule applied in *Long* start by saying that the power is not the donee's

"property"; its exercise is personal to the donee and cannot be exercised by another. As Lord Justice Fry once said: "The power of a person to appoint an estate to himself is, in my judgment, no more his 'property' than the power to write a book or to sing a song." In re Armstrong, 17 Q.B.D. 521, 531 (1886). But, then, if the donee exercises the power by appointing to another, the appointive assets somehow — according to the majority of courts — pass into the donee's hands (or estate) for a scintilla of time and, while in the donee's hands (or estate), equity seizes the assets for the benefit of creditors.

One may reasonably ask why, if the donee of a presently exercisable general power may reach the property simply by asking for it, the donee's creditors cannot reach it? How does the property differ in essence from money in the donee's checking account? In a number of states statutes enable creditors of a donee of a general power presently exercisable to reach the appointive property, usually with the qualification that the creditors must first exhaust the donee's own assets before resorting to the appointive property. See, e.g., Cal. Civ. Code §1390.3 (1989); Wis. Stat. Ann. §702.17 (1979). Under these statutes, the creditors of the donee of a general testamentary power can also reach the property but only at the donee's death. In New York, creditors of a general power presently exercisable can reach the appointive property, but creditors of a donee of a general testamentary power cannot. N.Y. Est., Powers & Trusts Law §§10-7.2, 10-7.4 (1967).

Under the federal bankruptcy act, a general power presently exercisable passes to the donee's trustee in bankruptcy, but a special power and a general testamentary power do not. 10 U.S.C. §541(b) (1979). See Note, Powers of Appointment Under the Bankruptcy Code: A Focus on General Testamentary Powers, 72 Iowa L. Rev. 1041 (1987).

If the donee of a general power is also the donor of the power, creditors may reach the appointive assets. Restatement (Second) of Property, supra, §13.3.

2. *Spouse of the donee.* As for the surviving spouse seeking to reach the appointive property at the donee's death under elective share statutes, the donee of a general power, as well as the donee of a special power, is not treated as owning the property. The surviving spouse has a claim against the donee's *probate* estate, and since the appointive assets are not in the donee's probate estate, the spouse may not reach them. This is true even in states that have statutes permitting the donee's creditors to reach appointive property subject to a general power. The surviving spouse is not given the rights of general creditors. See Mahoney, Elective Share Statutes: The Right to Elect Against Property Subject to a General Power of Appointment in the Decedent, 55 Notre Dame Law. 99 (1979).

3. Suppose that *W* has a general testamentary power of appointment over a trust created by her husband. At *W*'s death, can *W*'s executors

include the trust assets in figuring their commissions? See In re Wylie's Estate, 342 So. 2d 996 (Fla. App. 1977).

NOTE: TAX REASONS FOR CREATING POWERS

Powers of appointment are extensively employed in trusts to give the donee considerable control over the trust property while at the same time gaining some tax advantage. The federal tax laws provide that the holder of a general power of appointment over income or principal is treated as owner of the property. The income from the property is taxable to the donee (Internal Revenue Code of 1986, §678). If the donee exercises the power during life, the property transferred by exercise is subject to gift taxation (IRC §2514 and see infra pages 985-986). If the donee dies holding a general power, the property is included in the donee's federal gross estate and is subject to taxation (IRC §2041, discussed infra at pages 985-987). On the other hand, *property subject to a special power of appointment is not treated as owned by the donee.* Hence, if your client wants to transfer property and avoid estate taxation at the death of the donee, while giving the donee considerable control over the property, create a special power of appointment and not a general power.

By carefully tailoring the powers given a donee to fit the Internal Revenue Code, a donee can be given power to do almost anything an owner of property can do while not being treated as owner for federal estate and gift tax purposes. Let us see how this can be done. Suppose that *O* wishes to pass property to her son, *A*, for his life and then to *A*'s children. At the same time *O* wishes to give *A* as much power over the property as is possible without causing *A* to be treated as owner for tax purposes. Although *O* cannot escape taxation at her death, *O* is looking ahead and wishes to skip estate taxation on *A*'s death. To accomplish *O*'s wishes, *O*'s will can set up a trust along the following lines:

(1)   *O*'s will transfers the legal title to the property to *A* as trustee. *As trustee, A* has the power of management. *A* can decide when to sell and in what to reinvest. If the trustee's powers are broadly drafted, *A* can manage the property almost as if he owned it himself.

(2)   *O*'s will gives to *A, not as trustee but as a beneficiary*, the following rights and powers:
 (a)   the right to receive all the income,
 (b)   a special power of appointment exercisable by deed or will to appoint the trust property to anyone *A* desires except

himself, his creditors, his estate, and the creditors of his estate,

(c)   a power to consume the trust property measured "by an ascertainable standard relating to the health, education, support or maintenance"[6] of *A*, and

(d)   a power to withdraw each year $5,000 or 5 percent of the corpus, whichever is greater.[7]

(3)   If *O* desires to make sure that *A* will be able to use the entire property if he needs it, *O* can appoint an independent co-trustee and give this co-trustee the power to pay *A* the entire principal or to terminate the trust.

None of the above powers given *A*, individually or collectively, causes *A* to be treated as owner of the trust fund under the federal estate tax. Yet *A* has such broad control over the trust fund that in most instances he can do exactly with the trust funds as he could do if he had been bequeathed the property outright.

Prior to the Tax Reform Act of 1986, federal estate taxes could be avoided over several generations through the creation of successive life estates. To give the desired flexibility to cope with changing events, each successive life tenant could be given special powers of appointment as indicated above. This tax avoidance device has now been curtailed by the imposition of a tax on certain *generation-skipping transfers*. IRC §§2601-2663, discussed infra at pages 1022-1037. It is now Congress's policy to exact a transfer tax at every generation. Hence a generation-skipping transfer tax is imposed on the death of a life tenant of a younger generation than the settlor's (on *A*'s death in the above example).

Nonetheless, special powers of appointment remain useful and without adverse tax consequences in most intrafamily transfers of wealth. *O* can give a special power to her spouse to appoint among *O*'s descendants. This is not a generation-skipping transfer, since *O*'s spouse is deemed to be of *O*'s own generation. Also, each transferor can transfer up to $1 million in a trust, which will be exempt from generation-skipping transfer tax for the duration of a trust. Hence in the above example, *O* could create a trust of $1 million for her son *A* and his descendants, giving each generation special powers as outlined above, with the trust to endure until 21 years after the death of *O* and

---

6. Powers to consume measured by an ascertainable standard are not treated as general powers under the Code. See infra pages 986.

7. Under a "$5,000 or 5 percent" power, $5,000 or 5 percent of the corpus (whichever is greater) will be included in the estate of the donee to the extent the power is not exercised in the year of the donee's death. IRC §2041(b)(2), discussed infra at page 986-987. This is a small price to pay for the flexibility gained thereby. This is the type of power litigated in Irwin Union Bank & Trust Co. v. Long, supra.

all *O*'s living descendants (the perpetuities period). No generation-skipping transfer tax would be payable while the trust endured. If *O* were married, she and her husband (using his $1 million exemption) could transfer $2 million in such a G.S.T.-tax-exempt dynasty trust. See infra page 1029. Other uses of special powers of appointment in saving transfer taxes will be dealt with in Chapter 13 on federal wealth transfer taxes.

Although as a rule general powers should not be created if the donor is seeking favorable tax treatment, there is one exception. Property that passes to the surviving spouse in such a manner as to qualify for the *marital deduction* is not taxed upon the death of the first spouse to die. A life estate coupled with a general testamentary power in the surviving spouse qualifies for the marital deduction (IRC §2056(b)(5), discussed infra at page 1001) and is a common estate planning tool. Thus:

> *Case 3.* *H* devises property to *X* in trust to pay the income to *W* and on *W*'s death to distribute the principal to such person or persons as *W* by her will appoints. *H*'s devise qualifies for the marital deduction; no federal estate taxes are payable on the property at *H*'s death. However, since *W* has a general power, the property is subject to estate taxation on *W*'s death. In effect the marital deduction permits taxation to be postponed until the death of the surviving spouse.

Because of adverse tax consequences, general powers are rarely created in anyone except the surviving spouse.

It has been held that a lawyer who drafts wills and trusts is liable for malpractice if the lawyer does not know the tax consequences of powers of appointment. In Bucquet v. Livingston, 57 Cal. App. 3d 914, 129 Cal. Rptr. 514 (1976), the lawyer failed to recognize that a general power of appointment is the equivalent of ownership for tax purposes. In holding the lawyer liable, the court noted that the attorney had employed well-established tax saving devices, the marital deduction trust and the non-marital by-pass trust (see infra pages 1012-1017), and that the creation of general and special powers of appointment is a significant aspect of the law of trusts and estates. The court concluded that a reasonable, diligent, and competent attorney engaged in estate planning should be expected to know the potential tax consequences of creating or holding a general power of appointment.

SECTION B.   CREATION OF A POWER OF APPOINTMENT

1. *Intent to Create a Power*

To create a power of appointment, the donor must manifest an intent to do so, either expressly or by implication. No particular form of words is necessary. It is not necessary that the words "power of appointment" or "appoint" be used. A power of appointment confers discretion on the donee, who may choose to exercise the power or not, and is to be distinguished from a direct nondiscretionary disposition by the donor. Thus:

> *Case 4.*   Aunt Fanny executes a will in 1990 bequeathing her tangible personal property "to my sister Polly, to dispose of in accordance with a letter addressed to Polly dated January 4, 1989, which is in my safe deposit box." Aunt Fanny has incorporated the letter by reference and the tangible personal property must be distributed in accordance therewith. Polly does not have a power of appointment.

Words that merely express a wish or desire (*precatory words*) do not create a power of appointment in the absence of other circumstances indicating a contrary intent. If in Case 4 Aunt Fanny had left her tangible personal property to Polly "with the request that she give some of the property to my blood relatives," Polly would take a fee simple; the precatory words would not create a power of appointment. See Flynn v. Flynn, 469 S.W.2d 886 (Ky. 1971).

PROBLEMS

1.   *T* devises Blackacre "to my wife, *W*, with power to devise the same to my children as she may decide." *T*'s residuary devisee is *A*. *W* is *T*'s second wife and not the mother of his children. Subsequently *W* dies intestate, leaving *H* as her heir. Who owns Blackacre? See Restatement (Second) of Property, Donative Transfers §12.1, Comment c (1986).

2.   *T* devises property in trust for her husband *H* for life, and if *H* should die intestate, then to her son *S* in fee simple. Since *S* is to take only if *H* does not leave a will, by implication *H* has a general testamentary power of appointment. Restatement (Second) of Property, supra, §12.1, Comment f.

Now take this harder case. *T* devises property in trust "for *A* for life, and upon *A*'s death to pay the principal of the trust to *A*'s executor, provided *A* leaves a child or children living at his death." Does *A* have a general power or a special power or no power at all? See In re Clark, 274 A.D. 49, 80 N.Y.S.2d 1 (1948); Bredin v. Wilmington Trust Co., 42 Del. Ch. 563, 216 A.2d 685 (1965).

3.   In 1986 *T* executes a will devising her residuary estate "to such person or persons as my brother, *B*, shall by his last will appoint." In 1988 *B* dies, leaving a will executed in 1984 that devises "all my property, and all property over which I hold a power of appointment,

to *C*." In 1990 *T* dies. *C* claims the residue of *T*'s estate. Is *C* entitled to it? See Curley v. Lynch, 206 Mass. 289, 92 N.E. 429 (1910); Restatement (Second) of Property, supra §18.4.

2. Powers to Consume

One of the most frequently litigated problems in regard to creation of powers is whether a power to consume principal has been created and, if so, what standard governs the exercise of the power. Much of this litigation stems from homemade wills, but some litigation, alas, results from inadequate drafting by lawyers.

Sterner v. Nelson
Supreme Court of Nebraska, 1982
210 Neb. 358, 314 N.W.2d 263

KRIVOSHA, C.J.   The instant case involves the construction of the last will and testament of Oscar Wurtele, deceased. The appellants appeal from a summary judgment entered by the District Court for Otoe County, Nebraska, finding that the nature of the devise and bequest made by Oscar Wurtele to his wife, Mary Viola Wurtele, by his last will and testament was a fee simple absolute. We believe the trial court was correct and affirm the judgment.

As noted, the appeal herein arises out of the last will and testament of Oscar Wurtele, executed on August 4, 1939. While the will is simple and to the point, it is not a model for estate planners. It reads in total as follows:

> I, the undersigned, Oscar Wurtele do hereby make, publish and declare the following as and for my Last Will and Testament:
> I hereby give, devise and bequeath all of my property of every kind and nature to my wife Mary Viola Wurtele to be her property *absolutely with full power in her to make such disposition of said property as she may desire*; conditioned, however, that if any of said property is remaining upon the death of said Mary Viola Wurtele, or in the event that she predeceases me then and in such event such of said property as remains shall vest in my foster daughter Gladys Pauline Sterner and her children.
> I hereby nominate and appoint my said wife, Mary Viola Wurtele, of Nebraska City, Nebraska, as executrix of this My Last Will and Testament.
> Dated at Nebraska City, Nebraska, this 4th day of August, 1939. Oscar Wurtele. [Emphasis supplied.]

Following Oscar Wurtele's death in 1955 his will was admitted to probate in the county court of Otoe County, Nebraska, and all of the property which Oscar Wurtele owned at the time of his death was devised and bequeathed to his wife, Mary Viola Wurtele, to be hers absolutely. Certain of the property, including two commercial buildings, a farm, and a residence, were held in joint tenancy and passed to Mary Viola Wurtele by action of law and are not in any manner involved in this case. Two other commercial buildings, however, did pass to Mary Viola Wurtele by reason of the will of her husband, Oscar Wurtele, as well as certain personal property having an estimated value of $19,000. Mary Viola Wurtele thereafter married one Aaron Rose with whom she lived until her death on March 7, 1978. Mary Viola Rose died testate leaving her property to various individuals, including her husband, Aaron, and certain other nieces and nephews, but leaving no property to the appellants herein who are the foster daughter and her children referred to in the last will and testament of Oscar Wurtele. Aaron Rose died on June 24, 1979.

The evidence further discloses that in 1963 Mary Viola Rose sold the four commercial buildings for a total sale price of $70,000. No division of the sale price was made between the joint tenancy property and the property received under the will of her former husband. It is, however, clear from the evidence that none of the original property devised and bequeathed to Mary Viola Wurtele remained at the time of her death, though she did die owning property, some of which may have been purchased from the proceeds of either the personal property or the sale of the real estate. Following a hearing, the trial court found that the will of Oscar Wurtele devised and bequeathed all of his property to his wife, Mary Viola Wurtele, in fee simple absolute, and granted the personal representative's motion for summary judgment. The trial court's opinion provides in part as follows: "The Court is of the opinion that the language in the Oscar Wurtele will is so precise as to create a fee simple title in the wife, Mary Viola Wurtele."

Appellants have raised a number of errors, but the principal issue which needs to be addressed is whether the devise and bequest by Oscar Wurtele to Mary Viola Wurtele was a fee simple absolute or merely a life estate with authority to dispose of so much of the property as she chose during her lifetime. For, obviously, if we conclude, as the trial court did, that the devise and bequest was a fee simple absolute, then Mary Viola Rose was entitled to do whatever she wished with her property, both during her lifetime and upon her death, and Gladys Pauline Sterner and her children would not be entitled to any portions of the property remaining at the death of Mary Viola Rose. While the issue as so stated is clear, the decisions of our court concerning this matter are not so clear. It is appropriate that we examine this question in order to resolve the dispute.

The general and majority rule is as expressed in 28 Am. Jur. 2d Estates §94 at 198-99 (1966), wherein it provides in part:

It is a well-settled, general rule that where there is a grant, devise, or bequest to one in general terms only, expressing neither fee nor life estate, and there is a subsequent limitation over of what remains at the first taker's death, if there is also given to the first taker an unlimited and unrestricted power of absolute disposal, express or implied, the grant, devise, or bequest to the first taker is construed to pass a fee. The attempted limitation over, following a gift which is in fee with full power of disposition and alienation, is void. Most of the cases arriving at this conclusion are based upon the reasoning that the well-settled rule that a general or indefinite grant or gift, coupled with an absolute or unlimited power or disposition, passes a fee applies with full force and effect even though the will purports to make a gift over of whatever may remain at the death of the grantee or devisee, the purported gift over merely being an invalid repugnancy.

The American Jurisprudence annotation cited above then goes on to note that the general rule is consistently applied even in cases involving wills of slightly different but substantial tenor, a number of which are similar to the language of the Wurtele will.

One may likewise find cases in Nebraska and other jurisdictions to support the general view expressed in the American Jurisprudence citation. In the case of Moffitt v. Williams, 116 Neb. 785, 788, 219 N.W. 138, 139 (1928), we said: . . . "'The settled rule of law is that, if a deed or will conveys an absolute title in fee simple, an inconsistent clause in the instrument attempting merely to limit that title or convey to the same person a limited title in the same land will be disregarded.'"

Cases may likewise be found in a majority of the jurisdictions which support the general rule. In the case of Moran v. Moran, 143 Mich. 322, 323, 106 N.W. 206 (1906), the Michigan Supreme Court was presented a will which provided in part as follows: "'I give and bequeath to my beloved wife . . . all my property real and personal, of every name, nature and description to be hers absolutely, providing however, that if at her death any of the said property be still hers, then the residue still hers shall go to my, not her, nearest heir or heirs.'" The court held that such language created a fee simple absolute in the wife and the provision for the property remaining was void and unenforceable.

In Hicks v. Fairbanks' Heirs, 208 Okla. 346, 347, 256 P.2d 169, 169-70 (1953), the Oklahoma Supreme Court was presented a will which provided in part:

> . . . I give, devise and bequeath unto my beloved wife, Ada Fairbanks all of my estate real and personal and mixed to have and to hold to her and her heirs forever.
> . . . [S]hould any of my estate remain at the death of my said wife Ada Fairbanks undisposed of then in that event I give and bequeath such

remainder to my nephew. . . . This provision is not intended to restrain or hamper my said [wife] . . . in any manner . . . she is to have my entire estate as above provided — and this provision is only to take effect in case any of my estate remains undisposed of at the death of my said wife Ada Fairbanks.

The Supreme Court held that since the widow had been given an absolute power of disposition, she had taken a fee simple title and there was nothing remaining to be taken by the nephew. In so holding the Oklahoma court in Hicks v. Fairbanks' Heirs, supra at 350, 256 P.2d at 172, said:

It is a well-settled rule, firmly supported by a great numerical preponderance of the authorities, that where there is a devise or bequest to one in general terms only, expressing neither fee nor life estate, and there is a subsequent limitation over of what remains at the first taker's death, if there is also given to the first taker an unlimited and unrestricted power of absolute disposal, express or implied, the devise or bequest to the first taker is construed to pass a fee. . . .

In Langston v. Hunt, Adm'r, 269 Ark. 328, 329, 601 S.W.2d 833, 834 (1980), the Arkansas court was presented with a will which provided in part:

I give to my beloved wife, Ethel Deliah Jones, all of my property, both real and personal, of every kind and character, wherever situated. . . . At the death of my said wife . . . I desire that all of my property of which she dies seized of shall be divided among her nearest relatives and my nearest relatives, share and share alike.

Notwithstanding the language of the will, the court held that the devise was of a fee simple and that the remainder over to the heirs was unenforceable. In doing so the Arkansas court said in Langston v. Hunt, Adm'r, supra at 330, 601 S.W.2d at 834:

The present rule simply stated is that a testator cannot give an estate in fee simple by clear and concise language and subsequently diminish or destroy the devise by use of other language. In other words, once the fee is given to a person or class of persons or other devisee, it cannot be thereafter taken away or diminished unless the terms are clear, unequivocal, and demonstrate the intent to limit the prior devise.

To a similar effect see Hendrix v. Hester, 385 So.2d 990 (Ala. 1980); Quickel v. Quickel, 261 N.C. 696, 136 S.E.2d 52 (1964); Virginia National Bank v. United States, 307 F. Supp. 1146 (E.D. Va. 1969), aff'd 443 F.2d 1030 (4th Cir. 1971); Jackson v. Ku Klux Klan, 231 Ky.

370, 21 S.W.2d 477 (1929); Shaw v. Wertz, 369 S.W.2d 215 (Mo. 1963); Rawlings v. Briscoe, 214 Va. 44, 197 S.E.2d 211 (1973).

While this might at first blush seem to make the disposition of this matter relatively easy, unfortunately there are cases to be found in Nebraska which appear to hold to the contrary. The principal case is Merrill v. Pardun, 125 Neb. 701, 251 N.W. 834 (1933). In *Merrill*, supra at 703, 251 N.W. at 835, the testator's will provided in part as follows:

> I give and bequeath to my wife, Maggie Brown, all the rest, residue and remainder of my property of whatever kind and wherever situated to be hers absolutely. It is my request, however, that any of said property remaining on the death of my said wife, shall go to my daughter, Mildred I. Merrill, to be hers absolutely and in case of her prior death then to her children, share and share alike.

This court held that the conveyance was simply a life estate with the power to dispose during one's lifetime. In so holding, we said in *Merrill* at 706, 251 N.W. at 836:

> The general rule under the common law is that, where an estate in fee simple is given in one clause of a will, subsequent clauses attempting to cut down said estate would be void; but in Nebraska, on account of the *peculiar provisions* of our statute regarding the intentions of the testator, in construing a will it is held that, where a will in one clause makes an apparently absolute bequest of property, but in a subsequent clause makes a further bequest of the remainder after the death of the legatee taking under the first clause, the two clauses are to be construed and considered together to ascertain the true character of the estate in fact granted by the first clause; and in such case, contrary to the ancient rule at common law, the second clause is effective and operative to define and limit the estate granted by the first to and as a life estate with power of disposition, and the second is effective and operative to grant an estate in remainder in the unused, unexpended or undisposed property granted for life by the first. (Emphasis supplied.)

As support for such position the *Merrill* case cites the cases of In re Estate of Darr, 114 Neb. 116, 206 N.W. 2 (1925); Krause v. Krause, 113 Neb. 22, 201 N.W. 670 (1924); Heyer v. Heyer, 110 Neb. 784, 195 N.W. 109 (1923); and Grant v. Hover, 103 Neb. 730, 174 N.W. 317 (1919).

However, neither the rationale of the *Merrill* case nor the earlier decisions seems to justify abandoning the general common-law majority rule for what appears to have developed as the Nebraska rule.

In the first instance the *Merrill* decision maintains that we are *compelled* to reach a separate decision because of the "peculiar provisions of our statute regarding the intentions of the testator." The peculiar provisions apparently refer to what was then cited as Comp. Stat. §76-109 (1929), and which is now Neb. Rev. Stat. §76-205 (Reissue 1976). It reads:

> In the construction of every instrument creating or conveying, or authorizing or requiring the creation or conveyance of any real estate, or interest therein, it shall be the duty of the courts of justice to carry into effect the true intent [interest] of the parties, so far as such intent can be collected from the whole instrument, and so far as such intent is consistent with the rules of law.

While the *Merrill* opinion suggests that that statute creates some "peculiar" rule of law, in fact it merely codifies what has always been the common-law rule in both this jurisdiction and in others as well.

The most important aspect of both the statute and the common law was seemingly ignored by the court in Merrill v. Pardun, 125 Neb. 701, 251 N.W.2d 834 (1933). Both the statute, §76-205, and the common law provide that in attempting to ascertain the true intent of the testator you cannot ignore the rules of law applicable to a situation. A testator may intend to violate the rule against perpetuities in his will. The statute, nevertheless, cannot permit such action even if the testator's intent to that effect is absolute and clear. . . .

In the instant case it is not possible to reconcile the devise given by Oscar Wurtele to his wife, on the one hand, and the expression of desire concerning his foster daughter, on the other.

The grant to Mary Viola Wurtele was clear and unambiguous. She was to have the property to "be her property absolutely with full power in her to make such disposition of said property as she may desire." That intent is clear. By having the property as hers "absolutely" and with "full power" to "dispose" of the property as she may desire, she had not only the right to sell or give away the property during her lifetime but the right to will the property upon her death as well. Anything less would not have granted her the property "absolutely" with "full power in her to make such disposition" as she desired. The authority given was not limited to sale or disposition during her lifetime, but rather was to be *absolute*. . . .

No reason is given to us nor are we able to find any on our own as to why the majority rule following the common law should not be the rule in this jurisdiction. Certainly the reason suggested by the court in the *Merrill* decision, to wit, the particular nature of our statute, is not very persuasive. If the testator does not desire for the devisee to have a fee simple, it is easy enough to say so. But having once granted the devise or bequest in language which standing alone constitutes an absolute conveyance, the balance of the limitations should be disregarded, regardless of the intent of the testator, on the basis that the intent is in conflict with the first grant. Either a devisee has received the property absolutely or the devisee has not received the property absolutely. Like honesty, morality, and pregnancy, an absolute devise cannot be qualified.

To be sure, a testator can give less than absolute grant, as was done in the case of Annable v. Ricedorff, 140 Neb. 93, 95, 299 N.W. 373, 375 (1941), where the testator provided his property to his wife "'to her own use and benefit forever; and it is my desire and wish that after her death, that all the property remaining'" go to his children. In such a case it can be argued that only a life estate was granted to the wife for her use and benefit during her lifetime. But where, as here, the devise is "absolute," we can reach no other conclusion but that the grant was a fee simple. As such, it is without qualification regardless of what the testator may intend.

We, therefore, now adopt the majority rule to the effect that where there is a grant, devise, or bequest to one in general terms only, expressing neither fee nor life estate, and there is a subsequent limitation over of what remains at the first taker's death, if there is also given to the first taker an unlimited and unrestricted power of absolute disposal, express or implied, the grant, devise, or bequest to the first taker is construed to pass a fee. The attempted limitation over, following a gift which is in fee with full power of disposition and alienation, is void. To the extent that our previous decision in *Merrill* and cases of similar import are to the contrary, they are overruled.

Having thus concluded that the trial court was correct in ruling that the devise and bequest by Oscar Wurtele to his wife, Mary Viola Wurtele, was as a matter of law a fee simple absolute, there remained no question of fact to be resolved and the trial court was correct in granting summary judgment. . . . The judgment of the trial court, therefore, is affirmed.

Affirmed.

NOTES AND QUESTIONS

1. Oscar Wurtele's will appears to have been drafted by a lawyer. Should the lawyer be liable to Gladys for malpractice? See St. Mary's Church of Schuyler v. Tomek, 212 Neb. 728, 325 N.W.2d 164 (1982); Dukeminier, Cleansing the Stables of Property: A River Found at Last, 65 Iowa L. Rev. 151, 169-170 (1979). See also Fratcher, Bequest of Orts, 48 Mo. L. Rev. 475 (1983), for discussion of successful ways to make a gift over to B of whatever is left on A's death.

2. In Sterner v. Nelson, the court says, "No reason is given to us nor are we able to find any on our own as to why the majority rule following the common law should not be the rule in this jurisdiction."

If counsel and court had dug a bit deeper, they should have unearthed an extended, critical treatment of the rule of repugnancy in 3 L. Simes & A. Smith, The Law of Future Interests §§1481-1491 (2d ed. 1956), or the summary of criticisms, originating with Professor Gray, in 6 American Law of Property §26.43 (1952). The latter authority says, "Only in Nebraska has the rule been directly repudiated." Id. §26.45. Alas, that is no longer true. For more criticism of this senseless rule, see the dissenting opinion of Chief Justice Vanderbilt in Fox v. Snow, 6 N.J. 12, 76 A.2d 877 (1950). See also Note, Estates Coupled with Powers of Disposition in Tennessee, 15 Mem. St. U.L. Rev. 415 (1985).

3.   One thing can be said in favor of the rule of repugnancy applied in Sterner v. Nelson. It enables the court to avoid hard questions. If the devise over to Gladys were valid, could Mary Viola use the devised property to support her second husband, to take a round-the-world cruise, to spend the winter in Florida, to build a room on her house? Could she give away the property? Does Mary Viola have to give a bond to protect Gladys' interest in the personal property valued at $19,000? These questions often arise where the life tenant is given a power to consume, and litigation over ambiguous language is extensive. See Annots., 31 A.L.R.3d 6 (1970) (158 pages); id. at 169 (129 pages); id. at 309 (61 pages). Compare the rights of the survivor whose property is bound by a contract not to revoke a will, supra page 278.

A good attorney will never create a *legal* fee simple with the power to consume because of the danger of running afoul of the rule of repugnancy. Nor will a good attorney create a *legal* life estate at all; a trust with a life beneficiary is preferable in almost all situations (see supra page 444 for reasons why). If the life beneficiary of a trust is to have rights to consume the principal, the attorney drafting a will or trust should make it as clear as possible under exactly what circumstances the life tenant can reach the principal. See Andersen, Informed Decisionmaking in an Office Practice, 28 B.C.L. Rev. 225, 239-241 (1987) (recommending complete discussion between lawyer and client).

NOTE: TAXATION OF POWERS TO CONSUME

Property subject to a general power of appointment is in the donee's federal gross estate at death and subject to estate taxation (see page 985 infra). If a power to consume permits the donee to appoint the property to herself during life, it is a general power of appointment. However, there is an important exception in the tax laws. Internal Revenue Code of 1986, §2041(b)(1)(A) provides that "A power to consume, invade, or appropriate property for the benefit of the decedent which is limited by an ascertainable standard relating to the health, education, support, or maintenance of the decedent shall not be deemed a general power of appointment." Hence the tax question respecting each power to consume is: Is the power at hand limited by an ascertainable standard relating to the health, education, support, or maintenance of the decedent? If it is not so limited, the property subject to the power is included in the donee's gross estate. The lawyer drafting a power to consume must choose words very, very carefully and track the words of §2041(b)(1)(A) or the regulations. A power to consume for the donee's "comfort, welfare, or happiness" is not limited by the requisite standard. Nor, in the opinion of the Internal Revenue Service, is a power to invade corpus "to *continue* the donee's accustomed standard of living." A revenue ruling provides:

> A power to use property to enable the donee to continue an accustomed mode of living without further limitation, although predictable and measurable on the basis of past expenditures, does not come within the ascertainable standard prescribed in section 2041(B)(1)(A) of the Code since the standard of living may include customary travel, entertainment, luxury items, or other expenditures not required for meeting the donee's "needs for health, education or support." Nor does the requirement of a good faith exercise of a power create an ascertainable standard. Good faith exercise of a power is not determinative of its breadth. [Rev. Rul. 77-60, 1977-1 C.B. 282.]

On the other hand, a power to consume "to *maintain* the standard of living to which the donee is accustomed" is regarded as limited by the requisite standard. I.R.S. Letter Ruling 7914036 (Jan. 3, 1979), Fed. Est. & Gift Tax Rep. (CCH) ¶12,266. And a power to consume "as needed for his reasonable health, education, support and maintenance needs *consistent with a high standard and quality of living*" is measured by the requisite standard. I.R.S. Letter Ruling 7836008 (May 30, 1978), Fed. Est. & Gift Tax Rep. (CCH) ¶12,187. If the instrument says the donee of the power is the "sole judge" of the necessity of consuming corpus, very likely the donee will be held to have a general power of appointment. See Rev. Rul. 77-194, 1977-1 C.B. 283. See also infra pages 991-992.

The lawyer drafting a trust instrument may decide that rather than give the donee a power to consume, it is safer to give a trustee who is not the beneficiary a discretionary power to use corpus to maintain the beneficiary in the style of living to which she is accustomed.

SECTION C. RELEASE OF A POWER OF APPOINTMENT

The donor of a life estate coupled with a testamentary power usually intends to protect the donee from an indiscreet or unwise exercise of the power during life. A testamentary power has as one of its purposes keeping the donee free to exercise discretion up until the moment of death. Hence, the donee of a testamentary power of appointment cannot legally contract to make an appointment in the future. Such a contract cannot be specifically enforced nor can damages be awarded for breach. If the law were otherwise, the donee of a testamentary power could in effect exercise the power during life by contracting to exercise it. Courts will not allow the donor's intent to be defeated in this manner. The promisee of the contract may, however, obtain restitution of the value that the promisee gave the donee.

Although a contract to exercise a testamentary power is not enforceable, a result somewhat close to that which the donee wants to obtain by a contract may sometimes be obtained by releasing the power of appointment. If a power is released, the uncertainty it creates as to the ultimate takers is removed. Thus:

> *Case 5. T* devises property in trust for *A* for life, then as *A* by will appoints, and in default of appointment to *A*'s children equally. *A* releases her power of appointment. *A*'s children now have an indefeasibly vested remainder. *A* could not contract to appoint to her children, but she may achieve her objective by a release.

All powers of appointment except powers in trust or imperative powers have been made releasable in all jurisdictions either by judicial decision or by statute. A releasable power may be released with respect to the whole or any part of the appointive property and may also be released in such manner as to reduce or limit the permissible appointees. See Restatement (Second) of Property, Donative Transfers §§14.1, 14.2 (1986), including Statutory Notes and Reporter's Notes.

Seidel v. Werner

New York Supreme Court, Special Term, New York County, 1975
81 Misc. 2d 220, 364 N.Y.S.2d 963,
aff'd on opinion below, 50 A.D.2d 743, 376 N.Y.S.2d 139

SILVERMAN, J. Plaintiffs, trustees of a trust established in 1919 by Abraham L. Werner, sue for a declaratory judgment to determine who is entitled to one-half of the principal of the trust fund — the share in which Steven L. Werner, decedent (hereinafter "Steven"), was the life beneficiary and over which he had a testamentary power of appointment. The dispute concerns the manner in which Steven exercised his power of appointment and is between Steven's second wife, Harriet G. Werner (hereinafter "Harriet"), along with their children, Anna G. and

Frank S. Werner (hereinafter "Anna" and "Frank") and Steven's third wife, Edith Fisch Werner (hereinafter "Edith").

Anna and Frank claim Steven's entire share of the trust remainder on the basis of a Mexican consent judgment of divorce, obtained by Steven against Harriet on December 9, 1963, which incorporated by reference and approved a separation agreement, entered into between Steven and Harriet on December 1, 1963. That agreement included the following provision:

> 10.   The Husband shall make, and hereby promises not to revoke, a will in which he shall exercise his testamentary power of appointment over his share in a trust known as "Abraham L. Werner Trust No. 1" by establishing with respect to said share a trust for the benefit of the aforesaid Children, for the same purposes and under the same terms and conditions, as the trust provided for in Paragraph "9" of this Agreement, insofar as said terms and conditions are applicable thereto.

Paragraph 9 in relevant part provides for the wife to receive the income of the trust, upon the death of the husband, for the support and maintenance of the children, until they reach twenty-one years of age, at which time they are to receive the principal in equal shares.

On March 20, 1964, less than four months after entry of the divorce judgment, Steven executed a will in which instead of exercising his testamentary power of appointment in favor of Anna and Frank, he left everything to his third wife, Edith:

> First, I give, devise and bequeath all of my property . . . including . . . all property over which I have a power of testamentary disposition, to my wife, Edith Fisch Werner.

Steven died in April 1971 and his Will was admitted to probate by the Surrogate's Court of New York County on July 11, 1973.

(1) Paragraph 10 of the Separation Agreement is a contract to exercise a testamentary power of appointment not presently exercisable (EPTL 10-3.3) and as such is invalid under EPTL 10-5.3, which provides as follows:

> (a) The donee of a power of appointment which is not presently exercisable or of a postponed power which has not become exercisable, cannot contract to make an appointment. Such a contract, if made, cannot be the basis of an action for specific performance or damages, but the promise can obtain restitution of the value given by him for the promise unless the donee has exercised the power pursuant to the contract.

This is a testamentary power of appointment. The original trust instrument provided in relevant part that: ". . . Upon the death of such child [Steven] the principal of such share shall be disposed of as such child shall by its last will direct, and in default of such testamentary disposition then the same shall go to the issue of such child then surviving per stirpes. . . ." It is not disputed that New York law is determinative of the validity of Paragraph 10 of the Separation Agreement; the Separation Agreement itself provides that New York law shall govern.

The reasoning underlying the refusal to enforce a contract to exercise a testamentary power was stated by Justice Cardozo in the case of Farmers' Loan & Trust Co. v. Mortimer, 219 N.Y. 290, 293-4, 114 N.E. 389, 390 (1916):

> The exercise of the power was to represent the final judgment, the last will, of the donee. Up to the last moment of his life he was to have the power to deal with the share as he thought best. . . . To permit him to bargain that right away would be to defeat the purpose of the donor. Her command was that her property should go to her son's issue unless at the end of his life it remained his will that it go elsewhere. It has not remained his will that it go elsewhere; and his earlier contract cannot nullify the expression of his final purpose. "It is not, I apprehend, to be doubted," says Rolt, L.J., in Cooper v. Martin, L.R. [3 Ch. App.] 47, 58, "that equity . . . will never uphold an act which will defeat what the person creating the power has declared, by expression or necessary implication, to be a material part of his intention."

See also, In re Estate of Brown, 33 N.Y.2d 211, 351 N.Y.S.2d 655, 306 N.E.2d 781 (1973).

(2) The question then is whether entry of the Mexican divorce decree, incorporating the Separation Agreement, alters this result; I do not think it does. . . .

[The court held that the Mexican divorce decree was not controlling, because, first, it did not direct Steven to exercise his power of appointment but merely approved the separation agreement as fair and reasonable, and, second, the Mexican court did not pass on or consider rules of New York property law.]

(3) As indicated, the statute makes a promise to exercise a testamentary power in a particular way unenforceable. However, EPTL 10-5.3(b) permits a donee of a power to release the power, and that release, if in conformity with EPTL 10-9.2, prevents the donee from then exercising the power thereafter.

Under the terms of the trust instrument, if Steven fails to exercise his power of appointment, Anna and Frank (along with the children of Steven's first marriage) take the remainder, i.e., the property which is the subject of Steven's power of appointment. Therefore, Harriet, Anna and Frank argue that at a minimum Steven's agreement should be construed as a release of his power of appointment, and that Anna and Frank should be permitted to take as on default of appointment.

There is respectable authority — by no means unanimous authority, and none binding on this Court — to the effect that a promise to appoint a given sum to persons who would take in default of appointment should, *to that extent,* be deemed a release of the power of appointment. See Restatement of Property §336 (1940); Simes and Smith, The Law of Future Interests §1016 (1956).

This argument has the appeal that it seems to be consistent with the exception that the release statute (EPTL 10-5.3(b)) carves out of EPTL 10-5.3(a); and is also consistent with the intentions and reasonable expectation of the parties at the time they entered into the agreement to appoint, here in the separation agreement; and that therefore perhaps in these circumstances the difference between what the parties agreed to and a release of the power of appointment is merely one of form. Whatever may be the possible validity or applicability of this argument to other circumstances and situations, I think it is inapplicable to this situation because:

(a)   It is clear that the parties did not intend a release of the power of appointment. Cf. Matter of Haskell, 59 Misc. 2d 797, 300 N.Y.S.2d 711 (N.Y. Co. 1969). Indeed, the agreement — unlike a release of a power of appointment — expressly contemplates that something will be done by the donee of the power in the future, and that that something will be an exercise of the power of appointment. Thus, the agreement, in the very language said to be a release of the power of appointment, says (Par. 10): "the Husband *shall* make . . . a will in which he *shall exercise* his testamentary power of appointment. . . ." (emphasis added).

(b)   Nor is the substantial effect of the promised exercise of the power the same as would follow from release of, or failure to exercise the power.

(i)   Under the separation agreement, the power is to be exercised so that the entire appointive property shall be for the benefit of Anna and Frank; under the trust instrument, on default of exercise of the power, the property goes to all of Steven's children (Anna, Frank and two children of Steven's first marriage). Thus the agreement provides for appointment of a greater principal to Anna and Frank than they would get in default of appointment.

(ii)   Under the trust instrument, on default of exercise of the power, the property goes to the four children absolutely and in fee. The separation agreement provides that Steven shall create a *trust,* with *income* payable to *Harriet as trustee,* for the support of Anna and Frank until they both reach the age of 21, at which time the principal shall be paid to them or the survivor; and if both fail to attain the age of 21, then the principal shall revert to Steven's estate. Thus, Anna and

Frank's interest in the principal would be a defeasible interest if they did not live to be 21; and indeed at Steven's death they were both still under 21 so that their interest was defeasible.

(iii) Finally, under the separation agreement, as just noted, if Anna and Frank failed to qualify to take the principal, either because they both died before Steven or before reaching the age of twenty-one, then the principal would go to Steven's estate. Under the trust instrument, on the other hand, on default of appointment and an inability of Anna and Frank to take, Steven's share of the principal would not go to Steven's estate, but to his other children, if living, and if not, to the settlor's next of kin.

In these circumstances, I think it is too strained and tortuous to construe the separation agreement provision as the equivalent of a release of the power of appointment. If this is a release then the exception of EPTL 10-5.3(b) has swallowed and destroyed the principal rule of EPTL 10-5.3(a).

I note that in Wood v. American Security and Trust Co., 253 F. Supp. 592, 594 (D.D.C. 1966), the principal case relied upon by Harriet, Anna and Frank on this point, the Court said: "The Court finds that it is significant that the disposition resulting from the agreement is in accordance with the wishes of the testator in the event the power should not be exercised."[8]

Furthermore, the language of the instrument in that case was much more consistent with the non-exercise of the power of appointment than in the case at bar.

Accordingly, I hold that the separation agreement is not the equivalent of a total or partial release of the power of appointment.

(4) Anna and Frank also seek restitution out of the trust fund of the value given by them in exchange for Steven's unfulfilled promise. EPTL 10-5.3(a) provides that although the contract to make an appointment cannot be the basis for an action for specific performance or damages, "the promisee can obtain restitution of the value given by him for the promise unless the donee has exercised the power pursuant to contract."

Anna and Frank's remedy is limited, however, to the claim for restitution that they have (and apparently have asserted) against Steven's estate. They may not seek restitution out of the trust fund, even if their allegation that the estate lacks sufficient assets to meet this claim were factually supported, because the trust fund was not the property of

---

8. In the *Wood* case, *T* devised property in trust to pay the income to his four children, "the last survivor of my children to have the disposition of such property by will, and in case no will is made, the property to go according to the laws of inheritance." The children then entered into an agreement providing that on the death of the last child the corpus should be divided into four shares and distributed among their respective issue per stirpes. Subsequently the last surviving child died, appointing all the corpus to his wife. The court held the agreement was a valid release. — Eds.

Steven, except to the extent of his life estate, so as to be subject to the equitable remedy of restitution, but was the property of the donor of the power of appointment until it vested in someone else. Farmers' Loan & Trust Co. v. Mortimer, 219 N.Y. 290, 295, 114 N.E. 389, 390 (1916); see Matter of Rosenthal, 283 App. Div. 316, 319, 127 N.Y.S.2d 778, 780 (1st Dept. 1954); see also EPTL §§10-7.1 and 10-7.4.

(5)   Finally, Edith moves for summary judgment that she is entitled to receive Steven's share of the trust fund on the ground that Steven exercised his testamentary power in her favor in his will of March 20, 1964, in the provision quoted at the beginning of this decision.

Since there are no factual questions raised as to Steven's exercise of his testamentary power of appointment in Edith's favor in that will provision, and since each of the other defendants' conflicting claims to the share of trust principal has been dismissed, Edith's motion for summary judgment is granted.

(6)   Accordingly, on the motions for summary judgment I direct judgment declaring that defendant Edith Fisch Werner is entitled to the one-half share of Steven C. Werner in the principal of the Abraham L. Werner trust; to the extent that the counterclaims and cross-claims asserted by Harriet, Anna and Frank seek relief other than a declaratory judgment, they are dismissed.[9]

NOTE

How are remainders in default of appointment classified? Can they be vested subject to divestment by exercise of the power of appointment or are they always contingent because subject to the condition precedent of nonexercise of the power? The answer is the former. Powers of appointment are always viewed as involving the exercise of a condition subsequent, depriving the remaindermen of the property. For example, suppose that *T* devises property in trust "for *A* for life, then to such persons as *A* by will appoints, and in default of appointment to the children of *A*." *A* has one child, *B*. This conveyance is read as if it were "to *A* for life, then to *A*'s children, but if *A* otherwise appoints by will, to such appointees." Thus *B* has a vested remainder subject to open and also subject to complete defeasance by *A*'s exercise of his power of appointment. See Note, Remainders Over in Default of Exercise of Powers of Appointment and Revocation, 106 U. Pa. L. Rev. 420 (1958).

In Seidel v. Werner the remainder in default of appointment was given to the "issue of [Steven] then living per stirpes." It is a contingent remainder because the class of takers cannot be ascertained until Steven's death; his issue must survive him in order to take. It is not contingent on the ground that it is subject to nonexercise of a power of appointment.

9. The case is discussed in Fetters, Future Interests, 27 Syracuse L. Rev. 365, 366-377 (1976). — Eds.

SECTION D.   EXERCISE OF A POWER OF APPOINTMENT

1. *Exercise by Residuary Clause in Donee's Will*

Beals v. State Street Bank & Trust Co.
Supreme Judicial Court of Massachusetts, 1975
367 Mass. 318, 326 N.E.2d 896

WILKINS, J.   The trustees under the will of Arthur Hunnewell filed this petition for instructions, seeking a determination of the proper distribution to be made of a portion of the trust created under the residuary clause of his will. A judge of the Probate Court reserved decision and reported the case to the Appeals Court on the pleadings and a stipulation of facts. We transferred the case here.

Arthur Hunnewell died, a resident of Wellesley, in 1904, leaving his wife and four daughters. His will placed the residue of his property in a trust, the income of which was to be paid to his wife during her life. At the death of his wife the trust was to be divided in portions, one for each then surviving daughter and one for the then surviving issue of any deceased daughter. Mrs. Hunnewell died in 1930. One of the four daughters predeceased her mother, leaving no issue. The trust was divided, therefore, in three portions at the death of Mrs. Hunnewell. The will directed that the income of each portion held for a surviving daughter should be paid to her during her life and on her death the principal of such portion should "be paid and disposed of as she may direct and appoint by her last Will and Testament duly probated." In default of appointment, the will directed that a daughter's share should be distributed to "the persons who would be entitled to such estate under the laws then governing the distribution of intestate estates."

This petition concerns the distribution of the trust portion held for the testator's daughter Isabella H. Hunnewell, later Isabella H. Dexter (Isabella). Following the death of her mother, Isabella requested the trustees to exercise their discretionary power to make principal payments by transferring substantially all of her trust share "to the Dexter family office in Boston, there to be managed in the first instance by her husband, Mr. Gordon Dexter." This request was granted, and cash and securities were transferred to her account at the Dexter office. The Hunnewell trustees, however, retained in Isabella's share a relatively small cash balance, an undivided one-third interest in a mortgage and undivided one-third interest in various parcels of real estate in the Commonwealth, which Isabella did not want in kind and which the trustees could not sell at a reasonable price at the time. Thereafter, the trustees received payments on the mortgage and proceeds from occasional sales of portions of the real estate. From her one-third share of these receipts, the trustees made further distributions to her of $1,900 in 1937, $22,000 in 1952, and $5,000 in 1953.

In February, 1944, Isabella, who was then a resident of New York, executed and caused to be filed in the Registry of Probate for Norfolk County an instrument which partially released her general power of appointment under the will of her father. See G.L. c. 204, §§27-36, inserted by St. 1943, c. 152. Isabella released her power of appointment "to the extent that such power empowers me to appoint to any one other than one or more of the . . . descendants me surviving of Arthur Hunnewell."

On December 14, 1968, Isabella, who survived her husband, died without issue, still a resident of New York, leaving a will dated May 21, 1965.[10] Her share in the trust under her father's will then consisted of

---

10. N.Y. Times, Sept. 28, 1894, at 5, col. 4:

HARRIMAN — HUNNEWELL

Boston, Mass., Sept. 27. — The beautiful country seat of Mr. and Mrs. Arthur Hunnewell, at Wellesley, was a scene of joy and festivity yesterday, when their daughter, Miss Isabella, was married to Herbert M. Harriman of New-York. The ceremony was performed by the Rev. Leighton Parks, pastor of the Emanuel Church. There were no bridesmaids. The groom's brother, Joseph, was best man.

The ushers were Lawrence Kip of New-York, Belmont Tiffany of New-York, Edgar Scott of Philadelphia, Columbus Baldwin of New-York, Gordon Dexter, and W.S. Patten. Of the bridegroom's kinsfolk there were present: His mother, Mr. and Mrs. Border Harriman, and Mr. and Mrs. Oliver Harriman.

The wedding breakfast was spread beneath the grand old trees which dot the lawn before the mansion. At the expiration of a short wedding trip Mr. and Mrs. Harriman will reside in New-York.

A year after the wedding, Herbert Harriman obtained an $18-a-week clerkship in the West, through his cousin E.H. Harriman of the Union Pacific Railroad. But after a few months he abandoned his plan to work his way up in the railroad world and returned to New York, where he was a champion amateur golfer and a prominent figure in New York and Newport society. Herbert and Isabella identified themselves with the "Meadow Brook set." They were divorced in 1906. N.Y. Times, Jan. 4, 1933, at 17, col. 4 (Harriman's obituary).

N.Y. Times, Dec. 16, 1968, at 47, col. 1:

MRS. GORDON DEXTER

Mrs. Isabella Hunnewell Dexter, widow of Gordon Dexter, a Boston businessman, clubman and yachtsman, died Saturday in her home at 680 Madison Avenue. Her age was 97.

Mrs. Dexter's previous marriages, to Herbert M. Harriman and J. Searlo Barclay, ended in divorce.

— Eds.

an interest in a contract to sell real estate, cash, notes and a certificate of deposit, and was valued at approximately $88,000. Isabella did not expressly exercise her power of appointment under her father's will. The residuary clause of her will provided in effect for the distribution of all "the rest, residue and remainder of my property" to the issue per stirpes of her sister Margaret Blake, who had predeceased Isabella.[11] The Blake issue would take one-half of Isabella's trust share, as takers in default of appointment, in all events. If, however, Isabella's will should be treated as effectively exercising her power of appointment under her father's will, the Blake issue would take the entire trust share, and the executors of the will of Isabella's sister Jane (who survived Isabella and has since died) would not receive that one-half of the trust share which would go to Jane in default of appointment.

In support of their argument that Isabella's will did not exercise the power of appointment under her father's will, the executors of Jane's estate contend that (1) Massachusetts substantive law governs all questions relating to the power of appointment, including the interpretation of Isabella's will; (2) the power should be treated as a special power of appointment because of its partial release by Isabella; and (3) because Isabella's will neither expresses nor implies any intention to exercise the power, the applicable rule of construction in this Commonwealth is that a general residuary clause does not exercise a special power of appointment. The Blake issue, in support of their argument that the power was exercised, contend that (1) Isabella's will manifests an intention to exercise the power and that no rule of construction need be applied; (2) the law of New York should govern the question whether Isabella's will exercised the power and, if it does, by statute New York has adopted a rule that a special power of appointment is exercised by a testamentary disposition of all of the donee's property; and (3) if Massachusetts law does apply, and the will is silent on the subject of the exercise of the power, the principles underlying our rule of construction that a residuary clause exercises a general power of appointment are applicable in these circumstances.

    1.   We turn first to a consideration of the question whether Isabella's

---

11. The significant portion of the residuary clause reads as follows:

All the rest, residue and remainder of my property of whatever kind and wherever situated (including any property not effectively disposed of by the preceding provisions of this my will and all property over which I have or may have the power of appointment under or by virtue of the last will and testament dated November 27, 1933 and codicils thereto dated January 7, 1935 and January 8, 1935 of my husband, the late Gordon Dexter) . . . I give, devise, bequeath and appoint in equal shares to such of my said nephew George Baty Blake and my said nieces Margaret Cabot and Julia O. Beals as shall survive me and the issue who shall survive me of any of my said nephew or nieces who may predecease me, such issue to take per stirpes.

will should be construed according to the law of this Commonwealth or the law of New York.[12] There are strong, logical reasons for turning to the law of the donee's domicil at the time of death to determine whether a donee's will has exercised a testamentary power of appointment over movables. See Restatement 2d: Conflict of Laws, §275, comment c (1971); Scott, Trusts, §642, p.4065 (3d ed. 1967); Scoles, Goodrich's Conflict of Laws, §§175-177, p.346 (4th ed. 1964). Most courts in this country which have considered the question, however, interpret the donee's will under the law governing the administration of the trust, which is usually the law of the donor's domicil. . . . This has long been the rule in Massachusetts. . . . Fiduciary Trust Co. v. First Natl. Bank, 344 Mass. 1, 2, 181 N.E.2d 6 (1962) (inter vivos trust).[13]

If the question were before us now for the first time, we might well adopt a choice of law rule which would turn to the substantive law of the donee's domicil, for the purpose of determining whether the donee's will exercised a power of appointment. However, in a field where much depends on certainty and consistency as to the applicable rules of law, we think that we should adhere to our well established rule. Thus, in interpreting the will of a donee to determine whether a power of appointment was exercised, we apply the substantive law of the jurisdiction whose law governs the administration of the trust.

2.   Considering the arguments of the parties, we conclude that there is no indication in Isabella's will of an intention to exercise or not to exercise the power of appointment given to her under her father's will. A detailed analysis of the various competing contentions would not add to our jurisprudence.[14] In the absence of an intention disclosed by her

---

12. The applicable rules of construction where a donee's intention is not clear from his will differ between the two States. In the absence of a requirement by the donor that the donee refer to the power in order to exercise it, New York provides by statute that a residuary clause in a will exercises not only a general power of appointment but also a special power of appointment, unless the will expressly or by necessary implication shows the contrary. 17B McKinney's Consol. Laws of N.Y. Anno., E.P.T.L., c. 17-b, §10-6.1 (1967). See Matter of Hopkins, 46 Misc. 2d 273, 276, 259 N.Y.S.2d 565 (1964). "'Necessary implication'" exists only where the will permits no other construction. Matter of Deane, 4 N.Y.2d 326, 330, 175 N.Y.S.2d 21, 151 N.E.2d 184 (1958). In Massachusetts, unless the donor has provided that the donee of the power can exercise it only by explicit reference to the power, a general residuary clause in a will exercises a general power of appointment unless there is a clear indication of a contrary intent. . . . However, in Fiduciary Trust Co. v. First Natl. Bank, 344 Mass. 1, 6-10, 181 N.E.2d 6 (1962), we held that a general residuary clause did not exercise a special testamentary power of appointment in the circumstances of that case.

13. Of course, the law of the donee's domicile would be applied if the donor expressed such an intention. . . .

14. Isabella's residuary clause disposed of her "property." Because the trustees had agreed to distribute her trust portion to her and had largely done so and because, in a sense, she had exercised dominion over the trust assets by executing the partial release, a reasonable argument might be made that she regarded the assets in her portion of the trust as her "property." However, a conclusion that she intended by implication to include

will construed in light of circumstances known to her when she executed it, we must adopt some Massachusetts rule of construction to resolve the issue before us. The question is what rule of construction. We are unaware of any decided case which, in this context, has dealt with a testamentary general power, reduced to a special power by action of the donee.

3.   We conclude that the residuary clause of Isabella's will should be presumed to have exercised the power of appointment. We reach this result by a consideration of the reasons underlying the canons of construction applicable to general and special testamentary powers of appointment. Considered in this way, we believe that a presumption of exercise is more appropriate in the circumstances of this case than a presumption of nonexercise.

When this court first decided not to extend to a special power of appointment the rule of construction that a general residuary clause executes a general testamentary power (unless a contrary intent is shown by the will), we noted significant distinctions between a general power and a special power. Fiduciary Trust Co. v. First Natl. Bank, 344 Mass. at 6-10, 181 N.E.2d 6. A general power was said to be a close approximation to a property interest, a "virtually unlimited power of disposition," while a special power of appointment lacked this quality. We observed that a layman having a general testamentary power over property might not be expected to distinguish between the appointive property and that which he owns outright, and thus "he can reasonably be presumed to regard this appointive property as his own." On the other hand, the donee of a special power would not reasonably regard such appointive property as his own: "[h]e would more likely consider himself to be, as the donor of the power intended, merely the person chosen by the donor to decide who of the possible appointees should share in the property (if the power is exclusive), and the respective shares of the appointees."

Considering the power of appointment given to Isabella and her treatment of that power during her life, the rationale for the canon of construction applicable to general powers of appointment should be applied in this case. This power was a general testamentary power at its inception. During her life, as a result of her request, Isabella had the use and enjoyment of the major portion of the property initially placed in her trust share. Prior use and enjoyment of the appointive property is a factor properly considered as weighing in favor of the exercise of a power of appointment by a will. Fiduciary Trust Co. v.

---

assets over which she had a special power of appointment within the word "property" is not justifiable because her residuary clause refers expressly to other property over which she had a special power of appointment under the will of her husband.

First Natl. Bank, supra, at 10, 181 N.E.2d 6. Isabella voluntarily limited the power by selecting the possible appointees. In thus relinquishing the right to add the trust assets to her estate, she was treating the property as her own. Moreover, the gift under her residuary clause was consistent with the terms of the reduced power which she retained. In these circumstances, the partial release of a general power does not obviate the application of that rule of construction which presumes that a general residuary clause exercises a general power of appointment.

4. A decree shall be entered determining that Isabella H. Dexter did exercise the power of appointment, partially released by an instrument dated February 25, 1944, given to her by art. Fourth of the will of Arthur Hunnewell and directing that the trustees under the will of Arthur Hunnewell pay over the portion of the trust held under art. Fourth of his will for the benefit of Isabella H. Dexter, as follows: one-third each to George Baty Blake and Julia O. Beals; and one-sixth each to Margaret B. Elwell and to the estate of George B. Cabot. The parties shall be allowed their costs and counsel fees in the discretion of the probate court.

So ordered.

NOTES AND PROBLEMS

1. In White v. United States, 680 F.2d 1156 (7th Cir. 1982), the court held that the law of the donee's domicile governs issues concerning the donee's intention to exercise a power of appointment by will. The court said: "We recognize the special need for certainty and consistency in laws affecting trusts [citing *Beals*], but fail to see how that end is promoted by perpetuation of a legal fiction that confuses lawyers and laymen alike."

2. Considerable disagreement exists over whether a residuary clause should presumptively exercise a general or special power of appointment. The large majority of jurisdictions takes the position that a residuary clause does *not* exercise a power of appointment held by the testator. This is also the position of Uniform Probate Code §2-610 (1983), which provides:

> A general residuary clause in a will, or a will making general disposition of all of the testator's property, does not exercise a power of appointment held by the testator unless specific reference is made to the power or there is some other indication of intention to include the property subject to the power.

States adhering to the majority rule differ on whether the search for a contrary intent is limited to the face of the will or may be aided by extrinsic evidence. The Uniform Probate Code permits extrinsic evidence to be used to show intent. Restatement (Second) of Property, Donative Transfers §17.3 (1986), presumes that a residuary clause does not exercise a power because "the donee does not own the property subject to the power" but permits use of a wide variety of extrinsic evidence to show a contrary intent.

In a minority of jurisdictions a residuary clause exercises a general power of appointment unless a contrary intent affirmatively appears. In a few jurisdictions — New York is the leading example — a residuary clause exercises a special power of appointment if the residuary devisees are objects of the power.

At the time of the *Beals* case, Massachusetts adhered to the minority rule, but in 1978, Massachusetts enacted Uniform Probate Code §2-610. See Mass. Gen. Laws Ann. ch. 191, §1(A)(4) (1981). A number of other states that formerly adhered to the minority rule have in the recent past enacted statutes adopting the majority rule.

The positions of the various states are analyzed in detail in French, Exercise of Powers of Appointment: Should Intent to Exercise Be Inferred from a General Disposition of Property?, 1979 Duke L.J. 749.

3. *Requiring a specific reference.* To prevent an unintentional exercise of a power of appointment, the donor may provide that the power can be exercised only by an instrument, executed after the date of the creating instrument, that refers specifically to the power. However, different courts may have different ideas about whether general language in the donee's will exercising a power is a specific reference to the power. For example, in Clinton County National Bank & Trust Co. v. First National Bank of Cincinnati, 62 Ohio St. 2d 90, 403 N.E.2d 968 (1980), the donee's residuary clause provided: "All the rest, residue and remainder of my estate, of every kind and nature and wheresoever situated, *which I may own or have the power to dispose of at the time of my death*, I hereby give, devise and bequeath" to A. The court held that this was not a specific reference and the power was not exercised. But in Cross v. Cross, 559 S.W.2d 196 (Mo. App. 1977), a reference in the donee's residuary clause — *"including all property over which I have a power of appointment, which power I hereby exercise,"* — was held to be a specific reference to the power and hence the power was exercised. See also Annot., 15 A.L.R. 4th 810 (1982); Restatement (Second) of Property, supra, §17.1, Reporter's Note.

4. The lawyer drafting an instrument creating a power should consider whether it is wise to avoid possible conflict of laws problems by specifying in the trust instrument that the law of a particular state governs any question presented in connection with a power of appointment. If the appointive asset is land, the law of the jurisdiction where the land is located governs. But if the appointive assets are personal property, the donor of the power may be able to select the law to

govern the trust. If the power is created by an inter vivos trust, the donor may select the law of the domicile of the donor or the donee or of the state where the trust is administered. If the power is created by a testamentary trust, the states are split. Some states permit the donor's intention to control. See, e.g., the *Beals* case, supra, footnote 13. Other states apply the law of the donor's domicile to a testamentary trust and do not permit the donor's intention to control. See, e.g., N.Y. Est., Powers & Trusts Law §3-5.1(g) (1981), providing that a general testamentary power or a special power created by will is to be governed by the law of the donor's domicile.

5. *Lapse: Appointee dies before donee dies.*   In the *Beals* case, the court held that the donee, Isabella, exercised her power in favor of the issue of her sister, Margaret Blake, who had predeceased Isabella. Suppose that Isabella's will had been executed during Margaret's lifetime, and Isabella had exercised the power by appointing to Margaret. If Margaret had predeceased Isabella, would Margaret's issue take the appointive property under the anti-lapse statute? See Thompson v. Pew, 214 Mass. 520, 102 N.E. 122 (1913); French, Application of Antilapse Statutes to Appointments Made by Will, 53 Wash. L. Rev. 405, 421-428 (1978).

Suppose that Isabella had a special power to appoint among her nephews and nieces and that she exercised the power by appointing to the issue of a niece who had predeceased her. What result? See id. at 428-431. If Isabella could have appointed to the niece, with the issue of the niece taking the appointive property under the anti-lapse statute, why not permit Isabella to appoint directly to the issue? See Restatement (Second) of Property, supra, §18.6, providing that takers substituted by an anti-lapse statute are regarded as objects of the power.

Suppose that Isabella had a general testamentary power created by her husband's will and had appointed to her husband's nephew, who predeceased Isabella leaving issue. Would the issue of the nephew take under the anti-lapse statute? See French, supra, at 417-421; Restatement (Second) of Property, supra, §18.6, Comment b.

2.   *Limitations on Exercise of a Special Power*

In almost all jurisdictions, a donee of a *general* power of appointment can appoint outright or in further trust and can create new powers of appointment. Inasmuch as the donee of a general power could first appoint to himself or to his estate and then, by a second instrument or a second clause in his will, appoint in further trust, it makes no sense to forbid the donee to appoint in further trust when he uses only one piece of paper or one clause in his will. (Of course, in numerous other situations, property law requires the use of two pieces of paper to carry out the transferor's intent, but here we have refreshing sanity.) With respect to a *special* power of appointment, the donee's authority is more limited.

The donee of a special power may not be able to appoint in further trust unless the creating instrument expressly so permits. In some older cases, courts — influenced by the idea that the donee of a special power was a limited agent of the donor — read the donee's power narrowly. Without authorization, the donee could only select the persons among the designated class and determine the proportion each should take. These cases may still be viable in a few jurisdictions. See Loring v. Karri-Davies, 371 Mass. 346, 357 N.E.2d 11, 94 A.L.R.3d 884 (1976), changing the rule prospectively to allow donees of special powers created after the date of the opinion to appoint in further trust.

In addition to whether the donee of a special power can appoint in further trust, other questions about the donee's authority have resulted in considerable litigation. One of the most vexing questions is whether the donee of a special power can create a new power of appointment. For example, suppose *T* gives *A* a power to appoint among *A*'s issue. Can *A* exercise the power by creating in his daughter *B* a life estate plus either a general power[15] or a special power to appoint among *B*'s children (who are, of course, objects of the original power)? The answer clearly should be yes; since *A* could appoint outright to *B*, there is no persuasive reason for refusing to permit *A* to appoint to *B* something less than absolute ownership. Yet the cases are divided on this point. Some cases hold that the creation of a new power is an impermissible delegation of the special power. See 5 American Law of Property §23.49 (1952).

Restatement (Second) of Property, Donative Transfers §19.4 (1986), takes the position that the donee of a special power can create a general power in an object of the special power or create a special power in any person to appoint to an object of the original special power. The latter situation includes an appointment in further trust, giving the trustee discretionary power to appoint to the objects.

There are a number of other problems concerning the scope of special powers. The most important restriction involves the persons to

---

15. For tax reasons *A* should not exercise a *special* power by creating a *general power to appoint by deed or will* except upon the advice of *A*'s tax advisor. If a special power of appointment is exercised by creating "another power of appointment which under the applicable local law can be validly exercised so as to postpone the vesting of any estate . . . for a period ascertainable without regard to the date of the creation of the first power [i.e., in most states, a general power to appoint by deed or will]," the appointive property will be included in *A*'s federal gross estate. For an explanation of this tax trap, see infra page 806. A sophisticated tax planner may, however, find this tax trap useful in avoiding generation-skipping taxes. See infra page 1037.

whom the donee can appoint. The designation of the objects is usually by a class description, such as "children," "issue," or "heirs." Any appointment to a nonobject of the power is void. In determining who comes within the class designation, the law of powers relies heavily on the law of class gifts. It may be wise for the creating instrument to include a clause defining the intended class.

A special power may be exclusive or nonexclusive. If it is exclusive, the donee can exclude entirely one or more objects of the power. The donee can appoint all the property to one member of the class of permissible appointees, excluding the rest. If the power is nonexclusive, the donee must appoint some amount to each permissible object. Thus, suppose that *T* bequeaths a fund in trust for *A* for life, remainder as *A* shall appoint by will among his children. *A* has three children, *B*, *C*, and *D*. If the power is exclusive, *A* can appoint all the property to *C*. If the power is nonexclusive, *A* must give some amount each to *B*, *C*, and *D* if *A* exercises the power. You must readily see the great difficulty with nonexclusive powers: How much must the donee give each member of the class? Can *A* appoint $1 each to *B* and *D* and the remainder of the fund to *C*? In some states, the amount cannot be too small because of the "illusory appointment" rule requiring that each permissible appointee receive a "substantial" sum; in other states the illusory appointment rule has been repudiated. See 5 American Law of Property, supra, §23.58. Restatement (Second) of Property, supra, §21.1, provides that a special power is exclusive "unless the donor specifies the share of the appointive assets from which an object may not be excluded" (in other words, specifies the minimum share).

Whether a power is exclusive or nonexclusive depends upon the intention of the donor as revealed by the creating instrument. A power to appoint to "any one or more of *A*'s issue in such amount or amounts and for such estates and interests and upon such conditions and limitations as *A* shall designate" would create an exclusive power. If the creating instrument does not reveal the donor's intent, classification will turn upon the presumption adhered to in the jurisdiction. Restatement (Second) of Property, supra, §21.1, provides that, in the absence of a contrary intent, special powers of appointment are presumptively exclusive. As an abstract proposition, this position seems to have the support of most courts. However, there are cases holding that a contrary intent is shown by language creating a power to appoint "*among A*'s children as *A* shall by will appoint." (Compare this with the words, "*among such of A*'s children as *A* shall by will appoint," which would create an exclusive power.) The problem, as well as the other possible limitations on the scope of the power mentioned above, can and should be avoided by proper drafting.

PROBLEM

Appraise the following special power of appointment form: *O* creates a revocable trust to pay the income to *O* for life, then to *O*'s wife for life, then to *O*'s daughter for life. The trust instrument continues:

> On the death of such daughter, the trustees shall pay the then-remaining principal and undistributed income to, or hold the same for the benefit of, such one or more of such daughter's issue living at her death or born thereafter and such charitable organizations as such daughter shall appoint by a will, executed after the death of the survivor of the settlor and the settlor's said wife, which refers specifically to this power. The exercise of this power by such daughter, however, shall not apply to the proceeds of any life insurance on the life of such daughter payable to this trust. Subject to the above restrictions in the exercise of this power of appointment, the settlor's said daughter may appoint outright or in trust; she may select the trustee or trustees if she appoints in trust; she may create new powers of appointment in a trustee or trustees or in any other appointee; she may, if she appoints in trust, establish such administrative powers for the trustee or trustees as she deems appropriate; she may create life interests or other limited interests in some of the appointees with future interests in favor of other appointees; she may impose lawful conditions on an appointment; she may appoint to one or more of the objects of this power to the exclusion of other objects and she may appoint different types of interests to different objects; she may impose lawful spendthrift provisions; and generally she may appoint by will in any manner; provided always, however, that no appointment shall benefit, either directly or indirectly, one who is not an object of this power, and that nothing herein shall be construed as authorizing such daughter to appoint to herself, her creditors, her estate, or creditors of her estate. [5 A. Casner, Estate Planning §17.8 at 250 (5th ed. 1983).]

Would it be a good idea to include as objects of the power the spouse of the donee and spouses of issue, including spouses of issue who predecease the donee? Suppose that the donee desires to appoint a sum to her brother or his children. Should the objects of the power be broadened to include issue of the settlor? Should the power be further broadened to enable the donee to appoint to any person or persons (and charitable organizations) other than the estate of the donee and the creditors of the donee or of the donee's estate? Cf. id. at 244.

Why are the life insurance proceeds excluded from the power of appointment? See infra page 967.

3.   Fraud on a Special Power

An appointment in favor of a person who is not an object of the power is invalid. An appointment to an object for the purpose of circumventing the limitation on the power is a "fraud on the power," and is void to the extent it is motivated by such purpose. Thus: Elsa Milliken held a special testamentary power to appoint among her "kindred," and in default of appointment the property was to pass to Elsa's descendants or, if none, to the donor's heirs. Elsa, who had no issue, wanted to appoint $100,000 to her husband. She approached her cousin Paul Curtis and told him that she was going to leave him $150,000 and an additional $100,000, which she would like him to give to her husband. Paul said he would be happy to sign a paper to that effect. Elsa's attorney prepared a letter directed to her and signed by Paul which read: "I am informed that by your last will and testament you have given me and bequeathed to me the sum of Two Hundred and Fifty Thousand Dollars ($250,000). In the event that you should predecease me and I should receive the bequest before mentioned, I hereby promise and agree, in consideration of the said bequest, that I will pay to your husband, Foster Milliken, Jr., the sum of One Hundred Thousand Dollars ($100,000) out of the said bequest which you have given to me by your said will." Elsa died leaving a will appointing $250,000 to Paul. Is Paul entitled to $250,000, $150,000, or zero? See In re Carroll's Will, 274 N.Y. 288, 8 N.E.2d 864, 115 A.L.R. 923 (1937); Restatement (Second) of Property, Donative Transfers §20.2 (1986).

4. Ineffective Exercise of the Power

When the donee intends to exercise a power of appointment, but the exercise is ineffective for some reason, it may be possible to carry out the donee's intent through the doctrines of allocation and of capture.

a. Allocation of Assets

The doctrine of allocation (also known as marshaling) applies when *appointive assets* and *assets owned by the donee* are disposed of under a common dispositive instrument (usually the donee's will). Its purpose is to try to allocate these assets to different provisions under the donee's will to give effect to the donee's intent when the appointive assets cannot go where the donee intended. Typical cases applying allocation involve an ineffective appointment to a nonobject of a power or an appointment that violates the Rule against Perpetuities. It is important to realize that, where assets are allocated by a court, *the donee could have provided for the allocation in specific language and the court is merely doing what the donee would have done but for the ineptness of the donee's lawyer.*

The doctrine of allocation is: If the donee *blends* both the appointive property and the donee's own property in a common disposition, the blended property is allocated to the various interests in such a way as to increase the effectiveness of the disposition. Restatement (Second) of Property, Donative Transfers §§22.1, 22.2 (1986). Thus:

> *Case 6.*   *A* holds a special testamentary power created by her father to appoint trust property among *A*'s issue. The trust assets are worth $100,000. *A* also owns outright $350,000. *A*'s will provides:
>
>> I give all my property, including any property over which I have a power of appointment, as follows:
>> 1. I give $100,000 to my daughter-in-law, *B*, widow of my deceased son, *S*.
>> 2. I give all the rest to my daughter, *D*.
>
> Since *B* is not an object of the special power, the trust assets cannot be allocated to her. They will be allocated to *A*, and $100,000 of *A*'s owned assets will be allocated to *B*.

If, in Case 6, *A* had owned assets of only $50,000, *B* would receive only $50,000 because the trust assets cannot be allocated to *B*. Hence, allocation to satisfy completely the ineffective appointment requires that the donee have property of her own sufficient to substitute for the appointive property.

The blending requirement of the doctrine of allocation is met in Case 6 by the introductory clause of *A*'s will. The blending requirement may also be met by a residuary clause disposing of both appointive property and owned property. Suppose that, in Case 6, there had been no introductory clause, and *A* had bequeathed the appointive property to *B* and her own property to *D*. Since *A* did not blend the property but specifically bequeathed the appointive property to *B*, the appointment would fail and none of *A*'s owned assets would be allocated to *B*. See Restatement (Second) of Property, supra, §22.1, Comment g.

b.   Capture

If the donee of a power makes an ineffective appointment, and the donee's intent cannot be given effect through allocation of assets, to whom does the appointive property pass? The general rule is that the property passes in default of appointment or, if there is no gift in default, to the donor's estate. To this rule is one important exception: the doctrine of capture, which captures the property for the donee's estate.

Capture occurs when the donee of a *general* power "manifests an intent to assume control of the appointive property for all purposes and not merely for the limited purpose of giving effect to the expressed appointment." Restatement (Second) of Property, supra, §23.2. The doctrine of capture rests upon the conception that inasmuch as the donee of a general power could appoint to her estate, the appointive property will pass to her estate if she would prefer that in case of an ineffective appointment. Ineffective appointments raising the issue of whether capture applies usually involve lapse of an appointment to a dead appointee, or a violation of the Rule against Perpetuities, or failure of the donee to comply with some prescribed formality in exercising the power.

The intent of the donee to assume control of the appointive property for all purposes is most commonly manifested by provisions in the donee's will that *blend* the owned property of the donee with the appointive property. As with the doctrine of allocation, the requisite blending can occur in a residuary clause disposing of both the appointive property and the donee's own assets or in an introductory clause stating that the donee intends the appointive property to be treated as her own property. Thus:

> *Case 7.*   A is donee of a general power. A's will provides:
>
> I give all my property and any property over which I have a power of appointment as follows:
>   1. $10,000 to my friend B [who predeceases A, and no anti-lapse statute applies];
>   2. $15,000 in trust for my dog Trixie [which violates the Rule against Perpetuities];
>   3.   All the rest to C.
>
> A has captured the appointive property by blending it with her own. C takes everything, including the appointive property.

Capture applies only to general powers and only when the attempted exercise of the general power is ineffective or incomplete. See Jones, Consequences of an Ineffective Appointment — Capture, 18 Ala. L. Rev. 229 (1966).

SECTION E.   FAILURE TO EXERCISE A POWER OF APPOINTMENT

If the donee of a *general* power fails to exercise it, the appointive property passes in default of appointment. If there is no gift in default of appointment, the property reverts to the donor's estate. If the donee of a *special* power fails to exercise it, and there is no gift in default of appointment, the appointive property may — if the objects are a defined limited class — pass to the objects of the power.

Loring v. Marshall
Supreme Judicial Court of Massachusetts, 1985
396 Mass. 166, 484 N.E.2d 1315

WILKINS, J.   This complaint, here on a reservation and report by a single justice of this court, seeks instructions as to the disposition of the remainder of a trust created under the will of Marian Hovey. In Massachusetts Inst. of Technology v. Loring, 327 Mass. 553, 99 N.E.2d 854 (1951), this court held that the President and Fellows of Harvard College, the Boston Museum of Fine Arts, and Massachusetts Institute of Technology (the charities) would not be entitled to the remainder of the trust on its termination. The court, however, did not decide, as we now must, what ultimate disposition should be made of the trust principal.

Marian Hovey died in 1898, survived by a brother, Henry S. Hovey, a sister, Fanny H. Morse, and two nephews, John Torrey Morse, Third, and Cabot Jackson Morse. By her will, Marian Hovey left the residue of her estate in trust, the income payable in equal shares to her brother and sister during their lives. Upon her brother's death in 1900, his share of the income passed to her sister, and, upon her sister's death in 1922, the income was paid in equal shares to her two nephews. John Torrey Morse, Third, died in 1928, unmarried and without issue. His share of the income then passed to his brother, Cabot Jackson Morse, who remained the sole income beneficiary until his death in 1946.

At that point, the death of the last surviving income beneficiary, Marian Hovey's will provided for the treatment of the trust assets in the following language:

> At the death of the last survivor of my said brother and sister and my two said nephews, or at my death, if none of them be then living, the trustees shall divide the trust fund in their hands into two equal parts, and shall transfer and pay over one of such parts to the use of the wife and issue of each of my said nephews as he may by will have appointed; provided, that if his wife was living at my death he shall appoint to her no larger interest in the property possessed by me than a right to the income during her life, and if she was living at the death of my father, he shall appoint to her no larger interest in the property over which I have a power of disposition under the will of my father than a right to the income during her life; and the same limitations shall apply to the appointment of income as aforesaid. If either of my said nephews shall leave no such appointees then living, the whole of the trust fund shall be

paid to the appointees of his said brother as aforesaid. If neither of my said nephews leave such appointees then living the whole trust fund shall be paid over and transferred in in [sic] equal shares to the Boston Museum of Fine Arts, the Massachusetts Institute of Technology, and the President and Fellows of Harvard College for the benefit of the Medical School; provided, that if the said Medical School shall not then admit women to instruction on an equal footing with men, the said President and Fellows shall not receive any part of the trust property, but it shall be divided equally between the Boston Museum of Fine Arts and the Massachusetts Institute of Technology.[16]

The will thus gave Cabot Jackson Morse, the surviving nephew, a special power to appoint the trust principal to his "wife and issue" with the limitation that only income could be appointed to a widow who was living at Marian Hovey's death.[17] Cabot Jackson Morse was survived by his wife, Anna Braden Morse, who was living at Marian Hovey's death, and by his only child, Cabot Jackson Morse, Jr., a child of an earlier marriage, who died in 1948, two years after his father. Cabot Jackson Morse left a will which contained the following provisions:

Second: I give to my son, Cabot Jackson Morse, Jr., the sum of one dollar ($1.00), as he is otherwise amply provided for.

Third: The power of appointment which I have under the wills of my aunt, Marian Hovey, and my uncle, Henry S. Hovey, both late of Gloucester, Massachusetts, I exercise as follows: I appoint to my wife, Anna Braden Morse, the right to the income during her lifetime of all of the property to which my power of appointment applies under the will of Marian Hovey, and I appoint to my wife the right during her widowhood to the income to which I would be entitled under the will of Henry S. Hovey if I were living.

Fourth: All the rest, residue and remainder of my estate, wherever situated, real or personal, in trust or otherwise, I leave outright and in fee simple to my wife, Anna Braden Morse.

In Welch v. Morse, 323 Mass. 233, 81 N.E.2d 361 (1948), we held that the appointment of a life interest to Anna Braden Morse was valid, notwithstanding Cabot Jackson Morse's failure fully to exercise the power by appointing the trust principal. Consequently, the trust income following Cabot Jackson Morse's death was paid to Anna Braden Morse

---

16. The parties have stipulated that at the relevant time the Harvard Medical School admitted women to instruction on an equal footing with men.

17. We are concerned here only with "property possessed" by the testatrix at her death and not property over which she had "a power of disposition under the will of [her] father." That property was given outright to his widow under the residuary clause of the will of Cabot Jackson Morse.

until her death in 1983, when the principal became distributable. The trustees thereupon brought this complaint for instructions.

The complaint alleges that the trustees

> are uncertain as to who is entitled to the remainder of the Marian Hovey Trust now that the trust is distributable and specifically whether the trust principal should be paid in any one of the following manners: (a) to the estate of Cabot Jackson Morse, Jr. as the only permissible appointee of the remainder of the trust living at the death of Cabot Jackson Morse; (b) in equal shares to the estates of Cabot Jackson Morse, Jr. and Anna Braden Morse as the only permissible appointees living at the death of Cabot Jackson Morse; (c) to the estate of Anna Braden Morse as the only actual appointee living at the death of Cabot Jackson Morse; (d) to the intestate takers of Marian Hovey's estate on the basis that Marian Hovey failed to make a complete disposition of her property by her will; (e) to Massachusetts Institute of Technology, Museum of Fine Arts and the President and Fellows of Harvard College in equal shares as remaindermen of the trust; or (f) some other disposition.

Before us each named potential taker claims to be entitled to trust principal.

In our 1951 opinion, Massachusetts Inst. of Technology v. Loring, 327 Mass. at 555-556, 99 N.E.2d 854, we explained why in the circumstances the charities had no interest in the trust:

> The rights of the petitioning charities as remaindermen depend upon the proposition that Cabot J. Morse, Senior, did not leave an "appointee" although he appointed his wife Anna Braden Morse to receive the income during her life. The time when, if at all, the "whole trust fund" was to be paid over and transferred to the petitioning charities is the time of the death of Cabot J. Morse, Senior. At that time the whole trust fund could not be paid over and transferred to the petitioning charities, because Anna Braden Morse still retained the income for her life. We think that the phrase no "such appointees then living" is not the equivalent of an express gift in default of appointment, a phrase used by the testatrix in the preceding paragraph.

In Frye v. Loring, 330 Mass. 389, 393, 113 N.E.2d 595 (1953), the court reiterated that the charities had no interest in the trust fund.

It is apparent that Marian Hovey knew how to refer to a disposition in default of appointment from her use of the terms elsewhere in her will. She did not use those words in describing the potential gift to the charities. A fair reading of the will's crucial language may rightly be that the charities were not to take the principal unless no class member who could receive principal was then living (i.e., if no possible appointee of principal was living at the death of the surviving donee). Regardless of how the words "no such appointees then living" are construed, the express circumstances under which the charities were to take did not occur. The question is what disposition should be made of the principal in the absence of any explicit direction in the will.

Although in its 1951 opinion this court disavowed making a determination of the "ultimate destination of the trust fund," the opinion cited the Restatement of Property §367(2) (1940), and 1 A. Scott, Trusts §27.1 (1st ed. 1939)[18] to the effect that, when a special power of appointment is not exercised and absent specific language indicating an express gift in default of appointment, the property not appointed goes in equal shares to the members of the class to whom the property could have been appointed. For more recent authority, see 5 American Law of Property §23.63, at 645 (A.J. Casner ed. 1952 & Supp. 1962) ("The fact that the donee has failed to apportion the property within the class should not defeat the donor's intent to benefit the class"); Restatement (Second) of Property §24.2 (Tent. Draft No. 7, 1984).[19]

Applying this rule of law, we find no specific language in the will which indicates a gift in default of appointment in the event Cabot Jackson Morse should fail to appoint the principal. The charities argue that the will's reference to them suggests that in default of appointment Marian Hovey intended them to take. On the other hand, in Welch v. Morse, 323 Mass. at 238, 81 N.E.2d 361, we commented that Marian Hovey's "will discloses an intent to keep her property in the family." The interests Marian Hovey gave to her sister and brother were life

---

18.   In Restatement: Property, §367(2), it is said, with certain immaterial exceptions, that "where there is a special power and no gift in default of appointment in specific language, property not effectively appointed passes to those living objects to whom the donee could have appointed at the time of expiration of the power, unless the donor has manifested an intent that the objects shall receive the property only so far as the donee elects to appoint it to them." In Scott, Trusts, §27.1, the author says, "Where there is no express gift over in default of appointment the inference is that the donor intended the members of the class to take even though the donee should fail to exercise the power. The inference is that he did not intend that they should take only if the donee should choose to exercise the power. . . . The cases are numerous in which it has been held that the members of the class are entitled to the property in equal shares where the donee of a power to appoint among them fails to exercise the power." See also Farwell, Powers (3d ed. 1916) 528; Kales, Estates Future Interests (1920) §616.

327 Mass. at 556.

19. Section 24.4, concerning the disposition of unappointed property under a non-general power of appointment, states:

To the extent the donor of a non-general power has not specified in the instrument creating the power who is to take unappointed property, the unappointed property passes (1) In default of appointment to the objects of the power (including those who are substituted objects under an antilapse statute) living at the time of the expiration of the power as though they had been specified in the instrument creating the power to take unappointed property, if — (a) the objects are a defined limited class and (b) the donor has not manifested an intent that the objects shall receive the appointive property only so far as the donee elects to appoint it to them; or (2) To the donor or the donor's estate, if subsection (1) is not applicable.

interests, as were the interests given to her nephews. The share of any nephew who died unmarried and without issue, as did one, was added to the share of the other nephew. Each nephew was limited to exercising his power of appointment only in favor of his issue and his widow.[20] We think the apparent intent to keep the assets within the family is sufficiently strong to overcome any claim that Marian Hovey's will "expressly" or "in specific language" provides for a gift to the charities in default of appointment.[21]. . . .

[The charities argued that the principle of res judicata was not applicable because the attorney general, the supervisor of public charities, was not a party to Massachusetts Inst. of Technology v. Loring, 327 Mass. 553, 99 N.E.2d 854 (1951). The court rejected this argument and held that "the public interest in protecting the charities' rights was fully accommodated by the Justices of this court in its prior decision."]

What we have said disposes of the claim that the trust principal should pass to Marian Hovey's heirs as intestate property, a result generally disfavored in the interpretation of testamentary dispositions. . . . The claim of the executors of the estate of Anna Braden Morse that her estate should take as the class, or at least as a member of the class, must fail because Marian Hovey's will specifically limits such a widow's potential stake to a life interest.

A judgment shall be entered instructing the trustees under the will of Marian Hovey to distribute the trust principal to the executors of the estate of Cabot Jackson Morse, Jr. The allowance of counsel fees, costs, and expenses from the principal of the trust is to be in the discretion of the single justice.

So ordered.

NOTES AND PROBLEM

1. The Loring, Wolcott & Coolidge Office, which has been involved in many Massachusetts trust cases besides Loring v. Marshall, is an unincorporated firm of private professional trustees. Private trusteeship

---

20. The gift to any widow was to be a life interest if she were living at Marian Hovey's death.

21. The nominal distribution made to his son in the donee's will provides no proper guide to the resolution of the issues in this case. We are concerned here with the intention of Marian Hovey, the donor of the special power of appointment. The intentions of the donee of the power of appointment are irrelevant in constructing the donor's intent. Similarly, those who rely on language in Frye v. Loring, 330 Mass. 389, 113 N.E.2d 595 (1953), as instructive in resolving questions in this case miss the point that Cabot Jackson Morse's intention with regard to his exercise of the power of appointment is irrelevant in determining his aunt's intention concerning the consequences of his partial failure to exercise that power.

in Boston stems from the early nineteenth century when heirs to fortunes made in the slave trade, the China trade, and other foreign markets needed trust management and advice. The Loring office was founded by Nathaniel Bowditch in 1817.

Today the Loring office is comprised of 8 trustees and about 50 employees. The trustees are not lawyers, but most have M.B.A. degrees. They are responsible for approximately $1 billion in some 1,000 fiduciary accounts. The office operates much the same as a highly personalized trust company. It is office policy to have the same two trustees assigned to one trust indefinitely, so that the trustees become well acquainted with the particular family's needs and circumstances. The readiness to take pains with people is a major reason for the continuing appeal of private trusteeships today.

2. The theory of the court in Loring v. Marshall was that there was an implied gift in default of appointment to the potential appointees. This theory is adopted by Restatement (Second) of Property, Donative Transfers §24.2 (1986), referred to in footnote 19 of the court's opinion.

Another way of solving the problem in the case is to say that Cabot Jackson Morse had an *imperative* special power of appointment. A special power is imperative when the creating instrument manifests an intent that the permissible appointees be benefited even if the donee fails to exercise the power. If a special power is imperative, the donee must exercise it or the court will divide the assets equally among the potential appointees. The term *imperative power* is used in Cal. Civ. Code §1381.4 (1989) and N.Y. Est., Powers & Trusts Law §10-3.4 (1967).

In most cases it is not likely to make any difference whether a court adopts an implied gift in default theory or an imperative power theory. The same result is ordinarily reached under both because both are based on the inferred intent of the donor. But in other situations, the theory followed may make a difference. Consider Bridgewater v. Turner, 161 Tenn. 111, 29 S.W.2d 659 (1930). The testator's will provided:

> I bequeath to Eliza V. Seay during her life that portion of the old home tract and household furniture etc., which lies between the Trousdale Ferry turnpike road and the creek of Round Lick and Jennings Fork, and, at her death I desire it to go to one of my nephews and I leave it with her to decide which one it shall be. . . . It is my desire that the above described tract shall remain in the hands of the family as long as possible, for here sleeps my wife, my father and mother.

At the testator's death, he had four nephews, W.S., John C., W.R., and Richard. Richard died before the life tenant, Eliza, leaving as his heirs two children, Elizabeth and Carr. Eliza died without exercising her power of appointment. Who owns the old home tract? Cf. Waterman

v. New York Life Insurance & Trust Co., 237 N.Y. 293, 142 N.E. 668 (1923). If Elizabeth and Carr now share in ownership, could Eliza have appointed the old home tract to Elizabeth? If Richard had died before the testator, what result? See Restatement (Second) of Property, supra, §24.2, Illustration 3. See also id., §18.6, providing that takers substituted by an anti-lapse statute are regarded as objects of the power.

11

DURATION OF TRUSTS: THE RULE AGAINST PERPETUITIES

[A]rrangements for the distant future are likely to result in an inefficient use of resources brought about by unforeseen contingencies.

R. POSNER
Economic Analysis of Law
486 (3d ed. 1986)

That I have done my own sums correctly, I do not venture to hope. There is something in the subject which seems to facilitate error. Perhaps it is because the mode of reasoning is unlike that with which lawyers are familiar. The study and practice of the Rule against Perpetuities is indeed a constant school of modesty. A long list might be formed of the demonstrable blunders with regard to its questions made by eminent men, . . . and there are few lawyers of any practice in drawing wills and settlements who have not at some time either fallen into the net which the Rule spreads for the unwary, or at least shuddered to think how narrowly they have escaped it.

J. GRAY
The Rule Against Perpetuities
xi (4th ed. 1942)

SECTION A.   INTRODUCTION

1.   *Development of the Rule*

The classic statement of the Rule against Perpetuities, formulated with Delphic simplicity by John Chipman Gray, reads:

> No interest [in real or personal property] is good unless it must vest, if at all, not later than twenty-one years after some life in being at the creation of the interest. [J. Gray, The Rule Against Perpetuities §201, at 191 (4th ed. 1942).]

Although Gray put the Rule in this one sentence, to explain what it meant took Gray more than 400 scrupulously detailed pages in the first edition of his great work, The Rule Against Perpetuities (1886), expanded to more than 800 pages in the fourth edition (1942). By virtue of his erudition, his rigorous logic, his dogmatic style, and his position as a celebrated teacher of property law at Harvard, Gray became established as not just a leading authority on the Rule but as *the* authority.[1]

Because of the deference paid to Gray's work by the courts, the Rule has sometimes been treated as if it were laid down at one time by this one man. In fact, the Rule had a long and involved evolution. The Rule against Perpetuities is judicial legislation par excellence, and the case-by-case development of the Rule by the courts took several centuries. The origins of the Rule against Perpetuities are somewhat obscure because of the ambiguous nature of the concept *perpetuity*. The political and social evils attending on perpetual entails, permitted by the Statute de Donis (1285), led judges to become jealous of allowing any limitation tying up land in perpetuity. They defeated the Statute de Donis in 1472 by approving the common recovery, a bogus lawsuit that left the fee tail tenant with a fee simple. When lawyers for landowners tried new devices for keeping land within the family — principally by clauses restraining alienation and by creating executory interests in long terms of years that were indestructible by common recovery — the judges began to throw up new obstacles to limitations "tending to a perpetuity."

From the sixteenth until the nineteenth century, judges struggled against perpetuities, without ever defining exactly what a perpetuity was. There were several unrefined notions and ambiguous doctrines that might be called rules against perpetuities. It fell the lot of Lord

---

1. On the role of Gray, see Siegel, John Chipman Gray, Legal Formalism, and the Transformation of Perpetuities Law, 36 U. Miami L. Rev. 439 (1982).

Chancellor Nottingham[2] to clarify these ancient contradictory decisions and point the way for modern development of the Rule.

The Rule against Perpetuities as we know it began with the Duke of Norfolk's Case, 3 Ch. Cas. 1, 22 Eng. Rep. 931 (Ch. 1682). The Earl of Arundel had eight sons. Thomas, the eldest son and heir apparent, was *non compos mentis*, weak in body, and not expected to have children. Thus the earl assumed that after his own death and the death of Thomas, the earldom and the estates accompanying it would likely descend to his second son, Henry, and Henry's issue. If Henry did inherit the earldom at Thomas's death, the earl wanted the barony of Grostock, which he planned to give initially to Henry, to shift to his fourth son, Charles. The earl went to an experienced estate planner (known as a conveyancer in those days when land was the chief form of wealth), Sir Orlando Bridgman. This outstanding member of the bar, who later became Lord Keeper, drew up a set of highly complicated documents. They cannot be easily summarized inasmuch as they require an understanding of some very complex doctrines involving terms of years. It is enough to say that the limitation that brought on the Duke of Norfolk's Case boiled down to this: The barony of Grostock was given to Henry, but an executory limitation was created, providing that if the eldest son, Thomas, should die without issue in the lifetime of Henry, then the barony would go to Charles.

In 1652 the Earl of Arundel died and the earldom descended to the mentally defective son, Thomas. Henry then moved into action. He assumed full control of the properties accompanying the title, and he took Thomas to Padua in Italy where he was incarcerated until his death. Henry also engineered the restoration of the title, "Duke of Norfolk," to the family. In 1572 Queen Elizabeth I had beheaded the fourth duke for intrigues involving Mary, Queen of Scots, and by attainder all his honors were forfeited.[3] In 1660 Parliament, with the

---

2. Lord Nottingham, born Heneage Finch, was one of the greatest of English Chancellors and called the "Father of Equity" by Mr. Justice Story. He was equally devoted to the law and to his family. When he lost his wife, mother of his 14 children, he comforted himself by taking the Great Seal to bed with him. 4 J. Campbell, Lives of the Lord Chancellors 273 (1857).

3. The turbulence of the times is reflected in the history of the title of Duke of Norfolk, who is the premier duke, ranking just below the blood royal. The title goes back to the first Earl of Norfolk, one of the Breton followers of William the Conqueror. After several attainders and lapses of the earldom, the dukedom was created anew by Richard II in 1397 and given to his chief supporter Thomas Mowbray, perhaps best remembered for his quarrel with Henry Bolingbroke, Duke of Hereford (afterward Henry IV), which forms Act I of Shakespeare's Richard II and which resulted in Mowbray's banishment. After four Mowbray dukes, the title lapsed.

In 1483, after the murder of the princes in the Tower, Richard III conferred the dukedom on Sir John Howard, an heir of the Mowbray estates and the first of the Howard dukes. Two years later, "Jack of Norfolk" died fighting for Richard at Bosworth; the title and the estates were forfeited to the victorious Henry Tudor, who ascended the

consent of Charles II, restored the dukedom of Norfolk, and the incompetent Thomas became the premier duke of England. When Thomas died without issue in 1677, Henry became the sixth Duke of Norfolk.

After succeeding to the dukedom and its properties, Henry did not want to give up the barony of Grostock. Charles brought a bill in chancery to enforce his interest. Henry resisted, claiming the gift to Charles was in the nature of a perpetuity and hence void. Sympathetic to the rational estate planning of a landowner with an incompetent eldest son, Lord Chancellor Nottingham was of the opinion that Charles's interest would "wear itself out" in a single lifetime (Thomas's) and should not be regarded as a perpetuity. The sole matter of concern, ruled Nottingham, is the time at which a future interest will vest, and if a future interest must vest, if at all, during or at the end of a life in being, it is good. Upon appeal to the House of Lords, after two days of argument in a crowded house with King James II present, the Lords voted almost unanimously to affirm Nottingham's decision.

Lord Nottingham, disagreeing with other judges who favored maximum alienability of land, was willing to compromise to accommodate the desires of the landed class. Professor Haskins says this great case gave the increasingly dominant landed class "room to maneuver in order to secure its future. . . . [T]he new Rule was a clear victory for the dead hand, not for free alienability. The rule served the fathers, not the sons." Haskins, "Inconvenience" and the Rule *For* Perpetuities, 48 Mo. L. Rev. 451, 474 (1983).

In the Duke of Norfolk's Case, Lord Nottingham indicated the direction the Rule against Perpetuities should take, but he did not attempt a definitive statement. When asked, "Where will you stop?" he replied, "I will tell you where I will stop: I will stop wherever any visible Inconvenience doth appear." From this beginning of a single life in being, the judges gradually extended the permissible period of dead-

---

throne as Henry VII. The first duke's son regained royal favor by commanding, in his 70th year, the army that defeated the Scots at Flodden, and in 1514 Henry VIII restored the title. Two nieces of the third duke, Anne Boleyn and Catherine Howard, were wives of Henry VIII, both beheaded for infidelity. Subsequently, the Howard family fell from grace; the third duke's son was executed on a charge of treason, and the duke himself was arrested, stripped of his title, and ordered to be beheaded. During the night before the morning set for execution, Henry VIII died and the duke was spared. Seven years later, Queen Mary released him from prison and restored the dukedom to him. The third duke was succeeded by his grandson, who in turn was executed by Elizabeth I for plotting with Mary Stuart. His son Philip, through inheritance from Philip's mother, became the Earl of Arundel, whose disposition was at issue in the Duke of Norfolk's Case.

Since the fourteenth century, the Duke of Norfolk has been the hereditary earl marshal of England. The highest ranking Catholic lord of the realm, the duke attends the sovereign upon the opening of Parliament, walking at his or her right hand, and arranges state ceremonies such as coronations, royal marriages, and funerals.

hand rule until, 150 years later, they finally fixed it at lives in being plus 21 years. In Scatterwood v. Edge, 1 Salk. 229, 91 Eng. Rep. 203 (K.B. 1699), it was held that it was sufficient if an interest would vest within a considerable number of lives in being, not merely one or two, "For let the lives be never so many, there must be a survivor, and so it is but the length of that life; for Twisden used to say, the candles were all lighted at once."[4] In Thellusson v. Woodford, 11 Ves. 112, 32 Eng. Rep. 1030 (Ch. 1805), it was held that any number of lives reasonably capable of being traced could be used to measure the applicable perpetuities period.[5] Concurrently with the expansion of lives in being from one or two to a considerable number, the courts were adding, first, a minority period and, subsequently, a period of 21 years in gross. Finally, in Cadell v. Palmer, 1 Cl. & Fin. 372, 6 Eng. Rep. 956 (H.L. 1832, 1833), the period allowed by the Rule was settled: any reasonable number of lives in being plus 21 years thereafter plus any actual periods of gestation.

---

4. Justice Twisden's remark was made in Love v. Wyndham, 1 Mod. 50, 54, 86 Eng. Rep. 724, 726 (K.B. 1681).

Do You Rule Your Perpetuity?

Lives plus one-and-twenty years,
The learned fathers thought,
Should be the time for vesting
Or the gift would come to naught;

As many lives as are ascertained
Without undue delay,
For you light the candles all at once,
As Twisden used to say.

This was to keep the land well oiled
And free to come and go,
For a dead man's hand must idle be
And his mind works awful slow.
   — *Anonymous student at Harvard Law School 1932*
   (Reprinted from W. Leach, Langdell Lyrics of 1938 (1938))

5. The court in In re Villar, [1929] 1 Ch. 243, sustained a provision postponing vesting until 20 years after the death of the survivor of all descendants of Queen Victoria living at the testator's death. There were about 120 known descendants of Queen Victoria then living. The grand duchess Anastasia, youngest daughter of the last Czar of Russia, was such a descendant, but it was not known whether she escaped the firing squad of the Bolsheviks. See A. Summers & T. Mangold, The File on the Tsar (1976).

In Warren's Will Trusts, 105 Sol. J. 511 (1961), the testator postponed vesting until the expiration of 20 years after the death of descendants of Queen Victoria living at the testator's death (as in In re Villar). There were 194 legitimate issue of the good Queen then alive. The gift was held valid.

In re Moore, [1901] 1 Ch. 936, held void for uncertainty a trust for maintenance of a tomb for "the period of 21 years from the death of the last survivor of all persons who shall be living at my death," on the ground that it would be impossible to say when the period ended.

DUKE OF NORFOLK.

The Sixth Duke of Norfolk
by Gerard Soest, ca. 1677
Tate Gallery, London

Reproduced by permission of the Tate Gallery.

His greed brought on the case that originated the Rule against Perpetuities.

The First Earl of Nottingham, Lord Chancellor
after Godfrey Kneller, 1680
National Portrait Gallery, London

Reproduced by permission of the National Portrait Gallery.

His decision gave the rich the power to secure family wealth for another
generation.

Although Gray's book is the authority in the field, it is much too detailed and recondite for the student beginning a study of the Rule. The classic introduction to the Rule for students is Leach's deservedly famous article, Perpetuities in a Nutshell, 51 Harv. L. Rev. 638 (1938), brought up to date by Leach in Perpetuities: The Nutshell Revisited, 78 Harv. L. Rev. 973 (1965). This lucid article, written in a lively, piquant style, for two generations now has introduced students into the magic garden of perpetuities. For a more recent synopsis of the Rule, see Dukeminier, A Modern Guide to Perpetuities, 74 Calif. L. Rev. 1867 (1986). See also W. McGovern, S. Kurtz & J. Rein, Wills, Trusts and Estates §§13.1-13.7 (1988).

L. Simes, Public Policy and the Dead Hand
59-60 (1955)

... [The most] important reason for the Rule is this. It is socially desirable that the wealth of the world be controlled by its living members and not by the dead. I know of no better statement of that doctrine than the language of Thomas Jefferson, contained in a letter to James Madison, when he said: "The earth belongs always to the living generation. They may manage it then, and what proceeds from it, as they please during their usufruct." Sidgwick, in his Elements of Politics, also discusses the problem in the following words:

... it rather follows from the fundamental assumption of individualism, that any such posthumous restraint on the use of bequeathed wealth will tend to make it less useful to the living, as it will interfere with their freedom in dealing with it. Individualism, in short, is in a dilemma. ... Of this difficulty, there is, I think, no general theoretical solution: it can only be reduced by some practical compromise.

2. Summary of the Rule[6]

a. Introduction

(1) The Rule and Its Policies
We start with Gray's classic statement of the Rule: "No interest is good unless it must vest, if at all, not later than twenty-one years after

---

6. This summary of the rule is taken, with some changes, from Dukeminier, A Modern Guide to Perpetuities, 74 Calif. L. Rev. 1867 (1986).

some life in being at the creation of the interest." Although Gray's one sentence must be qualified in several ways, because of its brevity it is the most useful working description of the Rule.

The fundamental policy assumption of the Rule against Perpetuities is that vested interests are not objectionable, but contingent interests are. The Rule therefore limits the time during which property can be made subject to contingent interests to "lives in being plus 21 years."

The assumption that only *contingent* future interests are objectionable is questionable. The Rule has three basic purposes: (1) to limit "dead hand" control over the property, which prevents the present generation from using the property as it sees fit; (2) to keep property marketable and available for productive development in accordance with market demands; and (3) to curb trusts, which can protect wealthy beneficiaries from bankruptcies and creditors, decrease the amount of risk capital available for economic development, and after a period of time and change in circumstances, tie up the family in disadvantageous and undesirable arrangements. See Restatement (Second) of Property (Donative Transfers), Pt. 1, Introductory Note (1981); F. Lawson & B. Rudden, The Law of Property 185-186 (2d ed. 1982); L. Simes, Public Policy and the Dead Hand 36-60 (1955); Ogus, The Trust as Governance Structure, 36 U. Toronto L.J. 186, 214-220 (1986).

Whenever future interests, vested or contingent, exist, these three objectives are compromised. These objectives are fully realized only when a person owns an absolute fee simple free of trust. Hence, it is arguable that the Rule against Perpetuities should prohibit all future interests, and not merely contingent interests, that exist beyond the perpetuities period. But history has settled the question differently. The Rule prohibits only those interests that may remain contingent beyond the perpetuities period. Although the Rule is thus not finely tuned for carrying out the policies for which it was designed, it does, by and large, effectively prevent tying up property for an inordinate length of time.

All legal and equitable interests in property created in *transferees* are subject to the Rule against Perpetuities. Hence all remainders and executory interests come within the ambit of the Rule. Future interests retained by the *transferor* — reversions, possibilities of reverter, and rights of entry — are not subject to the Rule against Perpetuities.

(2)   Why Lives in Being Are Used to Measure the Period

Although no one can say for sure what was in the minds of English judges when they fixed on "lives in being" as the appropriate perpetuities period, history does suggest a reason. At the time of the formulation of the Rule against Perpetuities, heads of families — the fathers — were much concerned about securing the family land, perhaps acquired only a couple of generations earlier, from incompetent sons. In the

Duke of Norfolk's Case, Lord Chancellor Nottingham recognized this concern as legitimate, and he and his successor judges developed an appropriate period during which the father's judgment could prevail. The father could realistically and perhaps wisely assess the capabilities of *living* members of his family, and so, with respect to them, the father's informed judgment, solemnly inscribed in an instrument, was given effect. But the head of the family could know nothing of unborn persons. Hence, the father was permitted control only as long as his judgment was informed with an understanding of the capabilities and needs of persons alive when the judgment was made. This seems the most plausible reason for selecting "lives in being" as the perpetuities period.

Lord Hobhouse put it this way in his lectures on the dead hand:

> A clear, obvious, natural line is drawn for us between those persons and events which the Settlor knows and sees, and those which he cannot know or see. Within the former province we may trust his natural affections and his capacity of judgment to make better dispositions than any external Law is likely to make for him. Within the latter, natural affection does not extend, and the wisest judgment is constantly baffled by the course of events. I submit, then, that the proper limit of Perpetuity is that of lives in being at the time when the settlement takes effect. [A. Hobhouse, The Dead Hand 188 (1880).]

Professor Leach observed that the balance struck by the courts permitted "a man of property . . . [to] provide for all of those in his family whom he personally knew and the first generation after them upon attaining majority." 6 American Law of Property §24.16 (1952). There was no need, he thought, to add to "lives in being" a 21-year period in gross instead of an actual minority, or to permit wholly extraneous lives (such as "a dozen healthy babies selected at random") to be included among the "lives in being." Nonetheless, given the historical tendency of property law to forget the original reasons for its rules and to reduce principles to logic, it was perhaps inevitable that the Rule against Perpetuities would become firmly established in the nineteenth century as a purely logical theorem.

(3) The Rule Is a Rule of Proof

The essential thing to grasp about the Rule against Perpetuities is that *it is a rule of logical proof.* The donee of an interest must prove that his interest will vest upon creation or vest or fail thereafter within the applicable perpetuities period. If there is any possibility that the interest will remain contingent after the perpetuities period expires, the interest is void.

The perpetuities period for a particular interest begins at creation of the interest and continues until 21 years after the death of persons alive at the creation of the interest who can affect vesting of the interest. If the interest will not necessarily vest or fail within this period, it is void at the outset. Case 1 shows how to make the necessary proof that an interest will vest or fail within this period.

> *Case 1.*   *O* transfers a fund in trust "to pay the income to *A* for life, then to *A*'s children for their lives, then to pay the principal to *B*." *A*'s life estate is vested in possession *upon creation*. The remainder to *A*'s children for their lives will vest in possession or, if there are no children, fail *upon A's death*. *B*'s remainder is vested in interest *upon creation* and valid under the Rule. Thus all interests created by the transfer are valid.

As Case 1 shows, the crucial inquiry under the Rule is: When will the interest vest? An interest satisfies the Rule if it will necessarily vest, if at all, either *in possession* or *in interest* when it is created or thereafter within the perpetuities period. Observe that in Case 1, *B*'s remainder is valid because it vests in interest upon creation. It is valid despite the fact that it may vest in possession at the death of *A*'s children, which could be well beyond the relevant lives in being plus 21 years if *A* has children born after the transfer.

Observe also that Case 1 contains a trust that may endure for the lives of *A*'s children born after the date of the transfer. The trust thus possibly may last longer than lives in being at the date of the transfer plus 21 years. Nonetheless, the trust is not void. The Rule against Perpetuities does not directly limit trust duration. It is concerned only with the time when interests vest.[7] In Case 1, all interests in the trust either are presently vested or will vest, if at all, within the period allotted by the Rule. Therefore, the trust is valid in its entirety. If an interest in trust violates the Rule, only to that extent is a trust void.

Here are other illustrations of interests that can be proven valid because they will vest, or fail, within the perpetuities period:

> *Case 2.*   *T* bequeaths $10,000 "to *A*, when she marries" and $5,000 "to *A*'s first child." The bequest to *A* will vest during *A*'s *life*, if at all; it is valid. The bequest to *A*'s first child also will vest during *A*'s life, if at all; it is valid.

> *Case 3.*   *O*, a teacher, declares a trust of her first edition of Dickens's Bleak House "for the first student in *O*'s current wills class to be sworn in as a judge." The gift will vest or fail within the *lives of the students* in

---

7. Since all interests in a trust must be vested within the perpetuities period, a trust can be terminated by the beneficiaries, holding vested interests, at or before the expiration of the perpetuities period. In this indirect way, the Rule against Perpetuities limits the duration of trusts. See supra page 580.

the class. The condition precedent will necessarily be met, if it is ever met, before the last surviving student dies.

Case 4.   O transfers a fund in trust "to pay the income to *A* for life, then to pay the principal to *A*'s children who reach 21." The remainder is valid because it will vest, at the latest, *21 years after A's death*, for all *A*'s children must reach 21 within 21 years after *A* dies (plus a period of gestation).

The period of the Rule includes any actual periods of gestation involved. The Rule follows the general principle of property law that a person is in being from the time of conception, if later born alive. A child *en ventre sa mere* when the perpetuities period begins counts as a life in being, and a child *en ventre sa mere* when the perpetuities period ends can take as a beneficiary.

b.   When the Lives in Being Are Ascertained

Although Gray said the life in being must be a person alive *"at the creation of the interest,"* it is more accurate to say that the validating life or lives must be in being *when the perpetuities period starts to run.* Generally, the perpetuities period begins when the instrument takes effect. If an interest is created by *will,* the validating life or lives must be in being at the testator's death. If the interest is created by *deed* or *irrevocable trust,* the validating life or lives must be persons in being when the deed or trust takes effect.

Different rules for determining validating lives govern revocable trusts and interests created by exercise of a power of appointment. If the interest is created by an *inter vivos trust revocable by the settlor alone,* the validating life or lives must be persons in being when the power to revoke terminates. If the power to revoke terminates at the settlor's death, as will usually be the case, the validating lives must be persons alive at the settlor's death. The perpetuities period begins when the power to revoke terminates because, so long as one person has the power to revoke the trust and receive absolute title to the trust assets, the property is not tied up.

c.   The Validating Life

Because the Rule against Perpetuities is a rule of logical proof, you must look for a life that works in making the proof required. This person, if found, is sometimes known as the *measuring life,* but this term is the source of much confusion, particularly among persons beginning a study of the Rule. To the uninitiated, the term "measuring life or lives" appears to refer ambiguously both to the life or lives that measure or fix the perpetuities period applicable to the particular interest in question and to the life or lives among those that enable one to prove validity of the interest. To the cognoscenti, the term refers only to the latter. Because of this confusion, we use the term *validating life*.

The Rule is easier to understand if the two distinct types of lives involved in solving perpetuities problems are explicitly separated and defined. First, there are the *relevant* lives — that is, those persons who can affect vesting and therefore fix the perpetuities period applicable to the particular interest in question. Second, there may be a *validating* life — that is, a person from among the relevant lives about whom you can say, "The interest in question will necessarily vest or fail during this person's life or at his death or within 21 years after his death." The validating life is the person you are looking for in order to validate the interest.

In seeking a validating life, you must, of logical necessity, narrow the candidates to persons who might qualify in making the required proof. You will find a validating life, if you find one at all, *only among persons who can affect vesting*.[8] All other persons are irrelevant to the search. "Persons who can affect vesting" are given by the definition of a vested interest. An interest is vested when it either vests in possession or vests in interest. Any person who can affect the time a future interest vests in possession is related to vesting of the interest. An interest is vested in interest when (1) the beneficiary or beneficiaries are ascertained and (2) any condition precedent is satisfied. Accordingly, the persons who can affect vesting in interest are:

(a) The beneficiary or beneficiaries of the contingent interest;
(b) Any person who can affect the identity of the beneficiary or beneficiaries (such as *A* in a gift to *A*'s children); and
(c) Any person who can affect any condition precedent attached to the gift, or, in case of a class gift, any person who can affect a condition precedent attached to the interest of any class member.

You should test each of these relevant persons to see if the interest will vest or fail during the person's life or within 21 years after that person's death. If there is no person among this group of relevant lives by whom the requisite proof can be made, the interest is void unless it must vest or fail within 21 years. Thus:

---

8. "Such [validating] life or lives, if they exist, will be related to the occurrence of the events that lead to the vesting of the non-vested interest in question." Restatement (Second) of Property, Donative Transfers §1.3, Comment b (1981). Accord, J. Gray, supra, §219.2, n.2; R. Megarry & H. Wade, The Law of Real Property 251 (5th ed. 1984).

Case 5. *T* devises Blackacre "to *A* for life, remainder to *A*'s children who reach 25." The persons in being who can affect vesting are *A* and *A*'s children. (*A* can affect both the time the remainder vests in possession and, by procreating a child or children, the identity of the remaindermen.[9] *A*'s children supply the identity of the remaindermen and, in addition, can affect the condition precedent by reaching 25.) Test each of these persons to see if the remainder will vest or fail for *all* of the class members within 21 years after the death of such person.[10] None of them, you will find, permits the necessary proof to be made because this sequence of events might occur: *A* may die leaving an afterborn child under the age of four, which child may reach 25 more than 21 years after the death of *A* and all of *A*'s children in being at *T*'s death. Hence, *all* of *A*'s children will not necessarily reach 25 within 21 years of the death of *A* and *A*'s presently living children. (Observe that if the age condition were 21 rather than 25, the necessary proof could be made by reference to *A* (see Case 4 above).)

Although it is common to speak of validating lives in the plural, a single validating life can be identified from among this group. Whenever an interest must vest or fail at or before the death of a survivor of a group of persons, or within 21 years after the death of the survivor, the validating life is the survivor, "for [as] Twisden used to say, the candles were all lighted at once."

If you first identify all persons who can affect vesting, and then test each person, the logical process of the Rule becomes clear. For an interest to be valid, the necessary proof must be made from among persons who can affect vesting. Alternatively, the interest must vest at creation or vest, or fail, within 21 years after creation.

PROBLEMS

1. *T* bequeaths a fund in trust "for *A* for life, then to the first child of *A* to be admitted to the bar." Is the latter gift valid? If so, who is the validating life?

2. Compare the following bequests:
(a) To *A* for life, then to *B* if *B* goes to the planet Saturn.
(b) To *A* for life, then to *B* if any person goes to the planet Saturn.
(c) To *A* for life, then to *B* for life if any person goes to the planet Saturn.

Is *B*'s remainder good in each bequest? Who is the validating life?

3. *T* devises Blackacre "to *A* for life, then for life to *A*'s oldest child who survives *A*, then to the first child of that child for life, then to *B*."

---

9. *A*'s spouse and other potential sexual partners, who can become a parent of *A*'s child, can affect vesting, but they are redundant. You cannot prove anything by them that you cannot prove by *A*. Hence they do not qualify for testing in search of a validating life.

10. A class gift must be good for all members of the class or it is void for all. See infra page 787.

A, *B*, and *A*'s son, *S*, survive *T*. What interests, if any, violate the Rule against Perpetuities?

4.   Professor Leach illustrated the rigorous logic of the Rule in this imaginative and famous passage:

> The settled inclusion of twenty-one years in gross and the admission of extraneous lives bring it about that a testator or settlor, when motivated by vanity, is able to tie up his property, regardless of lives and deaths in his own family, for an unconscionable period — viz., twenty-one years after the deaths of a dozen or so healthy babies chosen from families noted for longevity, a term which, in the ordinary course of events, will add up to about a century. [6 American Law of Property §24.16, at 52 (1952).]

A trust to pay the income to the testator's issue per stirpes from time to time living until 21 years after the death of the survivor of Alice, Bob, Chuck, Dorothy, Ellie, Frances, Gary, Hank, Ira, Jimmy, Karen, and Lucy (12 healthy babies born last week in local hospitals), then to distribute the principal to the testator's issue per stirpes then living, is valid.

Can you imagine any situation where using extraneous lives might be useful? Can you see why lawyers do not create trusts to last for the lives of 12 healthy babies plus 21 years? See Dukeminier, The Uniform Statutory Rule Against Perpetuities: Ninety Years in Limbo, 34 UCLA L. Rev. 1023, 1030 (1987).

5.   For different ways of solving perpetuities problems, see Becker, A Methodology for Solving Perpetuities Problems Under the Common Law Rule, 67 Wash. U.L.Q. 949 (1989); Fletcher, Perpetuities: Basic Clarity, Muddled Reform, 63 Wash. L. Rev. 791 (1988).

SECTION B.   THE REQUIREMENT OF NO POSSIBILITY OF REMOTE VESTING: THE WHAT-MIGHT-HAPPEN RULE

> The Rule against Perpetuities is not a rule of construction, but a peremptory command of law. It is not, like a rule of construction, a test, more or less artificial, to determine intention. Its object is to defeat intention. Therefore every provision in a will or settlement is to be construed as if the Rule did not exist, and then to the provision so construed the Rule is to be remorselessly applied.
>
> J. Gray
> *The Rule Against Perpetuities*
> *§629 (4th ed. 1942)*

1. The Fertile Octogenarian

The poet Marianne Moore once wrote of an imaginary garden with real toads in it. Because of the rule that any possibility that an interest might vest too remotely invalidates the interest, the Rule against Perpetuities is much like Marianne Moore's garden. Developed by the active imagination of lawyers, the Rule is the abode of such fantastical characters as the fertile octogenarian, the unborn widow, and other imaginary beings with power to bring the Rule down hard on the head of any trespasser. The first of these characters we meet is the fertile octogenarian. In the following famous case, Jee v. Audley, be sure you understand why the gift is valid if we assume Elizabeth Jee cannot give birth to any more children — an assumption the court rejects. Also be sure you understand why — given the court's assumptions — none of the persons mentioned in the will, including Mary Hall and the four living Jee daughters, can be used as validating lives.

Jee v. Audley
Court of Chancery, England, 1787
1 Cox 324, 29 Eng. Rep. 1186

Edward Audley, by his will, bequeathed as follows,

> Also my will is that £1000 shall be placed out at interest during the life of my wife, which interest I give her during her life, and at her death I give the said £1000 unto my niece Mary Hall and the issue of her body lawfully begotten,[11] and to be begotten, and in default of such issue I give the said £1000 to be equally divided between the daughters then living of my kinsman John Jee and his wife Elizabeth Jee.

It appeared that John Jee and Elizabeth Jee were living at the time of the death of the testator, had four daughters and no son, and were of a very advanced age. Mary Hall was unmarried and of the age of about 40; the wife was dead. The present bill was filed by the four daughters of John and Elizabeth Jee to have the £1000 secured for their benefit upon the event of the said Mary Hall dying without leaving children. And the question was, whether the limitation to the daughters of John and Elizabeth Jee was not void as being too remote; and to prove it so, it was said that this was to take effect on a general failure of issue of Mary Hall; and though it was to the daughters of John and

---

11. A fee tail estate could not be created in personal property. "Unto Mary Hall and the issue of her body" gives Mary the equivalent of a fee simple in the £1000. — Eds.

Elizabeth Jee, yet it was not confined to the daughters living at the death of the testator, and consequently it might extend to after-born daughters, in which case it would not be within the limit of a life or lives in being and 21 years afterwards, beyond which time an executory devise is void.

On the other side it was said, that though the late cases had decided that on a gift to children generally, such children as should be living at the time of the distribution of the fund should be let in, yet it would be very hard to adhere to such a rule of construction so rigidly, as to defeat the evident intention of the testator in this case, especially as there was no real possibility of John and Elizabeth Jee having children after the testator's death, they being then 70 years old; that if there were two ways of construing words, that should be adopted which would give effect to the disposition made by the testator; that the case, which had decided that afterborn children should take, proceeded on the implied intention of the testator, and never meant to give an effect to words which would totally defeat such intention. . . .

KENYON, M.R.[12] Several cases . . . have settled that children born after the death of the testator shall take a share in these cases; the difference is, where there is an immediate devise, and where there is an interest in remainder; in the former case the children living at the testator's death only shall take; in the latter those who are living at the time the interest vests in possession; and this being now a settled principle, I shall not strain to serve an intention at the expense of removing the landmarks of the law; it is of infinite importance to abide by decided cases, and perhaps more so on this subject than any other. The general principles which apply to this case are not disputed: the limitations of personal estate are void, unless they necessarily vest, if at all, within a life or lives in being and 21 years or 9 or 10 months afterwards. This has been sanctioned by the opinion of judges of all times, from the time of the Duke of Norfolk's Case to the present: it is grown reverend by age, and is not now to be broken in upon; I am desired to do in this case something which I do not feel myself at liberty to do, namely to suppose it impossible for persons in so advanced an age as John and Elizabeth Jee to have children; but if this can be done in one case it may in another, and it is a very dangerous experiment,

---

12. Lord Ellenborough said of Lord Kenyon: "No man ever hit so often, who always shot flying." G. Kenyon, The Life of Lloyd, First Lord Kenyon, Lord Chief Justice of England, 319 (1873). Lord Kenyon did shoot flying but whether he hit the target so often is debatable. He is credited with fathering in this case the absolute certainty doctrine of the Rule, the conclusive presumption of fertility, and the all-or-nothing doctrine applicable to class gifts.

For an unflattering portrait of this black-letter judge, who strictly enforced the rules without consulting the purposes of substantial justice or convenience, see 1 W. Townsend, The Lives of Twelve Eminent Judges 33-128 (1846). — Eds.

and introductive of the greatest inconvenience to give a latitude to such sort of conjecture. Another thing pressed upon me, is to decide on the events which have happened; but I cannot do this without overturning very many cases. The single question before me is, not whether the limitation is good in the events which have happened, but whether it was good in its creation; and if it were not, I cannot make it so. Then must this limitation, if at all, necessarily take place within the limits prescribed by law? The words are "in default of such issue I give the said £1000 to be equally divided between the daughters then living of John Jee and Elizabeth his wife." If it had been to "daughters now living," or "who should be living at the time of my death," it would have been very good; but as it stands, this limitation may take in after-born daughters; this point is clearly settled by Ellison v. Airey, [1 Ves. 111], and the effect of law on such limitation cannot make any difference in construing such intention. If then this will extended to after-born daughters, is it within the rules of law? Most certainly not, because John and Elizabeth Jee might have children born ten years after the testator's death, and then Mary Hall might die without issue 50 years afterwards; in which case it would evidently transgress the rules prescribed. I am of opinion therefore, though the testator might possibly mean to restrain the limitation to the children who should be living at the time of his death, I cannot, consistently with decided cases, construe it in such restrained sense, but must intend it to take in after-born children. This therefore not being within the rules of law, and as I cannot judge upon subsequent events, I think the limitation void. Therefore dismiss the bill, but without costs.

NOTES AND PROBLEMS

1. In Jee v. Audley, the Jee daughters brought a suit against Mary Hall "to have the £1000 secured for their benefit." When future interests are created in personal property, without any trust, there is obviously a danger that the possessory owner will dispose of the property so that there is nothing left at her death. The court may, in its discretion, compel the possessory owner to execute a bond. Mary Hall's defense is that the Jee daughters have no interest to be protected because their interest violates the Rule against Perpetuities and is void.

2. Lord Kenyon held that "in default of such issue" of Mary Hall meant a *general failure of issue*, which is more commonly called an *indefinite failure of issue*. Indefinite failure of issue means the running out of Mary's line of issue at her death *or at any time thereafter*. See supra, page 689.

The indefinite failure construction made a good deal of sense when applied to a gift over following a fee tail. For example, in eighteenth-century England, if *T* devised blackacre "to *A* and the heirs of his body, but if *A* dies without issue to *B* and his heirs," *B* had a vested remainder following a fee tail. "If *A* dies without issue" simply referred to the termination of the preceding fee tail estate and meant "when *A*'s bloodline runs out." Where it was not possible to create a fee tail, as in personal property, an indefinite failure construction is rather hard to justify. Fourteen years before Jee v. Audley, Charles Fearne, the great authority on contingent remainders, wrote, "the courts, in the case of personal estates, will incline to construe a limitation after dying without issue, to be a dying without issue living at the death of the party, wherever any ground is afforded for such construction, in order to support the devise over." C. Fearne, Contingent Remainders 148 (2d ed. 1773). But Lord Kenyon was not so inclined in Jee v. Audley.

The court could have saved the gift over to the daughters of John and Elizabeth Jee if it had construed the gift to be effective only if Mary Hall left no issue living at her death. Given that construction, Mary Hall would be the validating life, and the gift over would be valid.

3. Lord Kenyon rejected all the arguments made to save the gift. The opinion also states that the court was urged "to decide on the events which have happened" between the testator's death and the lawsuit, without specifying what they were. Perhaps John or Elizabeth Jee had died. The court refused to take into account actual events. In recent years a number of states have adopted the wait-and-see doctrine (see infra pages 816-838), under which the validity of interests is judged by actual events happening after the date the instrument becomes effective, but the position of Lord Kenyon remains the orthodox one.

4. Although the indefinite failure of issue construction has been abolished in probably all states and is of very little modern importance, the principles involved in Jee v. Audley are still fundamental. "Indefinite failure of issue" is the equivalent of any remote event that may happen more than 21 years after the death of all living persons.[13] With the gift in Jee v. Audley, compare the following bequests. Which would be valid?

(a) To Mary Hall, but if the Bay Bridge falls, to John Jee.

(b) To Mary Hall, but if the Bay Bridge falls, to the daughters of

---

13. If you have a hard time imagining similar remote events, here are two: *T* devises his gravel pits to trustees to work them until the pits are exhausted and then to sell them and divide the proceeds among *T*'s issue then living (held void in In re Wood, [1894] 3 Ch. 381, even though the pits in fact were exhausted in six years). During World War II, *T* devises property to her husband's relatives in Germany who should survive the war (held void in Brownell v. Edmunds, 209 F.2d 349 (4th Cir. 1953), on ground World War II might not end within lives in being plus 21 years). Other remote events will appear in subsequent cases in this chapter.

John and Elizabeth Jee now living. (Note the dictum of Lord Kenyon on this question.)

(c) To Mary Hall, but if the Bay Bridge falls, to the daughters of John and Elizabeth Jee now living who are then living.

(d) To Mary Hall, but if the Bay Bridge falls, to John Jee for life, then to Elizabeth Jee for life, then to the daughters of John and Elizabeth Jee now living for life, then to the issue of John and Elizabeth Jee now living who are then living, per stirpes.

5. *T* devises Blackacre "to my good friend, *A*, for life, then in fee to such of *A*'s nephews and nieces as live to attain the age of 21." At the time of *T*'s death, *A* is living and has two brothers (*B* and *C*) and four nephews and nieces, all of whom are under age 21. Is the interest given to *A*'s nephews and nieces valid under the Rule against Perpetuities? (A clue: The answer is, "It depends.")

NOTE: THE PRESUMPTION OF FERTILITY

The Fertile Octogenarian. The Bible tells us that Sarah gave birth to Isaac when she was 90 years old and Abraham 100. Genesis 17:15 to 21:3. But modern verifiable medical records show no births to women over 60, and births to women over 50 are statistically insignificant. The Guinness Book of World Records 15 (27th ed. 1989) says:

> Medical literature contains extreme but unauthenticated cases of septuagenarian mothers such as Mrs Ellen Ellis, aged 72, of Four Crosses, Clwyd, Wales, who allegedly produced a stillborn 13th child May 15, 1776, in her 46th year of marriage. Many very late maternities are cover-ups for illegitimate grandchildren. The oldest recorded mother of whom there is satisfactory verification (provided by the doctor who attended her) was Mrs Ruth Alice Kistler . . . of Portland, Ore. She . . . gave birth to a daughter, Suzan, in Glendale, Calif, Oct. 18, 1956, when her age was 57 years 129 days.

Nonetheless, in spite of the evidence that women over 60 cannot bear children, the standard rule in perpetuities cases is that it is conclusively presumed that a person can have a child until death.

The Precocious Toddler. What is the youngest age of procreation presumed by the law? This has never been established. Only one known case has dealt with the issue. In Re Gaite's Will Trusts, [1949] 1 All E.R. 459 (Ch.), the court had before it a bequest that would be void only if it were assumed that a person under the age of five could have a child. The court validated the gift, not on the ground of physical impossibility of a person becoming a parent at an age under five, but on the ground that a child born to so young a person would necessarily be illegitimate, and hence excluded as a child. The Family Law Reform Act, 1969, §15(1), provides that thereafter it will be presumed, in dispositions of property, that references to children and other relatives of a person include illegitimate children. The constructional escape from the Rule used by the court is no longer available.

The youngest mother on record is Lina Medina of Lima, Peru. On May 14, 1939, at the age of five, she was delivered of a 6½-pound boy by caesarian section.[14] An investigation revealed that she had been raped by a mentally retarded teenage stepbrother. In a story in the New York Times, April 3, 1963, at 70, one of Lina's obstetricians, Dr. Rolando Colareta, recalled that he and his colleagues were astounded to discover that "although Lina had every aspect of a five-year-old infant, her sexual development corresponded to that of a young lady over 15 years old. . . . Surprising though it seems, we confirmed that Lina had menstrual periods since she was one-month old." Dr. Colareta went on to point out that cases of 12- and 13-year-old mothers were common in the Andes, where Lina came from. "As a matter of fact," he said, "I delivered a child to a 9-year-old girl here last week and it didn't even make the newspapers." The New York Times reported that Lina, then 28 and still unmarried, was working as a secretary. Her son Gerardo, then 23, was living with Lina's parents and studying accounting.

The Fertile Decedent (or The Child En Ventre Sa Frigidaire).   With the establishment of sperm and ova banks and the advent of frozen embryos medical science has made it possible for a person to become a genetic father or mother after death. The impact of this development on the Rule against Perpetuities has not yet been examined by the courts. Suppose that *T* bequeaths his residuary estate in trust to pay the income to his son (and sole heir) *A* for life, remainder to *A*'s children who reach 21. The gift to *A*'s children has been assumed to be valid because all of *A*'s children will be born before *A*'s death (or within a period of gestation thereafter) and they will all reach age 21 within 21 years thereafter. *A* is the measuring life in being. Is such a gift now to fail because medical science has made it possible for *A* to become a father

---

14. Occasionally a questionable story of an even younger mother appears. The National Examiner, Mar. 12, 1985, at 23, col. 1, reported that a 14-pound baby girl in the Philippines was born pregnant. According to the story, the baby girl had a male fetus growing in her uterus, in the fifth month of its development. A few days after the baby's birth, the fetus was removed by Caesarean section. The newspaper reported that the fetus lived a few hours in an incubator and was baptized Juan according to Catholic rites. The attending doctor said it seemed likely that the developing fetus was really the girl's fraternal twin brother. "Probably the two eggs were fertilized at the same time, but only one became properly implanted in the uterine wall, engulfing the other egg during its faster growth." Id. In medical journals, there have been a few dozen cases of *fetus-in-fetu* reported (as many in boys as in girls!) but no *fetus-in-fetu* has before been alleged to have been born alive. See 82 Am. J. Clinical Pathology 115 (1984).

of a child conceived after he is dead, who may reach 21 more than 21 years after *A*'s death? The answer to this question should be a resounding NO, but can that answer be reached through the application of principles consistent with the conclusive presumption of fertility? See Leach, Perpetuities in the Atomic Age: The Sperm Bank and The Fertile Decedent, 48 A.B.A.J. 942 (1962); 3 A. Casner, Estate Planning §11.4.11 at 258 n.12 (5th ed. 1986).

A few jurisdictions have modern statutes limiting the presumption of fertility in perpetuities cases to statistically significant child-bearing years (say, between 13 and 65) or permitting the introduction in any case of evidence of capacity to bear children. Ill. Ann. Stat. ch. 30, ¶194, §4(c)(3) (Supp. 1989); N.Y. Est., Powers & Trusts Law §9-1.3(e) (Supp. 1989); Tenn. Code Ann. §24-5-112 (1980). The Illinois and New York statutes provide that the possibility that a person may adopt a child shall be disregarded.

2. The Unborn Widow

Dickerson v. Union National Bank of Little Rock
Supreme Court of Arkansas, 1980
268 Ark. 292, 595 S.W.2d 677

SMITH, J.   The principal question on this appeal is whether a trust created by the holographic will of Nina Martin Dickerson, who died on June 21, 1967, is void under the rule against perpetuities, because it is possible that the interest of the various beneficiaries may not vest within the period allowed by that rule. Cecil H. Dickerson, Jr., one of the testatrix's two sons, attacks the validity of the trust. The chancellor rejected Cecil's attack on two grounds: First, Cecil should have raised the question of the validity of the trust in the probate court in connection with the probate of the will and the administration of the estate. His failure to do so makes the issue res judicata. Second, on the merits, the trust does not violate the rule against perpetuities. We disagree with the chancellor on both grounds.

The facts are not in dispute. The testatrix was survived by her two children. Cecil, 50, was single, and Martin 45, was married. At that time the two sons had a total of seven children, who of course were the testatrix's grandchildren.

The testatrix named the appellee bank as executor and directed that at the close of the administration proceedings the bank transfer to itself as trustee all the assets of the estate. The terms of the trust are quite long, but we may summarize them as follows:

The trust is to continue until the death of both sons and of Martin's widow, *who is not otherwise identified*. The income is to be divided equally between the two sons during their lives, except that Cecil's share is to be used in part to provide for a four-year college education for his two minor children, who are named, and for the support and education of any bodily heirs by a later marriage. When the two named minor children finish college, their share of the income is to revert to Cecil. Upon Martin's death his share of the income is to be paid monthly to his widow and children living in the home, but the share of each child terminates and passes to the widow when that child marries or becomes self-supporting. The trustee is given discretionary power to make advance payments of principal in certain cases of emergency or illness. If either son and his wife and all his bodily heirs die before the final distribution of the trust assets, that son's share in the estate and in the income passes to the other son and then to his bodily heirs.

As far as the rule against perpetuities is concerned, the important part of the will is paragraph VIII, from which we quote:

> VIII. This Trust shall continue until the death of both my sons and my son Martin's widow and until the youngest child of either son has reached the age of twenty-five years, then at that time, the Trust shall terminate and the Union National Bank Trustee shall distribute and pay over the entire balance of the Trust Fund in their hands to the bodily heirs of my son, Cecil H. Dickerson, and the bodily heirs of my son, William Martin Dickerson, in the same manner and in the same proportions as provided for by the general inheritance laws of Arkansas.

Upon the death of the testatrix in 1967, her will was presented to the Faulkner Probate Court by her son Cecil, who lived in Conway, Arkansas. (The other son, Martin, was living in Indiana.) The probate court entered a routine order reciting that the will had been properly executed, admitting the instrument to probate, and appointing the bank as executor, without bond. On May 31, 1968, the probate court entered another routine order approving the executor's first and final accounting, allowing fees to the executor and its attorneys, discharging the executor, and closing the administration of the estate. That order made no reference to the validity of the trust or to the manner in which the assets of the estate were to be distributed.

In fact, the assets of the estate, except for $18,000 set aside for administration expenses and estate taxes, had already been transferred by the bank to itself as trustee. On August 11, 1967, about a month after the probate of the will, the bank filed in the Faulkner Chancery Court an ex parte "Declaration of Trust," in which the bank expressed its desire to perform the trust and asked the court to find and decree that it held the property in trust for the beneficiaries of the testamentary trust. . . .

Nothing further appears to have taken place in the case until 1977, when Cecil Dickerson filed . . . the present complaint against the bank and its trust officer. The complaint, after reciting the background facts, asserts that the trust is void under the rule against perpetuities. The complaint charges the trust officer with violations of his fiduciary duties in failing to deliver all the assets of the estate to the heirs of the testatrix and in failing to ask the probate court to construe the will with respect to violations of the rule against perpetuities. The complaint charges that the trust officer concealed the trust's defects from the court and from the testatrix's two sons. The prayer is for an order restraining the trustee from making further transfers or distributions of the trust funds, for recovery of Cecil's half interest in the estate, for compensatory and punitive damages, and for other proper relief. The charges of negligence and wrong-doing on the part of the bank were later dismissed without prejudice. The other matters were heard upon stipulated facts, culminating in the decree dismissing Cecil's complaint. . . .

First, there is no merit in the argument that Cecil's failure to challenge the validity of the trust in the probate proceedings precludes him from raising that issue now. Under the Probate Code the probate court does have the power to construe a will, but the construction must be necessary to the determination of some issue properly before the court. Ark. Stat. Ann. §60-416 (Repl. 1971).

. . . The complications that may be presented by the rule against perpetuities are so numerous and difficult that even experienced lawyers and judges must usually consult the authorities to be certain about its application to a given set of facts. There was not the slightest reason for Cecil or Martin Dickerson to suspect a possible invalidity in their mother's testamentary trust, nor any duty on their part to raise such a question. To deprive them of their property on the basis of res judicata would actually be to deny them their day in court.

Indeed, if there was any duty on anyone to raise the issue, that duty rested on the bank. It was a fiduciary, both as executor and as trustee. It owed a duty of good faith and loyalty to all the beneficiaries of the estate and of the trust and a duty to act impartially as between successive beneficiaries. Restatement of Trusts (2d), §§170 and 232 (1959), and Arkansas Annotations (1939) to those sections. We do not imply any wrongdoing on the part of this appellee, but it is certainly not in a position to ignore the possible invalidity of the trust both in the probate court and in the ex parte chancery court case and then take advantage, to its own pecuniary benefit, of the beneficiaries' similar course of conduct. A contrary rule would compel the beneficiaries of an estate or trust to hire a lawyer to watch the executor or trustee, when the law actually permits them to rely upon the fiduciary.

Second, the trust is void because there is a possibility that the estate will not vest within a period measured by a life or lives in being at the testatrix's death, plus 21 years. A bare possibility is enough. "The interest *must* vest within the time allowed by the rule. If there is any possibility that the contingent event may happen beyond the limits of the rule, the transaction is void." Comstock v. Smith, 255 Ark. 564, 501 S.W.2d 617 (1973).

The terms of this trust present an instance of the "unborn widow," a pitfall that is familiar to every student of the rule against perpetuities. This trust is not to terminate until the deaths of Cecil, Martin, and Martin's widow, but the identity of Martin's widow cannot be known until his death. Martin might marry an 18-year-old woman twenty years after his mother's death, have additional children by her, and then die. Cecil also might die. Martin's young widow, however, might live for another 40 or 50 years, after which the interests would finally vest. But since Cecil and Martin would have been the last measuring lives in being at the death of the testatrix, the trust property would not vest until many years past the maximum time allowed by the rule. The rule was formulated to prevent just such a possibility — uncertainty about the title to real or personal property for an unreasonably long time in the future.

The violation of the rule, except for the interposition of a trust, is actually so clear that the appellee does not argue the point. Instead, it insists that the property would vest in Cecil and Martin's bodily heirs at their deaths, with only the right of possession of the property being deferred until the termination of the trust.

This argument overlooks the fact that the words "bodily heirs" were used in the decisive paragraph VIII of the will not as words of limitation, to specify the duration of an estate granted to Cecil and Martin, but as words of purchase, to specify the persons who would take at the termination of the trust. Obviously the identity of those persons cannot be determined until the death of Martin's widow; so the ownership would not vest until that time. . . .

Here the testatrix directed that at the termination of the trust the property be distributed as provided by the general inheritance laws of Arkansas. At the time of the deaths of Cecil and Martin it would be utterly impossible to say who would take, in the case we have supposed, at the death of Martin's young widow 50 years later. Under our law the surviving descendants would then take per capita if they were related to Cecil and Martin in equal degree, but per stirpes if in unequal degree. Ark. Stat. Ann. §§61-134 and -135 (Repl. 1971). If there were no surviving descendants of one brother, the entire property would go to the surviving descendants of the other. If there were no surviving descendants of either, the property would revert to the testatrix's estate and go to her collateral heirs. Thus it is really too plain for argument that the interest of every descendant (or "bodily heir") of Cecil or Martin would be contingent upon his surviving the death of Martin's widow, at which time — and only at which time — the title would finally vest. . . .

Reversed and remanded for further proceedings.

PROBLEMS AND NOTE

1. *T* bequeaths a fund in trust to pay the income "to my son for life, then to my son's widow, if any, for life; then to pay the principal to my son's children, but if no child of my son is alive at the death of the survivor of my son and his widow, then to pay the principal to the American Red Cross." Is any gift invalid? See J. Morris & W. Leach, The Rule Against Perpetuities 44 (2d ed. 1962).

2. Why did not the gift to Cecil's and Martin's bodily heirs vest at their deaths? See Note 3, supra page 664; Warren-Boynton State Bank v. Wallbaum, supra page 694.

3. California Civ. Code §715.7 (1982) provides: "In determining the validity of a future interest in real or personal property . . . [under the Rule against Perpetuities], an individual described as a spouse of a person in being at the commencement of a perpetuities period shall be deemed a 'life in being' at such time whether or not the individual so described was then in being." Similar provisions, but varying in detail, have been adopted in Ill. Ann. Stat. c. 30, §194 (c)(1)(C) (Supp. 1989), and N.Y. Est., Powers & Trusts Law §9-1.3(c) (1967).

NOTE: SPLIT CONTINGENCIES

In the *Dickerson* case the trust was to continue (1) "until the death of both of my sons and my son Martin's widow" or (2) "until the youngest child of either son has reached the age of twenty-five years," whichever happened later. Each of these events might happen beyond lives in being plus 21 years. Suppose, however, that the first event had read "until the death of both of my sons and my son's wife Lucy." In that case, if the trust actually terminates on the first event, the remainder to bodily heirs is valid, as it will happen at the end of lives in being.

The rule applicable to our hypothetical is known as the doctrine of split contingencies. If the testator expressly provides that a remainder will vest upon one of two events, one of which might occur too remotely (i.e., when the youngest child of Cecil and Martin reaches 25), and the other of which must occur, if at all, at the death of persons in being (i.e., Cecil, Martin, and Lucy), the testator is treated as making two separate gifts. Each gift of a remainder is tested separately under the Rule against Perpetuities. In our hypothetical, the remainder given to bodily heirs when Cecil's and Martin's children reach 25 would be void; the remainder given upon the death of Cecil, Martin, and Lucy would be valid.

3. Administrative Contingencies

Another unusual possibility, occasionally overlooked by the drafter, is that a will may not be probated, or an estate distributed, for many years after the testator's death. Although distribution of an estate ordinarily is completed within a few years of the testator's death, in a few cases an estate has been tied up for many years in litigation or the will has been found many years after the testator dies. See, for example, Estate of Garrett, 372 Pa. 438, 94 A.2d 357 (1953), supra page 111 (estate closed after 23 years); Richards v. Tolbert, 232 Ga. 678, 208 S.E.2d 486 (1974) (will found and probated 57 years after the testator's death).

The possibility of remote distribution gives rise to what are known as the administrative contingency cases. Thus:

> *Case 7. The Slothful Executor. T* devises property "to *T*'s issue living upon distribution of *T*'s estate." *T*'s purpose is to avoid extra administrative costs and possible taxation in the estates of any of *T*'s issue who die before *T*'s estate is distributed. Yet, because *T*'s estate may not be distributed for many years, perhaps after all *T*'s surviving issue are dead, the gift to *T*'s issue living at distribution may be held void. See In re Estate of Campbell, 28 Cal. App. 2d 102, 82 P.2d 22 (1938) (holding void a gift to officers of lodge in office at time of distribution of *T*'s estate).

There are at least two arguments that can be made to save the gift in Case 7. First, it can be argued that distribution of the estate will not be delayed beyond a reasonable time, which necessarily is less than 21 years. This argument was accepted in Belfield v. Booth, 63 Conn. 299, 27 A. 585 (1893). Second, it can be argued that since the testator did not intend the executor to have the power to select recipients by delaying distribution, the class of issue will close at the time distribution reasonably should be made. See Estate of Taylor, 66 Cal. 2d 855, 428 P.2d 301 (1967).

The administrative contingency involved in Case 7 is a true condition precedent: *T*'s will requires *T*'s issue to survive distribution in order to take. Some administrative contingency cases, however, involve language that ought not to be construed to create a condition precedent to vesting. Examples are "to *A* upon distribution of my estate," "to my issue when my debts are paid," and "to *A* upon probate of this will." Language of this sort, not requiring survival, should be construed as merely describing the natural course of events and not importing a condition precedent. Unfortunately, occasionally such language has been construed to create a condition precedent.

Deiss v. Deiss

Illinois Appellate Court, 1989
180 Ill. App. 3d 600, 536 N.E.2d 120

McCULLOUGH, J.   Plaintiff Katie B. Deiss appeals the circuit court's order denying her petition for declaratory judgment. Plaintiff contends the inter vivos trust of which she is a codonor is void because it violates the Rule against perpetuities and the circuit court's finding to the contrary is erroneous. We affirm.

Plaintiff Katie B. Deiss and her husband, Rudolph V. Deiss, established an irrevocable trust on January 29, 1969, with their son, Orville Deiss, as trustee. The corpus of this trust consists of a house in Mason City and farmland located in McLean, Logan, and Mason Counties in Illinois and farmland in Jewel County in Kansas. The trust provides that the trustee shall manage the real estate and pay the mortgages and other encumbrances on the property out of the income received from farming the property. Any net income is paid to Rudolph and Katie. The trustee is given the power to "lease and release" the real estate, including leasing the tract which the trustee then occupied to himself as well as leasing the remaining tracts to the other sons of the donors; Rudolph V. Deiss, Jr., Merle Deiss, and LeRoy Deiss. The trustee is also given the power to mortgage and remortgage the trust property.

At the first death of Rudolph and Katie, all of the income of the trust is paid to the survivor of them. Rudolph Deiss died on November 15, 1973. The trust continues until Katie's death and all of the mortgages on the trust property are paid in full. After both conditions are met, the corpus and accumulated income of the trust is divided as follows:

Orville Deiss	farmland in Mason County
Rudolph V. Deiss, Jr.	farmland in Logan County
Merle Deiss	farmland in McLean County
LeRoy Deiss	house in Mason City, Illinois and farmland in Kansas

Each child of the donor receives a life estate in the property and the remainder passes to the children of each named child (grandchildren of the donors), or to his children (great-grandchildren of the donors), should a grandchild predecease his parent.

On July 1, 1987, the plaintiff filed a complaint for declaratory judgment, praying that the trust be declared void because it violates the Rule against perpetuities and that the court declare that the defendants, the sons of the plaintiff as well as the present living grandchildren and great-grandchildren of the plaintiff, have no interest in the trust property. A guardian ad litem was appointed to represent the minor beneficiaries.

In the instant case, the remainder interest is described as follows:

> [U]pon the death of the survivor [of the donors] this trust shall continue until mortgages on the real estate . . . has [sic] been paid in full and both [d]onors are deceased. At the time that both of these conditions are met, the corpus and accumulated income of the trust shall be divided [with specific parcels going to each of the four sons for life] . . . with remainder [in such parcels] to his children, the children of any predeceased child to take the share their parent would have taken if living. . . . Should any of our children die leaving no child or children, or descendants of a child or children surviving, their share shall go, in equal shares, to their brothers or the children thereof per stirpes.

After hearing argument from the parties, the court found that the trust did not violate the Rule against perpetuities and denied plaintiff's petition.

Plaintiff argued in the trial court that the remainder interests are contingent because two conditions must be met before the interests vest: the mortgages must be paid in full and the children must survive the death of the life tenant of the property. Plaintiff argued that the mortgage condition *delayed* vesting and because it is possible that any of the children of the plaintiff, all lives in being at the creation of the interest, could die before the plaintiff and before the mortgages are paid, vesting may not occur within 21 years after their death. This violates the Rule against perpetuities and, therefore, the trust is void.

The defendants, Merle, Sr.; Stacia; Merle, Jr.; Lynette; Steve; LeRoy; and Susan argued in the trial court that the remainder interests were vested at the time the trust was created. These defendants urged that the payment of the mortgages affected the quantum or amount of the estate and not the time of its vesting. Because the remainder interests were vested, the defendants argued that the Rule against perpetuities does not apply and therefore the trust is valid.

Plaintiff now urges that the trial court erred in concluding that the remainder interests are vested and that the payment of mortgages does not delay vesting but refers to the quantum of the estate conveyed. Plaintiff urges that Johnson v. Preston (1907), 226 Ill. 447, 80 N.E. 1001, and Trabue v. Gillham (1951), 408 Ill. 508, 97 N.E.2d 341, govern this case. Plaintiff also represents that the so-called "quantum theory" does not apply to this case.

The guardian ad litem urges that the payment of mortages by the trustee affects the quantum of the estate received by the beneficiaries and does not prevent the vesting of the interest at the time of the creation of the trust. Thus, the remainder interests are vested and the Rule against perpetuities does not apply. Among other cases, the guardian ad litem directs our attention to Ducker v. Burnham (1893), 146 Ill. 9, 34 N.E. 558.

Similarly, several of the defendants on appeal urge that the interests are vested remainders because there is no uncertainty as to who takes the property after the retirement of the mortgages and the deaths of the plaintiff, as surviving donor, and all the named life tenants.

The Rule against perpetuities concerns the remoteness in the vesting of interest. It provides: "No interest is good unless it must vest, if at all, no later than twenty-one years after some life in being at the creation of the interest." (Gray, The Rule Against Perpetuities sec. 201, at 191 (4th ed. 1942).) The Rule against perpetuities does not apply to vested interests and the postponement of enjoyment or possession does not bring the interest within the rule. (Chicago Title & Trust Co. v. Shellaberger (1948), 399 Ill. 320, 334, 77 N.E.2d 675, 683.) Since the Rule against perpetuities does not apply to vested interests, it must be determined whether the language in the document before us created a vested or contingent remainder.

Initially, we note as did the supreme court in Warren-Boynton State Bank v. Wallbaum (1988), 123 Ill. 2d 429, 435-36, 123 Ill. Dec. 936, 939, 528 N.E.2d 640, 643, that the law of future interests is confusing at best. Moreover, while there is an abundance of reported cases, no case is ever factually identical to the issue then before the court and therefore, each case must be carefully examined. We have thoroughly reviewed those cases relied upon by the parties and conclude that the language in the instrument in this case describes a vested remainder.

Plaintiff urges that the payment of the mortgages before the division of the trust property is a condition precedent which makes the remainder interest contingent and subject to the Rule against perpetuities. Because the mortgages may never be paid in full, the remainder interests violate the rule and are void. As authority, plaintiff cites Johnson v. Preston (1907), 226 Ill. 447, 80 N.E. 1001.

In *Johnson*, the testatrix devised certain real estate in the residue of her estate to her executor "to have and to hold for a space of 25 years from and after the date of the probate of this will." Thereafter, the property so held was devised to several of the testatrix' grandsons in fee simple. During the 25 years, each named beneficiary was to share in the use, benefit and enjoyment of the property, and each was allowed to live and work on the property. The court held that the executor's interest was subject to a condition precedent — probate of the will — and since the condition could not be said to conclusively happen within 21 years, the devise to the executor was void.

We find *Johnson* distinguishable from the instant case. Significantly, the estate of the executor in *Johnson* was subject to a condition precedent, thus making it a contingent interest. The executor himself in *Johnson* had to fulfill a condition — probating the will — before his interest arose. In the instant case, there is no condition that the plaintiff's four sons must fulfill or plaintiff's grandchildren or great grandchildren must *personally* fulfill before their interest arises. It is the trustee in the case before us who is directed and therefore has a duty to pay the mortgages on the trust corpus before dividing the corpus among the plaintiff's four sons after her death. We do not find *Johnson* persuasive authority for this case. . . .

Plaintiff next argues that the language used to describe the remainders in this case also makes them contingent and therefore, subject to the Rule against perpetuities. Specifically, plaintiff contends that the remainderman cannot be ascertained until the death of the life tenants — plaintiff's four sons. Plaintiff cites Trabue v. Gillham (1951), 408 Ill. 508, 97 N.E.2d 341, in support of her argument. In *Trabue*, the remainder interest described as follows was found to be a contingent remainder. "'At the death of the said . . . , I devise the real estate herein given him for life, to his children and the descendants of any deceased child of his, in fee . . . , the descendants . . . to take the portion such deceased child would be entitled to if living.'" (*Trabue*, 408 Ill. at 508, 97 N.E.2d at 341.) The issue in *Trabue* concerned the meaning of the phrase "die leaving no issue," found in a later clause of the will. The court found that "die leaving no issue" evidenced the testator's intent that the remainderman be ascertained at the death of the life tenant. Thus, a condition precedent of surviving the life tenant was attached to the remainder interest. The court further supported its conclusion by looking specifically to the word "and" used by the testator in the above-quoted clause. The court stated: "The gift following the life estate is to the children *and* the descendants of any deceased child. The interest of the descendants is in terms given the same status as that of the children, and is to arise at the same moment the children's interest comes into existence." *Trabue*, 408 Ill. at 512, 97 N.E.2d at 343.

The language used in the instant case is distinct from that used in *Trabue*. Here, the donors stated that after the life estate to each son, "the remainder to his children, the children of any deceased child to take the share their parent would have taken if living." In a later clause, the trust provides: "Should any of our children die leaving no child or children, or descendants of a child or children surviving, their share shall go, in equal shares, to their brothers, or the children thereof per stirpes." Taken together, both clauses do not treat grandchildren and great-grandchildren equally. The great-grandchildren's interests arise when a grandchild dies, which death could occur before the death of a life tenant-child of the donors. In the present case, the class of the remainder beneficiaries is certain and ascertainable now, unlike in *Trabue*.

Similar language to that used in the instant case has been found to be a vested interest, subject to divestment during the life of a life tenant where a remainderman predeceases a life tenant. (Warrington v. Chester (1920), 294 Ill. 524, 526, 128 N.E. 549, 550) ("'[u]pon the re-marriage of my said wife . . . I give . . . to my children . . . to be equally divided among them . . . the issue of any child who may have then deceased taking the share to which such deceased child would be entitled to if living'"); Murphy v. Westhoff (1944), 386 Ill. 136, 139, 53 N.E.2d 931, 932 ("'all . . . real estate . . . to my said wife for and during her life, with remainder to my children [named] in fee . . . in the event of the death of one of them . . . then to the survivors or survivor of them'"); Fleshner v. Fleshner (1941), 378 Ill. 536, 537, 39 N.E.2d 9, 10 ("'[A]ll of my property . . . to beloved wife . . . for . . . life. After the death of my wife . . . to my beloved children [named] or the surviving heirs of their body, the residue of my estate.'") The language in the instant case does not require the survival of remainder beneficiary until the death of the donors' children as a condition precedent but contemplates that a child of any one of the four sons of the donors may die before their parent. We find the language used in the instant case describes a vested remainder.

The trial court held that the sons of the plaintiff will take an equitable life estate at the death of the plaintiff and their descendants will take equitable remainders with the trustee retaining legal title to accomplish the payment of the mortgages. This conclusion is supported by the decision in Scofield v. Olcott (1887), 120 Ill. 362, 11 N.E. 351, where the court held:

> [I]f such payment or distribution appear to be postponed for the convenience of the fund or property, as where the future gift is postponed . . . a direction to pay upon the decease of the legatee for life, or after payment of the debts, the gift in remainder vests at once, and will not be deferred until the period in question. But where the payment is deferred for reasons personal to the legatee, the gift will not vest till the appointed time. [Citations.] *Scofield*, 120 Ill. at 373, 11 N.E. at 353.

The *Scofield* court also held: "A devise to a person after the payment of debts and legacies is not contingent, until such debts and legacies are paid; such a devise confers an immediately vested interest; the words of apparent postponement are considered only as creating a charge. [Citations.]" *Scofield*, 120 Ill. at 376, 11 N.E. at 355.

The holding of *Scofield* was later reaffirmed in Ducker v. Burnham (1893), 146 Ill. 9, 34 N.E. 558, Hawkins v. Bohling (1897), 168 Ill. 214, 48 N.E. 94, and Mettler v. Warner (1910), 243 Ill. 600, 90 N.E. 1099. The *Ducker* court also noted that "[t]he law presumes, that words of postponement relate to the enjoyment of the remainder rather than to the vesting thereof, and the intent to postpone the vesting of the estate must be clear and manifest." *Ducker*, 146 Ill. at 22-23, 34 N.E. at 561.

We find that the instrument before us does not clearly and manifestly evidence an intent to postpone the vesting of the estates until the payment of the mortgages. What is postponed is full enjoyment of the property.

Lastly, plaintiff contends that the quantum theory referred to by the trial court has little meaning in the context of this case. Specifically, plaintiff urges that the quantum principle means nothing more than size and the size of the trust corpus, 940 acres of farmland, is not affected by the payment of the mortgages because the income from the farmland is used to pay these mortgages. Further, when and if the mortgages are paid in full, the size of the corpus will always be the same — 940 acres. Thus, according to the plaintiff, the quantum argument means nothing in this case. We cannot agree.

Plaintiff's quantum argument ignores the fact that the trust provides that after both conditions are met, the corpus *and accumulated income* are divided among the donors' children for life. While the number of acres of farmland remain the same, the value of the devise is increased due to the retirement of the mortgages thereon. Also, the devise of the trust property carries with it the income which the property produces and that income decreases over time because it is used to pay the mortgages. Plaintiff focuses on the number of acres involved and ignores the value of the devise, a fact noted by the court in *Mettler* when ascertaining a testator's intent.

For the foregoing reasons, we agree with the trial court's findings and order that the trust is not violative of the Rule against perpetuities. Therefore, the order of the trial court denying plaintiff's petition for declaratory judgment is affirmed.

Affirmed.

QUESTION

Under the rules in Clobberie's Case, supra page 669, a gift to a person payable at a designated age may be vested with possession postponed. Should the concept of vested with possession postponed be extended to apply to gifts upon an uncertain event other than reaching a designated age? Should a gift "to *A*, to be possessed when the big tree falls," be vested with possession postponed? If not, how can you distinguish it from a gift "when the mortgages are paid," held valid in Deiss v. Deiss?

4. Gifts to Charity

Like a gift to an individual, a gift to charity must vest or fail within lives in being plus 21 years. After a charitable gift has vested, however, it may endure indefinitely.

When a gift to a nonexistent charity is made by will, it may violate the Rule against Perpetuities. W.C. Field's will is useful in demonstrating this problem. A story has gone around that W.C. Fields in his will directed that on his tombstone be carved, "On the whole, I'd rather be in Philadelphia."[15] Inspection of Fields's will revealed the story to be apocryphal and also revealed a potential perpetuities problem. This legendary misanthrope devised his estate in trust to pay his brother Walter $75 a week for life, his sister Adel $60 a week for life, and his friend Carlotta Monti $25 a week for life, and upon their deaths, "I direct that my executors procure the organization of a membership or other approved corporation under the name of the W.C. Fields College for orphan white boys and girls, where no religion of any sort is to be preached. Harmony is the purpose of this thought. It is my desire the college will be built in California in Los Angeles County." Does this violate the Rule against Perpetuities? See First Camden National Bank & Trust Co. v. Collins, 114 N.J. Eq. 59, 168 A. 275 (1933) (holding void a gift to a charitable corporation to be organized under the laws of New Jersey, on the ground it might not be organized within lives in being plus 21 years); but cf. Rice v. Stanley, 42 Ohio St. 2d 209, 327 N.E.2d 774 (1975), noted in 37 Ohio St. L.J. 685 (1976), 43 Tenn. L. Rev. 166 (1975) (holding valid a bequest in trust for a charitable corporation to be organized after the testator's death; the court saying that the gift was "immediate" and that the court would direct the trustee to convey the property to the corporation if organized within a reasonable time, and, if not so organized, would frame a scheme for disposition under the doctrine of cy pres).

One difference between gifts to individuals and gifts to charity ought to be noted here. If a gift to Charity *A* is to be divested in favor of Charity *B* if a specified event happens, the gift over to Charity *B* is exempt from the Rule against Perpetuities. Thus if *T* devises Blackacre to the Board of Education, and if the land ceases to be used for school purposes, then to the County Hospital, the gift to County Hospital is

---

15. Other Fields stories have become garbled in the retelling. At a "roast" of Fields at the Masquers' Club in Hollywood in 1939, Leo Rosten, taken by surprise when called on to say a few words, said: "The only thing I can say about W.C. Fields, whom I have admired since the day he advanced upon Baby LeRoy with an ice pick, is this: any man who hates dogs and babies can't be all bad." Ever since then this crack has been credited to — W.C. Fields! Rosten, Diversions, Saturday Rev., June 12, 1976, at 12.

valid even though it may not vest for centuries. This exemption applies only if *both* the possessory estate and the future interest are in charitable organizations. It does not apply if either the possessory estate or the future interest is in a private individual. See 4A A. Scott, Trusts §§401.5-401.7 (W. Fratcher 4th ed. 1989).

PROBLEMS

1.   *T* devises Blackacre "to the City School District so long as used for school purposes, then to *A* and her heirs." *T*'s residuary devisee is *A*. Who has what interests in Blackacre? See Brown v. Independent Baptist Church of Woburn, 325 Mass. 645, 91 N.E.2d 922 (1950).

2.   *T* bequeaths a sum to Charity *A* with a proviso that if Charity *A* fails to maintain *T*'s family home for use by her family, the sum is to go to Charity *B*. What result? See 6 American Law of Property §24.40 (1952).

3.   *T* bequeaths the income of his real estate for 21 years to Charity *A* and directs that at the end of 21 years the real estate is to be sold and the proceeds are to be paid to Charity *A* to erect a building, provided that Charity *A* names the building the "Babbitt Memorial." The will provides that naming of the building is a condition precedent to payment of the proceeds to Charity *A*. Is the gift of the proceeds valid? See In re Kagan, [1966] Vict. Rep. 538.

SECTION C.   APPLICATION OF THE RULE TO CLASS GIFTS

1.   *The Basic Rule: All-or-Nothing*

Under the Rule against Perpetuities, a class gift cannot be partially valid and partially void. It must be valid for all members of the class, or it is valid for none. If the interest of any member possibly can vest too remotely, the entire class gift is bad. This rule was definitely established in Leake v. Robinson, 2 Mer. 363, 35 Eng. Rep. 979 (Ch. 1817), though it was tacitly assumed in Jee v. Audley.

The all-or-nothing rule requires that (a) the class must close and (b) all conditions precedent for every member of the class must be satisfied, if at all, within the perpetuities period. Case 8 illustrates a common class gift that is void according to these principles.

Case 8. T devises property "to A for life, then to A's children for life, remainder to A's grandchildren in fee." The remainder to A's grandchildren is void because every member of the class will not be ascertained until the death of A's children, some of whom might not be in being at T's death. If at T's death A has a grandchild, G, alive, G's gift is vested in interest subject to open up and let in after-born grandchildren, but it is not vested for purposes of the Rule, and it is therefore void. Repeat: A remainder that is vested subject to open is not vested for purposes of applying the Rule against Perpetuities. The class must be closed before a remainder in a class is vested under the Rule.

Some gifts to a class may be saved through the operation of the rule of convenience, which may close the class prior to the time it closes physiologically. Under the rule of convenience, the class will close when any member of the class is entitled to immediate possession and enjoyment. See supra page 671. Thus:

Case 9. O transfers property in an irrevocable trust "for my daughter A for life, then to distribute the principal to my grandchildren." At the time of the transfer O has one grandchild, G, alive. Under the rule of convenience, G or his administrator can demand possession of his share at A's death, closing the class and forcing distribution among the grandchildren then living and the estates of grandchildren then dead.[16] The gift thus is valid. If O had no grandchild alive at the date of the transfer, the gift to grandchildren would be void.

QUESTION

If the creating instrument in Case 9 were a will or a revocable trust rather than a deed, the gift to the transferor's grandchildren would be valid regardless of whether a grandchild were alive when the instrument became effective. Do you see why?

It does not necessarily follow from the closing of the class within the perpetuities period that the gift is valid. Every member of the class may be ascertained, but every member may not have satisfied some condition precedent, and this too is required. In a gift of a fee simple, the ultimate

---

16. Suppose that G is living in Argentina, doesn't learn of A's death until several years after A dies, and therefore doesn't appear at A's death to demand payment. Will the class nevertheless close at A's death? Yes. The class will close whenever a class member has the right to demand possession. See supra page 671. Were this not so, the rule of convenience could never save a class gift because it is possible that the qualified class member would not actually demand possession at the time the right to possession arises.

number of takers in the class must be fixed so that it neither increases nor decreases. Thus:

> *Case 10.*   *T* devises property "to *A* for life, remainder in fee to such of *A*'s children as attain the age of 25." The class will close physiologically at *A*'s death (a life in being), but the exact share each child of *A* will take cannot be determined until all of *A*'s children have passed 25 or have died under that age. Here is what might happen: Suppose, at *T*'s death, *A* has one child, *C*, age 10. After *T*'s death *A* might have another child, *D*. Before *D* reaches age 4, *A* and *C* might die. Since *D* might meet the condition precedent more than 21 years after the expiration of any relevant life in being at *T*'s death, the remainder fails.

QUESTION

Suppose that in Case 10 a child of *A* is age 25 at *T*'s death. Is the gift good? If you say yes, you have not mastered the principle illustrated by this case.

Ward v. Van der Loeff
House of Lords, United Kingdom, 1924
[1924] A.C. 653

[The testator, William John Dalzell Burnyeat, barrister and member of Parliament, died in 1916, survived by his wife Hildegard but no children, by his father and mother, age 67, and by two brothers and two sisters. Each of these brothers and sisters had children living at the testator's death. In 1921 the testator's widow married Mr. Van der Loeff, a Dutch subject. Another nephew of the testator, Philip Ponsonby Burnyeat, was born after the testator's death and after the remarriage of his widow.

The testator left a will executed in 1915, and a codicil executed in 1916. By the will, the testator left his estate in trust for his wife for life, with the remainder to his children. In the event that he had no children (which happened), he gave his wife a power to appoint the trust fund among the children of his brothers and sisters, and in default of appointment the trust fund was to go in equal shares to the children of his brothers and sisters.]

HALDANE, L.C. . . . About the validity of these trusts no question arises. But it is otherwise with the codicil made by the testator. It was in these terms:

> I declare that the life interest given to said wife by my said will shall be terminable on her remarriage unless such remarriage shall be with a

natural born British subject.[17] I revoke the power of appointment among the children of my brothers and sisters given to my said wife by my said will. And I declare that after her death my trustees shall stand possessed of the residuary trust funds in trust for all or any the children or child of my brothers and sisters who shall be living at the death of my wife or born at any time afterwards before any one of such children for the time being in existence attains a vested interest and who being a son or sons attain the age of twenty-one, or being a daughter or daughters attain that age or marry if more than one, in equal shares.

On the construction of the will and codicil, two questions arise. The first is, whether the limitation in favour of children, contained in the concluding words of the codicil, is valid, having regard to the rule against perpetuities. The second is whether, if invalid, this new limitation and the wording of the codicil have been at all events efficacious as expressing a revocation of his bequest to children contained in the will. If the limitation to children in the codicil be invalid, and that in the will has not been revoked, then a further question arises, whether the gift in the will operated in favour of any children of the brothers and sisters who were not born until after the testator's death. Philip Ponsonby Burnyeat, who is one of the parties to these appeals, was a son of the testator's brother, Myles Fleming Burnyeat, but was not born until after the testator's death and the remarriage of his widow. It is argued against his claim that the life interest of the widow was effectively determined by the provision in the codicil and that the class of children to take was finally ascertained at that date as the time of distribution. If this be so, Philip Ponsonby Burnyeat is excluded.

P.O. Lawrence J. was the judge before whom this summons came in the first instance. He decided that the gift in the codicil in favour of the children of the testator's brothers and sisters was so framed as to be void for perpetuity. He held further, that the codicil operated to revoke the residuary gift in the will only so far as the substituted provision in the codicil was valid, and that the gift in the will in favour of these children, therefore, took effect, but merely in favour of such of the children as were born before the remarriage of the testator's widow. Philip Ponsonby Burnyeat was thus excluded. A majority of the Court of Appeal, Lord Sterndale M.R. and Warrington L.J., agreed with him in holding that the gift in the codicil in favour of the children

---

17. The testator's widow, Hildegard Burnyeat (later Van der Loeff), was a Prussian. During the 1914-1918 war, she was interned on the Isle of Man. We thought this provision might have been inserted because Van der Loeff was waiting in the wings when Burnyeat executed his codicil, but Dr. Myles Fredric Burnyeat, the testator's great-nephew, thinks this provision in the codicil was due to the intensity of anti-German feeling at the time.

Dr. Burnyeat also informed us that Philip Ponsonby Burnyeat, who was closed out of the class in this case, had the terrible misfortune at the age of three to contract sleeping sickness, then incurable, and spent his life in an institution. Letter from Dr. Myles Fredric Burnyeat to Jesse Dukeminier, dated March 25, 1982. — Eds.

of brothers and sisters was void for perpetuity, but held that the codicil revoked the gift in their favour contained in the will, and that there was an intestacy as regarded the residuary estate of the testator as from the remarriage of his widow. Atkin L.J. dissented, holding that the testator must be taken, as matter of construction, to have been referring in his codicil only to the brothers and sisters of the whole blood in existence when he died, just as if he had designated them individually. The provision in the codicil was therefore valid, that in the will having been revoked.

My Lords, the principle to be applied in construing instruments for the purpose of ascertaining whether the direction they contain infringes the rule against perpetuity is a well settled one. It was repeated with emphasis in this House in Pearks v. Moseley [5 App. Cas. 714], where it was laid down that in construing the words the effect of the rule must in the first instance be left out of sight, and then, having in this way defined the intention expressed, the Court had to test its validity by applying the rule to the meaning thus ascertained. It is only therefore if, as matter of construction, the words in the codicil, taken in the natural sense in which the testator used them, do not violate the rule that they can be regarded as giving a valid direction. Looking at the language of the testator here, I am wholly unable to read it as not postponing the ascertainment of possible members of the class beyond the period of a life in being and twenty-one years afterwards. No doubt if we were warranted in interpreting the testator as having referred only to the children of those of his brothers and sisters who were alive at his death we might read his language in a way which would satisfy the law. But for so restricting the natural meaning of his words there is no justification in the language used in the context. He speaks of his brothers and sisters generally, and there is no expression which excludes the children of other possible brothers and sisters of the whole or half blood who might in contemplation of law be born. He has nowhere indicated an intention that his words are not to be construed in this, their natural meaning. I think, therefore, that the class to be benefited was not one all the members of which were, as a necessary result of the words used, to be ascertained within the period which the law prescribes, and that the gift in the codicil in favour of children of brothers and sisters is wholly void.

The next question is whether the codicil, although inoperative to this extent, was yet operative to revoke the gift to children of brothers and sisters contained in the will. After consideration, I have come to the conclusion that it was not so operative. There is indeed a revocation expressed in the codicil, but it is confined to the power of appointment given to the wife. It does not extend to what follows. That is, in terms, an attempt at a substantive and independent gift, and, as it is wholly void, I think, differing on this point from the Court of Appeal, that the provision in the will stands undisturbed. There is nothing else in the codicil which purports to affect it. It can make no difference that the class of children is a new and different class if the constitution of the new class is wholly inoperative in law. If it fails, then unless an independent and valid intention to revoke has been independently of it expressed, no revocation can take place. There is no such independent expression of intention here.

The only other point is at what period the class of children of brothers and sisters who took under the will is to be ascertained. I think that according to a well-known rule, the period is that of distribution; in other words, taking the valid alteration in the codicil into account, the remarriage of the widow with a foreign subject. Philip Ponsonby Burnyeat is thus excluded.

The result is that the judgment of P.O. Lawrence J. should be restored. As the difficulty has been entirely caused by the testator himself, I think that the costs here and below should be taxed as between solicitor and client and paid out of the residuary estate.

LORD DUNEDIN.   My Lords, the main question in this case seems to me to be determined by what was said in this House by Lord Cairns in the two cases of Hill v. Crook [L.R. 6 H.L. 265] and Dorin v. Dorin [L.R. 7 H.L. 568]. In the former of these cases that noble and learned Lord laid down that when you wish to vary the meaning of a word denoting a class of relations from what the prima facie meaning of that word is — he actually said it of the words legitimate children, but the application is obviously wider — there are two classes of cases only where the primary signification can be departed from. The one is where it is impossible in the circumstances that any person indicated by the prima facie meaning can take under the bequest. That is not the case here because probably in law, though scarcely in fact, the idea of other brothers and sisters to the testator coming into existence could not be excluded, but in any case the half-brother or sister was a real possibility. The second class of cases is where you find something in the will itself, that is, in the expressions used in the will, to exclude the prima facie interpretation. That also seems to be absent. He has used the words "brother and sister" without explanation or glossary, and I am afraid he must take the consequences.[18]

18. *He* must take the consequences?

In construing statutes, Lord Dunedin did not take such a strict, literal approach, but said that a statute should be interpreted to carry out its intent. "I have said before that I think in interpreting a statute a Court must take it that the statute is meant to work, and that it should not allow the statute to be defeated unless the words used are quite inadequate to have the desired effect." Ocean Coal Co. v. Davies, [1927] A.C. 271, 278 (dissenting opinion). Why should statutes be construed to work, but not wills? If the testator must "take the consequences," why not the legislature? The legislature at least has the opportunity of patching up faulty drafting, which the testator does not have. — Eds.

PROBLEMS

1. Do you see why the rule of convenience saves the gift to nephews and nieces in the will and does not save the gift in the codicil? Suppose there had been a nephew 22 years old at the testator's death. Would the gift to the nephews and nieces in the codicil be good?

2. *T* devises Blackacre "to such of the grandchildren of *A* as shall attain the age of 25." Unless otherwise stated, assume that no grandchild of *A* has reached age 25. Is the gift valid if at *T*'s death:

(a) *A* is dead?

(b) *A* and all of *A*'s children are dead?

(c) *A* is alive and one grandchild of *A* is 25?

(d) *A* is dead and one grandchild of *A* is 25?

(e) *A* is dead and one grandchild of *A* is 4?

3. *T* bequeaths a fund in trust "to pay the income to *A* for life, and then in trust for the grandchildren of *B*, their shares to be payable at their respective ages of 25." Is the gift valid if *T* is survived by *A* and *B* and,

(a) the eldest grandchild of *B* is 25 at *T*'s death?

(b) the eldest grandchild of *B* is 10 at *T*'s death?

(c) the eldest grandchild of *B* is 2 at *T*'s death?

Suppose that *B* survives *T*, but *A* predeceases *T*, and the eldest grandchild of *B* is 2 at *T*'s death. Is the gift valid?

Suppose that *A* survives *T*, but *B* predeceases *T*, and the eldest grandchild of *B* is 2 at *T*'s death. Is the gift valid?

4. *T* devises property "to *A* for life, remainder to such of *A*'s children as shall reach their respective twenty-first birthdays." Since a person reaches 21 at the first moment of the day before his or her twenty-first birthday,[19] is the gift valid? See Leach, The Careful Draftsman: Watch Out!, 47 A.B.A.J. 259 (1961).

NOTE: CONSEQUENCES OF VIOLATING RULE

The standard rule is: Any interest that violates the Rule against Perpetuities is struck out and the valid interests are left standing. We can illustrate this rule — as well as other possible solutions — with the two-generation trust. Thus:

---

19. The theory is that a person is in existence on the day of his birth, and that on the day before his first birthday he has completed one year. His birthday is the first day of the second year. See Erwin v. Benton, 120 Ky. 596, 87 S.W. 291 (1905); Annot., 5 A.L.R.2d 1143 (1949). But see Johnson v. Superior Court, 208 Cal. App. 3d 1093, 256 Cal. Rptr. 651 (1989), rejecting the common law rule and holding that a person reaches a given age on his birthday.

> *Case 11.* *T* bequeaths his residuary estate in trust "to pay the income to my children for their lives, then to my grandchildren for their lives, then to distribute the principal among my great-grandchildren." *T* is survived by children. The remainder to the great-grandchildren is void because the class will not close until the death of *T*'s grandchildren, who may not all be in being at *T*'s death. The standard rule is to leave the valid interests standing with a reversion in *T*'s heirs to become possessory upon the death of *T*'s grandchildren.

There is one exception to the standard rule known as the *doctrine of infectious invalidity*. The name is apt. The invalidity of one interest infects other valid estates and causes them to fail. It is applied where the invalid gift is thought to be an essential part of the testator's plan, and if it fails, the testator would prefer other gifts to fail. The doctrine may be applied to cause prior interests to fail or to cause other gifts in the will to fail. Thus:

> *Case 12.* *T* devises one-half of his estate in trust "for my daughter *D* for life, then to *D*'s children for their lives, then to *D*'s grandchildren in fee." The other one-half is devised outright to *T*'s son *S*. *D* and *S* are *T*'s only children and heirs. The remainder to *D*'s grandchildren violates the Rule and is void. The choice is this: Would *T* prefer for the one-half intended for his daughter's family to stay in trust for the lives of *D* and *D*'s children, and then pass equally to *D* and *S* as *T*'s heirs, which would result in *S* ultimately receiving three-fourths of *T*'s property? Or would *T* prefer an equal distribution between the children, which can only be accomplished by striking down the entire will? It has been held that *T* would prefer the latter. Taylor v. Dooley, 297 S.W.2d 905 (Ky. 1957).

There is another possible solution to Cases 11 and 12, which as far as we can tell has never been adopted by any state court, but it appears to us to be the best solution: When the void remainder is given to the children of the preceding life tenants, increase the preceding life estate to a fee simple. Most likely the children will inherit the property from their parents, and the chances are that this solution will carry the property ultimately to the intended recipients. This solution to Cases 11 and 12 would be reached in Georgia and Pennsylvania under statutes that give the void interest to the owner of the preceding estate. Ga. Code §44-6-1(a) (1982); Pa. Cons. Stat. Ann. tit. 20, §6105(c) (1975). The Georgia statute is criticized in Chaffin, The Rule Against Perpetuities as Applied to Georgia Wills and Trusts: A Survey and Suggestions for Reforms, 16 Ga. L. Rev. 235, 322-327 (1982), on grounds that fail to shake our belief in its soundness as applied to Cases 11 and 12.

2. Gifts to Subclasses

American Security & Trust Co. v. Cramer
United States District Court, District of Columbia, 1959
175 F. Supp. 367

YOUNGDAHL, J.   Six of the eleven defendants before the Court have moved for summary judgment. A hearing has been held and memoranda of points and authorities have been submitted. Plaintiff, trustee of a testamentary trust, is a stakeholder in this controversy among competing heirs. Since all the material facts have been stipulated, the Court is free to render summary judgment.

Abraham D. Hazen, a resident of the District of Columbia, died in the District on December 4, 1901. His will, executed on October 16, 1900, was admitted to probate on March 11, 1902.

Testator was survived by Hannah E. Duffey, who is referred to in his will as his "adopted daughter." At the time of the testator's death, Hannah had two children: Mary Hazen Duffey [now Cramer], born November 12, 1897, and Hugh Clarence Duffey, born July 11, 1899. After the testator's death, Hannah gave birth to two more children: Depue Hazen Duffey, born October 9, 1903, and Horace Duffey, born July 8, 1908.

The will provided for the payment of debts and certain specific bequests and then provided that the residue of the estate be put in trust for the benefit of testator's wife for life. At her death, one-half of the corpus was to be, and has been, given to testator's sister and brothers; the other half, composed of realty, remained in trust for Hannah for life. At Hannah's death, the income was to go to the children of Hannah "then living or the issue of such of them as may then be dead leaving issue surviving" Hannah, and then "upon the death of each the share of the one so dying shall go absolutely to the persons who shall then be her or his heirs at law according to the laws of descent now in force in the said District of Columbia."[20]

---

20. The seventh paragraph of testator's will reads [in part]:

I do direct that Mary Hazen Duffey, the daughter of my adopted daughter and the namesake of my wife and for whom my wife and I have the greatest affection, shall if living at the death of her mother take a share three times as large as the share of each of the other children of my said adopted daughter, which other children shall take in equal shares between and among themselves, and each of the children of said adopted daughter shall take only for and during the terms of their respective lives and upon the death of each the share of the one so dying shall go absolutely to the persons who shall then be her or his heirs at law according to the laws of descent now in force in the said District of Columbia.

Mary took a three-sixths share; each of the other three children took a one-sixth share.

Testator's widow died on October 31, 1916; Hannah died on May 21, 1915.

On October 5, 1917, the heirs of the testator brought an action in equity to have the provisions of the seventh paragraph of the will stricken as being in violation of the rule against perpetuities. The Supreme Court of the District of Columbia held that the interests of Hannah's children under the will were valid and the Court of Appeals affirmed. Hazen v. American Security & Trust Co., 1920, 49 App. D.C. 297, 265 F. 447. The validity of the remainders over, after the death of each child, was expressly not ruled upon as the life estates were not "so intimately connected with the gift over as to require us now to determine the validity of such gifts."

Hugh, one of the four life tenants after the death of the widow and Hannah, died on December 19, 1928, and shortly thereafter the trustee brought a bill for instructions; this time the validity of the remainder over to Hugh's heirs was in issue. On January 2, 1930, Judge Bailey ruled that "the remainder provided by the will after his [Hugh's] death to the persons who shall then be his heirs at law became vested within the period prescribed by law and is valid."

On December 13, 1954, Depue died and for the fourth time a suit concerning this trust was started in this court. The trustees desired instructions as to the disposition of Depue's one-sixth share. While this action was pending, on December 18, 1957, Horace died. A supplemental bill was then filed, asking for instructions as to the disposition of this one-sixth share as well. The remainder over after the death of the sole living life tenant, Mary, cannot yet take effect; however, due to the request of all the parties concerned, and in order to save both the time of this court and the needless expense it would otherwise cost the estate, the Court will also pass on the validity of this remainder. . . .

The effect of the rule [against perpetuities] is to invalidate ab initio certain future interests that might otherwise remain in existence for a period of time considered inimicable to society's interest in having reasonable limits to dead-hand control and in facilitating the marketability of property. The policy of the law is to permit a person to control the devolution of his property but only for a human lifetime plus twenty-one years and actual periods of gestation. With careful planning, this period could be as long as one hundred years — and this is long enough.

A gift to a class is a gift of an aggregate amount of property to persons who are collectively described and whose individual share will depend upon the number of persons ultimately constituting the class. Evans v. Ockershausen, 1938, 69 App. D.C. 285, 292, 100 F.2d 695, 702, 128 A.L.R. 177. The members of the class must be finally determined within a life or lives in being plus twenty-one years and actual periods of gestation, or the gift will fail. Put another way, the class must close within the period of the rule against perpetuities, if the class gift is to be valid. Unless a contrary intent is indicated by the testator, the class will close when any member of the class is entitled to immediate possession and enjoyment of his share of the class gift. Applying these basic principles to the trust here involved, it is seen that the life estates to Hannah's children had to vest, if at all, at the termination of the preceding life estates of the widow and Hannah. Since Hannah's children had to be born within Hannah's lifetime, and since Hannah was a life in being, the class (Hannah's children) physiologically had to close within the period of the rule. This has already been so held. Hazen v. American Security & Trust Co., supra. . . . Furthermore, the remainder over at Hugh's death has been held valid. The Court now holds that the remainder limited to the heirs of Mary is valid. Both Hugh and Mary were lives in being at the testator's death; the remainders limited to their heirs had to vest, if at all, within the period of the rule. Horace and Depue were born after the testator died; the remainders over at their deaths are invalid.

In applying the rule against perpetuities, it does not help to show that the rule might be complied with or that, the way things turned out, it actually was complied with. After the testator's death, Hannah might have had more children; one of these might have lived more than twenty-one years after the death of all the lives in being at the testator's death. The vesting of the remainder in this after-born's heirs would take place after the expiration of lives in being and twenty-one years, since the heirs could not be ascertained until the after-born's death and an interest cannot be vested until the interest holder is ascertained. Consequently, because of the possibility that this could happen, even though, in fact, it did not,[21] the remainders limited to the heirs of Horace and Depue (both after-borns) are invalid as a violation of the rule against perpetuities.

Counsel have not argued the point of whether the invalidity of the remainders to the heirs of Horace and Depue serves to taint the otherwise valid remainders to the heirs of Mary and Hugh. Of course, the remainder after Hugh's life estate has already been distributed and is not properly in issue. Nevertheless, as shall be demonstrated, it (and the remainder to the heirs of Mary) are not affected by the two invalid remainders, since the four remainders are to subclasses and stand (or fall) separately.

---

21. Mary, a life in being at testator's death, is still alive. Therefore, the heirs of Horace and Depue would *actually* be taking within the period of the rule, but in this area of imagination-run-wild, actualities do not count; what could happen is all that matters.

In this case, the above suppositions are not unreasonable since Hannah was in her middle thirties when the testator died. But cf. the cases of the "the fertile octogenarian," "the unborn widow," and "the magic gravel pit" in Professor Leach's classic article Perpetuities in a Nutshell, 51 Harv. L.R. 638, 642-645 (1938).

Beginning with Jee v. Audley, 1 Cox Eq. Cas. 324 (1787) and flowering with Leake v. Robinson, 2 Mer. 363, 35 Eng. Rep. 979 (Chancery 1817), there has been the curious anomaly in future interests law that if the interest of any potential member of a class can possibly vest too remotely, the interests of all the members of the class fail. . . . Fortunately, the Court need not apply it in this case because of the limitation put on it by a long line of cases beginning with Cattlin v. Brown, 11 Hare 372, 68 Eng. Rep. 1318 (Chancery, 1853).

In *Cattlin*, the devise was of mortgaged property to A for life, then to the children of A in equal shares during their lives, and after the death of any such child, his share to his children and their heirs. Some of A's children were in being at the time that the testator died; some were born after his death. Counsel conceded that the remainders over to the heirs of those children of A born after the testator's death were invalid. The question was whether those concededly invalid remainders tainted the otherwise valid remainders and rendered them invalid. The Court held that they did not; the remainders to the heirs of the children in being at the testator's death were valid. *Leake* was distinguished on the ground that it concerned remainders to *one* class (A's children that reach twenty-five) while the remainders involved in *Cattlin* were to a group of subclasses (the heirs of each of A's children was a subclass). In other words, the limitation placed on *Leake* by *Cattlin* is that if the ultimate takers are not described as a single class but rather as a group of subclasses, and if the share to which each separate subclass is entitled will finally be determined within the period of the rule, the gifts to the different subclasses are separable for the purpose of the rule.

In the instant case, the language of the will compels the Court to read it as a devise of remainders to subclasses and within the rule of *Cattlin*. The provision in issue reads, in part: ". . . and *each* of the children of said adopted daughter shall take only for and during the terms of their *respective* lives and upon the death of *each* the share of the *one* so dying shall go absolutely to the persons who shall then be *her or his* heirs at law . . ." (Emphasis supplied). . . .

When a remainder in fee after a life estate fails, there is no enlargement or diminution of the life estate; rather there is then a reversion in the heirs of the testator. . . . The two one-sixth shares held invalid shall pass to the successors in interest to the heirs of Abraham D. Hazen. . . .

One matter remains. The Court has been urged to terminate the trust and order distribution of three-sixths of the original corpus to the life tenant, Mary. This life tenant is presently sixty-two years of age; she is a widow and has three adult children. These three children and their wives have signed an "assignment" of their interests in the trust to Mary. Although the legal significance of this "assignment," standing alone, is questionable, in light of the fact that the children are not their mother's heirs but only presumptive heirs until she dies, nevertheless, it is significant to show that the only persons likely to become remaindermen are willing to have the income beneficiary take the corpus. The intent of the testator is clear: ". . . I do direct that Mary Hazen Duffey, the daughter of my adopted daughter and the namesake of my wife and for whom my wife and I have the greatest affection, shall if living at the death of her mother take a share three times as large as the share of each of the other children of my said adopted daughter. . . ." It seems obvious that the testator had Mary's interest uppermost in his mind. Last year, Mary's share of the income from the trust amounted to $750.51 which was hardly sufficient for her subsistence; her needs would be amply provided for were she to receive the share of the corpus. If General Hazen were now alive, there would seem to be little doubt but that he would wish to join with Mary's children to have the trust terminated and the corpus distributed to the one for whom he had "the greatest affection" and who was to receive "a share three times as large as the share of each of the other children." In light of the realities of the situation, the desire of all concerned to have the trust terminated, and the evident purpose of the will, the Court shall order the trust terminated and the corpus distributed to the life tenant. Cf. Wolcott's Petition, 1948, 95 N.H. 23, 56 A.2d 641, 1 A.L.R.2d 1323. This, however, is conditioned upon the furnishing of a bond to protect any unascertained remaindermen.

Defendant Blakelock's motion for summary judgment is granted. Defendant Mary Duffey Cramer's prayer for additional relief is granted to the extent of having her receive that portion of the corpus presently supplying the income to which she is entitled as a life tenant, conditioned on her furnishing a bond or undertaking with surety approved by the court.

Counsel will submit an appropriate order.

QUESTION

In the *Cramer* case, the court applied the doctrine of subclasses and saved the remainders to the heirs of Mary and Hugh, whereas the remainders to the heirs of Horace and Depue failed. If this carries out the intent of the testator, why are not all class gifts split into good and bad parts?

There is, of course, this difference: when the invalid gifts are struck out [under Cattlin v. Brown], the valid gift remains as it would be if all gifts were good, whereas in Leake v. Robinson, the elimination of the invalid gift causes the amount of the valid gift to be increased by eliminating the partial divestment which the testator intended. But as we have previously pointed out, this is no objection. Where property is devised to *A* in fee, but if the testator's grave falls into disrepair to *B* in fee, the invalidity of the executory devise to *B* causes *A* to get much more than the testator intended; yet it is well settled that *A* gets it. But in Leake v. Robinson and the cases which have followed it the courts failed, it is submitted, to recognize that they are dealing with a situation in which there is a valid interest subject to partial divestment by an invalid gift. [J. Morris & W. Leach, The Rule Against Perpetuities 130-131 (2d ed. 1962).]

The all-or-nothing rule of Leake v. Robinson is rejected in Carter v. Berry, 243 Miss. 321, 140 So. 2d 843 (1962), where the court said the good part of a class gift would be separated from the bad.

3. Specific Sum to Each Class Member

In addition to gifts to subclasses, there is another exception to the all-or-nothing class gift rule where there is a gift of a specific sum to each member of a class. In Storrs v. Benbow, 3 De Gex, M. & G. 390, 43 Eng. Rep. 153 (Ch. 1853), the testator bequeathed £500 apiece to each child of the children of his brothers, to be paid at age 21. The testator had two brothers living at his death. The court held that, as a matter of construction, applying the ordinary class closing rule applicable to per capita gifts (see supra page 672), the gift benefited only children living at the testator's death. The court went on to say, however, in a dictum that has been treated as law ever since, that if the testator meant to include children born after his death, the bequest would be valid for all children born to the testator's nephews and nieces living at his death and invalid for all children of the testator's afterborn nephews and nieces. The amount intended to be received by each member of the class is ascertainable without reference to the number of persons in the class, and hence each gift is tested separately under the Rule. Thus:

> *Case 13.* *T* bequeaths "$1,000 apiece to my nephews and nieces, whether born before or after my death." *T* is survived by his parents, his sister *A*, and *A*'s daughter *B*. After *T*'s death, a child, *C*, is born to *T*'s parents, and *A* has another child, *D*. Twenty years later, *C* marries and has a child, *E*. *B* is entitled to receive $1000 because her gift vests at *T*'s death. *D* is entitled to receive $1000 because, viewed at *T*'s death, her gift will necessarily vest during the life of *A*, a person in being at *T*'s death. *E* is not entitled to receive $1000 because her gift will not necessarily vest during the life of a person in being. The validity of each gift is judged separately since the amount each nephew or niece takes is fixed at $1000 and cannot increase or decrease by any fluctuation in the number of recipients.

PROBLEM

Clause 7 of the testator's will declares, "To all of my nieces and nephews, I wish that my Estate would provide a four-year college course to any wishing to accept such." Clause 8 devises the residue of the testator's estate to his mother, wife, and son in equal shares. The testator is survived by the residuary legatees, by several brothers and sisters, and by several nephews but no nieces. If you are representing the residuary legatees, how will you argue against the validity of the gift in clause 7? If you are representing the nephews, what arguments will you make in favor of sustaining the gift? See Crockett v. Crockett, 332 Mass. 564, 126 N.E.2d 363 (1955).

4. *Does vest = vest = vest?*

Now that you understand the meaning of vest as applied to class gifts, you are in a position to appreciate some of the difficulties hidden in that four-letter word. Many of these difficulties arise because orthodox doctrine has insisted that whether an interest is vested or contingent depends entirely upon the *form of words* set forth in the limitation. Orthodox doctrine further holds that an interest vested for one purpose is vested for all purposes (with one obvious exception, the vesting of class gifts under the Rule against Perpetuities). The practical problems and the purposes of the rules in which vest is a key word are ignored. Hence, the distinction made in Edwards v. Hammond, supra page 655, to deal with the practical problem of how to put into possession a 17-year-old remainderman whose interest looked distinctly contingent upon reaching 21 is applied in perpetuities cases where the problem and policies are very different. Similarly, the rules in Clobberie's Case, supra page 669, designed to carry out the average testator's intent as to whether survivorship to a designated age is required, are applied under the Rule against Perpetuities without taking into account the fact that they may continue dead-hand control in violation of the policy of the Rule against Perpetuities. Giving so much weight to the form of the limitation, and so little to policy, results in some strange and striking results.

Moving the word *vest* from one context to another without regard to the purposes of the rule in which it is used is an example of what Professor Moffatt Hancock called The Fallacy of the Transplanted Category, 37 Can. B. Rev. 535 (1959). It is not a fallacy limited to the law of future interests. As that renowned fallacy-hunter, Walter Wheeler Cook, pointed out years ago, "The tendency to assume that a word which appears in two or more rules, and so in connection with more than one purpose, has and should have precisely the same scope in all

A rose is a rose is a rose.

Drawing by Saul Steinberg.
Copyright © 1970 by The New Yorker Magazine, Inc.
Reproduced by permission.

of them runs all through legal discussions. It has all the tenacity of
original sin and must constantly be guarded against." W. Cook, Logical
and Legal Bases of the Conflict of Laws 159 (1942). Saul Steinberg, in
the drawing above, illustrates this fallacy in another guise. Steinberg, a
literalist of the imagination, is a kindred spirit of lawyers who for
centuries have reified abstractions.

PROBLEMS

1.   Apply the rules developed in Edwards v. Hammond, supra page
655, and Festing v. Allen, supra page 657, to the following bequests. *A*
survives *T*. *A* has no children at *T*'s death. Is the Rule against Perpetuities
violated? Are the results sound? See J. Morris & W. Leach, The Rule
Against Perpetuities 45 (2d ed. 1962).

(a)   To *A* for life, remainder in fee to *A*'s first-born child if he or
she reaches 25, but if the first-born child of *A* does not reach 25, then
to *B*.

(b)   To *A* for life, remainder in fee to such children of *A* as reach
25, but if no child of *A* reaches 25, then to *B*.

2.   Apply the rules laid down in Clobberie's Case, supra page 669, to the following bequests. *A* survives *T*. No child of *A* is 25 at *T*'s death. Is the Rule against Perpetuities violated? Are the results sound? See 6 American Law of Property §24.19 (1952).

(a)   To the children of *A* who shall reach 25.

(b)   To the children of *A* payable at 25.

3.   Compare "to *A* for life, then to *A*'s children who reach 25" with "to *A* for life, then to *A*'s children for their lives." The remainder in the first example is void, in the second valid. Will the property likely be tied up longer in the first example or the second?

4.   Should we require that an interest vest in possession or enjoyment within the perpetuities period? Should we subject vested remainders to the Rule? See Schuyler, Should the Rule Against Perpetuities Discard Its Vest?, 56 Mich. L. Rev. 887, 926-948 (1958); Waggoner, Reformulating the Structure of Estates: A Proposal for Legislative Action, 85 Harv. L. Rev. 729, 760-765 (1972). One difficulty with requiring an interest to vest in possession: How do you treat reversions? Can they be distinguished in policy from remainders vested in interest?

SECTION D.   APPLICATION OF THE RULE TO POWERS OF APPOINTMENT

In applying the Rule against Perpetuities to powers of appointment, it is necessary to separate powers into (a) general powers presently exercisable and (b) general testamentary powers and all special powers. The former are rarely created, except in the form of a power to revoke a trust. Hence our main concern is with testamentary and special powers.

1.   *General Powers Presently Exercisable*

a.   Validity of Power

General powers presently exercisable are treated as absolute ownership for purposes of the Rule. Nothing stands between the donee and absolute ownership except a piece of paper that can be signed at any time; hence the property is not tied up. In order to be a valid power, a general inter vivos power must *become exercisable*, or fail, within the perpetuities period. When the power becomes exercisable, the property becomes marketable and the policy of the rule is not offended. Hence, if a general inter vivos power will become exercisable, or fail, within lives in being plus 21 years, it is valid. See Restatement (Second) of

Property, Donative Transfers §1.2, Comment h (1983). For example, *T* devises property "to *A* for life, then to *A*'s children for their lives, with a general power in each child, exercisable by deed, to appoint a proportionate share of the corpus." Each child's power is valid. *A* is the validating life.

b. Validity of Exercise

Since the donee of a general power presently exercisable is treated as owner of the property, the validity of an interest created by exercise of the power is determined on the same basis as if the donee owned the property in fee. The perpetuities period runs from the exercise of the power.

An unconditional power to revoke in one person is treated the same as a general power presently exercisable if the holder can exercise the power to revoke for his or her own exclusive benefit. The perpetuities period runs from the termination of the power. See Restatement (Second) of Property, supra, §1.2.

PROBLEM

O creates a revocable trust "to pay the income to *O* for life, then to pay the income to *O*'s children for their lives, then to distribute the principal to *O*'s grandchildren." Does the gift to grandchildren violate the Rule against Perpetuities? Would it if the trust were irrevocable?

2.   *General Testamentary Powers and Special Powers*

General testamentary powers and all special powers are treated differently from a general power presently exercisable. A person holding one of these powers does not have an absolute and unlimited present right to alienate the property, and consequently the donee is not treated as owner. In applying the Rule to these powers, two questions arise: (a) Is the power itself valid? (b) Are the interests created by the exercise of the power valid?

a. Validity of Power

For a general testamentary power or a special power to be valid, it must not be possible for the power to be exercised beyond the perpetuities period. If it can possibly be exercised beyond the period, it is void ab initio. A testamentary or special power cannot be given to an afterborn person unless its exercise is limited to the perpetuities period. A discretionary power of distribution in a trustee is the equivalent of a special power of appointment.

Case 14. *T* bequeaths a fund in trust "to pay the income to *A* for life, then to *A*'s children for their lives, then to distribute the principal to such persons as the last surviving child shall appoint by will; in default of appointment, to *A*'s issue then living per stirpes." At the time of *T*'s death, *A* has no children. The secondary life estate in the children is valid since it will vest in interest, if at all, upon the death of *A*. However, the general testamentary power is void because it can be exercised by an afterborn person. The gift in default of appointment is void because it does not vest until the death of the last survivor of *A*'s children.

Case 15. *T* bequeaths a fund in trust "to pay the income to *A* for life; then in the trustee's *discretion* to pay the income to *A*'s children during their lives or to accumulate the income and add it to principal; then on the death of each child of *A* to pay a proportionate part of the principal equal to the number of children of *A* who survived *A* as such child shall appoint by will." The discretionary power in the trustee to pay or accumulate income is either partially or totally void. The testamentary powers given to children of *A* born after *T*'s death are void, but the powers given to children of *A* in being at *T*'s death are valid.

Gray took the position that a discretionary trust did not create one power that was either entirely valid or entirely void, but a succession of annual powers that were exercisable with respect to each year's income. Thus a discretionary power in a trustee exercisable during lives not in being, as during the lives of *A*'s children in Case 15, could be exercised for 21 years after *A*'s death but no longer. See J. Gray, The Rule Against Perpetuities §§410.1 to 410.5 (4th ed. 1942). However, in the few cases in which this issue has been directly before the court, the discretionary power has been held void in its entirety if it is capable of being exercised in favor of persons not in being. See Arrowsmith v. Mercantile-Safe Deposit & Trust Co., 313 Md. 334, 545 A.2d 674 (1988); Bundy v. United States Trust Co., 257 Mass. 72, 153 N.E. 337 (1926); Thomas v. Harrison, 24 Ohio Op. 2d 148, 191 N.E.2d 862 (1962). But see Tidex v. Trustees Executors & Agency Co. Ltd., [1971] 2 N.S.W.L.R. 463, agreeing with Gray.

b. Validity of Exercise

(1) Perpetuities Period Runs from Creation of Power
In the United States, general testamentary powers are treated like

special powers in determining the validity of the appointment. The donee of a testamentary power or a special power is regarded as an agent of the donor, not as the beneficial owner of the property. The appointments under testamentary and special powers are read back into the instrument creating the power. The perpetuities period runs from the creation of the power.

Although it is now well settled[22] in most of the states that general testamentary powers are to be treated like special powers under the Rule, the question was the subject of an historic debate between John Chipman Gray and his star pupil, Albert M. Kales. Gray maintained that general testamentary powers should be classified with special powers for purposes of the Rule against Perpetuities. Gray's view was that the donee of a general testamentary power "is not practically the owner; he cannot appoint to himself; he is, indeed, the only person to whom he cannot possibly appoint, for he must die before the transfer of the property can take place." J. Gray, supra, §526.2. Kales thought general testamentary powers should be classified with general inter vivos powers because at the moment of death the donee of a general testamentary power can do everything any absolute owner of property can do. Kales, General Powers and the Rule Against Perpetuities, 26 Harv. L. Rev. 64, 66-67 (1912). It is curious that Kales thought asking what the donee can do with the property before death is irrelevant. The donee of an inter vivos general power can sell the property and use the proceeds for a trip to Acapulco or for a new house. The donee can exchange the property for consumer goods and services. The quantum of wealth represented by the property is not withdrawn from commercial exchange. Thus, in a very real sense the donee of a general inter vivos power is the owner of the property since the donee can choose exactly what is to be done with it. The donee of a general testamentary power does not, as a practical matter, have this choice. The donee cannot sell the property and use the proceeds for consumer goods and services. Hence, property subject to a general testamentary power is withdrawn from commerce.

NOTE: THE "DELAWARE TAX TRAP"

In Delaware a statute provides that all interests created by the exercise of *all* powers, *special as well as general*, must vest within 21 years of the

---

22. Well, fairly well settled. In Industrial National Bank of Rhode Island v. Barrett, 101 R.I. 89, 220 A.2d 517 (1966), the court bought Kales' argument and held that the perpetuities period runs from the date of the exercise of a general testamentary power, not from the date of creation. See Jones, The Rule Against Perpetuities and Powers of Appointment: An Old Controversy Revived, 54 Iowa L. Rev. 456 (1968). In a few states by statute the perpetuities period runs from the exercise of a general testamentary power. See Del. Code Ann. tit 25, §501 (1975); S.D. Codified Laws Ann. §43-5-5 (1983); Wis. Stat. Ann. §700.16(c) (Supp. 1988).

death of some life in being at the time the power is *exercised*, not some life in being at the date of creation of the power. Del. Code Ann. tit. 25, §501 (1975). See also S.D. Codified Laws Ann. §43-5-5 (1983). Under the Delaware statute, it is possible to create a private trust that can last forever. *T* can set up a trust giving his child *A* the income for life and a special testamentary power to appoint outright or in further trust among *A*'s descendants. *A* can exercise the power by appointing in further trust for his child *B* for life, giving *B* a special testamentary power in favor of *B*'s descendants. *B* can exercise the power by appointing in further trust for his child — and so on down the generations.

Under the federal estate tax, property subject to a special power of appointment is not taxable at the death of the donee of the power. Although the property escapes estate taxation at that time, it will become subject to estate taxation within a generation or two thereafter because the standard Rule against Perpetuities ultimately calls a halt to successive life estates. In Delaware, however, life estates can be created in indefinite succession through the exercise of successive special powers of appointment.

Out of concern for estate tax avoidance through the use of Delaware trusts, Congress enacted §2041(a)(3) of the Internal Revenue Code. This statute taxes the appointive assets in the donee's estate if the donee exercises a special power "by creating another power of appointment which under the applicable local law can be validly exercised so as to postpone the vesting of any estate or interest in such property, . . . for a period ascertainable without regard to the date of the creation of the first power."

This provision plugs the tax loophole that would otherwise exist for Delaware trusts — but the general language of the statute creates a tax trap for residents of all states. In any jurisdiction, *if a donee by will exercises a special power in such a manner as to create a general inter vivos power, the property subject to the special power will be includible in the donee's gross estate.* Reread the quoted statutory provision, and you will see that this is so.

This statute is a clear indication that Congress regards the Rule against Perpetuities as an essential part of the tax structure whereby family wealth must be put through the tax wringer from time to time.

(2) The Second-Look Doctrine

Any interest created by exercise of a testamentary or special power is void unless it must vest, if at all, within 21 years after the death of some *life in being at the date the power was created.* The exercise of the power is read back into the original instrument — but facts existing on the date of exercise are taken into account. This is known as the *second-look doctrine*. This means we wait and see how the donee actually appoints the property, and then we determine on the basis of facts existing at the date of the appointment whether the appointive interests will vest within the period (computed from the date of creation of the power). Thus:

> *Case 16.*   *T* devises property "to *A* for life, remainder to such persons as *A* appoints by will, outright or in further trust." *A* appoints in further trust "to my children for life, remainder to my grandchildren in fee." We now read *A*'s appointment into the will that created the power; the disposition is treated as though *T*'s will read "to *A* for life, then to *A*'s children for life, then to *A*'s grandchildren in fee." However, under the second-look doctrine we are allowed to take into account facts existing at the time of *A*'s appointment. If at *A*'s death *A* leaves no children or the only children surviving *A* were born in *T*'s lifetime, the remainder to the grandchildren is valid because it will vest, if at all, at the death of persons in being at *T*'s death. Otherwise the remainder is void.

Second National Bank of New Haven v. Harris Trust & Savings Bank
Connecticut Superior Court, New Haven County, 1971
29 Conn. Supp. 275, 283 A.2d 226

SHEA, J.   In this action the plaintiff trustee seeks a determination of how the portion of a trust fund subject to a power of appointment is to be distributed; a judicial settlement of its accounts; an order fixing and allocating attorneys' fees; and other equitable relief. All of the defendants have appeared, and their answers admit paragraphs of the complaint alleging facts which may be summarized as follows:

In New Haven on April 21, 1922, Caroline Haven Trowbridge, a resident of that city, created an inter vivos trust with the plaintiff as trustee. The income of the trust was given to the settlor's daughter, Margaret Trowbridge Marsh, and she was also given a general testamentary power of appointment over one-half of the corpus. The remaining one-half, as well as the half subject to the power in default of its exercise, would be distributed to Margaret's surviving children or issue per stirpes or, if there were none, to another daughter of the settlor, Mary Brewster Murray, or her surviving issue per stirpes. During the life of the settlor, a power was reserved to "revoke, modify or alter" the terms of the trust "respecting the payment of income." The settlor, Caroline, died in New Haven on June 26, 1941, without having exercised this power.

Margaret, the life tenant and donee of the testamentary power, a resident of Winnetka, Illinois, died on April 13, 1969, leaving a will purporting to exercise the power by creating another trust, giving the income to her daughter, Mary Marsh Washburne, for a period of thirty years. At that time the trust estate would be distributed to Mary, if living, or, if not, to her surviving children or their descendants per stirpes, with outright distribution at age twenty-one. . . .

Mary, the named beneficiary of the power of appointment as exercised, was born on October 25, 1929. As one of the two surviving children of Margaret, she would share equally with her brother, Charles Allen Marsh, the half of the trust created by Caroline subject to the power, in default of its exercise. If Margaret's exercise of the power under her will is fully effective, the defendant Harris Trust and Savings Bank, as executor and trustee would receive this half of the trust to pay the income to Mary for thirty years following her mother's death, and ultimately to distribute the corpus to Mary. If she did not live that long, upon her death the defendant trustee would make distribution to Mary's surviving children or their surviving descendants.

It appears that all of the living persons having any interest in the trust have been made parties. A guardian ad litem has been appointed to represent any unborn or undetermined persons who may have an interest and also to represent the five children of Mary, all of whom are minors.

I

The first problem is whether the exercise of the testamentary power of appointment by Margaret's will is invalid because of a claimed violation of the rule against perpetuities.

It is well established that a donee of a power of appointment, in exercising the power, acts as a mere conduit of the donor's bounty. "Whenever such a power is in fact exercised, the validity of the appointment is determined by precisely the same rule as if the original testator, who created the power, had made in his own will the same provision in favor of the same appointee." Bartlett v. Sears, 81 Conn. 34, 42, 70 A. 33, 36. "The appointment is 'read back' into the instrument creating the power, as if the donee were filling in blanks in the donor's instrument." 6 American Law of Property §24.34.

So far as perpetuities are concerned, the period of the rule is reckoned from the date of creation of the power, not from the date of its exercise. Gray, Rule against Perpetuities (4th Ed.) §515, p.499. Where the power has been created by a will, the period is measured from the time of the death of the testator. Gray, op. cit. §520; Simes & Smith, Future Interests (2d Ed.) §1226. Where a deed is the source of the power, the date of delivery would ordinarily start the running of the period. Gray, loc. cit.; Simes & Smith, loc. cit.

In the case of inter vivos instruments, there is an exception for revocable transfers, for the reason that the policy of the rule is not violated where the grantor may at will terminate any future interests by revoking the grant. Where such an unconditional power of revocation is reserved, the period of perpetuities is calculated from the time the power of revocation ceased, usually at the death of the grantor unless the power was released earlier. 6 American Law of Property §24.59; Gray, op. cit. §524.1.

In this case, the defendants who seek to uphold the validity of the exercise of the power by Margaret's will claim that Caroline did retain a power to revoke the trust. The provision upon which they rely is paragraph (i) of the trust instrument, which reads as follows: ". . . as a measure of protection against possible contingencies, I hereby expressly reserve to myself power to revoke, modify or alter the terms hereof respecting the payment of income during my own life, by an instrument in writing, signed, dated and acknowledged, and delivered to the trustee." It seems clear that a power "to revoke, modify or alter the terms . . . respecting the payment of income" would not include a power to revoke the provisions for disposition of the principal of the trust. Such a partial power of revocation could affect only the life tenant, Margaret, during the life of the settlor, Caroline. Such a power would not qualify for the exception applicable to a full and unconditional power of revocation, because the remoteness of the future interests created could not be affected by any exercise of the power. 6 American Law of Property §24.59.

. . . As applied to this case the rule [against perpetuities] would bar any future interest which might not vest within twenty-one years after the life of some person in being on April 21, 1922, the date the trust was established. Since Mary was not born until October 25, 1929, she was not in being at the creation of the trust and her life cannot be taken as a measuring life under the rule against perpetuities. The only relevant life mentioned in the trust is that of Margaret, and, therefore, any valid future interest must vest no later than twenty-one years after her death on April 13, 1969.

In exercising the power of appointment, Margaret in her will used the language of an absolute gift to Mary of the income for thirty years and then a distribution to her of the principal of the trust.[23] The next

---

23. Article Three (b) of Margaret's will provided: "At the end of thirty (30) years after the date of my death, said Trustee shall pay over and deliver all of the corpus of the trust estate held under this Article Three to my daughter, Mary Marsh Washburne. In the event of the death of my daughter, Mary Marsh Washburne, prior to my death or prior to the expiration of said thirty (30) year period after my death, said Trustee shall pay over and distribute all of the corpus of the trust estate to" her issue then living per stirpes, with the share of any beneficiary under 21 to be vested in him and payable at age 21. — Eds.

sentence adds the provision that upon Mary's death within the thirty-year period (or prior to the death of the testatrix, Margaret) the principal of the trust would be distributed to Mary's children or descendants of deceased children surviving her. Such unconditional words of gift would ordinarily be construed as creating a vested interest subject to defeasance upon the occurrence of the condition subsequent contained in the later clause. Howard v. Batchelder, 143 Conn. 328, 336, 122 A.2d 307, 310. "If the conditional element is incorporated into the description of, or into the gift to, the remainderman, then the remainder is contingent; but if, after words giving a vested interest, a clause is added divesting it, the remainder is vested." Gray, op. cit. §108; Howard v. Batchelder, supra, 334, 122 A.2d 307. Such exaltation of verbalism over substance has been criticized, but it is rigidly adhered to in the legalistic sophistry which comprises much of the lore of future interests. As it was once remarked, "I am quite aware that this is all largely [a] matter of words, but so is much of the law of property; and unless we treat such formal distinctions as real, that law will melt away and leave not a rack behind." Commissioner of Internal Revenue v. City Bank Farmers' Trust Co., 2 Cir., 74 F.2d 242, 247.

"An interest is 'vested' for purposes of the Rule when the following conditions exist: a. any condition precedent attached to the interest is satisfied, and b. the taker is ascertained, and c. where the interest is included in a gift to a class, the exact amount or fraction to be taken is determined." 6 American Law of Property §24.18. The language creating the gift to Mary imposes no condition precedent, but rather a condition subsequent, i.e. her death within thirty years after Margaret's death. Since the gift is to a named person the identity of the taker is established. The third requirement (c) is not applicable to a gift to an individual.

The construction of the gift of the remainder to Mary as vested rather than contingent is reinforced by the intermediate gift of the income to her. 6 American Law of Property §24.19. A gift in favor of a named individual has historically been treated as vested and not subject to the rule unless it is expressly subject to a condition precedent. Restatement, 4 Property §370, comment g. The preference of the law for vested rather than contingent interests certainly dictates such a construction in this case, where even the grammatical form of a condition subsequent has been observed by the draftsman. . . .

The gift to Mary's children, following the same verbal formalism, is a contingent remainder,[24] because it is expressly subject to the condition that they survive their mother and that she not live until termination of the thirty-year trust. White v. Smith, 87 Conn. 663, 669-673, 89 A.

---

24. Contingent remainder or executory interest? Does it matter? — Eds.

272. It is also contingent because, as a gift to a class (surviving children and surviving descendants of deceased children), the fractional interest of each member of the class cannot be ascertained until the contingency (Mary's death) happens. Gray, op. cit. §§369-375.

It is well established that the rule against perpetuities does not affect vested interests, even though enjoyment may be postponed beyond the period of the rule. Connecticut Trust & Safe Deposit Co. v. Hollister, 74 Conn. 228, 232, 50 A. 750; Restatement, 4 Property §386, comment j. It would not operate therefore, to invalidate either the gift of the income to Mary for life or thirty years or the gift of the remainder after the thirty years. Colonial Trust Co. v. Brown, 105 Conn. 261, 272, 135 A. 555; Bartlett v. Sears, 81 Conn. 34, 44, 70 A. 33. Both of these gifts vested in interest at the death of Margaret within the period of the rule, and the postponement of enjoyment beyond the period of the rule would not invalidate them. Howard v. Batchelder, 143 Conn. 328, 336, 122 A.2d 307.

The permissible duration of a trust is not governed by the rule against perpetuities. Restatement, 4 Property §378; Gray, op. cit. §§232-246. It is no objection, therefore, that Mary's life estate may last beyond the period of the rule. It is also of no significance that her remainder interest may be defeated by her death, which may occur after that time. A vested remainder is exempt from the rule even though it may be subject to complete defeasance. Restatement, 4 Property §370. The rule does bar the contingent remainder to Mary's children because it may vest more than twenty-one years after the death of Margaret, whose life must be taken as the measuring life. This result, abhorrent to the rule, would occur if Mary should die more than twenty-one but less than thirty years after her mother. . . .

"If future interests created by any instrument are avoided by the Rule against Perpetuities, the prior interests become what they would have been had the limitation of the future estate been omitted from the instrument." Gray, op. cit. §247. . . . "Where a divesting interest is void, the interest which would otherwise have been divested becomes absolute." 6 American Law of Property §24.47, p.124. . . .

Under these principles, the gift of the remainder to Mary becomes indefeasibly vested because of the invalidation of the contingent remainder to her children.

In summary, the court has concluded that Mary has a valid income interest, in the half of the trust subject to the power of appointment, for thirty years and is then entitled to receive the principal. If she dies before then, the principal would be distributed to her estate, because her remainder has become indefeasibly vested.

Accordingly, it is ordered that the plaintiff trustee turn over to the defendant Harris Trust and Savings Bank one-half of the trust, to be held by that defendant to pay the income (including accumulated income) to the defendant Mary Marsh Washburne until April 13, 1999, when the principal shall be distributed to her. In the event of her earlier death, the principal shall be distributed to her estate. The court's advice is not sought with respect to any question pertaining to the remaining half of the trust fund. . . .

Judgment may enter accordingly.

QUESTION AND NOTES

1.   Do you see how, as lawyer for Margaret Trowbridge Marsh, you could have almost certainly carried out her wishes by a further appointment using extraneous lives to measure the perpetuities period?

2.   Margaret Trowbridge Marsh wanted the trust principal held in trust for her daughter Mary until Mary reached 70 years of age. Is this sound estate planning?

More famous as a controlling mother was the movie actress Joan Crawford. Crawford's will created trusts of $77,500 for her daughters Cathy and Cynthia, to distribute the principal to them at age 50. The residue of her estate was bequeathed to six charities. Crawford's will also disinherited two children: "TENTH: It is my intention to make no provision herein for my son Christopher or my daughter Christina for reasons which are well known to them." Of course, Christina settled the score in C. Crawford, Mommie Dearest (1978), which was made into a movie and reaped a profit far exceeding what her mother left her sisters.

3.   If a donee makes an invalid appointment, what are the consequences? The property passes in default of appointment to the takers in default or, if none, to the donor or the donor's estate unless the doctrine of capture applies. On capture, see supra page 744.

———————

The second-look doctrine permits facts existing at the date a testamentary or special power is exercised to be taken into account in determining the validity of the *exercise* of the power. But what if the donee does not exercise the power, and the assets pass to the takers in default of appointment? Can the second-look doctrine be invoked to sustain the validity of a gift in default of appointment? Thus:

> *Case 17.   T* devises property "to *A* for life, remainder as *A* shall appoint by will; in default of appointment, to *A*'s children for their lives, remainder to *A*'s grandchildren in fee." *A* dies without exercising the power. The facts existing at *A*'s death show that *A*'s only children (*B* and *C*) were alive

at *T*'s death. *If* the second-look doctrine can be invoked, the remainder to *A*'s grandchildren is valid; otherwise it is void.

In Sears v. Coolidge, 329 Mass. 340, 108 N.E.2d 563 (1952), the court applied the second-look doctrine to gifts in default of appointment. See 6 American Law of Property §24.36 (1952).

SECTION E.   SAVING CLAUSES

Because of the ease with which even experienced attorneys can overlook some remote possibility of untimely vesting, experienced estate planners today always incorporate in trusts they draft a perpetuities saving clause to take care of any possible violation. The perpetuities saving clause is not actually intended to govern the duration of the trust, except in the event some overlooked violation of the Rule unexpectedly extends the trust too long. The perpetuities saving clause's purpose is simply to make sure the Rule is not violated.

Here is an example of a saving clause:

> Notwithstanding any other provisions in this instrument, this trust shall terminate, if it has not previously terminated, 21 years after the death of the survivor of the beneficiaries of the trust living at the date this instrument becomes effective. In case of such termination the then remaining principal and undistributed income of the trust shall be distributed to the then income beneficiaries in the same proportions as they were, at the time of termination, entitled to receive the income.

Instead of terminating the trust on the death of the survivor of the "beneficiaries" in being when the trust becomes effective, the attorney can, if desired, expressly name the measuring lives. This alternative might be more useful in an inter vivos trust than in a testamentary trust because a will might become effective many years after execution when some of the named measuring lives are dead. Note also that the second sentence of the saving clause provides how the trust estate is distributed if the trust is terminated under this clause. This is essential, for it is not enough to "terminate" the trust without giving direction for distribution of the principal. The example given may be satisfactory if the trust is mandatory. If the trust is discretionary, however, the sentence would have to be reworded. It could provide that the trust estate is to be distributed to the settlor's issue then living, per stirpes. Almost every will and trust form book includes one or more forms of a perpetuities saving clause which the drafter can use. See W. McGovern, S. Kurtz & J. Rein, Wills, Trusts and Estates §13.4 at 524 (1988).

Insertion of a perpetuities saving clause is advisable even in jurisdictions that have adopted a cy pres or wait-and-see reform statute. These statutes do not eliminate perpetuities problems; they provide solutions for perpetuities problems that do arise. In a state that has a reform statute, litigation may be necessary (a) to determine whether the will or trust contains a perpetuities problem so as to invoke the operation of the statute and (b) to determine the remedy that is to be given by the statute.

As a result of the routine insertion of saving clauses, which began in the 1960s, trusts drafted by skilled lawyers almost never violate the Rule anymore. It is highly likely that violations of the Rule in the future in donative transfers will be found, with rare exceptions, in homemade wills or trusts, in instruments drafted by inexpert lawyers, or in instruments drafted before the 1960s. Bear this in mind as you evaluate the reforms of the Rule in the next section.

NOTE: ATTORNEY LIABILITY FOR VIOLATING RULE

In an increasing number of jurisdictions, attorneys are liable to intended beneficiaries of negligently drafted instruments. See supra page 73. Whether it is negligent to draft an instrument that violates the Rule against Perpetuities is not settled. In Lucas v. Hamm, 56 Cal. 2d 583, 364 P.2d 685 (1961), the court held the attorney who violated the Rule was not negligent on the specific facts of the case (involving an administrative contingency). *Lucas*, however, is a shaky precedent. It has been criticized by the Vice-Chancellor of England as an embarrassment to the profession. Note, 81 L.Q. Rev. 465, 478-481 (1965). A lower California court has warned that *Lucas* is of doubtful validity today, because the legendary traps of the Rule can be easily avoided by the insertion of a perpetuities saving clause. Wright v. Williams, 47 Cal. App. 3d 802, 809 n.2, 121 Cal. Rptr. 194, 199 n.2 (1975). See also Millwright v. Romer, 322 N.W.2d 30 (Iowa 1982), where the court appeared to assume that an attorney who violates the Rule is liable for malpractice but held the suit barred by the statute of limitations.

The threat of malpractice liability probably will be a strong force for reform of this intricate field. See Dukeminier, Cleansing the Stables of Property: A River Found at Last, 65 Iowa L. Rev. 151, 159-160 (1979).

SECTION F.   PERPETUITIES REFORM

In the last half of the twentieth century extensive debate has erupted over whether the Rule against Perpetuities needs reform and, if so, in what manner. The reformers' ideas and judicial and legislative changes in the law can be sorted into two basic kinds: The wait-and-see doctrine and the cy pres doctrine.

1.   *The Wait-and-See Doctrine*

The first attempt in modern times to change the requirement that there be no possibility that an interest might vest too remotely was a statute enacted in 1947 in Pennsylvania. Pa. Cons. Stat. Ann. tit. 20, §6014 (1975) provides:

> Upon the expiration of the period allowed by the common law rule against perpetuities as measured by actual rather than possible events any interest not then vested and any interest in members of a class the membership of which is then subject to increase shall be void.

In 1952 Professor W. Barton Leach began his attack upon the Rule against Perpetuities in its orthodox form. Dubbing the Pennsylvania approach "wait-and-see," Leach strongly approved it in a seminal article, Leach, Perpetuities in Perspective: Ending the Rule's Reign of Terror, 65 Harv. L. Rev. 721 (1952). Leach, writing with eloquence and wit, fired up a movement to adopt the wait-and-see doctrine. The essence of the wait-and-see doctrine, as suggested by the Pennsylvania statute, is that we wait and see what actually happens during the perpetuities period applicable to the interest; we do not invalidate an interest because of what might happen.

The proponents of wait-and-see argue that the what-might-happen test penalizes persons who do not consult skilled lawyers, who routinely insert saving clauses into trusts. As the Restatement (Second) of Property, Donative Transfers 13 (1983), puts it, "The adoption of the wait-and-see approach in this Restatement is largely motivated by the equality of treatment that is produced by placing the validity of all non-vested interests on the same plane, whether the interest is created by a skilled draftsman or one not so skilled." Implicit in this argument, however, is a recognition that the wait-and-see doctrine will mainly affect families whose ancestor consulted an unskilled lawyer or, worse, drew the will himself. The inept work of a bumbling drafter will be saved for the wait-and-see period.

In re Estate of Anderson
Supreme Court of Mississippi, 1989
541 So. 2d 423

ROBERTSON, J.

I

Today's testator, a bachelor during his lifetime, by will made substantial bequests to his favorite nephew. The rest of his estate he placed in trust to provide for the education of his nephews and nieces for the next twenty-five years, at the end of which the trust corpus and any undistributed income will also go to the favorite nephew.

We are told that the bequest in trust violates the Rule against Perpetuities, and by this we are told that testator has misjudged the nephew much more than the measure of the Rule.

The Chancery Court rejected the attack and upheld the trust. With but slight modification, we affirm.

II

Charles Maurice Anderson, late of Amite County, Mississippi, died December 12, 1984. Anderson was never married and had no children. Anderson was one of three children of Mr. and Mrs. Fred Alvin Anderson, Sr., the other two being Fred Alvin Anderson, Jr., his brother, and Helen J. Waitzman, his sister. Anderson was predeceased by both of his parents, and by his brother and his sister.

At the time of his death, Charles Maurice Anderson provided for a last will and testament which left a number of specific bequests to Howard W. Davis, his nephew, who is the son of testator's deceased sister. Davis is presently 53 years of age and is alive and well and living in Gloster, Mississippi. The portion of the will at issue today is Item IX which reads as follows:

> I hereby direct that the Deposit Guaranty National Bank of Jackson, Mississippi, take into its absolute control and handle as trustee the following described property, to-wit: (Then follows the description of approximately 960 acres of land.)
> The trustee shall use all of the income derived from the above described property, be it timber, minerals or other such income which may develop in the future, *for the education of the descendants of F.A. Anderson, Sr. for a*

period of twenty-five (25) years from the date of the admission of this last will and testament for probate. The trustee shall not be authorized to sell and dispose of the real property but only use the income therefrom and it shall do so without any limitation whatsoever. *Also to be used in the same manner for the same purpose, that being the education of the descendants of F.A. Anderson, Sr., for a period of twenty-five (25) years from the date of the admission of this last will and testament for probate shall be all of the income developed from my interests* in oil, gas and mineral rights including, but not necessarily limited to that portion of Magnolia State Oil & Land Company which I own and any other minerals which I own or in which I may have an interest, and minerals which may in the future become mine or part of my estate. I direct that my trustee not allow any one of the descendants of F.A. Anderson, Sr., to take advantage of the educational benefits which may be derived under this item but ask that the trustee be as liberal with each as possible. *At the conclusion of the twenty-five year period for which this trust is created, then I give, devise, and bequeath the real property and all of the oil, gas and minerals, which may then be in, on or under the property to Howard W. Davis and any money or securities which may still be in the educational fund at the end of the twenty-five years should likewise be delivered to Howard W. Davis, and in the event of his death prior to his taking, then to the heirs of his body.* [emphasis added]

The principal assets of the testator's estate consist of

(a)   960 acres of land and minerals, valued at the time of trial at $660,179.10, and devised in trust; [and]

(b)   a 41⅓% interest in Magnolia State Oil & Land Company valued at the time of trial at $86,136.05, devised in trust. . . .

The descendants of the testator's late father, Fred Alvin Anderson, Sr., a/k/a F.A. Anderson, Sr., living on December 12, 1984, included five grandchildren and ten great-grandchildren. Two more great-grandchildren have been born since that date.

The will of Charles Maurice Anderson was admitted to probate in the Chancery Court of Amite County, Mississippi, on December 21, 1984, nine days following Anderson's death. Subsequently, . . . Deposit Guaranty National Bank of Jackson, Mississippi, the executor of the will . . . , filed a petition for construction of will and for instructions. Specifically, the Executor requested interpretation of Item IX of the will of Charles Maurice Anderson, which has been quoted above.

On April 10, 1986, Howard W. Davis filed a response, arguing that (a) paragraph IX violates "the Rule against Perpetuities" . . . .

The matter came on for hearing before the Chancery Court of Amite County on August 12, 1986. . . .

In a decision rendered by letter dated December 26, 1986, and by declaratory judgment construing will entered April 10, 1987, the Court found that a valid and enforceable private educational testamentary trust has been created under Item IX of the will of Charles Maurice Anderson; that the term of said trust commenced on December 12,

1984, the date of the testator's death, and will continue thereafter for a period of twenty-five (25) years or twenty-one (21) years from and after the death of Howard W. Davis, whichever first occurs; that the trust will be unenforceable only to the extent that the term may exceed the lifetime of Howard W. Davis, plus twenty-one years; and, by reasons thereof, the term of the trust does not violate the Rule against Perpetuities and does not constitute an unlawful restraint on alienation. . . .

III

On April 17, 1987, Howard W. Davis gave his notice of appeal to this Court, where he makes essentially a three-part argument:

(1) The provision of the trust that gives educational benefits to the descendants of F.A. Anderson, Sr., creates executory interests in them. Thus, the interests are contingent. These interests may fail to vest within the period of the Rule against Perpetuities, so they are void. The Chancery Court below saved these interests by applying either cy pres or equitable approximation, and this was error.

(2) The alternative interest created in the heirs of Howard W. Davis' body upon the termination of the trust also violates the Rule against Perpetuities and also should not have been saved by either cy pres or equitable approximation.

(3) The trust is void because its terms are vague, ambiguous or indefinite.

IV. Does the Twenty-Five Year Private Educational Testamentary Trust Violate the Rule Against Perpetuities, and Thus Fail?

A. THE RULE DECLARED

That a person may by will devise his property as he or she sees fit is in our law a premise of the first rank, though not without qualification. The premise is an outgrowth of our law's respect for rights of private property. . . .

Yet our society has conflicting needs.

Public convenience today demands a rule of law (1) that will limit "dead hand" control over property which prevents the present generation from using the property as it sees fit, (2) that will keep property marketable and available for productive development in accordance with market demands, and (3) that will curb trusts which can protect wealthy beneficiaries from creditors, decrease the amount of risk capital available for economic development and, after a period of time and change in circumstances, tie up the family in disadvantageous and undesirable arrangements.[25]

One response our law has made to these concerns has been the promulgation and enforcement of the Rule against Perpetuities. Seen in its best light, the Rule represents a balancing of the interests of the present owner in controlling his property well into the future against the future owner's interests in unrestricted use and alienability. We approach the Rule as no other, having in mind Holmes' ideas of the historical development of law.[26] On the one hand, our experience with the Rule exemplifies the "historical tendency of property law to forget the original reason for its rules and to reduce principles to logic."[27] On the other hand, we regard the treatment of the Rule as a theorem, as a rule of logical proof, if you will, and the untoward, if not absurd, results so generated, as a major force fueling the flames of common sense and fidelity to principle and purpose which have marked this state's experience in recent times.

The Rule has its origins in common law England. See, e.g., Duke of Norfolk's Case, 3 Ch. Cas. 1, 22 Eng. Rep. 931 (1682); Jee v. Audley, 1 Cox 324, 29 Eng. Rep. 1186 (Ch. 1787). We need not recross the Atlantic on the Mayflower,[28] however, as what is important today is that the Rule has been posited among the law of this state via the articulate voice of this Court. Our cases afford a variety of forms of expression of the Rule.[29] While perfection in expression is an illusion no court should expect to achieve, we regard the best phrasing of the Rule as follows:

> No interest is good unless it vests within twenty-one years after the death of all persons in being when the interest is created who can affect the vesting of the interest.[30]

25. For further statement of and elaboration upon these policy statements, see Dukeminier, A Modern Guide to Perpetuities, 74 Calif. L. Rev. 1867, 1868-69 (1986); Restatement (Second) of Property (Donative Transfers), Pt. 1, Introductory Note (1981); Smith, Perpetuities in New Jersey: A Plea for Judicial Supremacy, 24 Rutgers L. Rev. 80, 81 (1969).

26. On page one of The Common Law (1881), Holmes wrote (shockingly at the time): "The life of the law has not been logic: it has been experience."

27. Dukeminier, A Modern Guide to Perpetuities, 74 Calif. L. Rev. 1867, 1870 (1986).

28. The antiquarian who wishes to pursue the history of the Rule would do well to begin with Haskins, Extending the Grasp of the Dead Hand: Reflections on the Origins of the Rule Against Perpetuities, 126 U. of Pa. L. Rev. 19 (1977).

29. The so-called classic statement of the Rule is that of John Chipman Gray: "No interest is good unless it must vest, if at all, no later than twenty-one years after some life in being at the creation of the interest." J. Gray, The Rule Against Perpetuities §201 at 191 (4th ed. 1942). This statement of the Rule has been quoted in Carter v. Berry, 243 Miss. 321, 358, 140 So. 2d 843, 846 (1962), and appears in our cases as early as 1922. . . .

30. See Dukeminier, Perpetuities: The Measuring Lives, 85 Colum. L. Rev. 1648, 1713 (1985). [This is the statement of the Rule in jurisdictions adopting wait-and-see for the common law perpetuities period.—Eds.]

... The very able brief of Appellant Davis concentrates upon Gray's traditional statement of the Rule and then struggles mightily to avoid the import of this state's three major modifications of the Rule:

(1)   Our shifting of emphasis from what-might-happen to wait-and-see, C & D Investment Co. v. Gulf Transport Co., 526 So. 2d 526, 530 (Miss. 1988); Phelps v. Shropshire, 254 Miss. 777, 785, 183 So. 2d 158, 162 (Miss. 1966);

(2)   the abolition of the all-or-nothing rule for class gifts, Carter v. Berry, 243 Miss. 321, 140 So. 2d 843 (1962), noted in 76 Harv. L. Rev. 1308 (1963); and

(3)   the empowerment of our courts to imply a savings clause[31] into any devise which would otherwise violate the Rule, to become operative only when it becomes apparent that remote vesting will otherwise occur.

Indeed, reflection upon the argument advanced by Appellant Davis makes clear that at least for today far greater inconvenience may result from the dead hand of John Chipman Gray than from the dead hand of Charles Maurice Anderson.

B.   THE RULE APPLIED

These general considerations before us, we turn to the elements of the Rule against Perpetuities, as modified, and their application to the

---

31. Our implied savings clause point requires explication, particularly in view of Davis' admonition that this Court should not be about the business of rewriting a testator's will, an admonition attended by citations to Ferguson v. Morgan, 220 Miss. 266, 271, 70 So. 2d 866, 867 (1954); and Jones v. Carey, 122 Miss. 244, 248, 84 So. 186, 187 (1920). The past three decades have produced case after case where we construed a devise, arguably technically deficient, to effect or approximate the testator's dominant intent. May v. Hunt, 404 So. 2d 1373, 1381 (Miss. 1981) (equitable approximation); In Re Estate of Kelly, 193 So. 2d 575, 578 (Miss. 1967) (equitable approximation); Carter v. Berry, 243 Miss. 321, 370-76, 140 So. 2d 843, 852-55 (1962) (cy pres and equitable approximation); see also In Re Estate of Hall, 193 So. 2d 587, 592 (Miss. 1967) (power to supplement provisions of testamentary charitable trust). The point is summed up in Estate of Bunch v. Heirs of Bunch, 485 So. 2d 284, 285 (Miss. 1986):

> Whatever may once have been the law in this state, it is much too late to question the authority and responsibility of this Court to *amend or supplement* the terms of a will — whether its devise be *private or charitable* in nature — where such is necessary to effect the testator's dominant intent and avoid a clearly unintended consequence.

Estate of Bunch, 485 So. 2d at 285 [Emphasis supplied]; see also Tinnin v. First Bank of Mississippi, 502 So. 2d 659, 664, 669 (Miss. 1987). The reason we may read these cases as authorizing an implied savings clause is simple. No sensible individual executes a will intending or anticipating that it will fail. . . . It defies common sense to suggest that the maker of a will does not contemplate and intend that his will be amended or supplemented where such is necessary to give effect to his dominant intent and avoid a discordant consequence. . . .

Thought of the content of such a savings clause is aided by perusal of actual savings clauses, see Leach and Logan, Perpetuities: A Standard Savings Clause to Avoid Violations of the Rule, 74 Harv. L. Rev. 1141 (1961); 2 Murphy's Will Clauses §F13, Form 6:80 (1988).

facts of this case. We first search for the measuring lives. The Rule tells us these must be persons who were alive when the interest was created. Which of the millions of persons who inhabited this earth on December 12, 1984 — the day Charles Maurice Anderson died — are the measuring lives? Our law is clear that we are not limited to persons whose names appear in the testator's will. Hughes v. Miller, 384 So. 2d 608, 610 (Miss. 1980); Carter v. Berry, supra, 243 Miss. at 362, 140 So. 2d at 848. Instead, we canvass those persons implied by the creating instrument, necessarily involved in the limitations contained therein, or, as we prefer to put it, who can affect the vesting of the interest.[32] We do not inquire whether the testator intended the particular lives in question to be the measuring lives, nor need those persons take anything under the instrument. Carter v. Berry, 243 Miss. at 362, 140 So. 2d at 848. Where there is a choice among more than one life in being at the creation of the interest, one who can save the interest must be selected.

The search for the measuring lives has been well summarized by Prof. Jesse Dukeminier:

> To find this validating life, logic requires us to use a two-step process of analysis. *First*, we start with this proposition: *If a validating life is found, it will necessarily be found among the lives that can affect vesting, and no others.* Hence, we assemble a pool of all persons alive who can affect vesting of the interest in some way. Persons who cannot affect vesting are irrelevant. *Second*, with respect to each person in the pool, we ask whether the interest will necessarily vest or fail within the life of such person or upon, or within twenty-one years after, such person's death. If we find a person in the pool by whom the necessary proof can be made, we have found the validating life. If, on the other hand, we cannot make the required proof by reference to any person in the pool, there is no life that validates the gift; the gift is void unless it must vest or fail within twenty-one years. *A conclusion that the gift is void implicitly says that all causally-related lives have been tested and found useless in making the requisite proof.*[33]

We add as a caveat: the conclusion that the gift is void is subject to the Mississippi modifiers: wait-and-see, abolition of all-or-nothing, and implied savings clause.

The Court below and the parties in their briefs appear to assume that Howard W. Davis is the measuring life, perhaps because his is the name mentioned in the will. No one articulates any reason why this should be so. But a moment's reflection upon our rules regarding the search for the measuring lives makes clear that all persons who are descendants of F.A. Anderson, Sr. and who were alive on December

32. Dukeminier, A Modern Guide to Perpetuities, 74 Calif. L. Rev. 1867, 1873 (1986); Dukeminier, Perpetuities: The Measuring Lives, 85 Colum. L. Rev. 1648, 1650 (1985); Restatement (Second) of Property (Donative Transfers) §1.3, comment b (1981).
33. Dukeminier, supra, 85 Colum. L. Rev. at 1650.

12, 1984, are eligible, measuring, validating lives. Will the interest vest within twenty-one years after the death of all descendants of F.A. Anderson who were in being on December 12, 1984?

By Item IX of his will, Charles Maurice Anderson created a trust for the "education" of the descendants of F.A. Anderson, Sr. The interests of each of these descendants will vest only upon his or her qualifying for the educational benefits provided by the trust. No wording in the will demands that each and every descendant receive a portion of the trust income. While all are potentially eligible for an interest, each must satisfy the stated requirement before receiving it. As each of the descendants of F.A. Anderson, Sr. must qualify for the educational benefits of the trust — according to guidelines to be developed by the trustee — before he or she becomes entitled to so much as a penny, we regard the interest of each as subject to a condition precedent and, accordingly, contingent, not vested.

Recall that the trust is to terminate "twenty-five years from the date of the admission of this last will and testament for probate," the termination date thus being December 21, 2009. As of December 12, 1984, the date of the death of Charles Maurice Anderson, it was theoretically possible that all of the descendants of F.A. Anderson, Sr. would die *more than twenty-one years before* the scheduled termination of the trust. It was also possible that no descendant of F.A. Anderson, Sr. would qualify for benefits within the term of the trust. If we turn back the clock to December 12, 1984, and look at the facts as they then existed, the conclusion was then inescapable the interest created by Item IX of the will might not vest within twenty-one years after the death of all persons in being on December 12, 1984, who could affect the vesting of the interest. From this conclusion, invoking the dead hand of John Chipman Gray, Appellant Davis argues that the Rule must be "remorselessly applied."[34] Our law demurs, and with authority.

One evil experience has revealed is that treating the Rule as a rule

---

34. The full quote from Gray is, "Every provision in a will or settlement is to be construed as if the Rule did not exist, and then to the provision so construed, the Rule is to be remorselessly applied." J. Gray, The Rule Against Perpetuities §629 (4th ed. 1942). We once followed Gray. Henry v. Henderson, 103 Miss. 48, 60 So. 33, 40 (1912). . . . Beyond this we cannot resist noting that Gray's grandson, Owen Tudor, has uttered upon the Rule, together with Prof. W. Barton Leach, in The Rule Against Perpetuities (1957), which is dedicated:

TO JOHN CHIPMAN GRAY
Grandfather of one of us
professional forebear of both
who in his juridical Valhalla
may well realize
that his "remorseless" Rule
was more appropriate
to his time than to ours

[Emphasis in original].

of logical proof and mechanical application produces distributions of property neither intended nor desired by the testator. See Carter v. Berry, 243 Miss. at 370, 140 So. 2d at 852. Established within our law is the principle that a person's will should be enforced so as to avoid clearly unintended consequences. Tinnin v. First Bank of Mississippi, 502 So. 2d 659, 669 (Miss. 1987); Estate of Bunch v. Heirs of Bunch, 485 So. 2d 284, 285 (Miss. 1986). Any reader of the will at issue may say with confidence that Charles Maurice Anderson did not intend[35] that Howard W. Davis take Anderson's entire estate to the exclusion of the educational needs of Anderson's nieces and nephews and their children. It is this conclusion that triggers the Court's responsibility to apply one or more of our ameliorative doctrines and save this testamentary trust.

West Virginia considered a legally analogous twenty-five year private educational testamentary trust in Berry v. Union National Bank, 164 W. Va. 258, 262 S.E.2d 766 (1980), and invoked "equitable modification" and reduced the term of the trust to twenty-one years. The West Virginia Court cites Carter v. Berry as evidence of "a developing trend to ameliorate the harsh consequences of 'remorseless application' of the rule." *Berry*, 164 W. Va. at 265, 262 S.E.2d at 770, n.8 and accompanying text. Carter v. Berry would indeed authorize a like result here.

Sufficient unto the day is our wait-and-see doctrine, an alternative to Carter v. Berry, which ought here [to] be employed as it may save all, not just most, of Charles Maurice Anderson's private educational testamentary trust. Under wait-and-see, the validity of an interest is not judged by what might happen, but rather by what does happen, by whether the interest in fact vests or fails within the perpetuities period. C & D Investment Co. v. Gulf Transport Co., 526 So. 2d at 530.

---

35. On the matter of Anderson's intent, we do not ignore Henry v. Henderson, 103 Miss. 48, 69, 60 So. 33, 40 (1912) to the point that the very object of the Rule "is to defeat intention." *Henry*, of course, relies upon Gray. Leach and Tudor have this to say:

> One sentence from Gray's pungent paragraph on this subject should be mentioned. He says, referring to the Rule against Perpetuities, "Its object is to defeat intention." We are well aware of what Gray had in mind in writing that sentence; unquestionably the Rule defeats the testator's intention when it invalidates an interest, and no expression of intention that the Rule shall not apply to his will is effective. Still, Gray's expression is unfortunate. The object of the Rule is to restrict the tying up of property to permissible limits. To attain this end it will defeat the intention of a particular testator, *if necessary*. The public interest must prevail over private wishes. But the Rule has no punitive aspect — indeed, if it did, the fact that the testator has already passed into the jurisdiction of a higher law would raise serious difficulties of enforcement. It is consistent with the status of the Rule as a precept of social policy that every possible measure should be taken to bring a testator's will into conformance with it rather than to find a violation of the law's prohibition.

Leach and Tudor, The Rule Against Perpetuities, §24.46, pp. 121-22 (1957) [Emphasis in original].

For one thing, the record reflects that by the time of trial (August, 1986), several beneficiaries had already qualified for and received substantial educational benefits. Some income and, of course, the entire principal remained untouched, in 1986 and, we presume, today as well. It is true that what remains may never vest in any member of the beneficiary class, as it is possible that no further descendants of F.A. Anderson, Sr., may qualify for educational benefits. That the interests thus remain contingent is no longer of concern, as the period of the Anderson testamentary trust will end on December 21, 2009, which is *less than twenty-one years from this day.* As there are now in being a host of measuring lives,[36] we may say with certainty that all interests created under the testamentary trust will *either vest or fail* within twenty-one years after the end of all measuring lives.[37] "There is no precedent in this state which compels us to close our eyes to the facts occurring after the death of the testat[or]." Phelps v. Shropshire, 254 Miss. at 785, 183 So. 2d at 162; quoted in *C & D Investment Co.,* 526 So. 2d at 529.

Davis' able counsel notes that the result we decree: that the trust be upheld, would allow this private educational testamentary trust to "go on for twenty-five years." Counsel tells us that this "not only violates the Rule against Perpetuities, it makes a shambles of it." The point revealed is that the Rule itself, at least without the Mississippi modifiers, is a shambles. But a moment's reflection reveals that an adept lawyer can tie up property "for an unconscionable period — viz., twenty-one years after the deaths of a dozen or so babies chosen from families noted for longevity, a term which, in the ordinary course of events, will add up to about a century."[38] If this be so, what sense does it make that the mere twenty-five years the Anderson trust will last are too much? Moreover, the twenty-five years these trust assets will be dominated by Charles Maurice Anderson's dead hand pale into insignificance when compared with the ninety year wait-and-see period which is the

36. The measuring lives under wait-and-see are the same lives relevant under what-might-happen: those causally related to vesting. Dukeminier, 74 Calif. L. Rev. at 1181-82.

[The court's list of the measuring lives — the five grandchildren and ten great-grandchildren of F.A. Anderson, Sr., living at Charles Anderson's death — is omitted.— Eds.]

37. Our cases have not yet fleshed out the meaning of our wait-and-see doctrine. One objection to wait-and-see is the practical problems that may result from not knowing whether an interest is valid or void, perhaps for several decades. See R. Powell, The Law of Real Property §§827[A]-827[H] (P. Rohan rev. ed. 1986); see also Simes and Smith, The Law of Future Interests §1230 (2d ed. 1956). Here we only had to wait and see for four years and nine days from December 12, 1984, a period which, alas, because of the slow pace of litigation, has come and gone. We have not concerned ourselves with the outer limits of wait-and-see and nothing said here should be taken as expressing a view on the point.

38. 6 American Law of Property §24.16, at 52 (A. Casner ed. 1952).

centerpiece of the new Uniform Statutory Rule Against Perpetuities promulgated in 1986 by the National Conference of Commissioners on Uniform State Laws.[39] 8A U.L.A. 80 (Supp. 1987).

Notions of wait-and-see and an implied savings clause may be found in our cases dating back at least two decades, and in that sense our decision this day is nothing new. On the other hand, we have never recognized the two so forcefully as today. We need not sacrifice civil justice on the altar of legal formalism or the purist's nostalgia, as it is beyond comprehension that Howard W. Davis, or any other citizen of this state, has in fact placed legally cognizable reliance — to his detriment — upon the dead hand Rule of John Chipman Gray. See Tideway Oil Programs, Inc. v. Serio, 431 So. 2d 454, 465-66 (Miss. 1983).

V. DO THE INTERESTS CREATED IN THE HEIRS OF HOWARD W. DAVIS VIOLATE THE RULE AGAINST PERPETUITIES?

Here Howard W. Davis claims that the remainder interests created in his heirs are executory, contingent on their surviving until the trust terminates with Howard W. Davis having already died. Davis' target is the language "at the conclusion of the twenty-five year period for which this trust is created *then I give*, devise and bequeath the real property . . . and in the event of his death prior to his taking, *then to the heirs of his body.*"

Howard W. Davis' remainder interest thus created is vested, subject to being defeated if he does not survive December 21, 2009. . . . The interests of the heirs of Davis' body are contingent upon Davis dying before December 21, 2009. In light of what we have said above, the answer is simple. We have waited and seen and Howard W. Davis is very much in being. The interests of the heirs of Davis' body, contingent though they are, will vest or fail on or before December 21, 2009, which is less than twenty-one years from this day.[40]

The assignment of error is denied.

39. It is no exaggeration to suggest that "there is agreement among virtually all of the commentators and experts in the field that the Rule against Perpetuities is in need of reform." Waggoner, Perpetuity Reform, 81 Mich. L. Rev. 1718 (1983). Out of exasperation with the continuing power of the dead hand of John Chipman Gray, many states have opted for statutory reform of the Rule, the new Uniform Statutory Rule being only the latest and most prominent of such efforts. With the three judicial ameliorations in being in this state — wait-and-see, abolition of all-or-nothing in class gifts, and implied savings clause — there would appear no need here for legislation on the subject. See Dukeminier, The Uniform Statutory Rule Against Perpetuities: Ninety Years in Limbo, 34 UCLA L. Rev. 1023 (1987); Smith, Perpetuities in New Jersey: A Plea for Judicial Supremacy, 24 Rutgers L. Rev. 80 (1969).

40. Davis' remainder vested upon creation. The gift over to his heirs, if Davis dies before the end of the trust, is valid under the old common law what-might-happen Rule *if the "heirs of his body" are ascertained at his death.* If Davis dies within twenty-five years, the

VI. WHETHER THE TERMS OF THE TRUST CREATED BY THE TESTATOR ARE SO VAGUE, AMBIGUOUS AND UNCERTAIN AS TO RENDER THE TRUST VOID

Here Davis asserts that the term "education" is ambiguous, citing numerous examples of "education" which are non-traditional and claiming the trust gives no guidance as to which pursuits are or are not education. . . .

We find no merit in Davis' challenge that "education" is too broad and ambiguous. We begin with the general premise that "If the trustee is to use trust funds to provide for the 'education' of a beneficiary, the type of education to be furnished will depend on his express directions or the reasonable implications arising from all the circumstances of the case." Bogert, Trusts and Trustees §811, p.28 (2d ed. 1981).

There is a wonderful, old case on point concerning Martha Washington's devise of stock in trust for "the proper education" of her three nephews and to fit them for some useful trade. Dandridge v. Washington's Executors, 2 Pet. (27 U.S.) 370, 7 L. Ed. 454 (1829). In part the dispute was whether the money should be limited to the pursuit of a mechanical trade or more broadly defined. Chief Justice Marshall wrote:

> But we do not think the bequest is confined to the expense of acquiring the trade so as to be enabled to exercise it in the common way. Such does not appear to have been the intent of the testatrix. Her bounty is extended to the proper education of three relatives so that they may be severally fitted and accomplished in some useful trade. Their education is a primary object, as well as their acquisition of the trade, and when we consider the situation and character of the parties and the language of the will, we cannot doubt that the testatrix intended such education as would fit her relatives to hold a distinguished place in that line of life in which she designed them to move. The sum allowed for the object ought to be liberal such as would accomplish it if the fund from which it was to be drawn would admit of it.

---

executory interest in his heirs will divest his vested remainder and become a vested remainder upon his death. Davis is the validating life. Wait-and-see is not necessary to save it.

If, on the other hand, the heirs of Davis' body *are not ascertained until twenty-five years after the testator's death,* the heirs' interest violates the common law Rule and wait-and-see is necessary to save it. Under the common law, validity depended upon the time when the heirs of Davis were ascertained.

Under the common law Rule, heirs were ascertained at an ancestor's death — not at some later time. But in some exceptional cases heirs were determined at the time of possession. See 5 American Law of Property §22.60(a) (standard rule) and (c) (exceptions) (A. Casner ed. 1952). None of the exceptions applies in this case.

In the view we take, it is unnecessary to determine when Davis' heirs are ascertained because in any case their interest is valid under wait-and-see.

Dandridge, 2 Pet. (27 U.S.) at 377, 7 L. Ed. at 457.

We have spoken directly to this issue. In Simpson v. Watkins, 162 Miss. 242, 139 So. 400 (1932), this Court was called upon to interpret provisions in what it deemed an "education will." One fourteen-year-old nephew then sued for expenses to attend a private boarding school as opposed to "the fine system of public schools" of Jackson, Mississippi. In affirming the trustee's allowance, the Court had this to say:

> Without further length of elaboration we will quote and adopt the resume of the question at issue as made by the chancellor in his decree which resume is in the following words:
>
>> That the trustees are vested with sufficient discretion by necessary implication to administer the trust estate with such reasonable and prudent economy as may be required to accomplish the ultimate goal and real intent to the testator, and to this end may adopt reasonable plans, regulations and schedules for the submission and allowance of educational expenses of beneficiaries.

Simpson, 162 Miss. at 251, 139 So. at 402. . . .

A trustee whose duty it was to apply the trust income and principal to the support and education of a minor, bought him an automobile and supplies for it in order that the boy could commute to school and live outside a large city. The trustee's action was held valid. Indianhead National Bank v. Theriault, 97 N.H. 212, 84 A.2d 828 (1952). Under a trust which permitted the trustee to spend up to $2,000.00 a year for the support and education of grandchildren, the trustee may expend $1800.00 a year to provide rearing and training for a "mongoloid" grandchild. In Re Besso's Estate, 220 N.Y.S.2d 475, 30 Misc. 2d 766 (1961).

The intent of Charles Maurice Anderson, as that intent may be gleaned from the words and expressions that appear in his will, is our touchstone. That intent signals a broad discretion vested in the trustee. While equity among beneficiaries is certainly a factor to be considered, the trustee has clear authority to consider as well the special needs, aptitude and diligence of each beneficiary — to be as liberal as possible without allowing unfair advantage. Nothing in the testator's plan mandates equality in distributions, nor are trust benefits restricted to college education, nor are they available only to the young. Should one of the descendants of F.A. Anderson, Sr., prove exceptionally talented in music, the trustee may well finance (a reasonable portion of) that child's education at Juilliard. And the same of another's pursuit of an M.B.A. at Wharton, or a third's attendance at Andover, or a young child's enrollment in a Montessori School. The trustee may purchase an Encyclopaedia Britannica for one beneficiary, a personal computer for another, athletic equipment for a third.

If perchance a problem of substance should arise regarding a particular expenditure, the Chancery Court, upon proper application, would have authority to afford such direction as may be needed. See Estate of Bunch v. Heirs of Bunch, 485 So. 2d 284, 285-87 (Miss. 1986); In Re Estate of Hall, 193 So. 2d 587, 591-92 (Miss. 1967). . . .

VII

In conclusion, we affirm the final declaratory judgment of the Chancery Court entered April 10, 1987, with but a single, slight modification. Because we have waited and seen and all interests now contingent will vest or fail in less than twenty-one years following the last of the measuring lives, certain language of Paragraph I thereof has been rendered moot. Paragraph I of the judgment below should be, and it hereby is, amended so that it reads:

> The objections to the validity of the trust interposed by Respondent, Howard W. Davis, are found to be without merit and the same are hereby dismissed; and the Court does now find and adjudicate that a valid trust was created under Item IX of the Last Will and Testament of Charles Maurice Anderson, and that the term of said trust commences on December 12, 1984, the date of the testator's death, and is to continue thereafter until December 21, 2009.[41]

The case is remanded for further proceedings in the execution of the last will and testament of Charles Maurice Anderson, deceased, and the administration of the estate and trust therein created, not inconsistent with this opinion.

Appellant's motion for modification of opinion granted in part, denied in part. Affirmed as modified.

NOTES AND QUESTIONS

1. *Waiting to see for the common law perpetuities period.*

(a)   The Rule against Perpetuities fixes for each contingent interest a period of time, applicable to it alone, within which the interest must be certain to vest or fail. This period — known as the perpetuities period — is determined by the lives in being that can affect vesting of the interest in question plus the addition of 21 years after those lives

---

41. The reason why the trust does not terminate until December 21, 2009, is found in the language of Item IX of Testator's will which provides that the twenty-five year period runs "from the date of the admission of this last will and testament for probate." The will was admitted for probate on December 21, 1984.

have expired (see supra page 765). The essence of wait-and-see is to say: "It is not fatal that you did not find a validating life among the lives that can affect vesting. You can wait out these lives and see if the interest vests within 21 years after their expiration."

Megarry & Wade explain it this way:

> The policy of the "wait and see" provisions . . . is not to alter the length of the perpetuity period, but to provide that gifts shall be valid if they do in fact vest within it rather than be void if they might by possibility vest outside it. The perpetuity period itself remains unchanged, and the lives in being which determine the period in any given case ought likewise to remain unchanged.
>
> . . .[T]he only lives in being which are significant under the rule at common law are those which in some way restrict the time within which the gift can vest, and which are expressly or impliedly connected with the gift by the donor's directions. The available perpetuity period must always be ascertained before it can be said whether the gift succeeds or fails. The conditions governing the vesting of the gift, and the lives implicated in those conditions, necessarily remain the same, whether or not the conditions are ultimately satisfied. . . .
>
> In order to introduce the "wait and see" principle, therefore, the most that [is] required [is] to enact that no extension of the familiar category of lives should be implied. [R. Megarry & H. Wade, The Law of Real Property 253-254 (5th ed. 1984).]

(b) Under wait-and-see, the term *measuring lives* does not refer to validating lives but to lives that measure the wait-and-see period. Who are the measuring lives for the trust in In re Estate of Anderson? How is it determined who can affect vesting or, to put it another way, who is causally related to vesting? If you don't know, go back and reread about "persons who can affect vesting" on page 765.

(c) Who are the wait-and-see measuring lives in the following cases?

(1) "To Mary Hall, and if her bloodline expires, to the daughters then living of John and Elizabeth Jee."

(2) "To the first child of A to become a lawyer."

(3) "To such of the grandchildren of A as reach 21."

(4) "To A for life, then to such of A's children as reach 25."

(5) "To A and her heirs, but if the property ever ceases to be used for residential purposes, to B and her heirs." (Careful! The hypothetical case involves the common law principle that if the number of persons who can affect vesting in the same way is so great that it is impracticable to say when the perpetuities period ends, none of such persons can be used as measuring lives. See In re Moore, supra page 759, footnote 5.) For answers, see Note 1(g), infra page 833.

See Dukeminier, Perpetuities: The Measuring Lives, 85 Colum. L. Rev. 1648, 1659-1674 (1985); Dukeminier, Wait-and-See: The Causal Relationship Principle, 102 L.Q. Rev. 250 (1986).

(d) In Fleet National Bank v. Colt, 529 A.2d 122 (R.I. 1987), the court had before it a trust established by the will of Samuel P. Colt. This was the fourth time since Colt's death in 1921 that his trust was litigated. In the first case, involving a claimed violation of the Rule against Perpetuities, the court decided that an instrument should be construed so as not to violate the Rule. It must be presumed, the court said, that the testator intended to make a valid devise. The opinion then proceeded, in a leavening style now out of fashion:

> Colonel Colt was a member of the bar of this State for many years and was attorney general for several years. It is presumed that he knew of the Rule against Perpetuities and that he would not knowingly make a will attempting to dispose of his property in violation of that Rule. Colonel Colt was prominent in the social, political and business life of the State, a man of vision, big deeds and generous impulses. He accumulated a large fortune; organized the Trust Company which he made executor of his will and trustee of his estate. By the 18th clause of his will he made a generous bequest to many persons in the employ of the Trust Company. See Industrial Trust Co. v. Alves, 46 R.I. 16. Colonel Colt was devoted to his family and wished to see them happy and prosperous. He lived in the homestead where his mother was born. In memory of his mother he erected The Colt Memorial High School for the town of Bristol on a portion of the Homestead Estate and in his will gave the town $100,000 in trust to use and employ the income therefrom in perpetuity for the maintenance of this memorial. He extended and developed the Colt Farm on the shores of Narragansett Bay and as a part of the development constructed a beautiful motor drive through the Farm and along the shore of the Bay and at the entrance to the drive erected a sign, "Colt Farm, Private Property. Public Welcome." This drive was used by thousands of motorists for many years preceding the death of the testator. [Colt v. Industrial Trust Co., 50 R.I. 242, 246-247, 146 A. 628, 630 (1929).][42]

In Fleet National Bank v. Colt, the court had to decide the application

---

42. In their casebook on Future Interests, Leach and Logan appended this sassy footnote to the 1929 *Colt* case:

> Other courts too get carried away in considering extraneous factors to determine whether the Rule against Perpetuities was violated. In Forman v. Troup, 30 Ga. 496 (1860), the court had under consideration the will of Governor George M. Troup and particularly a gift over in the event that any of his three children, Oralie, George, and Florida should "die without lineal heirs." The court seems to have felt that if an indefinite failure of issue was intended the Rule was violated. It found quite helpful the character of the testator: "And of all men, never would I impute such an intention to violate the laws of this State to a man who loved her, and every letter of her laws, and every inch of her soil with an energy and devotion that no soul could inspire but that of George M. Troup." [Perhaps, but he named his daughter Florida.] [W. Leach & J. Logan, Future Interests and Estate Planning 376 (1961).]

of the wait-and-see doctrine to a gift to subclasses (see supra, page 795). In 1983 the Rhode Island legislature adopted wait-and-see for a period measured by the lives causally related to vesting. R. I. Gen. Laws §34-11-38 (1984). The statute expressly provided that it was not retroactive. Nonetheless, the Rhode Island court decided that the statute was declaratory of the judicial policy of not ruling on the validity of remainders until the termination of preceding estates and applied the statute retroactively. The problem before the court essentially involved these facts. Colt bequeathed property in trust "to pay the income to Roswell Colt for life, then to pay the income to Roswell's children for their lives, and, upon the death of any child of Roswell leaving surviving issue, to pay the share of the trust principal upon which such child was receiving the income to such child's issue per stirpes, and if such child shall die without issue, to pay such child's share to my heirs." At Colt's death in 1921, Roswell had one child, Elizabeth, alive. Subsequently Caldwell, Melba, and Byron were born to Roswell. The remainders in the issue of Caldwell, Melba, and Byron violate the Rule against Perpetuities (see supra pages 795-800). At Caldwell's death in 1985, his sister Elizabeth, who was born before 1921, was still alive. Could Elizabeth be used as a life causally related to vesting of the remainder in Caldwell's issue? The court held she could, saying,

> She is causally connected not only to the vesting of the remainder in her own children, but also to the life estate of her siblings and thus to the remainder in her sibling's children. If, for example, Elizabeth had predeceased her father Roswell, the income that Roswell had been receiving as a first life tenant would have been divided into thirds rather than fourths and paid to Melba, Caldwell, and Byron, Roswell's surviving children. Thus, the amount of Caldwell's share, and consequently the amounts of his children's shares, were dependent upon the survival of Elizabeth.

For another examination of measuring lives for gifts to subclasses, coming to the same result as that reached by the Rhode Island court, see Dukeminier, 85 Colum. L. Rev. 1648, supra, at 1668 (Case 8). See also footnote 21, supra page 797, where the court seemingly suggests the same result.

(e) Statutes in a number of states adopting wait-and-see provide that the lives causally related to vesting are the measuring lives for wait-and-see. Alaska Stat. §34.27.010 (1986); Ky. Rev. Stat. Ann. §381.216 (1972); N.M. Stat. Ann. §47-1-17.1 (1987); R.I. Gen. Laws §34-11-38 (1984). In some other jurisdictions adopting wait-and-see, the measuring lives have not been specified by statute. Ohio Rev. Code Ann. §2131.08(c) (1987); Pa. Cons. Stat. Ann. tit. 20, §6104(b) (1975); S.D. Codified Laws Ann. §43-5-6 (1983); Vt. Stat. Ann. tit. 27, §501 (1975);

Va. Code Ann. §55-13.3 (1986). Nonetheless, the logic of wait-and-see implicitly suggests — as the Mississippi court holds — that the measuring lives are the lives relevant to vesting. See also North Bay Council, Inc., Boy Scouts of America v. Grinnell, 123 N.H. 321, 461 A.2d 114 (1983), apparently adopting the causal relationship principle to measure the wait-and-see period (wait-and-see has been judicially adopted in New Hampshire as well as in Mississippi). Almost all of these wait-and-see statutes also provide that if, after waiting to see, it turns out that an interest violates the Rule, it shall be reformed by a court to carry out the intention of the testator as far as possible within the perpetuities period. This is known as "delayed cy pres" to distinguish it from immediate reformation of a perpetuities violation at the testator's death, discussed in the next subsection.

(f) Two states have legislation applying wait-and-see to trusts but not to legal interests. See Ill. Ann. Stat. ch. 30, ¶195, §5 (Supp. 1988) (beneficiaries of trust are measuring lives); Wash. Rev. Code §11.98.130 (1987) (lives governing continuance of trust are measuring lives).

(g) Answers to Problem 1(c) supra. (1) Mary Hall, John and Elizabeth Jee, and the four Jee daughters now living. (2) A and any child of A now living. (3) A and any children and grandchildren of A now living. (4) A and any children of A now living. (5) B. The persons alive who can affect the condition precedent (everyone in the world to whom the property could be transferred) are too numerous to be measuring lives.

2. *Waiting for the duration of the preceding life estates.*   In two states limited wait-and-see statutes provide for waiting out the lives of preceding life tenants and determining validity of the remainder on the basis of facts existing at that time. Me. Rev. Stat. Ann. tit. 33, §101 (1988); Md. Est. & Trusts Code Ann. §11-103(a) (1974).

3. *Waiting during the lives of persons on an arbitrary list.*   The English wait-and-see statute proceeded on the premise, subsequently shown to be unfounded, that the common law did not furnish measuring lives for wait-and-see. The English statute provides an arbitrary list of persons, connected in some way with the gift and enumerated by statute, to measure the wait-and-see period. English Perpetuities & Accumulations Act, 1964, ch. 55, §3(4). This list proved quite controversial. Some found it unnecessary; others found it complex and ambiguous. See R. Megarry & H. Wade, supra, at 253-258; R. Maudsley, The Modern Law of Perpetuities 123-139 (1979). The Restatement (Second) of Property, Donative Transfers §1.4 (1983), adopts the wait-and-see doctrine and — like the English statute — lays down a list of persons related to the property involved to govern the wait-and-see period. The Restatement also provides for delayed cy pres. The Restatement list is examined in Dukeminier, 85 Colum. L. Rev. 1648, supra, at 1674-1701.

Iowa has followed the Restatement approach and adopted a wait-

and-see statute providing a list of measuring lives. Iowa Code Ann. 558.68 (Supp. 1989). See Kurtz, The Iowa Rule Against Perpetuities — Reform at Last, Restatement Style: Wait-and-See and Cy Pres, 69 Iowa L. Rev. 705 (1984).

4. *Waiting to see for 90 years.* The Uniform Statutory Rule Against Perpetuities, promulgated in 1986, rejects using measuring lives for wait-and-see and adopts a 90-year wait-and-see period instead. The drafters believed that the lives that can affect vesting might not be clear in every case, and, in any event, tracing measuring lives involved administrative costs avoidable by using a period of years. See Waggoner, Perpetuities: A Perspective on Wait-and-See, 85 Colum. L. Rev. 1714 (1985). Unlike the statutes adopting wait-and-see for the common law perpetuities period, which abolish the common law what-might-happen rule and replace it with a wait-and-see rule, ending up with one rule against perpetuities, the Uniform Statute provides *two* rules against perpetuities: (1) the what-might-happen rule of the common law, and (2) a wait-and-see rule of 90 years.

Under the Uniform Statute, the Rule against Perpetuities, with all its many distinctions and technicalities, is preserved. However, the Rule is put in abeyance for 90 years; it cannot strike down a contingent interest until 90 years have passed after the instrument creating the contingent interest becomes effective. Hence, all interests are valid for 90 years after creation. At the end of 90 years, the common law Rule swings into action. Any then-contingent interest that has not satisfied the Rule is declared void and is reformed by a court so as to best carry out the intention of the testator (dead some 90 years). (Question: Can you think of another rule of public policy that has been put in abeyance for 90 years?)

The Uniform Statute has proven to be even more controversial than the earlier wait-and-see statutes. In addition to the usual criticisms of wait-and-see, voiced in the next case, Pound v. Shorter, the 90-year period has drawn a number of objections. First, 90 years is a pretty close proxy for a period measured by Professor Leach's "dozen or so healthy babies chosen from families noted for longevity," a period Leach denounced as "an unconscionable period" of "little appropriateness."[43] Dead hand control is thus extended in those cases where the actual relevant lives are not so young. Second, the Uniform Statute abandons the ancient policy underlying the Rule of permitting the testator to control only during lives of persons he knew and assayed, not during lives of the afterborn. Third, the Uniform Statute will likely lead to abolition of the Rule against Perpetuities because knowledge of it will

---

43. See quotation from Leach, 6 American Law of Property §24.16, at 52, supra page 767.

be lost during its 90 years in the deep freeze. Fourth, by making it easy to create 90-year trusts, we invite 90-year trusts drawn by nonspecialists who unthinkingly straitjacket the families of clients with provisions unchangeable for 90 years, as well as 90-year dynasty trusts drawn by specialists or marketed by financial advisors for the rich seeking to take advantage of the $1 million exemption in the generation-skipping transfer tax.[44] See Bloom, Perpetuities Refinement: There Is an Alternative, 62 Wash. L. Rev. 23 (1987); Dukeminier, The Uniform Statutory Rule Against Perpetuities: Ninety Years in Limbo, 34 UCLA L. Rev. 1023 (1987). See also 1A A. Scott, Trusts §62.10 (W. Fratcher 4th ed. Supp. 1989), criticizing the Uniform Statute because it does not abolish infectious invalidity, leaving the possibility that after "90 years, a court might strike the entire trust down *ab initio,* making void the conveyances, mortgages and leases made by the trustee and subjecting the trustee to liability for all payments made to the beneficiaries."

Professor Waggoner defends the Uniform Statute as being a proxy for a perpetuities saving clause used by a skilled lawyer. Though there is no supporting empirical evidence, Waggoner believes it can be assumed that the youngest measuring life used in a perpetuities saving clause is, on average, 6 years old; a 6-year-old has a life expectancy of 69 years; 69 years plus 21 years equals 90 years. See Waggoner, The Uniform Statutory Rule Against Perpetuities: The Rationale of the 90-Year Waiting Period, 73 Cornell L. Rev. 157, 158 (1988); Waggoner, The Uniform Statutory Rule Against Perpetuities, 21 Real Prop., Prob. & Tr. J. 569 (1986).

For pros and cons, see King & Meiklejohn, The Uniform Statutory Rule Against Perpetuities: Wait-and-See for 90 Years, 17 Est. Plan. 24 (1990).

The Uniform Statutory Rule Against Perpetuities has been adopted by 1989 Conn. Acts H.B. 5985; Fla. Stat. Ann. §689.225 (Supp. 1989); 1990 Mass. Acts ch. 668 (with modifications); Mich. Stat. Ann. §26.48(1) (Supp. 1989); 1989 Mont. Acts S.B. 131; 1989 Neb. Acts L. 377; Nev. Rev. Stat. Ann. §111.1031 (1988); 1989 Or. Acts S.B. 297; S.C. Code Ann. §27-6-10 (Supp. 1988).

5. *Exemption of trusts from the Rule.*   In Wisconsin, if the trustee has a power to sell the trust assets, making them alienable, the trust is not subject to any perpetuities rule and may endure forever. Wis. Stat. Ann. §700.16 (1981). See also S.D. Codified Laws §43-5-8 (1983) to the same effect.

---

44. The Internal Revenue Code of 1986 imposes a generation-skipping transfer tax of 55 percent at the death of a younger generation life beneficiary of a trust when estate tax is not imposed on that event. IRC §§2601-2663. Section 2631(a) of the Code provides an exemption from generation-skipping transfer tax of $1 million ($2 million per married couple) settled in a trust for as long as the local perpetuities period allows. This tax-exempt trust is known as a *dynasty trust.* See infra page 1029.

Delaware has abolished the application of the common law Rule against Perpetuities to trusts. Del. Code Ann. tit. 25, §503 (Supp. 1988), provides that no trust can endure more than 110 years after it becomes irrevocable. At the end of 110 years, each trust must terminate, if it has not already terminated, and the principal is distributed as provided in the trust instrument or, if there is no provision, to the income beneficiaries.

The 110-year period was chosen because 110 years is longer than any life in this country. Hence, a trust for a baby can endure for the baby's life under a 110-year statute. If a shorter period of years is chosen, such as 90 years, then it might be necessary to keep the common law period of lives in being to validate the baby's trust. Delaware took the position that if the period permissible for dead hand control of trusts is to be a period of years, then the period should be long enough to permit complete abolition of the complexities of the Rule against Perpetuities with respect to trusts. The Delaware approach is approved by Haskell, A Proposal for a Simple and Socially Effective Rule Against Perpetuities, 66 N.C.L. Rev. 545 (1988).

Pound v. Shorter

Supreme Court of Georgia, 1989
259 Ga. 148, 377 S.E.2d 854

WELTNER, J. When Elizabeth Shorter died in 1929, her will created a trust that provided for her one unmarried son as follows:

> In trust further, should my son die, either before or after my death, leaving neither child, nor children of a deceased wife surviving him, but leaving a wife surviving him, to pay over the annual net income arising each year from said trust property, in quarterly installments each year, to the wife of my said son, during her life, and upon the death of the wife of my said son, to thereupon pay over, deliver and convey, in fee simple, the corpus of said trust property to the children and descendants of children of my brother . . . and sister. . . .

The son married in 1953 and died in 1987, survived by his widow. He left no descendants. After his death, the trustee bank filed a petition to determine the validity of the trust item. The trial court found that the item created a perpetuity and decreed that the trust be terminated and that the son's widow have fee ownership. Fifty-two lineal descendants of Elizabeth Shorter appeal.

1. The Rule against Perpetuities adopted first by the legislature in 1863, provides:

Limitations of estates may extend through any number of lives in being at the time when the limitations commence, and 21 years, and the usual period of gestation added thereafter. The law terms a limitation beyond that period a perpetuity and forbids its creation. When an attempt is made to create a perpetuity, the law will give effect to the limitations which are not too remote and will declare the other limitations void, thereby vesting the fee in the last taker under the legal limitations. OCGA §44-6-1.

2.   We have undertaken a study of both the rule against perpetuities and an alternative approach, commonly called "wait and see."[45] Fifteen states have adopted some form of the "wait and see" approach, and all have done so through legislation.[46] We conclude: (1) that the traditional rule against perpetuities has been effective so far in Georgia, judging by the few cases brought to invalidate grants, and the even fewer invalidations; and (2) that the alternative "wait and see" approach has many problems, including initial uncertainty (which is avoided by the traditional rule) and the necessity for selecting a method by which to determine the length of the waiting period.[47]

3.   We are not convinced that the goals of certainty and early vesting will be served by adopting the alternative, and accordingly decline to do so.

4.   As the will encompasses the possibilities that the son might marry a woman who was unborn in 1929 (a life *not* "in being") and then predecease her, it violated the rule against perpetuities.

Judgment affirmed.

All the Justices concur.

NOTES

1.   The debate over wait-and-see has produced a spate of scholarly articles ever since Professor Leach began his crusade for perpetuities

---

45. "The wait-and-see principle permits a court to consider the actual sequence of events occurring after the creation of the interest. Any interest that might possibly be too remote is valid, if under the facts as they actually occur, the interest vests within the period of the Rule." Chaffin, The Rule Against Perpetuities as Applied to Georgia Wills and Trusts: A Survey and Suggestions for Reform, 1982, 16 Ga. L. Rev. 235, 345.

46. See Chaffin, The Rule Against Perpetuities in Georgia (1984); Waggoner, Perpetuity Reform, 1983, 81 Mich. L. Rev. 1718.

47. The problems may be summarized as follows: (1) there is actually no severe problem of grants being invalidated due to a violation of the rule against perpetuities; (2) technical violations of the rule can be avoided by competent drafting, so only unwary counsel is trapped by the rule; (3) there is a big problem of expense and inconvenience during the waiting period; (4) there is an increase in litigation due to the alternative doctrine; (5) much of the testator's estate is diverted to lawyers' fees; (6) most alternative statutes provide for cy pres litigation at the end of the waiting period if the interest has neither vested nor failed, and that litigation is difficult and expensive due to the passage of time; and (7) the alternative does not simplify the perpetuities law. Bloom, Perpetuities Refinement: There Is an Alternative, 1987, 62 Wash. L. Rev. 23.

reform in 1952. Wait-and-see was strongly opposed by two leading treatise writers, Professors Lewis Simes and Richard Powell, largely on the grounds that it makes title uncertain for the waiting period and "is a long step in the direction of inalienability of property." Simes, Is the Rule Against Perpetuities Doomed? The "Wait and See" Doctrine, 52 Mich. L. Rev. 179, 188 (1953). When Professor Casner proposed wait-and-see for the second Restatement of Property, for which he was reporter, Professor Powell, the reporter for the first Restatement, rose out of retirement to attack it. Two annual meetings of the American Law Institute were given to the battle, at which Casner finally prevailed.

The passions continue; no controversy in property law since the founding of the Republic has been so spirited — and so divisive. For a comprehensive list of articles see 5A R. Powell, Real Property ¶¶827 A & G (P. Rohan rev. ed. 1988); 3 L. Simes & A. Smith, The Law of Future Interests §1230 (2d ed. 1956, Supp. 1989 by W. Fratcher).

2. In states that have adopted wait-and-see or cy pres, it is still necessary to know and apply the common law Rule. A good lawyer wants to draft a valid interest, not one that may turn out to be void or may have to be reformed. See Lynn, Perpetuities Literacy for the 21st Century, 50 Ohio L.J. 219 (1989); Becker, Estate Planning and the Reality of Perpetuities Problems Today: Reliance upon Statutory Reform and Saving Clauses Is Not Enough, 64 Wash. U.L.Q. 287 (1986).

Statutes adopting wait-and-see are generally not retroactive. The what-might-happen rule continues to apply to instruments effective before the date of the statute. However, in a few states, after a nonretroactive wait-and-see statute has been enacted, courts have declared wait-and-see to be the common law of the state applicable to earlier instruments. See Hansen v. Stroecker, 699 P.2d 871 (Alaska 1985); Warner v. Whitman, 353 Mass. 468, 233 N.E.2d 14 (1968); Fleet National Bank v. Colt, 529 A.2d 122 (R.I. 1987).

NOTE: THE USRAP TAX TRAP

In 1986, Congress enacted a tax on generation-skipping transfers (see infra page 1022). Irrevocable trusts created before 1986 are exempt from generation-skipping transfer tax; they are "grandfathered" in. However, if a special power of appointment in a grandfathered trust is exercised so as to violate the Rule against Perpetuities, and the Uniform Statutory Rule Against Perpetuities is applicable, the trust loses its exemption from the generation-skipping transfer tax. Temp. Treas. Reg. §26.2601-1(b)(v)(B)(2) (1989). The exemption is lost if the power is exercised so that vesting may be postponed beyond lives in being at the creation of the trust plus 21 years (which may happen under the 90-year wait-and-see period). The exemption is not lost if the jurisdiction has adopted wait-and-see for the common law perpetuities period or cy pres.

2. Cy Pres or Equitable Reformation

The second reform proposed by Professor Leach was to apply the cy pres doctrine, which developed in the law of charitable trusts, to reform perpetuities violations. Under this doctrine an interest violating the Rule is reformed so as to carry out the testator's intent as far as possible. Most wait-and-see statutes provide for reformation at the end of the wait-and-see period. Now we turn to statutes and judicial decisions providing for immediate reformation upon the testator's death.

Cal. Civ. Code §715.5 (1982)

No interest in real or personal property is either void or voidable as in violation of Section 715.2 of this code [the Rule against Perpetuities] if and to the extent that it can be reformed or construed within the limits of that section to give effect to the general intent of the creator of the interest whenever that general intent can be ascertained. This section shall be liberally construed and applied to validate such interest to the fullest extent consistent with such ascertained intent.

Estate of Chun Quan Yee Hop
Supreme Court of Hawaii, 1970
52 Haw. 40, 469 P.2d 183

LEVINSON, J.   This case presents the question whether the orthodox common law Rule Against Perpetuities will be strictly applied to nullify a testamentary trust which violates the Rule or whether some part of the trust or all of it will be allowed to take effect. We choose to resolve this issue by applying the doctrine of equitable approximation (also known as the cy pres doctrine) so that the trust will not violate the Rule or its underlying policies and the testator's expressed desires will be satisfied.

The facts have been stipulated by the parties. The testator, Chun Quan Yee Hop, died on August 11, 1954 leaving a will executed on September 28, 1953. His wife, who is still living, his four sons and twelve daughters survived him. When this action was filed in 1967 his issue including children, grandchildren, and great grandchildren numbered 135, of whom not less than 85 were living when the testator died.

The portion of the testator's will in question provided that: "This trust shall cease and determine upon the death of my wife, Chun Lai Shee, or thirty (30) years from the date of my death, whichever shall last occur. . . ." At the termination of the trust, the trust estate including principal and accumulated income was to vest in and be transferred to the beneficiaries with three-fourths of the trust estate going to the survivors of the four sons and the lawful issue of any deceased son, and the remaining one-fourth of the trust estate going to the survivors of the twelve daughters and the lawful issue of any deceased daughter.[48]

On the advice of counsel that the trust might be in violation of the Rule Against Perpetuities, the trustees filed a petition in the circuit court asking for instructions. After all interested parties were duly notified and represented and after a hearing, the trial court determined that there was a well-founded doubt . . . [and reserved the case to this court for decision].

In resolving an issue which has bedeviled lawyers and engaged legal scholars since Lord Nottingham began it all in the Duke of Norfolk's Case in 1682, we are aided by the very able briefs of counsel and a wealth of law review articles and treatises on the subject. Fortunately, we are not confronted by some of the more chimerical characters and situations dealt with by Professor Leach in his writings. We are simply dealing with a testamentary trust which might ultimately vest in the residuary legatees at a time beyond a specified life in being (the testator's widow) and twenty-one years thereafter. Since the testator's wife might have died within nine years after his death, there was no assurance at the time of his death that the trust estate would vest within the life of his wife or 21 years thereafter. The will expressly says that the trust is to cease and determine on the death of the testator's wife or thirty years from his death, *whichever shall last occur.* The trust, therefore, violated the orthodox Rule Against Perpetuities.[49]

The Rule Against Perpetuities is said to be part of the English common law and is therefore applicable in Hawaii. Fitchie v. Brown, 18 Haw. 52, 69 (1906), aff'd 211 U.S. 321 (1908) . . . (upholding the validity of a testamentary trust whose duration was measured by 42 lives in being plus 21 years). . . .

---

48. The division specified by the testator gives each son's family nine times the amount given each daughter's family. The testator, apparently of Chinese ancestry, may have been influenced by the traditional inheritance system of China. Prior to the Nationalist Revolution of 1911, overthrowing the Ch'ing Dynasty, only sons inherited property in China. A father could not by will deprive his sons of the bulk of his property. Daughters upon marriage became part of the husband's family, "sharing" the wealth of that family. Although the law was changed after the Nationalist Revolution, the traditional inheritance practice continued to be widely followed in China until the Communist era. In the New Territories of the Hong Kong Crown Colony, the traditional inheritance laws of the Ch'ing Dynasty were followed until very recent times. — Eds.

49. Since we decide the case on the grounds of equitable approximation (cy pres), we do not reach the merits of other forms of validating the trust which were ably presented by counsel. These included (a) holding the alternative contingencies "separable" and striking the invalid thirty year contingency; (b) applying the "wait and see" doctrine; (c) finding the gifts to the children and their respective issue to be separate gifts and treating each gift separately as to the time of vesting; and (d) holding the distribution of trust income to each of the children and their issue to be valid for at least twenty-one years on the basis that the trust provides for annual gifts of income. We do not intend to preclude such arguments and others from being raised in the future.

Since the Rule Against Perpetuities is a creature of judicial construction, any growth of the law with respect to it is purely one of judicial wisdom unless the state legislature chooses to act. As a judge-made rule of law, it is not so firmly ensconced in Hawaii that this court cannot deal with it like any other rule of judicial origin which must change with the times.

It should be no surprise that this court has held on several occasions that various testamentary trusts have complied with the common law Rule Against Perpetuities using accepted techniques of judicial construction to keep the trust from violating the Rule. Queen's Hospital v. Hite, 38 Haw. 494, 506 (1950) (ambiguity in will resolved in favor of trust's validity); Manufacturer's Life Ins. Co. v. Von Hamm-Young Co., 34 Haw. 288 (1937) (creation of interest under a life insurance trust at death of testator). Yet no case in this jurisdiction has heretofore presented the problem whether a testamentary trust, which clearly violates the Rule Against Perpetuities because of a term of years extending beyond the permissible twenty-one years, is to be judicially salvaged in order to effectuate the testator's intent.

We do not mean to say that the Rule Against Perpetuities has outlived its usefulness. Unlike so many rules of property which were handed down from feudal England, this rule is of continuing vitality. This court said in Manufacturer's Life Ins. Co. v. Von Hamm-Young Co., 34 Haw. 288, 293 (1937) of the Rule Against Perpetuities: "This rule was not of feudal origin but has its support in the practical needs of modern times, and was devised in order to restrain the tying up of property in future estates for an unreasonable period of time."

The policy against tying up of property in future estates has a number of important aspects. One is the freeing of wealth so that it can be channeled into open commerce without subjecting it to the limited discretion of a trustee. Another aspect is that the rule is conducive to giving the ultimate recipient complete power of management and disposition over that which is to be his. He may then sink or swim on his own rather than be subordinated to the paternalistic control of a trustee. The last and most important policy is that of letting the living control the wealth here on earth, rather than allowing those who once owned it and have since passed away to retain some powers over that wealth. These reasons all support the proposition that it is wise policy to loosen the dead hand's grip upon the wealth passed from one generation to the next. Dukeminier, Perpetuities Revision in California: Perpetual Trusts Permitted, 55 Calif. L. Rev. 678, 691 (1967); L. Simes, Public Policy and the Dead Hand 58 (1955).

The policy against the tying up of property in future estates is not inconsistent with the application of the doctrine of equitable approximation of a testamentary trust. Limiting an invalid term of thirty years to the twenty-one year period prescribed by the rule does no violence to any of the above policies or to the testator's general intent. The judicial recognition of a decedent's general testamentary intent has been recognized in an analogous body of law which applies the doctrine of equitable approximation to a charitable trust which would otherwise fail. If it is impossible, impractical or illegal to carry out the specific terms of a charitable trust in which the settlor has indicated a general charitable purpose, many courts will authorize the substitution of another charitable scheme within the testator's general purposes. Restatement (Second) of Trusts §399 (1959). . . .

Our decision should not be influenced by the fact that it was the testator's intent to distribute his estate among his children and their issue according to a plan which may appear to some as lopsidedly favoring his male progeny. This was, of course, his right. The wishes of the testator could have been accomplished exactly as he wished without violating the Rule if the attorney who drafted the will had specified that the trust was to continue until 21 years after the death of the last survivor of his wife and all of his issue living at the time of his death but not to exceed 30 years from the date of his death. Without the last mentioned limitation the trust could have continued for nearly 100 years from the date of his death without violating the Rule.

We are not alone in judicially adopting the doctrine of equitable approximation. The courts of New Hampshire and Mississippi have applied this doctrine in varying degrees and circumstances. The adoption of the rule of equitable approximation is further recommended by an overwhelming number of commentators[50] and, although the doctrine has judicial origins, it has been adopted by a number of state legislatures. We therefore hold that any interest which would violate the Rule Against Perpetuities shall be reformed within the limits of that rule to approximate most closely the intention of the creator of the interest. In the present case, where the testamentary trust violated the rule by providing that the trust "shall cease and determine upon the death of my wife, Chun Lai Shee, or thirty (30) years from the date of my death, whichever shall last occur . . . ," the thirty year period need only be reduced to twenty-one years in order to bring the trust within the rule. In response to the questions reserved to this court we may then answer that the trust is valid in its entirety and all provisions are to be carried

---

50. The cy pres doctrine was advanced by Judge James Quarles in 1946 in The Cy Pres Doctrine: Its Application to Cases Involving the Rule Against Perpetuities and Trusts for Accumulation, 21 N.Y.U.L. Rev.384 (1946). This was a revision of his earlier article in 1904, The Cy Pres Doctrine with Reference to the Rule Against Perpetuities — An Advocation of Its Adoption in All Jurisdictions, 38 Am. L. Rev. 683 (1904). A current exposition can be found in Professor Browder's article, Construction, Reformation, and the Rule Against Perpetuities, 62 Mich. L. Rev. 1 (1963). See also Fletcher, A Rule of Discrete Invalidity: Perpetuities Reform Without Waiting, 20 Stan. L. Rev. 459 (1968).

out in accordance with the language of the will with the exception that the trust shall cease and determine upon the death of the testator's wife, Chun Lai Shee, or twenty-one years from the date of the testator's death, whichever shall last occur.

It is so ordered.[51]

In Edgerly v. Barker, 66 N.H. 434, 31 A. 900 (1891), the testator gave the principal of a trust to such of his grandchildren as reached age 40. The court, in an opinion by Chief Justice Doe, reduced the age contingency to 21. John Chipman Gray sharply criticized this case.

J. GRAY, THE RULE AGAINST PERPETUITIES §§871, 872 (4th ed. 1942): "It is a dangerous thing to make such a radical change in a part of the law which is concatenated with almost mathematical precision. . . . The doctrine of the New Hampshire Court in this case involves a fallacy. It speaks of a primary intent to give to persons and a secondary intent to give to them at a particular time, and it purports to preserve the primary intent while discarding the secondary intent by substituting another time. This assumes that the persons remain the same, and only the time is changed. But that is precisely what does not occur; with the time, the persons are changed. Take the present case. The testator meant to give to those of his grandchildren who reached forty; the Court gives the property to those of the grandchildren who reach twenty-one. There may be six grandchildren who reach twenty-one, and only one who reaches forty. In such case shares would be given to five persons whom the testator never meant to have it. There may be some answer to this, but it is a real and a very serious objection, and deserves an answer, and it gets none from the New Hampshire Court. The case is dealt with throughout as if the only question were whether the same persons should get the property at forty or at twenty-one. . . ."

NOTES AND PROBLEMS

1. A handful of states have adopted the cy pres doctrine calling for reformation of an invalid interest at the time the instrument creating such interest becomes effective. Cal. Civ. Code §715.5 (1982); Idaho Code Ann. §55-111 (1988); Mo. Ann. Stat. §442.555 (1986); Okla. Stat.

---

51. Noted in 84 Harv. L. Rev. 738; 46 Wash. L. Rev. 785; 28 Wash. & Lee L. Rev. 184. — Eds.

Ann. tit. 60, §75 (Supp. 1989); Tex. Prop. Code Ann. §5.043 (1984); Berry v. Union National Bank, 262 S.E.2d 766 (W. Va. 1980); In re Foster's Estate, 190 Kan. 498, 503, 376 P.2d 784, 788 (1962) (semble). See also Atchison v. City of Englewood, 568 P.2d 13, 17-18 (Colo. 1977) (reforming commercial agreement so as to avoid violation of the Rule).

The main objections to cy pres are two: First, as Gray pointed out, reformation can be used to rewrite the will so as to give the property to persons not intended by the testator. See Merrill v. Wimmer, 481 N.E.2d 1294 (Ind. 1985), rejecting cy pres on this ground. Second, reformation requires a lawsuit; if we wait and see, no lawsuit may be necessary.

The first objection was dealt with in Browder, Construction, Reformation, and the Rule Against Perpetuities, 62 Mich. L. Rev. 1 (1963). Professor Browder suggests using the cy pres power to insert a perpetuities saving clause adapted to the particular possibility that causes the gift to be invalid. For example, in the Estate of Chun Quan Yee Hop, the contingency that caused the gift to be invalid was the possibility that the testator's wife and living issue might die within 9 years after his death. In that event, the trust would endure for a term of years more than 21 after the expiration of the relevant lives. Instead of reducing the length of the trust term to 21 years, the court might have inserted the following saving clause to cure the violation: "If the testator's wife and issue living at his death die within 9 years of the testator's death, the trust will cease 21 years after the death of the survivor of these persons." This saving clause would result in the least interference with the testator's wishes, and, since in fact the testator's wife did live more than nine years after the testator's death, the trust would have ended exactly when the testator intended. See also In re Estate of Anderson, supra page 817, at page 821 n.31, where the court authorizes the insertion of a saving clause in the exercise of cy pres.

Judicial insertion of a saving clause of this sort resembles wait-and-see, but the measuring lives for waiting are tailored to the particular invalidating circumstances. See Dukeminier, A Modern Guide to Perpetuities, 74 Calif. L. Rev. 1867, 1898-1901 (1986).

Immediate cy pres has engendered far less hostility among academics than wait-and-see. Almost all scholars have favored cy pres, though some prefer it at the end of a wait-and-see perpetuities period rather than immediately upon the testator's death.

2. Apply immediate cy pres to the following bequests:

(a) "To A for life, then to such children of A as reach 30." See Estate of Ghiglia, 42 Cal. App. 3d 433, 116 Cal. Rptr. 827 (1974).

(b) "To A for life, then to A's children for their lives, then to A's grandchildren in fee." See Estate of Grove, 70 Cal. App. 3d 355, 138 Cal. Rptr. 684 (1977).

3. *Specific correctives.* New York and Illinois have adopted by statute specific cy pres correctives for the most frequent violations of the Rule.

Age contingencies in excess of 21 that cause the gift to fail are reduced to 21 as to all persons subject to such contingency. The unborn widow is dealt with by a presumption that a gift to a spouse is a gift to a person in being. Administrative contingencies are presumed to be intended to occur within 21 years. The fertile octogenarian is dealt with by a presumption that a woman is incapable of bearing children after 55 and by the admission of evidence of infertility in any case of a living person. It is generally presumed in these states that the transferor intended the interest to be valid, so instruments are construed to avoid the Rule. Ill. Ann. Stat. ch. 30, ¶194(c) (Supp. 1989). N.Y. Est., Powers & Trusts Law §§9-1.2 & 9-1.3 (1967).

Professor Bloom recommends adopting the specific correctives authorized by the New York statutes plus, if these correctives do not apply, a general immediate cy pres power. See Bloom, Perpetuities Refinement: There Is an Alternative, 62 Wash. L. Rev. 23 (1987).

3. Why Not Abolish the Rule against Perpetuities?

Pax Vobiscum

> Rounding and turning and doubling back,
> Gray's rule runs — on a limitless track.
> Vest, ait, ordo tranquilitatis est,
> Those lucky Scots[52] are deemed thrice blest.
>
> Ubi nunc, O Domine,
> Sunt arbusta Academiae?
> Damn, tempus non fugit.
>
> Pax, pax, O benedicta pax:
>   Veni!
>
> —*Largely attributable to a learned student of the law who became a distinguished teacher of Torts.*

It is our misfortune that scholars and other experts could not, in the beginning of or during the reform movement, agree upon what, if any, reform of the Rule is desirable. Lacking harmonious guidance, Gray's great empire of one uniform Rule throughout the country has fallen apart. The majority of states have now reformed the Rule, adopting diverse types of amendments. Nonetheless, even though reformed, the common law Rule, with all its teasers and technicalities, remains with us in most states.

Why not get rid of this ancient learning and abolish the Rule against

---

52. The Rule against Perpetuities is not in force in Scotland. 4 D. Walker, Principles of Scottish Private Law 191 (3d ed. 1983).

Perpetuities? The problem of controlling the duration of legal future interests, which make land unmarketable, could be dealt with by converting legal future interests into equitable ones, as the English have done.[53] That leaves the problem of trust duration. There may be no need to control the duration of trusts if the beneficiaries can terminate the trust whenever they want to.

In 1983 the Canadian province of Manitoba abolished the Rule against Perpetuities entirely. Perpetuities & Accumulations Act of 1983, 1982-1983 Man. Rev. Stat. ch. 43. At the same time Manitoba transformed legal future interests into equitable interests and gave courts authority to alter or terminate any trust if this will benefit the beneficiaries. Manitoba Act of 1983 to Amend the Trustee Act, 1982-1983 Man. Rev. Stat. ch. 38. This approach to the problem of overlong trusts was recommended by the Manitoba Law Reform Commission, Report on the Rules Against Accumulations and Perpetuities, Pub. L. No. 49 (1982).

The essential idea underlying the Manitoba approach is that a variation of trusts act, giving a court power to consent on behalf of unborn or minor beneficiaries to vary, rearrange, or terminate trusts — despite the settlor's intent — is preferable to limiting trust duration. The Manitoba approach is approved by Deech, The Rule against Perpetuities Abolished, 4 Oxford J. Leg. Stud. 454 (1984), and disapproved by Glenn, Perpetuities to Purefoy: Reform by Abolition in Manitoba, 62 Can. B. Rev. 618 (1984).

The Manitoba approach is strikingly different from the practice in this country, where the settlor's intent cannot be set aside at the wish of the beneficiaries. See supra pages 573-575 on termination of trusts. It seems probable that one of the effects of the wait-and-see doctrine will be the development of more permissive doctrines allowing modification and termination of trusts by adult beneficiaries with court approval. Likely the law will find some way to undo extended dead-hand rule, if it proves inconvenient. See Bird, Trust Termination: Unborn, Living, and Dead Hands — Too Many Fingers in the Trust Pie, 36 Hastings L.J. 563 (1985).

SECTION G.   THE RULE AGAINST SUSPENSION OF THE POWER OF ALIENATION: NEW YORK LAW

1.   A Brief Explanation of the Suspension Rule

Although since the time of Gray it has been settled that the rule against remote vesting is *the* common law Rule against Perpetuities, it was not

---

53. See supra page 447.

clear before Gray whether there was also a common law rule against suspension of the power of alienation. Gray insisted there was not, and his view prevailed. However, in 1830 New York enacted statutes forbidding suspension of the power of alienation for more than a specified period.[54] Several other states copied or were influenced by this New York legislation. After Gray's book was published, establishing that the rule against suspension of the power of alienation was not the common law Rule against Perpetuities, these states were left with the problem of determining whether their statutes were declaratory of the common law, as Gray had later interpreted it, or were additions to or replacements of that law.[55]

The rule prohibiting suspension of the power of alienation is clearly distinguishable from the rule against remote vesting. The rule against remote vesting (the common law Rule against Perpetuities) is directed against contingent interests that may remain contingent beyond lives in being plus 21 years. The policy underlying it is that all contingent interests, assignable and nonassignable, impair marketability.

The power of alienation is suspended only when there are not persons in being who can convey an absolute fee. The rule assumes that legally unassignable interests make property unmarketable and should be struck down if they remain unassignable for more than the permitted period. Since all vested and contingent future interests are assignable or releasable if (1) the holders thereof are ascertainable and (2) there is no express restraint upon alienation, the only interests that suspend the power of alienation, absent an express restraint, are interests given to unborn or unascertained persons. To put it shortly, the rule against remote vesting applies to all contingent interests; the rule against suspension of the power of alienation applies only to interests that are contingent because the taker is unborn or unascertainable (or to interests where the transfer is restrained expressly or by law).

The suspension rule, like the Rule against Perpetuities, incorporates

---

54. In their present form, they are N.Y. Est., Powers & Trusts Law §9-1.1(a) (1967):

(1)   The absolute power of alienation is suspended when there are no persons in being by whom an absolute fee or estate in possession can be conveyed or transferred.
(2)   Every present or future estate shall be void in its creation which shall suspend the absolute power of alienation by any limitation or condition for a longer period than lives in being at the creation of the estate and a term of not more than twenty-one years. . . .

55. The rule against remoteness of vesting is also part of New York law. N.Y. Est., Powers & Trusts Law §9-1.1(b) (1967). Hence, New York has both the remoteness of vesting rule and the suspension rule, which has never been repealed.

Practically all of the other states that enacted a rule prohibiting suspension of the power of alienation have in time either reinstated the common law Rule against Perpetuities by statute or declared the suspension statute to be declaratory of the common law rule against remote vesting. See 5A R. Powell, Real Property ¶¶808-827 (P. Rohan rev. ed. 1988).

a possibilities test: If there is any possibility that the power of alienation will be suspended longer than lives in being plus 21 years, the interests causing such invalid suspension are void ab initio.

The rule against remoteness of vesting is the more inclusive. Except for a restrained interest, any interest that will violate the suspension rule will necessarily violate the rule against remoteness, but the converse is not true. Thus:

> *Case 18.   (Contingent remainder after term of years.)* T devises property "to A for 99 years, then in fee to B Church if it is then in existence." The power of alienation is never suspended since A, B Church, and T's heir (the reversioner) may join together and convey a fee simple. Under the suspension rule all interests are valid. However, the gift to B Church is contingent on its being in existence after 99 years, and this violates the rule against remote vesting. (If the gift over had been to A's issue whenever born living 99 years from now, the gift over would be to unascertained persons and would have violated both rules.)

> *Case 19.   (Shifting executory interest.)* O conveys land "to B Church, but if the land ever ceases to be used for church purposes, then to A." This disposition does not violate the suspension rule because B Church and A could join in a deed today and convey a fee simple. However, A's interest is contingent on an event that may occur beyond lives in being plus 21 years. Thus, it is void under the rule against remote vesting.

2.   Application of the Suspension Rule to Spendthrift Trusts

Even if the holders of all interests are ascertainable, or will be ascertainable within the permissible period, the suspension rule is violated if transferability of any interest in the property is restrained beyond the permissible period. If a transfer is made in trust, the power of alienation is suspended in New York if either the legal fee simple to the specific property held in trust cannot be transferred or the owners of all the equitable interests cannot convey an absolute fee in possession. Even if the trustee is given the power to sell the specific assets, the power of alienation is still suspended unless the beneficiaries of the trust can convey their interests. The policy of alienability is directed both at the specific assets in the trust and at the beneficial interests in the trust.

In New York, by statute, an income beneficiary's interest in trust is inalienable unless the settlor of the trust has expressly made it alienable. N.Y. Est., Powers & Trust Law §7-1.5 (Supp. 1989). If the income beneficiaries' interests are inalienable, the trust suspends the power of alienation during the income beneficiaries' lives. Hence the duration of a spendthrift trust is limited to the perpetuities period. Such a trust is partially or wholly invalid if it can exceed the perpetuities period in duration. Therein lies the most important difference today between the common law Rule (which does not directly restrict the duration of trusts) and the New York rule against suspension of the power of alienation. Thus:

> *Case 20.   T*, domiciled in New York, dies in 1990. She bequeaths a fund in a spendthrift trust "to pay the income to *A* for life, then to pay the income to *A*'s children for their lives, and then to pay the principal to New York University." The gift does not violate the Rule against Perpetuities. However, the income interests in *A* and *A*'s children are inalienable. Since the power of alienation might be suspended during the lifetime of afterborn persons (*A*'s children born after *T*'s death), the life income interests in *A*'s children are void. The remainder in New York University will be accelerated unless infectious invalidity applies.

If, in Case 20, *T* had by her will expressly provided that *A*'s children could alienate their interests, the trust would be wholly valid. The power of alienation would be suspended only during *A*'s lifetime, a life in being. At *A*'s death all of *A*'s children are in being and, together with New York University, they can convey a fee simple absolute.

On the suspension rule in New York, and other aspects of New York perpetuities law, see 5A R. Powell, supra, ¶¶791-807B; Powell, The Rule against Perpetuities and Spendthrift Trusts in New York, 71 Colum. L. Rev. 688 (1971).

12

TRUST ADMINISTRATION: THE
FIDUCIARY OBLIGATION

> For as a trust is an office necessary in the concerns
> between man and man, and which, if faithfully
> discharged, is attended with no small degree
> of trouble, and anxiety, it is an act of great
> kindness in any one to accept it.
>
> LORD CHANCELLOR HARDWICKE
> *in Knight v. Earl of Plymouth,*
> *Dick. 120, 126, 21 Eng. Rep.*
> *214, 216 (1747)*

SECTION A. GENERAL FIDUCIARY DUTIES AND LIABILITIES

1. *Duty of Loyalty: Herein of Self-dealing*

The office of trustee, on which the law has fastened many burdensome duties, is onerous. The most fundamental duty is the duty of undivided loyalty to the beneficiaries: The trustee must administer the trust solely in the interest of the beneficiaries. If the trustee puts or finds himself in a position of conflict of interest with the beneficiaries, the trustee must show that he acted in good faith and that his actions were fair to the beneficiaries.

If the trustee engages in self-dealing (i.e., bargains with himself in his individual capacity), good faith and fairness to the beneficiaries are not enough to save the trustee from liability. In case of self-dealing, *no further inquiry* is made; the trustee's good faith and the reasonableness of the transaction are irrelevant. The beneficiaries can hold the trustee accountable for any profit made on the transaction, or, if the trustee has bought trust property, can compel the trustee to restore the property to the trust, or, if the trustee has sold his own property to the trust, can compel the trustee to repay the purchase price and take back the property. The only defense the trustee has to self-dealing is that the beneficiaries consented after full disclosure; even then the transaction must be fair and reasonable.

The no-further-inquiry rule is based on a general principle of policy and morality formulated by Judge Cardozo in a famous passage in Meinhard v. Salmon, 249 N.Y. 458, 164 N.E. 545 (1928). Cardozo said:

> Many forms of conduct permissible in a work-a-day world for those acting at arms length, are forbidden to those bound by fiduciary ties. A trustee is held to something stricter than the morals of the market place. Not honesty alone, but the punctilio of an honor the most sensitive, is then the standard of behavior. As to this there has developed a tradition that is unbending and inveterate. Uncompromising rigidity has been the attitude of courts of equity when petitioned to undermine the rule of undivided loyalty by the "disintegrating erosion" of particular exceptions. . . . Only thus has the level of conduct for fiduciaries been kept at a level higher than that trodden by the crowd. It will not consciously be lowered by any judgment of this court. [Id. at 464, 164 N.E. at 546.]

Self-dealing occurs when the trustee sells his own property to the trust or buys the trust property. Self-dealing ordinarily includes the purchase by the trustee of trust property at auction, sale of trust property to the trustee's spouse, and sale to the trust of property owned by a corporation controlled by the trustee. If a corporate trustee purchases securities owned by the trustee or its officers or directors, that is self-dealing, but the sale by the trustee of assets of one trust to itself as trustee of another trust is not self-dealing. In determining what is self-dealing (to which the no-further-inquiry rule applies) and what is a conflict of interest but not self-dealing, courts must assess whether the danger of permitting the trustee to engage in the action is so great as to make the action wholly impermissible or only such as to make the action permissible if justifiable. On what is self-dealing, see 2A A. Scott, Trusts §§170-170.23 (W. Fratcher 4th ed. 1987).

In re Rothko
Court of Appeals of New York, 1977
43 N.Y.2d 305, 372 N.E.2d 291, 401 N.Y.S.2d 449

COOKE, J. Mark Rothko, an abstract expressionist painter whose works through the years gained for him an international reputation of greatness, died testate on February 25, 1970. The principal asset of his estate consisted of 798 paintings of tremendous value, and the dispute underlying this appeal involves the conduct of his three executors in their disposition of these works of art. In sum, that conduct as portrayed in the record and sketched in the opinions was manifestly wrongful and indeed shocking.

Rothko's will was admitted to probate on April 27, 1970 and letters testamentary were issued to Bernard J. Reis, Theodoros Stamos and Morton Levine.[1] Hastily and within a period of only about three weeks and by virtue of two contracts each dated May 21, 1970, the executors dealt with all 798 paintings.

By a contract of sale, the estate executors agreed to sell to Marlborough A.G., a Liechtenstein corporation (hereinafter MAG), 100 Rothko paintings as listed for $1,800,000, $200,000 to be paid on execution of the agreement and the balance of $1,600,000 in 12 equal interest-free installments over a 12-year period. Under the second agreement, the executors consigned to Marlborough Gallery, Inc., a domestic corporation (hereinafter MNY), "approximately 700 paintings listed on a Schedule to be prepared," the consignee to be responsible for costs covering items such as insurance, storage, restoration and promotion. By its provisos, MNY could sell up to 35 paintings a year from each of two groups, pre-1947 and post-1947, for 12 years at the best price obtainable but not less than the appraised estate value, and that it would receive a 50 percent commission on each painting sold, except

---

1. The executors were three of Rothko's most intimate companions during his last years. Bernard J. Reis, a certified public accountant who had graduated from law school but had not been licensed to practice law, had acted for years as Rothko's business and professional advisor and confidant. Reis drafted Rothko's will.

Theodoros Stamos was a fellow artist in whose family plot Rothko was buried. Stamos entered into a personal contract with Marlborough Gallery, Inc., on January 1, 1971, whereby Marlborough became Stamos's exclusive art dealer agent for four years at a commission of 50 percent. The Surrogate found "Executor Levine stated, and the court finds, that in a conversation in April, 1970, before the execution of the questioned agreements, executor Stamos related that Marlborough had evidenced interest in his paintings. The conversation led Levine to believe that Stamos was interested in entering into some contractual arrangement with Marlborough which indicated a conflict of interest on the part of Stamos. Levine testified that when he confronted Stamos with the impropriety of such motivation angry exchanges followed." In re Rothko, 84 Misc. 2d 830, 844, 379 N.Y.S.2d 923, 940 (Sur. Ct. 1975).

Morton Levine, professor of anthropology at Fordham University, was chosen by Rothko to act as guardian of his two children. Kate Rothko came of age soon after her father's death and, at her insistence, Levine was removed as guardian of Christopher Rothko. "It is recognized that Levine was neither an art expert nor an experienced fiduciary but he was an educated man who, despite his educational background and his position as a college professor, failed to exercise ordinary prudence in his performance of fiduciary obligations which he assumed. Levine's argument at best is a statement that he undertook a responsibility which he was unqualified to handle...." Id. at 846, 379 N.Y.S.2d at 942.

On the Rothko litigation, see L. Seldes, The Legacy of Mark Rothko (1979). — Eds.

Mark Rothko
Number 22 (1949)
Collection, The Museum of Modern Art, New York

Reproduced by permission of The Museum of Modern Art.

for a commission of 40 percent on those sold to or through other dealers.

Petitioner Kate Rothko, decedent's daughter and a person entitled to share in his estate by virtue of an election under EPTL §5-3.3,[2] instituted this proceeding to remove the executors, to enjoin MNY and MAG from disposing of the paintings, to rescind the aforesaid agreements between the executors and said corporations, for a return of the paintings still in possession of those corporations, and for damages. She was joined by the guardian of her brother Christopher Rothko, likewise interested in the estate, who answered by adopting the allegations of his sister's petition and by demanding the same relief. The Attorney General of the State, as the representative of the ultimate beneficiaries of the Mark Rothko Foundation, Inc., a charitable corporation and the residuary legatee under decedent's will, joined in requesting relief substantially similar to that prayed for by petitioner. . . .

Following a nonjury trial covering 89 days and in a thorough opinion, the Surrogate found: that Reis was a director, secretary and treasurer of MNY, the consignee art gallery, in addition to being a coexecutor of the estate; that the testator had a 1969 inter vivos contract with MNY to sell Rothko's work at a commission of only 10 percent and whether that agreement survived testator's death was a problem that a fiduciary in a dual position could not have impartially faced; that Reis was in a position of serious conflict of interest with respect to the contracts of May 21, 1970 and that his dual role and planned purpose benefited the Marlborough interests to the detriment of the estate; that it was to the advantage of coexecutor Stamos as a "not-too-successful artist, financially," to curry favor with Marlborough and that the contract made by him with MNY within months after signing the estate contracts placed him in a position where his personal interests conflicted with those of the estate, especially leading to lax contract enforcement efforts by Stamos; that Stamos acted negligently and improvidently in view of his own knowledge of the conflict of interest of Reis; that the third coexecutor, Levine, while not acting in self-interest or with bad faith, nonetheless failed to exercise ordinary prudence in the performance

---

2. Mark Rothko devised his residuary estate to the Mark Rothko Foundation, a charitable corporation, with Reis, Stamos, and Levine named as directors of the foundation. New York Est., Powers and Trusts Law §5-3.3 (1967), provided that a child of a testator may set aside a testamentary disposition to charity to the extent it exceeds one-half of the testator's estate. Kate Rothko elected to do this, with the result that one-half of the residuary gift passed to Rothko's heirs. By so electing, Kate Rothko — who otherwise was left nothing by Mark Rothko's will — obtained an interest in her father's estate and had standing to attack the action of the executors. New York Est., Powers & Trusts Law §5-3.3 was repealed in 1981. If Rothko had died after 1981, only the Mark Rothko Foundation and the state attorney general, the overseer of charitable trusts (see supra page 618) would have standing to sue the executors. — Eds.

of his assumed fiduciary obligations since he was aware of Reis' divided loyalty, believed that Stamos was also seeking personal advantage, possessed personal opinions as to the value of the paintings and yet followed the leadership of his coexecutors without investigation of essential facts or consultation with competent and disinterested appraisers, and that the business transactions of the two Marlborough corporations were admittedly controlled and directed by Francis K. Lloyd. It was concluded that the acts and failures of the three executors were clearly improper to such a substantial extent as to mandate their removal under section 711 of the Surrogate's Court Procedure Act as estate fiduciaries. The Surrogate also found that MNY, MAG and Lloyd were guilty of contempt in shipping, disposing of and selling 57 paintings in violation of the temporary restraining order dated June 26, 1972 and of the injunction dated September 26, 1972; that the contracts for sale and consignment of paintings between the executors and MNY and MAG provided inadequate value to the estate, amounting to a lack of mutuality and fairness resulting from conflicts on the part of Reis and Stamos and improvidence on the part of all executors; that said contracts were voidable and were set aside by reason of violation of the duty of loyalty and improvidence of the executors, knowingly participated in and induced by MNY and MAG; that the fact that these agreements were voidable did not revive the 1969 inter vivos agreements since the parties by their conduct evinced an intent to abandon and abrogate these compacts. The Surrogate held that the present value at the time of trial of the paintings sold is the proper measure of damages as to MNY, MAG, Lloyd, Reis and Stamos. . . . It was held that Levine was liable for $6,464,880 in damages, as he was not in a dual position acting for his own interest and was thus liable only for the actual value of paintings sold MNY and MAG as of the dates of sale, and that Reis, Stamos, MNY and MAG, apart from being jointly and severally liable for the same damages as Levine for negligence, were liable for the greater sum of $9,252,000 "as appreciation damages less amounts previously paid to the estate with regard to sales of paintings." . . . The liabilities were held to be congruent so that payment of the highest sum would satisfy all lesser liabilities including the civil fines and the liabilities for damages were to be reduced by payment of the fine levied or by return of any of the 57 paintings disposed of, the new fiduciary to have the option in the first instance to specify which paintings the fiduciary would accept.

The Appellate Division, in an opinion by Justice Lane, modified to the extent of deleting the option given the new fiduciary to specify which paintings he would accept. Except for this modification, the majority affirmed on the opinion of Surrogate Midonick, with additional comments. Among others, it was stated that the entire court agreed that executors Reis and Stamos had a conflict of interest and divided loyalty in view of their nexus to MNY and that a majority were in agreement with the Surrogate's assessment of liability as to executor Levine and his findings of liability against MNY, MAG and Lloyd. The majority agreed with the Surrogate's analysis awarding "appreciation damages" and found further support for his rationale in Menzel v. List (14 N.Y.2d 91). . . . Justices Capozzoli and Nunez, in separate dissenting in part opinions, viewed Menzel v. List as inapplicable and voted to modify and remit to determine the reasonable value of the paintings as of May 1970, when estate contracts with MNY and MAG had their inception in writing.

Since the Surrogate's findings of fact as to the conduct of Reis, Stamos, Levine, MNY, MAG and Lloyd and the value of the paintings at different junctures were affirmed by the Appellate Division, if there was evidence to support these findings they are not subject to question in this Court and the review here is confined to the legal issues raised. . . .

In seeking a reversal, it is urged that an improper legal standard was applied in voiding the estate contracts of May 1970, that the "no further inquiry" rule applies only to self-dealing and that in case of a conflict of interest, absent self-dealing, a challenged transaction must be shown to be unfair. The subject of fairness of the contracts is intertwined with the issue of whether Reis and Stamos were guilty of conflicts of interest.[3] Scott is quoted to the effect that "[a] trustee does not necessarily incur liability merely because he has an individual interest in the transaction. . . . In Bullivant v. First National Bank [246 Mass. 324], it was held that . . . the fact that the bank was also a creditor of the corporation did not make its assent invalid, *if it acted in good faith and the plan was fair* . . ." (emphasis added here) (II Scott on Trusts, §170.24, p.1384), and our attention has been called to the statement in Phelan v. Middle States Oil Corp. (220 F.2d 593, cert. den. sub nom Cohen v. Glass, 349 U.S. 929) that Judge Learned Hand found "no decisions that have applied [the no further inquiry rule] inflexibly to every occasion in which the fiduciary has been shown to have had a personal interest that might in fact have conflicted with his loyalty" (p.603).

These contentions should be rejected. First, a review of the opinions of the Surrogate and the Appellate Division manifests that they did not rely solely on a "no further inquiry rule," and secondly, there is more than an adequate basis to conclude that the agreements between the Marlborough corporations and the estate were neither fair nor in the best interests of the estate. . . . The opinions under review demonstrate

---

3. In New York, an executor, as such, takes a qualified legal title to all personalty specifically bequeathed and an unqualified legal title to that not so bequeathed; he holds not in his own right but as a trustee for the benefit of creditors, those entitled to receive under the will and, if all is not bequeathed, those entitled to distribution under the Estates, Powers and Trusts Law. . . .

that neither the Surrogate nor the Appellate Division set aside the contracts by merely applying the no further inquiry rule without regard to fairness. Rather they determined, quite properly indeed, that these agreements were neither fair nor in the best interests of the estate.

To be sure, the assertions that there were no conflicts of interest on the part of Reis or Stamos indulge in sheer fantasy. Besides being a director and officer of MNY, for which there was financial remuneration, however slight, Reis, as noted by the Surrogate, had different inducements to favor the Marlborough interests, including his own aggrandizement of status and financial advantage through sales of almost one million dollars for items from his own and his family's extensive private art collection by the Marlborough interests (see 84 Misc. 2d 843-844). Similarly, Stamos benefited as an artist under contract with Marlborough and, interestingly, Marlborough purchased a Stamos painting from a third party for $4,000 during the week in May 1970 when the estate contract negotiations were pending (see 84 Misc. 2d at 845). The conflicts are manifest. Further, as noted in Bogert, Trusts and Trustees (2d ed.), "The duty of loyalty imposed on the fiduciary prevents him from accepting employment from a third party who is entering into a business transaction with the trust" (§543[S], p.573). "While he [a trustee] is administering the trust he must refrain from placing himself in a position where his personal interest or that of a third person does or may conflict with the interest of the beneficiaries" (Bogert, Law of Trusts [Hornbook Series-5th ed.], p.343). Here, Reis was employed and Stamos benefited in a manner contemplated by Bogert (see, also, Meinhard v. Salmon, 249 N.Y. 458, 464, 466-467; Schmidt v. Chambers, 265 Md. 9, 33-38). In short, one must strain the law rather than follow it to reach the result suggested on behalf of Reis and Stamos.

Levine contends that, having acted prudently and upon the advice of counsel, a complete defense was established.[4] Suffice it to say, an executor who knows that his coexecutor is committing breaches of trust and not only fails to exert efforts directed towards prevention but

---

4. The three executors sought advice from their legal counsel about entering into the contracts with MAG and MNY. Counsel advised the executors that Reis had a conflict of interest.

> By the same letter, this law firm advised the executors that a petition for advance approval of any contracts for liquidation of the estate through Marlborough Galleries would not be entertained by a Surrogate. While it is true, as the law firm advised, that Surrogates do not usually give advance approval concerning matters of business judgment which are within the province of executors, no indication was given that the opposite rule governs when a fiduciary faces a conflict of interest.
> [In re Rothko, 84 Misc. 2d 830, 840, 379 N.Y.S.2d 923, 936 (Sur. Ct. 1975).]

Is the law firm liable to executor Levine for negligence? See Cremer, Should the Fiduciary Trust His Lawyer?, 19 Real Prop., Prob. & Tr. J. 786 (1984). — Eds.

accedes to them is legally accountable even though he was acting on the advice of counsel (Matter of Westerfield, 32 App. Div. 324, 344; III Scott, Trusts [3d ed.], §201, p.1657). When confronted with the question of whether to enter into the Marlborough contracts, Levine was acting in a business capacity, not a legal one, in which he was required as an executor primarily to employ such diligence and prudence to the care and management of the estate assets and affairs as would prudent persons of discretion and intelligence (King v. Talbot, 40 N.Y. 76, 85-86), accented by "[n]ot honesty alone, but the punctilio of an honor the most sensitive" (Meinhard v. Salmon, 249 N.Y. 458, 464, supra). Alleged good faith on the part of a fiduciary forgetful of his duty is not enough (Wendt v. Fischer, 243 N.Y. 439, 443). He could not close his eyes, remain passive or move with unconcern in the face of the obvious loss to be visited upon the estate by participation in those business arrangements and then shelter himself behind the claimed counsel of an attorney. . . .

Further, there is no merit to the argument that MNY and MAG lacked notice of the breach of trust. The record amply supports the determination that they are chargeable with notice of the executors' breach of duty.

The measure of damages was the issue that divided the Appellate Division (see 56 A.D.2d 500). The contention of Reis, Stamos, MNY and MAG, that the award of appreciation damages was legally erroneous and impermissible, is based on a principle that an executor authorized to sell is not liable for an increase in value if the breach consists only in selling for a figure less than that for which the executor should have sold. For example, Scott states:

> The beneficiaries are not entitled to the value of the property at the time of the decree if it was not the duty of the trustee to retain the property in the trust and the breach of trust consisted *merely* in selling the property for too low a price (emphasis added) (III Scott, Trusts (3d ed.), §208.3, p.1687).
>
> If the trustee is guilty of a breach of trust in selling trust property for an inadequate price, he is liable for the difference between the amount he should have received and the amount which he did receive. He is not liable, however, for any subsequent rise in value of the property sold (Id., §208.6, pp.1689-1690).

A recitation of similar import appears in comment d under Restatement, Trusts, §205:

> d. Sale for less than value. If the trustee is authorized to sell trust property, but in breach of trust he sells it for less than he should receive, he is liable for the value of the property at the time of the sale less the amount which he received. If the breach of trust consists *only* in selling it

for too little, he is not chargeable with the amount of any subsequent
increase in value of the property under the rule stated in Clause (c), as
he would be if he were not authorized to sell the property (see §208)
(emphasis added).

However, employment of "merely" and "only" as limiting words
suggests that where the breach consists of some misfeasance, other than
solely for selling "for too low a price" or "for too little," appreciation
damages may be appropriate. Under Scott (§208.3, pp.1686-1687) and
the Restatement (§208), the trustee may be held liable for appreciation
damages if it was his or her duty to retain the property, the theory
being that the beneficiaries are entitled to be placed in the same position
they would have been in had the breach not consisted of a sale of
property that should have been retained. The same rule should apply
where the breach of trust consists of a serious conflict of interest —
which is more than merely selling for too little.

The reason for allowing appreciation damages, where there is a duty
to retain, and only date of sale damages, where there is authorization
to sell, is policy oriented. If a trustee authorized to sell were subjected
to a greater measure of damages he might be reluctant to sell (in which
event he might run a risk if depreciation ensued). On the other hand,
if there is a duty to retain and the trustee sells there is no policy reason
to protect the trustee; he has not simply acted imprudently, he has
violated an integral condition of the trust.

"If a trustee in breach of trust transfers trust property to a person
who takes with notice of the breach of trust, and the transferee has
disposed of the property . . . [i]t seems proper to charge him with the
value at the time of the decree, since if it had not been for the breach
of trust the property would still have been a part of the trust estate"
(IV Scott, Trusts [3d ed.], §291.2; see also United States v. Dunn, 268
U.S. 121, 132). This rule of law which applies to the transferees MNY
and MAG also supports the imposition of appreciation damages against
Reis and Stamos, since if the Marlborough corporations are liable for
such damages either as purchasers or consignees with notice, from one
in breach of trust, it is only logical to hold that said executors, as sellers
and consignors, are liable also pro tanto.

Contrary to assertions of appellants and the dissenters at the Appellate
Division, Menzel v. List (24 N.Y.2d 91, supra) is authority for the
allowance of appreciation damages. There, the damages involved a
breach of warranty of title to a painting which at one time had been
stolen from plaintiff and her husband and ultimately sold to defendant.
Here, the executors, though authorized to sell, did not merely err in
the amount they accepted but sold to one with whom Reis and Stamos
had a self-interest. To make the injured party whole, in both instances
the quantum of damages should be the same. In other words, since the

paintings cannot be returned, the estate is therefore entitled to their value at the time of the decree, i.e., appreciation damages. These are not punitive damages in a true sense, rather they are damages intended to make the estate whole. Of course, as to Reis, Stamos, MNY and MAG, these damages might be considered by some to be exemplary in a sense, in that they serve as a warning to others (see Reynolds v. Pegler, 123 F. Supp. 36, 38, aff'd 223 F.2d 429, cert. den. 350 U.S. 846), but their true character is ascertained when viewed in the light of overriding policy considerations and in the realization that the sale and consignment were not merely sales below value but inherently wrongful transfers which should allow the owner to be made whole. . . .

The decree of the Surrogate imposed appreciation damages against Reis, Stamos, MNY and MAG in the amount of $7,339,464.72 — computed as $9,252,000 (86 works on canvas at $90,000 each and 54 works on paper at $28,000 each) less the aggregate amounts paid the estate under the two rescinded agreements and interest. Appellants chose not to offer evidence of "present value" and the only proof furnished on the subject was that of the expert Heller whose appraisal as of January 1974 (the month previous to that when trial commenced) on a painting-by-painting basis totaled $15,100,000. There was also testimony as to bona fide sales of other Rothkos between 1971 and 1974. Under the circumstances, it was impossible to appraise the value of the unreturned works of art with an absolute certainty and, so long as the figure arrived at had a reasonable basis of computation and was not merely speculative, possible or imaginary, the Surrogate had the right to resort to reasonable conjectures and probable estimates and to make the best approximation possible through the exercise of good judgment and common sense in arriving at that amount. . . . This is particularly so where the conduct of wrongdoers has rendered it difficult to ascertain the damages suffered with the precision otherwise possible. . . . Significantly, the Surrogate's factual finding as to the present value of these unreturned paintings was affirmed by the Appellate Division and, since that finding had support in the record and was not legally erroneous, it should not now be subjected to our disturbance. . . .

Accordingly, the order of the Appellate Division should be affirmed, with costs to the prevailing parties against appellants, and the question certified answered in the affirmative.

NOTES AND PROBLEMS

1. *Epilogue.* Bernard Reis, Theodoros Stamos, and Morton Levine were removed as executors of Mark Rothko's will, and Kate Rothko was appointed sole administrator c.t.a. of Rothko's estate. Kate Rothko

was not agreeable to the bill for legal services presented by her counsel in the amount of $7.5 million and hired another lawyer to resist its collection out of the estate. In view of the fact that her lawyers had successfully recovered paintings then worth $40 million for the estate, the surrogate allowed the firm a fee of $2.6 million, which was about twice the hourly rate usually charged by the firm. In re Rothko, 98 Misc. 2d 718, 414 N.Y.S.2d 444 (Sur. Ct. 1979).

Marlborough Gallery paid most of the $9.2 million assessed as damages in the principal case, but inasmuch as Reis, Stamos, and Levine were liable for the estate's legal fees and costs, Bernard Reis filed for bankruptcy in 1978. N.Y. Times, Jan. 26, 1978, at C-19, col. 6.

In 1977 Marlborough Gallery owner Frank Lloyd was indicted on charges of tampering with the evidence in the *Rothko* case by altering a gallery stock book containing the purchase and sale prices of Rothko works. Lloyd, a British subject, was outside the country when the indictment was handed up, and upon his return in 1982 he was tried and convicted on the charges. His sentence required him to set up a scholarship fund and art education programs at his gallery. N.Y. Times, Jan. 7, 1983, at 1, col. 5.

In 1983 a painting by Rothko sold for $1.8 million at an auction at Sotheby's in New York. This price equalled the amount Marlborough A.G. was to pay for 100 paintings under its agreement with Rothko's executors. It was, at the time, the highest price ever paid for a modern work by an American artist. In 1988 a Rothko painting sold at Christie's in New York for $2.5 million.

2. The measure of damages applied in the *Rothko* case is sharply criticized in Wellman, Punitive Surcharges Against Disloyal Fiduciaries — Is *Rothko* Right?, 77 Mich. L. Rev. 95 (1978). Professor Wellman would limit recovery against the two disloyal fiduciaries and the gallery to restitution (recovering all amounts received by the gallery for sales and resales of the paintings plus interest from sale dates). "Since the gallery received this amount under arrangements contemplating personal benefits of uncertain amounts for the disloyal executors, a lower award might have unjustly enriched persons who collaborated to compromise estate interests." Id. at 100. Wellman regards restitutionary liability as inapplicable to executor Levine, since he was not to profit personally from the breach, and would limit Levine's liability to the difference between the contract price and the market value as of the date of the contract selling the paintings to the gallery. Levine thus would be liable only for damages proximately caused by the breach, and the two disloyal fiduciaries would be liable for restitutionary damages.

Wellman's central point is that appreciation damages (a penalty) may be appropriate where a trustee sells an asset he has no authority to sell but are inappropriate where a trustee has authority to sell (as did Rothko's executors) but is guilty of disloyalty or self-dealing.

> [T]he wisdom of assessing any penalty can be questioned when a trustee has, or later may be said to have had, personal interests which conflict with his fiduciary duty. In such instances, it will usually be unclear whether the fiduciary has breached his duty of loyalty: liability is decided by hindsight and may arise in countless unforeseen ways. A penalty exceeding the liability of an insurer against controllable losses is simply an unjust remedy for conduct of only uncertain impropriety. Even in *Rothko*, the wrongfulness of the executors' conduct was not self-evident. For example, in 1969 Rothko sold a number of paintings to the gallery at prices comparable to those of the executors' 1970 sale and signed a long-term exclusive-consignment contract with the gallery. Further, Rothko knew that Reis and Stamos had personal ties to the gallery. These facts suggest that Rothko wanted his executors to deal with the gallery. Nor was it clear that executor Reis profited financially from his connection with the gallery: the surrogate found that his prestige was enhanced. Finally, while the court concluded that the 1970 sale and consignment was unfavorable in light of the gallery's highly profitable resales, much of the profit was generated by the gallery's vigorous promotion and by publicity from the litigation.
>
> The costs of penalty awards in cases where a fiduciary's conduct is not obviously wrongful are most severe for estates consisting of unique assets where potential conflicts of interest are common. Testators and settlors whose estates include real property, closely held corporate stock, stamps, books, automobiles, coins, or art understandably select as fiduciaries persons knowledgeable about those assets. As these persons accept fiduciary positions or deal with associates or potential associates who are fiduciaries, conflicts or potential conflicts of interest must arise. A rule which discourages the selection of persons who are experienced and successful in the handling of the testator's kind of assets is clearly unwise.
>
> *Rothko* will increase the complexity and cost of these trusteeships. As a precedent, it will encourage fiduciaries to consult their attorneys prior to any transaction possibly tainted with conflict of interest. And, if the attorneys read Surrogate Midonick's opinion carefully, the fiduciaries will be advised to seek a court proceeding with notice for and an opportunity to be heard by all persons interested in the estate, including appropriate state officials if charitable bequests are involved. What could be more wasteful? Expedited transactions will become impossible; transactions with the fiduciary's friends, associates, or any persons from whom some future favors might be predicted, no matter how favorable for the estate, will be too dangerous without test litigation and thus too expensive to be practical. For settlors and testators who would rather keep their estates out of court, the message of *Rothko* is obvious: they should either rearrange their estates so that they include only fungible and readily marketable assets or select fiduciaries without prior experience in handling the testator's unique assets. . . .
>
> Even if these considerations are unpersuasive and fail to end the judicial

thirst to penalize disloyal fiduciaries, a penalty measured by the value at
the time of trial of an asset that is beyond the defendant's control is a
bizarre punishment. When a court assesses appreciation damages, it
admits, contrary to the usual rule that the penalty fit the misdeed, that
the size of the penalty need not be related to the degree of culpability.
Yet, one violation of the duty of undivided loyalty is not necessarily as
unethical or immoral as another. There is a significant difference between
stealing another's property, thereby leaving him nothing, and partially
benefitting from a position of trust in a way that may have been
contemplated and condoned by a giftmaker. Rothko's executors, who
were guilty of guessing wrong about the legality of self-aggrandizing acts
that Rothko may have anticipated, were treated as thieves by the New
York courts. [Id. at 113-117.]

See also Harrow, Reflections on Estate of Rothko, 26 Clev. St. L. Rev.
573 (1977); Note, Trustee Liability for Breach of the Duty of Loyalty,
49 Fordham L. Rev. 1012 (1981).

3. Suppose that Mark Rothko's will had given each of his executors
an option to purchase one of his paintings. Would an executor be
permitted to enforce the option? Who would determine the price?
Options to purchase stock in a closely held corporation given to an
executor have generally been upheld, if the executor has no power to
set the price. See Estate of Bock, 198 Neb. 121, 251 N.W.2d 872 (1977);
cf. Goldman v. Rubin, 292 Md. 693, 441 A.2d 713 (1982).

4. In the Rothko estate, a number of paintings were disposed of by
Marlborough Gallery and Francis K. Lloyd before suit was brought
against them. Can the Rothko estate recover these paintings? Suppose
that the Gallery had swapped a Rothko painting for a Milton Avery
painting owned by a customer. Could the estate recover the Rothko
painting? Suppose that the Gallery had given a Rothko painting to The
Museum of Modern Art. Could the estate recover this painting?

One of the remedies afforded in equity for a breach of trust is known
as the "trust pursuit rule." This rule is stated in Restatement, Second,
Trusts §202 as follows:

§202. Following Trust Property into Its Product
(1) Where the trustee by the wrongful disposition of trust
property acquires other property, the beneficiary is entitled at his
option either to enforce a constructive trust of the property so
acquired or to enforce an equitable lien upon it to secure his claim
against the trustee for damages for breach of trust, as long as the
product of the trust property is held by the trustee and can be
traced.
(2) Except as stated in Subsection (1), the claim of the beneficiary
against the trustee for breach of trust is that of a general creditor.

The trust pursuit rule is also applied where the property purchased from misappropriated trust funds ends up in the hands of a third person. In that situation the remedy afforded the beneficiary of the trust depends upon whether or not the third person was a bona fide purchaser for value and without notice of the breach of trust. The rule is stated in the Restatement, Second, Trusts §284, p.47, as follows:

> (1)   If the trustee in breach of trust transfers trust property to, or creates a legal interest in the subject matter of the trust in, a person who takes for value and without notice of the breach of trust, and who is not knowingly taking part in an illegal transaction, the latter holds the interest so transferred or created free of the trust, and is under no liability to the beneficiary.

If the trustee in breach of trust transfers trust property to a person who takes with notice of the breach of trust, the transferee does not hold the property free of the trust, although he paid value for the transfer. (Restatement, Second, Trusts §288.) Likewise if the trustee in breach of trust transfers trust property and no value is given for the transfer, the transferee does not hold the property free of the trust, although he had no notice of the trust. (Restatement, Second, Trusts, §289.) [Kline v. Orebaugh, 214 Kan. 207, 211-212, 519 P.2d 691, 695-696 (1974).]

NOTE: CO-TRUSTEES

If there is more than one trustee, the trustees of a private, noncharitable trust must act as a group and with unanimity, unless the trust instrument provides to the contrary. One of several trustees does not have the power alone to transfer or deal with the property.[5]

One co-trustee may delegate to another co-trustee (or the trustees may delegate to a third-party agent) ministerial functions that do not require the exercise of discretion. A co-trustee may not delegate to another co-trustee discretionary powers, which can be exercised only by the co-trustees together. These powers include the purchase or sale of trust assets, investment of trust funds, allocation of receipts and disbursements between principal and income, and discretionary payments of income or principal to trust beneficiaries. Since co-trustees must act jointly, a co-trustee is liable for the wrongful acts of a co-trustee to which he has consented or which, by his negligence through

---

5. Statutes in some states provide that a majority of trustees can act if there are three or more trustees. For example, Uniform Trustees' Powers Act §6(a) (1985) provides that:

Any power vested in 3 or more trustees may be exercised by a majority, but a trustee who has not joined in exercising a power is not liable to the beneficiaries or to others for the consequences of the exercise; and a dissenting trustee is not liable for the consequences of an act in which he joins at the direction of the majority of the trustees, if he expressed his dissent in writing to any of his co-trustees at or before the time of the joinder.

inactivity or wrongful delegation, he has enabled the co-trustee to commit. It is improper for one trustee to leave to the others the custody and control of the trust property. See Report, The Co-Trustee Relationship — Rights and Duties, 8 Real Prop., Prob. & Tr. J. 9 (1973).

In the case of charitable trusts, unanimity of action is not required of the trustees. Action by a majority of the trustees is valid.

PROBLEMS

1.   *A* and *B* are co-trustees. While *A* is on a Caribbean cruise, a $10,000 government bond held in trust comes due. *B* collects the $10,000 and invests the proceeds in common stock of Zany Corporation, a pure speculation. Six months later Zany Corporation stock is worthless. The trust beneficiaries sue *A* and *B* for the $10,000 loss. Is *A* liable? Cf. Pank v. Chicago Title & Trust Co., 314 Ill. App. 53, 40 N.E.2d 787 (1942).

2.   What would you, as counsel for Levine in the estate of Mark Rothko, have advised him to do when the conflict of interest of Reis became apparent? See 3 A. Scott, Trusts §194 (W. Fratcher 4th ed. 1988). Could Levine have resigned as executor and trustee? See id., §169.

In re Heidenreich
New York Surrogate's Court, Nassau County, 1976
85 Misc. 2d 135, 378 N.Y.S.2d 982

BENNETT, S.   In these accounting proceedings the guardian ad litem interposed the following objections:

(1)   That the fiduciaries be surcharged for retaining convertible preferred stock of Franklin New York Corporation, the parent corporation of Franklin National Bank, a successor trustee herein;
(2)   That the fiduciaries should be surcharged for depositing trust funds in savings accounts at the Franklin National Bank;
(3)   That the fiduciaries should be surcharged for depositing $6,450 on August 25, 1972 in a checking account at a commercial bank where it remained until August 13, 1973.

The transcript of an examination before trial of a trust officer of the Franklin National Bank and affidavits from him, the surviving trustee and an attorney were submitted to the court together with a stipulation consenting that this matter be determined on the papers filed with the same effect as if a hearing had been held.

The decedent died on October 11, 1965 leaving a will and codicil which were admitted to probate. She nominated two individual executors and trustees and provided for the appointment of a successor trustee in certain events.

The residuary of her estate was held in trust with income payable to her daughter for life and upon her death the corpus of the trust then remaining was to be divided into three separate trusts for her daughter's three children, to be held until they each reached age 30. The guardian ad litem represents two of the infant grandchildren; the third has reached her majority and has not interposed any objections to the account.

At the time of the decedent's death in 1965 she owned 1,309 shares of common stock of Federation Bank and Trust Company. This stock had been acquired when the Citizens Bank of Brooklyn (of which she and her late husband had been principal stockholders and her husband also an officer and director since the bank was organized and incorporated) was merged with the Federation Bank and Trust Company. The latter was then merged after her death with Franklin National Bank. The Federation Bank and Trust Company stock was exchanged for 1,341 shares of convertible preferred stock of Franklin National Bank and these shares were subsequently exchanged for 1,341 shares of convertible preferred stock of Franklin New York Corporation when Franklin National Bank was reorganized in 1969. Franklin National Bank was appointed successor trustee on August 3, 1973 to take the place of one of the individual trustees who died. The income beneficiary of the trust has now died and the fiduciaries have submitted their intermediate account.

After Franklin National Bank became a successor trustee they reviewed their portfolio and decided at that time to retain the stock which had a current value of approximately $31-32 a share. The trustees reviewed the portfolio from time to time thereafter and decided to hold the stock until May 10, 1974 when trading of the stock was suspended and at the present time it appears that the stock has no value as a result of the collapse of the bank. It is the position of the guardian ad litem that the trustees of the bank held on to the stock in order not to embarrass the management of the Franklin National Bank and that there was a conflict of interest in that the corporate trustee was possibly more concerned with protecting the bank which had financial difficulties rather than concentrate all of its efforts to protect the portfolio of the trust.

The issue raised by the guardian ad litem regarding the retention of the bank stock is whether the fiduciaries were authorized to retain the stock because of a conflict of interest. There is no question that a taint existed in the retention in the portfolio of the trust of stock owned by one of the fiduciaries. It matters not whether the fiduciaries acted in good faith in retaining the stock for the courts must insist on rigid adherence to the principle that divided loyalties should be avoided so that all temptations can be removed from one acting as fiduciary unhindered with the possible desire to serve its own interests in conflict with its duty to act solely for the benefit of the trust (City Bank Farmers Trust Co. v. Cannon, 291 NY 125).

A fiduciary has an obligation to extricate itself from a conflict of interest by either not qualifying to act as trustee or selling an unauthorized retention of stock of its own corporation (Matter of Ryan, 291 NY 376). Even broad powers of investment authorized by the terms of decedent's will do not absolve a fiduciary from the conflict of interest of owning stock in its own corporation (Matter of Durston, 297 NY 64) and if the conflict of interest exists and a surcharge is to be levelled against the corporate fiduciary, the surcharge also must be levelled against the individual trustee who should have insisted that the stock be sold or not purchased (Matter of Durston, supra).

Under article Twelfth (a) the testatrix authorized the fiduciary to "retain any property . . . however acquired." Accordingly, had Federation Bank and Trust Company been an initial fiduciary and part of the estate portfolio consisted of stock of Federation Bank and Trust Company, they would have been authorized to retain these shares of stock. Since the rule of undivided loyalty as applied to the retention of corporate trustees of shares of its own stock is subject to the testatrix' authorization that they be retained, this authorization appears to cover instances where the stock is subsequently merged or consolidated with another corporation (Matter of Ridings, 297 NY 417; Matter of Read, 84 NYS2d 871).

Accordingly, the court finds that the trustees were authorized to retain the stock in spite of the conflict of interest. In spite of said power to retain, the court could surcharge a trustee if it found that the trustee acted recklessly or did not act in good faith. The power to retain removed the possibility of surcharge brought about by an automatic taint where a fiduciary acts in good faith. The authorization does not apply when the fiduciary does not act in good faith and a surcharge is still possible. However, based on the testimony submitted to the court, the court cannot find that the trustees acted in bad faith but that they made a considered judgment regarding the retention of the stock and they should not be second-guessed (Matter of Bank of N.Y., 35 NY2d 512).

As to the retention of assets in the bank's savings accounts, the record clearly demonstrates that the trustees were making short-term deposits in order to have liquid assets ready for investment and they have demonstrated that they used proper judgment in the investment of the cash in short-term deposits in order to have funds available for investment. The funds earned interest and the delay of having to transfer these funds to savings banks to earn additional interest would not be justified because of the need to have the funds readily available. The investment was secure and there is no basis for a surcharge. The guardian ad litem's objection concerning these deposits is overruled.

As to the funds retained in the checking account, these represented commissions due the fiduciaries. They elected to have the funds remain as trust assets for their own benefit to be taken at a subsequent date. The assets represent commissions earned from August 25, 1972 to August 13, 1973 as determined by the decree of August 3, 1973. The funds were earmarked for them and the court does not find any basis for a surcharge. Accordingly, the objection of the guardian ad litem concerning the failure to deposit these funds which were earmarked for commissions is overruled.

The account should be supplemented by affidavit and a supplemental report of the guardian ad litem should be filed.

NOTE AND QUESTION

1.   The retention or purchase of its own shares by a corporate trustee is not self-dealing. Nonetheless, because the trustee cannot approach the problem of selling or retaining its shares with the same detachment it applies to other trust assets, a special rule has developed that a corporate trustee cannot invest trust funds in purchasing its own shares. As for retaining its own shares where they were received by the trustee as part of the original trust estate, the majority of states (including New York) hold that retention is not proper unless authorized by the terms of the trust.

The testator may waive the undivided loyalty rule and authorize a corporate trustee to hold shares of its own stock as a trust asset. As stated in In re Heidenreich, waiver reduces the standard of duty to one of good faith and permits the court to weigh the merits of the transaction. An authorization to retain the securities coming into the trust at the time of its creation ordinarily raises a presumption of waiver. If the trustee is authorized to retain the initial investments in its own stock, the trustee may retain additional shares given as dividends on the theory that the trustee is maintaining the trust's authorized proportionate interest in the company. Similarly, if the corporate trustee participates in a merger resulting in a new corporation, the new corporate trustee can retain the new shares if they are substantially equivalent to the old. The theory is that the conflict of interest, present at the creation of the trust and then waived, may continue as long as it remains substantially the same. Is this the theory applied in In re Heidenreich?

2. Can a bank, authorized to hold its own stock as trustee, vote the shares of stock held in its fiduciary capacity? If the bank holds a large number of its shares as trustee, by voting them the bank may be able to perpetuate the bank management in power. On the other hand, if the bank does not vote the stock the trust beneficiaries are disenfranchised. The states are about evenly split on whether banks can vote their own stock held in trust. Several states have statutes prohibiting a fiduciary from voting its own shares in the election of directors. See Cleveland Trust Co. v. Eaton, 21 Ohio St. 2d 129, 256 N.E.2d 198 (1970), noted 54 Va. L. Rev. 327 (1968); Jennings v. Murdock, 220 Kan. 182, 553 P.2d 846 (1976); 12 U.S.C.A. §61 (1945, Supp. 1989) (national banks).

NOTE: INSIDER TRADING

SEC Rule 10b-5, as construed by the courts, provides that a person with inside information about a stock cannot buy or sell the stock unless he first discloses the information. An insider is one who has access to material corporate information not publicly disclosed and that is intended to be confidential. If an insider discloses nonpublic information to outsiders (*tippees*) for the purpose of protecting their investments in the stock, the insider and the tippee may be liable in damages. The damages may be all profits gained in the transaction (and possibly substantially more).

Suppose that a bank trustee learns through its commercial department, in processing an application for a loan, that the earnings of Day Corporation are likely to be considerably less this year; this information is not yet public. The commercial department communicates this information to the trust investment committee, which proceeds to sell substantial holdings of Day Corporation for $100 a share. Within a few days the bad news is made public, and the market price of the stock drops to $60 a share. Has the bank violated Rule 10b-5? If the trust investment committee, after receiving the information, did not sell the stock, has the bank violated its fiduciary duty of loyalty? The position of the SEC seems clear: "[T]here can be no doubt which is primary here; . . . the obligations of a fiduciary do not include performing an illegal act," i.e., violation of Rule 10b-5. Cady, Roberts & Co., 40 S.E.C. 907 (1961). It is not clear, however, that this view will completely supersede in all cases the ancient fiduciary standard that a trustee administer the trust solely in the interest of the beneficiaries. See Schuyler, From *Sulphur* to Surcharge? Corporate Trustee Exposure Under SEC Rule 10b-5, 67 Nw. U.L. Rev. 42 (1972).

Not all communications between the commercial and trust departments of a bank present this dilemma. The trust department is free to act on any information that is neither "inside" nor "material." These two words often represent the dividing line between violation or nonviolation of Rule 10b-5. "Inside" information is generally any information not yet available to the public. The definition of "material" has created the most uncertainty; almost every case involving Rule 10b-5 redefines it. A paraphrase of its current meaning is: Information is material if it significantly alters the total mix of information available to the investor.

The lack of objective standards has resulted in banks instituting protective measures to minimize the risk of violating Rule 10b-5. Many banks have established "Chinese walls" between their commercial and trust departments in order to prevent this internal flow of material inside information. These "walls" are not physical barriers but rather sets of rules that attempt to filter the communications flow. Clearly this not only creates administrative difficulties, but it also impedes the efficient functioning of a "full service" bank. Moreover, it is not certain that a "wall" will always shield the bank from liability. The SEC has stated that it will give weight to a "wall" or "Statement of Bank Policy," but "as a matter of Commission Policy, we do not, and indeed cannot, determine that the Statement of Policy will prove adequate in all circumstances that may arise."

Nor does a Chinese wall insure the bank against breach of the fiduciary obligation. In Estate of Pitzer, 155 Cal. App. 3d 979, 202 Cal. Rptr. 855 (1984), the court upheld a surcharge against a bank where the commercial department of another branch of the bank made a loan to the purchaser of trust assets, taking as security a mortgage on the trust property. The bank earned interest on its loan, which the court viewed as an impermissible dealing with trust property for the trustee's own profit. See comment by Johanson in 12 Prob. Notes 67, 71 (1986).

Even if authorized to hold its own stock, should a bank trustee do so in view of SEC Rule 10b-5?

2. Fiduciary Duties Relating to Care of the Trust Property

a. Duty to Collect and Protect Trust Property

A trustee has the duty of obtaining possession of the trust assets without unnecessary delay. What is unreasonable delay depends upon the circumstances. When a testamentary trust is established, the trustee should collect the assets from the executor as promptly as circumstances permit. In addition, a testamentary trustee owes a duty to the beneficiaries to examine the property tendered by the executor to make sure it is what the trustee ought to receive. This means the trustee must look at the acts of the executor and require the executor to redress any breach of duty which diminished the assets intended for the trust. See In re First National Bank of Mansfield, 37 Ohio St. 2d 60, 307 N.E.2d 23, 68 A.L.R.3d 1258 (1974) (trustee is liable to beneficiaries for not objecting to executor's overpayment of inheritance tax); Report, Duties and Responsibilities of a Successor Trustee, 10 Real Prop., Prob. & Tr. J. 310 (1975).

Once having obtained the trust property, a trustee must act as a prudent person in preserving it. If real property is involved, a trustee must keep buildings in repair, guard against theft, pay taxes, and insure against loss by fire.

b. Duty to Earmark Trust Property

A trustee has a duty to earmark trust property. The reason: If the property is not earmarked, a trustee might later claim that the investments that proved profitable were the trustee's own investments and the investments that lost value were made for the trust. An established exception is that a trustee may invest in bonds payable to bearer instead of registering the bonds in the name of the trustee.

Under the older view, where a trustee commits a breach of trust by failing to earmark a trust investment, a trustee is strictly liable for any loss resulting from the investment. Even though it clearly appears that the loss is not due to the failure to earmark, a trustee is liable for the actual loss sustained by the trust. The more modern view, adopted by the Restatement (Second) of Trusts §179, Comment d (1959), is that a trustee is liable only for such loss as results from the failure to earmark and is not liable for such loss as results from general economic conditions.

PROBLEMS

1. A trustee deposits money in Security Bank in the trustee's individual name. Security Bank fails. Is the trustee liable for the amount of the deposit? See 2A A. Scott, Trusts §180 (W. Fratcher 4th ed. 1987). Would it matter if the trustee were an officer or director of the bank and knew the bank was in difficulty? See Epworth Orphanage v. Long, 207 S.C. 384, 36 S.E.2d 37 (1945).

2. A trustee invests in Baker Company stock, taking title to the certificates in the trustee's individual name. The trustee did this to

facilitate later transfer since on subsequent sale the buyer might have to inquire into the terms of the trust if the buyer knew the shares were held in trust. Baker Company stock goes down in value. Is the trustee liable for the loss? Would it make any difference if the trustee had shown on the trustee's records that the stock was purchased for the trust? See White v. Sherman, 168 Ill. 589, 48 N.E. 128 (1897); Miller v. Pender, 93 N.H. 1, 34 A.2d 663, 150 A.L.R. 798 (1943). Would it make any difference if the trustee took title in the name of a nominee? See Potter v. Union & Peoples National Bank, 105 F.2d 437 (6th Cir. 1939).

c. Duty Not to Mingle Trust Funds with the Trustee's Own

A trustee is guilty of a breach of trust if the trustee commingles the trust funds with his own, even though the trustee does not use the trust funds for his own purposes. The reason: The trust funds become more difficult to trace and hence subject to the risk that personal creditors of the trustee can reach them. (The prohibition against commingling has been partially abrogated in almost all jurisdictions to permit a corporate fiduciary to hold and invest trust assets in a common trust fund. See 3 A. Scott, supra, §227.9.)

As with breach of the duty to earmark, there is a divergence of views regarding the extent of a trustee's liability for commingling. The older view is that a trustee is strictly liable, even though the loss would have occurred had there been no commingling. More recent authority holds a trustee liable only to the extent the commingling caused the loss.

PROBLEM

The trustee of a trust under the will of José Martinez places bearer bonds, bought for $10,000, in her individual safe-deposit box, in an envelope marked "Owned by José Martinez Trust." The trustee dies. The market value of the bonds is $9,500. Is the trustee's estate liable for the $500 loss? See Lavarelle's Estate, 13 D. & C. 703 (1930), aff'd, 101 Pa. Super. 448 (1931):

We freely concede that a trustee may illegally abstract assets from the box maintained in his own name, as trustee, quite as readily as he could by taking the securities from his individual box. On the other hand, either through accident or design, the envelope may become worn, dilapidated, or it may entirely disappear; the markings or writings on the envelope, in time, may fail to remain decipherable; the rubber bands surrounding the envelope may become hard and brittle and disintegrate, or the tape or string with which they are tied may break or disappear. In such event, the securities, unearmarked, may become commingled with those which the trustee may individually own. Should the trustee die under such circumstances, it may become impossible or difficult to segregate the trust securities from those of his own. Or should the trustee become insolvent, a contest with creditors may arise and jeopardize the trust assets. Furthermore, should a trustee keep assets in his individual box, *his* executor, on his death, may assume custody. Thus, securities come into possession of a stranger to the trust and without bond. Where, however, the box is in the name of the fiduciary as trustee, the appointment of a substituted trustee is requisite before access may be had to the box. This is an added protection to the trust estate. In our opinion, it is quite as reprehensible for a trustee to commingle trust (unregistered) securities with his own as it is to keep the cash of the estate in his own individual bank account.

d.   Duty Not to Delegate

A trustee has a duty not to delegate to others the doing of acts which the trustee can reasonably be required to perform personally. A trustee cannot delegate the entire administration of the trust, not even for a short period when the trustee is out of the country. If a trustee delegates to another the power to administer the trust, the trustee is personally liable for *any* loss that results to the trust estate and not merely for loss resulting from negligence of the delegate. On the other hand, some functions can be delegated. The authorities attempt to distinguish between discretionary functions, which require a trustee's personal attention, and ministerial functions, which can be delegated. Ministerial functions include hiring an attorney, accountant, stockbroker, or real estate agent when prudent. In many situations, the line between the two functions is rather unclear because almost every act involves the exercise of a certain amount of discretion. In spite of the uncertainty about many acts, one thing is (or was) clear. Although a trustee may employ an investment adviser, a trustee cannot properly delegate to an agent the power to select investments for the trust. See Restatement (Second) of Trusts §171, Comment h (1959).[6]

6. But see Langbein & Posner, Market Funds and Trust-Investment Law, 1976 A.B.F. Res. J. 1, 19-24, pointing out that "as a practical matter the duty of nondelegation [of investment power] is widely evaded in modern trust administration." Many trustees invest in mutual funds — an investment authorized by statute in many states and now thought to be proper almost everywhere. Also, the duty not to delegate can be waived in the trust instrument. See Note, Trustee's Power to Delegate: A Comparative View, 50 Notre Dame Law. 173 (1974).

e.   Liability for Contracts and Torts

In caring for the trust property, a trustee may make contracts respecting the property. The traditional rule is that a trustee is personally liable on any contract the trustee makes, in the absence of an express provision in the contract relieving the trustee of liability. This is true regardless of whether the trustee does or does not have power to enter into the contract. The mere fact that the contract is signed by a trustee in a fiduciary capacity (e.g., "X as trustee") is not ordinarily sufficient to relieve the trustee of liability.

If the contract is properly made by a trustee, the trustee is entitled to be indemnified out of the trust assets. However, if the trust estate is insufficient to indemnify the trustee, the trustee suffers the loss. A trustee should therefore be very careful to insert in the contract a provision excluding personal liability on the part of the trustee.

A trustee's liability for tort traditionally has followed a similar rule. A trustee is personally liable to the same extent a beneficial owner of the trust property would be liable. A trustee should take out insurance to cover his liability for torts committed by the trustee or an employee of the trustee.

If a trustee is held liable for tort but is not personally at fault, the trustee is entitled to indemnification out of the trust assets. As with contract liability, if the trust assets are insufficient to indemnify the trustee, the trustee suffers the loss.

Contract and tort creditors must sue the trustee personally. After they recover a judgment, they must try to collect the judgment from the trustee's own assets. If these are insufficient, the creditors may proceed to enforce the trustee's right of indemnification against the trust estate. In this proceeding for indemnification, the beneficiaries can assert setoffs against the trustee unrelated to the contract or tort claim. See Cook v. Holland, 575 S.W.2d 468 (Ky. App. 1978).

The traditional rules have been criticized by many commentators as putting unwarranted burdens on creditors and unfair liability on a trustee where the trustee is not personally at fault and the trust assets are insufficient for indemnification. See Johnston, Development in Contract Liability of Trusts and Trustees, 42 N.Y.U.L. Rev. 483 (1966). Many states have enacted statutes reversing the traditional rules, and permitting contract and tort creditors to sue a trustee in his representative capacity. Uniform Probate Code §7-306, reproduced below, is typical.

Uniform Probate Code (1983)

§7-306 [Personal Liability of Trustee to Third Parties]

(a)   Unless otherwise provided in the contract, a trustee is not personally liable on contracts properly entered into in his fiduciary capacity in the course of administration of the trust estate unless he fails to reveal his representative capacity and identify the trust estate in the contract.

(b)   A trustee is personally liable for obligations arising from ownership or control of property of the trust estate or for torts committed in the course of administration of the trust estate only if he is personally at fault.

(c)   Claims based on contracts entered into by a trustee in his fiduciary capacity, on obligations arising from ownership or control of the trust estate, or on torts committed in the course of trust administration may be asserted against the trust estate by proceeding against the trustee in his fiduciary capacity, whether or not the trustee is personally liable therefor.

(d)   The question of liability as between the trust estate and the trustee individually may be determined in a proceeding for accounting, surcharge or indemnification or other appropriate proceeding.

3.   Duty of Impartiality: Allocations to Income and Principal

A trustee has the duty to deal with both the income beneficiary and the remainderman impartially. The trust property must produce a reasonable income while being preserved for the remainderman. Because a trustee cannot favor the remainderman at the expense of the life beneficiary, a trustee cannot hold property that produces no income unless authorized to do so in the trust instrument. Hence, unless so authorized, a trustee cannot invest in raw land, gold, art, foreign currencies, jewels, or other nonproductive property.

The duty to invest in income-producing assets has sometimes caused grief (and financial loss) to persons who accept the office of trustee without being aware of the trustee's duties. In Witmer v. Blair, 588 S.W.2d 222 (Mo. App. 1979), the testator, dying in 1960, named his niece Jane as trustee for the education of his granddaughter Marguerite, age 7. Jane had no experience as a trustee and for ten years kept $6,000 (about half of the trust assets) in a checking account. She did this, she said, so that she could withdraw the money quickly if Marguerite needed it for college. The court held that failure to invest this sum before Marguerite became of college age was a breach of trust and that Jane was liable for the amount of interest that could have been earned on the money in the checking account. Jane's good faith and inexperience were not a defense.

In re Kuehn
Supreme Court of South Dakota, 1981
308 N.W.2d 398

JONES, J.   Max A. Kuehn, Sr., died testate on April 26, 1957, leaving a widow, Nell Carter Kuehn, and two sons, Carter and Max, Jr. Under the terms of his will, the residue of his estate was placed in trust. Included in the residue was a one-half interest in farm land adjacent to Sioux Falls.[7]

The sons were to receive the income from the trust. Carter died in 1960 without issue, and his interest in the trust went to Max, Jr., who died on September 11, 1971. The widow and daughter of Max, Jr., then became the income beneficiaries of this trust.

The will provided that upon the death of the sons of Max A. Kuehn, Sr., and their children and widows who were living at the time of his death, the trust would terminate and be distributed to the lineal descendants of his sons in existence, and if there were none, then to certain charities as contingent remaindermen. The daughter and only child of Max A. Kuehn, Jr., has had surgery rendering her incapable of having children, so it appears likely that the contingent remaindermen will receive the corpus of this trust. . . .

The trial court entered an order finding that the real estate that had been sold was underproductive, and allocated $49,374.43 of the sale proceeds to the income beneficiaries under the formula contained in Restatement (Second) of Trusts §241 (1959).

The trial court also entered an order allowing and denying certain requests for attorney fees and costs.

The primary issue in this appeal is whether under the facts of this case the income beneficiaries are entitled to share in the proceeds from five parcels of real estate heretofore sold by the trustee.

Normally, income beneficiaries do not share in the appreciation of value of trust assets. Restatement (Second) of Trusts §233(b) (1959); III A. Scott, The Law of Trusts §233 (3d ed. 1967). This creates an inequity where those assets consist of unproductive or underproductive property, and Restatement (Second) of Trusts §240 (1959) evolved to

---

7. The farms are known as the "West 41st Street farm" consisting of approximately 239 acres originally appraised at $200 per acre, some of which was sold for $6,000 per acre; the "West 12th Street farm" consisting of approximately 160 acres originally appraised at $125 per acre; and the "South Minnesota Avenue farm" consisting of approximately 152 acres originally appraised at $106.60 per acre, some of which was sold for $3,000 per acre. A total of 222 acres were sold in five separate sales between 1972 and 1977 for approximately $630,000, of which the trust received one-half.

do equity as between competing classes of beneficiaries.[8] This section provides in substance that where assets are unproductive or under-productive and likely to remain so, the trustee is under a duty to the income beneficiaries to sell such assets within a reasonable time, unless it is otherwise provided by the terms of the trust. Restatement (Second) of Trusts §241 (1959) sets out a formula for allocation of the net sale proceeds where the sale is delayed.[9]

Because the real estate assets of this trust were only fractional interests held jointly with other members of the Kuehn family, Max A. Kuehn, Sr., expressly authorized the trustees to hold such realty in order to protect the interests of the other owners and to consult with them before making any sales. The contingent remaindermen argue that this provision negates the duty to sell required by Restatement (Second) of Trusts §240 (1959). . . .

It appears from the evidence presented in the trial court that the income from the land sold ranged from 1% to 2% of the value of the property at a time when the trial court found that return achieved by trust institutions in Sioux Falls ranged from 5.02% to 5.86%. There is no real dispute that the property in question was underproductive.

The income beneficiaries argue that where the land sold was under-

---

8. *§240. Unproductive Property.*

> Unless it is otherwise provided by the terms of the trust, if property held in trust to pay the income to a beneficiary for a designated period and thereafter to pay the principal to another beneficiary produces no income or an income substantially less than the current rate of return on trust investments, and is likely to continue unproductive or under-productive, the trustee is under a duty to the beneficiary entitled to the income to sell such property within a reasonable time.

Restatement (Second) of Trusts §240 (1959).

9. *§241. Allocation on Delayed Conversion*

> (1) Unless it is otherwise provided by the terms of the trust, if property held in trust to pay the income to a beneficiary for a designated period and thereafter to pay the principal to another beneficiary is property which the trustee is under a duty to sell, and which produces no income or an income substantially less than the current rate of return on trust investments, or which is wasting property or produces an income substantially more than the current rate of return on trust investments, and the trustee does not immediately sell the property, the trustee should make an apportionment of the proceeds of the sale when made, as stated in Subsection (2).
>
> (2) The net proceeds received from the sale of the property are apportioned by ascertaining the sum which with simple interest thereon at the current rate of return on trust investments from the day when the duty to sell arose to the day of the sale would equal the net proceeds; and the sum so ascertained is to be treated as principal, and the residue of the net proceeds as income.
>
> (3) The net proceeds are determined by adding to the net sale price the net income received or deducting therefrom the net loss incurred in carrying the property prior to the sale.

Restatement (Second) of Trusts §241 (1959).

productive because of its great appreciation in value and since they are the primary objects of the testator's bounty, they should share in the sale proceeds even though the testator authorized the trustees to retain these assets. We agree. In re Jackson's Will, 258 N.Y. 281, 179 N.E. 496 (1932); In re Rowland's Estate, 273 N.Y. 100, 6 N.E.2d 393 (1937); Amerige v. Goddard, 316 Mass. 566, 55 N.E.2d 919 (1944).

The fact that the testator authorized the retention of the real estate assets does not relieve the trustees of the legal obligation to treat the income beneficiaries fairly. 76 Am. Jur. 2d Trusts §324 (1975); Restatement (Second) of Trusts §232 (1959); III A. Scott, The Law of Trusts, supra, §232; 51 Am. Jur. 2d Life Tenants and Remaindermen §26 (1978). When land held in trust appreciates in value to the point it becomes underproductive, and there are conflicting interests between income beneficiaries and remaindermen, the law will imply a duty to sell the land within a reasonable time, even in those instances where the testator authorized the trustee to retain the assets. Such a result is required in this case in order to carry out the clearly expressed intent and desires of the testator, and to treat the competing interests equitably.

We approve the formula set out in Restatement (Second) of Trusts §241 (1959) as a proper formula for making an equitable allocation of the sales proceeds.

The trial court held that because Max A. Kuehn, Jr., was both a co-trustee and beneficiary, the income beneficiaries' claim to apportionment of the sale proceeds cannot extend back beyond the date of his death on September 11, 1971. Max A. Kuehn, Jr., as co-trustee, either consented to or acquiesced in retention of this real estate. In re Trust Estate of Higgins, 83 S.D. 535, 162 N.W.2d 768 (1968). The present income beneficiaries are not entitled to an allocation of income predating their interest in this trust.

In determining the current rate of return on trust investments, the trial court derived the percentages used from the investment results of three Sioux Falls bank trust departments during the time involved herein. The income beneficiaries contend that good grades of corporate bonds would yield considerably higher income than the results achieved by the Sioux Falls banks. The trial court's finding is amply supported by the evidence and will be affirmed.

NOTES

1. The apportionment formula of the Restatement (Second) of Trusts §241(2) is set forth in footnote 9 in In re Kuehn. If you are

good in algebra, you will realize that the amount apportioned to principal is determined by the following equation:

$$\text{principal} = \frac{\text{net proceeds}}{1 + (\text{period of years})(\text{interest rate})}$$

If algebra is not your forte, perhaps the following illustration will help.

Testator devises Blackacre, unproductive land, in trust for *A* for life, remainder to *B*. After one year Blackacre is sold for $33,000. Taxes and other carrying charges for the year are $1,500; therefore the net proceeds are $31,500. If the current rate of interest on trust investments is 5 percent, the amount allocated to principal is $31,500 divided by 1.05, or $30,000. The amount allocated to income is $1,500. If Blackacre were sold after 3 years for $43,000 and the taxes and other carrying charges are $2,750, the amount of the net proceeds, $40,250, is divided by 1.15. (Why 1.15? The formula is 1 *plus* the number of years (3) times the interest rate (.05).) Hence, $35,000 is allocated to principal and $5,250 to income. Looking at this another way: $35,000 invested at 5 percent will produce $1,750 interest; multiply this sum by 3 (for 3 years) and you get $5,250.

The common law, as set forth by the Restatement, has been changed by the Uniform Principal and Income Act. The Act has two versions, the first promulgated in 1931 (adopted in nine states) and a revised one promulgated in 1962 (adopted in 30 states). Section 12 of the revised Uniform Principal and Income Act provides that, in the case of unproductive property that is sold, a portion of the net proceeds (to be determined by the Restatement formula) shall be allocated to trust income regardless of whether there was a duty to sell the nonproductive property. For a critique of the rules relating to nonproductive property, see Note, Underproductive Trust Property in Florida: Sacrificing Yearly Return for Administrative Convenience, 32 U. Fla. L. Rev. 247 (1980).

2. *Bond premium and discount.* Suppose that a trustee holds an 8 percent bond maturing in 10 years with a face or par value of $100 but which cost $103. The $3 is known as a premium, which must be paid by the purchaser because the interest rate of 8 percent on the bond is above the going market interest rate at the time of purchase. Similarly, if the $100 bond were purchased for $96, there is a $4 discount resulting from the fact that the interest rate of 8 percent on the bond is below the going market interest rate. The exact amount of premium or discount is determined by how greatly the bond's interest rate varies from the market interest rate and by the length of time to maturity. If the trustee takes $103 out of principal now to buy a bond that will return $100 to principal in 10 years, it is obvious that the amount of principal will drop $3 when the bond comes due. Similarly, if the bond costs $96, when the bond comes due principal will gain $4.

Under the common law, if a trustee purchases a bond at a premium, he may or must (jurisdictions differ) set aside from the bond income each year an amount sufficient to produce at the maturity of the bond an amount equal to the loss of the premium from principal (this is called *amortization*). Thus the income beneficiary does not receive the amount of interest paid on the bond but receives something less. Oddly enough, in the converse situation, where the bond is purchased at a discount, a trustee may not give the income beneficiary any part of the appreciation when the bond matures. The income beneficiary is entitled only to the actual interest received. It seems somewhat unfair to take away some of the interest from the income beneficiary when the bond is purchased at a premium but not make an adjustment in the income beneficiary's position when the bond is purchased at a discount. But the authorities support that position. See Old Colony Trust Co. v. Comstock, 290 Mass. 377, 195 N.E. 389, 101 A.L.R. 1 (1935); 3A A. Scott, Trusts §239.2 (W. Fratcher 4th ed. 1988).

The original Uniform Principal and Income Act, in §6, provides that all gain or loss realized on the maturity of a bond shall enure to principal; a trustee is not authorized to amortize a bond premium or accumulate for a bond discount. Section 7 of the revised uniform act continues this rule. The reason for the uniform act rule is that premiums and discounts tend to balance out generally and the allocation may be more trouble than it is worth.

First Wyoming Bank v. First National Bank & Trust Co. of Wyoming

Supreme Court of Wyoming, 1981
628 P.2d 1355

[In 1919 Charles W. Burdick, a lawyer in Cheyenne, executed his will. Some six months later, Burdick transferred 12,000 shares of stock of the Standard Oil Company of Indiana to his daughter, Margaret Hewlett, in trust to pay Burdick the income for life and upon his death to transfer "the said shares of stock to the trustee or trustees of the estate of said grantor who have been or may be named and designated by said grantor in his Last Will and Testament." Burdick died in 1927. His will appointed Margaret and her husband, George Hewlett, as "joint trustees of my estate." Burdick devised all his property to Margaret and George Hewlett "as joint trustees" to pay the income to Margaret for her life and, upon her death, to certain named remaindermen.

Margaret and George Hewlett were appointed executors. In 1929, before they filed a final accounting as executors, Standard Oil Company declared a 50 percent stock dividend on the 12,000 shares held in the inter vivos trust and issued a certificate for 6,000 shares to Margaret Hewlett, as trustee of that trust. In 1930, the executors filed a petition for final accounting. The petition listed as inventory of the estate 12,000 shares of Standard Oil and noted also that a 50 percent stock dividend had been declared on the shares and a certificate issued for 6,000 shares to Margaret Hewlett as trustee. The petition asked (1) that Margaret and George be appointed testamentary trustees, (2) that the 6,000 shares resulting from the stock dividend, held by certificate in the name of Margaret as trustee, be distributed to Margaret as income beneficiary of Burdick's estate, and (3) that 12,000 shares be transferred to Margaret and George to hold as testamentary trustees. The remaindermen were either minors or nonresidents of Wyoming; a guardian ad litem, a Cheyenne lawyer appointed to represent them, notified them of the petition. No party entered an objection, and the probate court entered a decree allowing the petition.

Upon the death of Margaret Hewlett in 1976, the remaindermen challenged the distribution of the 6,000 shares to Margaret on the theory that the probate court lacked jurisdiction over the assets of the inter vivos trust, which, they alleged, passed directly to the testamentary trustees and not through probate. The trial court ruled against the remaindermen on the ground of res judicata, and they appealed.]

RAPER, J. . . . In order to resolve this question, the language of the inter vivos trust must be analyzed and compared to that appearing in the will. The trust agreement provided:

> TO HAVE AND TO HOLD all and singular the said shares of stock, in trust nevertheless . . . and upon the death of the said grantor shall transfer, pay over and deliver the said shares of stock to the *trustee or trustees of the estate* of said grantor who have been or may be named and designated by said grantor in his Last Will and Testament. [Emphasis added.]

Mr. Burdick's will also used the term "joint trustees of my estate." . . . The probate court appointed the persons who were named joint trustees of the estate as the executors, apparently having concluded that the terms were intended to be synonymous. Since the trust agreement was executed six months after the will, the conclusion follows that the term "joint trustees of the estate" as used in that agreement in all probability would have the same meaning the court determined was ascribed to it in the will. Therefore, under the trust agreement, upon Charles Burdick's death, the trust property passed to the executors and into the estate, and from there, in accord with the provisions of the will, it passed on into the testamentary trust. Since the property would have first become a part of the estate, the conclusion then follows that it was subject to the probate court's jurisdiction [and the matter is res judicata].

. . . Accordingly, we must agree with the district court's determination that it is too late for appellants to object to the transfer of the 6,000 shares of Standard Oil of Indiana to Margaret Hewlett.

Between the years 1948 and 1963, Standard Oil of Indiana declared certain dividends to its stockholders, payable in shares of stock of Standard Oil of New Jersey. Standard Oil of Indiana had acquired these shares in 1932 when it transferred certain of its foreign properties to Standard Oil of New Jersey.

When paying on the dividends, Standard Oil of Indiana had designated that the value of distribution be of dividends in kind, payable in Standard Oil of New Jersey stock. The distribution was charged against the earned surplus of Standard Oil of Indiana. The dividends were not denominated as a return of capital. In every year in which such a dividend was paid, Standard Oil of Indiana sent notices to all stockholders receiving the dividends advising them to treat the dividends as income for the taxable year in which they were received.

Standard Oil Company of Indiana had sufficient earnings and earned surplus against which such charge was made. There is no evidence of record demonstrating that the stock dividend, in kind, of Standard of New Jersey, declared to the owners of Standard Oil Company of Indiana impinged upon the capital of Standard of Indiana, or amounted to a partial liquidation of Standard of Indiana. Further, the distribution of the stock dividend in kind of Standard Oil Company of New Jersey does not appear to have been made by Standard Oil Company of Indiana pursuant to a court decree or final administrative order by a government agency ordering distribution of the particular assets.

In Margaret Hewlett's estate, 18,298 shares of Standard Oil of New Jersey were attributable to dividends taken by Margaret Hewlett as income of the trust, the corpus of which was originally the 12,000 shares of Standard Oil of Indiana.

Currently, §34-18-106, W.S. 1977,[10] is the controlling statute for deciding whether the distribution of corporate stock is principal or

---

10. Section 34-18-106, W.S. 1977:

   (a)   Corporate distributions of shares of the distributing corporation, including distributions in the form of a stock split or stock dividend, are principal. A right to subscribe to shares or other securities issued by the distributing corporation accruing to stockholders on account of their stock ownership and the proceeds of any sale of the right are principal.
   (b)   Except to the extent that the corporation indicates that some part of a corporate distribution is a settlement of preferred or guaranteed dividends accrued since the trustee became a stockholder or is in lieu of an ordinary cash dividend, a corporate distribution is principal if the distribution is pursuant to:
      (i)   A call of shares;
      (ii)   A merger, consolidation, reorganization, or other plan by which assets of the corporation are acquired by another corporation; or

income. As part of the Uniform Principal and Income Act (1962 version), the statute was passed in 1963. . . . [I]t would be improper to apply the statute to the situation here since the legislation evinces a legislative intent that it not apply to receipts obtained before the effective date of the act. . . . Therefore, we are constrained to try and reconstruct what the law would have been before the passage of the statute.

The only Wyoming case which bears on the subject is Allith-Prouty Co. v. Wallace, 1925, 32 Wyo. 392, 233 P. 144, reh. den. 234 P. 504. There in dictum Justice Blume hinted that Wyoming would follow the Massachusetts rule. This rule was to the effect that dividends paid in stock of the declaring corporation were principal while dividends paid in either cash or in stock of another corporation were income unless they amounted to a partial liquidation of the corporate assets. The Massachusetts rule has long since the *Allith-Prouty Co.* decision become the majority rule and been embodied in the Restatement, Trust 2d §236. . . . We believe that the Restatement is consistent with *Allith-Prouty Co.* and also reflects the majority view of the country during the time in question. It is the law to be applied to the dividends paid in this case.

Turning to the facts in this case, since the dividends were distributed in stock of another corporation, the ultimate question for us to resolve is whether the payment of these dividends amounted to a partial liquidation of Standard Oil of Indiana.

. . . The dividends were charged against the earned surplus of Standard Oil of Indiana. There is no evidence that the capital of the corporation was impinged upon in any way. In light of the facts adduced

---

(iii) A total or partial liquidation of the corporation, including any distribution which the corporation indicates is a distribution in total or partial liquidation or any distribution of assets, other than cash, pursuant to a court decree or final administrative order by a government agency ordering distribution of the particular assets.

(c) Distributions made from ordinary income by a regulated investment company or by a trust qualifying and electing to be taxed under federal law as a real estate investment trust are income. All other distributions made by the company or trust, including distributions from capital gains, depreciation, or depletion, whether in the form of cash or an option to take new stock or cash or an option to purchase additional shares, are principal.

(d) Except as provided in subsections (a), (b), and (c), all corporate distributions are income, including cash dividends, distributions of or rights to subscribe to shares or securities or obligations of corporations other than the distributing corporation, and the proceeds of the rights or property distributions. Except as provided in subsections (b) and (c), if the distributing corporation gives a stockholder an option to receive a distribution either in cash or in its own shares, the distribution chosen is income.

(e) The trustee may rely upon any statement of the distributing corporation as to any fact relevant under any provision of this act concerning the source or character of dividends or distributions of corporate assets. [This Wyoming statute is taken verbatim from the revised Uniform Principal and Income Act §6 (1962).]

before the district court, we must conclude that the payment of Standard Oil of New Jersey stock as dividends by Standard Oil of Indiana did not amount to a partial liquidation; therefore, the dividends were properly treated as income.

At the time of his death, Charles Burdick was the owner of certain oil royalty interests located in Natrona County. These interests were overriding oil royalty interests arising out of federal leases. Prior to Mr. Burdick's death, oil wells had been drilled and he was receiving royalty payments. In accord with the provisions in the will, the royalty interests were placed in the testamentary trust. From the date of commencement of said trust down to the date of death of Margaret Hewlett, the total amount of royalties paid was in the sum of over six hundred thousand dollars. All of these payments were turned over to Margaret Hewlett and she treated the total amount thereof as income. No part of the payments were treated by her or accounted for by her as corpus of the trust and no reserve was set up for the benefit of the remaindermen of the trust.

The best statement of the law currently with respect to the rights of owners of successive legal interest in the mineral lands can be found in Scott on Trusts, Vol. III, §239.3. There it is stated:

> . . . Where the owner of such land creates a legal life estate in one person and a remainder in another, and it is not otherwise provided by the terms of the instrument by which the successive estates are created, it is held that if mines were opened prior to the creation of the estates the life tenant is entitled to continue to work the mines and to take the proceeds as his own without deduction for depletion. On the other hand, where no mines were opened prior to the creation of the estates, neither the life tenant nor the remainderman is entitled to open the mines without the consent of the other. If the life tenant does open mines, the proceeds will be treated as principal. . . . (Footnotes omitted.)

Here, the oil wells were producing before Mr. Burdick's death.

The purpose of the so-called "open mine" rule is to try and match testator's intent. Presumably where she/he has been receiving oil royalty payments she/he considers them to be income. Thus, absent some words of limitation in instrument creating a trust, it is assumed that testator intended the life tenant to enjoy the property in the same fashion and to the same extent it had been enjoyed by the testator. . . .

The Uniform Principal and Income Act does not dictate a different result. As stated in §34-18-109(b), W.S. 1977:

> (b) If a trustee, on the effective date of this act, held an item of depletable property of a type specified in this section he shall allocate receipts from the property in the manner used before the effective date of this act, but as to all depletable property acquired after the effective

date of this act by an existing or new trust, the method of allocation provided herein shall be used.

Thus, by its own terms, this trust was exempted from coverage since the corpus was acquired nearly forty years before the act.

Affirmed.

McCLINTOCK. J., dissenting in part. I agree that the "open-mine" principle should be applied if the mineral rights were producing royalties at the time the trust was created. I also agree that the "Massachusetts rule," espoused by this court in Allith-Prouty Co. v. Wallace, 32 Wyo. 392, 233 P. 144, 39 A.L.R. 513 (1925), reh. denied 234 P. 504, and essentially stated in Restatement of Trusts, Second, §236, that dividends "in property other than in shares of the holding corporation," should govern the treatment to be given the distribution of shares in New Jersey Standard by Indiana Standard.

However, the probate judge's ruling that the stock dividends consisting of 6,000 shares of Standard Oil Company of Indiana stock were income and should be distributed to Margaret Hewlett was contrary to the law of Wyoming. Four years prior to the probate court's ruling this court stated: "... Ordinarily a dividend declared in stock is to be deemed capital and not income. The interest of stockholders in a corporation remains unchanged upon the latter declaring a stock dividend. . . ." Allith-Prouty Company v. Wallace, supra, 32 Wyo. at 408 and 234 P. at 506.

As this court explained in *Allith-Prouty*, when a corporation declares a stock dividend it is merely increasing the number of shares that a stockholder owns without increasing the stockholder's interest in the corporation. By allowing Margaret Hewlett to treat the stock dividend as income, the probate judge reduced the percentage of the trust's ownership of the corporation. In other words, the principal of the trust and the contingent remaindermen's interest were substantially diminished. Therefore, the probate judge erred when he declared that the stock dividends were income of the trust and the remaindermen should be entitled to recover these shares of stock from Margaret Hewlett's estate.

The majority avoids this very logical and proper result by treating the action of the probate court of Laramie County as an error committed in the exercise of proper jurisdiction and, therefore, correctable only by timely appeal. I cannot agree . . . that the inter vivos trust property passed to the estate in accordance with the provisions of the will. While the 12,000 shares of Indiana were included in the inventory the probate judge did not treat them as part of the testamentary estate of Charles W. Burdick. What he did was to give effect to an instrument not before him and direct a person (the trustee of the inter vivos trust) likewise not before him to transfer part of the corpus of the trust to one entity (the testamentary trust) and another part of that corpus to another party (the life beneficiary). . . .

Appellees contend that appellants are barred from asserting the present claims by reason of the statute of limitations and laches. Once again, I cannot agree. Appellants did not have a right of action until the life estate was terminated. As a general rule neither the applicable statute of limitations nor laches will bar an action brought by remaindermen until the remaindermen are entitled to possession of the estate. . . . I find the theory behind this general rule particularly compelling in the case of contingent remaindermen like those in the case at bar because their interest may never become vested. Here the remaindermen's cause of action is not barred by the statute of limitations or laches.

NOTES

1.   The court in the principal case quotes Scott on Trusts §239.3, with regard to the open mines doctrine applicable to *legal* life estates and remainders. Should this doctrine apply to minerals held in trust? Section 9(a)(3) of the revised Uniform Principal and Income Act (1962) provides that 27½ percent of mineral royalties shall be added to income and the balance treated as income. The fractional share allotted to principal has been changed in several states adopting the act to "such portion of the gross receipts as shall be allowed as a deduction for depletion in computing taxable income for federal income tax purposes." See, e.g., N.Y. Est., Powers & Trusts Law §11-2.1(h)(1) (Supp. 1989).

On apportionment of wasting assets other than minerals (such as patents, copyrights, and artists' royalties), see Abravanel, Apportioning Receipts from Wasting Assets Under the Uniform Laws: A Proposal for Legislative Reform, 58 N.C.L. Rev. 255 (1980).

2.   For a comprehensive study of allocation of stock dividends before the triumph of the Massachusetts rule, see Flickinger, A Trustee's Nightmare: Allocation of Stock Dividends Between Income and Principal, 43 B.U.L. Rev. 199 (1963). While it has been adopted in nearly every jurisdiction, the Massachusetts rule on the allocation of stock dividends is not without its critics. See Comment, Effectuating the Settlor's Intent: A Formula for Providing More Income for the Life Beneficiary, 33 U. Chi. L. Rev. 783 (1966); Note, Range of Returns: A New Approach to the Allocation of Trust Gains and Losses, 21 Stan. L. Rev. 420 (1969); Comment, Trust Allocation Doctrine and Corporate Stock: The Law Must Respond to Economics, 50 Tex. L. Rev. 747 (1972).

3. Because of the insensitivity of the Massachusetts rule and the other allocation rules previously discussed, trusts are usually drafted with a provision that the trustee shall have discretion to allot receipts or expenses to principal or income. Courts are generally reluctant to interfere with the trustee's allocation and will uphold the trustee's action if it is made reasonably and in good faith. However, the existence of statutes or common law regulating allocation to principal and income has profoundly affected the latitude of discretion considered allowable for the trustee. Courts often read a discretionary clause narrowly. Even where there is a broad discretionary power, some cases have held that the legally permissible area of discretion is limited to those issues on which there is some doubt under state law. For example, in In re Clarenbach's Will, 23 Wis. 2d 71, 126 N.W.2d 614 (1964), noted in 50 Iowa L. Rev. 656, 48 Marq. L. Rev. 262, 1965 Wis. L. Rev. 391, the trustees had power to allocate receipts between principal and income "and the decision of the executors [trustees] shall be final and not subject to question by any court or by any beneficiary hereof." The trustees allocated half the capital gains realized upon sale of stock to income. Under the Uniform Principal and Income Act, adopted in Wisconsin, capital gain enures to principal. The court held, 4-3, that this allocation was an abuse of discretion. The dissent pointed out that the true nature of profits was a subject of much debate among economists and that one of the purposes of the discretionary clause was to permit flexibility in favoring the life tenant or remainderman in order to do equity between them. See also England v. First National Bank of Birmingham, 381 So. 2d 8 (Ala. 1980).

4. What effect should portfolio theory (see infra page 912) have on allocation of receipts between principal and income? Consider the following excerpt.

Gordon, The Puzzling Persistence of the Constrained
Prudent Man Rule
62 N.Y.U.L. Rev. 52, 99-107 (1987)

The most important aspect of trust law cast into doubt by . . . portfolio theory . . . is the traditional allocation of investment returns. No principle in the law of trusts seems more settled than the rule that income beneficiaries receive ordinary cash dividends from common stock ownership and remaindermen receive capital gains if the stock is sold. The only skirmishing is on the edges of the rule, regarding, for example, the allocation of extraordinary cash dividends or stock dividends. Acceptance of portfolio theory, however, would undermine the traditional rule. The economic models on which portfolio theory relies all calculate investment returns based on the total return during a specific period — cash payouts (dividends and interest) plus gain or loss. The analysis of covariance or comovement among securities returns, which provides the basis for determining the amount of risk a particular security adds to a portfolio, depends upon this total return definition.

A division of a firm's return between income and capital gain is highly artificial from the perspective of financial economics. Imagine two firms, *A* and *B*. For every hundred dollars of shareholders' equity, each earns ten dollars. *A*, thinking its primary business has reached a no-growth steady state, pays out all earnings as dividends. *B*, thinking its business provides additional investment opportunities, reinvests all earnings, which leads to an increase in the price of its shares. Each firm is providing comparable economic return to its shareholders; only the form is different. But a trustee holding *A* must pay out all dividends to income beneficiaries, even if, because of inflation, the purchasing power of the remainder interest, the *A* stock in the portfolio, is meanwhile depreciating. A trustee holding *B* can pay out nothing to income beneficiaries, even if the remainder interest is increasing in value because of *B*'s decision to reinvest earnings that would otherwise be available to an income beneficiary.

To assure fairness between income beneficiaries and remaindermen, the trustee may have to adopt an investment policy that mixes *A* and *B* stock. Alternatively, present law apparently allows the trustee to refuse to hold *B*. The result in either case will be a portfolio that is not optimally diversified; it has not been assembled with the objective of producing the greatest expected returns for the risk. It is easy to see why systematic exclusion of companies with low dividends but high reinvestment rates will upset a diversification scheme. But there is no assurance that a portfolio that emphasizes balance between high and low dividend-paying securities will be well-diversified in other respects. The allocation of total returns between income and principal compelled by settled trust law is profoundly inconsistent with the portfolio theory paradigm. . . .

The starting point must be certain assumptions about the customary intent of the settlor. What can we infer from the settlor's general instructions that the income from a property should go to certain people now alive and that the principal should go to others, who may or may not be alive, or which may be charitable institutions rather than individuals? The settlor's main object is most likely a continuous income stream to the life beneficiaries, but how should that stream be fashioned, and who should bear the risks of uneven returns? The focus should be on the stability in real terms of both the payouts and the corpus — payouts, because of the settlor's presumed desire to provide a constant level of support, and corpus, because stable payouts ultimately depend upon the corpus, and because of the settlor's presumed desire to transfer wealth dynastically. . . .

[After discussing alternative approaches, the author recommends a "payout of adjusted real yield" approach.]

An adjusted real yield approach contemplates that the life beneficiaries will receive payouts geared to the real yield of the portfolio. The payout is based on total portfolio returns for the period (income and capital gains) after correcting for any loss in the real value of the corpus, whether from inflation or capital loss. This approach requires no assumptions about the long-term portfolio yields or the rate of inflation. Moreover, preservation of the corpus follows automatically under the adjusted real yield approach, protecting the life beneficiary's income stream and the remainder interest.

The only problem is that the stability of corpus comes at the expense of a stable income stream, in nominal or real terms, to the life beneficiaries. The requirement that the value of the corpus be held constant even taking into account capital losses makes this problem particularly acute. It is easy to imagine periods in which the total real returns on a well-managed portfolio would be minimal, if not negative. Thus, a real yield approach would not always supply steady maintenance for the life beneficiaries.

How can this income stability problem be addressed? One way is to set a tentative payout assumption based on long-term average real yields and construct a stabilization account that reflects surpluses or shortfalls. In years of higher-than-average returns, the account would accumulate funds that would cover payouts in leaner years. The account could be bounded above and below; at a certain point, the payout assumption would change to reflect accumulated higher or lower returns. Thus the adjusted real yield approach suggested here is based on real portfolio yields, but it would use a stabilization fund to smooth out the variability in actual payouts.

Such an approach comes closest to effectuating the settlor's objective of a steady real income stream that nevertheless admits of some variation. It is almost certain that this approach will produce higher average sustainable real payouts for the life beneficiaries than either fixed payout approach. If the stabilization account is properly conceived, both the life beneficiaries and the remainder interest can be protected against dramatic shifts in conditions. This approach also underscores the proper emphasis of trustee investment management: producing a steady stream of real returns while managing the inevitable flux of market conditions.

Professor Langbein has furnished us with the University of Chicago's Total Return Investment Pool (TRIP) formula, which could be used in private trusts to smooth out fluctuations in total return from year to year and avoid the volatility of the stock market.

> Under this formula, the payout [from the endowment] to the budget [for current expenses] is 5 percent of a specially calculated ten-year average. The average is constructed by taking the year-end market values of the TRIP endowment for the preceding ten years (adjusted for new gifts), eliminating the highest two years and the lowest two years, and then averaging the remaining six years.

SECTION B.   POWERS OF THE TRUSTEE

1.   General Managerial Powers

In the absence of legislation, the administrative powers of a trustee are derived exclusively from the instrument creating the trust. There are supposedly no "inherent" powers in a trustee; the task of management differs from that of an executor, who has inherent powers to collect the decedent's property, pay debts, and distribute the property to the beneficiaries. The task of a trustee is to carry out the settlor's intent, which varies from trust to trust.

Although a trustee's administrative powers are to be ascertained initially from the trust instrument, a trustee is not limited to powers expressly conferred. Certain powers may be implied as necessary to accomplish the purposes of the trust. Under proper circumstances, a court of equity can confer powers on a trustee not expressly or impliedly provided in the trust instrument; a deviation from the terms of the trust may be permitted when, because of circumstances not known to the settlor and not anticipated, failure to grant relief would substantially impair the accomplishment of the purposes of the trust.

Having in mind the uncertainty of trustees' powers, legislatures in a large majority of states have enacted legislation to broaden trustees' powers. This legislation has usually taken one of three forms:

(a)   An act permits the settlor to *incorporate by reference* in the trust instrument all or some enumerated statutory powers similar to those found in Uniform Trustees' Powers Act §3(c) below.

(b)   A broad trustees' powers act *grants to trustees* basic powers set forth in the statute, as exemplified by Uniform Trustees' Powers Act §3(c).

(c)   A statute gives a trustee the power to act as a *prudent man* dealing with the property of another, as provided in Uniform Trustees' Powers Act §3(a) and Uniform Probate Code §7-302.[11]

See T. Shaffer, The Planning and Drafting of Wills and Trusts 103-107 (2d ed. 1979).

Uniform Trustees' Powers Act (1985)

§3 [Powers of Trustees Conferred by This Act]

(a)   From time of creation of the trust until final distribution of the assets of the trust, a trustee has the power to perform, without court authorization, every act which a prudent man would perform for the purposes of the trust including but not limited to the powers specified in subsection (c).

(b)   In the exercise of his powers including the powers granted by this Act, a trustee has a duty to act with due regard to his obligation as a fiduciary, including a duty not to exercise any power under this Act in such a way as to deprive the trust of an otherwise available tax exemption, deduction, or credit for tax purposes or deprive a donor of a trust asset of a tax exemption, deduction, or credit or operate to impose a tax upon a donor or other person as owner of any portion of the trust. "Tax" includes, but is not limited to, any federal, state, or local income, gift, estate, or inheritance tax.

(c)   A trustee has the power, subject to subsections (a) and (b):

(1)   to collect, hold, and retain trust assets received from a trustor until, in the judgment of the trustee, disposition of the assets should be made; and the assets may be retained even though they include an asset in which the trustee is personally interested;

(2)   to receive additions to the assets of the trust;

(3)   to continue or participate in the operation of any business or other enterprise, and to effect incorporation, dissolution, or other change in the form of the organization of the business or enterprise;

(4)   to acquire an undivided interest in a trust asset in which the trustee, in any trust capacity, holds an undivided interest;

(5)   to invest and reinvest trust assets in accordance with the provisions of the trust or as provided by law;

---

11. Uniform Probate Code §3-715 provides broad enumerated powers for the *personal representative* very similar to Uniform Trustees' Powers Act §3(c). UPC §7-302 provides that a *trustee* shall administer the trust as "a prudent man dealing with the property of another."

(6) to deposit trust funds in a bank, including a bank operated by the trustee;

(7) to acquire or dispose of an asset, for cash or on credit, at public or private sale; and to manage, develop, improve, exchange, partition, change the character of, or abandon a trust asset or any interest therein; and to encumber, mortgage, or pledge a trust asset for a term within or extending beyond the term of the trust, in connection with the exercise of any power vested in the trustee;

(8) to make ordinary or extraordinary repairs or alterations in buildings or other structures, to demolish any improvements, to raze existing or erect new party walls or buildings;

(9) to subdivide, develop, or dedicate land to public use; or to make or obtain the vacation of plats and adjust boundaries; or to adjust differences in valuation on exchange or partition by giving or receiving consideration; or to dedicate easements to public use without consideration;

(10) to enter for any purpose into a lease as lessor or lessee with or without option to purchase or renew for a term within or extending beyond the term of the trust;

(11) to enter into a lease or arrangement for exploration and removal of minerals or other natural resources or enter into a pooling or unitization agreement;

(12) to grant an option involving disposition of a trust asset, or to take an option for the acquisition of any asset;

(13) to vote a security, in person or by general or limited proxy;

(14) to pay calls, assessments, and any other sums chargeable or accruing against or on account of securities;

(15) to sell or exercise stock subscription or conversion rights; to consent, directly or through a committee or other agent, to the reorganization, consolidation, merger, dissolution, or liquidation of a corporation or other business enterprise;

(16) to hold a security in the name of a nominee or in other form without disclosure of the trust, so that title to the security may pass by delivery, but the trustee is liable for any act of the nominee in connection with the stock so held;

(17) to insure the assets of the trust against damage or loss, and the trustee against liability with respect to third persons;

(18) to borrow money to be repaid from trust assets or otherwise; to advance money for the protection of the trust, and for all expenses, losses, and liabilities sustained in the administration of the trust or because of the holdings or ownership of any trust assets, for which advances with any interest the trustee has a lien on the trust assets as against the beneficiary;

(19) to pay or contest any claim; to settle a claim by or against the trust by compromise, arbitration, or otherwise; and to release, in whole

or in part, any claim belonging to the trust to the extent that the claim is uncollectible;

(20)   to pay taxes, assessments, compensation of the trustee, and other expenses incurred in the collection, care, administration, and protection of the trust;

(21)   to allocate items of income or expense to either trust income or principal, as provided by law, including creation of reserves out of income for depreciation, obsolescence, or amortization, or for depletion in mineral or timber properties;

(22)   to pay any sum distributable to a beneficiary under legal disability, without liability to the trustee, by paying the sum to the beneficiary or by paying the sum for the use of the beneficiary either to a legal representative appointed by the court, or if none, to a relative;

(23)   to effect distribution of property and money in divided or undivided interests and to adjust resulting differences in valuation;

(24)   to employ persons, including attorneys, auditors, investment advisors, or agents, even if they are associated with the trustee, to advise or assist the trustee in the performance of his administrative duties; to act without independent investigation upon their recommendations; and instead of acting personally, to employ one or more agents to perform any act of administration, whether or not discretionary;

(25)   to prosecute or defend actions, claims, or proceedings for the protection of trust assets and of the trustee in the performance of his duties;

(26)   to execute and deliver all instruments which will accomplish or facilitate the exercise of the powers vested in the trustee.

PROBLEMS

1.   The testator devises his residuary estate to Security Bank in trust for his wife for life, remainder to his children. In the testator's residuary estate are 200 shares of Security Bank stock. May Security Bank retain this stock in the trust? See Uniform Trustees' Powers Act §3(c)(1); Hallgring, The Uniform Trustees' Powers Act and the Basic Principles of Fiduciary Responsibility, 41 Wash. L. Rev. 801, 813-816 (1966). Suppose the state has an incorporation by reference statute and the testator's will incorporates by reference all powers in the state act, one of which is similar to UTPA §3(c)(1). What result? See Note, The North Carolina Fiduciary Powers Act and the Duty of Loyalty, 45 N.C.L. Rev. 1141 (1967).

2.   Under Uniform Trustees' Powers Act §3(c)(20), can a trustee determine its own fee? Customarily, trustees' fees are fixed by statute or determined by a court. Is this provision of the Uniform Act wise? See Hallgring, Problem 1 supra, 816-818.

3.   Security Bank, acting as trustee, pays itself a fee for employing a bookkeeper to keep records and another fee for receiving investment advice from its investment advisory committee. Such fees would not be proper under the common law because of the prohibition against self-hiring. Are they proper under Uniform Trustees' Powers Act §3(c)(24)? See Hallgring, Problem 1 supra, 819-823; Haskell, Some Problems with the Uniform Trustees' Powers Act, 32 Law & Contemp. Prob. 168, 175-179 (1967).

4.   Read §3(b) of the Uniform Act carefully. Do you see any hazards to a trustee here? Many states adopting the Uniform Act declined to adopt §3(b).

Uniform Trustees' Powers Act (1985)

§7 [THIRD PERSONS PROTECTED IN DEALING WITH TRUSTEE]

With respect to a third person dealing with a trustee or assisting a trustee in the conduct of a transaction, the existence of trust power[s] and their proper exercise by a trustee may be assumed without inquiry. The third person is not bound to inquire whether the trustee has power to act or is properly exercising the power; and a third person, without actual knowledge that the trustee is exceeding his powers or improperly exercising them, is fully protected in dealing with the trustee as if the trustee possessed and properly exercised the powers he purports to exercise. A third person is not bound to assure the proper application of trust assets paid or delivered to the trustee.

Uniform Trustees' Powers Act §7 provides unusually broad protection for third persons who deal with the trustee. The common law puts a duty of inquiry upon the third person in certain circumstances. Scott says:

> Whether a person who deals with another who is in fact a trustee is under a duty to inquire whether he is a trustee and whether he is committing a breach of trust in making the transfer, and, if so, to what extent inquiry should be made, depends on the circumstances. A purchaser or mortgagee or pledgee of trust property may be under such a duty where persons dealing with the trustee in other ways would be under no such duty. So also a purchaser of land may be under a duty of inquiry where a purchaser of negotiable paper would be under no such duty. In other words, the existence and the extent of a duty of inquiry may depend on the character of the transaction, and may depend on the character of the trust property. [4 A. Scott, Trusts §297 (W. Fratcher 4th ed. 1988).]

PROBLEMS

1. *T* devises Blackacre to *X* in trust with power to sell Blackacre if *X* decides that such sale is necessary to raise money for the support of *A*. *X* sells Blackacre to *B*, who has notice of the trust (*T*'s will is recorded) but believes that the sale is necessary for the support of *A*, although in fact it is not necessary. Does *B* take Blackacre free of trust? See 2 Restatement (Second) of Trusts §297, Illustration 4 (1959). Would the result be different if the trust were an inter vivos trust of which *B* had no notice?

2. *X*, as trustee, has no power to invest in nonincome-producing property. *X* buys from *A* desert land, which produces no income. Must *A* refund the purchase price upon demand of the beneficiary? See 4 A. Scott, Trusts §321.1 (W. Fratcher 4th ed. 1988).

3. *X* is a co-trustee with *Y* of Whiteacre. *X* and *Y* have the power to sell Whiteacre; they sell it to *A*. *A* pays the purchase price to *Y* alone without the consent of *X*, and *Y* misappropriates the money. Can *A* be compelled to pay again? See Coxe v. Kriebel, 323 Pa. 157, 185 A. 770, 106 A.L.R. 102 (1936).

Allard v. Pacific National Bank
Supreme Court of Washington, 1983
99 Wash. 2d 394, 663 P.2d 104

DOLLIVER, J. Plaintiffs Freeman Allard and Evelyn Orkney are beneficiaries of trusts established by their parents, J.T. and Georgiana Stone. Defendant Pacific National Bank (Pacific Bank) is the trustee of the Stone trusts. Plaintiffs appeal a King County Superior Court decision dismissing their action against Pacific Bank for breach of its fiduciary duties as trustee of the Stone trusts. . . .

J.T. and Georgiana Stone, both deceased, established trusts in their wills conveying their property upon their deaths to Pacific Bank to be held for their chidren and the issue of their children. The Stones' children, Evelyn Orkney and Freeman Allard, are life income beneficiaries of the Stone trusts. Upon the death of either life income beneficiary, the trustee is to pay the income from the trust to the issue of the deceased beneficiary. When all the children of the deceased beneficiary reach the age of 21 years, the trusts direct the trustee to distribute the trust corpus equally among the issue of that beneficiary.

In 1978 the sole asset of the Stone trusts was a fee interest in a quarter block located on the northwest corner of Third Avenue and Columbia Street in downtown Seattle. The trust provisions of the wills gave Pacific Bank "full power to . . . manage, improve, sell, lease, mortgage, pledge, encumber, and exchange the whole or any part of the assets of [the] trust estate" and required Pacific Bank to "exercise the judgment and care under the circumstances then prevailing, which prudent men exercise in the management of their own affairs, not in regard to speculation but in regard to the permanent disposition of their funds, considering the probable income as well as the probable safety of their capital."

The Third and Columbia property was subject to a 99-year lease, entered into by the Stones in 1952 with Seattle-First National Bank (Seafirst Bank). The lease contained no rental escalation provision and the rental rate was to remain the same for the entire 99-year term of the lease. The right of first refusal to purchase the lessor's interest in the property was given to the lessee. The lease also contained several restrictive provisions. One paragraph required any repair, reconstruction, or replacement of buildings on the property by the lessee to be completed within 8 months from the date the original building was damaged or destroyed "from any cause whatsoever." Another paragraph provided that, upon termination of lease, the lessee had the option either to surrender possession of all improvements or to remove the improvements. The lease prohibited, without the lessor's consent, any encumbrance which would have priority over the lessor in case of the lessee's insolvency.

In June 1977 Seafirst Bank assigned its leasehold interest in the Third and Columbia property to the City Credit Union of Seattle (Credit Union). Eight months later, on February 14, 1978, Credit Union offered to purchase the property from Pacific Bank for $139,900. On April 25, 1978, Pacific Bank informed Credit Union it was interested in selling the property, but demanded at least $200,000. In early June 1978, Credit Union offered $200,000 for the Third and Columbia property. Pacific Bank accepted Credit Union's offer, and deeded the property to Credit Union on August 17, 1978. On September 26, 1978, Pacific Bank informed Freeman Allard and Evelyn Orkney of the sale to Credit Union.

On May 1, 1979, plaintiffs commenced the present action against Pacific Bank for breach of its fiduciary duties regarding management of the Stone trusts. . . .

At trial, the primary dispute was over the degree of care owed by Pacific Bank to the Stone trusts and to the Stone trust beneficiaries. . . .

At the culmination of the trial, the court entered judgment dismissing plaintiffs' action against Pacific Bank. It determined Pacific Bank acted in good faith and in conformance with its duties under the Stone trust instruments. The court concluded Pacific Bank neither had a duty to inform the trust beneficiaries prior to sale of the Third and Columbia property nor a duty to obtain an independent appraisal of the property or to place the property on the open market. . . . From this judgment plaintiffs bring appeal.

. . . Defendant contends it had full authority under the trust instrument to exercise its own judgment and impartial discretion in deciding how to invest the trust assets and a duty to use reasonable care and skill to make the trust property productive. It further contends the sale of the property was conducted in good faith and with honest judgment. Plaintiffs assert this discretion was limited by its fiduciary duties and that defendant in its management of the trusts breached its fiduciary duty.

Plaintiffs' argument regarding Pacific Bank's alleged breach of its fiduciary duties is twofold. First, Pacific Bank had a duty to inform them of the sale of the Third and Columbia property. Second, Pacific Bank breached its fiduciary duties by failing either to obtain an independent appraisal of the Third and Columbia property or to place the property on the open market prior to selling it to Seattle Credit Union. We agree with plaintiffs' position in both instances and hold defendant breached its fiduciary duty in its management of the trusts.

A

Initially, plaintiffs and amicus curiae the Attorney General of the State of Washington contend Pacific Bank should be held to a higher standard of care than the ordinary, prudent investor standard provided in R.C.W. 30.24.020. Plaintiffs and amicus curiae argue the ordinary, prudent investor standard is inappropriate where the trustee represents that it has greater skill than that of a nonprofessional trustee. They fail to mention, however, the terms of the Stone trust agreements which specifically adopt the prudent investor standard of care provided in R.C.W. 30.24.020.

R.C.W. 30.24.020 provides:

> In acquiring, investing, reinvesting, exchanging, selling and managing property for the benefit of another, a fiduciary shall exercise the judgment and care *under the circumstances* then prevailing, which *men of prudence*, discretion and intelligence exercise *in the management of their own affairs*, not in regard to speculation but in regard to the permanent disposition of their funds, considering the probable income as well as the probable safety of their capital. (Italics ours.)

Under the trust agreements, Pacific Bank is required as trustee to "exercise the judgment and care under the circumstances then prevailing, which prudent men exercise in the management of their own affairs, not in regard to speculation but in regard to the permanent disposition of their funds, considering the probable income as well as the probable safety of their capital."

Significantly, the statute recognizes the standard of care required of a trustee is "subject to any express provisions or limitations contained in any particular trust instrument." R.C.W. 30.24.020. Furthermore, the terms of the trust instrument control as to the investments made by a trustee. R.C.W. 30.24.070. Except where impossible, illegal, or where a change of circumstances occurs which would impair the purposes of the trust, the nature and extent of the duties and powers of a trustee are determined by the trust agreement. See Baldus v. Bank of Cal., 12 Wash. App. [621,] at 628, 530 P.2d 1350 [1975]; Steiner v. Hawaiian Trust Co., 47 Hawaii 548, 562-63, 393 P.2d 96 (1964). Although in some future cases we may be called upon to determine if a corporate professional trustee should be held to a higher standard because of the language in the trust instruments, this issue need not be decided here. Cf. Restatement (Second) of Trusts §227, comment d (1959).

B

The Stone trusts gave Pacific Bank "full power to . . . manage, improve, sell, lease, mortgage, pledge, encumber, and exchange the whole or any part of the assets of [the] trust estate." Under such an agreement, the trustee is not required to secure the consent of trust beneficiaries before selling trust assets. 3 A. Scott, Trusts §190.5 (3d ed. 1967). Accord, Bulla v. Valley Nat'l Bank, 82 Ariz. 84, 308 P.2d 932 (1957); In re Wellman Estate, 119 Vt. 426, 127 A.2d 279 (1956). The trustee owes to the beneficiaries, however, the highest degree of good faith, care, loyalty, and integrity. Esmieu v. Schrag, 88 Wash. 2d 490, 498, 563 P.2d 203 (1977); Monroe v. Winn, 16 Wash. 2d 497, 508, 133 P.2d 952 (1943).

Pacific Bank claims it was obligated to sell the property to Credit Union since Credit Union, as assignee of the lease agreement with Seafirst Bank, had a right of first refusal to purchase the property. Since it did not need to obtain the consent of the beneficiaries before selling trust assets, Pacific Bank argues it also was not required to inform the beneficiaries of the sale. We disagree. The beneficiaries could have offered to purchase the property at a higher price than the offer by Credit Union, thereby forcing Credit Union to pay a higher price to exercise its right of first refusal as assignee of the lease agreement. Furthermore, letters from the beneficiaries to Pacific Bank indicated their desire to retain the Third and Columbia property. While the beneficiaries could not have prevented Pacific Bank from selling the property, they presumably could have outbid Credit Union for the property. This opportunity should have been afforded to them.

On a previous occasion, we ruled the trustee's fiduciary duty includes the responsibility to inform the beneficiaries fully of all facts which would aid them in protecting their interests. Esmieu v. Schrag, supra. See United States v. Bennett, 57 F. Supp. 670 (E.D. Wash. 1944). We adhere to the view expressed in *Esmieu.* That the settlor has created a trust and thus required the beneficiaries to enjoy their property interests indirectly does not imply the beneficiaries are to be kept in ignorance of the trust, the nature of the trust property, and the details of its administration. G. Bogert, Trusts and Trustees §961 (2d ed. 1962). If the beneficiaries are able to hold the trustee to proper standards of care and honesty and procure the benefits to which they are entitled, they must know of what the trust property consists and how it is being managed. G. Bogert, Trusts and Trustees, supra.

The duty to provide information is often performed by corporate trustees by rendering periodic statements to the beneficiaries, usually in the form of copies of the ledger sheets concerning the trust. G. Bogert, Trusts §141 (5th ed. 1973). For example, such condensed explanations of recent transactions may be mailed to the beneficiaries annually, semiannually, or quarterly. G. Bogert, Trusts, supra. Ordinarily, periodic statements are sufficient to satisfy a trustee's duty to beneficiaries of transactions affecting the trust property. The trust provisions here, for example, provide the trustee "shall furnish on or before February 15 of each year to each person described in Section 1 of Article IV who is then a beneficiary . . . a statement showing how the respective trust assets are invested and all transactions relating thereto for the preceding calendar year."

The trustee must inform beneficiaries, however, of all material facts in connection with a nonroutine transaction which significantly affects the trust estate and the interests of the beneficiaries prior to the transaction taking place. The duty to inform is particularly required in this case where the only asset of the trusts was the property on the corner of Third and Columbia. Under the circumstances found in this case failure to inform was an egregious breach of fiduciary duty and defies the course of conduct any reasonable person would take, much less a prudent investor.

C

We also conclude Pacific Bank breached its fiduciary duties regarding management of the Stone trusts by failing to obtain the best possible price for the Third and Columbia property. Pacific Bank made no attempt to obtain a more favorable price for the property from Credit Union by, for example, negotiating to cancel the restrictive provisions in the lease originally negotiated with Seafirst Bank. Cf. Hatcher v. United States Nat'l Bank, 56 Or. App. 643, 643 P.2d 359 (1982) (trustee had not fulfilled its fiduciary duties by merely examining offer to purchase and altering the terms slightly). The bank neither offered the property for sale on the open market, see Rippey v. Denver United States Nat'l Bank, 273 F. Supp. 718 (D. Colo. 1967), nor did it obtain an independent outside appraisal of the Third and Columbia property to determine its fair market value. See Belcher v. Birmingham Trust Nat'l Bank, 348 F. Supp. 61 (N.D. Ala. 1968); Webb & Knapp, Inc. v. Hanover Bank, 214 Md. 230, 133 A.2d 450 (1957).

Washington courts have not yet considered the nature of a trustee's duty of care regarding the sale of trust assets. Other courts, however, generally require that a trustee when selling trust assets try to obtain the maximum price for the asset. E.g., Berner v. Equitable Office Bldg. Corp., 175 F.2d 218, 221 (2d Cir. 1949); Terry v. Midwest Ref. Co., 64 F.2d 428 (10th Cir.), cert. denied, 290 U.S. 660 (1933); Lockwood v. OFB Corp., 305 A.2d 636, 638 (Del. Ch. 1973); Ross v. Wilson, 308 N.Y. 605, 127 N.E.2d 697 (1955). The Oregon Court of Appeals required a trustee to determine the fair market value of trust property prior to selling the property by obtaining an appraisal or by "testing the market" to determine what a willing buyer would pay. Hatcher v. United States Nat'l Bank, 56 Or. App. at 652, 643 P.2d 359. Some courts specifically require trustees to obtain an independent appraisal of the property. See, e.g., Belcher v. Birmingham Trust Nat'l Bank, 348 F. Supp. 61 (N.D. Ala. 1968); Webb & Knapp, Inc. v. Hanover Bank, 214 Md. 230, 133 A.2d 450 (1957). Other courts merely require that a trustee determine fair market value by placing the property on the open market. See, e.g., Lockwood v. OFB Corp., supra; State v. Hartman, 54 Wis. 2d 47, 194 N.W.2d 653 (1972).

We agree with the Oregon Court of Appeals in *Hatcher* that a trustee may determine the best possible price for trust property either by obtaining an independent appraisal of the property or by "testing the market" to determine what a willing buyer would pay. The record discloses none of these actions were taken by the defendant. By its failure to obtain the best possible price for the Third and Columbia property, defendant breached its fiduciary duty as the prudent manager of the trusts.

. . . The case is remanded for a determination of the damages caused to plaintiffs by defendant's breach of its fiduciary duties as trustee of the Stone trusts. . . .

For a case where the trustees were surcharged $1.9 million for failing to make adequate efforts to determine the property's value before sale, see In re Green Charitable Trust, 172 Mich. App. 298, 431 N.W. 2d 492 (1988).

2. Powers of Investment

Fleming, Prudent Investments: The Varying Standards of Prudence
12 Real Prop., Prob. & Tr. J. 234-248 (1977)

A general rule of prudence in making investments has always been imposed on trustees of trusts. The difficulty through the years has come in its application to specific investments and in the yardstick to be used for the determination. By the late 18th century, the rule in England had largely crystallized to the effect that only government-backed investments . . . were sufficiently safe to justify their inclusion in trust portfolios.

When, in the early 19th century, American courts came to consider the question of what were prudent trustee investments, . . . they were obliged to consider whether American trustees should be limited to securities of the fledgling nation or be allowed a more expanded range.

In one of the earliest American cases, the Supreme Court of Massachusetts in Harvard College v. Amory, [26 Mass. (9 Pick.) 446 (1830),] decided in 1830, observed that do what a trustee would, the capital of a trust was always at risk, and sanctioned a flexible standard for trustee action embracing any category of investment, including common stocks, so long as it was within the bounds of good judgment and care. All that can be expected of a trustee, said the court, is that he "conduct himself faithfully and exercise a sound discretion," and heed how other men of prudence, discretion and intelligence manage their affairs, not for speculation, but for the permanent disposition of their funds.

In this view, the test of prudence is one of *conduct*, rather than of performance or result. It is how the trustee does his job and not particularly whether he succeeds or fails. Has he used the care and judgment that other prudent investors employ as to the permanent investment of their funds? If so, that is all the law can reasonably demand of him. In this frame of reference, common stocks were as much within the range of permissible investments as bonds and mortgages. . . .

No little responsibility for the failure of the Prudent Man [Rule to give sound investment guidance] . . . must be attributed to the text writers and commentators on trust subjects, particularly the Restatement of Trusts (Second) [§§227, 228]. The interpretation of the Prudent Man Rule and its implications to be found in the Restatement points away from the adaptability approach of *Harvard College* and toward the ancient standards of prudence of the English common law. Thus, . . . in Scott on Trusts [§227], and in the Restatement of Trusts, (Second) [§§227, 228] the phrase "men of prudence" becomes a hypothetical single "prudent man" and the concept of managing their own affairs becomes "safeguarding the property of others." The standard which a trustee must observe, says Scott, is not that which he would use in dealing with his own property but that of one who is a *trustee of another's property*.

Courts and commentators, in turn, reflected this slant. . . . [T]he court decisions and commentaries have breathed into the language the traditional rules of trusteeship, with a renewed emphasis on conservation and a distinction between "speculation" and "investment." The rule to be applied is that which is applicable to one who acts as *trustee* of the property of another. In recent cases this concept of *acting as trustee for another* has been enlarged upon by adding that if the trustee has special skills or expertise he will be judged by the standards of care and judgment appropriate to a professional trustee.

The Uniform Probate Code has been adopted in certain states and is under consideration in others. It provides in section 7-302 that "a trustee shall observe the standards in dealing with the trust assets that would be observed by a prudent man dealing with the property of another, and if the trustee has special skills or is named trustee on the basis of representations of special skills or expertise, he is under a duty to use those skills," thus mirroring the same observations.

To the uninitiated, these glosses may not seem significant departures, but it is submitted that there is a considerable difference between what businessmen are permitted to do in regard to their own affairs in a contemporary economic climate and what a person must do as trustee in managing the affairs of another. The *Harvard College* standard is capable of adapting to changing times and changing notions of investment opportunity and risk taking, whereas the concept of prudence reflected in Scott, in the Restatement of Trusts, (Second) and in the Uniform Probate Code is static. It imports conventional limitations for the preservation of capital and the avoidance of risk taking which the law of trusts has imposed on trustees for centuries. Further, the importation of a double standard depending on whether the trustee has or has not special skills or expertise as to investments, is unfortunate and in recent cases has lent itself as a justification for penalizing corporate trustees. Expertise is a relative quality at best. In today's fast-moving business milieu, factors beyond the control of any trustee, professional or nonprofessional, too often intervene to make expertise a fair or appropriate test for prudent conduct.

The effect of these strictures is to deter conscientious trustees from doing the best investment job they are capable of, and to limit their selections to "favorite fifty" lists and the like. This, in turn, leads to investment "tiers" and the overpricing of stocks of certain companies and underpricing those of others, even though of good investment quality. The emergence of so-called Index Funds — in reality a mutual fund concept — with the investments taken from Standard & Poor's 500 (on the theory that the averages outperform individually selected portfolios), is an over-reaction to a concern for the risk taking involved in individually selected investment portfolios.

Estate of Collins

California Court of Appeal, Second District, 1977
72 Cal. App. 3d 663, 139 Cal. Rptr. 644

KAUS, J.   Objectors ("plaintiffs") are beneficiaries under a testamentary trust established in the will of Ralph Collins, deceased. Carl Lamb and C.E. Millikan ("defendants") were, respectively, Collins' business partner and lawyer. They were named in Collins' will as trustees. In 1973 defendants filed a petition for an order approving and settling the first and final account and discharging the trustees. Plaintiffs objected on grounds that defendants had improperly invested $50,000 and requested that defendants be surcharged. After a hearing, the trial court ruled in favor of defendants, and approved the account, terminated the trust, and discharged the trustees. Plaintiff beneficiaries have appealed. . . .

The primary beneficiaries under the testamentary trust were Collins' wife and children; his mother and father were also named as beneficiaries. General support provisions were included; the will also specifically provided that the trustees pay his daughter $4,000 a year for five years for her undergraduate and graduate education.

The will authorized the trustees to purchase "every kind of property, real, personal or mixed, and every kind of investment, specifically including, but not by way of limitation, corporate obligations of every kind, and stocks, preferred or common, irrespective of whether said investments are in accordance with the laws then enforced in the State of California pertaining to the investment of trust funds by corporate trustees."

The will also provided:

> Unless specifically limited, all discretions conferred upon the Trustee shall be absolute, and their exercise conclusive on all persons interest[ed] in this trust. The enumeration of certain powers of the Trustee shall not limit its general powers, the Trustee, subject always to the discharge of its fiduciary obligations, being vested with and having all the rights, powers and privileges which an absolute owner of the same property would have.

Collins died in 1963 and his will was admitted to probate. In June 1965, the court ordered the estate to be distributed. After various other payments and distributions, defendant trustees received about $80,000 as the trust principal. After other distributions, such as the annual

$4,000 payment for the education of Collins' daughter, the trustees had about $50,000 available for investment.

Defendant Millikan's clients included two real property developers, Downing and Ward. In March 1965, Millikan filed an action on behalf of Downing and Ward against a lender who refused to honor a commitment to carry certain construction loans. In June 1965, defendants learned that Downing and Ward wanted to borrow $50,000. Millikan knew that the builders wanted the loan because of their difficulties with the lender who had withdrawn its loan commitment.

The loan would be secured by a second trust deed to 9.38 acres of unimproved real property in San Bernardino County near Upland. This property was subject to a $90,000 first trust deed; the note which secured the first trust deed was payable in quarterly installments of interest only, and due in full in three years, that is, in July 1968. The $50,000 loan to be made by defendants would be payable in monthly installments of interest only, at ten percent interest with the full amount due in 30 months, that is, in January 1968.

Defendants knew that the property had been sold two years earlier in 1963 for $107,000. Defendants checked with two real estate brokers in the area, one of whom said that property in that area was selling for $18,000 to $20,000 an acre. They did not have the property appraised, they did not check with the county clerk or recorder in either Los Angeles or San Bernardino County to determine whether there were foreclosures or lawsuits pending against the construction company. In fact, when defendants made the loan in July 1965, there were six notices of default and three lawsuits pending against Downing and Ward.

Defendants obtained and reviewed an unaudited company financial statement. This statement indicated that the Downing and Ward Company had a net worth in excess of $2,000,000.

Downing and Ward told defendants that they were not in default on any of their loans, that they were not defendants in any pending litigation, and that there had never been any liens filed on any of their projects. Defendants phoned the bank with whom Downing and Ward had a line of credit and learned that the bank had a satisfactory relationship with the builders.

Based on this information, on July 23, 1965, defendants lent Downing and Ward $50,000 on the terms described above. In addition to the second trust deed, Downing and Ward pledged 20 percent of the stock in their company as security. However, defendants neither obtained possession of the stock, placed it in escrow, nor placed a legend on the stock certificates. Defendants also obtained the personal guarantees of Downing and Ward and their wives. However, defendants did not obtain financial statements from the guarantors.

When the loan was made in July 1965, construction in the Upland area was, as the trial court said, "enjoying boom times, although the bubble was to burst just a few months later." From July 1965 through September 1966, the builders made the monthly interest payments required by the note. In October 1966, Downing & Ward Construction Corporation was placed in involuntary bankruptcy and thereafter Mr. and Mrs. Ward and Mr. and Mrs. Downing declared personal bankruptcies. Defendants foreclosed their second trust deed in June 1967, and became the owners of the unimproved real property. They spent $10,000 in an unsuccessful effort to salvage the investment by forestalling foreclosure by the holder of the first trust deed. In September 1968, the holder of the first trust deed did foreclose. This extinguished the trustees' interest in the property and the entire investment. In short, about $60,000 of the trust fund was lost.

The trial court made findings of fact and drew conclusions of law. As relevant, the court found that defendant trustees "exercised the judgment and care, under the circumstances then prevailing, which men of prudence, discretion and intelligence exercised in the management of their own affairs, not in regard to speculation, but in regard to the disposition of their funds, considering the probable income, as well as the probable safety of their capital."[12] In making the loan, "the cotrustees used reasonable care, diligence and skill. The cotrustees did not act arbitrarily or in bad faith." . . .

The trial court's finding that defendants exercised the judgment and care "which men of prudence, discretion and intelligence exercised in the management of their own affairs," reflects the standard imposed upon trustees by Civil Code section 2261. (See also, Rest. 2d Trusts, §227 ["Restatement"].)

Plaintiffs contend, and we agree, that contrary to the trial court's findings and conclusions, defendants failed to follow the "prudent investor" standard, first, by investing two-thirds of the trust principal in a single investment, second, by investing in real property secured only by a second deed of trust, and third, by making that investment without adequate investigation of either the borrowers or the collateral.

Although California does not limit the trustee's authority to a list of authorized investments, relying instead on the prudent investor rule (see 7 Witkin, Summary of Cal. Law (8th ed.) Trusts, §63, p.5424), nevertheless, the prudent investor rule encompasses certain guidelines applicable to this case.

First, "the trustee is under a duty to the beneficiary to distribute the risk of loss by reasonable diversification of investments, unless under the circumstances it is prudent not to do so." (Rest., §228. . . .)

---

12. This language is taken almost verbatim from Harvard College v. Amory, 26 Mass. (9 Pick.) 446, 461 (1830). — Eds.

Second, ordinarily, "second or other junior mortgages are not proper trust investments," unless taking a second mortgage is a reasonable method of settling a claim or making possible the sale of property. (Rest., §227, p.533.) Stated more emphatically:

> While loans secured by second mortgages on land are sometimes allowed, they are almost always disapproved by courts of equity. The trustee should not place the trust funds in a position where they may be endangered by the foreclosure of a prior lien. . . . In rare cases equity will sanction an investment secured by a second mortgage, but only when the security is adequate and unusual circumstances justify the trustee in taking this form of investment. (Bogert, Trusts & Trustees (2d ed.) §675, p.274.)

Third, in "buying a mortgage for trust investment, the trustee should give careful attention to the valuation of the property, in order to make certain that his margin of security is adequate. He must use every reasonable endeavor to provide protection which will cover the risks of depreciation in the property and changes in price levels. And he must investigate the status of the property and of the mortgage, as well as the financial situation of the mortgagor." (Bogert, supra, §674, at p.267.) Similarly, the Restatement rule is that "the trustee cannot properly lend on a mortgage upon real property more than a reasonable proportion of the value of the mortgage property." (Sec. 229.)

We think it apparent that defendants violated every applicable rule. First, they failed totally to diversify the investments in this relatively small trust fund. Second, defendants invested in a junior mortgage on unimproved real property, and left an inadequate margin of security. As noted, the land had most recently sold for $107,000, and was subject to a first trust deed of $90,000. Thus, unless the land was worth more than $140,000, there was no margin of security at all. Defendants did not have the land appraised; the only information they had was the opinion of a real estate broker that property in the area — not that particular parcel — was going for $18,000 to $20,000 an acre. Thus, any assumption that the property was worth about $185,000 — and therefore the $140,000 in loans were well-secured — would have been little more than a guess.

Third, the backup security obtained by defendants was no security at all. The builders pledged 20 percent of their stock, but defendants never obtained possession of the stock, placed it in escrow or even had it legended. They accepted the personal guarantees of the builders and their wives without investigating the financial status of these persons. They accepted at face value the claimed $2,000,000 value of the company shown in an unaudited statement. Defendant Millikan apparently ignored the fact that one lender had, for whatever reasons, reneged on a loan commitment to the builders.

Defendants contend that the evidence sustains the trial court's findings that they exercised the judgment and care under the circumstances then prevailing expected of men of prudence. They rely on the rule that the determination whether an investment was proper must be made in light of the circumstances existing at the time of the investment. (E.g., Witkin, supra, §63, p.5425.) That rule does not help defendants. Nothing that happened after the loan was made can change the fact that defendants invested two-thirds of the principal of the trust in a single second deed of trust on unappraised property, with no knowledge of the borrowers' true financial status, and without any other security. . . .

Defendants alternatively contend that the trust instrument conferred "absolute discretion" on them as trustees, and that the prudent-investor standard did not apply to their conduct. Rather, the only question is whether the trustee avoided arbitrary action and used his best judgment. (Coberly v. Superior Court (1965) 231 Cal. App. 2d 685, 689, 42 Cal. Rptr. 64.)

We leave aside the question whether even a trustee with "absolute discretion" would be permitted to make this kind of investment, consistent with the rule that an absolute discretion does not permit a "trustee to neglect its trust or abdicate its judgment." (Coberly, supra, at p.689, 42 Cal. Rptr. at p.67.) The instrument in this case conferred no such absolute discretion.

Defendants rely particularly on the rule that the prudent investor standard does not apply where the settlor himself specifies that the trustees of his trust are not limited by what the law provides are proper investments. (E.g., Stanton v. Wells Fargo Bank, etc. Co. (1957) 150 Cal. App. 2d 763, 777, 310 P.2d 1010.) Their reliance on that rule is misplaced.

First, the provision in the trust instrument to purchase every kind of property and make every kind of investment "irrespective of whether said investments are in accordance with the laws then enforced in the State of California pertaining to the investment of trust funds by corporate trustees" does not authorize the trustees to make improper investments.

Neither Civil Code section 2261 nor any other authority which we can locate authorizes different types of investments for "corporate trustees" and for amateur trustees. The difference, rather, is that the corporate trustee is held to a greater standard of care based on his presumed expertise. . . . Thus, defendants might have been protected by that clause had they deviated in some respects from the general rules — for example, had they accepted a well-secured second trust deed, or possibly had they accepted a first trust deed without careful investigation. Here, however, defendants did nothing right. Second, the "absolute discretion" in the trust instrument is "specifically limited" by the requirement that the trustee is "subject always to the discharge of its fiduciary obligations. . . ."

In conclusion, the evidence does not support the trial court's conclusion that defendants acted properly in investing $50,000 in the property.

Reversed.

NOTES

1.   Restatement (Second) of Trusts §228 (1959) imposes a duty of diversification upon trustees. The purpose of this duty is to minimize the risk of large losses. Some states follow the Restatement rule while in others such a duty does not exist. New York lower courts have held that diversification per se is not required, but investment of a large portion of trust funds in a single security, coupled with other elements of hazard, may be the basis of a finding of imprudence. In re Newhoff, 107 Misc. 2d 589, 435 N.Y.S.2d 632 (Sur. Ct. 1980). The New York Court of Appeals has not dealt with the issue.

Cases hold that a general authority to retain property originally transferred to the trust eliminates any duty to diversify by selling such property. Restatement (Second) §230, Comment j, says it is a question of interpretation whether such authorization dispenses with the requirement of diversification. Some cases have held that the duty of diversification does not apply to an executor because the executor's duty is to close out the estate as promptly as possible. In re Estate of Beach, 15 Cal. 3d 632, 542 P.2d 994, 123 Cal. Rptr. 570 (1975); Estate of Knipp, 489 Pa. 509, 414 A.2d 1007 (1980); Hamilton v. Nielsen, 678 F.2d 709 (7th Cir. 1982) (Illinois law).

2.   Exculpatory (or exoneration) clauses have been strictly construed by the courts. See Hatcher v. United States National Bank of Oregon, 56 Or. App. 643, 643 P.2d 359 (1982); Note, Directory Trusts and the Exculpatory Clause, 65 Colum. L. Rev. 138 (1965). They will not be given effect if the result is to allow a fiduciary to act in bad faith or with reckless indifference to the interests of the beneficiaries. See Rippey v. Denver United States National Bank, 273 F. Supp. 718 (D. Colo. 1967) (holding trustee liable for selling stock to an interested third party without first testing the market).

New York Est., Powers & Trusts Law §11-1.7(a) (1967) provides:

> The attempted grant to an executor or testamentary trustee, or the successor of either, of any of the following enumerated powers or immunities is contrary to public policy:
>
> (1)   The exoneration of such fiduciary from liability for failure to exercise reasonable care, diligence and prudence.

(2)   The power to make a binding and conclusive fixation of the value of any asset for purposes of distribution, allocation or otherwise.

Note that the New York statute does not apply to inter vivos trusts, in which exoneration provisions may protect a trustee from liability absent recklessness, fraud, or intentional wrongdoing. See Stark v. United States Trust Co. of New York, 445 F. Supp. 670, 683 (S.D.N.Y. 1978).

In Corpus Christi National Bank v. Gerdes, 551 S.W.2d 521 (Tex. Civ. App. 1977), where negligent conduct was alleged, the court gave effect to a broad exculpatory clause, relying upon a state statute that gave the settlor the power to change the duties and liabilities of trustees. The court said "the public policy prohibition is limited to exculpatory clauses which authorize self-dealing."

Young & Lombard, Fiduciary Responsibility in Investments
124 Trusts & Estates, June 1985, at 14-15

An early but respectable authority on fiduciary investment is the Gospel according to Saint Matthew.[13] A man about to leave on an extended trip called in his three servants. He gave five talents to the first, two to the second, and one to the third. On his return, the traveler asked for an accounting, much as would a modern beneficiary. The first servant said he had invested the money, earned an additional five talents, and presented the ten talents. This fiduciary was praised and rewarded, and given the ten talents back to further invest. The same story was repeated for the servant with two talents. But the third servant said he knew the traveler was risk averse. He didn't want to risk losing the money and so buried it in the ground, kept it safe, and returned the one talent. That servant was not praised as expected, he was castigated. Since he had not earned any return on the money, the talent was taken away and given to the servant with ten talents to continue to invest. The third servant was cast into outer darkness, there was much wailing and gnashing of teeth, and that was the first recorded fiduciary surcharge.

It also illustrates the problem that present day fiduciaries have of protecting the real value of money. Most of the litigation to date has dealt with protection of the nominal value of the trust corpus. But, at four percent inflation, one dollar is worth only 50 cents in purchasing power in 17 years. At 10 percent inflation, which is possible (we once thought we were getting used to it), a dollar becomes 50 cents in purchasing power in six years, and only six cents at the end of 28 years.

---

13. Matthew 25: 14-30.

The beneficiaries at the end of the 28-year period who are given in effect only six cents in purchasing power for every dollar in that trust, may well complain. Future litigation may deal with preservation of the real value. . . .

One thing we know is that the trustee shouldn't speculate. But speculation is not always easy to identify. It seems easier after the fact when things have gone wrong. But hindsight is infallible, and a trustee should only be judged on its knowledge and actions at the time. There is one case, In Re White,[14] which is clear. The cotrustee said the trust should invest in canned goods and store them; in coins, and bury them; and in puts and calls and commodities. He said he had been very successful personally in investing this way, why shouldn't the trust make money as well. The corporate cotrustee wisely resisted the temptation.

The basic rule of prudence is from Harvard College v. Amory.[15] . . .

But a rule stated in those terms does not always identify what is a proper investment and what is not. Recent opinions from Massachusetts and Alabama show how courts, taking the same rule, can come out with remarkably different results.

In the Massachusets case, Chase v. Pevear,[16] the trustee had managed to pick the three biggest bankruptcies of our time, CMI, W.T. Grant, and Penn Central Railroad. He had invested in REITS, had invested in securities that were rated as speculative or lower-medium grade by Moody's and Standard & Poor's and by his own investment rating service. For all of this, and for some other problems, he was surcharged and removed by the trial court. On appeal, the Massachusetts Supreme Judicial Court said that the trustee in investing cannot be bound by inflexible rules and categories, but has to be judged on the facts. The court had the facts mentioned, but those were swept aside. What the court focused on in reducing the amount of the surcharge was the fact that others, as shown by Standard & Poor's and the Common Trust Fund Report, had invested in the same securities. It is hard to miss under that standard. The court did surcharge the removed trustee for holding on to some questionable investments too long after "disquieting information was known." . . .

The situation is much different in Alabama. Applying the same prudent person rule (citing Harvard College v. Amory) the Supreme Court of Alabama in First Alabama Bank of Montgomery v. Martin[17] upheld surcharges in excess of $2.5 million on two common trust funds. Some of the purchases were in violation of the bank's own standards. The major evidence against the bank was the testimony of a business

14. 467 A.2d 1148 (Super. Ct. Pa. 1983), rev'd on other grounds, 484 A.2d 763 (1984).
15. 26 Mass. (9 Pick.) 446 (1830).
16. 383 Mass. 350, 419 N.E.2d 1358 (1981).
17. 425 So. 2d 415 (Ala. 1983), cert. denied, 461 U.S. 938 (1983).

school professor, who stated that safety of principal was the major consideration and he followed Benjamin Graham's tests for safety. He had reviewed all of the securities, they failed to meet Graham's tests in one or more respects, and so there should be surcharges. The court adopted this result even though on cross-examination the expert had to testify that of the thirty stocks in the Dow Jones Average, only five would have met all of the tests.

The opinion is also interesting for another reason. Sometimes when a court gets on a roll it goes all the way. The bank also was surcharged for selling some securities too soon. The court said that if, instead of selling in a depressed market, they had held on to the securities and sold them later they would have made more money, and they should be surcharged for failing to do that. That result is unique. Once you have seen in hindsight what happened to the curve you can tell that you were then at the bottom and things got better. But when you have to make the decision there is no one who knows with certainty how the market will move. After all, Bernard Baruch said he made his money by "selling too soon."

Under the classic formulation of the prudent investor rule, in Harvard College v. Amory, speculation is inappropriate for a trustee. Investment strategies viewed as speculation include entering a transaction with the purpose of a quick turnover or profit (*market timing*) and investing in a relatively unknown or unseasoned company that has high potential for capital gain as well as high risk. Buying or selling options (*puts* and *calls*) is risky for a fiduciary, although option trading is viewed as a sound strategy by many professional money managers.

In the last decade, economists and others have suggested that the legal distinction between investment and speculation does not make sense in the modern investment world. Contemporary investment analysts say the performance of the portfolio is what is important, whereas the prudent investor rule stresses the conduct of the trustee and not the performance. The following excerpts provide useful background information, some of which challenges commonly held beliefs about how to invest. In re Bank of New York, infra page 917, addresses the question of whether a trustee should be held responsible for particular "imprudent" investments when the trust portfolio shows an overall increase in value.

Note, *The Regulation of Risky Investments*
83 Harv. L. Rev. 603, 616-621 (1970)

Running throughout the disparate legal approaches to the regulation of risk is a consistent concern with one particular type of risk: the risk of loss. While this regulation may have other objectives, the leitmotiv is an attempt to minimize the probability that the capital value of each investment will be less at some future date than when bought.[18] . . . Statutory legal lists restricting institutional and trust portfolios are explicitly designed to prevent risk of loss by forbidding investment in securities supposedly too susceptible to capital depreciation. The distinction drawn by the modern prudent man rule between "investment" and "speculation" also emphasizes conservation rather than growth. A "speculative" security is one especially likely to be worth less than its cost at some future date.

While this notion of risk savors of common sense, it makes a very peculiar assumption about the proper concerns of investors, policyholders, and trust beneficiaries. The assumption is that these parties are exclusively concerned with the possibility that their investment will sell for less than cost, rather than with all possible future values of their investment. Accordingly, this view ignores the probabilities associated with these other possible future values.

In addition to focusing solely on risk of loss, current regulation is limited to minimizing that risk on each particular security, rather than on the portfolio as a whole. . . . In evaluating the investment of trust funds, the prudent man rule treats each investment separately, instead of considering the portfolio as a whole. As one court has declared, "losses in one investment can not be set off against other investments, and . . . each investment must stand or fall by itself."[19] Even if risk is viewed narrowly as risk of loss, this focus on individual securities ignores the fact that the risk of a portfolio is not the arithmetic sum of the risks of its component securities. The performance of many different securities may depend on the same future contingent event. A portfolio whose securities strongly covary — are each strongly affected by the same future events — will be riskier than a portfolio composed of securities which covary only slightly. For example, a portfolio consisting of fifty stocks, each of which has an even chance of doing very well or very poorly, carries relatively little risk as long as independent factors determine the success or failure of each security. On the other hand, if the same contingency — for example, the size of next year's defense budget — determines the fortunes of each security, security performance would covary strongly and portfolio risk would be quite large. Thus, concern should be directed not at the risk profile of each security, but at the marginal effect on total portfolio risk of acquiring each

18. It thus includes the risk of decline in capital value of an equity security, the risk of default on a debt obligation, and the risk of interest rate rise with a consequent decline in the capital value of a fixed income security (if the horizon date falls before maturity).

19. McKechnie v. Springfield, 311 Mass. 406, 414, 41 N.E.2d 557, 561 (1942); see Creed v. McAleer, 275 Mass. 353, 175 N.E. 761 (1931).

security. Even a security which is quite risky taken alone may decrease total portfolio risk and, accordingly, be a more prudent purchase than a security which appears less risky by itself. Therefore, current regulation necessarily ignores the real risk contributed by a security by insisting that each investment with a portfolio stand or fall on its own.

Finally, the law treats risk in isolation from the return an investment may contribute to a portfolio. . . . [T]rust beneficiaries . . . benefit from investments that increase the return to a portfolio just as they are harmed by investments that increase its risk. It has been noted that blue sky laws, legal lists, and the prudent man rule all neglect this trade-off between risk and return. Each security is evaluated solely by the probability that a capital loss will be incurred. If two securities carry equal risks and only one has a return high enough to justify its risk, current regulatory policy must accept or reject both. Whichever decision is made, the . . . trust beneficiary . . . is harmed, either by being denied a worthwhile investment or by being exposed to the dangers of a poor one.

Thus the legal concept of risk has three characteristics. It concerns itself solely with the risk of loss, focuses on the risk of particular securities rather than of portfolios, and views risk in isolation from return. Because of these characteristics, the legal concept is imprecisely related to the interests of those the current regulation is designed to protect.

Rigorous economic analysis has devised another concept of risk which may be a better guide to regulatory policy than the current legal concept. This economic concept views the risk of a portfolio as the uncertainty associated with its market value or expected rate of return at some future horizon date. Statisticians have quantified this concept by describing it as the width of the probability distribution of possible future values of the portfolio. If the portfolio has a wide range of possible future values at the appropriate horizon date, and no one value has a high level of probability, the portfolio is riskier than if all possible prices fell within a narrow range and one possible price was highly probable. One portfolio might thus be riskier than another even though it has a low probability of loss. This is because risk of loss considers only those possible future values which are less than cost. The economic concept considers every possible future value, and thus measures what the investor is actually worried about, the future value of his portfolio.

In addition to being a more appropriate index of risk than risk of loss, the economic concept of risk emphasizes the relationship between the risk of a particular security and the risk of the portfolio. The uncertainty risk of the portfolio is the aggregate of the uncertainty risks of the securities which compose it. This aggregation of risks is not an arithmetic total but recognizes that securities which strongly covary add more to portfolio risk than securities which do not. The relationship between the risk of a portfolio and that of its component securities can be expressed mathematically and reveals that the covariance of a security is as important to portfolio risk as the uncertainty risk of the security taken by itself; it also reveals that the addition of a speculative security may actually reduce the risk of the portfolio as a whole. Thus, because the economic approach to risk views the risk of particular securities in terms of the risk they contribute to the whole portfolio, it is more appropriate than the legal concept.

NOTES AND QUESTIONS

1. For an informative analysis of the prudent investor rule and its failure to respond to the development of portfolio theory, see Gordon, The Puzzling Persistence of the Constrained Prudent Man Rule, 62 N.Y.U.L. Rev. 52 (1987). See also Note, Contraditional Investments of Fiduciaries: Reexamining the Prudent Investor Rule, 33 Emory L.J. 1067 (1984).

2. The efficient market hypothesis asserts that prices set on national markets reflect all relevant information, both public and non-public. Under the efficient market hypothesis, should a trustee sell a stock that has continued to decline in price over a substantial period of time? Consider the following case. In In re Mendleson's Will, 46 Misc. 2d 960, 261 N.Y.S.2d 525 (Sur. Ct. 1965), the testator bequeathed to a bank in trust a large block of shares of stock in B.T. Babbitt Co., a closely held family corporation. The will specially requested the trustee to retain the shares of B.T. Babbitt Co. In 1950 the market value of the stock was $14, which it had been for two years. But changes began to occur in early 1950. Earnings were down, and the dividend was reduced from 30 cents to 15 cents a quarter. In 1952 the dividend was cut from 15 cents to 5 cents; the market value fell to $6 a share. The trustee decided to keep the stock on the ground that a public sale of management stock would be looked on suspiciously by prospective buyers, fearing a bail-out. The trustee was of a view that a private sale or merger was wisest, but the trustee made no reasonable effort to sell until 1956, and only in 1964 was the stock sold for around $1.50 a share. The court found that the trustee had a duty to sell within a reasonable time after the 1952 cut in dividend, and that July 1, 1953, was the day of default ("four years is simply too long to wait [for an effort to sell]"). The court held that the failure to diversify was not a breach of trust, as in New York diversification is not mandatory, but that retention after 1952 was imprudent.

Is the case correct if the trustee — watching the business — had inside information in 1952 not available to the market? Would it be lawful under SEC Rule 10b-5 (supra page 870) to use this information in deciding to sell? See Brudney, Insiders, Outsiders, and Informational Advantages Under the Federal Securities Laws, 93 Harv. L. Rev. 322 (1979); Anderson, Fraud, Fiduciaries, and Insider Trading, 10 Hofstra L. Rev. 341 (1982). If B.T. Babbitt had been a publicly held company, with stock traded on the New York stock exchange, and the trustee had no inside information, should the trustee be surcharged for not selling in 1952? See Stark v. United States Trust Co. of New York, 445 F. Supp. 670 (S.D.N.Y. 1978).

Is it more dangerous for a trustee to hold an over-the-counter security than a stock traded on a national stock exchange? See In re Berg, 91 Misc. 2d 939, 398 N.Y.S.2d 948 (Sur. Ct. 1977).

3.   Langbein & Posner, Market Funds and Trust-Investment Law, 1976 A.B.F. Res. J. 1 (1976):

> There is growing interest within the investment community in what are known as "index" or "market" funds. These are mutual or other investment funds that have abandoned the traditional attempt to "beat the market" by picking and choosing among securities — buying stocks or bonds that they believe to be undervalued and selling those they believe to be overvalued. Instead, they create and hold essentially unchanged a portfolio of securities that is designed to approximate some index of market performance such as the Standard & Poor's 500. The S&P 500 is a hypothetical portfolio consisting of 500 major nonfinancial companies on the New York Stock Exchange weighted by the market value of each company's total outstanding shares. . . .

If a trustee indexes all or part of the trust portfolio by buying the stocks in the Standard & Poor's 500, without investigating the individual securities, has the trustee improperly delegated his duty? Standard & Poor changes the stocks in its index from time to time, substituting one new stock for an old one. If the trustee sells the old stock and buys the new stock without investigating it, is the investment decision being made by someone other than the trustee? Compare investment by a trustee in a mutual fund, supra page 874, footnote 6.

4.   Suppose that the settlor directs the trustee to invest only in first mortgages and government bonds and forbids investment in corporate stock. If the trustee can show that in an inflationary economy the value of the trust estate will seriously decline by investing in fixed-value obligations, should the court authorize the trustee to invest in common stock? See In re Trusteeship Agreement with Mayo, 259 Minn. 91, 105 N.W.2d 900 (1960); Toledo Trust Co. v. Toledo Hospital, 174 Ohio St. 124, 187 N.E.2d 36 (1962).

5.   In 1985, California amended its prudent investor rule by statute to eliminate language proscribing "speculation" and authorize the

trustee to consider "individual investments as part of an overall invest-
ment strategy." Cal. Prob. Code §16040 (1989). See Wade, The New
California Prudent Investor Rule: A Statutory Interpretive Analysis, 20
Real Prop., Prob. & Tr. J. 1 (1985).

In re Bank of New York
Court of Appeals of New York, 1974
35 N.Y.2d 512, 323 N.E.2d 700, 364 N.Y.S.2d 164

JONES, J.   We hold that on the record in this case objections filed by
the guardian ad litem to certain investment decisions of a bank acting
as trustee of its own common trust fund were properly dismissed on a
motion for summary judgment.

In 1952 Empire Trust Company established a discretionary common
trust fund pursuant to section 100-c of the Banking Law, Consol. Laws,
c. 2.[20] In conformity with the provisions of that section The Bank of
New York (into which Empire was merged in 1966) as continuing
trustee of the common trust fund made a periodic accounting of the
proceedings of the trustee for the four-year period ending September
30, 1968. In his report the guardian ad litem and attorney for principal
questioned four investments made by the trustee. The trustee moved
to dismiss these objections. . . .

The Surrogate granted the trustee's motion for summary judgment
as to the objections of two investments (Harcourt, Brace & World, Inc.
and Mercantile Stores Company, Inc.) and denied it as to the objections
with respect to the other two investments (The Boeing Company and
Parke, Davis & Company). The majority at the Appellate Division
modified by granting summary judgment for the trustee with respect
to the objections which the Surrogate had reserved for trial. We now
affirm the determination at the Appellate Division, thus dismissing all
objections raised by the guardian.

We take occasion to commend the guardian for the thoroughness of
his investigation and, such investigation having been completed to his
satisfaction, for his further readiness to adopt what appears to be a
sensible procedural vehicle, at least in this case, for the disposition of

---

20. A common trust fund is one established by a corporate fiduciary for the collective
investment of funds held by the fiduciary in a fiduciary capacity. It has many advantages
to offer participating trusts, especially smaller ones. These advantages include greater
diversification and economies of scale. Although a common trust fund theoretically
violates the rule against commingling of the assets of separate trusts, statutes have been
passed in almost all states permitting the investment of trust money by a corporate trustee
in a common trust fund operated by the corporate fiduciary. See Report, Investment by
Fiduciaries in Common Trust Funds, 11 Real Prop., Prob. & Tr. J. 28 (1976); 3 A. Scott,
Trusts §227.9 (W. Fratcher 4th ed. 1988). — Eds.

the objections raised by him. The statutory requirement for accountings every four years with respect to common trust funds presents an occasion for the exercise of a particularly sagacious prudence. Primarily, we observe that most of the trust beneficiaries have so limited an economic interest in a common trust fund that it is unrealistic to place practical reliance on the disposition of any of them carefully to scrutinize a trustee's account. Thus the role of the guardian[21] takes on a special significance, for the trust beneficiaries must be assured that the trustee's accounts will receive careful and thorough review. At the same time if it is to serve the useful purpose for which it was designated, the common trust fund must be spared the adverse economic impact of the types of harassing litigation to which the mandatory four-year accounting requirement may expose it.

We turn then to the objections raised here. Initially we do not agree with what appears to have been in part the basis on which the majority at the Appellate Division reached its conclusion. The fact that this portfolio showed substantial overall increase in total value during the accounting period does not insulate the trustee from responsibility for imprudence with respect to individual investments for which it would otherwise be surcharged (cf. King v. Talbot, 40 N.Y. 76, 90-91; 3 Scott, Trusts [3d ed.], §213.1, pp.1712-1713). To hold to the contrary would in effect be to assure fiduciary immunity in an advancing market such as marked the history of the accounting period here involved. The record of any individual investment is not to be viewed exclusively, of course, as though it were in its own water-tight compartment, since to some extent individual investment decisions may properly be affected by considerations of the performance of the fund as an entity, as in the instance, for example, of individual security decisions based in part on considerations of diversification of the fund or of capital transactions to achieve sound tax planning for the fund as a whole. The focus of inquiry, however, is nonetheless on the individual security as such and factors relating to the entire portfolio are to be weighed only along with others in reviewing the prudence of the particular investment decisions.

. . . The record discloses that with respect to each investment the trustee acted in good faith and cannot be said to have failed to exercise "'such diligence and such prudence in the care and management [of the fund], as in general, prudent men of discretion and intelligence in such matters, employ in their own like affairs'" (Matter of Clark, 257 N.Y. 132, 136, 177 N.E. 397, 398; Costello v. Costello, 209 N.Y. 252,

---

21. The guardians ad litem are appointed not only to protect the interests of infants, incompetents and unknowns, as in the usual case, but also to represent all others who do not appear in the proceeding (Banking Law, §100-c, subd. 12).

261, 103 N.E. 148, 152; cf. EPTL, Consol. Laws, c. 17-b, 11-2.2). It was not shown in any instance that the losses to the trust fund resulted from imprudence or negligence. There was evidence of attention and consideration with reference to each decision made. Obviously it is not sufficient that hindsight might suggest that another course would have been more beneficial; nor does a mere error of investment judgment mandate a surcharge. Our courts do not demand investment infallibility, nor hold a trustee to prescience in investment decisions. (Matter of Hubbell, 302 N.Y. 246, 257, 97 N.E.2d 888, 893.)

Whether a trustee is to be surcharged in these instances, as in other cases, must necessarily depend on a balanced and perceptive analysis of its consideration and action in the light of the history of each individual investment, viewed at the time of its action or its omission to act. In our opinion no sufficiently useful purpose would be served by a detailed description of the analysis by which we reach the conclusion that there is no basis for surcharge with respect to any of the four investments here called into question. Procedures we now find acceptable with respect to these investments at the time of this accounting may not be satisfactory at another time in other circumstances. It suffices here to state that we do not find sufficient basis for surcharge in this case.

The order of the Appellate Division should accordingly be affirmed.

NOTE: BALANCING GAINS AND LOSSES

Can a trustee who commits a breach of trust in investing, which results in a loss to the trust in one stock (stock *A*) and a gain in another stock (stock *B*), balance the loss against the gain? Suppose that the trustee is not authorized to invest in common stock but buys common stock *A* for $10,000. The trustee then sells stock *A* for $8,000 and invests the proceeds in common stock *B*. Stock *B* rises to $14,000 in value and is sold. If the trustee can balance gain and loss, the trustee is accountable only for a $4,000 net gain. If the trustee cannot offset gain against loss, the trustee is chargeable for a $2,000 loss in stock *A* and a $6,000 gain in stock *B*: total $8,000. The rule is: If the breaches of trust are *separate and distinct*, the trustee is not permitted to balance gains and losses and is liable for $8,000. The gains belong to the trust; the loss is personal to the trustee.

In the above example, the breaches are probably not separate and distinct, so that the trustee is liable only for $4,000. See 3 A. Scott, Trusts §213.2 (W. Fratcher 4th ed. 1988). Would it make any difference if at the same time the trustee invested $5,000 in stock *A* and $5,000 in stock *B*, and then stock *A* were sold for a loss of $1,000 and stock *B* were sold for a gain of $3,000? See id. §213.1.

For discussion of how the anti-netting rule might apply under portfolio theory, see Gordon, The Puzzling Persistence of the Constrained Prudent Man Rule, 62 N.Y.U.L. Rev. 52, 96-97 (1987).

Langbein & Posner, Market Funds and Trust-Investment Law
1976 A.B.F. Res. J. 1, 24-26

The courts characteristically apply the prudent-man standard to each investment decision of the trustee rather than to the trust portfolio as a whole. . . . As we shall see, the individual investment standard continues to make good sense in the context in which it was developed. But when the purposes of a standard are properly understood, its inapplicability to the separate components of market portfolios becomes apparent.

The individual-investment standard derives from two distinct principles of trust law. One is the rule, codified in Section 213 of the Restatement, that a trustee cannot reduce his liability for wrongful investments that have resulted in losses by setting off profits earned on other trust investments. The justification for that rule is that the gains are not the trustee's to set off against his personal liability for wrongful conduct — they belong to the trust. Section 213 pertains only to *wrongful* investments. When losses result from prudent investments, the trustee is allowed to charge them to the trust and hence in effect to net the trust's investment losses and gains. Usually when the courts refer to their duty to review individual investments they are enforcing the rule against netting the losses from wrongful investments.

To be sure, courts have also examined trust investments on an individual basis for the purpose of deciding what is wrongful (imprudent). But since in traditional trust investment strategy the trustee selects investments on an individual basis, it is reasonable for courts to review them on that basis. Even then, the judicially developed duty of the trustee to diversify the investments of the trust reflects the courts' awareness that factors extrinsic to a particular security bear on its prudence as a trust investment. . . .

When, however, the trustee's investment strategy is to hold a market portfolio, which implies that he will not attempt to evaluate the merits of the individual securities in the portfolio, the rationale of the individual-investment standard is inapplicable, and we would not expect the courts to apply the standard to him. Since the trustee in such a case is not selecting individual stocks and is passing on to the trust the savings that result from his abstention from a conventional stock-picking investment strategy, the appropriate standard of prudence should be that of the reasonableness of the market portfolio in the light of the risk/return objectives of the particular trust. If the risk/return characteristics of the portfolio are at least as attractive as those of an individual security that would be considered a prudent investment for the trustee, there is no basis in logic — and we believe there is none in the law — for inquiring into the prudence of the individual securities constituting the portfolio.

NOTES

1. For more on trustees' investments in market funds, see Langbein & Posner, The Revolution in Trust Investment Law, 62 A.B.A.J. 887 (1976); Hambach & Dresch, Prudence, Information, and Trust Investment Law, id. at 1309; Langbein & Posner, Market Funds and Efficient Markets: A Reply, id. at 1616; Langbein & Posner, Market Funds and Trust-Investment Law: II, 1977 A.B.F. Res. J. 1 (1977).

2. On portfolio theory, see Bines, Modern Portfolio Theory and Investment Management Law: Refinement of Legal Doctrine, 76 Colum. L. Rev. 721 (1976); Cohen, The Suitability Rule and Economic Theory, 80 Yale L.J. 1604 (1971); Pozen, Money Managers and Securities Research, 51 N.Y.U.L. Rev. 923 (1976).

NOTE: ERISA

The Employee Retirement Income Security Act of 1974 (ERISA) governs investment of pension funds by the trustees managing the funds. The standard governing investments is the prudent investor rule. The act provides that a fiduciary shall discharge his duties

> with the care, skill, prudence, and diligence under the circumstances then prevailing that a prudent man acting in a like capacity and familiar with such matters would use in the conduct of an enterprise of a like character and with like aims; by diversifying the investments of the plan so as to minimize the risk of large losses unless under the circumstances it is clearly prudent not to do so. [29 U.S.C. §1104 (1982).]

Waiver of these limitations in the trust instrument is forbidden. 29 U.S.C. §1104(a)(1)(D) (1982).

On ERISA and the prudent investor rule, see Note, Fiduciary Standards and the Prudent Man Rule Under the Employment [sic] Retirement Income Security Act of 1974, 88 Harv. L. Rev. 960 (1975); Note, Fiduciary Responsibility: Prudent Investments Under ERISA, 14 Suffolk U.L. Rev. 1066 (1980).

ERISA also provides that the trustee

> shall discharge his duties with respect to a plan solely in the interest of
> the beneficiaries and ... for the exclusive purpose of ... providing
> benefits to participants and their beneficiaries. [29 U.S.C. §1104
> (a)(1)(A)(i)(1982).]

This is known as the exclusive benefit rule. The trust law analogue to
the exclusive benefit rule is the trustee's duty of loyalty.

Professors Fischel and Langbein believe the exclusive benefit rule
bedevils many of the main issues in modern pension trust administration, including social investing. It does not recognize, yet, the multiplicity
of interests that inhere in modern pension trusts. Fischel & Langbein,
ERISA's Fundamental Contradiction: The Exclusive Benefit Rule, 55
U. Chi. L. Rev. 1105 (1988).

On ERISA, see Symposium: ERISA Fiduciary Responsibility, 23 Real
Prop., Prob. & Tr. J. 561 (1988). The management of huge pension
and employee benefit funds will undoubtedly bring many changes in
the law of trusts dealing with trustees' powers and duties. Common law
rules, developed for family trusts, will be reshaped by these giant funds,
but only the twenty-first century will tell us exactly how.

NOTE: SOCIAL INVESTING

Can the trustees of a pension fund — or the trustees of a private
trust, for that matter — invest the trust assets to accomplish social
goals? Can the trustees refuse to invest in the stock of a corporation
that does business in South Africa, pollutes the atmosphere, or publishes
textbooks that teach the theory of evolution? Or can a labor union
pension fund invest in projects that provide jobs to the union members?
Do such investments breach the duty of undivided loyalty to the fund
beneficiaries? Are they prudent?

To date, only two cases in this country have come close to considering
this issue. In Blankenship v. Boyle, 329 F. Supp. 1089 (D.D.C. 1971),
aff'd mem., 511 F.2d 447 (D.C. Cir. 1975), the court held that trustees
of the United Mineworkers pension fund could not buy large blocks of
electric utility shares in an effort to induce the utility management to
buy union-mined coal, nor could the trustees allow excessive money to
remain in noninterest bearing accounts in a bank owned by the union.
The court took the position that the duty of loyalty to the beneficiaries
(pensioners) was breached by investments designed to increase the
power of the union (and the wages of the still-working). In Withers v.
Teachers' Retirement System, 447 F. Supp. 1248 (S.D.N.Y. 1978), aff'd
mem., 595 F.2d 1210 (2d Cir. 1979), the court approved the purchase
of New York City bonds by the New York City Teachers' Retirement
System as part of a plan to stave off bankruptcy of the city. The court

held that, inasmuch as New York City contributed annually 62 percent of the fund's revenue, the trustees acted in the sole interest of the beneficiaries of the fund and not to protect the jobs of city teachers nor the general public welfare. Although neither case sheds much light on the problem of social investing, both decisions are consistent with existing trust rules regarding the duty of loyalty and prudent investments. Fischel and Langbein, supra, at 1144-1147, criticize these cases for failing to recognize the conflict between the classes of beneficiaries — the older, who want retirement income, and the younger, who want employment. See also Cowan v. Scargill, [1984] 2 All E.R. 750 (Ch.), holding trustees of pension trust for coal miners may not refuse to invest in energy industries competing with coal but must diversify and seek maximum income.

The commentators are by no means in agreement on social investing and often do not distinguish between social investing that benefits "outsiders" at the expense of the plan beneficiaries and social investing that benefits only a subgroup of the plan beneficiaries. See J. Langbein, R. Schotland & A. Blaustein, Disinvestment: Is It Legal? Is It Moral? Is It Productive? (1985); Brand, Investment Duties of Trustees of Charitable Trusts and Directors of Nonprofit Corporations: Applying the Law to Investments That Acknowledge Social and Moral Concerns, 1986 Ariz. St. L.J. 631; Dobris, Arguments in Favor of Fiduciary Divestment of South African Securities, 65 Neb. L. Rev. 209 (1986); Jerry & Joy, Social Investing and the Lessons of South Africa Divestment: Rethinking the Limitations on Fiduciary Discretion, 66 Or. L. Rev. 685 (1987); Langbein & Posner, Social Investing and the Law of Trusts, 79 Mich. L. Rev. 72 (1980); Lynn, Investing Pension Funds for Social Goals Requires Changing the Law, 53 U. Colo. L. Rev. 101 (1981); Ravikoff & Curzan, Social Responsibility in Investment and the Prudent Man Rule, 68 Calif. L. Rev. 518 (1980); Zelinsky, The Dilemma of the Local Social Investment: An Essay on "Socially Responsible" Investing, 6 Cardozo L. Rev. 111 (1984).

SECTION C. ACCOUNTINGS

National Academy of Sciences v. Cambridge Trust Co.
Supreme Judicial Court of Massachusetts, 1976
370 Mass. 303, 346 N.E.2d 879

REARDON, J. This matter is before us for further appellate review, the Appeals Court having promulgated an opinion.

The facts which give rise to the case are essentially as follows. Leonard T. Troland died a resident of Cambridge in 1932 survived by his widow, Florence R. Troland. By his will executed in April, 1931, he left all of his real and personal property to be held in trust by the Cambridge Trust Company (bank) with the net income of the trust, after expenses, "to be paid to, or deposited to the account of [his wife], Florence R. Troland" during her lifetime so long as she remained unmarried. He further provided that

> [k]nowing my wife, Florence's, generosity and unselfishness as I do, I wish to record it as my intention that she should not devote any major portion of her income under the provisions of this will, to the support or for the benefit of people other than herself. It is particularly contrary to my will that any part of the principal or income of my estate should revert to members of my wife's family, other than herself, and I instruct the trustees to bear this point definitely in mind in making decisions under any of the options of this will.

The testator went on to provide in part that on his wife's death or second marriage the bank would transfer the trusteeship to The National Research Council of Washington, D.C., which the petition alleged to be an agency of the National Academy of Sciences (academy), to constitute a trust to be known as the Troland Foundation for Research in Psychophysics. . . .

The will was allowed, the trust was established as provided by the testator, and the bank paid the income thereof to the widow until her death in 1967. During the period from 1932 to 1945 the widow provided eighteen different mailing addresses for income checks to be transmitted to her by the bank. On February 13, 1945, she married Edward D. Flynn in West Palm Beach, Florida, and failed to advise the bank of her remarriage. Following her remarriage she lived in Perth Amboy, New Jersey. Commencing on April 14, 1944, she directed the bank to forward all her monthly checks to her in care of Kenneth D. Custance, her brother-in-law through marriage to her sister. Over the years these checks were forwarded to two Boston addresses and were made payable to "Florence R. Troland." Custance in turn forwarded the checks to Florence R. Flynn who indorsed them in blank "Florence R. Troland" and returned them to Custance who also indorsed them prior to depositing them in bank accounts in his name maintained at the State Street Bank and Trust Company in Boston and the National Bank of Wareham, Massachusetts. After Florence R. Flynn's death on December 25, 1967, the bank for the first time learned of her remarriage.[22]

---

22. A letter from Thomas Quarles, Jr., a lawyer in Manchester, New Hampshire, discloses some interesting information about the parties in this case. Quarles, who came upon this case while a law student using a prior edition of this book, writes:

Throughout her second marriage Florence R. Flynn lived with her husband who was able to provide support for her and who, although aware that she was receiving payments from the trust, was ignorant of the limitation on her rights to receive such payments. . . . The total of all checks collected by Florence R. Flynn following her marriage in 1945 up to the date of her death is $106,013.41. The twelfth through thirty-third accounts of the bank covering that period between her remarriage and October 8, 1966, were presented to the Probate Court for Middlesex County in separate proceedings and allowed. The academy had formal notice prior to the presentation of the twelfth through fourteenth accounts and the eighteenth through thirty-third accounts, and with respect to the fifteenth through seventeenth accounts assented in writing to their allowance. The academy, unaware of the widow's remarriage, did not challenge any of the accounts and they were duly allowed.

The petition brought in the Probate Court by the academy seeks revocation of the seven decrees allowing the twelfth through thirty-third accounts of the bank, the excision from those accounts of "all entries purporting to evidence distributions to or for the benefit of 'Florence R. Troland' . . . subsequent to February 13, 1945," the restoration by the bank to the trust of the amounts of those distributions with interest at the rate of six percent, a final account reflecting the repayments and adjustments, [and] appointment of the academy as trustee. . . .

Following hearing a judge of the Probate Court revoked the seven

---

My father, Thomas Quarles, Sr., was the trust officer at the Cambridge Trust Company in charge of the Troland trust at the time of Florence Troland's death in 1967. Leonard Troland, the settlor of the trust, was apparently quite a colorful individual. A professor of psychology at Harvard for many years, he was also one of a group that developed the Technicolor motion picture film process. Proceeds from the sale of this invention formed part of the principal of the Troland trust. Mr. Troland apparently had a flair for the theatrical in his personal life as well. In 1932, he reportedly committed suicide by driving his car off the rim of the Grand Canyon at sunset.

Florence Troland was aware of the limitation in the trust that cut off her interest if she remarried. So was her brother-in-law, Kenneth Custance. Nevertheless, after her remarriage in 1945, he convinced her to keep quiet and to endorse her trust income check over to him. He told her that the money was needed to support a succession of spiritualist churches that he headed in the Onset, Massachusetts area. When Florence died in 1967, Kenneth apparently felt guilty about the years of fraud. At her funeral, he gave Florence's latest trust check to her surviving husband, who contacted the Cambridge Trust Company asking what he should do with it. It was only at that point that the Bank realized that through Mrs. Troland and Mr. Custance's fraud it had paid the wrong beneficiary for 22 years. Fortunately, my father kept his job. He had only been with the Bank for a few years and had only recently taken over the Troland trust.

Letter from Thomas Quarles, Jr., to Jesse Dukeminier, dated Dec. 1, 1986. — Eds.

decrees allowing the twelfth through thirty-third accounts, ordered restoration to the trust of $114,314.18, representing amounts erroneously distributed to Florence R. Flynn plus Massachusetts income taxes paid on those amounts from trust funds, together with interest thereon in the sum of $104,847.17 through March 31, 1973, and interest thereafter at the rate of six percent per annum to the date of restoration in full. . . .

The issues before us have to do with the power of the Probate Court judge to order the revocation of the decrees allowing the twelfth through thirty-third accounts, and the propriety of charging the bank for the amounts erroneously disbursed. . . .

The bank recited in the heading of each of the challenged accounts that the trust was "for the benefit of Florence R. Troland," and stated in schedule E of each account (in the first four accounts specifically as "Distributions to Beneficiary") that monthly payments of $225 or more were made to "Florence R. Troland." The Appeals Court held that these recitals and statements "constituted a continuing representation by the bank to the academy and to the court that the widow remained 'Florence R. Troland' despite her (then unknown) remarriage to Flynn, and that she remained the sole income beneficiary of the trust." . . . The court further held that those representations were technically fraudulent in that "[t]hey were made as of the bank's own knowledge when the bank had no such knowledge and had made absolutely no effort to obtain it." . . . With these views we find ourselves substantially in accord.

The doctrine of constructive or technical fraud in this Commonwealth is of venerable origin. As we pointed out in Powell v. Rasmussen, 355 Mass. 117, 118-119, 243 N.E.2d 167 (1969), the doctrine here was developed in two opinions by Chief Justice Shaw. In Hazard v. Irwin, 18 Pick. 95, 109 (1836), it was defined in the following terms: "[W]here the subject matter is one of fact, in respect to which a person can have precise and accurate knowledge, and . . . he speaks as of his own knowledge, and has no such knowledge, his affirmation is essentially false." This rule was reiterated by Chief Justice Shaw in Page v. Bent, 2 Met. 371, 374 (1841): "The principle is well settled, that if a person make a representation of a fact, as of his own knowledge, in relation to a subject matter susceptible of knowledge, and such representation is not true; if the party to whom it is made relies and acts upon it, as true, and sustains damage by it, it is fraud and deceit, for which the party making it is responsible." In this case the marital status of Mrs. Troland/Flynn was a fact susceptible of precise knowledge, the bank made representations concerning this fact of its own knowledge when it had no such knowledge, and the academy to whom the representations were made relied on them to its detriment. While this standard of fraud in law has been developed primarily in the context of actions seeking rescission of contracts and of tort actions for deceit, we have indicated in past decisions that an analogous standard might be applicable to misrepresentations in the accounts of fiduciaries. See Greene v. Springfield Safe Deposit & Trust Co., 295 Mass. 148, 152, 3 N.E.2d 254 (1936); Welch v. Flory, 294 Mass. 138, 142-143, 200 N.E. 900 (1936); Brigham v. Morgan, 185 Mass. 27, 39-40, 69 N.E. 418 (1904). We hold today that "fraud" as used in G. L. c. 206, §24, contemplates this standard of constructive fraud at least to the extent that the fiduciary has made no reasonable efforts to ascertain the true state of the facts it has misrepresented in the accounts. This rule is not a strict liability standard, nor does it make a trustee an insurer against the active fraud of all parties dealing with the trust. Entries in the accounts honestly made, after reasonable efforts to determine the truth or falsity of the representations therein have failed through no fault of the trustee, will not be deemed fraudulent or provide grounds for reopening otherwise properly allowed accounts. However, in the instant case the probate judge found that the bank, through the twenty-two years covered by the disputed accounts, exerted "no effort at all . . . to ascertain if Florence R. Troland had remarried even to the extent of annually requesting a statement or certificate from her to that effect" and that "in administering the trust acted primarily in a ministerial manner and in disregard of its duties as a trustee to protect the terms of the trust." In these circumstances we have little trouble in concluding that the bank's representations as to the marital status of the testator's widow fully justified the reopening of the accounts.

Cases relied on by the bank in which this court refused to allow previously allowed accounts to be reopened are distinguishable in that either they did not involve representations of fact susceptible of precise knowledge but rather questions of judgment and discretion as to matters fully and frankly disclosed in the accounts . . . or that the alleged wrongful acts or mistakes of the trustee were discernible from an examination of the accounts, the trust documents and the law. . . . We adhere to our decisions that it is the duty of beneficiaries "to study the account presented to the Probate Court by the trustee, and to make their objections at the hearing." Greene v. Springfield Safe Deposit & Trust Co., supra, 295 Mass. at 154, 3 N.E.2d at 257. However, in this case the fact of the widow's remarriage was not discernible from the most scrupulous examination of the accounts, the trust documents and the relevant law, and the bank cannot avoid responsibility here for its misrepresentations by alleging a breach of duty on the part of the academy.

As to the propriety of surcharging the bank for the amounts erroneously disbursed, when a trustee makes payment to a person other than the beneficiary entitled to receive the money, he is liable to the proper beneficiary to make restitution unless the payment was authorized by a proper court. . . . Since, as we have held the decrees allowing the twelfth through thirty-third accounts were revoked properly, the bank thus became liable to the academy to restore to the trust corpus the payments it made to Mrs. Troland/Flynn when she was not entitled to receive them. In addition to the amounts erroneously disbursed, the bank was also properly charged by the Probate Court judge with simple interest on those payments at the legal rate of six percent per annum. . . .

[T]he decree is affirmed.

NOTE AND QUESTION

1. In order to avoid expensive accountings, provisions are often inserted in a trust instrument providing that judicial accountings should be dispensed with and accounts rendered periodically to the adult income beneficiaries of the trust. In the case of testamentary trusts, a few courts have indicated that a testator will not be permitted to dispense with statutorily required accountings.[23] In the case of inter vivos trusts, which are not placed under judicial supervision by statute, it would appear that a "no judicial accounting" provision does not contravene public policy. But here again, at least in New York, such a provision may run into trouble. In In re Crane, 34 N.Y.S.2d 9 (Sup. Ct. 1942), an irrevocable inter vivos trust provided: "The written acceptance of the beneficiary entitled to income of the correctness of any account rendered by the Trustee shall constitute a final and complete discharge to said Trustee in respect of the matters covered by such account." This clause was held not to divest the remaindermen of their right to question the actions of the trustee. The court said:

> It does not seem conscionable to me to hold that the life tenant, who enjoys merely the income and who does not own or directly control the principal, should be permitted to be placed in an immunized position where she might possibly squander, or indirectly control, principal, and thus not only cheat the remaindermen but flagrantly frustrate the settlor's intention. The possibilities for collusion are too obvious and manifold. The opportunities for squeezing every penny of income from the principal so as to shrink the principal — by fair means or foul — to the serious detriment of the vested remaindermen, are so manifest that, unless compelled by mandatory language, the opportunities should not be sanctioned or emboldened. Rather, equity should, I think, barricade the door against the possibilities. [Id. at 14.]

___

23. New York courts in particular have had a negative attitude toward "no judicial accounting" provisions. See In re Uran, 24 Misc. 2d 1069, 204 N.Y.S.2d 840 (Sur. Ct. 1960); In re Burden, 5 Misc. 2d 558, 160 N.Y.S.2d 372 (Sur. Ct. 1957).

This reasoning is criticized by Westfall, Nonjudicial Settlement of Trustees' Accounts, 71 Harv. L. Rev. 40, 61 (1957). Professor Westfall argues that if the income beneficiaries can be given a power of appointment that diminishes or destroys the remainder, there is no reason to refuse to give effect to a clause permitting the income beneficiary to absolve the trustee from further accountability. Westfall also contends that public policy does not require the protection of remaindermen when the settlor has implicitly withheld protection.

In Briggs v. Crowley, 352 Mass. 194, 224 N.E.2d 417 (1967), the court held that the clauses in an inter vivos trust instrument purporting to relieve the trustees of the duty to account to anyone were invalid as against public policy insofar as they purported to deprive a court of jurisdiction and the petitioner of standing to require the trustees to show that they had faithfully performed their duties.

2. *O* transfers property to *X* in trust to pay the income to *A* for life, remainder to *A*'s children. *A* is now 42 years old, is not married, and has no issue. To avoid expense, chargeable against the trust assets, *A* seeks to have the trustee account nonjudicially to her, agreeing to indemnify the trustee against any objections to its administration subsequently made by the remaindermen. Should the trustee agree to this?

NOTE: CHANGING TRUSTEES

Suppose that the beneficiaries are dissatisfied with the performance of the trustee or are dissatisfied with the fees charged. Can the beneficiaries remove the trustee and have a new trustee appointed? Unless the trustee has been guilty of breach of trust or has shown unfitness, the answer is No. The standard rule is that inasmuch as the settlor reposed special confidence in the designated trustee, the court will not change trustees merely because the beneficiaries want to. 2 A. Scott, Trusts §§107-107.3 (W. Fratcher 4th ed. 1987).

The inability of beneficiaries to change trustees lessens competition among trust companies and contributes to higher trustees' fees. Should this rule be changed?

In answering this question, consider the erosion of personal traditional fiduciary relationships in recent years. In some states, entire inventories of trust accounts are now routinely bought and sold between banks. Beneficiaries may currently be served by a bank or trust company never selected by the settlor. Should the beneficiaries now be offered the opportunity to change trustees if they are disadvantaged by these transactions? California Prob. Code §15642 (Supp. 1989) authorizes a court to remove a trustee where the trustee's compensation is excessive or for other good cause, upon petition by a beneficiary. To encourage out-of-court solutions, where a corporate trustee without good cause refuses to resign and transfer the trust property to a successor corporate trustee, and the court orders the transfer, Cal. Prob. Code §15645 (Supp. 1989) permits the beneficiaries to recover from the corporate trustee costs and attorneys' fees incurred in the proceedings.

13

WEALTH TRANSFER TAXATION: TAX PLANNING

SECTION A. INTRODUCTION

1. A Brief History of Federal Wealth Transfer Taxation

Death duties have an ancient history and were known to the Greeks, Romans, and even to the Egyptians. In this country until World War I federal death duties were only levied temporarily during times of urgent need for revenue. When relations with France deteriorated in 1797, Congress imposed stamp taxes on legacies; the taxes disappeared five years later when the revenue crisis had passed. During the Civil War Congress levied an inheritance tax, which was promptly repealed after the war. Again in the 1890s, seeking revenues to finance our military encounters with Spain, Congress imposed an inheritance tax, which was discarded upon victory. In 1916, with military expenditures mounting, Congress turned again to death duties as an untapped source of revenue and enacted an *estate* tax. (Generally speaking, an estate tax is imposed on the transferor's estate, an inheritance tax on the transferee.)

The 1916 estate tax was not repealed at the end of World War I because the tax had come to be seen as a means of levelling great fortunes as well as a source of revenue. Public hostility toward great wealth began to manifest itself in the late nineteenth century, soon after enormous fortunes had been amassed by John D. Rockefeller, Cornelius Vanderbilt, J.P. Morgan, and others during the "robber baron" era. Inheritance taxes were imposed by several states as a result of populist pressures, and soon after the turn of the century President Theodore Roosevelt proposed a steeply graduated inheritance tax on "swollen fortunes which it is certainly of no benefit to this country to perpetuate."[1] Thereafter the movement for an inheritance tax to break up hereditary accumulations gained many new supporters, even among conservatives. But Congress declined to act until the war required it to find new sources of revenue.

After World War I Congress was subjected to conflicting pressures. Some groups wanted to retain the estate tax to regulate hereditary wealth, others wanted to repeal this "socialistic" tax on capital. Congress responded by leaving the tax in place and reducing rates. In 1931, beset by the need to increase revenues in the Great Depression, Congress again turned to the estate tax. With President Hoover's blessing (Hoover regarded the estate tax as a means of striking at "the evils of inherited economic power"), Congress doubled the rates of the estate tax, pushing the tax on any estate in excess of $10 million to 45 percent. At the same time, Congress imposed a gift tax to prevent avoidance of death taxes by inter vivos gifts.

With the Franklin D. Roosevelt administration, the estate tax entered a new phase. The levelling of great inherited fortunes was formally accepted as an objective of the estate tax. In a message to Congress, President Roosevelt declared:

> The desire to provide security for one's self and one's family is natural and wholesome, but it is adequately served by a reasonable inheritance. Great accumulations of wealth cannot be justified on the basis of personal and family security. In the last analysis such accumulations amount to the perpetuation of great and undesirable concentration of control in a relatively few individuals over the employment and welfare of many, many others. . . . [I]nherited economic power is as inconsistent with the ideals of this generation as inherited political power was inconsistent with the ideals of the generation which established our government. [H.R. Rep. No. 1681, 74th Cong., 1st Sess. 2 (1935), 1939-1 Cum. Bull. (Part 2) 643.]

To level the rich and to raise money to finance the Second World War, Congress, during the 1930s and 1940s, kept raising the rates every few years. Finally, in the Internal Revenue Code of 1954, the exemption from estate taxes was fixed at $60,000; the rates went up to 77 percent on any estate in excess of $10 million.

Though the rates were high, the loopholes in the 1954 Code were several. The term *loopholes* describes both ways of avoiding estate taxation intentionally provided by Congress and ways subsequently discovered

---

1. 17 Works of Theodore Roosevelt 434 (Memorial ed. 1925). Our historical summary of the estate tax draws heavily from Eisenstein, The Rise and Decline of the Estate Tax, 11 Tax L. Rev. 223 (1956). This article is well worth reading in its entirety.

by imaginative lawyers. The gift tax rates were set at 75 percent of estate tax rates, thus providing an incentive to make gifts before death. Both gift and estate taxes provided an unlimited deduction for transfers to charity. A taxpayer in the 77 percent bracket might well choose to leave huge sums to charity rather than pay 77 percent to the government. The Ford Foundation, for example, was, like many other charitable foundations, established largely to avoid estate taxation. Other ways of avoiding the tax burden, intentionally provided by Congress, included devising property to the taxpayer's spouse (the marital deduction), buying life insurance (life insurance is not included in the gross estate unless the decedent possesses incidents of ownership over it), and creating a trust with successive life beneficiaries (the estate tax, imposed on transferable interests, does not apply on the death of a life tenant, who can transfer nothing). This last loophole in the 1954 Code, continued from the earliest estate tax days, was the foundation stone of dynastic trusts set up to avoid estate taxes for future generations. A rich person, *O*, could create a trust for *A* for life, then for *B* for life, then for *C* for life, and so on until the Rule against Perpetuities calls a halt (approximately 100 years later). Although *O* had to pay either a gift or estate tax upon creating the trust, no estate tax would be levied at the death of *A*, *B*, *C*, or any succeeding life tenant. If *O* created the trust back in, say, 1935, the trust would still be going on today, paying out income to successive life beneficiaries, without an estate tax ever having been levied since the creation of the trust.

The estate and gift tax scheme of the Internal Revenue Code of 1954, described above, lasted about a generation. Beginning in 1976, Congress began tinkering with the Code, first with moderate revisions, later with substantial restructuring that completely changed the life of estate planners. In the Tax Reform Act of 1976, the gift and estate taxes were unified. The same rate schedule was applied to both gifts and estates. The new rate schedule was applied to cumulative gifts and bequests; each taxable gift moved the taxpayer toward a higher bracket, and the estate tax bracket was determined by the sum of cumulative lifetime gifts and the decedent's gross estate at death, in effect making a bequest the final gift. However, though the gift and estate tax rates were unified, tax advantages in lifetime giving still remain (see infra page 938).

The 1976 change was minor. It took a Republican administration to redo completely the federal estate and gift tax system. The Economic Recovery Tax Act of 1981, enacted at the urging of President Reagan, provided considerable tax relief at both the lower and upper ends of the economic scale. The tax exemption (in the form of a credit) was increased to $600,000, thus eliminating estate tax worries of the vast majority of citizens. At the same time the top rate was lowered to 55 percent, to be lowered further, to 50 percent, in 1992. An unlimited marital deduction was also introduced into the tax system. A husband or wife can transfer to his or her spouse unlimited amounts of property tax free. Transfer taxes are not levied until the spouses' property is transferred outside the marital unit. With the unlimited marital deduction, and the exemption of estates under $600,000, tax planning became — after 1981 — estate planning for the rich. The middle class — which for more than 40 years had skewed its estate plans to avoid taxation on estates exceeding $60,000 — was removed by Congress from the estate taxation system.

A second tax act of the Reagan administration — the Tax Reform Act of 1986 — struck the rich a body blow. It closed the great loophole in the estate tax — the exemption of the life estate from taxation. History may record that this tax act did more damage to dynastic wealth in this country than any previous tax act. The Tax Reform Act of 1986 imposed a *generation-skipping transfer tax*, at the highest rate of the estate tax, upon any generation-skipping transfer (which is, generally speaking, a transfer that skips the estate tax for a generation). Hence, in the trust created by *O* above, a generation-skipping transfer tax is payable at the death of *A*, at the death of *B*, and at the death of *C*. Congress has now decided that a wealth transfer tax must be exacted once every generation from millionaire families. The tax saving possibilities of the dynastic trust have been severely curtailed.

Federal wealth transfer taxation now consists of three different taxes: (a) gift tax, (b) estate tax, and (c) generation-skipping transfer tax. We shall treat them in that order in this book.

NOTE: ESTATE AND INHERITANCE TAXES
DISTINGUISHED

As suggested at the beginning of this introduction, death duties can take several forms; the usual forms are an estate tax, an inheritance tax, or an accessions tax. The federal government imposes an estate tax, whereas many of the states impose an inheritance tax. What is the difference? An *estate tax* is a tax upon the privilege of transfer and is levied upon the decedent's estate (the transferor being dead and being unable to pay). The tax is levied on the total amount transferred or, to put it more technically, on the amount of the decedent's taxable estate. An *inheritance tax* is a tax imposed upon each beneficiary for the privilege of receiving property from the dead. The amount each beneficiary pays in tax depends upon the size of the bequest received and the relationship of the beneficiary to the decedent (spouses and children pay lower rates than more remote kindred and friends). Under the federal estate tax, if a person dies leaving $2 million to ten children, the amount of tax is the same as if there were only one child. Under an inheritance tax with progressive rates for each beneficiary's share, the total amount of tax would be less for a decedent with ten children than it would be for a decedent with one child.

Whether an estate tax is preferable to an inheritance tax is debatable. An estate tax is generally thought easier to administer since it avoids valuing the share each beneficiary receives (especially where a discretionary trust or contingent future interest is involved). On the other hand, an inheritance tax might seem fairer because it is based upon the amount each beneficiary receives (and not on the size of the donor's estate) and also offers preferential treatment for close relatives.

In recent years, a number of scholars have come to favor an *accessions tax*, which is a cumulative form of an inheritance tax. The tax on a given accession by gift or inheritance is calculated by applying the tax rate schedule to the cumulative tax base (consisting of prior taxable accessions plus the current accession), and deducting the tax paid on the prior accessions. Under an accessions tax, the progressive tax is based upon cumulative gratuitous receipts; under the present federal estate and gift taxes, the progressive tax is based upon cumulative gratuitous transfers. The arguments in favor of an accessions tax are that it more effectively breaks up undue wealth concentrations by taxing very heavily the individual who receives large inheritances, correlates the tax burden with each recipient's ability to pay, and resolves many of the difficulties in correlating the gift tax and the estate tax. See Halbach, An Accessions Tax, 23 Real Prop., Prob. & Tr. J. 211 (1988).

For proposals to further restructure the wealth transfer taxes, see Graetz, To Praise the Estate Tax, Not to Bury It, 93 Yale L.J. 259 (1983); Gutman, Reforming Federal Wealth Transfer Taxes After ERTA, 69 Va. L. Rev. 1183 (1983); Dodge, Beyond Estate and Gift Tax Reform: Including Gifts and Bequests in Income, 91 Harv. L. Rev. 1177 (1978) (proposing to treat gifts and inheritances as income taxable under the income tax law).

2.   The Unified Federal Estate and Gift Tax

One of the first things you need to do to understand the unified estate and gift tax system is to see how it works. If you understand the basic principles of the unified system, details and modifications that come later will be easier to understand. In this brief introduction, we want to concentrate on how a cumulative system works and how the unified credit works.

The Tax Reform Act of 1976 unified gift and estate taxes for estates of decedents dying after December 31, 1976, and for gifts made after that date. A single unified rate schedule applies to both gift and estate taxes. The rates are progressive on the basis of *cumulative* lifetime and death transfers. For lifetime gifts, the amount of the gift tax is determined by applying the unified rate schedule to cumulative gifts and then subtracting gift taxes payable on gifts made in earlier tax periods. The tentative estate tax is computed by applying the unified rate schedule to the aggregate of the decedent's taxable estate *plus* taxable gifts made after 1976. From this tentative tax are deducted gift taxes paid on the post-1976 gifts.

The unified credit applicable to gift and estate taxes in effect gives to taxpayers a certain number of "credits," which they can apply against gift taxes or, if not used during life, against estate taxes.[2] Generally speaking, a credit is the equivalent of an exemption. The unified credit is $192,800, which is the equivalent of an exemption of $600,000 from taxation.

The schedule below sets forth the transfer tax rates applicable to gifts made, and to decedents dying, between 1990 and 1992. After 1992, the maximum rate declines to 50 percent for transfers of $2,500,000 or more.

Unified Transfer Tax Rate Schedule

(A) Amount subject to tax more than —	(B) Amount subject to tax equal to or less than —	(C) Tax on amount in column (A)	(D) Rate of tax on excess over amount in column (A) Percent
—	$ 10,000	—	18
$ 10,000	20,000	$ 1,800	20
20,000	40,000	3,800	22
40,000	60,000	8,200	24
60,000	80,000	13,000	26
80,000	100,000	18,200	28
100,000	150,000	23,800	30
150,000	250,000	38,800	32
250,000	500,000	70,800	34
500,000	750,000	155,800	37
750,000	1,000,000	248,300	39
1,000,000	1,250,000	345,800	41
1,250,000	1,500,000	448,300	43
1,500,000	2,000,000	555,800	45
2,000,000	2,500,000	780,800	49
2,500,000	3,000,000	1,025,800	53
3,000,000	—	1,290,800	55

If you will apply the $192,800 credit to the taxes given in the schedule,

---

2. The use of the unified credit to offset gift tax liability is mandatory. A donor cannot use the credit as he sees fit or avoid using it where the donee agrees to pay the gift tax.

you will find that gift and estate tax rates will start at 37 percent on taxable gifts or estates worth $600,000 or more. (How to do this? Look in column (C) until you find $155,800, the tax on $500,000. Column (D) tells you that the tax on the excess over $500,000 (up to $750,000) is 37 percent. Therefore the tax on $100,000 in excess of $500,000 is $37,000. Add $37,000 and $155,800; the sum is $192,800, the maximum credit. Therefore, because of the credit, $600,000 is exempt from tax.)

Case 1 illustrates how the tax applies to cumulative gifts and also illustrates the tax credit.

Case 1. In 1990 W, a widow, gives Acme stock worth $100,000 to her daughter D. W is entitled to make a tax-free gift of up to $10,000 to any donee each year (see infra page 946); hence W is entitled to exclude $10,000 of this gift from taxable gifts. W makes no gifts of more than $10,000 to any other person in 1990. W has not made any taxable gifts in any earlier year. In 1990 W files a gift tax return showing:

$100,000	gift to D in 1990
− 10,000	annual exclusion
$ 90,000	taxable gift in 1990
+ 0	taxable gifts in earlier years
$ 90,000	cumulative taxable gifts
$ 21,000	tentative gift tax
− 21,000	unified gift tax credit used
$ 0	gift tax due

In 1991 W gives Beta stock worth $100,000 to D. W makes no gifts in excess of $10,000 to any other person in 1991. In 1991 W files a gift tax return showing:

$100,000	gift to D in 1991
− 10,000	annual exclusion
$ 90,000	taxable gift in 1991
+ 90,000	taxable gifts in earlier years (Acme stock in 1990)[3]
$180,000	cumulative taxable gifts
$ 48,400	tax on cumulative gifts
− 21,000	tax on preceding gifts (1990)
$ 27,400	tentative gift tax
− 27,400	unified gift tax credit used
$ 0	tax due

3. Taxable gifts in prior years are brought into the computation at their date-of-gift value. If Acme stock were worth $200,000 in 1991, it would still be included in the 1991 return at its previous taxable gift value ($90,000).

In Case 1, observe the effect of a rate schedule based on cumulative gifts. The 1990 gift of Acme stock is taxed at a marginal rate of 28 percent; the 1991 gift of Beta stock of the same value is taxed at a marginal rate of 32 percent. Under the cumulative transfer system, a donor does not start at the bottom rung of the tax rates for taxable gifts in any one year but starts on the rung where prior gifts left the donor. Similarly, a decedent starts on the rung he was on when he made his last inter vivos gift. Observe also that in Case 1 *W* has used $48,400 of her unified credit. If *W* dies in 1992 or thereafter, without making further gifts, *W* will have a credit of $144,400 to apply against the estate tax.[4]

QUESTION AND NOTE

1. Apart from taking advantage of the annual exclusion of $10,000 per donee, is there any transfer tax advantage in *W* making inter vivos gifts to her daughter, as in Case 1? If *W* has a choice of giving her daughter a $100,000 corporate bond, paying current market interest rates, due in the year 2010, or $100,000 worth of stock in a growth company, from the sole point of view of transfer taxes, which should she give?

2. One advantage of making a gift, which might not be obvious, results from the fact that the tax base for gifts is the value of the property transferred. If the transfer results in gift tax liability, the gift tax is not included in the gift tax base. On the other hand, the estate tax is levied on the decedent's assets at death, which include the amount that will be transferred to Uncle Sam as estate taxes. To express this difference, sometimes it is said that the gift tax is "tax-exclusive," whereas the estate tax is "tax-inclusive."

To illustrate, assume that *O* aims to transfer $1,000,000 to her daughter *A* and that this transfer is subject to a 50 percent rate. For *A* to receive by gift $1,000,000 subject to a tax of $500,000, *O* must part with a total of $1,500,000. Hence, the tax rate on the amount parted with is really $33\frac{1}{3}$ percent. In contrast, for *O* to transfer $1,000,000 to *A* at death, *O* must part with $2,000,000 (subject to a 50 percent rate) to get $1,000,000 in the hands of *A*. The tax preference for lifetime giving can be expressed as a rate reduction. If the maximum estate tax rate is 50 percent, the equivalent gift tax rate is $33\frac{1}{3}$ percent. To

---

4. Actually, it is not technically accurate to say that *W* will have a credit of only $144,400 to apply against the estate tax. Since the taxable gifts of $180,000 made in 1990 and 1991 must be added to *W*'s gross estate to determine *W*'s estate tax, the entire unified credit of $192,800 is available to *W*'s estate. Our explanation, however, is a simple way of indicating how much credit (and how much exemption) *W* has left.

eliminate the tax preference for lifetime giving, the gift tax itself would have to be included in the gift tax base.

The A.B.A. Section on Taxation Task Force on Transfer Tax Restructuring disagrees with a current Treasury proposal to make the gift tax base tax-inclusive. It says a tax preference for lifetime giving creates social and economic benefits by causing "business and investment capital to be moved into the hands of younger, more vigorous owners." A.B.A. Section on Taxation, Task Force Report on Transfer Tax Restructuring, 41 Tax Law. 395, 403 (1988). Do you agree? See Gutman, A Comment on the ABA Tax Section Task Force Report on Transfer Tax Restructuring, id. at 653, 656-657. See also Sims, Timing Under a Unified Wealth Transfer Tax, 51 U. Chi. L. Rev. 34 (1984); Isenbergh, Further Notes on Transfer Tax Rates, id. at 91.

Liability for payment of taxes.   The donor has the primary liability for paying the gift tax. If the donor does not pay, the donee is liable for unpaid gift tax. The executor or administrator of a decedent's estate has personal liability for payment of the estate tax but is entitled to reimbursement out of the decedent's estate. If there is no administration of the decedent's estate, persons in possession of the decedent's property are liable for the tax due.

Although the executor or administrator must pay the entire estate tax due, the executor or administrator is entitled to be reimbursed from life insurance beneficiaries for the portion of the tax resulting from the inclusion of life insurance in the decedent's estate. IRC §2206. Similarly, the executor is entitled to proportionate reimbursement from recipients of property over which the decedent had a general power of appointment. Id. §2207. With these two exceptions, the Code does not generally provide for apportionment of estate taxes to the recipients but leaves the matter to state law. A large majority of states follows the rule that federal estate taxes are apportioned and must be borne by each beneficiary pro rata, in the absence of a direction to the contrary in the testator's will. A minority of states follows the opposite rule: Unless the testator's will directs otherwise, the estate tax is paid out of the residuary estate. See Estate of Rosta, 111 Ill. App. 3d 786, 444 N.E.2d 704 (1982).

SECTION B.   THE FEDERAL GIFT TAX

1.   Nature of a Taxable Gift

Section 2501(a) of the Internal Revenue Code of 1986 imposes a gift tax on "the transfer of property by gift" during each calendar year by an individual. But nowhere in the Code is *gift* defined. The courts have decided that the question is not whether the donor has donative intent, but whether the donor gives up complete dominion and control. If the donor keeps dominion and control, the gift is not complete and no taxable gift has been made. Creation of a revocable trust does not effect a taxable transfer. The transfer is not complete until the power of revocation ceases. If the power of revocation ceases at the donor's death, no gift tax is due, but the trust property is included in the donor's gross estate under the estate tax.

Holtz's Estate v. Commissioner
United States Tax Court, 1962
38 T.C. 37

DRENNAN, J. . . . The principal issue for decision is whether taxable gifts resulted from transfers to a trust established by [Leon Holtz, the decedent] by deed of trust dated June 12, 1953, wherein Leon was the settlor and Land Title Bank and Trust Company, now Provident Tradesmens Bank and Trust Company, was the sole trustee. The trust instrument provided that the trustee should distribute the net income therefrom and the principal thereof as follows. During the lifetime of settlor the income should be paid to him, and as much of the principal as the trustee "may from time to time think desirable for the welfare, comfort and support of Settlor, or for his hospitalization or other emergency needs," should be paid to him or for his benefit. Upon the death of the settlor, if his wife survived him, the income of the trust was to be paid to her during her lifetime, and a similar provision was made for invasion of principal for her benefit during her lifetime. The trust was to terminate at the death of the survivor of settlor and his wife and the "then-remaining principal" was payable to the estate of the survivor.

On June 12, 1953, Leon transferred property having a value of $384,117 to the trust, and on January 18, 1955, he transferred an additional $50,000 in cash to the trust. Respondent determined that, as a result of these transfers, Leon made taxable gifts in 1953 in the amount of $263,277.63, and in 1955 in the amount of $35,570, computing the value of the taxable gifts by reducing the value of the property transferred in each instance by the actuarial value of Leon's life estate and reversionary interest in each transfer. Petitioner claims the transfers were not completed gifts and that no part of the value thereof was subject to gift tax. . . .

The Internal Revenue Codes of 1939 and 1954 provide no guideposts for determining when a gift becomes complete for gift tax purposes beyond the direction that "the tax shall apply whether the transfer is in trust or otherwise, whether the gift is direct or indirect, and whether the property is real or personal, tangible or intangible." [IRC §2511(a).] It is well settled in cases involving this issue, however, that the question whether a transfer in trust is a completed gift, and thus subject to gift tax, turns on whether the settlor has abandoned sufficient dominion and control over the property transferred to put it beyond recall. Burnet v. Guggenheim, 288 U.S. 280 (1933); Estate of Sanford v. Commissioner, 308 U.S. 39 (1939); Smith v. Shaughnessy, 318 U.S. 176 (1943).

Here we do not have a situation where the settlor either reserved the power in himself alone to modify, alter, or revoke the trust and thus revest the trust property in himself, as in Burnet v. Guggenheim, supra, or reserved the power to alter the disposition of the property or income therefrom in some way not beneficial to himself, as in Estate of Sanford v. Commissioner, supra, or reserved the power in conjunction with someone else to modify, alter, or revoke the trust, as in Camp v. Commissioner, 195 F.2d 999 (C.A. 1, 1952), reversing in part 15 T.C. 412 (1950). Leon reserved no rights in himself to change the disposition of the income or principal of the trust as fixed in the trust agreement. However, the trust agreement itself gave the trustee power to pay directly to Leon or for his benefit as much of the principal of the trust as the trustee thought desirable for Leon's welfare, comfort, and support, or for his hospitalization or other emergency needs. The question is whether this discretionary power placed in the trustee by the settlor under the terms of the trust agreement made the gifts of the remainder interests incomplete for gift tax purposes.

A number of cases decided by this and other courts have held that the placing of discretionary power in the trustee to invade corpus makes the gift of corpus incomplete under certain circumstances. The rule of thumb generally accepted seems to be that if the trustee is free to exercise his unfettered discretion and there is nothing to impel or compel him to invade corpus, the settlor retains a mere expectancy which does not make the gift of corpus incomplete. Herzog v. Commissioner, 116 F.2d 591 (C.A. 2, 1941), affirming 41 B.T.A. 509 (1940). But if the exercise of the trustee's discretion is governed by some external standard which a court may apply in compelling compliance with the conditions of the trust agreement, and the trustee's power to invade is unlimited, then the gift of corpus is incomplete, Commissioner v. Irving Trust Co., 147 F.2d 946 (C.A. 2, 1945), affirming 2 T.C. 1052 (1943), and this is true even though such words as "absolute" and "uncontrolled" are used in connection with the trustee's discretion, provided the external standards are clearly for the guidance of the trustee in exercising his discretion. Estate of John J. Toeller, 6 T.C. 832 (1946), affd. 165 F.2d 665 (C.A. 7, 1948); Estate of Lelia E. Coulter, 7 T.C. 1280 (1946).

The theory behind this rule seems to be that by placing such standards for guidance of the trustee's discretion in the trust agreement itself, the settlor has not actually lost all dominion and control of the trust corpus or put it completely beyond recall because to ignore the implications and purpose for writing the standards into the invasion clause would be an abuse of discretion on the part of the trustee which the trustee would neither desire to do nor be likely to risk doing under State laws. . . .

The rule of thumb appears to be a reasonable application of the general rule established in the *Guggenheim, Sanford,* and *Shaughnessy* cases because where there is a reasonable possibility that the entire corpus might be repaid to the settlor there can be no assurance that anyone else will receive anything in the form of a gift, and if the corpus should happen to be kept intact until the settlor's death, even though the transfer in trust was not subjected to a gift tax, the corpus of the trust will in all likelihood be subjected to the estate tax in the settlor's estate. See Estate of John J. Toeller, supra; Estate of Lelia E. Coulter, supra.

Applying the above principles to the facts under consideration here, we conclude that no part of or interest in the property transferred to the trust constituted a completed gift for gift tax purposes when transferred to the trust.

The form of the trust agreement indicates that the principal beneficiary of the income, and the principal if it became desirable for his welfare, comfort, support, or emergency needs, was the settlor. The first instructions to the trustee, as shown by the part of the deed of trust quoted in our Findings of Fact, were to distribute net income and principal to the settlor during his lifetime. Only upon the death of the settlor, and if she survived him, was any provision made for payment of either income or principal to the settlor's wife. And only upon the death of the survivor of settlor and his wife was any provision made for distribution of the "then-remaining principal." The trustee had the unfettered power to use all of the corpus for the benefit of settlor, if it thought that it was desirable for the welfare, comfort, or needs of the settlor. The words used were broad enough to cover about anything Leon might want or need. It is reasonable to assume that the trustee would invade corpus and that it would be required to do so by a court if the welfare, comfort, or needs of the settlor made it seem desirable. Otherwise, there would not have been much reason for including the paragraph giving the trustee power to invade principal. It was entirely possible that the entire corpus might be distributed during the settlor's lifetime and no one other than the settlor would receive any portion thereof. As long as that possibility was present, by reason of the language employed by the settlor, the settlor had not abandoned sufficient dominion and control over the property transferred to make the gift consummate. Estate of John J. Toeller, supra.

In addition to the trust agreement itself, the evidence indicates that the settlor, who was 80 years of age when the trust was established, expressed concern over whether he would have available sufficient funds to meet his needs. He asked the trust officer whether he would have enough money to buy an automobile and the trust officer reassured him by telling him that the trust agreement provided for the payment of all income to him and that he could also have money out of the principal, and that the trustee would be liberal in giving him money out of the principal. While the term "liberal" is not defined, the above conversation indicates the understanding of the parties was that the trustee recognized that principal should be distributed at any time the settlor's needs reasonably justified it. . . .

Decision will be entered for the petitioner.

NOTES AND PROBLEMS

1.   *O* transfers property in trust to pay income to her son *A* for life and on *A*'s death to pay the principal to *A*'s daughter *B*. *O* retains the power to revoke the trust. Because *O* retains the power to revoke the trust, the income from the trust property is taxed to *O* whether the income is paid to *O* or to *A*. See IRC §§676, 677 (income tax). Suppose that the trustee earns $10,000 during the calendar year after the trust is created and the trustee pays the $10,000 to *A*. Who pays income tax on the $10,000? Has a taxable gift been made to *A*?

Suppose that *O* did not reserve the power to revoke the trust but reserved only the power to change the owner of the remainder interest from *B* to *A* at any time during *A*'s life. (At the time of transfer, *O*'s granddaughter *B* was in her teens and was a rather willful, indeed rebellious, young lady experimenting with drugs.) Has *O* made a taxable gift to *A*? To *B*? Suppose that after reaching majority during *A*'s life, *B* irrevocably assigns her interest to a Hindu mystic, under whose influence she has fallen. Has *B* made a taxable gift to the mystic? If *A* dies, leaving *O* surviving, and the remainder passes then to the mystic, has *O* at that time made a taxable gift? See Macris, Open Valuation and the Completed Transfer: A Problem Area in Federal Gift Taxation, 34 Tax L. Rev. 273, 278 n.16 (1979).

If *O* cannot recover the transferred property, why should not *O* be treated as having made a completed gift? Has not *O*'s wealth been irrevocably depleted?

2.   *O* establishes an irrevocable trust that is funded with securities worth $200,000. Trust income is to be paid to *O* for life, "and on her death the trustee shall distribute the trust corpus to such of the Settlor's issue as she shall appoint by will; and in default of such appointment

the trustee shall distribute the corpus to the Settlor's issue then living, per stirpes." Has *O* made a taxable gift of a remainder? See Treas. Reg. §25.2511-2(b). Suppose that *O* releases the special power of appointment. Does the release result in a taxable gift of a remainder? If so, how is the remainder valued? See supra page 647.

Since *O* retained a life estate in the trust assets, the value of the trust assets will be taxable at *O*'s death under §2036 of the estate tax. Any gift tax paid by *O* on this transfer is later credited against *O*'s estate tax; double taxation is thereby avoided. Nonetheless, in view of the estate tax consequences of this transfer, what is the purpose of taxing the gift of a remainder during life?

3. *O* transfers property in trust to pay the income to *A* for life, and on *A*'s death to distribute the principal to *B*. *O* retains the power to revoke or amend the trust instrument in whole or in part with the consent of *A*. Has a taxable gift been made? See Camp v. Commissioner, 195 F.2d 999 (1st Cir. 1952).

4. Although a gift is not defined in the Code, §2512(b), dealing with "part gift — part sale," helps define what is a gift. It provides:

> Where the property is transferred for less than an adequate and full consideration in money or money's worth, then the amount by which the value of the property exceeded the value of the consideration shall be deemed a gift, and shall be included in computing the amount of gifts made during the calendar year.

From this section it is inferred that a gift is a transfer where full consideration in money or money's worth is not received. As the statute indicates, a transfer can be part gift and part sale. If *O* sells land worth $100,000 to her son for $50,000, for example, the transfer is treated as a gift of $50,000.

The statute taxes indirect as well as direct gifts. If *O* lends money to her son *A* and forgives the debt, *O* makes a gift to *A*. Indeed, if *O* lets the statute of limitations run, barring the debt, *O* makes a gift to *A*. See Rev. Rul. 81-264, 1981-2 C.B. 186. A loan to a child evidenced by a demand note bearing no interest has been held to be a gift of the value of using the loaned funds. Dickman v. Commissioner, 465 U.S. 330 (1984).

5. *Disclaimer.* Suppose that an heir or legatee disclaims his intestate share or the legacy. Has the heir or legatee made a taxable gift to the person who takes the disclaimed property? Internal Revenue Code §2518(b) provides that no taxable gift is made if the refusal to take is a "qualified disclaimer." A disclaimer is "qualified" if:

> (a)   the disclaimer is in writing, and made either within nine months after the interest is created or within nine months after the disclaimant reaches 21, whichever is later,

(b)   the disclaimant has accepted no interest in the property, and

(c)   the transfer is to persons entitled under local law to disclaimed property and not to persons designated by the disclaimant.

A disclaimer of an undivided portion may be a qualified disclaimer. See supra page 126. See also Frimmer, A Decade Later: Final Disclaimer Regulations Issued Under Section 2518, 21 U. Miami Inst. on Est. Plan. ¶600 (1987); Gans, Disclaimers, 46 Inst. on Fed Taxn., ch. 52 (1988); Ramlow, Qualified Disclaimers: Planning Considerations Under the Final Regulations, 24 Idaho L. Rev. 413 (1988).

NOTE: INCOME TAX BASIS

Under the Internal Revenue Code, income tax is levied upon capital gain realized upon the sale of property. The amount of capital gain is the difference between the taxpayer's "basis" and the selling price. Generally speaking, if the taxpayer purchased the property, his basis is the purchase price. If O buys land for $50,000, and sells it for $75,000, the capital gain of $25,000 is subject to income taxation.

In the case of property acquired by gift, for purpose of computing gain on any subsequent sale by the donee, the donee takes the donor's basis (with an upward adjustment for any gift taxes paid by reason of the gift). IRC §1015. If property is acquired from a decedent, the basis of the property is the value of the asset as valued in the decedent's gross estate. Id. §1014. The *stepped-up basis* at death means that any capital gain on property held until death escapes income taxation.

PROBLEMS

1.   O purchases 100 shares of IBM common stock for $50 per share. Over the years, the stock's value increases to $150 per share.

(a)   If O sells the stock for $150 per share, what are the income tax consequences?

(b)   If O gives the stock to her son A and then A sells the stock for $150 per share, what are the income tax consequences?

(c)   If O dies leaving a will that bequeaths the stock to A and then A sells the stock for $150 per share, what are the income tax consequences?

2.   Does the transfer tax preference for lifetime gifts roughly compensate for the fact that the donor's basis is carried over to the donee whereas estate distributees get a new basis? See Stephan, A Comment on Transfer Tax Reform, 72 Va. L. Rev. 1471, 1480-1490 (1986).

3.   *Net gifts.*   If a donor makes a gift to a donee with a provision that the donee must pay the gift tax, the donee has made a "net gift"

to the donee (market value of the property less the gift tax paid). A gift of this type must be advised cautiously, however, because the donor of a net gift realizes taxable income to the extent that the gift tax exceeds the donor's basis. The donor receives an economic benefit by the donee's assumption of the donor's legal obligation to pay the gift tax. See Diedrich v. Commissioner, 457 U.S. 191 (1982).

2. The Annual Exclusion

Under §2503(b) of the Code, a taxpayer is permitted to exclude from taxable gifts the first $10,000 given to any person during the calendar year. The purpose of the exclusion "is to obviate the necessity of keeping an account of and reporting numerous small gifts, and . . . to fix the amount sufficiently large to cover in most cases wedding and Christmas gifts and occasionally gifts of relatively small amounts." H.R. Rep. No. 708, 72d Cong., 1st Sess. 29 (1932), 1939-1 C.B. (part 2) 457, 478.[5] A donor must file a gift tax return only if gifts (other than marital deduction gifts) to any donee during the year exceed the $10,000 annual exclusion and must report on the return only gifts in excess of $10,000 to any one person. Thus:

> Case 2. A gives $12,000 each to B and C and $5,000 to D. A must file a tax return reporting the gifts to B and C, from which two annual exclusions are deducted, leaving $4,000 in taxable gifts. The gift to D is not reported on the return because it is covered by the annual exclusion. If A had given only $10,000 each to B and C, no gift tax return need be filed.

In addition to the annual exclusion of $10,000 per donee, §2503(e) of the Code allows an unlimited exclusion for *tuition payments* and *medical expenses* paid on behalf of any person. With the rising cost of education, the $10,000 annual exclusion might not cover college tuition and educational expenses of children who have reached majority. (A parent generally has no duty to support a child who has reached majority, which in most states is now age 18, and college tuition technically could be considered a gift.) Similarly, some taxpayers incur large medical expenses on behalf of an elderly relative, an adult child, or someone else. Congress has taken the view that such payments should be exempt from gift taxes without regard to the amounts paid for such purposes or to the relationship between the donor and the donee.

---

5. The annual exclusion was $5,000 from 1932 to 1939, $4,000 from 1939 to 1942, and $3,000 from 1943 to 1981. Because of inflation, the Economic Recovery Tax Act of 1981 raised the annual exclusion to $10,000, beginning in 1982.

The §2503(e) exclusion applies only to payments made directly to the service provider and does not cover payments to reimburse expenses incurred by the donee. Also, the exclusion for educational expenses covers only "tuition [paid] to an educational institution," and does not include payments for related expenses such as dormitory bills, books, or living expenses.

Gifts of future interests.   The annual exclusion is not available for gifts of future interests. The denial of an exclusion for a gift of a future interest rests upon the apprehended difficulty, in many instances, of determining the number of eventual donees and the value of their respective gifts.

> *Case 3.*   O gives property worth $100,000 to A for life, remainder to A's issue. Based upon A's life expectancy, A's life estate is worth $65,000; the value of the remainder is worth $35,000 (see supra page 647 on valuation of future interests). O is entitled to a $10,000 exclusion for the gift to A of a possessory life estate, but O is not entitled to an exclusion for the remainder given to A's issue.

> *Case 4.*   O creates a trust to pay the income among O's three children in such shares as the trustee in its uncontrolled discretion deems advisable. Even though all the net income must be distributed, since no beneficiary has a right to any ascertainable portion of the income, no beneficiary has a present interest. No exclusions are allowable with respect to the transfers in trust.

The denial of an exclusion for a gift of a future interest creates special problems when property is given to a minor. A child can be given possession of a doll or a toy; the doll or toy is not a future interest. But if the property is income-producing or requires management, ordinarily possession is not given the child. The child takes possession only upon reaching majority. Is, then, any gift of income-producing property to a child a gift of a future interest? The answer is no, with qualifications. If property is given outright to a minor, the gift qualifies for the exclusion. So too does a gift to a guardian of a minor. But guardianship is cumbersome, expensive, and not to the minor's advantage (see supra page 103), and estate planners tend to avoid passing property to guardians. Property can be given in trust for a minor but care must be taken to draft the trust so as not to create a future interest. To permit flexible property management of a minor donee's property, Congress has provided in §2503(c) of the Code a way to avoid having a gift to a minor classified as a future interest.

Sec. 2503(c).   Transfer for the Benefit of Minor

No part of a gift to an individual who has not attained the age of 21 years on the date of such transfer shall be considered a gift of a future

interest in property for purposes of subsection (b) if the property and
the income therefrom —

> (1) may be expended by, or for the benefit of, the donee before
> his attaining the age of 21 years, and
> (2) will to the extent not so expended —
>> (A) pass to the donee on his attaining the age of 21 years, and
>> (B) in the event the donee dies before attaining the age of 21
>> years, be payable to the estate of the donee or as he may appoint
>> under a general power of appointment as defined in section 2514(c).

To create a §2503(c) trust for a minor qualifying for the annual
exclusion, the donor must give the trustee power to expend *all* the
income and principal on the donee before the donee reaches 21, and
further provide that unexpended income and principal must pass to
the donee at 21 or, if the donee dies under 21, to the donee's estate or
as the donee appoints under a general power. No person other than
the minor can have a beneficial interest in the property.

Section 2503(c) is not limited to transfers in trust. Any transfer that
satisfies the statute's requirements qualifies for an exclusion. To provide
a convenient form for making gifts to minors, every state has enacted
the Uniform Transfers to Minors Act or its equivalent. Under the act
property can be transferred to a person (including the donor) as
custodian for the benefit of a minor. The custodian's powers over income
and principal, set forth in the act (see supra page 455), meet the
requirements of §2503(c).

For discussion of gifts that qualify for the annual exclusion, see
Bittker, The $10,000 Annual Per-Donee Gift Tax Exclusion, 44 Ohio
St. L.J. 447 (1983); Sherman, 'Tis a Gift to be Simple: The Need for a
New Definition of "Future Interest" for Gift Tax Purposes, 55 U. Cin.
L. Rev. 585 (1987).

PROBLEM

O creates a trust for a minor grandchild *A*. The trustees are directed
to use income and principal for *A*'s support and education until
A reaches 21, when *A* is to receive the principal. The trust also provides that if *A* dies under age 21, the trust assets are to be distributed
among such of *O*'s descendants as *A* appoints by will and if *A* fails
to exercise the power of appointment, to *A*'s heirs. Is *O* entitled to
the annual exclusion? See Ross v. Commissioner, 652 F.2d 1365 (9th
Cir. 1981).

Crummey v. Commissioner
United States Court of Appeals, Ninth Circuit, 1968
397 F.2d 82

BYRNE, J.   On February 12, 1962, the petitioners executed, as grantors, an irrevocable living trust for the benefit of their four children. The beneficiaries and their ages at relevant times are as follows:

	Age	*12/31/62*	*12/31/63*
John Knowles Crummey		22	23
Janet Sheldon Crummey		20	21
David Clarke Crummey		15	16
Mark Clifford Crummey		11	12

Originally the sum of $50 was contributed to the trust. Thereafter, additional contributions were made by each of the petitioners in the following amounts and on the following dates:

$ 4,267.77	6/20/62
49,550.00	12/15/62
12,797.81	12/19/63

The dispute revolves around the tax years of 1962 and 1963. Each of the petitioners filed a gift tax return for each year. Each petitioner claimed a $3,000 per beneficiary tax exclusion under the provisions of 26 U.S.C. §2503(b). The total claimed exclusions were as follows:

D.C. Crummey	1962 — $12,000	1963 — $12,000
E.E. Crummey	1962 — $12,000	1963 — $12,000

The Commissioner of Internal Revenue determined that each of the petitioners was entitled to only one $3,000 exclusion [in 1962 (for John) and to only two $3,000 exclusions in 1963 (for John and Janet).] ... This determination was based upon the Commissioner's belief that the portion of the gifts in trust for the children under the age of 21 were "future interests" which are disallowed under §2503(b). The taxpayers contested the determination of a deficiency in the Tax Court. ...

The Tax Court followed the Commissioner's interpretation. ...

The key provision of the trust agreement is the "demand" provision which states:

> THREE.   *Additions.*   The Trustee may receive any other real or personal property from the Trustors (or either of them) or from any other person or persons, by lifetime gift, under a Will or Trust or from any other source. Such property will be held by the Trustee subject to the

terms of this Agreement. A donor may designate or allocate all of his gift to one or more Trusts, or in stated amounts to different Trusts. If the donor does not specifically designate what amount of his gift is to augment each Trust, the Trustee shall divide such gift equally between the Trusts then existing, established by this Agreement. The Trustee agrees, if he accepts such additions, to hold and manage such additions in trust for the uses and in the manner set forth herein. *With respect to such additions, each child of the Trustors may demand at any time (up to and including December 31 of the year in which a transfer to his or her Trust has been made) the sum of Four Thousand Dollars ($4,000.00) or the amount of the transfer from each donor, whichever is less, payable in cash immediately upon receipt by the Trustee of the demand in writing and in any event, not later than December 31 in the year in which such transfer was made. Such payment shall be made from the gift of that donor for that year. If a child is a minor at the time of such gift of that donor for that year, or fails in legal capacity for any reason, the child's guardian may make such demand on behalf of the child. The property received pursuant to the demand shall be held by the guardian for the benefit and use of the child.* (emphasis supplied)

The whole question on this appeal is whether or not a present interest was given by the petitioners to their minor children so as to qualify as an exclusion under §2503(b). The petitioners on appeal contend that each minor beneficiary has the right under California law to demand partial distribution from the Trustee. In the alternative they urge that a parent as natural guardian of the person of his minor children could make such a demand. As a third alternative, they assert that under California law a minor over the age of 14 has the right to have a legal guardian appointed who can make the necessary demand. . . .

It was stipulated before the Tax Court in regard to the trust and the parties thereto that at all times relevant all the minor children lived with the petitioners and no legal guardian had been appointed for them. In addition, it was agreed that all the *children* were supported by petitioners and none of them had made a demand against the trust funds or received any distribution from them.

The tax regulations define a "future interest" for the purposes of §2503(b) as follows:

"Future interests" is a legal term, and includes reversions, remainder, and other interests or estates, whether vested or contingent, and whether or not supported by a particular interest or estate, which are limited to commence in use, possession or enjoyment at some future date or time. Treasury Regulations of Gift Tax, §25.2503-3.

This definition has been adopted by the Supreme Court. Fondren v. Commissioner of Internal Revenue, 324 U.S. 18 (1945); Commissioner of Internal Revenue v. Disston, 325 U.S. 442 (1945). In *Fondren* the court stated that the important question is when enjoyment begins. There the court held that gifts to an irrevocable trust for the grantor's minor grandchildren were "future interests" where income was to be accumulated and the corpus and the accumulations were not to be paid until designated times commencing with each grandchild's 25th birthday. The trustee was authorized to spend the income or invade the corpus during the minority of the beneficiaries only if need were shown. The facts demonstrated that need had not occurred and was not likely to occur.

Neither of the parties nor the Tax Court has any disagreement with the above summarization of the basic tests. The dispute comes in attempting to narrow the definition of a future interest down to a more specific and useful form.

The Commissioner and the Tax Court both placed primary reliance on the case of Stifel v. Commissioner of Internal Revenue, 197 F.2d 107 (2nd Cir. 1952). In that case an irrevocable trust was involved which provided that the beneficiary, a minor, could demand any part of the funds not expended by the Trustee and, subject to such demand, the Trustee was to accumulate. The trust also provided that it could be terminated by the beneficiary or by her guardian during minority. The court held that gifts to this trust were gifts of "future interests." They relied upon *Fondren* for the proposition that they could look at circumstances as well as the trust agreement and under such circumstances it was clear that the minor could not make the demand and that no guardian had ever been appointed who could make such a demand.

The leading case relied upon by the petitioners is Kieckhefer v. Commissioner of Internal Revenue, 189 F.2d 118 (7th Cir. 1951). In that case the donor set up a trust with his newly born grandson as the beneficiary. The trustee was to hold the funds unless the beneficiary or his legally appointed guardian demanded that the trust be terminated. The Commissioner urged that the grandson could not effectively make such a demand and that no guardian had been appointed. The court disregarded these factors and held that where any restrictions on use were caused by disabilities of a minor rather than by the terms of the trust, the gift was a "present interest." The court further stated that the important thing was the right to enjoy rather than the actual enjoyment of the property. . . .

Although there are certainly factual distinctions between the *Stifel* and *Kieckhefer* cases, it seems clear that the two courts took opposing positions on the way the problem of defining "future interests" should be resolved. As we read the *Stifel* case, it says that the court should look at the trust instrument, the law as to minors, and the financial and other circumstances of the parties. From this examination it is up to the court to determine whether it is likely that the minor beneficiary is to receive any present enjoyment of the property. If it is not likely, then the gift is a "future interest." At the other extreme is the holding in *Kieckhefer* which says that a gift to the minor is not a "future interest" if the only reason for a delay in enjoyment is the minority status of the donee and his consequent disabilities. The *Kieckhefer* court noted that under the terms there present, a gift to an adult would have qualified for the exclusion and they refused to discriminate against a minor. The court equated a present interest with a present right to possess, use or enjoy. The facts of the case and the court's reasoning, however, indicate that it was really equating a present interest with a present right to possess, use or enjoy except for the fact that the beneficiary was a minor. In between these two positions there is a third possibility. That possibility is that the court should determine whether the donee is legally and technically capable of immediately enjoying the property. Basically this is the test relied on by the petitioners. Under this theory, the question would be whether the donee could possibly gain immediate enjoyment and the emphasis would be on the trust instrument and the laws of the jurisdiction as to minors. . . .

Under the provisions of this trust the income is to be accumulated and added to the corpus until each minor reaches the age of 21, unless the trustee feels in his discretion that distributions should be made to a needy beneficiary. From 21 to 35 all income is distributed to the beneficiary. After 35 the trustee again has discretion as to both income and corpus, and may distribute whatever is necessary up to the whole thereof. Aside from the actions of the trustee, the only way any beneficiary may get at the property is through the "demand" provision, quoted above.

One question raised in these proceedings is whether or not the trust prohibits a minor child from making a demand on the yearly additions to the trust. The key language from paragraph three is as follows: "If a child is a minor at the time of such gift of that donor for that year, or fails in legal capacity for any reason, the child's guardian may make such demand on behalf of the child." The Tax Court interpreted this provision in favor of the taxpayers by saying that "may" is permissive and thus that the minor child can make the demand if allowed by law, or, if not permitted by law, the guardian may do it. Although, as the Commissioner suggests, this strains the language somewhat, it does seem consistent with the obvious intent in drafting this provision. Surely, this provision was intended to give the minor beneficiary the broadest demand power available so that the gift tax exclusion would be applicable.

There is very little dispute between the parties as to the rights and disabilities of a minor accorded by the California statutes and cases. The problem comes in attempting to ascertain from these rights and disabilities the answer to the question of whether a minor may make a demand upon the trustee for a portion of the trust as provided in the trust instrument.

It is agreed that a minor in California may own property. Estate of Yano, 188 Cal. 645, 206 P. 995 (1922). He may receive a gift. DeLevillain v. Evans, 39 Cal. 120. A minor may demand his own funds from a bank (Cal. Fin. Code, §§850 & 853), a savings institution (Cal. Fin. Code, §§7600 & 7606), or a corporation (Cal. Corp. Code, §§2221 & 2413). A minor of the age of 14 or over has the right to secure the appointment of a guardian, and one will be appointed if the court finds it "necessary or convenient." Cal. Prob. Code, §1406; Guardianship of Kentera, 41 Cal. 2d 639, 262 P.2d 317 (1953).

It is further agreed that a minor cannot sue in his own name (Cal. Civ. Code, §42) and cannot appoint an agent. (Cal. Civ. Code, §33). With certain exceptions a minor can disaffirm contracts made by him during his minority. Cal. Civ. Code, §35. A minor under the age of 18 cannot make contracts relating to real property or personal property not in his possession or control. Cal. Civ. Code, §33.

The parent of a child may be its natural guardian, but such a guardianship is of the person of the child and not of his estate. Kendall v. Miller, 9 Cal. 591; Cal. Civ. Code, §202. . . .

The Commissioner concentrated on the inability to sue or appoint an agent and concluded that none of the minors had anything more than paper rights because he or she lacked the capacity to enforce the demand.

. . . We cannot agree with the position of the Commissioner because we do not feel that a lawsuit or the appointment of an agent is a necessary prelude to the making of a demand upon the trustee. As we visualize the hypothetical situation, the child would inform the trustee that he demanded his share of the additions up to $4,000. The trustee would petition the court for the appointment of a legal guardian and then turn the funds over to the guardian. It would also seem possible for the parent to make the demand as natural guardian. This would involve the acquisition of property for the child rather than the management of the property. It would then be necessary for a legal guardian to be appointed to take charge of the funds. The only time when the disability to sue would come into play, would be if the trustee disregarded the demand and committed a breach of trust. That would not, however, vitiate the demand.

All this is admittedly speculative since it is highly unlikely that a demand will ever be made or that if one is made, it would be made in this fashion. However, as a technical matter, we think a minor could make the demand.

Given the trust, the California law, and the circumstances in our case, it can be seen that very different results may well be achieved, depending upon the test used. Under a strict interpretation of the *Stifel* test of examining everything and determining whether there is any likelihood of present enjoyment, the gifts to minors in our case would seem to be "future interests." Although under our interpretation neither the trust nor the law technically forbid a demand by the minor, the practical difficulties of a child going through the procedures seem substantial. In addition, the surrounding facts indicate the children were well cared for and the obvious intention of the trustors was to create a long term trust. No guardian had been appointed and, except for the tax difficulties, probably never would be appointed. As a practical matter, it is likely that some, if not all, of the beneficiaries did not even know that they had any right to demand funds from the trust. They probably did not know when contributions were made to the trust or in what amounts. Even had they known, the substantial contributions were made toward the end of the year so that the time to make a demand was severely limited. Nobody had made a demand under the provision, and no distributions had been made. We think it unlikely that any demand ever would have been made. . . .

Under the general language of *Kieckhefer* which talked of the "right to enjoy," all exclusions in our case would seem to be allowable. The broader *Kieckhefer* rule which we have discussed is inapplicable on the facts of this case. That rule, as we interpret it, is that postponed enjoyment is not equivalent to a "future interest" if the postponement is solely caused by the minority of the beneficiary. In *Kieckhefer*, the income was accumulated and added to the corpus until the beneficiary reached the age of 21. At that time everything was to be turned over to him. This is all that happened unless a demand was made. In our case, on the contrary, if no demand is made in any particular year, the additions are forever removed from the uncontrolled reach of the beneficiary since, with the exception of the yearly demand provision, the only way the corpus can ever be tapped by a beneficiary, is through a distribution at the discretion of the trustee.

We decline to follow a strict reading of the *Stifel* case in our situation because we feel that the solution suggested by that case is inconsistent and unfair. It becomes arbitrary for the I.R.S. to step in and decide who is likely to make an effective demand. Under the circumstances suggested in our case, it is doubtful that any demands will be made against the trust — yet the Commissioner always allowed the exclusion as to adult beneficiaries. There is nothing to indicate that it is any more likely that John will demand funds than that any other beneficiary will do so. The only distinction is that it might be easier for him to make such a demand. Since we conclude that the demand can be made by the others, it follows that the exclusion should also apply to them. In another case we might follow the broader *Kieckhefer* rule, since it seems least arbitrary and establishes a clear standard. However, if the minors have no way of making the demand in our case, then there is more than just a postponement involved, since John could demand his share of yearly additions while the others would never have the opportunity at their shares of those additions but would be limited to taking part of any additions added subsequent to their 21st birthdays.

. . . The petitioners should be allowed all of the exclusions claimed for the two year period.

The decision of the Tax Court denying the taxpayers' exclusions on the gifts is reversed. . . .

NOTE AND PROBLEM

1. The Commissioner acquiesced in the *Crummey* case, and trusts with *Crummey* powers have proliferated. The estate planner now has two basic options in drafting trusts for minors: (a) draft a §2503(c) trust, or (b) include a power in the minor, exercisable within a reasonably limited period, to withdraw the amount of the annual exclusion or less. Rev. Rul. 83-108, 1983-2 C.B. 168, holds that a 45-day period to exercise the right of withdrawal after receiving notice is a reasonable time. Letter Ruling 9004172 approves a 30-day period. See Rothberg, *Crummey* Powers Enhance the Usefulness of Trusts for Minors and Life Insurance Trusts, 15 Est. Plan. 322 (1988); Simmons, Drafting the *Crummey* Power, 15 U. Miami Inst. Est. Plan. ¶1770 (1981). For criticism of the *Crummey* case, see Pedrick, Crummey is Really Crummy!, 20 Ariz. St. L.J. 943 (1988). See also Atkinson, Gifts to Minors: A Roadmap, 42 Ark. L. Rev. 567 (1989).

2. *O* creates a trust to pay the income to her daughter *A* for life, remainder to *A*'s children. *A* is given the power to withdraw $5,000 out of the property *O* gives to the trust in any given year. If *A* does not exercise the power during a particular year, it lapses. *A* is 8 years old. No guardian has been appointed for *A*. *O* transfers $5,000 to the trust. Does this qualify for the annual exclusion? If you are curious as to why we use the figure $5,000 rather than $10,000 (the maximum annual exclusion), see infra page 986.

3.   Gifts Between Spouses and from One Spouse to a Third Person

Since 1981 the Code has permitted one spouse to take an *unlimited* marital deduction for gifts to the other spouse (see infra page 997). Any amount of property (except certain terminable interests) can now be transferred between the spouses, either during life or at death, without payment of a gift or estate tax. The policy is: Husband and wife are permitted to treat their property as assets of a marital unit, transferable between husband and wife without paying any transfer taxes. Only when the assets pass from one of the spouses to a third person is a transfer tax imposed.

The marital deduction is allowed only if a spouse makes transfers to the other spouse that qualify for the marital deduction. The policy of Congress is that if a transfer of property from one spouse to the other is to be exempt from transfer tax, the transfer must be in a form that is subject to taxation when the property is transferred by the donee spouse to a third party. Inasmuch as a terminable interest (e.g. a life estate) is not subject to transfer taxation when it terminates, a *terminable interest* does not qualify for the marital deduction, subject to certain exceptions. The two most important exceptions to the nondeductible terminable interest rule are set forth below as Cases 6 and 7. Inasmuch as we give extended treatment to the marital deduction in connection with the estate tax (see infra pages 997-1017), we only mention the nondeductible terminable interest rule here in passing. It is enough to say — with an explanation to come later — that the following property interests qualify for the marital deduction under the gift tax and the estate tax:

Case 5.   *Fee simple or absolute ownership.*   W gives H $1 million outright. No gift tax is payable by W. The $1 million will be included in H's taxable gross estate at death if H then owns it. If H gives the property to a third person a gift tax will be payable.

Case 6.   *Power of appointment trust.*   W transfers $1 million in trust to pay H the income for his life and upon H's death to distribute the principal as H appoints by will. H has a life estate coupled with a general testamentary power of appointment. H has a terminable interest (a life estate), but it qualifies for the marital deduction because H has in addition a general power of appointment. No gift tax is payable by W. The value of the trust fund will be included in H's taxable gross estate at death.

Case 7.   *QTIP (qualified terminable interest property) trust.*   W transfers $1 million in trust to pay the income to H for life and upon H's death to distribute the principal to W's children. W may elect under §2523(f) of the Code to take a marital deduction for the terminable interest given H; as a result of this election, the value of the trust fund will be included in H's taxable gross estate at death even though H has only a life estate.

Observe that in all three transfers above, the gift by the wife qualifies for the marital deduction, but when the property is transferred by the husband to a (noncharitable) third party during life or at death, a gift or estate tax becomes payable. (If you want to know more about the marital deduction and cannot contain your curiosity, skip to page 997 infra.)

When property is transferred by gift from one spouse to a third person, the transfer is subject to taxation. However, if the other spouse consents, §2513 of the Code permits the gift to be considered as made one half by each spouse. Thus if the wife transfers $200,000 to her daughter, this may be treated — with the husband's consent — as a transfer by the wife of $100,000 and a transfer by the husband of $100,000. One effect of §2513 is to double the available annual exclusions.

PROBLEMS

1. *W* gives property worth $100,000 to *A*, and her husband *H* signifies his consent to splitting the gift by signing at the appropriate point on the gift tax return filed by the donor. Neither *W* nor *H* has made taxable gifts in any earlier year. What is the amount of taxable gift made by *W*? By *H*?

2. *H* and *W* have three children. They want to know (a) what is the maximum amount they can give to each child tax free each year without using any of their unified gift tax credits, and (b) what is the maximum amount they can give the children tax free in one year, using their annual exclusions and their unified gift tax credits. Suppose that *H* dies after making these gifts, leaving all his property to *W*. Is any estate tax payable on *H*'s death?

SECTION C. THE FEDERAL ESTATE TAX

1. A Thumbnail Sketch of the Federal Estate Tax

The basic purpose of the federal estate tax is to tax the value of property owned or passing at death plus the value of property given away during lifetime. This is accomplished by imposing a graduated tax rate schedule on the aggregate of the decedent's *taxable estate* plus *adjusted taxable gifts*, against which various *credits* may be applied.

In determining the amount of the taxable estate, the first step is to compute the value of the decedent's *gross estate*. The federal estate tax attempts to subject to taxation all manner of transfers wherein an economic benefit is transferred from the decedent to another person at death. The Internal Revenue Code's definition of the gross estate encompasses three general categories of transfers: (a) transfers by will or intestacy, (b) certain lifetime transfers that, generally speaking, pass economic benefits at the death of the decedent, and (c) certain nonprobate transfers.

Section 2033 of the Code reaches the value of all *property owned at death*. It thus applies to all "probate assets," i.e., property that passes by will or intestacy and is subject to administration in the decedent's estate.

Sections 2035-2038 sweep into the gross estate certain lifetime transfers. Section 2035 reaches some *gifts made within three years of death* plus any gift taxes paid thereon. Sections 2036 to 2038 include in the gross estate transfers in which the decedent retained some interest or control, to wit, *transfers with a retained life estate or with a retained power to control beneficial enjoyment, transfers taking effect at death*, and *transfers where the decedent has the power to revoke, alter, amend, or terminate*. In addition, §2043 taxes *transfers for a partial consideration*, including lifetime sales having a gift component to which one of the lifetime transfer sections applies.

Sections 2039-2042 include in the gross estate several types of "nonprobate" property. They apply to certain *annuities and employee benefits*, property passing by *right of survivorship*, property over which the decedent held a *general power of appointment*, and the proceeds of *life insurance* on the decedent's life.

Section 2044 applies to certain *transfers for which a marital deduction was previously allowed*. This section includes property in the decedent's gross estate if the decedent was the beneficiary of a "qualified terminable interest" in the property for which a marital deduction was allowed in the estate of the decedent's spouse.

The taxable estate is computed by subtracting from the gross estate various deductions to which the estate may be entitled. Since the tax is on the decedent's net estate, under §2053 the estate is entitled to a *deduction for administration and funeral expenses, debts, and taxes*. Section 2054 grants a *deduction for casualty losses* for assets lost, stolen, or destroyed during the course of estate administration. Under §2055, charitable bequests qualify for a *charitable deduction*. Transfers to a decedent's spouse that take a certain form qualify for a *marital deduction* under §2056.

Gross estate minus allowable deductions equals taxable estate. To compute the tax, the taxable estate is added to the date-of-gift value of *adjusted taxable gifts*, defined as taxable gifts, made after 1976, of property not otherwise includable in the gross estate. (Why 1976? because the gift and estate taxes were unified in that year, and the post-1976 rate schedule applies to cumulative gifts and bequests.) Taxable estate plus adjusted taxable gifts equals the *tentative estate tax base*, against which the tax rate schedule is applied to produce a *tentative estate tax*. From the tentative tax as thus computed are deducted gift taxes paid on taxable gifts made after 1976, which may be viewed as an advance payment of estate taxes. Also deducted are various credits to which the estate may be entitled. These include a *credit for state death taxes*, a *credit for gift taxes on pre-1977 gifts* that are included in the gross estate under one of the lifetime transfer sections, a *credit for taxes on prior transfers* that were taxed in the estate of another decedent within the preceding ten years, and a *credit for foreign death taxes.*

The most important credit is the *unified credit against the estate tax, which is $192,800.* This is the equivalent of a $600,000 exemption from the tax, i.e., a tentative estate tax base of $600,000 produces a tentative estate tax of $192,800, fully covered by the unified credit.

Here follows an outline of the estate tax provisions of the Internal Revenue Code in table form:

	§2033	Property owned at death
+	§2035	Transfers of life insurance policies and certain other interests within three years of death
+	§2036	Transfers with a retained life estate or with retained controls
+	§2037	Transfers taking effect at death
+	§2038	Revocable transfers
+	§2039	Annuities and employee benefits
+	§2040	Property passing by right of survivorship (joint tenancy)
+	§2041	General powers of appointment
+	§2042	Life insurance
+	§2043	Transfers for a partial consideration
+	§2044	Certain property for which a marital deduction was previously allowed

= Gross Estate

−	§2053	Deduction for administration expenses, debts, funeral expenses
−	§2054	Deduction for casualty losses
−	§2055	Charitable deduction
−	§2056	Marital deduction

= Taxable Estate

+ Adjusted taxable gifts (taxable gifts made after 1976, other than gifts that are includable in the decedent's gross estate)

= Tentative Estate Tax Base

× §2001   Estate tax rate schedule

= Tentative Estate Tax

−		Gift taxes on gifts made after 1976
−	§2010	Unified estate tax credit
−	§2011	Credit for state death taxes
−	§2012	Credit for pre-1977 gift taxes on property included in gross estate
−	§2013	Credit for taxes on prior transfers
−	§2014	Credit for foreign death taxes

= Federal Estate Tax

2. The Gross Estate: Property Passing by Will or Intestacy

a. Section 2033: Property Owned at Death

Section 2033 of the Internal Revenue Code provides: "The value of the gross estate shall include the value of property to the extent of the interest therein of the decedent at the time of his death." Section 2033 reaches all property owned at death that passes by will or intestacy. This includes real and tangible personal property; transmissible future interests; intangibles such as securities, patents, and copyrights; interests in an incorporated or unincorporated business; and undivided interests in property (such as the decedent's share of property held in a tenancy in common). In other words, the gross estate includes, under §2033, all items in the decedent's probate estate.

Section 2033 also reaches property owned at death that passes under a payable-on-death provision of a contract (other than life insurance, annuities, or employee death benefits, which are governed by separate sections of the Code).

If the decedent owned a life estate created by another person,[6] nothing is includable in the decedent's gross estate under §2033. Since a life estate terminates at death, the decedent owned no interest that could pass by will or intestacy. This principle is of considerable importance in estate planning. It is possible to transfer property into a trust giving the beneficiary the income from the property for life without causing any *estate* tax to be levied on the life beneficiary's death. It is even possible to give the income beneficiary certain limited powers to invade the corpus of the trust for his or her benefit and a special power to appoint the remainder interest at death, all without estate tax cost (see infra page 986). However, if the income beneficiary is of a younger generation than the settlor, a *generation-skipping transfer tax* may be levied at the life tenant's death (see infra pages 1022).

PROBLEM

State law determines what rights constitute property. Commissioner v. Estate of Bosch, 387 U.S. 456 (1967). In a majority of states, wrongful death statutes give specified survivors the right to recover for a wrongful death. Connecticut, however, gives the executor the right to sue the tortfeasor for wrongful death and provides that the recovery shall be

---

6. If the decedent made an inter vivos transfer with a retained life estate, the value of the transferred property is includable in the decedent's gross estate under §2036. See infra page 969.

distributed in accordance with the will of the victim or, if there is no will, to the victim's heirs. Is the value of an action for wrongful death "property of the decedent at the time of his death" under this statute? See Connecticut Bank & Trust Co. v. United States, 465 F.2d 760 (2d Cir. 1972).

b.   Section 2034: Dower or Curtesy

Property includable under §2033 includes assets passing to the surviving spouse by operation of law and over which the decedent did not have the power of disposition at death. Under §2034, "the value of the gross estate shall include the value of all property to the extent of any interest therein of the surviving spouse, existing at the time of the decedent's death as dower or curtesy, or by virtue of a statute creating an estate in lieu of dower or curtesy." Section 2034 does not apply to community property. In community property states, each spouse is the owner of an undivided one-half interest in community assets and has the power of testamentary disposition over only that one-half share. Only the value of the decedent's community interest is includable as an owned interest under §2033.

3.   The Gross Estate: Nonprobate Property

a.   Section 2040: Joint Tenancy

The decedent's interest in a joint tenancy is not taxed under §2033 because the decedent's interest terminates at death. A joint tenancy interest is, however, taxed under §2040. In discussing §2040, together with the gift tax rules applicable to the creation of joint tenancies, we must distinguish between (1) a joint tenancy between persons other than spouses and (2) a joint tenancy or tenancy by the entirety between husband and wife.

(1)   Joint Tenancy Between Persons Other than Husband and Wife
(a)   *Gift tax.*   A joint tenancy is treated differently under the gift tax from the way it is treated under the estate tax. Different principles of taxation are applied by these two taxes. Under the gift tax, a joint tenancy is treated in the same manner as a tenancy in common is treated. Case 8 illustrates the treatment of a tenancy in common created by the donor with the donee.

Case 8.   In 1990 *O* pays $40,000 for securities, taking title in the name of O and A as *tenants in common*. O and A each acquire an undivided one-half interest in the securities. O has made a gift of one-half the value of the property, or $20,000, to A. Deducting the $10,000 annual exclusion, O has made a taxable gift of $10,000. (Because of the unified credit against the gift tax, however, no gift tax is actually payable unless O has used up his unified credit.)

Since a joint tenant can sever at any time the joint tenancy, destroying the right of survivorship and converting the tenancy into a tenancy in common, the gift tax law assumes the donee joint tenant receives the same economic benefit as does a donee tenant in common. Thus:

> *Case 9.* In 1990 O pays $40,000 for securities, taking title in the name of O and A as *joint tenants with right of survivorship*. O has made a gift to A of one-half the value of the property, or $20,000. The valuation of the gift does not turn upon the ages of the parties but upon the fractional share of the whole given. If O is 70 years old and A 20, A is likely to survive O, but the value of A's right of survivorship is not treated as a gift because O can destroy it by severing the joint tenancy at any time.

A joint and survivor bank account is treated somewhat differently. In such an account either party can withdraw all funds on deposit, whereas a common law joint tenant can, by partition, only acquire title in severalty to his or her fractional share. Since a depositor in a joint and survivor account can withdraw the amount deposited (in effect, revoking the transfer), no gift occurs until the amount is withdrawn by the non-depositing party. Thus:

> *Case 10.* In 1990 O deposites $30,000 in a joint and survivor bank account; money in the account is payable to O or A or the survivor. Since O can withdraw the $30,000, the gift is incomplete (see supra page 297). If A withdraws funds from the account, a gift is then made from O to A of the amount withdrawn. Similarly, if O and A each deposit $15,000 in a joint account, no gift is made until either O or A withdraws more than the $15,000 he or she deposited. Treas. Reg. §25.2511.1(h)(4).

The rules applicable to a joint bank account also apply to a United States government bond registered in the name of "O or A." Under this "or" form of ownership, either O or A can present the bond for payment. Thus there is no gift unless A cashes in the bond.

(b) *Estate tax.* A joint tenancy is not treated like a tenancy in common under the federal estate tax. Instead, the decedent's share of a tenancy in common is included in his gross estate under §2033 in an amount ascertained by multiplying the value of the property at death by the decedent's fractional share. If the decedent is one of two tenants in common, one-half the value of the property is included in the decedent's gross estate. Thus:

> *Case 8a.*   Refer back to Case 8, involving the creation of a tenancy in common in 1990. *O* dies in 1991. *O* is survived by *A*. On *O*'s death the securities are worth $60,000. The value of *O*'s one-half interest in the securities, or $30,000, is includable in *O*'s gross estate under §2033 as an interest owned at death. $10,000 is brought into the estate tax computation as an adjusted taxable gift.

With respect to a joint tenancy, the amount included in the decedent's gross estate is not the value of the decedent's fractional share of ownership. Where spouses are not involved, the portion to be included is based upon the percentage of the decedent's contribution to the total cost of the property. Section 2040(a) of the Code requires the inclusion of the entire value of the property held in joint tenancy, except such part of the entire value as is attributable to the amount of *consideration furnished* by the other joint tenant or was originally owned by the other joint tenant. This rule applies to property held in joint tenancy, joint bank accounts, and government bonds with survivorship provisions. Thus:

> *Case 9a.*   Refer back to Case 9, involving the creation of a joint tenancy in 1990. *O* dies in 1991. At *O*'s death the securities are worth $60,000. Under §2040, the full value of the securities, or $60,000, is includable in *O*'s gross estate. (There is no adjusted taxable gift inclusion because the property that was the subject of the gift is included in *O*'s gross estate under §2040.) If *O* paid a gift tax at the time the joint tenancy was created in 1990, there is no double taxation. Section 2001(b)(2) provides that the tentative estate tax is reduced by the amount of gift taxes paid on gifts made after 1976.

If, in Case 9a, *O* had contributed three-fourths of the purchase price of the securities ($30,000) and *A*, one-quarter ($10,000), three-fourths of the value of the securities at the date of *O*'s death, or $45,000, would be included in *O*'s gross estate. The burden of showing the amount contributed by the survivor is on the decedent's personal representative. The value of the entire property will be included in the gross estate unless the amount contributed by the survivor is proved. When title is taken in joint tenancy form, it is important to keep records showing the source of the funds with which the property was acquired. Failure to do this may result in needless taxation if the decedent"s personal representative cannot satisfactorily establish the amount of the contribution furnished by the survivor. With respect to joint bank owners, the decedent's personal representative must sustain the burden of showing the amount on deposit attributable to the survivor's contributions, or the full amount is included in the decedent's gross estate.

PROBLEMS

1.   *O* purchases Blackacre for $100,000 and takes title in the name of *O* and *A* as joint tenants with right of survivorship. *O* has used up her unified gift tax credit and therefore pays a gift tax on the $40,000 gift to *A* ($50,000 minus the $10,000 exclusion). A few years later *A* dies. Is *O* entitled to a return of the gift tax paid? Is *O*'s executor entitled to credit the gift tax paid against *O*'s estate tax when she dies? Suppose that *O* sells Blackacre before her death. Is *O*'s executor entitled to credit the gift tax paid against the estate tax?

2.   In 1980 *A* and *B* buy a house as joint tenants. The purchase price is $100,000. *A* and *B* each contribute $10,000 to the down payment of $20,000. The balance of $80,000 is financed by a mortgage on which *A* and *B* are jointly and severally liable. During the 1980s, *A* makes all the mortgage payments, in a total principal amount of $20,000. In 1990, *A* dies. The house is worth $180,000. The mortgage balance is $60,000. What amount is includable in *A*'s gross estate? Is any amount deductible under §2053 (infra page 1020)? See Rev. Rul. 79-302, 1979-2 C.B. 328.

3.   The who-furnished-the-consideration test was adopted by Congress at a time when the gift and estate taxes were separate and gift tax rates were 75 percent of estate tax rates. At the time, if only the fractional share owned by the decedent joint tenant were included in the decedent's gross estate, the joint tenancy would have offered a vehicle for avoiding the higher estate taxes on the surviving joint tenant's share of the property. Now that the gift and estate taxes have been unified and have the same rates, what is the justification for keeping the who-furnished-the-consideration test in the estate tax while using the fractional share of ownership test in the gift tax?

The who-furnished-the-consideration test raises difficult problems of measuring the respective contributions. Here are two examples: (a) where improvements are made by one co-tenant, either in cash outlay or in services; and (b) where jointly held property originally paid for by one joint owner is sold and the proceeds reinvested in new jointly held property. See J. Gaubatz, I. Bloom & L. Solomon, Federal Taxation of Estates, Trusts and Gifts 569-577 (1989).

4.   Suppose that the surviving joint tenant disclaims the percentage share of the joint tenancy property that is attributable to the decedent's contributions. Is this permissible? Would it be consistent with the common law notion that the survivor owned the whole property from

the beginning of the joint tenancy? See Morris, Disclaiming Joint Interests: One New Trick and No Longer a Dog?, 1983 Ariz. St. L.J. 45. See also Problem, supra page 305.

(2) Joint Tenancy and Tenancy by the Entirety Between Husband and Wife

(a) *Gift tax.* Internal Revenue Code §§2056 and 2523 provide for an unlimited marital deduction: Any amount of property may be transferred by one spouse to the other spouse as tenants in common, joint tenants, or tenants by the entirety tax free. Thus, if a wife buys property and takes title in the name of herself and her husband as joint tenants, a gift has been made to the husband of one-half the value of the property, as in Case 9, but the amount of the gift qualifies for the marital deduction and no gift tax is payable.

(b) *Estate tax.* The who-furnished-the-consideration test applicable to joint tenancies between nonspouses does not apply to a "qualified joint interest" held between spouses. A qualified joint interest is a tenancy by the entirety or a joint tenancy with right of survivorship where the spouses are the only joint tenants. With respect to both of these forms of property holding, each spouse owns an undivided one-half interest in the property.

Section 2040(b) of the Code provides that with respect to property held by the decedent and the decedent's spouse as joint tenants with right of survivorship or as tenants by the entirety, one-half the value of the property is includable in the decedent's gross estate regardless of which spouse furnished the consideration for the property's acquisition. Hence for both gift and estate tax purposes a joint tenancy or tenancy by the entirety owned by husband and wife is treated as owned one-half by each. The one-half interest includable in the decedent's gross estate that passes to the surviving spouse qualifies for the unlimited marital deduction. Therefore no estate taxes result from the inclusion of the decedent spouse's one-half interest.

NOTE: INCOME TAX BASIS

Since each spouse is deemed to own one-half the amount of a joint tenancy with right of survivorship or a tenancy by the entirety, the decedent spouse's one-half interest in the property that is included in his gross estate will receive a stepped-up basis at death. Case 11 illustrates this.

Case 11. *H* purchases Blackacre for $50,000, taking title in *H* and *W* as joint tenants with the right of survivorship. *H*'s income tax basis is $25,000 as is *W*'s. *H* dies. Blackacre is worth $90,000 at *H*'s death. One-half the value, $45,000, is included in *H*'s gross estate (but it qualifies for the marital deduction). *W*'s new tax basis for Blackacre is $70,000 (which is the sum of $25,000, *W*'s basis on her one-half, and $45,000, the stepped-up basis on *H*'s one-half). If *W* sells Blackacre thereafter for $90,000, *W* will have a capital gain of $20,000. The $20,000 gain on *H*'s one-half will never be taxed because it received a stepped-up basis.[7]

b.   Section 2039: Employee Death Benefits

Section 2039 of the Code provides that employee death benefits receivable by a beneficiary are includable in the gross estate of the decedent if the decedent "possessed the right to receive" any benefits during his lifetime. The type of right that usually causes §2039 to apply is the right of the decedent to an annuity or pension upon retirement. If the decedent has this right, and death benefits — usually in the form of an annuity or a lump sum payment — are payable to a surviving beneficiary, the value of the death benefits is includable in the decedent's gross estate. Individual Retirement Accounts (IRAs) and Keogh plans are included in the decedent's gross estate under §2039.

Section 2039 is inapplicable to "insurance under policies on the life of the decedent," which is governed by §2042.

If the decedent has no power to select the beneficiary of his employee benefits, because the death benefits are payable *by statute* to the decedent's spouse or children, the death benefits are not includable in the decedent's estate. Social Security benefits are excludable, for example.

Employee death benefits included in the decedent's estate and payable to the decedent's spouse ordinarily will qualify for the marital deduction.

Income tax treatment.   When employee death benefits are received by a beneficiary after the death of the employee or of the owner of an income-tax-deferred plan (such as IRA or Keogh), the receipts are treated as "income in respect of a decedent" under §691(a) of the Code. Essentially, this means the beneficiary stands in the income tax shoes of the decedent, with no step-up in basis. The beneficiary may deduct from his or her income tax return the estate tax attributable to the benefit. §691(c).

On taxation of employee death benefits, see J. Dodge, Wills, Trusts, and Estate Planning 85-92, 522-536 (1988).

---

7. If *H* and *W* had owned Blackacre as community property, one-half the value of Blackacre would be included in *H*'s gross estate. However, the entire interest in community property would receive a stepped-up basis at *H*'s death. IRC §1014(b). If *W* sells Blackacre after *H* dies for $90,000, *W* will pay no tax on the capital gain. Thus in community property states, holding property as community property rather than in joint tenancy has a potential income tax advantage.

PROBLEM

H, an employee of Standard Oil Co., has retired on a pension. As part of Standard's death benefits, the company has agreed to pay benefits to a survivor equal to 12 times the monthly retirement sum *H* receives. The plan is unfunded; its cost is borne entirely by Standard. *H* dies. Is the death benefit excluded from §2039 on the ground that it is insurance? See All v. McCobb, 321 F.2d 633 (2d Cir. 1963); Helvering v. LeGierse, 312 U.S. 531 (1941) ("Historically and commonly insurance involves risk-shifting and risk-distributing."). See also J. Dodge, supra, at 103:

> The term "life insurance" as used in §2042 refers to any kind of private contractual arrangement under which a sum is paid to one or more beneficiaries, by reason of the insured's death, out of an "actuarial pool" funded by premiums paid into the pool as a hedge against death. This definition of life insurance excludes most employee death benefits, which are made available without regard to the *risk* of death. It includes "accident insurance" which insures, inter alia, against the risk of death.

c. Section 2042: Life Insurance

Section 2042 of the Code provides that the gross estate shall include the value of insurance proceeds on the life of the decedent (1) if the decedent possessed at death any of the *incidents of ownership* under the policies, or (2) if the policy proceeds were *payable to the insured's executor or estate*. The incidents of ownership include such policy rights as the right to change the beneficiary, to surrender, cancel, or assign the policy, or to borrow against the cash surrender value in the policy. In the ordinary situation where a person takes out a policy on his own life and names some member of the family as beneficiary, the proceeds will be taxed in the insured's estate since he will hold whatever incidents of ownership are given by the policy. This is true of even a term insurance policy that has no investment features and hence no cash surrender value, for the insured has the right to change the beneficiary designation and also the right to assign or cancel the policy. The retention of only one incident of ownership causes the full value of the insurance proceeds to be taxed under §2042.

In community property states, life insurance policies that are owned as community property are taxed in the same manner as other community assets (i.e., as owned one-half by the husband and one-half by the wife). If the husband is the insured under a community policy that names the wife as primary beneficiary, and the husband predeceases his wife, only one-half the value of the proceeds is includable in his gross estate.

If an insurance policy owned by a decedent spouse (and therefore includable in the decedent's gross estate) is payable to the surviving spouse in a lump sum, the policy proceeds qualify for the unlimited marital deduction. No taxes result from the inclusion of the policy in the decedent's gross estate.

PROBLEMS

1. *H* is the insured under a $50,000 ordinary life insurance policy that names *W* as the owner of the policy and of all incidents of ownership therein. The policy was issued in *W*'s name as owner when it was taken out 10 years ago, and all policy premiums have been paid out of *W*'s funds. The policy names *W* as primary beneficiary and the couple's daughter, *D*, as contingent beneficiary. *H* dies and the policy proceeds are paid to *W*. *H* leaves a will that devises his entire estate to *W* and *D* in equal shares. The will names *W* as executor. Are the policy proceeds includable in *H*'s gross estate?

2. Consider the same facts as in Problem 1 except that *W* predeceases *H*, leaving a will that devises "all my property" to *H*. On the date of *W*'s death, the cash surrender value of the policy is $10,000. *H* dies a year later, and the $50,000 in policy proceeds are paid to the couple's daughter, *D*, as contingent beneficiary. What are the estate tax consequences in *W*'s estate? In *H*'s estate?

If the insurance policy is not owned by *W* but is community property owned by *H* and *W*, what are the estate tax consequences in *W*'s estate? In *H*'s estate?

3. *A* takes out an insurance policy on the life of her father, *F*. *A* owns the policy. Each year *F* gives *A* $10,000 to pay the premium on the policy. Does the $10,000 gift qualify for the annual exclusion or is it a gift of a future interest?

4. *W* owns a life insurance policy on *H*'s life. *W* dies, bequeathing her residuary estate, including the policy, to *H* as trustee for their daughter *D* for life, remainder to *D*'s issue. Under the trust, *H* is given discretionary power as trustee to invade principal for the benefit of *D*. *H* dies. Are the policy proceeds includable in *H*'s estate? See Estate of Skifter v. Commissioner, 468 F.2d 699 (2d Cir. 1972); Rev. Rul. 84-179, 1984-2 C.B. 195 (holding that "incidents of ownership" means the insurance equivalent of a general power of appointment under §2042, unless the power was "retained" by the insured, in which case the broader concept of a power found in §2038 would apply).

4.   The Gross Estate: Lifetime Transfers with Rights Retained

The gross estate includes certain lifetime transfers made by the decedent, where the decedent retained some rights over the transferred property. The relevant sections are 2036, 2037, and 2038. We take them up here in the order that, we think, makes them easiest to understand.

a.   Section 2036: Transfers with Life Estate or Power of Control Retained

Section 2036(a) provides:

The value of the gross estate shall include the value of all property to the extent of any interest therein of which the decedent has at any time made a transfer (except in case of a bona fide sale for an adequate and full consideration in money or money's worth), by trust or otherwise, under which he has retained for his life or for any period which does not in fact end before his death —

(1)   The possession or enjoyment of, or the right to the income from, the property, or

(2)   The right, either alone or in conjunction with any person, to designate the persons who shall possess or enjoy the property or the income therefrom.

Note that §2036 includes in the gross estate two types of lifetime transfers. Section 2036(a)(1) applies when the decedent retains a life estate in the transferred property. Although the life estate terminates at death, the transfer is subjected to estate taxation because the decedent retained the most important incident of property ownership: the right to possess and enjoy the property, or the right to its income, for life.

Section 2036(a)(2) reaches transfers in which the decedent retains the right to control beneficial enjoyment of the property even though the right cannot be exercised in a manner that would benefit the transferor personally. To take an obvious case, when the transferor designates himself as a co-trustee and the trustees have a discretionary power to accumulate trust income or distribute it to the beneficiary, or a power to distribute the income among several beneficiaries in such shares as the trustees shall determine, the transfer is taxed under this section. The transfer is also taxed even though the power is exercisable only with the consent of a person having an interest which could be adversely affected by the exercise of the power.[8]

To a considerable extent, as we shall see, §2036(a)(2) overlaps with §2038, which applies to lifetime transfers where the transferor possesses the power to alter, amend, or revoke.

For a complete discussion of §2036, see Bittker, Transfers Subject to Retained Right to Receive the Income or Designate the Income Beneficiary, 34 Rutgers L. Rev. 668 (1982).

PROBLEMS

1. *O* transfers property to *X* in trust to pay the income to *O* for life and on *O*'s death to distribute the trust assets to *A*. What are the gift and estate tax consequences of this transfer?

2. *O* transfers property to *X* in trust. The trustee has unfettered discretion to pay the income to *O* or to accumulate it and to invade the corpus for *O*'s benefit; on *O*'s death, the trustee is to distribute the trust assets to *A*. What are the gift and estate tax consequences? See Dodge, Retentions, Receipts, Transfers and Accumulations of Income and Income Rights: Ruminations on the Post-*Byrum* Role of Estate Tax Sections 2036, 2037, 2039, and 2043(a), 58 Tex. L. Rev. 1, 11-16 (1979).

3. *O* transfers property to *X* in trust to pay income for the support of *O*'s minor children. If *O* dies while her children are still minors, is the trust property includable in *O*'s estate under §2036(a)(1)? Would your answer be the same if the minor children did not have the right to the income but the trustee had discretion to use it for their support? See Newman, Discharges of Legal Obligations, Section 2036 and Consideration in Estate and Gift Taxation, 35 Wash. & Lee L. Rev. 107 (1978).

---

8. Sections 671-677 of the Internal Revenue Code spell out the circumstances under which the settlor of a trust is taxable on trust *income* on grounds of dominion and control. The income tax provisions are not entirely consistent with the estate tax provisions. A settlor may have succeeded in eliminating the trust income from his gross income but not the principal from his gross estate. For example, if the settlor has the power to control beneficial enjoyment of the income only with the consent of an *adverse party*, the income is not taxable to the settlor. IRC §674(a). But the value of the principal is includable in the settlor's gross estate at death because §§2036 and 2038 do not distinguish between a power held with an adverse party and a power held with a nonadverse party. Or if the settlor as trustee has only a discretionary power to pay income to, or accumulate it for, the life beneficiary, the settlor is not taxable on the income. Id. §674(b)(6). But the value of the trust property will be included in the settlor's gross estate. If your client wishes to create a trust and retain any power over income or principal, both income tax and estate tax sections must be explored if the settlor is to successfully eliminate the income from his gross income and the principal from his gross estate. See supra pages 545-547.

Estate of Linderme v. Commissioner
United States Tax Court, 1966
52 T.C. 305

TANNENWALD, J.   Respondent determined a deficiency in petitioner's estate tax in the amount of $11,075.89. . . .

The sole issue confronting us is whether the decedent retained the "possession or enjoyment" of his residence so as to bring its value within his gross estate for purposes of the Federal estate tax pursuant to section 2036(a)(1).

Petitioner insists that respondent's assertion of the applicability of section 2036(a)(1) constitutes an unwarranted attempt to create a statutory presumption of retention of "possession or enjoyment" from the mere fact of occupancy of the residence by the decedent from the time of the quitclaim deed in favor of his three sons in 1956 until his removal to a nursing home. We do not thus interpret respondent's position. Rather, we understand respondent to argue that, based upon an evaluation of all the facts and circumstances herein, there are adequate grounds for inferring an agreement or understanding on the part of decedent and his three sons sufficient to bring the transfer within the sweep of section 2036(a)(1). We agree with respondent.

The facts involved herein are clear. Decedent executed a quitclaim deed to the residence to his three sons in 1956. At that time, he delivered the deed to his son Emil. While the other two sons were not made aware of the delivery until after the father's death, we think it a reasonable assumption that Emil's actions in accepting the deed and in dealing with the decedent in respect of subsequent treatment of the property coincided with their views. Although the deed had been recorded prior to delivery, it was put into a file with decedent's other papers — a factor perhaps of more significance if there were an issue as to whether any gift was made, but also having some bearing on the existence, of an understanding with respect to decedent's interest in the property. Decedent continued in *exclusive* possession of the residence until he entered the nursing home. The residence was unoccupied from that time until his death about a year and a half later. There was neither consideration of any sale or rental of, nor any effort to sell or rent, the residence during that interval, thus indicating that the property was being held available for decedent's possible return. From the date of the quitclaim deed until his death, decedent's funds were used to pay all the expenses relating to the property, including real estate taxes, insurance premiums, and costs of maintenance. Even after the property was sold, part of the proceeds of sale were used to pay the obligations of decedent's estate. While this factor also would have greater bearing on the "any gift" issue . . . , it is a further indication, when taken into account with the other elements involved herein, of a retained interest in decedent.

Petitioner claims that the application of section 2036(a)(1) under the foregoing circumstances would unjustifiably extend the frontiers of that section contrary to the mandate of the decided cases and particularly our decision in Estate of Allen D. Gutchess, 47 T.C. 554 (1966), acq. 1967-1 C.B. 2. We disagree. Petitioner correctly concludes that it is neither necessary that the proscribed retained interest be expressed in the instrument of transfer nor necessary that the decedent have a legally enforceable right to possession or enjoyment. Petitioner, however, points out that, in all of the decided cases in which section 2036(a) was held applicable to situations similar to that involved herein, the property was income-producing . . . and that, in all of the decided cases which refused to apply that section, the property involved was non-income-producing. . . . Petitioner then seeks to parlay the foregoing decisions into the negative proposition that, unless income-producing property is involved, no agreement or understanding with respect to a decedent's retention of "possession or enjoyment" can be inferred.

To be sure, the factual distinction emphasized by petitioner does exist in these cases. But a more significant element seems to have been the fact that there was no withholding of occupancy from the donee. In the absence of such withholding, the continued co-occupancy of the property by the donor with the donee was considered, in and of itself, an insufficient basis for inferring an agreement as to retained possession or enjoyment. See Estate of Allen D. Gutchess, 46 T.C. at 556-557. The presence of income from the property was simply a useful ancillary tool for decision rather than a limiting principle imposed as a matter of law. The retention of income was thus only an example, albeit a very clear one, of "possession or enjoyment." Moreover, most of the cases decided in favor of the taxpayer involved a husband-wife relationship where the crosscurrent of section 2040 was at work. See concurring opinion in Estate of Allen D. Gutchess, 46 T.C. at 558.

In the instant case, the decedent continued to occupy the residence to the exclusion of the donees or anyone else whose status stemmed from their rights to the property. Surely that occupancy was as much an "economic benefit" as if decedent had rented the property and obtained the income therefrom. See Estate of Daniel McNichol, 29 T.C. at 1184. Additionally, such *exclusive* occupancy, while not necessarily determinative, should be accorded greater significance than co-occupancy in the process of evaluating the various facets of a particular situation in order to determine whether an understanding existed whereby a decedent would retain possession or enjoyment.

In Commissioner v. Estate of Church, 335 U.S. 632 (1949), the Supreme Court, in dealing with the predecessor of section 2036, in the context of transfers in trust, cut the shackles of earlier decisions and stated (335 U.S. at 645-646):

> [A]n estate tax cannot be avoided by any trust transfer except by a bona fide transfer in which the settlor, absolutely, unequivocally, irrevocably, and without possible reservations, parts with all of his title and all of his possession and all of his enjoyment of the transferred property. After such a transfer has been made, the settlor must be left with no present legal title in the property, no possible reversionary interest in that title, and no right to possess or to enjoy the property then or thereafter. In other words such a transfer must be immediate and out and out, and must be unaffected by whether the grantor lives or dies.

We take our cue from this mandate for a broad inclusion within the gross estate pursuant to section 2036(a)(1). The burden of proof is on the taxpayer and, in cases of this type, that burden may be a heavy one. Skinner's Estate v. United States, 316 F.2d 517, 520 (C.A. 3, 1963); cf. Estate of Henry Wilson, 2 T.C. 1059, 1091 (1943). But such difficulty does not justify exclusion from the operation of section 2036(a)(1). On the basis of the entire record herein, we are satisfied as our ultimate finding of fact reflects that, beyond the mere existence of the family relationship and the mere occupancy of the premises, decedent did have an understanding whereby he retained the exclusive use of the residence until his death. The property in question is thus includable in decedent's gross estate under section 2036(a)(1). . . .

Decision will be entered under Rule 50.

PROBLEMS

1.   The Bennetts own a cabin and lake property worth $80,000 in a neighboring state. They spend three or four weeks at the cabin every summer and make occasional visits during the rest of the year. The Bennetts' two daughters and their families also use the cabin during their vacations and for holiday visits. The Bennetts, who are both in their sixties, have been advised that substantial legal costs may be incurred in transferring title to the property at their deaths. They want to know: Can they save estate taxes and avoid the "ancillary adminis-tration" problem if they give the property to their daughters? (The Bennetts want to continue to visit and use the cabin as they have in the past.) Advise them.

2.   Joseph Grace executes a trust instrument providing for payment of income to his wife, Janet, for her life, with payment to her of any part of the principal which a majority of the trustees think advisable. Mrs. Grace is given a special testamentary power of appointment over

the trust estate. Named as trustees are Joseph, his nephew, and a third party. Shortly thereafter Janet Grace, at Joseph's request, executes a virtually identical trust instrument naming Joseph as life beneficiary. Upon Joseph's death is the corpus of either of the trusts includable in Joseph's gross estate? See United States v. Estate of Grace, 395 U.S. 316 (1969), noted in 50 B.U.L. Rev. 321 (1970), 17 UCLA L. Rev. 436 (1969), and 1970 Wis. L. Rev. 571.

In the *Grace* case, the court held that, under the reciprocal trust doctrine, the value of the Janet Grace trust must be included in Joseph's estate. "[A]pplication of the reciprocal trust doctrine requires only that the trusts be interrelated, and that the arrangement, to the extent of mutual value, leaves the settlors in approximately the same economic position as they would have been in had they created trusts naming themselves as life beneficiaries."

3. Under the Uniform Transfers to Minors Act, supra page 454, if the donor names himself as custodian and dies while serving in that capacity, the value of the custodial property is included in the donor's gross estate for federal estate tax purposes. Because the donor-custodian's discretionary power to distribute the custodial property to the minor is a retained power to alter the time of enjoyment, the value of the custodial property is included in the donor's estate under §2038.

In Exchange Bank & Trust Co. of Florida v. United States, 694 F.2d 1261 (Fed. Cir. 1982), a husband transferred stock to his wife to hold as custodian for their children under the Florida Gifts to Minors Act. At the same time the wife transferred stock to her husband to hold as custodian for the benefit of their children under the Florida Gifts to Minors Act. The husband died. Is any of the stock included in the husband's gross estate?

If a parent wants to make a gift of income-producing assets to a minor child and be either the trustee or the custodian, is a trust or a custodianship preferable if estate taxes are a concern?

Old Colony Trust Co. v. United States
United States Court of Appeals, First Circuit, 1970
423 F.2d 601

ALDRICH, J. The sole question in this case is whether the estate of a settlor of an inter vivos trust, who was a trustee until the date of his death, is to be charged with the value of the principal he contributed by virtue of reserved powers in the trust. The executor paid the tax and sued for its recovery in the district court. All facts were stipulated. The court ruled for the government, 300 F. Supp. 1032, and the executor appeals.

The initial life beneficiary of the trust was the settlor's adult son. Eighty percent of the income was normally to be payable to him, and the balance added to principal. Subsequent beneficiaries were the son's widow and his issue. The powers upon which the government relies to cause the corpus to be includable in the settlor-trustee's estate are contained in two articles. . . .

Article 4 permitted the trustees to increase the percentage of income payable to the son beyond the eighty percent, "in their absolute discretion . . . when in their opinion such increase is needed in case of sickness, or desirable in view of changed circumstances." In addition, under Article 4 the trustees were given the discretion to cease paying income to the son, and add it all to principal, "during such period as the Trustees may decide that the stoppage of such payments is for his best interests."

Article 7 gave broad administrative or management powers to the trustees, with discretion to acquire investments not normally held by trustees, and the right to determine what was to be charged or credited to income or principal, including stock dividends or deductions for amortization. It further provided that all divisions and decisions made by the trustees in good faith should be conclusive on all parties, and in summary, stated that the trustees were empowered, "generally to do all things in relation to the Trust Fund which the Donor could do if living and this Trust had not been executed."

The government claims that each of these two articles meant that the settlor-trustee had "the right . . . to designate the persons who shall possess or enjoy the [trust] property or the income therefrom" within the meaning of section 2036(a)(2) of the Internal Revenue Code of 1954, 26 U.S.C. §2036(a)(2), and that the settlor-trustee at the date of his death possessed a power "to alter, amend, revoke, or terminate" within the meaning of section 2038(a)(1) (26 U.S.C. §2038(a)(1)).

If State Street Trust Co. v. United States, 1 Cir., 1959, 263 F.2d 635, was correctly decided in this aspect, the government must prevail because of the Article 7 powers. There this court, Chief Judge Magruder dissenting, held against the taxpayer because broad powers similar to those in Article 7 meant that the trustees "could very substantially shift the economic benefits of the trusts between the life tenants and the remaindermen," so that the settlor "as long as he lived, in substance and effect and in a very real sense . . . 'retained for his life . . . the right . . . to designate the persons who shall possess or enjoy the property or the income therefrom. . . .'" 263 F.2d at 639-640, quoting 26 U.S.C. §2036(a)(2). We accept the taxpayer's invitation to reconsider this ruling.

It is common ground that a settlor will not find the corpus of the trust included in his estate merely because he named himself a trustee. Jennings v. Smith, 2 Cir., 1947, 161 F.2d 74. He must have reserved a power to himself[9] that is inconsistent with the full termination of ownership. The government's brief defines this as "sufficient dominion and control until his death." Trustee powers given for the administration or management of the trust must be equitably exercised, however, for the benefit of the trust as a whole. Blodget v. Delaney, 1 Cir., 1953, 201 F.2d 589; United States v. Powell, 10 Cir., 1962, 307 F.2d 821; Scott, Trusts §§183, 232 (3d ed. 1967); Rest. 2d, Trusts §§183, 232. The court in *State Street* conceded that the powers at issue were all such powers, but reached the conclusion that, cumulatively, they gave the settlor dominion sufficiently unfettered to be in the nature of ownership. With all respect to the majority of the then court, we find it difficult to see how a power can be subject to control by the probate court, and exercisable only in what the trustee fairly concludes is in the interests of the trust and its beneficiaries as a whole, and at the same time be an ownership power.

The government's position, to be sound, must be that the trustee's powers are beyond the court's control. Under Massachusetts law, however, no amount of administrative discretion prevents judicial supervision of the trustee. Thus in Appeal of Davis, 1903, 183 Mass. 499, 67 N.E. 604, a trustee was given "full power to make purchases, investments and exchanges . . . in such manner as to them shall seem expedient; it being my intention to give my trustees . . . the same dominion and control over said trust property as I now have." In spite of this language, and in spite of their good faith, the court charged the trustees for failing sufficiently to diversify their investment portfolio.

The Massachusetts court has never varied from this broad rule of accountability, and has twice criticized *State Street* for its seeming departure. Boston Safe Deposit & Trust Co. v. Stone, 1965, 348 Mass. 345, 351, n.8, 203 N.E.2d 547; Old Colony Trust Co. v. Silliman, 1967, 352 Mass. 6, 8-9, 223 N.E.2d 504. See also, Estate of McGillicuddy, 54 T.C. No. 27, 2/17/70, CCH Tax Ct. Rep. Dec. 29, 1965. We make it a further observation, which the court in *State Street* failed to note, that the provision in that trust (as in the case at bar) that the trustees could "do all things in relation to the Trust Fund which I, the Donor, could do if . . . the Trust had not been executed," is almost precisely the provision which did not protect the trustees from accountability in Appeal of Davis, supra.

We do not believe that trustee powers are to be more broadly construed for tax purposes than the probate court would construe them

---

9. The number of other trustees who must join in the exercise of that power, unless the others have antagonistic interest of a substantial nature is, of course, immaterial. Treas. Reg. §20.2036-1(a)(ii), (b)(3)(i) (1958); §20.2038-1(a) (1958).

for administrative purposes. More basically, we agree with Judge Magruder's observation that nothing is "gained by lumping them together." State Street Trust Co. v. United States, supra, 263 F.2d at 642. We hold that no aggregation of purely administrative powers can meet the government's amorphous test of "sufficient dominion and control" so as to be equated with ownership.

This does not resolve taxpayer's difficulties under Article 4. Quite different considerations apply to distribution powers. Under them the trustee can, expressly, prefer one beneficiary over another. Furthermore, his freedom of choice may vary greatly, depending upon the terms of the individual trust. If there is an ascertainable standard, the trustee can be compelled to follow it.[10] If there is not, even though he is a fiduciary, it is not unreasonable to say that his retention of an unmeasurable freedom of choice is equivalent to retaining some of the incidents of ownership. Hence, under the cases, if there is an ascertainable standard the settlor-trustee's estate is not taxed, . . . but if there is not, it is taxed. . . .

The trust provision which is uniformly held to provide an ascertainable standard is one which, though variously expressed, authorizes such distributions as may be needed to continue the beneficiary's accustomed way of life. . . . On the other hand, if the trustee may go further, and has power to provide for the beneficiary's "happiness," Merchants Nat'l Bank v. Com'r of Internal Revenue, 1943, 320 U.S. 256, or "pleasure," Industrial Trust Co. v. Com'r of Internal Revenue, 1 Cir., 1945, 151 F.2d 592, cert. denied 327 U.S. 788, or "use and benefit," Newton Trust Co. v. Com'r of Internal Revenue, 1 Cir., 1947, 160 F.2d 175, or "reasonable requirement[s]," State Street Bank & Trust Co. v. United States, 1 Cir., 1963, 313 F.2d 29, the standard is so loose that the trustee is in effect uncontrolled.

In the case at bar the trustees could increase the life tenant's income "in case of sickness, or [if] desirable in view of changed circumstances." Alternatively, they could reduce it "for his best interests." "Sickness" presents no problem. Conceivably, providing for "changed circumstances" is roughly equivalent to maintaining the son's present standard of living. . . . The unavoidable stumbling block is the trustees' right to accumulate income and add it to capital (which the son would never receive) when it is to the "best interests" of the son to do so. Additional payments to a beneficiary whenever in his "best interests" might seem to be too broad a standard in any event. In addition to the previous cases see Estate of Yawkey, 1949, 12 T.C. 1164, where the court said,

---

10. See, e.g., Old Colony Trust Co. v. Rodd, 356 Mass. 584, N.E.2d 886 [supra page 539], trustee of trust to provide "comfortable support and maintenance," rebuked for "parsimonious" exercise of judgment.

at p.1170, "We can not regard the language involved ['best interest'] as limiting the usual scope of a trustee's discretion. It must always be anticipated that trustees will act for the best interests of a trust beneficiary, and an exhortation to act 'in the interests and for the welfare' of the beneficiary does not establish an external standard." Power, however, to decrease or cut off a beneficiary's income when in his "best interests," is even more troublesome. When the beneficiary is the son, and the trustee the father, a particular purpose comes to mind, parental control through holding the purse strings. The father decides what conduct is to the "best interests" of the son, and if the son does not agree, he loses his allowance. Such power has the plain indicia of ownership control. The alternative, that the son, because of other means, might not need this income, and would prefer to have it accumulate for his widow and children after his death, is no better. If the trustee has power to confer "happiness" on the son by generosity to someone else, this seems clearly an unascertainable standard. Cf. Merchants Nat'l Bank v. Com'r of Internal Revenue, supra, 320 U.S. at 261-263.

The case of Hays' Estate v. Com'r of Internal Revenue, 5 Cir., 1950, 181 F.2d 169, is contrary to our decision. The opinion is unsupported by either reasoning or authority, and we will not follow it. With the present settlor-trustee free to determine the standard himself, a finding of ownership control was warranted. To put it another way, the cost of holding onto the strings may prove to be a rope burn. State Street Bank & Trust Co. v. United States, supra.

Affirmed.[11]

NOTES

1. It might be thought that application of §2036(a)(2) to retained powers can be avoided by not naming the settlor as trustee or co-trustee. This alone is not enough, however. If the named trustee has these powers, and if the settlor has the power to remove the trustee and appoint himself as successor trustee, the settlor is deemed to possess the powers, and estate taxation results. Treas. Reg. §2036-1(b)(3) (1958). Even if the settlor, upon removing the trustee, can appoint only a trustee other than himself, the settlor is deemed to have a §2036 power. Rev. Rul. 79-353, 1979-2 C.B. 325. Moreover, if the settlor has the power — either under the trust instrument or under local law — to name himself a successor trustee upon a contingency beyond his control (e.g., death of the trustee), the settlor has a §2036 power. Rev. Rul. 73-

---

11. Noted in 49 N.C.L. Rev. 811. — Eds.

21, 1973-1 C.B. 405; Estate of Farrel v. United States, 553 F.2d 637 (Ct. Cl. 1977). The only safe course of action to avoid §2036 is to create a trust where the settlor is not the trustee, cannot remove the trustee, and cannot be appointed a successor trustee. If the settlor has only the power to appoint a successor trustee other than himself upon the death or resignation of the trustee, the settlor does not have a §2036 or §2038 power. Rev. Rul. 77-182, 1977-1 C.B. 273.

2.   Section 2036(b) provides that, "For purposes of subsection (a)(1), the retention of a right to vote (directly or indirectly) shares of stock in a controlled corporation shall be considered to be a retention of the enjoyment of transferred property." A controlled corporation is defined as a corporation in which the decedent, after the transfer, owned or had the right to vote "stock possessing at least 20 percent of the total combined voting power of all classes of stock." Hence if a trust settlor retains the right to vote stock in a controlled corporation, transferred to the trust, the trust corpus is includable in the settlor's gross estate under §2036.

3.   Professor Isenbergh suggests that if the Code were amended to blunt the effect of the tax base being tax-exclusive for the gift tax and tax-inclusive for the estate tax, §2036 should be repealed. Isenbergh, Simplifying Retained Interests, Revocable Transfers, and the Marital Deduction, 51 U. Chi. L. Rev. 1 (1984).

b.   Section 2038: Revocable Transfers

Section 2038(a) provides that the value of the gross estate shall include the value of all property —

> To the extent of any interest therein of which the decedent has at any time made a transfer (except in case of a bona fide sale for an adequate and full consideration in money or money's worth), by trust or otherwise, where the enjoyment thereof was subject at the date of his death to any change through the exercise of a power (in whatever capacity exercisable) by the decedent alone or by the decedent in conjunction with any other person (without regard to when or from what source the decedent acquired such power), to alter, amend, revoke or terminate, or when any such power is relinquished during the three-year period ending on the date of the decedent's death.

To a considerable extent, §2038 applies to the same transfers caught within §2036(a)(2). However, there are situations covered exclusively by §2038. Section 2036(a)(2) covers only a retained right to designate the *persons* who shall enjoy the property. Section 2038 is applicable if the transferor has the power to effect any change, including the *time* of enjoyment. Hence §2038 alone applies where the settlor may terminate a trust and accelerate enjoyment by a beneficiary. Note also that §2038, like §2036(a)(2), is applicable even though the power is held in conjunction with an adverse party or is held by the settlor as trustee.

If the power to alter, amend, revoke, or terminate is given to some third person, the transfer is not taxed under §2038 even if the person given the power is a nonadverse party. It is for this reason that a trustee who is not the settlor can be given broad discretionary powers, including the power to distribute a portion or all of the trust corpus (thereby terminating the trust), without adverse tax consequences. This last statement is subject to the same qualification that was made in the discussion of §2036. If a trustee has such a power, and if the transferor has the right to remove the trustee and appoint himself as trustee, the transferor is treated as having the power and §2038 is applicable. Treas. Reg. §20.2038-1(a)(3).

Although §2038 is generally referred to as the provision that includes in the gross estate revocable transfers, it reaches transfers over which the decedent held any one of the enumerated powers, even though the power cannot be exercised in such a way as to benefit the transferor. If *O* creates an irrevocable trust in which *O*, as co-trustee, has a discretionary power to accumulate or distribute trust income, or a discretionary power to distribute corpus to the income beneficiary, the property is included in *O*'s gross estate under §2038; *O*'s discretionary power is a power to alter or amend. (*O*'s reserved power would of course also cause inclusion under §2036(a)(2).)

PROBLEMS

1. *O* transfers property to the First National Bank in trust to pay the income to *O*'s daughter, *A*, for life, and on *A*'s death to pay the trust principal to *O*'s granddaughter, *B*. The trust is irrevocable. *O* retains the power to invade corpus for the benefit of *B*. On *O*'s death, is any portion of the value of the trust corpus includable in *O*'s gross estate?

2. What result if, on the facts in Problem 1, *O* has no power to invade corpus but retains the power to direct that all or a portion of trust income be accumulated and added to corpus?

3. *O* transfers property to the Second National Bank in trust to pay the income to *O*'s daughter, *D*, until she reaches 25, and when *D* reaches 25 or, if *D* dies before reaching 25, when *D* would have reached 25 had she lived, to pay the trust principal to *D* or *D*'s estate. The trust is irrevocable. *O* retains the power to direct that all or a portion of the trust income be accumulated until *D* reaches 25 and also the power to

invade corpus for the benefit of *D*. *O* dies; *D* is 19 years old. Is any portion of the value of the trust corpus includable in *O*'s gross estate? See Lober v. United States, 346 U.S. 335 (1953).

c.   Section 2037: Transfers with Reversionary Interest Retained

Under §2037 of the Code, the value of property transferred during life is includable in the transferor's gross estate if

(1)   possession or enjoyment of the property can . . . be obtained only by surviving the decedent, and

(2)   the decedent has retained a reversionary interest in the property . . . , and the value of such reversionary interest immediately before the death of the decedent exceeds five percent of the value of the property.

Both of the above conditions must be present for §2037 to apply. Thus:

Case 12. *H* conveys $100,000 to *X* in trust, to pay income to *W* for life, then to distribute the trust principal to *H* if *H* is then living, and if *H* is not then living to his daughter *A* or her estate. Condition (1) above is met. *A* cannot obtain possession or enjoyment without surviving *H*. Therefore if the value of *H*'s reversionary interest exceeded 5 percent of the value of the property, the value of the trust assets, less *W*'s life estate, will be includable in *H*'s gross estate if *H* predeceases *W*. (The value of *H*'s reversionary interest would be measured by the actuarial probability of *H* outliving *W*.)

If no beneficiary's enjoyment of the property depends upon surviving the decedent, §2037 is inapplicable. Thus in Case 12 if there were no gift over to *A*, §2037 would not apply. Only the value of *H*'s reversionary interest would be included under §2033.

Since instruments are seldom drawn that meet both conditions of §2037, this section is of little concern to the practitioner. For the attorney drafting an irrevocable inter vivos trust, §2037 can be avoided by eliminating any possibility that the trust property will revert to the settlor or the settlor's estate. This can be accomplished by making sure that some person other than the settlor or the settlor's estate will take the property regardless of what contingencies occur. The attorney may include an end-limitation to charity to take effect if all of the designated beneficiaries die before they become entitled to their interests. See Problem 4, supra page 635.

5. The Gross Estate: Transfers Within Three Years of Death

Section 2035 brings into the decedent's gross estate certain inter vivos transfers made within three years prior to death. The purpose of this section is to close some tax avoidance opportunities that would otherwise exist in the few years prior to death. Section 2035 has undergone numerous alterations since 1916, when its predecessor section was first enacted. In 1916, the section taxed transfers "in contemplation of death," with Congress first creating a rebuttable presumption that a transfer within two years of death was in contemplation of death. After ten years, Congress changed the section to create a conclusive presumption, but after another six years, the presumption again became rebuttable. Later Congress lengthened the presumptive period to three years. Because the question of whether a transfer was in contemplation of death turned on the subjective state of mind of the transferor, much litigation resulted. In 1976, Congress eliminated the contemplation of death language — and the subjective test. It reworded §2035 to require that all gifts made within three years of death be included in the gross estate. Upon reflection, this did not seem necessary inasmuch as the gift and estate taxes were unified in 1976, and any gift made within three years of death would be taxed at the same rate as a bequest. In 1981, the Economic Recovery Tax Act changed §2035 again, this time to eliminate its application to all gifts except those, generally speaking, that have a lower valuation as a gift than they have at death.

Under §2035, any of the following transfers made within three years of death is included in the decedent's gross estate:

(1) Any gift tax paid by the decedent or his estate on gifts made within three years of death. [The purpose of this subsection is to prevent a person from giving property away immediately prior to death, and removing the amount of gift tax from the gross estate.]

(2) Any transfer or release of an interest in property when, had such interest been retained, the property would have been included in the decedent's gross estate under any of the following sections of the Internal Revenue Code: section 2036 (transfers with retained life estate); section 2037 (transfers taking effect at death); section 2038 (revocable transfers); or section 2042 (life insurance).[12] [The purpose of this subsection is to prevent persons from avoiding taxes by making gifts soon before death of property that balloons in value at death.]

Unless an inter vivos transfer is referred to above, it is not includable

---

12. Other transfers made within three years of death are included in the decedent's gross estate for certain very limited purposes relating to the executor's election to redeem stock to pay estate taxes or to use a special use valuation of a farm, or relating to whether property is subject to estate tax liens. IRC §2035(d)(3).

in the decedent's gross estate even though made within three years of death. Hence, if *O* gives Blackacre to *A* two months before *O*'s death, a taxable gift is made at the time of transfer, and Blackacre is not included in *O*'s gross estate at death. (The amount of gift tax paid is included in *O*'s gross estate, however.)

It is apparent that Congress' major purpose is to deter taxpayers, in the few years before death, from giving away property that increases greatly in value by reason of the person's death. A gift of a life insurance policy will illustrate this.

> *Case 13.*   *O* owns a life insurance policy on her life with a face value of $100,000. The cash surrender value is $45,000. *O* gives the policy to her son *A*, paying a gift tax on $35,000 ($45,000 minus the annual exclusion of $10,000). *O* dies one year later, and $100,000 is payable to *A*. If the policy proceeds were not included in *O*'s gross estate, *O* could transfer this asset to *A* at a low gift tax valuation immediately prior to death. Section 2035 requires the inclusion of the policy proceeds in *O*'s gross estate.

But for §2035, the owner of a life insurance policy on the owner's life would have a strong tax incentive to give the policy away prior to death, perhaps on the deathbed. So too would exist a strong tax incentive to release a life estate when death appeared imminent. Thus:

> *Case 14.*   In 1984, *O* creates an irrevocable trust of securities worth $300,000, retaining a life estate, with remainder to *O*'s son *A*. This results in a taxable gift to *A* of the value of the remainder in assets worth $300,000. In 1990, the trust assets are worth $500,000, and *O*, ill with cancer, releases her life estate. The release is a taxable gift to *A* of the value of *O*'s life estate in $500,000. *O* dies in 1991. If there were no §2035, *O*'s 1990 release would have eliminated transfer tax on the value of a remainder in $200,000 worth of assets. But §2035 prevents *O* from doing this by requiring the inclusion of the entire $500,000 worth of assets in *O*'s gross estate. (The gift tax paid in 1984 is credited against estate taxes payable at *O*'s death.)

PROBLEMS

1.   Your client, a 72-year-old widow with a $750,000 estate, has been diagnosed as having terminal cancer. Her present will leaves her entire estate to her two children in equal shares. The client has a daughter, a son, two in-laws, and five grandchildren. What advice would you give her?

2.   The same client's will includes a bequest of $20,000 to her church.

Would there be any advantage in the client's making the $20,000 gift to the church during life in lieu of the testamentary gift?

3.   *H*, a widower, is the insured under a $100,000 life insurance policy that names his daughter *D* as a primary beneficiary. In 1990, *H* irrevocably assigns the policy and all of its incidents of ownership to *D*; thereafter, *D* pays all premiums needed to keep the policy in force. At the time of the transfer, the cash surrender value of the property is $20,000. What are the estate tax consequences in *H*'s estate (a) if *H* dies in 1992 and (b) if *H* dies in 1994?

4.   Consider the same facts as in Problem 3 except that the policy that *H* assigned to *D* was a $25,000 policy and the cash surrender value at the time of the transfer was $4,000. What are the estate tax consequences in *H*'s estate (a) if *H* dies in 1992 and (b) if *H* dies in 1994?

5.   John Bel purchased a $250,000 accidental death policy on his own life, paying the premium with his own funds and naming his children as owners and beneficiaries. Bel died two months later. What amount is includable in Bel's estate under §2035? Or, what did Bel "transfer" — the amount of the premium or the amount of the proceeds? In Bel v. United States, 452 F.2d 683 (5th Cir. 1971), cert. denied, 406 U.S. 919 (1972), the court held that the entire $250,000 in proceeds (and not merely the premium paid) is includable in Bel's gross estate under §2035.

> We recognize, of course, that John Bel never formally possessed any of the incidents of ownership in an accidental death policy. . . . [H]owever, we conclude that section 2042 and the incidents-of-ownership test are totally irrelevant to a proper application of section 2035. We think our focus should be on the control beam of the word "transfer." The decedent, and the decedent alone, beamed the accidental death policy at his children, for by paying the premium he designated ownership of the policy and created in his children all the contractual rights to the insurance benefits. These were acts of transfer. . . . Had the decedent, within three years of his death, procured the policy in his own name and immediately thereafter assigned all ownership rights to his children, there is no question but that the policy proceeds would have been included in his estate. In our opinion the decedent's mode of execution is functionally indistinguishable. [452 F.2d at 691-692.]

Suppose that Bel had taken out the policy more than three years before death and had continued to pay the premiums. Is any amount includable in Bel's estate under §2035? See Estate of Coleman v. Commissioner, 52 T.C. 921 (1969).

Suppose that Bel's wife had taken out the policy within three years before Bel's death, naming herself as owner and beneficiary, and Bel had paid the premiums. What result? See Estate of Leder v. Commissioner, 89 T.C. 235 (1987).

6.   The Gross Estate: Powers of Appointment Given Decedent by Another

Sections 2036 and 2038 are the "grantor power" sections of the Internal Revenue Code. Under those sections, the value of property transferred during life is taxed in the grantor's estate because of retained benefits or controls. By contrast, §2041 is the "grantee power" section of the Code. This provision sets forth the circumstances under which property is taxed in the estate of a decedent who never owned the property and never transferred it, but was given by another a general power to appoint it.

Under §2041, the gross estate includes the value of property over which the decedent at the time of his death held a general power of appointment. A general power of appointment is defined as a power exercisable in favor of the decedent, his creditors, his estate, or the creditors of his estate. The assets subject to the general power are taxed in the decedent's estate whether the power was exercisable during lifetime or by will, and (if the power was created after October 21, 1942[13]), whether the decedent actually exercised the power.

> *Case 15.*   *H*'s will creates a testamentary trust providing for the payment of trust income to *H*'s wife *W* for life and on her death "to pay the trust principal to such person or persons as *W* appoints by her will." On *W*'s subsequent death, the value of the trust corpus is includable in her gross estate regardless of whether *W* exercised the power of appointment by her will. Although *W* was restricted to the income from the trust, and she could not exercise the power of appointment in such a way as to benefit herself or her creditors during her lifetime, she held at death a power of appointment that was exercisable in favor of her estate or the creditors of her estate.

The donee of a general power of appointment is treated, under the Code, as owner of the property subject to the power. If a donee exercises or releases a general power of appointment, the donee makes a taxable gift. If a donee exercises or releases the power under circumstances that would have resulted in taxability if the property had been the donee's own (such as releasing a general power and reserving a life

---

13. Property subject to a general power created on or before October 21, 1942, is taxed in the estate of the holder of the power only if the power is exercised. IRC §2041(a)(1).

estate), estate tax liability results. A donee of a general power of appointment is treated as owner under the generation-skipping transfer tax (see infra page 1030).

If the decedent held a special power of appointment, the property subject to the power is not taxed under §2041.[14] A special power of appointment is a power to appoint among a restricted class of persons that does not include the decedent, her creditors, her estate, or the creditors of her estate.

> *Case 16.* H's will creates a testamentary trust providing for the payment of trust income to H's wife W for life and on her death "to pay the trust principal to such one or more of her descendants as she shall appoint by her will." On W's subsequent death, the trust corpus is not subject to taxation in her estate. Since W's life estate terminated at her death, nothing is taxed under §2033. Since W's power of appointment was not a general power, nothing is taxed under §2041.

As Case 16 demonstrates, it is possible to give a beneficiary a life income interest in property and also a limited power to control devolution of the property at death without subjecting the property to estate taxation in the beneficiary's estate. It is also possible to give the beneficiary certain limited powers to appoint property to herself during her lifetime without adverse estate tax consequences. Under §2041(b)(1)(A), "[a] power to consume, invade, or appropriate property for the benefit of the decedent which is limited by an ascertainable standard relating to the health, education, support, or maintenance of the decedent shall not be deemed a general power of appointment." Hence a power in the donee to appoint to the donee limited by the quoted standard is not a general power of appointment.

In addition to a power limited by a standard, a donee may be given a "$5,000 or 5 percent" power with little tax cost. Section 2041(b)(2) provides that if the decedent held a power to consume or invade that was limited to the greater of $5,000 or 5 percent of corpus each year, the maximum amount includable in the donee's gross estate is $5,000 or five percent of the corpus. If the donee has fully exercised the power in the year of death, withdrawing $5,000 or 5 percent from the trust, nothing is included in the donee's estate.

Under §2041(b)(2), a lapse of a power in any calendar year is considered a release (with resulting gift tax liability) to the extent that the property over which the power existed exceeded the greater of $5,000 or five percent of the value of the assets which could be appointed. Thus:

---

14. Treas. Reg. §20.2041-1(c)(1) (1958). There is one important exception to this general rule. See the "Delaware Tax Trap," supra page 806.

Case 17. In 1990, *T* bequeaths $500,000 in trust to pay income to *A* for life. *A* is given a power to withdraw $5,000 or 5 percent of the corpus of the trust in any given year. The right is noncumulative, so that *A* can never withdraw more than $25,000 in any one year, even though *A* fails to withdraw the full amount in a preceding year. In 1991, *A* does not exercise the power. The power lapses, but no taxable gift results. In 1992, *A* withdraws $25,000. In 1993, *A* dies, after withdrawing $10,000 in that year. The amount still subject to *A*'s power of withdrawal at death — $15,000 — is included in *A*'s gross estate.

Special powers of appointment and limited invasion powers (measured by a standard or "$5,000 or 5 percent"), and also discretionary powers given to a trustee, can be employed to create a flexible estate plan that accommodates the foreseen needs of the grantor's family and yet allows for adjustments if future events should warrant. Contrast such a flexible plan with an old-fashioned settlement of property "to my wife for life, and on her death remainder to my descendants per stirpes." At the time the transfer is made, the income from the property may appear to ensure that the wife's support and other needs will be met. But if the wife (or one of the couple's children) should encounter unusual medical or other expenses, or if inflation erodes the real value of the income interest, the income from the property may be insufficient to meet the wife's needs. If, on the other hand, the trustee is given a discretionary power to distribute corpus to the wife whenever it is needed to supplement the trust's income, and if the wife is given an "ascertainable standard" or "$5,000 or 5 percent" invasion power, the corpus of the trust can be used to satisfy the wife's support and other needs whenever trust income proves insufficient.

Upon the wife's death, a distribution of the remainder in stipital shares may, and ordinarily will, be appropriate. Yet it may turn out that life will have been kinder to some of the children (or the descendants of a deceased child) than to the others, and various factors may point toward an unequal, rather than an equal, distribution. Through the use of a special testamentary power of appointment, a final decision on how the remainder should be distributed can be postponed until the income beneficiary's death.

Under §2041, all of these powers can be given to the income beneficiary and trustee with little or no estate tax cost.

Miller v. United States
United States Court of Appeals, Third Circuit, 1968
387 F.2d 866

FREEDMAN, J. This case presents the recurring problem of the taxability as part of a decedent's estate of a power of appointment over trust corpus which the decedent possessed but did not exercise. Here, as in other such cases, the legal question is mixed with the apparent injustice of the imposition of an estate tax on a power which was never exercised and which would clearly have been exempt from tax as a limited power had the words of grant been more narrowly chosen.

Decedent's husband created by his will a residuary trust whose net income was to be paid to decedent for life with remainder on her death to their children. The testamentary trust contained a provision authorizing the trustees, who were the decedent and a trust company, to make disbursements out of the principal of the trust to decedent "at such times and in such amounts as my said Trustees, in their discretion, shall deem necessary or expedient for her proper maintenance, support, medical care, hospitalization, or other expenses incidental to her comfort and well-being."

Decedent died three years after her husband's death. She had lived modestly, had substantial assets of her own and in the period following her husband's death she had not received nor had she requested any payment from the corpus of the trust. Her executors did not include the value of the trust in her gross estate for federal estate tax purposes. The Commissioner of Internal Revenue, however, assessed a deficiency on the ground that the trust was property over which the decedent had held a general power of appointment at the time of her death and that it therefore was includable in her gross estate under §2041 of the Internal Revenue Code of 1954. The executors paid the assessment and brought this suit for refund in the district court. On cross-motions for summary judgment and a stipulation of facts the district court entered judgment for the executors. 267 F. Supp. 182 (W.D. Pa. 1967). The United States has appealed.

The standard of taxability of a general power of appointment, which includes a power to consume, and the extent of the exceptions thereto are explicitly laid down in §2041 of the Code. Section 2041(a)(2) provides that the value of the gross estate of the decedent shall include the value of property with respect to which the decedent at the time of his death possesses a general power of appointment created after October 21, 1942. A general power of appointment is defined in subsection (b)(1) as "a power which is exercisable in favor of the decedent, his estate, his creditors, or the creditors of his estate," but an exception is made by subsection (b)(1)(A) that a "power to consume, invade, or appropriate property for the benefit of the decedent which is limited by an ascertainable standard relating to the health, education, support, or maintenance of the decedent shall not be deemed a general power of appointment."

The Regulations provide that a power is limited by an ascertainable standard "if the extent of the holder's duty to exercise and not to exercise the power is reasonably measurable in terms of his needs for health, education, or support (or any combination of them)," deeming maintenance to be synonymous with support.

It is by this measuring rod that we must judge whether the trust provision here falls within the exception or outside it. It is clear, and indeed it is conceded by the government, that the power to consume for decedent's "proper maintenance, support, medical care, hospitalization," as the trust provides, if there were nothing more, would bring the case clearly within the exception from taxability. The dispute, therefore, revolves around the remaining phrase, "or other expenses incidental to her comfort and well-being."

We had occasion not long ago in Strite v. McGinnes, 330 F.2d 234 (3d Cir. 1964), affirming 215 F. Supp. 513 (E.D. Pa. 1963), cert. denied, 379 U.S. 836, rehearing denied 379 U.S. 910 (1964), to consider a problem quite similar, although not precisely identical. There the power to consume was exercisable "at any time necessary or advisable in order to provide for the reasonable needs and proper expenses or the benefit or comfort" of decedent, and there were indicia in the will itself that the decedent had been the main object of the testatrix's bounty and that the power to invade principal should therefore be given its broadest meaning. We held that the power to consume when necessary or advisable for the decedent's "benefit" fell outside the exception and we therefore found it unnecessary to decide the effect of the word "comfort," which the district court had held was also beyond the exception.

The extent of the decedent's interest in the testator's estate under the power to consume must be determined by Pennsylvania law, although the taxability of the interest will be determined by federal law. In ascertaining the extent of decedent's property interest under Pennsylvania law we recognize its guiding principles that each will is unique and that the intention of the testator must be found within the four corners of the instrument. We must determine this meaning uninfluenced by our present knowledge that decedent died without ever having sought to invade the principal of the trust and we must view the trust in the same way that a Pennsylvania court would have done in considering an application by the decedent for the consumption of principal in her lifetime. Of course, we may not disregard the plain meaning of words used in a testamentary trust on any representation or plea that they may have been selected without a discriminating understanding of their meaning. In Strite v. McGinnes the district court said:

> In ascertaining the meaning of [the language of the power to consume] . . . we may not dismiss the language used as "boiler plate," although it is so characterized by plaintiff's counsel, perhaps with some justice. Boiler plate it may be, in the sense that the words may have been chosen

indiscriminately by the scrivener without that imaginative understanding which is the hallmark of the skillful draftsman. Executors confronted with substantial tax liability because of the carefree use of words in a will, especially words which never were put to use, must view a scrutiny of their meaning as an academic intrusion into the world of reality. But we deal here with the *power* to consume property, regardless whether the power was exercised or lay dormant. The grant of power in the will is the test of taxability, and the reality which governs is the language of the grant rather than the extent of its exercise. 215 F. Supp. at 515-516.

The district court, applying the rule of *ejusdem generis*, considered "incidental" as the significant word, so that the phrase "or other expenses *incidental* to her comfort and well-being" should be made to read as if it had provided for expenses incidental to her maintenance, support, medical care or hospitalization, and thus "comfort or well-being" was to be limited to such items.

This construction is erroneous. The word "incidental" relates to the decedent's "comfort and well-being," and not to her maintenance, support, medical care or hospitalization. To read the phrase "or other expenses incidental to her comfort and well-being" as limited by what has gone before would cut down to meaninglessness the words "comfort and well-being." It is impossible to adopt such a meaning in reading the language, as we must, as a Pennsylvania court would have done if decedent in her lifetime had sought to exercise the power to consume granted by her husband, rather than with the eyes of a reversioner's lawyer poring over the language of a condition subsequent. An artificial rule of construction such as the doctrine of *ejusdem generis* has very limited application and is to be exercised with caution, and in any event is applicable to a will only where the intention of the testator is ambiguous. The words "comfort and well-being" must be given their ordinary meaning and as such go far beyond support and medical and hospital care. In *Strite* we found it unnecessary to determine the meaning of "comfort" in the phrase "benefit or comfort." Here "comfort" is joined with "well-being" and without referring to dictionary definitions or authorities which have considered one or the other of the words, it is clear that much like the words "benefit or comfort" in the *Strite* case, they conferred a power to consume which extended beyond the statutory exception of an ascertainable power for health, education and support. Indeed, the Regulations make this plain beyond doubt. They provide: "A power to use property for the comfort, welfare, or happiness of the holder of the power is not limited by the requisite standard."[15]

The power to consume in the present case therefore exceeds the

_____

15. 26 C.F.R. §20.2041-1(c)(2).

limit fixed for exception from a general power of appointment which is taxable to the estate of the holder of the power.

Appellant argues that in any event the power is not taxable to the decedent's estate because it falls within the exception of §2041 (b)(1)(C)(ii) as a power not exercisable by the decedent except in conjunction with a person "having a substantial interest in the property, subject to the power, which is adverse to the exercise of the power in favor of the decedent." Here a trust company was co-trustee with decedent. The power to invade principal was granted to the trustees jointly and not to the decedent alone, and it was exercisable "at such times and in such amounts as my said Trustees, in their discretion, shall deem necessary or expedient. . . ."

The corporate trustee had no substantial interest in the property of the trust adverse to the decedent's exercise of the power. Its only interest was in the administration of the trust as trustee; it was not a beneficiary of the trust and would have lost no right to obtain any property that might have been turned over to the decedent on the exercise of the power. The trust company's right to compensation for serving as a trustee, even though dependent to some extent on the amount of the corpus of the trust, is not a substantial adverse interest within the meaning of the statute. The substantial adverse interest must be one, as the statute declares, "in the property itself" and not an interest in continuing in the office of trustee. Otherwise there would be no need to describe, as the statute does in the subdivision (ii), the existence of a substantial adverse interest, for subsection (C) which speaks of a power exercisable by a decedent only in conjunction with another person, would alone be enough. Subdivision (ii) has limited this, however, to cases where the co-trustee, in addition to its status as a co-trustee and the incidental compensation as such, has a substantial interest in the property which is adverse to the beneficiary.

The judgment therefore will be reversed and the cause remanded with direction that judgment be entered in favor of the United States. . . .

PROBLEMS

1. *T*'s will creates a trust to pay the income to *A* for life and on *A*'s death to distribute the trust principal to *A*'s descendants. *A* is given the power to invade corpus "in cases of emergency or in situations affecting her care, maintenance, health, welfare, and well-being." Does *A* hold a general power of appointment? See Estate of Jones v. Commissioner, 56 T.C. 35 (1971), aff'd per curiam, 1973-1 U.S. Tax Cas. (CCH) ¶12,914 (3d Cir. 1973), cert. denied, 414 U.S. 820 (1973); Pennell, Estate Planning: Drafting and Tax Considerations in Employing Individual Trustees, 60 N.C.L. Rev. 799, 803-810 (1982).

Suppose, instead, that *A* is given the power to invade corpus "as desired to continue her accustomed standard of living." Does *A* hold a general power? See Rev. Rul. 77-60, 1977-1 C.B. 282; supra page 725.

Suppose, instead, that *A* is given the power to invade corpus "for her comfortable care, support, and maintenance." Does *A* hold a general power? See Treas. Reg. §20.2041-1(c)(2) (1961).

2.   Suppose that soon after the testator's death, the life beneficiary, *A*, comes to you for advice. You read the trust set up by *T* in Problem 1, drafted by another lawyer. Would you recommend that *A* partially disclaim her power?

Reg. §25.2518-3(a)(2) takes the position that

> all interests in the corpus of a trust are treated as a single interest [and] in order to have a qualified disclaimer of an interest in corpus the disclaimant must disclaim all such interests, either totally or as to an undivided portion. Thus, if a disclaimant has a testamentary power of appointment over the trust corpus coupled with either an inter vivos power to invade corpus or an interest as discretionary appointee, a disclaimer by that person can constitute a qualified disclaimer only if both such interests are disclaimed.

De Oliveira v. United States
United States Court of Appeals, Ninth Circuit, 1985
767 F.2d 1344

SNEED, J.   Jose de Oliveira, Jr., executor of the estate of Serafina de Oliveira, appeals from a judgment entered in proceedings for the determination of entitlement to an estate tax refund. The district court held that estate taxes were properly assessed against Serafina's estate and granted the Internal Revenue Service's (IRS) motion for summary judgment. . . . We affirm.

I.   FACTS AND PROCEEDINGS BELOW

Jose de Oliveira, Sr. (the testator) died testate in 1956. His last will and testament created a testamentary trust to hold his half of the community property and named his wife, Serafina, as lifetime beneficiary and trustee. The will also gave the trustee certain powers. The nature and scope of those powers are the principal matters of dispute between the parties in this action.

In 1972, Serafina executed a document entitled "Power of Attorney." Under that document Serafina agreed to confer with the family members and to abide by a majority vote on any proposed sale, lease, loan or transaction regarding any of the family property.

Serafina died testate in 1978. Her son, Jose Jr., was appointed executor of her estate. A timely federal estate tax return was filed for the estate. This return did not include as assets of the estate the property in the testamentary trust established by the testator, Jose Sr.

On audit, the IRS determined that the provisions of the testator's will creating the trust gave Serafina the power, exercisable in favor of herself, to consume, appropriate, or dispose of the corpus of the trust. Based on this determination the IRS concluded that Serafina possessed a general power of appointment and that the trust assets were required to be included in her gross estate for estate tax purposes under the provisions of 26 U.S.C. §2041.

In February 1982, the executor paid the assessed deficiency plus penalties and interest in the total sum of $179,893.91. On September 16, 1982 he filed a claim for refund of this sum in district court. The parties then filed cross-motions for summary judgment. On July 9, 1984, the district court granted the government's motion and on July 23, 1984, entered judgment for the government.

The provisions of the testator's will that gave rise to this dispute are the sixth, seventh, and ninth paragraphs.

Paragraph six reads in part:

Said estate to be held and administered thereafter by said Trustee in trust . . .

a) *for the benefit of my said wife* so long as she lives,

b) with all the powers and subject to the conditions specifically designated hereinafter in paragraph Ninth for my said Trustee and/or Executrix.

c) and shall continue until the death of my said wife. Upon the death of my said wife, this trust to cease and terminate and all the rest, residue and remainder of my trust estate I hereby give, devise and bequeath to my ten children. . . . (emphasis added).

Paragraph nine gives the trustee various powers "[i]n addition to any inherent or implied or statutory powers" and places no limitations on the use of the trust assets.[16]

---

16. Paragraph nine provides in part:

In addition to any inherent or implied or statutory powers my Executrix and/or Trustee may have in either capacity, I grant the following powers to such Executrix and Trustee and her successor: . . .

(b) During the continuance of the administration of my estate, and for the trust herein created, my Trustee shall own, control, possess and use the said trust estate and all property therein; shall collect and receive the rents, issues and profits thereof and shall apply them to the uses and purposes of said trust; said Trustee is hereby empowered to sell, convey, lease, mortgage, hypothecate, encumber by deed of trust and/or convert the property of said trust as from time to time shall be deemed necessary or convenient; to invest and reinvest the trust estate in any property or securities . . . hereby giving to my said Trustee every power and discretion in the management of the trust estate that she would have if she were the absolute, unqualified and unlimited owner thereof . . .

Paragraph seven contains the following language: "I hereby direct that *all provisions for support herein* are intended to take effect as of the date of my death." (emphasis added).

II. DISCUSSION

To determine whether the trust assets were properly included in Serafina's gross estate, we must determine whether the testator's will created a general power of appointment in the trustee (Serafina), and, if so, whether this power was terminated by Serafina's execution of the "Power of Attorney" document in a manner that removed the trust assets from Serafina's gross estate. . . .

THE EXISTENCE OF A GENERAL POWER OF APPOINTMENT

The executor argues that the language in the testator's will creating the trust did not expressly grant to Serafina a general power of appointment. If such a power might be implied, he argues, the will is latently ambiguous since this was not the testator's intent. The executor maintains that certain extrinsic evidence offered below proves that the testator intended that the trust could be invaded only for Serafina's support.

Our analysis begins by recognizing that state law determines the property rights and interests created by a will, but federal law determines the tax consequences of those rights and interests. Morgan v. Commissioner, 309 U.S. 78, 80 (1940); Little v. United States, 704 F.2d 1100, 1105 (9th Cir. 1983). No one disputes this principle.

The district court concluded that the will created a power of appointment under California law. The executor does not contest that conclusion on appeal. Rather, the issue on appeal is whether the power of appointment created by the will was a general power of appointment within the meaning of the federal estate tax law.

Section 2041 of the Internal Revenue Code includes within the gross estate of a decedent the value of property over which the decedent possessed a general power of appointment. Such a general power is defined by section 2041(b)(1), relevant portions of which are set forth in the margin.[17] Serafina's power of appointment is derived from

---

17. The term "general power of appointment" means a power exercisable in favor of the decedent, his estate, his creditors, or the creditors of his estate; except that —

(A) A power to consume, invade, or appropriate income or property for the benefit of the decedent which is limited by an ascertainable standard relating to the health, education, support, or maintenance of the decedent shall not be deemed a general power of appointment. . . .

(C) In the case of a power of appointment created after October 21, 1942, which is exercisable by the decedent only in conjunction with another person — . . .

(ii) If the power is not exercisable by the decedent except in conjunction with a person having a substantial interest in the property, subject to the power, which is adverse to the exercise of the power in favor of the decedent — such power shall not be deemed a general power of appointment.

paragraphs six and nine of the testator's will. Paragraph six provides that the trust was "for the benefit" of Serafina. In addition, paragraph nine grants extensive powers to Serafina as trustee to own, control, possess and use the trust assets, to collect and receive rents, issues and profits for the benefit of the trust, and to sell, convey, lease or mortgage property of the trust as deemed necessary or convenient.[18] Serafina's power to consume, invade, or appropriate property is limited only by the requirement that it be exercised for her "benefit."

The executor does not deny that "benefit" is not an "ascertainable standard" sufficient to bring the power within the exception stated in subsection 2041(b)(1)(A). See, e.g., Lehman v. United States, 448 F.2d 1318 (5th Cir. 1971) holding that the words "comfort" and "welfare" rendered a power of appointment general); Treas. Reg. §20.2041-1(c)(2) (1954). Accordingly, Serafina's power remains one exercisable in her favor, her estate, or the creditors of her estate.

Paragraph seven of the will states that "all provisions for support herein" shall take effect on the day of the testator's death and directs the executrix "to make the same provisions for the beneficiary [Serafina] as provided in said trust" during the probate administration of the estate. This does not alter the conclusion that Serafina's power was a general power. The purpose of paragraph seven was to free Serafina from the need to seek court-ordered maintenance pursuant to Cal. Prob. Code §§680-684 (West 1956).

Nonetheless, the executor argues that the use of the "provisions for support" creates an ambiguity which requires that extrinsic evidence be examined to determine the testator's intent. The extrinsic evidence offered below, the executor insists, shows that the testator intended that the trust could be invaded only for Serafina's support. Thus, her power was not general because limited by an "ascertainable standard."

We are not persuaded. . . .

The essence of the executor's argument is that the testator intended to create an arrangement that would allow the trust assets to pass to the children without being taxed as part of Serafina's estate. In an affidavit, the attorney who drafted the testator's will stated that both he and the testator intended to limit Serafina's use of the trust assets to the funds necessary for her "support." In effect, the executor is urging this court to rewrite the will to effectuate the testator's intent. California law does not permit us to construe a will in that fashion.

> [W]hether or not resort is had to extrinsic evidence, the court must determine the intent of the testator from the language used. The court in interpreting the will may not decide what the testator should have done or even that the testator desired to accomplish a particular objective.

---

18. See footnote [16].

The court only determines what the testator did do by the manner in which he expressed himself. In short, the court, under the guise of interpretation, may not write a will for the testator.

Estate of Casey, 128 Cal. App. 3d 867, 871, 198 Cal. Rptr. 170, 172 (1982) (citations omitted); see Estate of Cleaver, 126 Cal. App. 3d 341, 346, 178 Cal. Rptr. 729, 732 (1981). While it is possible the testator intended to limit Serafina's power over the trust assets by an ascertainable standard, he did not do so. Accordingly, the will should not be construed to limit Serafina's power to invade the trust assets to "support." The federal estate tax consequences must be determined on the basis of the testator's will as it is written, not on the basis of how it might have been written.

"POWER OF ATTORNEY" DOCUMENT

The executor also argues that the power of attorney document eliminated the general power of appointment by requiring that Serafina exercise the power only upon the authorization by a majority of her children. While it is true that the power of appointment would not have been general if that requirement had been in the testator's will, the subsequent creation of the requirement does not achieve the legal effect that the executor desires. Section 2041(a)(2) of the Code states that the decedent's gross estate includes the value of all property "with respect to which the decedent has at any time . . . released [a general] power of appointment by a disposition which is of such nature that if it were a transfer of property owned by the decedent, such property would be includible in the decedent's gross estate under Sections 2035 to 2038, inclusive." The document constituted a release of Serafina's general power of appointment. See Treas. Reg. §20.2041-3(d) (1954). Section 2036(a) states:

> The value of the gross estate shall include the value of all property to the extent of any interest therein of which the decedent has at any time made a transfer . . . under which he has retained for his life . . .
>   (1) the possession or enjoyment of, or the right to the income from, the property, or
>   (2) the right, either alone or in conjunction with any person, to designate the persons who shall possess or enjoy the property or income therefrom.

If the power of attorney document had been a transfer of property owned by Serafina, it is obvious that property would have been includible in Serafina's estate under section 2036(a). Her retained powers fit snugly within that section. Accordingly, the value of the trust assets is includible in Serafina's estate pursuant to section 2041(a)(2). The fact that Serafina perhaps was not aware that she had a general power of appointment when she executed the power of attorney document is irrelevant. Serafina had a general power of appointment regardless of whether she was aware of that fact. It follows that the property subject to the general power of appointment was includible in Serafina's gross estate both before and after the execution of the power of attorney document.

Affirmed.

QUESTION

Is the attorney who drafted de Oliveira's will liable for the additional estate taxes resulting from the court's holding that Serafina had a general power of appointment? See Bucquet v. Livingston, 57 Cal. App. 3d 914, 129 Cal. Rptr. 514 (1976), supra page 715.

7.   The Marital Deduction

a.   Introduction

Section 2056 allows a marital deduction for certain dispositions of property to a decedent's spouse. Before 1982 the primary purpose of the marital deduction was to equalize the tax treatment of couples residing in separate property and community property states. The marital deduction enabled spouses to split their gifts and estates for transfer tax purposes, in effect having them taxed the same as community property is taxed. Generally speaking, if the couple's wills were properly drafted, one-half of the couple's total property would be taxable at the husband's death and one-half at the wife's death.

The marital deduction provisions of the Economic Recovery Tax Act of 1981 were based on an altogether different policy: Interspousal transfers should not be subject to taxation. The act adopted an unlimited marital deduction rule under both the estate tax and the gift tax. Thus, unlimited amounts of property (other than certain "terminable interests") now can be transferred between spouses without the imposition of either a gift tax or an estate tax.[19]

---

19. The unlimited marital deduction rule applies to estates of persons dying after December 31, 1981 — with two important exceptions. First, if a will executed or trust created before September 12, 1981, gives the surviving spouse the "maximum allowable" marital deduction, the marital deduction will be limited to one-half the adjusted gross estate unless (a) the will is thereafter amended to refer to the unlimited marital deduction, or (b) the state enacts a statute providing that a gift of the maximum allowable marital deduction refers to the unlimited marital deduction available after 1981.

Second, no marital deduction is allowed if the spouse of the transferor is not a citizen

For many couples, the changes made by the 1981 act eliminated any concerns about transfer taxes in the estate of either spouse. Because of the unlimited marital deduction, a husband or wife can leave his or her estate to the other spouse without the imposition of an estate tax. Taxes in the estate of the surviving spouse are not a concern unless the projected value of the survivor's estate is greater than $600,000.

PROBLEMS

1. *H* has an estate worth about $750,000. *H* is married to *W*, and the couple has three adult children. *W* has little property of her own. *H* presently has a will that devises his entire estate outright to *W*, with an alternate gift to the couple's children. What will be the estate taxes (a) in *H*'s estate and (b) in *W*'s estate if *H* dies in 1991 and *W* dies one year later? Assume that deductions for administration expenses, debts, and funeral expenses allowable in *H*'s estate total $30,000, that the value of the property passing from *H* to *W* neither increases nor decreases in value from *H*'s death to *W*'s death, and that deductions for administration expenses, debts, and funeral expenses allowable in *W*'s estate total $20,000.

2. *H* devises his entire estate in equal shares to his two daughters, *A* and *B*, subject to the condition that they provide and care for their mother, *W*. In an attempt to create a marital deduction, *A* and *B* execute a disclaimer. Under state law, a disclaimed interest passes as though the disclaimant predeceased the decedent. Whether *H*'s estate is entitled to the marital deduction turns upon the application of another state statute of a kind that almost all states have. What kind of statute do you want to look for (you studied it in Chapter 5), and what is the crucial fact under most such statutes?

b. Interests that Qualify for the Deduction

(1) The Nondeductible Terminable Interest Rule

For an interest to qualify for the marital deduction, five requirements must be met.

---

of the United States. §§2056(d)(1). The citizenship requirement does not apply to any property passing to the surviving spouse in a "qualified domestic trust." §2056(d)(2). A "qualified domestic trust" is one where *all* trustees of the trust are citizens of the United States or domestic corporations. This citizenship requirement means that the lawyer must investigate the citizenship of the client's spouse. In view of the increasing immigration population of recent years, it is not uncommon for a decedent to leave a substantial estate to a surviving spouse who is not a citizen of the United States.

(1) The decedent must have been a citizen or resident of the United States at the time of death.

(2) The decedent must have been survived by his or her spouse.

(3) The value of the interest deducted must be includable in the decedent's gross estate.

(4) The interest must pass from the decedent to the surviving spouse.

(5) The interest must be a deductible interest. More precisely, it must not be a "nondeductible terminable interest" within the meaning of §2056(b).

The first three of these requirements are straightforward. As for the "passing" requirement, this is defined rather broadly in §2056(c) to include interests passing by will, by inheritance, by right of survivorship, by dower or elective share, by the exercise or nonexercise of a power of appointment held by the decedent, or pursuant to a life insurance beneficiary designation. An interest is considered to have passed from the decedent to the spouse if "such interest has been transferred to such person at any time." Thus, lifetime transfers includable in the decedent's gross estate under §§2035 to 2038 can qualify for the deduction. In fact, a commonly used means of satisfying the marital deduction is a gift by way of a revocable trust funded with assets during lifetime, with decedent's will making a "pour-over" gift of testamentary assets to the inter vivos trust.

The fifth requirement is the most important and the most productive of litigation. In general, to qualify for the marital deduction the interest passing to the surviving spouse must be such that it is subject to taxation in the spouse's estate (to the extent not consumed or disposed of by the spouse during his or her lifetime). The marital deduction permits deferral of estate taxation until the surviving spouse's death. In effect, Congress has said: "We won't tax your property in your estate, as long as you leave it to your spouse in a form that exposes it to taxation in your spouse's estate on his or her death." The clearest example of an interest that qualifies for the deduction is an outright (or "fee simple") gift of property to the spouse.

From this it does not follow that any interest that will be taxed in the surviving spouse's estate qualifies for the deduction. To qualify, the interest must not run afoul of the *nondeductible terminable interest rule:*

Where, on the lapse of time, on the occurrence of an event or contingency, or on the failure of an event or contingency to occur, an interest passing to the surviving spouse will terminate or fail, no deduction shall be allowed under this section with respect to such interest —

(A) if an interest in such property passes or has passed (for less than an adequate and full consideration in money or money's worth) from the decedent to any person other than such surviving spouse (or the estate of such spouse); and

(B) if by reason of such passing such person (or his heirs or assigns) may possess or enjoy any part of such property after such termination or failure of such interest so passing to the surviving spouse. [IRC §2056(b)(1).]

Absent special exception, the clearest example of a terminable interest is a life estate given to a surviving spouse, with the remainder to pass to other persons on the spouse's death. On the occurrence of an event or contingency — the spouse's death — the interest will terminate or fail. Upon such termination, an interest in the property — the remainder interest — will pass from the decedent to persons other than the surviving spouse or her estate. By reason of such passing, the remaindermen may possess or enjoy the property on the termination of the spouse's life estate. See Abrams, A Reevaluation of the Terminable Interest Rule, 39 Tax L. Rev. 1 (1983).

PROBLEM

H buys a commercial annuity contract providing for payments to himself for life and then to his wife *W* for life if *W* survives *H*. On the death of *H* and *W*, all payments will cease. *H* dies, and the value of the annuity (i.e., the discounted value of the remaining annuity payments to which *W* is entitled) is included in *H*'s gross estate under §2039. Does the value of this interest qualify for the marital deduction? See Treas. Reg. §20.2056(b)-1(g), example (3).

There are four important exceptions to the nondeductible terminable interest rule.

> The purpose of these exceptions is to prevent the marital deduction prejudicing the prudent disposition of an estate. Standing alone, the nondeductible terminable interest rule creates considerable pressure to give property outright to a surviving spouse in order to take advantage of the marital deduction, although wisdom might dictate a more conservative disposition. The exceptions to the terminable interest rule seek to ease this pressure by providing that certain restrictions upon the interest passing to the surviving spouse will not disqualify the interest given to her for the marital deduction. [C. Lowndes, R. Kramer, & J. McCord, Federal Estate and Gift Taxes 465 (3d ed. 1972).]

(2) Limited Survivorship Exception

In drafting wills, it is a common practice to include a clause requiring that a legatee must survive the testator by a stated period (e.g., 30 or 60 days) in order to take under the will. The purpose of this type of condition is to avoid determining who survived in a common disaster (see supra page 79). Section 2056(b)(3) provides that a devise with a limited survival requirement is not a nondeductible terminable interest if (a) the condition of survival is for a period not exceeding six months and (b) the contingency (the spouse's death within the period) does not in fact occur. In short, a requirement of survival for up to six months can be attached to the interest passing to the spouse without disqualifying it for the marital deduction. (If the spouse does not survive for the stated period, no marital deduction will be available since no interest will actually pass from the decedent to the surviving spouse.)

To take advantage of the marital deduction when the couple dies in a common disaster, one spouse may include in his will a provision along these lines: "For purposes of the gift to my wife in Article III, if my wife and I die under circumstances such that the order of our deaths cannot be established by proof, my wife shall be deemed to have survived me." In other words, the presumption of nonsurvival can be reversed. It may be very desirable to do so if one spouse is considerably richer than the other. For example, suppose that the husband has $1 million and the wife has $200,000. To take advantage of each spouse's unified credit, the husband must leave the wife $400,000. If the husband's will leaves the wife $400,000 and provides that the wife is presumed to survive in a common disaster, and the couple does die in a common disaster, then $600,000 passes tax-free under the husband's will and $600,000 passes tax-free under the wife's will.

(3) Life Estate Plus General Power of Appointment Trust Exception

In originally enacting the marital deduction in 1948, Congress permitted one form of trust disposition to qualify for the marital deduction even though the surviving spouse is given only a life estate. If the spouse is given a life estate and also a general power of appointment over the property, §2056(b)(5) declares that the interest passing to the spouse qualifies for the marital deduction — provided that five technical requirements imposed by the statute are met:

(1) The surviving spouse must be entitled to all income for life.

(2) The income must be payable to the spouse annually or at more frequent intervals.

(3) The power of appointment must be exercisable in favor of the spouse or his estate. In other words, the power must be a general power of appointment. The power may be exercisable during lifetime or by will.

(4) The power must be exercisable by the spouse "alone and in all events." A general testamentary power of appointment satisfies the "all events" requirement even though it cannot be exercised by the spouse during lifetime.

(5) The spouse's interest must not be subject to a power in anyone else to divert the property to someone other than the spouse. Thus the trustee cannot be given a discretionary power to distribute trust corpus to, for example, the couple's children.

This important exception to the nondeductible terminable interest rule led to widespread use of the *life estate plus general power of appointment trust,*[20] commonly referred to in the legal literature and in the practice as simply the "marital deduction power of appointment trust."

In the early years of the marital deduction, there was considerable litigation over whether particular trust dispositions qualified for the deduction, most notably over the requirement that a power of appointment be exercisable by the spouse "alone and in all events." More than a few attorneys apparently failed to grasp that, as a functional matter, Congress had drafted all of the terms of a marital deduction power of appointment trust, and that such a trust should not be drafted without the book open to the relevant pages in the Internal Revenue Code and the pertinent regulations.

Estate of Mittleman v. Commissioner
United States Court of Appeals, District of Columbia Circuit, 1975
522 F.2d 132

ROBINSON, J. Jerome Mittleman died testate on October 13, 1965, while resident and domiciled in the District of Columbia. His duly probated will makes bequests to his son and others, and in its ninth paragraph creates a trust of the residuary estate "[t]o provide for the proper support, maintenance, welfare and comfort" of Henrietta Mittleman, his wife, "for her entire lifetime."[21] The trustees, who are also

---

20. It is not necessary to use a trust in order to qualify for the marital deduction under §2056(b)(5). A legal life estate coupled with a general power of appointment qualifies for the deduction if the five technical requirements of the statute are satisfied. As a practical matter, though, legal life estates are rarely used in estate planning. See supra page 444.

21. The ninth paragraph reads:

I give, devise and bequeath all of the rest, residue and remainder of my property and estate of every nature whatsoever, that I may own or have any interest in at the time of my death, to my hereinafter named Trustees and their successors, in trust nevertheless, for the following purposes:

a. To provide for the proper support, maintenance, welfare and comfort of my beloved wife, Henrietta Mittleman, for her entire lifetime.

b. To invade the corpus of the trust estate from time to time in the sole and exclusive discretion of the Trustees and to use all or any portion of the said corpus for the proper support, maintenance and welfare of my wife, Henrietta Mittleman.

c. Upon the death of my said wife, Henrietta Mittleman, the balance of the trust estate created under this article is to be paid or turned over to such person or persons or corporation or corporations as my said wife may by will appoint. If the power of appointment is for any reason not validly exercised by my said wife in whole or in part, then upon her death such portion or all of the principal of the trust or such interests or estates therein as shall not have been validly appointed by her shall be paid or turned over to my son, Stephen Mittleman, but if my son, Stephen Mittleman, does not survive my wife, such portion shall be paid or turned over to the blood or adopted children, if any, of my son, Stephen Mittleman, in equal shares, per stirpes.

the executors of the estate, are authorized in their sole discretion to invade the corpus of the trust partially or wholly, and upon the wife's death the balance of the corpus is to be distributed to those whom by will she may appoint. If for any reason the power of appointment is not fully exercised, the unappointed estate is to pass to the testator's son if he survives, and otherwise to the son's children.

Mittleman's executors filed a federal estate tax return claiming a marital deduction based on the value of the estate left in the trust. The Commissioner disallowed the deduction and assessed a deficiency. The Tax Court sustained the Commissioner. We reverse. We hold that the relevant features of the trust, ascertained by interpretation of the ninth paragraph of the will, qualify the trust res for the deduction sought.

I

Interests in property passing from a decedent to the surviving spouse may qualify for a deduction from the gross estate, to a maximum of one-half of its value, in determining the taxable estate. The purpose underlying the deduction is equalization of the tax burden on taxpayers in common law states vis-à-vis those in community property jurisdictions. While the surviving spouse is relieved of the tax on the deductible portion of the decedent's estate, that portion may eventually be taxed either as a part of the surviving spouse's estate or as a gift in the event of a gratuitous inter vivos transfer.

Consistently with the theme of uniformity, Congress has limited the availability of the deduction to interests approximating the outright ownership which the surviving spouse acquires under the community property system. Accordingly, the deduction is unavailable for "terminable interests" — those which will expire by lapse of time or on the occurrence or nonoccurrence of a contingency. The trust before us may, however, fall within an apparent — though hardly a real — exception to the terminable-interest rule. When a trust instrument confers a life estate — a terminable interest — and couples it with a general power of appointment over the trust principal, the life interest, though less than outright ownership, may nonetheless win the deduction. To qualify for this exception, the trust must meet specific standards, including requirements that the surviving spouse be entitled to the entire income from the trust or some part thereof, and that the income be payable no less frequently than annually.

In the Tax Court's view, Ms. Mittleman's right did not extend to all of the income from the trust created by her husband's will, or to income distributions annually or more often. The court reached these conclusions by the process of "[f]ocusing on the first two requirements of the regulation, and comparing them with the language of the ninth paragraph of the decedent's will. . . ." The court felt that "[a]ccording to the plain terms of the will provision, [Ms. Mittleman] is entitled to support and maintenance for her remaining life, not to 'all of the income' from the residue of the estate. Nor is she entitled to the income 'annually or at more frequent intervals.'" The court was unable to "agree with [appellants] that the wife had such command over the income that it was virtually hers." "If," the court said, "the trust's income exceeded that which was sufficient for her 'support, maintenance, welfare and comfort,' she would have no right to receive excess income. In such event, the power to invade corpus lodged in subparagraph b of the ninth paragraph would not come into play."

We think the Tax Court erred in its decision, primarily because of the limited scope of its inquiry. The court probed no deeper than the bare language of the ninth paragraph of the will, and grounded its interpretation of that paragraph on what it took to be "the plain terms of" that provision. Had the court delved further and considered additional manifestations of testamentary intent, it would have been readily apparent that the terms of paragraph nine were not nearly as plain as at first blush they might seem to be, and that other factors speak more eloquently than the testator's pen.

On the critical issues of income entitlement and frequency of distribution, the testator's intent is dispositive. To ascertain that intent, we must look first to the words he used — not to particular passages in isolation, but to the language of the will as a whole. If the intent is not then clearly disclosed on the face of the document, we must examine relevant extrinsic evidence including the circumstances surrounding the formulation of the will. Local law, not federal law, governs the solution of any legal problems arising as to the meaning of the will. In the quest for intent, however, prior decisions are of little value because each case hinges on its own peculiar facts.

Hence, the task on this appeal is a full-scale interpretation of Jerome Mittleman's will to resolve the question whether his wife is entitled to distribution of all of the income from the trust at intervals no greater than annually. After responding to that call, we answer the question in the affirmative. The factors we identify and discuss establish beyond peradventure that the testator intended a gift of the entire trust income to the wife, and distribution thereof promptly enough to qualify the trust property for the marital deduction.

II

The Commissioner's argument, like the Tax Court's ruling, is founded wholly on the premise that Ms. Mittleman is not entitled to all of the income generated by the trust, but only to such amounts as may be needed for her "proper support, maintenance, welfare and comfort." To be sure, a trust instrument explicitly directs the trustee to distribute just so much of the income as is actually required for the beneficiary's support.[22] But the Mittleman will imposes no such restriction expressly, nor in our view does it do so impliedly. Rather, when examined in its full context, the provision on which the Commissioner and the Tax Court rested their respective rulings emerges as a mere declaration of the purpose of the trust, and not as a ceiling on the life beneficiary's entitlement. We are brought to this conclusion by a number of circumstances, some within and some outside the four corners of the will.

Nowhere does the ninth paragraph of the will expressly refer to the trust income. Since, however, the stated goal of the trust is "to provide for the proper support, maintenance, welfare and comfort of [the wife] . . . for her entire lifetime," it is evident that a gift of income to fully serve that purpose was intended. The amount of income to be paid to the wife is not limited in terms, not is it conditioned upon the judgment of the trustees. In contrast, by the next following subparagraph the trust corpus can be invaded only "in the sole and exclusive discretion of the [t]rustees." The compelling inference is that the intent was to make an unqualified disposition of the income to the wife.

Had the testator envisioned a surplus of income after expenditures for his wife's maintenance, he likely would have told the trustees what to do with it. There is, however, no direction to accumulate the income,[23] or to dispose of it otherwise than for the benefit of his wife. Additionally, the power of appointment conferred upon Ms. Mittleman extends to "the balance of the trust estate" without the slightest hint as to its makeup; but in the event of a default in exercise of power, the will disposes of "such portion or all of the *principal* of the trust or such interests or estates therein as shall not have been validly appointed. . . ."[24] This language indicates the more clearly that the testator contemplated no accumulation of income.

In addition, the testator gave the trustees discretion to invade the corpus of the trust for his wife's benefit, thus demonstrating an acute awareness of the possibility that the trust income might not be sufficient to satisfy the support needs of the beneficiary. Moreover, the discretion to invade corpus is more limited than the stated objective of the gift of

22. See G. Bogert, Trust & Trustees §229 (2d ed. 1965); 2 A. Scott, Trusts §128.4 (3d ed. 1967).

23. "Strong and clear language would be necessary to permit that result," for "[t]he law does not favor the implication of a direction to accumulate income. All considerations are adverse to accumulation." Grabois v. Grosner, 124 U.S. App. D.C. 247, 250, 363 F.2d 979, 982 (1966).

24. If we accepted the Commissioner's interpretation of the will, there would be no testamentary disposition of any income accumulated should Ms. Mittleman fail to exercise her power of appointment. To this extent, that interpretation collides with the construction canon disfavoring intestacy where a testamentary disposition of the entire estate appears to have been made.

the income; "comfort"' is deleted, further denoting a purpose to treat income differently from principal.

Should these indicia of testamentary intent fail to define with sufficient certainty Ms. Mittleman's right to the trust income, we must resort to the surrounding circumstances and other evidence extrinsic to the will. When that is done, the intent is displayed beyond any doubt. To begin with, the relatively small size of the trust itself readily substantiates the thesis that the beneficiary is entitled to all of the income. The corpus of the trust is not large,[25] and by the same token the income it can produce is modest,[26] and falls far short of the family income before Mr. Mittleman died.[27] In contemplating the proper level of support and maintenance, a very important consideration is the recipient's station in life when the trust is created, and there is nothing whatever to suggest that the testator expected a surplus after his wife's needs were met. Indeed, the evidence showed, and the Tax Court found, that "[i]n the course of administration of the trust established in decedent's will, substantially all of the income, and to some extent its principal, have been distributed to Ms. Mittleman upon her request." The strong inference here is that the testator felt that the entire trust income was necessary to enable his wife to maintain the standard of living to which she was accustomed.

Moreover, it is well known that wills and testamentary trusts are customarily prepared in light of their probable tax consequences, and that, particularly where the testator is married, they are usually written to take advantage of the marital deduction. In light of the all-pervasive influence of the tax laws on estate planning, it seems entirely reasonable for courts to presume, absent contrary language, that testamentary provisions in favor of spouses are designed to qualify for the marital deduction.

In this case, however, it is unnecessary to indulge in presumption, for the evidence demonstrates that Mr. Mittleman had exactly that in mind. At the trial in the Tax Court, the attorney who drafted the will testified that when the will was drawn Mittleman voiced concern as to whether the trust would qualify for the marital deduction, and that he, the attorney, advised Mittleman that in his considered opinion it would. On this testimony, the Tax Court found that "Jerome Mittleman's

---

25. The gross estate, as adjusted by the Commissioner, is approximately $265,000. Subtracting expenses and debts of $39,000 and specific bequests of $67,000, the residuary estate is reduced to about $159,000 even prior to payment of federal estate and local inheritance taxes.

26. We understand that the trust yielded an income averaging only $5,200 during the period 1968 to 1971.

27. In both 1963 and 1964, Mr. Mittleman received a salary of $10,400. On his federal income tax returns for those years, he also reported dividends of about $5,600 and $7,600, respectively. The will was drafted in June 1965, and he died four months later.

primary concern in this matter was to provide for his wife's future well-being and to insure that she would be free from want, as much as possible," and, further, that Mittleman "was advised by his attorneys that his will gave the estate the benefit of the marital deduction; that was his wish." Mittleman's intent in that regard, then, could hardly be clearer.

As the Supreme Court has observed, "Congress' intent to afford a liberal 'estate-splitting' possibility to married couples, where the deductible half of the decedent's estate would ultimately — if not consumed — be taxable in the estate of the survivor, is unmistakable." So, in interpreting a will ostensibly within this policy, courts should give due weight to the testator's desire to secure the marital deduction. We recognize that the mere intention to garner a tax benefit is not decisive, or even necessarily relevant, in deciding whether a deduction is available. We hold, however, that where a testator intends to create a trust qualifying for the marital deduction, ambiguities in his will should, if possible, be resolved in favor of success in that endeavor.

The Commissioner also contends that Ms. Mittleman does not have the right to receive the income annually or at more frequent intervals. To the extent that this position rests upon the assumption that she is entitled to less than all of the income, it is refuted by what we have already said on that score. And to the extent that the argument proceeds from the absence of a provision specifying the times at which payments to the beneficiary are to be made, it dishonors the Commissioner's own regulations, which provide that "silence of a trust instrument as to the frequency of payment will not be regarded as a failure to satisfy the condition . . . that income must be payable to the surviving spouse annually or more frequently unless the applicable law permits payment to be made less frequently than annually." Indubitably, the Commissioner is bound by the regulation, and our attention has not been directed to, nor have we found, any provision of local law that would exempt this case from its operation.[28]

---

28. Lastly, the Commissioner asserts that the power conferred upon Ms. Mittleman does not enable an appointment of the trust property to her estate, a qualification for testamentary powers of appointment demanded both by statute and administrative regulation. The reason the Commissioner assigns is that no authority to appoint her own estate is expressly granted. The Tax Court, ruling for the Commissioner on other grounds, found it unnecessary to pass on this contention.

We deem the Commissioner's position untenable. The power is clearly general, see D.C. Code §45-1002 (1973); it is subject only to the condition that it be exercised by will — a characteristic of all testamentary powers — and that circumstance does not embarrass the marital deduction sought by appellants. See 26 C.F.R. §20.2056(b)-5(g)(ii) (1975). The authority of the donee of a power is effectively circumscribed only by restrictions that are clearly expressed, 3 Powell, Real Property ¶398 and 378.40 (1974); Restatement of Property ¶324 (1940), and here we perceive none affecting Ms. Mittleman's ability to make an appointment in favor of her estate.

We hold then, that the trust created by Jerome Mittleman's will in favor of his wife satisfies the prerequisites for the marital deduction. The order of the Tax Court is accordingly reversed, and the case is remanded for recomputation of the deficiency.

Reversed and remanded.

NOTES

1.   In Estate of Foster v. Commissioner, 725 F.2d 201 (2d Cir. 1984), the testator, a dairy farmer, left his wife his property for her lifetime with power to invade principal "for her needs and the needs of my children as she in her discretion may deem necessary," with remainder over to the children. The court held the bequest did not qualify for the marital deduction because the wife's power to consume was not equivalent to a power to appoint "in all events." A power to consume is limited by a standard of good faith on the part of the donee of the power. See supra page 724.

2.   It is desirable to state, in drafting a will, that the testator intends the gift to the spouse to qualify for the marital deduction. If the testator's intention in this regard is made clear, the court will in all likelihood interpret any ambiguities in favor of the marital deduction. See Cal. Prob. Code §§21522 and 21524 (1989), requiring a court to do so.

(4)   Estate Trust Exception

The *estate trust* exception to the nondeductible terminable interest rule is included within the statement of the rule (see supra page 999). An interest is a nondeductible terminable interest only if, on termination of the spouse's interest, the property passes *to someone other than the surviving spouse or the spouse's estate*. Consequently, a disposition of property "to my husband for life, and on his death to his estate," whether in the form of a legal life estate or in a trust settlement, qualifies for the marital deduction.

The estate trust is seldom used as a means of qualifying for the deduction because of its relative inflexibility. Also, an estate trust causes the assets to be subject to creditors' claims and administration expenses in the spouse's estate. However, there is one situation in which an estate trust might be desirable, stemming from the requirement that, under a marital deduction power of appointment trust or a qualified terminable interest property trust (QTIP trust, see below), all trust income must be paid to the surviving spouse for life. If the testator's estate includes *unproductive property*, a marital deduction power of appointment trust or QTIP trust must include a provision authorizing the surviving spouse to compel the trustee to (a) convert the unproductive assets to income-producing property or (b) pay the spouse a reasonable amount out of other trust assets to compensate for lost income. See Treas. Reg. §20.2056(b)-5(f)(5). This could raise a potentially serious problem if, for example, the testator owns closely held stock that does not pay dividends or owns unimproved real estate that is being held for future development. An estate trust might be useful in this situation.

(5) Qualified Terminable Interest Property Trust Exception

Until 1982, as a practical matter only three forms of transfer could be used to secure the marital deduction for an estate: an outright disposition, a marital deduction power of appointment trust, and an estate trust.[29] All of these forms of transfer had the effect of giving the surviving spouse the unrestricted power of disposition over the property, either during lifetime or at death. When the unlimited marital deduction was enacted in 1981, Congress recognized that, under the existing law,

> the decedent cannot insure that the spouse will subsequently pass the property to his children. Because the maximum marital deduction is limited under present law to one-half of the decedent's adjusted gross estate, a decedent may at least control disposition of one-half of his estate and still maximize current tax benefits. However, unless certain interests that do not grant the spouse total control are eligible for the unlimited marital deduction, a decedent would be forced to choose between surrendering control of his entire estate to avoid imposition of estate tax at his death or reducing his tax benefits at his death to insure inheritance by the children. The committee believes that the tax laws should be neutral and that tax consequences should not control an individual's disposition of property. Accordingly, the committee believes that a deduction should be permitted for certain terminable interests. [H.R. Rep. No. 4242, 96th Cong., 2d Sess., 161 (1981).]

In 1981 Congress enacted §2056(b)(7), which allows a marital deduction for a *qualified terminable interest*. To qualify for the deduction under this section, three requirements must be met.

---

29. Many persons have established during life a revocable trust to avoid probate or to secure other advantages. See supra pages 532-538. Suppose that *H* has established such a trust. A devise by *W* to *H*'s revocable trust might not qualify for the marital deduction. The revocable trust must be carefully examined. As for qualifying the trust as a marital deduction power of appointment trust, the power to revoke may not be the equivalent of a general power exercisable "in all events" if, under the trust instrument, it ceases to be exercisable in the event of the settlor's incapacity. If the revocable trust contains a provision that in the event of incapacity of the settlor the trustee may make gifts to members of the family qualifying for the annual $10,000 gift tax exclusion, the revocable trust is disqualified as a marital deduction power of appointment trust and as a QTIP trust because the trustee has power to appoint trust property to persons other than the spouse.

(1) The spouse must be entitled to all income for life.
(2) The income must be payable to the spouse annually or at more frequent intervals.
(3) No person (including the spouse) can have the power to appoint the property during the spouse's lifetime to any person other than the spouse. The spouse may, but need not, be given a special or general power to appoint the property *by will*, and such power can be as broad or as limited as the creator of the trust deems appropriate.

Since the purpose of the marital deduction is to permit deferral of estate taxes until the death of the surviving spouse, allowance of a marital deduction for a qualified terminable interest is conditioned on the donor (if a lifetime gift) or the decedent's executor (if a death transfer) making an election to have the property taxed in the surviving spouse's estate. If such an election is made, the value of the property in which the spouse had an income interest is includable in the spouse's gross estate under §2044. To prevent the tax attributable to this interest from increasing the tax burden on the spouse's own heirs, the tax is borne by the persons receiving the qualified terminable interest property on the spouse's death. Thus, if a trust is involved, the tax attributable to the interest (measured by the difference between the estate tax actually paid in the spouse's estate and the tax that would have been due if the property had not been included in the spouse's gross estate) is paid out of the corpus of the trust.

Since the beneficiary of a qualified terminable interest trust is treated as owner for gift and estate tax purposes, if the surviving spouse makes a lifetime gift of his qualified terminable interest, the value of the entire property (and not just the value of the spouse's income interest) is treated as a taxable gift.

A qualified terminable interest can be either a life estate in trust or a legal life estate. Since legal life estates are rarely used in estate planning, creating a qualified terminable interest to secure the marital deduction usually takes the form of a qualified terminable interest property trust (known as a QTIP trust). In comparing the QTIP trust with a marital deduction power of appointment trust, it will be noted that both require that all income must be payable to the surviving spouse at least annually *for life*. If the spouse's income interest terminates on remarriage, this disqualifies both a marital deduction power of appointment trust and a QTIP trust. However, there are two important differences. Under a QTIP trust, there is no requirement that the surviving spouse be given a general power of appointment exercisable in all events. On the spouse's death, the remainder interest can pass outright or in further trust to any beneficiary or by exercise of a special power or a conditional general power. Second, under a QTIP trust there can be no power in any person *including the spouse* to appoint the property to anyone other than the spouse during his lifetime. Invasions of trust principal by the spouse or by a trustee for the spouse are permitted. The standards for determining such invasions may be as liberal or restrictive as the settlor desires.[30] If the spouse wants to reduce the corpus of the trust by making gifts (since the corpus of the trust will be taxed in his estate), a two-step process is involved. The spouse must invade the corpus of the trust (if the trust gives him an invasion power) or the trustee must distribute corpus to him (if the instrument gives the trustee such a power), and then the spouse must make the gift directly to the donee.

The permissible terms of a qualified terminable interest trust are so attractive that the traditional marital deduction power of appointment trust will probably be far less frequently used in the future. A QTIP trust is particularly useful if the spouses have different natural beneficiaries (e.g., children by a former marriage) or if the testator is concerned about the prospect that his spouse may remarry and then favor the new spouse.

There are other advantages in using a QTIP trust. In several states, following the Internal Revenue Code, property over which the decedent held a general power of appointment is taxed at the powerholder's death whether or not the power is exercised. If a QTIP trust, rather than a marital deduction power of appointment trust, is used to secure the deduction, state death taxes in the estate of the surviving spouse may be lower.

The testator may direct his executor to elect to qualify a terminable interest trust for the marital deduction. Or the testator may direct his executor *not* to so elect. Or the testator may leave the election to the executor's discretion. If the testator leaves it up to the executor, the testator should be careful not to create any conflicts of interest so as to raise difficult questions of fiduciary obligations. See Ascher, The Quandary of Executors Who Are Asked to Plan the Estates of the Dead: The Qualified Terminable Interest Property Election, 63 N.C.L. Rev. 1 (1984); Schain, Marital Trust v. QTIP: Advice for Estate Planners, 49 Mo. L. Rev. 741 (1984); Report, The Qualified Terminable Interest Trust Election, 18 Real Prop., Prob. and Tr. J. 1 (1983).

c.   Tax Planning

In a compendious treatment of estate taxation such as this, we cannot cover in detail the more complicated tax avoidance devices developed

---

30. However, if the invasion power is unrestricted, i.e., exercisable in all events, it will be treated as a general power of appointment, and the trust will be not a QTIP trust but a marital deduction power of appointment trust.

for spouses. However, there are certain basic strategies and devices with which you should be familiar. The more complex and refined arrangements build on these.

(1)   Using the Exemptions of Both Spouses

Each spouse has an exemption from estate and gift taxation, in the form of a unified credit, which is $600,000. It is possible for a spouse to leave his or her entire estate to the other spouse, deferring all taxation until the death of the surviving spouse. However, if this is done, the first spouse's exemption is lost since *all* of his or her assets will be subject to taxation on the surviving spouse's death. Thus:

> *Case 18.* W owns property worth $1,200,000. H owns no property. H and W have made no taxable gifts. W dies, devising all her property to H. Because of the unlimited marital deduction, no taxes are paid at W's death. At H's death, H leaves an estate of $1,200,000; $600,000 is exempt from taxation. An estate tax of $235,000 is payable on the remaining $600,000. (For ease of illustration, we keep the asset values the same in the estates of W and H and ignore deductions for administration expenses, debts, and funeral expenses, and various credits.)

By devising everything to H, W in Case 18 did not use her $600,000 exemption applicable to property taxable in her estate. To use this exemption, W must leave a taxable estate of $600,000, which means that $600,000 worth of property should *not* qualify for the marital deduction. Case 18a illustrates how this can be done:

> *Case 18a.* Refer back to Case 18. W dies, bequeathing $600,000 in trust for H for life, remainder as H appoints by will among W's issue, and in default of appointment to W's issue per stirpes. This bequest would qualify for the marital deduction as a QTIP trust if W's executor so elected, but W's will directs her executor not to elect the marital deduction for this trust. This $600,000 is taxable at W's death, but because of W's $600,000 exemption in the form of a credit, no taxes are paid (hence this trust is known as a *credit shelter trust*). The assets in the credit shelter trust are not taxable at H's death because H has only a life estate coupled with a special power of appointment.
>
> The remainder of W's assets (worth $600,000) is bequeathed by W's residuary clause outright to H. These assets are taxable at H's death, but no taxes are paid because the total is not more than $600,000.

By taking advantage of both spouses' exemptions, as is done in Case 18a, $1,200,000 can be passed to the couple's children, free of estate taxation. If the spouses desire that the surviving spouse have all the income from the property, this can be arranged as in Case 18a. The key to taking advantage of both exemptions is that $600,000 worth of property must not qualify for the marital deduction in the estate of the first spouse to die. Putting $600,000 in a credit shelter trust will reduce death taxes payable on the surviving spouse's death by an amount equal to at least 37 percent of the value of the trust assets on the surviving spouse's death. (If the value of the assets remains the same at the surviving spouse's death, the tax saving of the estate plan in Case 18a, as compared to Case 18, is $235,000.)

The credit shelter trust does not, of course, have to give all the income to the surviving spouse. Case 18a is merely an illustration of a situation where the couple wants all the income to go to the surviving spouse. The credit shelter trust could give discretion to the trustee to spray the income among family members, thus reducing income taxes during the surviving spouse's remaining life. Or the first spouse to die could use his or her $600,000 exemption by bequeathing that amount to children or persons other than the surviving spouse.

In discussing Case 18, we have assumed that W, the richer of the spouses, will die first. But suppose that H dies first. In that case, H's exemption will be lost to the extent of $600,000 because H owns nothing. At W's death $600,000 ($1,200,000 minus W's $600,000 exemption) will be taxable. In order to take advantage of H's exemption, W must transfer to H during life property worth $600,000. W can give H property outright or in a trust. The trust can be either a marital deduction power of appointment trust or a QTIP trust, which W elects to be taxable at H's death. No gift tax is payable upon the transfer because any of these transfers qualifies for the gift tax marital deduction. Thus:

> *Case 18b.* W creates an inter vivos QTIP trust with all income to be paid to H for his life and upon his death to pay the principal to W's children. W transfers $600,000 to this trust and on her gift tax return elects to take the marital deduction. This results in the trust principal being taxable in H's gross estate, but because of H's exemption, no taxes are payable.[31] W has reduced her taxable estate to $600,000, which is exempt from taxation. (If W wants to have the income on the $600,000

---

31. The income tax basis of the trust assets is stepped up on H's death to the value at the date of H's death. Hence if it is likely that W will survive H by several years, it may be wise for W to transfer into the QTIP trust assets that have the lowest basis. These assets will become saleable without paying a capital gains tax after H's death, which (we assume) will occur before W's death. If the wealth position of the parties is reversed, if it is H who is rich and W who is poor, and W is expected to outlive H, H should put in the inter vivos QTIP trust for W those of his assets with the highest basis, saving for himself the assets with the lowest basis. In other words, the spouse who is expected to die first should own the assets with the lowest basis in order to free the assets earlier of potential capital gain liability.

As a general rule property that has depreciated in value should be held by the spouse who has the longer life expectancy.

come back to *W* after *H* dies, *W* can create an inter vivos marital deduction power of appointment trust with *H* as the beneficiary, and *H* by will can exercise the general power of appointment by appointing the trust funds to *W* for life, directing his executor not to elect the marital deduction.)

(2) Equalizing Estates

Because of the graduated tax rates, the total estate tax payable on the death of a husband and wife will be lower if the two estates are equal. Suppose that *W* has $2,000,000 and *H* nothing. To equalize the estates if *W* dies first, *W* can bequeath $1,000,000 in a marital deduction trust (taxable at *H*'s death) and $1,000,000 in a trust that does not qualify for the marital deduction (taxable at *W*'s death and not taxable at *H*'s death). However, equalization is not possible if *H*, who has no assets, dies first, unless *W* gives *H* one-half of her assets during life. She can do this by creating a QTIP trust for *H* for life, remainder to *W*'s children. But of course *W* may be unwilling to give substantial property to her spouse.

Equalization is not necessarily the best solution in all cases. If the spouses own more than $1,200,000, and the estates are equalized, the estate of the spouse first to die must pay some estate tax. If, on the other hand, the first spouse to die took complete advantage of the marital deduction, postponing all estate taxes until the death of the surviving spouse, income could be earned on the property that would otherwise go for estate taxes on the death of the first spouse to die. Also, capital gains may accrue on the property that picks up a new basis at the second death. In deciding whether equalization is better than tax deferral, this lost income and possible lost gain must be taken into consideration. (Of course to the extent that it is not spent or given away by the surviving spouse, it will be included in the gross estate and taxed at the second death.) The surviving spouse may consume the property or give it away in $10,000 annual gifts to various members of the family. On the other hand, if all the income of property is paid to (and is taxable to) the surviving spouse, who does not need it, wasteful income taxation in the spouse's high bracket may be incurred. See Kasner, The "Optimum" Marital Deduction — Pay Now or Pay Later?, 43 N.Y.U. Tax Inst. ch. 54 (1984).

(3) Formula Clauses

Prior to the Economic Recovery Tax Act of 1981, when the maximum marital deduction was the greater of $250,000 or one-half the decedent's adjusted gross estate, estate planners used a fine-tuned *formula clause* to produce precisely the maximum amount allowed for the marital deduction. In 1981 the tax laws were amended to allow an unlimited marital deduction. Thereafter formula clauses designed to produce a *maximum* marital deduction became useless, for the maximum (unlimited) marital deduction can now be produced by a bequest of "everything I own to my spouse" (or to *X* in trust for the spouse in a marital deduction power of appointment trust, estate trust, or QTIP trust). Formula clauses remain useful, however, in producing precisely the right amount to put in a credit shelter trust or a marital deduction trust. As indicated above, a credit shelter trust is a trust designed to hold an amount equal to the exemption of the first spouse to die (and therefore not taxable on his death) in such a manner as not to be taxable on the surviving spouse's death. Thus:

> *Case 19.* *H*, owning assets worth $1,500,000, wants to leave all the income on his property to his wife for life, remainder to his children. *W* has very little property of her own. *H* has made no taxable gifts during life. *H*'s will creates a credit shelter trust of $600,000, giving *W* the income for life, remainder to *H*'s children. The will directs *H*'s executor not to elect to treat this as a QTIP trust. The sum of $600,000 is taxable in *H*'s estate but is sheltered from taxation because of the unified credit. *H*'s will devises the remainder of his assets in either a marital deduction power of appointment trust or a QTIP trust. *H*'s children are given the remainder after *W*'s life estate. The assets in the marital deduction trust will be taxable at *W*'s death.

So far in this discussion we have assumed that a decedent has a $600,000 tax exemption in the form of a tax credit. This is true, but for reasons we must now go into the actual amount of property that will be taxable in the decedent's estate but pass free of taxation may turn out to be somewhat more or somewhat less than $600,000. Because we cannot during the client's life predict absolutely accurately what amount should or will be sheltered from taxation, we use a formula clause in drafting a will to fix the sheltered amount. We do not create a credit shelter trust of $600,000, as is done in Case 19, but a credit shelter trust of an amount determined by a formula. Why cannot we say now that $600,000 will exactly equal the amount exempt? Go back and look at page 959, where we show how the estate tax is calculated by deducting deductions and credits. There are a number of matters, presently unknown, that enter into the final tax calculation. To return to Case 19, *H* may make inter vivos gifts, using up some of the unified credit during life. After *H*'s death, *H*'s executor may make tax elections under §2053 that affect the amount of the taxable estate and the amount of the unified credit. The amount of state death taxes and the amount of the credit for state death taxes cannot accurately be calculated during *H*'s life. Enter the *formula bequest*. It solves all these problems. Here is an example of a *pecuniary credit shelter formula* bequest:

If my wife survives me,[32] I give to *X* as trustee [of a credit shelter trust]

---

32. This form is useful for the facts in Case 19, where *W* owns little property. Another

a sum equal to the largest amount, if any, that can pass free of federal estate tax under this Article by reason of the unified credit and the state death tax credit (provided use of this credit does not require an increase in the state death taxes paid) allowable to my estate but no other credit,[33] and after deducting the value of property disposed of by previous Articles of this will and property passing outside of this will that is includable in my gross estate and does not qualify for the marital or charitable deduction[34] and after deducting charges to principal that are not allowed as deductions in computing my federal estate tax.[35] For the purpose of establishing the sum disposed of by this Article the values finally determined for federal estate tax purposes shall be used.

If a pecuniary credit shelter disposition is made in a will, the residuary estate is usually devised to the surviving spouse in a marital deduction trust (power of appointment, estate, or QTIP).

We have set forth above a pecuniary credit shelter formula. An alternative is a *fractional share* credit shelter disposition. A pecuniary formula clause makes a disposition of a fixed dollar amount of property, whereas a fractional share formula clause makes a gift of a fractional share of the residue. The numerator of the fraction is the amount of the credit shelter, and the denominator is the residuary estate. The primary difference between a pecuniary bequest and a fractional share bequest is that the latter receives a fractional share of gains and losses during the period of administration whereas a pecuniary bequest remains constant in value. If a pecuniary amount trust is funded with an asset that has appreciated in value above its estate tax value, capital gain to the estate will result. A fractional share bequest will avoid any capital gains tax to the estate when the trust is funded, but administration of fractional share formula bequests is complicated because the fraction cannot be ascertained until administration is complete, which may be several years after the testator's death. Also, a fractional share bequest, giving the credit shelter trust a fractional share of each asset in the

---

provision in *H*'s will should provide that if *H* and *W* die under circumstances where the order of deaths cannot be established by proof, *W* shall be deemed to have survived *H*. Such a provision will result in a marital deduction being allowed in *H*'s estate for the amount not going into the credit shelter trust. See supra page 1001.

33. If the shelter covers both the unified credit and the credit for state death taxes, the maximum credit shelter will be $626,728. See IRC §2011.

34. The formula clause adjusts to take into account dispositions of property not covered by the will but includable in the gross estate and not qualifying for the marital deduction, e.g., life insurance payable to a child.

35. The credit shelter formula requires a reduction for charges to principal not allowed as deductions in computing the estate tax. Most frequently, these charges are administration expenses used as income tax deductions rather than as estate tax deductions (see infra pages 1021). Since these items reduce the value of the property passing under the will and are not deductible against the estate tax, they must be deducted from the credit shelter amount.

residuary estate, prevents the executor from allocating specific assets to the credit shelter trust and other specific assets to the marital deduction trust. The executor must make pro-rata distributions of property to implement a fractional share bequest, and a pro-rata distribution of every item can lead to some sticky situations. Largely because of the problem of making a pro-rata distribution, most estate planners favor the pecuniary formula clause.

In addition to credit shelter formula dispositions, practitioners use marital deduction formula dispositions. The marital deduction gift can be, like the credit shelter disposition, either of a pecuniary amount or of a fractional share of the residue. For comparison of these different arrangements, see R. Covey, Marital Deductions and Credit Shelter Dispositions and the Use of Formula Provisions (1984); Kurtz, Marital Deduction Estate Planning Under the Economic Recovery Tax Act of 1981: Opportunities Exist, but Watch the Pitfalls, 34 Rutgers L. Rev. 591, 611-632 (1982).

8. The Charitable Deduction

Section 2055 of the Internal Revenue Code allows an unlimited deduction for transfers for public, charitable, or religious purposes. There is no limitation on the amount that can qualify for a charitable deduction.

A principal question is whether a particular bequest is for uses that qualify for the charitable deduction. The statute and regulations provide guidelines that, while taking care of the clear cases, leave the harder cases for resolution by revenue ruling or case decision. If a bequest is made to a corporation, to qualify as a "charity" the corporation must be

> organized and operated exclusively for religious, charitable, scientific, literary, or educational purposes, including the encouragement of art, or to foster national or international amateur sports competition (but only if no part of its activities involve the provision of athletic facilities or equipment), and the prevention of cruelty to children or animals, no part of the net earnings of which inures to the benefit of any private stockholder or individual, which is not disqualified for tax exemption under §501(c)(3 by reason of attempting to influence legislation, and which does not participate in, or intervene in (including the publishing or distributing of statements), any political campaign on behalf of any candidate for public office. . . . [IRC §2055(a)(2).]

If a bequest is made to trustees, or to a fraternal society or lodge, the trust or association need not be organized and operated exclusively for charitable purposes, but the bequest itself must be used exclusively for these purposes. See id. §§2055(a)(3) and 2055(a)(4).

To qualify for a deduction, the bequest must be for public charity, not private charity. Some examples: A deduction was disallowed for a trust created to provide scholarships for the decedent's children, grandchildren, nephews, and nieces and for a trust providing for the maintenance of a park-like memorial for the family burial plot. A deduction was allowed for a trust providing for scholarships for student nurses and for a trust to provide relief for the needy — even though, in the latter case, preference was to be given to the decedent's friends and relatives.

It is important to identify the charitable beneficiary with precision and by its exact legal name. Failure to do so may, at best, lead to litigation to determine the identity of the intended recipient and may, at worst, cause the gift to fail for indefiniteness. IRS Publication 76, published biannually, lists the official names of all "section 501" organizations: Nonprofit organizations exempt from taxation under the federal income tax.

If a client wants to make a gift of a *remainder* to charity, unusual care must be taken by the drafter lest the gift fail to qualify for the charitable deduction. A charitable deduction for a remainder is disallowed under the federal income, gift, and estate tax laws unless the remainder is in an *annuity trust* or a *unitrust* or unless the gift is to a *pooled income fund*. IRC §§664(d), 2055(e)(2), and 2522(c)(2). A bequest in trust "to pay all the income to A for life, remainder to the Y charity" does *not* qualify for the charitable deduction because such a trust is not an annuity trust or a unitrust.

A charitable remainder *annuity trust* is one under which a fixed sum, which can be no less than 5 percent of the *original value* of the trust corpus, is paid at least annually to the private beneficiary or beneficiaries. The "income" beneficiary of an annuity trust thus receives a fixed and constant amount each year. A *unitrust* is one under which a fixed percentage, which cannot be less than 5 percent of the trust corpus, *valued annually*, is paid to the beneficiary. The "income" beneficiary of a unitrust thus will receive an annual amount that will fluctuate as the value of the trust changes. A *pooled income fund* is set up by a charitable organization to meet certain specific requirements of the Code. If the trustee or private beneficiary of an annuity trust, a unitrust, or a pooled income fund has a discretionary power to invade principal, the trust does not qualify for a charitable remainder deduction. The objectives of these rules are to reduce the uncertainty involved in valuing the future interest given to charity and to increase the likelihood that an interest will in fact pass to charity on the private beneficiary's death. However, the rules governing the drafting of these trusts are extremely technical and stringent, so much so that they create a trap for the nonspecialist attorney who attempts to draft such a trust.

We mention only one technicality to illustrate and underscore the need for caution in drafting gifts to charitable remainder trusts. If estate taxes may be paid from a charitable remainder trust, no charitable deduction is allowable. Rev. Rul. 82-128, 1982-27 I.R.S. 7. If taxes are apportioned by state law or by a clause in the decedent's will, a deduction may be denied. The will should provide that the charitable bequest pass free of all taxes.

For discussion of annuity trusts, unitrusts, and pooled income funds, see Darling, The Charitable Remainder Trust as an Estate Planning Tool, 44 Inst. Fed. Tax'n ch. 57 (1986); McCue & Gary, Split Interest Charitable Giving — Down But Not Out, 20 U. Miami Inst. Est. Plan. ch. 8 (1986); Comment, It Pays to Give It Away — Sometimes: Inter Vivos Charitable Remainder Unitrusts in Estate Planning, 15 Pepperdine L. Rev. 367 (1988).

PROBLEMS

1. *H* bequeaths $10,000 to *W*, "with the request, which is not legally binding, that *W* give the $10,000 to the American Red Cross." What are the tax consequences of this bequest?

2. *W* bequeaths $200,000 in trust to pay the income to *H* for life, remainder to Smith College. The gift to Smith College does not qualify for the charitable deduction in *W*'s estate because the trust is not an annuity trust or a unitrust. *W*'s net estate is worth $800,000. *H* elects to take against the will a surviving spouse's elective share, which is one-half of *W*'s estate. *H*'s elective share is $400,000. What effect does *H*'s disclaimer of his life estate have on the charitable deduction? See First National Bank of Fayetteville v. United States, 82-2 U.S. Tax Cas. (CCH) ¶13,478 (W.D. Ark. 1982).

If *H* had not elected to take against the will and *W*'s executor had claimed the marital deduction for the trust as a QTIP trust, would a charitable deduction be allowed in *H*'s estate upon *H*'s death? See IRC §2044.

3. Sometimes courts have reformed defective charitable remainder unitrusts to qualify under §2055 as a charitable unitrust, when the intent to obtain the charitable deduction is manifest. See In re Woods, N.Y.L.J., Dec. 5, 1988, at 31 (Sur. Ct.); Cal. Prob. Code §21540 (1989).

9. Executor's Elections: Post-Death Tax Planning

The executor or administrator has a number of elections that can affect both the estate and income taxes paid by the estate.

a. Valuation of Estate Assets

For estate tax purposes, assets are valued at their fair market value as of the date of death or, if the decedent's personal representative elects, as of the *alternate valuation date*. The alternate valuation date is the date six months after death except for assets "distributed, sold, exchanged, or otherwise disposed of" during the six-month period, for which it is the date of distribution or sale. IRC §2032. The purpose of the alternate valuation date option is to give some protection against the hardship that could result if estate assets decline in value shortly after the decedent's death. The personal representative must select either the date-of-death valuation date or the alternate valuation date for all assets. Election of one date for some assets and the other date for the remaining assets is not permitted.

Selection of the valuation date has income tax as well as estate tax consequences. Under §1014 of the Code, property acquired from a decedent is given a new basis for federal income tax capital gain purposes. The new basis is the value of the assets as of the decedent's death or as valued in the decedent's gross estate. Section 1014 applies to all property included in the gross estate, including transfers taxed under §§2035-2038. The alternate valuation date election is available only if a federal estate tax return is required to be filed on behalf of the estate. The stepped-up basis rule does not apply to gifts nor to assets brought into the estate tax computation as adjusted taxable gifts.

Section 2032A of the Code grants special relief to estates that include farm or ranch land or real estate devoted to a family business. Section 2032A permits farm and wood land and real estate devoted to business purposes to be valued by a method tied to the land's actual use value, rather than to its market value. See Harl, Special Use Valuation of Farmland Under IRC Section 2032A with Emphasis on Planning to Meet Predeath Requirements, 16 U. Miami Inst. Est. Plan. ¶1500 (1982).

b. Sections 2053 and 2054 Deductions

Section 2053 allows a deduction "(1) for funeral expenses, (2) for administration expenses, (3) for claims against the estate, and (4) for unpaid mortgages on, or any indebtedness in respect of, property where the value of the decedent's interest therein, undiminished by such mortgage or indebtedness, is included in the value of the gross estate."[36] Administration expenses include such items as the commission paid to

---

36. In community property states only one-half of a claim that is classified as a community obligation is deductible under §2053.

the personal representative as compensation for administering the estate, attorneys' fees, court costs and appraisers' fees, and expenses incurred in preserving and distributing the estate assets. Claims deductible under §2053 are "personal obligations of the decedent existing at the time of death, whether or not matured, and interest thereon which has accrued at the time of death." Treas. Reg. §20.2053-4. Obligations incurred by the estate after the decedent's death are not deductible. If, for example, the decedent dies in September, and property taxes on real estate owned by the decedent accrue and become payable on October 1, the taxes are an obligation of the estate, not of the decedent, and they are not deductible under §2053. Taxes owed by the decedent at death are deductible as claims against the estate.

Section 2054 allows a deduction for "losses incurred during the settlement of estates arising from fires, storms, shipwrecks, or other casualties, or from theft, when such losses are not compensated for by insurance or otherwise." The losses deductible under this section are limited to casualty losses. No deduction is allowed, for example, for a loss resulting from the sale of securities that have depreciated in value due to market conditions.

Administration expenses and casualty losses are also deductible against estate income under the income tax. Section 212 of the Internal Revenue Code of 1954 allows a deduction for expenses incurred "for the production or collection of income," and "for the management, conservation, or maintenance of property held for the production of income." The executor's commission and such items as attorneys' fees, appraisers' fees and court costs qualify for deduction under §212. Not surprisingly, the tax laws do not permit deduction of a single expense (or loss) against both the estate tax and the income tax. Under §642(g), the personal representative is given an election. These items can be taken as deductions from the gross estate in computing the estate tax or as deductions against estate income. The personal representative can split the deductions, taking some against the gross estate and the rest against estate income. How the deductions are taken will depend on which treatment produces the lowest overall tax bill.

See generally Kasner, Post-Mortem Tax Planning (1982), particularly §§11.100-11.132 on distributions to satisfy a marital deduction bequest under a formula clause.

PROBLEMS

1. Section 2054 deductions are rarely encountered in practice. Why do you suppose this is so?

2. On June 1, *O* borrows $10,000 from his local bank and signs a

note promising to pay the principal amount, together with interest at 16 percent per annum, on December 1. *O* dies on September 1. On December 1, *O*'s executor pays the bank $10,800 in satisfaction of the obligation. What portion of this amount, if any, is deductible under §2053? Would it make any difference if the executor selects the alternate valuation date as the date for valuing estate assets? See Treas. Reg. §20.2053-4.

SECTION D.   THE GENERATION-SKIPPING TRANSFER TAX

1.   *The Nature of the Tax*

Until 1986 it was possible for wealthy persons to make transfers in trust, either during lifetime or by will, in a manner that would insulate the transferred property from estate or gift taxation over several generations. We call this the "dynastic trust." *O* might transfer property worth (say) $5,000,000 to a trust under which the income was payable to *O*'s children for *their lives*, then to the children's children for *their lives*, then to the grandchildren's children for *their lives*, and so on down the generations until the local version of the Rule against Perpetuities, if any, called a halt. Each beneficiary could be given, in addition to a share of the income, a power to consume principal measured by an "ascertainable standard," a "$5,000 or 5 percent" withdrawal power, and a special testamentary power of appointment over his or her share of the trust corpus, all without estate or gift tax cost to the beneficiary. In addition, an independent trustee could be given an unlimited power to distribute trust principal to the beneficiaries with no transfer tax consequences. As each beneficiary died, nothing would be taxed in the beneficiary's estate because the beneficiary held only a life estate and limited powers of appointment. See supra pages 713-715. Through careful drafting to comply with the Rule against Perpetuities, the trust might continue — and be removed from the transfer tax rolls — for several generations. When the assets "resurfaced" on termination of the trust, the new owners could turn around, pay a gift or estate tax on the value of the assets, and make another generation-skipping transfer for another long period of time.

In the Tax Reform Act of 1986, Congress put an end to this tax-avoidance technique by enacting what is titled a "Tax on Generation-

Skipping Transfers."[37] Although the rules governing imposition of generation-skipping taxes can become enormously complicated, a general understanding of the generation-skipping tax is not difficult and is essential for the ordinary estate planner. Our treatment here is designed to give you a basic understanding. The fine details will have to be left to a course in tax planning.

The loophole in the estate and gift taxes that brought on the generation-skipping tax is the exemption of the life estate from transfer taxation at the death of the life tenant. The essential idea underlying the generation-skipping tax is that a transfer tax (gift, estate, or generation-skipping) should be paid *once a generation*, and that it should not be possible for an owner of property to avoid a generational transfer tax by giving the next generation only a life estate or skipping its members entirely. To implement this idea, the Code imposes a tax on any *generation-skipping transfer*, which is defined in §2611(a) as —

(1) a *taxable termination*,
(2) a *taxable distribution*, and
(3) a *direct skip*.

Generally, a generation-skipping transfer is a transfer to a *skip person* (a new term invented by Congress in imposing this tax). A skip person is a grandchild, great-grandchild, or any other person assigned to a generation that is two or more generations below the transferor's generation (§2613(a)). A spouse or a child (or other person in the transferor's generation or the generation just below the transferor's) is a nonskip person. As you will see, it is transfers from a grandparent to a grandchild, either direct or as a future interest, which avoid estate taxation at the death of the donor's children, that are the central concern of the generation-skipping tax.

There are three types of generation-skipping transfers. A *taxable termination* is the "termination (by death, lapse of time, release of power, or otherwise) of any interest in property held in a trust unless —

(A) immediately after such termination, a non-skip person has an interest in such property, or
(B) at no time after such termination may a distribution (including

---

37. The generation-skipping tax provisions, Chapter 13 of the Internal Revenue Code, comprise a separate and distinct tax from the estate tax (Chapter 11) and the gift tax (Chapter 12). The relevant sections are 2601-2663. Another version of the generation-skipping tax was written into the Code by Congress in 1976, but its effective date was annually postponed until 1986, when the earlier generation-skipping tax was retroactively repealed.

distributions on termination) be made from such trust to a skip person." (§2612(a)(1))

Here is an example:

> *Case 20.* T bequeaths $5,000,000 in trust for her son A for life, remainder to A's children. At A's death a "taxable termination" takes place. A's life interest terminates and only skip persons (A's children) have an interest in the property. A generation-skipping tax must be paid. If the income were payable to T's daughter B after A's death, there would be no taxable termination upon A's death; there would, however, be a taxable termination upon B's death, when only skip persons would have an interest in the trust.

The purpose of the exceptions in the definition of a taxable termination ((A) and (B) above) is to limit to *one* the number of taxable terminations, per dollar of property, that can occur in each generation below the transferor's. Where, for example, T bequeaths the income from a trust to her children, with principal to be distributed to her grandchildren upon the death of her *last* surviving child, a taxable termination occurs only at the death of the last surviving child. On the other hand, if at the death of one child his or her share is distributed to his or her children, then a taxable termination of a fractional share of the trust principal has occurred (§2612(a)(2)). Each dollar of a generation-skipping transfer is to be taxed once a generation.

A *taxable distribution* takes place whenever any distribution is made from a trust to a skip person (other than a taxable termination or a direct skip). Thus, if in Case 20, A had a (special) power to distribute income or corpus to A's children, a taxable distribution would take place when and if such distribution were made. In a discretionary trust a taxable distribution takes place whenever a distribution is made to a skip person.[38]

It is easy to see, from the explanation of a taxable termination and a taxable distribution, that the old-fashioned dynastic trust, described above in introducing the generation-skipping tax, generally will not work any longer in avoiding wealth transfer taxes. At the death of the transferor's children, holding life estates, or upon earlier distribution to the transferor's grandchildren, generation-skipping taxes must be paid. It is important to note, however, that the 1986 generation-skipping tax does not apply to any irrevocable trust created before the date of

---

38. An income tax deduction is provided for any generation-skipping tax imposed on any income distributions. This deduction prevents the same amount being subject to both income tax and the generation-skipping tax. But observe that the generation-skipping tax rate is considerably higher than the income tax rate.

the act. All those trusts already established by the Rockefellers, the DuPonts, and the Gettys, as well as lesser millionaires — with life estates and special powers of appointment in succeeding generations — will continue untaxed until after the termination of the trust. Hence the impact of the generation-skipping tax may not be felt on old money for a couple of generations.

To prevent the rich from bypassing one generation and making untaxed gifts to grandchildren or more remote descendants, Congress also has imposed a tax on direct skips. A *direct skip* is a transfer of property directly to a skip person. Case 21 illustrates a direct skip:

> *Case 21.* *T* leaves surviving her son *A* and *A*'s daughter *B*. *T* bequeaths $3,000,000 to her granddaughter *B*. This is a direct skip. A generation-skipping tax (in addition to the estate tax payable on *T*'s death) is due on *T*'s death. This "double taxation" follows from the principle that a transfer tax must be paid once per generation. Similarly, if *T* had given *B* $3,000,000 during life, a gift tax *and* a generation-skipping tax would be due.

Exceptions. Observe that the principle underlying taxation of a direct skip is that a transfer tax (be it an estate tax, gift tax, or generation-skipping tax) must be paid once a generation *regardless of whether any person assigned to a particular generation has any present interest or power*. This principle has two important exceptions.

(a) *Multiple skips.* First, skipping over two or more generations is permitted with the payment of only one generation-skipping tax. An owner can transfer property to a great-grandchild, paying a generation-skipping tax for the direct skip. Although two generations are skipped over, only one tax is paid.

(b) *Predeceased child.* The second exception relates to transfers to descendants of predeceased children. If a child of the transferor is dead at the time of the transfer, the children of that child are treated as the children of the transferor. Thus in Case 21 suppose that *A* had predeceased *T*. If this had happened, there would be no direct skip. The child of a predeceased child is treated as the child of the transferor; he or she is moved up a generation (§2612(c)(2)). The children of this child — really *T*'s great-grandchildren — are treated as grandchildren. This makes sense. Since no estate taxes could be levied on this property at *A*'s death, prior to *T*'s death, a generation-skipping tax (the functional equivalent of an estate tax) should not be levied upon a gift by *T* to the children of *T*'s dead son.

When generation-skipping tax imposed. No doubt you have observed one important difference between a direct skip on the one hand, and a taxable termination or distribution on the other. A direct skip occurs (and is taxable) on the day the transfer is effective; a taxable termination or taxable distribution occurs in the future, sometime after the original transfer in trust. In some cases it will be certain when the trust is established that the trust will produce a generation-skipping tax in the future. In other cases it will not be. Case 22 is an example.

> *Case 22.*   *T*'s will bequeaths property in trust to pay the income to *T*'s child *A* until *A* attains the age of 30, at which time the trustee is to distribute the trust principal to *A*. If *A* dies before reaching age 30, the trustee is to distribute the principal to *A*'s children in equal shares. Whether this trust will produce a generation-skipping transfer will turn on the events that actually occur — and for this purpose we wait to see what happens. If *A* lives to age 30 and receives the trust principal, it will turn out that *T* did not make a generation-skipping transfer. If *A* dies under age 30, and the trust principal is distributed to *A*'s children, a taxable termination will occur.

If a trust turns out to produce a generation-skipping transfer, the tax is payable in the future when such transfer occurs.

PROBLEM

If a person makes a qualified disclaimer (see supra page 126), for purposes of federal gift, estate, and generation-skipping taxes, the disclaimed interest in property is treated as if it had never been transferred to the person making the disclaimer. The disclaimant is *not* treated as having predeceased the transferor, as occurs under many state disclaimer statutes (see UPC §2-801(c), supra page 123). *T* bequeaths $1.2 million to her son *A*. If *A* disclaims, is a generation-skipping tax imposed?

2.   Rate and Base of Tax

Rate.   All generation-skipping transfers are taxed at a flat rate, which is the highest rate applicable under the federal estate tax. The highest estate tax rate currently is 55 percent, which is scheduled to decline to 50 percent in 1993. Therefore the generation-skipping tax is 55 percent today or 50 percent after 1992.

Base.   The amount taxed and the person liable for the tax depend upon the type of transfer. Where there is a *direct skip*, the transferor must pay the tax on the amount received by the transferee. In this way the direct skip resembles the gift tax. The base excludes the amount of tax levied; a direct skip is said to be "tax exclusive" (see supra page 938). Thus for a transferor to pass $1 million directly to a grandchild, the transferor must part with $1.5 million, if the tax rate is 50 percent, in addition to the gift or estate tax imposed. The gift tax is imposed on the amount of the gift and on the amount of the generation-skipping tax paid.

Taxable terminations and *taxable distributions* are treated differently. The tax in these events is imposed on a "tax-inclusive" basis (i.e., the taxable amount includes the tax). In this respect, taxable terminations and distributions resemble the estate tax. Upon a taxable termination, the tax base is the entire property with respect to which the termination occurred. The tax is to be paid out of the trust.[39] Upon a taxable distribution, the tax base is the amount received by the beneficiary, who is liable for the tax. Thus if a generation-skipping trust terminates and the principal is $2 million, the trustee must pay $1 million to Uncle Sam (assuming a 50 percent rate) and $1 million is distributed to the beneficiary. Similarly, if a trustee distributes $2 million to a skip person, the donee is liable for $1 million in generation-skipping tax, leaving a net transfer of $1 million.

PROBLEM

O makes a $1 million gift to a grandchild, allocating no exemption to it. Assuming the maximum (and applicable) gift and estate tax rate is 50 percent, what is the cost of this transfer to *O*? To put the question a different way, how much does *O* have to part with to put $1 million in a grandchild's hands?

What would be the cost to *O* of a $1 million *bequest* to a grandchild?

3.   Exemption and Exclusions

Exemption.   Section 2631(a) provides an exemption of up to $1 million for each person making generation-skipping transfers. In the case of inter vivos transfers by a married person, the transferor and his or her spouse may elect to treat the transfer as made one-half by each spouse (as under §2513 of the gift tax, see supra page 957). A husband and wife can give away $2 million in generation-skipping transfers without incurring any tax. Thus:

Case 23.   During life *W* transfers $2,000,000 to a trustee to pay the

---

39. If the $1 million exemption is allocated to this trust at *T*'s death, no generation-skipping tax is payable at *A*'s death, even though the principal has appreciated. See discussion of exemption, infra.

income to *W*'s children for their lives, then to distribute the principal to *W*'s grandchildren. *H* consents to treating this transfer as having been made half by him, thus using up his $1,000,000 exemption. A gift tax is payable by *W* at the time of the transfer. At the death of *W*'s children, no generation-skipping tax is due.

If, in Case 23, *W* had not made an inter vivos transfer but had bequeathed $2 million in trust, only $1 million would be exempt from generation-skipping tax. The split-gift provision applies only to inter vivos gifts. In case of a death transfer, to take advantage of the spouse's generation-skipping tax exemption, it is necessary to make the spouse a "transferor" for estate tax purposes. This can be done by bequeathing the spouse outright ownership, or a life estate coupled with a general power of appointment, or a life estate in a QTIP trust. If, in Case 23, the trust had been a testamentary trust and *H* had been bequeathed a life estate in half of $2 million transferred by *W* into trust, *H*'s generation-skipping tax exemption of $1 million could be used up too.

If the transferor creates more than one generation-skipping trust, or makes generation-skipping transfers in excess of $1 million, the transferor or his personal representative can allocate the exemption as he sees fit. If not so allocated, §2642 provides some rather complex "default" rules. Generally, under these rules, the exemption is first allocated to direct skips and then to taxable terminations and taxable distributions. The exemption is allocated to the "property" transferred and not, in the case of taxable terminations and taxable distributions, to specific generation-skipping transfers that occur in the future. This means that with respect to trusts that might produce taxable terminations or taxable distributions, the entire exemption or a fraction thereof must be allocated to the trust *at the time of the transfer into trust.* Here is an example of a fractional allocation[40] of the exemption.

> *Case 24.* *T* bequeaths $5 million into a trust. The trustee is given discretion to pay income or corpus among *T*'s living descendants (which means the trust may produce taxable distributions). At the death of the survivor of *T*'s children, or when the youngest grandchild of *T* living at *T*'s death reaches 35, whichever happens later, the remaining trust property is to be divided among *T*'s descendants then living, per stirpes (which will produce a taxable termination if the corpus is not earlier distributed). At *T*'s death, two children of *T*, *A* and *B*, are alive. *A* has two children, *A¹* and *A²*, alive. *B* has one child, *B¹*, alive. *T*'s executor

---

40. The resulting fraction applicable to the property transferred to determine the generation-skipping tax is called the "inclusion ratio" by §2642. If $1 million is transferred into trust, and the entire exemption allocated to it, the inclusion ratio is zero. If none of the exemption is allocated to it, the inclusion ratio is 1. In Case 24 the inclusion ratio is .80.

allocates T's entire exemption to the trust. Any distributions of income or principal to A^1, A^2, or B^1 are partially exempt from the generation-skipping tax. The exempt portion is 20 percent ($1 million divided by $5 million), thus the taxable portion is 80 percent. As a result, distributions from the trust are subject to a generation-skipping tax (after 1992) at an effective rate of 40 percent (80 percent × tax rate of 50 percent). If, at the termination of the trust, the principal is worth $9 million, a generation-skipping tax of $3.6 million is then levied. Once the allocation of the exemption has been made, any subsequent appreciation in the value of the exempt property is also exempt from generation-skipping tax.

The allocation, once made, is irrevocable. Therefore it is important to allocate the exemption so as not to waste it on a trust that is uncertain to produce a generation-skipping transfer, when it could be allocated more effectively elsewhere. It is usually best to allocate the exemption first to direct skips, for this reason and for the additional reason that a tax postponed is better than a tax paid.

Under §2653(b)(1), the exempt fraction of the trust property — determined when the trust is created — remains the same for the duration of the trust. If the trust produces successive skips, the transferor's exemption can eliminate or reduce the generation-skipping tax generation after generation. If, for example, a trust provides for payment of income to T's children for their lives, then to T's grand-children for their lives, and then to distribute the principal to T's great-grandchildren, the transferor's $1 million exemption will shelter the trust, wholly or partially, from generation-skipping tax for its entire duration. This tax-shelter trust is known as a *dynasty trust*.

PROBLEM

T's will creates one trust of $1 million for the benefit of child A, with principal to be paid to A at age 35, and if A dies before 35 to pay the principal to A's issue. A similar trust is created for child B. You are T's executor. How will you allocate the $1 million exemption? Suppose that A dies thereafter at age 32 but that B lives to 35. In retrospect, was any of the exemption wasted? If A had been given the $1 million outright, the estate tax upon A's death on $1 million would be $153,000. What would the generation-skipping tax be?

Exclusions.   Certain transfers are excluded from the generation-skipping tax. Section 2612(c)(1) excludes any transfer not subject to the gift tax because of the annual exclusion (see supra page 946). Hence transfers of $10,000 or less annually to grandchildren will not produce a generation-skipping tax. Section 2611(b)(2) excludes from the term "generation-skipping transfer" any inter vivos transfers excluded under §2503(e) of the gift tax, relating to the direct payment of tuition and medical expenses (see supra page 946). Hence a grandparent can pay tuition for a grandchild without making a generation-skipping transfer, or a trust can make tuition or medical payments for a skip person without subjecting such distributions to the generation-skipping tax.

Section 2611(b)(1) provides that the term "generation-skipping transfer" does not include any transfer from a trust, to the extent such transfer is subject to estate or gift taxes with respect to a person in the first generation below that of the transferor. If property is transferred for the benefit of a child, and the property is subject to estate taxes at the child's death (or gift taxes if the child gives away the property), no generation-skipping tax is assessed at the child's death. This exclusion has important estate planning implications. *Each person can avoid the generation-skipping tax by transferring property to a child in such a manner as to subject the property to estate taxes at the child's death.* The cost of avoiding the generation-skipping tax is to involve the child with the gift and estate taxes. In view of the fact that the effective federal gift and estate tax rates range from 37 percent to 55 percent, and the child has a $600,000 exemption from these taxes, it may save tax dollars to give the property to the child in such a way as to cause inclusion of the property in the child's federal gross estate.

4. Definitions

To round out our picture of how the generation-skipping tax operates, it is necessary to look at some definitions in the Code.

a. Transferor

Generally, a transferor is a person who is treated as owner (or transferor) under the federal gift and estate taxes. A person transferring a fee simple is a transferor. A person who possesses a general power of appointment is a transferor when the power is exercised or when it lapses or is released. A person possessing a special power of appointment is not treated as a transferor. In case of a QTIP trust, the transferee spouse is the deemed transferor if the transferor spouse (or his executor) so elects. However, by a special provision in §2652(a)(3), the transferor spouse in a QTIP trust can elect to be the transferor for generation-skipping purposes (thus using his generation-skipping tax exemption), while at the same time electing to take the estate tax marital deduction.

As noted above, gift-splitting by married couples is permitted. Gift-splitting doubles the effect of any exemption or exclusion applicable to inter vivos transfers.

Successive skips. If a trust is created for several generations (for example, for children for their lives, then to grandchildren for their lives, then to great-grandchildren), a taxable termination occurs on the death of the first generation and again on the death of the second generation. This result follows from §2653(a), which provides that in such a trust, *after* a generation-skipping transfer at the death of the children, the "transferor" is dropped down to the children's level for any portion of the trust subject to generation-skipping tax. (However, any portion of the trust that has been allocated part of the original settlor's exemption remains exempt for the duration of the trust (see supra page 1028). Thus a dynasty trust of $1 million, allocated the transferor's entire exemption, pays no generation-skipping tax for its duration.)

b. Skip Person; Ascertaining Generations

Since a skip person is defined as an individual who is two or more generations below the transferor, it is necessary to define generation. With respect to descendants, the definition is naturally by generations. A grandchild or more remote descendant is a skip person. Similarly, for first and second line collaterals, the generations are natural. Nephews and nieces are treated as of the same generation as children; children of nephews and nieces are skip persons. §2651(b)(1). (See Table of Consanguinity, supra page 109, for a picture of second line collaterals who are on the same generational level as grandchildren.) Descendants and first and second line collaterals of spouses of the transferor are assigned to the same generation they would be assigned to if related to the transferor. §2651(b)(2).

A person who has at any time been married to the transferor is assigned to the transferor's generation. A person who has been married to a descendant (or to a first or second line collateral) of the transferor or the transferor's spouse is assigned to the generation of the individual married. §2651(c).

With respect to a beneficiary who is not a lineal descendant of a grandparent of the transferor or of the transferor's spouse, §2651(d) provides for an assignment of generation based on the beneficiary's age in relation to that of the transferor. A person born not more than 12½ years after the transferor is assigned to the transferor's generation.

A person born more than 12½ years but not more than 37½ years after the transferor is assigned to the generation of the transferor's children. Thereafter, generation assignments are made in successive 25-year periods. Hence a gift to someone more than 37½ years younger is treated the same as a gift to a grandchild (a skip person).

PROBLEMS

1. *T*, a bachelor, dies leaving a will that devises his residuary estate in trust, to pay the income to *T*'s sister, *S*, for life, and on *S*'s death to distribute the trust principal to *S*'s descendants then living per stirpes. Some years later *S* dies; she is survived by a daughter and by three grandchildren, the children of her deceased son. Does the generation-skipping tax apply?

2. *O*, your client, wants some advice. *O* wants to leave $1 million to her sister *S*. Is there any transfer tax advantage in leaving $1 million to *S* for life, remainder to *S*'s son *A*, rather than leaving $1 million to *S* outright?

c. Interest

We have noted above that a taxable termination occurs when an "interest" in property terminates and certain other conditions are present. A person has an interest if he has "a *right* (other than a future right) to receive income or corpus from the trust" or "is a *permissible current* recipient of income or corpus from the trust." §2652(c). A person who has a future interest, vested or contingent, does not have an interest for purposes of the generation-skipping tax. When an owner of a future interest dies, no taxable termination takes place. Thus:

> *Case 25.*   *T* bequeaths property in trust for her son *A* for life, remainder to *A*'s daughter *B* if *B* is then alive, and if *B* is not then alive to *B*'s children (*T*'s great-grandchildren). Subsequently *B* dies during the life of *A*. A generation-skipping transfer tax is not levied at *B*'s death. Upon the subsequent death of *A*, a generation-skipping tax is levied, but a tax at *B*'s generation has been skipped. The same result would be reached if *B* held an indefeasibly vested remainder and bequeathed it to her children during *A*'s life.

The treatment of future interests is consistent with, though not compelled by, the predeceased child exception (supra page 1025) and the exception for multiple skips (supra page 1025). It is not, however, consistent with estate taxation of remainders. If, in Case 25, *B* holds a transmissible remainder, the value of the remainder is includable in *B*'s gross estate if *B* dies during *A*'s lifetime. *B* is a transferor for estate tax purposes but not for generation-skipping purposes. Thus it remains important, for estate tax reasons, not to create transmissible remainders.

A person who is a potential appointee (or object) of a power *currently* exercisable by another has an interest. A discretionary trust will illustrate this type of interest.

> *Case 26.* *T* bequeaths property in trust to pay income to *T*'s son *A* or *A*'s daughter *B* in such amount as the trustee shall determine, or accumulate it, and at the death of *A* and *B* to distribute the principal to *T*'s issue then living, per stirpes. At the death of *A*, a taxable termination occurs and a tax is due. So too at the death of *B*. If the trustee distributes income to *B* during *A*'s life, a taxable distribution occurs.

If the trust in Case 26 had been a discretionary trust for *T*'s issue until the perpetuities period expires, a taxable termination would occur upon the death of the last survivor of each generation. Under §2653(a), once a generation-skipping transfer occurs (at the death of the last survivor of *T*'s children), the transferor of the trust is then considered to be a member of the first generation above any person then having an interest in the trust (see supra page 1031). In other words, the children are then treated as transferors, and the generation-skipping rules start over again.

Although the definitions of taxable termination and taxable distribution refer explicitly to property held in trust, which is the usual arrangement, the generation-skipping tax also applies to trust equivalents, such as legal life estates and remainders, estates for years, and insurance and annuity contracts. §2652(b).

5. Tax Strategies

To reduce or avoid the generation-skipping tax, certain strategies are fairly obvious:

(a) Use the annual gift tax exclusion of $10,000 per transferee ($20,000 for a married couple). See supra page 946.
(b) Use the gift tax exclusions for tuition and medical expense payments for grandchildren made directly to the educational institution or medical supplier. See supra page 946.
(c) Use the predeceased child exception, if applicable to the particular family. See supra page 1025.
(d) Use the generation-skipping tax exemption of $1 million. See supra page 1027.

(e) Arrange the assets of a married couple so as not to waste the generation-skipping tax exemption of either spouse. Where the couple's assets exceed $2 million, each spouse should be made the "transferor" of at least $1 million. To illustrate this, let us assume *H* is very rich and *W* has no assets. *H* should transfer (at least) $1 million in a QTIP trust for *W* for life, then to *H*'s children for their lives, then to *H*'s grandchildren. This qualifies for the marital deduction *and* makes *W* the transferor for generation-skipping taxes. An estate tax will be payable at *W*'s death on the amount of property exceeding her unified credit, but no generation-skipping tax will be payable when the assets are distributed to grandchildren.

(f) Create a trust of life insurance for the benefit of skip persons, paying the premiums in an annual amount qualifying for the annual exclusion (perhaps using *Crummey* provisions, see supra page 949).

(g) Make multiple skips in a direct skip, thus skipping more than one generation (for example, make gifts to great-grandchildren rather than grandchildren). See supra page 1025. This is sometimes called "layering."

(h) Use the transferor's $1 million exemption ($2 million for a married couple) to establish a dynasty trust for successive generations for as long as the perpetuities period allows, thus avoiding generation-skipping tax for the duration of the trust. See supra page 1029.

(i) Give children enough property in a form subject to estate taxes in their estates to use up the $600,000 exemption from estate tax (unified credit) each child has. (This credit can be expanded to $1.2 million when the child is married.) Consider giving more property to children outright, subjecting property to estate taxes, rather than generation-skipping taxes, at their deaths. This may produce these tax advantages at their deaths: lower graduated estate tax rates, a credit for previously taxed property,[41] and use of $1 million exemptions children have for generation-skipping transfers.

---

41. One tax disadvantage of paying the generation-skipping tax, as opposed to the estate tax, is that no credit is available on a generation-skipping tax for a transfer tax imposed previously within a few years. Such a credit is available for estate taxes paid in a prior estate, on the same property, ranging from 100 percent where the second transferor dies within two years of the first transferor to 20 percent where the time between the two deaths is ten years. Thus if *T* devises property to child *A*, who dies a year later devising the property to *A*'s child *B*, *A*'s estate is entitled to a credit against its estate taxes in the amount of estate tax *T*'s estate paid on the property. If *T* devises property to *A* for life, remainder to *B*, and *A* dies within a year, no credit on the generation-skipping tax due at *A*'s death is available.

Doubtless tax planners for the very rich will scrutinize the Code intensely, seeking other ways to reduce or eliminate generation-skipping transfer taxes. At this point, however, it is doubtful that any terribly large loopholes in the generation-skipping tax will be found. Congress adopted a principle of exacting one transfer tax per generation, and, except for the exemptions and exclusions mentioned above, it appears that the estate, gift, and generation-skipping taxes quite effectively implement that principle.

It must be understood that in this sketch we have touched upon only elementary principles applicable to the generation-skipping tax. For more explanation of the generation-skipping tax, see J. Dodge, Wills, Trusts, and Estate Planning 223-248 (1988); Abrams, Rethinking Generation-Skipping Transfers, 40 Sw. L.J. 1145 (1987); Bloom, Federal Generation-Skipping Transfer Taxation: How Should the States Respond, 51 Alb. L. Rev. 817 (1987); Plant & Wintriss, Generation-Skipping Transfer Tax, 17 U. Balt. L. Rev. 271 (1988).

6.   Consequences on Estate Planning of Generation-Skipping Transfer Tax

The generation-skipping tax is likely to have a profound impact on estate planning, though, as yet, this impact is more or less speculative. Many lawyers may choose not to draft generation-skipping trusts for clients with only a few millions, except to the extent they come within the exemptions from generation-skipping tax. They may deem it most desirable to give succeeding generations in the client's family flexibility to deal with transfer taxation. The greatest flexibility usually comes from absolute ownership. The cost of flexibility is a gift or estate tax payable in the next generation. But estate and gift taxes can be lowered by the owner giving away property expected to appreciate greatly in value, or by consuming the property, or by spending capital on education and other enhancers of the next generation's human capital, or, possibly, depleting capital by making income payments from it (taxed at a lower rate) to the next generation. And there may be an income tax advantage available to owners of property. They can decide whether to hold on to the property until death, giving the next generation a stepped-up basis,[42] or give it away now. A generation-skipping trust may deprive the next generation of that flexibility.

---

42. As pointed out at page 945 supra, any property acquired from a decedent receives a stepped-up basis, whereas property received by gift carries the donor's basis. The Code attempts to harmonize the generation-skipping tax with this treatment. If a taxable *termination* occurs at the same time and as the result of the death of an individual (which is comparable to receiving property at the death of the owner), the basis of the property transferred receives a new stepped-up basis, which is the value of the property at the time of the taxable termination. §2654(a)(2). In any other case where a generation-skipping tax is levied, the transferor's old basis continues, as with a gift, but is adjusted upward by the amount of generation-skipping tax attributable to the transfer. §2654(a)(1).

The total *amount* of wealth in dynastic trusts may decline as existing dynastic trusts are terminated and rich persons decide that absolute ownership in their children gives them the advantage of flexibility, including the possibility of taking up domicile in some place with no or low wealth transfer taxes. Yet even if the total amount of wealth in dynastic trusts declines, the *number* of such trusts will probably rise. This will likely happen because a $1 million ($2 million per married couple) generation-skipping trust is exempt from generation-skipping tax for its entire duration. With an eye to taxation, each new and old millionaire ought to create a dynasty trust of $1 million for his or her descendants. Such a trust will escape generation-skipping tax for the perpetuities period and, after the initial transfer, also escape gift and estate taxation for this period. One million dollar dynasty trusts may become common among millionaires.

It should be noted that in states having high state inheritance or estate tax rates, a tax incentive for creating new dynastic trusts may continue to exist. State inheritance or estate taxes on the next generation, together with federal estate taxes, may exceed the tax payable under the generation-skipping tax. In New York, for example, graduated estate and gift tax rates go up to 21 percent. Persons of great wealth there may find it cheaper for the next generation to pay a generation-skipping tax (50 percent) than to pay a federal estate tax (50 percent) and state estate tax (21 percent).

PROBLEM

A desirable position for a child to be in is to be able to decide whether to pay estate taxes or to pay generation-skipping taxes on his death. As indicated above, this flexibility may give the child the advantage of making use of his and his spouse's exemptions, unified credits, and graduated rates. Can a parent pass property to the child in such a way as to give the child this option, to be elected as future events unfold? Consider giving either a trustee or the child a power of appointment along the following lines: O transfers property in trust for her son A for life, then to A's children. (1) O gives the trustee power to pay any or all of the corpus to A. If it later appears wise for A to own the property at death, subjecting it to estate taxes, the trustee can appoint it to A during A's life. (2) O gives A a special power to appoint the property to one or more of A's descendants. If A wants the property in his federal gross estate at death, thereby avoiding generation-skipping tax, A can by will exercise the special power by creating a *general* power in his daughter B. This exercise causes the property subject to the general power to be includable in A's federal gross estate. See Note:

The "Delaware Tax Trap," supra page 806. Are these wise powers to create? See Blattmachr & Pennell, Adventures in Generation-Skipping, or How We Learned to Love the "Delaware Tax Trap," 24 Real Prop. Prob. & Tr. J. 75 (1989).

The result of the Reagan transfer tax revolution is to exempt the middle class and most of the moderately wealthy from involvement in wealth transfer taxes. The exemption from estate taxes was increased from $175,625 to $600,000 and an exemption of $1 million from generation-skipping tax was granted. On the other hand, in the future, with the imposition of a generation-skipping tax, wealth transfer taxes will hit far harder than in the past persons who have several million dollars or more. When the full impact of the generation-skipping tax is felt, a generation or so from now, Congress may be hard put to maintain its resolve. But for now, with President Reagan's assent, Congress has given us what Presidents Theodore and Franklin Roosevelt and Herbert Hoover wanted but could never impose — an effective tax to break up swollen fortunes and inherited economic power (see supra pages 932). The future of the great fortunes in this country is in some doubt.

SECTION E.   STATE WEALTH TRANSFER TAXES

All states except Nevada have death taxes, but less than a dozen impose a gift tax on lifetime transfers.[43] State death taxes fall into one of three general categories. The first category is the *pick-up tax*. This is a tax equal to the maximum credit for state death taxes under the federal estate tax. The maximum credit is fixed by §2011 of the Internal Revenue Code. In the 1920s, when an effort was made to repeal the federal estate tax on the ground that this source of revenue should be reserved to the states, Congress enacted a law allowing a credit against the federal estate tax for death taxes paid a state. Most states responded by enacting death taxes to take full advantage of the credit, since it permitted diversion of federal revenues to the state without increasing

---

43. The death tax laws of all states are compiled in CCH Inheritance, Estate, & Gift Tax Reporter, a multivolume looseleaf service. See also Report, Procedure for Objections to the Determination of State Death Taxes and Valuation, 18 Real Prop., Prob., & Tr. J. 34 (1983), surveying all state statutes.

the tax burden on the state's residents. The amount of the credit in 1928 was 80 percent of the federal tax, but the amount of the credit has been drastically reduced by Congress over the years. The maximum tax credits set out in §2011(b) of the Code range from 1 percent to 16 percent of the federal estate tax due.

In addition to the pick-up tax, about one-half the states have inheritance taxes under which a tax is levied on the amount passing to each legatee, heir, or other beneficiary of decedent's property. The tax rates and exemptions are determined by the beneficiary's relationship to the decedent. While the decedent's personal representative is responsible for filing the tax return and paying the tax to the state taxing authority, absent a contrary will provision the "burden" of the tax is borne by each beneficiary and is deducted from the amount passing to the beneficiary.

Although the usual state inheritance tax is imposed on many of the same items as are subject to federal estate taxation, often there are differences. It suffices to mention the three most common: joint tenancy, powers of appointment, and life insurance. Under most state inheritance taxes, a fractional share of a joint tenancy is taxed; the federal who-furnished-the-consideration test is not followed. The states vary considerably on how they treat property subject to a power of appointment. Some follow the federal law, others tax general powers that are exercised, and some tax special powers as well as general powers. Under most state inheritance tax laws, life insurance proceeds are not taxed if they are paid to some beneficiary other than the decedent's executor or estate.

Typically the inheritance tax rates and exemptions turn on whether the beneficiary is a Class A, Class B, or Class C beneficiary. Class A beneficiaries might include the spouse and descendants. Class B beneficiaries might include parents and descendants of parents. All other persons and organizations are Class C beneficiaries, and they pay the highest rates.

Less than a dozen states have an estate tax rather than an inheritance tax. These state estate tax laws do not follow any one pattern, although each incorporates some features of the federal estate tax. New York and Michigan closely pattern their estate tax laws after the federal estate tax, including an unlimited marital deduction for which a QTIP trust qualifies. But other state estate tax laws may not provide for any marital deduction or limit it in some way.

Inasmuch as the federal estate tax burden has been considerably lessened by the Economic Recovery Tax Act of 1981, planning for state inheritance and estate taxes has become more important. The unlimited marital deduction, which is so attractive in avoiding federal estate taxation, may have state death tax disadvantages. See Schaeffer, Avoiding the State Death Tax Disadvantages of the Unlimited Marital

Deduction in Large Estates, 10 Est. Plan. 36 (1983). For a discussion of the problems of coordinating federal tax planning with the state death tax laws of New York, New Jersey, Pennsylvania, and Florida, see Colloquium on Paradigmatic State Inheritance, State Estate and Gift Taxation, and the ERTA, 34 Rutgers L. Rev. 699 (1982).

TABLE OF CASES

Principal cases are in italic.

INDEX